# ANGLICANISM

## THE THOUGHT AND PRACTICE OF THE CHURCH OF ENGLAND, ILLUSTRATED FROM THE RELIGIOUS LITERATURE OF THE SEVENTEENTH CENTURY

COMPILED AND EDITED BY THE LATE

### PAUL ELMER MORE,

SOMETIME FELLOW OF THE AMERICAN ACADEMY OF ARTS AND LETTERS

AND

### FRANK LESLIE CROSS,

LADY MARGARET PROFESSOR OF DIVINITY IN THE UNIVERSITY OF OXFORD AND CANON OF CHRIST CHURCH

*"We have a vast inheritance, but no inventory of our treasures. All is given in profusion; it remains for us to catalogue, sort, distribute, select, harmonize, and complete."*—JOHN HENRY NEWMAN in "Lectures on the Prophetical Office of the Church" (1837).

LONDON

S · P · C · K

1962

*First published in* 1935
*Reprinted* 1951, 1957, 1962
S·P·C·K
*Holy Trinity Church*
*Marylebone Road*
*London, N.W.*1

PRINTED IN GREAT BRITAIN BY OFFSET LITHOGRAPHY BY
BILLING AND SONS LTD., GUILDFORD AND LONDON

# PREFACE

THE origin of this work goes back to a conversation some four years ago with Bishop Rhinelander, of the College of Preachers in Washington. At that time I chanced to remark that it had long been in my mind to make a collection of passages from the ecclesiastical writers of the Seventeenth Century which would set forth the doctrine and discipline,—what might be called in a broad sense the genius,—of the Church of England in that age of adjustment after the first confusions of the Reformation, but that other occupations had compelled me to abandon the project. It seemed to Bishop Rhinelander, as it had seemed to me, that such a compilation would have value for those concerned with the religious issues of the present day as well as for students of the past. For that reason he asked me to lay the plan before a committee which he called together in New York, and which included among others Dean Fosbroke and Professor Gavin of the General Theological Seminary, Dean Washburn of the Episcopal Theological School in Cambridge, Mass., and Dean Ladd of the Berkeley Divinity School.

At this meeting various aspects of the scheme were discussed, and the chairman, with the guile doubtless engendered by episcopal experience, suggested that I might be induced to take up the task if it were shared by an associate editor and if a certain amount of money were raised for incidental expenses. To these proposals the committee assented, but beyond such concurrence they are not responsible for the character of the work as actually carried out. We were fortunate enough to engage the interest of Dr. Cross in the project, and it is only fair to say that much the heavier part of the burden of reading and editing has been borne by him, and that he alone has assumed the labour of collating the texts and seeing the volume through the press.

For the purpose in view the selections have been drawn preferably from the more authoritative and better known writings of the period. Even so the field to be covered was immense and the need of discrimination very exacting. The editors cannot hope that their judgement will meet with universal approval, but they believe that the documents here assembled represent what was clearly the dominant teaching of the Anglican Church in that age. Those familiar with the vastness and variety of the literature will, they trust, be the slowest to find fault with any particular omission or insertion. In some cases the extract as printed is composed of passages strung together out of a long treatise, and in one or two instances the order of sequence has been changed; but all lacunae are indicated by points. The editors believe that a considerable number of the passages they have included have not been reprinted since the century in which they were written.

A major problem for the editors was the fact that often two or three subjects were entangled in a single passage, so that the same extract might have been placed with almost equal propriety under more than one heading. The arrangement of the passages under any particular caption was determined sometimes by chronology, sometimes by similarity of theme, as convenience dictated.

It was felt that some readers might welcome a connected account of the theological literature of the period from which the following extracts have been drawn, and accordingly Mr. F. R. Arnott, of Keble College, Oxford, who had already rendered generous assistance in the preparation of the bulky manuscript for the press, was invited to contribute the essay which stands after his name. The rich store of Dr. Darwell Stone's learning, seemingly inexhaustible in all branches of theology, enabled the editors to get on the track of a number of the passages they have included, though of course they themselves assume sole responsibility for the use made of them. In varying stages of the work, valuable help was received from Mr. C. S. Nye, of St. Peter's Hall; from Messrs. G. Watson and D. M. Mackinnon, both of New College, Oxford; and from Mr. G. L. Phillips, of Brasenose College. To all these gentlemen the editors tender their sincere gratitude.

The editors also desire to express their indebtedness to the author and to Messrs. Longmans, Green and Co., for permission to use the translation of some passages of William Forbes' *Considerationes Modestae*, contained in Dr. Stone's *History of the Doctrine of the Holy Eucharist;* and to Messrs. P. J. and A. E. Dobell for allowing them to reprint two extracts from Traherne's *Centuries of Meditations.*

P. E. M.

# CONTENTS

## I. THE ANGLICAN FAITH

## II. THE CHURCH

### (1) HOLY AND CATHOLIC

### (2) VISIBLE AND INVISIBLE

### (3) THE MARKS OF THE CHURCH

## III. SEPARATED CHURCHES

### (1) ROMAN CATHOLICISM

# VI. NATURAL THEOLOGY

# VII. REVEALED THEOLOGY

## VIII. SOTERIOLOGY

## IX. ESCHATOLOGY

# X. THE CHRISTIAN MINISTRY

# XI. THE SACRAMENTS

## XIV. OTHER RELIGIOUS PRACTICES

## XV. PRAYER

## XVI. ETHICS

## XVII. KING AND STATE

# THE SPIRIT OF ANGLICANISM

BY

PAUL ELMER MORE

The documents from which this compilation is drawn fall within the period from 1594 to 1691, for which the " seventeenth century " will pass as a convenient and sufficiently accurate term. On the earlier of these dates Hooker published the first four books of his *Ecclesiastical Polity*, which in the quiet living of Boscombe he had written out in memory of his controversy with Travers in the Temple. They were intended primarily to be a defence against the servile submission to Geneva that threatened to reduce the English reformation to a mere echo of the radical Protestantism of the Continent. In effect the finished product went far beyond any such defensive intention. Here first the Anglican Communion was made aware of itself as an independent branch of the Church Universal, neither Roman nor Calvinist, but at once Catholic and Protestant, with a positive doctrine and discipline of its own and a definite mission in the wide economy of Grace. As it has been well said, " Hooker was the father of Anglo-Catholic theology " ; [1] for it was he who laid the foundation upon which the majestic edifice of Caroline divinity was built. The publication of the *Ecclesiastical Polity* is thus the given *terminus a quo* for any compilation designed to illustrate the specific genius of Anglicanism.

For the *terminus ad quem* the year 1691 has been chosen as dating the schismatic activity of the Non-Jurors, and as marking a notable break in English ecclesiastical history. As a result of that schism we see on the one side a succession of writers who in the main, though with some lack of balance, follow the true line of development from Hooker and Laud, but whose place in an exposition of Anglicanism might be challenged on the ground that they can hardly be called members of the National Church. On the other side the theology of those who continued within the Establishment becomes irrelevant to our purpose for another reason. The extrusion of so large a body of the more Catholic elements left the rest of the Church for several decades a prey to the rising tide of rationalism and deism, so that the apologetic literature of the orthodox took, perforce, a new turn. The aim, for instance, of such a work as Bishop Butler's *Analogy* is not so much to define the peculiar position of the Church of England as to

[1] L. S. Thornton, *Richard Hooker*, p. 101. Cf. H. M. Gwatkin, " If Jewel is the apologist of the Reformation, Hooker is the apologist of the Church of England " (*Church and State in England to the Death of Queen Anne*, pp. 263 f.).

defend Christianity against the open or disguised attacks of infidelity. Thus the special task of the seventeenth century may be said to have been accomplished by the date 1691.

## I

Within this period of nearly a hundred years a considerable diversity of opinion may be discovered among admittedly Anglican writers on points of doctrine and discipline, and something of that uncertainty may be felt in the selections here brought together. England, it is important to remember, did not produce at that time, and indeed has never produced, a single theologian to whom appeal can be made for a final sentence in disputed questions, as the Germans could appeal to Luther and the Presbyterians to Calvin, nor had she any such ultimate court of authority as the Counter-Reformation possessed in the Council of Trent. Possibly Hooker, had he written at the conclusion of our century, might have summed up the scattered thought of his predecessors in quasi-definitive form ; but that is conjecture, and as a matter of fact no such legislator did appear. Of this condition the apologists of the age were well aware ; they could even turn it into a boast, as when Chillingworth declared proudly that we " call no man master on the earth."

Diversity of opinion and diffusion of authority are patent on the surface of the Caroline literature. But withal an attentive student of the whole movement will be more impressed by the unity within the variety and by the steady flow of the current beneath all surface eddies towards a definite goal. What we have to look for in the ecclesiastical literature of England is not so much finality as direction ; and if this implies a degree of inconsistency among those groping for the way, such pliancy of mind in approaching the mysteries of revelation may prove safer than premature fixation. The finished system of Calvin fell into ruins as soon as a single flaw was detected in its chain of logic, and a single discrepancy between fact and theory may bring the " fundamentalism " [1] of Rome to the same doom. In Aubrey de Vere's account of his conversion to Rome there is a passage that bears on this point. " Carlyle," he says, " was one of those who gave me the most curious form of warning : ' I have ridden over here to tell you not to do that thing. You were born free. Do not go into that hole.' I answered : ' But you used always to tell me that the Roman Catholic Church was the only Christian body that was consistent, and could defend her position.' He replied : ' And so I say still. But the Church of England is much better notwithstanding, because her face *is turned in*

---

[1] I use this term in its modern connotation to describe those who cling to a belief in the complete inerrancy of the Bible. It signifies a position the very opposite of the Anglican instance on the " fundamentals " of faith, of which later.

*the right direction.' "* [1] The word " right " may be a begging of the question, but it was in establishing a certain " direction " and in avoiding a premature fixation that Anglican theology in its formative period showed at once its character and wisdom and its underlying consistency.

## II

If challenged to state the motive that started the Church of England on her peculiar course, the historian is likely to reply that it was political rather than religious. The first impulse towards independence was given by the Papal refusal to admit the annulment of Henry the Eighth's marriage to Catherine of Aragon, and this conflict, however much it may have concerned that monarch's taste in wives, was presented to the people as though the monarchy and national autonomy were at stake. Henry was a Catholic still. He applied the " Whip with the Six Strings " (the Six Articles) with an inquisitorial zest that must have been infinitely distressing to the cautious Cranmer. And then no sooner was the jurisdiction of the Bishop of Rome discredited than there arose a new party, influenced from Geneva, which denied the authority of all bishops whatsoever. And again the issue, as presented to the people, became confused with politics. It was henceforth the cry of the Court and the Church that episcopacy and monarchy were indissolubly bound together: No Bishop, no King! Between these opposite intrusions from the Continent the Church of England was thus directed, primarily by reasons of State, to the *via media* which has been her watchword from that day to this. And the secular aspect of the cause persisted, in somewhat changed form, until the Revolution. We see it in Sanderson's theory of ecclesiastical laws : " In this, as in many other debates, the *mean* between the two *extremes* seems to be the truer opinion, and safer to follow,"—that is the middle way between " Romanists who would exempt the clergy from all jurisdiction of the civil magistrates " and " the Puritanical Reformers, . . . who . . . take away all power, authority, and ecclesiastical jurisdiction from the Crown and confine it wholly to their own classes and conventions."

It is in the light of this thrust of civil influences from abroad that we should interpret the special form which the Erastianism of the age took in England, and should consider the disabilities imposed upon Romanist and Nonconformist alike which were not removed until well into the nineteenth century. How far Erastianism is right or wrong in principle, what should be the exact relation between Church and State, is a question still *sub judice*. It flared up after the Vatican Council between Gladstone and Newman ; it flared up again recently in a presidential election in the United States, and is ablaze now on the

---

[1] *Recollections*, p. 321. (The Italics are in the original.)

Continent of Europe. The issue is not dead. Manifestly it is not the business of the present writer to express an opinion on the peculiar form of the problem as it confronts Great Britain to-day ; but those who may care to know the natural bent of the English mind will find matter for reflection in the arguments and distinctions of the older controversialists arranged under Section XVII.

That, however, is by the way. For our purpose the point of interest is the manner in which the Church gradually disentangled her theology from these secular disputes as she became more aware of her separate mission and function. And it is characteristic of this evolution that at the beginning so much heat was expended upon what might be called the furniture of religion. To turn from the contemporary debates on the Continent over the metaphysics of faith to the bickerings in England over the adjuncts of worship is to enter a different world— to the uninstructed reader a world wherein the more spiritual aspects of the conflict are lost in matters at once petty and materialistic. But that is the Englishman's way, to talk about what lies on the surface and to avoid as long as possible the deeper concerns of the heart. At any rate, not only were the vexed problems of faith involved in the wrangling over surplices and posture, communion table and altar, but we can see them in the literature from Hooker onwards slowly coming out into the open.[1]

### III

Such quite clearly is the external origin of the *via media* which was to become the very charter of the Church. It may have begun as a protest against the political claims of Rome on the one side and the Genevan theories of State on the other. It may have looked at the outset like a shift to avoid difficulties, a *modus vivendi*, at the best a " middle way " as commended by Donne because " more convenient and advantageous than that of any other Kingdom." But behind it all the while lay a profounder impulse, pointing in a positive direction, and aiming to introduce into religion, and to base upon the " light of reason," that love of balance, restraint, moderation, measure, which from sources beyond our reckoning appears to be innate in the English temper. Thus Hooker, at the inception of the great work which opened our era, carried this principle up to that first eternal law which is no less than the nature of God Himself, and then showed how from it depends as a golden chain the second eternal law, stretching down, link by link, to the humanly devised polity of Church and State :

> " If therefore it be demanded why, God having power and
> ability infinite, the effects notwithstanding of that power are all

---

[1] This subject has been treated amply and acutely by Principal Tulloch in the Introduction to his *English Puritanism and Its Leaders.*

so limited as we see they are, the reason hereof is the end which
He hath proposed, and the law whereby His wisdom hath stinted
the effects of His power, in such sort that it doth not work infinitely,
but correspondently unto that end for which it worketh, even
' all things χρηστῶς, in most decent and comely sort,' all things in
Measure, Number, and Weight."

That is the note struck by the master musician, and it gives the key
to all that follows. We shall find Joseph Hall exalting measure as
that which guides the celestial bodies in their harmonious courses, and
as " the centre wherein all, both divine and moral philosophy meet,
the rule of life, the governess of manners, the silken string that runs
through the pearl-chain of all virtues, the very ecliptic-line under
which reason and religion move without any deviation." And Fuller,
who employs the same metaphor of the silken chord through the pearl-
chain of the virtues, is careful to explain that " moderation is not
an halting betwixt two opinions, when the thorough-believing of one
of them is necessary to salvation," nor is it mere " luke-warmness " in
matters divine, but a law and an ideal whereupon all a man's soul may
be set, even to martyrdom.

So understood, the principle of measure is at once English and
Greek. One is reminded of Aristotle's definition of the ethical mean
as both a limit and unlimited. Courage, for instance, in relation to
the vices of rashness and cowardice is a measured avoidance of excess
in either direction ; but in itself, as a motive of conduct, it has its own
direction to which there is no limit. A man cannot be too courageous ;
there is no such thing as excess of virtue. Quite consciously, as could
be shown by specific passages, the Anglican divines were expanding
this Greek precept of ethics into a spiritual law of Christianity.

The point is, that though in matters of human expediency measure
and restraint may seem to result in compromise, in the sphere of religion,
where ultimate principles are involved, they depend upon a positive
choice of direction which is intrinsically different from compromise.
And this difference can be illustrated by the heretical and the orthodox
attitude towards the primary doctrine of Christianity. Here the
Fathers were confronted by the plain fact that the Founder of their
faith was presented to them by a tradition going back to those who had
lived with Him, as at once, in some unique manner, both divine and
human, both God and man. Reason was thunderstruck by such
a paradox ; the wisdom of the schools could make nothing of it. Logic
could deal with Him as God only or as man only, and indeed as one or
the other He did so appear to the docetic or humanitarian philosophy
of Gnostics and Adoptionists. But theology was bound to discover
a path between these two exclusions ; and the great heresy, the first

to threaten the very existence of Christianity as a religion, was an attempt to explain the *via media* as a compromise.   To the Arians Christ was neither quite God nor quite man, but a something intermediary which resembled the natures of both without being purely either.   Against this plausible and seemingly reasonable escape between the horns of faith's dilemma (which in fact possessed the virtues neither of reason nor of paradox), the Church, by the Definition of Chalcedon, simply thrust its way through the middle by making the personality of the Incarnate so large as to carry with it *both* natures.[1]   Evidently in this case at least the principle of measure does not produce a diminished or half truth, but acts as a law of restraint preventing either one of two aspects of a paradoxical truth from excluding the other.   Nor is the middle way here a mean of compromise, but a mean of comprehension.

Now the dogma of the Incarnation, so conceived, is not specially Anglican, since it is held by Roman and Reformed and Anglican alike so far as they adhere to the Catholic faith—indeed, so far as they remain Christian.   The Abbé Bardy, for instance, in a work published with the full *imprimatur* of Rome, concludes his account of the early Christological controversies with just such an exposition of the *voie moyenne*, which he declares to be the criterion of Catholic orthodoxy not only for the mystery of the Incarnation, but for the Trinity and other dogmas *de fide*.[2]   The course of the Anglicans was peculiar in this, that deliberately and courageously they clung to the principle of mediation in regions of doctrine and discipline, where, as they contended, the Romanist and the radical Protestant did in fact stray aside into vicious extremes of exclusion.

If we follow this contention through its ramifications we shall find that it revolves about the nature of authority in Tradition and Scripture as bearing upon two main points :  (1) the practical distinction between fundamentals and accessories of religion, and (2) the axiomatic rejection of infallibility.

## IV

The distinction between fundamentals and accessories, or, in the more usual language of the day, between things necessary for salvation and things convenient in practice, was clearly drawn by Hooker and recurs constantly through the ensuing literature.   The fundamentals are few and revealed, the accessories are indeterminate and more or

---

[1] The reader who wishes further to consider the character of the path thus cleft may be referred to Dr. Quick's works—notably his *Liberalism, Modernism and Tradition* and his *Gospel of Divine Action.*   It is fashionable to-day to pour scorn on the Christology of Chalcedon.   But Dr. Quick in the books referred to (particularly in the latter, where he interprets the purpose of the Incarnation in terms of the twin concepts of Symbol and Instrument) seems completely to vindicate the conclusions of the Fathers.

[2] *En lisant les Pères*, 2nd ed., pp. 35 and 43.

less dependent on human invention. So Jeremy Taylor declares that the " intendment " of his discourse on *The Liberty of Prophesying* is that men should " not make more necessities than God made, which indeed are not many." For the Anglicans of the seventeenth century those few things necessary for salvation were summed up conveniently in the Creeds, particularly in the so-called Apostles' Creed. And for the truth of this Creed they appealed, as did other Christians, to the double authority of Tradition and Scripture. They held the common belief that the twelve articles of the Creed went back to the actual Apostles, each one of whom made his individual contribution to the formula, and so handed on the deposit of the faith to the keeping of successive generations. But behind the Creed, guaranteeing its truth and in general confirming the authority of tradition where right and correcting it when astray, was the sacred canon of written books. For this reason Chillingworth, while allowing due weight to tradition in its place, could speak of the Bible as the religion, and, in case of dispute, the sole religion, of Protestants. " I am fully assured," he wrote, " that God does not and therefore that men ought not to require any more of any man than this, to believe Scripture to be God's Word, to endeavour to find the true sense of it, and to live according to it." And he who looks for the plain indisputable sense of the Bible will discover that it consists, not in a complicated web of theological propositions nor in subtleties of definition, but simply in the presentation of Jesus Christ as the Son of God who was born and lived and died for the salvation of the world.

Certainly no Anglican divine of the seventeenth century, if questioned, would have admitted that faith in the Incarnation as the one thing necessary could be divested of such accessories as the Virgin Birth and the literal Ascension into heaven which are included in the Creed and based on the record of Scripture ; but three quotations, from the beginning, the middle, and the end of our period, will show how the continued emphasis on what is fundamental was leading the Church in the direction of an utter simplicity. Hooker, commenting on the text, *These things are written that ye might believe that Jesus is the Christ the Son of God*, declares that the drift of Holy Scripture is to make men wise for salvation, the Old Testament by teaching of Him Who should come, the New by teaching that the Saviour is actually come. In the same vein, and more emphatically, Cudworth asserts that " the Gospel is nothing else but God descending into the world in our form and conversing with us in our likeness," in order " that He might deify us, that is (as St. Peter expresseth it), make us *partakers of the divine Nature*." And South, carrying on and, so to speak, closing the process of simplification, affirms that the fundamentals are embraced in a single article of faith : " Jesus Christ is the Son of God."

Just how literally such statements should be taken may be a matter of debate, but the direction in which the leading divines of England were moving cannot be missed by any unprejudiced reader of the literature. And it is certain that in thus isolating the few things, or the one thing, in the Bible necessary for salvation they saw themselves placed between the two fires of Romanist and Puritan.  In their controversy with the former it was a question of tradition.  To the Anglicans the value of tradition was measured by its tenacity of the original *depositum fidei*.  It was not that they rejected the principle of development utterly, but that in matters fundamental they limited its competence to an interpretation of dogma held strictly at every step to the test of Scripture. Ussher, for instance, is definite on this point, when he denies that "any traditions should be accepted for parcels of God's word [that is as demanding implicit belief] beside the Holy Scriptures and such doctrines as are either expressly therein contained or by sound inference may be deduced from thence."  Now the admission of "sound inference" as a canon of truth may seem to transfer the weight of authority from the book itself to the interpreter of the book, but practically the issue was clear and sharp.  The quarrel with Rome was because of her practice of extending the fundamentals of faith by increments on the warrant of her own inspired authority, and so of creating, as it were, instead of obeying tradition.  South was voicing the common view of all Protestants when he made the specific charge : "The Church of Rome has (in this respect) sufficiently declared the little value she has for the old Christian Truth, by the *new, upstart* articles she has added to it."  And Newman was merely repeating what he had learned from he Caroline divines when he criticized the Council of Trent and the Creed of Pope Pius IV, because, "after adding to it [*i.e.* to the Apostles' Creed] the recognition of the seven Sacraments, Transubstantiation, Purgatory, the Invocation of Saints, Image-worship, and Indulgences, the Romanist declares, 'This true Catholic Faith, *out of which no one can be saved*, . . . do I promise, vow, and swear . . . most constantly to retain and confess, whole and inviolate, to the last breath of life.'" [1]

We have seen how a modern Roman Catholic apologist applies the law of the *voie moyenne* to the Christological formula drawn up at Chalcedon. There is in the same author an eloquent passage [2] in which he shows how the Catholic of to-day is united by the long continuity of tradition with the ancient Fathers, holding the same articles of faith, worshipping in essentially the same forms, employing many of the same words to express the deeper emotions of his heart before the majesty of God.  It is a stirring appeal to the imagination intended to enforce

---

[1] *Prophetical Office of the Church*, 1st ed., p. 268.  The words in italics contain the real sting of the charge.

[2] Bardy, *op. cit.*, pp. 50 ff.

the attraction of Rome as against the aridity of the merely Protestant service. But reading it, one asks what, if these pages had fallen under his eyes, would have been the response of an Anglican Protestant of the seventeenth century, who claimed also to be genuinely Catholic, to whom the unsurrendered memories of the past were as the very breath of life, and who was passionately devoted to the liturgy and forms of adoration so marvellously transferred to his own native tongue in the Prayer Book. Certainly he would have been moved by the nobility of the French Abbé's sentiment; certainly he would have accepted the perpetuity of tradition as a power that confirms the truth, while it enhances the grace and poetry, of worship; but with equal certainty he would have contended that the obstinate retention by Rome of discordant elements added in the darker ages enveloped the core of truth to such an extent as to obscure what had been handed down from the beginning. To the Roman apologist for continuity he might have uttered the Virgilian retort: *Sic vos non vobis !*

In their repudiation of the Roman efforts to cover her dogmatic innovations under the authority of tradition, and in their insistence on the Bible as the sole final criterion of orthodoxy, the Anglicans stood with the Protestants; but on the other side they departed from the Reformers of the Continent and from the Puritans at home in their rejection of what they regarded as an illegitimate extension of Scriptural authority. Again it was a question of fundamentals and accessories. Certain inferences from the central dogma of the Incarnation they allowed as self-evident, even in a way as essential to the faith that saves; but they hesitated over, and with the passing of time drew back more resolutely from, the doctrines of absolute predestination, effectual calling, justification by faith alone, imputed righteousness, and the whole scaffolding of rationalized theology which Luther and Calvin had constructed about the central truth out of an unbalanced exposition of isolated texts. Not that way lay the simplicity of the faith.

Also, and even more unhesitatingly, they followed Hooker in his protest against the Puritan denunciation of all the accessories of ritual and discipline for which specific warrant could not be found in Scripture. Here they stood with Rome in so far as they would admit the immense value of tradition in much that was vital to religious observance, though it might not be necessary to salvation.

The true thread of continuity, the Anglicans held, was broken either by superimposing new and disputable dogmas upon the divine revelation after the manner of Rome, or by disallowing due weight in the practical sphere of religion to the wisdom of accumulated human experience after the manner of Geneva.

## V

Closely connected with the distinction between fundamentals and accessories was the axiomatic denial of infallibility. One of the surprises awaiting a student of the ecclesiastical literature of the seventeenth century is the frequency with which this word " infallibility " occurs in unexpected places. It was the veritable bugbear of the English mind of that age as it has become again since the Vatican Council, and upon the attitude to all that is conveyed by those fatal syllables hangs the ultimate philosophic difference, or let us say incompatibility of temper, between Roman and Anglican Catholicism and, in a fashion less sharply defined, between radical and Anglican Protestantism. " Two things there are," says Hooker, " which trouble greatly these later times : one that the Church of Rome cannot, another that Geneva will not, err." And in a sweeping assertion Hales sums up the Anglican position thus : " Infallibility either in judgement, or interpretation, or whatsoever, is annext neither to the See of any Bishop, nor to the Councils, nor to the Church, nor to any created power whatsoever." Now such a statement, which might be supplemented by quotations from other and more authoritative, at least more Catholic writers, if taken superficially would seem to leave religion a prey to the universal flux of uncertainty ; but not if full weight be given to the phrase " created power." Evidently this does not exclude from infallibility those necessary truths which proceed directly from a divine and uncreated source. What Hales had in mind is exactly the addition to these fundamentals by tradition or their expansion by reason. So Laud, replying to the Romanists' usurpation of the text, *I will send you the Spirit of Truth, which will lead you into all truth*, is quite explicit : " ' All ' is not always universally taken in Scripture. Nor is it here simply for ' all truth ' ; for then a General Council could no more err in matter of fact than in matter of faith, in which yet yourselves grant it may err. But ' into all truth ' is a limited ' all ' : ' into all truth absolutely necessary to salvation.' . . . A Church may err, and dangerously too, and yet not fall from the foundation." On the same ground Chillingworth drew his distinction between " being *infallible in fundamentals* and being an *infallible guide in fundamentals*," and adds, " that there shall be always a Church infallible in fundamentals, we easily grant ; for it comes to no more but this, *that there shall be always a Church*."

Taking together then the two axioms in regard to fundamentals and infallibility, we can see that the Anglicanism of the seventeenth century comes to something like this : The means divinely ordained for the salvation of mankind is plainly set forth in the Bible in the story of the birth and life and death and resurrection of Jesus

Christ, the Son of God. This truth, as Chillingworth maintained, is
of such " admirable simplicity "—though its simplicity and plainness
rather enhance than diminish its significance—as to need no inspired
interpreter. But there are recorded in the same book other facts
and doctrines, a vast body enveloping, so to speak, the central truth,
which, however great their importance, are not necessary to salvation,
and do not open their meaning so immediately. For the interpreting
of these secondary truths, and for the drawing of inferences therefrom,
upon which rests the whole structure of disputable theology, there is
no oracular organ of infallibility appointed among men or in any human
institution. This distinction is made clearly by Chillingworth in
words that might be taken as the charter of Anglican liberalism :
" Though we pretend not to certain means of not erring in interpreting
all Scripture, particularly such places as are obscure and ambiguous,
yet this, methinks, should be no impediment but that we may have
certain means of not erring in and about the sense of those places
which are so plain and clear that they need no interpreters ; and in such
we say our Faith is contained." The Anglicans believed and declared
that, however the human mind might go astray in its efforts to interpret
and unfold the whole mystery of God's economy of salvation, yet by
the office of the Holy Ghost the truth in its simplicity should not be
lost or ever utterly obscured, and the Church as the instrument of
Grace should not fail from the earth.

## VI

At this point the Anglican attitude towards infallibility raises a
question to which only a tentative answer can be given, in accordance
with one's notion of what was implicit in the direction of Caroline
theology. All branches of the Church in the seventeenth century
held the Bible to be infallibly inspired by God ; if, then, the more
liberal of the Anglicans at that time had been faced by the results of
modern Biblical scholarship, how would they have reacted ? Popes,
they knew, were against Popes, Councils against Councils, some
Fathers against others, age against age ; what then if they had been
compelled to extend this *sic et non* to the ultimate source of all authority,
and to admit that the Bible also was a " created power " and therefore
to the same degree and in the same manner subject to error ? Practically, indeed, they had come very close to such an admission,—how
close we can see from Chillingworth's admission that the Bible, though
*infallible in fundamentals* is not an *infallible guide in fundamentals*. The
distinction was directed against the claim of Rome that she was the
inspired guardian and unerring interpreter of Scripture. But its
implications go beyond any such purpose of apology ; for quite mani-

festly in practice an oracle that offers no infallible guide to its meaning
is itself for any who consult it fallible.　So far Chillingworth, and those
for whom he spoke, would have been driven by the force of logic to go.
But would they have yielded the next step?　Would they, in submission to the evidence of critical examination, have been ready to
acknowledge inconsistencies and contradictions in the Bible itself as a
" created power," while yet holding fast to the belief that it contains
the record of a fundamental truth upon which the assurances of faith
may be built?　This is not an idle question.　Upon an affirmative
answer to it depends the identity of the Anglican spirit as manifested
in that day and in ours.　Thus much is at stake, namely whether
the Church can be said to have moved in a straight direction, whether,
in a word, it is proper to speak of any such thing as Anglicanism.

Now no one is likely to dispute the statement that the eighteenth
century failed in the main to carry on the line of development indicated
by Hooker and Laud and Beveridge and Ken, and historians have
pretty well agreed in holding the significance of the Oxford Movement
to be exactly this, that it brought theology back to the path from which
it had deviated in the arid intervening years.　The renewed emphasis
on the Church as a divine institution, on the continuity of the Catholic
tradition as overleaping the more radical and destructive elements of
the Reformation, the enrichment of public worship, and the deepening
of individual religious experience,—these were common to the leaders
of the Movement, and they were a deliberate regression to the seventeenth century.　All this abides, and Newman's part in the great
*instauratio ecclesiae* will not be forgotten.　But it may still be asked
whether in the thought of him who is by common consent the greatest
of the Tractarians there were not also certain traits which would
have diverted the Church from its true course, had they completely
dominated the Movement as they finally did prevail in his own life.

The question first arises as to whether Newman's *Prophetical
Office of the Church*, avowedly a defence of the Anglican *via media*,
was conceived in loyalty to the spirit of the Caroline divines.　So the
author thought it to be, and on the face of it the animus of the book
would appear to support his view.　The attack on Romanism is powerful, indeed in places unmeasured if not virulent.　In no modern work
will one find a more eloquent exposition of the Anglican attitude
towards fundamentals and infallibility.　In the chapters dealing directly
with these subjects he speaks with a philosophical consistency and
clarity to which the older theologians seldom attained.　Under the
influence of Butler he even went beyond what the seventeenth century
would have granted in its revolt from the pretensions of infallibility.
" We, for our part," he declares categorically, " have been taught to
consider that faith in its degree as well as conduct, must be guided by

probabilities, and that doubt is ever our portion in this life." Nevertheless there are passages in the book which awaken a suspicion that his apology for Anglicanism was dictated more by affection (a perfectly sincere sentiment) for the Communion of his birth than by the native propension of his mind, and that his hostility to Rome was caused in part by misunderstanding and in part by an unconscious impulse of self-defence. And this apprehension is confirmed by his attitude towards the higher criticism of the Bible which was before very many years to trouble the sleepy conscience of the Church.

Now historically considered Newman's conservatism may not be of much importance, since it was shared by most of his countrymen. But one gets the impression that his " fundamentalism " (in the modern, not the Caroline, sense of the word) was not due to ignorance of German, and would have been as strong were he living to-day as it was in the mid-nineteenth century ; that it was in fact symptomatic of a deep-seated craving for the support of an absolute external authority which, from the beginning and despite all his protests, he was dimly conscious of needing for his faith. It is significant that in the *Prophetical Office*, after his large, if not too large, concessions to probability, after his dismission of " the claim of infallibility " as " an expedient [*i.e.* a cunning device of Rome] for impressing strongly upon the mind the necessity of hearing and of obeying the Church," he proceeds to plead for an infallible organ of authority, compounded of " Scripture, Antiquity, and Catholicity," of which the Church of England is the sacred custodian. It is a disputable thesis, but one for which a good case might be made, that Newman, deep down in his heart, was never in full sympathy with the liberal spirit of the seventeenth century, and that the Oxford Movement, so far as it was swayed by his genius, has not been without danger of leading the Church away from the line of its normal development.

Certainly at least any one who comes fresh from reading the Caroline divines to Gore and the other essayists of *Lux Mundi* will feel that here, rather than in Newman, he has picked up again the straight continuity of direction. That book of essays is not final, it is rather a new beginning ; but in its determination to face the results of increased knowledge (particularly as shown by the editor in his Preface to the tenth edition), and in its frank extension of fallibility to the Bible, while insisting on the Personality of Christ and on the Incarnation as the fundamental dogma on which the whole fabric of Christianity rests, one breathes again that air of larger freedom which frightened Newman into the prison-house of absolutism. It would be interesting, if space permitted, to show in detail how exultantly the leaders of Anglican thought since the appearance of *Lux Mundi* have responded to this reacquired note of intellectual liberty. We know what has happened in the other great branches of the Church. The Roman Curia has condemned both the good and the bad of " modernism " unflinchingly and, it would seem, irredeemably. For their part the radical Protestants have either clung to an impossible theory of Scriptural inerrancy, and so have put themselves hopelessly out of court, or else, bowing to the results of the higher criticism, have seen their faith in the fundamentals of religion go down in ruins along with their anti-catholic bibliolatry. With the recent literature of " fundamentalism " on the one side and of the *liberalische Theologie* (I use the phrases technically) on the other side one need only compare such works, to name a few out of many, as *Essays Catholic and Critical*, Canon Quick's *Christian Sacraments*, Sir Edwyn Hoskyns' and Mr. Noel Davey's *Riddle of the New Testament*, Dr. K. E. Kirk's *Vision of God*, Prof. A. E. Taylor's *Faith of a Moralist*, and the more recent essays on *Northern Catholicism*, to see the advantage of this line of the *via media* upon which the Church of England started out more than three centuries ago.

## VII

Looking backwards, then, upon the theology of the Caroline divines, we can see that their manifest intention was to steer a middle course between the excesses of Romanist and Radical Protestant. Clearly also such a middle course was not in the nature of compromise or of hesitation to commit themselves to conviction, but was governed by a positive determination to preserve the just balance between fundamentals and accessories which was threatened by an authority vested in the infallibility whether of Tradition or of Scripture. So far there can be no doubt in regard to the guiding principle of the Anglican *via media*. And at this point, if our sense of direction be right, we may venture upon a further step in definition, in the light of the continuity of the two movements instituted by Hooker and Gore. Here indeed we must proceed warily. But if we are looking for a single term to denote the ultimate law of Anglicanism, I do not see that we can do better than adopt a title which offers itself as peculiarly descriptive, despite the unsavoury repute it may have acquired from its usurpation by certain modern sects of philosophy ; I refer to the title " pragmatism." The self-styled " pragmatist " of to-day is commonly one who, pretending to eschew what he regards as unverifiable theory, limits his assent to " facts," and whose criterion of fact is " that which works "—works, that is, by the test of *physical* experience. But etymologically there is no reason why the word " pragmatism " should be so narrowed in its meaning as to include only one half of human experience. Rightly understood it may be said that among philosophers Plato was the supreme pragmatist, in so far as he sought to defend his belief in " Ideas " as facts more real than the objects of nature by showing that there, is a spiritual intuition larger, deeper, more positive and trustworthy, more truly scientific, than the clamorous rout of physical sensations. And by the same token there is no reason why we should shrink from describing the genius of Anglicanism as supremely pragmatic.

Such a pragmatism, then, if the word be allowed and if the more recent theology since the publication of *Lux Mundi* be the true heir and interpreter of the Caroline age, would come to this. Let us consider some questions. In the first place did the person Jesus ever live, was He born as our records assert and did He suffer death on the Cross? Secondly, did He, again as the records assert, think and speak of Himself as the Messiah, the Son of God? Now these, plainly, are questions of simple history the answer to which depends on the weighing of documentary evidence, exactly as in the case of any other recorded event of the past. So far the truth of the narrative may be granted without committing one's self to any supernatural creed. The real problem of Christianity begins with a question of a different order: When Jesus thought and spoke of Himself as the Messiah, the Son of God, was He what He proclaimed Himself to be or was He suffering a delusion? This also comes down to a simple question of fact, *pragma*, as do finally all questions of truth; but quite obviously the answer is to be sought otherwise than in the mere weighing of documentary evidence. We have passed from the province of history to that of philosophy and religion. All Christians of course believe in the actuality of this fact. If the Anglican differs from the Romanist or the radical Protestant, it is because more definitely and consciously than either he justifies his belief by the pragmatic test of experience, namely: " Does it work? " It is not that he rejects authority for an unchecked individualism; he sees that his personal experience is no more than a fragment of the larger experience of mankind, and must be controlled at every step by that accumulation of wisdom which is the voice of the Church. What he rejects is the Absolute of authority based on *a priori* theories of infallibility. Rather, looking within and without, he asks the consequences of believing or not believing. How does acceptance of the dogma of the Incarnation work out in practice? Does faith bring with it any proof of its objective validity?

Now pragmatism of this sort may seem to leave religion exposed to the shifting winds of human opinion, and, not to mention the charges brought against the Church of England by infallibilists of both branches, we have seen how Newman in his Anglican days confessed that faith must be guided by probabilities and that doubt is always our portion in this life. But Newman, it may be maintained, was here under a mistaken notion of the function and scope of probability, a mistake which helps to explain his later defection from the body he was defend-

3

ing. Historic evidence can never rise above the probable, though unprejudiced scholarship can and does say that the external evidence for Jesus' own avowed pretensions to the Messianic rôle is so convincing as to leave no sound warrant for doubt. But it does not follow that the pragmatic test of our faith in Jesus as in very truth the Incarnate Word is subject to the same conditions. Except in those cases of miraculously sudden conversion, of which the Anglican is temperamentally suspicious, though he would not deny their occasional happening, it may be that the Christian convert must begin with the probabilities with which history ends. It may be that he will never attain to that ecstasy of immediate knowledge claimed by the mystics, of which again the Anglican is inclined by nature to be sceptical. But, quickly or slowly, the experiment of believing may pass into experience, and the result of experience may be of such a kind as to bring the believer, however incapable he may be of convincing others, to a sure conviction that he has chosen the right way. He may come to know by effects which leave for him no doubt of their cause that the Christ in whom he trusts is not dead but living, and that faith has brought him into touch with fact. Nor is it arrogant to suggest that the Anglican insistence on distinguishing the fundamentals, or the one fundamental, of Christian theology may help to clarify this fundamental of Christian experience. At any rate the pragmatist may be aware of the working of divine Grace and certified of revelation, and this without leaning for support on the theory of an oracular infallibility committed to any visible organ of speech. Such, very nearly, would appear to be the meaning of Chillingworth in his retort upon the Romanists:

> "You content not yourselves with a moral certainty of the things you believe, nor with such a degree of assurance of them as is sufficient to produce obedience to the condition of the new Covenant, which is all that we require. God's spirit, if He please, may work more, a certainty of adherence beyond a certainty of evidence; but neither God doth, nor man may, require of us as our duty to give a greater assent to the conclusion than the premises deserve." [1]

## VIII

But perhaps the full force of the word pragmatic as applied to the Church of England can be seen even better in her attitude towards the priesthood and its sacramental function. We may concede that the Anglicans, particularly at the early stage of the controversy over

---

[1] Compare the statement of Professor Williams in *Northern Catholicism*, p. 233: " The final and clinching proof of Christian truth, which raises ' probability ' to *certainty*, for intellectual and simple alike, lies in its verification through first-hand experience of God in Christ, and of Christ in the Church and the Sacraments." That, I take it, is in the line, the direction, from Hooker through Gore.

the eucharistic sacrifice, rather shunned the term "priest" and even went so far as to deny that a "minister" should in any true sense be so called. This Hooker declares explicitly; and the "pious and profoundly learned Joseph Mede" defines "priest" as the English for *presbyter*, not *sacerdos*, as being a "minister" rather than a "sacrificer." It is fair, however, to add that the direction of Anglican theology was towards a more Catholic, even a more Roman view; and Hickes, in his monumental treatise on *The Christian Priesthood Asserted* (which as the work of a Non-Juror falls out of our period), was in the true line of development from Laud and Cosin and Thorndike.

But the acuteness of the debate centred not so much on the priesthood itself as on the various orders of ministry, more especially on the episcopate. Here, as we have seen, the Anglicans held primarily to a view that might be regarded as a sort of compromise. With Rome they adhered to the historic authority of bishops against the immoderate hostility of the Protestants to any distinction of orders; while at the same time they stood with the Reformation in disavowing the equally immoderate pretensions of the Bishop of Rome. The pragmatic note is felt in the kind of arguments by which they defended their medial position. Here indeed we encounter some differences in method. Certain controversialists contend that the distinct order of the episcopate can be justified by statements in the Bible; others, including notably Hooker, prefer to base their defence on the usage of sub-apostolic antiquity and on the continuous tradition of the Church since then. But in either case their ultimate appeal is to expedience and thus " pragmatic," though pragmatic in the sense that the values discovered by practice are spiritual as well as physical. It is in harmony with such arguments that the most convinced Episcopalians hesitated to rank the Divine origin of episcopacy among the *credenda*; and thus it was a common opinion among them that the Protestant communions on the Continent, which possessed no bishops at all, or at best no unbroken succession of bishops, should not for that reason be denied their place as a true, though errant, branch of the Church Universal. But they were insistent on the demonstrably historic fact that the integrity of the Church has been sustained chiefly by the recognition of episcopal authority, and their vast scholarship was nowhere better displayed than in their fierce rebuttal of the Roman efforts to deprive the English Church of its catholicity by discovering flaws in the consecration of the Elizabethan bishops. Very definitely they held that the spiritual function of the priesthood was proved by experience to depend for its higher and purer efficacy on the Apostolic Succession of the bishops. And from this pragmatic argument they could go on to infer that episcopacy, even though devised by man rather than commanded by revelation, was sanctioned by Providence to be the means of preserving the Church as the channel of Grace.

Whatever uncertainty may hover about the earlier conception of the priesthood there was practical unanimity in regard to the importance of the Eucharist administered by sacerdotal hands. Here, plainly, was a fundamental of religion which, standing parallel with the Incarnation, is the prime factor in the sacramental function of the Church as that is of its dogmatic theology; or, rather, it might be said that the two are not so much parallel factors as twin aspects of the one divine economy of salvation. The Anglicans widely admitted the " real presence," not corporal but spiritual, of the body and blood of Christ in the Eucharist. In so far, they tended away from Reformation Eucharistic theology towards the Objectivism of Rome. But in a different respect, namely in their emphasis on the need for the coöperation of faith in the communicant, they leaned towards the Protestant position. In regard to the spiritual fact behind the Eucharistic rite they were thus in the line of the *via media* between the extremes, to speak locally, of Rome and Zürich, and their departure from the one might be measured by their comprehension of the other. The radical difference from both appears when we touch the question of theory.

In so far as the Anglicans theorized at all about the *how* of the Sacrament, the prevalent view would seem to have followed Calvin and one side of St. Augustine in using the language of dynamic or instrumental symbolism. The physical participation, as Hooker expresses it, is " instrumentally a cause of that mystical participation "; and a favourite metaphor for the symbolic power of the consecration was to liken the elements to a legal document before and after the attachment of the royal seal. But they were not entirely coherent or, one gathers, very deeply concerned in such explanations. Hooker avowedly adopts his instrumentalism as a kind of common denominator upon which Lutheran and Roman and Anglican might agree in peace, since it " hath in it nothing but what the rest do all approve." And in general such theories, when they occur, have the air of half-hearted attempts to find a substitute for the Tridentine dogma of transubstantiation, which is denounced quite whole-heartedly as bad theology and bad philosophy and as a legacy of error under which the Roman Church, owing to its presumption of infallibility, must stagger on for ever. Oftener and more characteristically the Anglican theologians refused *on principle* to theorize at all on the how of sacramental efficacy. So Andrewes: " Christ said, *This is My body*; He did not say, This is My body in this way." So Ussher, scorning the untenable metaphysics of Trent, declares that the real presence must be left an inexplicable mystery. And Bramhall sums up the whole contention with the theorists of either party, Roman or Protestant, finally and definitely.

We know not, he insists, whether the real presence is by transubstantiation or consubstantiation, by production or conservation or adduction or assumption; and he quotes the great dictum attributed to Durandus of Troarn : *Motum sentimus, modum nescimus, praesentiam credimus.*

Why God should choose this special channel of sacramental grace we know not, any more than we know why His eternal purpose for the redemption of mankind should have necessitated the awful fact of the Incarnation; how the sacrament works we know not any more than we know how the death of His Son is made the instrument of eternal life. In such matters we are brought face to face with the causes and operation of Providence which reach up into the vast, transcendental, all-surrounding circle of the supernatural. But we do know by experience (*motum sentimus*) what faith and practice effect in our own souls. Here is not a reckoning of probabilities, but an immediate impress of reality growing ever from less to more distinctness; and, perceiving that the eucharistic elements do so operate, we believe in a supernatural power imparted to them (*praesentiam credimus*).

This is the pragmatic argument from effect to cause which permeates the theology of Anglicanism. Not only in the seventeenth century but from the time of Henry VIII to the present day, if there is any outstanding note of the English temper it is a humility of awe before the divine mysteries of faith and a recognition of the incompetence of language to define the ultimate paradox of experience. It is a pragmatism not of the lips only, as with the scholastics of the past or the present, but from a deep conviction that the rationalization of the supernatural is always in danger of pushing on to a formula which magnifies one half of the truth to an Absolute by excluding the other half. As Cudworth, one of the most metaphysical of the Caroline theologians, expressed it, "neither are we able to inclose in words and letters the life, soul, and essence of any spiritual truth, and as it were to incorporate it in them."

It is not fanciful to say that in the Anglican writers of the seventeenth century we find the Chalcedon of eucharistic theology. The perils alike of transubstantiation and receptionism are avoided: the one because it implies a docetic view of the divine operation in the Eucharist utterly inconsistent with that operation in the sacramental processus considered as a whole; the other because it points to what in the language of the present day might be called sacramental epiphenomenalism. And here again, as in the Christology of Chalcedon, the middle way is not compromise; it is direction.[1]

[1] To see how this direction has been carried on in Anglican Eucharistic theology compare the contribution of Will Spens to *Essays Catholic and Critical* ; O. C. Quick, *The Christian Sacraments*; the *Report of the Anglo-Catholic Congress*, 1927; the Report of the Farnham Conference on *Reservation*, 1925; and F. C. N. Hicks, *The Fullness of Sacrifice*.

## IX

It may appear to some who have followed this essay in its endeavour, admittedly tentative, to get at the principles directing the course of the Anglican Church that the outcome is a " diminished " Christianity. Such was not the intention of the essayist.   Nor is it the belief of the joint editors of this volume.   Rather, as they have collected these documents from the stalwart divinity of a past age, they have been impressed by the richness and depth and beauty of the religious life to which that literature as a whole bears witness.   In particular they have discovered no trace of " diminution " in a theology which aimed at separating the accretions to the faith from the dogmas necessary for salvation.   It might seem that in so insisting on the kernel of truth as distinguished from its accessories, the Church was playing into the hands of a Lord Herbert of Cherbury and the others who were laying the foundation of deism upon an elemental set of beliefs which, as they supposed, were common to all the religions of the world ; and it cannot be denied that after the schism of the Non-Jurors a portion of the established Church fell for a time under the chilling sway of that movement.   But in reality the refrigeration of the eighteenth-century theologians was owing to their loss of grip on the very dogma which their predecessors had singled out.   The fact of the Incarnation, with its corollary in the Sacramental life, was the one thing that could find no place in the five points of Lord Herbert's universal religion and that was inimical to the whole trend of deism,—as it is to the kindred " religiosity " of the present day.   As for the caviller vho would admit this distinction yet would criticize the Anglican position as tending to narrow the scope of Christianity, it may be proper to ask whether he has ever really considered the infinite riches of the Incarnation and the Eucharist, their inexhaustible meaning, the depth and breadth of their transforming power upon conduct and character, the glory of their promise.   The Anglicans were here in the great tradition of antiquity ; they, as Cudworth and others knew, were but taking up the doctrine of Irenaeus and Athanasius : ὁ Θεὸς γέγονεν ἄνθρωπος, ἵνα ἡμᾶς ἐν ἑαυτῷ θεοποιήσῃ.   Concentration may bring gain rather than loss ; to intensify may be to move towards more of strength and certainty.   We can remember the words of Christ Himself, His last perhaps upon the Cross : *It is finished.*   It was the utter simplicity of the Christian faith concentrated upon an act of God's merciful condescension that inspired one of the most modern and most Caroline of George Herbert's poems :

Could not that wisdom which first broach'd the wine
    Have thicken'd it with definitions ?
And jagg'd His seamless coat, had that been fine,
    With curious questions and divisions ?

But all the doctrine which He taught and gave,
    Was clear as heav'n from whence it came,
At least those beams of truth which only save,
    Surpass in brightness any flame.

It was a favourite thesis of Baron von Hügel that the English Church, with all its excellencies, has failed in producing the variety and depth of the saintly life to be found within the Roman Communion. And this in a manner may be conceded. Naturally, in the matter of variety, it could not be expected that Christianity manifested through the temperament of a single people at a given time should produce as many different types of holiness as a Communion embracing a number of divergent nationalities. But if one will compare the lives in Walton with, let us say, the biographies of contemporary saints and mystics of a neighbouring country collected by Abbé Bremond, it is not at all clear that the advantage lies with Roman Catholicism. And if to the little group commemorated in Walton's inimitable pages one adds Andrewes and Barrow and Taylor and Traherne and Henry More and Sir Thomas Browne and Ken, one will have a striking variety ranging through the man of prayer, the great scholar, the golden-mouthed orator, the romantic dreamer, the Platonic idealist, the devout physician, and the irreproachable prelate.

We may grant that among them all there is no one who stirs the poetic imagination quite as does St. Francis of Assisi. But, in the first place, such a character as St. Francis, coming before the Reformation, does in a sense belong to England of the seventeenth century almost as much as to France or Catholic Germany of the same age ; for the Anglicans, though in the heat of controversy they may have spoken uncharitably of Romanism, did not forget that, as Hooker reminded the Puritans, their fathers had served God and found salvation in communion with the Pope. And secondly they might say, or we may say for them, that, though a St. Francis could scarcely be expected in England at any time, neither could a Hooker or a Ken be imagined in Italy. One star differs from another in glory, and the galaxy of English saints sheds a light very precious for the world.

It might even be argued with plausibility that the saintly type of the future, as the mediatorial work of Christ is better understood, will conform rather to the Anglican than to the medieval model. Anglicanism will never become formally the religion of the world, nor has Canterbury any ambition to usurp the place claimed by Rome ; but there is reason to believe that a liberal *ethos* of Christianity, resembling that developed by Englishmen in their clear-eyed opposition to the pseudo-antiquity of the Reformation and to the tenacious medievalism of the Counter-Reformation, will more and more prevail in the Holy Catholic Church. The image of the Anglican branch of that brotherhood, rising before a mind imbued in the literature from which the following documents are compiled, is of one that *rejoiceth as a giant to run his course.*

# ANGLICANISM IN THE SEVENTEENTH CENTURY

BY

## FELIX R. ARNOTT

# I

On March 24th, 1603, Queen Elizabeth passed to her rest. For forty-five years she had ruled autocratically; but by force of character she had made England strong, and won the favour of all classes of the English nation. Her dying words,—" Far above all earthly treasure I esteem my people's love,"—were typical of her ideals. Just over a month later she was buried beside her unhappy sister in that magnificent chapel at Westminster which had been raised by the piety, and the extortions, of the first of her dynasty. Whitgift, the Archbishop of Canterbury, conducted the funeral service, and Andrewes, the Dean of the Abbey, preached the sermon. Ten years afterwards, in an anniversary sermon preached at St. Paul's Cross, Joseph Hall paid fitting tribute to her memory :—" O, Blessed Queen, the mother of this nation, the nurse of this Church, the glory of womanhood, the envy and example of foreign nations, the wonder of times; how sweet and sacred shall thy memory be to all posterities! . . . And though the foul mouths of our adversaries stick not to call her *miseram feminam*, as Pope Clement did . . . yet, as we say, she never prospered so well as when she was most cursed by their Pius V." [1]

With the passing of the great Queen, there passed also a completed era of English History. Henry VII had succeeded to the throne of a country in which feudal government had broken down under the stress of internal warfare. The new learning, which had followed upon the capture of Constantinople by the Saracens in 1453, had changed the whole character of European thought and art. Close in its train had followed the Reformation, and the Sixteenth Century throughout its course had been an age of turmoil and uneasiness both in politics and religion. But the first years of the Seventeenth Century inaugurated a new epoch. The spirit of mediæval England gradually yielded before a more philosophical point of view, and Bacon, Burton and Hobbes are the typical thinkers of the new era. The adventurous seamen and the chivalrous courtiers of earlier days found a fresh outlet for their enterprise in a whole-hearted devotion to commerce, the pursuit of which has earned England the gibes and the jealousy of many other countries. After the defeat of the Spanish Armada had ended any danger of foreign invasion, James I found himself at the head of a country which the genius of Wolsey and his successors had raised to a

[1] Strype, *Annals of the Reformation*, Vol. IV, Doc. cclxx.

first-class power. Indeed, it was now even possible to hope for a marriage alliance between the royal houses of England and Spain.

The new policy of government in Church as well as in State is admirably represented in the position taken up by the " judicious " Richard Hooker in his *Ecclesiastical Polity*. Hooker succeeded in rescuing theological controversy from the filth of the market place, and investing it with a new and dignified splendour. When we pass from the scurrility of the Marprelate Tracts to Hooker's breadth of religious vision, we find ourselves in an altogether different *milieu*, where bickering about *minutiae* has given place to the reasoned examination of principles.[1] In his writings we can trace the germ of the characteristic Anglican doctrine of *aurea mediocritas* laid down against the claims of both Rome and Geneva. Hallam justly described the *Ecclesiastical Polity* as the first great original prose work in our language, pointing out that its author " not only opened the mine, but explored the depths of our native eloquence." [2] The *Polity* formed the stylistic basis on which most of the later divines built, and its long and straightforward periods are constantly re-echoed in the magnificent language of the Authorized Translation of the Bible. Hooker's spirit permeated almost all that was best in subsequent English religious thought, and his ideas were worked out to their full conclusions by Andrewes, Laud and Sanderson; for it was his task *serere arbores, quae alteri saeculo prosint*. His fame penetrated even the walls of the Vatican itself, as Pope Clement VIII's eloquent eulogy of the *Ecclesiastical Polity* testifies. " There is no learning that this man hath not searched into, nothing too hard for his understanding. . . . His books will get reverence by age, for there are in them such seeds of eternity, that, if the 'rest be like this, they shall last till the last fire shall consume all learning." [3]

The Seventeenth-Century divines grew up and flourished in a period of great artistic activity. The same year that saw James VI of Scotland become James I of England saw also William Shakespeare writing the tragedy of *Hamlet*, Francis Bacon receiving a knighthood for his *Essays*—the first edition of which had been published in 1597— and John Donne, then a young Oxford student, composing some of the sweetest of English love lyrics. The flower of poetry blossomed abundantly throughout the Seventeenth Century; and though the splendour of John Milton has tended to overshadow the work of his contemporaries, it must not be forgotten that many of them wrote poetry of the highest quality, especially in the sphere of lyrical verse.

In the realm of music, Orlando Gibbons carried on the great tradi-

---

[1] On Hooker, cp. especially F. Paget, *An Introduction to the Fifth Book of Hooker's Treatise of the Laws of Ecclesiastical Polity*, 1899.
[2] Hallam, *Constitutional History*, Vol. I, ch. iv.
[3] Quoted in Anthony Wood, *Athenae Oxonienses*, ed. 1691, Vol. I, p. 262. Walton, *Life of Hooker*, ed. 1927, p. 212.

tion of madrigals and motets inherited from Tallis and Merbecke, both of whom had died some twenty years before the century opened.   The Puritans strongly objected to music, especially when played by the organ, and we find Prebendary Peter Smart [1] indicting John Cosin for erecting two organs in Durham Cathedral and causing them to be played during the administration of the Lord's Supper.   The Puritans would consent to sing the Psalms only if transposed into doggerel verse, and there is a striking absence of really great hymns written during this century.   In opposition to Puritan attacks we find John Gauden [2] writing in praise of music : " If there be not music in Heaven, sure there is a kind of heaven in music. . . . Certainly music is of all sensible human beauty the most harmless and divine.   Nor did I ever see any reason why it should be thought to deform us Christians, or be wholly excluded from making a part in the beauty of holiness."   With the appointment of Henry Purcell as organist of Westminster Abbey in 1680, English music found its full vindication, and flourished more splendidly than it has ever done until the dawn of the present century.

Similarly, the art of painting, which had lain dormant since the days of Holbein, was given fresh inspiration from the visit of Sir Anthony Van Dyck, who first came to London in 1621.   In 1626 he was followed by his master, Peter Paul Rubens, as an ambassador from the King of France.   The new influence speedily revealed itself in the work of the Royalist painters, William Dobson and Godfrey Kneller, and there were thus sown the seeds of the school of English portrait painting which was to bloom so luxuriantly in the following century.   Charles I was a liberal patron and himself an ardent collector of pictures, though his collection was dispersed, for the most part on the continent, during the Puritan régime.   Architecture in no way dallied behind the plastic arts, and this century saw the rebuilding of London on a magnificent scale. In the reign of James I Inigo Jones built the Banqueting Hall in White-hall and the pleasant Ashburnham House within the precincts of Westminster, while the Great Fire of 1666 gave Sir Christopher Wren his opportunity for crowning the city with the splendid dome of St. Paul's.   Such is the artistic background, against which we must view the lives and characters of the Seventeenth-Century divines.

The political background of the age was less exalted.   We have already remarked that Hooker found a common basis of law for both Church and State.   It was a primary consideration of Stuart policy that the Church should maintain its existence in close dependence upon the Crown.   At the head of all stood the King, whose word must be supreme both in Convocation and in Parliament.   The Tudors had acted on this hypothesis, but it was left for James I to defend such absolutism with the new philosophy of the divine prerogative of monarchy.   In a

---

[1] Cp. Document No. 254.          [2] Cp. Document No. 279.

speech to his judges in the Star Chamber, he asserted: " That which concerns the mystery of the King's power is not lawful to be disputed; for that is to wade into the weakness of princes, and to take away the mystical reverence that belongs unto them that sit in the throne of God." [1]  Such a theological basis being found for absolutism, it was only natural that the leaders of the National Church should closely ally themselves with the claims of the Crown.   At first, both Papists and Puritans expected favours from James.   But when these were withheld, the former almost at once resorted to the Gunpowder Plot; while the latter, biding their time until the autocracy of Charles' rule without a Parliament for the eleven years, 1629–1640, enabled them to disguise their revolutionary religious aspirations with the fair cloak of being defenders of English liberty, entered the Civil War with the express intention of overthrowing both the monarchy and the Anglican Church as settled by Elizabeth.   With the melancholy story of the struggle of Anglicanism against both Puritans and Romanists we shall deal in later sections.   The execution of the King in 1649 was, however, a defeat only in appearance.   Events soon revealed that the English people were determined not to submit to a pleasureless Puritanism which was every whit as tyrannical as the rule of any king.   It required but the death of Cromwell in 1658 to make even such staunch Parliamentarians as Monk and Prynne begin clamouring for the restoration of the Monarchy.

On May 29, 1660, Charles II entered London in triumph.   The exiled bishops were recalled, and William Juxon was summoned from his retirement in the little village of Chastleton in Oxfordshire to the throne of St. Augustine.   In 1661 the Savoy Conference was convened, which led in the following year to the publication of the revised Prayer Book, annexed to an Act of Uniformity.   With this Act the English Reformation may be said to have ended.   The doctrine of *aurea mediocritas* had prevailed over either extreme, and, sanctified by the blood of an archbishop and a king—the latter the only Saint she had canonized since the Reformation [2]—*Ecclesia Anglicana* had embarked on that course by which she might hope to become the " bridge Church " of all Christendom.

The years extending from the passing of the Prayer Book by Parliament on April 16, 1662, to the end of the period covered by the documents of this book is one of the sadder epochs of English Church History.   The tolerance which Charles II had promised at Breda was overshadowed by the triumphant zeal of the Church leaders and the Royalist Parliament, which proceeded to persecute Nonconformist

[1] *Works of James I* (ed. 1616), p. 557.
[2] See the discussion in W. H. Hutton, *The Influence of Christianity upon National Character, Illustrated by the Lives and Legends of the English Saints* [2], pp. 349–52.

and Papist alike.  The reign of James II (1685–88) showed Puritan iconoclasm at its worst in the acts wrought by Monmouth's soldiers in Wells Cathedral and elsewhere in the West of England; but it also proved once and for all that England would not tolerate a Catholicism which involved the acceptance of the papal claims.  On the accession of William and Mary, Archbishop Sancroft, and six bishops, including the saintly Ken of Bath and Wells and Lloyd of Norwich, refused, out of a rather narrow conception of the Oath of Allegiance which they had taken to the House of Stuart, to swear loyalty to another sovereign, and in 1691 they seceded from the Church, followed by about 400 clergy and many of the laity.  These so-called " Non-Jurors " included the very cream of the Church of England, and their schism involved a loss of piety and learning which might have proved an effective counterblast to the Latitudinarian and often semi-Deistic rationalism that characterized the Eighteenth Century.

## II

If the Civil War occupies the chief field of interest to students of English political history in the Seventeenth Century, the struggle between Anglicanism and Puritanism fills the corresponding place for the Church historian.

The Puritans met James I on his way from Scotland to London in April, 1603, with the " Millenary Petition." [1]  Compared with Cartwright's *Full and Plain Declaration of Ecclesiastical Discipline* it was a mild document.  It made no sweeping demands for a Presbyterian ministry, but merely set forth the stock objections to the Book of Common Prayer, attacking such things as the Cross at Baptism, the Ring in Matrimony, Lessons from the Apocrypha, and the wearing of the surplice.  At first James was sympathetic.  But when the University of Oxford successfully brought to his notice that the framers of the Petition were men who wished to limit the power of the Monarchy, the King's sympathies moved towards the anti-Puritan views of Whitgift, then Archbishop of Canterbury, and of Bancroft, the Bishop of London. The following January (1604) he summoned a Conference at Hampton Court, at which he took the chair himself, and thoroughly enjoyed lecturing on theology to the assembled divines.  The leaders on the Puritan side were Reynolds, the Dean of Lincoln, and Knewstubbs, a minister from Cockfield in Suffolk, while Bancroft was the fiery and uncompromising spokesman of the Bishops.  On the first day discussion centred in the usual Puritan objections to the Prayer Book and the use of excommunication, to which was added the somewhat strange subject of

---

[1] No original copy of the Petition survives.  The text is given in Fuller, *Church History* (ed. 1655, pp. 21 ff.), and in Gee-Hardy, *Documents Illustrative of History of English Church*, No. 88

the provision of clergy for Ireland.   It at once became clear, however, that the ceremonial demands of the Puritans were only a cloak for introducing into England Presbyterian government.   This discovery very quickly alienated James from the Puritan cause, and he delivered a sermon on his favourite text " No Bishop, no King," in the course of which he stated " A Scottish Presbytery . . . as well agreeth with a monarchy as God and the devil." [1]   His experience of Presbyterians in Scotland was indeed an exceedingly bitter memory.   " While I am in England," he said, " I will have bishops, for I had not been so quietly settled in my seat but for them," adding that he had " sufficiently tasted of the mischiefs thereof of a presbytery in Scotland . . . as some here in England already have begun to deal with me.   For at the first they prayed for me as supreme governor over all causes and persons, but after they began to abate their terms of my superiority." [2]

Such an attitude on the part of the King made further progress impossible, and the Conference was dismissed without any considerable results being attained other than the provision for the publication of the Authorized Translation of Holy Scripture, and the addition to the Catechism of the section on the Sacraments, probably the work of Overall, the then Dean of St. Paul's.   The Bishops for their part had decided beforehand to concede nothing, and treated the King with an almost repulsive attitude of adulation.   The petulant tone of the Conference can well be judged from a statement made by Sir John Harington, who was himself present.   " I was by and heard much discourse; the King talked much Latin and disputed with Doctor Reynolds at Hampton, but he rather used upbraidings than argument, and told the petitioners that they wanted to strip Christ again, and bid them away with their snivelling. . . . The Bishops seemed much pleased, and said his majesty spoke by the power of inspiration.   I wist not what they mean, but the Spirit was rather foul mouthed." [3]

After their rebuff at Hampton Court, the Puritans grew more open in their demands.   Matters of ritual became of secondary importance, and the struggle entered upon a more dogmatic phase.   Bancroft, an avowed opponent of Puritanism, succeeded Whitgift as Archbishop of Canterbury in 1604 ; but when he in turn died in 1611, George Abbot, already well known as a staunch adversary to Laud's reforming zeal at Oxford, was chosen to fill the vacant see.   The appointment of this mild and somewhat insignificant man must be ascribed to James' strong Calvinist views ; for however little patience the King might have with the ceremonial grievances of the Puritans, he deeply disliked the " Arminianism " now prevalent among the High Church party.   In fact,

[1] Quoted in William Barlow, *The Sum and Substance of the Hampton Court Conference*, p. 79.
[2] Harleian MSS. 828, f. 32.
[3] *Nugae Antiquae* (ed. 1779), Vol. II, pp. 227 f.

he himself sent Joseph Hall and three other English representatives to the Synod of Dort, summoned in 1618 for the express purpose of condemning the Arminian doctrines, with their insistence upon man's free will.    The Canons to which the Synod gave its assent were favourable to an extreme form of Calvinist teaching about the total depravity of human nature and God's inscrutable election to salvation of the chosen alone. It is an unhappy thought that eminent Anglican theologians should have expressed their agreement with the proposition : " Election is the unchangeable purpose of God whereby, before the foundation of the world, He hath out of mere grace, according to the sovereign good pleasure of His Own Will, chosen from the whole human race, which had fallen through their own fault from their primitive state of rectitude into sin and destruction, a certain number of persons to redemption in Christ, Whom He from eternity appointed the Mediator and Head of the Elect, and the foundation of salvation " (First Head of Doctrine, Art. vii).

An incident which occurred shortly before the death of James I led the controversy with Puritanism to enter a new stage.    Political considerations are now seen more and more to be superseding purely religious questions ; and even the King began to transfer his support to the High Church party.    Some " Romish Rangers " had visited the flock of Richard Montague at Petworth in Sussex, and caused a disturbance. In defence Montague, who was at that time also Dean of Hereford and Canon of Windsor (even the greatest of Anglicans were not afraid to accept pluralities), drew up three propositions against Rome, which were answered in turn by one, Matthew Kellison, in a book called *A Gag for the New Gospel*.    To this attack Montague replied in 1624 with *No, a New Gag for an Old Goose*, in which he declared that the Roman Church, though not itself the Catholic Church, nor even a sound member of it, was yet a real part of that Church.    The foreign Reformed Churches, on the other hand, were not members of the true Church at all : for *non est sacerdotium nisi in ecclesia; non est ecclesia sine sacerdotio*.[1] This indirect attack on the Protestant Churches aroused the fury of the English Puritans, especially in view of Montague's style, which sparkled with witty thrusts and epigrams.    As Fuller, the Church Historian, observed of him, " his great parts were attended with tartness of writing ; very sharp the nib of his pen, and much gall in his ink against such as opposed him." [2]   Further fuel was added to the flames by Montague publishing in the same year a book in defence of the Invocation of Saints, for teaching which doctrine he had been attacked three years before by the infamous Antonio de Dominis, Archbishop of Spalatro.[3]   On a petition from two Ipswich ministers,

---

[1] *Origines Ecclesiasticae*, p. 464.    [2] Fuller, *Church History*, Book XI, chap. vii.
[3] This unscrupulous trimmer had abandoned his see (and also incidentally his faith) and fled to England, where he was made Dean of Windsor.    Later he returned to Italy, was arrested by the Inquisition, and died in prison at Rome in 1624.

4

John Yates and Samuel Ward, the whole matter was laid before Parliament. Montague appealed to James I, who voiced his regard for Montague by writing to Abbot, " If that is to be a Papist, so am I a Papist." In the next year (1625) Montague made a new defence of himself, addressed to the King, *Appello Caesarem*, in which he repudiated the charges of both Popery and Arminianism. " I am none of that fraternity," he asserted, " no Calvinist, no Lutheran, but a Christian." [1] This hint that Calvinists were not Christians moved the Commons to arrest him, but he was saved by Charles I, who had just succeeded to the Crown. Charles, having thus at the very beginning of his reign irritated the Parliament, committed the further indiscretion of making him his chaplain, and in 1628 appointed him Bishop of Chichester.

The translation of William Laud to Canterbury in 1633 brought the crisis to a head. He was known to be a very ardent advocate of High Church Anglicanism, and in his career at Oxford as President of St. John's, and later as Chancellor, he had shown himself determined to purge the University of Calvinism as Andrewes and Whitgift had succeeded in doing at Cambridge. The suppression of the Genevan theology, coupled with the attempt to restore the outward dignity of public worship, became the dominant aim of his archiepiscopate. He attempted to enforce the observance of the Prayer Book by means of the Court of High Commission. " This I have observed," he said, " that no one thing hath made conscientious men more wavering in their own minds or more apt and easy to be drawn aside from the sincerity of religion professed in the Church of England, than the want of uniform and decent order in too many churches of the kingdom . . . and a great weakness it is not to see the strength which ceremonies, —things weak enough in themselves, God knows,—add even to religion itself." [2] The Visitation Articles for the Diocese of Winchester [3] show a desire to impose order and morality upon Church and State alike, and to recover for the English Church some of the rights of which she had been deprived by the avariciousness of the Tudors. " Laud intended," said Clarendon, " that the discipline of the Church should be felt as well as spoken of." [4]

It was the Court of High Commission, a sign of the close ties which bound Charles and Laud together, that incurred for Laud the undying hatred of the Puritans. It was regarded as an English counterpart of the Inquisition, encouraging Popery in belief and frivolity in daily life. If Charles had no use for Calvinism, Laud had none for demo-

[1] *Appello Caesarem* (ed. 1625), p. 45.
[2] Wm. Laud, *Epistle Dedicatory to the King*, in *Conference with Fisher the Jesuit*, edit. Simpkinson, p. xxix.
[3] See Document No. **334**.
[4] *History of the Great Rebellion*, ed. 1702, Bk. I, Vol. I, p. 73.

cracy. *Fluctus populi fluctus maris* he said in 1625 in a sermon before Charles' Second Parliament : hence the people need a King to keep them in control.[1] It was inevitable that the proceedings of the High Commission should have led to persecution. Puritan parsons were deprived for refusing to wear the surplice, to kneel at Communion, to restore the altar to its proper place at the East End, or to observe the Rubrics of the Prayer Book in their entirety. Even civil cases came under its jurisdiction. Thus in 1632 Prynne, who in his *Histriomastix* had attacked Queen Henrietta Maria in the coarsest and most unseemly language for taking part in a rehearsal of a Shepherd's Pastoral, was ordered by the Court to be fined and branded.

In 1642, the smouldering flames were kindled into open warfare, and King and Parliament took the field against each other. In the following year the Solemn League and Covenant was made between Parliament and the Scots, involving the adoption of a Presbyterian form of ministry in England. The King, when the fortunes of war turned against him, and when his money chests began to run dry, yielded first Strafford and then Laud to his enemies. Laud was impeached for High Treason before the House of Commons, and executed on Tower Hill, on January 10, 1645. In the same year the use of the Book of Common Prayer was made a penal offence, and the Presbyterian Directory for fifteen years was forced upon the country. Finally the King threw himself upon the mercy of the Scots, and was surrendered to Cromwell and his Ironsides. A mock remnant of the Long Parliament after a mere pretence at a trial condemned him as " a tyrant, a murderer, and a public enemy to the Commonwealth of England." On January 30, 1649, Charles was executed outside his palace of Whitehall.

Under the Commonwealth, the Anglican Faith was suppressed by force of law. The Bishops had been driven abroad, or had sought refuge in remote country parishes. The faithful clergy were deprived, churches were despoiled and desecrated, the use of the Prayer Book became a crime. In 1657 a congregation which had assembled in London for the observance of Christmas was arrested and imprisoned by Cromwell's soldiers. Hence the parishes lapsed into a state of complete anarchy, and were subject to an even more rigorous inquisition than any they had suffered under Laud's Court of High Commission. So great was the disorder that even the Puritan Baxter could write : " The disorderly tumultuous cries and petitions of such ignorant zealots for extremes under the name of Reformation had so great a part in our sin and misery from 1641-1660, as I must give warning to posterity to avoid the like and love moderation." [2]

With the Restoration of the Monarchy the exiled supporters of

[1] *Works, L. A. C. T.*, Vol. I, p. 85.     [2] *Reliquiae Baxterianae*, No. VIII, p. 125.

Anglicanism flocked back into popularity, and steps were immediately taken to place the English Church on a firm foundation.   Seldom has England seen a gathering of such learned theologians as came together for the conference which met at the Savoy on April 15, 1661, to revise the Prayer Book.   Gilbert Sheldon, the Bishop of London, presided ; John Cosin, who had been appointed Bishop of Durham in 1660, introduced into the new Book many liturgical changes in a Catholic direction, and advocated yet more ; Robert Sanderson, Bishop of Lincoln, wrote the new Preface ; William Sancroft, who was later to become Archbishop of Canterbury, superintended the printing. Three other important members of the Revisers' Committee were Matthew Wren, the Bishop of Ely, Peter Gunning, who succeeded him at Ely in 1675, and Anthony Sparrow, later Bishop of Norwich. The Puritans, led by Richard Baxter, were represented at the Conference, but they exercised practically no influence over its decisions. Their leader, who had declined the See of Hereford, proceeded to draw up a rival book, full of " weak and pettish criticisms," as Coleridge rather aptly described them : he quite failed to see any difference between public and private prayers, and objected to many such Anglican fundamentals as the historic Episcopate, Baptismal Regeneration, and the Real Presence.   Although there were some six hundred changes altogether in the Prayer Book of 1662, few were of great importance. Among the more significant was the re-insertion of the Black Rubric of 1552, with, however, the words " real and essential " altered to " corporal," and a large number of rubrical directions, including explicit orders for the Fraction in the Eucharistic Canon.

The Prayer Book of 1662 may well be regarded as the triumph of the cause for which Laud and Charles had died.   By it, the Anglican position was definitely secured against Puritanism.   The kneeling at Communion, the use of vestments, the Cross at Baptism, the Ring at Marriage, Absolution for the Sick,—all these things to which the Puritans had objected were not only retained in the new Book, but also enforced by Parliament, which required ministers to adopt the new Services, to submit to Episcopal Ordination, and to acknowledge the irregularity of their former conduct.   The Declaration at the end of the Baptismal Service that " children which are baptized, dying before they commit actual sin, are undoubtedly saved " closed the door to the Calvinist ideas of reprobation, " which doctrine," as Laud had so strongly insisted to Lord Saye and Sele in the House of Lords, " my very soul abominates ; for it makes God, the God of all mercies, to be the most fierce and unreasonable tyrant in the world." [1]

It must also not be forgotten that the memory of Charles' martyrdom did much to secure the Restoration of the Monarchy and the

[1] Laud, *Works*, L. A. C. T., Vol. VI, Part i, p. 133.

re-establishment of the Anglican position. Parliament might revile him as a public enemy, but the crowd who mourned in Whitehall that winter morning knew otherwise. It was because he would not surrender the Anglican Faith as settled by Elizabeth and by Hooker that he died, in his own words, " a Christian according to the profession of the Church of England." *Bona agere, et mala pati, regium est.*

## III

The opposition which the English Church had to encounter at the hands of Rome in the Seventeenth Century was as persistent though not as dangerous as that which confronted her from Puritanism.

James I was at first inclined to take up an attitude of toleration, but the " Bye Plot " of Watson and the " Main Plot " of Lord Cobham, followed by the far more serious Gunpowder Plot, made such a policy quite impossible. As early as February 22, 1604, a proclamation was issued ordering " all Jesuits, seminaries and other priests to depart the realm by the day appointed." [1] A little later all Roman Catholics were forced to take an Oath of Allegiance to the Throne. This led to theological controversy in two directions. It was alleged by the Papists that the priest Garnet, who had been executed for his conspiracy with Catesby, had been required to reveal information gleaned from the Confessional, and the issue was debated whether confessors were justified in concealing political crimes. A more far-reaching controversy centred upon the actual Oath, in which the protagonist on the Roman side was Cardinal Bellarmine, the most distinguished and learned exponent of the Tridentine theology. In 1607 James himself proceeded to defend the Oath with a book entitled *Triplici Nodo Triplex Cuneus*, in which he attacked the two *Breves* of Pope Clement VIII and Bellarmine's Letter to Blackwell, maintaining that Roman Catholics could lawfully take the Oath without any disloyalty to the Pope. Bellarmine replied under the name of his chaplain, Matthaeus Tortus. James, finding that the dispute had now entered an arena of European importance, and thinking that the subject was beyond his own rather pedantic capabilities, called upon Andrewes to answer him, on the pretence that a monarch could not lower himself to controvert a mere chaplain. Andrewes stated his case in his *Tortura Torti*, in which he diverted the argument from the Oath to the wider ground of the Papal primacy. He contended that the primacy of the Pope was not held by the Primitive Church, and hence that the Oath, even if the taking of it were proved incompatible with the papal primacy, was not incompatible with the Catholic Faith. He also rebutted the Cardinal's statement that " the authority of the head of

[1] For the full text, see E. Cardwell, *Documentary Annals*, Vol. II, pp. 50 ff.

the Church had been transferred in England from the successor of
St. Peter to the successor of Henry VIII," by defining the exact relationship of Church and State in this country. Bellarmine having made a
further retort with an *Apologia* in his own name, Andrewes showed
his scholarship at its best in his *Responsio ad Apologiam Cardinalis
Bellarmini.* Here the argument takes a much more positive tone,
and the Catholicity of the English Church is shown to be true to the
Vincentine Canon and the claims of the Primitive undivided Church.
Both Andrewes' books were written in Latin, in a scintillating style,
broken by many delightful touches of satire. In the year 1610 a
fresh contribution to the controversy came from the pen of John
Donne, who, at the King's request, published his *Pseudo-Martyr*,
in which he denied the Papal claims and the recusants' title to martyrdom. His work was the more valued, since he came from a family
of staunch Papists, being a direct descendant on his mother's side
of Elizabeth, the sister of Sir Thomas More. Study, however, at
both Universities had convinced him that Anglicanism was the natural
faith of Englishmen, and the remainder of his life, as Dean of St.
Paul's, he devoted to its cause. The King's own interest in the controversy never flagged. He had his own exegesis of the Petrine texts,
and had declared that he did not deny all supremacy to the Pope,
since the Pope, like himself, was a Western Monarch.[1] Against this
higher level of controversy must be set the more unpleasant picture
of cruel persecution, burning, and torturing, which marked the end
of James' reign—Pound and Latham being but two out of many
victims.

Shortly before the accession of Charles I, the theological controversy broke out again. Lady Villiers, the mother of the Duke of
Buckingham, had been converted to Romanism by a famous Jesuit,
Percy, who wrote under the name of Fisher. The Duke himself was
wavering, and, at his wish, a conference was held between Fisher and
Francis White, then Rector of St. Peter's, Cornhill, and later Bishop
of Ely. At the third meeting held on May 24, 1622, William Laud,
then Bishop of St. David's, was ordered by the King to defend the
English position. A lively series of attacks and retorts continued
to come from the press, until in 1639 Laud published his *Conference with
Fisher the Jesuit*, in which he dissected, criticized and demolished
each sentence of Fisher's book. In the course of this controversy
Laud argued that the Church of England had not erred in fundamentals, and he went on to discuss the true nature of the Catholic
Church. From such an ideal the Romanists had sadly departed with
their claim to infallible faith, reposing in the Pope ; they were " fishermen [a play, of course, on the Jesuit's name] which pretend St. Peter,

[1] See Document No. **1**, p. 7.

but fish not with his net." [1]   The English Church, on the other hand, deserves the complete confidence of the Christian world : for "to believe the Scripture and the Creeds, to believe these in the sense of the ancient primitive church, to receive the four great General Councils, to believe all points of doctrine generally received as fundamental in the Church of Christ, is a faith in which to live and die, cannot but give salvation." [2]

The controversy with Roman Catholicism was also waged over a period of years on foreign shores.   John Bramhall, Bishop of Derry since 1634, wrote a polemical treatise against the Jesuit, Sylvester Norris, in which he defended the Anglican Articles of Faith, and the validity of her orders against such absurdities as the Nag's Head Fable, [3] which had first appeared in print as far back as 1604.   While an exile in France during the Commonwealth, he had an opportunity to prove to De la Milletière, a French lay convert to Roman Catholicism, that the Church of England was not a Calvinist body, although she differed in much from the Church of Rome, as, for instance, in repudiating the doctrine of Transubstantiation, and reverting to the more primitive and scriptural doctrine of the Real Presence.

The Roman question again caused great alarm in the country when the news of Charles II's secret " Treaty of Dover " (1670) began to leak out.   The terms of this treaty were that Charles should change his faith, issue an act of Indulgence, and then join Louis XIV in a war with Holland.   It was known that several members of the Cabal were in favour of such a policy.   When, however, on March 15, 1672, the King actually issued the Declaration of Indulgence, Parliament promptly declared it illegal, and forced its withdrawal.   The next year they followed up their victory with the iniquitous Test Act, demanding that in future no one should be admitted to any office or public position unless he abjured the doctrine of Transubstantiation, and declared that in the Sacrament after Consecration there is the substance of bread and wine. [4]   It also required that the holder of any public office should produce a certificate stating that he had received the Sacrament of the Lord's Supper according to the usage of the Church of England.   This Act made toleration impossible for Papists and Nonconformists alike, and was at least partly responsible for the low value attached to the Eucharist throughout the Eighteenth Century. Of the persecution which followed the abominable lie of Titus Oates concerning a Popish plot, and of the miserable reign of James II,

---

[1] " Epistle Dedicatory to the King," in *Conference with Fisher the Jesuit*, edit. Simpkinson, p. xxiv.
[2] W. Laud, *Conference with Fisher the Jesuit*, edit. Simpkinson, p. 379.
[3] See Document No. **164**.
[4] The text of the Act is printed in H. Gee and W. J. Hardy, *Documents Illustrative of English Church History*, No. CXX.

nothing need be said here. Whereas the Nonconformists began to receive toleration almost immediately after the Revolution of 1689, the Roman Catholics had to wait until 1829 for their emancipation.

A study of the Controversy in all its stages makes it clear that Anglican theologians throughout the Century were hostile to all compromise with Rome. Thus Laud not only saved the Duke of Buckingham from secession, but converted no less than twenty-two Roman Catholics, including the great scholar, William Chillingworth, to the Anglican Faith. Joseph Mede was followed by most other writers in interpreting the prophecies of *Daniel* and the *Apocalypse* as referring to the Papacy. When Montague and Cosin ventured to assert that the great Turk was foretold by the title of Anti-Christ as much as the Pope, they were attacked for their supposed partiality to Rome. Joseph Hall and Jeremy Taylor both wrote *Dissuasives from Popery* in no measured terms. The extent of the hostility to Rome was largely dependent upon the theology of the individual divine. Thus Hooker sharply criticizes those "which measure religion by dislike of the Church of Rome " and " think every man so much the more sound, by how much he can make the corruptions thereof to seem more large." [1] On the other hand, Thomas Jackson, Dean of Peterborough, the most vehement, perhaps, of all the anti-Roman divines, wrote in his huge *Commentary on the Apostles' Creed* : " Whosoever steadfastly believes the absolute authority of the Romish Church, as now it is taught, doth truly and properly believe no article of Christian Faith, no God, no Trinity, no Christ, no Redemption, no Resurrection, no Heavenly joys, no Hell." [2]

## IV

The Seventeenth Century was an age of vast erudition. The number of marginal references to the Scriptures and the writings of the Fathers is amazing to one reading the folio editions for the first time. It is true that as yet the historical and critical faculties of scholars were not highly developed, even though Henry More doubted the Pauline authorship of *Hebrews*, and Jeremy Taylor was more or less certain that St. Athanasius had nothing to do with the creed called by his name. But passages from the Bible and the Fathers are quoted by controversialists at every turn, often without much regard to their contexts or real meaning. Texts were useful foils to gain advantage over one's adversary. Scholarship was ponderous rather than brilliant, and with a few notable exceptions used mainly in order to lay low theological opponents.

Of the many examples of erudition, we can here select only a few

---

[1] *Ecclesiastical Polity*, Book IV, chap. viii, § 2.   Ed. J. Keble, Vol. I, p. 443.
[2] *Works*, edit. Oxford, 1844, Vol. II, p. 501.

typical cases.  Our first instance shall be King James I.  He is chiefly remembered by posterity in the words of Henry IV's aphorism, " the wisest fool in Christendom."  It has been customary to dwell upon his folly, his want of tact, his bad statecraft, and to forget his wisdom. Yet he is almost certainly the most learned monarch that has ever sat on the English Throne, and his learning was predominantly theological.  Indeed, Lord Cecil remarked at the end of the second day of the Hampton Court Conference that he had now seen the truth of the statement *Rex est mixta persona cum sacerdote*.[1]  In the year 1597 James had written a book on Demonology : in 1603 he put forward his theory of kingship in *Basilikon Doron*, and further expounded it in *The True Law of Free Monarchies*, also 1603.  The versatility of his interests was proved when in the following year he published *A Counterblast to Tobacco*.  William Barlow well described him in the words of Eunapius as $\beta\iota\beta\lambda\iotao\theta\eta\kappa\eta$ $\tau\iota\varsigma$ $\check{\epsilon}\mu\psi\upsilon\chi o\varsigma$ $\kappa\alpha\grave{\iota}$ $\pi\epsilon\rho\iota\pi\alpha\tau o\hat{\upsilon}\nu$ $\mu o\upsilon\sigma\epsilon\hat{\iota}o\nu$.[2]

From the many learned Bishops of the Seventeenth Century, three may be singled out for mention here.  Of James Ussher (1581–1656), appointed Primate of Ireland 1625, Selden well remarked that he " was learned to a miracle."  In his theology he was much influenced by Calvin, and in 1615 drew up for the Church of Ireland a set of 104 Articles of Religion of a distinctively Calvinistic nature, while later he proposed a scheme for a modified episcopacy.  Yet he was a great friend of Laud's, and reproached Charles for yielding to Strafford's execution. His defence of prayers for the Dead was reprinted in 1836 as one of the *Tracts of the Times*.  In 1644 he had shown his historical scholarship at its best in his *Polycarpi et Ignatii Epistolae*, in which work he attempted to prove the genuineness of six of the Ignatian Epistles. His work in this direction was ably carried on by John Pearson, Bishop of Chester, our second instance.  In opposition to Presbyterian views on the ministry, he published his *Vindiciae Epistolarum Sancti Ignatii*, in which he showed all seven Epistles to be genuine.  His work earned the approbation of Bishop Lightfoot for its critical ability and its moderation of tone.  Pearson's greatest work, however, was his *Exposition of the Creed* (1659).  It is packed with references to Scripture and the Fathers, and is written with a fine sense of proportion and relevant reasoning.  The third of this important triad of scholars was George Bull (1634–1710), whose two greatest works were the *Harmonia Apostolica* and the *Defensio Fidei Nicaenae*.  In the former he dealt with Justification, and his arguments formed the basis of Newman's *Lectures* on the subject.  But this book was thought by his enemies to savour of Socinianism ; hence in his *Defence of the*

---

[1] William Barlow, *The Sum and Substance of the Conference, Second Day*, p. 84.
[2] *Ibid.*

*Nicene Faith*, Bull proceeded to vindicate the orthodoxy of the Ante-Nicene Fathers on the doctrine of the Trinity with a vast display of learning and much common sense, which earned him the congratulations of Bossuet and the French Church.

One of the most individualistic of Seventeenth-Century scholars was Herbert Thorndike (1598–1672), who attempted to give a fuller and more comprehensive treatment of theology than most of his contemporaries.   He alone approximates in outlook to the Schoolmen of earlier centuries in desiring to produce a *Summa Theologiae*.   Thorndike had been deprived by the Puritans of his living at Barley in Hertfordshire and of his fellowship at Trinity College, Cambridge, in 1643, and was prevented from being elected Master of Sidney Sussex by the Roundheads forcibly removing some of the Fellows.   In the dark days which marked the end of the Commonwealth he wrote his *Epilogue to the Tragedy of the Church of England*, and published it in 1659.   It consists of three large volumes, written in mazes of complex sentences, which make the work singularly difficult to read.   From a study of his arguments, it is clear that Thorndike is one of the most Catholically minded of the Seventeenth-Century divines, defending the Epiclesis in the Eucharist, the practice of Reservation, and Prayers for the Dead.   His characteristic doctrines, however, found little acceptance in the pages of the 1662 Prayer Book.

Two groups of scholars, each united among themselves by close personal ties, also call for notice.   The first was the brilliant company which frequented the house of the witty and pious Lucius Cary (Viscount Falkland) at Great Tew in Oxfordshire.[1]   Cary's mother was a staunch recusant, and to secure himself against her arguments he read the whole of the Greek and Latin Fathers, and made himself thoroughly conversant with the history of the great Councils.   Among those who frequently made Great Tew their *rendezvous* may be mentioned Hammond, Sheldon, Morley, Earle, Chillingworth and Hales.   Earle, in turn Bishop of Worcester and Salisbury, " would frequently profess that he had got more useful learning at Tew than he had at Oxford." [2] Izaak Walton said of him, " since Mr. Hooker died, none have lived whom God hath blessed with more innocent wisdom, more sanctified learning, or a more pious, peaceable, primitive temper." [3]   His most famous work was the *Microcosmography*, a series of " witty and sharp " discourses on typical characters of the day.   William Chillingworth was converted from Romanism in 1632 by Laud, whose spirit penetrates almost every page of his great work, *The Religion of Protestants*,

---

[1] *Vid*. Clarendon, *Life*, edit. 1759, pp. 21–3, and Document No. **343**.
[2] Clarendon, *Life*, edit. 1759, pp. 26–7.
[3] *Life of Hooker*, ed. 1927, p. 214.

*a Safe Way to Salvation.* The method of the book is polemical, and Chillingworth drives home his arguments for liberty against the exclusiveness of Rome with a force which reminds one of a woodsman felling a tree. Yet, with all its roughness, the book reveals deep thinking on the nature of the Church, and we meet occasional short sentences which impress themselves indelibly on the mind. Not the least interesting scholar in this group was " the ever memorable Mr. John Hales," Professor of Greek at Oxford, and Provost of Eton. In his early life he had been a Calvinist, but as an Oxford don he became a firm friend of Laud, and after the Synod of Dort declared, " There I bid John Calvin good night." He was possessed of a kindly and tolerant disposition, and Clarendon tells us he " would often say that he would renounce the religion of the Church of England to-morrow if it obliged him to believe that any other Christians should be damned."[1] He had a great desire for Reunion, and at one time suggested a scheme, comparable to that of Thomas Arnold two centuries later, for uniting all Englishmen by a Liturgy, " as might bring them into one Communion, all doctrinal points upon which men differed in their opinions, being to have no place in any Liturgy."[2] Hales was by temperament a recluse, with the nature of a philosopher, who loved to be alone with his books, and he was fittingly chosen to pronounce the funeral oration over Sir Thomas Bodley. Yet he fully understood the difficulties of life, warning his Eton boys of the responsibilities of riches and the wickedness of duelling. He was the loved and admired friend of the great ones of his day; " he tells men how to know, and love and worship God as one whose simple object it was to find it out."[3]

Of the famous Cambridge Platonists, perhaps the four most illustrious were Whichcote, More, Cudworth and Smith. They were the first English divines to attempt a philosophy of religion and to set forth in clear terms the divine inspiration of human reason. On these grounds, they hoped to overthrow the materialism of such thinkers as Thomas Hobbes, who published his *Leviathan* in 1651. They also desired to destroy all divisions amongst Protestants; for " all the differences in Christendom," said Whichcote, " are about institutions not about morals." With this group we may also number Robert Boyle and Isaac Newton, who found a new approach to religion through the wonders of the universe and the power of natural science. The writings both of Boyle and Newton have much literary distinction, particularly in their descriptions of the significance of natural phenomena. Whilst they had a real love of the Anglican Church, they

---

[1] Clarendon, *Life*, p. 28.   For a full account of Hales' impression of the Conference, see his *Golden Remains.*
[2] Clarendon, *ibid.*, p. 28.
[3] W. H. Hutton, *Cambridge History of English Literature*, Vol. VII, p. 152.

formed, however, the stepping stone to the Latitudinarian and Deistic thought of the Eighteenth Century.[1]

## V

The Seventeenth Century has a strong claim to be called the golden age of English Prose, and it is significant that the period produced both the Authorized Version of the Bible and the Book of Common Prayer, two of the foundations upon which the modern English language is built.  The translation of the Bible, published in 1611, was a response to the Puritan appeal at Hampton Court, and its main instigator was James himself, who " wished that some special pains should be taken in that behalf for one uniform translation, professing that he could never yet see a Bible well translated in English." [2]  Moreover, he had a personal objection to the King's Bible : " for where it is said that Asa deposed his mother Maachah,[3] some have it in the margin that he should rather have put her to death, and accordingly (said his Majesty) some in Scotland upon that ground would have had him in such sort to have proceeded against his grandmother, which he liked not of." [4]  James stipulated, therefore, that there should be no marginal notes, since those in the Genevan Version appeared to him " very partial, untrue, seditious and savouring too much of dangerous and traiterous deceits." [5]  It is, as Sir Arthur Quiller Couch has pointed out,[6] well-nigh a miracle that forty-seven men, otherwise unknown for any particular literary talent, should have produced a work " with a rhythm so personal, so constant, that our Bible has the voice of one author speaking through its many mouths."  Sometimes the effect is gained through sheer simplicity, by the use of strings of monosyllables, as in much of the discourse in the Upper Room in *St. John's Gospel*.  At other times the grand style is achieved by a succession of rolling polysyllables, as in Our Lord's condemnation of the Pharisees (*St. Matt.* xxiii), and the splendid Fifteenth Chapter of the *First Epistle to the Corinthians*. A subtle interplay of vowel sounds adds melody and variety to the style, and the translators showed extraordinary felicity in the selection of exactly the right word to express their meaning.

That the Prayer Book is likewise a masterpiece of English prose becomes only too clear when it is compared with many modern compositions, such as some of the " Occasional Prayers " in the 1928 Book.[7]  As has already been pointed out, most of the 1662 Prayer

[1] Cp. F. L. Cross, *The Oxford Movement and the Seventeenth Century*, pp. 22 f.
[2] So William Barlow, quoted in E. Cardwell, *A History of Conferences*, p. 188.
[3] *II Chronicles*, xv, 16.           [4] Harleian MSS., 828, f. 32.
[5] Barlow, *ibid.*, p. 188.           [6] *The Art of Writing*, p. 122.
[7] Cf. W. K. Lowther Clarke, " The Prayer Book as Literature " in *Liturgy and Worship*, pp. 806–12.

Book was inherited from Cranmer and the two Prayer Books of Edward VI ; but among the additions are such an admirable Collect as that for the Sixth Sunday after Epiphany, and the beautiful General Thanksgiving. The Prayers for Parliament, and for All Sorts and Conditions of Men, were also new, as well as the two Prayers for the Ember Weeks, taken from the Scottish Book of 1637. It is to be regretted that the Revisers did not take more notice of the Scottish Book, particularly its fine prayer for the Church and its Eucharistic Canon. The Psalms in the translation of the Great Bible of 1540 were for the first time bound up with the Prayer Book in 1662. In spite of many inaccuracies of translation, their simple and melodious rhythm has made them a religious classic, and our Psalter remains for all time an ideal example of what a translation of ancient verse should be. In the flowing cadences of our Prayer Book we hear again and again the echoes of Cicero's eloquent periods, passing down through the Latin Fathers. The Prayer Book preserves in language and doctrine the peculiar and splendid tradition of the national faith which it enfolds. As such, it has been finely suited to become a ceaseless source of inspiration and the prototype of the Prayer Books of the daughter Churches of the Anglican Communion.

The glories of the Bible and Prayer Book are reflected in much of the other literature of the period. W. H. Hutton has well written, " Nothing is more remarkable in an age of fading literary excellence than the way in which the thoughts and methods of the great poets and prose writers of the preceding generation were taken up and handled by the clergy of the National Church." [1]   Of the Seventeenth-Century theological prose writers, far the greatest is Jeremy Taylor (1613–67). Coleridge [2] placed him among the geniuses of the age, alongside Shakespeare, Milton and Bacon. He is one of the most individual of writers, and his style is full of an almost oriental splendour of colour and imagery. Each sentence is composed with an ear to its music, and even the most controversial and the most technical of his writings are written with a beautiful and harmonious freedom which becomes very apparent when compared with the laboured and often harsh prose style of his great contemporary, John Milton. Normally his style followed the Ciceronian model, but at times his imagination soared on high, and then he seems to dip his pen into an enchanted ink, so that the words dance to his music, and echo like the fading notes of a symphony in the mind. A fine example of his combination of sound and rhythm is to be found in his description of the fallen angels, " They grew vertiginous, and fell from the battle-

---

[1] *Cambridge History of English Literature*, Vol. VII, p. 142.
[2] *Table Talk*, edit. Oxford, 1917, p. 110, *Letters* (1895), p. 640.   Taylor's prose may be conveniently studied in L. P. Smith's collection, *The Golden Grove* (Oxford, 1930).

ments of heaven." [1]   What could excel his description of the Virgin's grief at the Crucifixion for brilliance of simile and depth of poetic imagination : " deep as the water of the abyss, but smooth as the face of a pool " ? [2]   For longer passages illustrating his power to pile up clauses and words and similes and epithets into one great diapason of splendour, one might study the description of sunrise [3] or of the soul in sickness.[4]  Jeremy Taylor, however, deserves a place among the immortals for his learning and his piety, apart from any literary qualities.  He was a typical example of the great Anglican priest of the period, and his style is never more than the instrument by which he registers the passionate sincerity of his convictions.

## VI

Much of the best Seventeenth-Century prose remains in the form of sermons ; [5] for preaching was then a great and solemn art, in which every divine was expected to excel.  Thus Hooker says of preaching : We esteem it " as the blessed ordinance of God, sermons as keys to the kingdom of heaven, as wings to the soul, as spurs to the good affections of man, unto the sound and healthy as food, as physick unto diseased minds." [6]  Some of the sermons are important to us for their intrinsic merits, in which class the work of Donne and Jeremy Taylor is pre-eminent.  Izaak Walton, in referring to Donne's first sermon before the Court, described him as " a preacher in earnest ; weeping sometimes for his auditory, sometimes with them ; always preaching to himself like an angel from a cloud, but in none ; carrying some, as St. Paul was, to Heaven in holy raptures, and enticing others by a sacred Art and Courtship to amend their lives." [7]  Others are of interest for the occasion on which they were preached, or for their historical effect.  Thus Bishop Beveridge's *Salvation in the Church only under the Sacred Ministry*, preached in Latin before the Convocation of Canterbury, resulted in the complete failure of William III's Plan of Comprehension, and his scheme for a new revision of the Prayer Book in 1689.

From the many great preachers, we may here take four examples. Of the older style Lancelot Andrewes was called by his contemporaries he *Stella Praedicantium*.  To us his sermons seem fastidious in the extreme.  They usually begin with a highly detailed and almost pedantic analysis of the text, which is followed by a very intellectual and precise

---

[1] *Works*, ed. Heber, Vol. VI, p. 80.
[2] *The Great Exemplar*, Part III (ed. Heber), Vol. III, p. 382.
[3] *Holy Dying*, Jeremy Taylor's *Works*, ed. Heber, Vol. IV, p. 350.
[4] *Ibid.*, p. 409.
[5] For a full account, see W. F. Mitchell, *English Pulpit Oratory from Andrewes to Tillotson*, S.P.C.K., 1932.
[6] Hooker, *Ecclesiastical Polity*, Bk. V, xxii, 1.
[7] Walton, *Life of Donne*, ed. 1927, p. 49.

exegesis of the subject in hand. They are full of quotations from the Fathers and from modern apologists, usually in the original tongue. That they were prepared with great care is clear from Buckeridge's assertion that few of them but were thrice between the anvil and hammer before they were preached, and " he ever misliked often and loose preaching without study of antiquity." [1]  Moreover, the preacher's delivery must have possessed a force which we cannot recapture, since it fascinated Elizabeth and James, both of them astute critics. With all his learning, there remains a charming vein of wit and humour, and a skilful use of word-play, as, for instance, the pun on Immanu-el, Immanu-hell, and Immanu-all, in one of his Christmas sermons preached before the King at Whitehall in 1614.[2]

When we pass to the sermons of Henry Hammond, we find ourselves in a quieter and less learned atmosphere. He had held various country livings until 1643, when he became Archdeacon of Chichester, and shortly afterwards Canon of Christ Church and Public Orator in the University of Oxford. Charles I said he was the most natural orator he had ever heard. In his sermons we discover no rhetorical purple passages, but a simple, restrained style which appeals through its very clarity. His life was spent apart from controversy, and with a broad and noble spirit, he pleads for religious toleration and denounces persecution as alien to the spirit of Christianity.

As representatives of the later preachers of the Century, we may instance Robert Sanderson and Isaac Barrow. In these writers we find neither the pedantry of Andrewes nor the elaborate conceits which had distinguished Donne and Jeremy Taylor. Their model was the severe simplicity characteristic of John Bunyan and Izaak Walton. Wealth of metaphor and illustration gives way to a directness of style, which avoids the strained sense, but also lacks some of the individuality of earlier writers. The Restoration prose is, however, capable of a splendid dignity for the treatment of serious themes. Robert Sanderson had at one time been a chaplain to Charles I, who said of him, " I carry my ears to hear other preachers, but I carry my conscience to hear Mr. Sanderson." [3]  His sermons, some of them reaching nearly 25,000 words in length, are sober in tone, and full of kindly argument and modest learning ; here, as Walton notes, we have " no improper rhetoric," but " his learning was methodical and exact, his wisdom useful, his integrity visible." [4]  The dignity of his style is nowhere better exemplified than in the language of the General Thanksgiving and the Preface to the Book of Common Prayer.

---

[1] Andrewes' *Works*, L. A. C. T., Vol. V, p. 295.
[2] *Ibid.*, Vol. I, p. 145.  On Andrewes' preaching, cp. T. S. Eliot's notable essay in *For Lancelot Andrewes*.
[3] Walton, *Life of Sanderson*, ed. 1927, p. 368.          [4] *Ibid.*, p. 397.

Isaac Barrow, Master of Trinity College, Cambridge, who died at the early age of forty-seven in 1677, was another illustrious preacher. Aubrey in his *Brief Lives* tells us he was " pale as the candle he studied by." He had travelled extensively ; and as he lay dying he kept murmuring, " I have seen the glories of the world." His sermons reflect an original mind and a broad thinker. He argues with the clarity of a mathematician and writes with the easy and unextravagant flow of a classical scholar. He begins as a rule by stating an hypothesis of some opponent, real or imagined, and allows him to make a full defence of his position, and then demolishes it with a series of rapid and irresistible blows. Thus Barrow presents us with a thoroughly solid and massive structure, reminding us somewhat of an elaborate geometrical problem which has been satisfactorily proved. He took extraordinary care over his style, with the result that his long and often complex sentences yet run smoothly. Coleridge declares that " he closes the first great period of the English language," and William Pitt the Elder was accustomed to learn his sermons by heart, and declaim them as a useful preparation for public speaking. This was no small feat since Barrow, like Sanderson, preached at a length which even for its age was inordinate. His sermon at the Spital on *Bountifulness to the Poor* took three hours and a half. Indeed, Charles II remarked that he was a very unfair speaker, since he never left any one else anything to say. It is recorded that on one occasion his eloquent flow in Westminster Abbey was only stopped by a noisy outburst on the organ, the organist being constrained to interrupt by the pleadings of the Vergers, who were missing their fees for escorting visitors round the church.

## VII

As has already been hinted, the Seventeenth Century saw a considerable output of religious poetry, in which art the Anglicans produced distinguished examples, even if none of them rivalled the great Puritan, Milton. John Donne, the first to break the supremacy of the Petrarchian tradition in English Literature, wrote much excellent mystical verse. His wit was essentially serious, and his gloomy brooding reminds the reader of Propertius, both in its love of melancholy and the magnificence of the language in which it is expressed. In his poems, as in his sermons, we find swift reasoning, a quaint but impressive imagery, a love of rare words and odd expressions, and a wide background of learning to which St. Augustine, Calvin, the Spanish mystics and secular chroniclers have all contributed their share. Something of a Puritan in his art, he despised mere verbal beauty. His verse is full of arguing, often in the subtlest forms, as, for instance, about the incorporeal nature of love in *Our Angels*. His love of the bizarre is, however, always pleasantly tempered with that admiration for *aurea mediocritas* which Donne had possibly inherited from one of Horace's *Odes*. Unfortunately, when subsequent verse-makers, particularly Crashaw and Traherne, tried to imitate him, their work was full of a grotesque bathos, relieved only by occasional flashes of genius. Just as Leonardo and Raphael were the culmination of their schools of Italian art, and stumbling-blocks to their slavish imitators, so was Donne to his poetical heirs.

Of the one or two exceptions to the decay which set in after the death of Donne, the most notable is that of Henry Vaughan, who was born in 1622. He ascribed his conversion to practising Christianity to " that blessed man, Mr. George Herbert, whose holy life and verse gained many converts, of whom I am the least." He had a genius for forcible epithets, as, for instance,

> " The fruitful flocks fill every dale
> And purling corn doth clothe the vale." [1]

or again,

> " Condemning thoughts—like sad eclipses—scowl
> Upon his soul." [2]

His use of metaphor and simile is daring, but wonderfully effective. The first poem of *Silex Scintillans* provides an excellent example.

> " And as a pilgrim's eye
>     Far from relief,
> Measures the melancholy sky
>     Then drops and rains for grief." [3]

Another instance may be taken from his poem, *The Lamp*.

> " Stars nod and sleep
> And through the dark air spin a fiery thread
> Such as doth gild the lazy glow-worm's bed."

He modelled his style on Herbert, but his spirit is the melancholy air of Donne. He loved to brood wistfully over man's relations with the unseen and eternal, and he could express the profoundest thoughts with an almost magical simplicity of language, as in the opening lines of his poem, *The World* :—

> " I saw eternity the other night
> Like a great ring of pure and endless light
>     All calm, as it was bright ;
> And round beneath it, Time in hours, days, years,
>     Driv'n by the spheres,
> Like a vast shadow moved, in which the world,
>     And all her train were hurled."

The Elizabethans, like the ancients, had regarded Nature as an ornamental appendage to human life ; but for Vaughan, as for Herbert, Nature yielded through her beauties both a mirror of God's mysteries and a pledge of His unfailing goodness. Vaughan was led to see in

---

[1] Paraphra. of Psalm LXV.    [2] *The World*.    [3] *Regeneration*, Stanza II.

her a new atmosphere of mystery, the link between earth and heaven, and it was at this point that he influenced so profoundly Wordsworth, Shelley, and the poets of the Romantic Revival.

Of all the poets of the Seventeenth Century, George Herbert represents most markedly the Anglican spirit. His greatest composition was *The Temple*, which he sent on his death-bed to Ferrar. There are 169 poems in the book, and 116 different metres are employed. Sometimes, especially in his use of simile, he is apt to descend to bathos, though he never fell to such depths of absurdity as did Crashaw. The book is marred by a frequent obscurity, and attempts to be clever with puns and trite sayings, of which the following anagram on the name of the Virgin Mary is typical :—

$$\text{Ana}\left\{\begin{array}{c}\text{Mary}\\\text{Army}\end{array}\right\}\text{Gram.}$$

" How well her name an ARMY doth present,
In whom the Lord of Hosts did pitch His tent."

Then again, some poems are written in a quaint shape, such as an altar, or a pair of wings, or the Echo in Heaven. Yet, with his faults, Herbert could rise to great heights of imagination, and many of his poems convey an impression of musical simplicity and profound religious thought which perfectly reflect the character of their author. Of such a type we may instance *The Elixir* or *The Quip*. Possibly, however, his finest couplet comes at the end of *The Agony*.

" Love is that liquor sweet and most divine
Which my God feels as blood, but I as wine."

Herbert imbibed, as did Keble later, the full beauty of the English countryside, and all things spoke to him of God. The poems of both reflect sorrow for sin, as surely as joy in communion with God, all the more intensified by the spiritual struggle which has preceded it. Both, too, had a deep affection for the English Church, which called forth the whole-hearted devotion of their art and their lives. This affection is well expressed in the final verse of Herbert's poem, *The British Church*.

" But, dearest mother (what those miss),
The mean Thy praise and glory is
And long may be.
Blessed be God, Whose love it was
To double-moat thee with His grace
And none but thee."

## VIII

It must ever be remembered that the Seventeenth Century was an age of Anglican piety, and remains a standing contradiction to those controversialists who have argued that the Church of England has produced no saints since the Reformation.   Charles I set a noble example to his country, and we find the quiet and spiritual manner of his life reflected in all classes of the community.   The diaries of Mary, Countess of Warwick, and Evelyn's biography of Margaret Blagge show how deep and religious lives could be spent even in the corrupt atmosphere of Charles II's Court.   We have a vast amount of devotional literature, varying from Lancelot Andrewes's *Preces Privatae* to John Bunyan's *Pilgrim's Progress*.   Both Cavalier and Roundhead entered battle with a prayer upon their lips.   Cromwell led his Ironsides to Naseby with a sword in one hand and a Bible in the other, while before the same battle, Sir Jacob Astley, one of the Royalist commanders, could utter this simple and sincere prayer, " Lord, I shall be very busy this day, and I may forget Thee, but do not Thou forget me."

To read the story of Charles' captivity and death, as related, for example, in Sir Thomas Herbert's *Memoirs*, is to recapture the spirit of the *Acta* of the primitive Christian martyrs.   We learn that during his imprisonment at Holmby House, and later at Carisbrooke and St. James' Palace, his favourite books were the Bible, Hooker's *Ecclesiastical Polity*, Andrewes' *Sermons*, Shakespeare, Spenser, Herbert, and translations of Tasso and Ariosto.   The day before his execution, Bishop Juxon preached a sermon to him,[1] and then gave him his Communion. The rest of the day he spent in prayer and meditation, eating and drinking almost nothing.   The Princess Elizabeth, who, with her small brother, the Duke of Gloucester, visited him in the course of the day, wrote down at her father's dictation his last message : " He wishes me not to grieve and torment myself for him.   For that would be a glorious death that he would die, it being for the laws and liberties of his land, and for maintaining the true Protestant religion.   He bid me read Bishop Andrewes' *Sermons*, Hooker's *Ecclesiastical Polity* and Bishop Laud's *Book against Fisher*, which would ground me against Popery." [2] He also wrote a long letter to the Prince of Wales urging him to meditate frequently on the Bible, " which in all the time of his affliction had been his best instructor and delight." [3]   On the morning of the 30th, Charles was much moved on learning that the Proper Lesson for the day was *St. Matt.*, xxvii, the story of Our Saviour's Passion.   He then made his last Confession to Juxon, and received his viaticum, and, thus comforted, went forth to the scaffold, exclaiming as he went : " This is my second marriage day.   I would be as trim to-day as may be.   For before night, I hope to be espoused to my blessed Jesus." [4]   He gave Juxon his Bible as a keepsake, and taking off his George Order, he commended it to the Bishop, and charged him to deliver it to Prince

[1] On the text *Rom.* ii, 16.
[2] Quoted in G. S. Stevenson, *Charles I in Captivity*, pp. 254 f.
[3] *Ibid.*, p. 279.
[4] *Ibid.*, p. 278.

Charles, saying : " I have a good and gracious God,—Remember." [1] After a short address to the crowd, he turned to the faithful Juxon and said : " I go from a corruptible to an incorruptible crown where no disturbance can be, but peace and joy for evermore." [2]

The popular feeling for Charles is well exemplified by the success of *Eikon Basilike*, written probably by John Gauden, one of Charles' chaplains; and published less than a month after the King's death. It contained some of the King's prayers, which the author had secured from Juxon, and preserved with remarkable fidelity the picture of the Saint preparing to meet his God in a spirit of penitent humility. In its pages Charles is portrayed at his best, as the simple and great-hearted Christian who desired peace and prayed for it earnestly, while here the Anglican Church is painted as Laud and Hooker longed to see her, quite free from party strife. If the book contained many arguments for kingship, it contained still more for Anglicanism. The following is typical : " I do require and entreat of you as your Father and your King, that you never suffer your heart to receive the least check against or disaffection from the true religion established in the Church of England." [3]

Of the many saintly Anglicans who have left us a legacy of their piety in their writings, we can select only a few examples. Here once more Lancelot Andrewes set the tune to which all the later divines sang in harmony. His *Preces Privatae*, originally composed in Greek, reveal the wide extent of his love and sympathy towards God and man. We are told that this book was seldom out of his hands as he lay dying, and Richard Drake adds : " Had you seen the original manuscript, happy in the glorious deformity thereof, watered with his penitential tears, you would have been forced to confess that book belonged to no other than pure and primitive devotion." [4] In 1627, John Cosin, at the King's request, published his *Collection of Private Devotions*, a manual based on the Mediæval Hours, and intended as an Anglican substitute for the somewhat profane Roman books, then popular in the Court of Henrietta Maria. The real character of Laud is best revealed in his book of *Devotions*, where we find prayers for the unity of Christ's mystical Body and the peace and happiness of the English people. It is ironical, in view of his death, to remember that Laud almost certainly composed our fine " Prayer for the High Court of Parliament." One last book we may mention here is *Centuries of Meditations* by Thomas Traherne. This is a more mystical work, and its author seems to have aimed at providing an *Imitatio Christi* for the Anglicans of his day. He was a splendid literary artist, who to the simplicity of Bunyan's

---

[1] *The Life and Death of King Charles I*, 1676, pp. 287 f.     [2] *Ibid.*, p. 288.
[3] *Eikon Basilike*, ed. 1648 [= 9], p. 171. Cp. especially chs. xvi, xxiv, and xxviii.
[4] Preface to first published Edition, 1648.

prose added the rich imagery of Jeremy Taylor ; and he presents us with a wonderful combination of mysticism and common sense. To Traherne no beauty of the natural world could be left outside the Kingdom of God. " You never enjoy the world aright till the sea itself floweth in your veins, till you are clothed with the heavens and crowned with the stars : and perceive yourself to be the sole heir of the whole world. . . . Till you can sing and rejoice and delight in God, as misers do in gold, and Kings in sceptres, you never enjoy the world." [1]

Approximating more to the science of ascetic and moral theology, we may count the writings of Jeremy Taylor, and his two contemporaries Joseph Hall and Robert Sanderson. Taylor's *Holy Living* and *Holy Dying* are English counterparts to the *Introduction to the Devout Life* by the great French Saint of the period, Francis de Sales. Here many of the melancholy notes we have remarked in Donne and Vaughan re-occur in the form of meditations upon mortality and death. In his *Ductor Dubitantium*, Taylor advises priests how to cultivate the fruits of the Spirit in the lives of their penitents, and presents us with discussions on Tutiorism, Probabilism and other matters of casuistry.[2] Indeed, these three divines almost alone among Anglicans until the present day have attempted to give any systematic treatment of moral theology, based on sound philosophical and psychological principles, and yet essentially practical in their application.

In one of the loneliest and dullest parts of England, some ten miles from Huntingdon, a narrow lane runs off the Great North Road to the village of Little Gidding.[3] Yet this obscure place saw the only attempt at Community life in England between the Reformation and the middle of the Nineteenth Century, and the fame of it travelled through the length of the land and leavened its whole life. Its founder was one Nicholas Ferrar, who, after a busy life as a Fellow of Clare College, Cambridge, and much travelling in the service of his father, a wealthy merchant, was ordained Deacon by Laud, and together with his family and a few friends to the number of thirty in all devoted himself to religion. They passed the day in religious exercises, saying the offices in the little village church, or in the oratory they had furnished within the Manor House. Often the nights too were devoted to prayer and meditation ; they fasted frequently, and gave alms with great liberality to the poor. At first John Williams, the kindly Bishop of Lincoln, would not allow the daughters to take a vow of celibacy, but he relented after his visit in 1640, and both Mary and Anna Collett took their vows. Much time was also devoted to study, and the

---

[1] *Centuries of Meditations*—First Century, Meditation No. 29, ed. B. Dobell, 1927, p. 19; cf. also Document No. **358**.
[2] See Jeremy Taylor, *Works*, ed. Heber, Vol. XII, pp. 87 ff. and 127 ff.; cp. Documents Nos. **310, 309**.
[3] See Walton's *Lives*, ed. 1927, pp. 309–12, and Document No. **339**.

women-folk of the house wrote harmonies of the Gospels which they bound in the most beautiful style of the day. A different kind of literature was a series of moral dialogues and tales, all of them with a pleasant touch of romance, which were read round the fireside in the evenings. It was in this retreat that Charles I spent the night in hiding, before he gave himself up to the Scots on May 5, 1646. The little Community had already been rudely attacked by the Puritans in 1641 with a pamphlet entitled *The Arminian Nunnery*.[1] Before the end of 1646 the Parliamentary soldiers broke up the community,—Nicholas having died in 1637,—and sacked the church and house. The plate was carried away, and the lectern and beautiful chased font of brass, both of them presents from Nicholas Ferrar, were thrown into a nearby duck-pond, whence they were recovered many years later, and restored to their former use.

Two further Anglican saints were great friends of the Little Gidding Community, George Herbert and Izaak Walton. With Herbert as a poet we have dealt. As a writer of prose he also excelled, his manner expressing the same open-air atmosphere as his poetry; we have the same characteristic simplicity and beauty of style, while the words used are almost all common ones and his metaphors homely in the extreme. The best known of his prose writings is *A Priest to the Temple* (1632) or, as it is more often entitled, *The Country Parson*.[2] It might well be a description of the writer's own life as a parish priest, and is remarkable for its high ideals, its evident sincerity, and its abundant common sense. One quotation must here suffice us : " The Country Parson is not only a father to his flock, but also professeth himself thoroughly of the opinion, carrying it about with him as fully as if he had begot his whole parish." [3] We cannot better Izaak Walton's appreciation of its value : " a book so full of plain, prudent, and useful rules that that country parson that can spare 12*d*. and yet wants it, is scarce excusable ; because it will both direct him what he ought to do, and convince him for not having done it." [4]

Izaak Walton himself is a charming example of the pious country gentleman. Originally a linen draper in London, he gained through his wife, Anne Ken, the friendship of many of the most famous divines of the day. In his *Lives* of Donne, Wotton, Hooker, Herbert, and Sanderson, we have a delightful picture of simple and good-tempered Christian practice. Walton's prose, like Bunyan's, gains its whole force through its essential directness, although Walton had the advantage over Bunyan of possessing an abundant fount of humour. By a happy chance three of his friends were keen fishermen. In *The Complete*

[1] See Document No. **340**.
[2] For extracts, see Document No. **335**.
[3] *The Country Parson*, Chap. XVI.
[4] *Life of Herbert*, ed. 1927, p. 294.

*Angler*, first published in 1653, we see the kindly old gentleman fly-fishing in beautiful Dovedale, listening intently to the bubbling of the river and the trilling of the lark, and watching the flowers unfolding their beauty in the sun.   All Nature deserved respect and admiration, since it was God's handiwork ; hence Walton could say of the frog : " Use him as though you loved him ; that is, harm him as little as you may possibly, that he may live the longer." [1]   It is possibly true, as an over-zealous Puritan rival hastened to point out to him, that Walton's method of casting flies was not the best.   We turn to his pages, how-ever, for other delights than learning the best methods of catching fish.

Of the important and permanent contribution of the Seventeenth Century towards the restoration of the Beauty of Holiness in Church worship little can here be said.   Prynne, in his *Canterbury's Doom*, has left us a detailed description of the beautiful chapel of Andrewes,[2] with its carefully furnished altar, and Ussher gives us a glowing account of Laud's private chapel at Lambeth.   The *Injunctions* of Peter Smart, Prebendary of Durham, against John Cosin well reveal how the Cathe-dral was improved with new altars, placed in their proper position at the East End, carved oak screens, vestments and altar lights.   It is recorded that on the evening of Candlemas Cosin burned over 300 candles in the Cathedral in honour of Our Lady.[3]   The inventories of William Dowsing, Commissioner under the Earl of Manchester in Suffolk 1643–4, and of other Puritan iconoclasts show how much of the pre-Reformation decorations still survived in parish churches until the Civil War.   Dowsing's account of his work at Clare is typical. " At Clare, Jan. 6, we brake down 1000 pictures superstitious.   I broke down 200 ;  three of God the Father and three of Christ and the Holy Lamb, and three of the Holy Ghost like a Dove with wings ; and the 12 Apostles were carved in wood on the top of the roof, which we gave orders to take down ;  and 20 Cherubims to be taken down ; and the Sun and Moon by the King's Arms to be. taken down." [4] This appalling destruction of England's artistic wealth under Puritan domination is too sad a subject to dwell upon.   We may be thankful that the cautious people of Fairford removed and buried their glorious Fifteenth-Century glass until the danger was past, and that Cromwell himself restrained one of his generals, who desired to pull down the West Tower of Ely and use it to build houses for his soldiers.

---

[1] *The Complete Angler*, ed. 1824, Vol. I, ch. viii, p. 239.
[2] W. Prynne, *Canterbury's Doom* (1646), pp. 121–4.
[3] Cosin, *Articles*, Edit. Surtees Society, Vol. LII, pp. 161–97.
[4] *Journal*, Edited by Evelyn White, in *Proceedings of Suffolk Institute of Archæology*, Vol. VI, 1883, p. 248.

## IX

The Seventeenth Century thus saw the English Church firmly established on the two-fold basis of Scripture and ancient tradition. The Anglican divines, whose writings comprise this book, had an uncompromising faith in the Catholicity of the English Church, and refused to bow to the claims of Rome, or to admit the revolutionary ideas of the Continental Reformers. They saw the Church of England as Catholic and as Protestant, as ancient and as reformed. " She has a plenary authority within herself, and has no need to recur to any other Church to direct her what to retain and what to do." So wrote Archbishop Wake.[1] This spirit of independence did not prove incompatible with many schemes for Reunion throughout the Century; Andrewes, Laud, and Stillingfleet all attempted negotiations with the Eastern Orthodox Church, and would also have welcomed negotiations with the rest of the West, if only Rome had been content to hold herself aloof from political ambitions and alliances, and if she had been content to reform herself, otherwise than by the Canons of the Council of Trent. Laud was twice offered a Cardinal's hat, but his answer was, " that somewhat dwelled within [him] which would not suffer that till Rome were other than it is." [2]

In this brief review we have attempted to show something of the essential greatness of the Seventeenth Century. The age was pre-eminently one of stress and storm, and the ideals of Anglicanism were necessarily forged upon the hard anvil of controversy. It was only as the result of a prolonged struggle against both Puritanism and Rome that the independent position of the English Church was at last attained by the Prayer Book of 1662. What is most remarkable against such a tumultuous background, is the fact that the age has bequeathed to posterity so positive and so permanent a contribution in learning, literature and art. May we, however, attribute this to that deep piety which we have seen to be reflected in the personal lives of every class of the community, clergy and laity alike ? It was the religious aspirations of the Seventeenth-Century divines which made the *Via Media* become a glorious reality instead of a barren philosophical theory. They desired to gather up all that was best in the Church's past, and to adapt it for English use, their aim being " to do that which to [their] best understandings [they] conceived might most tend to the preservation of peace and unity in the Church, the procuring of reverence, and exciting of piety and devotion in the public worship of God."[3] It was not the purpose of the Seventeenth-Century divines to imitate in a slavish spirit the doctrine or the ceremonial of other Churches. Their ideal of the Catho-

---

[1] Quoted in Perry, *Church History*, Vol. III, p. 46.
[2] Laud, *Works, L. A. C. T.*, Vol. III, p. 219.
[3] Preface to *The Book of Common Prayer*, 1662. Cp. Document No. **78**.

lic Church was of a body universal, which could yet contain within her fold divers independent Churches with peculiar national characteristics of faith and worship.    The Caroline divines would almost unanimously have agreed to Mr. Inglesant's verdict : " I am not blind to the peculiar dangers that beset the English Church.    Nevertheless, as a Church it is unique ; if suffered to drop out of existence, nothing like it can ever take its place." [1]

[1] J. H. Shorthouse, *John Inglesant*, ch. xxxix.

# EDITORIAL NOTE

FOR the text of the passages included in this *corpus*, the editions which have been used are named in the introductory note preceding each extract. Where good modern reprints existed, these have usually been preferred to the Seventeenth-Century originals for the purpose of page references on the ground that they are likely to be more accessible to the student. The inconsistencies of Seventeenth-Century orthography made any attempt to reproduce the original capitalization, punctuation and spelling a quite profitless task. No hesitation was felt, therefore, about modifying them in order to bring them, as far as possible, into conformity with modern practice. Only where differences in spelling were believed to imply differences in pronunciation has present usage in these matters been abandoned, though the long and often complicated structure of Seventeenth-Century sentences has probably tended to make our punctuation somewhat heavy. For the most part, footnotes and marginal references have been silently excised; but the editors have used complete discretion in this matter. In cases where emendations in the text have been ventured or explanatory notes added, they have been included in square brackets. Obvious misprints have been corrected. Considerable pains have been taken to secure an accurate text, in order to permit of the quotation of extracts without recourse to the (in some cases, rather scarce) original treatises. As we hardly dare hope, however, that complete exactitude has been attained, we make our own the request of Thomas Thompson which we print below.

It is less easy to summarize the principles which have determined the selection of the extracts themselves. As stated in the Preface, the primary purpose of this volume is to present the genius of Anglicanism as it found expression in the Seventeenth Century; and this end has never been long out of sight. Like all historical study which is more than the discovery and presentation of mere facts, such a task calls at every turn for discrimination and judgement. No purely mechanical method of selection could have been devised. It would clearly have been impossible, for instance, to have sought " objectivity " by including the first extract that was met with on each Subject. Apart from the inherent objections to such a plan, it must be remembered that a Table of Subjects itself presupposes a prior study of the literature. It would have been equally undesirable for the editors to have chosen only such extracts as expressed their own views on each particular theme. A *catena* composed on such principles would have been foreign to their purpose, which was not to bring together a number of proof texts, but to illustrate the ethos of a phase of English religion wherein (as in all historical manifestations of the Spirit) the permanent and the transitory were closely intertwined.  The Seventeenth Century itself did not attain complete consistency; and occasionally the editors have illustrated this fact by setting side by side passages which give expression to opposing religious attitudes or beliefs.  It was also felt desirable that as large a number as possible of representative Divines should be included in this *corpus*.  Herein will be found the explanation of the presence (and absence) of several passages.

The extended Table of Contents, when taken in conjunction with the Outline Biographies at the end of the volume, seemed to make an index quite unnecessary.                                        F. L. C.

" *If any faults be in printing, as it may be some few thou hast, as you read amend them, always remembering that as men we may slip, but as Christians we would not.*"—THOMAS THOMPSON, in a note affixed to a work published in A.D. 1612.

# I. THE ANGLICAN FAITH

## No. 1. KING JAMES I

[From *A Premonition to All Most Mighty Monarchs, Kings, Free Princes, and States of Christendom*. *Works*, ed. by James Montague, Bp. of Winchester (1616), pp. 301–308. This was the first collected edition of James I's *Works*. In 1619 a Latin translation of them was issued, also by Montague. The *Premonition* was sent in the first place to the Emperor Rudolf II. It was published in Latin at Basle in 1609.]

I WILL never be ashamed to render an accompt of my profession and of that hope that is in me, as the Apostle prescribeth. I am such a CATHOLIC CHRISTIAN as believeth the three Creeds, that of the Apostles, that of the Council of Nice, and that of Athanasius, the two latter being paraphrases to the former. And I believe them in that sense as the ancient Fathers and Councils that made them did understand them, to which three Creeds all the ministers of England do subscribe at their Ordination. And I also acknowledge for Orthodox all those other forms of Creeds that either were devised by Councils or particular Fathers, against such particular heresies as most reigned in their times.

I reverence and admit the Four First General Councils as Catholic and Orthodox. And the said Four General Councils are acknowledged by our Acts of Parliament, and received for orthodox by our Church.

As for the Fathers, I reverence them as much and more than the Jesuits do, and as much as themselves ever craved. For whatever the Fathers for the first five hundred years did with an unanime consent agree upon, to be believed as a necessary point of salvation, I either will believe it also, or at least will be humbly silent, not taking upon me to condemn the same. But for every private Father's opinion, it binds not my conscience more than Bellarmine's, every one of the Fathers usually contradicting others. I will therefore in that case follow St. Augustine's rule in judging of their opinions as I find them agree with the Scriptures. What I find agreeable thereto I will gladly embrace. What is otherwise I will (with their reverence) reject.

As for the Scriptures, no man doubteth I will believe them. But even for the Apocrypha, I hold them in the same accompt that the Ancients did. They are still printed and bound with our Bibles, and publicly read in our churches. I reverence them as the writings of holy and good men. But since they are not found in the Canon, we accompt them to be *secundae lectionis* or *ordinis* (which is Bellarmine's own distinction) and therefore not sufficient whereupon alone to

3

ground any Article of Faith, except it be confirmed by some other place of Canonical Scripture; concluding this point with Rufinus (who is no Novelist, I hope) that the Apocryphal books were by the Fathers permitted to be read, not for confirmation of doctrine, but only for instruction of the people.

As for the Saints departed, I honour their memory, and in honour of them do we in our Church observe the days of so many of them as the Scripture doth canonize for saints; but I am loath to believe all the tales of the legended saints.

And first for the Blessed Virgin Mary, I yield her that which the Angel Gabriel pronounced of her, and which in her Canticle she prophecied of herself, that is, That she is blessed among women, and That all generations shall call her blessed. I reverence her as the Mother of Christ, of whom our Saviour took His flesh, and so the Mother of God, since the Divinity and Humanity of Christ are inseparable. And I freely confess that she is in glory both above angels and men, her own Son (that is both God and man) only excepted. But I dare not mock her, and blaspheme against God, calling her not only *Diva* but *Dea*, and praying her to command and control her Son, Who is her God and her Saviour. Nor yet not, I think, that she hath no other thing to do in Heaven than to hear every idle man's suit and busy herself in their errands, whiles requesting, whiles commanding her Son, whiles coming down to kiss and make love with priests, and whiles disputing and brawling with devils. In Heaven she is in eternal glory and joy, never to be interrupted with any worldly business; and there I leave her with her blessed Son, our Saviour and hers, in eternal felicity.

As for prayer to Saints, Christ, I am sure, hath commanded us to come all to Him that are loaden with sin, and He will relieve us; and St. Paul hath forbidden us to worship angels, or to use any such voluntary worship, that hath a shew of humility in that it spareth not the flesh. But what warrant we have to have recourse unto these *Dii Penates* or *Tutelares*, these Courtiers of God, I know not; I remit that to these philosophical Neoteric Divines. It satisfieth me to pray to God through Christ, as I am commanded, which I am sure must be the safest way; and I am sure the safest way is the best way in points of salvation. But if the Romish Church hath coined new Articles of Faith, never heard of in the first 500 years after Christ, I hope I shall never be condemned for an heretic, for not being a Novelist. Such are the Private Masses, where the Priest playeth the part both of the Priest and of the People. And such are the Amputation of the one half of the Sacrament from the people; the Transubstantiation, Elevation for Adoration, and Circumportation in procession of the Sacrament; the Works of Supererogation, rightly named *Thesaurus*

*Ecclesiae* ; the Baptizing of Bells and a thousand other tricks, but above all, the Worshipping of Images. If my faith be weak in these, I confess I had rather believe too little than too much. And yet since I believe as much as the Scriptures do warrant, the Creeds do persuade, and the ancient Councils decreed, I may well be a schismatic from Rome, but I am sure I am no heretic.

For Relics of Saints, If I had any such I were assured were members of their bodies, I would honourably bury them and not give them the reward of condemned men's members, which are only ordained to be deprived of burial. But for worshipping either them or images, I must account it damnable idolatry.

I am no *Iconomachus*. I quarrel not with the making of images, either for public decoration or for men's private uses. But that they should be worshipped, be prayed to, or any holiness attributed unto them, was never known of the ancients. And the Scriptures are so directly, vehemently, and punctually against it, as I wonder what brain of man or suggestion of Satan durst offer it to Christians. And all must be salved with nice philosophical distinctions as *Idolum nihil est* ; and They worship (forsooth) the Images of things in being and the Image of the true God. But the Scripture forbiddeth to worship the Image of anything that God created. It was not a *nihil* then that God forbade only to be worshipped, neither was the Brazen Serpent nor the body of Moses a *nihil* ; and yet the one was destroyed and the other hidden for eschewing of idolatry. Yea, the Image of God Himself is not only expressly forbidden to be worshipped, but even to be made. The reason is given, That no eye ever saw God ; and how can we paint His Face, when Moses (the man that was ever most familiar with God) never saw but His back parts ? Surely, since He cannot be drawn to the *vive*, it is a thankless labour to mar it with a false representation ; which no Prince, nor scarcely any other man, will be contented with in their own pictures. Let them therefore that maintain this doctrine answer it to Christ at the latter day, when He shall accuse them of idolatry. And then I doubt if He will be paid with such nice sophistical distinctions. . . .

As for Purgatory, and all the trash depending thereupon, it is not worth the talking of ; Bellarmine cannot find any ground for it in all the Scriptures. Only I would pray him to tell me, If that fair green meadow that is in Purgatory have a brook running through it, that in case I come there I may have hawking upon it. But as for me, I am sure there is a Heaven and a Hell, *praemium et poena*, for the Elect and Reprobate ; how many other rooms there be, I am not on God His council. *Multae sunt mansiones in domo Patris mei*, saith Christ, Who is the true purgatory for our sins. But how many chambers and ante-chambers the Devil hath, they can best tell that go to him.

But in case there were more places for souls to go to than we know of, yet let us content us with that which in His Word He hath revealed unto us, and not inquire further into His secrets. Heaven and Hell are there revealed to be the eternal home of all mankind. Let us endeavour to win the one and eschew the other; and there is an end.

Now in all this discourse have I yet left out the main article of the Romish faith, and that is, the Head of the Church or Peter's Primacy; for who denieth this, denieth *fidem Catholicam*, saith Bellarmine. That Bishops ought to be in the Church, I ever maintained it as an Apostolic institution and so the ordinance of God,—contrary to the Puritans, and likewise to Bellarmine, who denies that Bishops have their jurisdiction immediately from God. (But it is no wonder he takes the Puritans' part, since Jesuits are nothing but Puritan-Papists.) And as I ever maintained the state of Bishops and the Ecclesiastical Hierarchy for order sake, so was I ever an enemy to the confused anarchy or parity of the Puritans, as well appeareth in my Βασιλικὸν Δῶρον. Heaven is governed by order, and all the good angels there. Nay, Hell itself could not subsist without some order. And the very devils are divided into legions and have their chieftains. How can any society, then, upon earth subsist without order and degrees? And therefore I cannot enough wonder with what brazen face this Answerer could say, That I was a Puritan in Scotland and an enemy to Protestants,—I that was persecuted by Puritans there, not from my birth only, but even since four months before my birth? I that in the year of God 84 [*i.e.*, 1584] erected Bishops and depressed all their popular parity, I then being not 18 years of age? I that in my said Book to my Son do speak ten times more bitterly of them nor of the Papists, having in my second edition thereof affixed a long Apologetic Preface, only *in odium Puritanorum*? And I that for the space of six years before my coming into England laboured nothing so much as to depress their parity and re-erect Bishops again? Nay, if the daily commentaries of my life and actions in Scotland were written (as Julius Caesar's were) there would scarcely a month pass in all my life, since my entering into the thirteenth year of my age, wherein some accident or other would not convince the Cardinal of a lie in this point. And surely I give a fair commendation to the Puritans in that place of my book, where I affirm that I have found greater honesty with the highland and border thieves than with that sort of people. But leaving him to his own impudence, I return to my purpose.

Of Bishops and Church Hierarchy I very well allow (as I said before) and likewise of ranks and degrees amongst bishops. Patriarchs I know were in the time of the Primitive Church, and I likewise reverence that institution for order sake; and amongst them was a contention for the first place. And for myself (if that were yet the question) I would with all my heart give my consent that the Bishop of Rome should have the first seat; I being a Western King would go with the Patriarch of the West. And for his temporal principality over the Signory of Rome, I do not quarrel it either. Let him in God His Name be *Primus Episcopus inter omnes Episcopos*, and *Princeps Episcoporum*, so it be no otherwise but as Peter was *Princeps Apostolorum*. But as I well allow of the hierarchy of the Church for distinction of orders (for so I understand it), so I utterly deny that there is an earthly Monarch thereof, whose word must be a law, and who cannot err in his sentence, by an Infallibility of Spirit. Because earthly Kingdoms must have earthly Monarchs, it doth not follow that the Church must have a visible Monarch too. For the world hath not one earthly temporal Monarch. Christ is His Church's Monarch, and the Holy Ghost His Deputy, *Reges Gentium dominantur eorum, vos autem non sic*. Christ did not promise before His Ascension to leave Peter with them to direct and instruct them in all things. But He promised to send the Holy Ghost unto them for that end.

And as for these two before cited places, whereby Bellarmine maketh the Pope to triumph over kings, I mean *Pasce oves* and *Tibi dabo claves*, the Cardinal knows well enough that the same words of *Tibi dabo* are in another place spoken by Christ in the plural number. And he likewise knows what reason the ancients do give why Christ bade Peter *pascere oves*, and also what a cloud of witnesses there is, both of ancients, and even of late Popish writers, yea divers Cardinals, that do all agree, that both these speeches used to Peter were meant to all the Apostles represented in his person. Otherwise, how could Paul direct the Church of Corinth to excommunicate the incestuous person *cum spiritu suo*, whereas he should then have said, *cum spiritu Petri*? And how could all the Apostles have otherwise used all their censures only in Christ's Name, and never a word of His Vicar? Peter, we read, did in all the Apostles' meetings sit amongst them as one of their number. And when chosen men were sent to Antiochia from that great Apostolic Council at Jerusalem (*Acts* xv), the text saith, *It seemed good to the Apostles and Elders with the whole Church to send chosen men*; but no mention made of the Head thereof. And so in their Letters no mention is made of Peter, but only of the Apostles, Elders, and Brethren. And it is a wonder why Paul rebuketh the Church of Corinth for making exception of persons, because some followed Paul, some Apollos, some Cephas, if Peter was their visible Head! For then those that followed not Peter or Cephas renounced the Catholic Faith. But it appeareth well that Paul knew little of our new doctrine, since he handleth Peter so rudely, as he not only compareth, but preferreth, himself unto him. But our Cardinal proves Peter's superiority by Paul's going to visit him.    Indeed Paul saith, He went to Jerusalem to visit Peter and confer with him.    But he should have added, " And to kiss his feet." . . .

Thus have I now made a free Confession of my Faith.   And, I hope, I have fully cleared myself from being an Apostate ; and, as far from being an heretic as one may be, that believeth the Scriptures, and the three Creeds, and acknowledgeth the four first General Councils. If I be loath to believe too much, especially of novelties, men of greater knowledge may well pity my weakness.   But I am sure none will condemn me for an heretic, save such as make the Pope their God, and think him such a speaking Scripture as they can define heresy no otherwise, but to be whatsoever opinion is maintained against the Pope's definition of faith.   And I will sincerely promise, that whenever any point of the Religion I profess shall be proved to be new, and not Ancient, Catholic, and Apostolic (I mean for matter of faith), I will as soon renounce it, closing up this head with the maxim of Vincentius Lirinensis, that I will never refuse to embrace any opinion in divinity necessary to salvation which the whole Catholic Church with an unanime consent have constantly taught and believed even from the Apostles' days, for the space of many ages thereafter without any interruption.

## No. 2.   FRANCIS WHITE

[From *A Treatise of the Sabbath Day, Containing a Defence of the Orthodoxal Doctrine of the Church of England Against Sabbatarian Novelty*, London, 1635, pp. 11 f. Cp. note on No. **67**.]

The Church of England in her public and authorized Doctrine and Religion proceedeth in manner following.

It buildeth her faith and religion upon the Sacred and Canonical Scriptures of the holy Prophets and Apostles, as upon her main and prime foundation.

Next unto the Holy Scripture, it relieth upon the consentient testimony and authority of the Bishops and Pastors of the true and ancient Catholic Church ; and it preferreth the sentence thereof before all other curious or profane novelties.

The Holy Scripture is the fountain and lively spring, containing in all sufficiency and abundance the pure Water of Life, and whatsoever is necessary to make God's people wise unto salvation.

The consentient and unanimous testimony of the true Church of Christ, in the Primitive Ages thereof, is *Canalis*, a conduit pipe, to derive and convey to succeeding generations the celestial water contained in Holy Scripture.

The first of these, namely the Scripture, is the sovereign authority and for itself worthy of all acceptation. The latter, namely the voice and testimony of the Primitive Church, is a ministerial and subordinate rule and guide, to preserve and direct us in the right understanding of the Scriptures.

## No. 3. RICHARD MONTAGUE

[From *Appello Caesarem. A Just Appeal from Two Unjust Informers. Part I, Chapter v*, London, 1625, p. 48. The circumstances connected with the publication of this work are well known. In 1624 Montague had issued two treatises—*A New Gagg for an Old Goose* and *Immediate Address unto God Alone*. The former was a reply to a Roman Catholic controversialist named Kellison, the latter a work dealing with Invocation of Saints (cp. note on No. 237). The views set forth in these two treatises provoked a storm of hostility from the Puritans, and the book on Invocation was delated to Abbot the Archbishop of Canterbury by two Ipswich ministers, Yates and Ward, the " unjust informers " referred to on the title-page. Montague secured the support of James I, and wrote the *Appello Caesarem* as a public appeal. Abbot, however, refused to license the work, and Montague had to be content with an Imprimatur from Francis White, the Dean of Carlisle.]

What that Church [*i.e.*, the Church of England] believeth, I believe ; what it teacheth, I teach ; what it rejecteth, I reject ; what it doth not tender, I am not tied unto. I was bred a member of the Church of England, brought up a member of the Church of England ; therein, by the means and ministry of that Church, I received that earnest of my salvation, when by Baptism I was inserted into Christ. In the union and communion of that Church I have lived, not divided with Papist nor separated with Puritan. Through the assistance of the grace of God's Spirit, which is never wanting unto any that seek Him, I hope to live and die in the Faith and Confession of that Church, than which I know none, nor can any be named, in all points more conformable unto purest Antiquity in the best times ; which I trust to make good against any and all those brethren in evil, Papists and Puritans, whosoever ; who looking and running two several ways do, like Samson's foxes, join together in the tail.

## No. 4. THOMAS BROWNE

[From *Religio Medici*, Part I. Ed. Everyman's Library, pp. 3–5. Sir Thomas Browne probably wrote his famous treatise in 1635 during his residence at Shipden Hall, Halifax. Though it had received a considerable circulation in MS., apparently it was not intended for publication ; but a surreptitious printing of it in 1642 led the author to issue the first authorized edition of the work in the following year (1643). A Latin translation of this edition, the work of John Merryweather, was published in 1644 ; and in this form the work secured an immediate success on the Continent. Not unnaturally its unorthodox and quaint views on many religious topics led it to provoke much criticism ; and in 1645 Alexander Ross issued a reply, *Medicus Medicatus ; or the Physician's Religion Cured by a Lenitive or Gentle Potion*. In spite of its commonly alleged Roman Catholic leanings, Browne's treatise was placed on the *Index Expurgatorius*.]

Because the Name of a Christian is become too general to express our Faith (there being a Geography of Religions as well as Lands, and every clime distinguished not only by their laws and limits, but circumscribed by their Doctrines and Rules of Faith), to be particular, I am of that Reformed new-cast Religion, wherein I dislike nothing but the Name, of the same belief our Saviour taught, the Apostles disseminated, the Fathers authorized, and the Martyrs confirmed; but by the sinister ends of Princes, the ambition and avarice of Prelates, and the fatal corruption of times, so decayed, impaired, and fallen from its native beauty, that it required the careful and charitable hands of these times to restore it to its primitive integrity. Now the accidental occasion whereupon, the slender means whereby, the low and abject condition of the person by whom so good a work was set on foot, which in our adversaries beget contempt and scorn, fills me with wonder, and is the very same objection the insolent pagans first cast at Christ and His Disciples.

Yet have I not so shaken hands with those desperate resolutions (who had rather venture at large their decayed bottom, than bring her in to be new trimmed in the dock; who had rather promiscuously retain all, than abridge any, and obstinately be what they are, than what they have been) as to stand in diameter and swords point with them. We have reformed from them, not against them; for (omitting those improperations and terms of scurrility betwixt us, which only difference our affections, and not our cause) there is between us one common name and appellation, one faith and necessary body of principles common to us both; and therefore I am not scrupulous to converse and live with them, to enter their Churches in defect of ours, and either pray with them, or for them. I could never perceive any rational consequence from those many texts which prohibit the Children of Israel to pollute themselves with the Temples of the Heathens; we being all Christians, and not divided by such detested impieties as might profane our prayers, or the place wherein we make them; or that a resolved conscience may not adore her Creator any where, especially in places devoted to His Service; where, if *their* Devotions offend Him, mine may please Him; if theirs profane it, mine may hallow it. Holy-water and Crucifix (dangerous to the common people) deceive not my judgement nor abuse my devotion at all. I am, I confess, naturally inclined to that which misguided zeal terms *Superstition*. My common conversation I do acknowledge austere, my behaviour full of rigour, sometimes not without morosity; yet at my devotion I love to use the civility of my knee, my hat, and hand, with all those outward and sensible motions which may express or promote my invisible devotion. I should violate my own arm rather than a Church; nor willingly deface the name of Saint or Martyr. At the sight of a Cross or Crucifix I can dispense with my hat, but scarce with the thought or memory of my Saviour. I cannot laugh at, but rather pity, the fruitless journeys of Pilgrims, or contemn the miserable condition of Friars; for, though misplaced in circumstances, there is something in it of devotion. I could never hear the Ave-Mary Bell without an elevation; or think it a sufficient warrant, because *they* erred in one circumstance, for me to err in all, that is, in silence and dumb contempt. Whilst, therefore, they directed their devotions to *Her*, I offered mine to God, and rectified the errors of their prayers by rightly ordering mine own. At a solemn Procession I have wept abundantly, while my consorts, blind with opposition and prejudice, have fallen into an excess of scorn and laughter. There are, questionless, both in Greek, Roman, and African Churches, solemnities and ceremonies, whereof the wiser zeals do make a Christian use, and stand condemned by us, not as evil in themselves, but as allurements and baits of superstition to those vulgar heads that look asquint on the face of truth, and those unstable judgements that cannot consist in the narrow point and centre of virtue without a reel or stagger to the circumference.

## No. 5.  GEORGE  HERBERT

[From *The Temple : or Sacred Poems and Private Ejaculations. Works*, ed. G. H. Palmer (1905), Vol. III, pp. 101–103. George Herbert's *Poems*, like *The Country Parson* (cp. note on No. **335**), did not see the light during Herbert's lifetime. They were first published by Nicholas Ferrar in 1633 soon after their author's death, and at once secured great popularity. On the text and order of the poems see G. H. Palmer, *op. cit.*, Vol. I, pp. 171–191.]

### The British Church.

I joy, dear Mother, when I view
Thy perfect lineaments and hue
    Both sweet and bright.
Beauty in thee takes up her place,
And dates her letters from thy face,
    When she doth write.

A fine aspect in fit array,
Neither too mean, nor yet too gay,
    Shows who is best.
Outlandish looks may not compare,
For all they either painted are,
    Or else undrest.

She on the hills which wantonly
Allureth all, in hope to be
    By her preferr'd,
Hath kiss'd so long her painted shrines
That ev'n her face by kissing shines
    For her reward.

She in the valley is so shy
Of dressing that her hair doth lie
          About her ears ;
While she avoids her neighbour's pride,
She wholly goes on th' other side,
          And nothing wears.

But dearest Mother, (what those miss,)
The mean thy praise and glory is,
          And long may be.
Blessed be God, Whose love it was
To double-moat thee with His grace
          And none but thee.

## No. 6.  SIMON PATRICK

[From *An Account of the New Sect of Latitude-Men Together with some Reflections upon the New Philosophy. By S. P. of Cambridge, In answer to a Letter from his friend at Oxford.* London, 1662, pp. 7 f.  In his earlier years, Simon Patrick had many close relationships with the Cambridge Platonists ; and it seems to be fairly certain that he was the author of this pamphlet.  In the preceding year he had been elected President of Queens' College, Cambridge, but a Royal Mandate overrode the election, and Anthony Sparrow filled the office.]

Our Latitudinarians [with whom the author identified himself], therefore, are by all means for a Liturgy, and do prefer that of our own Church before all others, admiring the solemnity, gravity, and primitive simplicity of it, its freedom from affected phrases or mixture of vain and doubtful opinions.  In a word, they esteem it to be so good that they would be loath to adventure the mending of it, for fear of marring it.

As for the Rites and Ceremonies of Divine Worship, they do highly approve that virtuous mediocrity which our Church observes between the meretricious gaudiness of the Church of Rome and the squalid sluttery of fanatic conventicles.  Devotion is so overclad by the Papists that she is oppressed and stifled with the multitudes of her own garments.  *Pars minima est ipsa puella sui.*  Some of our modern Reformers to make amends have stripped her stark naked, till she is become in a manner cold and dead.  The Church of England only hath dressed her as befits an honourable and virtuous matron.  There are few men so abstractedly intellectual but that their devotion had need to be advanced with something that may strike upon their outward senses and engage their affections ; and therefore while we live in this region of mortality, we must make use of such external helps, and recommend religion to the people by those ornaments which the Church hath according to her prudence thought fittest for those ends. The Church of Rome is a luxuriant vine, full of superfluous branches and overrun with wild grapes from whence many a poisonous and intoxicating potion is pressed forth; but the greatest part of the Reformers have done like the rude Thracian in the apologue who, instead of moderate pruning and dressing his vines, as his more skilful Athenian neighbours did, cut them up by the roots. But the Church of England is the only well ordered vineyard.

## No. 7. JOHN GAUDEN

[From 'Ιερὰ Δάκρυα; *Ecclesiae Anglicanae Suspiria, or The Tears, Sighs, Complaints, and Prayers of the Church of England* (1659), Book I, Chapter i, p. 24. Cp. note on No. 41.]

By the name of the Church of England it is not imported or implied that we judge every particular person in this nation to be inwardly a good Christian or a true Israelite, that is, really sanctified or spiritually a member of Christ and His mystical Body, the Church Catholic, invisible. No, we are not so rude understanders or uncritical speakers. But we plainly and charitably mean that part of mankind in this polity or nation, which having been called, baptized, and instructed by lawful ministers in the mysteries and duties of the Gospel maketh a joint and public profession of the Christian Faith and reformed religion in the name, and as the sense, of the whole nation; as it is grounded upon the Holy Scriptures, guided also and administered by that uniform order, due authority, and holy ministry, for worship and government, which according to the mind of Christ, the pattern of the Apostles, and the practice of all primitive churches, hath been lawfully established by the wisdom and consent of all estates in this nation in order to God's glory, the public peace, and the common good of men's souls.

## No. 8. JOHN COSIN

[From Cosin's Last Will. The translation was made and published by Isaac Basire in his *Dead Man's Real Speech* (1673). It was reprinted in the *L. A. C. T.* edition of Cosin, Vol. IV. The following extract is from pp. 526–528.]

But whatsoever heresies or schisms heretofore, by what names soever they be called, the ancient Catholic and Universal Church of Christ with an unanimous consent hath rejected and condemned, I do in like manner condemn and reject, together with all the modern fautors of the same heresies, sectaries and fanatics, who, being carried on with an evil spirit, do falsely give out they are inspired of God :— the heresies and schisms, I say, of all these, I also, as most addicted to the symbols, synods, and confessions of the Church of England, or rather the Catholic Church, do constantly renounce, condemn, and reject. Among whom I rank not only the Separatists, the Anabaptists, and their followers, (alas) too too many, but also the new Independents and Presbyterians of our country, a kind of men hurried away with the spirit of malice, disobedience, and sedition, who by a disloyal attempt (the like whereof was never heard since the world began) have of late committed so many great and execrable crimes, to the contempt and despite of religion and the Christian Faith : which, how great they were, without horror cannot be spoken or mentioned.

Moreover I do profess, with holy asseveration and from my very heart, that I am now, and have ever been from my youth, altogether free and averse from the corruptions and impertinent new-fangled or papistical (so commonly called) superstitions and doctrines, and new superadditions to the ancient and primitive religion and faith of the most commended, so orthodox, and Catholic Church, long since introduced, contrary to the Holy Scripture and the rules and customs of the ancient Fathers.

But in what part of the world soever any Churches are extant, bearing the name of Christ, and professing the true Catholic Faith and religion, worshipping and calling upon God, the Father, the Son, and the Holy Ghost, with one heart and voice, if any where I be now hindered actually to be joined with them, either by distance of countries, or variance amongst men, or by any other let whatsoever, yet always in my mind and affection I join and unite with them ; which I desire to be chiefly understood of Protestants, and the best reformed Churches. For, where the foundations are safe, we may allow, and therefore most friendly, quietly, and peaceably suffer, in those Churches where we have not authority, a diversity, as of opinion, so of ceremonies, about things which do but adhere to the foundations, and are neither necessary or repugnant to the practice of the universal Church. As for all them, who through evil counsel have any way inveighed against, or calumniated me, and even yet do not forbear their invectives, I freely pardon them, and earnestly pray to God, that He also would be pleased to forgive them, and inspire them with a better mind. In the meanwhile, I take it to be my duty, and of all my brethren, especially the Bishops and Ministers of the Church of God, to do our utmost endeavours, according to the measure of grace which is given to every one of us, that at last an end may be put to the differences of religion, or at least that they may be lessened, and that we may *follow peace with all men, and holiness*; which, that it may be accomplished very speedily, God, *the Author of peace and concord*, grant : Whose infinite mercy I humbly beseech, that He would cleanse me, who was conceived in sin and iniquity, from every spot and corruption of human frailty ; and that through His great clemency He would make me, who am unworthy, to become worthy, and that He would apply to me the Passion and infinite merits of His most beloved Son, Jesus Christ our Lord, to the expiating of all mine offences ; that at the last hour of my life, which I daily look for, I may be carried by His holy Angels into Abraham's bosom, and, being placed in the fellowship of His saints and elect, may fully enjoy eternal felicity.

## No. 9. ROBERT SANDERSON

[According to Christopher Wordsworth (*Bishop Sanderson's Lectures on Conscience and Human Law*, p. vii), the following extract is from a passage written by Sanderson shortly before his death. Wordsworth reprints it in his Preface (on pp. viii f.) to his translation of those Lectures. Cp. also note on No. **330**.]

And here I do profess, that as I have lived, so I desire and, by the grace of God, resolve to die, in the communion of the Catholic Church of Christ, and a true son of the Church of England; which, as it stands by law established, to be both in doctrine and worship agreeable to the Word of God, and in the most [?] and most material points of both, conformable to the faith and practice of the godly churches of Christ in the primitive and purer times I do firmly believe; led so to do not so much from the force of custom and education, to which the greatest part of mankind owe their particular different persuasions in point of religion, as upon the clear evidence of truth and reason after a serious and impartial examination of the grounds as well of Popery as Puritanism, according on that measure of understanding and those opportunities which God hath afforded me. And herein I am abundantly satisfied, that the schism which the Papists on the one hand and the superstition which the Puritans on the other hand, lay to our charge, are very justly chargeable to themselves respectively. Wherefore I humbly beseech Almighty God, the Father of Mercies, to preserve this Church by His power and providence in truth, peace, and godliness evermore unto the world's end. Which doubtless He will do if the wickedness and security of a sinful people, and particularly those sins that are so rife, and seem daily to increase among us, of unthankfulness, riot, and sacrilege, do not tempt His patience to the contrary.

## No. 10. JEREMY TAYLOR

[From *A Letter to a Gentlewoman Seduced to the Church of Rome*. *Works*, ed. R. Heber, Vol. XI, p. 185 (ed. C. P. Eden, Vol. VI, pp. 646 f.).]

What can be supposed wanting [in the Church of England] in order to salvation? We have the Word of God, the Faith of the Apostles, the Creeds of the Primitive Church, the Articles of the four first General Councils, a holy liturgy, excellent prayers, perfect Sacraments, faith and repentance, the Ten Commandments, and the sermons of Christ, and all the precepts and counsels of the Gospel. We teach the necessity of good works, and require and strictly exact the severity of a holy life. We live in obedience to God, and are ready to die for Him, and do so when He requires us so to do. We speak honourably of His most Holy Name. We worship Him at the mention of His Name. We confess His attributes, We love His servants. We pray for all men. We love all Christians, even our most erring brethren. We confess our sins to God and to our brethren whom we have offended, and to God's ministers in cases of scandal or of a troubled conscience. We communicate often. We are enjoined to receive the Holy Sacrament thrice every year at least. Our priests absolve the penitent. Our Bishops ordain priests, and confirm baptized persons, and bless their people and intercede for them. And what could here be wanting to salvation?

## No. 11. GEORGE BULL

[From the *Examen Censurae; or An Answer to Certain Strictures before Un-published on a Book entitled "Harmonia Apostolica,"* Answer to the Preface, § 5. Ed. *L. A. C. T.* (" On Justification," Parts II and III), p. 5. Bull's *Harmonia Apostolica* (1670), which sought to interpret the Pauline doctrine of Justification in the light of *St. James* (cp. note on No. 129), had raised a storm of opposition from the more Calvinistically-minded theologians. Among his opponents was Charles Gataker, who attacked Bull in a set of unpublished " Animadversions." These strictures Gataker communicated to Nicholson, Bishop of Gloucester, who sent them on to Bull; and the *Examen Censurae* was Bull's reply. It was published in 1675. The translation is that made for the *L. A. C. T.* edition. In 1670, Charles Gataker had edited *An Antidote against Error concerning Justification; or the True Notion of Justification and of Justifying Faith, cleared by the Light of Scripture and . . . Reason,* an unfinished treatise of his father, Thomas Gataker (*d.* 1654).]

Lastly, whatever I may have written, either in this or other books, most humbly and most willingly do I submit it to the judgement of our holy mother, the English Church, her to whom I have hitherto devoted myself in all filial obedience, and to whom, while I live, by God's help I will devote myself.

## No. 12. THOMAS KEN

[From *Ichabod, or The Five Groans of the Church, Prudently Foreseeing and Passion-ately Bewailing her Second Fall, Threatened by these Five Dangerous, though Undiscerned Miscarriages, that Caused her* 1. *Undue Ordination;* 2. *Loose Profaneness;* 3. *Un-conscionable Simony;* 4. *Careless Non-Residence;* 5. *Encroaching Pluralities; Humbly presented to her Supreme Head and Governor, the King's Most Excellent Majesty, and His Great Council, the Parliament of England,* Chapter I. *Prose Works,* ed. W. Benham (" Ancient and Modern Library of Theological Literature "), pp. 3–6. This treatise first appeared anonymously in 1663. In 1689 it was reprinted with the title *Lachrymae Ecclesiae,* though, as its preface indicates, not by its author. Two months after Ken's death (1711), a third edition appeared, with yet another title—*Expostulatoria,* this time claiming to be the work of Ken. Though Hawkins, Ken's great nephew, denied that Ken had written it, Dean E. H. Plumptre (*The Life of Thomas Ken, D.D.,* Vol. I, pp. 55–59) has drawn out strong reasons for attributing it to him.]

O all you that pass by me, stand and see if there be any sorrow like unto my sorrow; if it hath been done to any Reformed or Protestant Church under heaven, as it is done unto me! O, now my wounds were ready to be closed, my ruins to be repaired, my desolations and wastes to be finished; when the barbarous was checked, the licentious was restrained, the usurpers were removed, the professed enemies of different interests and religion which persecuted me were subdued, and I ready to settle upon the eternal foundations of sound doctrine, of primitive government, of an holy and pure worship, of a decent and comely order, to the amazement of the world, to the honour of religion, to the glory of God, to the peace of the whole earth, and for good will among men. Behold! my children are discontent, my government is complained of, my ordinances are neglected, my ministers are despised, my peace is disturbed, and my safety endangered. Hear, O heavens, and give ear, O earth! What could I have done that I have not done? Have I not taught the truth of God sincerely, giving milk to babes, and stronger meat to them that were able to bear it, and the oracles of God to all in a language they best understood? Have I concealed any part of God's sacred counsel from you? Have I not set forth with all plainness and freedom the blessed fulness and excellences of my Lord Jesus Christ, in such a manner and measure as I received from the Word and Spirit? Have I not administered all the ordinances of God faithfully? Have I not enjoyed and taught all virtue and all grace, carefully recommending to my children *Whatsoever things are good, whatsoever things are true, whatsoever things are honest, whatsoever things are just, whatsoever things are pure, whatsoever things are lovely, whatsoever things are of good report ;* every holy duty, every necessary rule, and every imitable example ; with all the advantages of sound knowledge, powerful preaching, which at once was able to inform the weak, to reclaim the most erroneous, to reform the most debauched, to satisfy the most curious, and to silence the most refractory? Have I not prepared with much study and industry, with many prayers and tears, with long education and diligent care, reverend bishops, orderly presbyters, able ministers, workmen that need not be ashamed, duly ordained, and called after an uninterrupted and Catholic succession through all ages, agreeable to that original institution which was from Jesus Christ, the great High Priest, the true Prophet, the sovereign King of the Church, the chief Preacher of righteousness, and Bishop of our souls? Have I not, I say, taken an holy care of a succession of ministers about holy things, who might divide the Word aright by solid preaching, might wait upon God solemnly by a devout and discreet praying, might convince gainsayers by acute disputing, might instruct the world by exact writing, might maintain peace and order by wise governing, might reform the world by holy living? Hath it not been my care and endeavour to keep up the soundness, power, and life of Christian religion? Have not I laboured that my good people might everywhere have what is necessary and wholesome for their soul's good, in devout prayers, in Holy Sacraments, in powerful sermons ; whereby I desired (God knoweth) to preserve wholesome and saving truth, to promote true holiness, to set up an holy decency, to maintain the wholesome form and power

of godliness in truth, peace, order, and unity ?   Have not I held forth
an holy light, rule, and life, in the plain parts of Scripture everywhere
read, in the Articles everywhere acknowledged, in the Creeds and
Catechism every year explained, in the Liturgy constantly used,
whereby poor souls had a plain, easy, and sure way to Heaven, through
an unfeigned faith, sincere repentance, a catholic charity, a devout
humility, a good conscience, and an holy obedience to God and man,
according to the will of God unto all well-pleasing ?   Do not I take
care to instruct the ignorant diligently, to comfort the weak-hearted
tenderly, to raise up them that fall compassionately, to visit those
that are sick charitably, to relieve those that want mercifully, to bury
my dead that sleep in Jesus solemnly, to punish those that do amiss
severely, to restore them that have gone astray pitifully, to instruct
them that oppose themselves meekly, to frame a way of peace, order,
and communion (in which brethren might happily dwell together in
unity) prudently, rationally, and discreetly ?   O what failings of mine,
then, have occasioned these impatient murmurs which I hear ?
What faults of mine have raised those bitter reproaches which I bear ?
What enormities of mine have provoked those imminent dangers
which I fear ?   O, why is it that ye who own my God as Saviour,
who have submitted to my doctrine as your rule, who have partaken
of my Sacrament as your refreshment and comfort ;  O, why is it that
ye hate and despise me, that ye strip and wound me, that ye tear and
mangle me, that ye impoverish and debase me, that ye make me a
scorn, an abomination, an hissing and astonishment to all that see me,
a derision and a mocking to my enemies round about me ?

Alas, all men of weight and worth, for parts and piety, for judgement and ingenuity, for conscience and integrity, for grace, learning,
and renown, know my innocency thus far, that as to the foundation of
faith and rule of holiness, I have only adhered to God's blessed Word.
As for the circumstances and ceremonies of religion, I use in them
prudently and charitably that liberty and power which I suppose is
allowed here for peace, order, and decency, by that blessed God Who
is not the author of confusion, but of peace, as in all the Churches of
the saints.   If we may believe the integrity of those Reformers that
settled this Church, whose learning, worth, and piety have been confirmed by the testimony of so many wise and religious princes, by
the approbation of so many honourable and unanimous Houses of
Parliament, by the suffrages of so many learned and reverend Convocations, by the applauses of so many other Reformed Churches ;  if
we may believe the preaching, living, and dying, of so many hundred
excellent bishops and ministers, or the prayers and proficiencies of so
many thousand of godly Christians ;  or if we may believe the wonderful blessings and special graces of a merciful God, attesting the verity,

integrity, and sanctity of my Christian constitution for many happy years, or if you will believe all men in England, who have, by oaths and subscriptions, by vows and protestations, resolved to maintain the Protestant religion as it was established in the Church of England ; who despair anywhere to find the way of truth and peace, of holiness and happiness, but in the use of those holy means and in the exercise of those divine graces which accompany salvation, within me professed and enjoyed,—. I know nothing excellent in any Church for outward policy, inward tranquillity, and eternal felicity ; nothing that was pious or peaceable, moral or virtuous, ritual or spiritual, orderly or comely, or any way conducing to truth and holiness, to· grace or virtue, to the soul's edification and comfort, which was not by me entertained with competent maintenance, noble encouragements, ingenuous honours, peaceable serenity, and munificent plenty ; in which I flourished so many years by God's goodness and man's indulgence.

Alas, whatever I have done in the settlements of the rites, circumstances, and decencies of religion, I have observed that modesty, wisdom, and humility that became a Church of Christ, in discreetly and ingenuously complying with sober, primitive, and venerable antiquity in the Church, as far as it observed the rules of God's Word, and went not beyond the liberty allowed it in point of order and decency. O, you are too knowing to be ignorant, and too ingenious to be insensible, of your duty to God, and your respect to me, who was heretofore so much loved by my children, applauded by my friends, reverenced by my neighbours, feared and envied by mine enemies for those spiritual gifts, ministerial, devotional, and practical, which were evidently seen in me, those heavenly influences which people received from me, those gracious examples and frequent good works set forth by me, the blessed experiences men enjoyed with me, the charitable simplicities exercised by my members, the numerous assemblies, the frequent devotions, the reverent attentions, the unanimous communions, the well-grounded hopes, and unspeakable comforts which thousands enjoyed, both living and dying, in obedience to and communion with me ; which to impartial men were most impregnant evidences and valid demonstrations of true religion and a true Church, settled by the joint consent and public piety of a Christian nation.

# II. THE CHURCH

# (1) HOLY AND CATHOLIC

## No. 13.  JOHN PEARSON

[From *An Exposition of the Creed*, Article IX (" The Holy Catholic Church "). Ed. Oxford (E. Burton), 1864, pp. 589–620. This classic was first printed in 1659. Further editions appeared in the author's lifetime in 1662, 1669, 1676, and 1683; and there has been an almost continuous succession of reprints ever since. That of Edward Burton, Regius Professor of Divinity at Oxford, which was first issued in 1833, is a model of care and accuracy. A Latin version appeared in 1691; and it has also been translated into several other languages. The *Exposition* was based upon a set of lectures which the learned author had delivered to his parishioners at St. Clement's, Eastcheap, and to them the work was dedicated. The extensive notes contain a fund of Patristic learning.]

IN this Ninth Article [of the Apostles' Creed] we meet with some variety of position, and with much addition. For whereas it is here the Ninth, in some Creeds we find it the last; and whereas it consisteth of two distinct parts, the latter is wholly added, and the former partly augmented; the most ancient professing no more than to believe *the Holy Church*: and the Greeks having added, by way of explication or determination, the word *Catholic*, it was at last received into the Latin Creed.

To begin then with the first part of the Article, I shall endeavour so to expound it, as to show what is the meaning of the Church, which Christ hath propounded to us; how that Church is *holy*, as the Apostle hath assured us, how that holy Church is *Catholic*, as the Fathers have taught us. For when I say, *I believe in the Holy Catholic Church*, I mean that there is a Church which is holy, and which is Catholic; and I understand that Church alone which is both Catholic and holy; and being this holiness and catholicism are but affections of this Church which I believe, I must first declare what is the true nature and notion of the Church; how I am assured of the existence of that Church; and then how it is the subject of those two affections.

For the understanding of the true notion of the Church, first we must observe that the nominal definition or derivation of the word is not sufficient to describe the nature of it. If we look upon the old English word now in use, *Church* or *Kirk*, it is derived from the Greek, and first signified the house of the Lord, that is, of Christ, and from thence was taken to signify the people of God, meeting in the house of God. The Greek word, used by the Apostles to express the Church, signifieth *a calling forth*, if we look upon the origination; a congregation of men, or a company assembled, if we consider the use of it.

23

But neither of these doth fully express the nature of the Church, what it is in itself, and as it is propounded to our belief.

Our second observation is, that the Church hath been taken for the whole complex of men and angels worshipping the same God; and again, the angels being not considered, it hath been taken as comprehending all the sons of men believing in God ever since the foundation of the world. But being Christ took not upon Him the nature of angels, and consequently did not properly purchase them with His Blood, or call them by His Word; being they are not in the Scriptures mentioned as parts or members of the Church, nor can be imagined to be built upon the Prophets or Apostles; being we are at this time to speak of the proper notion of the Church, therefore I shall not look upon it as comprehending any more than the sons of men. Again, being though Christ was the Lamb slain before the foundation of the world, and whosoever from the beginning pleased God were saved by His Blood; yet because there was a vast difference between the several dispensations of the Law and Gospel, because our Saviour spake expressly of building Himself a Church when the Jewish Synagogue was about to fail, because Catholicism, which is here attributed unto the Church, must be understood in opposition to the legal singularity of the Jewish nation, because the ancient Fathers were generally wont to distinguish between the Synagogue and the Church, therefore I think it necessary to restrain this notion to Christianity.

Thirdly, therefore, I observe that the only way to attain unto the knowledge of the true notion of the Church, is to search into the New Testament, and from the places there which mention it, to conclude what is the nature of it. To which purpose it will be necessary to take notice that our Saviour first speaking of it, mentioneth it as that which then was not, but afterwards was to be; as when He spake unto the great Apostle, *Thou art Peter, and upon this rock I will build My Church*; but when He ascended into Heaven, and the Holy Ghost came down, when Peter had converted *three thousand souls* which were added to the *hundred and twenty* Disciples, then was there a Church (and that built upon Peter, according to our Saviour's promise), for after that we read, *The Lord added to the Church daily such as should be saved.* A Church then our Saviour promised should be built, and by a promise made before His death; after His ascension, and upon the preaching of St. Peter, we find a Church built or constituted, and that of a nature capable of a daily increase. We cannot then take a better occasion to search into the true notion of the Church of Christ than by looking into the origination and increase thereof; without which it is impossible to have a right conception of it.

Now what we are infallibly assured of the first actual existence of a

Church of Christ is only this: there were twelve Apostles with the Disciples before the descent of the Holy Ghost, and *the number of the names together were about an hundred and twenty*. When the Holy Ghost came after a powerful and miraculous manner upon the blessed Apostles, and St. Peter preached unto the Jews, that they should *repent and be baptized in the name of Jesus Christ for the remission of sins; they that gladly received his word were baptized, and the same day there were added unto them about three thousand souls*. These being thus added to the rest, *continued stedfastly in the Apostles' doctrine and fellowship, and in breaking of bread, and in prayers*; and all these persons so continuing are called the Church. What this Church was is easily determined, for it was a certain number of men, of which some were Apostles, some the former Disciples, others were persons which repented, and believed, and were baptized in the name of Jesus Christ, and continued hearing the Word preached, receiving the Sacraments administered, joining in the public prayers presented unto God. This was then the Church, which was daily increased by the addition of other persons received into it upon the same conditions, making up *the multitude of them that believed, who were of one heart and one soul, believers added to the Lord, multitudes both of men and women*.

But though the Church was thus begun, and represented unto us as one in the beginning, though that Church which we profess to believe in the Creed be also propounded unto us as one, and so the notion of the first Church in the *Acts of the Apostles* might seem sufficient to express the nature of that Church which we believe; yet because that Church was one by way of origination, and was afterwards divided into many, the actual members of that one becoming the members of several Churches; and that Church which we believe is otherwise one by way of complexion, receiving the members of all Churches into it; it will be necessary to consider, how at the first those several Churches were constituted, that we may understand how in this one Church they are all united. To which purpose it will be farther fit to examine the several acceptions of this word, as it is diversely used by the Holy Ghost in the New Testament; that, if it be possible, nothing may escape our search, but that all things may be weighed, before we collect and conclude the full notion of the Church from thence.

First then, That word which signifies the Church in the original Greek is sometimes used in the vulgar sense according as the native Greeks did use the same to express their conventions, without any relation to the worship of God or Christ, and therefore is translated by the word *Assembly*, of as great a latitude. Secondly, It is sometimes used in the same notion in which the Greek translators of the Old Testament made use of it, for the Assembly of the people of God under the Law, and therefore might be most fitly translated the *Congre-*

*gation*, as it is in the Old Testament. Thirdly, It hath been conceived that even in the Scriptures it is sometimes taken for the place in which the members of the Church did meet to perform their solemn and public services unto God; and some passages there are which seem to speak no less, but yet are not so certainly to be understood of the place, but that they may as well be spoken of the people congregated in a certain place. Beside these few different acceptions, the Church in the language of the New Testament doth always signify a company of persons professing the Christian faith, but not always in the same latitude. Sometimes it admitteth of distinction and plurality; sometimes it reduceth all into conjunction and unity. Sometimes the Churches of God are diversified as many; sometimes, as many as they are, they are all comprehended in one.

For first in general there are often mentioned *the Churches* by way of plurality, *the Churches of God, the Churches of the Gentiles, the Churches of the saints.* In particular we find a few believers gathered together in the house of one single person, called a Church, as the Church in the house of Priscilla and Aquila, the Church in the house of Nymphas, the Church in the house of Philemon; which Churches were nothing else but the believing and baptized persons of each family, with such as they admitted and received into their house to join in the worship of the same God.

Again, When the Scripture speaketh of any country where the Gospel had been preached, it nameth always by way of plurality the Churches of that country, as the Churches of Judaea, of Samaria, and Galilee, the Churches of Syria and of Cilicia, the Churches of Galatia, the Churches of Asia, the Churches of Macedonia. But notwithstanding there were several such Churches or congregations of believers in great and populous cities, yet the Scriptures always speak of such congregations in the notion of one Church; as when St. Paul wrote to the Corinthians, *Let your women keep silence in the Churches*; yet the dedication of his Epistle is *Unto the Church of God which is at Corinth.* So we read not of the Churches, but the Church at Jerusalem, the Church at Antioch, the Church at Caesarea, the Church at Ephesus, the Church of the Thessalonians, the Church of Laodicea, the Church of Smyrna, the Church of Pergamus, the Church of Thyatira, the Church of Sardis, the Church of Philadelphia. From whence it appeareth that a collection of several congregations, every one of which is in some sense a Church, and may be called so, is properly one Church by virtue of the subordination of them all in one government under one ruler. For thus in those great and populous cities where Christians were very numerous, not only all the several Churches within the cities, but those also in the adjacent parts, were united under the care and inspection of one Bishop, and therefore was accounted one Church, the number of the Churches following the number of the angels, that is, the rulers of them, as is evident in the *Revelation*.

Now as several Churches are reduced to the denomination of one Church, in relation to the single governor of those many Churches, so all the Churches of all cities and all nations in the world may be reduced to the same single denomination in relation to one supreme Governor of them all, and that one Governor is Christ the Bishop of our souls. Wherefore the Apostle, speaking of that in which all Churches do agree, comprehendeth them all under the same appellation of one Church; and therefore often by the name of Church are understood all Christians whatsoever belonging to any of the Churches dispersed through the distant and divided parts of the world. For the single persons professing faith in Christ are members of the particular Churches in which they live, and all those particular Churches are members of the general and universal Church, which is one by unity of aggregation; and this is the Church in the Creed which we believe, and which is in other Creeds expressly termed *one, I believe in one Holy Catholic Church*.

It will therefore be farther necessary for the understanding of the nature of the Church, which is thus one, to consider in what that unity doth consist. And being it is an aggregation not only of many persons, but also of many congregations, the unity thereof must consist in some agreement of them all, and adhesion to something which is one. If then we reflect upon the first Church again, which we found constituted in the *Acts*, and to which all other since have been in a manner added and conjoined, we may collect from their union and agreement how all other Churches are united and agree. Now they were described to be believing and baptized persons, converted to the Faith by St. Peter, *continuing stedfastly in the Apostles' doctrine and fellowship, and in breaking of bread, and in prayers*. These then were all built upon the same Rock, all professed the same faith, all received the same Sacraments, all performed the same devotions, and thereby were all reputed members of the same Church. To this Church were added daily such as should be saved, who became members of the same Church by being built upon the same Foundation, by adhering to the same doctrine, by receiving the same Sacraments, by performing the same devotions.

From whence it appeareth that the first unity of the Church considered in itself (beside that of the Head, which is one Christ, and the life communicated from that Head, which is one Spirit) relieth upon the original of it, which is one; even as an house built upon one foundation, though consisting of many rooms, and every room of many stones, is not yet many, but one house. Now there is but one foundation upon which the Church is built, and that is Christ: *for other*

*foundation can no man lay, than that is laid, which is Jesus Christ.*
And though the Apostles and the Prophets be also termed the foundation, yet even then the unity is preserved, because as they are stones
in the foundation, so are they united by one Corner-stone; whereby
it comes to pass that such persons as are of the Church, being *fellow-
citizens with the saints, and of the household of God, are built upon the
foundation of the Apostles and Prophets, Jesus Christ Himself being the
chief corner-stone, in Whom all the building fitly framed together, groweth
unto a holy temple in the Lord.* This *stone* was *laid in Zion for a foundation, a tried stone, a precious corner-stone, a sure foundation*: there was
the first Church built, and whosoever have been, or ever shall be converted to the true Christian Faith, are and shall be added to that Church,
and laid upon the same foundation, which is the unity of origination.
Our Saviour gave the same power to all the Apostles, which was to
found the Church; but He gave that power to Peter, to shew the unity
of the same Church.

Secondly, The Church is therefore one, though the members be
many, because they all agree in one faith. There is *one Lord*, and *one
faith*, and that faith *once delivered to the saints*, which whosoever shall
receive, embrace, and profess, must necessarily be accounted one in
reference to that profession. For if a company of believers become a
Church by believing, they must also become one Church by believing
one truth. If they be one in respect of the foundation, which is
ultimately one; if we look upon Christ, which is mediately one; if we
look upon the Apostles united in one Corner-stone; if those which
believe be therefore said to be built upon the foundation of the Apostles,
because they believe the doctrine which the Apostles preached, and the
Apostles be therefore said to be of the same foundation, and united
to the Corner-stone, because they all taught the same doctrine which
they received from Christ; then they which believe the same doctrine
delivered by Christ to all the Apostles, delivered by all the Apostles
to believers, being all professors of the same faith, must be members of
the same Church. And this is the unity of faith.

Thirdly, Many persons and Churches, howsoever distinguished by
time or place, are considered as one Church because they acknowledge
and receive the same Sacraments, the signs and badges of the people of
God. When the Apostles were sent to found and build the Church,
they received this commission, *Go and teach all nations, baptizing them
in the Name of the Father, and of the Son, and of the Holy Ghost.* Now
as there is but *one Lord*, and *one faith*, so also there is but *one Baptism*;
and consequently they which are admitted to it, in receiving it are one.
Again, At the institution of the Lord's Supper, Christ commanded,
saying, *Eat ye all of this, Drink ye all of this*; and all, by communicating
of one, become as to that communication one. *For we being many are*

*one bread and one body; for we are all partakers of that one bread.* As therefore the Israelites *were all baptized unto Moses in the cloud and in the sea, and did all eat the same spiritual meat, and did all drink the same spiritual drink,* and thereby appeared to be the one people of God; so all believing persons, and all Churches congregated in the Name of Christ, washed in the same laver of regeneration, eating of the same bread, and drinking of the same cup, are united in the same cognizance, and so known to be the same Church. And this is the unity of the Sacraments.

Fourthly, Whosoever belongeth to any Church is some way called; and all which are so *are called in one hope of their calling*: the same reward of eternal life is promised unto every person, and *we* all *through the Spirit wait for the hope of righteousness by faith.* They therefore which depend upon the same God and worship Him all for the same end, *the hope of eternal life, which God, that cannot lie, promised before the world began,* having all the same expectation, may well be reputed the same Church. And this is the unity of hope.

Fifthly, They which are all of one mind, whatsoever the number of their persons be, they are in reference to that mind but one; as all the members, howsoever different, yet being animated by one soul, become one body. Charity is of a fastening and uniting nature; nor can we call those many, who *endeavour to keep the unity of the Spirit in the bond of peace.* By this, said our Saviour, *shall all men know that ye are My Disciples, if ye have love one to another.* And this is the unity of charity.

Lastly, All the Churches of God are united into one by the unity of discipline and government, by virtue whereof the same Christ ruleth in them all. For they have all the same pastoral guides appointed, authorized, sanctified, and set apart by the appointment of God, by the direction of the Spirit, to direct and lead the people of God in the same way of eternal salvation. As therefore there is no Church where there is no order, no ministry, so where the same order and ministry is there is the same Church. And this is the unity of regiment and discipline.

By these means and for these reasons millions of persons and multitudes of congregations are united into one body, and become one Church. And thus under the name of *Church* expressed in this Article, I understand a body, or collection of human persons, professing faith in Christ, gathered together in several places of the world for the worship of the same God, and united into the same corporation by the means aforesaid. And this I conceive sufficient to declare the true notion of the Church as such, which is here the object of our faith. It remaineth therefore that we next consider the existence of the Church, which is acknowledged in the act of faith applied to this object. For when I profess and say, *I believe a Church*, it is not only an acknowledgment of a Church which hath been, or of a Church which shall be, but also of that which is. When I say, *I believe in Christ dead*, I acknowledge that death which once was, and now is not: for Christ once died, but now is not dead. When I say, *I believe the resurrection of the body*, I acknowledge that which never yet was, and is not now, but shall hereafter be. Thus the act of faith is applicated to the object according to the nature of it; to what is already past, as past; to what is to come, as still to come; to that which is present, as it is still present. Now that which was then past, when the Creed was made, must necessarily be always past, and so believed for ever; that which shall never come to pass until the end of the world, when this public profession of faith shall cease, that must for ever be believed as still to come. But that which was when the Creed began, and was to continue till that Creed shall end, is proposed to our belief in every age as being; and thus ever since the first Church was constituted, the Church itself, as being, was the object of the faith of the Church believing.

The existence therefore of the Church of Christ (as that Church before is understood by us) is the continuation of it in an actual being, from the first collection in the Apostles' times unto the consummation of all things. And therefore to make good this explication of the Article, it will be necessary to prove that the Church, which our Saviour founded and the Apostles gathered, was to receive a constant and perpetual accession, and by a successive augmentation be uninterruptedly continued in an actual existence of believing persons and congregations in all ages unto the end of the world.

Now this indeed is a proper object of faith, because it is grounded only upon the promise of God; there can be no other assurance of the perpetuity of this Church, but what we have from Him that built it. The Church is not of such a nature as would necessarily, once begun, preserve itself for ever. Many thousand persons have fallen totally and finally from the faith professed, and so apostatized from the Church. Many particular Churches have been wholly lost, many candlesticks have been removed; neither is there any particular Church which hath any power to continue itself more or longer than others; and consequently, if all particulars be defectible, the universal Church must also be subject of itself unto the same defectibility.

But though the providence of God doth suffer many particular Churches to cease, yet the promise of the same God will never permit that all of them at once shall perish. When Christ spake first particularly to St. Peter, He sealed His speech with a powerful promise of perpetuity, saying, *Thou art Peter, and upon this rock will I build My Church, and the gates of hell shall not prevail against it*. When He spake generally to all the rest of the Apostles to the same purpose, *Go teach all nations, baptizing them in the Name of the Father, and of the Son, and of the Holy Ghost*, He added a promise to the same effect, *And, lo, I am with you alway, even to the end of the world*. The first of these promises assureth us of the continuance of the Church, because it is built upon a rock; for our Saviour had expressed this before, *Whosoever heareth these sayings of Mine, and doeth them, I will liken him unto a wise man which built his house upon a rock: and the rain descended, and the floods came, and the winds blew, and beat upon that house; and it fell not: for it was founded upon a rock*. The Church of Christ is the house of Christ; for He hath *builded the house*, and is as a *Son over His own house, Whose house are we*; and as *a wise man*, He hath built His house upon a rock, and what is so built shall not fall. The latter of these promises giveth not only an assurance of the continuance of the Church, but also the cause of that continuance, which is the presence of Christ. *Where two or three are gathered together in the Name of Christ, there He is in the midst of them*, and thereby they become a Church; for they are as a builded house, and the Son within that house. Wherefore, being Christ doth promise His presence unto the Church, even to the end of the world, He doth thereby assure us of the existence of the Church until that time of which His Presence is the cause. Indeed, this is *the city of the Lord of Hosts, the city of our God, God will establish it for ever*; as the great Prophet of the Church hath said.

Upon the certainty of this truth, the existence of the Church hath been propounded as an object of our faith in every age of Christianity; and so it shall be still unto the end of the world. For those which are believers are the Church; and therefore if they do believe, they must believe there is a Church. And thus having shewed in what the nature of a Church consisteth, and proved that a Church of that nature is of perpetual and indefectible existence by virtue of the promises of Christ, I have done all which can be necessary for the explication of this part of the Article, *I believe the Church*.

After the consideration of that which is the subject in this Article followeth the explication of the affections thereof; which are two, sanctity and universality; the one attributed unto it by the Apostles, the other by the Fathers of the Church. By the first the Church is denominated Holy, by the second Catholic. Now the Church which we have described may be called Holy in several respects, and for several reasons. First, in reference to the vocation by which all the members thereof are called and separated from the rest of the world to God, which separation in the language of the Scriptures is a sanctification: and so the calling being holy (*for God hath called us with an holy calling*), the body which is separated and congregated thereby may well be termed *holy*. Secondly, in relation to the offices appointed and the

powers exercised in the Church, which by their institution and operation
are holy, that Church for which they were appointed, and in which
they are exercised, may be called *holy*.   Thirdly, because whosoever
is called to profess faith in Christ is thereby engaged to holiness of
life, according to the words of the Apostle, *Let every one that nameth
the Name of Christ depart from iniquity* : for those namers of the Name,
or named by the Name, of Christ, are such as called on His Name,
and that was the description of the Church ; as when Saul did persecute
the Church, it is said he had *authority from the chief priests to bind all that
called upon the Name* of Christ ; and when he *preached Christ in the
synagogues, all that heard him said, Is not this he who destroyed them
which called on this Name in Jerusalem ?*   Being then all within the
Church are by their profession obliged to such holiness of life, in respect
of this obligation, the whole Church may be termed *holy*.   Fourthly,
in regard the end of constituting a Church in God was for the purchasing an holy and a precious people ; and the great design thereof
was for the begetting and increasing holiness, that as God is originally
holy in Himself, so He might communicate His sanctity to the sons of
men, whom He intended to bring unto the fruition of Himself, unto
which, without a previous sanctification, they can never approach,
because *without holiness no man shall* ever *see God*.

     For these four reasons, the whole *Church of God*, as it containeth
in it all the persons which were called to the profession of the faith of
Christ, or were baptized in His Name, may well be termed and believed
*holy*.   But the Apostle hath also delivered another kind of holiness which
cannot belong unto the Church taken in so great a latitude.   *For,*
saith he, *Christ loved the Church, and gave Himself for it, that He might
sanctify and cleanse it by the washing of water, by the word, that He might
present it to Himself a glorious Church, not having spot or wrinkle, or any
such thing, but that it should be holy and without blemish.*   Now though
it may be conceived that Christ did love the whole Church, as it did
any way contain all such as ever called upon His Name, and did give
Himself for all of them ; yet we cannot imagine that the whole body
of all men could ever be so holy, as to be without spot, wrinkle, blemish,
or any such thing.   It will be therefore necessary, within the great
complex body of the Universal Church, to find that Church to which
this absolute holiness doth belong : and to this purpose it will be fit
to consider both the difference of the persons contained in the Church,
as it hath been hitherto described, while they continue in this life,
and their different conditions after death ; whereby we shall at last
discover in what persons this holiness is inherent really, in what condition it is inherent perfectly, and consequently in what other sense
it may be truly and properly affirmed that the Church is holy.

     Where first we must observe that the Church, as it embraceth all the professors of the true faith of Christ, containeth in it not only such as do truly believe and are obedient to the Word, but those also which are hypocrites, and profane. Many profess the Faith, which have no true belief; many have some kind of faith, which live with no correspondence to the Gospel preached. Within therefore the notion of the Church are comprehended good and bad, being both externally called, and both professing the same Faith. For *the Kingdom of Heaven is like unto a field in which wheat and tares grow together unto the harvest; like unto a net that was cast into the sea, and gathered of every kind*; like unto *a floor* in which is laid up *wheat* and *chaff*; like unto *a marriage-feast*, in which some have on the *wedding-garment*, and some not. This is that ark of Noah in which were preserved beasts clean and unclean. This is that *great house* in which *there are not only vessels of gold and of silver, but also of wood and of earth, and some to honour and some to dishonour*. There are *many called*, of all which the Church consisteth, but there are *few chosen* of those which are called, and thereby within the Church. I conclude therefore, as the ancient Catholics did against the Donatists, that within the Church, in the public profession and external communion thereof, are contained persons truly good and sanctified, and hereafter saved, and together with them other persons void of all saving grace, and hereafter to be damned: and that Church containing these of both kinds may well be called *holy*, as St. Matthew called Jerusalem *the holy city*, even at that time when our Saviour did but begin to preach, when we know there was in that city a general corruption in manners and worship.

Of these promiscuously contained in the Church, such as are void of all saving grace while they live, and communicate with the rest of the Church, and when they pass out of this life, die in their sins, and remain under the eternal wrath of God; as they were not in their persons holy while they lived, so are they no way of the Church after their death, neither as members of it, nor as contained in it. Through their own demerit they fall short of the glory unto which they were called, and being by death separated from the external communion of the Church, and having no true internal communion with the members and the head thereof, are totally and finally cut off from the Church of Christ. On the contrary, such as are efficaciously called, justified, and sanctified, while they live are truly holy, and when they die are perfectly holy; nor are they by their death separated from the Church, but remain united still by virtue of that internal union by which they were before conjoined both to the members and the head. As therefore the Church is truly holy, not only by an holiness of institution, but also by a personal sanctity in reference to these saints while they live, so is it also perfectly holy, in relation to the same saints glorified in Heaven. And at the end of the world, when all the wicked shall be turned into hell, and consequently all cut off from the communion of the Church, when the members of the Church remaining being perfectly sanctified, shall be eternally glorified, then shall the whole Church be truly and perfectly holy.

Then shall that be completely fulfilled, that Christ shall *present unto Himself a glorious Church*, which shall *be holy and without blemish*. Not that there are two Churches of Christ, one, in which good and bad are mingled together, another, in which there are good alone; one, in which the saints are imperfectly holy, another, in which they are perfectly such; but one and the same Church, in relation to different times, admitteth or not admitteth the permixtion of the wicked, or the imperfection of the godly. To conclude, the Church of God is universally holy in respect of all, by institutions and administrations of sanctity; the same Church is really holy in this world, in relation to all godly persons contained in it, by a real infused sanctity; the same is farther yet at the same time perfectly holy in reference to the saints departed and admitted to the presence of God; and the same Church shall hereafter be most completely holy in the world to come, when all the members actually belonging to it shall be at once perfected in holiness and completed in happiness. And thus I conceive the affection of sanctity sufficiently explicated.

The next affection of the Church is that of universality, *I believe the holy CATHOLIC Church*. Now the word Catholic, as it is not read in the Scriptures, so was it not anciently in the Creed (as we have already shewn); but, being inserted by the Church, must necessarily be interpreted by the sense which the most ancient Fathers had of it, and that sense must be confirmed, so far as it is consentient with the Scriptures. To grant then that the word was not used by the Apostles, we must also acknowledge that it was most anciently in use among the primitive Fathers, and that as to several intents. For, first, they called the Epistles of St. James, St. Peter, St. John, St. Jude, the Catholic Epistles, because when the Epistles written by St. Paul were directed to particular Churches congregated in particular cities, these were either sent to the Churches dispersed through a great part of the world, or directed to the whole Church of God upon the face of the whole earth. Again, we observe the Fathers to use the word *Catholic* for nothing else but general or universal, in the originary or vulgar sense, as the catholic resurrection is the resurrection of all men, the catholic opinion the opinion of all men. Sometimes it was used as a word of state, signifying an officer which collected the Emperor's revenue in several provinces, united into one diocese; who, because there were particular officers belonging to the particular provinces, and all under him, was therefore called the *Catholicus*, as general Procurator of them all, from whence that title was by some transferred upon the Christian Patriarchs.

When this title is attributed to the Church, it hath not always the same notion or signification; for when by the Church is understood the house of God, or place in which the worship of God is performed, then by the *Catholic Church* is meant no more than the common Church into which all such persons as belonged to that parish in which it was built were wont to congregate. For where monasteries were in use, as there were separate habitations for men, and distinct for women, so were there also Churches for each distinct; and in the parishes, where there was no distinction of sexes, as to habitation, there was a common Church which received them both, and therefore called *Catholic*.

Again, When the Church is taken for the persons making profession of the Christian Faith, the *Catholic* is often added in opposition to heretics and schismatics, expressing a particular Church continuing in the true faith with the rest of the Church of God, as the Catholic Church in Smyrna, the Catholic Church in Alexandria. Now being these particular Churches could not be named Catholic as they were particular, in reference to this or that city in which they were congregated, it followeth that they were called Catholic by their coherence and conjunction with that Church which was properly and originally called so; which is the Church taken in that acception which we have already delivered. That Church which was built upon the Apostles as upon the foundation, congregated by their preaching and by their baptizing, receiving continued accession, and disseminated in several parts of the earth, containing within it numerous congregations, all which were truly called Churches, as members of the same Church; that Church, I say, was after some time called the *Catholic Church*, that is to say, the name *Catholic* was used by the Greeks to signify the whole. For being every particular congregation professing the name of Christ was from the beginning called a Church; being likewise all such congregations considered together were originally comprehended under the name of the Church; being these two notions of the word were different, it came to pass that for distinction sake at first they called the Church, taken in the large and comprehensive sense, by as large and comprehensive a name, the Catholic Church.

Although this seem the first intention of those which gave the name *Catholic* to the Church, to signify thereby nothing else but the whole or universal Church, yet those which followed did signify by the same that affection of the Church which floweth from the nature of it, and may be expressed by that word. At first they called the whole Church *Catholic*, meaning no more than the Universal Church; but having used that term some space of time, they considered how the nature of the Church was to be universal, and in what that universality did consist.

As far then as the ancient Fathers have expressed themselves, and as far as their expressions are agreeable with the descriptions of the Church delivered in the Scriptures, so far, I conceive, we may safely conclude that the Church of Christ is truly Catholic, and that the truly Catholic Church is the true Church of Christ, which must necessarily be sufficient for the explication of this affection, which we acknowledge when we say, we *believe the Catholic Church*.

The most obvious and most general notion of this Catholicism consisteth in the diffusiveness of the Church, grounded upon the commission given to the builders of it, *Go teach all nations*, whereby they and their successors were authorized and empowered to gather congregations of believers, and so to extend the borders of the Church unto the utmost parts of the earth. The synagogue of the Jews especially consisted of one nation, and the public worship of God was confined to one country. *In Judah* was *God known, and His name* was *great in Israel ; in Salem* was *His tabernacle, and His dwelling-place in Zion. He shewed His word unto Jacob, His statutes and His judgements unto Israel ; He hath not dealt so with any nation.* The temple was the only place in which the sacrifices could be offered, in which the priests could perform their office of ministration ; and so under the Law there was an inclosure divided from all the world besides. But God said unto His Son, *I will give the heathen for Thine inheritance, and the uttermost parts of the earth for Thy possession.* And Christ commanded the Apostles, saying, *Go ye into all the world, and preach the Gospel to every creature : that repentance and remission of sins should be preached in His Name among all nations, beginning at Jerusalem.* Thus the Church of Christ, in its primary institution, was made to be of a diffusive nature, to spread and extend itself from the city of Jerusalem, where it first began, to all the parts and corners of the earth. From whence we find them in the *Revelation* crying to the Lamb, *Thou wast slain, and hast redeemed us to God by Thy blood, out of every kindred, and tongue, and people, and nation.* This reason did the ancient Fathers render why the Church was called *Catholic*, and the nature of the Church is so described in the Scriptures.

Secondly, They called the Church of Christ the Catholic Church, because it teacheth all things which are necessary for a Christian to know, whether they be things in Heaven or things in earth, whether they concern the condition of man in this life or in the life to come. As the Holy Ghost did lead the Apostles *into all truth*, so did the Apostles leave all truth unto the Church which, teaching all the same, may well be called Catholic, from the universality of necessary and saving truths retained in it.

Thirdly, The Church hath been thought fit to be called Catholic in reference to the universal obedience which it prescribeth ; both in respect of the persons, obliging men of all conditions, and in relation to the precepts, requiring the performance of all the evangelical commands.

Fourthly, The Church hath been yet further called or reputed Catholic, by reason of all graces given in it; whereby all diseases of the soul are healed, and spiritual virtues are disseminated, all the works and words and thoughts of men are regulated, till we become perfect men in Christ Jesus.

In all these four acceptions did some of the ancient Fathers understand the Church of Christ to be Catholic, and every one of them doth certainly belong unto it. Wherefore I conclude that this Catholicism, or second affection of the Church, consisteth generally in universality, as embracing all sorts of persons, as to be disseminated through all nations, as comprehending all ages, as containing all necessary and saving truths, as obliging all conditions of men to all kind of obedience, as curing all diseases, and planting all graces, in the souls of men.

The necessity of believing the Holy Catholic Church appeareth first in this, that Christ hath appointed it as the only way unto eternal life. We read at the first, that *the Lord added to the Church daily such as should be saved*; and what was then daily done hath been done since continually. Christ never appointed two ways to Heaven, nor did He build a Church to save some, and make another institution for other men's salvation. *There is no other Name under Heaven given among men whereby we must be saved*, but the Name of Jesus; and that Name is no otherwise given under Heaven than in the Church. As none were saved from the deluge but such as were within the ark of Noah, framed for their reception by the command of God; as none of the first-born of Egypt lived, but such as were within those habitations, whose door posts were sprinkled with blood by the appointment of God for their preservation; as none of the inhabitants of Jericho could escape the fire or sword, but such as were within the house of Rahab, for whose protection a covenant was made; so none shall ever escape the eternal wrath of God, which belong not to the Church of God. This is the congregation of those persons here on earth which shall hereafter meet in Heaven. These are the vessels of the tabernacle carried up and down, at last to be translated into, and fixed in, the temple.

Secondly, It is necessary to believe the Church of Christ which is but one, that being in it we may take care never to cast ourselves, or be ejected, out of it. There is a power within the Church to cast those out which do belong to it; for if any *neglect to hear the Church*, saith our Saviour, *let him be unto thee as an heathen man and a publican*. By great and scandalous offences, by incorrigible misdemeanours, we may incur the censure of the Church of God; and while we are shut out by them, we stand excluded out of Heaven. For our Saviour said to His Apostles, upon whom He built His Church, *Whosoever sins ye remit, they are remitted unto them; and whosoever sins ye retain, they are retained*. Again, a man may not only passively and involuntarily

8

be ejected, but also may by an act of his own cast out or eject himself, not only by plain and complete apostasy, but by a defection from the unity of truth, falling into some damnable heresy; or by an active separation, deserting all which are in communion with the Catholic Church, and falling into an irrecoverable schism.

Thirdly, It is necessary to believe the Church of Christ to be holy, lest we should presume to obtain any happiness by being of it, without that holiness which is required in it. It is not enough that the end, institution, and administration of the Church are holy; but, that there may be some real and permanent advantage received by it, it is necessary that the persons abiding in the communion of it should be really and effectually sanctified. Without which holiness, the privileges of the Church prove the greatest disadvantages; and the means of salvation neglected tend to a punishment with aggravation. It is not only vain but pernicious to attend at the marriage-feast without a wedding-garment; and it is our Saviour's description of folly to cry, *Lord, Lord, open unto us*, while we are without oil in our lamps. We must acknowledge a necessity of holiness, when we confess that Church alone which is holy can make us happy.

Fourthly, There is a necessity of believing the Catholic Church, because except a man be of that, he can be of none. For being the Church which is truly Catholic containeth within it all which are truly Churches, whosoever is not of the Catholic Church cannot be of the true Church. That Church alone which first began at Jerusalem on earth will bring us to the Jerusalem in Heaven; and that alone began there which always embraceth the *faith once delivered to the saints*. Whatsoever Church pretendeth to a new beginning pretendeth at the same time to a new Churchdom, and whatsoever is so new is none, so necessary it is to believe *the Holy Catholic Church*.

Having thus far explicated the first part of this Article, I conceive every person sufficiently furnished with means of instruction what they ought to intend when they profess to believe *the Holy Catholic Church*. For thereby every one is understood to declare thus much: I am fully persuaded, and make a free confession of this, as of a necessary and infallible truth, that Christ, by the preaching of the Apostles, did gather unto Himself a Church, consisting of thousands of believing persons and numerous congregations, to which He daily added such as should be saved, and will successively and daily add unto the same unto the end of the world: so that by the virtue of His all-sufficient promise, I am assured that there was, hath been hitherto, and now is, and hereafter shall be, so long as the sun and moon endure, a Church of Christ one and the same. This Church I believe in general holy in respect of the Author, end, institution, and administration of it; particularly in the members here I acknowledge it really, and in the same hereafter perfectly, holy. I look upon this Church not like that of the Jews, limited to one people, confined to one nation, but by the appointment and command of Christ, and by the efficacy of His assisting power, to be disseminated through all nations, to be extended to all places, to be propagated to all ages, to contain in it all truths necessary to be known, to exact absolute obedience from all men to the commands of Christ, and to furnish us with all graces necessary to make our persons acceptable, and our actions well-pleasing, in the sight of God. And thus *I believe the Holy Catholic Church.*

## No. 14.  WILLIAM NICHOLSON

[From *A Plain but Full Exposition of the Catechism of the Church of England.* " Of the Creed " (" Holy Catholic Church "). Ed. *L. A. C. T.*, p. 60. Cp. note on No. 204.]

To believe the Catholic Church . . . is to believe that there is a society of Christians dispersed into all quarters of the world, who are united under Christ their Head, formalized and moved by His Spirit, matriculated by Baptism, nourished by the Word and Supper of the Lord, ruled and continued under Bishops and Pastors lawfully called to these offices, who succeed those upon whom the Holy Ghost came down, and have the power of the keys committed to them, for administration of doctrine and discipline, and who are bound to preach the Word, to pray with, and intercede for the people, to administer the Sacraments, to ordain ministers, and to use the Church censures.

## No. 15.  JOHN SHARP

[From *Sermons Against Popery preached in the Reign of King James II, and other Papers wrote in the Popish Controversy.* Sharp's Collected *Sermons*, Vol. VII, London, 1735, Sermon v (" Of the Church and Number of its Sacraments "), pp. 114 f., 118 f. The Sermons contained in this, the last, volume, were published then for the first time.]

*Go*, says He, *and make disciples of all nations, baptizing them in the Name of the Father and of the Son and of the Holy Ghost ; and teaching them to observe whatever I have commanded you. And lo ! I am with you alway, even unto the end of the world.*

This commission of Our Saviour we may properly enough style the Charter of the Church ; and mind, I pray, what is contained in it. Our Saviour here declares the extent of His Church, and of what persons He would have it constituted. It was to extend throughout all the world, and to be made up of all nations. He here declares by whom He would have it built and constituted, viz., the Apostles. He here declares upon what grounds He would have it constituted, or upon what conditions any person was to be received into it, viz., their becoming the disciples of Jesus Christ, and undertaking to observe all that He had commanded. He here likewise declares the form or the method by which persons were to be admitted into this Church, and that was by being baptized in the Name of the Father, and of the Son, and of the Holy Ghost. And lastly, He here promises the perpetual presence of His Holy Spirit, both to assist the Apostles and their successors in the building and governing this Church, and to actuate and enliven all the members of it. . . .

Thus, I am sure, I have given you the true notion of the Church which the Scripture always intends when it mentions the Church in general; when it speaks of the Church as the *Body of Christ*; when it speaks of the Church which Christ *purchased with His Blood*; when it speaks of *the Church into which we are baptized*; when it speaks of the Church to which all those glorious promises are made of the forgiveness of sins, of the perpetual presence and assistance of the Holy Spirit; of *the gates of hell never prevailing against it*, and of *everlasting salvation in the world to come*. I say, that Church is always meant of the whole company of Christians dispersed over all the world, that profess the common Faith (though perhaps none of them without mixture of errors), and enjoy the Administration of the Word and Sacraments under their lawful pastors and governors; all these people, wherever they live, or by what name soever they call themselves, make up together that one Body of Christ which we call the Catholic Church.

## No. 16. WILLIAM SHERLOCK

[From *A Vindication of the Doctrine of the Trinity* (1690), pp. 35 f. Cp. note on No. **58**.]

The Catholic Faith, I grant, is so called with relation to the Catholic Church, whose Faith it is, and the Catholic Church is the Universal Church, or all the true churches in the world, which are all but one whole Church, united in Christ their Head. The profession of the true Faith and Worship of Christ makes a true Church, and all true churches are the One Catholic Church, whether they be spread over all the world, or shut up in any one corner of it, as at the first preaching of the Gospel the Catholic Church was nowhere but in Judaea. Now as no Church is the Catholic Church of Christ, how far soever it has spread itself over the world, unless it profess the true Faith of Christ, no more is any Faith the Catholic Faith, how universally soever it be professed, unless it be the true Faith of Christ. Nor does the true Christian Faith cease to be Catholic, how few soever there be who sincerely profess it. It is downright Popery to judge of the Catholic Church by its multitudes or large extent, or to judge of the Catholic Faith by the vast numbers of its professors. Were there but one true Church in the world, that were the Catholic Church, because it would be the whole Church of Christ on earth, and were the true Christian Faith professed but in one such Church it would be the Catholic Faith still, for it is the Faith of the whole true Church of Christ, the sincere belief and profession of which makes a Catholic Church.

## (2) VISIBLE AND INVISIBLE

### No. 17. RICHARD HOOKER

[From *The Laws of Ecclesiastical Polity*, Book III, Chapter i, § 14. *Works*, ed. J. Keble, Vol. I, p. 351. Cp. note on No. 148.]

BY the Church . . . we understand no other than only the visible Church. For preservation of Christianity there is not any thing more needful, than that such as are of the visible Church have mutual fellowship and society one with another. In which consideration, as the main body of the sea being one, yet within divers precincts hath divers names, so the Catholic Church is in like sort divided into a number of distinct Societies, every of which is termed a Church within itself. In this sense the Church is always a visible society of men; not an assembly, but a Society. For although the name of the Church be given unto Christian assemblies, although any multitude of Christian men congregated may be termed by the name of a Church, yet assemblies properly are rather things that belong to a Church. Men are assembled for performance of public actions; which actions being ended, the assembly dissolveth itself and is no longer in being, whereas the Church which was assembled doth no less continue afterwards than before.

### No. 18. RICHARD FIELD

[From *Of the Church*, Book I, Chapter x. Ed. *E. H. S.*, Cambridge, 1847. Vol. I, pp. 31–36. Cp. note on No. 72.]

Hence it cometh that we say there is a visible and invisible Church, not meaning to make two distinct Churches, as our adversaries falsely and maliciously charge us, though the form of words may serve to insinuate some such thing, but to distinguish the divers considerations of the same Church; which though it be visible in respect of the profession of supernatural verities revealed in Christ, use of holy Sacraments, order of Ministry, and due obedience yielded thereunto, and they discernible that do communicate therein; yet in respect of those most precious effects, and happy benefits of saving grace, wherein only the elect do communicate, it is invisible; and they that in so happy, gracious and desirable things have communion among themselves are not discernible from others to whom this fellowship is denied, but are known only unto God. That Nathaniel was an Israelite all men knew; that he was *a true Israelite, in whom was no guile*, Christ only knew.

The persons, then, of them of whom the Church consisteth are visible; their profession known even to the profane and wicked of the world; and in this sort the Church cannot be invisible, neither did any of our men teach that it is or may be. For seeing the Church is the multitude of them that shall be saved, and no man can be saved unless he make confession unto salvation (for faith hid in the heart and concealed doth not suffice), it cannot be but they that are of the true Church must by the profession of the truth make themselves known in such sort, that by their profession and practice they may be discerned from other men.

Notwithstanding, because the truth and excellence of the faith and profession of Christians is not discerned by the light of nature, but by faith alone, the excellency of this society of Christians above other profane companies in the world, and their happiness that are of it, is invisible, hidden and unknown to natural men, and is known only to them that are spiritual. And who they are that have fellowship among themselves, not only in the profession of heavenly verities and outward means of salvation, but also in the benefits of effectual and saving grace, is known neither to the natural nor spiritual man, but to God alone.

If a man shall further urge that Luther, and some other that were in the beginning of the Reformation of the Church, did think the Church to be sometimes invisible, not only in those respects above specified, but even in the truth of profession and practice of those things that to salvation are necessary, we deny that any such thing can be collected out of any of their writings which they have left unto posterity. For how should there be a Church in the world, the perpetuity whereof they almost constantly defend, and none found to profess the saving truth of God, which all are bound to do that look for salvation? But this surely both they and we do teach, that though always the open, known, and constant profession of saving truth be preserved and found amongst men, and the ministry of salvation continued and known in the world (for how should there be a Church gathered without a ministry?); that yet sometimes errors and heresies so much prevail, that the most part, not only of them that apparently are without, but even of them also that hold and possess great places of office and dignity in the Church of God, either for fear, flattery, hope of gain, or honour, or else misled through simplicity, or directly falling into error or heresy, depart from the soundness of Christian faith, so that the sincerity of religion is upholden and the truth of the profession of Christians defended and maintained but only by some few, and they molested, persecuted, and traduced, as turbulent and seditious men, enemies to the common peace of the Christian world. In this sense then the Church is said to be sometimes invisible, not because there are none seen, known, or found that possess the truth of God; but because even in that company which is the true Church of God, many, and those the greatest, are carried into error, so that but some few, and they such, as (if we should judge by outward appearance) are most unlike to uphold and maintain the truth, are left to defend the same; multitude, authority, reputation and opinion of greatness in others, obscuring them in such sort, that they which measure things by outward appearance, can possibly take no notice of them. This was the state of the Christian world in the time of Athanasius, when in the Council of Seleucia and Ariminum the Nicene faith was condemned; and all the Bishops of the whole world (carried away with the sway of time) fell from the soundness of the faith, only Athanasius excepted, and some few confessors that *sub Athanasii nomine exulabant*; as Hierome noteth, writing against the Luciferians, *Ingemuit totus orbis, et miratus est se factum esse Arianum*, "the world poured forth sighs, marvelling how it was become an Arian."

At that time it was, when Hilarius writing against Auxentius, Bishop of Milan, complained that the Arian faction had confounded all, and therefore admonished all men to take heed how they suffered themselves to be led with outward appearances : *Male [enim] vos parietum amor cepit, male Ecclesiam Dei in tectis aedificiisque veneramini ; male sub his pacis nomen ingeritis. Anne ambiguum est in his Antichristum esse sessurum ? Montes mihi, et sylvae, et lacus, et carceres, et voragines sunt tutiores, in his enim prophetae [aut] manentes, aut demersi, Dei spiritu prophetabant.* "It is not well," saith he, "that you are in love with walls, that you esteem the Church in respect of houses and buildings and in and under those shows and outward appearances pretend and urge the name of peace. Is there any doubt of Antichrist's sitting in these places ? The mountains, the woods, the lakes, the prisons, the deep pits and devouring gulfs seem to me more safe. For in these the prophets either remaining, abiding and making them their dwelling-places, or, as it were drowned and overwhelmed in them, prophesied in old time." And to this purpose it is that Augustine writeth, most aptly distinguishing between the stars of heaven and the sands of the sea, according to the number whereof God promised Abraham that his seed should be. "The Church of God," saith he, "sometimes is obscured, darkened, and, as it were, overshadowed with the multitude of offences and scandals that are found in it, yet even then doth it appear and show itself in those worthies of most strong and constant resolution, which are as the stars of heaven among those of Abraham's seed and posterity ; but for the multitude of weak and carnal Christians, which is like to the sand on the sea-shore, in peaceable times they are free and quiet, but in dangerous times troubled, covered, and hidden with the waters and raging waves of tribulation and temptation."

This and no other thing our Divines meant, that affirmed the Church to be sometimes invisible; and, therefore, it is most true that Bellarmine noteth, that many of his companions have taken much needless pain in proving against us the perpetuity of the Church, which, as he confesseth, none of us ever denied; but it is as true that he also laboureth in vain, in proving that there is, and always hath been, a visible Church, and that not consisting of some few scattered Christians without order or ministry or use of Sacraments; for all this we do most willingly yield unto, howsoever perhaps some few have been of opinion, that though all others failing from the faith, the truth of God should remain only in some few of the laity, yet the promise of Christ concerning the perpetuity of His Church might still be verified.

This question was disputed by Occam and Cameracensis, long before our times, and who knoweth not that Cardinal Turrecremata and other great Divines have been of opinion that during the time that Christ was touching His body in the grave, all the Apostles being fallen from the faith, the same continued in the blessed Virgin alone. But these disputes we leave to them that are delighted in them, resting in the assured and undoubted persuasion of the truth of these things which we have delivered touching the visibility and invisibility of the Church; by which it may easily appear, in what sense the Church may be said to be sometimes invisible, and how the same Church is at the same time both visible and invisible in divers respects.

### No. 19.  JOSEPH HALL

[From *A Plain and Familiar Explication, by Way of Paraphrase, of all the Hard Texts of the Whole Divine Scripture of the Old and New Testament.* On *Matt.* xiii. 47–49. *Works*, ed. Peter Hall (1837), Vol. IV, p. 151. This treatise, the result of arduous labours stretching over many years, was first published in 1633 and was dedicated to Charles I; it fills the whole of Vols. III and IV of Peter Hall's edition. It must be admitted that a very large number of Hall's " paraphrases " contribute little towards the elucidation of the " hard places."]

As the Church, or Spiritual Kingdom of God here upon earth, is thus largely diffused through efficacy of His Gospel, so it may not be conceived to be pure and free from all sinful mixtures while it is here below. Rather it is like unto a drag-net, which is cast into the sea and fetches up much variety, not of great and little fishes only, but of stones and seaweed and shells and mud, altogether; which when it is drawn to the shore, is disburdened of all the unprofitable loan thereof and yieldeth the good provision of fish unto the vessels of the owner. So doth the Church of God. Here for the outward and visible composition of it, it containeth not only sound and holy and faithful men, but even the secretly vicious, sly hypocrites, hollow and faithless professors. But at the end of the world, when this great net is drawn up to the shore, the angels shall come forth and make a due separation of the wicked from among the just.

# (3) THE MARKS OF THE CHURCH

## No. 20. RICHARD FIELD

[From *Of the Church*, Book II, Chapter ii. Ed. *E. H. S.*, Cambridge, 1847. Vol. I, p. 65. Cp. note on No. **72**.]

THIS entire profession of the truth revealed in Christ, though it distinguish right believers from heretics, yet it is not proper to the happy number and blessed company of Catholic Christians, because schismatics may and sometimes do hold an entire profession of the truth of God revealed in Christ. It remaineth, therefore, that we seek out those things that are so peculiarly found in the companies of right believing and Catholic Christians, that they may serve as notes of difference to distinguish them from all, both Pagans, Jews, heretics and schismatics. These are of two sorts; for either they are such as only at some times and not perpetually, or such as do perpetually and ever, sever the true Church from all conventicles of erring and seduced miscreants. Of the former sort was multitude, largeness of extent, and the name of " Catholic," esteemed a Note of the Church in the time of the Fathers. The Notes of the latter sort, that are inseparable, perpetual, and absolutely proper and peculiar, which perpetually distinguish the true Catholic Church from all other societies of men and professions of religions in the world, are three: First, the entire profession of those supernatural verities, which God hath revealed in Christ His Son; Secondly, the use of such holy ceremonies and Sacraments as He hath instituted and appointed to serve as provocations to godliness, preservations from sin, memorials of the benefits of Christ, warrants for the greater security of our belief, and marks of distinction to separate His Own from strangers; Thirdly, an union or connexion of men in this profession and use of these Sacraments under lawful pastors and guides, appointed, authorized, and sanctified, to direct and lead them in the happy ways of eternal salvation. That these are Notes of the Church it will easily appear by consideration of all those conditions that are required in the nature of Notes. They are inseparable, they are proper, and they are essential, and such things as give being to the Church, and therefore are in nature more clear and evident, and such as that from them the perfect knowledge of the Church may and must be derived.

## No. 21. FRANCIS WHITE

[From *A Reply to Jesuit Fisher's Answer*, pp. 54, 102. Cp. note on No. **228**.]

The qualities of unity, holiness, verity, Apostolical Succession, and other the like, are not always found in the true Church equally or in the same degree and measure of perfection, but according to a latitude and inequality of intention and remission, and more or less; so that although the sounder part of the Church hath always the substance of truth, sanctity, and unity, yet this verity of doctrine, unity of charity, sanctity of manners, is greater, larger and more sincere and perfect in some persons and ages of the Church than in others. These qualities were in their greatest perfection when the Apostles themselves lived; they were in great measure in the ages immediately abutting upon the Apostles. But the holy Fathers complain of the decrease and decay of them in after times; and Papists deplore the extreme diminution of them in their days. . . .

Although the true Church is always holy for doctrine, yet it is not perfectly and in the highest degree ever so. And it is most inconsequent to argue: Christ which is the Truth is ever with the Church, *Ergo* the Church cannot err or teach any falsehood; for Christ is always with the faithful (*Eph.* iii, 17), yet just and faithful people may err. Because Christ was with the Apostles by miraculous inspiration, therefore they could not err or deliver any falsehood, great or small. But He is present with the sounder part of the Church militant since the Apostles by ordinary grace and assistance, which freeth the same from damnable and malicious error, but not from all error. And this assistance of grace is greater or less, according to the good pleasure of Christ, and the disposition of His people, which are compassed about with ignorance and infirmity, and at some times better or worse qualified than at other.

## No. 22. JEREMY TAYLOR

[From *A Dissuasive from Popery, Part II*, Book I, § 1. *Works*, ed. R. Heber. Vol. X, pp. 377–381 (ed. C. P. Eden, Vol. VI, pp. 375–378). Cp. note on No. **50**.]

Bellarmine reckons fifteen Notes of the Church. It is a mighty hue and cry after a thing that he pretends is visible to all the world. 1. The very name " Catholic " is his first Note. He might as well have said the word " Church " is a note of the Church; for he cannot be ignorant but that all Christians who esteem themselves members of the Church think and call themselves members of the Catholic Church; and the Greeks give the same title to their Churches. Nay, all conventions of heretics anciently did so; and, therefore, I shall quit Bellarmine of this note by the words of Lactantius, which himself also (a little forgetting himself) quotes *Sed tamen singuli quique haereticorum coetus, se potissimum Christianos, et suam esse catholicam ecclesiam putant.* 2. " Antiquity," indeed, is a Note of the Church, and Salmeron proves it to be so from the example of Adam and Eve, most learnedly. But the certainty that God had a Church in Paradise is as good an argument for the Church of England and Ireland, as for Rome ; for we derive from them as certainly as do the Italians, and have as much of Adam's religion as they have. But a Church might have been very ancient, and yet become no Church ; and without separating from a greater Church. The Church of the Jews is the great example ; and the Church of Rome, unless she takes better heed, may be another. St. Paul hath plainly threatened it to the Church of Rome. 3. " Duration " is made a note. Now this respects the time past or the time to come. If the time past, then the Church of Britain was Christian before Rome was [1] ; and, blessed be God, is so at this day. If Duration means the time to come—for so Bellarmine says, *Ecclesia dicitur catholica, non solum quia semper fuit, sed etiam quia semper erit*—so we have a rare note for us who are alive to discern the Church of Rome to be the Catholic Church, and we may possibly come to know it by this sign, many ages after we are dead, because she will last always. But this sign is not yet come to pass ; and when it shall come to pass, it will prove our Church to be the Catholic Church, as well as that of Rome, and the Greek Church as well as both of us ; for these Churches, at least some of them, have begun sooner, and for aught they or we know, they all may so continue longer. 4. " Amplitude " was no Note of the Church when the world was Arian, and is as little now, because that great part of Europe is papal. 5. " Succession of Bishops " is an excellent conservatory of Christian doctrine ; but it is as notorious in the Greek Church as in the Roman and therefore cannot signify which is the true Church, unless they be both true, and then the Church of England can claim by this tenure, as having, since her being Christian, a succession of Bishops never interrupted but, as all others have been, in persecution. 6. " Consent in doctrine with the Ancient Church " may be a good sign or a bad, as it happens ; but the Church of Rome hath not, and never can prove, the pure and prime Antiquity to be of her side. 7. " Union of members among themselves and with their Head," is very good, if the members be united in truth (for else it may be a conspiracy), and if by Head be meant Jesus Christ ; and indeed this is the only true sign of the Church. But if by head be meant the Roman Pope, it may be *ecclesia malignantium*, and Antichrist may sit in the chair. But the uncertainty of this Note, as it relates to this question, I have already manifested ; and what excellent concord there is in the Church of Rome, we are taught by the question of supremacy of Councils or Popes ; and now also by the strict and loving concord

---

[1] [Having been founded, as many Seventeenth-Century Divines believed, at an earlier date than that at which St. Peter arrived in Rome.]

between the Jansenists and Molinists, and the abettors of the Immaculate Conception of the blessed Virgin Mother with their antagonists. 8. " Sanctity of Doctrine " is an excellent note of the Church. But that is the question among all the pretenders, and is not any advantage to the Church of Rome, unless it be a holy thing to worship images, to trample upon kings, to reconcile a wicked life with the hopes of heaven at the last minute, by the charm of external ministries; to domineer over consciences, to impose useless and intolerable burdens, to damn all the world that are not their slaves, to shut up the fountains of salvation from the people; to be easier in dispensing with the laws of God than the laws of the Church; to give leave to princes to break their oaths, as Pope Clement VII did to Francis I of France to cozen the Emperor, and as Pope Julius II did to Ferdinand of Aragon, sending him an absolution for his treachery against the King of France, not to keep faith with heretics; to find out tricks to entrap them that trusted to their letters of safe conduct; to declare that Popes cannot be bound by their promises—for Pope Paul IV in a Conclave, A.D. 1555, complained of them that said he could make but four Cardinals, because (forsooth) he had sworn so in the Conclave, saying this was to bind the Pope, whose authority is absolute; that it is an article of faith that the Pope cannot be bound, much less can he bind himself; that to say otherwise was a manifest heresy; and against them that should obstinately persevere in saying so, he threatened the Inquisition. These, indeed, are holy doctrines, taught and practised respectively by their Holinesses at Rome, and, indeed, are the Notes of their Church—if by the doctrine of the head, to whom they are bound to adhere, we may guess at the doctrine of their body. 9. " The prevalency of their doctrine " is produced for a good note. And yet this is a greater note of Mahometanism than of Christianity, and was once of Arianism; and yet the argument is not now so good at Rome, as it was before Luther's time. 10. That " the chiefs of the Pope's Religion lived more holy lives than others " gives some light that their Church is the true one. But I had thought that their Popes had been the chiefs of their religion, till now; and if so, then this was a good note, while they did live well—but that was before Popery. Since that time, we will guess at their Church by the holiness of the lives of those that rule and teach all; and then if we have none to follow amongst us, yet we know whom we are to fly amongst them. 11. " Miracles " were in the beginning of Christianity a note of true believers; Christ told us so. And He also taught us that Antichrist should be revealed in lying signs and wonders, and commanded us by that token to take heed of them. And the Church of Rome would take it ill, if we should call them, as St. Austin did the Donatists, *mirabiliarios*, " miracle-mongers "; concerning which, he that pleases to read that excellent tract of St. Austin, *De Unitate Ecclesiae*, cap. 14, will be sufficiently satisfied in this particular, and in the main ground and foundation of the Protestant Religion. In the meantime, it may suffice that Bellarmine says, "miracles are a sign of the true Church," and Salmeron says that "they are no certain signs of the true Church, but may be done by the false." 12. "The Spirit of Prophecy" is also a pretty sure note of the true Church, and yet, in the dispute between Israel and Judah, Samaria and Jerusalem, it was of no force, but was really in both. And at the day of judgement Christ shall reject some who will allege that they prophesied in His Name. I deny not but there have been some prophets in the Church of Rome: Johannes de Rupe Scissa, Anselmus Marsicanus, Robert Grosthead (Bishop of Lincoln), St. Hildegardis, Abbot Joachim, whose prophecies and pictures prophetical were published by Theophrastus Paracelsus and John Adrasder, and by Paschalinus Regiselmus at Venice, 1589. But (as Ahab said concerning Micaiah) these do not prophesy good concerning Rome, but evil; and that Rome should be reformed *in ore gladii cruentandi* was one of the prophecies; and, *universa sanctorum ecclesia abscondetur*, "that the whole Church of the Saints shall be hidden," viz. in the Days of Antichrist; and that in the days of darkness the elect of God shall have that faith, or wisdom, to themselves, which they have, and shall not dare to preach it publicly, was another prophecy, and carries its meaning upon the forehead, and many more I could tell. But whether such prophecies as these be good signs that the Church of Rome is the true Church, I desire to be informed by the Roman doctors before I trouble myself any further to consider the particulars. 13. Towards the latter end of this catalogue of wonderful signs, the "Confession of Adversaries" is brought in for a note; and no question they intended it so! But did ever any Protestant, remaining so, confess the Church of Rome to be the true Catholic Church? Let the man be named, and a sufficient testimony brought, that he was *mentis compos*, and I will grant to the Church of Rome this to be the best note they have. 14. But since "the enemies of the Church have all had tragical ends," it is no question but this signifies the Church of Rome to be the only Church. Indeed, if all the Protestants had died unnatural deaths, and all the Papists, nay, if all the Popes had died quietly in their beds, we had reason to deplore our sad calamity and inquired after the cause. But we could never have told by this: for, by all that is before him, a man cannot tell whether he deserves love or hatred. And all the world finds that, as dies the Papist, so dies the Protestant; and the like event happens to them all, excepting only some Popes have been remarked by their own histories for funest and direful deaths. 15. And lately, "Temporal Prosperity" is brought for a Note of the true Church. And for this there is great reason; because the Cross is the highway to Heaven, and Christ promised to His disciples for their lot in this world great and lasting persecutions, and the Church felt His Blessing for three hundred years together. But this had been a better argument in the mouth of a Turkish mufti than a Roman Cardinal.

## No. 23.  JOHN HALES

[From *Miscellanies*, § i (" How to know the Church "). *The Works of the Ever Memorable Mr. John Hales of Eaton*, Glasgow, 1765, Vol. I, p. 104.]

Marks and notes to know the Church there are none, except we will make true profession—which is the form and essence of the Church —to be a mark. And as there are none, so it is not necessary there should be. For to what purpose should they serve ? That I might go seek and find out some company to mark. This is no way necessary; for glorious things are in the Scriptures spoken of the Church. Not that I should run up and down the world to find the persons of the professors; but that I should make myself of it. This I do by taking upon me the profession of Christianity and submitting myself to the rules of belief and practice delivered in the Gospel— though besides myself I know no other professor in the world.

# III. SEPARATED CHURCHES

# (1) ROMAN CATHOLICISM

## No. 24.  JOHN COSIN

[From a Letter written by Cosin to the Countess of Peterborough. *Works*, ed. *L. A. C. T.*, Vol. IV, pp. 332–336. It was first printed in 1705 in a volume entitled *Several Letters which passed between Dr. George Hickes and a Popish Priest, upon Occasion of a young Gentlewoman's departing from the Church of England to that of Rome ; With an Appendix of Papers.*]

*The Differences, in the Chief Points of Religion, between the Roman Catholics and us of the Church of England ; together with the Agreements, which we for our parts profess, and are ready to embrace, if they for theirs were as ready to accord with us in the same.*

### The Differences

We that profess the Catholic Faith and Religion in the Church of England do not agree with the Roman Catholics in any thing whereunto they now endeavour to convert us.  But we totally differ from them (as they do from the ancient Catholic Church) in these points :

1. That the Church of Rome is the Mother and Mistress of all other Churches in the world.

2. That the Pope of Rome is the vicar-general of Christ, or that he hath an universal jurisdiction over all Christians that shall be saved.

3. That either the Synod of Trent was a General Council or that all the canons thereof are to be received as matters of Catholic Faith under pain of damnation.

4. That Christ hath instituted seven true and proper Sacraments in the New Testament, neither more nor less, all conferring grace and all necessary to salvation.

5. That the priests offer up our Saviour in the Mass, as a real, proper, and propitiatory sacrifice for the quick and the dead, and that whosoever believes it not is eternally damned.

6. That, in the Sacrament of the Eucharist, the whole substance of bread is converted into the substance of Christ's Body, and the whole substance of wine into His Blood, so truly and properly, as that after Consecration there is neither any bread nor wine remaining there ; which they call Transubstantiation, and impose upon all persons under pain of damnation to be believed.

7. That the communion under one kind is sufficient and lawful (notwithstanding the institution of Christ under both), and that whosoever believes or holds otherwise is damned.

8. That there is a purgatory after this life, wherein the souls of the dead are punished, and from whence they are fetched out by the prayers and offerings of the living; and that there is no salvation possibly to be had by any that will not believe as much.

9. That all the old saints departed, and all those dead men and women whom the Pope hath of late canonized for saints or shall hereafter do so, whosoever they be, are and ought to be invocated by the religious prayers and devotions of all persons; and that they who do not believe this as an article of their Catholic Faith cannot be saved.

10. That the relics of all these true or reputed saints ought to be religiously worshipped; and that whosoever holdeth the contrary is damned.

11. That the images of Christ and the Blessed Virgin and of the other saints ought not only to be had and retained, but likewise to be honoured and worshipped, according to the use and practices of the Roman Church; and that this is to be believed as of necessity to salvation.

12. That the power and use of indulgences, as they are now practised in the Church of Rome, both for the living and the dead, is to be received and held of all, under pain of eternal perdition.

13. That all the ceremonies used by the Roman Church in the administration of the Sacraments (such as are spittle and salt at Baptism, the five crosses upon the Altar and Sacrament of the Eucharist, the holding of that Sacrament over the Priest's head to be adored, the exposing of it in their churches to be worshipped by the people, the circumgestation and carrying of it abroad ·in procession upon their Corpus Christi Day, and to their sick for the same, the oil and chrism in Confirmation, the anointing of the ears, the eyes, and noses, the hands, the reins, of those that are ready to die, the giving of an empty chalice and paten to them that are to be ordained Priests, and many others of this nature now in use with them) are of necessity to salvation to be approved and admitted by all other Churches.

14. That all the ecclesiastical observations and constitutions of the same Church (such as are their laws of forbidding all Priests to marry, the appointing several orders of monks, friars, and nuns, in the Church, the service of God in an unknown tongue, the saying of a number of Ave-Marias by tale upon their chaplets, the sprinkling of themselves and the dead bodies with holy water as operative and effectual to the remission of venial sins, the distinctions of meats to be held for true fasting, the religious consecration and incensing of images, the baptizing of bells, the dedicating of divers holidays for the Immaculate Conception and the Bodily Assumption of the blessed Virgin, and for Corpus Christi or Transubstantiation of the Sacrament, the making of the Apocryphal books to be as Canonical as any of the rest of the holy and undoubted Scriptures, the keeping of those Scriptures from

the free use and reading of the people, the approving of their own Latin translation only, and divers other matters of the like nature) are to be approved, held, and believed, as needful to salvation; and that whoever approves them not is out of the Catholic Church, and must be damned.

All which, in their several respects, we hold, some to be pernicious, some unnecessary, many false, and many fond, and none of them to be imposed upon any Church, or any Christian, as the Roman Catholics do upon all Christians and all Churches whatsoever, for matters needful to be approved for eternal salvation.

## Our Agreements

If the Roman Catholics would make the essence of their Church (as we do ours) to consist in these following points, we are at accord with them in the reception and believing of:

1. All the two and twenty canonical books of the Old Testament, and the twenty-seven of the New, as the only foundation and perfect rule of our faith.

2. All the apostolical and ancient Creeds, especially those which are commonly called the Apostles' Creed, the Nicene Creed, and the Creed of St. Athanasius; all which are clearly deduced out of the Scriptures.

3. All the decrees of faith and doctrine set forth, as well in the first four General Councils, as in all other Councils, which those first four approved and confirmed, and in the fifth and sixth General Councils besides (than which we find no more to be General), and in all the following Councils that be thereunto agreeable, and in all the anathemas and condemnations given out by those Councils against heretics, for the defence of the Catholic Faith.

4. The unanimous and general consent of the ancient Catholic Fathers and the universal Church of Christ in the interpretation of the Holy Scriptures, and the collection of all necessary matters of Faith from them during the first six hundred years, and downwards to our own days.

5. In acknowledgment of the Bishop of Rome, if he would rule and be ruled by the ancient canons of the Church, to be the Patriarch of the West, by right of ecclesiastical and imperial constitution, in such places where the kings and governors of those places had received him, and found it behooveful for them to make use of his jurisdiction, without any necessary dependence upon him by divine right.

6. In the reception and use of the two blessed Sacraments of our Saviour; in the Confirmation of those persons that are to be strengthened in their Christian Faith, by prayer and imposition of hands, according to the examples of the holy Apostles and ancient Bishops of the Catholic

Church ; in the public and solemn benediction of persons that are to
be joined together in Holy Matrimony ; in public or private absolution
of penitent sinners ; in the consecrating of Bishops, and the ordaining of Priests and Deacons, for the service of God in His Church by a
lawful succession ; and in visiting the sick, by praying for them, and
administering the Blessed Sacrament to them, together with a final
absolution of them from their repented sins.

7. In commemorating at the Eucharist the Sacrifice of Christ's
Body and Blood once truly offered for us.

8. In acknowledging His sacramental, spiritual, true, and real
Presence there to the souls of all them that come faithfully and de-
voutly to receive Him according to His own institution in that Holy
Sacrament.

9. In giving thanks to God for them that are departed out of this
life in the true Faith of Christ's Catholic Church ; and in praying to
God, that they may have a joyful resurrection, and a perfect consummation of bliss, both in their bodies and souls, in His eternal kingdom of
glory.

10. In the historical and moderate use of painted and true stories,
either for memory or ornament, where there is no danger to have them
abused or worshipped with religious honour.

11. In the use of indulgences, or abating the rigour of the canons
imposed upon offenders, according to their repentance, and their
want of ability to undergo them.

12. In the administration of the two Sacraments, and other rites of
the Church, with ceremonies of decency and order, according to the
precept of the Apostle, and the free practice of the ancient Christians.

13. In observing such Holy days and times of fasting as were in
use in the first ages of the Church, or afterwards received upon just
grounds, by public or lawful authority.

14. Finally, in the reception of all ecclesiastical constitutions and
canons made for the ordering of our Church ; or others which are
not repugnant either to the Word of God, or the power of kings, or
the laws established by right authority in any nation.

## No. 25.  WILLIAM LAUD

[From *A Relation of the Conference between William Laud and Mr. Fisher the
Jesuit.* Sections XX, XXV (*bis*). Ed. C. H. Simpkinson (1901), pp. 145 f.,
191 f., 211–214.  Cp. note on No. **54**.]

There is a great deal of difference, especially as Romanists handle
the question of the Church, between *the* Church and *a* Church.  And
there is some between a *true* Church and a *right* Church, which is
the word you use, but no man else that I know ; I am sure not I.

For " the Church " may import in our language " the only true

Church"; and, perhaps, as some of you seem to make it, "the root and the ground of the Catholic." And this I never did grant of the Roman Church, nor ever mean to do. But "a Church" can imply no more than that it is a member of the whole. And this I never did nor ever will deny, if it fall not absolutely away from Christ. That it is a "true Church" I granted also; but not a "right," as you impose upon me. . . .

He [*i.e.* Fisher] tells us this is so [viz. that Rome has the right of judging other Churches], "because the Church of Rome hath more powerful principality than other particular Churches, and that her bishop is pastor of the whole Church." To this I answer, that it is most true indeed; the Church of Rome hath had, and hath yet, "more powerful principality" than any other particular Church: but she hath not this power from Christ. The Roman patriarch, by ecclesiastical constitutions, might perhaps have a primacy of order; but for principality of power, the patriarchs were as even, as equal, as the Apostles were before them. The truth is, this "more powerful principality" the Roman bishops got under the emperors, after they became Christian; and they used the matter so, that they grew big enough to oppose, nay to depose, the emperors, by the same power which they had given them. And after this, other particular Churches, especially here in the West, submitted themselves to them for succour and protection's sake. And this was one main cause which swelled Rome into this "more powerful principality," and not any right given by Christ to make that prelate pastor of the whole Church. . . .

He [*i.e.* Fisher] tells us "the Bishop of Rome is St. Peter's successor," and therefore to him we must have recourse. The Fathers, I deny not, ascribe very much to St. Peter; but it is to St. Peter in his own person. And among them Epiphanius is as free and as frequent in extolling St. Peter as any of them, and yet did he never intend to give an absolute principality to Rome in St. Peter's right. There is a noted place in that Father, where his words are these: "For the Lord Himself made St. Peter the first of the Apostles, a firm rock, upon which the Church of God is built, and the gates of hell shall not prevail against it, etc. For in him the faith is made firm every way, who received the key of heaven, etc. For in him all the questions and subtleties of the faith are found." This is a great place at first sight, too, and deserves a marginal note, to call young readers' eyes to view it. And it hath this note in the old Latin edition, at Paris, 1564: *Petri principatus et praestantia.* "Peter's principality and excellency." The place, as much show as it makes for the Roman principality, I shall easily clear, and yet do no wrong either to St. Peter or the Roman Church. For most manifest it is that the authority of St. Peter is urged here to prove the Godhead of the Holy Ghost. And then follow the eulogies given to St. Peter, the better to set off and make good that authority: as that he was "*princeps apostolorum*, ' the Prince of the Apostles,' and pronounced blessed by Christ, because as God the Father revealed to him the Godhead of the Son, so did the Son the Godhead of the Holy Ghost." After this, Epiphanius calls him " *solidam petram*, ' a solid rock,' upon which the Church of God was founded, and against which the gates of hell should not prevail." And adds, " That the faith was rooted and made firm in him every way, in him who received the key of Heaven." And after this he gives the reason of all : " Because in him,"—mark, I pray, it is still, " in him," as he was blessed by that revelation from God the Father, *St. Matt.* xvi.—" were found all the λεπτολογήματα, ' the very niceties ' and exactness of the Christian faith." For he professed the Godhead of the Son, and of the Holy Ghost ; and so, *omni modo*, every point of faith was rooted in him. And this is the full meaning of that learned father in this passage. Now, therefore, " building the Church upon St. Peter," in Epiphanius's sense is not as if he and his successors were to be monarchs over it for ever ; but it is the edifying and establishing the Church in the true faith of Christ, by the confession which St. Peter made. And so he expresses himself elsewhere most plainly : " St. Peter," saith he, " who was made to us indeed a solid rock, firming the faith of our Lord ; on which rock the Church is built *juxta omnem modum*, ' every way.' First, that he confessed Christ to be the Son of the living God ; and by and by he heard, ' Upon this rock of solid faith I will build My Church.' And the same confession he made of the Holy Ghost." Thus was St. Peter a solid rock, upon which the Church was founded *omni modo*, " every way " ; that is, the faith of the Church was confirmed by him in every point. But that St. Peter was any rock or foundation of the Church, so as that he and his successors must be relied on in all matters of faith, and govern the Church like princes or monarchs, that Epiphanius never thought of. And that he did never think so, I prove it thus. For besides this apparent meaning of his context, as is here expressed, how could he possibly think of a supremacy due to St. Peter's successor, that in most express terms, and that twice repeated, makes St. James, the brother of our Lord, and not St. Peter, " succeed our Lord in the principality of the Church " ? And Epiphanius was too full both of learning and industry to speak contrary to himself in a point of this moment.

## No. 26. FRANCIS WHITE

[From *A Reply to Jesuit Fisher's Answer*, pp. 157 f. Cp. note on No. **228**.]

Protestants deny not the Primacy of St. Peter ; but they yield unto him, both, as he was an Apostle, primacy of spiritual authority and jurisdiction over the Universal Church (*Matt.* xxviii, 20 ; *Jn.* xx,

21), and also respectively to the other Apostles (which were his compeers and equals in regard of all Apostolical authority) primacy of calling, order, grace, gifts, etc.

## No. 27.  ISAAC BARROW

[From *A Treatise of the Pope's Supremacy*. From the refutation of Supposition V (" That the Bishops of Rome, according to God's Institution and by Original Right derived thence, should have an Universal Supremacy and Jurisdiction over the Christian Church "). *Works*, ed. A. Napier (Cambridge, 1859), Vol. VIII, pp. 269–271, 273–278, 284–286, 288 f., 362–365, 380–382. Of the libraries of treatises, pamphlets, and sermons, which have been written by Anglican theologians on the subject of the Roman claims, this is probably the most famous. A closely reasoned whole, it does not easily lend itself to excerpts. It first appeared, posthumously, in 1680, edited by John Tillotson; and ever since has been constantly reprinted.]

Whereas divers of the Fathers purposely do treat on methods of confuting heretics, it is strange they should be so blind or dull as not to hit on this most proper and obvious way of referring debates to the decision of him, to whose office of universal pastor and judge it did belong. Particularly one would wonder at Vincentius Lirinensis, that he on set purpose, with great care, discoursing about the means of settling points of faith, and of overthrowing heresies, should not light upon this notable way, by having recourse to the Pope's magisterial sentence; yea, that indeed he should exclude it; for he (" after most intent study, and diligent inquiry, consulting the best and wisest men ") could find but two ways of doing it : " I," saith he, " did always, and from almost every one, receive this answer; That if either I or any other would find out the frauds and avoid the snares of upstart heretics, and continue sound and upright in the true faith, he should guard and strengthen his faith, God helping him, by these two means; viz: first by the authority of the divine law, and then by the tradition of the Catholic Church." And again, " We before have said that this hath always been, and is at present, the custom of Catholics, that they prove their faith by these two ways; first, by authority of the divine canon; then by the tradition of the universal Church."

Is it not strange that he (especially being a western man, living in those parts where the Pope had got much sway, and who doth express great reverence to the apostolic see) should omit that way of determining points, which of all (according to the modern conceits about the Pope) is most ready and most sure ? . . .

It is odd, that even old popes themselves in elaborate tracts disputing against heretics (as Pope Celestine against Nestorius and Pelagius, Pope Leo against Eutyches) do content themselves to urge testimonies of Scripture, and arguments grounded thereon; not alleging their own definitive authority, or using this parlous argumentation : I, the supreme Doctor of the Church and judge of controversies, do assert thus; and therefore you are obliged to submit your assent.

It is matter of amazement, if the Pope were such as they would have him to be, that in so many bulky volumes of ancient Fathers, living through many ages after Christ, in those vast treasuries of learning and knowledge wherein all sorts of truth are displayed, all sorts of duty are pressed, this momentous point of doctrine and practice should nowhere be expressed in clear and peremptory terms (I speak so, for that by wresting words, by impertinent application, by straining consequences, the most ridiculous positions imaginable may be deduced from their writings).

It is strange that somewhere or other, at least incidentally, in their commentaries upon the Scripture, wherein many places concerning the Church and its hierarchy do invite to speak of the Pope; in their treatises about the priesthood, about the unity and peace of the Church, about heresy and schism; in their epistles concerning ecclesiastical affairs; in their historical narrations about occurrences in the Church; in their concertations with heterodox adversaries, they should not frequently touch it, they should not sometimes largely dwell upon it.

Is it not marvellous, that Origen, St. Hilary, St. Cyril, St. Chrysostom, St. Jerome, St. Austin, in their commentaries and tractates upon those places of Scripture (*Tu es Petrus. Pasce oves*) whereon they now build the papal authority, should be so dull and drowsy, as not to say a word concerning the Pope?

That St. Austin in his so many elaborate tractates against the Donatists (wherein he discourseth so prolixly about the Church, its unity, communion, discipline) should never insist upon the duty of obedience to the Pope, or charge those schismatics with their rebellion against him, or allege his authority against them?

If we consider that the Pope was Bishop of the imperial city, the metropolis of the world, that he thence was most eminent in rank, did abound in wealth, did live in great splendour and reputation; had many dependencies, and great opportunities to gratify and relieve many of the clergy; that of the Fathers, whose volumes we have, all well affected towards him, divers were personally obliged to him for his support in their distress (as Athanasius, Chrysostom, Theodoret) or as to their patrons and benefactors (as St. Jerome), divers could not but highly respect him as patron of the cause wherein they were engaged (as Basil, Gregory Nazianzen, Hilary, Gregory Nyssen, Ambrose, Austin), some were his partisans in a common quarrel (as Cyril), divers of them lived in places and times wherein he had got much sway (as all the Western Bishops); that he had then improved his authority much beyond the old limits; that all the Bishops of the western or Latin Churches had a peculiar dependence on him (especially after that by advantage of his station, by favour of the court, by colour of the Sardican Canons, by voluntary deferences and submissions, by several

tricks, he had wound himself to meddle in most of their chief affairs);
that hence divers Bishops were tempted to admire, to court, to flatter
him; that divers aspiring Popes were apt to encourage the commenders
of their authority, which they themselves were apt to magnify and
inculcate; considering, I say, such things, it is a wonder, that in so
many voluminous discourses so little should be said favouring this
pretence, so nothing that proveth it (so much that crosseth it, so much
indeed, as I hope to shew, that quite overthroweth it).

If it be asked how we can prove this, I answer, that (beside who
carefully peruseth those old books will easily see it) we are beholden
to our adversaries for proving it to us, when they least intended us such
a favour: for that no clear and cogent passages for proof of this pretence
can be thence fetched is sufficiently evident from the very allegations,
which after their most diligent raking in old books they produce; the
which are so few, and fall so very short of their purpose, that without
much stretching they signify nothing.

It is monstrous that in the code of the Catholic Church (consisting
of the decrees of so many synods, concerning ecclesiastical order and
discipline) there should not be one canon directly declaring his authority;
nor any mention made of him, except thrice [? twice] accidentally;
once upon occasion of declaring the authority of the Alexandrine
Bishop, the other upon occasion of assigning to the bishop of Constantinople the second place of honour, and equal privileges with
him.

If it be objected that these discourses are negative, and therefore
of small force, I answer that therefore they are most proper to assert
such a negative proposition. For how can we otherwise better shew
a thing not to be, than by shewing it to have no footstep there, where
it is supposed to stand? How can we more clearly argue a matter
of right to want proof, than by declaring it not to be extant in the laws
grounding such right; not taught by the masters who profess to instruct in such things; not testified in records concerning the exercise
of it? Such arguments indeed in such cases are not merely negative,
but rather privative; proving things not to be, because not affirmed
there, where in reason they ought to be affirmed; standing therefore
upon positive suppositions, that Holy Scripture, that general tradition
are not imperfect and lame toward their design; that ancient writers
were competently intelligent, faithful, diligent; that all of them could
not conspire in perpetual silence about things, of which they had often
fair occasion and great reason to speak. In fine, such considerations,
however they may be deluded by sophistical wits, will yet bear great
sway, and often will amount near to the force of demonstration with
men of honest prudence. However we shall proceed to other discourses more direct and positive against the popish doctrine. . . .

It was to be sure a visible headship which St. Gregory did so eagerly impugn and exclaim against; for he could not apprehend the Bishop of Constantinople so wild as to affect a jurisdiction over the Church mystical or invisible.

Indeed upon this very account the Romish pretence doth not well accord with Holy Scripture, because it transformeth the Church into another kind of body than it was constituted by God, according to the representation of it in Scripture. For there it is represented as a spiritual and heavenly society, compacted by the bands of *one faith, one hope, one spirit* of charity. But this pretence turneth it into a worldly frame, united by the same bands of interest and design; managed in the same manner by terror and allurement; supported by the same props of force, of policy, of wealth, of reputation, and splendour, as all other secular corporations are.

You may call it what you please; but it is evident, that in truth the papal monarchy is a temporal dominion, driving on worldly ends by worldly means; such as our Lord did never mean to institute: so that the subjects thereof may with far more reason, than the people of Constantinople had, when their Bishop Nestorius did stop some of their priests from contradicting him, say, We have a king; a bishop we have not: so that upon every Pope we may charge that, whereof Anthimus was accused, in the Synod of Constantinople, under Menas; " That he did account the greatness and dignity of the priesthood to be, not a spiritual charge of souls, but as a kind of politic rule."

This was that which seeming to be affected by the Bishop of Antioch, in encroachment upon the Church of Cyprus, the Fathers of the Ephesine Synod did endeavour to nip; enacting a canon against all such invasions, " lest under pretext of holy discipline the pride of worldly authority should creep in." And what pride of that kind could they mean beyond that which now the Popes do claim and exercise? Now, do I say, after that the papal empire hath swollen to such a bulk: whereas so long ago, when it was but in its bud and stripling age, it was observed of it by a very honest historian, " that the Roman episcopacy had long since advanced into a high degree of power beyond the priesthood." . . .

This pretence doth thwart the Holy Scripture, not only by trampling down the dignity of Bishops (which according to St. Gregory doth imply great pride and presumption), but as really infringing the rights granted by our Lord to His Church and the governors of it.

For to each Church our Lord hath imposed a duty and imparted a power of maintaining Divine truth and so approving itself *a pillar and support of truth,* of deciding controversies possible and proper to be decided with due temper ultimately without farther resort—for that he who will not obey or acquiesce in its decision is to be *as a heathen or publican* ; of censuring and rejecting offenders (in doctrine or demeanour)—*Those within*, saith St. Paul to the Church of Corinth, *do not ye judge ? But them that are without God judgeth : wherefore put away from among yourselves that wicked person* ; of preserving order and decency, according to that rule prescribed to the Church of Corinth, *Let all things be done decently and in order* ; of promoting edification ; of deciding causes.

All which rights and privileges the Roman Bishop doth bereave the Churches of, snatching them to himself ; pretending that he is the sovereign doctor, judge, regulator of all Churches ; overruling and voiding all that is done by them, according to his pleasure.

The Scripture hath enjoined and empowered all Bishops to feed, guide, and rule their respective Churches, as the *ministers, stewards, ambassadors, angels of God ; for the perfecting of the saints, for the work of the ministry, for the edification of the Body of Christ* ; to whom God hath committed the care of their people, so that they are responsible for their souls.

All which rights and privileges of the episcopal office the Pope hath invaded, doth obstruct, cramp, frustrate, destroy ; pretending (without any warrant) that their authority is derived from him ; forcing them to exercise it no otherwise, than as his subjects, and according to his pleasure. . . .

The ground of that eminence which the Roman Bishop did obtain in the Church, so as in order to precede other bishops, doth shake this pretence.

The Church of Rome was indeed allowed to be " the principal Church," as St. Cyprian calleth it : but why ? Was it preferred by Divine institution ? No surely ; Christianity did not make laws of that nature, or constitute differences of places. Was it in regard to the succession of St. Peter ? No ; that was a slim, upstart device, that did not hold in Antioch, nor in other apostolical Churches.

But it was for a more substantial reason, the very same on which the dignity and pre-eminency of other Churches was founded ; that is, the dignity, magnitude, opulency, opportunity of that city in which the Bishop of Rome did preside ; together with the consequent numerousness, quality, and wealth of his flock ; which gave him many great advantages above other his fellow-Bishops. It was, saith Rigaltius, called by St. Cyprian the principal Church, "because constituted in the principal city."

That Church in the very times of severest persecutions, " by the providence of God " (as Pope Cornelius said in his Epistle to Fabius) " had a rich and plentiful number, with a most great and innumerable people " ; so that he reckoneth forty-four presbyters, seven deacons (in imitation of the number in the *Acts*), seven sub-deacons, forty-two acoluthi, fifty-two others of the inferior clergy, and above fifteen hundred alms-people.

To that Church there must needs have been a great resort of Christians, going to the seat of the empire in pursuit of business; as in proportion there was to each other metropolis; according to that Canon of the Antiochene Synod which ordered that " the Bishop of each metropolis should take care of the whole province, because all that had business did resort to the metropolis."

That Church was most able to yield help and succour to them who needed it; and accordingly did use to do it, according to that of Dionysius, Bishop of Corinth, in his Epistle to Bishop Soter of Rome: " This," saith he, " is your custom from the beginning, in divers ways to do good to the brethren, and to send supplies to many Churches in every city, so refreshing the poverty of those who want."

Whence it is no wonder that the head of that Church did get most reputation and the privilege of precedence without competition.

" To this Church," said Irenaeus, " it is necessary that every Church (that is, the faithful who are all about) should resort, because of its more powerful principality." What is meant by that *resort* will be easy to him who considereth how men here are wont to go up to London, drawn thither by interests of trade, law, etc. What he did understand by " more powerful principality," the words themselves do signify, which exactly do agree to the power and grandeur of the imperial city, but do not well suit to the authority of a Church; especially then when no Church did appear to have either principality or puissance. And that sense may clearly be evinced by the context wherein it doth appear that St. Irenaeus doth not allege the judicial authority of the Roman Church, but its credible testimony, which thereby became more considerable because Christians commonly had occasions of recourse to it. . . .

The whole Church then was a body consisting of several confederations of Bishops, acting in behalf of their Churches under their respective metropolitans, who did manage the common affairs in each province; convoking synods at stated times and upon emergent occasions; in them deciding causes and controversies incident, relating to faith or practice; framing rules serviceable to common edification and decent uniformity in God's service; quashing heresies and schisms; declaring truths impugned or questioned; maintaining the harmony of communion and concord with other provinces adjacent or remote.

Such was the state of the Church, unto which the Apostolical Canons and Constitutions do refer, answerable to the times in which they were framed; and which we may discern in the practice of ancient synods.

Such it did continue, when the great Synod of Nice was celebrated, which by its authority (presumed to represent the authority of all Bishops in the world, who were summoned thereto), backed by the imperial authority and power, did confirm those orders, as they found them standing by more general custom and received rules in most provinces; reducing them into more uniform practice; so that what before stood upon reason, customary usage, particular consent, by so august sanction did become universal law; and did obtain so great veneration, as by some to be conceived everlastingly and immutably obligatory, according to those maxims of Pope Leo.

It is here further observable that whereas divers provinces did hold communion and intercourse, so that upon occasion they did (by their formed letters) render to one another an account of their proceedings, being of great moment, especially of those which concerned the general state of Christianity and common faith; calling, when need was, for assistance one of another, to resolve points of faith, or to settle order and peace; there was in so doing a special respect given to the metropolites of great cities. And to prevent dissensions, which naturally ambition doth prompt men to, grounded upon degrees of respect, an order was fixed among them, according to which in subscriptions of letters, in accidental congresses, and the like occasions, some should precede others (that distinction being chiefly and commonly grounded on the greatness, splendour, opulency of cities; or following the secular dignity of them); whence Rome had the *first* place, Alexandria the *second*, Antioch the *third*, Jerusalem the *fourth*, etc.

## No. 28.  JOHN BRAMHALL

[From *Schism Guarded*, Section I. chapter i.  *Works*, ed. *L. A. C. T.*, Vol. II, pp. 371 f.  Among the Roman Catholic critics of Bramhall's *Just Vindication of the Church of England from the Unjust Aspersion of Criminal Schism*, which was published in 1654, was one John Sergeant.  Sergeant attacked the Bishop of Derry in two separate treatises, *Schism Disarmed* and *Schism Despatched*.  In the greater part of the former treatise, indeed, Sergeant is concerned with answering Hammond, though Bramhall is attacked at the end in a sort of appendix which is entitled *Down Derry, or Bishop Bramhall's Just Vindication of the Church of England refuted*.  In *Schism Despatched*, however, Bramhall came in for a much fuller refutation, and it was to this treatise that Bramhall replied in his *Schism Guarded*.  The quotations in the extract are from *Schism Despatched*.]

Let him [*i.e.* St. Peter] be " first, chief, or prince of the Apostles " in that sense wherein the ancient Fathers styled him so.  Let him be the " first " ministerial " mover."  And why should not the Church have recourse to a prime Apostle or Apostolical Church in doubtful cases ?  The learned Bishop [*i.e.* Andrewes] of Winchester (of whom it is no shame for him to learn) might have taught him thus much, not only in his own name, but in the name of the king and Church of England.  " Neither is it questioned among us whether St. Peter had a primacy, but what that primacy was ; and whether it were such an one as the Pope doth now challenge to himself, and you challenge to the Pope: but the king doth not deny Peter to have been the prime and prince of the Apostles." I wonder how it cometh to pass that he, who commonly runneth over in his expressions, should now on a sudden become so dry upon this subject. If this be all, he needed not to have forsaken the communion of the Church of England, for any great devotion that he beareth to St. Peter more than we.

But yet we dare not rob the rest of the Apostles to clothe St. Peter. We say clearly with St. Cyprian, *Hoc erant utique et caeteri Apostoli quod fuit Petrus, pari consortio praediti et honoris et potestatis ; sed exordium ab unitate proficiscitur, primatus Petro datur, ut una Christi Ecclesia et una Cathedra monstretur.* "The rest of the Apostles were even the same thing that Peter was, endowed with an equal fellowship both of honour and power; but the beginning cometh from unity, the primacy is given to Peter, to signify one Church and one Chair." It is well known that St. Cyprian made all the Bishoprics in the world to be but one mass, *Episcopatus unus est Episcoporum multorum concordi numerositate diffusus*; "whereof every Bishop had an entire part,"— *cujus a singulis in solidum pars tenetur.* All that he attributeth to St. Peter is this "beginning of unity," this primacy of order, this pre-eminence to be the chief of Bishops, to be Bishop of "the principal Church from whence Sacerdotal unity did spring." Yet I esteem St. Cyprian as favourable an expositor to the See of Rome, as any they will find out of their own Chair, that was no more interested in that See. This primacy neither the ancients nor we do deny to St. Peter— of order, of place, of pre-eminence. If this "first movership" would serve his turn, this controversy were at an end for our parts. But this primacy is over lean; the Court of Rome have no gusto to it. They thirst after a visible monarchy upon earth, an absolute ecclesiastical sovereignty, a power to make canons, to abolish canons, to dispense with canons, to impose pensions, to dispose dignities, to decide controversies by a single authority. This was that which made the breach, not the innocent primacy of St. Peter.

## No. 29. GILBERT BURNET

[From *A Discourse wherein is held forth the Opposition of the Doctrine, Worship, and Practice of the Roman Church to the Nature, Designs, and Characters of the Christian Faith*, pp. 34–36. *Enchiridion Theologicum Anti-Romanum* (ed. E. Cardwell), Vol. III, pp. 31 f. Cp. note on No. 105.]

I advance to another invasion of Christ's regal authority, committed by him who pretends to be the Universal Bishop of the Church and to have authority over all Churchmen, whom he makes swear obedience to him and looks on them but as his delegates. It was unluckily done of Gregory the Great to be so severe on this head as to condemn the title of Universal Bishop as Antichristian. But little dreamed he in how few years his successor would aspire to that height of ambition. Now by this pretence all these officers, whom Christ hath appointed to rule and feed His Church, are turned out of their authority and made subject to him ; and with how much pride he treads on his fellow-Bishops the histories of many ages do declare. It is true, at first, as being Bishop of the imperial city, the Bishops of Rome were highly esteemed ; but pride and ambition began soon to leaven them. Yet they were for the first four ages looked upon by the other Bishops but as their fellow-Bishops ; and by the decrees of two General Councils, the Bishops of Constantinople were in all things, except the precedency, made equal to them ; and by the decree of the Council of Nice, other metropolitans are levelled with them. And here I must tell of a shameful forgery of three Bishops of Rome who, one after another, would have obtruded on the African Churches a decree of allowing of appeals from them to the Roman See, as if it had been made at Nice ; which they of Afric rejected, and upon trial found it to be none of the appointments at Nice, but a decree of the Council of Sardica.

But by degrees the Bishops of that city got up to the height they are now at ; and not content with their usurping over their brethren and fellow-Churchmen, their next attempt was upon princes, who, deriving their authority from Jesus Christ, the *King of kings, by Whom kings do reign*, it was an invasion of His power to attempt against His vicegerents on earth. But the Popes made no bones of this. For being now held Christ's vicars on earth, with other blasphemous titles, as *vice-God*, yea, and *Lord God*, they thought their power was limited as long as kings and emperors were not even in temporals subject to them. And therefore from the days of Pope Gregory the Seventh they pretended to a power of deposing princes, disposing of their dominions to others, and dispensing with the oaths of fidelity their subjects had sworn to them ; and it was easy for them to make crowns change their masters as they pleased. For there were always other ambitious princes ready, for their own ends, to invade the dominions of these deposed kings, upon the Pope's warrant. And the generality of the people were so possessed with the Pope's power of releasing souls from purgatory, and from the punishments due to sin, that they were easily prevailed upon to follow his thunders : and by that time the Popes had swarms of emissaries of the begging orders, who, under shows of austere piety, gained much reverence and esteem in the world, and so got all subjected to the papal tyranny. Now, should I instance this in particulars, I should transgress the limits of a short discourse by a long history ; but the lives of Gregory the Seventh, Alexander the Third, Boniface the Eighth, and Julius the Second, to mention no more, will sufficiently convince any who will be at the pains to read them, as they are written by those who lived in that

communion.   And Matthew of Paris will at length inform his reader
how much and how often England smarted under this tyranny.

## No. 30.  GEORGE HICKES

[From *The Spirit of Enthusiasm Exorcized*, London, 1680, p. 37.   This was a
Sermon preached before the University of Oxford on Act Sunday, July 11, 1680, and
was " printed at the request of Mr. Vice-Chancellor, and many others who heard it
preached."   A second edition appeared in 1681, a third in 1683, and a fourth in
1709.]

I proceed to show you what a sandy foundation the Pope's Infallibility is grounded upon.   For it must be resolved into this enthusi-
astical principle of immediate inspiration, which according to the doctrine
I have now preached, neither he nor any other Bishop or Presbyter
of the Church hath warrant from the Scriptures to pray for or expect.
I say it is a most dangerous and fanatical pretension, which is so far
from having any ground in Scripture, that it makes it a most imperfect
and useless Rule of Faith, destroys the certainty of the Christian belief,
which was fixed above 1600 years ago, and instead of being a means of
ending controversies, as Papists pretend, it introduces everlasting
scepticism into all the parts of Divinity, by making truth or [? and]
falsehood, good and evil, light and darkness, sweet and bitter, nay—
what shall I say?—by making right and wrong, God and Belial,
Christ and Anti-Christ, depend upon the breath of a single man.

## No. 31.  GEORGE HICKES

[From *The Spirit of Enthusiasm Exorcized*, London, 1680, pp. 35 f.   Cp. note on
No. **30**.]

I proceed to show what little reasons the Romish doctors have to
make miracles a sign of the true Church.   For miracles were formerly
wrought for signs to confirm the authority of the Apostles and their
assistants and successors, and to seal the truth of that new doctrine
which they were to preach about the world.   Therefore, to suppose
that the Church stands always in need of miracles is to suppose her to
be still in a state of minority and her doctrine to be always a publishing
to the world, or else to suppose that infinite wisdom may become impertinent and seal the same truths, ten thousand times over.   Indeed,
as they argue, in the Church of the Jews there were always miracles
to be found, because their Theocratical constitution of Church and
State was miraculous, God as their King being obliged to make known
His pleasure in civil and military, as well as in Ecclesiastical, matters
unto them by Voices from Heaven, Oracles, and Prophecies (as other
Princes do by Proclamations and messages), and their prophets were
always to work signs and wonders to prove the truth of their mission,
and sometimes the certainty of what they foretold should come to pass.
But then besides the miracles which belonged to the nature of their

Theocratical government, God wrought others for them and among them, to render Himself and that particular Church more conspicuous in the eyes of the Gentile world.   Hither we may refer their miraculous victories by single men or armies over their enemies, which God wrought to convince them by sensible experiments of His Omnipotence, that of all the Divinity of the Eastern world, He alone was the true God. But had the Law been published among all nations, like the Gospel, and Judaism become the Universal Religion of the world, miracles at length would have grown out of use, as indeed they grew very rare after the Jews were dispersed among the nations and their Law was translated into Greek, which at the time of the translation was become the most general language of the world.

## No. 32.  JAMES USSHER

[From *A Body of Divinity ; or the Sum and Substance of Christian Religion*, ed. 1649, pp. 438, 439–441.  This work was first published in 1645 by John Downham, who asserted that it was the work of Archbishop Ussher; but immediately on its appearance Ussher wrote to Downham, disclaiming the authorship of it.  It seems to have been based on a catena of passages from earlier Divines, including Cartwright and Crooke.  On the circumstances connected with its publication, see C. R. Elrington, *Life of Ussher*, pp. 248 f. ; because Ussher denied that he had written it, Elrington did not include the treatise in his edition of Ussher.  The extreme violence and deplorable tone of some passages of the following extract were unhappily only too common in some quarters in the Seventeenth Century.]

*Who is that Antichrist ?*

He is one who under the colour of being for Christ, and under title of His Vicegerent, exalteth himself above and against Christ, opposing himself unto Him in all his offices and ordinances, both in Church and Commonwealth ;  bearing authority in the Church of God ;  ruling over that City with seven Hills, which did bear rule over nations and put our Lord to death ; a Man of Sin, a harlot, a mother of spiritual fornications to the kings and people of the nations, a child of perdition, and a destroyer, establishing himself by lying miracles and false wonders.  All which marks together do agree with none but. the Pope of Rome. . . .

*What learn you of this ?*

That the calling of the Pope is unlawful.   For every office or calling which the Lord doth not bless or wherein none occupying the place groweth in piety is to be esteemed for an unlawful calling : for in a lawful calling some (at the least) are found in all ages profitable to the Church or Commonwealth.

*What is the use of all this doctrine ?*

That whosoever are partakers of the sins of Rome are also under the same curse.  And therefore such of us as have lived in Popery should examine ourselves if we have truly repented us of it ;  first, by the change of our understanding as whether we have grown in

10

the knowledge of the truth : and secondly, by the change of our affections, as whether we hate Popery, and love the truth unfeignedly ;
and so let every one judge himself, that he be not judged, and that with
harder judgement, according as God hath been the longer patient
towards us.

*What further ?*

That there can be no sound agreement betwixt Popery and the
profession of the Gospel ; no more than betwixt light and darkness,
falsehood and truth, God and Belial ; and therefore no reconciliation
can be devised betwixt them. For if the members of Antichrist
shall be destroyed, we cannot in any sort communicate with them in
their errors, unless we will bear them company in their destruction also.

*Doth every error destroy the soul ?*

No verily.  For as every wound killeth not a man, so every error
depriveth not a man of salvation : but as the vital parts, being wounded
or infected, bring death, so those errors that destroy the fundamental
points and heads of faith bring everlasting destruction ; in which kind
is Popery, which sundry ways overthroweth the principles and grounds
of our holy faith, and therefore is termed an Apostasy, or departing
from the faith.

*Is it then impossible for a Pope to be saved ?*

No ; it is not impossible, his sin being not necessarily against
the Holy Ghost, to which only repentance is denied.  For some (in
likelihood) have entered into, and continued in that See ignorantly,
and therefore may possibly find place to repentance.  But if any be
saved, it is a secret hidden with God ; for concerning any thing that
appears by the end of any Pope since he was lift up in the Emperor's
chair and discovered to be the Man of Sin, there is no grounded
hope given to persuade that any one of them is saved.

*So much of Antichrist, what he is towards others.  What is he in
himself ?*

That is set down in two points.  First, in that (contrary to right,
and by mere usurpation) he seateth himself in the Temple of God,
as if he were Christ's Vicar, being indeed His enemy ; both which the
word Antichrist noteth.

Secondly, in that he is here expressly named an adversary, and one
that is contrary to Christ.

*Wherein is the Pope adversary unto Christ ?*

Every way ;  in life, and in office.

*How in life ?*

In that Christ being most pure and holy, yea holiness itself, the
Popes many of them are, and have been, most filthy and abominable
n blaspheming, conjuring, murdering, covetousness, whoring, and
that incestuously and Sodomitically ;  and yet will they in their

ordinary titles be called holy, yea holiness itself, which is proper only to Christ.

*How in office?*

First, in his Kingdom. Christ's Kingdom is without all outward shew or pomp. But the Pope's Kingdom consisteth wholly in pomp and shows, as imitating his predecessors the Emperors of Rome in his proud, stately, and lordly offices, princely train, and outrageous expences in every sort.

Secondly, in his Priesthood; in raising up another sacrifice than Christ's, another Priesthood than His, other Mediators than Him.

Thirdly, in his Prophetical Office; in that he teacheth clean contrary to Him. Christ taught nothing but what He received of His Father; the Pope setteth out his own Canons and Decrees of Councils, and in them he teacheth such doctrine as overthroweth the main foundation of that which Christ taught.

*What is the second effect?*

That he is exceedingly lifted up against all that is called God.

*How doth this agree to the Pope?*

More fitly than to any other person. For Christ being very God, abaseth Himself unto the assuming of the nature of man: the Pope a vile man, advanceth himself to the Throne of God. Christ, being above all secular power, paid tribute, and was taxed, and suffered Himself to be crowned with a Crown of Thorns, and bear His Own Cross; but the Pope, being under all secular power, exalteth himself above all secular powers, exacteth tribute of kings, setteth his foot on the neck of Emperors, carrieth a triple crown of gold, and is borne upon men's shoulders.

*But he calleth himself the servant of servants?*

Though he do, yet (by the confession of his own canonists) he doth it but dissemblingly and in hypocrisy, which is double iniquity. For they say that he doth in humility only say so; not that he is indeed so as he saith.

## No. 33. EDWARD REYNOLDS

[From *An Explication of the Hundred and Tenth Psalm, Wherein the Several Heads of Christian Religion Therein Contained touching the Exaltation of Christ, the Sceptre of His Kingdom, the Character of His Subjects, His Priesthood, Victories, Sufferings, and Resurrection are largely explained and applied. Works*, ed. London (1826), Vol. II, pp. 256 f. This treatise, which was published in 1632, was dedicated to Lord Coventry. The author described its contents as " the substance of several sermons preached at Lincoln's Inn." A second edition came out in 1635.]

And this giveth a full answer to that question, "Where our Church was before the late Reformation began by Luther?"—for that Reformation did not new make the Church, but purge it. And that it stood in need of purging, the Papists themselves were fain to confess and declare to the world in their Council of Trent. Only herein is the difference, the Council pretended a Reformation in points of discipline and manners; and we made a Reformation in points of doctrine too. When Christ purged the temple of buyers and sellers, it was the same temple after, which before. When a man separateth the wheat from the chaff, it is the same corn which before. In these corrupter ages, then, the pure professors of Christ who denied not His faith did dwell where Satan had his seat. The members of Christ were amongst the rulers of Anti-Christ. We are not another Church, newly started up, but the same which before from the Apostles' times held the common and necessary grounds of faith and salvation; which grounds being in latter ages perverted and overturned by Anti-Christianism, have been by valiant champions for the faith of Christ therefrom vindicated, who have only pruned the Lord's vine, and picked out the stones and driven the boars out of His vineyard, but have not made either one or other new.

## No. 34.  HENRY DODWELL

[From *An Account of the Fundamental Principle of Popery as it is a Distinct Communion*, 1688, p. xii. This *Account* was first published in 1676 in *Two Short Discourses Against the Romanists*.]

The God of Peace allay the heats and destroy the dividing principles of Christendom, among which perhaps there are no principles more malignant than false pretences to infallibility. This has made them to define things upon very insufficient evidence when they have fancied themselves entitled to a greater infallibility in their conclusions than their premises could rationally account for. And this makes it impossible for them to recede, in ages of learning and more exact knowledge of the originals, of tradition, from the decrees of very wicked and withal very unskilful ages, and that in instances so very gross and manifest as hardly anything could hinder them from seeing and acknowledging but strong prejudices to the contrary of a Judicial Infallibility in those who introduced them. Whilst such opinions as these prevail and are received, in vain can anyone expect any candour in acknowledging the most pregnant convictions from them who are possessed by them. In vain does anyone offer sufficient reasons for conviction to persons already resolved and prejudged against conviction. In vain can such persons expect any illumination or assistance from God, who are not disposed to receive the truth in the love of it. And therefore the opposing and convicting of errors so mischievous and embroiling, and so incurable in persons resolved to stand by them, will deserve the utmost zeal and diligence of all true lovers of souls and all hearty well-wishers to Catholic Communion and the Peace of Christendom.

# (2) THE EASTERN CHURCH

## No. 35. WILLIAM LAUD

[From *A Relation of the Conference between William Laud and Mr. Fisher the Jesuit*, Section IX, Ed. C. H. Simpkinson (1901), pp. 29 f. Cp. note on No. 54.]

IT ought to be no easy thing to condemn a man of heresy in foundation of faith, much less a Church, least of all so ample and large a Church as the Greek, especially so as to make them no Church. Heaven gates were not so easily shut against multitudes, when St. Peter wore the keys at his own girdle. And it is good counsel which Alphonsus a Castro, one of your own, gives: " Let them consider that pronounce easily of heresy how easy it is for themselves to err."

## No. 36. ANTONIO DE DOMINIS

[A Letter sent by de Dominis to the Patriarch of Alexandria. Reprinted from *Marcus Antonio de Dominis Archbishop of Spalatro, His Shiftings in Religion*, London, 1624 (by R. Neile, Bishop of Durham), pp. 85–88. It is (inaccurately) reprinted in H. Newland, *The Life and Contemporaneous Church History of Antonio de Dominis*, pp. 213–215. This letter was composed to accompany a presentation copy to the Patriarch of Alexandria of the writer's *De Republica Ecclesiastica*, published in 1617.]

*To the Most Holy Father and beloved of our Saviour Jesus Christ, the Lord Cyril, Patriarch of Alexandria, Oecumenical Judge, the lowest of God's servants, Marcus Antonio de Dominis, Archbishop of Spalata, otherwise of Salona.*

Most Reverend Father and most worthy all observance. Your Egypt hath sometime felt most gross and palpable darkness under Pharaoh's hardened heart, and the people of God served with most intolerable bondage under a cursed tyrant, who both vexed the bodies of those miserable men with cruel afflictions and hindered them from the true worship of God, which was the proper food of their souls. But yet in those times God Himself did at length overcome the stubbornness and hard-heartedness of them, and revenged Himself of their wickedness by drowning them in the Red Sea, and so tamed and repressed all their impiety. It hath now happened that you and your most religious Christian Church (whose case we much commiserate) groan under another Pharaoh, under whom ye suffer oftentimes all extremities both in body and goods. But yet he doth not offer to take the service of God from you, nor use any such impediments of it, but that you may offer to God entire and pure sacrifice (though not with pomp and splendour to the sight of men) and enjoy peace and content

73

in your exercises of religion which I hear of with much delight. But as for our Western Churches, the most of them being subject to the Bishop of Rome, are in regard of temporal estate over-glorious; and whereas they were famous heretofore in regard of the purity and sincerity of their love and all internal virtues, even under the persecutions and oppressions of tyrants that were infidels, yet now in this age they, exceeding in all riot and excess, by God's most just though secret judgement, are oppressed under your old Pharaoh and brought again to a most miserable bondage. I therefore being born and bred and promoted within the Romish verge and having of long time endured that ancient Egyptian darkness under the Western Egypt and accursed Pharaoh, did a long time study how to convey myself to the land of Goshen where the light of the Gospel shineth most clearly, which at length by God's help I have happily accomplished; and now a year since or thereabouts I renounced the Pope and came into England, where I have liberty to write in defence of truth freely and safely, as in a place where the cause of Christ triumpheth under a most godly and most wise King, a true defender of the true, ancient and Catholic Faith. Now of these my works, the *De Republica Ecclesiastica*, the first birth being lately published, I send herewith to your Lordships (most religious Father) as a pledge of my hearty desire to enter communion with your Fatherhoods. In this Tractate, I strive to defend and vindicate your Oriental Churches, and that of Constantinople especially, from all Romish calumniations. I defend, moreover, the ancient rights of Patriarchs, and reduce the Bishop of Rome to his right place by taking away from him his absolute supremacy. So that I hope you shall find in this my book a ready armour of defence against the Jesuitical weapons. Accept of me then, most blessed Father, as of your most obedient brother and servant. And I pray and beseech you in all the bowels of Christ that you will enter into serious consideration of uniting your Eastern Churches with this most noble and flourishing Church of England. For by making such an union against Pharaoh, or rather Anti-Christ, we shall more easily prevail against him and remove his tyranny far from the Church of Christ. Stir up your zeal then, most Holy Father, and embrace an enterprise so befitting and worthy so great a Patriarch. And if you meet with any difficulty in the business, I pray and beseech you that after mature consideration of it you will be pleased to signify it either to myself or to the Lord Archbishop of Canterbury, Primate of England, a man most wise and most studious of propagating the glory of Christ. Cast then all the care and strength of your mind to take away, and utterly abolish so inveterate a schism. And so farewell in the Lord. God preserve you long in safety for the good of His Church, most holy and most religious Father, as one of the most noble and principal

members of His Holy Church. And God keep you in true charity
and true zeal of preserving the unity of the Church.

## No. 37.  PAUL RICAUT

[From *The Present State of the Greek and Armenian Churches, Anno Christi, 1678,*
Preface (unpaged), the concluding paragraphs.  This treatise was published in 1679
by the command of Charles II.  As Consul of the Levant Company from 1667 to
1679, Ricaut had had unique opportunities of observing religious conditions in the
Near East.]

It will not be difficult to conjecture under what notion the Eastern
apprehends the Western Reformed Churches ; for they, taking notice that
the English neither keep Fasts, nor practise Confession, nor ordinarily
make the Sign of the Cross, and that the Dutch Nation at Smyrna
rehearse no prayers at the burial of the dead, are not only scandalized
thereat, but also Jews and Turks take offence at the silence of prayers
when the dead are buried, wondering what sort of Heresy or Sect
is sprung up in the world, so different from the Religion of all the
Prophets ; at which undecent practice, the Roman Clergy taking advantage to disparage the Protestants, represent them to the Greeks
under the notion of Calvinists, whom they characterize to be such as
condemn all order in the Church, the authority of Priesthood, abolish
Fasts, abhor the Cross, condemn the Saints, besides a thousand other
heresies and schisms, in which they report we are at odds amongst
ourselves.  And in reality, were it not that the English Nation by
the orderly use of their Liturgy and discipline of their Church, observing the Lord's Day and the Grand Festivals, did vindicate themselves
of these aspersions, it were impossible to persuade the Oriental Countries
that those which we call Reformed were Christians, or at least to retain
anything of Ancient and Apostolical Institution.  Upon which score
the Greeks detest that Confession of Faith, supposed to be wrote by
Cyrillus, their Patriarch of Constantinople, in the year 1629, and printed
and confuted in the year 1631 by Matthæus Caryophilus, Archbishop
of Iconium ; for that Confession, agreeing wholly with the doctrine
of Calvin in every particular, is believed in a great measure to have
been fathered on him by the Jesuits, who, to justify their inhuman
persecutions of that worthy prelate, by making Turks and Infidels
the instruments of their rage, formed and vented anything which might
procure the curses and anathemas of the Old and New Rome.  I am
persuaded that this Cyrillus, having spent some time in England,
and there observed that purity of our doctrine and the excellency of
our discipline which flourished in the beginning of the Reign of King
Charles the Martyr, and viewed our Churches trimmed and adorned
in a modest medium, between the wanton and superstitious dress of
Rome and the slovenly and insipid Government of Geneva, entertained
a high opinion of our happy Reformation ; intending thence perhaps to

draw a pattern, whereby to amend and correct the defaults of the Greek Church, retrenching the length of their Services and the multitude of their Ceremonies, and also by that exemplar to reduce their Festivals to a moderate number, to create a right apprehension of the state of souls after separation, and wholly to take away certain conceits both superstitious and savouring of Gentilism, and confirm his Church in a reverend opinion of the Holy Sacrament of the Eucharist, without launching so far into the explication of that Mystery, as of late they have done both in the Anatolian Confession, which was generally owned and confirmed in the year 1672, by the Subscription of the four Oriental Patriarchs, and of the Metropolites then present, at the instance of Monsieur de Nointel, Ambassador for his Most Christian Majesty, a very intelligent and ingenious gentleman. And had not this good Patriarch been thus maliciously prosecuted, and his life taken from him by unhappy wiles, he might, with God's assistance, have accomplished a work of reformation, and piloted the Church into that state of Apostolical purity, which King James, Erasmus, Cassander, Melancthon, Bucer, the Archbishop of Spalatro, and others did design.

But God, it seems, hath not as yet ordained the time for so happy a conversion and reformation, which is a blessing rather to be wished for at present than to be expected ; till when, it is the duty of all good men, and the elect of God to offer a continual sacrifice of prayer on the altar of their hearts, that He would be pleased to grant us unity of faith in our Religion, and peace and concord in all Christian Governments, that being one sheepfold under one Shepherd, the Lord Jesus, we may imitate the example of Him Who is the Prince of Peace.

## No. 38.  EDWARD STILLINGFLEET

[From *A Rational Account of the Grounds of the Protestant Religion ; being a Vindication of the Lord Archbishop of Canterbury's " Relation of a Conference, etc." from the pretended Answer by T. C.*, Part I, Chapter i (" The Defence of the Greek Church "). Second edition, London, 1681, pp. 22, 25 f. This treatise was originally published in 1665. Laud's *Relation of a Conference, etc.* had appeared in 1639 (cp. note on No. 54), and provoked a number of replies, Puritan and Roman Catholic. Among the latter was *Labyrinthus Cantuariensis, or Dr. Laud's Labyrinth.* It purported to have been printed at Paris in 1658, and to be the work of T. C[arvell]. The author's real name was Thorold, a man of a Lincolnshire family, who died in 1664. Stillingfleet asserts that the *Labyrinthus* did not really appear until 1663.]

Having thus discovered that this opinion [*i.e.* the Greek teaching on the Procession of the Spirit] you condemn for heresy in the Greek Church was otherwise esteemed both by Fathers, Ecumenical Councils, and Popes, I come to that which you seem to rely on for making it heretical, namely that the Greeks and Latins both together condemned it for heretical in the General Council at Florence ; although it might be worth our while to enquire how far any General Council can either make or declare that to be a necessary Article of Faith which was determined to be otherwise by former General Councils. But omitting that at present. . . . I therefore come to examine the matter of fact in the Florentine Council concerning the determination of this opinion there as heretical. Wherein, if we consider the time in which and the occasion upon which this Council was called, if we consider the way of the managery of it, the arts whereby the Greeks were drawn to this consent, the manner of proposing the Decrees of it, or the acceptance which it found in the Greek Church, upon none of these respects we shall have cause to look upon it as a free and General Council, determining that opinion as heretical which you say was so determined here. In all which we must profess how much we are obliged to that faithful and impartial account of all the proceedings relating to this Council, written by Sylvester Sguropulus, one present at the most secret negotiations of it, transcribed out of the manuscript in the King of France his Library by Claudius Serravius, and first published for the general good of the world by our learned Dean of Wells [Robert Creighton]. . . .

This is the short account of the management of those affairs at Florence which are more particularly and largely prosecuted by the author [*i.e.* Sguropulus], wherein we see what clandestine arts, what menaces and insinuations, what threats and promises, were used to bring the poor Greeks to consent to this pretended Union. For it afterwards appeared to be no more than pretended; for the infinitely greater number of Bishops at home refused it, and these very Bishops themselves, when they saw what arts were used in it, fell off from it again, and the Emperor found himself at last deceived in his great expectations of help from the Latins. Must we then acknowledge this for a free and General Council, which hath a promise of Infallibility annexed to the Definitions of it? Shall we from hence pronounce the Greeks' Doctrine to be heretical, when for all these proceedings yet at last no more was agreed on than that they did both believe the Procession from the Son, without condemning the other opinion as heretical, as you pretend, which the Greeks would never have consented to; or anathematizing the persons who denied it, as was usual in former General Councils, who did suppose it not enough to have it virtually done by the positive Definition, but did expressly and formally do it? For when this anathematizing dissenters was propounded among the Greeks by Bessarion of Nice and Isidore of Russia (who, for their great service to the Pope in this business, were made Cardinals), it was refused by the rest who were zealous promoters of the Union. Thus have I at large, more out of a design to vindicate the Greek Church than being necessitated to it by anything you [*i.e.* the author of the *Labyrinth*] produce, shewed that there is no reason from authority, either before or after the Council of Florence, to charge the Greek Church with heresy.

# (3) PURITANISM AND PRESBYTERIANISM

## No. 39.  JOSEPH HALL

[From *Episcopacy by Divine Right Asserted*, Introduction, § 2.  *Works*, ed. Peter Hall (1837), Vol. X, pp. 147–149.  Joseph Hall, who had been consecrated Bishop of Exeter in 1627, though of Puritan sympathies, was a staunch believer in Episcopacy. Accordingly in 1637 Laud requested him to compose a defence of Episcopal Government.  Hall consented.  The MS. was submitted to Laud, who having examined it, returned it with some suggested modifications which Hall readily incorporated.  The redrafted treatise was again modified by Laud, in this case in a strongly anti-Puritan direction.  Hall again acquiesced and the treatise finally appeared in February 1639–40, with a dedication to Charles I.  From that moment onwards Hall took a prominent part in the controversy on the subject of Episcopacy.]

### *The Difference of the Condition of Foreign Churches and Divines from those of our Northern Neighbours.*

BUT, first, ere we enter these lists, let me advise you and your now-master the Faction not to deceive yourselves vainly, with the hope of hiding your heads, under the skirt of the authority of those Divines and Churches abroad which retain that form of government whereto you have submitted.

For, know, their case and yours is far enough different.  They plead to be, by a kind of necessity, cast upon that condition which you have willingly chosen.  They were not, they could not be, what you were, and might still have been.  Did any of them forsake and abjure that function of Episcopacy, which he might freely have enjoyed with the full liberty of professing the Reformed Religion ?  It is true many Bishops have been faulty in their own persons, and condemned too justly of exorbitance in managing their calling.  But, where the calling is, as it should be, severed from these exceptions to the person, did ever any wise man or Christian Church condemn that calling for itself ?

Yea, if the last Bishop of Geneva had become a Protestant, and consented in matter of doctrine to Calvin, Farel, Viret, have you or any man living just cause to think that the city would not gladly have retained his government still, and thought themselves happy under such a protection ?  Would they have rejected him as an enemy, whom they might have enjoyed as a patron ?  Would they have stood upon his Episcopacy, while they had his concurrence in the truth of religion ?  No man that hath either brain or forehead will affirm it, since the world knows the quarrel was not at his dignity but at his opposition to the intended Reformation.

But, because this is only a suggestion of a then-future-conditionate contingency and may perhaps meet with some stubborn contradiction, hear what Calvin himself saith for himself and his co-partners. " If they would," saith he, " bring unto us a Hierarchy, wherein the Bishops shall so rule as that they refuse not to submit themselves to Christ, that they depend upon Him, as their Only Head, etc., then, surely, if there shall be any that shall not submit themselves to that Hierarchy reverently and with the greatest obedience that may be, I confess there is no Anathema of which they are not worthy." Thus he, in the *Treatise of the Necessity of Reforming the Church.*

Do you hear your doom from your own oracle ? Lo, such, and no other was that Hierarchy, wherein you lately bore a part, and which you have now condemned ! Make account, therefore, of the merit and danger of Calvin's just Anathema !

Yet, again, the same author, in his Confession of Faith, written in the name of all the French Churches, speaking of the depraved estate of the Roman Church, then in the *fieri* of reforming, plainly writes thus : *Interea, tamen,*—" Yet, in the mean time, we would not have the authority of the Church, or of those Pastors, or Super-intendents, to whom the charge of governing the Church is committed, taken away. We confess, therefore, that these Bishops or Pastors are reverently to be heard, so far forth as, according to their function, they teach the Word of God."

And yet more plainly : " Certainly," saith he, speaking even of Popish Bishops, " if they were true Bishops, I would yield them some authority in this case,—not so much as themselves desire, but so much as is required to the due ordering of the policy or government of the Church."

Lastly, for it were easy to heap up this measure, in an Epistle of his wherein the question is purposely discussed, What is to be done if a Popish Bishop shall be converted to the reformed religion, he so de-termines it ? That it is fit such an one, first, renounce his Popish power of sacrificing, and profess to abstain from all the superstitions and fœdities of the Romish Religion ; then, that he must do his utmost endeavour that all the Churches which belong to his Bishopric may be purged from their errors and idolatry ; and, at last, concludes, that both his possessions and authority too should be left him, by virtue whereof, he must take order that the Ministers under him do duly preach God's Word, as himself also must do. Thus he, wisely and moderately ; not first of all stripping him of his Episcopal power, and discharging all his Clergy of their respects and obedience to him, and reducing him to the rank of the meanest plebeian Presbyter, as some hot heads would have done.

You hear how judicious and moderate Calvin's opinion was, then ; and, had he been in your late pretended Assembly at Glasgow or this of Edinburgh, what vote he would have given ?   Had he had the casting voice, your coat had not been cast for him.   How happy were it for your Churches, if all among you who so much honour his name would as readily submit to this his judgement!   Sure I am, had it been so with you, you had been as far from defying Episcopacy in holy professors, as you are now from truth and peace.

## No. 40.   JOHN BRAMHALL

[From *A Fair Warning to take Heed of the Scottish Discipline, as Being of all Others Most Injurious to the Civil Magistrate, Most Oppressive to the Subject, Most Pernicious to Both*, Chapter i.   *Works*, ed. L. A. C. T., Vol. III, pp. 242, 243.   This treatise, first printed in Holland in 1649, was issued at the moment when Robert Baillie was fiercely rating the French Huguenots for admitting the lawfulness of a "moderate" episcopacy.]

It is time to let the world see that this Discipline, which they so much adore, is the very quintessence of refined Popery, or a greater tyranny than ever Rome brought forth ;   inconsistent with all forms of civil government, destructive to all sorts of policy, a rack to the conscience, the heaviest pressure that can fall upon a people, and so much more dangerous, because, by the specious pretence of Divine institution, it takes away the sight but not the burden of slavery.   Have patience, reader, and I shall discover unto thee more pride and arrogancy through the holes of a threadbare coat than was ever found under a Cardinal's cap or a triple crown. . . .

If it were not for this Disciplinarian humour, which will admit no latitude in religion, but makes each nicety a fundamental, and every private opinion an article of Faith, which prefers particular errors before general truths, I doubt not but all Reformed Churches might easily be reconciled.   Before these unhappy troubles in England, all Protestants, both Lutherans and Calvinists, did give unto the English Church the right hand of fellowship.   The Disciplinarians themselves, though they preferred their own Church as more pure (else they were hard-hearted), yet they did not, they durst not, condemn the Church of England, either as defective in any necessary point of Christian piety, or redundant in any thing that might virtually or by consequence overthrow the foundation.

## No. 41.   JOHN GAUDEN

[From Ἱερὰ Δάκρυα; *Ecclesiae Anglicanae Suspiria, or The Tears, Sighs, Complaints, and Prayers of the Church of England, Setting forth her former Constitution, Compared with Her present Condition ; Also the Visible Causes and Probable Cures of her Distempers*, London, 1659.   Book I, Chapter xiii, pp. 105 f.   As the date indicates, this large folio treatise appeared on the eve of the Restoration.]

The first and second generation of Nonconformists were more excusable and more modest in their dissentings.   For, coming newly out of not only the dungeon of Papal superstition and darkness to a marvellous light of Reformation, they were jealous of any cloud or shadow which they suspected as threatening to eclipse that light. But coming also out of the fiery furnace of Romish persecution, they were jealous of everything that had once passed the Pope's fingers, lest it might be too hot for them. These good and warm men (to whose martyrly courage much might be indulged), while yet Reformation was an embryo (in the formation and birth) were in time much worn out. Men afterward began more coolly to consider the nature of the things, no less than their own fears or other men's prejudices, especially after they saw those things three times solemnly determined and settled by the public wisdom and authority both of this Church and State. The few remains of the old stock of pious dissenters which in my time I have known, were grown so calm and moderate as to the Ceremonies of the Church of England, that I never found they persuaded others against them. As for Liturgy and Episcopacy, I am sure they justly asserted them as to the main, as wishing only some small sweetening of the first as to a few darker expressions, and the softening of the other as to some more equable regulations, which were as far from extirpation of either of them as wiping the eyes is from pulling them out, and washing the hands from cutting them off.

Yea, I know by long experience that when the graver and more learned sort of Nonconformists perceived how mightily the Reformed Religion grew and prospered in England, amidst the Liturgy, Bishops, and Ceremonies, against which some fiercer spirits have so excessively inveighed; when they saw what buds and leaves, blossoms and ripe fruit Aaron's rod brought forth, what eminent gifts and graces God was pleased to dispense by Bishops and presbyters that were piously conformable to the Church of England, they wholly laid aside their former heats and youthful eagernesses; which sometimes fed high and were kept warm by the hopes and flatteries of those who expected that party should long ago have prevailed; yea, many of them, now aged, both repented of and recanted their more juvenile and indiscreet fervours, advising others, now beginners, to conform to the good orders, and to study the peace of the Church of England, which they saw so blessed of God as none in the world exceeded her.

Nor did I ever hear of any sober Christian or truly godly minister who, being in other things prudent, unblameable, and sincere, did ever suffer any penitential strokes or checks of conscience, either upon his death-bed, or before, merely upon the account of their having been conformable to, and keeping communion with, the Church of England. Nor did they ever find or complain of Ceremonies, Liturgy, or Episcopacy, as any damps to their real graces, or to their holy communion with God's blessed Spirit. At last, both good ministers and people generally submitted themselves in all peaceableness for many years to the order and uniformity of the Church of England, until the late Northern Earthquake scared many by a panic fear from their former steadfastness in practices and judgements which had been taken up by many ministers, not suddenly and easily, but after serious and mature deliberations, against which nothing new hath as yet been alleged to alter their minds, only old rusty arguments have been wrapped up in new furbished arms, and the strongest sword, it seems, makes the best proofs and impressions on some men's consciences, even in matters of religion.

## No. 42. WILLIAM BEVERIDGE

[From *Sermon LI. Works*, ed. *L. A. C. T.*, Vol. II, p. 439. The subject of this sermon was " Stedfastness to the Established Church Recommended," and the text *I Cor.* xv, 58. Another extract from this sermon is given as No. **51.**]

But if you leave the Communion or fellowship of our Church, and join yourselves to any of the sects which are risen up amongst us, as you will be certain to want many of the means of grace which you here enjoy, you will be uncertain whether you shall enjoy any of them, so as to attain the end for which they are appointed, even the salvation of your souls; for you will be uncertain whether they who administer them be lawfully called and sent by Christ to do it, as be sure many of them are not. You will be uncertain whether you can join with them in prayer; for in some places they know not what they say, in other places they themselves know not what they intend to say, until they have said it, and how then can you know it? You will be uncertain whether you shall ever receive any benefit from the Sacrament of the Lord's Supper; for some never administer it at all, others do it either so imperfectly or so irregularly, that the virtue and efficacy of it is very much impaired, if not quite destroyed; you will be uncertain, whether they preach the true doctrine of the Gospel, for they never subscribe to it, nor solemnly promise to preach that and no other; neither are they ever called to account for any thing they say or teach, be it never so false or contrary to what Christ and His Apostles taught, so that they may lead you blindfold whithersoever they please, without control; and after all, you will be uncertain whether they seek you or yours, for they have no more obligation upon them to take care of your souls than you have to take care of theirs; and therefore the most favourable and the most charitable construction that can be put upon the separation from our Church, is, that it is leaving a certainty for an uncertainty, which no wise man would do in any thing, much less in a matter upon which his eternal happiness and salvation depends; from whence ye may easily observe, that it is your wisdom and interest, as well as duty, to be steadfast as in the doctrine, so likewise in fellowship or communion with the Church, as the first Disciples were.

## No. 43. GEORGE MORLEY

[From the ' Preface ' to *Several Treatises Written upon Several Occasions*, London 1683, p. viii. In spite of his great learning Morley wrote little, and this collection of treatises appeared only when the author was 85 years of age. " How little forward," he remarked at the outset of the Preface, " I have been to trouble the press or the public with any scribbling of mine needs no other proof but that I was past my great ' climacterical ' before anything of mine was published with mine own privity and consent." Cosin, who is referred to in the extract, had been less rigid in his attitude towards the French Calvinists than was Morley. Cp. his letter to Mr. Cordel at Blois (No. **167**.)]

When I was in France [*i.e.* during the Commonwealth] I did at Paris assist Dr. Cosins [= Cosin], late Bishop of Durham, in preaching to the English Protestants there at Sir Richard Brown's house, then Resident there for our King, but never went to the French Presbyterian Church at Charenton, no more than I did afterwards to that of Caen in Normandy, whilst I was there. For which being asked the reason of the chief pastor of the Church, the learned Monsieur Bouchart, my answer was that I forbore to come to their Church, First because we had at my Lady Ormond's house there a congregation of our own, wherein we had not only preaching as they had but a Liturgy or Solemn Form of Worshipping God by Prayers, Praises, and Thanksgivings, which (as I was informed) they had not in their Churches. Secondly because, though I understood their language when I read it, yet I did not understand it when I heard it spoken so well as, though the matter were never so good, to be at all edified by it. And thirdly because if they did not favour and encourage, yet they did not, at least they had not hitherto, condemned or reproved the scandalous and rebellious proceedings of their Presbyterian brethren in England against the King and against the Church ; which until they should do by some public act or manifestation of their judgement to the contrary, I could not choose but think they approved, or at least did not dislike, what our Presbyterians in England had done and were still a-doing. And therefore I did forbear for the present to join in communion with them there at Caen, as I had done formerly for the very same reasons with those at Charenton.

## (4) THE QUAKERS

### No. 44.  RICHARD BAXTER

[From *The True Catholic, and Catholic Church Described ; and the Vanity of the Papists and all other Schismatics that confine the Catholic Church to their Sect discovered and shamed*, Sect. III, § 1.  Ed. 1660, pp. 79–81.  *Works*, ed. W. Orme (1830), Vol. XVI, p. 308.  Ed. London, 1838, Vol. IV, p. 738.  This treatise is a disquisition on the text *I Cor.* xii, 12 : " For as the body is one, and hath many members, and all members of that one body, being many, are one body, so also is Christ."  It was written in 1659, just before the Restoration.]

THE Quakers are but a few distempered people, risen up within a few years in this corner of the world : and yet they are not ashamed to condemn the most godly Christians, Ministers, and Churches of the world that are not of their way, as if the Church were confined to these few poor, distracted, erroneous persons.  I do not think that they are all of a mind among themselves ; some of them plainly deny the very essentials of Christianity.  And for these to reproach the Church is no wonder : but to appropriate it to themselves that are no members of it, is as if Turks or heathens should have persuaded the world that they are the only Christians.  In the meantime I thank God that Christianity is in so much esteem, that even the enemies of it do pretend to it : but for those that go under that name, and deny not the fundamentals let them consider what I said before to the Seekers : if there be no Church, there is no Christ, no body, no head : and no Church, no Christians, and no justification or salvation.  And therefore I would know of them, where was the true Church before the other day that the Quakers rose ?  If there were any, where was it ?  If there were none, then there was no Christ, no head !  I remember what a boy told them lately near us, " Your Church and religion (saith he) cannot be the right for I can remember since it first begun."  Surely Christ had a Church before the Quakers.

### No. 45.  GEORGE HICKES

[From *The Spirit of Enthusiasm Exorcized*, London, 1680, pp. 40 f.  Cp. note on No. **30**.]

Let us a little more particularly reflect upon that blasphemous doctrine of the Quakers (now by the industry of the emissaries no contemptible sect) concerning a Spiritual Ministry and Spiritual Worship, whereby they pretend that the Holy Ghost now comes down upon their assemblies, as it did in the Apostles' time, and moves them to preach and pray by inspiration without any regard to condition or sex. Hence when they meet together they sit hanging their heads in a silent dumb manner, till the Spirit, as they pretend, shall move somebody, it is indifferent be it man or woman, to preach or pray. Accordingly they call their preaching Prophesying, and precariously say that they have the *Spirit of Adoption, by which they call God Father*, and that the Spirit in the inspired minister *maketh Intercession for them with unutterable groans.* That they groan sufficiently, we grant; for sometimes in their meetings they do nothing else. But if their groaning or vocal devotions be from the Spirit, how comes it to pass that the Spirit never moves them, as it did in the Apostles' days, to pray and prophesy in unknown tongues? When we shall see in their assemblies, as the unbelieving Jews and Gentiles did in the Primitive Christian meetings, that they have the gift of tongues and the gift of interpreting thereof, when together with the gift of tongues we shall see that they have, as the Christians had, all the other miraculous gifts, when we shall see that they shew themselves to be Prophets and spiritual in receiving what this Apostle hath written (in particular, that a woman should not speak in the Church) as the commandments of God, and lastly, when with all this they shall preach no other doctrine than what the Apostle hath preached, and the Catholic Church received; then we will believe, if they be lawfully baptized, that it is the Spirit which is speaking in them, and that God is in them and among them of a truth. But till then we must believe them all to be Impostors, or Enthusiasts, and Blasphemers of the Holy Ghost.

# (5) SOCINIANISM

## No. 46. ROBERT SOUTH

[From *Twelve Sermons Upon Several Subjects and Occasions* (Vol. III of South's *Sermons*), London (1698), pp. 361–363. The Sermon from which the extract is taken is entitled " Jesus of Nazareth Proved the True and Only Promised Messiah," and was preached before the University of Oxford in St. Mary the Virgin's on Christmas Day, 1665. The text was *John* i, 11.]

I CANNOT think it directly requisite to the prosecution of these words (nor will the time allotted for it permit) to assert and vindicate the foregoing verses from the perverse interpretations of that false pretender to reason, and real subverter [of] all Religion, Socinus, who in the exposition of this chapter [i.e. *John* i.], together with some part of the eighth (both of them taken from the Posthumous Papers of his Uncle Lelius) laid the foundation of that great babel of blasphemies with which he afterwards so amused and pestered the Christian World, and under colour of reforming and refining (forsooth) the best of Religions, has employed the utmost of his skill and art to bring men indeed to believe none. And therefore no small cause of grief must it needs be to all pious minds that such horrid opinions should find so ready a reception and so fatal a welcome in so many parts of the world as they have done, considering both what they tend to, and whom they come from. For they tend only to give us such a Christ and Saviour as neither the Prophets nor Evangelists know, nor speak anything of; and as for their original, if we would trace them up to that, through some of the chief branches of their infamous pedigree, we must carry them a little backward from hence,—first to the fore-mentioned Faustus Socinus and his Uncle Lelius, and from them to Gentilis, and then to Servetus, and so through a long interval to Mahomet and his sect, and from them to Photinus, and from him to Arius, and from Arius to Paulus Samosatenus, and from him to Ebion and Cerinthus, and from them to Simon Magus and so in a direct line to the Devil himself; under whose conduct in the several ages of the Church these wretches successively have been some of the most notorious opposers of the Divinity of Our Saviour, and would un-doubtedly have overthrown the belief of it in the world, could they by all their arts of wresting, corrupting and false interpreting the Holy Text, have brought the Scriptures to speak for them, which they could never yet do. And amongst all the Scriptures, no one has stood so directly and immoveably in their way, as this First Chapter of St. John's Gospel,—a chapter carrying in it so bright and full an asser-tion of the Eternal Godhead of the Son, that a man must put common sense and reason extremely upon the rack before he can give any tolerable exposition of it to the contrary.

# IV. THE BIBLE

# (1) SCRIPTURE AS THE RULE OF FAITH

## No. 47. RICHARD HOOKER

[From *The Laws of Ecclesiastical Polity*, Book II, Chapter viii, § 7. *Works*, ed. J. Keble, Vol. I, pp. 335 f. Cp. note on No. **148**.]

Two opinions therefore there are concerning sufficiency of Holy Scripture, each extremely opposite unto the other, and both repugnant unto truth. The schools of Rome teach Scripture to be so unsufficient, as if, except traditions were added, it did not contain all revealed and supernatural truth, which absolutely is necessary for the children of men in this life to know that they may in the next be saved. Others justly condemning this opinion grow likewise unto a dangerous extremity, as if Scripture did not only contain all things in that kind necessary, but all things simply, and in such sort that to do any thing according to any other law were not only unnecessary but even opposite unto salvation, unlawful and sinful. Whatsoever is spoken of God or things appertaining to God otherwise than as the truth is, though it seem an honour, it is an injury. And as incredible praises given unto men do often abate and impair the credit of their deserved commendation, so we must likewise take great heed, lest in attributing unto Scripture more than it can have, the incredibility of that do cause even those things which indeed it hath most abundantly to be less reverently esteemed. I therefore leave it to themselves to consider, whether they have in this first point or not overshot themselves; which God doth know is quickly done, even when our meaning is most sincere, as I am verily persuaded their's in this case was.

## No. 48. RICHARD HOOKER

[From *The Laws of Ecclesiastical Polity*, Book I, Chapter xiv, §§ 1, 4. *Works*, ed. J. Keble, Vol. I, pp. 267 f., 270. Cp. note on No. **148**.]

Although the Scripture of God therefore be stored with infinite variety of matter in all kinds, although it abound with all sorts of laws, yet the principal intent of Scripture is to deliver the laws of duties supernatural. Oftentimes it hath been in very solemn manner disputed, whether all things necessary unto salvation be necessarily set down in the Holy Scriptures or no. If we define that necessary unto salvation, whereby the way to salvation is in any sort made more plain, apparent, and easy to be known, then is there no part of true philosophy, no art of account, no kind of science rightly so called but the Scripture must contain it. If only those things be necessary, as surely none else are, without the knowledge and practice whereof it is not the will and pleasure of God to make any ordinary grant of salvation, it may be notwithstanding and oftentimes hath been demanded, how the books of Holy Scripture contain in them all necessary things, when of things necessary the very chiefest is to know what books we are bound to esteem holy; which point is confessed impossible for the Scripture itself to teach. Whereunto we may answer with truth, that there is not in the world any art or science, which proposing unto itself an end (as every one doth some end or other) hath been therefore thought defective, if it have not delivered simply whatsoever is needful to the same end; but all kinds of knowledge have their certain bounds and limits; each of them presupposeth many necessary things learned in other sciences and known beforehand. He that should take upon him to teach men how to be eloquent in pleading causes, must needs deliver unto them whatsoever precepts are requisite unto that end; otherwise he doth not the thing which he taketh upon him. Seeing then no man can plead eloquently unless he be able first to speak, it followeth that ability of speech is in this case a thing most necessary. Notwithstanding every man would think it ridiculous, that he which undertaketh by writing to instruct an orator should therefore deliver all the precepts of grammar; because his profession is to deliver precepts necessary unto eloquent speech, yet so that they which are to receive them be taught beforehand so much of that which is thereunto necessary, as comprehendeth the skill of speaking. In like sort, albeit Scripture do profess to contain in it all things that are necessary unto salvation, yet the meaning cannot be simply of all things which are necessary, but all things that are necessary in some certain kind or form; as all things which are necessary, and either could not at all or could not easily be known by the light of natural discourse; all things which are necessary to be known that we may be saved; but known with presupposal of knowledge concerning certain principles whereof it receiveth us already persuaded, and then instructeth us in all the residue that are necessary. In the number of these principles one is the sacred authority of Scripture. Being therefore persuaded by other means that these Scriptures are the oracles of God, themselves do then teach us the rest, and lay before us all the duties which God requireth at our hands as necessary unto salvation. . . .

The main drift of the whole New Testament is that which St. John setteth down as the purpose of his own history, *These things are written, that ye might believe that Jesus is Christ the Son of God, and that in believing ye might have life through His Name.* The drift of the Old that which the Apostle mentioneth to Timothy, *The Holy Scriptures are able to make thee wise unto salvation.* So that the general end both of Old and New is one; the difference between them consisting in this, that the Old did make wise by teaching salvation through Christ that should come, the New by teaching that Christ the Saviour is come, and that Jesus Whom the Jews did crucify, and Whom God did raise again from the dead, is He. When the Apostle therefore affirmeth unto Timothy, that the Old was able to make him wise to salvation, it was not his meaning that the Old alone can do this unto us which live sithence the publication of the New. For he speaketh with presupposal of the doctrine of Christ known also unto Timothy; and therefore first it is said, *Continue thou in those things which thou hast learned and art persuaded, knowing of Whom thou hast been taught them.*

## No. 49.  PETER GUNNING

[From *The Paschal or Lent Fast, Apostolical and Perpetual ; At first delivered in a Sermon preached before His Majesty in Lent, and since enlarged, Wherein the Judgement of Antiquity is laid down.* Ed., *L. A. C. T.*, 1845, p. 18.  This Sermon, on *Luke* v, 35–38, dates from 1662.]

Reason, and experience, and the direction of all wise men in the Church of God ancient and modern (the house of wisdom), Councils, reverend Fathers and writers, and our Church in particular, have directed and commanded us not to interpret Scripture in things of public concernment to the Church's rule of believing and doing, but as we find it interpreted by the Holy Fathers and Doctors of the Church, as they had received it from those before them.  For that the leaving of every man to make anything of any text, upon any device out of his own head, to the founding any new and strange doctrine or practice, as necessary therefrom, or to the opposing of any constantly received doctrine or practice of the Church universal (for in other matters they may happily with leave quietly abound in their own sense) leaves all bold innovators which can but draw away disciples after them, to be as much lawgivers to the Church by their uncontrollable law-interpreting, as any Pope or enthusiast can or need pretend to be ; and hath been, and ever will be to the end of the world, the ground of most heresies and schisms brought into the Church by men who, departing from the teaching and stable interpretation of the Church, in their own instability and science falsely so called, pervert the Scriptures to their own and others' (their obstinate followers') destruction.

## No. 50.  JEREMY TAYLOR

[From *A Dissuasive from Popery*, Part II, Book I, § 2.  *Works*, ed. R. Heber, Vol. X, pp. 384–386 (ed. C. P. Eden, Vol. VI, pp. 380–382).  The first part of the *Dissuasive* which had come out in 1664, had been fiercely attacked by several Roman Catholics, including their well-known protagonist John Sergeant. Accordingly Taylor wrote a second part to the *Dissuasive* in which he replied to these attacks.  It appeared in 1667, the year of Jeremy Taylor's death.]

That the Scripture is a full and sufficient rule to Christians in faith and manners, a full and perfect declaration of the Will of God, is therefore certain, because we have no other. For if we consider the grounds upon which all Christians believe the Scriptures to be the Word of God, the same grounds prove that nothing else is. These indeed have a testimony that is credible as any thing that makes faith to men, the universal testimony of all Christians; in respect of which St. Austin said *Evangelio non crederem, etc.*, " I should not believe the Gospel, if the authority of the Church " (that is, of the Universal Church) " did not move me." The Apostles at first owned these writings; the Churches received them; they transmitted them to their posterity; they grounded their faith upon them; they proved their propositions by them; by them they confuted heretics; and they made them the measure of right and wrong. All that collective body of doctrines, of which all Christians consentingly made public confessions, and on which all their hopes of salvation did rely, were all contained in them; and they agreed in no point of faith, which is not plainly set down in Scripture. And all this is so certain, that we all profess ourselves ready to believe any other article which can pretend and prove itself thus proved, thus descended. For we know a doctrine is neither more nor less the Word of God for being written or unwritten. That is but accidental and extrinsical to it, for it was first unwritten and then the same thing was written; only when it was written, it was better conserved, and surer transmitted, and not easily altered, and more fitted to be a rule. And indeed only can be so. Not but that every Word of God is as much a rule as any Word of God; but we are sure that what is so written, and so transmitted, is God's Word; whereas concerning other things which were not written, we have no certain records, no evident proof, no sufficient conviction; and, therefore, it is not capable of being owned as the rule of faith or life, because we do not know it to be the Word of God. If any doctrine which is offered to us by the Church of Rome and which is not in Scripture be proved as Scripture is, we receive it equally. But if it be not, it is to be received according to the degree of its probation; and if it once comes to be disputed by wise and good men, if it came in after the Apostles, if it rely but upon a few testimonies, or is to be laboriously argued into a precarious persuasion, it cannot be the true ground of faith, and salvation can never rely upon it. The truth of the assumption in this argument will rely upon an induction, of which all Churches have a sufficient experience, there being in no Church any one instance of doctrine of faith or life that can pretend to a clear, universal, tradition and testimony of the first and of all ages and Churches, but only the doctrine contained in the undoubted Books of the Old and New Testament. And in the matter of good life, the case is evident and certain, which makes the other also to be like it; for there is no original or primary commandment concerning good life, but it is plainly and notoriously found in Scripture. Now faith being the foundation of good life upon which it is most rationally and permanently built it is strange that Scripture should be sufficient to teach us all the whole superstructure, and yet be defective in the foundation.

Neither do we doubt but that there were many things spoken by Christ and His Apostles which were never written; and yet those few only that were written are, by the Divine providence and the care of the Catholic Church of the first and all descending ages, preserved to us and made our Gospel. So that as we do not dispute whether the words which Christ spake and the miracles He did and are not written be as holy and as true as those which are written, but only say, they are not our rule and measures, because they are unknown: so there is no dispute, whether they be to be preferred or relied upon, as the written or unwritten Word of God; for both are to be relied upon, and both equally; always provided that they be equally known to be so. But that which we say is, That there are many which are called traditions which are not the unwritten Word of God; at least not known so to be: and the doctrines of men are pretended and obtruded as the commandments of God; and the testimonies of a few men are made to support a weight as great as that which relies upon universal testimony; and particular traditions are equalled to universal, the uncertain to the certain; and traditions are said to be apostolical if they be but ancient; and if they come from we know not whom, they are said to come from the Apostles; and if postnate, they are called primitive; and they are argued and laboriously disputed into the title of Apostolical traditions by not only fallible but fallacious arguments.

## No. 51. WILLIAM BEVERIDGE

[From *Sermon LI*. *Works*, ed. *L. A. C. T.*, Vol. II, p. 435. The title of the sermon is " Steadfastness to the Established Church Recommended," and the text *I Cor.* xv, 58.]

Wherefore, as ever ye desire to be saved, ye must be sure to be steadfast in the doctrine which the Apostles of Christ by His order and commission delivered at first by word of mouth, and afterwards in writing, that all generations might know it, by which means we are now as fully assured of what the Apostles taught, as they could be which heard them speak it,—their doctrine being transmitted to us by the infallible testimony of the Holy Ghost, by which they spake and writ it in that Holy Book which we call the "New Testament." So that whatsoever we there read, as taught by the Apostles, we are sure was their doctrine and therefore are bound steadfastly to believe it and diligently to frame our lives according to it; but what we do not find there written, we can never be sure that they taught it and therefore cannot be obliged to believe or observe it.

And hence appears the excellency of our Church, in that it requires nothing to be believed, as an article of faith or as necessary to salvation, but what the Apostles first taught, and what the Church of Christ in all ages hath believed to be consonant to the doctrine contained in their writings. But whatsoever opinion hath no ground or foundation in the said Apostolical writings, that ours, together with the Catholic Church, rejecteth as either utterly false or at best not necessary to be believed; and therefore in order to your continuing steadfast as the first Christians did in the Apostles' doctrine, the surest way is to keep close to the doctrine of our Church, which is plainly the same with that of the Apostles in all points, without any addition, diminution, or alteration whatsoever; which is the great glory of our Church, and should make us not only to continue firm and dutiful to it, but likewise to thank God that we live in such a Church, wherein we are duly instructed in all the great truths which our Saviour and His Apostles taught and are not required to believe anything else as necessary to our being saved. By which means, as our minds may be enlightened and our hearts purified by that faith which was once delivered to the Saints, so we are secure from falling into any damnable heresy and from being corrupted or perplexed with any of those new and dangerous opinions which the ignorance and superstition of after ages have brought into the Church.

What this doctrine of our Church is you may easily understand, as from the Holy Scriptures themselves, so likewise from the Liturgy and Articles of our Church, which are all taken out of the said Scriptures, or grounded upon them; and therefore whatsoever doctrine is contradicted by anything contained in our Liturgy or Articles, you may be sure it is contrary to something asserted in the Holy Scriptures; whatsoever doctrine is nowhere taught or declared there, you may be as confident that the Apostles never declared or taught it; and by consequence you are so far from being obliged to believe it, that you are rather obliged not to believe it, as a necessary Article of our Christian faith, howsoever specious or plausible it may seem to you. But whatsoever doctrine you find to be clearly propounded, asserted, or suggested, either in our Articles or Common-Prayer Book, you may and ought to rest fully satisfied in your minds that that is the true doctrine of the Apostles, which you ought to continue firm and steadfast in.

### No. 52. WILLIAM BEVERIDGE

[From *Ecclesia Anglicana Ecclesia Catholica. Works*, ed. L. A. C. T., Vol. VII, pp. 191 f. This treatise, which was an exposition of the Thirty-Nine Articles, was published posthumously, incompletely in 1716 and in full in the *L. A. C. T.* in 1846. " It is not unlikely . . . that as Bishop Burnet, his contemporary, was known to be engaged in his *Exposition of the Thirty Nine Articles*, Bishop Beveridge, with his characteristic modesty, kept back his own work in deference to another who was engaged in the same pursuit. Bishop Burnet's work first appeared in 1699 " (Advertisement to *L. A. C. T.* edition). The extract is from Beveridge's exposition of Article vi.]

This Holy Scripture, thus written in Hebrew and Greek, in those languages wherein it was written, containeth nothing but the will of

God and the whole will of God; so that there is nothing necessary to be believed concerning God, nor done in obedience unto God by us, but what is here revealed to us; and therefore all traditions of men which are contrary to this Word of God are necessarily to be abhorred, and all traditions of men not recorded in this Word of God are not necessarily to be believed. What is here written we are bound to believe because it is written; and what is not here written we are not bound to believe because it is not written. I say we are not bound to believe it, but I cannot say we are bound not to believe it; for there be many truths which we may believe, nay, are bound to believe, because truth, which notwithstanding are not recorded in the Word of God. But though there be many things we may believe, yet is there nothing we need believe in order to our everlasting happiness which is not here written; so that if we believe all that is here spoken, and do all that is here commanded, we shall certainly be saved, though we do not believe what is not here spoken, nor do what is not here commanded.

## No. 53. WILLIAM BEVERIDGE

[From *Ecclesia Anglicana Ecclesia Catholica* [= On the Thirty-Nine Articles], Vol. VII, pp. 378 f. Cp. note on No. **52**.]

Now that the Church hath authority in controversies is a truth which, should it not be granted, it would be impossible for any controversies to be ever ended. I know the Scripture is the rule of faith and the supreme judge of all controversies whatsoever, so that there is no controversy of faith ought to be determined but from the Scriptures. But I know also, that as all controversies of faith are to be determined by the Scripture, so there are no controversies of faith but what are grounded upon the Scriptures. What is not grounded upon the Scriptures I cannot be bound to believe, and by consequence it cannot be any controversy of faith. Hence it is, that as there is scarce an article of our Christian religion but hath been some time controverted, so there is no controversy that ever arose about it but still both parties have pretended to Scripture. As for example, that great controversy betwixt Arius and Athanasius, whether Christ was very God of the same substance with the Father. Arius, he pretended to Scripture in that controversy as well as Athanasius: and so for all other controversies, both sides still make as if the Scripture was for them. Now in such cases the question is, how the question must be decided, whether the Scripture is for the one or for the other side of the controversy. The Scripture itself cannot decide the controversy, for the controversy is concerning itself: the parties engaged in the controversy cannot decide it, for either of them thinks his own opinion to be grounded upon Scripture. Now how can this question be decided better or otherways, than by the whole Church's exposition of the Scripture, which side of the controversy it is for, and which side it is against? That it is lawful for the Church thus to expound the Scripture is plain. For it is lawful even for every particular person to pass his judgement upon any place of Scripture; otherwise the Bereans would not have been commended for searching the Scriptures to see whether those things which the Apostles preached were so or no (*Acts* xvii). And if the particular persons which the Church consisteth of may give the exposition of the Scripture, much more the Church itself that consisteth of those particular persons. And as the exposition that any particular person passeth upon the Scripture is binding to that person so that he is bound to believe and act according to it, so whatsoever exposition of Scripture is made by the Church in general, it is binding to the Church in general.

# (2) SCRIPTURE AND REASON

## No. 54.  WILLIAM LAUD

[From *A Relation of the Conference between William Laud, Then Lord Bishop of St. David's, Now Lord Archbishop of Canterbury, and Mr. Fisher, the Jesuit ; by the Command of King James of Ever Blessed Memory.  With an Answer to such Exceptions as A. C.* [i.e. " *Mr. Fisher* "] *takes against it*, Section XVI.  Ed. C. H. Simpkinson in the " English Theological Library " (1901), pp. 119–132, 86–88.  The Conference took place on May 24, 1622.  Though there was no intention of publishing an account of the Conference at the time, in 1624 a narration of it under the initials of one of Laud's Chaplains, R[ichard] B[aily], was brought out, Fisher's own narration of the Conference having been previously circulated in MS.  The subsequent literary history of the relation of the Conference is highly complex ;  a careful account of it may be found in the edition of Laud's *Works* in the *L. A. C. T.*, Vol. II, Editor's Preface.  The treatise from which the extract is drawn was issued by Laud himself in 1639 ; it was dedicated to Charles I.  Cp. note on No. **228**.]

To gather up whatsoever may seem scattered in this long discourse to prove that Scripture is the Word of God, I shall now, in the last place, put all together, that so the whole state of the question may the better appear.

First, then, I shall desire the reader to consider, that every rational science requires some principles quite without its own limits, which are not proved in that science, but presupposed.  Thus rhetoric presupposes grammar ;  and music, arithmetic.  Therefore it is most reasonable that Theology should be allowed to have some principles also, which she proves not, but presupposes.  And the chiefest of these is, That the Scriptures are of Divine authority.

Secondly, That there is a great deal of difference in the manner of confirming the principles of Divinity, and those of any other art or science whatsoever.

For the principles of all other sciences do finally resolve, either into the conclusions of some higher science, or into those principles which are *per se nota*, " known by their own light," and are the grounds and principles of all science.  And this is it, which properly makes them sciences, because they proceed with such strength of demonstration as forces reason to yield unto them.  But the principles of Divinity resolve not into the grounds of natural reason,—for then there would be no room for faith, but all would be either knowledge or vision,— but, into the maxims of Divine knowledge supernatural.  And of this we have just so much light, and no more, than God hath revealed unto us in the Scripture.

Thirdly, That though the evidence of these supernatural truths, which Divinity teaches, appears not so manifest as that of the natural, yet they are in themselves much more sure and infallible than they. For they proceed immediately from God, that Heavenly Wisdom, which being the fountain of ours, must needs infinitely precede ours, both in nature and excellence. *He that teacheth man knowledge, shall not He know?* And therefore, though we reach not the order of their deductions, nor can in this life come to the vision of them, yet we yield as full and firm assent, not only to the articles, but to all the things rightly deduced from them, as we do to the most evident principles of natural reason. This assent is called faith; and *faith being of things not seen*, would quite lose its honour, nay itself, if it met with sufficient grounds in natural reason whereon to stay itself. For faith is a mixed act of the will and the understanding; and the will inclines the understanding to yield full approbation to that whereof it sees not full proof. Not but that there is most full proof of them, but because the main grounds which prove them are concealed from our view and folded up in the unrevealed counsel of God, God in Christ resolving to bring mankind to their last happiness by faith, and not by knowledge, that so the weakest among men may have their way to blessedness open. And certain it is, that many weak men believe themselves into heaven, and many over-knowing Christians lose their way thither, while they will believe no more than they can clearly know. In which pride and vanity of theirs they are left, and have these things *hid from them*.

Fourthly, That the credit of the Scripture, the book in which the principles of faith are written, as of other writing also, depends not upon the subservient inducing cause that leads us to the first knowledge of the author, which leader here is the Church, but upon the author himself, and the opinion we have of his sufficiency, which here is the Holy Spirit of God, whose penmen the Prophets and Apostles were. And therefore the mysteries of Divinity contained in this book, as the Incarnation of our Saviour, the Resurrection of the Dead, and the like, cannot finally be resolved into the sole testimony of the Church, who is but a subservient cause to lead to the knowledge of the author, but into the wisdom and sufficiency of the author, Who, being omnipotent and omniscient, must needs be infallible.

Fifthly, That the assurance we have of the penmen of the Scriptures, the holy Prophets and Apostles, is as great as any can be had of any human authors of like antiquity. For it is morally as evident to any pagan, that St. Matthew and St. Paul writ the Gospel and Epistles, which bear their names, as that Cicero or Seneca wrote theirs. But that the Apostles were divinely inspired whilst they writ them, and that they are the very Word of God expressed by them, this hath ever been a matter of faith in the Church, and was so even while the

Apostles themselves lived, and was never a matter of evidence and knowledge, at least as knowledge is opposed to faith. Nor could it at any time then be more demonstratively proved than now. I say, not *scientifice*, not demonstratively. For, were the Apostles living, and should they tell us that they spake and writ the very oracles of God, yet this were but their own testimony of themselves, and so not alone able to enforce belief on others. And for their miracles, though they were very great inducements of belief, yet were neither they evident and convincing proofs, alone and of themselves, both because there may be counterfeit miracles, and because true ones are neither infallible nor inseparable marks of truth in doctrine.

Not infallible, for they may be marks of false doctrine in the highest degree; not proper and inseparable, for all which wrote by inspiration did not confirm their doctrine by miracles. For we do not find that David, or Solomon, with some other of the prophets, did any; neither were any wrought by St. John the Baptist. So, as credible signs, they were, and are still, of as much force to us as it is possible for things on the credit of relation to be: for the witnesses are many, and such as spent their lives in making good the truth which they saw. But that the workers of them were Divinely and infallibly inspired in that which they preached and writ was still to the hearers a matter of faith, and no more evident, by the light of human reason, to men that lived in those days than to us now. For, had that been demonstrated or been clear, as prime principles are, in its own light, both they and we had apprehended all the mysteries of Divinity by knowledge, not by faith. But this is most apparent was not. For, had the Prophets or Apostles been ordered by God to make this demonstratively or intuitively, by discourse or vision, appear as clear to their auditors as to themselves it did, that whatsoever they taught was divine and infallible truth, all men which had the true use of reason must have been forced to yield to their doctrine. Isaiah could never have been at *Domine quis? Lord, who hath believed our report?* Nor Jeremy at *Domine, factus sum, Lord I am in derision daily*. Nor could any of St. Paul's auditors have *mocked at him*, as some of them did, for *preaching the resurrection*, if they had had as full a view as St. Paul himself had in *the assurance*, which God gave of it, in and by *the resurrection of Christ*. But the way of knowledge was not that which God thought fittest for man's salvation. For man having sinned by pride, God thought fittest to humble him at the very root of the tree of knowledge, and make him deny his understanding, and submit to faith, or hazard his happiness. The credible object all the while, that is, the mysteries of religion and the Scripture which contain them, is Divine and infallible; and so are the penmen of them by revelation. But we and all our fore-fathers, the hearers and readers of them, have neither knowledge nor vision of the prime principles in or about them, but faith only. And the revelation, which was clear to them, is not so to us, nor therefore the prime tradition itself delivered by them.

Sixthly, That hence it may be gathered that the assent which we yield to this main principle of Divinity, " that the Scripture is the Word of God," is grounded upon no compelling or demonstrative ratiocination, but relies upon the strength of faith more than any other principle whatsoever. For all other necessary points of Divinity may, by undeniable discourse, be inferred out of Scripture itself, once admitted; but this concerning the authority of Scripture not possibly, but must either be proved by revelation, which is not now to be expected, or presupposed and granted as manifested in itself, like the principles of natural knowledge, which reason alone will never grant; or by tradition of the Church both prime and present, with all other rational helps, preceding or accompanying the internal light in Scripture itself, which though it give light enough for faith to believe, yet light enough it gives not to be a convincing reason and proof for knowledge. And this is it which makes the very entrance into Divinity inaccessible to those men, who, standing high in the opinion of their own wisdom, will believe nothing but that which is irrefragably proved from rational principles. For as Christ requires a denial of a man's self, that he may be able to follow Him, so as great a part as any of this denial of his whole self, for so it must be, is the denial of his understanding, and the composing of the unquiet search of this grand inquisitor into the secrets of Him that made it, and the overruling the doubtfulness of it by the fervency of the will.

Seventhly, That the knowledge of the supreme cause of all, which is God, is most remote, and the most difficult thing reason can have to do with. The *quod sit*, that there is a God, blear-eyed reason can see; but the *quid sit*, what that God is, is infinitely beyond all the fathoms of reason. He is a light indeed, but such as no man's reason can come at for the brightness. If anything, therefore, be attainable in this kind it must be by revelation, and that must be from Himself; for none can reveal but he that comprehends, and none doth or can comprehend God but Himself. And when He doth reveal, yet He is no further discernible than Himself pleases. Now, since reason teaches that the soul of man is immortal and capable of felicity; and since that felicity consists in the contemplation of the highest cause, which again is God Himself; and since Christ therein confirms that dictate, that man's eternal happiness is to know God, and Him Whom He hath sent; and since nothing can put us into the way of attaining to that contemplation but some revelation of Himself and of the way to Himself; I say, since all this is so, it cannot reasonably be thought by any udent man that the all-wise God should create man with a desire

37306

of felicity, and then leave him utterly destitute of all instrumental helps to make the attainment possible, since " God and nature do nothing but for an end," and help there can be none sufficient but by revelation. And once grant me that revelation is necessary, and then I will appeal to reason itself, and that shall prove abundantly one of these two : That either there was never any such revelation of this kind from the world's beginning to this day,—and that will put the *frustra* upon God in point of man's felicity ; or, that the Scriptures which we now embrace as the Word of God is that revelation. And that is it we Christians labour to make good against all atheism, profaneness, and infidelity.

Last of all, To prove that the Book of God, which we honour as His Word, is this necessary revelation of God and His truth, which must, and is alone able to, lead us in the way to our eternal blessedness, or else the world hath none, comes in a cloud of witnesses, some for the infidel and some for the believer, some for the weak in faith and some for the strong, and some for all. For then first comes in the tradition of the Church,—the present Church, so it is no heretical or schismatical belief; then the testimony of former ages, so it is no new belief; then the consent of times, so it is no divided or partial belief; then the harmony of the prophets and them fulfilled, so it is not a " devised " but a forespoken belief; then the success of the doctrine contained in this Book, so it is not a belief stifled in the cradle, but it hath spread through the world in despite of what the world could do against it, and increased from weak and unlikely beginnings to incredible greatness ; then the constancy of this truth, so it is no moon-belief, for in the midst of the world's changes, it hath preserved its creed entire through many generations ; then, that there is nothing carnal in the doctrine, so it is a chaste belief. And all along it hath gained, kept, and exercised more power upon the minds of men, both learned and unlearned, in the increase of virtue and repression of vice, than any moral philosophy or legal policy that ever was. Then comes the inward light and excellency of the text itself, and so it is no dark or dazzling belief. And it is an excellent text. For see the riches of natural knowledge which are stored up there as well as supernatural. Consider how things quite above reason consent with things reasonable. Weigh it well what majesty lies there hid under humility : what depth there is with a perspicuity unimitable : what delight it works in the soul that is devoutly exercised in it : how the sublimest wits find in it enough to amaze them, while the simplest want not enough to direct them : and then we shall not wonder, if,—with the assistance of God's Spirit, Who alone works faith and belief of the Scriptures and their Divine authority, as well as other articles,—we grow up into a most infallible assurance ; such an assurance as hath made many lay down their lives

12

for this truth : such as that, *though an angel from Heaven should preach unto us another Gospel*, we would not believe him or it.   No, though we should see as great and as many miracles done over again to dissuade us from it as were at first to win the world to it.   To which firmness of assent, by the operation of God's Spirit, the will confers as much or more strength than the understanding clearness, the whole assent being an act of faith and not of knowledge.   And therefore the question should not have been asked of me, by F. " How I knew ? " but " Upon what motives I did believe Scripture to be the Word of God ? "   And I would have him take heed lest hunting too close after a way of knowledge, he lose the way of faith, and teach other men to lose it too.

So then the way lies thus, as far as it appears to me, The credit of Scripture to be Divine resolves finally into that faith which we have touching God Himself, and in the same order.   For as that, so this, hath three main grounds, to which all other are reducible.   The first is, the tradition of the Church : and this leads us to a reverend persuasion of it.   The second is, the light of Nature : and this shows us how necessary such a revealed learning is, and that no other way it can be had.   Nay more, that all proofs brought against any point of faith, neither are nor can be demonstrations but soluble arguments. The third is, the light of the Text itself, in conversing wherewith, we meet with the Spirit of God inwardly inclining our hearts, and sealing the full assurance of the sufficiency of all three unto us.   And then, and not before, we are certain that the Scripture is the Word of God, both by Divine and by infallible proof.   But our certainty is by faith, and so voluntary ; not by knowledge of such principles as in the light of nature can enforce assent, whether we will or no. . . .

Though reason without grace cannot see the way to heaven nor believe this Book in which God hath written the way, yet grace is never placed but in a reasonable creature, and proves by the very seat which it hath taken up that the end it hath is to be spiritual eye-water, to make reason see what " by nature only it cannot," but never to blemish reason in that which it can, " comprehend."   Now the use of reason is very general, and man, do what he can, is still apt to search and seek for a reason why he will believe ; though, after he once believes, his faith grows stronger than either his reason or his knowledge. And great reason for this, because it goes higher, and so upon a safer principle, than either of the other can in this life.

In this particular the books called the Scripture are commonly and constantly reputed to be the Word of God, and so infallible verity to the least point of them.   Doth any man doubt this ?   The world cannot keep him from going to weigh it at the balance of reason, whether it be the Word of God or not.   To the same weights he brings the Tradition of the Church, the inward motives in Scripture itself, all testimonies within, which seem to bear witness to it; and in all this there is no harm. The danger is when a man will use no other scale but reason, or prefer reason before any other scale. For the Word of God, and the Book containing it, refuse not to be weighed by reason. But the scale is not large enough to contain, nor the weights to measure out, the true virtue and full force of either. Reason, then, can give no supernatural ground into which a man may resolve his faith that Scripture is the Word of God infallibly; yet reason can go so high, as it can prove that Christian Religion, which rests upon the authority of this Book, stands upon surer grounds of nature, reason, common equity, and justice, than anything in the world which any infidel or mere naturalist hath done, doth, or can adhere unto, against it, in that which he makes, accounts, or assumes as religion to himself.

## No. 55. WILLIAM CHILLINGWORTH

[From *The Religion of Protestants. A Safe Way to Salvation.* Chap. VI, §§ 56–71; Preface, § 12; Chap. II, §§ 115, 116; II, §§ 150–154; II, § 11; III, § 39; II, § 46; II, § 89. Ed. London, 1719, pp. 271–274; [preface unpaged]; 70; 80–82; 41; 109; 50; 61. The treatise from which this passage is taken was one of the most famous of the century. Chillingworth, who had been the intimate friend of Lucius Cary, was led in (or about) 1629 to join the Roman Church. He soon developed doubts, however, as to the claims of the Church to which he had given his allegiance. In the meantime a fierce controversy had sprung up which centred in the names of Knott and Potter. Knott, a Jesuit, had in 1630 written a book *Charity Mistaken, with the want whereof Catholics are unjustly charged for affirming, as they do with grief, that Protestancy unrepented destroys salvation.* To this Potter, the Provost of Queen's College, Oxford, replied in a book *Want of Charity justly charged on all such Romanists as dare (without truth or modesty) affirm that Protestancy destroyeth Salvation* (1633). The Jesuit replied in the following year with *Mercy and Truth, or Charity maintained by Catholics.* Chillingworth, who had become interested in this controversy, went to Cary's residence at Great Tew in order to prepare a refutation of Knott's book. It appeared in 1638 with the title *The Religion of Protestants, a Safe Way to Salvation, or an Answer to a Book entitled Mercy and Truth, or Charity Maintained by Catholics.* Its great merits were at once recognized. In it, Chillingworth developed at length his view on Scripture. He criticized the Tridentine doctrine that Scripture and Tradition were co-ordinate sources of revelation, contending that "Scripture is a perfect Rule of Faith" and that "the Bible and the Bible only" is "the Religion of Protestants." The latter of these assertions, remembered apart from its context, had led to Chillingworth being widely regarded as a literalist in his interpretation of Scripture. In point of fact, he was far removed from literalism, and, as the following passage shows, insisted, like Hooker and Laud, upon the need for interpreting the authority of Scripture by reason. Oxford Univ. Press, 1838, Vol. II, pp. 409–417; Vol. I, pp. 14 f., 238 f., 264–269, 167 f., 349 f., 218.]

It remains now, that I should shew that many reasons of moment may be alleged for the justification of Protestants which are dissembled by you and not put into the balance. Know then, Sir, that when I say the Religion of Protestants is in prudence to be preferred before yours, as on the one side, I do not understand by your Religion the doctrine of Bellarmine, or Baronius, or any other private man amongst you; nor the doctrine of the Sorbonne, or of the Jesuits, or of the Dominicans, or of any other particular company among you, but that wherein you all agree, or profess to agree, the Doctrine of the Council of Trent; so accordingly on the other side, by the "Religion of Protestants," I do not understand the Doctrine of Luther, or Calvin, or Melancthon, nor the Confession of Augusta, or Geneva, nor the Catechism of Heidelberg, nor the Articles of the Church of England, no nor the Harmony of Protestant Confessions, but that wherein they all agree, and which they all subscribe with a greater harmony, as a perfect rule of their faith and actions; that is, the BIBLE. The BIBLE, I say, the BIBLE only, is the Religion of Protestants. Whatsoever else they believe besides it, and the plain irrefragable, indubitable consequences of it, well may they hold it as a matter of opinion: but as matter of Faith and Religion, neither can they with coherence to their own grounds believe it themselves, nor require the belief of it of others, without most high and most schismatical presumption. I, for my part, after a long and (as I verily believe and hope) impartial search of the true way to eternal happiness, do profess plainly that I cannot find any rest for the sole of my foot but upon this rock only. I see plainly and with mine own eyes that there are Popes against Popes, Councils against Councils, some Fathers against others, the same Fathers against themselves, a Consent of Fathers of one Age against a Consent of Fathers of another Age, the Church of one Age against the Church of another Age. Traditive Interpretations of Scriptures are pretended, but there are few or none to be found. No Tradition but only of Scripture can derive itself from the fountain, but may be plainly proved either to have been brought in, in such an age after Christ, or that in such an age it was not in. In a word, there is no sufficient certainty but of Scripture only, for any considering man to build upon. This, therefore, and this only I have reason to believe; this I will profess; according to this I will live; and for this, if there be occasion, I will not only willingly, but even gladly lose my life, though I should be sorry that Christians should take it from me. Propose me any thing out of this Book, and require whether I believe it or no, and seem it never so incomprehensible to human reason, I will subscribe it with hand and heart, as knowing no demonstration can be stronger than this: "God hath said so, therefore it is true." In other things, I will take no man's liberty of judgement from him; neither shall any man take mine from me. I will think no man the worse man, nor the worse Christian; I will love no man the less for differing in opinion from me. And what measure I mete to others, I expect from them again. I am fully assured that God does not and therefore that men ought not to require any more of any man than this, to believe the Scripture to be God's Word, to endeavour to find the true sense of it, and to live according to it.

This is the Religion which I have chosen after a long deliberation, and I am verily persuaded that I have chosen wisely, much more wisely than if I had guided myself according to your Church's authority. For the Scripture being all true, I am secured, by believing nothing else, that I shall believe no falsehood as matter of faith. And if I mistake the sense of Scripture, and so fall into error, yet am I secure from any danger thereby, if but your grounds be true; because endeavouring to find the true sense of Scripture, I cannot but hold my error without pertinacy, and be ready to forsake it when a more true and a more probable sense shall appear unto me. And then, all necessary truth being, as I have proved, plainly set down in Scripture, I am certain by believing Scripture to believe all necessary Truth. And he that does so, if his life be answerable to his faith, how is it possible he should fail of salvation?

Besides, whatsoever may be pretended to gain to your Church the credit of a guide, all that and much more may be said for the Scripture. Hath your Church been ancient? The Scripture is more ancient. Is your Church a means to keep men at Unity? So is the Scripture, to keep those that believe it and will obey it, in Unity of Belief, in matters necessary or very profitable; and in Unity of Charity, in points unnecessary. Is your Church universal for time or place? Certainly the Scripture is more universal. For all the Christians in the world (those I mean, that in truth deserve this name) do now, and always have believed the Scripture to be the Word of God, so much of it at least, as contains all things necessary; whereas only you say, that you only are the Church of God, and all Christians besides you deny it.

Thirdly, following the Scripture, I follow that whereby you prove your Church's Infallibility. Whereof, were it not for Scripture, what pretence could you have, or what notion could we have? And by so doing, [you] tacitly confess that yourselves are surer of the truth of the Scripture than of your Church's authority. For we must be surer of the proof than of the thing proved; otherwise it is no proof.

Fourthly, following the Scripture, I follow that which must be true, if your Church be true; for your Church gives attestation to it. Whereas if I follow your Church, I must follow that which, though Scripture be true, may be false, nay which, if Scripture be true, must be false, because the Scripture testifies against it.

Fifthly, to follow the Scripture I have God's express warrant and command and no colour of any prohibition. But to believe your Church infallible, I have no command at all, much less an express command. Nay I have reason to fear that I am prohibited to do so in these words, *Call no man Master on the earth; They fell by infidelity, Thou standest by faith; Be not high-minded, but fear; The Spirit of Truth the world cannot receive.*

Following your Church I must hold many things not only above reason, but against it, if any thing be against it; whereas following the Scripture I shall believe many mysteries, but no impossibilities; many things above reason, but nothing against it; many things which had they not been revealed, reason could never have discovered, but nothing which by true reason may be confuted; many things which reason cannot comprehend how they can be, but nothing which reason can comprehend that it cannot be. Nay I shall believe nothing which reason will not convince that I ought to believe it; for reason will convince any man, unless he be of a perverse mind, that the Scripture is the Word of God. And then no reason can be greater than this, " God says so, therefore it is true."

Following your Church, I must hold many things which to any man's judgement that will give himself the liberty of judgement, will seem much more plainly contradicted by Scripture, than your Infallibility of the Church appears to be confirmed by it; and consequently must be so foolish as to believe your Church exempted from error upon less evidence rather than subject to the common condition of mankind upon greater evidence. Now if I take the Scripture only for my guide, I shall not need to do anything so unreasonable.

If I will follow your Church, I must believe impossibilities, and that with an absolute certainty, upon motives which are confessed to be but only prudential and probable; that is, with a weak foundation I must firmly support a heavy, a monstrous heavy building. Now following the Scripture, I shall have no necessity to undergo any such difficulties.

Following your Church, I must be Servant of Christ, and a Subject of the King, but only *ad placitum Papae*. I must be prepared in mind to renounce my allegiance to the King, when the Pope shall declare him an heretic and command me not to obey him, and I must be prepared in mind *to esteem Virtue Vice, and Vice Virtue, if the Pope shall so determine*. Indeed, you say, it is impossible he should do the latter; but that you know is a great question, neither is it fit my obedience to God and the King should depend upon a questionable foundation. And howsoever, you must grant, that if by an impossible supposition, the Pope's commands should be contrary to the Law of Christ, that they of your Religion must resolve to obey rather the commands of the Pope than the Law of Christ. Whereas if I follow the Scripture, I may, nay I must, obey my Sovereign in lawful things, though an heretic, though a Tyrant; and though I do not say the Pope, but the Apostles themselves, nay, *an Angel from Heaven should teach any thing against the Gospel of Christ*, I may, nay I must denounce Anathema to him.

Following the Scripture, I shall believe a Religion, which being contrary to flesh and blood, without any assistance from worldly power, wit, or policy, nay against all the power and policy of the world, prevailed and enlarged itself in a very short time all the world over; whereas it is too too apparent, that your Church hath got, and still maintains her authority over men's consciences, by counterfeiting false miracles, forging false stories, by obtruding on the world supposititious writings, by corrupting the monuments of former times, and defacing out of them all which any way makes against you, by wars, by persecutions, by massacres, by treasons, by rebellions, in short, by all manner of carnal means, whether violent or fraudulent.

Following the Scripture, I shall believe a Religion, the first Preachers and Professors whereof, it is most certain, could have no worldly ends upon the world; that they should not project to themselves by it any of the profits, or honours, or pleasures of this world, but rather were to expect the contrary, even all the miseries which the world could lay upon them. On the other side, the Head of your Church, the pretended Successor of the Apostles, and Guide of Faith, it is even palpable, that he makes your Religion the instrument of his ambition, and by it seeks to entitle himself directly or indirectly to the Monarchy of the World. And besides, it is evident to any man that has but half an eye, that most of those doctrines which you add to the Scripture, do make one way or other, for the honour or temporal profit of the teachers of them.

Following the Scripture only, I shall embrace a Religion of admirable simplicity, consisting in a manner wholly in the Worship of *God in Spirit and in Truth*. Whereas your Church and Doctrine is even [? ever] loaded with an infinity of weak, childish, ridiculous, unsavoury superstitions and ceremonies, and full of that *righteousness* for which *Christ shall judge the World*.

Following the Scriptures [= Scripture ?], I shall believe that which universal, never failing Tradition assures me, that it was by the admirable supernatural Works of God confirmed to be the Word of God; whereas never any miracle was wrought, never so much as a lame horse cured in confirmation of your Church's Authority and Infallibility. And if any strange things have been done, which may seem to give attestation to some parts of your doctrine, yet this proves nothing but the truth of the Scripture, which foretold that (God's Providence permitting it, and the wickedness of the world deserving it) *strange signs and wonders should be wrought to confirm false doctrine, that they which love not the Truth may be given over to strong delusions.* Neither does it seem to me any strange thing that God should permit some true wonders to be done, to delude them who have forged so many to deceive the world.

If I follow the Scripture, I must not promise myself salvation without effectual dereliction and mortification of all vices, and the effectual practice of all Christian Virtues. But your Church opens an easier and broader way to Heaven; and though I continue all my life long in a course of sin, and without the practice of any virtue, yet gives me assurance that I may be let into Heaven at a Postern Gate, even by an act of attrition at the hour of death, if it be joined with confession, or by an act of contrition without confession.

Admirable are the precepts of piety and humility, of innocence and patience, of liberality, frugality, temperance, sobriety, justice, meekness, fortitude, constancy and gravity, contempt of the world, love of God, and the love of mankind, in a word, of all Virtues, and against all Vice, which the Scriptures impose upon us to be obeyed under pain of damnation.   The sum whereof is in a manner comprised in Our *Saviour's Sermon upon the Mount*, recorded in the 5th, 6th, and 7th of *St. Matthew*, which if they were generally obeyed could not but make the world generally happy, and the goodness of them alone were sufficient to make any wise and good man believe, that this Religion, rather than any other, came from God, the Fountain of all Goodness.   And that they may be generally obeyed, Our Saviour hath ratified them all in the close of His Sermon with these universal sanctions : *Not every one that saith, Lord, Lord, shall enter into the Kingdom, but he that doth the Will of My Father which is in Heaven.*   And again, *Whosoever heareth these Sayings of Mine, and doth them not, shall be likened unto a foolish man which built his house upon the sand, and the rain descended, and the flood came, and the winds blew, and it fell, and great was the fall thereof.*   Now your Church, notwithstanding all this, enervates, and in a manner dis- . solves and abrogates, many of these precepts, teaching men that they are not laws for all Christians, but counsels of perfection and matters of Supererogation ;  that a man shall do well if he observe them, but he shall not sin if he observe them not ;  that they are for them who aim at high places in Heaven, who aspire with the two sons of Zebedee to the right hand, or to the left hand of Christ.   But if a man will be content barely to go to Heaven, and to be a Door-keeper in the House of God, especially if he will be content to taste of Purgatory in the way, he may obtain it at an easier purchase.   Therefore the Religion of your Church is not so holy nor so good as the doctrine of Christ delivered in Scripture, and therefore not so likely to come from the Fountain of Holiness and Goodness. . . .

You say again confidently, that *if this infallibility be once impeached every man is given over to his own wit and discourse.*   Which, if you mean discourse not guiding itself by Scripture, but only by Principles of Nature, or perhaps by prejudices and popular errors and drawing consequences not by rule but chance, is by no means true.   If you mean by discourse right Reason, grounded on Divine Revelation and common notions, written by God in the hearts of all men, and deducing, according to the never failing Rules of Logic, consequent deductions from them ; if this be it which you mean by discourse, it is very meet, and reasonable, and necessary that men, as in all their actions, so especially in that of greatest importance, the choice of their way to happiness, should be left unto it.   And he that follows this in all his opinions and actions, and does not only seem to do so, follows always God ;  whereas he that followeth a company of men, may ofttimes follow a company of beasts. . . .

And whereas you say that a *Protestant admits of Fathers, Councils, Church, as far as they agree with Scripture, which upon the matter is himself,* I say, you admit neither of them, nor the Scripture itself, but only so far as it agrees with your Church ; and your Church you admit, because you think you have reason to do so.   So that by you as well as Protestants all is finally resolved into your own reason.

Nor do heretics only, but Romish Catholics also, set up as many judges as there are men and women in the Christian World.   For do not your men and women judge your Religion to be true before they believe it, as well as the men and women of other Religions ?   Oh, but you say, *They receive it, not because they think it agreeable to Scripture but because the Church tells them so.*   But then, I hope they believe the Church, because their own Reason tells them they are to do so.   So that the difference between a Papist and a Protestant is this, not that the one judges and the other does not judge, but that the one judges his guide to be infallible, the other his way to be manifest. . . .

Neither in saying thus have I only cried quittance with you.   But that you may see how much you are in my debt, I will shew unto you that for your sophism against our way, I have given you a demonstration against yours.   First, I say, your argument against us is a transparent fallacy.   The first part of it lies thus :  " Protestants have no means to interpret, without error, obscure and ambiguous places of Scripture ; therefore plain places of Scripture cannot be to them a sufficient ground of Faith."   But though we pretend not to certain means of not erring in interpreting all Scripture, particularly such places as are obscure and ambiguous, yet this methinks should be no impediment but that we may have certain means of not erring in and about the sense of those places, which are so plain and clear that they need no interpreters ; and in such we say our Faith is contained.   If you ask me how I can be sure that I know the true meaning of these places, I ask you again, Can you be sure that you understand what I or any man else says ?   They that heard our Saviour and the Apostles preach, could they have sufficient assurance, that they understood at any time what they would have them do ?   If not, to what end did they hear them ?   If they could, why may we not be as well assured that we understand sufficiently what we conceive plain in their writings ?

Again, I pray tell us, whether you do certainly know the sense of these Scriptures, with which you pretend you are led to the knowledge of your Church ?   If you do not, how know you that there is any Church infallible, and that these are the notes of it, and that this is the Church that hath these notes ?   If you do, then give us leave to have the same means and the same abilities to know other plain places, which you have to know these.    For, if all Scripture be obscure, how come you to know the sense of these places ?    If some places of it be plain, why should we stay here ?

And now to come to the other part of your Dilemma.    In saying, *If they have certain means, and so cannot err*, methinks you forget your self very much and seem to make no difference between having certain means to do a thing, and the actual doing of it.    As if you should conclude because all men have certain means of Salvation, therefore all men certainly must be saved, and cannot do otherwise ; as if whosoever had a horse must presently get up and ride ; whosoever had means to find out a way could not neglect those means and so mistake it.    God be thanked, that we have sufficient means to be certain enough of the truth of our Faith.    But the privilege of not being in possibility of erring, that we challenge not, because we have as little reason as you to do so : and you have none at all.    If you ask, seeing we may possibly err, " How can we be assured we do not ? ", I ask you again, seeing your eye-sight may deceive you, " How can you be sure you see the sun when you do see it ? "    Perhaps you may be in a dream, and perhaps you, and all the men in the world have been so, when they thought they were awake, and then only awake, when they thought they dreamt.    But this I am sure of, as sure as that God is good, that He will require no impossibilities of us : not an infallible nor a certainly unerring belief, unless He hath given us certain means to avoid error ; and if we use those which we have, He will never require of us that we use that which we have not.

Now from this mistaken ground, That it is all one to have means of avoiding error and to be in no danger nor possibility of error, you infer upon us an absurd conclusion, *That we make ourselves able to determine controversies of Faith with Infallibility, and judges of controversies.*    For the latter part of this inference, we acknowledge and embrace it.    We do make ourselves judges of controversies, that is, we do make use of our own understanding in the choice of our Religion.    But this, if it be a crime, is common to us with you (as I have proved above), and the difference is, not that we are choosers, and you not choosers, but, that we, as we conceive, choose wisely, but you being wilfully blind, choose to follow those that are so too, not remembering what Our Saviour hath told you, *When the blind lead the blind, both shall fall into the ditch.*    But then again I must tell you, You have done ill to confound together *judges* and *infallible judges* ; unless you will say, either that we have no judges in our Courts of Civil Judicature, or that they are all infallible.

Thus have we cast off your dilemma and broken both the horns of it.    But now my retortion lies heavy upon you, and will not be turned off.    For first, you content not yourselves with a moral certainty of the things you believe, nor with such a degree of assurance of them, as is sufficient to produce obedience to the condition of the new Covenant, which is all that we require. God's Spirit, if He please, may work more, a certainty of adherence beyond a certainty of evidence. But neither God doth, nor man may, require of us as our duty to give a greater assent to the conclusion than the premises deserve, to build an infallible Faith upon motives that are only highly credible, and not infallible, as it were a great and heavy building upon a foundation that hath not strength proportionable. But though God require not of us such unreasonable things, you do, and tell men, They cannot be saved, unless they believe your proposals with an infallible Faith. To which end they must believe also your propounder, your Church, to be simply infallible. Now how is it possible for them to give a rational assent to the Church's infallibility, unless they have some infallible means to know that she is infallible ? Neither can they infallibly know the infallibility of this means, but by some other, and so on for ever : unless they can dig so deep as to come at length to the Rock, that is to settle all upon something evident of itself, which is not so much as pretended. But the last resolution of all is into motives, which indeed upon examination will scarce appear probable, but are not so much as avouched to be any more than very credible. For example, if I ask you, Why do you believe Transubstantiation ? What can you answer but Because it is a Revelation of the prime Verity ? I demand again, How can you assure yourself or me of that, being ready to embrace it if it may appear to be so ? And what can you say, but that you know it to be so, because the Church says so, which is infallible ? If I ask, What mean you by your Church ? You can tell me nothing but the Company of Christians which adhere to the Pope. I demand then further, Why should I believe this company to be the infallible propounder of Divine Revelation ? And then you tell me, that there are many motives to induce a man to this belief. But are these motives, lastly, infallible ? No, say you, but very credible. Well, let them pass for such, because now we have not leisure to examine them. Yet methinks, seeing the motives to believe the Church's infallibility are only very credible, it should also be but as credible that your Church is infallible ; and as credible, and no more, perhaps somewhat less, that her proposals, particularly Transubstantiation, are Divine Revelations. And methinks you should require only a moral, and modest assent to them, and not a Divine, as you call it, and infallible Faith. But then of these motives to the Church's infallibility, I hope you will give us leave to consider and judge whether they be indeed motives, and sufficient ; or whether they be not motives at all, or not sufficient ; or whether these motives or inducements to your Church be not impeached and opposed with compulsives and enforcements from it ; or lastly, whether these motives which you use be not indeed only motives to Christianity, and not to Popery,—give me leave for distinction-sake to call your Religion so. If we may not judge of these things, How can

my judgement be moved with that which comes not within its cognizance ?  If I may, then at least I am to be a judge of all these Controversies.  1. Whether every one of these motives be indeed a motive to
any Church ?  2. If to some, whether to Yours ?  3. If to Yours,
whether sufficient or insufficient ?  4. Whether other Societies have
not as many and as great motives to draw me to them ?  5. Whether I
have not greater reason to believe you do err than that you cannot ?
And now Sir, I pray let me trouble you with a few more questions.
Am I a sufficient judge of these controversies, or no ?  If of these, why
shall I stay here, why not of others ?  Why not of all ?  Nay, doth not
the true examining of these few contain and lay upon me the examination
of all ?  What other motives to your Church have you, but your notes
of it ?  Bellarmine gives some 14 or 15.  And one of these fifteen contains in it the examination of all Controversies ; and not only so, but of all
uncontroverted Doctrines.  For how shall I, or can I, know the Church
of Rome's conformity with the Ancient Church, unless I know first what
the Ancient Church did hold, and then what the Church of Rome doth
hold ?  And, lastly, whether they be conformable, or, if in my judgement
they seem not conformable, I am then to think the Church of Rome not
to be the Church, for want of the note, which she pretends is proper and
perpetual to it ?  So that, for aught I can see, Judges we are and must
be of all sides ; every one for himself and God for us all. . . .

In your second paragraph, you sum up those arguments wherewith
you intend to prove that *Scripture alone cannot be judge in controversies.*
Wherein I profess unto you before-hand that you will fight without an
adversary.  For though Protestants, being warranted by some of the
Fathers, have called Scripture *the judge of controversy* ;  and you, in
saying here, *That Scripture alone cannot be judge,* imply that it may be
called in some sense a judge, though not alone ;  yet to speak properly
(as men should speak when they write of controversies in Religion) the
Scripture is not a judge of controversies, but a *Rule only, and the only
Rule for Christians to judge them by.*  Every man is to judge for himself
with the judgement of discretion and to choose either his religion first,
and then his Church as we say ;  or, as you, his Church first, and
then his Religion.  But, by the consent of both sides, every man is to
judge and choose.  And the Rule whereby he is to guide his choice,
if he be a natural man, is Reason ; if he be already a Christian, Scripture ;
which we say is the Rule to judge controversies by.  Yet not all simply,
but all the controversies of Christians, of those that are already agreed
upon this first Principle, that *the Scripture is the Word of God.*  But
that there is any man, or any company of men, appointed to be a judge
for all men, that we deny, and that I believe you will never prove.  The
very truth is, we say no more in this matter, than evidence of Truth hath
made you confess in plain terms in the beginning of this chapter, viz.,

*That Scripture is a perfect Rule of Faith, forasmuch as writing can be a Rule.* . . .

But the *Church's infallible direction, extending only to fundamentals, unless I know them before I go to learn of her, I may be rather deluded than instructed by her.*  The reason and connexion of this consequence I fear neither I nor you do well understand.  And besides, I must tell you, you are too bold in taking that which no man grants you, *That the Church is an infallible director in fundamentals.*  For if she were so, then must we not only learn fundamentals of her but also *learn of her what is fundamental, and take all for fundamental which she delivers to us as such.*  In the performance whereof, if I knew any one Church to be infallible, I would quickly be of that Church.  But, good Sir, you must needs do us this favour, to be so acute as to distinguish between being *infallible in fundamentals*, and being an *infallible Guide in fundamentals.*  That there shall be always a Church infallible in fundamentals, we easily grant ; for it comes to no more but this, *that there shall be always a Church.*  But that there shall be always such a Church which is an infallible Guide in fundamentals this we deny.  For this cannot be without settling a known infallibility in some one known Society of Christians (as the Greek or the Roman, or some other Church), by adhering to which Guide, men might be guided to believe aright in all fundamentals.  A man that were destitute of all means of communicating his thoughts to others, might yet, in himself and to himself, be infallible ; but he could not be a guide to others.  A man or a Church that were invisible, so that none could know how to repair to it for direction, could not be an infallible guide, and yet he might be in himself infallible.  You see, then, there is a wide difference between these two, and therefore I must beseech you not to confound them, nor to take one for the other. . . .

The conclusion of your tenth section is, That *the Divinity of a writing cannot be known from itself alone, but by some extrinsical Authority* ; which you need not prove for no wise man denies it.  But then, this Authority is that of Universal Tradition, not of your Church.  For to me it is altogether as αὐτοπιστόν that the Gospel of St. Matthew is the Word of God as that all which your Church says is true. . . .

If there be any traditive interpretation of Scripture, produce it and prove it to be so, and we will embrace it.  But the tradition of all ages is one thing ; and the authority of the present Church, much more of the Roman Church, which is but a part, and a corrupted part, of the Catholic Church, is another.  And therefore, though we are ready to receive both Scripture and the sense of Scripture upon the authority of Original Tradition, yet we receive neither the one nor the other upon the Authority of your Church. . . .

## No. 56.  ROBERT BOYLE

[From *Some Considerations Touching the Style of the Holy Scriptures, Extracted from Several Parts of a Discourse Concerning Divers Particulars belonging to the Bible, Written Divers Years Since to a Friend. Works*, ed. London (1772), Vol. II, pp. 260 f. This treatise was first published at London in 1661 (T. Birch, *Life of Boyle*, p. 143, and *D. N. B.*, *s.v.* 'Boyle,' wrongly give 1663). A Latin translation appeared at Oxford in 1665. The *Discourse* referred to in the title was an 'Essay on Scripture' which the author had composed in about 1652 at the request of his brother.]

We should carefully distinguish betwixt what the Scripture itself says, and what is only said in the Scripture. For we must not look upon the Bible as an oration of God to men, or as a body of laws like our English Statute Book, wherein it is the legislator that all the way speaks to the people, but as a collection of composures of very differing sorts and written at very distant times; and of such composures that though the holy men of God, as St. Peter calls them, were acted by the Holy Spirit, Who both excited and assisted them in penning the Scripture, yet there are many others besides the Author and the penmen introduced speaking there. For besides the Books of *Joshua*, *Judges*, *Samuel*, *Kings*, *Chronicles*, the Four Evangelists, the *Acts of the Apostles*, and other parts of Scripture that are evidently historical and wont to be so called, there are in the other books many passages that deserve the same name, and many others wherein, though they be not mere narratives of things done, many sayings and expressions are recorded that either belong not to the Author of the Scripture or must be looked upon as such, wherein His secretaries personate others. So that, in a considerable part of the Scripture, not only prophets, and kings, and priests being introduced speaking, but soldiers, shepherds and women, and such other sorts of persons from whom witty or eloquent things are not (especially when they speak *extempore*) to be expected, it would be very injurious to impute to the Scripture any want of eloquence that may be noted in the expressions of others than its Author. For though not only in romances, but in many of those that pass for true histories, the supposed speakers may be observed to talk as well as the historian; yet that is, but either because the men so introduced were ambassadors, orators, generals, or other eminent men for parts as well as employments; or because the historian does, as it often happens, give himself the liberty to make speeches for them, and does not set down indeed what they said, but what he thought fit that such persons on such occasions should have said. Whereas the penmen of the Scripture, as one of them truly professes, having *not followed cunningly devised fables* in what they have written, have faithfully set down the sayings as well as actions they record, without making them rather congruous to the conditions of the speakers than to the laws of truth.

Nor is it only the style of very many passages of Scripture that may be justified by our second consideration; but, with the same distinction well applied, we may silence some of their malicious cavils who accuse the Scripture of teaching vice by the ungodly sayings and examples that are here and there to be met with in it.   But as the Apostle said, that *they are not all Israel, that are of Israel*, so we may say that is not [all] Scripture that is in the Scripture.   For many wicked persons and their perverter Satan, are there introduced whose sayings the Holy Ghost doth not adopt, but barely registers.   Nor does the Scripture affirm that what they said was true, but that it is true they said it.   And if I had not reduced some of those cavillers to confess that they never did themselves read those pieces of the Bible, at some of whose passages they cavil, I should much more admire than I do, to find them father as confidently as they do all they hear cited from it upon the enditer of it ; as if the devil's speeches were not recorded there, and as if it were requisite to make a history divinely inspired, that all the blasphemies and crimes it registers should be so too.   As for the ills recorded in the Scripture, besides that wicked persons were necessary to exercise God's children and illustrate His providence and, besides the allegations commonly made on that subject, we may consider that there being many things to be declined, as well as practised, it was fit we should be taught as well what to avoid as what to imitate ; and the known rocks and shelves do as well guide the seamen as the pole-star.   Now, as we could not be armed against the tempter's methods, if we ignored them, so could we never safelier nor better learn them than in His Book Who can alone discover the wiles and fathom the *depths of Satan*, and track him through all his windings and otherwise untraceable labyrinths ; and in that Book, where the antidote is exhibited with the poison, and either men's defeat or victory may teach us at others' costs, and without our hazard, the true art of what warfare we are all so highly concerned in.   And, as chemists observe in the book of nature that those simples that wear the figure or resemblance (by them termed signature) of a distempered part are medicinal for that part of that infirmity whose signature they bear ; so, in God's other Book, the vicious persons there mentioned still prove, under some notion, or upon some score or other, antidotal against the vices notorious in them, being (to present it you also in a Scripture simile) like the brazen serpent in the wilderness, set up to cure the poison infused by those they resemble.   *Whatsoever things were written aforetime*, says the Apostle, *were written for our instruction*.   And, to make further use of our former comparison, those to whom the Scripture gives the names of lions, wolves, foxes, and other brutes, by God's assistance prove to His saints as instructive beasts, as doth the northern bear [1] unto the wandering pilot.   And as anciently God fed His servant Elias, sometimes by an Angel, sometimes by a woman, and sometimes too by ravens, so doth He make all persons in the Bible, whether good,

---

[1] [*I.e.*, the Constellation.]

or bad, or indifferent, supply His servants with that instruction which is the aliment of virtue and of souls, and makes them and their examples contribute to the verification of that passage of St. Paul, wherein he says that *all things co-operate for good to them that love God.*

## No. 57.  DANIEL WHITBY

[From Δὸς ποῦ στῶ ; *or An Answer to Sure Footing, So far as Mr. Whitby is concerned in it ; Wherein the Rule and Guide of Faith, the Interest of Reason, and the Authority of the Church in Matters of Faith are fully handled and vindicated from the Exceptions of Mr. Serjeant and Petty Flirts of " Fiat Lux " ; together with an Answer to Five Questions propounded by a Roman Catholic,* Chapter II (" Of The Guide of Faith "). Oxford, 1666, pp. 28 f., 30 f. The contents of this small early treatise of Whitby are sufficiently described in its programmatic title. In 1664, Whitby had written *Romish Doctrines not from the Beginning*; and in 1665 John Sergeant, one of the leading English Roman Catholic controversialists of the Restoration period (cp. note on No. 28), had replied in *Sure Footing in Christianity ; or Rational Discourses on the Rule of Faith. With three short Animadversions on Dr. Pierce's Sermon ; also on some Passages in Mr. Whitby and Mr. Stillingfleet which concern that Rule.*]

Reason in judging of the sense of Scripture is regulated partly by principles of Faith, partly by Tradition, partly by Catholic maxims of her own.

First, By principles of Faith. For Scripture is to be interpreted *secundum analogiam Fidei* ; that is (say we) particular Texts of Scripture, when dubious, are so to be interpreted as not to contradict the Fundamentals of Faith, or any doctrine which evidently and fully stands asserted in the Word of God. And secondly since Scripture cannot contradict itself, when any paragraph of Scripture absolutely considered is ambiguous, that sense must necessarily obtain which is repugnant to no other paragraph, against what may be so ; and thus may Scripture regulate me in the sense of Scripture, and what I know of it lead me to the sense of what I do not.

Secondly, By Tradition. For since Tradition is necessary to assure us that there were once such men as the Apostles who delivered that Christianity and these Scriptures to us which we now embrace, to question the sufficiency of the like tradition, to assure me of the sense of Scripture is virtually to call in question the motives which induce us to believe it such. This then would be an excellent help unto the sense of Scripture ; only the mischief is that where it can be had we do not want it, and where we want it it is but too visible it cannot be had. Note only that I speak here of a " like tradition," to which two things are requisite. First, That it be as general as that of Scripture. And Secondly, That it be such as evidenceth itself by reason to have been no forgery (as here it doth, it being morally impossible that the whole Church, in the delivery of Scripture to us, should deceive or be deceived). For the infallibility of Tradition doth not consist entirely in the delivery of such a doctrine, but in the assurance which it gives my reason that it could not possibly have been embraced upon other terms. The Baptism of

Infants is at present (as the Communicating of Infants was of old) the tradition of the Church, but this gives no unquestionable assurance of the truth or derivation of these customs from our Lord and His Apostles, for haply the Church embraced them upon other motives,—the first from a conceived analogy therein to Circumcision, the second from a mistake of that of the Evangelist, *Except you eat my flesh, etc.* . . .

Thirdly, Reason is herein guided by her proper maxims and cannot rationally admit of anything as the sense of Scripture which is apparently repugnant to them. For seeing it is impossible to yield a rational assent without reason, it must be more impossible to do it against reason. Besides, right reason must be true; and therefore should a revelation be manifestly repugnant unto right reason, it must equally be opposed to truth.

## No. 58. WILLIAM SHERLOCK

[From *A Vindication of the Doctrine of the Trinity* (1690), p. 151. Sherlock's work was written against the Socinian theology which made itself increasingly felt in England in the later years of the Seventeenth Century. The Socinian interpretation of Scripture was notoriously rationalistic.]

We must believe nothing that contradicts the plain and express dictates of natural reason, which all mankind agree in, whatever pretence of revelation there be for it. Well, say they,[1] then you must expound Scripture so as to make it agree with the necessary principles and dictates of reason. No, say I, that does not follow. I must expound Scripture according to the use and signification of the words, and must not force my own sense on it, if it will not bear it. But suppose then that the natural construction of the words import such a sense, as is contrary to some evident Principle of Reason? Then I won't believe it. How? Not believe Scripture? No, no. I will believe no pretended Revelation which contradicts the plain dictates of reason, which all mankind agree in; and were I persuaded that those Books which we call the Holy Scriptures did so, I would not believe them; and this is a fairer and honester way than to force them to speak what they never intended, and what every impartial man who reads them must think was never intended, that we may believe them. To put our own sense on Scripture, without respect to the use of words, and to the reason and scope of the text, is not to believe Scripture, but to make it, is not to learn from Scripture, but to teach it to speak our language, is not to submit to the authority of Scripture, but to make Scripture submit to our reason, even in such matters as are confessedly above reason, as the infinite Nature and Essence of God is.

[1] [*I.e.,* Sherlock's Unitarian adversaries.]

13

## (3) THE APOCRYPHA

### No. 59.  JOHN COSIN

[From *A Scholastical History of the Canon of the Holy Scripture*, Chap. XIX. § cxcix.  *Works*, ed. *L. A. C. T.*, Vol. III, pp. 284 f.  This treatise was published in 1657 when its author was in exile in France.  Its purpose was to defend " that ancient Canon of Scripture, which by the Church of England, and by all other Reformed and Christian Churches abroad (except the Roman only) is now received " (Table of Contents to ch. I).  It is thus directed against the First Decree of the Fourth Session of the Council of Trent.  The treatise consists mainly of a long string of references to the Canon of Scripture from the earliest times to the Sixteenth Century, arranged chronologically.]

THE conclusion therefore of all this discourse will be,—That the religion of the Church of England, in her Article concerning the Holy Scriptures [*i.e.* Article vi] (whereunto the public Confessions of the Reformed and Protestant Churches abroad, besides the Christians of the East and South parts of the world, be agreeable), is truly Catholic ; That the ancient Church of the Old Testament acknowledged no other books to be canonical than we do ;  That our Blessed Saviour, and His Apostles after Him, received no other ;  That the several ages following adhered to the same Canon ;  That the authors of the Books of *Tobit*, and *Judith*, and the rest of that order, were no prophets inspired of God to write His authentical Scriptures ;  That they who first put these Deutero-canonical or Ecclesiastical books into the volume of the Bible, did not thereby intend to make them equal to the Books of Moses and the Prophets, but only to recommend them unto the private and public reading of the Church, both for the many excellent precepts and examples of life that be in them, and for the better knowledge of the history and estate of God's people from the time of the Prophets to the coming of Christ ;  That it is not in the power of the Roman Church, nor any other, either to make new articles of Faith, or to make any books sacred and Canonical Scriptures (so as to be the binding rules of our Faith and Religion) which were not such in their own nature before, that is, certainly inspired by God, and by His authority only ordained to be such, from the time when they were first written ; and, lastly, That adhering to the ancient Catholic Faith and Doctrine of the Church, we cannot admit or approve any such new decree as it hath lately pleased the masters of the Council at Trent to make, who have not only obtruded these books upon their own people, to be received as true and authentical parts of the ancient Testament, but have likewise damned all the world besides that will not recede from the universal consent of the Christian Church, and subscribe to that horrid anathema, whereby they have most rashly condemned so many ages of Fathers and writers before them.   And, if there were no other cause to reject the pretended authority of this late and exorbitant assembly (as there be many more), this only is enough.

# V. STANDARDS OF FAITH

# (1) CREEDS

## No. 60.  JOHN PEARSON

[From *An Exposition of the Creed*. The final sentences of his exposition of the words " I believe." Ed. Oxford (E. Burton), 1864, pp. 25 f.  Cp. note on No. **13**.]

ALTHOUGH those things [*i.e.* the Articles of the Apostles' Creed] which I am ready to affirm be not apparent to my sense, so that I cannot say I see them; although they be not evident to my understanding of themselves, nor appear unto me true by the virtue of any natural and necessary cause, so that I cannot say I have any proper knowledge or science of them; yet being they are certainly contained in the Scriptures, the writings of the blessed Apostles and Prophets; being those Apostles and Prophets were endued with miraculous power from above, and immediately inspired with the Holy Ghost, and consequently what they delivered was not the word of man, but of God Himself; being God is of that universal knowledge and infinite wisdom that it is impossible He should be deceived; of that indefectible holiness and transcendent rectitude that it is not imaginable He should intend to deceive any man, and consequently whatsoever He hath delivered for a truth must be necessarily and infallibly true; I readily and steadfastly assent unto them as most certain truths, and am as fully and absolutely, and more concerningly persuaded of them, than of any thing I see or know.  And because that God Who hath revealed them hath done it, not for my benefit only, but for the advantage of others, nor for that alone, but also for the manifestation of His own glory; being for those ends He hath commanded me to profess them, and hath promised an eternal reward upon my profession of them; being every particular person is to expect the justification of himself, and the salvation of his soul, upon the condition of his own Faith; as with a certain and full persuasion, I assent unto them, so with a fixed and undaunted resolution I will profess them; and with this faith in my heart and confession in my mouth, in respect of the whole body of the CREED, and every Article and particle in it, I sincerely, readily, resolvedly say, *I believe.*

## No. 61.  JOHN OVERALL

[From *The Convocation Book of* 1606, usually known as *Bishop Overall's Convocation Book Concerning the Government of God's Catholic Church and the Kingdoms of the Whole World*. Ed. *L. A. C. T.*, pp. 82–86.  This book was first published in 1690. The Convocation which met in 1603 continued, with many prorogations, to sit until

1610; and it set itself to frame a further set of Canons and a treatise expounding them. The compilation of the treatise was put into the hands of Overall, as Prolocutor of the Lower House. James I believed that his Royal Prerogative was being challenged by the Canons, some of which dealt with the King's authority, and thus the Canons incorporated in the *Book* never received the Royal Assent.]

We do therefore for ourselves, and in the name of all the rest of the Church of England, acknowledge and profess from the bottom of our hearts the truth of all that is written in the Sacred Scriptures ; and consequently, and in more particular manner, whatsoever is written in the same that doth appertain to the Most Holy and Blessed Trinity. Out of the doctrine of which sacred writings, because the Apostles and Churches of God, moved thereunto by sundry sorts of heretics, have long since most faithfully and learnedly deduced into certain summaries rightly termed Creeds, all those points of true doctrine which do concern God the Father, God the Son, and God the Holy Ghost and are necessarily to be believed under pain of condemnation, we do resolutely embrace and steadfastly believe all and every one the articles of the Apostles' Creed, and all and every one the articles of the other Creeds, made by sundry Councils for the further declaration of the Christian faith and Apostolic Creed, as of the Nicene Creed, made by the Council of Nice against Arius, who denied the Divinity of the Son of God ; and of the next Creed, made in the First Council of Constantinople, ratifying and further declaring the Nicene Creed against Eudoxius the Arian, and Macedonius, who denied the Holy Ghost to be God ; and of the Creed made in the First Council of Ephesus against Nestorius, who taught that the two natures in Christ were not united together personally, but that the Word, which did take our nature upon Him for our redemption, did only assist Christ our Saviour, as one friend may assist another ; and of the Creed made in the Council of Chalcedon against Eutyches, who did confound the two natures of Christ. Against any of which articles whosoever doth oppose himself, and doth wilfully continue in such his opposition, we hold and judge them to be worthily subject to all those censures and anathematisms, which the several constitutions and canons of the said councils have justly laid upon them.

Also, with the same resolution and faith before mentioned, we receive and believe all and every one the several points and articles of Athanasius' Creed, made a little after the Council of Nice, against such blasphemous opinions as in those times were either directly, or indirectly published in corners, and spread here and there to the seducing of many. According to some articles of the which Creed that do more nearly concern our course, we steadfastly believe and confess " that our Lord Jesus Christ, the Son of God, is both God and man ; God, of the substance of the Father, begotten before all worlds ; and man, of the substance of His Mother, born in the world ; perfect

God, and perfect man, of a reasonable soul and human flesh subsisting; equal to the Father as touching His Godhead, and inferior to the Father, [as] touching His manhood; Who although He be both God and man, yet He is not two, but one Christ; one, not by conversion of the Godhead into flesh, but by taking [of] the manhood into God; one altogether, not by confusion of substance, but by unity of person." In respect of which personal union of the two natures of our Saviour Christ, without confusion or mixture of either of them, thus described by Athanasius, whatsoever is affirmed in the Scriptures, as well of the one nature as of the other, the same is also truly to be affirmed *de toto composito*, that is, of His most sacred Person being both God and man; the essential proprieties of them both remaining, notwithstanding, distinguished.

For, as the said Personal or Hypostatical Union of the said two natures doth not make the one nature to be the other, the Divine nature to be the human nature, or the human nature to be the Divine nature, so doth it not make the essential proprieties of the one nature to be the essential proprieties of the other nature; but as well the proprieties and actions as the natures themselves do remain distinguished, though united in one person; both of them concurring together, the Deity in working that which appertaineth to the Deity, and the humanity executing those essential proprieties and actions which do belong unto the humanity. For example, the Divine nature appeared in Christ by miracles, when His human nature was subject to many opprobries and injuries. In that our Saviour Christ did satisfy five thousand persons with five loaves, did give water of life to the woman of Samaria, did walk upon the sea with dry foot, did by His commandment calm the winds, He shewed thereby some effects and works of His Divine nature, because they were, as one well saith, *Verbi propria, non carnis*, the proprieties of the Word, and not of the flesh. Again, in that Christ brake bread, this was an office of His human nature; but in that He multiplied it, the same did appertain to His Divine nature. In that He cried out *Lazarus, come forth*, that was the office of His human nature; but in that He quickened him and raised him from death, that did belong unto His Divine nature. In that He said, *Thy sins are forgiven thee*, that was an office of His human nature; but in that such sins were indeed remitted, the same did appertain to His Divine nature. In that our Saviour Christ died, the same did proceed from the flesh; but in that by His death He did expiate our sins, that did proceed from the Spirit. In that He was buried, did proceed from the flesh; but in that He did raise Himself from the dead, that was the office of His Divinity. In that He gave bread to His Apostles in His Last Supper, He did it as man; but in that He made them partakers of His Blessed Body, He did the same as He was God. In that now being in Heaven, He doth possess that kingdom in the name and behalf of His elect, that doth appertain unto His human nature; but that He doth now remain with us and dwell in our hearts, that is an office of His Divine nature. In that He maketh intercession for us, that doth belong to His human nature; but in that He doth justify us, regenerate us, work in us both to will and to perform, in that He ruleth us and leadeth us in the way of His commandments, all these offices do appertain unto His Divinity. Lastly, in that He shall come in the clouds, and say unto one sort of persons, *Come, ye blessed*, and unto the other sort, *Depart, ye cursed*, He shall do the same according to His human nature; but in that He shall judge every man according to His knowledge of all men's hearts, their cogitations, desires and works, that He shall do as God.

Nevertheless, any thing thus by us affirmed notwithstanding, Christ Himself is not divided, though the proprieties and actions of His two natures are in this sort to be distinguished, as God Himself is not divided, although the three persons in Trinity are rightly held to be indeed distinguished; and yet all the said actions and proprieties of the two natures of Christ, distinguished, as we have expressed, they are, notwithstanding, very truly to be affirmed of His sacred Person. The reason whereof hath been before touched, and it is this; because seeing that both the natures are joined together in the person of the Son by an hypostatical, and consequently by a true and essential union, so as Christ is thereby both true God in regard of His Divine nature, and true man in respect of His human nature. Whatsoever is the propriety of the Divine nature and of the human nature, the same is wholly and altogether in Christ, and is necessarily therefore to be affirmed of Him, both essentially and properly. In respect whereof, we say that Christ was dead and that He could not die; that He is both finite and infinite; eternal and temporal; in every place and yet circumscribed in one place. For of necessity whatsoever are the proprieties of the human nature, the same are truly and properly to be affirmed *de vero homine*; and whatsoever are the proprieties of the Divine nature, the same are likewise to be affirmed *de vero Deo*, Christ being, out of all controversy amongst the children of God, *et verus homo et verus Deus*. And thus we have, after a sort, both briefly and truly set down the force and efficacy of the Hypostatical Union of the two natures of Christ, being distinguished, but no ways confounded; as the same, together with the true doctrine of all other necessary articles concerning the blessed Trinity, doth by the Scriptures most truly expounded in the Creeds above mentioned many ways very notably appear.

To this purpose much more might have here been added by us if, our course considered, we had thought it necessary. Only we have thought it fit, furthermore to profess and make it thereby known to all men, that there are some other Creeds made by other councils and particular bishops, like to Athanasius', and other worthy persons; as Irenæus' Creed, Tertullian's Creed, as we may so term it, Damasus' Creed, the Creed ascribed to St. Ambrose and St. Augustine "*Te Deum laudamus, etc.*," the Creed of the First Council of Toledo, St. Jerome's Creed, the Creed ascribed to Leo which was approved by the Council of Chalcedon, and the Creed of the Sixth Council of Constantinople against the Monothelites, holding that in Christ both God and man there was but one will; all of them tending to the setting forth the orthodoxal and true doctrine of " One God in Trinity and Trinity in Unity, not confounding the Persons nor dividing the substance; and of one Christ, true God, and true man, not confounding His natures nor dividing His person." Which Creeds we do receive, embrace, and reverence in such sort as they have been received, embraced and reverenced hitherto by all the particular Churches of the Christian world; inasmuch as they agree, both with the Scriptures, with the Apostles' Creed, with the four Creeds mentioned of the first four General Councils, and with Athanasius's Creed; which contain in them that faith which was then, and so still ought to be accounted the true, Catholic faith; nothing, in effect, being contained in all the Creeds before by us specified, which may not be deduced by necessary consequences out of the Creed which Athanasius made; the conclusion of which Creed is in these words expressed, " This is the Catholic faith, which except a man believe faithfully he cannot be saved." To which conclusion that, in sense, is very consonant wherewith Damasus doth end his Creed in these words, " Read these things, believe them, retain them; to this faith submit thy soul, and thou shalt obtain life and reward from Christ."

## No. 62.  HENRY HAMMOND

[From *Of Fundamentals in a Notion Referring to Practice*, Chapter ix, §§ 1–4. *Miscellaneous Theological Works*, ed. L. A. C. T., pp. 110–112. Hammond's treatise on Fundamentals, which appeared in 1654, went through a number of editions in the Seventeenth Century.]

Having viewed the Apostles' Creed, and of it premised this one thing, that it was a complete catalogue of all that they, being directed by the Holy Ghost in their ministry, thought fit, to lay the foundation of Christian obedience in every Church, and consequently that there was no more in their opinion necessary in order to this end of working reformation in the world; it will from this datum demonstratively follow, either that there is in the two other Creeds, the Nicene and Athanasian, nothing materially different from that which the Apostles' Creed had contained, nothing really superadded to it, or else that that superaddition was not, in the Apostles' estimation, necessary to this end, and consequently that if, at the forming of them, it were by the following Church thought necessary to be thus made or still continues to be so, this must arise from some fresh emergent, one or more, which had been observable in the Church after the Apostles' time.

And which of these two is the truth it will not be uneasy to define. For though the omission of some words which had been retained in the Apostles' Creed do not signify much ; for it is certain that they were, while retained in that, and are still, now they are left out in following Creeds, eternally and unquestionably true, in the sense wherein the Apostles and their successors understood them,—not indeed any more, than that they were virtually contained in other words still continued,—as the Descent to Hades under that of His suffering and burial and not rising till the third day, and the Communication of Saints, under the Catholic Church, with the epithet of Apostolic added to it ; or else that they were not necessary to be repeated, because already familiarly known and confessed, and not questioned by those heretics against whom the variations were designed,—as in the Athanasian Creed, the articles of the Holy Ghost, so largely set down in four branches in the Nicene Creed, and the three articles attending that of the Holy Ghost in the Apostles' Creed, are all omitted ; yet those words which in the later Creeds were superadded to the former were apparently designed by the compilers for some special use, either by way of addition or interpretation, to fence the Catholic Orthodox Faith from the corruptions and depravations, or else from the doubtings and contradictions, of heretics.

Thus in the Nicene Creed, the two additions in the first article, the ἕνα, " one," prefixed to " God," and the καὶ πάντων τῶν ὁρατῶν καὶ ἀοράτων " and of all things visible and invisible," were upon prudent deliberation and consideration interposed, the first of them on occasion of the Arians, in one respect, and both of them, in another respect, by reason of the Gnostic and Valentinian, and such like following heretics, whose heathen and poetical theology taken from Hesiod, and Orpheus, and Philistion, had rendered them necessary. For that those heretics, beginning with their Simon and Helena, had introduced a plurality of gods, and so made the profession of the unity part of the *symbolum* that should discriminate the orthodox from them, and affirm that their *æones* or " angels " were begotten by Helena, Simon's πρώτη ἔννοια " first cogitation," and that the world was created by them, and that the God of the Jews was but one of those angels, and a great deal of the like, appears by Irenæus ; and these two insertions were clear explications of the Apostles' old form, *God the Father, Ruler of All, Maker of Heaven and Earth*, which sufficiently contained an acknowledgment of the unity—for how else could He be Monarch, or Ruler of All ?—and also asserted Him the Creator of all the angels, who were certainly comprehended under the " Heaven and Earth," the phrase of Scripture to denote the world, but yet was capable of more light, by these more explicit words, "visible and invisible," to exclude the contradictions of heretics.

And though the Creed in the ancient Apostolic form were sufficient for any man to believe and profess, yet when the Church hath thought meet to erect that additional bulwark against heretics, the rejecting or denying the truth of those their additions may justly be deemed an interpretative siding with those ancient or a desire to introduce some new heresies ; and though good life might have been founded without those additions, if on such occasions they had never been made, yet the pride or singularity or heretical design of opposing or questioning them, now they are framed, being themselves irreconcileable with Christian charity and humility, are destructive of the fabric directly and interpretatively of the very foundation, and is therefore justly deemed criminous and liable to censures in the Church of God.

## No. 63.   PETER HEYLYN

[From *Theologia Veterum*; or *The Sum of Christian Theology, Positive, Polemical, and Philological, contained in the Apostles' Creed or reducible to it, according to the Tendries of the Ancients, both Greeks and Latins.* London, 1654. Introduction, pp. |5] f. (This Preface is paged separately.) The treatise examines the twelve Articles of the Creed in turn, and may be considered a precursor of Pearson's *Exposition of the Creed* (Cp. note on No. 13). On the title page it has the Vincentian Canon, *In ipsa item Catholica Ecclesia magnopere curandum est ut id teneamus quod Ubique, quod Semper, quod Ab Omnibus creditum est.*]

But being the writings of the Evangelists and Apostles were of too great a bulk to be committed unto memory and that there were some things in them so obscure and difficult that many ignorant and unstable but well meaning men both might and did wrest them to their own destruction, other things which related rather unto moral duties than to points of faith, it was thought fit by the Apostles to draw the points of saving faith such as were necessarily to be believed of all Christian people into a brief and narrower compass. It was not for the ordinary sort of men to trouble themselves with doubtful disputations, as St. Paul calleth them, whereof many do occur in his Epistles,—disputes of too great difficulty and sublime a nature for every man, especially the weak in faith, either to understand or conceive aright. Nor was it possible that men of mean parts and laborious callings, of which the Church consisted for the most part in the first beginning, should either have so much leisure as to read over their writings, or so much judgement as to gather and collect from thence what of necessity was to be believed that they might be saved, what not ; or so much memory as to treasure up and repeat by heart the infinite treasures of Divine knowledge, which are comprehended in the same. And if it were so (as no doubt it was) when the Apostles and Evangelists had left those excellent monuments of themselves in writing which the

Church has ever since enjoyed, to which men might resort, as occasion was, for their information and instruction, how necessary then must we think it was for some such Summary and Abstract of the Christian Faith to be resolved upon amongst them, which men of weak memories might repeat by heart and men of shallow comprehensions rightly understand. Those blessed souls knew well, none better, how to apply themselves to the capacities of the weakest men; that there were many babes in Christ to be fed with milk and not with meats; and that if they became not all things unto all men, they must resolve amongst themselves to save but few. Upon this ground (than which what juster could there be to induce them to it ?) it is conceived they drew up that brief Abstract of the Christian Faith which we call the Creed; and couched therein whatever point was necessary for all sorts of men, in all times and all places of the world, both to believe in their hearts as also to profess and confess upon all occasions, though to the apparent hazard of their lives and fortunes. And why this might not be that ὑποτύπωσις ὑγιαινόντων λόγων, that *form of sound words* whereof St. Paul saith to Timothy *Hold fast that form of sound words thou hast heard of me,* I must confess that I could never yet see a convincing reason.

### No. 64. WILLIAM CHILLINGWORTH

[From *Sermon II*, §§ 14, 18–20. *Works*, ed. Oxford (1838), Vol. III, pp. 41, 43 f. The text of this Sermon was *Psalm* xiv, 1. We have been unable to trace the work from which the long quotation in the first paragraph is taken.]

It is a pretty observation that the author of the Narration of the English Seminary founded in Rome has, concerning the method and order the Devil has used in assailing and disturbing the peace and quiet of the Church with heresies and schisms. He began (saith he) with the First Article of our Creed, concerning " one God, the Father Almighty, Creator of Heaven and Earth "; against which, in the first three hundred years, he armed the Simonians, Menandrians, Basilidians, Valentinians, Marcionites, Manichees, and Gnostics. After the three-hundredth year he opposed the Second Article, concerning the Divinity of our Lord Jesus Christ, by his beloved servants the Noetians, Sabellians, Paullians, Photinians, and Arians. After the four hundredth year he sought to undermine the Fourth, Fifth, Sixth, and Seventh Articles of the Incarnation, Passion, Resurrection, Ascension, and the Second Coming to Judgement, by the heresies of Nestorius, Theodorus, Eutyches, Dioscorus, Gnapheus, Sergius, etc. After the eight hundred and sixtieth, he assailed the Eighth Article concerning the Holy Ghost, by the heresy and schism of the Greek Church. Lastly, since the year one thousand till these times, his business and craft has especially expressed itself in seeking to subvert the Ninth and Tenth, concerning the Holy Catholic Church

and Forgiveness of Sins, by the aid and ministry of the Ponti-
ficians, Anabaptists, Familists, and the like; and with the deceits
and snares of these his cunning ministers hath he entangled the greatest
part of the now Christian World. . . .

The art and cunning whereby this great work of the Devil's is brought
about is clearly detected by our Saviour in His exposition of the
Parable of the Sower, in these words, *When they have heard, then
cometh the Devil, and taketh away the Word out of their hearts*, i.e.,
the Devil will give such people leave freely to hear the Word of God
preached, to study it, dispute it, to know and be acquainted with all
the curious intricate subtilties of it, upon condition that they will
promise to resolve not to be a jot the better disposed for it in their
lives. He can well suffer it to swim in the brain, that the understanding
should be enlightened, the fancy affected and pleased with it, so that
he may have leave to stop the secret intercourse and passages thence
to the heart. It troubles him not to have the precious seed of the word
entertained by a man, so that it may be kept up safe in granaries,
and not multiply, so that the heart be not ploughed up and furrowed
for the receiving of it. As long as there is no fruitful harvest there,
all goes well.

He will be so far from hindering such from going to the Church,
so that their errand be to learn what they may be able to talk of, and
maintain discourse with, that he could wish every day were a Sunday
for them, that they might be able by abundance of knowledge, fruitless,
and void of practice, to hasten and aggravate their own damnation.

## No. 65. JEREMY TAYLOR

[From Θεολογία 'Εκλεκτική, or *A Discourse of the Liberty of Prophesying*, Section ii,
§ 36. *Works*, ed. R. Heber, Vol. VII, pp. 491–493 (ed. C. P. Eden, Vol. V, pp. 405–
407). Cp. note on No. **87**.]

If I should be questioned concerning the Symbol of Athanasius
(for we see the Nicene Symbol was the father of many more, some
twelve or thirteen symbols in the space of an hundred years), I confess
I cannot see that moderate sentence and gentleness of charity in his
preface and conclusion, as there was in the Nicene Creed. Nothing
there but damnation and perishing everlastingly, unless the article
of the Trinity be believed, as it is there with curiosity and minute
particularities explained. Indeed, Athanasius had been soundly
vexed on one side, and much cried up on the other; and, therefore,
it is not so much wonder for him to be so decretory and severe in his
censure; for nothing could more ascertain his friends to him, and dis-
repute his enemies, than the belief of that damnatory appendix; but
that does not justify the thing. For the articles themselves, I am most
heartily persuaded of the truth of them, and yet I dare not say all that

are not so, are irrevocably damned; because *citra hoc symbolum*, the faith of the Apostles' Creed is entire; and *he that believeth and is baptized, shall be saved*, that is, he that believeth such a belief as is sufficient disposition to be baptized, that faith with the sacrament is sufficient for Heaven. Now the Apostles' Creed does one; why, therefore, do not both entitle us to the promise? Besides, if it were considered concerning Athanasius's Creed, how many people understand it not, how contrary to natural reason it seems, how little the Scripture says of those curiosities of explication, and how tradition was not clear on his side for the article itself, much less for those forms and minutes, how himself is put to make an answer and excuse for the fathers speaking in excuse of the Arians, at least so seemingly that the Arians appealed to them for trial, and the offer was declined; and after all this, that the Nicene Creed itself went not so far, neither in article, nor anathema, nor explication; it had not been amiss if the final judgement had been left to Jesus Christ, for He is appointed Judge of all the world, and He shall judge the people righteously; for He knows every truth, the degree of every necessity, and all excuses that do lessen, or take away the nature or malice of a crime; all which I think Athanasius, though a very good man, did not know so well as to warrant such a sentence; and put case, the heresy there condemned be damnable (as it is damnable enough), yet a man may maintain an opinion that is in itself damnable, and yet he, not knowing it so, and being invincibly led into it, may go to Heaven; his opinion shall burn, and himself be saved. But, however, I find no opinion in Scripture called damnable, but what are impious *in materia practica*, or directly destructive of the faith, or the body of Christianity; such of which St. Peter speaks: *Bringing in damnable heresies, even denying the Lord that bought them; these are the false prophets, who out of covetousness make merchandise of you through cozening words.* Such as these are truly heresies, and such as these are certainly damnable. But because there are no degrees either of truth or falsehood, every true proposition being alike true; that an error is more or less damnable is not told us in Scripture, but is determined by the man and his manners, by circumstances and accidents; and, therefore, the censure in the preface and end are arguments of his zeal and strength of his persuasion; but they are extrinsical and accidental to the articles, and might as well have been spared. And, indeed, to me it seems very hard to put uncharitableness into the creed, and so to make it become as an article of faith, though perhaps this very thing was no faith of Athanasius, who, if we may believe Aquinas, made this manifestation of faith, *non per modum symboli, sed per modum doctrinae*, that is, if I understand him right, ' not with a purpose to impose it upon others, but with confidence to declare his own belief '; and that it was prescribed to others as a creed was the act of the Bishops of Rome, so he said. Nay, possibly it was none of his. So said the Patriarch of Constantinople, Meletius, about one hundred and thirty years since, in his epistle to John Douza, *Athanasio falso adscriptum symbolum, cum Pontificum Romanorum appendice illa adulteratum, luce lucidius contestamur.* And it is more than probable that he said true, because this Creed was written originally in Latin, which in all reason Athanasius did not, and it was translated into Greek, it being apparent that the Latin copy is but one, but the Greek is various, there being three editions or translations rather, expressed by Genebrard, *lib. iii. de Trinit.* But in this particular, who list may better satisfy himself in a disputation *de symbolo Athanasii*, printed at Wertzburg, 1590, supposed to be written by Serrarius or Clencherus.

# (2) ANTIQUITY AND TRADITION

## No. 66. FRANCIS WHITE

[From *A Treatise of the Sabbath Day*, pp. 97 f. Cp. note on No. **67**.]

REFORMED Churches reject not all Traditions, but such as are spurious, superstitious, and not consonant to the prime rule of faith, to wit, the Holy Scripture. Genuine Traditions agreeable to the Rule of Faith, subservient to piety, consonant with Holy Scripture, derived from the Apostolical times by a successive current, and which have the uniform testimony of pious Antiquity, are received and honoured by us. Now such are these which follow: The historical tradition concerning the number, integrity, dignity, and perfection of the Books of Canonical Scriptures, The Catholic exposition of many sentences of Holy Scripture, The Holy Apostles' Creed, The Baptism of Infants, The perpetual Virginity of the Blessed Virgin Mary, The religious observation of the Lord's Day and of some other Festivals, as Easter, Pentecost, etc., Baptizing and administration of the Holy Eucharist in public assemblies and congregations, The Service of the Church in a known language, The delivering of the Holy Communion to the people in both kinds, The superiority and authority of Bishops over Priests and Deacons in jurisdiction and power of Ordination, etc.

## No. 67. FRANCIS WHITE

[From *A Treatise of the Sabbath Day containing a Defence of the Orthodoxal Doctrine of the Church of England Against Sabbatarian Novelty*, London, 1635, pp. 99–103. Francis White, who had been consecrated Bishop of Ely in 1631, shortly afterwards held a conference with Theophilus Brabourne on the question of the Sabbath at Ely House in Holborn. His *Treatise* was the outcome of this discussion. It was written at the command of Charles I, and dedicated to Laud. Its production was closely connected with the reissue of the *Book of Sports* (No. **261**) in 1633.]

### *An Observation Concerning the quality of Ecclesiastical Precepts and Constitutions.*

Although the Ecclesiastical precepts and constitutions of the rulers in the Church are not Divine by miraculous and immediate inspiration in such manner as the precepts of God's written Law, yet when they are composed according to the rules and canons of Holy Scripture and are apt and convenient means to the better fulfilling of the Commandments of God, delivered in Holy Scripture, they are by conformity and subordination to the Divine Law and by Divine approbation sacred and venerable. For

i. Their immediate authors and composers are sacred persons, called and authorized by the Holy Ghost to rule and order the Church of Christ (*Acts* xx, 28 ; *Luke* xii, 42).

ii. The matter of these precepts, being ordered and framed according to the Apostolical rules (*Rom.* xiv, 19 ; *I Cor.* xiv, 26, 40) and according to precedent examples, and precedents of Holy Scripture, and the equity and analogy of former Divine Laws (*I Cor.* ix, 9, 13), and maxims and conclusions of natural reason rectified by grace (*I Cor.* ix, 7, 10 and xi, 14, 15), and the end of such precepts being godly edification, order, decency, and reverent administration of sacred and religious things ; the precepts and constitutions of the Church (I say) being thus qualified, are sacred and venerable, and their observation is an act of religion and of obedience to the general commandment of God. For the Holy Ghost commandeth : *Obey them that have the rule over you and submit yourselves* (*Heb.* xiii, 17), *Hear the Church* (*Matt.* xviii, 17). And if children, servants and subjects are bound by Divine Law, natural and positive, to obey their parents, worldly masters, and temporal princes in things human and secular, when the same are reasonable, honest, and just, and by performance thereof they serve and obey the Lord Christ (*Col.* iii, 14 ; *Eph.* vi, 1 ; *I Pet.* ii, 15) ; in like manner, when Christian people submit themselves to conformable observance of the lawful and religious constitutions of their spiritual rulers, this conformity and submission of theirs is pleasing to God.

iii. The Holy Apostle's common rule to all Christian people is (*Phil.* iv., 8) *Whatsoever things are true, whatsoever things are honest, whatsoever things are just, whatsoever things pertain to love, whatsoever things are of good report, these things do.* But peaceable and conformable observation of the lawful constitutions of the Church touching decent and reverent exercising religious offices is honest and just and appertaining to peace and love.

Therefore the Apostle's common rule, given to all Christian people (*Phil.* iv, 8), obligeth everyone to a peaceable and conformable observation of the lawful precepts and constitutions of the Church, as well as it doth to the obedience and observation of the commands of temporal lords, masters, officers, governors, parents, etc.

iv. In the Primitive Age, when Christian people excelled in virtue and piety, they generally observed the constitutions and precepts of the Church which were ordained for decency, order, and good government ; and if any frowardly and contemptuously disobeyed the same, they were censured as malefactors. It was a law of the Church in Ignatius' and Tertullian's days that people should not make the Lord's

14

Day a fasting day; and the wilful transgressing this ecclesiastical constitution was esteemed a nefarious offence.

Betwixt Easter and Whitsuntide and upon every Lord's Day the Law and Canon of the Church was: That people at public prayer and in time of Divine offices should stand upright on their legs and not sit or kneel.

It was likewise a general constitution to adore Christ with bodies and faces turned towards the East.

To receive the Holy Eucharist in the forenoon and when people were fasting; and to receive the same from the Bishop's, Priest's or Deacon's hands, and not for the people, being participants, to take it from off the Altar or Communion Table with their own hands; mixing some water with the wine of the Holy Communion.

In the administration of Baptism, *trina immersio*, thrice dipping or sprinkling in water.

Observation of certain yearly Festivals and Holy Days, among which were Easter and Whitsuntide; and likewise annual and weekly times of fasting.

In all these, and the like ecclesiastical observances, Christian people were very obsequious to the precepts and constitutions of the rulers of the Church.

But in our times it is otherwise. For our Disciplinarian guides, with their arguments,—*Ab authoritate Scripturae negative*: The Holy Scripture hath commanded none of these Rites and observations in particular; therefore they are Popish traditions, will-worship, and superstition—have made our people wild; and many are so perverse that they esteem it an high degree of purity and sanctity to perform all religious duties overwhart [= overthwart] to the way of the Church. And whereas in times past it was a general maxim among Christians, *Non habet Dei charitatem qui Ecclesiae non diligit unitatem*, " the love of God abideth not in them which do not love and observe the unity of the Church," now they are reputed most pure and holy who with greatest boldness bequarrel and cavil against the authority, government, and lawful precepts and constitutions of the Church. But Irenaeus said long since of such, That the Lord will judge those which cause schism and who, wanting the true love of God, upon very slender exceptions and occasions (to wit, *straining at a gnat and swallowing a camel*) tear and divide, and as much as in them lieth kill and destroy, the Body of Christ.

### No. 68.  JAMES USSHER

[From *An Answer to a Challenge made by a Jesuit in Ireland Wherein the Judgement of Antiquity in the Points Questioned is truly delivered, and the Novelty of the Now Romish Doctrine Plainly Discovered*, Chapter II. *Works*, ed. C. R. Elrington (1864), Vol. III, pp. 41-47. This treatise was published in 1625. It was a reply to a challenge made by William Malone some six years earlier, who enquired which of the Bishops of Rome it was who had altered the religion which Protestants admitted to be truly continued for the first 400 years of the Christian era.]

To begin . . . with traditions, which is your forlorn hope that in the first place we are to set upon, this must I needs tell you before we begin, that you much mistake the matter if you think that traditions of all sorts promiscuously are struck at by our religion. We willingly acknowledge that the Word of God, which by some of the Apostles was set down in writing, was both by themselves and others of their fellow-labourers delivered by word of mouth ; and that the Church in succeeding ages was bound, not only to preserve those sacred writings committed to her trust, but also to deliver unto her children, *viva voce*, the form of wholesome words contained therein. Traditions, therefore, of this nature come not within the compass of our controversy ; the question being betwixt us *de ipsa doctrina tradita*, not *de tradendi modo*, touching the substance of the doctrine delivered, not of the manner of delivering it. Again, it must be remembered that here we speak of the doctrine delivered as the Word of God, that is, of points of religion revealed unto the Prophets and Apostles for the perpetual information of God's people, not of rites and ceremonies and other ordinances which are left to the disposition of the Church, and consequently be not of Divine but of positive and human right. Traditions, therefore, of this kind likewise are not properly brought within the circuit of this question.

But that traditions of men should be obtruded unto us for articles of religion and admitted for parts of God's worship ; or that any traditions should be accepted for parcels of God's Word, beside the Holy Scriptures and such doctrines as are either expressly therein contained or by sound inference may be deduced from thence, I think we have reason to gainsay ; as long as for the first we have this direct sentence from God Himself, *In vain do they worship Me, teaching for doctrines the commandments of men* ; and for the second, the express warrant of the Apostle in the third chapter of the *Second to Timothy*, testifying of the Holy Scriptures, not only that they *are able to make us wise unto salvation* (which they should not be able to do if they did not contain all things necessary to salvation), but also that by them *the man of God*, that is the minister of God's Word unto whom it appertaineth *to declare all the counsel of God*, may be *perfectly instructed to every good work* ; which could not be if the Scriptures did not contain all the counsel of God which was fit for him to learn, or if there were any other word of God which he were bound to teach that should not be contained within the limits of the Book of God.

Now whether herein we disagree from the doctrine generally received by the Fathers, we refer ourselves to their own sayings. For ritual traditions unwritten, and for doctrinal traditions, written indeed, but preserved also by the continual preaching of the pastors of the

Church successively, we find no man a more earnest advocate than Tertullian. Yet he, having to deal with Hermogenes the heretic in a question concerning the faith, whether all things at the beginning were made of nothing, presseth him in this manner with the argument *ab authoritate negative*; for avoiding whereof the Papists are driven to fly for succour to their unwritten verities. " Whether all things were made of any subject matter, I have as yet read nowhere. Let those of Hermogenes his shop shew that it is written. If it be not written, let them fear that Woe, which is allotted to such as add or take away."

In the two Testaments, saith Origen, " every word that appertaineth to God may be required and discussed, and all knowledge of things out of them may be understood. But if anything do remain which the Holy Scripture doth not determine, no other third Scripture ought to be received for to authorize any knowledge, but that which remaineth we must commit to the fire, that is, we must reserve it to God. For in this present world, God would not have us to know all things."

Hippolytus the Martyr, in his *Homily against the Heresy of Noetus* : " There is one God, Whom we do not otherwise acknowledge, brethren, but out of the Holy Scriptures. For as he that would profess the wisdom of this world cannot otherwise attain hereunto, unless he read the doctrine of the philosophers, so whosoever of us will exercise piety toward God, cannot learn this elsewhere but out of the Holy Scriptures. Whatsoever, therefore, the Holy Scriptures do preach, that let us know ; and whatsoever they teach, that let us understand."

Athanasius, in his *Oration against the Gentiles*, toward the beginning : " The Holy Scriptures given by inspiration of God are of themselves sufficient to the discovery of truth."

St. Ambrose : " The things which we find not in the Scriptures, how can we use them ? " And again : " I read that he is the first, I read that he is not the second ; they who say he is the second, let them shew it by reading."

" It is well," saith St. Hilary, " that thou art content with those things which be written." And in another place he commendeth Constantius the Emperor for " desiring the faith to be ordered only according to those things that be written."

St. Basil : " Believe those things which are written ; the things which are not written, seek not." " It is a manifest falling from the faith and an argument of arrogancy, either to reject any point of those things that are written, or to bring in any of those things that are not written." He teacheth further " that every word and action ought to be confirmed by the testimony of the Holy Scripture, for confirmation of the faith of the good, and the confusion of the evil " ; and " that it is the property of a faithful man to be fully persuaded of the truth of those things that are delivered in the Holy Scripture, and not to dare either to reject or to add anything thereunto. For if whatsoever is not of faith be sin, as the Apostle saith, and faith is by hearing and hearing by the Word of God, then whatsoever is without the Holy Scripture, being not of faith, must needs be sin." Thus far St. Basil.

In like manner, Gregory Nyssen, St. Basil's brother, layeth this for a ground " which no man should contradict, that in that only the truth must be acknowledged wherein the seal of the Scripture testimony is to be seen." And accordingly in another book, attributed also unto him, we find this conclusion made : " Forasmuch as this is upholden with no testimony of the Scripture, as false we will reject it."

Thus also St. Hierome disputeth against Helvidius. " As we deny not those things that are written, so we refuse those things that are not written. That God was born of a virgin, we believe, because we read it. That Mary did marry after she was delivered we believe not, because we read it not."

" In those things," saith St. Augustine, " which are laid down plainly in the Scriptures, all those things are found which appertain to faith and direction of life." And again : " Whatsoever ye hear from the Holy Scriptures, let that savour well unto you ; whatsoever is without them, refuse, lest you wander in a cloud." And in another place : " All those things which in times past our ancestors have mentioned to be done toward mankind, and have delivered unto us, all those things also which we see and do deliver unto our posterity, so far as they appertain to the seeking and maintaining of true religion, the Holy Scripture hath not passed in silence."

" The Holy Scripture," saith St. Cyril of Alexandria, " is sufficient to make them which are brought up in it wise and most approved, and furnished with most sufficient understanding." And again, " That which the Holy Scripture hath not said, by what means should we receive, and account it among these things that be true ? "

Lastly, in the writings of Theodoret we meet with these kind of speeches. " By the Holy Scripture alone am I persuaded." " I am not so bold as to affirm anything which the sacred Scripture passeth in silence." " It is an idle and a senseless thing to seek those things that are passed in silence." " We ought not to seek those things which are passed in silence, but rest in the things that are written."

By the verdict of these twelve men you may judge what opinion was held in those ancient times of such traditions as did cross either the verity or the perfection of the sacred Scripture ; which are the traditions we set ourselves against. Whereunto you may add, if you please, that remarkable sentence delivered by Eusebius Pamphili, in the name of the three hundred and eighteen fathers of the First General Council of Nice : " Believe the things that are written ; the things that are not written, neither think upon nor enquire after."

## No. 69.  HERBERT THORNDIKE

[From *An Epilogue to the Tragedy of the Church of England*.  Book I, Chapter vii, §§ 15–21.  *Works*, ed. L. A. C. T., Vol. II, Part i, pp. 120–124.  This monumental treatise, which contained the expression of its author's most mature thoughts, was first published in 1659.  It consisted of three books, entitled respectively *The Principles of Christian Truth*, *The Covenant of Grace*, and *The Laws of the Church* ; in the L. A. C. T., the whole work fills no less than six volumes (Volumes II–IV, each volume being in two separate parts).  It was conceived and written under the Commonwealth, and drew out, at times with great discursiveness, and in a singularly obscure style, a plan for the reconstitution of the Church of England.  T. A. Lacey well described the whole work as approximating to a *Summa de Ecclesia* (*H. Thorndike*, p. 86).]

Whatsoever then is said of the Rule of Faith in the writings of the Fathers is to be understood of the Creed ; whereof, though it be not maintained that the words which pretenders were required to render by heart were the same, yet the substance of it and the reasons and grounds which make every point necessary to be believed, were always the same in all Churches and remain unchangeable.

I would not have any hereupon to think that the matter of this rule is not, in my conceit, contained in the Scriptures.  For I find St. Cyril (*Catech.* v) protesting, that it contains nothing but that which concerned our salvation the most, selected out of the Scriptures.  And, therefore, in other places he tenders his scholars evidence out of the Scriptures, and wishes them not to believe that whereof there is no such evidence.  And to the same effect, Eucherius, Paschasius, and after them Thomas Aquinas, all agree that the form of the Creed was made up out of the Scriptures, giving such reasons as no reasonable Christian can refuse ;  not only because all they whose salvation is concerned have not leisure to study the Scriptures, but because they that have cannot easily or safely discern wherein the substance of faith, upon the profession whereof our salvation depends, consisteth, supposing that they were able to discern between true and false in the meaning of the Scriptures.

To which I will add only that which Tertullian and others of the Fathers observe of the ancient heretics, that their fashion was to take occasion, upon one or two texts, to overthrow and deny the main substance and scope of the whole Scriptures ;  which, whether it be seen in the sects of our time or not I will not say here (because I will not take any thing for granted which I have not yet principles to prove), but supposing it only a thing possible, I will think I give a sufficient reason why God should provide Tradition as well as Scripture, to bound the sense of it ;  as St. Cyril also cautioneth in the place aforenamed, where he so liberally acknowledgeth the Creed to be taken out of the Scripture. . . . "For" (saith he) "the Faith was not framed as it pleased men, but the most substantial matters collected out of the Scripture do make up one doctrine of the Faith."  For, I beseech you, what had they, whosoever they were that first framed the Creed, but Tradition, whereby to distinguish that which is substantial from that which is not ?

Hear Origen in the Preface to his books περὶ ἀρχῶν . . . . " There being many that think their sense to be Christian, and yet the sense of some differs from their predecessors ; but that which the Church preaches, as delivered by order of succession from the Apostles, being preserved and remaining the same in the Churches, that only is to be believed for truth, which nothing differs from the Tradition of the Church.   This, notwithstanding, we must know, that the Holy Apostles, preaching the Faith of Christ, delivered some things (as many as they held necessary) most manifestly to all believers, even those whom they found the duller in the search of Divine knowledge, leaving the reason why they affirmed them to the search of those that got to receive the eminent gifts of the Holy Ghost, especially of utterance, wisdom, and knowledge, by the Holy Ghost.   Of other things they said that they are ;  but how, or wherefrom they are, they said not.   Forsooth, that the more studious of their successors, loving wisdom and knowledge, might have some exercise wherein to show the fruit of their wit ;  to wit, those that should prepare themselves to be worthy and capable of wisdom.   Now, the particulars of that which is manifestly delivered by the preaching of the Apostles are these," which he proceedeth to set down.   But Vincentius Lirinensis hath written a discourse on purpose to show that this rule of Faith, being delivered by succession to the principal [ ?], as St. Paul requires Timothy to do, and by them to those that were baptized, was the ground upon which all heresies, attempting upon the Faith, were condemned.   So that, so many heresies as historical truth will evidence to have been excluded the Church from the Apostles' time, for matter of belief, so many convictions of this rule , which, because all agreed that they transgressed, therefore they were excluded the Church.   But Vincentius, beside this, advanceth another mark to discern what belongs to the Rule, that is, what the ground and scope of our Creed requires.   For it might be said that perhaps something may come in question whether consistent with the rule of Faith or not, in which there hath passed no decree of the Primitive Church, because never questioned by that time ;  wherein therefore we shall be to seek, notwithstanding the decrees passed by the Church upon ancient heresies.   Which to meet with, Vincentius saith further, that whatsoever hath been unanimously taught in the Church by writing, that is, always, by all, everywhere, to that no contradiction is ever to be admitted in the Church.   Here the style changes ;  for whereas Irenaeus, Tertullian, and others of former time, appeal only to that which was visible in the practice of all Churches, by the time of the Council at Ephesus (the date of Vincentius' book) so much had been written upon all points of Faith, and upon the Scriptures that he presumeth, evidence may be made of it all, what may stand with that which the whole Church had taught, what may not.

## No. 70. WILLIAM PAYNE

[From *The Sixth Note of the Church Examined, viz. Agreement in Doctrine with the Primitive Church*, pp. 113–115. This essay was part of a composite work published in 1687 with the title, *The Notes of the Church, as laid down by Cardinal Bellarmine, Examined and Confuted*. The refutation of the several notes was assigned to different theologians; and the contributions were anonymous. A *Brief Discourse* introducing the whole subject was written by William Sherlock.]

We are very willing to own this for a true mark of the Church [namely] its agreeing with the doctrine of the Primitive Church; and we are so far from confuting Bellarmine for his giving of it, that we do not doubt but he has hereby confuted himself and the whole cause of the Roman Church. For if we may be allowed to go back to the Primitive Church and to examine the doctrine and belief of that in order to find out what is the true Church at present, then the pretended infallibility of the present Church and the necessity of receiving and believing all that she imposes must be set by, till it appears that she requires the same doctrine and no other than what was taught and believed by the Primitive Church. For according to this Note it does not appear which is the true Church till it first appears that it agrees with the doctrine of the Primitive; and till it appears that it is a true Church, it cannot sure appear to be an infallible one. For it cannot be pretended that Infallibility belongs to any but the true Church, and therefore it must be first known that the present Church agrees with the Primitive before it can be known that she is an infallible guide or teacher. So that we manifestly gain this first by this Note of the Church, that all those big and blustering claims to infallibility must be postponed and laid aside till that of agreeing with the doctrine of the Primitive Church be made out, and when that is done we shall not have quite so much reason to question her infallibility. We desire nothing more than to have the matter brought to this issue whether the doctrines of the Reformed or the Romish Church do agree best with the Primitive? Since, for reasons well known to themselves and very much suspected by others, they are so willing to go off from Scripture and to decline the judgement of that as incompetent and insufficient in most of the controversies between us, we are very ready to leave them to be decided by any other indifferent arbitrator. For we think it is a little odd and unreasonable that they should make themselves the only judges of what is in difference between us; and therefore we are very ready to stand to the award and umpirage of the Primitive Church, and we are not in the least afraid to venture our whole cause to the sentence and decision of that. For though the Scripture be our only Rule of Faith and Doctrine necessary to be believed by us, because we know of no other revelation but that, and nothing but revelation makes any doctrine necessary to be believed, yet we are very willing to take the sense and meaning of Scripture both from itself and from the Primitive Church too. So, according to Vincentius Lirinensis, to have the line of Scriptural Interpretation be directed by the rule of Ecclesiastical and Catholic judgement; that is, to have the Primitive Church direct us in interpreting Scripture where it stands in need of it, or there is any controversy about its meaning. Let the Scripture, therefore, as sensed by the Primitive Church, and not by the private judgement of any particular man, be allowed and agreed by us to be the Rule of our Faith; and let that be accounted the true Church, whose Faith and Doctrine is most conformable and agreeable with the Primitive.

## No. 71.  SIMON PATRICK

[From *The Second Note of the Church Examined, viz. Antiquity*, pp. 55 f. This essay appeared originally as part of a composite work published in 1687 with the title *The Notes of the Church, as laid down by Cardinal Bellarmine, Examined and Confuted.* Cp. note on No. **70**.]

The Religion of the Church of England, by Law established, is the true Primitive Christianity; in nothing new, unless it be in rejecting all that novelty which hath been brought into the Church. But they [*i.e.* the Roman Catholics] are the cause of that. For if they had not introduced new Articles, we should not have had occasion for such Articles of Religion as condemn them. Which cannot indeed be old because the doctrines they condemn are new, though the principle upon which we condemn them is as old as Christianity,—we esteeming all to be new, which was not from the beginning. . . .

And who dare say that this is a new Religion, which is as old as Christ and His Apostles? With whom whosoever agree, they are truly ancient Churches, though of no longer standing than yesterday; as they that disagree with them are new, though they can run up their pedigree to the very Apostles.

# (3) COUNCILS

## No. 72.  RICHARD FIELD

[From *Of the Church*, Book V, chs. xlviii–lii (in part).  Ed. Ecclesiastical History Society, Cambridge, 1852, Vol. IV, pp. 2–11, 15, 16–18, 24, 43 f., 45–48, 51, 59–63, 64 f., 66 f.  This classic was first published in 1606 with the title *Of the Church, Five Books by Richard Field, Doctor of Divinity*, though in actual fact the original edition contained only four books.  The fifth and last book did not appear until 1610.  The author was a personal friend of Hooker, and Field's work can claim a place in English theology hardly less exalted than the *Ecclesiastical Polity*.  Though Field's mind was less philosophical than Hooker's, he thought deeply about the principles of theology, and his style, if not so distinguished as that of Hooker, is much easier.  When a friend attempted to discourage Field from embarking on his work on the ground that he was provoking a controversy of which the issue might be doubtful, he observed " I will so write, as they shall have no great mind to answer me " (ed. *E. H. S.*, Vol. I, p. xii).]

WHEREFORE now it remaineth that we speak of General Councils. Wherein first, we are to consider the utility and necessity of such synodal assemblies and meetings ; secondly, of whom they must consist ; thirdly, what assurance they have of Divine assistance and direction ; and fourthly, who must call them.

Touching the first, the causes why General Councils are called are three.  The first is, the suppressing of new heresies, formerly not condemned.  The second, a general and uniform reformation of abuses crept into the Church.  The third, the taking away of schisms grown into patriarchical Churches, about the election of their pastors and the rejecting of intruders, violently and disorderly possessing themselves of those patriarchical thrones.  And so we find that the Council of Nice was called by Constantine, for the suppressing of the damnable heresy of the Arians ; the eighth General Council by Basilius, for the ending of the difference that was grown into the Church of Constantinople about Ignatius and Photius contending for the episcopal chair ; and that all General Councils intended and sought the reformation of abuses, there being scarce any one wherein canons were not made for the reformation of disorders ; insomuch that the fathers of the sixth General Council, having only condemned the heresy of the Monothelites, and made no canons, met afterwards again many of them, and made those canons that are now extant, and are the chief direction of the Greek Church unto this day.  These being the causes for which Councils are called, it is evident that the holding of them is not absolutely and simply necessary, but in a sort only.  For heresies may be suppressed by the concurrence of provincial synods, holden in the several parts of the world, as they were in the first three hundred years, when there were no General Councils : but one part of the Christian Church seeking the help of another in common dangers, and one part readily concurring with another (as for the extinguishing of a dangerous fire threatening all, or the repressing and repelling of a common enemy), by mutual intelligence passing from one to another, they abandoned heresies newly springing up, and preserved the unity of the common faith. Neither was this course holden only in the time of persecution during the first three hundred years, but afterwards also, in the time of the Church's peace, we find the same course to have been followed, in the suppressing of the Pelagians ; and therefore Austin affirmeth that there were but some few heresies of that nature that a General Council of all the Bishops of the East and West was necessarily to be called for the suppressing of them. And indeed we find, that if some five or six heresies have been condemned by the censure of General Councils, an hundred have been suppressed and extinguished by other means. And of those for the condemning whereof General Councils were holden, some were not extinguished for a long time after. For that of the Arians grew stronger after than ever it was before, and those of Nestorius and Eutyches continued some hundreds of years after the ending of those Councils in which they received the sentence of condemnation. How is it then that Isidore saith, the Church before Constantine's time was divided and rent into divers factions and sects, because there was no General Council ? as if there were no other means to preserve unity but General Councils, and that wheresoever they may be had, peace were presently established. For the clearing hereof we say, that such new opinions, as growing up in those times, found a concurring dislike in the several Churches, seeking one to another, were then suppressed, when yet there could be no General Councils, as the heresies of the Marcionites, Valentinians, and the like. But they, wherein there grew difference among the chief pastors and Bishops of the Churches, could not be determined in those times, as the errors of the Millenaries, of those that kept Easter after the Jewish observation, and of those that held the necessity of re-baptizing of such as were baptized by heretics : in which point many worthy pastors and Bishops of the Church did err in the first ages of the Church ; neither could their error be extinguished, as Austin noteth, nor the truth so cleared, as that all dissenters should incur the note of heresy, till the decree of a Council passed about it. *Quaestionis hujus obscuritas*, saith Austin, *prioribus Ecclesiae temporibus ante schisma Donati, magnos viros et magna charitate praeditos, patres et episcopos, ita inter se compulit, salva pace, disceptare et fluctuare, ut diu conciliorum in suis quibusque regionibus diversa statuta nutaverint, donec plenario totius orbis concilio, quod saluberrime sentiebatur, etiam remotis dubitationibus formaretur*, that is, " The obscurity of this question in former ages of the Church, before the schism of Donatus, did cause great men, and fathers, and bishops, endued with great charity, so to strive among themselves, and to waver as doubtful and uncertain without breaking the bond of peace, that for a long time the decrees of Councils in several regions were diverse and different, without any settled certainty; till that which was most wholesomely conceived was fully formed, settled, and established by a plenary Council of the Bishops of the whole world, and no place left for doubting and uncertainty any longer." Thus we see that some heresies may easily be suppressed without troubling all the Bishops of the world to meet in a General Council, and that some others cannot easily be suppressed without General Councils. And as heresies may be suppressed by the mutual concurrence of several Churches, so by the like correspondence, the severity of discipline may be upholden uniformly, and schisms prevented. When Cornelius was elected and ordained Bishop of Rome, at the first, because there was some opposition, Cyprian and others were fearful to write unto him as to the Bishop of Rome. But afterward being fully informed touching the lawfulness of his election and ordination, they rejected his competitors, and communicated with him only; and the like we shall find to have been practised generally by all Bishops, carefully seeking to be certified out of other provinces and parts of the Church, by such Bishops as were known to be Catholics, who came lawfully into places of ministry, and being so come, held the unity of faith and charity, that so they might hold communion with them, and reject those that entered otherwise. Whereupon Cyprian telleth Cornelius, Bishop of Rome, to whom in Africa he might write as to Catholic Bishops, and from whom he might receive letters, as from Catholics. Notwithstanding, General Councils are the best means for preserving of unity of doctrine, severity of discipline, and preventing of schisms when they may be had; and though they be not absolutely necessary to the being of the Church, yet are they most behoveful for the best, readiest, and most gracious governing of the same : and howsoever there may be a kind of exercise of the supreme jurisdiction that is in the Church by the concurrence of particular synods, and the correspondence of several pastors, upon mutual intelligence of the sense, judgement, and resolution of every of them, yet the highest and most excellent exercise of the supreme ecclesiastical jurisdiction is in General Councils. Here the Papists are wont to argue that the Protestants, having no General Councils, have not the exercise of the supreme ecclesiastical jurisdiction, and consequently they are not that Church out of which no salvation is found. But this is a very silly trifling and playing with their own shadows ; neither is it any thing else but a mere abusing of themselves and others, thus idly and fondly to jangle. For first, the Protestants being but a part of the Christian Church, never challenged to themselves the authority that belongeth to the whole, as the Papists do, who, excluding all the Christians of Graecia, Armenia, Russia, and Ethiopia, out of the fellowship and communion of saints, and (as much as in them lieth) casting them into hell, suppose a general meeting of those of their own faction to be a General Council. And secondly, if the Protestants did think themselves to be the whole Church, yet their argument were of no force, seeing the whole Church may be without the benefit of General Councils much longer than the Protestants have been since the division between them and the Papists ; for the Christians of the primitive Church had no General Council for the space of three hundred years after Christ. But to return to the point from which we are a little digressed (occasioned so to do by this frivolous objection of the Papists) touching the good and profitable use of General Councils, there is no difference between us and our adversaries ; but it is agreed on both sides, that though they be not absolutely necessary, yet they are very behoveful, and much to be desired in divers cases. Neither ever was there any man of judgement that thought otherwise. For that which Nazianzen hath, that he never saw good end of any Council, is not to be understood as spoken generally and absolutely, but respectively to the turbulent times wherein he lived, and the Arian faction so prevailed, that many synods were holden for the overthrow of the Nicene faith, without all respect to the good of the Church.

Having spoken of the necessity, profit, and use of General Councils, it remaineth that we proceed to see who they are that may be present in such Councils, and of whom do they consist. The persons that may be present are of divers sorts. For some are there with authority to teach, define, prescribe, and to direct ; others are there to hear, set forward, and consent unto that which is there to be done. In the former sort, none but only ministers of the Word and Sacraments are present in Councils, and they only have deciding and defining voices ; but in the latter sort, laymen also may be present. Whereupon, we shall find that Bishops and Presbyters subscribe in this sort : *Ego N. definiens, subscripsi*, that is, " I, as having power to define and decree, have subscribed." But the Emperor, or any other lay-person, *Ego N. consentiens, subscripsi*, that is, " I, as one giving consent to that which is agreed on by the spiritual pastors, have subscribed." That the Emperor and other laymen of place and sort may be present in General Councils, no man maketh doubt. For though Pope Nicolas seems to deny that the Emperors may be present in other Councils, where matters of faith are not handled, yet he confesseth they may be present in General Councils, where the faith, which is common to all, and pertaineth not to clergymen alone, but to laymen and all Christians generally, is treated of ; it being a rule in nature and reason, *Quod omnes tangit, ab omnibus tractari debere* : that is, that " that which concerneth all, may be handled and meddled with by all," so far forth as conveniently it may, and as there is no manifest reason in respect of the disturbance and hindrance of the deliberation to repel them from such intermeddling. For in such cases there may be a repelling of men having interest in such business and affairs ; and therefore Pulcheria, the Empress, commanded the captain of Bithynia with violence to drive out of the Council of Chalcedon such monks, clerks, and laymen as, being of no use, did but pester the Council, and to leave none there but such as the Bishops brought with them.

But our adversaries say, the Protestants affirm that laymen ought not only to be present in General Councils, but also to have decisive voices, as well as they of the clergy, and thereupon charge us with great absurdity. Wherefore, for the answering of this objection, we must observe that there is a threefold decision of things doubtful and questionable. The one, such as every one upon the knowledge of it must yield unto, upon peril of damnation, upon the bare word of him that decideth. The second, to which every one must yield upon like peril, not upon the bare word of him that decideth, but upon the evidence of proof he bringeth. The third, such as every one must yield unto, not upon peril of damnation, but of excommunication, and the like censure ecclesiastical. In the first sort the Protestants say that only Christ the Son of God hath a decisive voice. In the second sort, that any laymen as well as clergymen ; for whosoever it is that bringeth convincing proofs, decideth a doubt in such sort as that no man ought to resist against it. Whereupon Panormitan saith, that the judgement of one private man is to be preferred before the sentence of the Pope, if he have better authorities of the Old and New Testament to confirm his judgement. And Gerson saith, that any learned man may and ought to resist against a whole Council, if he discern it to err of malice or ignorance ; and whatsoever Bishops determine, their determinations bind not the conscience further than they approve that they propose some other way than by their authority only. So that in this sense the Protestants truly say that Bishops must not proceed praetor-like, but that all that they do must be but in the nature of an inquiry, and their decrees no farther of force than reason doth warrant them. For howsoever the Son of God hath promised to be with His Church to the end of the world, which shall be fulfilled in respect of His elect and chosen who cannot err damnably and finally, yet hath He not tied Himself to any one sort or company of men, neither is it certainly known but that all they that meet in a Council may err, notwithstanding Christ's promise. To which purpose it is that Brentius and others say, we cannot be certain of the determination of Councils, because every company of men professing Christ is not the true Church, seeing that all that so profess are not elect ; neither do they deny all authority and jurisdiction to such as are not known to be elect, nor give it all to such as no man can know who they be (as Bellarmine untruly saith they do), for in the third sort they willingly acknowledge that Bishops have deciding voices and power so to judge of things as to subject all those that shall think and teach otherwise than they do, to excommunication and censures of like nature. And that therefore they are properly judges ; that their course of proceeding is not a bare inquiry and search, but a binding determination, and that they have a praetor-like power to bind men to stand to that they propose and decree ; and in this sort we all teach that laymen have no voice decisive, but Bishops and pastors only ; which may be confirmed by many reasons. First, because, when the question is, in what pastures it is fit the sheep of Christ should feed, and in what pastures they may feed without danger, the duty of consulting is principally, and the power of prescribing wholly, in the pastors ; though the sheep of Christ, being reasonable, have and must have a kind of discerning whether they be directed into wholesome and pleasant pastures or not. Secondly, none but they, whom Paul saith *Christ, going up into heaven, gave for the gathering together of the saints, for the work of the ministry* have authority to teach and to prescribe unto others what they shall profess and believe ; of whom the Lord said by Jeremy the prophet : *I will give you pastors that shall feed you with knowledge and doctrine.* Thirdly, because in all Councils, Bishops and pastors only are found to have subscribed to the decrees made in them, as defining and decreeing ; howsoever other men testified their consent by subscription, and Princes and Emperors, by their Royal authority, confirmed the same, and subjected the contemners and violaters thereof to imprisonment, banishment, confiscation of goods, and the like civil punishments, as the Bishops did to excommunication and censures spiritual.

So that it is agreed on that Bishops and ministers only have decisive voices in Councils, in sort before expressed ; but the question is only whether all ministers of the Word and Sacraments have such decisive voices, or none but Bishops. The Papists think that this is the peculiar right of Bishops. But they are clearly refuted by the universal practice of the whole Church from the beginning. For in all provincial and national synods presbyters did ever give voice and subscribe in the very same sort that Bishops did, whether they were assembled to make canons of discipline, to hear causes, or to define doubtful points of doctrine, as I have before shewed at large ; and that they did not anciently sit and give decisive voices in General Councils, the reason was, not because they have no interest in such deliberations and resolutions, but because, seeing all cannot meet in Councils that have interest in such businesses, but some must be deputed for and authorized by the rest, therefore it was thought fit that Bishops, who are the chiefest among such as have interest in deliberation of this nature, should, in giving decisive voices, supply the places of the rest; especially seeing the manner was ever in all the first Councils that the chief Patriarchs, being acquainted with the matter that should be debated, sent to all the Metropolitans subject to them, who calling provincial synods, consisting of their Bishops and presbyters, discussed such doubts, and then, by common consent, choosing out certain principal Bishops to go to the General Council in their name, sent by them their resolutions. So that in effect, presbyters did subscribe as well as Bishops, seeing they that went and subscribed were not to vary from the instructions they carried with them. . . .

Touching the order that must be kept in General Councils. First, the Book of God must be laid in the midst of them that are present. Secondly, the meeting must be openly and not in secret. Thirdly, it must be free, and every man must be permitted boldly to speak what he thinketh. . . .

Touching the Presidentship of General Councils, it pertained in a sort to all the Patriarchs; and therefore Photius, in his discourse of the seven synods, in divers of them, nameth all the Patriarchs, and their vicegerents, presidents, as having an honourable pre-eminence above and before other Bishops in such assemblies; yet we deny not, but that as these were over all other Bishops, so even amongst these also there was an order, so that one of them had a pre-eminence above and before another. For the Bishop of Alexandria was before the Bishop of Antioch, and the Bishop of Rome before him, anciently, even before the time of the Nicene Council; and afterwards the Bishop of Constantinople, made a Patriarch, was set before the other two, next unto the Bishop of Rome. And as these were thus one before another in order and honour, so they had pre-eminence of honour in synodal assemblies accordingly, in sitting, speaking, and subscribing, though this were not always precisely observed. For in the Council of Nice, there being two ranks of seats, the one in the one side of the hall, and the other in the other, where the Council met, the Emperor sitting in the midst in the upper part of the hall, Eustathius, Bishop of Antioch, sat in the highest seat in that rank that was on the right hand, and made the oration to the Emperor; but in subscribing many were before him. And Hosius, the Bishop of Corduba in Spain, a man of great fame, was chief president, composed the form of faith there agreed on, and subscribed it first, and then, in the second place, the presbyters, that were the vicegerents of the Bishop of Rome, who in respect of his old age could not be present, subscribed to the same form of faith, and after them Alexander, the Bishop of Alexandria. That Hosius was president of the Council of Nice, and of many other Councils besides, we have the testimony of Athanasius. The reason why he, being a Bishop of so mean a place, should be so honoured and set before all other, was the good opinion that all men held of him, being a man famous and renowned throughout the world ; which moved Constantine, after he heard of the differences in the Church of Alexandria between Alexander and Arius, to send him thither before ever he thought of calling this Council, hoping that by his wisdom and authority he might quiet all.   But our adversaries, lest any prejudice might grow to the Church of Rome by this ill precedent of the Council of Nice, in admitting so mean a Bishop to be her president and neglecting the Bishop of Rome, adventure to say, that Hosius was not president in his own right, but as the Bishop of Rome's vicegerent, and supplying his place, though they be no way able to prove the same and the clear evidence of the thing itself reprove them. . . .

So that we find that neither the Bishop of Rome had the president-ship in all Councils, nor that there was any certain and uniform course holden in giving pre-eminences to the chief Bishops in the first seven General Councils. . . .

Having shewed who have decisive voices in General Councils, what presence of Bishops is necessary to the being of them, what order is to be observed in their proceedings, who is president in them, and what his authority is, it remaineth that we proceed to see what assurance they have of finding out the truth, and who is to call them.   Touching the first of these two, some have been of opinion, that the Bishops and Fathers in Councils are so guided by the Spirit of Truth, that their decrees and determinations may be joined to the Canonical Scripture, and reckoned parts of it.   This position Melchior Canus saith [that] a man excellently learned, and that had so profited in divinity that he might be thought matchable with great and eminent divines, feared not to hold in his hearing : and addeth, that Gratian seemeth to have been of the same opinion, where he affirmeth that the Decretal Epistles of Popes are Canonical Scripture, and allegeth Austin for proof thereof. But the same Canus refuteth that opinion as absurd, and sheweth that Gratian mistook St. Austin. . . .

But whatsoever we think of Gratian, we shall find that not only our divines, but the best learned among our adversaries also, put a great difference between the Sacred Scriptures of the Holy Canon and the Decrees of Councils.   For, first they say, the Scripture is the Word of God revealed immediately, and written in a sort from His own mouth ; according to that of St. Peter, *The holy men of God spake as they were moved by the Holy Ghost* ; and that of St. Paul, *All Scripture is by divine inspiration.*   Which is not so to be understood as if always the holy writers had had new revelations, and had always written that which before they were ignorant of : for it is certain that the Evangelists Matthew and John wrote those things which they saw, and Mark and Luke those things they heard from others, as Luke himself confesseth

15

In the beginning of his Gospel. But the holy writers are therefore said to have had immediate revelation and to have written the words of God Himself, because either some new things, and not known before, were revealed to them by God, or because God immediately inspired and moved the writers to write those things which they had seen and heard, and directed them that they should not any way err in writing; whereas Councils neither have nor write immediate revelations or words of God, but only declare which is that Word of God uttered formerly to the Prophets and Apostles, how it is to be understood, and what conclusions may be deduced from it by discourse of reason.

Secondly, the holy writers performed that which they did, without any further labour or travail, than that in writing and calling to mind what they had seen and heard. But in Councils the Bishops and Fathers, with great pain and travail, seek out the truth by discourse, conference, reading and deep meditation; and therefore the holy writers were wont to attribute all to God only, and the Prophets were wont often to repeat, *The Lord saith*.

Thirdly, in the Scriptures, not only the whole sentences, but every word pertaineth to faith: for no word is therein vain or ill-placed. But in Councils there are many disputations going on before resolution, many reasons brought for confirmation of things resolved on, many things added for explication and illustration, many things uttered *obiter* and in passage, that men are not bound to admit as true and right: nay, many things are defined in Councils, that men are not bound to stand unto. For it is the manner of Councils, sometimes to define a thing as certainly and undoubtedly true, pronouncing them heretics that think otherwise, and subjecting them to curse and anathema; and sometimes as probable only, and not certain, as the Council of Vienna decreed that it is more probable that both grace and virtues accompanying grace are infused into infants when they are baptized than when they are not, and yet is this no matter of faith in the Church of Rome.

Fourthly, in the Scripture all things (as well concerning particular persons, as in generality) are undoubtedly true. For it is as certain that Peter and Paul had the Spirit of God as that no man can be saved without the illumination and sanctification of the Spirit. But in the determinations and decrees of Bishops assembled in a General Council, it is not so. For they may err in judging of the persons of men, and therefore there is no absolute certainty in the canonization of saints, as both Thomas and Canus do confess.

Fifthly, in Scriptures there are no precepts touching manners either concerning the whole Church or any part of it, that are not right, equal, and just. But Councils may err, if not in prescribing things evil instead of good, yet in prescribing things not fitting nor expedient, if not to the whole Church, yet to some particular part of it, as not knowing the condition of things therein. Yea, some there are that think it not heretical to believe that General Councils may prescribe some laws to the whole Church that are not right, profitable, and just: as to honour such a one for a saint, who is indeed no saint; to admit such orders of religious men as are not profitable; to receive the communion only in one kind; and the like. And there are many that confidently pronounce that General Councils may decree such things as may breed inconvenience and may savour of too great severity and austerity, which the guides of the Church in the execution of the same must be forced to qualify and temper. So that the only question is, Whether a General Council may certainly define any thing to be true in matter of faith that is false; or command the doing of any act as good and an act of virtue that in deed and in truth is an act of sin. Touching this point, there are that say, that all interpretations of Holy Scriptures agreed on in General Councils, and all resolutions of doubts concerning things therein contained, proceed from the same Spirit from which the Holy Scriptures were inspired; and that therefore General Councils cannot err either in the interpretation of Scriptures or resolving of things doubtful concerning the Faith. But these men should know that though the interpretations and resolutions of Bishops in General Councils proceed from the same Spirit from which the Scriptures were inspired, yet not in the same sort, nor with like assurance of being free from mixture of error. For the Fathers assembled in General Councils do not rely upon immediate revelation in all their particular resolutions and determinations, as the writers of the books of Holy Scripture did, but on their own meditation, search and study, the general assistance of Divine grace concurring with them. . . .

It is no way necessary to think that the Fathers are any otherwise directed by the Spirit of Truth in General Councils than in patriarchical, national, or provincial; seeing General Councils consist of such as come with instructions from provincial, national, and patriarchical synods, and must follow the same in making decrees, as has been shewed before; and, consequently, that they are not led to the finding out of the truth in any special sort or manner beyond the general influence that is required to the performance of every good work. So that as God assisting Christian men in the Church only in a general sort to the performance of the works of virtue, there are even [? ever] some well-doers, and yet no particular man doth always well; and there is no degree or kind of moral virtue commanded in the law but is attained by some one or other, at one time or other, one excelling in one thing, and another in another; yet no particular man, or company of men, hath all degrees and perfections of virtue, as Hierome fitly noteth against the Pelagians. So in like sort God, assisting Christian men in the Church in seeking out the truth only in general sort, as in the performance of the actions of virtue, and not by immediate revelation and inspiration as in the Apostles' times, there are ever some that hold and profess all necessary truth; though no one man or company of men, do find the truth ever, and in all things, nor any assurance can be had of any particular men that they should always hold all necessary truths.

And therefore we may safely conclude that no man can certainly pronounce that whatsoever the greater part of Bishops assembled in a General Council agree on is undoubtedly true. . . .

Yet when there is a lawful General Council according to the former description, to wit, wherein all the Patriarchs are present, either in person or by their deputies, and the synod of Bishops under them signify their opinion, either by such as they send or by their provincial letters, if there appear nothing to us in it that may argue an unlawful proceeding, nor there be no gainsaying of men of worth, place, and esteem, we are so strongly to presume that it is true and right that with unanimous consent is agreed on in such a Council, that we must not so much as profess publicly that we think otherwise, unless we do most certainly know the contrary; yet may we in the secret of our hearts remain in some doubt, carefully seeking by the Scripture and monuments of Antiquity to find out the truth. Neither is it necessary for us expressly to believe whatsoever the Council hath concluded, though it be true, unless by some other means it appear unto us to be true, and we be convinced of it in some other sort than by the bare determination of the Council only. But it sufficeth that we believe it *implicite*, and *in praeparatione animi*, that out of the due respect we bear to the Council's decree we dare not resolve otherwise, and be ready expressly to believe it, if it shall be made to appear unto us. But concerning the General Councils of this sort that hitherto have been holden, we confess that in respect of the matter about which they were called, so nearly and essentially concerning the life and soul of the Christian Faith, and in respect of the manner and form of their proceeding, and the evidence of proof brought in them, they are and ever were expressly to be believed by all such as perfectly understand the meaning of their determination. And that therefore it is not to be marvelled at if Gregory profess that he honoureth the first four Councils as the Four Gospels; and that whosoever admitteth them not, though he seem to be a stone elect and precious, yet he lieth beside the foundation and out of the building. Of this sort there are only six; the First, defining the Son of God to be coessential, coeternal, and coequal with the Father. The Second, defining that the Holy Ghost is truly God, coessential, coeternal, and coequal with the Father and the Son. The Third, the unity of Christ's person. The Fourth, the distinction and diversity of His natures, in and after the personal union. The Fifth, condemning some remains of Nestorianism, more fully explaining things stumbled at in the Council of Chalcedon, and accursing the heresy of Origen and his followers touching the temporal punishments of devils and wicked castaways. And the Sixth, defining and clearing the distinction of operations, actions, powers, and wills in Christ, according to the diversity of His natures. These were all the lawful General Councils (lawful, I say, both in their beginning, and proceeding, and continuance) that ever were holden in the Christian Church touching matters of faith. For the Seventh, which is the Second of Nice, was not called about any question of faith, but of manners; in which our adversaries confess there may be something inconveniently prescribed, and so as to be the occasion of great and grievous evils; and surely that is our conceit of the Seventh General Council, the Second of Nice: for howsoever it condemn the religious adoration and worshipping of pictures and seem to allow no other use of them but that which is historical, yet in permitting men by outward signs of reverence and respect towards the pictures of saints to express their love towards them, and the desire they have of enjoying their happy society, and in condemning so bitterly such as upon dislike of abuses wished there might be no pictures in the Church at all, it may seem to have given some occasion and to have opened the way unto that gross idolatry which afterwards entered into the Church. The Eighth General Council was not called about any question of faith or manners, but to determine the question of right between Photius and Ignatius, contending about the Bishopric of Constantinople. So that there are but Seven General Councils that the whole Church acknowledgeth called to determine faith and manners. For the rest that were holden afterwards, which our adversaries would have to be accounted general, they are not only rejected by us, but by the Grecians also, as not general, but patriarchical only; because either they consisted only of the Western Bishops, without any concurrence of those of the East, or, if any were present (as in the Council of Florence there were), they consented to those things which they agreed unto, rather out of other respects than any matter of their own satisfaction. And therefore, howsoever we dare not pronounce that lawful General Councils are free from danger of erring (as some of our adversaries do), yet do we more honour and esteem, and more fully admit all the General Councils that ever hitherto have been holden, than they do; who fear not to charge some of the chiefest of them with error, as both the Second, and the Fourth, for equalling the Bishop of Constantinople to the Bishop of Rome; which I think they suppose to have been an error in faith.

From the assurance of truth which lawful General Councils have, let us proceed to see by whom they are to be called. The state of the Christian Church, the good things it enjoyeth, and the felicity it promiseth, being spiritual, is such that it may stand, though not only forsaken, but grievously oppressed, by the great men of the world, and doth not absolutely depend on the care of such as manage the great affairs of the world and direct the outward course of things here below. And therefore it is by all resolved on that the Church hath her guides and rulers distinct from them that bear the sword, and that there is in the Church a power of convocating these her spiritual pastors to consult of things concerning her welfare, though none of the princes of the world do favour her nor reach forth unto her their helping hands. Neither need we to seek far to find in whom this power resteth.   For there is no question but that this power is in them that are first, and before other, in each company of spiritual pastors and ministers ; seeing none other can be imagined from whom each action of consequence, and each common deliberation should take beginning but they who are in order, honour, and place before other, and to whom the rest that govern the Church in common have an eye, as to them that are first in place among them.   Hereupon we shall find that the calling of Diocesan Synods pertaineth to the Bishop ;  of Provincial, to the Metropolitan ; of National, to the Primate ;  and of Patriarchical, to the Patriarch ; in that they are in order, honour, and place before the rest ;  though some of these (as Bellarmine truly noteth) have no commanding authority over the rest. . . .

That we may see to whom the calling of General Councils doth pertain in the times of persecution, and when there are no Christian Princes, we must observe that among the Patriarchs, though one be in order before another (as the Patriarch of Alexandria is before the Patriarch of Antioch and the Patriarch of Rome before the Patriarch of Alexandria) yet is not one of them superior to another in degree, as Bishops are to Presbyters, nor so in order, honour, and place, as Metropolitans are to Bishops, or Patriarchs to Metropolitans, whom they are to ordain, or at the least to confirm ; and therefore no one of them singly and by himself alone hath power to call unto him any Patriarch, or any Bishop subject to such Patriarch ;  but as in case when there groweth a difference between the Patriarchs of one see and another, or between any of the Patriarchs and the Metropolitans and Bishops subject to them, the superior Patriarch, not of himself alone, but with his Metropolitans and such particular Bishops as are interested, may judge and determine the differences between them, if without danger of a further rent it may be done (as in the case of Chrysostom and Theophilus it could not) ; so if there be any matter of faith, or any thing concerning the whole state of the Christian Church, wherein a common deliberation of all the pastors of the Church is necessary, he that is in order the first among the Patriarchs, with the synods of Bishops subject to him, may call the rest together as being the principal part of the Church, whence all actions of this nature do take beginning. . . .

Thus we see to whom the calling of Councils pertaineth when there is no Christian magistrate to assist the Church. But when there is a Christian magistrate, it pertaineth to him to see that these assemblies be duly holden accordingly as the necessity of the Church requireth and the canons prescribe. And therefore we shall find, that though Christian Emperors, Kings, and Princes, within their several dominions, oftentimes permitted Bishops, Metropolitans, and Patriarchs to hold Episcopal, Provincial, National, or Patriarchical Councils, without particular intermeddling therein, when they saw neither negligence in those of the clergy in omitting to hold such Councils when it was fit, nor intrusion into their office; yet, so often as they saw cause, they took into their own hands the power of calling these more particular synods. And, touching General, there was never any that was not called by the Emperor.

## No. 73. WILLIAM LAUD

[From *A Relation of the Conference between William Laud and Mr. Fisher the Jesuit*, Section XXXIII. Ed. C. H. Simpkinson (1901), pp. 263–271; 278–280; 288 f. Cp. note on No. **54**.]

Upon this occasion, I shall not hold it amiss a little more at large to consider the point of General Councils. How they may or may not err; and a little to look into the Roman and Protestant opinion concerning them; Which is more agreeable to the power and rule which Christ hath left in His Church; and, Which is most preservative of peace established, or ablest to reduce perfect unity into the Church of Christ, when that poor ship hath her ribs dashed in sunder by the waves of contention. And this I will adventure to the world, but only in the nature of a consideration, and with submission to my mother, the Church of England, and the mother of us all, the Universal Catholic Church of Christ: as I do most humbly all whatsoever else is herein contained.

First, then, I consider, Whether all the power that an Ecumenical Council hath to determine, and all the assistance it hath not to err in that determination, it hath it not all from the Catholic Universal Body of the Church, and clergy in the Church, whose representative it is? And it seems it hath. For the government of the Church being not monarchical, but as Christ is Head, this principle is inviolable in nature;—Every body collective that represents, receives power and privileges from the body which is represented; else a representation might have force without the thing it represents, which cannot be. So there is no power in the council, no assistance to it, but what is in and to the Church. But yet then it may be questioned, Whether the representing body hath all the power, strength, and privilege which the represented hath? And suppose it hath all the legal power, yet it hath not all the natural, either of strength or wisdom, that the whole hath. Now, because the representative hath power from the whole—

and the main body can meet no other way—therefore the acts, laws, and decrees of the representative, be it ecclesiastical or civil, are binding in their strength; but they are not so certain, and free from error, as is that wisdom which resides in the whole: for in assemblies merely civil, or ecclesiastical, all the able and sufficient men cannot be in the body that represents. And it is as possible so many able and sufficient men, for some particular business, may be left out, as that they which are in may miss or misapply that reason and ground upon which the determination is principally to rest. Here, for want of a clear view of this ground, the representative body errs; whereas the represented, by virtue of those members which saw and knew the ground, may hold the principle inviolated.

Secondly, I consider, That since it is thus in nature and in civil bodies, if it be not so in ecclesiastical too, some reason must be given why; "for that body also consists of men"; those men, neither, all equal in their perfections of knowledge and judgements, whether acquired by industry, or rooted in nature, or infused by God; not all equal, nor any one of them perfect and absolute, or freed from passion and human infirmities. Nor doth their meeting together make them infallible in all things; though the act which is hammered out by many together must in reason be perfecter than that which is but the child of one man's sufficiency. If, then, a General Council have no ground of not erring from the men or the meeting, either it must not be at all, or it must be by some assistance and power upon them when they are so met together; and this, if it be less than the assistance of the Holy Ghost, it cannot make them secure against error.

Thirdly, I consider, That the assistance of the Holy Ghost is without error. That is no question; and as little there is, That a council hath it. But the doubt that troubles is, Whether all assistance of the Holy Ghost be afforded in such a high manner as to cause all the definitions of a Council in matters fundamental in the Faith, and in remote deductions from it, to be alike infallible?

Now the Romanists, to prove there is "infallible assistance," produce some places of Scripture; but no one of them infers, much less enforces, an infallibility. The places which Stapleton there rests upon, are these: *I will send you the Spirit of Truth, which will lead you into all truth.* And, *This Spirit shall abide with you for ever.* And, *Behold, I am with you to the end of the world.* To these others add, *The founding of the Church upon the rock, against which the gates of hell shall not prevail.* And Christ's prayer for St. Peter, *That his faith fail not.* And Christ's promise, *that where two or three are gathered in His name, He will be in the midst of them.* And that in the *Acts, It seemed good to the Holy Ghost and to us.*

For the first, which is, *leading into all truth*, and that *for ever*, " all," is not always universally taken in Scripture. Nor is it here simply for *all truth* : for then a General Council could no more err in matter of fact than in matter of faith, in which yet yourselves grant it may err. But *into all truth* is a limited *all* :—*into all truth absolutely necessary to salvation*, and this, when they suffer themselves to be led by the Blessed Spirit, by the Word of God ; and all truth which. Christ had before, at least fundamentally, delivered unto them : *He shall receive of Mine, and show it unto you.* And again, *He shall teach you all things, and bring all things to your remembrance, which I have told you.* And for this necessary truth, too, the Apostles received this promise, " not for themselves and a council, but for themselves and the whole Catholic Church," of which a council, be it never so general, is a very little part. Yea, and this very assistance is not so absolute, nor in that manner to the whole Church, as it was to the Apostles ; neither doth Christ in that place speak directly of a council, but of His Apostles' preaching and doctrine.

As for Christ's *being with them unto the end of the world*, the Fathers are so various that, in the sense of the ancient Church, we may understand Him present in majesty, in power, in aid and assistance against the difficulties they should find for preaching Christ ; which is the native sense, as I take it : and this promise was made to support their weakness. As for His presence " in teaching by the Holy Ghost," few mention it ; and no one of them which doth, speaks of any infallible assistance, farther than the succeeding Church keeps to the word of the Apostles, as the Apostles kept to the guidance of the Spirit. Besides, the Fathers refer their speech to the Church Universal, not to any council or representative body. And Maldonate adds, " That this His presence by teaching is, or may be, a collection from the place, but is not the intention of Christ."

For *the rock upon which the Church is founded*, which is the next place, we dare not lay any other foundation than Christ : Christ laid His Apostles, no question, but upon Himself. With these St. Peter was laid, no man questions, and in prime place of order (Would his claiming successors be content with that ?), as appears and divers Fathers witness, by his particular designment, *Tu es Petrus*. But yet the *rock* even there spoken of is not St. Peter's person, either only or properly, but the faith which he professed. And to this, besides the evidence which is in text and truth, the Fathers come in with very full consent. And this *that the gates of hell shall not prevail against it* is not spoken of the not erring of the Church principally, but of the not falling away of it from the foundation. Now, a Church may err, and dangerously too, and yet not fall from the foundation, especially if that of Bellarmine be true, " that there are many things, even *de fide*, ' of the faith,' which yet are not necessary to salvation." Besides, even here again, the promise of this stable edification is to the whole Church, not to a council; at least no farther than a council builds as a Church is built—that is, upon Christ. . . .

And for all the places together, weigh them with indifferency, and either they speak of the Church, including the Apostles, as all of them do—and then, all grant the voice of the Church is God's voice, divine and infallible;—or else they are general, unlimited, and appliable to private assemblies as well as General Councils, which none grant to be infallible but some mad enthusiasts;—or else they are limited, not simply into "all truth," but "all necessary to salvation"; in which I shall easily grant a General Council cannot err, suffering itself to be led by this Spirit of Truth in the Scripture, and not taking upon it to lead both the Scripture and the Spirit. For, suppose these places or any other did promise assistance, even to infallibility, yet they granted it not to every General Council, but to the Catholic body of the Church itself; and if it be in the whole Church principally, then is it in a General Council but by consequent, as the Council represents the whole. And that which belongs to a thing by consequent doth not otherwise nor longer belong unto it than it consents and cleaves to that upon which it is a consequent. And therefore a General Council hath not this assistance, but as it keeps to the whole Church and Spouse of Christ, whose it is to hear His Word and determine by it. And therefore if a General Council will go out of the Church's way, it may easily go without the Church's truth.

Fourthly, I consider, that all agree, That the Church in general can never err from the faith necessary to salvation; no persecution, no temptation, no *gates of Hell*, whatsoever is meant by them, can ever so *prevail against it*. For all the members of the militant Church cannot err, either in the whole faith, or in any article of it; it is impossible. For if all might so err, there could be no union between them as members and Christ the Head; and no union between head and members, no body; and so no Church; which cannot be. But there is not the like consent, That General Councils cannot err. And it seems strange to me, the Fathers having to do with so many heretics, and so many of them opposing Church authority, that in the condemnation of those heretics, this proposition, even in terms, "A General Council cannot err," should not be found in any one of them, that I can yet see. Now suppose it were true, that no General Council had erred in any matter of moment to this day—which will not be found true—yet this would not have followed, That it is therefore infallible, and cannot err. I have no time to descend into particulars; therefore to the general, still. St. Augustine puts a difference between the rules of Scripture and the definitions of men. This difference is, *Praeponitur Scriptura*, " That the Scripture hath the prerogative." That prerogative is, " That whatsoever is found written in Scripture may neither be doubted nor disputed whether it be true or right. But the letters of Bishops may not only be disputed, but corrected, by Bishops that are more learned and wise than they, or by National Councils; and National Councils, by Plenary or General; and even Plenary Councils themselves may be amended, the former by the later." It seems it was no news with St. Augustine, that a General Council might err; and therefore inferior to the Scripture, which may neither be doubted nor disputed where it affirms. And if it be so with the " definition " of a Council too, as Stapleton would have it, that that may neither be doubted not disputed, where is then the Scripture's prerogative ? . . .

Your fellows tell us, and you can affirm no more, " That the voice of the Church determining in Council is not human, but divine." That is well; " divine," then sure " infallible " : yea, but the proposition sticks in the throat of them that would utter it. It is not divine simply, but " in a manner divine." Why, but then, sure, not " infallible," because it may speak loudest in that manner in which it is not divine. Nay more: " The Church, forsooth, is an infallible foundation of faith, in a higher kind than the Scripture: for the Scripture is but a foundation in testimony, and matter to be believed, but the Church as [is?] the efficient cause of faith, and in some sort the very formal." Is not this blasphemy ? Doth not this knock against all evidence of truth, and his own grounds that says it ? Against all evidence of truth: for in all ages, all men that once admitted the Scripture to be the Word of God, as all Christians do, do with the same breath grant it most undoubted and infallible. But all men have not so judged of the Church's definitions, though they have in greatest obedience submitted to them. And against his own grounds that says it: for the Scripture is absolutely and every way divine; the Church's definition is but *suo modo*, " In a sort or manner," divine. But that which is but in a sort can never be a foundation in a higher degree than that which is absolute and every way such. Therefore neither can the definition of the Church be so infallible as the Scripture, much less *in altiori genere*, " in a higher kind," than the Scripture. But because, when all other things fail, you fly to this, That the Church's definition in a General Council is by inspiration, and so divine and infallible, my haste shall not carry me from a little consideration of that too.

Sixthly, then, if the definition of a General Council be infallible then the infallibility of it is either in the conclusion, and in the means that prove it; or in the conclusion, not the means; or in the means, not the conclusion. But it is infallible in none of these. Not in the first—the conclusion and the means: for there are divers deliberations in General Councils, where the conclusion is Catholic, but the means by which they prove it not infallible. Not in the second—the conclusion and not the means: for the conclusion must follow the nature of the premises or principles out of which it is deduced; therefore if those which the Council uses be sometimes uncertain, as is proved before, the conclusion cannot be infallible. Not in the third—the means and not the conclusion: for that cannot but be true and necessary, if the means be so. And this I am sure you will never grant; because if you should, you must deny the infallibility which you seek to establish.

## No. 74. WILLIAM LAUD

[From *A Relation of the Conference between William Laud and Mr. Fisher the Jesuit*, Section XXVII. Ed. C. H. Simpkinson (1901), pp. 244–247. Cp. note on No. **54**.]

It is true that you [*i.e.* Fisher] replied for the Council of Trent; and my answer was, not only that the Council was not legal in the necessary conditions to be observed in a General Council, but also that it was no General Council, which again you are content to omit. Consider it well. First, Is that Council legal, the abettors whereof maintain publicly that it is lawful for them to conclude any controversy, and make it be *de fide*, and so in your judgement fundamental, though it have not—I do not say now, the written Word of God for warrant, either in express letter or necessary sense and deduction (as all unerring Councils have had, and as all must have that will not err), but—not so much as probable testimony from it, nay, quite *extra*, "without" the Scripture? Nay, secondly, Is that Council legal where the Pope, the chief person to be reformed, shall sit president in it, and be chief judge in his own cause, against all law, divine, natural, and human? In a place not free, but in, or too near, his own dominion? To which all were not called that had deliberative or consultative voice? In which none had suffrage but such as were sworn to the Pope and the Church of Rome, and professed enemies to all that called for reformation or a free council? And the Pope himself, to show his charity, had declared and pronounced the appellants heretics, before they were condemned by the Council? I hope an assembly of enemies are no lawful council; and I think the decrees of such a one are *omni jure nulla*, and carry their nullity with them through all law.

Again: Is that Council general, that hath none of the Eastern Churches' consent, nor presence there? Are all the Greeks so become *non ecclesia*, "no church," that they have no interest in General Councils? It numbers, indeed, among the subscribers six Greeks. They might be so by nation, or by title, purposely given them; but dare you say they were actually Bishops of, and sent from, the Greek

Church to the Council? Or is it to be accounted a General Council, that in many sessions had scarce ten Archbishops, or forty or fifty Bishops, present? And for the West of Christendom, nearer home, it reckons one English, St. Asaph. But Cardinal Poole was there too; and English indeed he was by birth, but not sent to that Council by the King and Church of England, but as one of the Pope's legates; and so we find him in the Fifth Session of that Council, but neither before nor after. And at the beginning of the Council he was not Bishop in the Church of England; and after he was Archbishop of Canterbury, he never went over to the Council. And can you prove that St. Asaph went thither by authority? There were but few of other nations, and, it may be, some of them reckoned with no more truth than the Greeks. In all the sessions under Paul the Third, but two Frenchmen, and sometimes none—as in the sixth under Julius the Third, when Henry the Second of France protested against that Council; and in the end it is well known how all the French, which were then a good part, held off till the Cardinal of Lorraine was got to Rome. As for the Spaniards, they laboured for many things upon good grounds, and were most unworthily overborne.

### No. 75. THOMAS BARLOW

[From *A Few Plain Reasons Why a Protestant of the Church of England should not turn Roman Catholic*, by 'A Real Catholic of the Church of England.' London, 1688, pp. 8 f., 11. This pamphlet was published anonymously.]

That a General Council is not infallible is a truth from many cogent and undeniable reasons so evident that as there is no need I should, so it is not my purpose to say much. Only I shall, in short, say a few things and refer them to your prudence to make use of all or any of them as to you, circumstances considered, may seem convenient. Here then I desire it may be considered.

1. That a General Council is never so much as named in Scripture, nor any promise of Infallibility given to it. The Council of the Apostles (which was no General Council) was Infallible and might truly say *Sic visum est Spiritui Sancto et nobis*, because the Apostles had the infallible assistance of the Holy Ghost. But that any General Council had any such assistance truly to say after their decrees, *Sic visum est Spiritui Sancto et nobis*,—though that of Trent and others do vainly pretend to it,—is an assertion without all proof or probability.

2. But there is no necessity of such an infallible guide as a General Council; because Christians for several ages have attained Heaven and eternal Salvation who never had any General Council to be their guide. For it is certain and on all sides confessed, that the first Nicene Council, which was held *Anno Christi* 325, was the first General Council the Christian Church ever had. Now I desire to know—and you may ask

those who endeavour to seduce your parishioners,—whether the Christians in those 325 years when there was no General Council were saved or not? If they were saved, then it is evident that a General Council is not necessary to guide us to Heaven, seeing Christians for 325 years obtained salvation, yet in all that time there was no General Council to guide them.

But if it be said Christians, for want of a General Council to guide them, were not saved in those three centuries, then

3. They contradict the sense of Christendom and the constant testimony of Fathers and historians, who universally tell us of thousands not only of pious Christians but of many hundred thousands of pious confessors and martyrs. Now to say that they were not saved, who laid down their lives for Christ and His Gospel, is such an uncharitable and unchristian censure as no sober Christian ever did or, I believe, ever will be guilty of. . . .

4. Is it not irrational for them to boast of the Infallibility of their General Councils, when their greatest writers and publishers of their councils ridiculously contradict themselves and give us this distinction of General Councils;—1. *Generalia Concilia approbata;* 2. *Concilia Generalia reprobata;* 3. *Concilia Generalia partim appro-bata, partim reprobata;* 4. *Concilium Generale nec approbatum, nec reprobatum?*[1] They mean[2] the first of Pisa, about the year 1409, which they will not approve nor reject. In short, if General Councils may be reprobate and rejected, then sure they are not infallible.

### No. 76. JEREMY TAYLOR

[From *A Dissuasive from Popery, Part II.* Book I. § 1, *Works*, ed. R. Heber, Vol. X, p. 358 (ed. C. P. Eden, Vol. VI, p. 360). Cp. note on No. **50**.]

The Church of England receives the four first Generals [*i.e.* General Councils] as of highest regard, not that they are infallible, but that they have determined wisely and holily.

### No. 77. ROBERT NELSON

[From *Life of Bull*, Section 53, Bull's *Works*, ed. Oxford, 1827, pp. 250–256. Robert Nelson, who became a Non-juror, was a pupil of George Bull, and on Bull's death in 1710 undertook to write his life. The work was published in 1713. It was Nelson who had sent to Bossuet the copy of Bull's *Judicium Ecclesiae Catholicae* which led to the incident referred to in our note on No. **109**. Nelson's *Life* can claim a place among the most notable of the biographies of the Seventeenth-Century Divines. It criticized the use made by Samuel Clarke of Bull's *Defensio*, and thus involved Nelson in a controversy with him.]

It is hence plain that the late Bishop of Meaux [*i.e.* J. B. Bossuet], with whom I had the honour to be acquainted and who is known to have had a particular esteem for our author [*i.e.* Bishop Bull], is mistaken

---

[1] Cp. Bellarmine, *De Conciliis*, etc. Book I, chs. 6, 7.
[2] [*I.e.*, by the last of these distinctions.]

in supposing him to hold the *infallibility* of this Council of Nice; for had the Bishop but proved this once, all that Mr. Bull had written in defence of the Faith there established would have been altogether superfluous.

He had, it is true, a very great regard for Councils truly General, and in particular for the *Nicene* and the *Constantinopolitan*, not seeing any sufficient reason to object against their testimony: whence, allowing them to be competent witnesses of the faith and practice of the Church at that time, as in the several parts of it acknowledged and received, he concluded that the solemn attestation of above three hundred witnesses at once must needs be more authoritative than the single asseveration of here and there one occasionally, and perhaps not accurately expressing himself. For having in his *Proœmium* taken notice, that the matter treated of in this first General Council was the capital article of the whole Christian religion, namely the Divinity of our Saviour's Person, as whether He were truly God, or only a creature, he addeth, " If in a question of so vast importance as this, we can imagine that all the governors of the Church could fall into error so prodigiously, and deceive the people under them, how shall we be able to vindicate the veracity of our Blessed Lord, promising to be with His Apostles and in them with their successors to the end of the world? A promise which could not be true, seeing the Apostles were not to live so long, unless their successors be here comprehended in the persons of the Apostles themselves." Which he afterwards confirmeth, by a passage out of Socrates concerning some of the devout Fathers of this Council, which saith, that *even the unlearned* (ἰδιῶται) *of the Council were illuminated by God, and the grace of the Holy Ghost, so as they could not depart from the truth.* Whereupon the late Bishop of Meaux, reciting this and the former passage, doth triumph over his adversary not a little, whom he sendeth to be instructed by our author, in the infallibility of the Council of Nice, in order to bring in that of Trent. For the Bishop, concluding it to be our author's opinion that it was impossible for the Fathers of that Council to fall into error, because they were enlightened with the light of God's Spirit, without attending as he ought to what went before, and to what followeth afterwards, which might have undeceived him, he inferreth, " Hence he [Mr. Bull] shews at once the Infallibility of General Councils, both by Scripture and by the tradition of the ancient Church: God bless [continueth he] the learned Bull, and reward him for this sincere confession as also for the zeal which he hath made appear in defending the Godhead of Jesus Christ: may he be delivered from those prejudices which hinder him from opening his eyes to the lights of the Catholic Church and to the necessary consequences of the truth by him confessed." Thus far the Bishop.

Now the plain truth of the matter is no more than this. The aforementioned author [Daniel Zuicker] of the *Irenicum Irenicorum* had the confidence to call the Nicene Fathers *Novae fidei conditores* and by such other names, and by a great number of passages collected out of the more ancient Fathers had undertaken to make good his charge ; Curcellaeus, writing his *Quaternio* immediately after him, had therein declared that these testimonies did seem to him unanswerable, as to the preeminence at least of the Father above the Son ; Sandius had gone yet much farther, labouring to heap up all the scandal that was possible against this Council ; and many others of inferior name, borrowing their weapons from these authors, had been pelting at it as hard as they could. All which our Mr. Bull knew not how to digest, he saith ; but as often as he considered the incredibility that such a number of the pastors of this Church, met together from all the parts of the world where Christianity was planted, could in a matter of the greatest moment, even in the very foundation itself of Christian faith and worship, be either deceived or deceivers ; or that Christ should not so far remember His promise, as by His Spirit to abide with the Apostles and their successors to the end of the world, so as to guard them at least from laying another foundation than what He Himself had laid ; but reflecting hereupon, could not forbear expressing a sort of horror and indignation, for *their stupendous ignorance, or rather, impious madness, who were not afraid furiously to rail at those venerable Fathers in public, as if they had either maliciously or ignorantly corrupted the Catholic doctrine concerning Christ, which was taught by the Apostles, and constantly professed in the Church for three centuries, and had imposed a new faith upon the Christian world.* This was so very shocking to all pious ears, in the opinion of Mr. Bull, that he could not bear the thoughts of it with any patience ; and thence he falleth sometimes into expressions, that to some will seem to have more of fire in them than they ought to have, when he is speaking of these men, whom he considereth as the professed adversaries to the dignity and prerogative of our Saviour, and who are treated accordingly by him every where as such. And whereas Sabinus the Macedonian had anciently attacked the credit of this Council, by disparaging the Fathers that sat in it for a company of rude and illiterate persons, who understood not what they came thither about (though by the account which Eusebius hath given, we may be certain there were not wanting in it men of sense and capacity), Mr. Bull thought it not amiss to answer Sabinus and his followers in the very words which the historian Socrates had done before ; thereby implying, that notwithstanding they might be simple and plain persons, without much learning, yet they were never the worse witnesses for that, and especially since it was piously credible, that God would also readily assist their honest endeavours after the truth, and preserve them by His grace from falling into any pernicious mistake, wherein the whole Church would necessarily be involved.

Neither did Mr. Bull say, that he was of the opinion of Socrates, but only did declare what he took to be his meaning, which yet doth not come up at all to that of the Bishop of Meaux. And having told this, Mr. Bull then concludeth : " But if any be not willing to admit this hypothesis [of the illuminating grace of the Holy Spirit, assisting a Council of Bishops that is *truly universal* in the *necessary* articles of faith] the argument of Socrates may be put into this form following : Suppose the *Nicene* Fathers to have been never so ignorant and unlearned, yet the greatest part of them were pious men : and it is unreasonable to believe, that so many holy and approved men, being met together out of all parts of the Christian world, could wickedly conspire together to innovate the publicly received faith in the very principal article of Christianity ; it being not possible to suppose that the simplest there could be·so very ignorant as not to understand the very first rudiments concerning the Holy Trinity, which were wont to be delivered to the very catechumens, or not to know what they themselves had received concerning it from their predecessors." Since how defective soever they might be in any other part of knowledge, he concluded it impossible for them to be uninstructed in the first and most fundamental doctrine of their religion. This was then, and continued afterwards, to be the true sense of our author concerning *General Councils*, and in particular concerning this of *Nice* : let the advocates of the Church of Rome make the best of it they can. And if this be not thought a sufficient vindication, taken from the very book itself by the Bishop appealed to, let the reader farther consider that it is the whole scope of his most learned defence of the First General Council to shew that the Fathers thereof did not err in the determination of the article by them examined, both because this their determination was supported by the more ancient testimonies of their predecessors, and because it was morally impossible for them, under their circumstances, to have erred therein ; and much less for them to have conspired amongst themselves, to change and new model the faith, which had been universally received in all the churches. All which would have been perfectly needless, had he designed to prove the infallibility of this Council ; for this once proved, all the rest must have been a superfluous labour, and consequently his whole book would have been to no purpose. Nay, even supposing that he was fully of the opinion that there is an infallible assistance of the Holy Spirit which attendeth every Council that is truly General, so as to keep them from erring in matters of faith, yet could he not, for this, be ever the nearer to the Church of Rome, or to the communion of the Gallican

16

Bishop, as that Church is at present limited by the Council of Trent;
since in the very same premonition he afterwards saith expressly
*That the Trent Convention is to be called by any other name, rather than
by that of a General Council*; and greatly complaineth of such Romish
writers and advocates for the decrees thereof, as make no conscience
of building up thereby there [? their] pseudo-Catholic Faith, upon
the ruins of the truly Catholic Faith. Nothing in the world can be
more express than this, especially all things being laid together. But
if to any one this be not yet satisfactory, let him but for his farther
information carefully read over his whole introduction, and our author's
answer to the Bishop of Meaux's queries, printed in the first volume
of Dean Hickes's Controversial Letters.

# (4) THE BOOK OF COMMON PRAYER

## No. 78.  THE BOOK OF COMMON PRAYER

[The 'Preface' to the *Book of Common Prayer* (1661). This was in the main the work of Robert Sanderson, though it was revised by a committee of Bishops. See Izaak Walton's *Life of Sanderson* (ed. "World's Classics," p. 405); and cp. E. Cardwell, *Synodalia*, Vol. II, p. 655. The Preface sets out the principles upon which the revision made at the Savoy Conference had been carried through.]

IT hath been the wisdom of the Church of England, ever since the first compiling of her Public Liturgy, to keep the mean between the two extremes of too much stiffness in refusing, and of too much easiness in admitting, any variation from it.  For, as on the one side common experience sheweth, that where a change hath been made of things advisedly established (no evident necessity so requiring) sundry inconveniences have thereupon ensued ; and those many times more and greater than the evils, that were intended to be remedied by such change ; so on the other side, the particular forms of Divine worship, and the Rites and Ceremonies appointed to be used therein, being things in their own nature indifferent and alterable, and so acknowledged, it is but reasonable that upon weighty and important considerations, according to the various exigency of times and occasions, such changes and alterations should be made therein, as to those that are in place of Authority should from time to time seem either necessary or expedient. Accordingly we find, that in the reigns of several Princes of blessed memory since the Reformation, the Church, upon just and weighty considerations her thereunto moving, hath yielded to make such alterations in some particulars as in their respective times were thought convenient ; yet so as that the main body and essentials of it (as well in the chiefest materials, as in the frame and order thereof) have still continued the same unto this day, and do yet stand firm and unshaken, notwithstanding all the vain attempts and impetuous assaults made against it, by such men as are given to change, and have always discovered a greater regard to their own private fancies and interests than to that duty they owe to the public.

By what undue means and for what mischievous purposes the use of the Liturgy (though enjoined by the Laws of the Land, and those Laws never yet repealed) came, during the late unhappy confusions, to be discontinued, is too well known to the world, and we are not willing here to remember.  But when, upon His Majesty's happy Restoration, it seemed probable that, amongst other things, the use of the Liturgy also would return of course (the same having never been legally abolished) unless some timely means were used to prevent it, those men who under the late usurped powers had made it a great part of their business to render the people disaffected thereunto, saw themselves in point of reputation and interest concerned (unless they would freely acknowledge themselves to have erred, which such men are very hardly brought to do) with their utmost endeavours to hinder the restitution thereof. In order whereunto divers pamphlets were published against the *Book of Common Prayer*, the old objections mustered up, with the addition of some new ones, more than formerly had been made, to make the number swell. In fine, great importunities were used to His Sacred Majesty that the said Book might be revised, and such alterations therein and additions thereunto made, as should be thought requisite for the ease of tender consciences. Whereunto His Majesty, out of his pious inclination to give satisfaction (so far as could be reasonably expected) to all his subjects of what persuasion soever, did graciously condescend.

In which review we have endeavoured to observe the like moderation as we find to have been used in the like case in former times. And therefore of the sundry alterations proposed unto us, we have rejected all such as were either of dangerous consequence (as secretly striking at some established doctrine or laudable practice of the Church of England, or indeed of the whole Catholic Church of Christ), or else of no consequence at all but utterly frivolous and vain. But such alterations as were tendered to us (by what persons, under what pretences, or to what purpose soever so tendered) as seemed to us in any degree requisite or expedient, we have willingly and of our own accord assented unto; not enforced so to do by any strength of argument, convincing us of the necessity of making the said alterations; for we are fully persuaded in our judgements (and we here profess it to the world) that the Book as it stood before established by law doth not contain in it any thing contrary to the Word of God or to sound doctrine, or which a godly man may not with a good conscience use and submit unto, or which is not fairly defensible against any that shall oppose the same; if it shall be allowed such just and favourable construction as in common equity ought to be allowed to all human writings, especially such as are set forth by authority, and even to the very best translations of the Holy Scripture itself.

Our general aim therefore in this undertaking was, not to gratify this or that party in any their unreasonable demands, but to do that which to our best understandings we conceived might most tend to the preservation of peace and unity in the Church, the procuring of reverence and exciting of piety and devotion in the public worship of God, and the cutting off occasion from them that seek occasion of cavil or quarrel against the Liturgy of the Church. And as to the several variations from the former Book, whether by alteration, addition, or otherwise, it shall suffice to give this general account, That most of the alterations were made, either first, for the better direction of them that are to officiate in any part of Divine Service, which is chiefly done in the Calendars and Rubrics ; or secondly, for the more proper expressing of some words or phrases of ancient usage in terms more suitable to the language of the present times, and the clearer explanation of some other words and phrases that were either of doubtful signification, or otherwise liable to misconstruction ; or thirdly, for a more perfect rendering of such portions of Holy Scripture, as are inserted into the Liturgy ; which, in the Epistles and Gospels especially, and in sundry other places, are now ordered to be read according to the last Translation : and that it was thought convenient, that some Prayers and Thanksgivings fitted to special occasions, should be added in their due places, particularly for those at Sea, together with an Office for the Baptism of such as are of Riper Years : which, although not so necessary when the former Book was compiled, yet by the growth of Anabaptism, through the licentiousness of the late times crept in amongst us, is now become necessary, and may be always useful for the baptizing of natives in our plantations, and others converted to the Faith. If any man, who shall desire a more particular account of the several alterations in any part of the Liturgy, shall take the pains to compare the present Book with the former, we doubt not but the reason of the change may easily appear.

And having thus endeavoured to discharge our duties in this weighty affair, as in the sight of God, and to approve our sincerity therein (so far as lay in us) to the consciences of all men, although we know it impossible (in such variety of apprehensions, humours and interests, as are in the world) to please all, nor can expect that men of factious, peevish, and perverse spirits should be satisfied with anything that can be done in this kind by any other than themselves, yet we have good hope that what is here presented, and hath been by the Convocations of both Provinces with great diligence examined and approved, will be also well accepted and approved by all sober, peaceable, and truly conscientious sons of the Church of England.

## No. 79.  JEREMY TAYLOR

[From *An Apology for Authorized and Set Forms of Liturgy*, Preface, §§ 5–20, 33–37, 47. *Works*, ed. R. Heber, Vol. VII, pp. 286–293, 301–304, 311 f. (ed. C. P. Eden, Vol. V, pp. 233–239, 245–248, 254). The *Apology*, which was first published anonymously in 1646 with the title *A Discourse concerning Prayer Ex Tempore, or by Pretence of the Spirit*, was an attack on the *Directory*, which Parliament had authorized in 1644–5 in substitution for the *Book of Common Prayer*. In 1649, it was reissued with the author's name. The Preface, however, from which all the following extracts are taken, was not added until 1673. Internal evidence indicates that it was written before the Restoration ; and as it is absent from an edition which appeared in 1657, it was written presumably between 1657 and 1660.]

The Liturgy of the Church of England hath advantages so many and so considerable, as not only to raise itself above the devotions of other Churches, but to endear the affections of good people to be in love with liturgy in general.

For to the Churches of the Roman Communion we can say that ours is reformed ; to the Reformed Churches we can say that ours is orderly and decent ; for we were freed from the impositions and lasting errors of a tyrannical spirit, and yet from the extravagancies of a popular spirit too. Our Reformation was done without tumult, and yet we saw it necessary to reform. We were zealous to cast away the old errors, but our zeal was balanced with the consideration and the results of authority : not like women or children when they are affrighted with fire in their clothes ; we shaked off the coal indeed, but not our garments, lest we should have exposed our churches to that nakedness, which the excellent men of our sister-churches complained to be among themselves.

And, indeed, it is no small advantage to our Liturgy that it was the offspring of all that authority, which was to prescribe in matters of religion. The king and the priest, which are the *antistites religionis*, and the preservers of both the tables joined in this work, and the people, as it was represented in Parliament, were advised withal, in authorizing the form after much deliberation ; for the rule, *Quod spectat ad omnes, ab omnibus tractari debet*, was here observed with strictness, and then, as it had the advantages of discourse, so also of authorities,—its reason from one, and its sanction from the other, that it might be both reasonable, and sacred, and free, not only from the indiscretions but (which is very considerable) from the scandal of popularity.

And in this, I cannot but observe the great wisdom and mercy of God in directing the contrivers of the Liturgy with the spirit of zeal and prudence, to allay the furies and heats of the first affrightment. For when men are in danger of burning, so they leap from the flames, they consider not whither, but whence : and the first reflexions of a crooked tree are not to straightness, but to a contrary incurvation. Yet it pleased the Spirit of God so to temper and direct their spirits, that in the first Liturgy of King Edward, they did rather retain something that needed further consideration, than reject any thing that was certainly pious and holy ; and in the second Liturgy, that they might also thoroughly reform, they did cast out something that might, with good profit, have remained, than not satisfy the world of their zeal to reform, of their charity in declining every thing that was offensive, and the clearness of their light in discerning every semblance of error or suspicion in the Roman Church.

The truth is, although they framed the Liturgy with the greatest consideration that could be, by all the united wisdom of this Church and State, yet, as if prophetically to avoid their being charged in after ages with a *crepusculum* of religion, a dark, 'twilight,' imperfect reformation, they joined to their own star all the shining tapers of the other reformed Churches, calling for the advice of the most eminently learned and zealous reformers in other kingdoms, that the light of all together might show them a clear path to walk in. And this their care produced some change ; for, upon the consultation, the first form of King Edward's Service Book was approved with the exception of a very few clauses, which upon that occasion were reviewed and expunged, till it came to that second form and modest beauty it was in the edition of MDLII., and which Gilbertus, a German, approved of as a transcript of the ancient and primitive forms.

It was necessary for them to stay somewhere. Christendom was not only reformed, but divided too, and every division would, to all ages, have called for some alteration, or else have disliked it publicly ; and since all that cast off the Roman yoke thought they had title enough to be called reformed, it was hard to have pleased all the private interests and peevishness of men that called themselves friends, and, therefore, that only in which the Church of Rome had prevaricated against the Word of God, or innovated against Apostolical tradition, all that was pared away. But at last she fixed, and strove no further to please the people, who never could be satisfied.

The painter that exposed his work to the censure of the common passengers, resolving to mend it as long as any man could find fault, at last had brought the eyes to the ears, and the ears to the neck, and for his excuse subscribed, *Hanc populus fecit* : but his *hanc ego*, that which he made by the rules of his art and the advice of men skilled in the same mystery, was the better piece. The Church of England should have pared away all the Canon of the Communion, if she had mended her piece at the prescription of the Zwinglians ; and all her Office of Baptism, if she had mended by the rules of the Anabaptists ; and kept up altars still by the example of the Lutherans ; and not have retained decency by the good will of the Calvinists ; and now another new light is sprung up, she should have no Liturgy at all, but the worship of God be left to the managing of chance and indeliberation and a petulant fancy.

It began early to discover its inconvenience ; for when certain zealous persons fled to Frankfurt, to avoid the funeral piles kindled by the Roman bishops in Queen Mary's time, as if they had not enemies enough abroad, they fell foul with one another, and the quarrel was about the Common Prayer-Book ; and some of them made their appeal to the judgement of Mr. Calvin, whom they prepossessed with strange representments, and troubled phantasms concerning it ; and yet the worst he said upon the provocation of those prejudices was, that even its vanities were tolerable. *Tolerabiles ineptias* was the unhandsome epithet he gave to some things, which he was forced to dislike by his over earnest complying with the brethren of Frankfurt.

Well! upon this, the wisdom of this Church and State saw it necessary to fix where, with advice, she had begun,—and with counsel, she had once mended. And to have altered in things inconsiderable, upon a new design or sullen mislike, had been extreme levity and apt to have made the men contemptible, their authority slighted, and the thing ridiculous, especially before adversaries that watched all opportunity and appearances to have disgraced the Reformation. Here, therefore, it became a law, was established by an Act of Parliament, was made solemn by an appendant penalty against all that, on either hand, did prevaricate a sanction of so long and so prudent consideration.

But the Common Prayer-Book had the fate of St. Paul. For when it had scaped the storms of the Roman sea, yet a viper sprung out of Queen Mary's fires, which at Frankfurt first leaped upon the hand of the Church; but since that time, it hath gnawn the bowels of its own mother, and given itself life by the death of its parent and nurse.

For as for the adversaries from the Roman party, they were so convinced by the piety and innocence of the Common Prayer-Book, that they could accuse it of no deformity, but of imperfection, of a want of some things which they judged convenient, because the error had a wrinkle on it, and the face of Antiquity. And, therefore, for ten or eleven years they came to our churches, joined in our devotions, and communicated without scruple, till a temporal interest of the Church of Rome rent the schism wider and made it gape like the jaws of the grave.

And let me say, it adds no small degree to my confidence and opinion of the English Common Prayer-Book, that, amongst the numerous armies sent from the Roman seminaries (who were curious enough to inquire, able enough to find out, and wanted no anger to have made them charge home any error in our Liturgy, if the matter had not been unblameable, and the composition excellent), there was never any impiety or heresy charged upon the Liturgy of the Church: for I reckon not the calumnies of Harding, for they were only in general, calling it ' darkness,' etc., from which aspersion it was worthily vindicated by Mr. Dering. The truth of it is, the compilers took that course which was sufficient to have secured it against the malice of a Spanish Inquisitor or the scrutiny of a more inquisitive Presbytery; for they put nothing of controversy into their prayers, nothing that was then matter of question; only because they could not prophesy, they put in some things which, since then, have been called to question by persons, whose interest was highly concerned to find fault with something. But that also hath been the fate of the penmen of Holy Scripture, some of which could prophesy, and yet could not prevent this. But I do not remember that any man was ever put to it to justify the Common Prayer against any positive, public, and professed charge by a Roman adversary : nay, it is transmitted to us by the testimony of persons greater than all exceptions, that Paulus Quartus, in his private inter-courses and letters to Queen Elizabeth, did offer to confirm the English Common Prayer-Book, if she would acknowledge his primacy and authority, and the reformation derivative from him. And this lenity was pursued by his successor, Pius Quartus, with an *omnia de nobis tibi polliceare* ; he assured her she should have any thing from him, not only things pertaining to her soul, but what might conduce to the establishment and confirmation of her royal dignity ; amongst which, that the Liturgy, new established by her authority, should not be rescinded by the Pope's power, was not the least considerable.

And possibly this hath cast a cloud upon it in the eyes of such persons who never will keep charity, or so much as civility, but with those, with whom they have made a league offensive and defensive against all the world. This hath made it to be suspected of too much compliance with that Church and her offices of devotion, and that it is a very cento composed out of the Mass-book, Pontifical, Breviaries, Manuals, and Portuises of the Roman Church.

I cannot say but many of our prayers are also in the Roman offices. But so they are also in the Scriptures, so also is the Lord's prayer ; and if they were not, yet the allegation is very inartificial, and the charge peevish and unreasonable, unless there were nothing good in the Roman books, or that it were unlawful to pray a good prayer, which they had once stained with red letters. The objection hath not sense enough to procure an answer upon its own stock, but by reflexion from a direct truth, which uses to be like light manifesting itself and discovering darkness.

It was first perfected in King Edward VI.'s time, but it was, by and by, impugned, through the obstinate and dissembling malice of many ; they are the words of Mr. Foxe in his *Book of Martyrs*. Then it was reviewed and published with so much approbation that it was accounted the work of God ; but yet, not long after, there were some persons, *qui divisionis occasionem arripiebant*, saith Alesius, *vocabula et pene syllabas expendendo*, 'they tried it by points and syllables, and weighed every word,' and sought occasions to quarrel : which being observed by Archbishop Cranmer, he caused it to be translated into Latin, and sent it to Bucer, requiring his judgement of it ; who returned this answer, "That although there are in it some things *quae rapi possunt ab inquietis ad materiam contentionis*, 'which, by peevish men may be cavilled at,' yet there was nothing in it but what was taken out of the Scriptures, or agreeable to it, if rightly understood ; that is, if handled and read by wise and good men." The zeal which Archbishop Grindal, Bishop Ridley, Dr. Taylor, and other the holy martyrs and confessors in Queen Mary's time expressed for this excellent Liturgy, before and at the time of their death, defending it by their disputations, adorning it by their practice, and sealing it with their bloods, are arguments which ought to recommend it to all the sons of the Church of England for ever, infinitely to be valued beyond all the little whispers and murmurs of argument pretended against it. And when it came out of the flame and was purified in the martyr's fires, it became a vessel of honour, and used in the house of God in all the days of that long peace, which was the effect of God's blessing, and the reward, as we humbly hope, of a holy religion. And when it was laid aside, in the days of Queen Mary, it was " to the great decay of the due honour of God, and discomfort to the professors of the truth of Christ's religion,"—they are the words of Queen Elizabeth, and her grave and wise Parliament.

Archbishop Cranmer, in his purgation, A.D. 1553, made an offer, if the Queen would give him leave, to prove all that is contained in the Common Prayer-Book to be conformable to that order which our blessed Saviour Christ did both observe and command to be observed. And a little after, he offers to join issue upon this point that the order of the Church of England, set out by authority of the innocent and godly prince Edward VI., in his High Court of Parliament, is the same that was used in the Church fifteen hundred years past.

And I shall go near to make his words good. For very much of our Liturgy is the very words of Scripture. The Psalms and Lessons and all the Hymns, save one, are nothing else but Scripture, and owe nothing to the Roman Breviaries for their production or authority. So that the matter of them is, out of question, holy and true. As for the form, none ever disliked it, but they that will admit no form; for all admit this that admit any. But that these should be parts of liturgy needs not be a question when we remember that Hezekiah and the princes made it a law to their Church, to sing praises to the Lord *with the words of David, and of Asaph, the seer*, and that Christ Himself did so, and His apostles, after the manner of the Jews, in the Feast of Passover, sung their Hymns and portions of the great Allelujah in the words of David, and Asaph, the seer, too, and that there was a song in heaven made up of the words of Moses and David and Jeremy, the seer, and that the Apostles and the Church of God always chose to do so, according to the commandment of the Apostle, that we sing Psalms and Hymns to God. I know not where we can have better than the Psalms of David and Asaph, and these were ready at hand for the use of the Church insomuch that in the Christian synaxes, particularly in the churches of Corinth, St. Paul observed that *every man had a psalm*. It was then the common devotion and

Liturgy of all the faithful, and so for ever ; and the Fathers of the Fourth Council of Toledo justified the practice of the Church, in recitation of the Psalms and Hymns by the example of Christ and His Apostles, who, after supper, sung a Psalm.  And the Church did also make Hymns of her own in the honour of Christ and sung them, such as was the *Te Deum* made by St. Ambrose and St. Austin ; and they stood her in great stead, not only as acts of direct worship to Christ, but as conservators of the articles of Christ's Divinity, of which the Fathers made use against the heretic Artemon, as appears in Eusebius, *Eccles. Hist.*, lib. v, c. 28. . . .

I shall therefore press these things no further, but note, that since all Liturgy is, and ever was, either prose or verse, or both, and the Liturgy of the Church of England, as well as most others, is of the last sort,—I consider that whatsoever is in her devotions besides the Lessons, Epistles, and Gospels (the body of which is no other thing, than was the famous *lectionarium* of St. Jerome) is a compliance with these two dictates of the Apostle for liturgy : the which, one for verse, the other for prose,—*in psalms and hymns and spiritual songs*, for verse ; for prose, *deprecations, and prayers, and intercessions, and giving of thanks*,—will warrant and commend, as so many parts of duty, all the portions of the English Liturgy.

If it were worth the pains, it were very easy to enumerate the authors, and especially the occasions and time, when the most minute passages, such I mean as are known by distinct appellatives, came into the Church ; that so it may appear, our Liturgy is as ancient and primitive in every part as it is pious and unblameable, and long before the Church got such a beam in one of her eyes, which was endeavoured to be cast out at the Reformation.  But it will not be amiss to observe that very many of them were inserted as antidotes and deletories to the worst of heresies, as I have discoursed already : and such was that clause, " Through Jesus Christ our Lord, Who liveth and reigneth with Thee, in the unity of the Holy Spirit, ever one God " ; and some other phrases parallel were put in, in defiance of the Macedonians, and all the species of the Anti-trinitarians, and used by St. Ambrose in Milan, St. Austin in Africa, and Idacius Clarus in Spain ; and in imitation of so pious precedents, the Church of England hath inserted divers clauses into her offices.

There was a great instance in the administration of the Blessed Sacrament.  For upon the change of certain clauses in the Liturgy, upon the instance of Martin Bucer, instead of ' the Blood of our Lord Jesus Christ, Which was given for you, preserve your body and soul unto everlasting life,' was substituted this, ' take and eat this in remembrance,' etc. ; and it was done lest the people, accustomed to the opinion of Transubstantiation and the appendant practices, should retain the same doctrine upon intimation of the first clause. But in the beginning of Queen Elizabeth's reign, when certain persons of the Zwinglian opinion would have abused the Church with Sacramentary doctrine and pretended the Church of England had declared for it in the second clause of 1552, the wisdom of the Church thought it expedient to join both the clauses; the first, lest the Church should be suspected to be of the Sacramentary opinion; the latter, lest she should be mistaken as a patroness of Transubstantiation: and both these with so much temper and sweetness, that by her care she rather prevented all mistakes than by any positive declaration in her prayers engaged herself upon either side, that she might pray to God without strife and contention with her brethren. For the Church of England had never known how to follow the names of men, but to call Christ only ' her Lord and Master.'

But from the inserting of these and the like clauses, which hath been done in all ages, according to several opportunities and necessities, I shall observe this advantage, which is in many, but is also very signally in the English Liturgy. We are thereby enabled and advantaged in the meditation of those mysteries *de quibus festivatur in sacris*, as the casuists love to speak;—which, upon solemn days, we are bound to meditate and make to be the matter and occasion of our address to God. For the offices are so ordered that the most indifferent and careless cannot but be reminded of the mystery in every anniversary, which, if they be summed up, will make an excellent creed: and then let any man consider what a rare advantage it will be to the belief of such propositions, when the very design of the Holiday teaches the hardhanded artisan the name and meaning of an article, and yet the most forward and religious cannot be abused with any semblances of superstition. The life and death of the saints, which is very precious in the eyes of God, is so remembered by His humble and afflicted handmaid, the Church of England, that by giving Him thanks and praise God may be honoured, the Church instructed by the proposition of their example, and we give testimony of the honour and love we owe and pay unto religion by the pious veneration and esteem of those holy and beatified persons.

Certain it is that there is no part of religion, as it is a distinct virtue, and is to be exercised by interior acts and forms of worship, but is in the offices of the Church of England. For if the soul desires to be humbled, she hath provided forms of confession to God before His Church. If she will rejoice and give God thanks for particular blessings, there are forms of thanksgiving described and added, by the King's authority, upon the Conference at Hampton Court, which are all the public, solemn, and foreseen occasions, for which, by law and order, provision could be made. If she will commend to God the public and private necessities of the Church and single persons, the whole body of collects and devotions supplies that abundantly. If her devotion be high and pregnant and prepared to fervency and importunity of congress with God, the litanies are an admirable pattern of devotion, full of circumstances proportionable for a quick and an earnest spirit. When the revolution of the anniversary calls on us to perform our duty of special meditation and thankfulness to God for the glorious benefits of Christ's Incarnation, Nativity, Passion, Resurrection, and Ascension (blessings, which do as well deserve a day of thanksgiving as any other temporal advantage, though it be the pleasure of a victory), then we have the offices of Christmas, the Annunciation, Easter, and Ascension.   If we delight to remember those holy persons whose bodies rest in the bed of peace and whose souls are deposited in the hands of Christ till the day of restitution of all things, we may, by the collects and days of anniversary-festivity, not only remember, but also imitate them too in our lives, if we will make that use of the proportions of Scripture allotted for the festival which the Church intends.   To which if we add the advantages of the whole Psalter, which is an entire body of devotion by itself and hath in it forms to exercise all graces by way of internal act and spiritual intention, there is not any ghostly advantage which the most religious can either need or fancy, but the English Liturgy in its entire constitution will furnish us withal.   And certainly it was a very great wisdom, and a very prudent and religious constitution, so to order that part of the Liturgy, which the ancients called the *lectionarium*, that the Psalter should be read over twelve times in the year, the Old Testament once, and the New Testament thrice, besides the Epistles and Gospels, which renew with a more frequent repetition, such choice places as represent the entire body of faith and good life. There is a defalcation of some few chapters from the entire body of the order.   But that also was part of the wisdom of the Church not to expose to public ears and common judgements some of the secret rites of Moses' Law or the more mysterious prophecies of the New Testament, whose sense and meaning the event will declare, if we, by mistaken and anticipated interpretations, do not obstruct our own capacities, and hinder us from believing the true events, because they answer not those expectations with which our own mistakes have prepared our understandings; as it happened to the Jews in the case of Antiochus, and to the Christians in the person of Antichrist. . . .

And yet this excellent book hath had the fate to be cut in pieces with a pen-knife and thrown into the fire, but it is not consumed. At first it was sown in tears and is now watered with tears; yet never was any holy thing drowned and extinguished with tears. It began with the martyrdom of the compilers, and the Church hath been vexed ever since by angry spirits, and she was forced to defend it with much trouble and unquietness; but it is to be hoped that all these storms are sent but to increase the zeal and confidence of the pious sons of the Church of England. Indeed, the greatest danger that ever the Common Prayer Book had, was the indifferency and indevotion of them that used it but as a common blessing; and they who thought it fit for the meanest of the clergy to read prayers, and for themselves only to preach, —though they might innocently intend it, yet did not, in that action, consult the honour of our Liturgy, except where charity or necessity did interpose. But when excellent things go away, and then look back upon us, as our blessed Saviour did upon St. Peter, we are more moved than by the nearer embraces of a full and an actual possession. I pray God it may prove so in our case, and that we may not be too willing to be discouraged; at least, that we may not cease to love and to desire what is not publicly permitted to our practice and profession.

### No. 80. WILLIAM LAUD

[From *The History of the Troubles and Trial of the Most Reverend Father in God, William Laud, Lord Archbishop of Canterbury, Wrote by Himself during his Imprisonment in the Tower*, Chapter XIX. *Works*, ed. L. A. C. T., Vol. IV, p. 29. This treatise was first published in 1694 by Henry Wharton from a MS. in Laud's own handwriting in the possession of St. John's College, Oxford.]

I shall for my part never deny but that the Liturgy of the Church of England may be made better; but I am sure withal it may easily be made worse.

### No. 81. JOHN SELDEN

[From *Table Talk*, Section LXXXI (" Liturgy "). Ed. S. H. Reynolds (Oxford, 1892), p. 105. Cp. note on No. 117.]

To know what was generally believed in all ages, the way is to consult the Liturgies, not any private man's writing. As if you would know how the Church of England serves God, go to the Common Prayer Book, consult not this or that man. Besides, Liturgies never compliment, nor use high expressions. The Fathers oft times speak oratoriously.

### No. 82. JOHN GAUDEN

[From Ἱερὰ Δάκρυα; *Ecclesiae Anglicanae Suspiria, or The Tears, Sighs, Complaints, and Prayers of the Church of England* (1659), Book I, Chapter xii, p. 88. Cp. note on No. 41.]

As for the English Liturgy's symbolizing with the Popish Missal, as some have odiously and falsely calumniated, it doth no more than our Communion or Lord's Supper celebrated in England doth with the Mass at Rome; or our doctrine about the Eucharist doth with theirs about Transubstantiation; or our humble veneration of our God and Saviour in that mystery doth with their strange gesticulations and superstitions. In all which particulars how much the Church of England differed both in doctrine and devotion from that of Rome, no man that is intelligent and honest can either deny or dissemble.

I am sure we differ as much as English doth from Latin, truth from error, true antiquity from novelty, completeness from defect, sanctity from sacrilege, the giving of the cup to the people from the denying of it; as much as the holy use of things doth from the superstitious abuse of them; as much as Divine faith doth from human fancy or Scripture plainness and proportions from Scholastic subtleties and inventions.

That the Church of England retained many things pious and proper to several occasions, which the Roman Devotionals had received and retained from the ancient Liturgies is no more blameable than that we use and preserve those Scriptures, Sacraments, and other holy services which the Church of Rome doth now profess to celebrate and use. The wisdom of the Church of England did freely and justly assert to its use and to God's glory whatever upon due trial it found to have the stamp of God's truth and grace, or the Church's wisdom and charity upon it, as what it thought most fit for this Church's present benefit; finding no cause peevishly to refuse any good, because it had been mixed with some evil; but trying all things, it held fast that which it judged good, as it is commanded; never thinking that the usurpations of error ought to be made any obstructions to truth; or that human inventions are any prejudice to Divine institutions. It knew that, though the holy vessels of the Temple had been captive at Babylon, and there profaned by Belshazzar, yet they might well be restored again and consecrated by Ezra to the service of God.

## No. 83. JOHN DUREL

[From *The Liturgy of the Church of England Asserted in a Sermon* [on *I Cor.* xi, 16] *Preached at the Chapel of the Savoy, before the French Congregation which usually assembles in that place, upon the first day that Divine Service was there celebrated according to the Liturgy of the Church of 'England*, London 1662, pp. 20–24. The translation is said to have been the work of " G. B., Doctor in Physic." The sermon was appended to Durel's *View of the Government and Public Worship of God in the Reformed Churches beyond the Seas, Wherein is shewed their Conformity and Agreement with the Church of England, as it is established by the Act of Uniformity*, which appeared in the same year. The sermon reached a second edition in 1688.]

Our Liturgy is an admirable piece of devotion and instruction. It is the marrow and substance of all that the piety and experience of the first five centuries of Christianity found most proper to edification in the public assemblies. It is a compound of texts of Scripture, of exhortations to repentance, of prayers, hymns, psalms, doxologies, lessons, creeds, and of thanksgivings; of forms for the administration of Sacraments and for other public duties of Christians in the Church; and of comminations against impenitent sinners. And all this mixed and diversified with great care expressly to quicken devotion and stir up attention.

The Instructions consist in the order which is set for the reading of the Holy Scripture every day in the year, and in the choice made of

certain chapters of the Old Testament and of certain portions of the
Gospel and of the Epistles of the New for Sundays and for Festival
Days, which are called Proper Lessons; and the Gospel and the
Epistles for the day. All this ordered with so wise an economy that
those who have devotion and leisure enough to come to church, and
be present at Divine Service every day, morning and evening, may
hear the whole Bible read every year, the Old Testament once, and
the New (wherein we ought to be more conversant) no less than thrice.
And the Book of Psalms (which is so excellently useful for the consolation, sanctification, as also instruction, of all believers in any
condition whatsoever, but especially in adversity) no less than twelve
times. And for other places, where people cannot meet but upon
Sundays and Holy Days, are extracted out of the Old Testament for
the first Lessons, Morning and Evening, all the most remarkable
histories and chief prophecies of the same. And out of the New
(besides the instructions which our Saviour gave to His Disciples
in His Sermon upon the Mount and His other Divine exhortations)
are selected the most illustrious miracles of His life, and these are called
the Gospels; as also the principal places, either for doctrine or manners,
of the Epistles of St. Paul and of the rest of the holy Apostles, and of the
*Revelation*, which are termed the Epistles. And although the Church
of England makes that distinction which ought to be made between
Canonical Books and those which are called Apocrypha, declaring
that no article of faith can be grounded upon them, but upon the first
only, yet she hath selected certain chapters, and even whole Books,
of the latter to be read after that the former, which she holds to be
alone of Divine Inspiration, have been read in that order which I
have now represented. But nevertheless she orders them to be read
by reason they contain some histories, which are part of the History
of the Jewish Church and a continuation of the same, as in the Thirty
Nine Articles it is expressed, *For the example of life, and for the
instruction of manners, and not to establish any doctrine.* So as the
Church of England causeth them to be read publicly only for the
same reasons for which the Primitive Church read them and for which
they are commonly bound up in one volume with the Canonical Books
in the Reformed Churches of France and in all others, none, that I
know, having ever left them out wholly before the late Empirics of
this Church.

   To these we may also add the three Creeds, that of the Apostles,
the Nicene, and that of Athanasius, which our Church orders to be
publicly recited among other means which she useth for the instruction
of believers. To the Apostles' Creed is added that of Nice, because
it doth more especially teach the Godhead of the Son and of the Holy
Ghost. And to these two she joins that of Athanasius, where in a

wonderful manner is expressed whatsoever the Scripture doth teach concerning the incomprehensible mystery of the most glorious Trinity and that of the Incarnation of the Son of God, the depth of which is no less unsearchable; because upon these two most wonderful mysteries the whole sum of Christianity doth depend, which in the said Creed are set out in as clear terms as so sublime a subject can permit. All that this Liturgy contains besides is proper to teach humility, zeal, and devotion, especially the Litany, and all that is comprised in the several lessons, prayers, confessions of sins, and in the forms of thanksgiving which is appointed for the Celebration of the Lord's Supper. But your own experience being better able to instruct you in these particulars than all I can say upon this subject, I shall only speak a word of the manner wherein the Church orders the recital of the Decalogue. He that pronounceth it must be a minister, as another Moses sent from God, the whole congregation devoutly kneeling all the while, making a serious reflexion upon the commandments of God, upon the want of care they have in time past been guilty of to obey the same, and upon their unability, as of themselves, to do better for the time to come; and thereupon they ought to beg His pardon and implore His assistance, saying with a loud though humble voice, *Lord have mercy upon us, and incline our heart to keep this law.* There can be nothing more powerful to touch sinners to the quick and to draw them from their evil courses than the Commination, to which the whole congregation is bound to say *Amen*, after every particular denunciation of God's curse upon all sorts of sinners who persist in their sins. Not to wish them cursed (as ignorant and contentious spirits affirm, contrary to truth), but as it is expressly set down there, *To the intent that everyone being admonished of the great indignation of God against sinners may the rather be called to earnest and true repentance and may walk more warily in these dangerous days, eschewing such vices for the which they affirm with their own mouths the curse of God to be due.* For the words are not *cursed be*, but *cursed is*, he who commits such or such a sin,—which saying doth not import any imprecation of a curse, but declares it only. And then the *Amen*, which every one saith, is not an expression of any wish made that the thing may come to pass, but only an intimation that it is so. For in truth it signifies in this case not *So be it*, as it usually doth, but *So it is*,—which would be so nevertheless, though it were not pronounced.

Our Liturgy hath also set forms of Administering Baptism, Marriage, and the Visitation of the Sick, all very proper and fitted to their subject. It hath also a form for the Confirmation of children, which binds the parents and ministers to bring them to their Bishop, to render him an account of their faith when they are capable, to make a solemn and public profession that they will live and die in the belief and observation

17

of those things their Godfathers and Godmothers promised for them at their Baptism that they should believe and do, and after that to receive the blessing from their pastor, who gives it them solemnly with the imposition of hands and with prayers. And all this without chrism, or box on the ear, or without any such superstitious or superfluous ceremony. And as children are the gift of God, and as they are formed in the womb, and come out of it into the light of the living, through His wonderful goodness, wisdom, and power, the Church commands that the mothers being risen out of child-bed come upon their first going-abroad into the public assembly, there to return thanks to God for so signal a mercy and prescribes the manner wherein to do it. Finally, it is therein ordered that the dead be buried in a decent and solemn manner, in hope of a blessed Resurrection. And to the intent that Ministers who together with their relations and friends come to perform this their last duty to them may not be silent in an occasion wherein so much may be said, and that they may comfort them who survive, and lay before them the shortness and vanity of this life, and exhort them to improve it to their best advantage, while God suffers them to enjoy it, there are certain places of Scripture appointed, such as are fit for that purpose, which they are enjoined to read; whereunto they are to add certain Prayers, not for the dead, to whom they are useless, but for the living, that they may profit by the example that is set before their eyes.

It is required of the people that they repeat aloud the Confession of Sins, that they may be the more sensibly affected therewith. Which custom ought to be the less wondered at in this country, by how much (besides the benefit which I now observed, that pious souls do always reap by it) everyone knows it is the custom in public transactions, which concern only some particular person, as in tendering of an oath, that everyone is bound to repeat aloud, word after word, the forms of it, that the thing may be the more express and may make a deeper impression into the minds of men. But as for the Confession of Sins to God Whom we have offended, if we had a lively sense of them it would be needless to bind us to do it with a loud voice, when we stand before His Tribunal. Did you never read in history in what manner whole towns and armies, having committed some great offence, have come together in a body to their magistrates or generals, to beg their pardon, crying all with one voice for mercy? The great resentment of their crime, and their earnest desire to have the same remitted, causing every particular man to utter that speech which they intended one man only should make in their behalf. And as often as this hath happened, the event hath manifested that supplications thus united, reinforced, and uttered with such violence of affection, have moved to compassion those to whom they made their addresses. In like manner we are enjoined by the Church to lift up our voice to God with one accord, to the end that the Confession of our Sins and the Prayers we join therewith may obtain pardon for them, and produce the same effect in moving His tender compassions towards us. And these joint supplications of ours will infallibly have this effect, if the heart which sends them and the mouth which utters them doth at the same time stir up the bowels and the whole man to a true compunction according to the intention of our wise and pious Reformers.

### No. 84. HUMPHREY PRIDEAUX

[From *A Letter to a Friend relating to the Present Convocation*. Ed. Norwich (C. N. Wodehouse), 1834, pp. 52–55. This pamphlet, which has been erroneously ascribed to Tillotson, was first published in 1690. As is well known, proposals were rampant at the Revolution for a revision of the Prayer Book; it was believed that a modification of it in a Protestant direction might lead the majority of the Nonconformists to reunite themselves with the Church of England. These proposals, however, led to nothing.]

As to the Liturgy of our Church, I freely acknowledge, and I think no man can contradict me therein, that it is the best which was ever yet used in any Christian Church, but that it should therefore be so perfect as not to be capable of amendments or alterations for the better, doth by no means follow. For nothing of human composure can be such, especially in a thing of this nature, where process of time and alteration of circumstance frequently produce a necessity of correction, as most certainly in our Liturgy they very often do. For the language in which it is wrote being constantly *in fluxu*, as all the living languages are, in every age some words that were in use in the former grow obsolete, and some phrases and expressions formerly in grace and fashion through disuse become uncouth and ridiculous; and always to continue these in our Liturgy without correction would be to bring a disparagement upon the whole and expose to contempt the worship of God among us. Besides, there are several things which in one age may conduce to devotion which, through variation of times and circumstances, may not be borne in another; several things which may be the proper matter of prayer at one time, which may not be so in another; and all those things call for alterations and amendments whenever they happen. And therefore I am so far from assenting with some of our brethren in this particular, that our Liturgy ought not to be altered, that I think it absolutely necessary from the above mentioned particulars, that it be always at least once in thirty years brought to a review for this purpose. And I am sure this hath been the judgement of the whole Christian Church from the beginning to this time. The Greek Church hath so often altered as to this, and made so many different forms of their Liturgies, that a collection of them in a late auction amounted to twenty volumes; and the Latin Church, who brag most of their constancy in these matters,

have rather exceeded than come behind them herein, as in old manu-
scripts of their Liturgies will sufficiently appear to any that will take
the pains to look into them. Nay, they were so far from continuing
one age in conformity with another herein, that they observed none
at all in this matter, but almost every province had its different Liturgy,
and it is well known that there were five different forms of them in
this kingdom till the Reformation, and the like was also practised in
other parts of the Latin or Romish Church; and a general agreement
as to this was so far from being thought necessary, that the Act of King
Edward the Sixth was the first law for a uniform Liturgy in any Church
that was ever enacted from the beginning of Christianity to that time.
But neither did that exclude all varying from it in after times. The
Liturgy that was first established in that King's reign, within a very
little while after underwent a review, which produced considerable
alterations in it. And when Queen Elizabeth came to the Crown,
many others were made therein. And those who compute the late
alterations decreed in the Convocation of 1662 tell us they amount to
the number of four hundred. And why we only of this present time
should be debarred the privilege of bettering ourselves in this matter,
which all other times of the Church before us have enjoyed, I would
fain know a reason.

# (5) THE THIRTY NINE ARTICLES

## No. 85. PETER HEYLYN

[From *Historia Quinquarticularis ; or a Declaration of the Judgement of the Western Churches and more particularly of the Church of England in the Five Controverted Points reproached in these last times by the Name of Arminianism ; Collected in the Way of an Historical Narration out of the public Acts and Monuments and Most Approved Authors of those Several Churches*, p. 555 (ed. 1681). This treatise, the first edition of which appeared in 1660, was an historical account of the Calvinist controversy, and is a sustained polemic against the Calvinist position. The ' Five Articles ' referred to in the title were, of course, the propositions of the Remonstrants which were first put forward in 1610. The official Dutch text will be found in J. Tideman, *De Remonstrantie en het Remonstrantisme* (Haarlem, 1851); an English version of them is printed in *The Creeds of Christendom* (ed. P. Schaff, 1882), Vol. III, pp. 545–549. In 1619, at the Synod of Dort, these five articles were condemned.]

THUS have we seen the doctrine of the Church of England in the five controverted points,[1] according as it is delivered in the Book of Articles. But in what sense we ought to understand it hath been made a question. Some take the Articles in the literal and grammatical sense, which is the fairest and most approved way of interpretation, according to the saying of an ancient writer, that if the *literal* sense of Holy Scripture will stand with the analogy of faith and piety, it is to be preferred before any other. Others there are (of which his late Majesty [2] complained) who draw the Articles aside and put their own sense or comment to be the meaning of the Articles, fashioning them to their own fancies as they please themselves. Each of the parties in those curious points in which the present differences do most consist conceive the Articles of the Church to speak for them, exclusive wholly of the other, but with a notable difference in the application. The Calvinists, by which name they love to be called, endeavour to captivate the sense of the Article and bring it to the bent of their own understanding; but the true English Protestants (whom for distinction sake we may call Confessionists) accommodate, though they do not captivate, their own sense to the sense of the Church, according to the plain and full meaning of the Articles in the points disputed. But because possibly both parties may not be agreed on a rule or medium by which the proper sense and meaning of the Articles may be best discovered, it will not be amiss to follow the directions of the Civil Laws, in cases of like doubtful nature, which is briefly this, viz. *Si de interpretatione Legis quaeritur, imprimis inspiciendum est, quo*

---

[1] [*I.e.*, of the Remonstrants.]
[2] [*I.e.*, Charles I in the Declaration prefixed in 1628 to the Articles.]

*jure Civitas retro in hujusmodi casibus usa fuit.* And this we shall the better do if we enquire into the doctrine of these learned, religious, and godly men, who either had a principal hand in the Reformation or were most conversant with them; and beloved of them in their several stations, taking along with us the authority of the Homilies and Public Liturgy, to which all parties have subscribed.

## No. 86. JOHN BRAMHALL

[From *Schism Guarded*, Section I, Chapter xi. *Works*, ed. *L. A. C. T.*, Vol. II, p. 470. Cp. note on No. 28.]

We do not suffer any man " to reject " the Thirty-Nine Articles of the Church of England " at his pleasure "; yet neither do we look upon them as essentials of saving faith or " legacies of Christ and of His Apostles "; but in a mean, as pious opinions fitted for the preservation of unity. Neither do we oblige any man to believe them, but only not to contradict them.

# (6) RELIGIOUS TOLERATION

## No. 87. JEREMY TAYLOR

[From Θεολογία Εκλεκτική ; *or A Discourse of the Liberty of Prophesying,* From the Epistle Dedicatory. *Works*, ed. R. Heber, Vol. VII, pp. 401–407, 409–412, 413, 416–421, 421–423 (ed. C. P. Eden, Vol. V, pp. 345–348, 349 f., 351, 353–356, 356 f.). This work appeared on June 28, 1647; the long Dedication, from which the extract is taken, was to Lord Hatton of Kirby. At a time when men's religious passions were deeply stirred and intolerance almost everywhere prevailed, this treatise advocated a more liberal attitude to religious differences.]

IT is a hard case that we should think all Papists and Anabaptists and Sacramentaries to be fools and wicked persons. Certainly, among all these sects, there are very many wise men and good men as well as erring. And although some zeals are so hot and their eyes so inflamed with their ardours that they do not think their adversaries look like other men, yet certainly we find by the results of their discourses and the transactions of their affairs of civil society that they are men that speak and make syllogisms, and use reason, and read Scripture; and although they do no more understand all of it than we do, yet they endeavour to understand as much as concerns them, even all that they can, even all that concerns repentance from dead works and faith in our Lord Jesus Christ. And, therefore, methinks this also should be another consideration distinguishing the persons. For, if the persons be Christians in their lives and Christians in their profession, if they acknowledge the eternal Son of God for their Master and their Lord and live in all relations as becomes persons making such professions, why then should I hate such persons whom God loves, and who love God, who are partakers of Christ and Christ hath a title to them, who dwell in Christ, and Christ in them, because their understandings have not been brought up like mine, have not had the same masters, they have not met with the same books nor the same company, or have not the same interest, or are not so wise, or else are wiser ; that is, for some reason or other, which I neither do understand nor ought to blame, have not the same opinions that I have, and do not determine their school-questions to the sense of my sect or interest ?

But now I know beforehand that those men who will endure none but their own sect, will make all manner of attempts against these purposes of charity and compliance and, say I or do I what I can, will tell all their proselytes that I preach indifferency of religion ; that

I say it is no matter how we believe, nor what they profess, but that they may comply with all sects, and do violence to their own consciences ; that they may be saved in all religions, and so make way for a *colluvies* of heresies, and by consequence, destroy all religion.   Nay, they will say worse than all this ;  and, but that I am not used to their phrases and forms of declamation, I am persuaded I might represent fine tragedies beforehand.   And this will be such an objection that although I am most confident I shall make it apparent to be as false and scandalous as the objectors themselves are zealous and impatient ; yet, besides that I believe the objection will come where my answers will not come, or not be understood, I am also confident that, in defiance and incuriousness of all that I shall say, some men will persist pertinaciously in the accusation, and deny my conclusion in despite of me.   Well, but however, I will try.

And, first I answer, that whatsoever is against the foundation of Faith or contrary to good life and the laws of obedience or destructive to human society and the public and just interests of bodies politic is out of the limits of my question, and does not pretend to compliance or toleration.   So that I allow no indifferency, nor any countenance to those religions whose principles destroy government, nor to those religions (if there be any such) that teach ill life ; nor do I think that any thing will now excuse from belief of a fundamental article, except stupidity or sottishness, and natural inability.   This alone is sufficient answer to this vanity ;  but I have much more to say.

Secondly, the intendment of my discourse is, that permissions should be in questions speculative, indeterminable, curious, and un-necessary ; and that men would not make more necessities than God made, which indeed are not many.   The fault I find and seek to remedy is, that men are so dogmatical and resolute in their opinions and impatient of others disagreeing, in those things wherein is no sufficient means of union and determination ; but that men should let opinions and problems keep their own forms, and not be obtruded as axioms, nor questions in the vast collection of the system of divinity be adopted into the family of faith.   And, I think, I have reason to desire this.

Thirdly, it is hard to say that he who would not have men put to death or punished corporally for such things for which no human authority is sufficient, either for cognizance or determination, or competent for infliction, that he persuades to an indifferency, when he refers to another judicatory, which is competent, sufficient, infallible, just, and highly severe.   No man, or company of men, can judge or punish our thoughts or secret purposes, whilst they so remain.   And yet it will be unequal to say that he who owns this doctrine, preaches it lawful for men to think or purpose what they will.   And so it is in matters of doubtful disputation, such as are the distinguishing articles of most of the sects of Christendom; so it is in matters intellectual, which are not cognizable by a secular power; in matters spiritual, which are to be discerned by spiritual authority, which cannot make corporal inflictions; and in questions indeterminate, which are doubtfully propounded, or obscurely, and, therefore, may be *in utramque partem* disputed or believed. For God alone must be Judge of these matters, Who alone is Master of our souls, and hath a dominion over human understanding; and he that says this does not say that indifferency is persuaded, because God alone is Judge of erring persons.

Fourthly, no part of this discourse teaches or encourages variety of sects and contradiction in opinions, but supposes them already in being. And therefore, since there are, and ever were, and ever will be, variety of opinions, because there is variety of human understandings and uncertainty in things, no man should be too forward in determining all questions, nor so forward in prescribing to others, nor invade that liberty which God hath left to us entire, by propounding many things obscurely, and by exempting our souls and understandings from all power externally compulsory. So that the restraint is laid upon men's tyranny, but no licence given to men's opinions; they are not considered in any of the conclusions, but in the premises only, as an argument to exhort to charity. So that if I persuade a licence of discrediting any thing which God hath commanded us to believe and allow a liberty where God hath not allowed it, let it be shown and let the objection press as hard as it can. But to say that men are too forward in condemning where God hath declared no sentence, nor prescribed any rule, is to dissuade from tyranny, not to encourage licentiousness; is to take away a licence of judging, not to give a licence of dogmatizing what every one pleases, or as may best serve his turn. And for the other part of the objection,

Fifthly; this discourse is so far from giving leave to men to profess anything, though they believe the contrary, that it takes order that no man shall be put to it. For I earnestly contend that another man's opinion shall be no rule to mine, and that my opinion shall be no snare and prejudice to myself; that men use one another so charitably and so gently, that no error or violence tempt men to hypocrisy; this very thing being one of the arguments I use to persuade permissions, lest compulsion introduce hypocrisy, and make sincerity troublesome and unsafe.

Sixthly; if men would not call all opinions by the name of religion, and superstructures by the name of fundamental articles, and all fancies by the glorious appellative of faith, this objection would have no pretence or footing. So that it is the disease of the men, not any cause that is ministered by such precepts of charity, that makes them perpetually clamorous. And it would be hard to say that such physicians are incurious of their patients, and neglectful of their health, who speak against the unreasonableness of such empirics that would cut off a man's head, if they see but a wart upon his cheek, or a dimple upon his chin, or any lines in his face to distinguish him from another man. The case is altogether the same, and we may as well decree a wart to be mortal as a various opinion *in re alioqui non necessaria* to be capital and damnable.

For I consider that there are but a few doctrines of Christianity that were ordered to be preached to all the world, to every single person, and made a necessary article of his explicit belief. Other doctrines, which are all of them not simply necessary, are either such as are not clearly revealed, or such as are. If they be clearly revealed, and that I know so too, or may but for my own fault,—I am not to be excused: but for this I am to be left to God's judgement, unless my fault be externally such as to be cognizable and punishable in human judicatory. . . .

But . . . it is observable that this, with its appendant degrees, I mean restraint of prophesying, imposing upon other men's understanding, being masters of their consciences, and lording it over their faith, came in with the retinue and train of Antichrist; that is, they came as other abuses and corruptions of the Church did, by reason of the iniquity of times, and the cooling of the first heats of Christianity, and the increase of interest, and the abatements of Christian simplicity when the Church's fortune grew better and her sons grew worse and some of her Fathers worst of all. For, in the first three hundred years, there was no sign of persecuting any man for his opinion, though at that time, there were very horrid opinions commenced, and such which were exemplary and parallel enough to determine this question; for they then were assaulted by new sects, which destroyed the common principles of nature, of Christianity, of innocence, and public society; and they who used all the means, Christian and spiritual, for their disimprovement and conviction, thought not of using corporal force, otherwise than by blaming such proceedings. And, therefore, I do not only urge their not doing it, as an argument of the unlawfulness of such proceeding, but their defying it and speaking against such practices, as unreasonable, and destructive of Christianity. For so Tertullian is express: *Humani juris et naturalis potestatis est, unicuique quod putaverit, colere ; sed nec religionis est cogere religionem, quae suscipi debet sponte, non vi.* The same is the doctrine of St. Cyprian, Lactantius, St. Hilary, Minucius Felix, Sulpicius Severus, St. Chrysostom, St. Jerome, St. Austin, Damascene, Theophylact, Socrates Scholasticus, and St. Bernard, as they are severally referred to and urged, upon occasion, in the following discourse.

To which I add, that all wise princes, till they were overborne with faction or solicited by peevish persons, gave toleration to differing sects, whose opinions did not disturb the public interest. But, at first, there were some heretical persons that were also impatient of an adversary, and they were the men, who at first entreated the Emperors to persecute the Catholics; but till four hundred years after Christ no Catholic persons, or very few, did provoke the secular arm, or implore its aid against the heretics, save only that Arius behaved himself so seditiously and tumultuarily that the Nicene Fathers procured a temporary decree for his relegation; but it was soon taken off, and God left to be his judge; Who indeed did it to some purpose, when He was trusted with it, and the matter wholly left to Him.

But as the ages grew worse, so men grew more cruel and unchristian. And in the Greek church, Atticus, and Nestorius of Constantinople, Theodosius of Synnada, and some few others, who had forgotten the mercies of their great Master, and their own duty, grew implacable and furious and impatient of contradiction. It was a bold and an arrogant speech, which Nestorius made in a sermon before Theodosius the younger, *Da mihi, O imperator, terram ab haereticis repurgatam, et ego tibi vicissim coelum dabo : Disperde mecum haereticos, et ego tecum disperdam Persas.* It was as groundless and unwarrantable, as it was bloody and inhuman. . . .

And indeed there is great reason for princes to give toleration to disagreeing persons, whose opinions, by fair means, cannot be altered. For if the persons be confident, they will serve God according to their persuasions; and if they be publicly prohibited, they will privately convene; and then all these inconveniences and mischiefs, which are arguments against the permission of conventicles are arguments for the public permissions of differing religions, because the denying of the public worship will certainly produce private conventicles, against which all wise princes and commonwealths have, upon great reasons, made edicts and severe sanctions. . . .

But, in the Church of Rome, the Popes were the first preachers of force and violence in matters of opinion, and that so zealously that Pope Vigilius suffered himself to be imprisoned and handled roughly by the Emperor Justinian, rather than he would consent to the restitution and peace of certain disagreeing persons. But as yet it came not so far as death. The first that preached that doctrine was Dominic, the founder of the begging Orders of Friars, the friar-preachers; in memory of which the Inquisition is intrusted only to the friars of his Order. And if there be any force in dreams or truth in legends (as there is not much in either), this very thing might be signified by his mother's dream, who, the night before Dominic was born, dreamed she was brought to bed of a huge dog with a firebrand in his mouth. Sure enough, however his disciples expound the dream, it was a better sign that he should prove a rabid, furious, incendiary than any thing else. Whatever he might be in the other parts of his life, in his doctrine he was not much better, as appears in his deportment towards the Albigenses, against whom he so preached, *adeo quidem ut centum haereticorum millia ab octo millibus catholicorum fusa et interfecta fuisse perhibeantur*, saith one of him; and of those who were taken, one hundred and eighty were burnt to death, because they would not abjure their doctrine. This was the first example of putting erring persons to death that I find in the Roman Church. For about one hundred and seventy years before, Berengarius fell into opinion concerning the Blessed Sacrament, which they called heresy, and recanted, and relapsed, and recanted again, and fell again two or three times, saith Gerson, writing against ' Romant of the Rose,' and yet he died *sicca morte*, his own natural death, and with hope of Heaven; and yet Hildebrand was once his judge, which shows that, at that time, Rome was not come to so great heights of bloodshed. In England, although the Pope had as great power here as anywhere, yet there were no executions for matter of opinion known till the time of Henry IV, who, because he usurped the crown, was willing by all means to endear the clergy by destroying their enemies, that so he might be sure of them to all his purposes. And indeed, it may become them well enough, who are wiser in their generations than the children of light,—it may possibly serve the policies of evil persons,—but never the pure and chaste designs of Christianity, which admits no blood but Christ's, and the imitating blood of martyrs, but knows nothing how to serve her ends by persecuting any of her erring children.

By this time, I hope it will not be thought reasonable to say, he that teaches mercy to erring persons teaches indifference in religion; unless so many Fathers and so many Churches and the best of Emperors and all the world (till they were abused by tyranny, popery, and faction) did teach indifference. For I have shown that Christianity does not punish corporally persons erring spiritually, but indeed Popery does; the Donatists, and Circumcellians and Arians, and the Itaciani, they of old did: in the Middle Ages the patrons of images did, and the Papists at this day do, and have done, ever since they were taught it by their St. Dominic.

Seventhly; And yet after all this, I have something more to exempt myself from the clamour of this objection. For let all errors be as much and as zealously suppressed as may be (the doctrine of the following discourse contradicts not that); but let it be done by such means as are proper instruments of their suppression, by preaching and disputation (so that neither of them breed disturbance), by charity and sweetness, by holiness of life, assiduity of exhortation, by the Word of God and prayer.

For these ways are most natural, most prudent, most peaceable and effectual. Only let not men be hasty in calling every disliked opinion by the name of heresy; and when they have resolved that they will call it so, let them use the erring person like a brother, not beat him like a dog, or convince him with a gibbet, or vex him out of his understanding and persuasions.

And now if men will still say " I persuade to indifferency," there is no help for me, for I have given reasons against it; I must bear it as well as I can; I am not yet without remedy, as they are; for patience will help me, and reason will not cure them. Let them take their course, and I will take mine.

Only I will take leave to consider this, and they would do well to do so too, that unless faith be kept within its own latitude, and not called out to patrocinate every less necessary opinion, and the interest of every sect or peevish person; and if damnation be pronounced against Christians believing the Creed, and living good lives, because they are deceived, or are said to be deceived, in some opinions less necessary; there is no way in the world to satisfy unlearned persons in the choice of their religion or to appease the unquietness of a scrupulous conscience. For suppose an honest citizen, whose employment and parts will not enable him to judge the disputes and arguings of great clerks, sees factions commenced and managed with much bitterness by persons, who might, on either hand, be fit enough to guide him; when if he follows either, he is disquieted and pronounced damned by the other (who also, if he be the most unreasonable in his opinion, will perhaps be the more furious in his sentence), what shall this man do? Where shall he rest the sole of his foot? Upon the doctrine of the Church where he lives? Well, but that he hears declaimed against perpetually, and other Churches claim highly and pretend fairly for truth, and condemn his Church. If I tell him that he must live a good life, and believe the Creed, and not trouble himself with their disputes, or interest himself in sects and factions, I speak reason; because no law of God ties him to believe more than what is of essential necessity, and whatsoever he shall come to know to be revealed by God. Now if he believes his Creed, he believes all that is necessary to all or of itself; and if he does his moral endeavour beside, he can do no more toward finding out all the rest, and then he is secured. But then, if this will secure him, why do men press further and pretend every opinion as necessary, and that in so high a degree, that if they all said true, or any two indeed of them, in five hundred sects which are in the world (and for aught I know there may be five thousand), it is five hundred to one but that every man is damned; for every sect damns all but itself, and that is damned of four hundred and ninety-nine, and it is excellent fortune then if that escape. And there is the same reason in every one of them, that is, it is extreme unreasonableness in all of them to pronounce damnation against such persons, against whom clearly and dogmatically Holy Scripture hath not. *In odiosis, quod minimum est sequimur; in favoribus, quod est maximum*, saith the law; and therefore we should say any thing, or make any excuse, that is in any degree reasonable, rather than condemn all the world to hell; especially if we consider these two things,—that we ourselves are as apt to be deceived, as any are; and that they who are deceived, when they used their moral industry, that they might not be deceived, if they perish for this they perish for what they could not help. . . .

And then, if we look abroad and consider how there is scarce any Church but is highly charged by many adversaries in many things, possibly we may see a reason to charge every one of them in some things, and what shall we do then? The Church of Rome hath spots enough and all the world is inquisitive enough to find out more and to represent these to her greatest disadvantage. The Greek Churches deny the Procession of the Holy Ghost from the Son. If that be false doctrine, she is highly to blame; if it be not, then all the Western Churches are to blame for saying the contrary. And there is no Church that is in prosperity, but alters her doctrine every age, either by bringing in new doctrines, or by contradicting her old; which shews that none are satisfied with themselves, or with their own confessions. And since all Churches believe themselves fallible, that only excepted, which all other Churches say is most of all deceived,—it were strange if, in so many articles, which make up their several bodies of confessions, they had not mistaken, every one of them, in some thing or other. The Lutheran Churches maintain Consubstantiation, the Zwinglians are Sacramentaries, the Calvinists are fierce in the matters of absolute predetermination; and all these reject Episcopacy, which the Primitive Church would have made no doubt to have called heresy. The Socinians profess a portentous number of strange opinions; they deny the Holy Trinity, and the satisfaction of our blessed Saviour. The Anabaptists laugh at Paedo-Baptism: the Ethiopian churches are Nestorian. Where then shall we fix our confidence, or join communion? To pitch upon any one of these is to throw the dice, if salvation be to be had only in one of them, and that every error that by chance hath made a sect, and is distinguished by a name be damnable.

If this consideration does not deceive me, we have no other help in the midst of these distractions and disunions, but all of us to be united in that common term, which as it does constitute the Church in its being such, so it is the medium of the Communion of Saints; and that is the Creed of the Apostles; and, in all other things an honest endeavour to find out what truths we can, and a charitable and mutual permission to others that disagree from us and our opinions. I am sure this may satisfy us, for it will secure us. But I know not any thing else that will; and no man can be reasonably persuaded or satisfied in any thing else, unless he throws himself upon chance, or absolute predestination, or his own confidence, in every one of which it is two to one, at least, but he may miscarry.

## No. 88.  THOMAS BROWNE

[From *Religio Medici*, Part I.  Ed. Everyman's Library, pp. 7 f.  Cp. note on No. 4.]

I could never divide myself from any man upon the difference of an opinion, or be angry with his judgement for not agreeing with me in that from which perhaps within a few days I should dissent myself. I have no genius to disputes in Religion, and have often thought it wisdom to decline them, especially upon a disadvantage, or when the cause of truth might suffer in the weakness of my patronage.  Where we desire to be informed, 'tis good to contest with men above our selves; but to confirm and establish our opinions, 'tis best to argue with judgements below our own, that the frequent spoils and victories over their reasons may settle in ourselves an esteem and confirmed opinion of our own.  Every man is not a proper champion for truth, nor fit to take up the gauntlet in the cause of verity:  many, from the ignorance of these maxims, and an inconsiderate zeal unto truth, have too rashly charged the troops of error, and remain as trophies unto the enemies of truth.  A man may be in as just possession of truth as of a city, and yet be forced to surrender:  'tis therefore far better to enjoy her with peace, than to hazard her on a battle.  If, therefore, there rise any doubts in my way, I do forget them, or at least defer them till my better settled judgement and more manly reason be able to resolve them, for I perceive every man's own reason is his best Œdipus, and will, upon a reasonable truce, find a way to loose those bonds wherewith the subtleties of error have enchained our more flexible and tender judgements.  In philosophy, where truth seems double-faced, there is no man more paradoxical than myself: but in divinity I love to keep the road, and, though not in an implicit, yet an humble faith, follow the great wheel of the Church, by which I move, not reserving any proper Poles or motion from the Epicycle of my own brain.  By this means I leave no gap for heresies, schisms, or errors, of which at present I hope I shall not injure truth to say I have no taint or tincture.

# VI. NATURAL THEOLOGY

# (1) THE USE OF NATURAL THEOLOGY

## No. 89. ROBERT BOYLE

[From *Some Considerations Touching the Usefulness of Experimental Natural Philosophy, Proposed in a Familiar Discourse to a Friend, By way of Invitation to the Study of it.* Part I, Essays II, III, IV, V. *Works*, ed. London (1772), Vol. II, pp. 15 f., 16–18, 18 f., 20, 21 f., 25–27, 29 f., 31–33, 36 f., 55 f. The First Part of this treatise appeared in 1663; a good deal of it, however, had been written many years previously. It was followed by a Second Part in 1671. The editing of it was entrusted to Robert Sharrock.]

THE next advantage, Pyrophilus, that we mentioned the knowledge of nature to bring to the minds of men is that therein it excites and cherishes devotion; which when I say, Pyrophilus, I forget not that there are several Divines (and some of them eminent ones) that out of a holy jealousy (as they think) for religion, labour to deter men from addicting themselves to serious and thorough inquiries into nature, as from a study unsafe for a Christian, and likely to end in atheism, by making it possible for men (that I may propose to you their objection as much to its advantages as I can) to give themselves such an account of all the wonders of nature, by the single knowledge of Second Causes, as may bring them to disbelieve the necessity of a First. And certainly, Pyrophilus, if this apprehension were well grounded, I should think the threatened evil so considerable that instead of inviting you to the study of natural philosophy, I should very earnestly labour to dissuade you from it. For I, that had much rather have men not philosophers than not Christians, should be better content to see you ignore the mysteries of nature than deny the Author of it. But though the zeal of their intentions keep me from harbouring any unfavourable opinion of the persons of these men, yet the prejudice that might redound from their doctrine (if generally received) both to the glory of God from the creatures, and to the empire of man over them, forbids me to leave their opinion unanswered; though I am sorry that the necessity of vindicating the study I recommend to you from so heinous a crime as they have accused it of, will compel me to theologize in a philosophical discourse: which that I may do, with as much brevity as the weight and exigency of my subject will permit, I shall content myself only in the explication of my own thoughts, to hint to you the grounds of answering what is alleged against them.

And first, Pyrophilus, I must premiss, that though it may be a presumption in man (who, to use a Scripture expression, *is but of yesterday,*

199

*and knows nothing, because his days upon the earth are but as a shadow*)
precisely and peremptorily to define all the ends and aims of the omniscient God in His great work of the creation, yet perhaps, it will be
no great venture to suppose, that at least in the creating of the sublunary
world and the more conspicuous stars, two of God's principal ends
were the manifestation of His own glory and the good of men.   For
the first of these, *The Lord hath made all things for Himself*, says the
Preacher; *for of Him, and through Him, and to Him, are all things*,
says the Apostle.   And, *Thou hast created all things, and for Thy
pleasure they are and were created*, say the twenty-four prostrate elders
(representatives, perhaps, of the whole Church of both Testaments,
propagated by the Twelve Patriarchs, and the like number of Apostles)
to their Creator; which truth, were it requisite, might be further
confirmed by several other texts, which, to decline needless prolixity,
I here forbear to insist on.   Consonantly to this, we hear the Psalmist
proclaiming that *the Heavens declare the glory of God, and the firmament
sheweth His handiworks*.   To which purpose we may also observe, that
though man were not created till the close of the sixth day (the resident's
arrival being obligingly suspended till the palace was made ready to
entertain him), yet that none of God's works might want intelligent
spectators and admirers, the Angels were created the first day, as Divines
generally infer from the words of God in *Job*; *Where wast thou, when
I laid the foundations of the earth?* and a little after: *When the morning
stars sang together, and all the sons of God shouted for joy*.   Where, by
the morning stars and sons of God, are supposed to be meant the newly
created Angels, one of whose earliest exercises was, it seems, to applaud
the creation, and take thence occasion to sing hymns to the Almighty
Author of it. . . .

And to proceed to that which we have formerly assigned for the
second end of the creation; that much of this visible world was made
for the use of man, may appear not only from the time of his creation
(already taken notice of) and by the commission given to the first progenitors of mankind to replenish the earth and subdue it, and to have
dominion over the fish of the sea, and over the fowls of the air, and
over all the earth, and over every living thing that creepeth or moveth
on the earth, but also by God's making those noble and vast luminaries
and other bodies that adorned the sky, to give light upon the earth,
though inferior to them in dimensions, and to divide between the day
and between the night, and to be for signs, and for seasons, and for days,
and for years.   To this agrees that passage in the Prophet, *Thus saith
the Lord that created the heavens, God Himself that formed the earth and
made it, He hath established it, He created it not in vain, He formed it to
be inhabited, etc.*   And the inspired poet speaks of man's dignity in very
comprehensive terms, *For Thou* (says he to his Maker) *hast made him
little lower than the Angels and hast crowned him with glory and honour ;*

*Thou madest him to have dominion over the works of Thy hands, Thou hast put all things under his feet.*

The same truth may be confirmed by divers other texts which it might here prove tedious to insist on.   And therefore I shall rather observe, that consonantly thereunto, God was pleased to consider man so much more than the creatures made for him, that He made the sun itself at one time to stand still and at another time to go back, and divers times made the parts of the universe forget their nature or act contrary to it ; and has (in sum) vouchsafed to alter by miracles the course of nature, for the instruction or relief of man (as when the fire suspended its destructive operation, whilst the three resolute Jews, with their protector, walked unharmed in the midst of those flames that destroyed the kindlers ; and as the heavy iron, emerged up to the swimming piece of wood, miraculously by Elisha made magnetical).   And you may also, Pyrophilus, take notice that when Adam had transgressed, immediately the ground was cursed for his sake.   And as it is not unusual in human justice to raze the very houses of regicides and resembling traitors, so when the provocations of Sodom swelled high enough to reach Heaven, God did not only destroy the inhabitants from the face of the earth, but for the inhabitants' sins destroyed the very face of the earth.   So when in Noah's time, a deluge of impiety called for a deluge of waters, God, looking upon the living creatures, as made for the use of man, stuck not to destroy them with him and for him, but involved in his ruin all those animals that were not necessary to the perpetuation of the species and the sacrifice due for Noah's preservation.   And so, when (in the last days) the earth shall be replenished with those scoffers mentioned by St. Peter, who will walk after their own lusts, and deride the expectation of God's foretold coming to judge and punish the ungodly, their impiety shall be as well punished as silenced by the unexpected flames (perhaps hastened by that very impiety) that shall either destroy or transfigure the world. For as by the law of Moses, the leprous garment, which could not be recovered by being washed in water, was to be burned in the fire, so the world, which the Deluge could not cleanse, a general conflagration must destroy.

Nor is reason itself backward to countenance what we teach.   For it is no great presumption to conceive that the rest of the creatures were made for man, since he alone of the visible world is able to enjoy, use, and relish many of the other creatures, and to discern the Omniscience, Almightiness, and Goodness of their Author in them, and return Him praises for them.   It is not for themselves that the rubies flame, other jewels sparkle, the bezoar-stone is antidotal, nor is it for their own advantage that fruitful trees spend and exhaust themselves in annual profusions. The light, which he diffuses through the world, is useless to the sun himself, whose inanimate being makes him incapable of delighting in his own splendour, which he receives but to convey it to the earth, and other by him illuminated globes: whence probably the Hebrews called him *Shemesh*, which grammarians derive from the root *Shemash*, signifying, in the Chaldean tongue, "to serve," or "minister to," the sun being the great minister of nature and fervent general of the universe. And as animals alone among the creatures seem to have a proper sense of, and complacency in, their own being, so man alone among animals is endowed with reason, at least such a pitch of it, as by which he can discern God's creatures to be the gifts of God and refer them to their Creator's glory. This truth I find not only embraced by Christians, but assented to even by Jews and Heathens. . . .

Having thus premised, Pyrophilus, that two of God's principal aims in the Creation were the manifestation of His own glorious attributes, and the welfare of His noblest visible creature, man, it will not be perhaps difficult for you to discern, that those, who labour to deter men from sedulous enquiries into Nature, do (though, I grant, designlessly) take a course, which tends to defeat God of both those mentioned ends.

For to speak, first, to the last of them, that man's external fruition of the creatures and the delight and accommodation which they may afford him, must be highly prejudiced and impaired by his ignorance of that natural philosophy wherein his dominion over the creatures chiefly consists, what we shall say hereafter concerning the usefulness of the knowledge of nature to human life will sufficiently evince. But such an animal fruition (if I may so call it) of the works of nature affords not man all the good that God designed him in them. For religion being not only the great duty of man, but the grand instrument of his future happiness, which consists in an union with and fruition of God, during that endless term that shall succeed the expiration of his transitory life on earth, whatever increases or cherishes his religion deserves to be looked on as a great contributor to his happiness. And we may therefore venture to affirm that the knowledge of the creatures does less advantage man, as it enables him to master them, than as it assists him, by admiring and serving Him, to become acceptable to their Author. And whatever our distrustful adversaries are pleased to surmise to the contrary, certainly God intended that His creatures should afford not only necessaries and accommodations to our animal part, but instructions to our intellectual. The world is wont to be styled not unfitly by Divines, the Christian's inn; but perchance it may be altogether as properly called his ship. For whereas both appellations suppose him a traveller, the inn, though it refresh him in his journey, does not further him in it, but rather retard his progress, by detaining him in one place; whereas a ship not only serves the passenger for an inn when he is weary, but helps to convey him towards his journey's end. And according to this notion, to suppose that God hath placed in the world innumerable things to feed man and delight him, and none to instruct him, were a conceit little less injurious to God than it were to a wise merchant, that sends persons he loves to a far country, to think that he would furnish their cabinets with plenty of provisions, soft beds, fine pictures, and all other accommodations for their voyage, but send them to sea disprovided of sea-charts, and mariner's compasses, and other requisite helps to steer their course by to the desired harbour. . . .

Now if you should put me upon telling you, Pyrophilus, what those attributes of God are, which I so often mention to be visibly displayed in the fabric of the world, I can readily answer you, that though many of God's attributes are legible in His creatures, yet those, that are most conspicuous there, are His power, His wisdom, and His goodness, in which the world, as well as the Bible, though in a differing, and in some points a darker way, is designed to instruct us; which, that you may not think to be affirmed gratis, we must insist a while on each of the three.

At first, how boundless a Power, or rather what an Almightiness is eminently displayed in God's making out of nothing all things, and without materials or instruments constructing this immense fabric of the world, whose vastness is such that even what may be proved of it can scarcely be conceived, and after a mathematical demonstration its greatness is distrusted! Which yet is, I confess, a wonder less to be admired, than the power expressed by God in so immense a work, which nevertheless some modern philosophers (whose opinions I find some Cabalists to countenance) suppose to be not the only production of God's Omnipotence. . . .

The next attribute of God that shines forth in His creatures is His Wisdom, which to an intelligent considerer appears very manifestly expressed in the world, whether you contemplate it as an aggregate or system of all natural bodies, or consider the creatures it is made up of, both in their particular and distinct natures, and in relation to each other and the universe which they constitute. In some of these the Wisdom of God is so conspicuous, and written in such large characters, that it is legible even to a vulgar reader. But in many others the lineaments and traces of it are so delicate and slender, or so wrapt up and covered with corporeity, that it requires an attentive and intelligent peruser. So numberless a multitude and so great a variety of birds, beasts, fishes, reptiles, herbs, shrubs, trees, stones, metals, minerals, stars, etc., and every one of them plentifully furnished and endowed with all the qualifications requisite to the attainment of the respective ends of its creation, are productions of a Wisdom too limitless not to be peculiar to God: to insist on any one of them in particular (besides that it would too much swell this discourse) might appear injurious to the rest; which do all of them deserve that extensive exclamation of the Psalmist, *How manifold are Thy works, O Lord ; in wisdom hast Thou made them all.* And therefore I shall content myself to observe in general that, as highly as some naturalists are pleased to value their own knowledge, it can at best attain but to understand and applaud, not emulate the productions of God. For as a novice, when the curiousest watch the rarest artist can make is taken in pieces and set before him, may easily enough discern the workmanship and contrivance of it to be excellent, but had he not been shewn it, could never have of himself devised so skilful and rare a piece of work ; so, for instance, an anatomist, though when by many and dextrous dissections of human bodies, and by the help of mechanical principles and rules (without a competent skill wherein, a man can scarce be an accomplished and philosophical anatomist), he has learned the structure, use, and harmony of the parts of the body, he is able to discern that matchless engine to be admirably contrived, in order to the exercise of all the motions and functions, whereto it was designed ; and yet this artist, had he never contemplated a human body, could never have imagined or devised an engine of no greater bulk, anything near so fitted to perform all that variety of actions we daily see performed either in or by a human body. Thus the circular motion of the blood and structure of the valves of the heart and veins (the consideration whereof, as himself told me, first hinted the circulation to our famous Harvey), though now modern experiments have for the main (the modus seeming not yet so fully explicated) convinced us of them, we acknowledge them to be very expedient, and can admire God's wisdom in contriving them. Yet those many learned anatomists that have for many succeeding ages preceded both Dr. Harvey and Columbus, Cesalpinus, Padre Paulo, and Mr. Warner (for each of these four last are supposed by some to have had some notion of the circulation), by all their diligent contemplation of human bodies never dreamed (for aught appears) of so advantageous an use of the valves of the heart, nor that nimble circular motion of the blood, of which our modern circulators think they discern such excellent use, not to say, necessity. . . .

The last of the three properties of God which we mentioned Him to have manifested in the Creation is His Goodness, of which all His creatures do in their due measure partake, partly by their having a being vouchsafed them, and partly by their being preserved in it, as long as their subordination to higher purposes and to more powerful creatures do permit, by that supporting influence of God, which keeps them from relapsing into their first nothing ; according to that memorable passage where Nehemiah, having mentioned God as the Creator of the Heavens, the earth, the seas, and all the creatures belonging to them, he calls Him the Preserver, or (as the original has it) *the Enlivener of them all.* And as for animals, who are more capable of enjoying, though not most of them of discerning His bounty, His Goodness to them is more conspicuous. For besides that in Scripture He is called the Preserver both of man and beast, and accordingly is said to give food even to the young ravens that cry, and to have, after the Flood, remembered not only Noah, but every living thing that was with him in the ark, His goodness to them is apparent by the plentiful and easily attainable provision He makes according to the exigence of their several natures, for that innumerable swarm of various birds, beasts, fishes, reptiles and other animals that people the terrestrial globe and the contiguous parts of the world, and by His endowing each of them with all the qualifications requisite to the perpetuation of their species, and the preservation of their lives, as far forth as is consistent with His ends in their creation. But most resplendent does the goodness of God appear towards His favourite creature, man, whom having vouchsafed to ennoble with His own image, He makes most of the creatures of the world visible to us pay homage to him, and in some manner or degree do him service, God's liberality at once bestowing on him all those creatures, by endowing him with a reason enabling him to make use of them ; so that even those creatures which he is not able to subdue by power he is able to make serviceable to him by his knowledge,—as those vast globes of light, which are so far above him, that their immensity and brightness can scarce render them visible to him, are by man's mathematics forced to give him an account of all their motions, and waiting upon his dials keep time for him ; and even the defects of such works of nature are by man's skill made serviceable to him, as the eclipses of the moon serve geographers notably in that difficult and useful work of finding longitudes. The stars serve for candles to give man light, and the celestial orbs are his candlesticks. He breathes the air, the fire warms him, and serves him not only in his kitchen, but to master most other bodies in his furnaces. The clouds water his land, the earth supports him and his buildings, the sea and winds convey him and his floating houses to the remotest parts of the world and enable him to possess every where almost all that nature or art has provided for him anywhere. The earth produces him an innumerable multitude of beasts to feed, clothe, and carry him ; of flowers and jewels to delight and adorn him ; of fruits, to sustain and refresh him ; of stones and timber, to lodge him ; of simples to cure him ; and in sum, the whole sublunary world is but his magazine. And it seems the grand business of restless nature so to constitute and manage his productions, as to furnish him with necessaries, accommodations, and pleasures.

Of such a number of plants, animals, metals, minerals, etc., that people and enrich the terrestrial globe, perhaps there is not anyone, of which man might not make an excellent use, had he but an insight into its nature ; nor are the most abject and despicable therefore the least useful. There is not any stone, no not the sparkling diamond itself, to whom man is so much beholden as he is to the dark and unpromising loadstone; without which the new world probably had never been detected, and many regions of the old world would have little or no commerce with each other. Nor have the lion, the eagle, and the whale joined all together (though reputed the chief of birds, beasts, and fishes), been so serviceable to man, as that despicable insect, the silkworm. And if we impartially consider the lucriferousness (if I may speak in My Lord of St. Alban's style) of the properties of things and their medical virtues, we shall find that we trample upon many things for which we should have cause to kneel and offer God praises, if we knew all their qualities and uses. But of this subject we may elsewhere purposely treat.

To which I must only add, Pyrophilus, that you will injure nature if you suppose either that all the concretes, endowed with excellent properties, have long since been notorious, or that all the medicinal virtues of simples, commonly used, are already known, or that all those concretes are destitute of considerable properties, to whom none have been yet ascribed by eminent authors. For almost every day either discloses new creatures or makes new discoveries of the usefulness of things, almost each of which hath yet a kind of *terra incognita*, or undetected part in it. How many new concretes, rich in medicinal virtues, does the new world present the inquisitive physicians of the old ? . . . .

Nor can we, without listening to these sermons, derive the entire (perhaps not the chiefest) benefit designed us in the creatures. For sure that God, Who hath composed us both of body and soul, hath not confined the uses of so many admirable creatures, and so much inimitable workmanship, to that ignoble part of man which coupleth him to the beasts, with the neglect of that Diviner portion which allies him to the Angels, vouchsafing to the lord of the creatures, in the fruition of this his palace, no higher prerogative than He is pleased to allow to the brutes, that serve but to complete the variety requisite for its embellishment. Of this opinion I lately found that excellent writer, St. Austin, to have been before me; for *non debes uti oculis*, says he, *ut pecus, tantum ut videas, quae addas ventri, non menti : utere, ut homo, intende caelum, et intende facta et quaere factorem ; aspice quae vides et quaere quem non vides, crede in eum quem non vides, propter ista quae vides. Nolite fieri sicut equus et mulus*, etc. " You ought not to use your eyes as a brute, only to take notice of provisions for your belly, and not for your mind : use them as a man; pry up into heaven; see the things made, and enquire the Maker; look upon those things you can see, and seek after him, whom you cannot see, and believe on him you cannot see, because of those things you see : and be not like the horse and mule, etc."

Nor can the creatures only inform man of God's being and attributes (as we have already seen), but also instruct him in his own duties; for we may say of the world, as St. Austin did of the Sacraments, that it is *verbum visibile*. And certainly God hath never so confined Himself to instruct men by words or types, as not to reserve Himself the liberty of doing it by things. Witness His appointing the rainbow to preach His goodness to all nations, and fortify the faith of mankind against the fear of a second deluge. It is something too high a saying for an heathen, that of Plato, where he teaches, " That the world is God's Epistle written to mankind." For by Solomon God sends *the sluggard to school to the ant*, to learn a provident industry. Christ commands His disciples to *learn of serpents and pigeons* prudence and inoffensiveness. The same Divine Teacher enjoins His Apostles to *consider the lilies*, or (as some would have it) *the tulips of the field*, and to learn thence that difficult virtue of a distrustless reliance upon God. And St. Paul seems almost angry with the Corinthians that their faith, in so abstruse mysteries as that of the Resurrection, was not informed and strengthened, by considering the meliorating death of corn committed to the earth. And the royal poet learns humility, by the contemplation of the most elevated parts of nature. *When I consider*, says he, *the heavens, the work of Thy fingers, the moon and stars, which Thou hast ordained, what is man, that Thou visitest him?* Thus you may see that God intended the world should serve man, not only for a palace to live in and to gaze on, but for a school of virtue, to which His philanthropy reserves such inestimable rewards, that the creatures can on no account be so beneficial to man, as by promoting his piety, by a competent degree of which, God's goodness hath made no less than eternal felicity attainable. . . .

Very like a philosopher, methinks, does the great Mercurius Trismegistus (if we grant him to be author of the books ascribed to him) speak, when he tells his son, " There can be no religion more true or just than to know the things that are, and to acknowledge thanks for all things to Him, that made them; which things I shall not cease to do." He continues, " Be pious and religious, O my son! For he, that does so is the best and highest philosopher; and without philosophy, it is impossible ever to attain to the height and exactness of piety and religion." And it was perhaps, Pyrophilus, to engage us to an industrious indagation of the creatures that God made man so indigent and furnished him with such a multiplicity of desires; so that whereas other creatures are content with those few obvious and easily attainable necessaries that nature has almost everywhere provided for them, in man alone every sense has store of greedy appetites, for the most part of superfluities and dainties, that to relieve his numerous wants or satisfy his more numerous desires, he might be obliged with an inquisitive industry to range, anatomize, and ransack nature, and by that concerned survey come to a more exquisite admiration of the omniscient author. To illustrate this subject yet a little further, Pyrophilus, give me leave to observe to you that philosophers of almost all religions have been, by the contemplation of the world, moved to consider it under the notion of a temple. *Ne adoremus*, says Plutarch, *elementa, caelum, solem, lunam, etc., specula sunt haec, in quibus artem illius singularem intueamur, qui mundum condidit et adornavit ; nec est alius mundus quam templum ejus.* "Let us not venerate the elements, the heaven, the sun, the moon, etc. These are but mirrors, wherein we may behold His excellent art, Who framed and adorned the world : nor is the world anything else but His temple." *Homines*, says Cicero, *tuentur illum globum, quem in templo hoc medium vides, qui terra dicitur.* "Men abide upon that globe, which you see in the middle of this temple, and is called the earth." Which Macrobius handsomely thus expounds: *Quicquid humano aspectui subjicitur, templum ejus vocavit, qui sola mente concipitur, ut qui haec veneratur ut templa, cultum tamen maximum debeat Conditori, sciatque quisquis in usum templi hujus inducitur, ritu sibi vivendum sacerdotis:* "All that human view reaches, He terms His temple, Who is apprehended by the mind alone ; to the end, that whoso reverences these things as temples might render the greatest worship to the Maker : and everyone, that is brought to converse in this temple, might know himself obliged to live like a priest."

And the lofty Seneca (to mention now no other heathens), in divers passages of his excellent writings, styles the world a temple ; and I remember, in his treatise *De Beneficiis*, he avers in terms not unworthy his mind or his subject, *Totum mundum deorum esse immortalium templum, solum quidem amplitudine illorum ac magnificentia dignum :* "That the whole world is the temple of the immortal gods, being alone worthy of their grandeur and magnificence." The assent of the Jewish philosophers to this notion you may be pleased to receive from their eloquent Philo, who not only gives the world the name of temple, but gives us this account of that appellation : *Templum Dei supremum et vere tale existimare totum hunc mundum, qui sacrarium quidem habet, purissimam rerum naturae partem, caelum ; ornamenta, stellas ; sacerdotes, administros potentiae ejus, angelos et incorporeas animas :* "The whole world is to be accounted the chiefest temple of God ; *the Sanctum Sanctorum* of it is of the purest part of the universe, heaven ; the ornaments, the stars ; the priests, the ministers of His power, angels and immaterial souls." And as for Christian philosophers, I suppose it would be needless to enumerate the passages wherein they adopt the notion of the world already mentioned ; and therefore I shall content myself to add, that the Scripture itself seems to authorise it by representing to us, in the eighth or [? and] ninth chapters of the Epistle to the Hebrews, the

Mosaical tabernacle, as an adumbration of that great temple of the world; and particularly there is a signal text in the latter of those chapters, where it is said, that Christ is not entered into holy places made with hands (χειροποίητα ἅγια) which are copies of the true, (ἀντίτυπα τῶν ἀληθινῶν) but into Heaven itself, now to appear in the presence of God for us.

Upon what account, Pyrophilus, I esteem the world a temple, I may elsewhere have occasion to declare; but this for the present it will not be rash to infer, that if the world be a temple, man sure must be the priest, ordained (by being qualified) to celebrate Divine service not only in it, but for it. For as in schools, when the prince or some munificent benefactor confers some large possession or rich annuity upon the foundation, though all the boys be concerned in the benefit, yet because most of them are too young to be sensible of it, or too unlearned to be able to make the retribution of a handsome acknowledgêment, either the master or that other person of the society who is most capable and the best spokesman, is by a kind of natural right engaged to the duty of returning praise and thanks, not for himself alone, but in the name of all the rest; so in the world, where there are so many inanimate and irrational creatures, that neither understand how much they owe to their Creator, by owing Him even themselves, nor are born to a condition enabling them to acknowledge it, man, as born the priest of nature, and as the most obliged and most capable member of it, is bound to return thanks and praises to his Maker, not only for himself, but for the whole creation. In which sense, we may reconcile those two current assertions, That God made all things for His own glory, and that God made all things for man, and man for Himself. Since whether or no man be a microcosm or little world in Paracelsus's sense, if not as a resembler, yet as a representer of the macrocosm or great world, he presents with his own adorations the homages of all the creatures to their Creator, though they be ignorant of what is done, as infants under the law were of the sacrifices offered on their account. And in this relation may the creatures answer the solemn invitation made them in the whole 148th Psalm and numerous other Scriptures; which they may do (to borrow a barbarous, but significant school-term) objectively, though not formally, I mean, by proving occasions, though not fingers, of His praises; being such objects as prompt and invite man to pay God that praise upon their score, which they cannot actually pay Him themselves; even God's mutest works being capable of being said to praise Him in the same sense (though in an incomparably transcendenter degree) that Solomon says of his virtuous woman (in the last verse of the *Proverbs*) *Let her own works praise her in the gates*,—that is, give the considerers of them occasion to extol her. And thus by man's referring the knowledge of the creature to the Creator's glory, it becomes in some sense and congruously to its own nature the praiser of its Maker, as may seem intimated in this Economy of the last part of one of the *Psalms, Bless the Lord, all ye His hosts, the ministers of His that do His pleasure. Bless the Lord, all His works, in all places of His dominion ; bless the Lord, O my soul.* Where, by shutting up the rest of God's creatures betwixt angels and man's soul, he seems to insinuate that the irrational creatures bless the Lord by the mouth of those that are intelligent. . . .

I ignore not, that not only Leucippus, Epicurus, and other Atomists of old, but of late some persons, for the most part adorers of Aristotle's writings, have pretended to be able to explicate the first beginning of things and the world's phenomena without taking in, or acknowledging any divine Author of it. And therefore, though we may elsewhere, by the assistance of that author, have an opportunity to give you an account of our unsatisfiedness with the attempts made by some bold wits in favour of such pretensions, yet since the main truth we plead for in this discourse is so nearly concerned in what hath been taught by those that would keep God from being thought to have any share in the production of the universe, I can scarce forbear (as unwilling as I am to digress) to represent to you on the present occasion a few considerations, which may assist you, if not to lessen the arrogance of such persons, at least, to keep yourself from thinking their evidence as great, as their confidence is wont to be. Now of the philosophers we speak of, some being Atomists, and others not, it will be requisite to say something to each of the two sorts. And because we not long since, in an illustrious company, where you, Pyrophilus, are not unknown, met with one of them, who avowedly grounded his opinions on the Aristotelian or vulgar physiology, we shall first recommend to you two or three considerations concerning such arrogant Peripatetics (for I speak not of that sect in general, of which I know there are divers excellent men).

First, then, you will in many passages of the following essays find that divers things that have been very magisterially taught and confidently believed among the followers of Aristotle are errors or mistakes ; and that as several, even of the obvious phenomena of nature, do contradict the common Peripatetic doctrine, so divers, at least of those, that are more abstruse, are not explicable by it ; and as confidently as these his followers talk of the expounding the very riddles of nature ; yet I remember, that he himself somewhere (for I cannot call to mind the place) did not scruple to confess that " As the eyes of owls are to the splendour of the day, so are those of our minds even to things obvious and manifest."

I shall next take notice that philosophers who scorn to ascribe anything to God, do often deceive themselves in thinking they have sufficiently satisfied our inquiries, when they have given us the nearest and most immediate causes of some things; whereas oftentimes the assignment of those causes is but the manifesting that such and such effects may be deduced from the more catholic affections of things, though these be not unfrequently as abstruse as the phenomena explicated by them, as having only their effects more obvious, not their nature better understood: as when, for instance, an account is demanded of that strange supposed sympathy betwixt quicksilver and gold; in that we find that whereas all other bodies swim upon quicksilver, it will readily swallow up gold, and hide it in its bosom. This pretended sympathy the naturalist may explicate by saying that gold being the only body heavier than quicksilver of the same bulk, the known laws of the hydrostatics make it necessary that gold should sink in it, and all lighter bodies swim on it. But though the cause of this effect be thus plausibly assigned, by deducing it from so known and obvious an affection of bodies as gravity, which every man is apt to think he sufficiently understands; yet will not this put a satisfactory period to a severe inquirer's curiosity, who will, perchance, be apt to allege, that though the effects of gravity indeed be very obvious, yet the cause and nature of it are as obscure as those of almost any phenomenon it can be brought to explicate; and that therefore he that desires no further account desists too soon from his inquiries, and acquiesces long before he comes to his journey's end. And indeed, the investigation of the true nature and adequate cause of gravity is a talk of that difficulty, that in spite of aught I have hitherto seen or read, I must yet retain great doubts whether they have been clearly and solidly made out by any man. And sure, Pyrophilus, there are divers effects in nature, of which though the immediate cause may be plausibly assigned, yet if we further inquire into the causes of those causes, and desist not from ascending in the scale of causes till we are arrived at the top of it, we shall perhaps find the more catholic and primary causes of things to be either certain, primitive, general, and fixed Laws of Nature (or rules of action and passion among the parcels of the universal matter), or else the shape, size, motion, and other primary affections of the smallest parts of matter, and of their first coalitions or clusters; especially those endowed with seminal faculties or properties, or (to dispatch) the admirable conspiring of the several parts of the universe to the production of particular effects; of all which it will be difficult to give a satisfactory account, without acknowledging an intelligent Author or Disposer of things. . . .

In the fourth place, I consider that the universal experience of all ages manifests that the contemplation of the world has been much more prevalent to make those that have addicted themselves to it believers than deniers of a Deity. For it is very apparent that the old philosophers, for the most part, acknowledged a God; and as evident it is, by their want of revelation, by many passages in their writings and by divers other things not now to be insisted on, that the consideration of the works of nature was the chief thing that induced them to acknowledge a Divine Author of them. This truth I could easily make out, were I at leisure to transcribe testimonies, which, because I am not, I shall content myself to mention to you one which may well serve for many, it being a confession made by Aristotle, or whatever other learned philosopher it was, who writ the book *De Mundo*, that God's being the architect and upholder of the world was the general belief of the ages that preceded his. *Vetus* (says he) *sermo est a majoribus proditus, inter omnes homines, universa tum ex Deo tum per Deum constituta fuisse atque coagmentata, nullamque naturam satis instructam ad salutem esse posse, quae citra Dei praesidium, suae ipsa demum tutelae permissa sit :* " It is an ancient tradition " (saith he) " diffused amongst all mankind from our ancestors, that all things were made and produced of God, and by God ; and that no nature can be sufficiently furnished for its own safety, which is left without the support of God, to its own protection." And as for both the opinion of that eminent author himself, and the grounds of it, he speaks of God and the creation almost in the terms of St. Paul : *Proinde* (says he) *haec etiam de Deo sentienda nobis sunt, illo quidem, si vim spectes, valentissimo ; si decorem, formosissimo ; si vitam, immortali ; denique, si virtutem, praestantissimo. Quapropter cum sit inconspicabilis naturae omni interiturae, ipsis nihilominus ipse cernitur ab operibus, atque ea quidem quae aere quoquo modo affecto, quae in terra, quae in aqua, ea certe Dei opera esse merito dixerimus : Dei inquam opera, cum imperio summo mundum, ac pro potestate obtinentis, ex quo Deo, ut inquit Empedocles physicus :*

> *Omnia quotquot erunt, quot sunt praesentia, quotque*
> *Orta fuere antehac stirpes, hominesque feraeque,*
> *Inde etiam volucres, piscesque humoris alumni.*

" Thus therefore we ought to conceive of God. If we consider His power, He is omnipotent ; if His shape, most beautiful ; if His life, immortal ; and finally, if His virtue, most excellent. Wherefore though undiscernible by any corruptible nature, yet He is perceived by such in His works ; and indeed those things, which are produced in the air, by any mutation whatsoever, in the earth or in the water, we ought deservedly to term the works of God ; which God is the absolute and sovereign Lord of the world, and out of Whom (as saith Empedocles the naturalist),

> All things beginning have, which e'er shall be,
> Are present or to come, plants, men, and beasts,
> And fowl, and fish the off-spring of the sea."

And those few philosophers (if ever there have been any at all) that have been really atheists, are no ways considerable for their number, in respect of those that have asserted a Deity; and their paradoxes have been looked upon as so irrational, that as soon as they have been proposed, they have been disdainfully rejected and condemned by all the rest of mankind, who have looked upon the patrons of them as monsters, rather than philosophers. And if there be, at this day, any nations (as navigators inform us there are in Brazil, and some other parts of the Indies) that worship no God, they consist not of naturalists, but brute and irrational barbarians, who may be supposed rather to ignore the being of God than deny it; and who, at least, are little less strangers to the mysteries of nature than to the Author of it. And if it be a truth that there are really such atheistical people, it may serve to recommend to us the study of physiology, by shewing us, that without the help of any such innate belief or persuasion of a God, as is supposed connatural to man, reason exercised upon the objects the creation presents us with, is sufficient to convince philosophers of a Deity. And indeed such a care has God taken, to make His Being conspicuous in His creatures, that they all seem loudly and unanimously to speak to their attentive considerers in the Psalmist's language, *Know ye, that the Lord He is God; it is He, that hath made us, and not we ourselves.* . . .

## No. 90. BENJAMIN WHICHCOTE

[From *Several Discourses. Works*, ed. Aberdeen, 1751, Discourse XXIII. Vol. I., pp. 370 f. This sermon was the second of a pair on *Phil*. iii, 12 called " The Exercise and Progress of a Christian." As one of the Cambridge Platonists, Whichcote was a keen advocate of the use of reason in matters of religion.]

They are not to be blamed, or looked upon as neglecters of God's grace, or undervaluers of it, or to abate it in the least, who vigorously and with all imaginable zeal call upon men to use, employ, and improve the principles of God's creation, that charge it upon men as a point of religion and conscience, to use, employ, and improve the principles of God's creation. I find that some men take offence to hear reason spoken of out of a pulpit, or to hear those great words of natural light, of principles of reason, and conscience. They are doubtless in a mighty mistake; for these two things are very consistent, as I shall shew you by and by; and there is no inconsistency between the grace of God and the calling upon men carefully to use, improve, and employ the principles of God's creation, and the telling men they shall meet with no discouragement from God, forasmuch as He will not leave them, till they first leave Him. And indeed this is a very profitable work to call upon men, to answer the principles of their creation, to fulfil natural light, to answer natural conscience, to be throughout rational in what they do; for these things have a Divine foundation. *The spirit in man is the candle of the Lord, lighted by God, and lighting men to God.* It is from God by way of efficiency, and to God finally.

19

# (2) FAITH AND REASON

## No. 91. LANCELOT ANDREWES

[From *A Pattern of Catechistical Doctrine*, Part I, ch. ii, § 2. *Minor Works*, ed. L. A. C. T., pp. 19–22. This treatise is probably derived from the notes of the lectures which Andrewes gave while at Pembroke College, Cambridge, where he had been appointed " Catechist " in 1578. It was published posthumously in 1630; a second edition appeared in 1641. Two other works, entitled respectively *The Moral Law expounded* (1642) and *The Pattern of Catechistical Doctrine at Large* (1650), were based on the same lectures. That the work consists of lecture notes and that it was never prepared for publication by the author explain its epigrammatic and unfinished style.]

To come to God there are two ways—by reason, or by faith.

The Manichees held that error, that by cunning and reason we should come to God, and not by faith. Which opinion is next unto Atheism. This the Manichees held in a bravery against Christians, because they well knew that the philosophers would rather submit to their sect, opening *fontem sciendi*, 'the fountain of knowledge,' than to the Christians, laying on them *jugum credendi*, 'the yoke of belief'; and this was the cause that some philosophers, who became Christians, were first drawn into Manicheeism, and afterwards were won thence to the orthodox doctrine of Christ. And such be they whom the learned in our days call *quaeristae*, which will have a reason for every thing: as, Why thus, and not rather thus? and therefore so far as they see reason, so far they will go, and no further.

Now then we must prove that faith is the best way, and reason the worst.

### We cannot come to God by reason.

1. If by knowledge only and reason we could come to God, then none should come but they that are learned and have good wits, and so the way to God should be as if many should go one journey, and because some can climb over hedges and thorns, therefore the way should be made over hedges and thorns; but God hath made His way *viam regiam*, 'the king's highway.'

2. Many are weak natured, and cannot take the pains that is needful to come to knowledge, and many are detained by the affairs of the commonwealth.

3. Many are cut off before they come to age to understand reason and to attain knowledge.

And so we see that few by reason can come to God.

*Faith not a sign of lightness.*

*Objection.* And whereas they object against faith, as Porphyry did against the Christians in his time, that it is a sign of lightness and credulity, which might breed occasion of doubting whether they were in the truth or no; which objection hindered many in that time.

*Answer* 1. We answer them by themselves; for they say themselves, that *nemo credulus nisi qui credit stulto aut improbo,* 'no man is counted credulous but he that believes a fool or a knave'; which two things are both excluded from God, and it were blasphemy to say otherwise; and so remaineth no place for credulity in believing of God. Besides, our believing is grounded on the Word of God, which Word, though it was delivered by the ministry of men, yet was of great power, as plainly appeareth; for those very men, first, healed leprosies, dropsies, men possessed with foul spirits, palsies, etc., all diseases,—cures far beyond the strength of physic's skill; secondly, they raised divers from death; thirdly, they shook the powers of Heaven; fourthly, unlettered and plain men in one day became skilful in all tongues. Therefore what was done by them had the Divine power working by their ministry, and was far above all human abilities.

2. Lightness is more in reason than in faith; for when there were two hundred and forty-eight sects of philosophers, and every one had a diverse felicity and divers reasons, there must needs be many crooked ways, and so, much doubting of the one side and credulity on the other.

3. In the knowledge of *prima entia,* 'first essences,' they are in the dark; for the principles of reason are from the sense, but God is above sense and reason, and beyond both.

4. Themselves dispute that God is above all reason of man. And therefore we cannot come to God by reason.

*We cannot come to God save by belief.*

Now to shew that there is no other way to come to God, but belief.

1. If they should in any matter be driven to prove every thing by reason, it would drive them into madness.

2. No man can make demonstration of every thing, no not in matters of the world; a man cannot make a demonstration that his father is his father, or that he is his son; so that there must needs be belief.

3. If a man should say he hath seen such and such a place, he can make no demonstrative reason of it; for the circumstances are not capable of demonstration, and no more is God, being the end of our journey.

*Of belief.*

Thus much for the necessity of belief;—now for belief itself.

1. *Oportet discentem credere,* 'a learner must believe'; we must

lay hold of that we hear; but this belief at the first is not perfect, *nam quod recipitur in imperfectum est primo imperfectum*, 'for that which is received in an imperfect body is at the first imperfect'; wood in the fire is first warm before it burn; it hath *calorem alienum*, 'heat from another,' before it have *proprium* 'its own' heat; so the learner must first take *ex aliena fide*, 'of another man's credit.' *Esay* vii, 9, *nisi credideritis non stabiliemini* 'unless you believe ye shall not be established.'

2. We must try and prove those things which we thus receive, either *à priori*, or *à posteriori; quia ut virtutum reliquarum, ita et religionis principia nobis innata habemus*, 'by what is precedent or consequent,' 'for we have inbred in us the principles, as of other virtues, so of religion'; and reason uncorrupt always agreeth with God's Word, and so God sends us often to nature; so the Apostle, *Acts* xvii, 24, etc.; *Rom.* i, 20 : *the invisible things of Him from the creation of the world are clearly seen, being understood by the things that are made.*

3. When we have thus strengthened our faith, we must yet look for a higher teacher; for though faith be a perfect way, yet we walk unperfectly in it, and therefore *in iis quae sunt supra naturam soli Deo credendum*, 'in things above nature we must believe God only'; so that we must look to God for His Spirit and inspiration.

4. This inspiration cometh not at the first, and therefore we must, as they say, *festinare lente*, 'make haste with leisure,' to avoid rashness; as *Esay* xxviii, 16, *qui crediderit non festinabit*, 'he that believes maketh not haste,' so we must wax perfect by little and little, and ever be building *to our faith, virtue ; to our virtue, knowledge ; to our knowledge, temperance ; with temperance, patience ; with patience, godliness ; with godliness, brotherly kindness ; with brotherly kindness, love (II Pet.* i, 5 f.); and though we build slowly, yet ever be sure to build on the rock.

Thus much for the second point, that the way to come to God is by belief.

## No. 92.  THOMAS BROWNE

[From *Religio Medici*, Part I.  Ed. Everyman's Library, pp. 10 f., 11 f., 17–19, 53 f.  Cp. note on No. 4.]

As for those wingy Mysteries in Divinity and airy subtleties in Religion, which have unhinged the brains of better heads, they never stretched the *Pia Mater* of mine.  Methinks there be not impossibilities enough in Religion for an active faith; the deepest Mysteries ours contains have not only been illustrated, but maintained, by syllogism and the rule of reason.  I love to lose my self in a mystery, to pursue my reason to an *O altitudo* !  'Tis my solitary recreation to pose my apprehension with those involved enigmas and riddles of the Trinity, with Incarnation, and Resurrection.  I can answer all the objections of Satan and my rebellious reason with that odd resolution I learned of Tertullian, *Certum est, quia impossibile est*. I desire to exercise my faith in the difficultest point; for to credit ordinary and visible objects is not faith, but persuasion. Some believe the better for seeing Christ's Sepulchre; and, when they have seen the Red Sea, doubt not of the Miracle. Now, contrarily, I bless my self and am thankful that I lived not in the days of Miracles, that I never saw Christ nor His Disciples. I would not have been one of those Israelites that passed the Red Sea, nor one of Christ's patients on whom He wrought His wonders; then had my faith been thrust upon me, nor should I enjoy that greater blessing pronounced to all that believe and saw not. It is an easy and necessary belief to credit what our eye and sense hath examined. I believe He was dead, and buried, and rose again; and desire to see Him in His glory, rather than to contemplate Him in His Cenotaph or Sepulchre. . . .

It is true there is an edge in all firm belief, and with an easy metaphor we may say, the *Sword* of Faith; but in these obscurities I rather use it in the adjunct the Apostle gives it, a *Buckler*; under which I conceive a wary combatant may lie invulnerable. Since I was of understanding to know we knew nothing, my reason hath been more pliable to the will of Faith; I am now content to understand a mystery without a rigid definition, in an easy and Platonic description. That allegorical description of Hermes pleaseth me beyond all the metaphysical definitions of Divines. Where I cannot satisfy my reason, I love to humour my fancy: I had as live you tell me that *anima est angelus hominis, est Corpus Dei*, as *Entelechia;—Lux est umbra Dei*, as *actus perspicui*. Where there is an obscurity too deep for our Reason, it is good to sit down with a description, periphrasis, or adumbration; for by acquainting our Reason how unable it is to display the visible and obvious effects of nature, it becomes more humble and submissive unto the subtleties of faith; and thus I teach my haggard and unreclaimed reason to stoop unto the lure of faith. . . .

Thus there are two Books from whence I collect my Divinity; besides that written one of God, another of His servant Nature, that universal and public manuscript that lies expansed unto the eyes of all. Those that never saw Him in the one have discovered Him in the other. This was the Scripture and Theology of the Heathens: the natural motion of the Sun made them more admire Him than its supernatural station did the Children of Israel; the ordinary effects of Nature wrought more admiration in them than in the other all His Miracles. Surely the Heathens knew better how to join and read these mystical letters than we Christians, who cast a more careless eye on these common Hieroglyphics, and disdain to suck Divinity from the flowers of Nature. Nor do I so forget God as to adore the name of Nature; which I define not, with the Schools, to be the principle of motion and rest, but that straight and regular line, that settled and constant course the Wisdom of God hath ordained the actions of His creatures, according to their several kinds. To make a revolution every day is the Nature of the Sun, because of that necessary course which God hath ordained it, from which it cannot swerve but by a faculty from that voice which first did give it motion. Now this course of Nature God seldom alters or perverts, but, like an excellent Artist, hath so contrived His work, that with the self same instrument, without a new creation, He may effect His obscurest designs. Thus He sweetneth the water with a wood, preserveth the Creatures in the Ark, which the blast of His mouth might have as easily created; for God is like a skilful Geometrician, who, when more easily and with one stroke of his compass he might describe or divide a right line, had yet rather do this in a circle or longer way, according to the constituted and fore-laid principles of his art. Yet this rule of His He doth sometimes pervert, to acquaint the world with His prerogative, lest the arrogancy of our reason should question His power, and conclude He could not. And thus I call the effects of Nature the works of God, Whose hand and instrument she only is; and therefore to ascribe His actions unto her, is to devolve the honour of the principal agent upon the instrument; which if with reason we may do, then let our hammers rise up and boast they have built our houses, and our pens receive the honour of our writings. I hold there is a general beauty in the works of God, and therefore no deformity in any kind or species of creature whatsoever. I cannot tell by what Logic we call a toad, a bear, or an elephant ugly, they being created in those outward shapes and figures which best express the actions of their inward forms, and having past that general Visitation of God, Who saw that all that He had made was good, that is, conformable to His Will, which abhors deformity, and is the rule of order and beauty. There is no deformity but in monstrosity, wherein, notwithstanding, there is a kind of beauty,—Nature so ingeniously contriving the irregular parts, as they become sometimes more remarkable than the principal fabric. To speak yet more narrowly, there was never any thing ugly or mis-shapen, but the chaos, wherein, notwithstanding (to speak strictly), there was no deformity, because no form; nor was it yet impregnant by the voice of God. Now Nature is not at variance with art, nor art with Nature, they being both servants of His providence. Art is the perfection of Nature. Were the world now as it was the sixth day, there were yet a chaos. Nature hath made one world, and art another. In brief, all things are artificial; for Nature is the art of God. . . .

How shall the dead arise, is no question of my Faith; to believe only possibilities is not Faith, but mere Philosophy. Many things are true in Divinity, which are neither inducible by reason, nor confirmable by sense ; and many things in philosophy confirmable by sense, yet not inducible by reason. Thus it is impossible by any solid or demonstrative reasons to persuade a man to believe the conversion of the Needle to the North, though this be possible and true and easily credible, upon a single experiment unto the sense. I believe that our estranged and divided ashes shall unite again, that our separated dust, after so many pilgrimages and transformations into the parts of minerals, plants, animals, elements, shall at the Voice of God return into their primitive shapes, and join again to make up their primary and predestinate forms. As at the Creation there was a separation of that confused mass into its species ; so at the destruction thereof there shall be a separation into its distinct individuals. As at the Creation of the World, all the distinct species that we behold lay involved in one mass, till the fruitful Voice of God separated this united multitude into its several species, so at the last day, when those corrupted reliques shall be scattered in the wilderness of forms, and seem to have forgot their proper habits, God by a powerful Voice shall command them back into their proper shapes, and call them out by their single individuals. Then shall appear the fertility of Adam, and the magic of that sperm that hath dilated into so many millions. I have often beheld as a miracle that artificial resurrection and revivification of mercury, how being mortified into a thousand shapes, it assumes again its own, and returns into its numerical self. Let us speak naturally and like philosophers. The forms of alterable bodies in these sensible corruptions perish not, nor, as we imagine, wholly quit their mansions, but retire and contract themselves into their secret and unaccessible parts, where they may best protect themselves from the action of their antagonist. A plant or vegetable consumed to ashes, to a contemplative and school-philosopher seems utterly destroyed, and the form to have taken his leave for ever. But to a sensible artist the forms are not perished, but withdrawn into their incombustible part, where they lie secure from the action of that devouring element. This is made good by experience, which can from the ashes of a plant revive the plant, and from its cinders recall it into its stalk and leaves again. What the art of man can do in these inferior pieces, what blasphemy is it to affirm the finger of God cannot do in these more perfect and sensible structures ! This is that mystical Philosophy, from whence no true scholar becomes an Atheist, but from the visible effects of nature grows up a real Divine, and beholds not in a dream, as Ezekiel, but in an ocular and visible object, the types of his resurrection.

## No. 93.  JOSEPH HALL

[From *Meditations and Vows, Divine and Moral, Serving for Directions in Christian and Civil Practice.* Century II, No. xv.  *Works*, ed. Peter Hall (1837), Vol. VIII, p. 32.  Cp. note on No. **282**.]

The School of God and Nature require two contrary manners of proceeding.  In the School of Nature, we must conceive, and then believe ; in the School of God we must first believe, and then we shall conceive.  He that believes no more than he conceives can never be a Christian ; nor he a Philosopher that assents without reason.  In Nature's school, we are taught to bolt out the truth by logical discourse.  God cannot endure a logician.  In His School, he is the best scholar that reasons least and assents most.  In Divine things, what I may, I will conceive ; the rest I will believe and admire.  Not a curious head, but a credulous and plain heart, is accepted with God.

## No. 94.  HENRY HAMMOND

[From *The Reasonableness of Christian Religion*, Chapter II, §§ 6–8, 16, 17.  *Miscellaneous Theological Works*, ed. *L. A. C. T.*, pp. 29 f., 32 f.  The treatise was written in 1649 and published in the following year.  The execution of the King had seemed to many Anglicans to put an end to their hopes.  The uncertainty of the future was leading some towards the Roman Church, others towards Presbyterianism, and yet others in the direction of unbelief altogether.  It was to the last of these classes that *The Reasonableness of Christian Religion* was addressed.]

For a thing to be good morally (for metaphysical goodness is all one with truth) depends, by sure connexion, from that eternal justice which is primarily in God,—that being the Rule, as it is the Fountain, of all moral goodness in men or things ; every thing being good, more or less, as it more or less partakes of that justice which is in God.

Now this being one of the attributes of God which are called communicable, it is truly affirmed that that justice which is in God is the very same in substance communicated to men, though in a lower degree.  And therefore it follows . . . that man, by the light of nature and general impressions, *i.e.* by a power of seeing whatsoever is within his sphere, is enabled by God to judge what is just, what not, what morally good, what bad.  And no man judges amiss in these things but he that hath his judgement corrupted by some prepossession or habitual vice or present prevailing temptation ; and therefore of moral controversies, *i.e.* whether a thing naturally, or in itself, be good or bad, just or not, right reason is a judge.

Yet this with this caution or limitation, that it be not extended to those things wherein the law of nature hath been elevated higher by any positive law of Christ.  For, as right reason cannot judge what is lawful in any particular kingdom, because what nature hath made lawful, the municipal laws of that place may have forbidden and made unlawful, and that right reason cannot take notice of, unless it be told so, so in Christ's kingdom, the Church, when He hath forbidden what nature had left free and unforbidden, reason, untaught by Christ, cannot say that that is unlawful, yet generally will be found to bear that testimony to Christ, that what Christ hath superadded to the law of nature, right reason will of its own accord commend as best or most laudable and excellent in them that do it; though, not knowing any precept for it, it will not affirm that it is necessary, so as it cannot be omitted without sin. . . .

Hence the conclusion is, that right reason is able to judge of all merely moral objects, whether anything be good or bad morally,—of natural objects in matter of fact, whether such a thing be done or no, by the help of the means specified, and by discourse, and analogy from things that we see are done, to judge that such another thing is possible. But of supernatural truths, such things as it never discerned in nature, either in the kind or the like, it cannot judge any further than thus : Either first, that though we cannot do it, yet for aught we know, it is possible (nay it hath a being) with God ; or secondly, that God hath affirmed it so, therefore I am sure it is ; or thirdly, what comes to me from authority, that I have no reason to suspect, but, on the contrary, concurrence of all reasons to be persuaded by it ; nay, there are some inward characters in the thing itself, that make me cast off all jealousy or doubt of such affirmations, and therefore I believe it is so. But generally, and *in thesi*, it is no way judge of these last kind of controversies.

And therefore though God, in moral actions, even in Himself, submits and appeals to man's reason, yet in these latter He derides all those that go about to judge of them by reason. And agreeably St. Paul in his preaching the Gospel, for the proving the truth of Christianity was fain, saith Origen, to use a peculiar way of demonstration, first, by comparing of prophecies in the Old Testament concerning Christ; secondly, by miracles: but in practical matters he appeals to that which was *written in every one's heart*.

## No. 95. DANIEL WHITBY

[From Λόγος τῆς πίστεως, *An Endeavour to evince the Certainty of the Christian Faith* (Oxford, 1671). Preface. Cp. note on No. **118**.]

If then you do reject a Providence because you are not able to conceive God's Omnipresence or any other attribute on which this Providence depends, if you renounce the Mysteries of Christian Faith because you cannot apprehend them, have you not equal reasons to reject the notions of infinite unbounded space, of an eternal flux of time, or an indivisible eternity, which yet your reason must acknowledge? Must you not question the existence of the souls of men and brutes, as being not sufficient to conceive that spirits, if confined to points, can perform any of those actions which we ascribe to them, or that they can diffuse themselves through bodies, receive impressions from them, or make impressions on them, or that mere matter should perceive, reflect, and reason, or have any sense of pain and pleasure? Lastly, must not this principle oblige you to question the existence of all material compounds? For who is able to conceive that indivisibles can be united? Or that a grain of sand can be for ever divisible and have as many parts as the whole world?

If you do question or dispute the truth of any miracle, revelation, or prediction, because you are not able to perceive the manner how it was or may be done, this will oblige you to deny the ebb and flowing of the sea, till you are able to acquaint us with the true causes of it, and to distrust that ever you were born, because you never can explain the manner of your own production. *For as thou knowest not the way of the wind, nor how the bones do grow in the womb of her that is with child, even so thou knowest not the works of God, Who maketh all things* (Eccles. xi, 5).

If you are tempted to disown these revelations, because you are not able to conceive God's ends and reasons in them, why He Who hath proclaimed Himself the God of Mercy should threaten an eternal punishment to finite transitory sins, why He should leave the world so long in darkness and the like, might not a subject on the like account reject the precepts of his sovereign because not able to perceive the wisdom of them or the necessity of all the sanctions he annexeth to them? Is it not certain that if there be a God, He must be infinite in His perfections and so incomprehensible, and then His wisdom must exceedingly transcend the reach of finite apprehensions? The secrets of it must be double to that which doth appear to us, and there must be such depths both in His judgements and His acts of mercy as we can never fathom. So that unless the notion of an infinite and all-wise Being includes a contradiction in the terms, we cannot doubt but that He may reveal what we can never apprehend. Besides, we cannot understand the beauty or wisdom of Divine transactions, but we must be acquainted with the ends and motives, the tendence and result of all He doth. For otherwise what seems absurd to us may admirably comply with the designs of Providence, what seems confused in the beginning may conclude in order and the greatest beauty. Since then we do not know the mind of God, since we are not acquainted with the designs and purpose nor are we able to look forward to the results of Providence, it is sure we cannot pass a judgement on the wisdom of them.

## No. 96. JOHN SMITH

[From *Select Discourses* (1673), pp. 2-4. The author was one of the leading writers of the famous Cambridge Platonist group. Very little is known of him. He died in 1652 at the early age of 34; and his ten Discourses were edited later by John Worthington. The following extract is from the first of them, entitled " Of the True Way or

[Method of attaining to Divine knowledge." A marked strain of ' Moralism ' such as
is to be seen in this extract, was characteristic of the whole Cambridge Platonist
school.]

They are not always the best skilled in Divinity that are the most
studied in those Pandects which it is sometimes digested into, or that
have erected the greatest Monopolies of Art and Science. He that
is most practical in Divine things hath the purest and sincerest knowledge of them, and not he that is most dogmatical. Divinity indeed
is a true efflux from the Eternal Light, which, like the sun-beams,
does not only enlighten, but heat and enliven; and therefore Our
Saviour hath in His Beatitudes connected purity of heart with the
Beatifical Vision. And as the eye cannot behold the sun, ἡλιοειδὴς μὴ
γινόμενος, unless it be sunlike, and hath the form and resemblance
of the sun drawn in it, so neither can the soul of man behold God,
θεοειδὴς μὴ γινομένη, unless it be Godlike, hath God formed in it,
and be made partaker of the Divine Nature. And the Apostle St.
Paul, when he would lay open the right way of attaining to Divine
Truth, he saith that *Knowledge puffeth up*, but it is *Love that edifieth*.
The knowledge of Divinity that appears in Systems and Models
is but a poor wan light, but the powerful energy of Divine knowledge
displays itself in purified souls: here we shall find the true πεδίον
ἀληθείας, as the ancient philosophy speaks, the land of Truth.

To seek our Divinity merely in books and writings, is to seek the
living among the dead. We do but in vain seek God many times
in these, where His Truth too often is not so much enshrined as
entombed. No. *Intra te quaere Deum*, seek for God within thine
own soul; He is best discerned νοερᾷ ἐπαφῇ, as Plotinus phraseth it,
by an intellectual touch of Him: we must see with our eyes, and
hear with our ears, and our hands must handle the Word of Life, that
I may express it in St. John's words. Ἔστι τῆς ψυχῆς αἴσθησίς τις,
the soul itself hath its sense, as well as the body: and therefore, David
when he would teach us how to know what the Divine Goodness is,
calls not for speculation but sensation, *Taste and see how good the Lord
is*. That is not the best and truest knowledge of God which is
wrought out by the labour and sweat of the brain, but that which is
kindled within us by an heavenly warmth in our hearts. As in the
natural body it is the heart that sends up good blood and warm spirits
into the head, whereby it is best enabled to its several functions, so
that which enables us to know and understand aright in the things of
God, must be a living principle of Holiness within us. When the Tree
of Knowledge is not planted by the Tree of Life, and sucks not up sap
from thence, it may be as well fruitful with evil as with good, and bring
forth bitter fruit as well as sweet. If we would indeed have our
knowledge thrive and flourish, we must water the tender plants of it
with holiness. When Zoroaster's scholars asked him what they should

do to get winged souls, such as might soar aloft in the bright beams of Divine Truth, he bids them bathe themselves in the waters of Life : they asking what they were, he tells them, the four cardinal virtues, which are the four rivers of Paradise. It is but a thin, airy knowledge that is got by mere speculation, which is ushered in by syllogisms and demonstrations; but that which springs forth from true goodness is θειότερόν τι πάσης ἀποδείξεως, as Origen speaks, it brings such a Divine light into the soul, as is more clear and convincing than any demonstration. The reason why, notwithstanding all our acute reasons and subtle disputes, Truth prevails no more in the world, is, we so often disjoin Truth and true Goodness, which in themselves can never be disunited. They grow both from the same root, and live in one another.

# (3) THE EXISTENCE OF GOD

## No. 97. FRANCIS BACON

[From *Essays* ; No. XVI, " Of Atheism " (ed. ' World's Classics,' pp. 43–46). The textual history of the famous *Essays* is highly complicated. Many details may be found in Edward Arber, *A Harmony of the Essays, etc., of Francis Bacon* (London, 1871), Introduction. The first edition of the Essays (containing only ten) appeared in 1597; that on " Atheism " was not published until 1612. The enumeration and text of the 1625 edition is that usually followed (*e.g.* by the edition in the ' World's Classics ').]

I HAD rather believe all the fables in the Legend and the Talmud and the Alcoran, than that this universal frame is without a mind ; and, therefore, God never wrought miracle to convince Atheism, because His ordinary works convince it. It is true, that a little philosophy inclineth man's mind to Atheism ; but depth in philosophy bringeth men's minds about to religion. For while the mind of man looketh upon second causes scattered, it may sometimes rest in them, and go no further ; but when it beholdeth the chain of them confederate, and linked together, it must needs fly to Providence and Deity. Nay, even that school which is most accused of atheism doth most demonstrate religion, that is, the school of Leucippus and Democritus and Epicurus ; for it is a thousand times more credible that four mutable elements, and one immutable fifth essence, duly and eternally placed need no God, than that an army of infinite small portions, or seeds unplaced, should have produced this order and beauty without a Divine marshal. The Scripture saith, *The fool hath said in his heart, there is no God*; it is not said, *The fool hath thought in his heart*. So as he rather saith it by rote to himself as that he would have, than that he can thoroughly believe it or be persuaded of it ; for none deny there is a God, but those for whom it maketh that there were no God. It appeareth in nothing more that Atheism is rather in the lip than in the heart of man than by this, that Atheists will ever be talking of that their opinion, as if they fainted in it within themselves, and would be glad to be strengthened by the consent of others ; nay more, you shall have Atheists strive to get disciples as it fareth with other sects, and—which is most of all—you shall have of them that will suffer for Atheism, and not recant ; whereas, if they did truly think that there were no such thing as God, why should they trouble themselves ? Epicurus is charged that he did but dissemble for his credit's sake when he affirmed there were blessed natures, but such as enjoyed themselves without having respect to the government of the world; wherein they say he did temporise, though in secret he thought there was no God. But certainly he is traduced, for his words are noble and divine : *Non Deos vulgi negare profanum ; sed vulgi opiniones Diis applicare profanum*. Plato could have said no more; and although he had the confidence to deny the administration, he had not the power to deny the nature. The Indians of the West have names for their particular gods, though they have no name for God : as if the heathens should have had the names *Jupiter*, *Apollo*, *Mars*, etc., but not the word *Deus*, which shows that even those barbarous people have the notion, though they have not the latitude and extent of it; so that against Atheists the very savages take part with the very subtlest philosophers. The contemplative Atheist is rare—a Diagoras, a Bion, a Lucian perhaps, and some others. And yet they seem to be more than they are; for that all that impugn a received religion, or superstition, are by the adverse part branded with the name of Atheists. But the great Atheists indeed are hypocrites, which are ever handling holy things but without feeling; so as they must needs be cauterized in the end.

The causes of Atheism are, divisions in religion, if they be many; for any one main division addeth zeal to both sides, but many divisions introduce Atheism. Another is, scandal of priests, when it is come to that which St. Bernard saith, *Non est jam dicere ut populus, sic sacerdos ; quia nec sic populus, ut sacerdos*. A third is, custom of profane scoffing in holy matters which doth by little and little deface the reverence of religion. And lastly, learned times, specially with peace and prosperity; for troubles and adversities do more bow men's minds to religion. They that deny a God destroy man's nobility; for certainly man is of kin to the beasts by his body; and if he be not of kin to God by his spirit, he is a base and ignoble creature. It destroys likewise magnanimity, and the raising of human nature; for take an example of a dog, and mark what a generosity and courage he will put on when he finds himself maintained by a man, who to him is instead of a God, or *melior natura* ; which courage is manifestly such as that creature, without that confidence of a better nature than his own, could never attain. So man, when he resteth and assureth himself upon Divine protection and favour, gathereth a force and faith which human nature in itself could not obtain. Therefore, as Atheism is in all respects hateful, so in this, that it depriveth human nature of the means to exalt itself above human frailty. As it is in particular persons, so it is in nations : never was there such a state of magnanimity as Rome. Of this state hear what Cicero saith, *Quam volumus, licet, Patres conscripti, nos amemus, tamen nec numero Hispanos, nec robore Gallos, nec calliditate Pœnos, nec artibus Græcos, nec denique hoc ipso hujus gentis et terræ*

*domestico nativoque sensu Italos ipsos et Latinos ; sed pietate, ac religione,*
*atque hac una sapientia, quod Deorum immortalium numine omnia regi,*
*gubernarique perspeximus, omnes gentes, nationesque superavimus.*

## No. 98. ROBERT SANDERSON

[From the former of *Two Sermons Preached at Paul's Cross*, London, the One
*November* 21 [1624], the *Other April* 15, 1627. *Sermons*, ed R. Montgomery (1841),
Vol. I, pp. 445 f.; *Works*, ed. W. Jacobson (1854), Vol. III, pp. 151–153. It is
numbered ' Sermon V *Ad Populum.*' The text was *I Tim.* iv, 4. Sanderson's
sermons were long even for his age. This one extends to some 24,000 words.]

From the goodness of the least creature guess we at the excellent
goodness of the great Creator. *Ex pede Herculem.* God hath imprinted,
as before I said, some steps and footings of His goodness in the creatures,
from which we must take the best scantling we are capable of, of those
admirable, and inexpressible, and inconceivable perfections that are
in Him. There is no beholding of the body of this sun who dwelleth
in such a glorious light as none can attain unto ; that glory would
dazzle with blindness the sharpest and most eagly eye that should dare
to fix itself upon it with any steadfastness. Enough it is for us, from
those rays and glimmering beams which He hath scattered upon the
creatures, to gather how infinitely He exceedeth them in brightness
and glory. *De ipso vides, sed non ipsum*, we see His, but not Him ;
His creatures they are our best, indeed our only, instructors. For
though His revealed Word teach us what we should never have learned
from the creatures without it, yet (fitted to our capacity) it teacheth no
otherwise than by resemblances taken from the creatures. τὸ γνωστὸν τοῦ
θεοῦ, as St. Paul calleth it ; the whole latitude of that which may be known
of God is manifest in the creatures, and the invisible things of God
not to be understood but by things that are made. St. Basil therefore
calleth the world, θεογνωσίας παιδευτήριον, the very school where
the knowledge of God is to be learned ; and there is a double way of
teaching, a twofold method of training us up into that knowledge in
that school ; that is to say, *per viam negationis* and *per viam eminentiæ.*
First *via negationis.* Look whatsoever thou findest in the creature,
which savoureth of defect or imperfection, and know God is not such.
Are they not limited, subject to change, composition, decay, etc. ?
Remove these from God, and learn that He is infinite, simple, unchangeable, eternal. Then *via eminentiæ.* Look whatsoever perfection
there is in the creature, in any degree, and know that the same, but
(infinitely and incomparably more eminently) is in God. Is there
wisdom, or knowledge, or power, or beauty, or greatness, or goodness,
in any kind, or in any measure, in any of the creatures ? Affirm the
same, but without measure, of God, and learn that He is infinitely
wiser, and skilfuller, and stronger, and fairer, and greater, and better ;
in every good thing so differently excellent above and beyond the

creatures, as that, though yet they be good, yet compared with Him, they deserve not the name of good ; *there is none good but one, that is God.* None good as He, simply, and absolutely, and essentially, and of Himself such.

The creatures that they are good, they have it from Him ; and their goodness dependeth upon Him ; and they are good but in part, and in some measure, and in their own kinds. Whensoever, therefore, we find any good from, or observe any goodness in any of the creatures, let us not bury our meditations there, but raise them up by those stairs, as it were, of the creatures to contemplate the great goodness of Him their Creator. We are unhappy truants, if, in this so richly furnished school of God's good creatures, we have not learned from them at the least so much knowledge of Him and His goodness, as to admire and love, and depend upon it and Him. Look upon the workmanship, and accordingly judge of the workman. *Every creature of God is good* ; surely, then, the Creator must needs excel in goodness.

## No. 99.  JOHN TILLOTSON

[From *The Wisdom of Being Religious. A Sermon Preached at St. Paul's* [on *Job* xxviii, 28], London, 1664. *Works*, ed. London (1728), Vol. I, pp. 16 f. In 1663, not long before this sermon was delivered, Tillotson had been appointed " Preacher to the Honourable Society of Lincoln's Inn " (Title page). In the noteworthy dedication to Anthony Bateman, the Lord Mayor of London, Tillotson deplores the anti-religious tendencies of the times.]

Speculative Atheism is absurd, because it requires more evidence for things than they are capable of. Aristotle hath long since well observed how unreasonable it is to expect the same kind of proof and evidence for every thing, which we have for some things. Mathematical things, being of an abstracted nature, are capable of the clearest and strictest demonstration. But conclusions in natural philosophy are capable of proof by an induction of experiments ; things of a moral nature by moral arguments ; and matters of fact by credible testimony. And though none of these be capable of that strict kind of demonstration which mathematical matters are, yet have we an undoubted assurance of them when they are proved by the best arguments that things of that kind will bear. No man can demonstrate to me, unless we will call every argument that is fit to convince a wise man a demonstration, that there is such an island in America as Jamaica. Yet upon the testimony of credible persons who have seen it and authors who have written of it, I am as free from all doubt concerning it as I am from doubting of the clearest mathematical demonstration. So that this is to be entertained as a firm principle by all those who pretend to be certain of anything at all. That when any thing in any of these kinds is proved by as good arguments as a thing of that kind is capable of, and we have as great assurance that it is as we could possibly have supposing it were, we ought not in reason to make any doubt of the existence of that thing.

Now to apply this to the present case. The Being of a God is not *mathematically* demonstrable, nor can it be expected it should, because only mathematical matters admit of this kind of evidence. Nor can it be proved immediately by sense, because God being supposed to be a pure Spirit cannot be the Object of any corporeal sense. But yet we have as great assurance that there is a God as the nature of the thing to be proved is capable of, and as we would in reason expect to have, supposing that He were. For let us suppose there were such a Being as an Infinite Spirit, clothed with all possible perfection, that is as good and wise and powerful, etc., as can be imagined. What conceivable ways are there whereby we should come to be assured that there is such a Being, but either by an internal impression of the notion of a God upon our minds, or else by such external and visible effects as our reason tells us must be attributed to some cause and which we cannot without great violence to our understandings attribute to any other cause but such a Being as we conceive God to be, that is, One that is infinitely good and wise and powerful? Now we have this double assurance that there is a God, and greater or other than this the thing is not capable of. If God should assume a body and present Himself before our eyes, this might amaze us, but could not give us any rational assurance that there is an Infinite Spirit. If He should work a miracle, this could not in reason convince an Atheist more than the arguments he already hath for it. If the Atheist, then, were to *ask a sign in the heaven above or in the earth beneath*, what could he desire God to do for his conviction more than He hath already done? Could he desire Him to work a greater miracle than to make a world? Why, if God should carry this perverse man out of the limits of this world, and shew him a new heaven and a new earth springing out of nothing, he might say that innumerable parts of matter chanced just then to rally together and to form themselves into this new world, and that God did not make it. Thus you see that we have all the rational assurance of a God that the thing is capable of, and that Atheism is absurd and unreasonable in requiring more.

## No. 100.  ISAAC NEWTON

[From *Philosophiae Naturalis Principia Mathematica*, Concluding paragraphs of Book III. English translation, ed. 1729, Vol. II, pp. 388–393. The Third Book of this epoch-making treatise was presented by Isaac Newton to the Royal Society on April 6, 1687, when the two preceding Books were already in the press. The work appeared in the summer of that year. It was dedicated to the Royal Society, and a set of Latin hexameters, addressed to Halley, was prefixed to it. The book created an immediate sensation throughout the length and breadth of Europe.]

The six primary Planets are revolved about the Sun, in circles concentric with the Sun, and with motions directed towards the same

20

parts and almost in the same plane.  Ten Moons are revolved about
the Earth, Jupiter, and Saturn, in circles concentric with them, with
the same direction of motion and nearly in the planes of the orbits of
those Planets.  But it is not to be conceived that mere mechanical
causes could give birth to so many regular motions, since the Comets
range over all parts of the heavens, in very eccentric orbits.  For by
that kind of motion they pass easily through the orbs of the Planets and
with great rapidity ;  and in their aphelions, where they move the
slowest, and are detained the longest, they recede to the greatest
distances from each other and thence suffer the least disturbance from
their mutual attractions.  This most beautiful System of the Sun,
Planets, and Comets, could only proceed from the counsel and
dominion of an intelligent and powerful Being.  And if the fixed Stars
are the centres of other like Systems, these being formed by the like
wise counsel, must be all subject to the dominion of One, especially
since the light of the fixed Stars is of the same nature with the light
of the Sun, and from every System light passes into all the other
Systems.  And lest the Systems of the fixed Stars should by their
gravity, fall on each other mutually, He hath placed those Systems at
immense distances one from another.

This Being governs all things, not as the soul of the world but as
Lord over all.  And on account of His dominion, He is wont to be
called *Lord God*, παντοκράτωρ or *Universal Ruler*.  For God is a
relative word, and has respect to servants ;  and *Deity* is the dominion
of God, not over His own body, as those imagine who fancy God to be
the soul of the world, but over servants.  The supreme God is a Being
eternal, infinite, absolutely perfect.  But a being, however perfect,
without dominion cannot be said to be Lord God ;  for we say, my God,
your God, the God of Israel, the God of Gods and Lord of Lords,—
but we do not say, My Eternal, your Eternal, the Eternal of Israel,
the Eternal of Gods ;  we do not say, My Infinite, or my Perfect.  These
are titles which have no respect to servants.  The word *God* usually
signifies *Lord* ;  but every lord is not a God.  It is the dominion of a
spiritual being which constitutes a God ;  a true, supreme, or imaginary
dominion makes a true, supreme, or imaginary God.  And from His
true dominion it follows that the true God is a living, intelligent, and
powerful Being ;  and from His other perfections that He is supreme or
most perfect.  He is eternal and infinite, omnipotent and omniscient ;
that is, His duration reaches from eternity to eternity, His presence
from infinity to infinity ;  He governs all things and knows all things
that are or can be done.  He is not eternity or infinity, but eternal and
infinite.  He is not duration or space, but He endures and is present.
He endures for ever and is everywhere present ;  and by existing always
and everywhere, He constitutes duration and space.  Since every

particle of space is always, and every indivisible moment of duration
is everywhere, certainly the Maker and Lord of all things cannot be
never and nowhere. Every soul that has perception is, though in
different times and in different organs of sense and motion, still the
same indivisible person. There are given successive parts in duration,
co-existent parts in space, but neither the one nor the other in the
person of a man or his thinking principle; and much less can they be
found in the thinking substance of God. Every man, so far as he is a
thing that has perception, is one and the same man during his whole
life, in all and each of his organs of sense. God is the same God,
always and everywhere. He is omnipresent, not *virtually* only but
also *substantially*; for virtue cannot subsist without substance. In
Him are all things contained and moved; yet neither affects the other.
God suffers nothing from the motion of bodies; bodies find no resistance from the omnipresence of God. It is allowed by all that the
supreme God exists necessarily, and by the same necessity He exists
always and everywhere. Whence also He is all similar, all eye, all ear,
all brain, all arm, all power to perceive, to understand, and to act;
but in a manner not at all human, in a manner not at all corporeal,
in a manner utterly unknown to us. As a blind man has no idea of
colours, so have we no idea of the manner by which the all-wise God
perceives and understands all things. He is utterly void of all body
and bodily figure, and can therefore neither be seen nor heard nor
touched; nor ought He to be worshipped under the representation
of any corporeal thing. We have ideas of His attributes, but what
the real substance of anything is, we know not. In bodies we see only
their figures and colours, we hear only the sounds, we touch only their
outward surfaces, we smell only the smells and taste the savours; but
their inward substances are not to be known, either by our senses or by
any reflex act of our minds. Much less then have we any idea of the
substance of God. We know Him only by His most wise and excellent
contrivances of things, and final causes; we admire Him for His
perfections; but we reverence and adore Him on account of His
dominion. For we adore Him as His servants; and a God without
dominion, providence, and final causes is nothing else but Fate and
Nature. Blind metaphysical necessity, which is certainly the same
always and everywhere, could produce no variety of things. All that
diversity of natural things which we find, suited to different times
and places, could arise from nothing but the ideas and will of a Being
necessarily existing. But by way of allegory, God is said to see, to
speak, to laugh, to love, to hate, to desire, to give, to receive, to rejoice,
to be angry, to fight, to frame, to work, to build. For all our notions
of God are taken from the ways of mankind, by a certain similitude
which, though not perfect, has some likeness however. And thus much

concerning God ; to discourse of Whom from the appearances of things does certainly belong to natural philosophy.

Hitherto we have explained the phenomena of the heavens and of our sea by the power of gravity, but have not yet assigned the cause of this power. This is certain, that it must proceed from a cause that penetrates to the very centres of the sun and planets, without suffering the least diminution of its force ; that operates, not according to the quantity of the surfaces of the particles upon which it acts (as mechanical causes use to do), but according to the quantity of the solid matter which they contain and propagates its virtue on ail sides, to immense distances, decreasing always in the duplicate proportion of the distances. Gravitation towards the Sun is made up out of the gravitations towards the several particles of which the Body of the Sun is composed ; and in receding from the Sun, decreases accurately in the duplicate proportion of the distances, as far as the orb of Saturn, as evidently appears from the quiescence of the aphelions of the Planets, nay, and even to the remotest aphelions of the Comets, if those aphelions are also quiescent. But hitherto I have not been able to discover the cause of those properties of gravity from phenomena, and I frame no hypotheses. For whatever is not deduced from the phenomena is to be called an hypothesis, and hypotheses, whether metaphysical or physical, whether of occult qualities or mechanical, have no place in experimental philosophy. In this philosophy particular propositions are inferred from the phenomena, and afterwards rendered general by induction. Thus it was that the impenetrability, the mobility, and the impulsive force of bodies, and the laws of motion and of gravitation, were discovered. And to us it is enough that gravity does really exist, and act according to the laws which we have explained, and abundantly serves to account for all the motions of the celestial bodies, and of our sea.

And now we might add something concerning a certain most subtle Spirit, which pervades and lies hid in all gross bodies ; by the force and action of which Spirit, the particles of bodies mutually attract one another at near distances, and cohere, if contiguous ; and electric bodies operate to greater distances, as well repelling as attracting the neighbouring corpuscles ; and light is emitted, reflected, refracted, inflected, and heats bodies ; and all sensation is excited, and the members of animal bodies move at the command of the will, namely by the vibrations of this Spirit, mutually propagated along the solid filaments of the nerves, from the outward organs of sense to the brain, and from the brain into the muscles. But these are things that cannot be explained in few words, nor are we furnished with that sufficiency of experiments which is required to an accurate determination and demonstration of the laws by which this elastic Spirit operates.

# (4) MIRACLES

## No. 101.  ISAAC BARROW

[From *Theological Works*, ed. A. Napier, Cambridge, 1859, Vol. III, pp. 479 f. The sermon from which the following extract is taken is No. 48.   Its title is " The Unsearchableness of God's Judgements " :  and the text *Rom.* xi, 33.]

GOD commonly doth not intend to exert His hand notoriously; for that whereas every special interposition of His hand is in effect a miracle (surmounting the natural power, or thwarting the ordinary course of inferior causes), it doth not become Him to prostitute His miraculous power, or to exert it otherwise than upon singular occasions and for most weighty causes.  It is not conformable to the tenor of His administrations to convince men against their will, or by irresistible evidence to wring persuasion from stubborn or stupid minds; but to exercise the wisdom and to prove the ingenuity of well-disposed persons, who upon competent intimations shall be capable to spell out, and forward to approve His proceedings.

He will not glare forth in discoveries so bright as to dazzle, to confound our weak sight.   Therefore He veileth His face with a cloud and wrappeth His power in some obscurity ; therefore *clouds and darkness are round about Him : He maketh darkness His secret place ; His pavilion round about Him is dark waters and thick clouds of the sky.*

He meaneth thereby to improve and exalt our faith, being the less seen that He may be the more believed,—faith never rising higher than when it doth soar to objects beyond our sight; when we can approve God's wisdom and justice in occurrences surmounting our conceit, when we can rely upon God's Word and help, although the stream of His proceedings seemeth to cross our hopes.

## No. 102.  THOMAS BROWNE

[From *Religio Medici*, Part I.   Ed. Everyman's Library, pp. 32 f.   Cp. note on No. 4.]

That miracles are ceased, I can neither prove nor absolutely deny, much less define the time and period of their cessation.   That they survived Christ is manifest upon the record of Scripture ; that they outlived the Apostles also and were revived at the conversion of nations many years after, we cannot deny, if we shall not question those writers whose testimonies we do not controvert in points that make for our own opinions.   Therefore that may have some truth in it that is reported

233

by the Jesuits of their miracles in the Indies; I could wish it were true, or had any other testimony than their own pens. They may easily believe those miracles abroad, who daily conceive a greater at home, the transmutation of those visible elements into the Body and Blood of Our Saviour. For the conversion of Water into Wine, which He wrought in Cana, or, what the Devil would have had Him done in the wilderness, of stones into bread, compared to this, will scarce deserve the name of a miracle: though indeed, to speak properly, there is not one miracle greater than another, they being the extraordinary effects of the hand of God, to which all things are of an equal facility; and to create the world, as easy as one single creature. For this is also a miracle, not only to produce effects against or above Nature, but before Nature; and to create Nature, as great a miracle as to contradict or transcend her. We do too narrowly define the Power of God, restraining it to our capacities. I hold that God can do all things; how He should work contradictions, I do not understand, yet dare not therefore deny. I cannot see why the Angel of God should question Esdras to recall the time past, if it were beyond His own power; or that God should pose mortality in that which He was not able to perform Himself. I will not say God cannot, but He will not, perform many things, which we plainly affirm He cannot. This, I am sure, is the mannerliest proposition, wherein, notwithstanding, I hold no paradox; for, strictly, His power is the same with His will, and they both, with all the rest, do make but one God.

# (5) THE NEW PHILOSOPHY

## No. 103.  ROBERT BOYLE

[From *The Christian Virtuoso, Shewing that by being addicted to Experimental Philosophy, a Man is rather assisted than indisposed to be a good Christian, The First Part. Works*, ed. London (1772), Vol. V, pp. 516 f.  This treatise, which appeared in 1690, was one of the last which Boyle published.  He did not live to complete the projected second part of it.]

IN reference to this matter, we may confidently say that the Experimental Philosophy has a great advantage of the Scholastic.  For in the Peripatetic schools, where things are wont to be ascribed to certain substantial forms and real qualities (the former of which are acknowledged to be very abstruse and mysterious things, and the latter are many of them confessedly occult), the accounts of nature's works may be easily given in a few words that are general enough to be applicable to almost all occasions.  But these uninstructive terms do neither oblige nor conduct a man to deeper searches into the structure of things, nor their manner of being produced, and of operating upon one another ; and consequently are very insufficient to disclose the exquisite wisdom, which the omniscient Maker has expressed in the peculiar fabrics of bodies, and the skilfully regulated motions of them or of their constituent parts.  From the discernment of which things nevertheless it is, that there is, by way of result, produced in the mind of an intelligent contemplator a strong conviction of the being of a divine Opificer, and a just acknowledgment of His admirable wisdom.  To be told that an eye is the organ of sight, and that this is performed by that faculty of the mind which from its function is called visive, will give a man but a sorry account of the instruments and manner of vision itself, or of the knowledge of that Opificer, Who, as the Scripture speaks, *formed the eye*.  And he that can take up with this easy theory of vision will not think it necessary to take the pains to dissect the eyes of animals, nor study the books of mathematicians, to understand vision ; and accordingly will have but mean thoughts of the contrivance of the organ and the skill of the Artificer, in comparison of the ideas that will be suggested of both of them to him that, being profoundly skilled in anatomy and optics, by their help takes asunder the several coats, humours, and muscles, of which that exquisite dioptrical instrument consists ; and having separately considered the figure, size, consistence, texture, diapheneity, or opacity, situation, and connexions of each

of them, and their coaptation in the whole eye, shall discover, by the
help of the laws of Optics, how admirably this little organ is fitted to
receive the incident beams of light, and dispose them in the best manner
possible for completing the lively representation of the almost infinitely
various objects of sight.

## No. 104.  ROBERT BOYLE

[From *Tracts Containing New Experiments touching the Relation betwixt Flame and
Air, and about Explosions. An Hydrostatical Discourse, Occasioned by the Objections
of the learned Dr. Henry More Against some Explications of New Experiments made
by Mr. Boyle*, London, 1672.   From the Preface to the Reader.  *Works*, ed. London
(1772), Vol. III, pp. 597 f.   In his *Enchiridion Metaphysicum* (1671), an attack upon
Cartesianism, More had contended for the existence of an *Anima Mundi*, and maintained that herein was to be found the principle of atmospheric pressure.  Boyle
argued against the introduction of " any such unphilosophical principle " into
mechanics.  See F. I. Mackinnon, *The Philosophical Writings of Henry More* (New
York, 1925), p. 305.]

But though I have declined the delivering my opinion of the Doctor's
[*i.e.* Henry More's] book, yet I dare not forbear owning my not being
satisfied with that part of his preface, which falls foul upon Monsieur
*Des Cartes* and his philosophy.   For though I have often wished that
learned gentleman had ascribed to the Divine Author of Nature a more
particular and immediate efficiency and guidance, in contriving the
parts of the universal matter into that great engine we call the world;
and though I am still of opinion that he might have ascribed more than
he has to the supreme Cause, in the first origin and production of
things corporeal, without the least injury to truth, and without much,
if any, prejudice to his own philosophy; and though not confining
myself to any sect, I do not profess myself to be of the Cartesian; yet
I cannot but have too much value for so great a wit as the founder of it,
and too good an opinion of his sincerity in asserting the existence of a
Deity, to approve so severe a censure as the Doctor is pleased to give
of him.   For I have long thought that in tenets about religion, though
it be very just to charge the ill consequences of men's opinions upon the
opinions themselves, yet it is not just, or at least not charitable, to charge
such consequences upon the persons, if we have no pregnant cause to
think they discern them, though they disclaim them.  And since men have
usually the fondness of fathers for the offspring of their own brains,
I see not why Cartesius himself may not have overlooked the bad inferences that may be drawn from his principles (if indeed they afford
any such), since divers learned, and not a few pious persons and professed Divines of differing Churches, have so little perceived that the
things objected are consequent to such principles, that they not only
absolve them as harmless, but extol them as friendly and advantageous
to natural religion.   And I see not why so great and radiant a truth as
that of the existence of a God, that has been acknowledged by so many
mere philosophers, might not as well impress itself on so capable an

intellect as that of Monsieur *Des Cartes*; or that so piercing a wit may not really believe he had found out new mediums to demonstrate it by. And since the learned Gassendus, though an ecclesiastic, had been able, as well safely as largely to publish the irreligious philosophy of Epicurus himself, it seems not likely that so dexterous a wit as that of Monsieur *Des Cartes* could not have proposed his notions about the mechanical philosophy without taking so mean a course to shelter himself from danger, as in the most important points that can fall under man's consideration, to labour with great skill and industry to deceive abundance of ingenious men, many of whom appeared to be lovers of truth, and divers of them lovers of him also. And I am the more averse from so harsh an opinion of a gentleman, whose way of writing, even in his private letters, tempts me very little to it, because I cannot think him an Atheist and an hypocrite, without thinking him (what Dr. More has too much celebrated him) to call him a weak head, and almost as bad a philosopher as a man. For, as far as I understand his principles, some of the most important points of his philosophy (which, if it were needful, I could name) are interwoven with the truth of the existence of a God, or do at least suppose it, and are not demonstrable without it. But I must not prevent the Cartesians, who, now he cannot do it for himself, I doubt not will apologize for their master; though looking upon him as a great benefactor to, though not the first founder of the mechanical philosophy, I could not consent by a total silence upon such an occasion to become any way accessory to the blemishing of his memory.

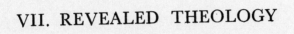

# VII. REVEALED THEOLOGY

# (1) THE CHRISTIAN RELIGION
## No. 105. GILBERT BURNET

[From *A Discourse Wherein is held forth the Opposition of the Doctrine, Worship, and Practices of the Roman Church to the Nature, Designs, and Characters of the Christian Faith*, London, 1688. A second edition of this pamphlet was issued in the same year. *Enchiridion Theologicum Anti-Romanum*, ed. Oxford (E. Cardwell), 1837, Vol. III, pp. 2–6.]

THE designs of the Christian Religion run betwixt these four heads : The first, is to give us right apprehensions of the nature and attributes of God, that we may conceive aright of Him, and adore Him suitably to His nature and according to His will, and thereby be admitted to a free converse with Him, and become partakers of the Divine Nature. How little of God was known by the twinklings of Nature's light, even to the better and wiser part of the world, Tully's Books of *The Nature of the Gods* do sufficiently inform us. But if the philosophers were so much to seek in it, what shall we expect from the vulgar ? And indeed Homer's *Iliad* and Ovid's *Metamorphoses* were wretched systems of Divinity ; and yet such, and such like, were the sentiments of the nations about the Godhead. It is true, the seed of Abraham were delivered from that darkness, and knew God by His Name Jehovah, and had laws and ordinances given them by God ; yet their worship was so carnal, and did so strike upon and affect the senses, that we will be soon satisfied it was not so sublime and free as became the spirituality of the Divine Nature, and so was only fitted for the infancy of the people of God. But by Christ *the mystery that lay hid from ages and generations was revealed ; for He declared the Father, and revealed Him*, and taught us to *renounce idols and vanities and to serve the living God, commanding all men everywhere to repent, the times of ignorance, wherein God winked at idolatry*, being then over ; that so mankind, being *God's offspring, might feel after Him*, and not worship Him any more in the blinding grossness of idolatry, but in a pure spiritual manner. And whereas *the law came by Moses, by Christ came grace and truth* ; grace in opposition to the severity of the law ; and truth, as opposed, not to falsehood, but to the figures and shadows of Moses his law ; and therefore God is to be worshipped in spirit and truth, in opposition to the carnal ordinances and typical rites, which shadowed out the truth in the law.

The second branch of the Christian religion is, to hold forth the method of man's reconciliation with his Maker. For the sense of all mankind agrees in this, that sin is an indignity done God, which deserveth punishment, and cannot be expiated by any service man can do. It was therefore necessary there should be a mean found for encouraging sinners to embrace a religious life ; of which all had reason to despair, without pardon were offered to penitents, upon the change of their lives. Now this was what the heathen could not dream how to procure. It is true the Jews had sacrifices for expiating of sin, but these could never quiet their consciences, since the common sense of mankind tells that the blood of beasts cannot appease God. The mystery therefore of the reconciliation of sinners to God is the proper character of the Christian Religion, which holds forth to us how the Eternal Word was made man, and endured unspeakable sufferings for the sins of men, even to the death of the Cross ; and was raised up by God, and carried to Heaven, where He is vested with all power and authority, and by the merits of His death hath a right to grant pardon, give grace, and confer eternal life on all that believe on Him ; by Whom God conveys all things to us, and through Whom we are to offer up all our worship to God, He being the *Mediator betwixt God and man.*

The third head of the Christian Religion is, to teach the perfectest, clearest, and most Divine rules, for advancing of the souls of men to the highest perfection of their natures. It is true noble pieces of morality were acknowledged and taught by the heathen philosophers ; and the books of the Old Testament have the doctrine of virtue, purity, humility, and meekness laid open very fully ; but without derogating from these, it must be acknowledged, that as the doctrine of Christianity teacheth all these precepts with clearer rules and fuller directions, so they were in it recommended by the example of its author, backed with the strongest motives, and enforced with the greatest arguments. In these are the lessons of purity, chastity, ingenuity, humility, meekness, patience, and generosity, so clearly laid down, and so fully evinced that no man, who is so much a man as to love those things whereby his mind may be improved to all that is truly great and noble, but must be enamoured of the Christian Religion, as soon as he is taught it.

The fourth design of religion is, to unite mankind in the closest bonds of peace, friendship, and charity, which it doth not only by the rules prescribed for the tempering our passions, forgiving of injuries, and loving our enemies, and by the doctrine of obedience to those in authority over us ; but likewise by associating us into one body, called " the Church " ; wherein we are to worship God jointly, and to be coupled in one by the use of the Sacraments, which are the ligaments of this body.

Having thus viewed the great designs of the Christian Religion in the several branches and parts thereof, I shall add to this the main distinguishing characters of our religion, which are also four.

The first is, its verity; that it is not founded on the tattles of persons concerned, nor on the reveries of dotards, nor received with a blind credulity, being founded on the authority of the great God, which appeared visibly in those that published it, chiefly in the person of Jesus Christ, Who by His miracles that were wrought in sight of all the people, even His enemies looking on, and not being able to deny them, but chiefly by His Resurrection from the dead, was declared to be the Son of God, Which was seen and known by many, who followed not cunningly devised fables, but were the eyewitnesses of His Majesty, who went in His Name and published it to the world, confirming it by miracles and mighty wonders, attesting it notwith-standing all the persecutions they met with, most of them confirming it with their blood : and this doctrine was received and believed by the better part of mankind, though it being contrary to all the interests of the flesh, whose mortification it teacheth, its reception cannot be imputed to credulity or interest.

The second character of our religion is, its genuine simplicity and perspicuity, that all its doctrines and rules are clearly and distinctly held out to us, not like the heathen divinity, much whereof lay in dark oracles in the Books of the Sibyls, and in other pretended mysteries, which none but the priests might handle and expound. The Jewish Religion was also veiled with types and figures, so that it was not easy to see the substance and truth through all these foldings and shadows. But the glory of the Christian Religion, as to this particular, is nobly laid out by St. Paul in these words (*II Cor.* iii, 18) *But we all, with open face as in a glass beholding the glory of the Lord, are changed into the same image from glory to glory, as by the Spirit of the Lord.*

The third character is, the reasonableness of the Christian Religion, it containing none of these absurd incredible things, which abounded among the heathens ; nor of these rites of Judaism, the reasons whereof, besides the Will of God in enjoining them, could not be assigned. But both the doctrines and precepts of the Christian Religion are fitted for mankind, and so congenial to his nature, that they well deserve the designation of *reasonable service*, or rational worship, God having made our souls and them of a piece.

And the fourth character of our religion is, its easiness ; *Christ's yoke is easy, and His burden light* (*Matt.* xi, 30). Wherein we are freed from all the barbarous and cruel rites of Gentilism, and from the oppressive bondage of Judaism, *which was a law of ordinances* and *a yoke that our fathers were not able to bear* ; but that we are called to by Christ is so simple, so easy, and so plain, that well may we say *His commandments are not grievous* (*I John* v, 3).

## (2) THE DOCTRINE OF GOD

### No. 106. RICHARD HOOKER

[From *The Laws of Ecclesiastical Polity*, Book I, Chapter ii, §§ 2, 3. *Works*, ed. J. Keble, Vol. I, pp. 200–203. Cp. note on No. 148.]

ALL things therefore do work after a sort according to law: all other things according to a law, whereof some superior, unto Whom they are subject, is Author; only the works and operations of God have Him both for their Worker, and for the law whereby they are wrought. The being of God is a kind of law to His working; for that perfection which God is, giveth perfection to that He doth. Those natural, necessary, and internal operations of God, the Generation of the Son, the Proceeding of the Spirit, are without the compass of my present intent: which is to touch only such operations as have their beginning and being by a voluntary purpose, wherewith God hath eternally decreed when and how they should be. Which eternal decree is that we term an eternal law.

Dangerous it were for the feeble brain of man to wade far into the doings of the Most High, Whom although to know be life, and joy to make mention of His Name, yet our soundest knowledge is to know that we know Him not as indeed He is, neither can know Him: and our safest eloquence concerning Him is our silence, when we confess without confession that His glory is inexplicable, His greatness above our capacity and reach. He is above, and we upon earth; therefore it behoveth our words to be wary and few.

Our God is one, or rather very Oneness, and mere unity, having nothing but itself in itself, and not consisting (as all things do besides God) of many things. In which essential Unity of God a Trinity Personal nevertheless subsisteth, after a manner far exceeding the possibility of man's conceit. The works which outwardly are of God, they are in such sort of Him being one, that each Person hath in them somewhat peculiar and proper. For being Three, and they all subsisting in the essence of one Deity; from the Father, by the Son, through the Spirit, all things are. That which the Son doth hear of the Father, and which the Spirit doth receive of the Father and the Son, the same we have at the hands of the Spirit as being the last, and therefore the nearest unto us in order, although in power the same with the second and the first.

244

The wise and learned among the very heathens themselves have all acknowledged some First Cause, whereupon originally the being of all things dependeth.  Neither have they otherwise spoken of that cause than as an Agent, which knowing what and why it worketh, observeth in working a most exact order or law.  Thus much is signified by that which Homer mentioneth, Διὸς δ᾽ ἐτελείετο βουλή.  Thus much acknowledged by Mercurius Trismegistus, Τὸν πάντα κόσμον ἐποίησεν ὁ δημιουργὸς οὐ χερσὶν ἀλλὰ λόγῳ.  Thus much confessed by Anaxagoras and Plato, terming the Maker of the world an *intellectual* Worker.  Finally the Stoics, although imagining the first cause of all things to be fire, held nevertheless, that the same fire having art, did ὁδῷ βαδίζειν ἐπὶ γενέσει κόσμου.  They all confess therefore in the working of that First Cause that counsel is used, reason followed, a way observed; that is to say, constant order and law is kept, whereof itself must needs be author unto itself.  Otherwise it should have some worthier and higher to direct it, and so could not itself be the first.  Being the first, it can have no other than itself to be the author of that law which it willingly worketh by.

God therefore is a law both to Himself, and to all other things besides.  To Himself He is a law in all those things, whereof Our Saviour speaketh, saying, *My Father worketh as yet, so I.*  God worketh nothing without cause.  All those things which are done by Him have some end for which they are done;  and the end for which they are done is a reason of His will to do them.  His will had not inclined to create woman, but that He saw it could not be well if she were not created.  *Non est bonum, It is not good man should be alone; therefore let us make a helper for him.*  That and nothing else is done by God, which to leave undone were not so good.

If therefore it be demanded, why God having power and ability infinite, the effects notwithstanding of that power are all so limited as we see they are, the reason hereof is the end which He hath proposed, and the law whereby His wisdom hath stinted the effects of His power in such sort, that it doth not work infinitely, but correspondently unto that end for which it worketh, even " all things χρηστῶς, in most decent and comely sort," all things in Measure, Number, and Weight.

## No. 107.  JOHN PEARSON

[From *On the Creed*.  The concluding sentences of his exposition of the words " I believe in God the Father Almighty."  Ed. Oxford (E. Burton), 1864, pp. 83 f.  Cp. note on No. **13**.]

As I am persuaded of an infinite and independent Essence, which I term a God, and of the mystery of an eternal generation by which that God is a Father, so I assure myself that Father is not subject to infirmities of age, nor is there any weakness attending on the *Ancient of days*;

21

but, on the contrary, I believe Omnipotency to be an essential attribute of His Deity, and that not only in respect of operative and active power (concerning which I shall have occasion to express my faith hereafter), but also in regard of power authoritative, in which I must acknowledge His antecedent and eternal right of making what, and when, and how He pleased, of possessing whatsoever He maketh by direct dominion, of using and disposing as He pleaseth all things which He so possesseth. This dominion I believe most absolute in respect of its independency, both in the original and the use or exercise thereof; this I acknowledge infinite for amplitude or extension, as being a power over all things without exception; for plenitude or perfection, as being all power over every thing without limitation; for continuance or duration, as being eternal without end or conclusion. Thus *I believe in God the Father Almighty*.

# (3) THE HOLY TRINITY

## No. 108. RICHARD HOOKER

[From *The Laws of Ecclesiastical Polity*, Book V, Chapter li, § 1. *Works*, ed. J. Keble, Vol. II, pp. 220 f. Cp. note on No. 148.]

*The Lord our God is but one God.* In which indivisible unity, notwithstanding we adore the Father as being altogether of Himself, we glorify that Consubstantial Word which is the Son, we bless and magnify that co-essential Spirit eternally proceeding from Both, which is the Holy Ghost. Seeing therefore the Father is of none, the Son is of the Father, and the Spirit is of Both, they are by these their several properties readily distinguishable each from other. For the substance of God with this property *to be of none* doth make the Person of the Father; the very selfsame substance in number with this property *to be of the Father* maketh the Person of the Son; the same substance having added unto it the property of *proceeding from the other Two* maketh the Person of the Holy Ghost. So that in every Person there is implied both the substance of God which is one, and also that property which causeth the same Person really and truly to differ from the other two. Every Person hath His own subsistence which no other besides hath, although there be others besides that are of the same substance. As no man but Peter can be the person which Peter is, yet Paul hath the selfsame nature which Peter hath. Again, Angels have every of them the nature of pure and invisible spirits, but every Angel is not that Angel which appeared in a dream to Joseph.

## No. 109. GEORGE BULL

[From *Defensio Fidei Nicaenae*. The extract which follows is reprinted from the " Index of the Propositions demonstrated in this Work," which was affixed to Bull's *Defensio*. The treatise, which was first published in 1685, is deservedly a classic. The circumstances which led to its composition are noteworthy. In his earlier writings (cp. note on No. 129), Bull had made some incisive criticisms of the Lutheran doctrine of Justification and was accused in consequence of Socinianism; this was a charge currently made against those who held " Arminian " views on Justification. It was in order to repel the suspicions thus raised as to his orthodoxy that Bull conceived and wrote the *Defensio*. This work took the form of an analysis of the theology of the Church Fathers prior to the Council of Nicaea (A.D. 325), in which he sought to prove the conformity of their teaching with the Nicene Formula. The author found further grounds for doing this, because in 1643 the Jesuit theologian, Dionysius Petavius, had published the first three volumes of his *Dogmata Theologica* (these were dated actually 1644), in which he had questioned the orthodoxy of the ante-Nicene writers, judged by the standard of the teaching of the Council, and justified them on the grounds of a theory of ' development '; and Bull mockingly attacked Petavius in his *Proemium*. When the *Defensio* appeared in 1685, its merits were immediately recognized. It was supplemented later, in 1694, by the *Judicium Ecclesiae Catholicae trium primorum Seculorum de Necessitate Credendi quod Dominus Noster Jesus Christus sit verus Deus, assertum contra S. Episcopium aliosque.* A copy of the *Judicium* sent to Bossuet procured for Bull "the unfeigned congratulations of the whole clergy of France, assembled at St. Germain's, for the great service he had done to the Catholic Church."

An English translation of the *Defensio* by Dr. F. Holland was published in 1725. A second version, made for the *L. A. C. T.*, was published in 1851. From this translation the present and the following extracts are taken.]

## On the Pre-existence of the Son of God

The Catholic Doctors of the First Three Centuries all with one accord taught that Jesus Christ, that is, He Who was afterwards called Jesus Christ (before He was made man, that is, before His birth, according to the flesh, of the most Blessed Virgin), existed in another nature far surpassing the human; that He appeared to holy men, as a prelude to His Incarnation; that He always presided over and provided for that Church which He was afterwards to redeem with His Own Blood; and that thus from the beginning the " whole order of the Divine Administration" (as Tertullian expresses it) " had its course through Him"; and that, moreover, before the foundations of the world were laid He was present with God His Father, and that through Him this universe was created.

## On the Consubstantiality of the Son

It was the settled and unanimous opinion of the Catholic Doctors who flourished in the First Three Centuries that the Son of God was of one substance, or consubstantial, with God the Father; that is, that He was not of any created or mutable essence, but of altogether the same Divine and unchangeable Nature with His Father, and therefore very God of very God.

## On the Co-eternity of the Son

### The First Proposition

The more authoritative and larger part of the Doctors, who lived before the Council of Nice, unambiguously, openly, clearly, and perspicuously taught and professed the co-eternity of the Son, that is, His co-eternal existence with God the Father.

### The Second Proposition

There are some Catholic writers, more ancient than the Council of Nice, who seem to have attributed to the Son of God, even in that He is God, a certain nativity, which began at a certain time, and immediately preceded the creation of the world. And yet they were very far removed from the opinion of Arius. For, if their expressions be more accurately weighed, it will appear that they spoke not of a true and properly so called nativity in which, that is, the Son received the beginning of His hypostasis and subsistence, but of a figurative and metaphorical one; that is, they merely intended this, that the Word, Who before all ages (when nothing existed besides God) did exist in and with God the Father, as the co-eternal offspring of the Eternal Mind itself, went forth in operation from God the Father Himself at the time when He was about to form the world, and proceeded to create the universe, and to manifest both Himself and His Father to the creatures ; and that, in consequence of this going forth and manifestation, He is called in the Scriptures the Son of God and the First-begotten.

### The Third Proposition

Certain Catholic Doctors who lived after the rise of the Arian Controversy, and resolutely opposed themselves to the heresy of the Ariomanites, did not shrink from the view of the Primitive Fathers, whom we last mentioned, or rather the mode in which they explained their view. For they themselves also acknowledged that going forth of the Word, Who existed always with God the Father, from the Father (which some of them also called His Condescension) in order to create this universe ; and confessed that, with respect of that going forth also the Word Himself was, as it were, born of God the Father, and is in the Scriptures called the first-begotten of every creature.

### The Fourth Proposition

Tertullian, indeed, has in one passage ventured to write expressly that there was a time, when the Son of God was not. But, in the first place, it is certain, that that writer, though in other respects a man of great ability and equal learning, fell off from the Catholic Church to heresy. And it is very uncertain, which books he wrote when a Catholic, which when inclining to heresy, and which, lastly, when a decided heretic. Secondly, Tertullian appears to have used that expression in a controversial way and in disputation with his adversary, playing on the word Son ; so that, although he seems to have absolutely denied the Eternity of the Son, still he really meant no more than what those Fathers meant, whom we have cited in Chaps. 5–8 of this Book : [1] namely, that the Divine Person, Who is called the Son of God, although He always existed with the Father, was then first declared to be the Son, when He went forth from the Father to make the universe. Certainly the same Tertullian has in many other passages treated of the co-eternity of the Son in a clearly Catholic sense, if we regard the main drift of his doctrine. As for Lactantius, who also in one passage attributes, not obscurely, a beginning of existence to the Son of God, his estimation and authority is but of little weight in the Church of God, inasmuch as he was almost entirely uninstructed in Holy Scripture and Christian Doctrine. And secondly, it must

---

[1] [The Fathers referred to are Athenagoras, Tatian, Theophilus of Antioch, Hippolytus, and "Novatian, or the author of the *Treatise on the Trinity*, published among and under the name of Tertullian."]

necessarily be held, either that those passages in the writings of Lactantius which seem to make against the Eternity of the Son have been corrupted by some Manichaean heretic; or at any rate that Lactantius himself was infected with the heresy of Manes. Lastly, he has himself in other passages expressed a more sound opinion concerning the eternity of the Word.

## On the Subordination of the Son to the Father

### The First Proposition

That Decree of the Council of Nice in which it is laid down that the Son of God is ' God of God ' is confirmed by the voice of the Catholic Doctors, both those who wrote before and those who wrote after that Council. For they all with one accord taught that the Divine Nature and perfections belong to the Father and the Son, not collaterally or co-ordinately, but subordinately; that is to say, that the Son has indeed the same Divine Nature in common with the Father, but communicated by the Father; in such sense, that is, that the Father alone hath the Divine Nature from Himself, in other words, from no other, but the Son from the Father; consequently that the Father is the Fountain, Origin, and Principle of the Divinity which is in the Son.

### The Second Proposition

The Catholic Doctors, both those who preceded and those who lived after the Council of Nice, with unanimous consent determined tnat God the Father, even in respect of His Divinity, is greater than the Son; that is to say, not in Nature indeed, or in any essential perfection, so that it should be in the Father, and not in the Son; but in Authorship alone, that is to say, in Origin; forasmuch as the Son is from the Father, not the Father from the Son.

### The Third Proposition

This Doctrine respecting the subordination of the Son to the Father as to His Origin and Principle was regarded by the ancient Doctors as very useful and absolutely necessary to be known and believed for this reason, that by means of it especially the Divinity of the Son is so asserted, as that the Unity of God and the Divine Monarchy, is nevertheless preserved unimpaired. For although the Name and the Nature be common to the two, namely the Father and the Son of God, still, inasmuch as the One is the Principle of the Other, from Which He is propagated, and that by an internal not an external production, it follows that God is rightly said to be only one. This reason those Ancients believed to be equally applicable to the Divinity of the Holy Ghost.

## No. 110. GEORGE BULL

[From *Defensio Fidei Nicaenae*, Introduction §§ 1, 2, 4, 7-10, 11. Ed. *L. A. C. T.*, Vol. I, pp. 1-3, 5 f., 9-13, 14. Cp. note on No. **109**.]

The first Oecumenical Council, which was held at Nice, has ever been regarded by all Catholics as of the highest authority and esteem, and indeed deservedly so. For never since the death of the Apostles has the Christian world beheld a synod with higher claims to be considered universal and free, or an assembly of Bishops and Prelates more august and holy. "For at that Council," as Eusebius says, "there were assembled out of all the Churches, which had filled the whole of Europe, Asia, and Africa, the very choicest from amongst the ministers of God : and one sacred building, expanded as it were by the Divine command, embraced at once within its compass both Syrians and Cilicians, Phoenicians and Arabians, and Christians of Palestine ; Egyptians too, Thebans and Libyans, and some who came out of Mesopotamia. A Bishop also from Persia was present at the Council, and even Scythia was not wanting to that company. Pontus also and Galatia, Pamphylia and Cappadocia, with Asia and Phrygia, contributed the choicest of their prelates. Moreover Thracians, Macedonians, Achaians and Epirotes, and inhabitants of still more remote districts, were, notwithstanding their distance, present. Even from Spain itself, that most celebrated man [Hosius] took his seat along with the rest. The prelate of the imperial city " (of Rome, that is), " was indeed absent on account of his advanced age, but presbyters of his were present to supply his place. Constantine is the only Emperor from the beginning of the world, who, by convening this vast assembly, an image, as it were, of the company of the Apostles, presented to Christ His Saviour a garland such as this, twined and knit together by the bond of peace, as a sacred memorial of his gratitude for the victories which he had gained over his foreign and domestic enemies. . . . In this company more than two hundred and fifty Bishops were present," (Athanasius, Hilary, Jerome, Rufinus, Socrates, and many others, assert that three hundred and eighteen Bishops sat in this Council), " whilst the number of the Presbyters who accompanied them, with the deacons, acolytes, and crowds of others, can scarcely be computed. Moreover of these ministers of God some were eminent for their wisdom and eloquence, others for their gravity of life and patient endurance of hardships, whilst others again were adorned with modesty and gentleness of demeanour. Some also among them were held in the highest honour from their advanced age ; others were young and vigorous in body and mind," etc.

The subject treated of in this Council concerned the chief doctrine of the Christian Religion, namely, the dignity of the Person of Jesus Christ Our Saviour, whether He is to be worshipped as true God, or to be reduced to the rank and condition of creatures and of things subject to the true God.   If we imagine that in this question of the very utmost moment the whole of the rulers of the Church altogether erred and persuaded the Christian people to embrace their error, how will the promise of Christ Our Lord hold good, Who engaged to be present, even to the end of the world, with the Apostles, and consequently with their successors ?   For, since the promise extends to the end of the world, and yet the Apostles were not to continue alive so long, Christ must most certainly be regarded as addressing, in the persons of the Apostles, their successors also in that office. . . .

Faustus Socinus of Siena, in his Second Letter to Radecius, asserts that the knowledge of the true doctrine concerning God, namely, that the Father alone is very God, continued down to the time of the Council of Nice.   " This knowledge," he says, " without any controversy ceased not to exist even until the period of the Council of Nice and for some time afterwards, among those who professed the Name of Christ.   For throughout the whole of that period, as is clear from the writings of all who then lived, the Father of Jesus Christ alone was believed to be that one true God, of Whom the Holy Scriptures everywhere make mention."   In this passage, when he says that this was the belief of all the Ancients down to the Council of Nice " that the Father of Jesus Christ alone is the one true God," if it be understood of that special prerogative of the Father, by which He alone is of Himself very God, then we acknowledge it to be most true.   But this does not make anything in favour of Socinus ; and it is certain that the knowledge of this doctrine not only " continued until the time of the Council of Nice, or some time after," but has ever continued in the Church of Christ. But if, on the other hand, this proposition, " The Father of Jesus Christ alone is the one true God," be taken altogether exclusively, so as to take away from Christ His true Divinity and to deny what was defined by the Nicene Council, namely, that the Son is very God of very God (and it is but too evident that this was what Socinus meant), then we contend that it is manifestly false that " all the Ancients, down to the Council of Nice, did so believe."   Nay, we shall shew that they all taught that the Son is of the same nature with the Father, and therefore is very God, equally with the Father.   Accordingly even Socinus himself in another place, i.e. in his Third Letter to this same Matthew Radecius (contradicting himself, as he is apt to do), confesses " that almost from the very earliest period of the existence of the Church, even to our own time, so many men most distinguished for piety no less than for learning, so many most holy martyrs of Christ, as to be past numbering, have followed that error, in other respects most serious, that Christ is the one true God, Who created all things, or, at least, was begotten of His proper substance."   But surely, that the Son of

God was begotten of the proper substance of God, and is, therefore, very God of very God, is the sum and substance of the doctrine, which the Nicene Fathers asserted against Arius. . . .

There is, however, one great man fully furnished with learning of every kind, Dionysius Petavius, at whom I cannot sufficiently wonder. For, whilst he professes the utmost reverence for the Nicene Council, and on all occasions declares that he receives the Faith therein affirmed against the Arians as truly Catholic and Apostolic, still he freely gives up to the Arians that which (if true) would very greatly tend to confirm their heresy and to disparage, nay rather, utterly to overthrow, the credit and authority of the Council of Nice; I mean, that almost all the Bishops and Fathers before the Council of Nice held precisely the same opinions as Arius. For thus he writes (*Of the Trinity*, I, v, 7) " Accordingly there was this settled opinion in the minds of some of the Ancients touching the Godhead and the diversity of Persons in It, viz., that there is One supreme, unbegotten, and invisible God, Who put forth, without, from Himself, as vocal and sounding, that Logos, that is, that Word which He had laid up within (ἐνδιάθετον), yet not, like a voice of sound, passing away and capable of being dissipated, but of such sort as that, as though embodied and subsisting, It might in turn afterwards create all other things. Moreover, they said that the Word was put forth by the Supreme God and Father at the time when He determined on creating this universe, in order that He might use Him as His assisting minister. This opinion some intimate more clearly, others more obscurely. But these may be specially mentioned, —Athenagoras, Tatian, Theophilus, Tertullian, and Lactantius. Both these authors, however, and the rest whom I have mentioned " (and which of the Primitive Fathers had he not before mentioned ?) " thought that the Father was superior to the Word, in age, dignity, and power; and although they asserted that the Son was of the Substance or Nature of the Father (in which point alone they made His mode of existence to differ from that of all other beings, which are properly called creatures), still they conceived that He had a beginning no less than the creatures; in other words, that He had by no means been a distinct Person from eternity." But in the Second Section of the Eighth Chapter of the same book he speaks still more plainly. " It is most clear," he says, " that Arius was a genuine Platonist, and that he followed the opinions of those ancient writers who, while as yet the point had not been developed and settled, had fallen into the same error.. For they also taught that the Word was produced by God the Father, yet not from eternity but before He formed the world, in order that He might use Him as His assisting Minister for the accomplishment of that work. For they conceived that He had not created all things by Himself and without the intervention of any one, a doctrine which Philo also followed in his Book *On the Creator of the World*. And therefore I take it to have been in a rhetorical and exaggerated way of expression that Alexander in his Epistle, and others of the Fathers who wrote against this heresy, complained that Arius had been the author of that opinion, the like to which had been unheard of before his time; inasmuch as we have brought forward a great number of early writers who previously taught the same doctrine as Arius."

If, therefore, reliance is to be placed on Petavius, we shall have to lay down, first, that the heresy of Arius which was condemned by the Nicene Fathers agreed, in the most important points, with the commonly received view of the ancient Catholic Doctors who preceded him. Secondly, that the doctrine concerning the true Divinity of the Son was not settled and developed before the Council of Nice. Thirdly, that Alexander and the other Catholics who accused Arius as the author of a doctrine which was new and unheard of previously in the Catholic Church, said this in a rhetorical and an exaggerated way; that is to say (if the thing is to be more plainly stated), that they uttered a notable falsehood, I suppose in the Jesuit fashion, to subserve the Catholic cause. Unlucky Arius! that Petavius was not yet born, to become the patron and advocate of his cause in the conflict at Nicæa. It is not, however, easy to say what Petavius had in view when he wrote thus. Some suspect that in his heart he cherished the Arian heresy himself, and wished craftily to pass on the cup to others. This was the opinion of Sandius, whom I have just before mentioned, who thus remarks of Petavius: " But when I recollect that Petavius asserts that the Ante-Nicene Fathers taught the same doctrines as Arius, and also that the articles of the Faith are to be proved by traditions, I think it impossible but that Petavius must have been persuaded of the truth of the conclusion, which infallibly follows from these premises, namely, that the Trinity which the Arians hold, and not the Consubstantial Trinity, is an article of the Faith. And as to his wresting the argument to a contrary conclusion, I presume he did this with a twofold view: 1. To escape the inconveniences which commonly fall on those who secede from the Roman Catholic to the Arian party; 2. That the Arians might be able to derive a stronger proof of their doctrine from a Father of the Society of Jesus, as from an adversary; especially since it is sufficient to prove premises, from which any person of sound mind can draw such a conclusion, as will make it plain what his opinion is about the Trinity." These are the words of Sandius. In my opinion, however, it is most clear from the writings of Petavius himself that the conjecture of this most vain writer is entirely false. If indeed it must be said that Petavius wrote thus with any sinister purpose and not merely from that bold and reckless temper which is his wont in criticizing and commenting on the Holy Fathers, I should say that, being a

Jesuit, he wished to promote the Papal, rather than the Arian, interest. For, from the fact (for which Petavius contends) that almost all the Catholic doctors of the first three centuries fell into the self-same error which the Nicene Council afterwards condemned as heresy in the case of Arius, these two things will easily follow: 1. That little authority is to be assigned to the Fathers of the First Three Centuries,—to whom Reformed Catholics are wont to make their chief appeal,—as being persons to whom the principal articles of the Christian Faith were not as yet sufficiently understood and developed; 2. That Oecumenical Councils have the power of framing, or, as Petavius says, of settling and developing new articles of Faith,—by which principle it may seem that sufficient provision is made for those additions, which the Fathers of Trent patched on to the Rule of Faith and thrust upon the Christian world; though not even in this way will the Roman Faith stand good, since the assembly at Trent is to be called any thing rather than a General Council.

But so it is. The masters of that school have no scruples in building their Pseudo-catholic Faith on the ruins of the Faith which is truly Catholic. The Divine oracles themselves must, forsooth, be found guilty of too great obscurity and the most Holy Doctors, Bishops, and Martyrs of the Primitive Church be accused of heresy in order that, by whatever means, the faith and authority of the degenerate Roman Church may be kept safe and sound. And yet these sophists (of all things) execrate us as if we are so many accursed Hams, and deriders and despisers of the venerable Fathers of the Church, whilst they continually boast that they themselves religiously follow the Faith of the ancient Doctors and reverence their writings to the utmost. That Petavius, however, wrote those passages with this wicked design, I would not venture to affirm for certain, leaving it to the judgement of that God Who knoweth the hearts. At the same time, what the Jesuit has written, as it is most pleasing to modern Arians (who on this account with one consent look up to and salute him as their patron), so we confidently pronounce it to be manifestly repugnant to the truth, and most unjust and insulting to the Holy Fathers, whether those of the Council of Nice or those who preceded it.

For this is the plan of the work which I have undertaken,—to shew clearly that what the Nicene Fathers laid down concerning the Divinity of the Son, in opposition to Arius and other heretics, was in substance (although sometimes perhaps in other words and in a different mode of expression) taught by all the approved Fathers and Doctors of the Church, without a single exception, who flourished before the period of the Council of Nice down from the very age of the Apostles.

And, O most holy Jesus, the Co-eternal Word of the Eternal Father, I, the chief of sinners and the least of Thy servants, do humbly beseech

Thee that Thou wouldest vouchsafe to bless this labour of mine, undertaken (as Thou O searcher of hearts, dost know) for Thine honour and the good of Thy Holy Church; and to succour and help mine infirmity in this most weighty work, for Thine infinite mercy and most ready favour towards them that love Thee. Amen!

The Nicene Creed, as it is quoted by Eusebius in his Epistle to his own Diocese of Cæsarea, by Athanasius in his Letter to Jovian *De Fide*, and by other writers, is as follows: [Here follows the text in Greek and Latin (English) of the Creed of the Council of Nicæa of A.D. 325.] . . .

The doctrine respecting the Son of God, contained in this Creed, so far as it concerns our present design, may be reduced to these heads.

The First; concerning the προΰπαρξις, or Pre-existence, of the Son of God before [His Incarnation of] the blessed Virgin Mary, nay rather, before the foundation of the world; and concerning the creation of the universe through the Son.

The Second; concerning the ὁμοούσιον ("of one substance"), or Consubstantiality, of the Son; that He is not of any such essence as is created or subject to change, but a nature altogether the same with His Father, that is, that He is very God.

The Third; concerning the συναΐδιον, the Co-eternity of the Son; that is, His existence co-eternal with His Father.

The Fourth; concerning the subordination of the Son to the Father, as to Him Who is His Author and Principle, which is expressed by the Nicene Fathers in two ways,—in that, first, they call the Father "One God"; and then, in that they say that the Son is "God of God, Light of Light," etc.

On all these points we shall make it manifest that the Faith of the Ante-Nicene Fathers is quite in harmony with the Nicene Creed; going through each particular in the order in which we have just proposed them.

# (4) CREATION

## No. 111. JAMES USSHER

[From *Annales Veteris Testamenti a Prima Mundi Origine Deducti*, Aetas Mundi I
—the year 1. *Works*, ed. C. R. Elrington (1864), Vol. VIII, pp. 13–15. This treatise
is a sort of 'Dictionary of Dates,' stretching from the Creation downwards. The
year of Christ's Birth is given as 4000 (*i.e.* reckoned from the Creation). The first
part of the *Annales*, extending as far as the time of Antiochus Epiphanes, was published
in 1650; the second part carried the history to the Fall of Jerusalem, and appeared in
1654. Ussher did not live to complete the work.]

In principio creavit Deus coelum et terram, quod temporis prin-
cipium, juxta nostram chronologiam, incidit in noctis illius initium,
quae vigesimum tertium diem Octobris praecessit, in anno periodi
Julianae 710.

Primo igitur saeculi die, Octobris vigesima tertia, feria prima, cum
supremo coelo creavit Deus Angelos; deinde summo operis fastigio
primum perfecto, ad ima mundanae hujus fabricae fundamenta pro-
gressus mirandus Artifex, infimum hunc globum ex abysso et terra
conflatum constituit; concinentibus et collaudantibus Eum simul
omnibus ipsius Angelis. Cumque terra esset inanis et vacua, et
tenebrae essent in superficie abyssi, in ipso primi diei medio creata
est lux; quam a tenebris distinguens Deus, illam appellavit diem,
has noctem.

Secundo die, Octobris vigesimo quarto, feria secunda, creato
expanso, quod coelum est appellatum, distinctio est facta inter aquas
superiores et inferiores terrae circumfusas.

Tertio die, Octobris vigesimo quinto, feria tertia, aquis inferioribus
in locum unum confluentibus, emersit terra arida. Aquas in mare
congregavit Creator; emissis interim fluviis, qui in mare refluerunt.
Terram, omne genus herbae et plantae, cum seminibus et fructibus,
germinare fecit. Prae aliis autem locis, Paradisum in Edene plantis
ornavit; in quibus, arbor vitae et arbor scientiae boni ac mali.

Quarto die, Octobris vigesimo sexto, feria quarta, sol, luna, et
reliqua sidera creata sunt.

Quinto die, Octobris vigesimo septimo, feria quinta, aquatilia et
volatilia animantia producta sunt; et foecunditate donata.

Sexto die, Octobris vigesimo octavo, feria sexta, terrestria animalia
creata sunt; tum gradientia, tum repentia. Demum vero homo, ad
imaginem Dei in Divina mentis scientia et genuina voluntatis sanctitate
praecipue consistentem, conditus est. Ille statim reliquis animalibus,

257

divinitus ad se adductis, ut dominus eorum designatus, nomina imposuit. In quibus cum adjutricem sibi similem non inveniret; ne socia necessaria careret, Deus, costa ex dormientis latere desumpta, mulierem formavit atque in uxorem illi tradidit, conjugii lege instituta. Tum conjugibus benedicens, foecunditatem eis tribuit, et dominium in animantia; eisque omnibus de cibo liberaliter providit. Denique, peccato in mundum hucusque non ingresso, *inspexit Deus quicquid fecerat, ecce autem bonum erat valde. Sic fuit vespera et fuit mane diei sexti.*

Septimo die, Octobris vigesimo nono, feria septima, cum perfecisset Deus opus suum quod fecerat, quievit ab omni opere; et diei septimo benedicens, Sabbatum instituit et consecravit. Quippe in quo *respiravit* (ut humano more Ipse de Se loquitur), *et recreavit Se*; nec dum (ut videtur) peccato admisso, aut poena sontibus, vel angelis, vel hominibus, a Deo inflicta. Unde dies hic postea constitutus est, signum tum sanctificationis nostrae in hoc saeculo, tum aeterni illius sabbatismi, quo in futuro ab omnibus peccati et reliquiis et poenis plenam liberationem expectamus.

# (5) CHRISTOLOGY

## No. 112.  RICHARD HOOKER

[From *The Laws of Ecclesiastical Polity*, Book V, Chapter liv. *Works*, ed. J. Keble, Vol. II, pp. 231–238.  Cp. note on No. 148.]

IF then both Natures do remain with their properties in Christ thus distinct as has been shewn, we are for our better understanding what either Nature receiveth from other, to note, that Christ is by three degrees a Receiver : First, in that He is the Son of God ; Secondly, in that His human Nature hath had the honour of union with Deity bestowed upon it ; Thirdly, in that by means thereof sundry eminent graces have flowed as effects from Deity into that nature which is coupled with it.  On Christ, therefore, there is bestowed the gift of eternal generation, the gift of union, and the gift of unction.

By the gift of eternal generation, Christ hath received of the Father one and in number the selfsame Substance, which the Father hath of Himself unreceived from any other.  For every beginning is a Father unto that which cometh of it ; and every offspring is a Son unto that out of which it groweth.  Seeing therefore the Father alone is originally that Deity which Christ originally is not (for Christ is God by being of God, light by issuing out of light), it followeth hereupon that whatsoever Christ hath common unto Him with His Heavenly Father, the same of necessity must be *given* Him, but naturally and eternally given, not bestowed by way of benevolence and favour, as the other gifts both are.  And therefore where the Fathers give it out for a rule, that whatsoever Christ is said in Scripture to have *received*, the same we ought to apply only to the manhood of Christ, their assertion is true of all things which Christ hath received *by grace*, but to that which He hath received of the Father by eternal nativity or birth, it reacheth not.

Touching union of Deity with manhood, it is by grace, because there can be no greater grace shewed towards man than that God should vouchsafe to unite to man's nature the Person of His only begotten Son.  Because *the Father loveth the Son* as man, He hath by uniting Deity with manhood *given all things into His hands*.  It hath *pleased* the Father that in Him *all fullness should dwell*.  The *Name* which He hath *above all names* is *given* Him.  *As the Father hath life in Himself*, the *Son in Himself hath life also* by the *gift* of the Father.  The gift whereby God hath made Christ a Fountain of Life is that

259

" conjunction of the nature of God with the nature of man " in the person of Christ, *which gift*, saith Christ to the woman of Samaria, *if thou didst know and in that respect understand Who it is which asketh water of thee, thou wouldest ask of Him that He might give thee living water.* The union therefore of the flesh with Deity is to *that flesh* a gift of principal grace and favour. For by virtue of this grace, man is really made God, a creature is exalted above the dignity of all creatures, and hath all creatures else under it.

This admirable union of God with man can enforce in that higher nature no alteration, because unto God there is nothing more natural than not to be subject to any change. Neither is it a thing impossible that the Word being made flesh should be that which it was not before as touching the manner of subsistence, and yet continue in all qualities or properties of nature the same it was; because the Incarnation of the Son of God consisteth *merely in the union* of natures, which union doth add perfection to the weaker, to the nobler no alteration at all. If therefore it be demanded what the Person of the Son of God hath attained by assuming manhood, surely the whole sum of all is this, to be as we are truly, really, and naturally man, by means whereof He is made capable of meaner offices than otherwise His Person could have admitted; the only gain He thereby purchased for Himself was to be capable of loss and detriment for the good of others.

But may it rightly be said concerning the Incarnation of Jesus Christ, that as our nature hath in no respect changed His, so from His to ours as little alteration hath ensued? The very cause of His taking upon Him our nature was to change it, to better the quality, and to advance the condition thereof, although in no sort to abolish the substance which He took nor to infuse into it the natural forces and properties of His Deity. As therefore we have shewed how the Son of God by His Incarnation hath changed the manner of that personal subsistence which before was solitary, and is now in the association of flesh, no alteration thereby accruing to the Nature of God; so neither are the *properties of man's nature* in the Person of Christ by force and virtue of the same conjunction so much altered as not to stay within those limits which our substance is bordered withal; nor the *state and quality* of our substance so unaltered, but that there are in it many glorious effects proceeding from so near copulation with Deity. God from us can receive nothing, we by Him have obtained much. For albeit the natural properties of Deity be not communicable to man's nature, the supernatural gifts, graces, and effects thereof are.

The honour which our flesh hath by being the flesh of the Son of God is in many respects great. If we respect but that which is common unto us with Him, the glory provided for Him and His in the Kingdom of Heaven, His right and title thereunto even in that He is man, differeth from other men's, because He is that man of whom God is Himself a part. We have right to the same inheritance with Christ, but not the same right which He hath, His being such as we cannot reach, and ours such as He cannot stoop unto.

Furthermore, to be the Way, the Truth, and the Life; to be the Wisdom, Righteousness, Sanctification, Resurrection; to be the Peace of the whole world, the Hope of the righteous, the Heir of all things; to be that supreme Head whereunto all power both in heaven and in earth is given: these are not honours common unto Christ with other men, they are titles above the dignity and worth of any which were but a mere man, yet true of Christ even in that He is man, but man with whom Deity is personally joined, and unto whom it hath added those excellencies which make Him more than worthy thereof.

Finally, sith God hath Deified our nature, though not by turning it into Himself, yet by making it His own inseparable habitation, we cannot now conceive how God should without man either exercise Divine power, or receive the glory of Divine praise. For man is in both an associate of Deity.

But to come to the grace of unction. Did the parts of our nature, the soul and body of Christ, receive by the influence of Deity wherewith they were matched no ability of operation, no virtue or quality above nature? Surely as the sword which is made fiery doth not only cut by reason of the sharpness which simply it hath, but also burn by means of that heat which it hath from fire, so there is no doubt but the Deity of Christ hath enabled that nature which it took of man to do more than man in this world hath power to comprehend; forasmuch as (the bare essential properties of Deity excepted) He hath imparted unto it all things, He hath replenished it with all such perfections as the same is any way apt to receive, at the least according to the exigence of that economy or service for which it pleased Him in love and mercy to be made man. For as the parts, degrees, and offices of that mystical administration did require which He voluntarily undertook, the beams of Deity did in operation always accordingly either restrain or enlarge themselves.

From hence we may somewhat conjecture how the powers of that soul are illuminated, which being so inward unto God cannot choose but be privy unto all things which God worketh, and must therefore of necessity be endued with knowledge so far forth universal, though not with infinite knowledge peculiar to Deity itself. The soul of Christ that saw in this life the face of God was here through so visible presence of Deity filled with all manner graces and virtues in that unmatchable degree of perfection, for which of Him we read it written, *That God with the oil of gladness anointed Him above His fellows.*

And as God hath in Christ unspeakably glorified the nobler, so

22

likewise the meaner part of our nature, the very bodily substance of man. Where also that must again be remembered which we noted before concerning degrees of the influence of Deity proportionable unto His own purposes, intents, and counsels. For in this respect His body which by natural condition was corruptible wanted the gift of everlasting immunity from death, passion, and dissolution, till God which gave it to be slain for sin had for righteousness' sake restored it to life with certainty of endless continuance. Yea in this respect the very glorified Body of Christ retained in it the scars and marks of former mortality.

But shall we say that in Heaven His glorious Body by virtue of the same cause hath now power to present itself in all places and to be everywhere at once present ? We nothing doubt but God hath many ways above the reach of our capacities exalted that Body which it hath pleased Him to make His own, that Body wherewith He hath saved the world, that Body which hath been and is the root of eternal life, the instrument wherewith Deity worketh, the sacrifice which taketh away sin, the price which hath ransomed souls from death, the leader of the whole army of bodies that shall rise again. For though it had a beginning from us, yet God hath given it vital efficacy, Heaven hath endowed it with celestial power, that virtue it hath from above, in regard whereof all the Angels of Heaven adore it. Notwithstanding a body still it continueth, a body consubstantial with our bodies, a body of the same both nature and measure which it had on earth.

To gather therefore into one sum all that hitherto hath been spoken touching this point, there are but four things which concur to make complete the whole state of our Lord Jesus Christ, His Deity, His manhood, the conjunction of both, and the distinction of the one from the other being joined in one. Four principal heresies there are which have in those things withstood the truth : Arians by bending themselves against the Deity of Christ; Apollinarians by maiming and misinterpreting that which belongeth to His human nature ; Nestorians by rending Christ asunder, and dividing Him into two persons ; the followers of Eutyches by confounding in His person those natures which they should distinguish. Against these there have been four most famous ancient General Councils : the Council of Nice to define against Arians, against Apollinarians the Council of Constantinople, the Council of Ephesus against Nestorians, against Eutychians the Chalcedon Council. In four words, ἀληθῶς, τελέως, ἀδιαιρέτως, ἀσυγχύτως, truly, perfectly, indivisibly, distinctly ; the first applied to His being God, and the second to His being Man, the third to His being of both One, and the fourth to His still continuing in that one Both ; we may fully by way of abridgment comprise whatsoever Antiquity hath at large handled either in declaration of Christian belief, or in refutation of the foresaid heresies. Within the compass of which four heads, I may truly affirm that all heresies which touch but the Person of Jesus Christ, whether they have risen in these later days, or in any age heretofore, may be with great facility brought to confine themselves.

We conclude therefore that to save the world it was of necessity the Son of God should be thus Incarnate, and that God should so be in Christ as hath been declared.

# (6) THE INCARNATION

## No. 113.  WILLIAM SHERLOCK

[From W. Sherlock, *A Vindication of the Doctrine of the Trinity* (1690), pp. 238–240.  Cp. note on No. 58.]

THE fundamental mystery of the Christian Religion is the stupendous Love of God in giving His own Son, His only begotten Son, for the redemption of mankind.  This Our Saviour lays great stress on.  *God so loved the world, that He gave His only begotten Son, that whosoever believeth in Him should not perish, but have everlasting life.*  By this, one would have thought that Christ had been the Son, the only begotten Son of God, before He gave Him,—as Isaac, who was a type of Christ, was Abraham's son, before he offered him at God's command ; for that is the argument of love, when we part with what we have and what is dear to us.  But this is not the case if Socinianism be true.  God did not give us any Son He had before, but made an excellent Man, Whom He was pleased to call His only begotten Son,—(though He might have made as many such only begotten Sons as He pleased), and Him He gave for us,—that is, made a man on purpose to be Our Saviour.  God's love, indeed, in redeeming sinners is very great, be the means what they will.  But His love in giving His only begotten Son for our Redemption, which Our Saviour fixes on as the great demonstration of God's love, is not so wonderful, if this giving His Son signifies no more than making a man on purpose to be Our Saviour.

In the next place, the Apostles mightily insist on the great love of Christ in dying for us, and His great humility in submitting to the condition of human nature, and suffering a shameful and accursed death, even the death of the Cross.  *Ye know the grace of Our Lord Jesus Christ that for your sakes He became poor, that ye through His poverty might be rich.  For the love of Christ constraineth us, because we thus iudge, that if one died for all, then were all dead.  Let this mind be in you, which was in Christ Jesus, Who being in the form of God thought it not robbery to be equal with God, but made Himself of no reputation, and took upon Him the form of a Servant, and was made in the likeness of men ; and being found in fashion as a man, He humbled Himself and became obedient unto death, even the death of the Cross.*  Now supposing Christ to be but a mere man, Who had no being before He was born of the Virgin, Who knew nothing of His own coming into the world nor for what end He came, Whose undertaking was not His own voluntary choice but God's appointment, where is the great love, where is the great humility of this? How did He become poor for our sakes, Who was never rich? "Yes," says our historian,[1] "He could have lived in the greatest splendour, dignity, and plenty. He that could multiply the loaves and fishes and the wine at the wedding of Cana, need not have wanted any comforts of life." Right! If he can prove that God would have enabled Him to work miracles, to have made Himself rich and great, and to have ministered to secular pomp and luxury, if He had so minded; but He being a mere creature could work no miracles, nor to any other ends or purposes than God pleased. And therefore, if by God's decree, He was to live a mean life here, and die an accursed death, and He was made for this purpose, He neither ever was rich, nor ever could be rich, and therefore did not make Himself poor for our sakes. He could not by the constitution of God have done otherwise than He did, if He would be the Saviour of Mankind; and therefore if He was not rich before He came into the world, and voluntarily chose His poverty for us, I do not understand the great grace of His becoming poor, for He never was rich, nor ever could be in this world.

## No. 114.  ROBERT SOUTH

[From *Twelve Sermons Upon Several Subjects and Occasions* (Vol. III of South's Sermons), London (1698), pp. 367 f.  From the Sermon entitled " Jesus of Nazareth Proved the True and Only Promised Messiah."  Cp. note on No. 46.]

But now was there ever any wonder comparable to this! To behold Divinity thus clothed in Flesh! The Creator of all things humbled not only to the company, but also to the cognation of His creatures! It is as if we should imagine the whole world not only represented upon, but also contained in, one of our little artificial globes; or the body of the sun inveloped in a cloud as big as a man's hand, all which would be looked upon as astonishing impossibilities,—and yet as short of the other as the greatest finite is of an infinite, between which the disparity is immeasurable. For that God should thus in a manner transform Himself, and subdue and master all His glories to a possibility of human apprehension and converse, the best reason would have thought it such a thing as God could not do, had it not seen it actually done. It is as it were to cancel the essential distances of things, to remove the bounds of Nature, to bring Heaven and Earth, and (what is more) both ends of the contradiction, together.

[1] [*I.e.*, Sherlock's Socinian opponent.]

# (7) THE DESCENT INTO HELL

## No. 115.  ISAAC BARROW

[From *An Exposition* [= *Sermon 28* (ed. 1818)] *on the Creed*. *Works*, ed. A. Napier
(1859), Vol. VII. pp. 274 f., 275 f., 287–291. Ed. Oxford (1818), Vol. V, pp. 26 f.,
27 f., 35–37, 38.  The following extract is taken from the exposition of the clause
"He descended into Hell"; the text of the Sermon was *Acts*, ii, 27.  The meaning
of the words in the Apostles' Creed "He descended into Hell" was the subject of
endless discussion in the Seventeenth Century, largely stimulated by Calvin's interpretation of them (cp. *e.g. Institutes*, Book II, c. xvi, § 8).]

### *He descended into Hell.*

THIS article is of later standing in the Creed and doth not appear
to have had place in any of the most ancient ones public or private,
excepting that of Aquileia, into which also perhaps it might have been
inserted not long before Rufinus's time; and the meaning thereof
hath always (both in more ancient times among the Fathers, and
afterwards among the Schoolmen, and lately among modern Divines)
been much debated, having yielded occasion to many prolix and elaborate
discourses.  To recite the several opinions about it, or different
explications thereof, with the reasons produced to maintain or disprove
them, were a matter of greater time and pains than I can well afford;
and to decide the controversies about it, a matter of greater difficulty
than I could hope to achieve.  Wherefore (both upon these accounts,
and because I rather choose to insist upon matters more clear in their
nature and more practical in consequence) I should be willing altogether
to wave this obscure and perplexed subject.  Yet however somewhat
to comply with expectation, I shall touch briefly upon some things
seeming conducible to the clearing, or to the ending of the controversies
about it. . . .

It seems needless to dispute what meaning they, who placed the
words here, did intend, since, i. It is possible, and by many like instances
might be declared so, and perhaps not unlikely, that they might both
themselves upon probable grounds believe, and for plausible ends
propound to the belief of others, this proposition, without apprehend-
ing any distinct sense thereof; as we believe all the Scriptures, and
commend them to the faith of others, without understanding the sense
of many passages therein. And since, ii. Perhaps they might by
them intend some notion not certain, or not true, following some
conceits then passable among divers, but not built upon any sure
foundation (like that of the Millennium, and the necessity of infants
communicating, etc., which were anciently in great vogue, but are

now discarded). And since, iii. To speak roundly, their bare authority, whoever they were (for that doth not appear), could not be such as to oblige us to be of their minds, whatever they did mean or intend; they perhaps were such to whom we might owe much reverence, but should not be obliged to yield entire credence to their opinions. But further, iv. Were I bound to speak my sense, I should say that, supposing they had any distinct meaning, they did intend to affirm that Our Saviour's soul did, by a true and proper kind of motion, descend into the regions infernal or beneath the earth, where they conceived the souls of men were detained: for this appears to have been the more general and current opinion of those times, which it is probable they did comply with herein, whencesoever fetched, however grounded. . . .

I add that, seeing it is a most certain truth that Our Saviour's soul did immediately go into the place appointed to receive happy souls after their recession from the body and resignation into God's hands, if we take " hell " in a general and common sense for the place or the state of souls departed, and " descending " for passing thereinto (by a falling, as it were, from life, or by going away together with the descent of the body, and thence styled " descending,"—what appeareth visibly happening to the body being accommodated to the soul); if, I say, we do thus interpret Our Saviour's " descent into hell " for His soul's going into the common receptacle and mansion of souls, we shall so doing be sure not substantially to mistake. And this sense, I conceive, if the words can handsomely bear it, would be very proper to this place as signifying somewhat distinct from what is otherwise expressed, and serving to the further establishment of those great articles adjoining, Our Lord's Death and Resurrection,—it implying the perfect accomplishment of death for the soul to have deserted the body, and to have been translated into that ἀδύνατον ᾅδην (as the Book of Wisdom calls it), that invisible region, so far distant hence, whence revocare gradum superasque evadere ad auras is a labour indeed, and a work not to be effected, but by the power of Him, Whose prerogative it is to kill, and make alive ; to bring down to Hell, and to bring up ; to lead unto the gates of Hell, and to bring back again.

This is all that I shall say about this intricate point; for I cannot well be at the pain to consider or examine those conceits which pretend to acquaint us why and to what effect Our Saviour descended into hell,—

That Our Lord went thither to preach unto, convert, and redeem from thence all, or some of the damned souls (for some say, that He depopulated and emptied that region of darkness; others are not so liberal as to free all thence, but only the fitter objects of compassion and favour; both saying that which hath very weak or no reasons to maintain, very strong and plain objections to assail it).

That He went to rescue and conduct into glory the souls of the Patriarchs and other good persons from that infernal *Limbus*, in which till then they were detained (a place by no likely means to be proved existent otherwhere than in the fancy of its inventors); or, that He went to deliver the souls of the just, and Prophets, from the wicked powers into whose power they had fallen (as Justin Martyr, in his *Dialogue with Tryphon*).

That He went to affront, triumph over, and terrify the powers of darkness upon their own ground, or in their own dominions.

These and the like conceits seem enough discountenanced by saying the Scriptures nowhere plainly declare any such thing, and that therefore they have no good ground to stand upon. . . . But let it suffice to have discoursed thus far about this endless question ; except we will end it with that saying of St. Austin : *Melius est dubitare de occultis, quam litigare de incertis* or with that more peremptory saying of Calvin : *Atqui stultum et temerarium est de rebus incognitis altius inquirere, quam Deus nobis scire permittit.*

## No. 116.  RICHARD FIELD

[From *Of the Church*, Book V, ch. xix.  Ed. Cambridge, *E.H.S.*, 1850, Vol. III, pp. 114 f.  Cp. note on No. 72.]

Thus then our Divines deny the Descending of Christ into purgatory, *limbus puerorum* and *limbus patrum*, persuading themselves that there are no such places.  But His descending into the Hell of the damned they all acknowledge, though not to deliver men thence, yet to fasten condemnation to them that are there; to bind Satan the prince of darkness, that he may not prevail against them that believe in Christ, and to keep them from sinking down into that devouring pit into which He went and out of which He so triumphantly returned.  Only this difference may seem to be amongst them, that some of them think He went personally and locally, others, only virtually, in power and operation.  Which diversity of opinions is likewise amongst the Papists,—Bellarmine and some other in our time teaching that He went locally into the lowest Hell; and the Schoolmen, that He went not locally into the lowest hell, but virtually only in the manifestation of His virtue and power, and into *limbus patrum* locally and personally. So that all the controversy between them and us standeth in two points, the descending of Christ into *limbus patrum* and the suffering of hellish pains.

## No. 117.  JOHN SELDEN

[From *Table Talk, Being the Discourses of John Selden Esquire ; Or his Sense of Various Matters of Weight and High Consequence, Relating Especially to Religion and State.*  Section LI (" Hell ").  Ed. S. H. Reynolds (Oxford, 1892), pp. 76 f.  The " Table Talk " was recorded by Richard Milward, a secretary of Selden (1609–1680; see the article on him in *D.N.B.*) who himself died, however, some nine years before the first publication of it in 1689. Selden had died in 1654. See the Introduction and Notes to Reynolds' edition; and also A. W. Ward in "Cambridge History of English Literature," Vol. VIII, pp. 321–327.]

*He descended into Hell.* This may be the interpretation of it. He may be dead and buried, then His soul ascended into heaven. Afterwards He descended again into hell, that is, into the grave, to fetch His body and to rise again. The ground of this interpretation is taken from the Platonic learning, who held a metempsychosis; and when a soul did descend from heaven to take another body, they called it κατάβασιν εἰς ᾅδην, taking ᾅδης for the lower world, the state of mortality. Now the first Christians, many of them, were Platonic philosophers, and no question spoke such language as was then understood amongst them. To understand by *hell* "the grave," is no tautology; because the Creed first tells what Christ suffered, "He was crucified, dead, and buried"; then it tells us what He did, "He descended into Hell, the third day He rose again, He ascended, etc."

# (8) THE RESURRECTION

## No. 118. DANIEL WHITBY

[From D. Whitby, Λόγος τῆς πίστεως, *An Endeavour to evince the Certainty of Christian Faith in General, and of the Resurrection of Christ in particular*, Oxford, 1671, pp. 394–400. This treatise was one of the heralds of the vast mass of apologetic literature which was to appear in the following century.]

OUR second demonstration of the Resurrection of Our Saviour will arise from three conclusions. First that Our Saviour's Body was removed from the grave. For its continuance there must surely have discovered the falsehood of this bold assertion and made all other ways of confirmation of it not only needless, but absurd ; whilst by an ocular demonstration anyone might have perceived the truth, and discovered the impudent folly of all those who durst affirm that it was risen from the dead.

Secondly, the disciples of Our Saviour cannot be justly charged with its conveyance from the sepulchre ; for, besides the no advantage, nay the assurance of the worst of miseries which could attend the promulgation of this doctrine, they dreamed of a Messiah Who should sway the sceptre and subdue the nations under them ; and when they found it otherwise, their hopes lay buried in His grave, and expired together with Him. After such manifold experience of their Master's power to assist them by an Almighty hand, after their solemn protestations made to own Him in the sharpest trials, they shamefully deserted Him, and at first assault betook themselves to their heels ; their prolo-cutor renounced Him, and seconded His denial with an oath ; they barred their doors and hid their heads, dreading everything they heard or saw. And can it be imagined that persons so extremely timorous should hazard their lives to rescue His dead Body from the grave, who after all obligement both of faith and duty did so little to preserve Him from it, against a watch so vigilant and zealously concerned to prevent the mischiefs of a second and therefore more pernicious error ? After commands so strict and peremptory to secure the sepulchre, in vain must they attempt to rifle it ; which, if any say they did whilst the watchmen slept, how came they privy to it, what credit can their word deserve ? If whilst they waked, what could induce those watchmen to make lies their refuge and wilfully permit the cheat ? Besides it is a timorous trade to play the thief, much more to rob the grave of its inhabitants, and they might well expect that vengeance should arrest them in a fact designed to delude the world and to entitle God unto the worst of villanies, and hence not only their respect unto their Master, but their own safety, must have taught them to despatch their business, and not to spend their time in the uncasing of His Body and rolling up the napkins that were about His Head, and to do things of such needless curiosities.

But thirdly, more incredible it is that persons unconcerned for this Jesus should run so great an hazard or be concerned to remove His Body thence, or that the Apostles should bottom all their hopes on such a tottering foundation and trust to the fidelity of those men who in this very business in which their silence could alone befriend them, were the worst of cheats. It is lastly most incredible that persons of this temper should still go on to stifle and conceal the matter and not be tempted by the pleasure of the thing, the service they might do to their religion, the hopes of a considerable reward, or by the hatred of a cheat so gross and palpable, to manifest the shame and infamy of those that forged it. Besides, how could His own disciples hope by mighty signs and wonders, by gifts and graces of the Holy Spirit, great and numerous, to give in evidence unto His Resurrection (which they confidently pretended) had He been still reserved under the power of death, and only by their own or other's arts removed from His sepulchre? How is it that they never thought within themselves, He could not save Himself, and whence shall we expect salvation? He could not by His miracles of power and goodness prevail upon one nation to believe His doctrine; and can we, though destitute of all that power which resided in Him, think to reduce the world into obedience or to impart the Holy Ghost to others, when we ourselves have the spirit of delusion only? Nay, might not the example of Theudas, Judas, and many others (both of their own and other nations), all whose endeavours (although their hopes and their abilities were greater and their undertaking less) proved unsuccessful, and ended in the ruin of those bold adventurers, be sufficient to deter them from such bold attempts? Lo, here a testimony which gives the greatest evidence of itself, and yet asserted by such men, who neither would deceive nor were deceived in this particular, and consequently whose attestation could be no deceit. Which, that it may appear with greater evidence,

Consider first, That they pretended to many and infallible convictions of the truth, to frequent apparitions of this Jesus, attended with some signal circumstance to evidence their truth unto them, and gave it out that they conversed with Him forty days, saw many miracles done by Him, received instructions from His mouth to feed His sheep, to teach all nations and baptize them. Yea that they were endowed with power from Him to confirm the testimony by mighty signs and wonders; and for the truth of this they frequently appealed unto their adversaries and the experience of those who did embrace their doctrines, —in all which confident appeals and attestations requiring little more than eyes and ears to certify the truth unto them, 'tis equally incredible they should deceive or be deceived.

Did they give credit to this Jesus, they must conclude Him risen according to His own prediction, and therefore could not be deceivers in asserting it. Did they conclude Him an impostor, what motives could they have to publish Him the Saviour of the World, Who after He had called them to leave all and follow Him, and made such ample promises unto them of judging the twelve tribes of Israel, left them so sadly in the lurch, exposed unto shame and infamy? Did they give credit to the Sacred Oracles, and reverence the Law of Moses, why did they not dread those judgements which God proclaimed against the false and lying prophet? If they did not believe it, why were they so concerned for the truth of the predictions of the Law concerning the Messias, as to assert them with the loss both of the freedom and safety of their lives?

Should we ascribe the cheat unto the powers of imagination (since they pretended to be eyewitnesses of the Resurrection and to deliver nothing but what they saw and heard), is it not strange to think that fancy should create a person to them frequently appearing, preaching, and instructing, giving out commissions, administering of Holy Ordinances and the like; that it should draw them out unto the Mount of Olives after an aery phantasm, and then present it, carried up into Heaven? In short, they were certain His Body was not privately conveyed away by their endeavours and that this only was pretended to disgrace their testimony and what could farther be required to assure both them and us that they were not deceived? To conclude,

If this relation were untrue, either they were beside their senses when they did believe, or beside their wits when they affirmed it, and did endeavour to confirm what they did not believe with loss of life and fortunes. And if so, what shall we say to the world of Christians, that maugre all temptations to the contrary, did steadfastly believe these men, who had so little reason to believe themselves? It is prodigious to think that a poor ignorant young man, of meanest birth and breeding of a most hateful nation, and hated by that nation to the death, because pretending that He was a prophet sent from God, and after this His death, only avouched to be so by twelve fishermen, pretending with loud boasts of miracles, false as God is true, to testify His Resurrection through a greater falsehood, and promising to all that would believe it nothing besides this power of working miracles but death and miseries at present, which their experience proved to be true; I say, it is prodigious to think that He and His disciples should with no other charms work such a lasting faith in all the wisest part of men, that neither time nor vice, though most concerned to do so, should ever be able to deface it. And yet what's so prodigiously incredible must be certain truth, or else the Resurrection must be so.

## (9) THE ASCENSION

### No. 119. PETER HEYLYN

[From *Theologia Veterum* (1654), p. 270. (' Of the Seventh Article of the Creed, Ascribed to St. Bartholomew,'—" He Ascended into Heaven "; near the end). Cp. note on No. 63.]

IT was then in His natural Body that Christ ascended into Heaven ; in it He hath acquired for it all those high pre-eminences which have been formerly expressed,—not altering thereby the nature which before it had, but adding a perfection of that glory which before it had not, and making it, though a natural Body still, yet a Body glorified. And this is generally agreed upon by all the Fathers, affirming with a joint consent this most Catholic truth, that notwithstanding the accessions of immortality and glory to the Body of Christ, yet it reserved still all the properties of a natural Body. " Christ," saith St. Hierome, " ascended into Heaven and sitteth at the right hand of the Father, *manente ea natura carnis*, the very same nature of His Body remaining still, in which He was born, suffered, and did rise again." And then, *non enim exinanita est humanitatis substantia, sed glorificata.* The substance of His Body was not done away, but only glorified. St. Augustine as fully, but in fewer words, *Christum corpori suo majestatem dedisse, naturam tamen corporis non ademisse,*—" that Christ, by giving majesty to His Body, did not destroy the nature of it." As plainly, but more fully in another place, *Huic corpori immortalitatem dedit, naturam non abstulit.* " Christ," saith the Father, " hath apparelled His flesh with immortality, but He hath not taken from it the nature of flesh." And therefore it concerneth us to take good heed, *ne ita divinitatem astruamus hominis, ut veritatem corporis auferamus,* " not to maintain His Divinity on such faulty grounds as utterly ruin His humanity "; or so advance the man as to spoil His Body. Pope Leo to this purpose also, *Caro Christi ipsa est per essentiam, non ipsa per gloriam*—" the flesh or Body of Christ in substance is the same it was, in glory it is not the same." Others might be produced to the same effect, were not these three sufficient to confirm a point so little subject to dispute amongst men of reason.

273

## (10) THE HOLY GHOST

### No. 120.  ISAAC BARROW

[From *A Brief Exposition of the Creed, the Lord's Prayer, and the Decalogue. Works*, ed. Oxford (1818), Vol. V, pp. 464 f.  Ed. Napier (1859), Vol. VII, pp. 336 f.  The following extract is from Barrow's exposition of the article in the Creed "I believe in the Holy Ghost."  Required by the statutes of Trinity College, Cambridge, to compose some theological discourses, he wrote his *Brief Exposition of the Creed* in 1669; in the same year he resigned his Lucasian Professorship of Mathematics in favour of Isaac Newton.]

THAT there is an essential union between the Holy Ghost and the other Divine Persons is both by evident consequence deducible from, and is immediately asserted in Scripture.  For that there is but one God is there continually taught and inculcated upon us, and how it calls the Holy Ghost we have seen; therefore necessarily the Holy Ghost doth partake of that One Divine Essence.  Also, that the Holy Ghost is God is inferred from that comparison of St. Paul between the spirit of man in respect to man, and the Spirit of God in respect to God.  As the spirit of man is intrinsical to man, so the Spirit of God is to Him : and by reason of the perfect simplicity of the Divine Nature, that which subsists in God must necessarily be God.  In fine, St. John expressly tells us, *That there are Three which bear record in Heaven, the Father, the Word, and the Holy Ghost : and these Three are one.*  They are one.

And yet there is a personal distinction of the Holy Ghost from the Father and the Son ; for they are three, three Persons.  For that not only distinct names, but peculiar operations are assigned to them ; which should not be done without good reason, if there were no personal distinction,—that which also appears from His being said to *proceed from the Father, and to be sent from Him;* from *His being an Advocate* and *interceding with the Father; His crying within us, Abba, Father,* our having *access in Him to the Father:* as also, *His being sent by the Son, His glorifying Him, receiving of His,* His *not speaking from Himself;*— which expressions plainly argue a personal distinction, as do also Our Saviour's Birth by Him, His performing miracles by Him ; in a word, God's executing all His purposes of grace and power by Him.

Lastly, That the Holy Spirit doth derive the common Divine Essence from the Father and the Son is thence sufficiently apparent, for that He is called the *Spirit of the Father*, and also *the Spirit of the Son* : the Spirit of the Father, because He doth ἐκπορεύεσθαι,—in a manner incomprehensible doth proceed and emanate from the Father,

274

is of Him, is sent by Him ; for the same reason is He the Spirit of the Son, wherefore He is also expressly said to be *sent by the Son*.

## No. 121.  ISAAC BARROW

[From *Works*, ed. Oxford (1818), *Sermon 77*, Vol. III, pp. 475–478 ; ed. Napier (1859), *Sermon 63*, Vol. IV, pp. 433–438.  This was a " Whitsunday Sermon, of the Gift of the Holy Ghost " on *Acts* ii, 38.  Cp. note on No. **344**.]

Almighty God, seeing the generality of mankind alienated from Himself by gross ignorance of its duty toward Him, and by habitual inclinations to violate His holy laws (originally implanted by Him in our nature, or anciently revealed to our first parents), immersed in error, enslaved to vice, and obnoxious to the woeful consequences of them, severe punishment and extreme misery, was pleased in His immense goodness and pity to design its rescue from that sad condition ; and, in pursuance of that gracious design, did resolve upon expedients the most admirable and most efficacious that could be.  For to redeem men from the tyranny of sin and hell, to reconcile them to Himself, to recover them into a happy state, He sent His own only beloved Son out of His bosom into this world, clothed with our nature ;  by Him, as by a Plenipotentiary Commissioner from Himself, inviting all men to return unto Him, declaring Himself, by the meritorious obedience, the expiatory passion, the effectual intercession of His dear Son, abundantly satisfied for, and ready to grant a full pardon of, all offences committed against Him in their state of error and estrangement ;  to admit them into a state of present indemnity and peace, yea to settle them in perpetual alliance and friendship with Himself, upon most fair and gentle terms ;   namely, that, renouncing their erroneous principles, and reforming their vicious courses of life, they cheerfully would embrace His merciful overtures, and thereafter conform their lives to His righteous laws ;  the which, together with all His good intentions concerning them, He, by the same blessed agent, clearly discovered to them, fully by Him instructing them in their duty, and strongly encouraging them to the performance thereof by the promise of most bountiful rewards,—His certain love and favour attended with endless joy and bliss.  Thus *did*, as St. Paul expresseth it, *the saving grace of God appear unto all men, teaching us, that, denying ungodliness and worldly lusts, we should live soberly, righteously, and godly in this present world, expecting that blessed hope.*

But to render this wonderfully gracious design successful, in a way of wisdom and reasonable proceeding, accommodated to the capacities of human nature, it was requisite that there should be provided convincing arguments to persuade men of the truth and reality of these things (that indeed such an extraordinary agent, with such a message, was come from Heaven), effectual means of admonishing and exciting men to a heedful advertency toward them, competent motives to a cordial acceptance of them, a power also sufficient, notwithstanding their natural impotency and instability to continue them in the belief, to uphold them in the practice of the duties prescribed, in the performance of the conditions required.

For if it were not very credible, that God had truly those intentions toward us, or if we did not much regard the overture of them, or if we did not conceive the business highly to concern us ; or if, resolving to comply with the Gospel, we yet were unable to discharge the conditions thereof, the design would totally be frustrated, and of itself come to nothing. To prevent which disappointment of His merciful intentions, Almighty God did abundantly provide, in a manner and measure suitable to the glorious importance of them ; for to the ministry of His eternal wisdom, He adjoined the efficacy of His eternal love and Blessed Spirit, the which not only conducted God our Saviour into His fleshy tabernacle, and with *unmeasurable communications* of Himself did continually reside within Him, but also did attend Him in the conspicuous performance of numberless miraculous works, implying Divine power and goodness, as exceeding not only any natural, but all created power (such as were by mere word and will healing the sick and restoring the maimed, ejecting evil spirits, discerning the secret thoughts of men, foretelling contingent events, reviving the dead, raising Himself from the grave) ; which works, some expressly, others by parity of reason, are ascribed to the Holy Spirit ; for, *If*, saith Our Lord, *I by the Spirit of God cast out devils—and God*, saith St. Peter, *anointed Him with the Holy Ghost, and with power ; Who went about doing good, and healing all that were oppressed by the devil* : and, *Who*, saith St. Paul, *was declared to be the Son of God, according to the Holy Spirit, by the resurrection from the dead* : so did God afford the most evident attestation that could be to the truth of our Saviour's quality, commission, and doctrine, by so clear and rousing significations did God invite men to take notice of these things.

But farther to induce them heartily to comply with these gracious overtures, and to render them thoroughly available to the purpose designed, the salvation of men, according to the terms prescribed, of faith in God and obedience to His commandments, God was pleased farther to resolve, and He faithfully did promise, that He would impart the same Blessed Spirit, as a continual guide and assistant to all those, who seriously would entertain those tenders of mercy, sincerely resolving the performance of the conditions.

Now although the natural and ordinary manner of this Divine Spirit's operation, like that of all spirits and more subtle substances, is not by violent and sensible impressions, but rather in way of imperceptible penetration or gentle insinuating of itself into the subject upon which it worketh, hardly discovering itself otherwise than by the notable effects resulting from it ; and although likewise the proper and principal effects thereof, according to Divine designation, do relate to the furthering our performance of the said conditions requisite toward our salvation, that is, to the cherishing our faith and quickening our obedience, disposing men to perform virtuous actions, rather than to achieve wondrous exploits ; yet more fully to satisfy the doubtful, to convince the incredulous, to confound the obstinate, world about the truth of His intentions, more illustriously to manifest the completion of His promise, more surely to fortify the faithful against the scandals and temptations which their profession would incur, God was pleased after our Lord's Ascension, and when the Apostolical promulgation of the Christian doctrine did commence, to dispense both to the teachers and the disciples thereof more liberal communications of that Holy Spirit, attended with notorious, strange, and wonderful effects, apt to provoke the admiration of men, to persuade their judgements, to prevail upon their affections, to produce within them strong desires of partaking so high a privilege and excellent endowment.

The memorial therefore of that most gracious and glorious dispensation, the Christian Church wisely and piously hath continually preserved, obliging us at this time peculiarly to bless God for that incomparable and inestimable gift, conferred then most visibly upon the Church, and still really bestowed upon every particular member, duly incorporated thereinto.

### No. 122.  WILLIAM LAUD

[From *A Relation of the Conference between William Laud and Mr. Fisher the Jesuit*, Section IX.  Ed. C. H. Simpkinson (1901), p. 27.  Cp. note on No. 54.]

I know and acknowledge that error [of the Eastern Church] of denying the Procession of the Holy Ghost from the Son to be a grievous error in Divinity.  And sure, it would have grated the foundation, if they had so denied the Procession of the Holy Ghost from the Son as that they had made an inequality between the Persons.  But since their form of speech is, That the Holy Ghost proceeds from the Father by the Son, and is the Spirit of the Son, without making any difference in the consubstantiality of the Persons, I dare not deny them to be a true Church for this, though I confess them an erroneous Church in this particular.

### No. 123.  WILLIAM SHERLOCK

[From *A Vindication of the Doctrine of the Trinity* (1690), pp. 16 f.  Cp. note on No. 58.]

The Holy Ghost is of the Father and of the Son, not made nor created, for no Creature ; not begotten, for no Son ; but proceeding, ἐκπορευόμενος, the manner of which we understand no more than

23

the manner of the Eternal Generation.    But there is this plain difference
between being begotten and proceeding, that though the Holy Spirit
have the same Nature with the Father and the Son, yet He represents
the Person of neither, as the Son does the Person of the Father, as
being the brightness of His Father's glory and the express Image of
His Person ; and therefore is said not to be begotten, but to proceed.

But the difficulty of this is with reference to the dispute between
the Greek and Latin Church about the *Filioque*, or the Spirit's proceeding from the Father and from the Son.   The reason why the Latin
Church insists on this is to preserve the Unity and subordination
of the Divine Persons to each other.   The Son is united and subordinate to the Father, as begotten by Him ; the Holy Ghost is united
and subordinate to Father and Son, as proceeding both from the
Father and from the Son.   But if the Holy Spirit proceeded only
from the Father, not from the Son, there would be no union and
subordination between the Son and the Spirit, and yet the Spirit is
the Spirit of the Son, as well as of the Father, and that these Three
Persons be one God, it is necessary that there should be an union of
Persons, as well as One Nature.   But then the Greek Church confesses,
that the Spirit proceedeth from the Father *by* the Son, though not
*from* the Son ;   and *by* and *from* are such niceties when we confess we
understand not the manner of this Procession of the Holy Spirit,
as ought to have made no dispute, much less a schism, between the
two Churches.   The Greek Church acknowledges the Distinction
of Persons, and their Unity and Subordination ;   that there is One
Father, not Three Fathers, One Son, not Three Sons, One Holy
Ghost, not Three Holy Ghosts ;   that the Unity in Trinity and the
Trinity in Unity is to be worshipped ;   which is all this Creed requires
as necessary to salvation.

# (11) ANGELS

## No. 124.  ROBERT BOYLE

[From *Some Motives and Incentives to the Love of God, Pathetically Discoursed of in a Letter to a Friend.  Works*, ed. London (1772), Vol. I, p. 295.  (This treatise is termed in the running title " Seraphic Love.")  This Letter first appeared in 1659, addressed to the Countess of Warwick ; but it was not until the fourth edition (1665) that the passage containing the following extract was added.  It comes from an Appendix entitled " An Occasional Reflexion upon a Letter Received in April, 1662, Containing an Account of what passed on the King's Coronation Day in a little Country Town."]

AND now I must on this occasion confess to you, Pyrocles, that I have (on other rises) several times been revolving in my thoughts what the Angels think of those praises and descriptions of God that men devise (for I intend not here to speak of those the Scripture suggests), and wherein we are most applauded by others and do oftentimes, perchance, applaud ourselves.  For those celestial courtiers (if I may so call them) have several advantages to assist them in the celebration of our Common Master, which we poor mortals want.  For first, they are free from those selfish and inordinate affections that too often hinder us either from discerning the excellency of divers of God's attributes and ways, or from duly acknowledging it.  They have no sins to keep them from descrying the justness of what He does ;  they have no ingratitude to oppose the fuller resentments of His goodness ;  and they are not tempted not to discern and adore His wisdom, for fear they should appear culpable for repining at His dispensations.  And indeed, their longevity allowing them the full prospect from end to end of those intricate transactions of Providence, of which short-lived mortals do commonly see but a part, they are questionless far more satisfied with the incomparably better contrivances they discern in the management of human affairs, than we are with the conduct or plots of the most skilfully written plays and romances.  Besides, those happy spirits, of whom the Scripture tells us that they *stand before God*, and that they *continually see His face*, have by that privilege the blessed opportunities of discovering in the Deity they contemplate and serve many excellences, which even they could never but by experience have formed any thoughts of ;  and they see in one another's solemn adorations and praises a way of honouring the Object of them so much transcending the utmost of what we here aim at, that their homages to their Creator may well be supposed of a far nobler kind than ours.  And lastly when I consider,

how much less unworthy thoughts and expressions touching things
Divine the same person may have, when come to his full maturity of
age and parts, and whilst he was but a child in both ; and when I
consider how much more advantageous conceptions of the wisdom
displayed in the universe, and particularly in the contrivance of a
human body, one that is a true philosopher and a skilful anatomist may
have, in comparison of a man illiterate and unacquainted with dissections ; when, I say, I consider these things, and compare the dim
twilight of human intellects in this life with that clear and radiant light,
which the Scripture ascribes to angels ; I cannot but think that, having
to the privilege of a much nearer access than is allowed us to contemplate God's perfections, the advantage of having incomparably more
illuminated intellects to apprehend them with, they must frame otherguise conceptions of the Divine attributes, and glorify the possessor
at an otherguise rate, than is allowed to those whose understandings
are so dim, and whose residence is so remote from that blessed place
where the perfections they would extol are most displayed.

# VIII.   SOTERIOLOGY

# (1) THE ATONEMENT

## No. 125. JOHN PEARSON

[From *An Exposition of the Creed.* On the words of Article II, " And in Jesus Christ, His Only Son, Our Lord." Ed. Oxford (E. Burton), 1864, pp. 131–135. Cp. note on No. **13**.]

I⟨T⟩ remaineth therefore that we should explain how and for what reasons Christ truly is, and properly is called, Our Saviour. First then, I conceive, one sufficient cause of that appellation to consist in this, that He hath opened and declared unto us the only true way for the obtaining eternal salvation, and by such patefaction can deserve no less than the name of Saviour. For if those Apostles and Preachers of the Gospel, who received the way of salvation from Him, which they delivered unto others, may be said to save those persons which were converted by their preaching, in a far more eminent and excellent manner must He be said to save them, Who first revealed all those truths unto them. St. Paul *provoked to emulation them which were his flesh, that he might save some of them ;* and *was made all things to all men, that he might by all means save some.* He exhorted Timothy *to take heed unto himself, and unto the doctrine, and continue in them ; for in doing this, he should both save himself and them that heard him.* And St. James speaks in more general terms : *Brethren, if any of you do err from the truth, and one convert him, let him know, that he which converteth a sinner from the error of his way, shall save a soul from death.* Now if these are so expressly said to save the souls of them which are converted by the doctrine which they deliver, with much more reason must Christ be said to save them, Whose ministers they are, and in Whose name they speak. For it was He Which *came and preached peace to them which were afar off, and to them that were nigh.* The will of God concerning the salvation of man was revealed by Him. *No man hath seen God at any time : the only-begotten Son, which is in the bosom of the Father, He hath declared Him.* Being then *the Gospel of Christ is the power of God unto salvation to every one that believeth,* being they which preach it at the command of Christ are said to save the souls of such as believe their word, being it was Christ alone *Who brought life and immortality to light through the Gospel,* therefore He must in a most eminent and singular manner be acknowledged thereby to save, and consequently must not be denied, even in this first respect, the title of Saviour.

283

Secondly, this Jesus hath not only revealed, but also procured, the way of salvation, not only delivered it to us, but also wrought it out for us ; and so *God sent His Son into the world, that the world through Him might be saved.* We were all concluded under sin, and, being the wages of sin is death, we were obliged to eternal punishment, from which it was impossible to be freed except the sin were first remitted. Now this is the constant rule, that *without shedding of blood is no remission. It was therefore necessary that Christ should appear to put away sin by the sacrifice of Himself.* And so He did, for He *shed His blood for many for the remission of sins,* as Himself professeth in the sacramental institution ; He *bare our sins in His own body on the tree,* as St. Peter speaks ; and so in Him *we have redemption through His blood, even the forgiveness of sins.* And if *while we were yet sinners, Christ died for us ; much more then, being now justified by His blood, we shall be saved from wrath by Him.* Again we were all enemies unto God, and having offended Him, there was no possible way of salvation, but by being reconciled to Him. If then we ask the question, as once the Philistines did concerning David, *Wherewith should we reconcile ourselves unto our master?* we have no other name to answer it but Jesus. For *God was in Christ reconciling the world unto Himself, not imputing their trespasses unto them.* And as under the Law *the blood of the sin-offering was brought into the tabernacle of the congregation to reconcile withal in the holy place,* so it pleased the Father through the Son, *having made peace by the blood of His Cross, by Him to reconcile a'l things unto Himself.* And thus it comes to pass, that *us who were enemies in our mind by wicked works, yet now hath He reconciled in the body of His flesh through death.* And upon this reconciliation of our persons must necessarily follow the salvation of our souls. *For if, when we were enemies, we were reconciled unto God by the death of His Son, much more, being reconciled, we shall be saved by His life.* Furthermore, we were all first enslaved by sin, and brought into captivity by Satan, neither was there any possibility of escape but by way of redemption. Now it was the law of Moses, that if *any were able he might redeem himself*: but this to us was impossible, because absolute obedience in all our actions is due unto God, and therefore no act of ours can make any satisfaction for the least offence. Another law gave yet more liberty, that he which *was sold might be redeemed again ; one of his brethren might redeem him.* But this in respect of all the mere sons of men was equally impossible, because they were all under the same captivity. Nor could they satisfy for others, who were wholly unable to redeem themselves. Wherefore there was no other brother, but that Son of man which is the Son of God, Who was like unto us in all things, sin only excepted, Which could work this redemption for us. And what He only could, that He freely did perform. For *the Son of man came to give His life a ransom for many*; and as He came to give, so He *gave Himself a ransom for all.* So that in Him *we have redemption through His blood, the forgiveness of sins.* For we are *bought with a price*; for we are *redeemed, not with corruptible things, as silver and gold, but with the precious blood of Christ, as of a lamb without blemish and without spot.* He then Which hath obtained for us remission of sins, He Who through Himself hath reconciled us unto God, He Who hath given Himself as a ransom to redeem us, He Who hath thus wrought out the way of salvation for us, must necessarily have a second and a far higher right unto the name of *Jesus*, unto the title of our *Saviour*.

Thirdly, beside the promulging and procuring, there is yet a farther act, which is conferring of salvation on us. All which we mentioned before, was wrought by virtue of His death, and His appearance in the Holy of Holies ; but we must still believe He *is able also to save them to the uttermost that come unto God by Him, seeing He ever liveth to make intercession for them.* For now being set down at the right hand of God, He hath received all power both in Heaven and earth, and the end of this power which He hath received is, to confer salvation upon those which believe in Him. For the Father gave the Son *this power over all flesh, that He should give eternal life to as many as He hath given Him ; that He should raise our bodies out of the dust, and cause our corruptible to put on incorruption, and our mortal to put on immortality* : and upon this power we are to expect salvation from Him. For we must *look for the Saviour, the Lord Jesus Christ, from Heaven, Who shall change our vile body, that it may be fashioned like unto His glorious body, according to the working whereby He is able even to subdue all things unto Himself.* And *unto them that* thus *look for Him shall He appear the second time, without sin unto salvation.* Being then we are all to endeavour that our *spirits may be saved in the day of the Lord Jesus*, being St. Peter hath taught us that *God hath exalted Christ with His right hand to be a Prince and a Saviour*, being the conferring of that upon us which He promised to us, and obtained for us, is the reward of what He suffered, therefore we must acknowledge that the actual giving of salvation to us is the ultimate and conclusive ground of the title *Saviour*.

Thus by the virtue of His precious blood Christ hath obtained remission of our sins, by the power of His grace hath taken away the dominion of sin, in the life to come will free us from all possibility of sinning, and utterly abolish death the wages of sin : wherefore well said the Angel of the Lord, *Thou shalt call His name Jesus, for He shall save His people from their sins* ; well did Zacharias call Him *an horn of salvation* ; Simeon, *the salvation of God* ; St. Paul, *the captain and author of eternal salvation* ; St. Peter, *a Prince and a Saviour*, correspondent to those judges of Israel, raised up by God Himself to deliver His people from the hands of their enemies, and for that reason called *Saviours*.

## No. 126.   JAMES USSHER

[From *Sermons*, ed. C. R. Elrington (1864), Vol. XIII, pp. 509-513. This Sermon, taken from a MS. of 36 Sermons in the Library of Balliol College, was first published by Elrington (No. IX of his enumeration of the Balliol MS. Sermons). The text was *Gal.* iv, 4. Ussher himself desired that none of his sermon notes should be published after his death.]

Thus stood the case betwixt God and us. We were at variance with God, without any means of reconcilement on our part. There cometh in in the meantime the Middle-man to take up the matter by assuming unto Himself these two offices. First, He becometh our intercessor, to solicit and make peace for us; secondly, He becometh our advocate, to plead the justice of our cause. He must in this (you see) first seek God's mercy, and then also challenge God's justice, what it can exact.

This variance betwixt God and man, Job well sheweth, where he affirmeth that, though he were righteous, yet he would submit himself to his judge, not answer and make replication. And again, *He is not a man as I am, that I should answer him if we come together to judgement, neither is there any umpire that should lay his hand upon both.* Old Eli also reproving his sons to this purpose telleth them if one man sin against another, the judge shall judge it; but if a man sin against the Lord, who will plead for him, who will lay his hand upon both? This is an hard and a strange matter. There must then of necessity be an Emmanuel to plead our cause, Who will not be ashamed for us to appear before the throne of justice, clothed with our nature, and there challenge righteousness for us, laying His hand upon both, one hand upon the Father, Whose wrath He appeaseth, keeping it from us, and the other upon us, whom He cherisheth from sinking under so great a burden, upholding us by His reconcilement. Yea, such a one He must needs be, Who first for intercession must be high in favour with God, Who in Himself or for Himself hath no spot or blemish, Who hath nothing to do for Himself, but all for us; Whose person in the Father's sight is already accepted, and He well pleased therein, etc. Again such a one He must be, Who is tender-hearted to us, in a compassionate feeling of our sorrows, taking part with us (as the Apostle speaks) that we might obtain so much the surer deliverance and victory by His fellow-feeling with us. The angels they could not, for they have enough ado to keep in for themselves, and we see those of them who have fallen have not the power to rise again and intercede for themselves, much less for others.

But our Emmanuel and elder brother Christ Jesus, He taketh us by hand, and presenteth Himself with us before the Father, saying,

" Behold, O Father, here am I, and the children which Thou hast given Me, be pleased for My sake to pardon these, they are My brethren and Thou canst not be angry with them unless Thou be also angry with Me, Who am Thy well-beloved Son. Here am I ready to satisfy Thy justice for them." Neither was this indeed an easy matter thus to appear before God for us ; for indeed if God in the work of our redemption had intended only one thing, viz. to be merciful, then it had not been so much. But as those who have eyes may easily see, God intended in this great work to set not only His mercy but also all His other attributes on work,—His justice, His power, His greatness, His anger, His goodness, etc. To this purpose the Apostle reasoneth for the law, that the law, notwithstanding of mercy and forgiveness of sins, must have the [? its] own work and not be in vain, and that the redemption purchased must not make void His justice, where after he had spoken of *that redemption and reconciliation set forth by God, through faith in Christ's Blood, and the declaration of that righteousness by forgiveness of sins passed [over] through the patience of God,* he addeth, *to show at this time, this righteousness, that He might be just, and a justifier of him who is of the faith of Jesus.* Although, therefore, the Lord intend mercy, yet He will have us appear guilty ; and as He is just, so His justice must not be in vain. Christ therefore thus standing for us, before His Father thus pleadeth our cause.

*Plea* :—

These men indeed, O Father, stand indebted unto Thy justice ; but such is their misery, that they are not able to satisfy Thee, Another therefore shall give Thee satisfaction. I, O Father, will undertake to pay their debt ; destroy not therefore the work of Thine hands. Thou art not so rigorous, that the party indebted, since He is not able, must needs give satisfaction. I, Thy Wisdom, will in their nature pay all. The perfection of My obedience shall outstrip their disobedience, etc. And the parties thus relieved must have such an interest in Him, Who is the Mediator, that in justice God cannot deny to impute unto them whatsoever He hath done, that all be as though themselves had done it. They must be mystically knit and joined unto Him by a secret conjunction of faith and love by His Spirit. Again for Him, He must have these properties : 1. He must be our Mediator and satisfy our debt with all satisfaction ; 2. He must be such a one Who is able to transfer and convey His estate from Himself unto them who are of the blood royal, and of His kindred ; He must interest them in His right.

First, then, He must satisfy our debts by justice. Many think not so, but that His mere death without obedience and satisfaction to the law was sufficient. But we here see the contrary ; we see Christ tied to the law, *born of a woman and made under the law.* Now in the law must be considered two things,—1. strict obedience, sound payment; 2. the penalty due to the breach of the law. First, there must be full account, as at the beginning was due. By reason of our insufficiency, Christ giveth us a bill under His hand unto the Father, that all our debts are satisfied, all are reckoned up upon His score, and therefore now being in Him we need not fear.

Neither must we account of Adam's fall, as of a light confused sin, but as an heavy great sin, distinct (by reason of a breach). A particular thing, which must have a particular remedy. Christ, therefore, because Adam did not fulfil the law, He (*sic*) undertook to fulfil the same to relieve us, and that God's justice should not be in vain.

Secondly, the penalty due to the breach of the law, Christ, He also doth this: the Godhead and the manhood performeth this work, the Deity assisting the humanity, therein not to be overcome. And because the law in our weak nature could never thus have been satisfied (as the Apostle speaketh) *for that which was impossible to the law, God sending His own Son in the similitude of sinful flesh, and for sin, condemned sin in the flesh, that the righteousness of the law might be fulfilled in us*, etc. First, then, the law exacteth satisfaction of the nature trespassing; that nature which transgressed must satisfy. Christ, therefore, He taketh upon Him our nature, bindeth Himself unto all, to satisfy whatsoever might be exacted of us by His cleanness and pureness, blotting out whatsoever stains or spots we are infected with in our nature. For it pleaseth Him, as from Adam all of us are infected with the leprosy of sin, sending forth a spring of filthy corruptions which cry for judgement and provoke God's vengeance, so from Him He sendeth forth a counter spring of His merits, obedience, and righteousness, satisfaction, and the like, which outrunning ours and being of so infinite a value and perfect, standeth betwixt God's wrath and us, making perfect atonement and peace, being as it were the mirror through which God beholdeth us and our actions, whom He also by degrees transformeth into His image little and [? by] little, until at last this river of our corruptions be quite dried up in the ocean of His righteousness, as it were, hiding us in the holds of the rock, until by dissolution we be fully glorified.

## No. 127.  ISAAC BARROW

[From *Sermon 27 on the Creed*. *Works*, ed. Oxford (1818), Vol. V, pp. 5, 9 f., 13 f., 17, 18 (*bis*), 19, 20, 20–22; ed. Napier (1859), Vol. VI, pp. 311, 316 f., 321–323, 326 f., 328, 329, 330, 331, 331–333. The text of this Sermon, on the words "Dead and buried," was 1 *Cor.* xv, 3. Cp. note on No. **344**.]

Our Saviour's death then was a true, real, and proper death suitable to that frail, passible, and mortal nature, which He vouchsafed to undergo for us; to the condition of *sinful flesh, in the likeness whereof He did appear*, severing His soul and body, and remitting them to their original sources; His passion was indeed *ultimum supplicium*, an extreme capital punishment, the highest, in the last result, which in this world either the fiercest injustice or the severest justice could inflict: for, *to kill the body* is, as Our Lord Himself taught, the utmost limit of all human power and malice, the most and worst that men can do; they have not περισσότερόν τι, anything beyond that which they can attempt upon us; and so far did they proceed with Our Lord. Such was the nature of His death; such indeed as was requisite for the accomplishment of the ends and effects designed thereby. . . .

The High Priest's entrance once a year into the Holy of Holies, *not without blood to atone for his own and the people's ignorances* (or miscarriages), did imply that our great High Priest should make one bloody atonement for the offences of mankind and, passing through the veil of mortal flesh, should enter into the true *sanctum sanctorum* of Heaven, there to *appear in the presence of God for us*, exhibiting the virtue of His meritorious passion, together with His effectual intercession for mercy toward us. Especially the Paschal Lamb, in its substance (as a lamb, meek and gentle), in its quality (as without blemish and spot, pure and innocent), in its manner of preparation and dressing (being killed by all the assembly, having its blood sprinkled upon the doors of every house, being roasted with fire having bitter herbs for its sauce), with other observable circumstances about it, was a most apposite emblem of *Christ our passover*; Who not only by His death did signify, and mind us of, but did really achieve our deliverance from the mystical Egypt, our state of spiritual bondage. So did ancient types exhibit and represent. Plain predictions also did express the same death and suffering of our Lord: *Those things*, saith St. Peter, *which God before had shewed by the mouth of all His prophets, that Christ should suffer, He hath so fulfilled*;—not one Prophet only, not some few, but *all*, saith he (that is, either plainly or covertly, either directly or by consequence), have foreshewed (or foretold) it. It is our negligence or stupidity if we do not discern it in them, as Our Lord intimated, when He thus spake to His disciples: *O fools, and slow of heart to believe all that the prophets have spoken! ought not Christ* (ought He not, according to their presignifications and predictions) *to have suffered these things, and so to enter into His glory?* . . .

Let us now consider the causes and principles whence it proceeded, which moved God to determine it and Our Lord to undertake it. They were, in Both, acts most voluntary and free. Of the Father it is said, *It pleased the Lord to bruise Him*; and, *Behold*, saith Our Lord in the Psalm, *I come to do Thy will, O God*; that is, as the Apostle to the Hebrews expoundeth it, to offer, not the blood of beasts in sacrifice, but My own Body, according to Thy will and appointment: and, *This commandment*, saith He in St. John, *I received of My Father, to lay down My life* : and, *The cup*, saith He again, *which My Father hath given Me, shall I not drink it?* So on the Father's part, and on our Saviour's likewise, it was no less voluntary; for, *None*, saith He, *taketh My life from Me* (that is, it is not from any necessity or compulsion that I do part with it), *but I lay it down of Myself* (with absolute choice and freedom) ; *I have power to lay it down, and I have power to resume it* : and, *The bread*, saith He, *which I shall give, is My flesh, which I shall give for the life of the world : The Son of man came to give His life a ransom for many.* The yielding His flesh to death, the paying His life to ransom were deeds of gift, perfectly free: and that both in regard to God the Father and the Son this performance was voluntary, St. Paul together thus expresseth, *Who gave Himself for our sins, that He might deliver us from this present evil world, according to the will of God and our Father* : so this death issued from the joint wills of God and His Son. But as the volitions of every intelligent and wise agent do always proceed from some principle inclining, or are directed according to some impulsive cause moving to them, so divers principles and causes of these voluntary acts are declared in Scripture; the chief of which are reducible to these two; one internally disposing God's goodness; the other externally inviting man's distress. The case stood thus: mankind lying in a sad and forlorn estate, oppressed by Satan, enslaved to sin, subject to a rigorous law, exposed to the severity of justice, tormented by the sense of guilt, fearful of divine wrath and due vengeance, in short, by the sentence of Heaven and by the suffrage of conscience within, condemned to punishment unavoidable, and to intolerable misery; man, I say, lying in so desperately uncomfortable a condition, God's infinite goodness regarded His poor creature, His *bowels of compassion* yearned toward him, a desire of relieving sprang up in His will; thence was He moved to provide such a remedy, suitable and sufficient for his delivery, for the removing all those mischiefs and curing all those distempers. The main source of all this wonderful performance (as of all other providential dispensations and works, *ad extra*), was that most excellent perfection of God, which, in regard to this matter, is sometime termed χρηστότης, benignity, or bounty; implying the great benefit and advantage we do thence receive; sometimes grace, or favour, signifying the pure freeness in dispensing it, without any design of profit to Himself, or any desert on our part (*By the grace of God He tasted death for every man*); sometimes mercy, denoting our bad deserts, or obnoxiousness to justice and punishment; sometimes pity, signifying the great need we had thereof, by reason of our extreme distress and misery. Commonly also it is, by the most obliging and endearing name styled love, and philanthropy, intimating the earnest regard and benevolence God had to us as His creatures, and as capable of being benefited and bettered by Him; *Herein*, saith St. Paul, *God commended His love toward us, in that we being yet sinners, Christ died for us ; and, God*, saith St. John, *loved us, and sent His Son to be a propitiation for us ; and, God*, saith our Lord Himself, *so loved the world, that He gave His only begotten Son—that the world might be saved by Him.* . . .

Now for the ends which our Lord's death aimeth at, and the effects which it produceth (these we join, because in reality they are the same), they in Scripture reckoning and expression are various and many : the most general are these, comprehending divers others subordinate to them.

1. The illustration of God's glory, by demonstrating and displaying therein His most excellent attributes and perfections. So doth St. Paul teach us ; *Whom God*, saith he, *hath set forth a propitiation by faith in His blood*, εἰς ἔνδειξιν τῆς δικαιοσύνης αὐτοῦ, *for a demonstration of His righteousness* ; that is, as I take it, of His goodness, His justice, His fidelity, His constancy, of all those commendable perfections, which are expressed in dealing with others. And Our Lord, His Passion being instantly to follow, made this reflection,—*Now is the Son of man glorified, and God is glorified in Him ;* and, *I have glorified Thee upon earth; I have finished the work which Thou gavest Me to do.* . . .

2. The dignifying and exaltation of our Lord Himself ; by acquiring unto Him in a manner a new right unto, and instating Him in an universal dominion, in a transcendent glory, in perfect joy accruing to Him by remuneration for so excellent an instance of submission and obedience to God's will. . . .

3. The salvation of mankind ; the which He was designed to procure by His death, and in many respects He did promote it thereby.

He did it by appeasing that wrath of God which He naturally beareth toward iniquity, and reconciling God to men, who by sin were alienated from Him, by procuring a favourable disposition and intentions of grace toward us. . . .

Again, it furthered our salvation, by purchasing the remission of our sins, and justification of our persons, our freedom from condemnation and punishment, our appearance as upright and acceptable in God's sight, upon the conditions of faith and repentance propounded in the Gospel ; in regard to which effects He is said thereby to redeem us from our sins, to bear them, to take them away, to expiate them, to cleanse, to purge, to sanctify us from them : *Who shall lay anything to the charge of God's elect? Who shall condemn them? It is Christ that died ;* that is, Christ's death hath freed them from all liableness to guilt and condemnation. . . . Our Lord also by His death procured our salvation, as having thereby purchased for us means sufficient to free us from the power and dominion of sin, to purify our hearts, and sanctify our lives ; for, *He gave Himself for us, that He might redeem us from all iniquity, and purify to Himself a peculiar people, zealous of good works. . . .*

In subordination to, coincidence or concurrence with, the principal designs and effects, our Lord also died for the reparation of God's honour, which we by contempt of His authority and violation of His law had impaired, but our Saviour by so signal an obedience thereto did repair ; for the recovery of God's right, which was infringed by withdrawing so great and noble a part of His creation from its due allegiance and service, the which He recovered and restored to Him, for the satisfaction to God's justice, provoked by so heinous impieties and iniquities, the which was abundantly performed by so infinitely valuable a compensation and sacrifice offered thereto.

Also for ratification of the New Covenant between God and us ; whence His Blood is called, *the Blood of the Covenant, the Blood of the New Testament.*

For the pacifying and reconciling all things in Heaven and earth ; removing all causes of dissension and distance ; inducing obligations to concord and charity.

For pulling out *the sting,* and removing the terrors *of death; destroying* (or defeating) *him that had the power of death, and delivering them who through the fear of death are all their lifetime subject to death.*

For the suppressing, vanquishing, and *triumphing over the powers of hell* and darkness, the which He did, as St. Paul telleth us, achieve *upon His cross* : and by His death He telleth us, that *the prince of this world was condemned, and cast out.*

For engaging us to the practice of all righteousness and obedience (especially to the most excellent, high and hard parts thereof, charity, humility, meekness, patience, self-denial, utmost constancy and perseverance), both from our obligation in regard to what He suffered for us, and in imitation of His example ; for, *We should run with patience the race that is set before us, looking unto Jesus, the author and finisher of our faith, Who for the joy that was set before Him endured the cross, despising the shame :* and, *Christ having suffered for us in the flesh, we should,* saith St. Peter, *arm ourselves with the same mind,—so as no longer to live the rest of our time in the flesh to the lust of men, but to the will of God.*

Lastly, for attestation unto and confirmation of Divine truth ; sealing by His Blood that Heavenly Doctrine which He taught, *and witnessing before Pontius Pilate a good confession.* He was the Prince of martyrs Who, *as He for this end,* as He told Pilate, *was born, and for this end came into the world, that He might bear witness to the truth,* so He especially did accomplish that glorious design by His death, *enduring the contradiction of sinners against Himself, resisting unto blood in combating against sin; by His blood* indeed all other witnesses of truth did, as it is said in the Revelation, accomplish their warfare, and *obtain victory* :

His blood purchased for them their resolution and strength; His promises supported them, His example did animate them, to the profession and maintenance of truth, in the greatest dangers and most violent assaults.

Such ends did the death of our Lord regard, such fruits did grow from it, which the time permitteth us but thus cursorily to touch.

## No. 128.  ISAAC BARROW

[From *Sermons*.  *Works*, ed. Oxford (1818), *Sermon 32*, § V, 1, 4, 5, 11. Vol. II, pp. 228–230, 231, 234, 235 f., 240.   Ed. A. Napier (1859), *Sermon 2*, Vol. I, pp. 128–130, 131, 135 f., 137 f., 143 f.  The title of this Sermon was " Upon the Passion of Our Blessed Saviour," and the text *Phil.* ii, 8.  Cp. note on No. **344**.]

Lastly, the consideration of Our Lord's suffering [the death on the Cross] is very useful in application to our practice.  No point is more fruitful of wholesome instruction, none is more forcible to kindle devout affections, none can afford more efficacious inducements and incentives to a pious life.  For what virtue will not a serious meditation on the Cross be apt to breed and to cherish ?  To what duty will it not engage and excite us ?

Are we not hence infinitely obliged, with most humble affection and hearty gratitude, to adore each Person of the Blessed Trinity ?

That God the Father should design such a redemption for us, *not sparing His own Son*, (*the Son of His love*, dear to Him as Himself,) but *delivering Him up for us*, to be thus dealt with for our sake: that God would endure to see His Son in so pitiful a condition, to hear Him groaning under so grievous pressures, to let Him be so horribly abused; and that for us, who deserved nothing from Him, who had demerited so much against Him; for us, who were no friends to Him, (for *even when we were enemies, we were reconciled to God by the death of His Son ;*) who were not any ways commendable for goodness or righteousness: (for *Christ did suffer for sinners, the just for the unjust* ; and *God commended His love to us, that while we were sinful, Christ died for us :* ) that God thus should *love us, sending His Son to be a propitiation for our sins*, in so dismal a way of suffering, how stupendous is that goodness!  How vast an obligation doth it lay upon us to reciprocal affection !  If we do owe all to God, as our Maker, from Whose undeserved bounty we did receive all that we have, how much farther do we stand indebted to Him as the author of our redemption, from Whose ill-deserved mercy we receive a new being, and better state ; and that in a way far more obliging !  For God created us with a word, without more cost or trouble, but to redeem us stood Him in huge expenses and pains, no less than the debasing of His only Son to our frailty, the exposing Him to more than our misery, the withdrawing His face and restraining His bowels from His best beloved.  If a Jew then were commanded by law, if a Gentile were obliged by nature, to *love God*

24

*with all his heart and all his soul* ; what affection doth a Christian, under the law and duty of grace, owe unto Him ? By what computation can we reckon that debt ? What faculties have we sufficient to discharge it ? What finite heart can hold an affection commensurate to such an obligation ?

And how can it otherwise than inflame our heart with love toward the blessed Son of God, our Saviour, to consider that, merely out of charitable pity towards us, He purposely came down from Heaven, and took our flesh upon Him, that He might therein undergo those extreme acerbities of pain, and those most ugly indignities of shame for us ? *Greater love,* said He, *hath no man than this, that a man lay down his life for his friends.* But that God should lay down His life, should pour forth His blood, should be aspersed with the worst crimes, and clothed with foulest shame, should be executed on a cross as a malefactor and a slave, for His enemies and rebellious traitors, what imagination can devise any expression of charity or friendship comparable to this ? Wherefore if love naturally be productive of love, if friendship justly meriteth a correspondence in good-will, what effect should the consideration of so ineffable a love, of so unparalleled friendship, have upon us ? . . .

Nor should we forget, that also upon this account we do owe great love and thanks to God the Holy Ghost, who, as He did originally conspire in the wonderful project of our redemption, as He did executively by miraculous operation conduct our Saviour into His fleshly tabernacle, as He did by unmeasurable communications of divine virtue assist His humanity through all the course of His life, so in this juncture He did inspire Him with charity more than human, and did support Him to undergo those pressures with invincible patience ; and so did sanctify all this sacerdotal performance, that our Lord, as the Apostle doth affirm, *did through the eternal Spirit offer Himself without spot to God.* . . .

This consideration is most useful to render us very humble and sensible of our weakness, our vileness, our wretchedness. For how low was that our fall, from which we could not be raised without such a depression of God's only Son ? How great is that impotency, which did need such a succour to relieve it ? How abominable must be that iniquity, which might not be expiated without so costly a sacrifice ? How deplorable is that misery, which could not be removed without commutation of so strange a suffering ? Would the Son of God have so *emptied* and abased Himself for nothing ? Would He have endured such pains and ignominies for a trifle ? No, surely ; if our guilt had been slight, if our case had been tolerable, the divine wisdom would have chosen a more cheap and easy remedy for us. . . .

But farther, while this contemplation doth breed sober humility, it also should preserve us from base abjectness of mind; for it doth evidently demonstrate, that, according to God's infallible judgement, we are very considerable, that our souls are capable of high regard; that it is a great pity we should be lost and abandoned to ruin. For surely, had not God much esteemed and respected us, He would not for our sakes have so debased Himself, or deigned to endure so much for our recovery; divine justice would not have exacted or accepted such a ransom for our souls, had they been of little worth. We should not therefore slight ourselves, nor demean ourselves like sorry contemptible wretches, as if we deserved no consideration, no pity from ourselves; as if we thought our souls not worth saving, which yet our Lord thought good to purchase at so dear a rate. By so despising or disregarding ourselves, do we not condemn the sentiments, do we not vilify the sufferings of our Lord; so with a pitiful meanness of spirit joining the most unworthy injustice and ingratitude? . . .

But furthermore, what can be more operative than this point toward breeding a disregard of this world, with all its deceitful vanities and mischievous delights, toward reconciling our minds to the worst condition into which it can bring us, toward supporting our hearts under the heaviest pressures of affliction which it can lay upon us? For can we reasonably expect, can we eagerly affect, can we ardently desire great prosperity, whenas the Son of God, our Lord and Master, did only taste such adversity? How can we refuse, in submission to God's pleasure, contentedly to bear a slight grievance, whenas our Saviour gladly did bear a cross, infinitely more distasteful to carnal will and sense than any that can befall us? Who now can admire those splendid trifles, which our Lord never did regard in His life, and which at His death only did serve to mock and abuse Him? Who can relish those sordid pleasures, of which He living did not vouchsafe to taste, and the contraries whereof He dying chose to feel in all extremity? Who can disdain or despise a state of sorrow and disgrace, which He, by voluntary susception of it, hath so dignified and graced, by which we so near resemble and become conformable to Him; by which we concur and partake with Him; yea, by which in some cases we may promote, and after a sort complete His designs, *filling up*, as St. Paul speaketh, *that which is behind of the afflictions of Christ in our flesh?*

# (2) JUSTIFICATION

## No. 129.   GEORGE BULL

[From *Harmonia Apostolica ; or Two Dissertations in the Former of which the Doctrine of St. James on Justification by Works is Explained and Defended, in the latter, the Agreement of St. Paul with St. James is clearly shewn.* Diss. I, ch. i, § 2 ; ch. ii, §§ 8, 9 ; ch. iv, § 8 ; ch. vi, § 12 ; Diss. II, ch. i, §§ 1, 2 ; Diss. II, ch. iv, § 2 ; xi, § 4. These dissertations were composed in Latin. The translation here printed is from that in the *L. A. C. T.* (²1844), pp. 6, 16–18, 27 f., 40, 43, 57, 138 ; this was based upon one by Thomas Wilkinson, published in 1801. Bull's treatise appeared originally in 1669–70 ; and its publication immediately provoked a storm. As the following extracts shew, he repudiated any teaching on justification which depreciated the value of good works, and was thus accused of Arminianism. In 1675 Bull wrote two replies to his opponents—his *Examen Censurae* (an answer to Charles Gataker ; cp. note on No. **11**) and *Apologia pro Harmonia* (an answer to Thomas Barlow).]

THE word ' to justify,' δικαιοῦν (to which the Hebrew הצדק answers), is used by him [*i.e.*, by St. James] in its more usual sense, that is, as a term of law, meaning ' to acquit,' or ' pronounce guiltless.' Every unprejudiced person must know this to be the most obvious and common meaning of that word in the Holy Scriptures, and especially in the New Testament. So that it is strange to find a most learned man who in other respects has with great truth explained this doctrine of justification, denying it, and contending that the word justification generally signifies, especially when connected with the word faith, a ' purifying from vice,' or a ' freedom from the habit of sinning.' Grotius, indeed, does allow (for him I mean) that to ' justify ', in the Second Chapter of St. James, signifies ' to treat anyone as just ', and adds that the whole context of his argument renders this meaning absolutely necessary. Still he entirely denies that this is its general sense, especially in the Epistles of St. Paul. But we will easily prove, though perhaps a better opportunity may appear hereafter, that this word constantly, and almost always, has the above-mentioned meaning in the New Testament. . . . .

It is wonderful how those who acknowledge these truths,—and none but a professed libertine dare deny them,—can defend their paradox of justification by faith alone, faith being understood by them as separated from the works of repentance. They will say, perhaps, as indeed they are accustomed to say, that repentance is only required as *a preceding disposition*, by which a sinner is prepared for the forgiveness of sins, but faith is the sole *instrument* by which that forgiveness is received, as by a hand, and therefore it is not improperly said, we are justified by faith alone. But here they are egregiously wrong, and that in two respects. In the first place, they clearly suppose that the works of repentance precede faith, which is a great mistake ; for no man either can or will grieve for sin, detest it, determine upon a better conduct in future, or perform the other works of repentance, *works meet for repentance*, as the Baptist says, except he first had a firm faith in the Gospel of Christ. We may therefore press them with this dilemma. If faith alone and by itself justifies, it performs this office either before the works of repentance are produced, or not until after them. If they say *before*, how then can they call repentance a disposition preceding justi- fication ; or how can the works of repentance be required by the Holy Spirit, as necessary to his justification, who hath been already justified by faith alone ? But if they answer that faith does not justify until *after* these works are produced, they must necessarily fall into one of these two absurdities, either that faith does not exist before the works of repentance, or that it does not operate towards effecting our justification. You will say, that although faith is the source of repentance, and therefore, in the order of nature be prior to repentance, yet still faith and repentance may begin to exist together at one and the same instant. I answer that this is very absurd, and besides perfectly impossible. It cannot be that faith should produce repentance in an instant. For that anyone should grieve for his sins, detest them, humble himself under the hand of God, should produce an act of love to God, should conceive a design of newness of life, requires some time, and some length of pious contem- plation. These things, I confess, are subtleties. But the cover is worthy of the dish ; the answer squares with the objection. It was absolutely necessary to split hairs with those who do the same.

Secondly, what they advance respecting the instrumentality of faith in the matter of justification is a trifling piece of sophistry. For besides having no warrant in Scripture for what they say, if the word ' instru- ment ' be taken in its strict and proper sense for the secondary efficient cause, it is evident that faith can in no sense be called the instrument of justification. For, in the first place, since justification is the act of God alone, and produced entirely without us, how our faith or any action of ours can give any physical assistance in effecting our justification, is altogether inconceivable. And, in the next place, every instrumental cause, as we have already hinted, operates according to its own peculiar nature, and the production of the effect may be properly attributed to it. Now, since justification is entirely the gracious act of God, by which He pardons our sins and grants us salvation, it is extremely absurd to say, that either our faith or our works, or anything else of ours, forgives our sins, or makes us ac- ceptable. Which, however, is said by those who call faith the instru- mental cause of justification. You may ask, Is it not right to say, " By faith we accept Christ, and embrace the benefit of justification obtained by Him "? I answer, although many, with great reason, suppose that this acceptation of Christ is an act rather of love than of faith, yet, for the present at least, we will not contend about it. Let it therefore be taken for granted. What I insist upon is this, this act of embracing Christ wholly and entirely differs, and is distinct from, the act of justification. The one is our own act; the other the act of God alone. Although, therefore, we should allow that the habit of faith is the instrument of that act, by which we embrace Christ, yet whoever should infer from thence that faith is also the instrument of justification, would argue contrary to all the rules of reasoning. Upon the whole, therefore, faith can be an instrument only in this sense, because it is a work commanded by God, and performed by His grace. For a condition being performed may in a certain sense be called the means or instrument by which we obtain what is promised upon that condition. And this is called by some, the moral instrument. And if in this sense the word instrument is taken as the condition or moral instrument, we pointedly deny that faith is the only instrument of justification. Since, as we have already shown, the works of repentance also are positively insisted upon by the Holy Spirit as no less necessary to obtain justification. . . .

I will conclude the whole subject in a few words. Confidence in Christ, whether conditional or absolute, little signifies, is common to the good and the bad, so that, if this be the last step and *perfection* of justifying faith, certainly every wicked man may boast of his salvation. For it is, alas, too well known, that the greatest part of those who call themselves Christians, secure of the mercy of God, the merits of Christ, and of their own salvation, pass their days without the least anxiety, being at the same time very far short of a true Christian life. Their good works, which they never perform, they renounce, acknowledge themselves the worst of sinners, and then tranquilly depend on Christ, the Mediator, to obtain salvation for them. You may persuade them to do this without any difficulty; they rush on headlong into this confidence. Those who have the cure of souls find no difficulty so great as the convincing unhappy men of this error, deluded by which they carelessly give up all care of their souls.

But, you will say, they are not sincere. This confidence is greatly different from that which is peculiar to the justified. How, I pray, do they pretend a confidence which they have not? You will never persuade them so. They both know and congratulate themselves, that they truly, and unfeignedly trust in the merits of Christ. This facts prove, for in this confidence they live and are ready to die; nay, too often really do so die. They therefore truly trust in Christ, but not as they ought, because they do it without any grounds. They depend on the merits of Christ, but despise His commands; they eagerly embrace the promises of the Gospel, but care nothing for its precepts. This is the only difference between the confidence of the good and the wicked. It is in vain to seek any other. Lastly, St. John clearly informs us what is true and Christian confidence : *And hereby we know (i.e.,* by love) *that we are of the truth, and shall assure our hearts before Him. For if our heart condemn us, God is greater than our heart, and knoweth all things. Beloved, if our heart condemn us not, then have we confidence toward God.* For surely a secure confidence of mind is the daughter of a good conscience and arises from good works, so far is it from being of any profit without good works. . . .

· It is very wonderful that they who acknowledge the necessity of good works to attain salvation on the promise of God, should be so averse from our opinion, that good works are also necessarily required to justification. For by the same arguments through which they are induced to reject this, they must necessarily reject the other also, if they would only be consistent with themselves. For why do they deny that good works are necessary to justification ? First, because this opinion detracts from the merits of Christ ; secondly, because it contradicts St. Paul. But who does not perceive that these arguments equally militate against the other opinions which they support ? With respect to the merits of Christ, to them our salvation, no less than our justification, is entirely due. Freely are we saved, freely are we justified. With respect to St. Paul, it is manifest that the works concerning which he treats are removed by him just as far from having any effect in our salvation as in our justification. Works which are excluded from either are so from both ; this appears from many passages of St. Paul, particularly from that in the *Epistle to Titus,* iii, 5, compared with that in the *Epistle to the Ephesians,* ii, 8, 9. . . .

St. James says thus : *Ye see then how that by works a man is justified, and not by faith only.* The conclusion of St. Paul is directly opposite to this. *We conclude therefore that a man is justified by faith without the deeds of the law.* What a difference do we here behold and how greatly opposed are they to each other !

But let not the reader be discouraged ; with a little patience he will certainly find these Apostles, though apparently disagreeing, in the most perfect harmony with each other. I will, moreover, venture to promise, however incredible it may appear, that from what St. Paul hath said concerning works, I will bring additional proofs for the doctrine of St. James, of justification by works. . . .

From what we have already said, this may be laid down as a foundation : that it is more agreeable to reason, to explain St. Paul by St. James than the contrary. For besides that the words of St. James are so very express, clear, and evident, that he who hesitates about their sense may well be said to seek a knot in a bulrush, it also deserves particular attention, that many of the ancients, and among them Augustine,

supposed this Epistle of St. James with the first of St. John, that of
St. Jude and the second of St. Peter, to have been written against those
who wrongly interpreting St. Paul's Epistles held that faith without
good works were sufficient for salvation. Which opinion is greatly
confirmed by St. Peter, where he says that in the Epistles of St. Paul
may be found some things hard to be understood, which by bad men
are perverted to the worst sense, and to their own destruction. For
certainly if you attend to the subject, you will find no doctrine in the
Epistles of St. Paul which is more liable to false interpretations, or
which, indeed, from the first ages of Christianity to the present, has
suffered more, than this very dispute concerning justification by faith
alone without works. What adds a farther degree of probability is,
that St. James uses the same example of Abraham, to prove works are
required for justification, from which St. Paul in the whole of the
fourth chapter of his Epistle to the Romans deduces that man is justified
by faith without works. . . .

Hence too another question may be answered, whether namely the
Holy Spirit was given in the times of the Old Testament ? Undoubtedly
it was, for otherwise there could not have been so many pious and holy
men under the Mosaic law. But, first, the Spirit was indeed given
under the law, but not by, or through the law, since this grace was
mutually given and received as derived from the grace of the Gospel.
Hence the promise of the Spirit is called by St. Paul in the passage already
noticed, *the blessing of Abraham*, not of Moses, because that great
blessing arose from the promise made to Abraham, and not from the
Mosaic covenant, that is, from the Gospel, and not from the law.

Secondly, although God indeed bestowed His Holy Spirit on those
who asked for it under the Old Testament, as well as under the New,
still there was a great difference made ; for in the times of the Old
Testament, God gave the grace of His Holy Spirit in small and moderate
portions, under the Gospel, abundantly and bountifully. Hence in
the times of the New Testament, God is said to *give the Spirit not
by measure* but to pour it out first upon Christ the Head, and then
upon the Church His body : for now has *He shed on us abundantly the
Spirit*. To this, too, I refer that remarkable passage in St. John's Gospel
where those who live under the gospel are said to receive *of the fulness
of Christ* ($\chi\acute{\alpha}\rho\iota\nu$ $\dot{\alpha}\nu\tau\grave{\iota}$ $\chi\acute{\alpha}\rho\iota\tau\sigma\varsigma$), *grace for grace*, that is, *abundant grace, or
grace heaped upon grace*. For so I think the words should be interpreted,
as here ' *grace for grace* ' is clearly the same as what the Son of Sirach
says, *A shamefaced and faithful woman is a double grace* ($\chi\acute{\alpha}\rho\iota\varsigma$ $\dot{\epsilon}\pi\grave{\iota}$ $\chi\acute{\alpha}\rho\iota\tau\iota$),
that is, modesty in a wife is a great grace of God ; but if fidelity be
also added, such a wife is an accumulated grace, since to her modesty,
a treasure of itself sufficiently great, fidelity also, an uncommon virtue
among women, is added as it were over and above.

## No. 130. JOHN SELDEN

[From *Table Talk*, Section XLII (" Faith and Works "). Ed. S. H. Reynolds (Oxford, 1892), p. 69. Cp. note on No. **117.**]

It was an unhappy division that has been made betwixt faith and works,—though in my intellect I may divide them, just as in the candle I know there is both heat and light. But yet put out the candle, and they are both gone; one remains not without the other. So it is betwixt faith and works. Nay, in a right conception, *fides est opus* ; if I believe a thing because I am commanded, that is *opus*.

## No. 131. ISAAC BARROW

[From *Sermon 5 on the Apostles' Creed. Works*, ed. Oxford (1818), Vol. IV, pp. 119 f., 137–140; ed. A. Napier, Vol. V, pp. 152, 175–180. Cp. note on No. **344.**]

To each person sincerely embracing the Gospel and continuing in steadfast adherence thereto, God doth afford His Holy Spirit as a principle productive of all inward sanctity and virtuous dispositions in his heart, enabling also and quickening him to discharge the conditions of faith and obedience required from him and undertaken by him, that which is by some termed making a person just, infusion into his soul of righteousness, of grace, of virtuous habits; in the Scripture style it is called *acting by the Spirit*, bestowing the gift of the Holy Ghost, renovation of the Holy Ghost, creation to good works, sanctification by the Spirit, etc., which phrases denote partly the collation of a principle enabling to perform good works, partly the design of religion tending to that performance. . . .

So much may suffice for a general explication of the notion; but for a more full clearing of the point, it may be requisite to resolve a question concerning the time when this act is performed or dispensed. It may be inquired, when God justifieth, whether once, or at several times, or continually. To which question I answer briefly:

(1). That the justification which St. Paul discourseth of, seemeth in his meaning only or especially to be that act of grace which is dispensed to persons at their baptism, or at their entrance into the Church, when they openly professing their faith, and undertaking the practice of Christian duty, God most solemnly and formally doth absolve them from all guilt, and accepteth them into a state of favour with Him: that St. Paul only or chiefly respecteth this act, considering his design, I am inclined to think, and many passages in his discourse seem to imply.

If his design were (as I conceive it probable) to vindicate the proceeding of God, peculiarly declared in the Gospel, in receiving the most notorious and heinous transgressors to grace in baptism, then especially must the justification he speaketh of relate to that; to confirm which supposition, we may consider that,

1. In several places justification is coupled with baptismal regeneration and absolution : *Such were some of you ; but ye have been washed, ye have been sanctified, ye have been justified in the name of Christ Jesus* : (where, by the way, being sanctified and being justified seem equivalent terms ; as in that place where Christ is said to *have given Himself for the Church, that He might sanctify it, and cleanse it with the washing of water by the Word*, sanctification, I conceive, importeth the same thing with justification). Again, *He saved us by the laver of regeneration, that having been justified by His grace, we may be made heirs of everlasting life.*

2. St. Paul in expressing this act, as it respecteth the faithful, commonly doth use a tense referring to the past time : he saith not δικαιούμενοι, *being justified*, but δικαιωθέντες, *having been justified* ; not δικαιοῦσθε, *ye are justified*, but ἐδικαιώθητε, *ye have been justified* ; namely, at some remarkable time, that is, at their entrance into Christianity. (Our translators do render it according to the present time ; but it should be rendered as I say, in our text, and in other places.)

3. St. Paul in the 6th to the Romans discourseth thus : Seeing we in baptism are cleansed and disentangled from sin, *are dead to it, and so justified from it*, God forbid that we should return to live in the practice thereof, so abusing and evacuating the grace we have received ; which discourse seemeth plainly to signify, that he treateth about the justification conferred in baptism.

4. He expresseth the justification he speaketh of by the words πάρεσις τῶν προγεγονότων, ἁμαρτημάτων, the passing over foregoing sins, which seemeth to respect that universal absolution, which is exhibited in baptism. *Being*, saith he, *justified freely by His grace, through the redemption that is in Christ Jesus ; Whom God hath set forth to be a propitiation through faith in His blood, to declare His righteousness, for the remission of sins, that are past, through the forbearance of God.*

5. The relation this justification hath to faith, being dispensed in regard thereto, (or upon condition thereof,) doth infer the same : Faith is nothing else but a hearty embracing Christianity, which first exerteth itself by open declaration and avowal in baptism, (when we *believe with our hearts to righteousness, and confess with our mouth to salvation ;*) to that time therefore the act of justification may be supposed especially to appertain : then, when the evangelical covenant is solemnly ratified, the grace thereof especially is conferred. Upon such considerations I conceive that St. Paul's justification chiefly doth respect that act of grace, which God consigneth to us at our baptism. But farther,

(2). The virtue and effect of that first justifying act doth continue (we abide in a justified state) so long as we do perform the conditions imposed by God, and undertaken by us at our first justification; *holding fast the profession of our hope without wavering; keeping faith, and a good conscience,* so long as we do not forfeit the benefit of that grace by making shipwreck of faith and a good conscience relapsing into infidelity, or profaneness of life. Our case is plainly like to that of a subject, who having rebelled against his prince, and thence incurred his displeasure, but having afterward upon his submission, by the clemency of his prince, obtained an act of pardon, restoring him to favour and enjoyment of the protection and privileges suitable to a loyal subject, doth continue in this state, until by forsaking his allegiance, and running again into rebellion, he so loseth the benefit of that pardon, that his offence is aggravated thereby: so if we do persevere firm in faith and obedience, we shall (according to the purport of the evangelical covenant) continue in a state of grace and favour with God, and in effect remain justified; otherwise the virtue of our justification ceaseth, and we in regard thereto are more deeply involved in guilt.

(3). Although justification chiefly signifieth the first act of grace toward a Christian at his baptism, yet (according to analogy of reason, and affinity in the nature of things) every dispensation of pardon granted upon repentance may be styled justification. For as particular acts of repentance, upon the commission of any particular sins, do not so much differ in nature, as in measure or degree, from that general conversion practised in embracing the Gospel; so the grace vouchsafed upon these penitential acts is only in largeness of extent and solemnity of administration diversified from that, especially considering that repentance after baptism is but a reviving of that first great resolution and engagement we made in baptism; that remission of sin upon it is only the renovation of the grace then exhibited; that the whole transaction in this case is but a reinstating the covenant then made (and afterward by transgression infringed) upon the same terms, which were then agreed upon; that consequently, by congruous analogy, this remission of sins, and restoring to favour, granted to a penitent, are only the former justification reinforced; whence they may bear its name. But whether St. Paul ever meaneth the word to signify thus, I cannot affirm.

Now according to each of these notions all good Christians may be said to have been justified; they have been justified by a general abolition of their sins, and reception into God's favour in baptism; they so far have enjoyed the virtue of that gracious dispensation, and continued in a justified state, as they have persisted in faith and obedience; they have, upon falling into sin, and rising thence by repentance, been justified by particular remissions. So that *having been justified by faith, they have peace with God, through our Lord Jesus Christ.*

## No. 132.  RALPH CUDWORTH

[From *Mr. Cudworth's Sermon preached before the House of Commons*.   Cambridge, 1852, pp. 5–10.   Cp. note on No. 362.]

First, then, if this be the right way and method of discovering our knowledge of Christ, by our keeping of His commandments, then we may safely draw conclusions concerning our state and condition from the conformity of our lives to the will of Christ.   Would we know whether we know Christ aright, let us consider whether the life of Christ be in us.   *Qui non habet vitam Christi, Christum non habet.*   He that hath not the life of Christ in him, he hath nothing but the name, nothing but a fancy of Christ, he hath not the substance of Him.   He that builds his house upon this foundation,— not an airy notion of Christ, swimming in his brain, but Christ really dwelling and living in his heart,—as Our Saviour Himself witnesseth, he *buildeth his house upon a rock* ; and when the floods come, and the winds blow, and the rain descends and beats upon it, it shall stand impregnably.   But he that builds all his comfort upon an ungrounded persuasion that God from all eternity hath loved him and absolutely decreed him to life and happiness, and seeketh not for God really dwelling in his soul, he builds his house upon a quicksand, and it shall suddenly sink and be swallowed up.   *His hope shall be cut off, and his trust shall be a spider's web.   He shall lean upon his house, but it shall not stand, he shall hold it fast, but it shall not endure.*   We are no where commanded to pry into these secrets, but the wholesome counsel and advice given us is this, *to make our calling and election sure.*   We have no warrant in Scripture to peep into these hidden rolls and volumes of eternity and to make it our first thing that we do when we come to Christ to spell out our names in the stars, and to persuade ourselves that we are certainly elected to everlasting happiness, before we see the *image of God* in righteousness and true holiness, shaped in our hearts.   God's everlasting decree is too dazzling and bright an object for us at first to set our eye upon.   It is far easier and safer for us to look upon the rays of His goodness and holiness as they are reflected in our own hearts, and there to read the mild and gentle characters of God's love to us in our love to Him, and our hearty compliance with His Heavenly will ; as it is safer for us if we would see the sun, to look upon it here below in a pail of water than to cast up our daring eyes upon the body of the sun itself, which is too radiant and scorching for us.   The best assurance that anyone can have of his interest in God is doubtless the conformity of his soul to Him.   Those Divine purposes, whatsoever they be, are altogether unsearchable and unknowable by us, they lie wrapt up in everlasting darkness and covered in a deep abyss.   Who is able to fathom the bottom of them ?   Let us not therefore make this our first attempt towards God and religion, to persuade ourselves strongly of these everlasting decrees; for if at our first flight we aim so high, we shall haply but scorch our wings and be struck back with lightning as those giants of old were, that would needs attempt to invade and assault Heaven. And it is indeed a most gigantical essay to thrust ourselves so boldly into the lap of Heaven. It is the prank of a Nimrod, of a mighty hunter, thus rudely to deal with God and to force Heaven and happiness before His face whether He will or no. The way to obtain a good assurance indeed of our title to Heaven is not to clamber up to it by a ladder of our own ungrounded persuasions, but to dig as low as hell by humility and self-denial in our own hearts; and though this may seem to be the furthest way about, yet it is indeed the nearest and safest way to it. We must ἀναβαίνειν κάτω and καταβαίνειν ἄνω as the Greek epigram speaks,—ascend downward and descend upward,—if we would indeed come to Heaven or get any true persuasion of our title to it. The most gallant and triumphant confidence of a Christian riseth safely and surely upon this low foundation that lies deep underground, and there stands firmly and stedfastly. When our heart is once turned into a conformity with the Word of God, when we feel our will perfectly to concur with His will, we shall presently perceive a *spirit of adoption* within ourselves, teaching us to cry *Abba, Father*. We shall not then care for peeping into those hidden records of eternity to see whether our names be written there in golden characters. No, we shall find a copy of God's thoughts concerning us written in our own breasts. There we may read the characters of His favour to us, there we may feel an inward sense of His love to us, flowing out of our hearty and unfeigned love to Him, and we shall be more undoubtedly persuaded of it than if any of those winged " Watchmen " above, that are privy to Heaven's secrets, should come and tell us that they saw our names enrolled in those volumes of eternity. Whereas on the contrary, though we strive to persuade ourselves never so confidently that God from all eternity hath loved us and elected us to life and happiness, if we do yet in the meantime entertain any iniquity within our hearts and willingly close with any lust, do what we can, we shall find many a cold qualm ever now and then seizing upon us at approaching dangers; and when death itself shall grimly look us in the face, we shall feel our hearts even to die within us and our spirits quite faint away, though we strive to raise them and recover them never so much, with the strong waters and *aqua vitae* of our own ungrounded presumptions. The least inward lust willingly continued in will be like a worm, fretting the gourd of our jolly confidence, and presumptuous persuasion of God's love, and always gnawing at the root of it; and though we strive to keep it alive and continually besprinkle it with

some dews of our own, yet it will always be dying and withering in
our bosoms. But a good conscience within will be always better to
a Christian than *health to his navel and marrow to his bones*. It will
be an everlasting cordial to his heart. It will be softer to him than
a bed of down, and he may sleep securely upon it in the midst of
raging and tempestuous seas, when the winds bluster and the waves
beat round about him. A good conscience is the best looking-glass
of Heaven, in which the soul may see God's thoughts and purposes
concerning it, as so many shining stars reflected to it. *Hereby we know
that we know Christ, hereby we know that Christ loves us, if we keep
His Commandments.*

# (3) PREDESTINATION

## No. 133.  HENRY HAMMOND

[From *Of Fundamentals*, Chapter XIV " Of Christ's Dying for None but the Elect." *Miscellaneous Theological Works*, ed. *L. A. C. T.*, pp. 133–140.  Cp. note on No. 62.]

Now for that doctrine of Christ's dying for none but the elect,—i.e. according to the opinion of those which thus teach, for a small remnant of the world,—as it is asserted without any pretence or colour of Scripture proof, nay, in opposition to as plain distinct affirmations as can be produced for any Article in the Creed, so is it of very ill consequence to the superstructing of good life.

That Christ's dying for all is the express doctrine of the Scripture is elsewhere manifested by the phrases of the greatest latitude used in this matter.  First, κόσμος, the *world*, which is a word of the widest extent ; and although it be sometimes used more restrainedly, yet never doth nor can in any reason be interpreted to signify a far smaller disproportionable part of the world.  Secondly, *all*, which word, though it be sometimes restrained by the matter, and doth not always signify every person or thing, yet generally it must be extended as far as the matter is capable of, and must not be restrained without some considerable reason for doing so.  Thirdly, *every man*, a form of speaking which excludes all exceptions, of which some general phrases are oft capable.  Fourthly, *those that perish*, those that are damned, those that deny Christ, and *purchase to themselves swift damnation*, which being added to the number of those which are saved by His death, and acknowledged by all opposers to be so, make up the whole unlimited number of all mankind.  Fifthly, *as many as are fallen in Adam and dead through him*, which phrase is by all but Pelagius and his followers supposed to comprehend every son of Adam, every branch of his progeny.

And accordingly, though the Apostles' Creed make no other mention of this than is contained in styling Jesus Christ ' Our Lord,'—i.e. the Lord, by title of redemption, of us all indefinitely, and particularly of every person who is appointed to make that confession of his Faith, i.e. every one that is admitted to Baptism,—yet the Nicene Creed hath inserted some words for the further explication of that Article " Who for us men and for our salvation came down," etc., which signify all mankind to have their interest in it.

Nay if it be observed in the Apostles' Creed that the two first Articles are corresponding and proportionable one to the other,—to ' God ' in the First Article, ' Jesus Christ ' in the Second ; to ' Father Almighty ' in the First, ' His only Son ' in the Second ; to ' Maker of Heaven and Earth ' in the First, ' Our Lord ' in the Second,— we shall have reason to infer that as ' Heaven and Earth ' in the First Article signify in the greatest latitude all and every creature in the world to have been created by the Father, so the ' Our ' in the Second Article is set to denote all and every one of us, every man in the world without any exception, to be redeemed by God the Son.

And accordingly the Catechism of the Church of England estab-lished by law, and preserved in our Liturgy as a special part of it, expounds the Creed in this sense, " I believe in God the Father which made me and all the world ; 2. In God the Son Who redeemed me and all mankind ; 3. In God the Holy Ghost Who sanctifieth me and all the elect people of God ; " where, as creation is common to more creatures than redemption, and redemption than sanctification, so mankind, to which redemption belongs, as it is far narrower than the world, or the works of God's creation, so it is far wider than the catalogue of " all the elect people of God," to whom sanctification belongs.

So in other parts of our Liturgy, in consecrating the Eucharist, we have this Form of prayer, " Almighty God . . . Which didst give Thine only Son Jesus Christ to suffer death upon the Cross for our redemption, and made there, by His one oblation of Himself once offered, a full, perfect, and sufficient sacrifice, oblation, and satis-faction for the sins of the whole world ; " and accordingly in the Administration of that Sacrament, the elements are delivered to every communicant in this Form, " The Body of our Lord Jesus Christ which was given for thee," and " The Blood of our Lord Jesus Christ which was shed for thee, preserve thy body and soul unto everlasting life ; " which supposeth it the doctrine of our Church, avowed and professed, that Christ's death was not only sufficient for all, if God would have so intended and designed it, but that He was actually designed and given for all, not only as many as come to that Sacra-ment,—which yet is wider than the elect,—but us men, or mankind in general, whose salvation was sought by God by this means.

So in our Articles also, " Christ suffered for us . . . that He might be a sacrifice not only for original sin, but also for all the actual sins of men " (Art. 2). And, " By Christ who is the only Mediator of God and men . . . eternal life is promised to mankind " (Art. 7). And, " Christ came as a lamb . . . that by the offering of Himself once made He might take away the sins of the world " (Art. 15). And, " The oblation of Christ once made is a perfect redemption, pro-pitiation, and satisfaction for all the sins of the whole world " (Art. 31).

All which I have thus largely set down to shew the perfect consonancy of our persecuted Church to the doctrine of Scripture and Antiquity in this point, whereon so much depends for the stating and determining other differences, which have also a special influence on practice.

As for the ill consequences toward the obstructing of good life, which are considerable to attend this one doctrine of Christ's dying for none but the elect, they will be most discernible by attempting the reformation and change of any vicious Christian that believes that doctrine, or the comfort of any disconsolate despairing Christian that hath gotten into this hold and remains fortified in the belief of it.

For the former, it is evident, and that which he is supposed to believe, if he believe the foundation,—as I presume him now to do when I set the case of a vicious Christian,—that there is no salvation to be had for any sinner but only by the sufferings of Christ and that redemption by Him wrought for such. If therefore a vicious liver, believing that Christ died for none but the elect, shall have any attempt made on him to reform and amend his life, it is certain that one medium to induce him to it must be a tender of mercy from Christ, of present pardon and future bliss upon his reformation. But if he be able to reply that that mercy belongs only to the elect, and he is none of them, it necessarily follows that he that would reduce this stray sheep, must either prove convincingly to him that he is one of the elect, or else hath no further to proceed in this attempt.

And if he thus attempt to persuade the vicious Christian that he is one of the elect, then, first, the very attempt confesses to him that a vicious person, remaining such, may be in the number of the elect, and from thence he will presently be able to infer that then he needs not reformation of life to constitute him such, and if so, then reformation of life is not the condition on which only bliss is to be expected, and without which it is not to be had, it being supposed and acknowledged by both parties that all the elect shall have it, and so the medium which was thought necessary to persuade his reformation,—the tender of mercy from Christ upon reformation,—is already vanished, and consequently it is to no purpose to persuade him that he is one of the elect, which was useful only for the enforcing this medium ; and so the very making this attempt is destructive to the only end of it.

But if this were not the result of this attempt yet, secondly, it is in the progress agreed to be necessary that he persuade this person that he is one of the elect ; and what possible medium can he use to prove that to a vicious person ? *A priori*, from any secret decree of God's it is certain he cannot demonstrate it, for he hath never entered into God's secrets and it is sure the Scripture hath revealed nothing of it, whatsoever it saith of the Book of Life, never affirming that particular man's name is written there ; and then the one possible

25

way of attempting it is *a posteriori* from the fruits of election, and those are not supposable in him who is supposed a vicious liver, who lives in that estate,—and is by him acknowledged to do so, for otherwise why should he think it necessary to reduce him?—wherein he that lives *shall not inherit the Kingdom of God*. For his proof, whatever it is, will easily be retorted, and the contrary proved by interrogating, *Shall the adulterer, the drunkard, the vicious Christian, inherit the Kingdom of God?* If he shall, what need I that am now exhorted to reform my life, reform it? If he shall not, then certainly I that am such am none of the elect, for all that are elect shall certainly *inherit the Kingdom of God*.

The only reserve imaginable is that this vicious Christian be persuaded to believe in Christ; and if he do so, he shall by that know that he is one of the elect, and so that his sins shall be pardoned, etc. But if this be the method made use of, then, first, this is not the attempting to reform, to work repentance, which was the thing proposed in this first case, but to work faith in him; and with men of those opinions these are two distinct things, faith and repentance, and the former must be before the other, and is resolved to do the whole business without the other, and consequently this is not the way to bring the sinner to repentance, but rather to assure him that he hath no need of it, his business may be done without it.

Secondly, this very attempt of persuading him to believe in Christ, as that signifies the full persuasion that the promises of Christ belong to him, is, supposing that Christ died for none but the elect, as desperate an attempt as the former. For why should he believe that Christ died for him, Who died only for the elect, when he hath no means to persuade him that he is one of the elect, but great and strong presumptions to the contrary; for to believe that Christ died for him for whom He died not, is to believe a downright falsity, and such is the believing Christ died for him, who both believes that He died only for the elect, and that he himself is none of that number.

And in like manner the former inconvenience returns again; for if the vicious Christian be advised to believe that Christ died for him, remaining such,—and that must be the case if this faith must precede repentance,—it is by that advice presupposed and granted to him, that Christ, Which died only for the elect who shall certainly *inherit the Kingdom of God*, died for this vicious person, of whom the Scripture saith, that he shall not *inherit the Kingdom*. And again, if he may believe what he is advised to believe, that Christ died for him as now he is, an unreformed Christian, then what needs he reformation to make him capable of the benefits of His death? And so still it is impossible, where this opinion is imbibed and unremoved, to found any convincing argument to reform a vicious Christian.

But this hath no such appearance of difficulty to him that hath received the doctrine of universal, but conditional, redemption, i.e. of Christ dying for all, if all will take care to perform the condition required by Him, and to which His grace is ready to enable him. For then, how great soever the sins of any unreformed person are, it is evident that Christ died for him, because He died for all; that He died for those sins of his, because He died for all sins; only he must reform, and forsake his sins, or else he shall never receive the benefit of His death. And then, though there be that pleasure in sin, which the habitual sinner cannot be persuaded to part with, unless he must,—unless he discern the danger of retaining, and the advantage of parting with it,—yet when he hath such arguments as these proposed to him, eternal bliss in exchange for short temporary pleasures, assurance of this upon reformation, and an impossibility and absolute desperation without it, the vicious Christian, if he have advanced no further than so and if his habit of sin have not corrupted his principles, may think it reasonable to reform and amend upon such terms as these, the preacher may hope to superstruct good life upon such a foundation.

And the like inconveniences are found to be consequent to this opinion of Christ's dying for none but the elect, whensoever any comfort is offered to a disconsolate despairing Christian. For it is not possible to give him any comfort but by fetching it from Christ; and that he shall receive no benefit from Christ is the affirmation whereon all his despair is founded, and the one way of removing this dismal apprehension is to convince him that Christ's death and the benefits thereof, either do, or, if he perform the condition required of him, shall certainly belong to him.

This upon the belief of universal redemption is presently so far done, that if he set industriously and sincerely to perform the commands of Christ, he can have no ground or pretence of doubting but it shall prove successful to him, and so all that he hath to do is to endeavour by prayer and use of the means, and by good hope, of which he hath such clear grounds, to qualify himself for this blessed condition, and in the mean time hath no excuse to continue in this melancholy mournful posture, who hath so cheerful a prospect before him.

But to him that believes Christ died for none but the elect, and whose comforter is of that opinion also, there is no possible reply to his objections, or satisfaction to his sad bodings. For that no mercy doth or can belong to him, he is resolved upon this ground, because Christ died not for him; and the doctrine that Christ died for the elect yields him no relief, because he is verily persuaded that he is none of the elect. And when the number of the elect is defined to be so small and disproportionable to the number of the reprobates, and so there is really all odds against him that he is not of the number of the few ; when his fears shall help to increase that odds, and make him less capable of believing what is so much less probable ; when his present despairs, being so contrary to that faith, assurance of his salvation, which alone can justify, in his opinion, or bear witness to his election, shall by necessary consequence bear witness against him ; and when the Scripture, that should, and in this case alone can interpose for his relief, doth certainly affirm nothing of his particular election ; and lastly, when what it saith of Christ's dying for all, is by him misunderstood to belong but to a few, it is not imaginable what can be said to this man to persuade him that this progress is not rational, that he doth not well to despair, who hath so slight grounds to build any hope, and so much weightier to comply with and assist his fears in overwhelming him.

And then, as necessary as hope is to labour, encouragement to quickening of action, so necessary is the belief of universal redemption to the superstructing Christian life, where the foundation of Christian belief is already laid.

## No. 134. GEORGE BULL

[From *Harmonia Apostolica*, Dissertation II, Chapter xviii, §§ 13, 14. Ed. L. A. C. T., *On Justification*, Vol. I, pp. 217-219. Cp. note on No. 129.]

Whilst we avoid Pelagianism by acknowledging the necessity of grace, let us take care, on the other hand, that we fall not into the abyss of Manichæan folly, by taking away free will and the co-operation of human industry. The middle, the royal way must here be chosen, so as to turn neither to the left hand nor to the right, which will be done if we suppose that with grace, but in subjection to it, the freedom of the will amicably unites. This saying of Augustine is common and well known : " If there be no grace of God, how can He save the world ? and if there be no free will, how can He judge it ? " In like manner Bernard : " Take away free will, and nothing is left to be saved : take away grace, and there is nothing left which can save." Therefore we must not so urge the liberty of the will as to be hostile to grace, nor so preach up grace as to take away free will. It is hard to say from which of these two errors the greatest dangers arise. " Let not," Vossius well observes, " Let not our idleness be increased by him who denies free will, nor our pride by him who is ignorant of the gift of grace. In answer to both there must be equally preached the justice of God, which assuredly cannot exist without free will, and His mercy, which the enemies of grace would undermine." But greater danger seems to be threatened by a denial of free will than of grace, as that learned man observes : " For this last error is so very gross as always to be evident; and the light of the Gospel is so clearly given on this subject that it can infect none but the unlearned and profane, whom ignorance and self-confidence easily seduce, especially if the pride of worldly glory be added. But all modest and pious men are more subject to the heresies of those who, like the Chaldeans concerning whom John of Salisbury speaks in his *Polycraticon*, ' impose a kind of fatal necessity on affairs, under pretence of humility and reverence to God, fearing lest His providence should be destroyed, unless a necessity accompanied the course of affairs.' Which error, concealed by the veil of humility and piety, has in proportion to its secrecy the more dangerous effect upon the minds of men." Excellent, indeed, are the words of Augustine, which are praised by the same great man, " Some are exalted to be proud by a too great confidence in their own will, and some are cast into negligence by a too great diffidence of their will. The former say, Why should we beg of God that we be not conquered by temptation, when this is in our power? The latter, Why should we endeavour to live well since this is in the power of God only? O God and Father, Which art in heaven, lead us into neither of these temptations, but deliver us from evil." Truly then, and according to the sense of all the Fathers (in Grotius's opinion) hath Tertullian said, " It is not the part of a good and sound faith to be perpetually referring to the will of God, and so to flatter one's self by saying that nothing is done without His permission, as if we knew not that there was something in ourselves. But everything will be excused if we maintain that nothing is done in us without the will of God," that is, as Grotius rightly says, without His predisposing will.

But perfectly divine is that advice of St. Paul's to the Philippians, *Work out your own salvation with fear and trembling ; for it is God Which worketh in you, both to will and to do of His good pleasure* ; which is, Work out your salvation with the greatest modesty and humility of mind,—for so some of the Fathers interpret *with fear and trembling*, as if it were the same as, with lowliness (μετὰ ταπεινοφροσύνης)— since you can do nothing of yourselves in the work of your salvation, but it is necessary that the grace of God should work in you and with you. Or, Work out your salvation with great fear and anxiety, lest you should be wanting to the grace of God, and extinguish His Spirit, Which, if It should desert and leave you, would entirely destroy your salvation. Or, Work out your salvation with care and diligence, and be not afraid lest you should not have strength to fulfil what I recommend, for God worketh with you in this matter and is ready of His goodness to assist you in overcoming all difficulties. In whatever manner you interpret these words of the Apostle, they totally overturn the irresistible operation of grace ; for unto what purpose would be this grave exhortation of the Apostle's that we should work out our own salvation, if we could not work?

## No. 135. WILLIAM BEVERIDGE

[From *Ecclesia Anglicana Ecclesia Catholica.* [= On the Thirty-Nine Articles.] On Article XVII, " Of Predestination and Election." *Works*, ed. *L. A. C. T.*, Vol. VII, pp. 343 f. Cp. note on No. 52.]

Though in the other [*i.e.* of the Thirty Nine] Articles we may make use of reason as well as Scripture and Fathers, yet in this [XVIIth] we must make use of Scripture and Fathers only, and not of reason. For as the ordinary priests were not to enter into the Holy of Holies, so neither is carnal reason to venture upon this mystery of mysteries. For it concerns God's Predestination, which must needs be infinitely above man's apprehension. So that a cockle-fish may as soon crowd the ocean into its narrow shell, as vain man ever comprehend the decrees of God. And hence it is that both in public and private I have still endeavoured to shun discourses of this nature; and now that I am unavoidably fallen upon it, I shall speak as little as possibly I can unto it, especially considering how many other truths are still behind to be insisted upon. And in that little that I shall speak, I shall labour to make use of as few of my own words as by any means I can, speaking nothing concerning this great mystery but what Scripture and Fathers have expressly delivered unto me.

## No. 136. PETER HEYLYN

[From *Historia Quinquarticularis*, ed. 1681, pp. 520 f. Cp. note on No. 85.]

For the better carrying on of my design, I must go back again to Calvin, whom I left under a suspicion of making God the author of sin; from which, though many have taken much pains (none more than industrious Dr. Field) to absolve and free him, yet by his doctrine of Predestination, he hath laid such grounds as have involved his followers in the same guilt also. For not content to travel a known and beaten way, he must needs find out a way by himself which neither the Dominicans nor any other of the followers of St. Augustine's rigours had found out before, in making God to lay on Adam an unavoidable necessity of falling into sin and misery, that so He might have opportunity to manifest His mercy in the electing of some few of his posterity, and His justice in the absolute rejecting of all the rest. In which, as he can find no countenance from any of the ancient writers, so he pretendeth not to any ground for it in the Holy Scriptures. For whereas some objected on God's behalf, *De certis verbis non extare*, That the decree of Adam's fall, and consequently the involving of his whole posterity in sin and misery, had no foundation in the express words of Holy Writ, he makes no other answer to it than a *quasi vero*, as if (saith he) God made and created man the most exact piece of His heavenly workmanship, without determining of his end. And on this point he was so resolutely bent, that nothing but an absolute decree for Adam's fall, seconded by the like for the involving of all his race in the same prediction, would either serve his turn or preserve his credit. For whereas others had objected on God's behalf that no such unavoidable necessity was laid upon mankind by the Will of God, but rather that he was created by God unto such a perishing estate because He foresaw to what his own perverseness at the last would bring him, he answereth that this objection proves nothing at all, or at least, nothing to the purpose ; which said, he tells us further out of Valla, though otherwise not much versed (as he there affirmeth) in the Holy Scriptures, That this question seems to be superfluous, because both Life and Death are rather the acts of God's Will than of His Prescience or Foreknowledge. And then he adds as of his own, That if God did but foresee the successes of men and did not also dispose and order them by His Will, then this question should not without cause be moved (namely), Whether His foreseeing anything availed to the necessity of them. But since (saith he) He doth no otherwise foresee the things which shall come to pass, than because He hath decreed that they should so come to pass, it is in vain to move any controversy about God's foreknowledge where it is certain that all things do happen rather by Divine ordinance and appointment. Yet notwithstanding all these shifts, he is forced to acknowledge the decree of Adam's Fall to be *Horribile Decretum*, a cruel and horrible decree, as indeed it is a cruel and horrible decree to preordain so many millions to destruction and consequently unto sin, that He might destroy them. And then what can the wicked and impenitent do but ascribe all their sins to God, by Whose inevitable Will they are lost in Adam, by whom they were particularly and personally necessitated to death, and so by consequence to sin,—a doctrine so injurious to God, so destructive of piety, of such reproach among the Papists, and so offensive to the Lutherans, of what sort soever, that they profess a greater readiness to fall back to Popery than to give way to this Predestinarian Pestilence (by which name they call it) to come in amongst them.

## No. 137.  RICHARD MONTAGUE

[From *Appello Caesarem. A Just Appeal from Two Unjust Informers*, Part I, Chapter xi, London, 1625, pp. 107 f.  Cp. note on No. 3.  On the Synod of Dort, cp. note on No. 85.]

You, or any Puritan or Papist, make it plain that anything by me disclaimed for being the public, established, doctrine of our Church is yet the doctrine of the Church, and I am ready to recant. If the

Synod of Dort hath determined otherwise, let their determinations stand for me; I quarrel them not, I meddle not with them. Those that like the Decrees of that Synod, or are bound to maintain the Decrees of that Synod, let them maintain them if they like them. *Non equidem invideo.* I have no part nor portion in them. I am not tied to uphold them farther than they consent unto that which I am bound to maintain, the doctrine of the Church of England. And if it were true, which is most false, wherewith I am charged by these honest men, yet I might answer (and what if I do?), Who bound the Church of England, or me, a priest and a member of the Church of England, unto defence of all the Decrees or Determinations of that Synod? Hath Prince? Or Parliament? Or Convocation? Edict? Statute? Or Canon? I know none; I have heard of none; nor ever shall, I hope. And till I hear of such (*quod μὴ γένοιτο*) I answer, Let them that are interested plead for themselves. For my part, I nor have, nor ever will, subscribe that Synod absolutely and in all points (for in some, it condemneth, upon the bye, even the discipline of the Church of England), but so far forth only, as their determinations shall be found and made conformable unto the doctrine of our Church; nor I think will the ferventest amongst you subscribe it in every point. For sure I am your Divines, as you call them, have disavowed sometimes some things resolved of in that Synod; as, for instance, Co-operation of Free-Will and Grace, Reprobation negative rather than positive. But, as I said, the Synod of Dort is not *my* rule, and your magisterial conclusions are no rule.

# IX.  ESCHATOLOGY

# (1) IMMORTALITY

## No. 138.  GEORGE BULL

[From the *Harmonia Apostolica*, Dissertation II, Chapter x, §§ 13–16.  Ed.
L. A. C. T. (' On Justification,' Part I), pp. 127–130.  The *L. A. C. T.* translation
has been slightly altered.  Cp. note on No. **129**.]

FROM the last answer a new question arises.  In what sense then
is Christ said to have *brought life and immortality to light through the
Gospel*, since it appears from what has been said that the doctrine
of a future life was commonly received among the Jews many years
before the coming of Christ ?  In the first place I answer, that this
text may perhaps be referred to the Gentiles only, who were before
described by the Apostle as *having no hope, and being without God in the
world* ; his words in the eleventh verse evidently incline to this meaning,—
*Whereunto I am appointed a preacher and an Apostle and a teacher of the
Gentiles.*  You will say, But even among the Gentiles there were some
who had hopes of a life after this.  This is true ; and indeed among all
the civilized, and even barbarous nations, some notion or, as it were,
report of the immortality of souls had prevailed.  But first, not a few
of the philosophers thought otherwise.  Epicurus, for example, and his
herd openly laughed at the notion of a future life, and even Aristotle
either says nothing, or that very obscurely, on the soul's immortality.
Secondly, those who most favoured this doctrine hesitated greatly
about it, and it was rather an opinion than a belief.  Thirdly, in explaining it, their opinions were various and discordant ; the Stoics
thought that the souls remained for a certain time, but not beyond the
period of ' *conflagration.*'  The Pythagoreans defended the doctrine of
metempsychosis of which a certain poet says :

> " The souls are free from death, their former seat,
> Relinquished, they dwell in new abodes " etc.

And

> " He compels them to endure the forms of mute beasts
> He makes the cruel, bears, the rapacious, wolves,
> The crafty, foxes.  And when he has driven them
> Through many years and thousand shapes,
> At length he again recalls them, purged
> By Lethe's stream, to the first elements
> Of the human form."

And finally, the Platonists, the most religious sect of philosophers, imagined a kind of rotation, and that the souls of men were for ever by turns happy and miserable. So that Justin Martyr, in his *Dialogue with Trypho*, said truly of all the philosophers, " that they knew nothing on this subject, and could not tell what the soul was." Fourthly, and lastly, those among the Gentiles who have said any thing concerning a future life, have restricted it to the soul only, never dreaming of the resurrection of the body. Hence we read that when St. Paul at Athens spoke of the resurrection of the body, the philosophers mocked him as if he taught a direct absurdity.

Again, the words of the text above quoted may be most strictly applied to the Jews themselves ; for Christ enlightened their understandings upon this doctrine in three different points. First, by the light of a decisive determination ; for as among the Gentile philosophers some denied, and others asserted the immortality of the soul, so among the Jews many doubted this doctrine, of such vast importance to piety. The Pharisees affirmed it : the Sadducees denied it, admitting nothing but what was laid down in Scripture in express words, while the Pharisees on the other hand had no other means of proving their opinions, than by the authority of the *cabala*, or tradition. The Pharisees could indeed produce that passage from Daniel, and the Sadducees durst not reject his authority. (For Scaliger, I think, has clearly proved that it is quite erroneous to suppose that the Sadducees rejected all the Prophetical Books, except the Pentateuch, and has also shewn that this error arose from a misapprehension of the words of Josephus the historian.) But a single passage, and such as might be easily eluded under pretence of the luxuriance of the prophetic style, and might be understood of a release from the Babylonish captivity, was an argument scarcely sufficient to stop the mouth of an obstinate sophist. To the multitude, thus fluctuating between the opinions of contending sects, Christ, the chief of prophets, proclaimed in express terms, and in the Name of God, the doctrine of the resurrection and a future world, and publicly declared it to all men as a thing indubitable and certain.

Christ, secondly, added to this doctrine the light of a clear and plain explanation. For as to the nature of a future life, the masters of the Jews themselves were shamefully ignorant, of which Maimonides is a sufficient witness, who in his exposition of the tenth chapter of *The Sanhedrin* thus speaks : " You will find that the opinions of those who embrace the law concerning the happiness to be obtained by him who performs the commandments of God given by Moses, and the misery which will follow upon us who transgress them, are very discordant, according to the difference of understandings. For there is much confusion and misunderstanding on this subject, so that you will scarcely find one to whom the matter is clearly known, neither will you find a treatise of any one, who hath fully discoursed upon it, who is not exceedingly confused." So that what the learned Pococke hath said of the Rabbins who lived after Maimonides, may be said no less truly of those who preceded him, namely, " That you will hardly find any other subject on which you might assert that they were more generally agreed amongst themselves than that there was something to be believed and expected which was called a resurrection. On the nature of it, nearly each one had his own separate opinion." Of the fate of the wicked they were entirely in the dark, as they are at this day; some thought that they would rise again, others that they would not. As to the happiness of the good, many thought it would be of long duration, but not eternal. Then they supposed that happiness to be of a gross earthly nature, arising from an abundance of corporal delights. For as now the Talmudists pretend they are to have banquets, in which they will feast on the behemoth, leviathan, and bariuchne, an ox, a fish, and a bird, so in the time of Christ the Jews supposed there would be a happy state hereafter, but exactly similar to our present life. Hence Josephus, mentioning the opinion of the Essenes (the most spiritual sect among the Jews) concerning future happiness, uses almost the same words as the Greeks did when speaking of the Fortunate Islands. For he says, to the good were granted, " beyond the ocean, habitations free from storms, and heat and cold, but where gentle zephyrs from the sea perpetually refresh the air." Whence arose the captious question of the Sadducees, proposed to Christ, concerning the woman who had married seven brothers successively, whose wife should she be at the resurrection. For the Sadducees, the opponents of the Pharisees, supposed that Christ taught the resurrection on the same principles as the Pharisees did; but these, among other corporal pleasures, supposed that conjugal love would remain to us in a future state. These gross and dark ideas Christ illumined by heavenly light, teaching openly the punishment of the wicked, and declaring that the rewards of the pious were not only lasting, but eternal; and not of every kind, but such as consisted in the company of angels and the beatific vision and fruition of God Himself.

Thirdly, Christ gave to His doctrine what was of the greatest consequence, the light of firm and sufficient testimony, by enforcing its belief on men by many and great miracles, of which the chief was, that He openly recalled the dead to life, and after His Own death shewed Himself alive again to many. After which, nothing more to confirm this point could be reasonably expected. For it was now certain, as the Apostle argues, that *God hath appointed a day in the which He will judge the world in righteousness, by that Man Whom He hath ordained, whereof He hath given assurance unto all men, in that He hath raised Him from the dead.*

## No. 139.  JOSEPH GLANVILL

[From *Lux Orientalis ; or an Enquiry into the Opinion of the Eastern Sages Concerning the Pre-Existence of Souls. Being a Key to unlock the Grand Mysteries of Providence,* 1662. Chapter X, pp. 96 f., 98 f., 102 f. The author, who was also a great admirer of Baxter, was an enthusiastic disciple of Henry More, the Cambridge Platonist; and the treatise from which this extract is taken was a defence of More's teaching about Pre-existence. The *Lux Orientàlis* was one of the earliest of Glanvill's long series of publications.]

If we do but reflect upon what was said above against the soul's daily creation from that enormous pravity which is so deeply rooted in some men's natures, we may thence have a considerable evidence of Pre-existence. For as this strong natural propensity to vice and impiety cannot possibly consist with the hypothesis of the soul's coming just out of God's Hands, pure and immaculate, so doth it most aptly suit with the doctrine of its pre-existence, which gives a most clear and apposite account of the phenomenon. For let us but conceive the souls of men to have grown degenerate in a former condition of life, to have contracted strong and inveterate habits to vice and lewdness, and that in various manners and degrees, we may then easily apprehend when some men's natures had so incredibly a depraved tincture and such impetuous, ungovernable, irreclaimable inclinations to what is vicious; while others have nothing near such wretched propensions, but by good education and good discipline are mouldable to virtue. This shews a clear way to unriddle this amazing mystery, without blemishing any of the Divine attributes, or doing the least violence to our faculties. . . .

But yet besides. We might another way enforce this argument from the strange difference and diversity that there is in men's wits and intellectual craseis (*sic*), as well as in the dispositions of their wills and appetites. Even the natural tempers of men's minds are as vastly different as the qualities of their bodies. As 'tis easy to observe in things purely speculative and intellectual, even where neither education or custom have interposed to sophisticate the natural νοήματα, that some men are strangely propense to some opinions which they greedily drink in as soon as they are duly represented; yea, and find themselves burdened and oppressed while their education hath kept them in a contrary belief; when as others are as fatally set against these opinions and can never be brought favourably to resent them. . . .

Besides, it is easy to observe the strange and wonderful variety of our geniuses, one man's nature inclining him to one kind of study and employment, another's to what is very different. Some almost from their very cradles will be addicted to the making of figures and in little mechanical contrivances. Others love to be rhyming almost as soon as they can speak plainly and are taken up in small essays of poetry. Some will be scrawling pictures, and others take as great delight in some pretty offers at music and vocal harmony. Infinite almost are the ways in which this pure natural diversity doth discover itself. Now to say that all this variety proceeds primarily from the mere temper of our bodies is methinks a very poor and unsatisfying account. For those that are the most like in the temper, air, complexion, of their bodies are yet of a vastly differing genius. Yea, they that have been made of the same clay, cast in the same mould, and have lain at once in the same natural bed the womb, yea, whose bodies have been as like as their state and fortunes, and their education and usages the same, yea even they do not unfrequently differ as much from each other in their genius and dispositions of the mind, as those that in all these particulars are of a very different condition. Besides, there are all kinds of makes, forms, dispositions, tempers, and complexions of body, that are addicted by their natures to the same exercise and employments; so that to ascribe this to any peculiarity in the body is, meseems, a very improbable solution of the phenomenon. And to say all these inclinations are from custom or education is the way not to be believed, since all experience testifies the contrary.

## No. 140. JOHN PEARSON

[From *An Exposition of the Creed*. On Article XII (" The Life Everlasting "). Ed. Oxford (E. Burton), 1864, p. 691. Cp. note on No. 13.]

To conclude this branch of the Article, I conceive these certain and infallible doctrines in Christianity: That the wicked after this life shall be punished for their sins, so that in their punishment there shall be a demonstration of the justice of God revealed against all unrighteousness of men. That to this end they shall be raised again to life, and shall be judged and condemned by Christ, and delivered up under the curse, to be tormented with the devil and his angels. That the punishment which shall be inflicted on them shall be proportionate to their sins, as a recompense of their demerits, so that no man shall suffer more than he hath deserved. That they shall be tormented with a pain of loss, the loss from God, from Whose presence they are cast out, the pain from themselves, in a despair of enjoying Him, and regret for losing Him. That they farther shall be tormented with the pain of sense inflicted on them by the wrath of God which abideth upon them, represented unto us by a lake of fire. That their persons shall continue for ever in this remediless condition, under an everlasting pain of loss, because there is no hope of Heaven, under an eternal pain of sense, because there is no means to appease the wrath of God which abideth on them. Thus the Athanasian Creed, " They that have done good shall go into life everlasting, and they that have done evil into everlasting fire."

# (2) HEAVEN

## No. 141.  RICHARD BAXTER

[From *The Saint's Everlasting Rest*, Part I, ch. iv, §§ 1–4, 5, 6, 7, 8 (*bis*) ; Part III, ch. i, §§ 4, 4 f. ; Part III, ch. vi, § 2 ; Part IV, ch. iii, § 1.  *Works*, ed. W. Orme (1830), Vol. XXII, pp. 46–50, 54–56, 56–58, 60 f., 62, 63 f., 367, 368 f., 456 f. ; Vol. XXIII, pp. 217 f.  Ed. London, 1838, Vol. III, pp. 16–18, 19 f., 20 f., 21 f., 22, 22 f., 127, 128, 159, 263 f.  This is the most famous of all of Baxter's voluminous devotional works.  The greater part of it was written at Sir Thomas Rouse's home in Worcestershire in 1647, when the author believed himself to be on his death-bed.]

But all this is only the outward court, or at least not the holiest of all.  Now we have ascended the steps, may we look within the veil ? May we show what this rest [*i.e.* the Saint's Everlasting Rest, viz. Heaven] containeth, as well as what it presupposeth ?  But alas ! how little know I of that whereof I am about to speak.  Shall I speak before I know ?  But if I stay till I clearly know, I shall not come again to speak.  That glimpse which Paul saw, containeth that which could not, or must not, be uttered, or both.  And if Paul had had a tongue to have uttered it, it would have done no good, except his hearers had ears to hear it.  If Paul had spoke the things of Heaven in the language of Heaven, and none understood that language, what the better ?  Therefore, I will speak, while I may, that little, very little which I do know of it rather than be wholly silent.  The Lord reveal it to me, that I may reveal it to you ; and the Lord open some light, and show both you and me His inheritance, not, as to Balaam only, whose eyes the vision of God opened, to see the goodliness of Jacob's tents and Israel's tabernacles, where he had no portion, but from whence must come his own destruction ; nor as to Moses, who had only a discovery, instead of possession, and saw the land which he never entered ; but as the pearl was revealed to the merchant in the gospel, who rested not till he had sold all he had, and bought it, and as Heaven was opened to blessed Stephen, which he was shortly to enter, and the glory showed him, which should be his own possession.

There is contained in this rest, a cessation from motion or action ; not of all action, but of that which hath the nature of a means, and implies the absence of the end.  When we have obtained the haven, we have done sailing.  When the workman hath his wages, it is implied he hath done his work.  When we are at our journey's end, we have done with the way.  All motion ends at the centre, and all means cease when we have the end.  Therefore, *prophesying ceaseth, tongues fail, and knowledge shall be done away*, that is, so far as it had the nature

324

of a means, and was imperfect. And so faith may be said to cease : not all faith, for how shall we know all things past, which we saw not but by believing ? How shall we know the last judgement, the resurrection of the body beforehand, but by believing ? How shall we know the life everlasting, the eternity of the joys we possess but by believing ? But all that faith, which, as a means referred to the chief end, shall cease. There shall be no more prayer, because no more necessity, but the full enjoyment of what we prayed for. Whether the soul pray for the body's resurrection, for the last judgement, etc., or whether the soul and body pray for the eternal continuance of their joys, is to me unknown ; otherwise, we shall not need to pray for what we have, and we shall have all that is desirable. Neither shall we need to fast, and weep, and watch any more, being out of the reach of sin and temptations. Nor will there be use for instructions and exhortations : preaching is done, the ministry of man ceaseth, sacraments useless, the labourers called in because the harvest is gathered, the tares burned, and the work done, the unregenerate past hope, the saints past fear for ever : much less shall there be any need of labouring for inferior ends, as here we do, seeing they will all devolve themselves into the ocean of the ultimate end, and the lesser good be wholly swallowed up of the greatest.

This rest containeth a perfect freedom from all the evils that accompanied us through our course, and which necessarily follow our absence from the chief good ; besides our freedom from those eternal flames and restless miseries, which the neglecters of Christ and grace must remedilessly endure, an inheritance which, both by birth and actual merit, was due to us as well as to them. As God will not know the wicked so as to own them, so neither will Heaven know iniquity to receive it : for *there entereth nothing that defileth, or is unclean* ; all that remains without. And, doubtless, there is not such a thing as grief and sorrow known there : nor is there such a thing as a pale face, a languid body, feeble joints, unable infancy, decrepit age, peccant humours, dolorous sickness, griping fears, consuming care, nor whatsoever deserves the name of evil. Indeed, a gale of groans and sighs, a stream of tears, accompanied us to the very gates, and there bid us farewell for ever. *We did weep and lament, when the world did rejoice ; but our sorrow is turned into joy, and our joy shall no man take from us.* God were not the chief and perfect good, if the full fruition of Him did not free us from all evil. But we shall have occasion to speak more fully of this in that which follows.

This rest containeth the highest degree of the saints' personal perfection, both of soul and body. This necessarily qualifies them to enjoy the glory, and thoroughly to partake the sweetness of it. Were the glory never so great, and themselves not made capable by a personal perfection suitable thereto, it would be little to them. There is necessary a right disposition of the recipient, to a right enjoying and affecting. This is one thing that makes the saints' joys there so great. Here *Eye hath not seen, nor ear heard, nor heart conceived, what God hath laid up for them that wait for Him.* For this eye of flesh is not capable of seeing it, nor this ear of hearing it, nor this heart of understanding it; but there the eye and ear and heart are made capable; else how do they enjoy it? The more perfect the sight is, the more delightful the beautiful object. The more perfect the appetite, the sweeter the food. The more musical the ear, the more pleasant the melody. The more perfect the soul, the more joyous those joys, and the more glorious to us is that glory. Nor is it only our sinful imperfection that is here to be removed; nor only that which is the fruit of sin, but that which adhered to us in our pure naturals. Adam's dressing the garden was neither sin nor the fruit of sin: nor is either to be less glorious than the stars or the sun in the firmament of our Father: yet is this the dignity to which the righteous shall be advanced. There is far more procured by Christ than was lost by Adam. It is the misery of wicked men here, that all without them is mercy, excellent mercies, but within them a heart full of sin shuts the door against all and makes them but the more miserable. When all is well within, then all is well indeed. The near good is the best, and the near evil and enemy the worst. Therefore will God, as a special part of His saints' happiness, perfect themselves, as well as their condition.

This rest containeth, as the principal part, our nearest fruition of God, the chiefest good. And here, reader, wonder not if I be at a loss, and in my apprehensions receive but little of that which is in my expressions. If to the beloved disciple that durst speak and inquire into Christ's secrets and was filled with His revelations, and saw the new Jerusalem in her glory, and had seen Christ, Moses, and Elias, in part of theirs, if it did not appear to him what we shall be, but only in general, that when Christ appears we shall be like Him, no wonder if I know little. When I know so little of God, I cannot know much what it is to enjoy Him. When it is so little I know of mine own soul, either its quiddity or quality, while it is here in this tabernacle, how little must I needs know of the infinite Majesty, or the state of this soul when it is advanced to that enjoyment! If I know so little of spirits and spirituals, how little of the Father of Spirits! Nay, if I never saw that creature which contains not something unsearchable, nor the worm so small, which affordeth not matter for questions to puzzle the greatest philosopher that ever I met with, no wonder, then, if mine eyes fail, when I would look at God, my tongue fail me in speaking of Him, and my heart in conceiving. As long as the Athenian superscription doth so too well suit with my sacrifices, *To the unknown God*, and while I cannot contain the smallest rivulet, it is little I can contain of this immense ocean. We shall never be capable of clearly knowing, till we are capable of fully enjoying, nay, nor till we do actually enjoy Him. What strange conceivings hath a man born blind, of the sun, and its light, or a man born deaf, of the nature of sounds and music! So do we yet want that sense by which God must be clearly known. I stand and look upon a heap of ants and see them all with one view, very busy to little purpose. They know not me, my being, nature, or thoughts, though I am their fellow-creature; how little, then, must we know of the great Creator, though He with one view continually beholds us all. Yet a knowledge we have, though imperfect, and such as must be done away. A glimpse the saints behold, though but in a glass, which makes us capable of some poor, general, dark apprehensions of what we shall behold in glory. If I should tell a worldling but what the holiness and spiritual joys of the saints on earth are, he cannot know it; for grace cannot be clearly known without grace: how much less could he conceive it, should I tell him of this glory! But to the saints I may be somewhat more encouraged to speak; for grace giveth them a dark knowledge and slight taste of glory.

As all good whatsoever is comprised in God, and all in the creature are but drops of this ocean; so all the glory of the blessed is comprised in their enjoyment of God and if there be any mediate joys there, they are but drops from this. If men and angels should study to speak the blessedness of that estate in one word, what can they say beyond this, That it is the nearest enjoyment of God? Say, They have God, and you say, They have all that is worth the having. Oh the full joys offered to a believer in that one sentence of Christ's! I would not, for all the world, that one verse had been left out of the Bible: *Father, I will that those whom Thou hast given Me, be with Me where I am, that they may behold My glory which Thou hast given Me* (*John* xvii, 24). . . .

This rest containeth a sweet and constant action of all the powers of the soul and body in this fruition of God. It is not the rest of a stone, which ceaseth from all motion when it attains the centre. The senses themselves, as I judge, are not only passive in receiving their object, but partly passive and partly active. Whether the external senses, such as now we have, shall be continued and employed in this work, is a great doubt. For some of them, it is usually acknowledged they shall cease, because their being importeth their use, and their use implieth our estate of imperfection: as there is no use for eating and drinking so neither for the taste. But for other senses the question will be harder; for Job saith, *I shall see Him with these eyes.*

But do not all senses imply our imperfection? If Job did speak of more than a redemption from this present distress, as it is like he did, yet certainly these eyes will be made so spiritual that whether the name of sense, in the same sense as now, shall befit them, is a question. This body shall be so changed, that it shall be no more flesh and blood, for *that cannot inherit the Kingdom of God (I Cor. xv, 50), but a spiritual body* (ver. 44). *That which we sow, we sow not that body that shall be ; but God giveth it a body as it hath pleased Him, and to every seed his own body (I Cor.* xv, 37, 38). As the ore is cast into the fire a stone, but comes forth so pure a metal that it deserves another name, and so the difference betwixt it and the gold exceeding great, so far greater will the change of our bodies and senses be, even so great as now we cannot conceive. If grace make a Christian differ so much from what he was, that the Christian could say to his companion, *Ego non sum ego,* ' I am not the man I was '; how much more will glory make us differ! We may then say much more, This is not the body I had, and these are not the senses I had. But because we have no other name for them let us call them senses, call them eyes and ears, seeing and hearing: but thus conceive of the difference ; that as much as a body spiritual, above the sun in glory, exceedeth these frail, noisome, diseased lumps of flesh or dirt that now we carry about us, so far shall our senses of seeing and hearing exceed these we now possess: for the change of the senses must be conceived proportionable to the change of the body. And, doubtless, as God advanceth our sense and enlargeth our capacity; so will He advance the happiness of those senses, and fill up with Himself all that capacity. And certainly the body should not be raised up and continued, if it should not share of the glory: for as it hath shared in the obedience and sufferings, so shall it also do in the blessedness; and as Christ bought the whole man, so shall the whole partake of the everlasting benefits of the purchase. The same difference is to be allowed for the tongue. For, though perhaps, that which we now call the tongue, the voice, the language, shall not then be ; yet, with the forementioned, unconceivable change, it may continue. Certain it is, it shall be the everlasting work of those blessed saints, to stand before the throne of God and the Lamb, and to praise Him for ever and ever. As their eyes and hearts shall be filled with His knowledge, with His glory, and with His love, so shall their mouths be filled with His praises. Go on, therefore, O ye saints, while you are on earth, in that divine duty. Learn, O learn, that saint-beseeming work ; for in the mouths of His saints His praise is comely. Pray, but still praise: hear and read, but still praise: praise Him in the presence of His people; for it shall be your eternal work : praise Him, while His enemies deride and abuse you : you shall praise Him, while they shall bewail it, and admire you. . . .

And if the body shall be thus employed, oh how shall the soul be taken up! As its powers and capacities are greatest, so its actions strongest and its enjoyments sweetest. As the bodily senses have their proper aptitude and action, whereby they receive and enjoy their objects, so doth the soul in its own action enjoy its own object, by knowing, by thinking and remembering, by loving, and by delightful joying: this is the soul's enjoying. By these eyes it sees, and by these arms it embraceth. If it might be said of the disciples with Christ on earth, much more that behold Him in His glory, *Blessed are the eyes that see the things that ye see, and the ears that hear the things that ye hear ; for many princes and great ones have desired, and hoped, to see the things that ye see, and have not seen them*, etc. (*Matt.* xiii, 16, 17).

Knowledge of itself is very desirable, even the knowledge of some evil, though not the evil itself. As far as the rational soul exceeds the sensitive, so far the delights of a philosopher, in discovering the secrets of nature, and knowing the mystery of sciences, exceed the delights of the glutton, the drunkard, the unclean, and of all voluptuous sensualists whatsoever; so excellent is all truth. What then is their delight, who know the God of truth! What would I not give, so that all the uncertain, questionable principles in logic, natural philosophy, metaphysics, and medicine, were but certain in themselves, and to me; and that my dull, obscure, notions of them were but quick and clear! Oh, what then should I not either perform or part with to enjoy a clear and true apprehension of the most true God! How noble a faculty of the soul is the understanding! It can compass the earth; it can measure the sun, moon, stars, and Heaven; it can foreknow each eclipse to a minute many years before: yea, but this is the top of all its excellency, it can know God, Who is infinite, Who made all these; a little here, and more, and much more hereafter. Oh the wisdom and goodness of our blessed Lord! He hath created the understanding with a natural bias and inclination to truth and its object; and to the prime truth, as its prime object: and lest we should turn aside to any creature, He hath kept this as His own Divine prerogative, not communicable to any creature, viz. to be the prime truth. And though I think not, as some do, that there is so near a close between the understanding and truth, as may produce a proper union or identity, yet, doubtless, it is no such cold touch or disdainful embrace, as is between these gross, earthly heterogeneals. The true, studious, contemplative man knows this to be true; who feels as sweet embraces between his intellect and truth, and far more than ever the quickest sense did in possessing its desired object. But the true, studious, contemplative Christian knows it much more; who sometimes hath felt more sweet embraces between his soul and Jesus Christ than all inferior truth can afford. . . .

And, doubtless, the memory will not be idle or useless in this blessed work, if it be but by looking back to help the soul to value its enjoyment. Our knowledge will be enlarged, not diminished; therefore, the knowledge of things past shall not be taken away; and what is that knowledge, but remembrance? Doubtless, from that height, the saint can look behind him and before him; and to compare past with present things must needs raise, in the blessed soul, an inconceivable esteem and sense of its condition. To stand on that mount, whence we can see the wilderness and Canaan both at once; to stand in Heaven, and look back on earth, and weigh them together in the balance of a comparing sense and judgement, how must it needs transport the soul, and make it cry out, Is this the purchase that cost so dear as the blood of God? No wonder: O blessed price, and thrice blessed love, that invented and condescended! Is this the end of believing? Is this the end of the Spirit's workings? Have the gales of grace blown me into such a harbour? Is it hither that Christ hath enticed my soul? O blessed way, and thrice blessed end! Is this the glory which the Scriptures spoke of, and ministers preached of so much? Why, now I see the gospel indeed is good tidings, even tidings of peace and good things; tidings of great joy to all nations. Is my mourning, my fasting, my sad humblings, my heavy walking, groanings, complainings, come to this? Are all my afflictions, sickness, languishing, troublesome physic, fears of death, come to this? Are all Satan's temptations, the world's scorns and jeers, come to this? . . .

But oh the full, the near, the sweet enjoyment is that of the affections, love, and joy! It is near; for love is of the essence of the soul, and love is the essence of God: *for God is love.* How near, therefore, is this blessed closure! The Spirit's phrase is, *God is love ; and he that dwelleth in love dwelleth in God, and God in him* (*I John* iv, 8, 16). The acting of this affection, wheresoever, carrieth much delight along with it, especially when the object appears deserving, and the affection is strong; but oh, what will it be when perfect affections shall have the strongest, perfect, incessant acting upon the most perfect object, the ever-blessed God! . . .

And if this were all, what a high favour that God will give us leave to love Him; that He will vouchsafe to be embraced by such arms, that have embraced lust and sin before Him! But this is not all. He returneth love for love; nay, a thousand times more: as perfect as we shall be, we cannot reach His measure of love. Christian, thou wilt be then brimful of love; yet love as much as thou canst, thou shalt be ten thousand times more beloved. Dost thou think thou canst overlove Him? What! love more than love itself? Were the arms of the Son of God open upon the cross, and **an open passage** made to His heart by the spear, and will not arms and heart be open to thee in glory? Did He begin to love before thou lovedst, and will not He continue now? Did He love thee, an enemy, thee, a sinner, thee, who even loathedst thyself, and own thee when thou didst disclaim thyself; and will He not now immeasurably love thee, a son; thee, a perfect saint, thee, who returnest some love for love? Thou wast wont injuriously to question His love; doubt of it now if thou canst. As the pains of hell will convince the rebellious sinner of God's wrath, who would never before believe it, so the joys of heaven will convince thee thoroughly of that love which thou wouldst so hardly be persuaded of. . . .

But the great loss of the damned will be their loss of God; they shall have no comfortable relation to Him, nor any of the saints' communion with Him. As they did not like to retain God in their mind, but said to Him, *Depart from us, we desire not the knowledge of Thy ways* (*Rom.* i, 28; *Job* xxi, 14), so God will abhor to retain them in His household, or to give them entertainment in His fellowship and glory. . . .

And, as they would not consent that God should by His Spirit dwell in them, so shall not these evil-doers dwell with Him. The tabernacles of wickedness shall have no fellowship with Him, nor the wicked inhabit the city of God: for without are the dogs, the sorcerers, whoremongers, murderers, idolaters, and whatsoever loveth and maketh a lie. For God knoweth the way of the righteous, but the way of the wicked leads to perishing. God is first enjoyed in part on earth, before He be fully enjoyed in Heaven. It is only they that walked with Him here, who shall live and be happy with Him there. Oh, little doth the world now know what a loss that soul hath, who loseth God! What were the world but a dungeon, if it had lost the sun? What were the body but a loathsome carrion, if it had lost the soul? Yet all these are nothing to the loss of God; even the little taste of the fruition of God, which the Saints enjoy in this life, is dearer to them than all the world. As the world, when they feed upon their forbidden pleasures, may cry out with the sons of the prophet, *There is death in the pot!* (*II Kings* iv, 40); so when the Saints do but taste of the favour of God, they cry out with David, *In His favour is life!* (*Psal.* xxx, 5). Nay, though life be naturally most dear to all men, yet they that have tasted and tried do say with David, *His loving-kindness is better than life!* (*Psal.* lxiii, 3). So that, as the enjoyment of God is the Heaven of the Saints, so the loss of God is the hell of the ungodly. And, as the enjoying of God is the enjoying of all, so the loss of God is the loss of all.

Thirdly. Moreover, as they lose God, so they lose all those spiritual, delightful affections and actions, by which the blessed do feed on God ; that transporting knowledge ; those ravishing views of His glorious Face ; the unconceivable pleasure of loving God ; the apprehensions of His infinite Love to us ; the constant joys which His Saints are taken up with, and the rivers of consolation wherewith He doth satisfy them. Is it nothing to lose all this ? The employment of a king in ruling a kingdom doth not so far exceed the employment of the vilest scullion or slave, as this heavenly employment exceedeth his. . . .

Consider, our affections and actions should be somewhat answerable to the greatness of the ends to which they are intended. Now the ends of a Christian's desires and endeavours are so great, that no human understanding on earth can comprehend them ; whether you respect their proper excellency, their exceeding importance, or their absolute necessity.

These ends are, the glorifying of God, the salvation of our own and other men's souls, in our escaping the torments of Hell, and possessing the glory of Heaven. And can a man be too much affected with things of such moment ? Can he desire them too earnestly, or love them too violently, or labour for them too diligently ? When we know that if our prayers prevail not, and our labour succeeds not, we are undone for ever, I think it concerns us to seek and labour to the purpose. When it is put to the question, Whether we shall live for ever in Heaven or in Hell ?—and the question must be resolved upon our obeying the gospel or our disobeying it, upon the painfulness or the slothfulness of our present endeavours,—I think it is time for us to bestir ourselves, and to leave our trifling and complimenting with God. . . .

Is there a rest, and such a rest, remaining for us ? Why then are our thoughts no more upon it ? Why are not our hearts continually there ? Why dwell we not there in constant contemplation ? Sirs, ask your hearts in good earnest, What is the cause of this neglect ? Are we reasonable in this, or are we not ? Hath the eternal God provided us such a glory, and promised to take us up to dwell with Himself, and is not this worth the thinking on ? Should not the strongest desires of our hearts be after it, and the daily delights of our souls be there ? Do we believe this ; and can we yet forget and neglect it ? What is the matter ? Will not God give us leave to approach this light ? Or will He not suffer our souls to taste and see it ? Why, then, what mean all His earnest invitations ? Why doth He so condemn our earthly mindedness and command us to set our affections above ? Ah, vile hearts, if God were against it, we were likelier to be for it. When He would have us to keep our station, then we are aspiring to be like God and are ready to invade the Divine prerogatives. But when He commands our hearts to heaven, then they will not stir an inch, like our predecessors, the sinful Israelites. When God would have them march for Canaan, then they mutiny and will not stir; either they fear the giants or the walled cities or want necessaries. Something hinders them. But when God bids them not go, then will they needs be presently marching, and fight they will, though it be to their overthrow. If the forethoughts of glory were forbidden fruits, perhaps we should be sooner drawn unto them, and we should itch, as the Bethshemites, to be looking into this ark. Sure I am, where God hath forbidden us to place our thoughts and our delights, thither it is easy enough to draw them. If He say, *Love not the world, nor the things of the world,* we dote upon it nevertheless. We have love enough if the world require it, and thoughts enough to pursue our profits. How delightfully and un-wearidly can we think of vanity, and day after day employ our minds about the creature! And have we no thoughts of this our rest? How freely and how frequently can we think of our pleasures, our friends, our labours, our flesh, our lusts, our common studies, our news; yea, our very miseries, our wrongs, our sufferings, and our fears! But where is the Christian whose heart is on his rest? Why, sirs, what is the matter? Why are we not taken up with the views of glory, and our souls more accustomed to these delightful medita-tions? Are we so full of joy that we need no more? Or, is there no matter in Heaven for our joyous thoughts? Or rather, are not our hearts carnal and blockish? Earth will to earth. Had we more spirit, it would be otherwise with us. . . .

## No. 142.  JOSEPH HALL

[From *Susurrium Cum Deo* [*i.e.*] *Soliloquies, or Holy Self-Conferences of the Devout Soul upon Sundry Choice Occasions ; with Humble Addresses to the Throne of Grace,* Soliloquy No. XXXIII. *Works,* ed. Peter Hall (1837), Vol. VIII, p. 262. Cp. note on No. **346**.]

### The All-Sufficient Knowledge.

I find much inquiry of curious wits, whether we shall know one another in Heaven ; there is no want of arguments on both parts, and the greatest probabilities have seemed to be for the affirmative. But, O Lord, whether or no we shall know one another, I am sure we shall all like Thy glorified Saints know Thee ; and in knowing Thee we shall be infinitely happy. And what would be more? Surely, as we find here, that the sun puts out the fire, and the greater light ever extinguisheth the less, so why may we not think it to be above? When Thou art all in all to us, what can the knowledge of any creature add to our blessed-ness? And if when we casually meet with a brother, or a son before some great prince, we forbear the ceremonies of our mutual respects, as being wholly taken up with the awful regard of a greater presence, how much more may we justly think that, when we meet before the glorious throne of the God of Heaven, all the respects of our former earthly relations must utterly cease, and be swallowed up of that beatifical presence, Divine Love, and infinitely blessed fruition of the Almighty ?

O God, it is my great comfort here below to think and know that I have parents, or children, or brothers and sisters, or friends, already in possession of glory with Thee, and to believe assuredly that in my time I shall be received to the association of their blessedness. But, if upon the dissolution of this earthly tabernacle, I may be admitted to the sight of Thy all-glorious essence, and may set eye upon the face of my blessed Saviour, now sitting at the right-hand of Thy incomprehensible Majesty, attended with those millions of His heavenly Angels, I shall neither have need nor use of enquiring after my kindred according to the flesh. What can fall into my thoughts or desires beside or beyond that which is infinite ?

## No. 143. JOSEPH HALL

[From *A Treatise of Christ Mystical ; or the Blessed Union of Christ and His Members*, Section XXIV (" The Union of the Saints on Earth with Those in Heaven "). *Works*, ed. Peter Hall (1837), Vol. VII, pp. 261 f. (This edition has the treatise divided into chapters, and prints the present extract in Chapter VII, § 3.) It was written by the author in his great age as Bishop of Norwich, and first published in 1647.]

As there is a perfect union betwixt the glorious Saints in heaven, and an union, though imperfect, betwixt the Saints on earth, so there is an union, partly perfect and partly imperfect, between the Saints in heaven and the Saints below upon earth, perfect in respect of those glorified Saints above, imperfect in respect of the weak returns we are able to make to them again.

Let no man think that because those blessed souls are out of sight far distant in another world, and we are here toiling in a vale of tears, we have therefore lost all mutual regard to each other. No ; there is still, and ever will be, a secret but unfailing correspondence between Heaven and earth. The present happiness of those Heavenly citizens cannot have abated ought of their knowledge and charity, but must needs have raised them to a higher pitch of both. They, therefore, who are now glorious comprehensors cannot but, in a generality, retain the notice of the sad condition of us poor travellers here below, panting towards our rest together with them, and in common wish for the happy consummation of this our weary pilgrimage in the fruition of their glory. That they have any perspective whereby they can see down into our particular wants is that which we find no ground to believe. It is enough, that they have an universal apprehension of the estate of Christ's warfaring Church upon the face of the earth ; and fellow-members of the same mystical body long for a perfect glorification of the whole.

As for us wretched pilgrims that are yet left here below to tug with many difficulties, we cannot forget that better half of us that is now triumphant in glory.   O ye blessed Saints above, we honour your memories so far as we ought ;  we do with praise recount your virtues ; we magnify your victories ;  we bless God, for your happy exemption from the misery of this world, and for your estating in that blessed immortality ;  we imitate your holy examples ;  we long and pray for a happy consociation with you.   We dare not raise temples, dedicate altars, direct prayers to you ;  we dare not, finally, offer any thing to you which you are unwilling to receive, nor put any thing upon you which you would disclaim as prejudicial to your Creator and Redeemer.   It is abundant comfort to us that some part of us is in the fruition of that glory, whereto we, the other poor labouring part, desire and strive to aspire ;  that our head and shoulders are above water, while the other limbs are yet wading through the stream.

# (3) HELL

## No. 144.   JOHN DONNE

[From ' Sermon LXXVI ' in *LXXX Sermons*, 1640, pp. 776 f.   *Donne's Sermons. Selected Passages*, ed. L. P. Smith, Oxford (1919), pp. 208–211.]

THAT God should let my soul fall out of His hand into a bottomless pit, and roll an unremoveable stone upon it, and leave it to that which it finds there,—and it shall find that there which it never imagined till it came thither,—and never think more of that soul, never have more to do with it ; that of that providence of God, that studies the life of every weed and worm and ant and spider and toad and viper, there should never, never, any beam flow out upon me ; that that God Who looked upon me when I was nothing, and called me when I was not as though I had been, out of the womb and depth of darkness, will not look upon me now when, though a miserable and a banished and a damned creature, yet I am His creature still and contribute something to His glory, even in my damnation ;  that that God, Who hath often looked upon me in my foulest uncleanness, and when I had shut out the eye of the day, the sun, and the eye of the night, the taper, and the eyes of all the world, with curtains and windows and doors, did yet see me and see me in mercy, by making me see that He saw me and sometimes brought me to a present remorse and, for that time, to a forbearing of that sin, should so turn Himself from me, to His glorious Saints and Angels, as that no Saint nor Angel, nor Christ Jesus Himself, should ever pray Him to look towards me, never remember Him that such a soul there is, that that God, Who hath so often said to my soul " *Quare morieris?*   Why wilt thou die ? "   and so often sworn to my soul, " *Vivit Dominus*, As the Lord liveth, I would not have thee die but live," will neither let me die nor let me live, but die an everlasting life and live an everlasting death ;  that that God Who when He could not get into me by standing and knocking, by His ordinary means of entering, by His Word, His mercies, hath applied His judgements and hath shaked the house, this body, with agues and palsies, and set this house on fire with fevers and calentures, and frighted the master of the houses, my soul, with horrors and heavy apprehensions, and so made an entrance into me; that that God should frustrate all His Own purposes and practices upon me, and leave me, and cast me away, as though I had cost Him nothing ;  that this God at last should let this soul go away,

336

as a smoke, as a vapour, as a bubble, and that then this soul cannot be a smoke, a vapour, nor a bubble, but must lie in darkness as long as the Lord of Light is light itself, and never spark of that light reach to my soul ; What Tophet is not Paradise ? What brimstone is not amber ? What gnashing is not a comfort ? What gnawing of the worm is not a tickling ? What torment is not a marriage bed, to this damnation to be secluded eternally, eternally, eternally from the sight of God ? Especially to us. For as the perpetual loss of that is most heavy with which we have been best acquainted and to which we have been most accustomed, so shall this damnation, which consists in the loss of the sight and presence of God, be heavier to us than others, because God hath so graciously and so evidently and so diversely appeared to us in His pillar of fire, in the light of prosperity, and in the pillar of the Cloud, in hiding Himself for a while from us. We that have seen Him in all the parts of this commission, in His Word, in His Sacraments, and in good example, and not believed, shall be further removed from His sight, in the next world than they to whom He never appeared in this. But *Vincenti et Credenti*, to him that believes aright, and overcomes all tentations to a wrong belief, God shall give the accomplishment of fullness, and fullness of joy, and joy rooted in glory, and glory established in eternity, and this eternity is God. To him that believes and overcomes, God shall give Himself in an everlasting presence and fruition, Amen.

## No. 145. " CONTEMPLATIONS ON THE STATE OF MAN."

[From Book II, Chapter vi (" Considerations of Eternal Evils, and of the Miserable State of the Damned "). *Works of Jeremy Taylor*, ed. R. Heber, Vol. III, p. 517. This treatise, which was first published in 1684, was attributed to Jeremy Taylor (who had died in 1667); but Edward Churton has shown it to be really an abridgement of a Spanish work by J. E. Nieremberg, entitled *De la diferencia entre lo temporal y eterno*. (See Eden's edition of Jeremy Taylor, Vol. I, p. vii of the ' Life '.) The treatise was widely welcomed, and reached a seventh edition in 1707.]

If one were cast into some deep dungeon, without clothes, exposed to the inclemency of the cold and moisture of the place, where he should not see the light of Heaven, should have nothing to feed on, but once a day some little piece of hard barley-bread ; and that he were to continue there six years without speaking or seeing of anybody ; and not to sleep on other bed but the cold ground ; what a misery were this ! One week of that habitation would appear longer than a hundred years. Yet compare this with what shall be in the banishment and prison of hell, and you shall find the miserable life of that man to be an happiness ; there in all his troubles, he should not meet with any to scoff at his misfortune, none to torment, and whip him, but in hell he shall find both ; the devils shall not cease to deride, whip, and cruelly torment him : there should be no horrid sights, no fearful noises of howlings, groanings, and lamentations ; in hell the eyes and ears of the damned shall never be free from such affrights : there should be no flames of fire to scorch him ; in hell they shall burn into his bowels : there he might move and walk ; . in hell, not stir a foot : there he may breathe the air without stink ; in hell he shall suck in nothing but flames, stink, and sulphur : there he might hope for coming forth ; in hell there is no redemption : there that little piece of hard bread would seem every day a dainty ; but in hell, in millions of years, his eyes shall not behold a crumb of bread, nor a drop of water, but shall eternally rage with hunger, and a burning thirst : this is to be the calamity of that land of darkness.

## No. 146.  THOMAS BROWNE

[From *Religio Medici*, Part I.   Everyman's edition, p. 58.   Cp. note on No. 4.]

I thank God, and with joy I mention it, I was never afraid of Hell, nor never grew pale at the description of that place.   I have so fixed my contemplations on Heaven, that I have almost forgot the idea of Hell, and am afraid rather to lose the joys of the one, than endure the misery of the other : to be deprived of them is a perfect Hell, and needs, methinks, no addition to complete our afflictions.   That terrible term hath never detained me from sin, nor do I owe any good action to the name thereof.   I fear God, yet am not afraid of Him :  His mercies make me ashamed of my sins, before His judgements afraid thereof.   These are the forced and secondary method of His wisdom, which He useth but as the last remedy, and upon provocation ; a course rather to deter the wicked, than incite the virtuous to His worship. I can hardly think there was ever any scared into Heaven ;  they go the fairest way to Heaven that would serve God without a Hell ;  other mercenaries, that crouch into Him in fear of Hell, though they term themselves the servants, are indeed but the slaves, of the Almighty.

# (4) PURGATORY

## No. 147.  WILLIAM WAKE

[From *A Discourse of Purgatory*.  Section V (" That the Doctrine of Purgatory is contrary to Scripture, Antiquity, and Reason ").  First issued anonymously with another treatise as *Two Discourses ; Of Purgatory, and Prayers for the Dead*, London, 1687.  *Enchiridion Theologicum Anti-Romanum* (Miscellaneous Tracts ;  No. X), Oxford, 1837, Vol. III, pp. 526-531.]

### *That the Doctrine of Purgatory is contrary to Scripture, Antiquity and Reason.*

HITHERTO we have seen how little grounds the Church of Rome has to establish this doctrine as an article of faith ;  we will now go yet further, and shew, not only that there is no obligation upon us, either from Scripture or antiquity or reason, to believe this doctrine ;  but that according to the principles of every one of these, we ought not to do it.

First, for Scripture.

It is not a little to be considered, in opposition to this doctrine, that these sacred writings not only every where represent to us this present life as the time of trial and exercise of sufferings and afflictions, but also encourage us on this very consideration to bear them with patience and resignation, that as soon as we die they shall all end, and we shall receive the blessed reward which God has prepared for them that bear them as they ought to do.  *I look upon it*, says St. Paul, (*Rom.* viii, 18) *that the sufferings of this present life are not worthy to be compared with the glory which shall be revealed.*  And again, (*II Cor.* iv, 17) *For the sufferings of this present life work out for us a far more exceeding and eternal weight of glory.*  Many other places of this kind there are, in which our present sufferings are compared with and opposed to our future reward.  Now if when all these encounters are ended, there will be still another and a more dreadful sort of trial to be undergone elsewhere, how could the apostle have used those kind of antitheses, and have encouraged us to a constancy in our present afflictions, from the prospect of a time, when, according to these men, there are yet greater and more severe ones to be undergone by us ?

And this then may be a second observation, That the Scripture always speaks of the death of good men as a blessing, an immediate rest from their labours ;  and therefore, sure understood nothing of those torments to which the Church of Rome now condemns them.  So *Rev.* xiv, 13.  *I heard a voice from Heaven saying unto me, Write, Blessed are the dead which die in the Lord from henceforth ; Yea, saith the Spirit, that they may rest from their labours.* It was this assurance made the holy men of old so desirous of their dissolution, that they might find an end of all those labours and evils which they suffered here. (*Phil.* i, 23) *I am in a strait,* says St. Paul, *betwixt two, having a desire to depart, and to be with Christ ; which is far better,* etc. Surely St. Paul never thought of purgatory when he talked thus of going to Christ ; nor would he have appeared so desirous of his dissolution, had he known he should have been cast into such a fire as the Romanists suppose to be in this infernal region.

Nor can it here be reasonably said that this was the apostle's peculiar happiness ; and therefore, that though he indeed was secure of going immediately to Christ, yet others were not therefore to expect the like favour. For (*II Cor.* v, 1) we find him promising the very same to all Christians indifferently : *We know,* says he, *that if our earthly house of this tabernacle were dissolved, we have a building of God, an house not made with hands, eternal in the heavens.* And again, verse 6, *when we are absent from the body,* says he, *we are present with the Lord* : by all which it appears, that when good men die they go to the Lord, to Christ, to their heavenly house ; and that sure is not purgatory.

To this agree those few instances we have of just men's dying in the New Testament. Lazarus in the parable was in *Abraham's bosom ;* the penitent thief on the cross was promised that he should be that day with Christ in paradise : and we have good reason to believe that the same is the state of all others, not only from the passages already mentioned, and many more of the like kind that might have been offered, but also from this, that we have not in all the Holy Scripture the least intimation of any such place as purgatory : that there is neither precept nor example of any one, that either prayed for the delivery of their friends departed out of these pains, or any directions left for any one hereafter so to do. Now certainly it is not easy to be imagined that the holy penmen should have been so perfectly silent in this matter, had there been so great a cause for it as the delivery of their souls out of purgatory undoubtedly would have been, or had they then esteemed it so excellent and necessary a piece of Christian charity as it is now pretended to be.

And this presumption against purgatory the Holy Scriptures will afford us. If we look, secondly, to the holy Fathers,

We shall find them proceeding exactly upon the same principles : they thought the just, when they were departed, were presently in a state of happiness ; that it was injurious to Christ, to hold that such as died in His faith were to be pitied, that Christians therefore ought not by any means to be afraid of dying. " It is for him," says St. Cyprian, " to fear death, that is unwilling to go to Christ. It is for him to be unwilling to go to Christ, who doth not believe that he beginneth to reign with Christ.—Simeon said, *Lord, now lettest Thou Thy servant depart in peace*, proving and witnessing that the servants of God then have peace, then enjoy free and quiet rest, when, being drawn from these storms of the world, we arrive at the haven of our everlasting habitation and security.—Let us therefore embrace the day that bringeth every one to his own house, which having taken us away from hence, and loosed us from the snares of this world, returneth us to Paradise, and to the Kingdom of Heaven."

I shall leave it to any one to consider, whether this holy Father, who discoursed thus of our dying, believed any thing of these tormenting purgatory fires that now keep men in anxiety, and make the best Christians afraid to die. And the same is the language of all the rest. St. Chrysostom particularly enforces the same considerations from those Psalms that were usually said at the burial of the dead. *Return to thy rest, O my soul, for the Lord hath been gracious unto thee.* "You see," says that holy Father, "how that death is a blessing, a rest,—God calls it a blessing, and dost thou lament? What couldst thou have done more, if thou hadst been His enemy?"

But to put this matter, as to the point of antiquity, beyond all doubt, I will remark distinctly two or three things:

First, That several of the most ancient Fathers not only believed the souls of the faithful to be in happiness immediately upon their departure, but to be carried immediately into Heaven. 1. So Athenagoras, 2. St. Cyprian, 3. Origen, 4. Gregory Nazianzen, 5. Chrysostom, 6. Cyril Alexandrinus, 7. St. Hierome and others. Now, certainly they who believed that just men when they die go straight to Heaven, could not have believed that they were for a long while after their death tormented in purgatory; and therefore all these, at least, must have been of an opinion different from the Church of Rome in this matter.

Secondly, Another thing remarkable in some of the ancient Fathers is, that they utterly deny that the soul is capable of being purged in another world; and this is, to be sure, expressly contrary to the present doctrine of the Romanists in this point. Thus Gregory Nazianzen speaking of the judgement after death: "It is better," says he, "to be now chastised and purged, than to be delivered over to that torment, when it shall be no longer a time of purgation but of punishment." Where we see the Father expressly opposes the time of purgation in this life to the time, not of purgation, but of punishment in the next. And St. Chrysostom, "If the soul be purged here" (*i.e.* from sin), "that fire shall not hurt it when it departs hence; but the soul that goes hence in sin, that fire" (not of purgatory, but of hell) "shall receive." This was the doctrine of those times; the soul that was clear of sin, by God's pardon and forgiveness, no fire could hurt;

27

that which was not, no fire could cleanse; but it was to remain in torments of hell for ever.

Nor may we omit to observe, thirdly, that the Fathers take no notice of purgatory in such places, as had they believed it, they could not well have omitted it. Hence we see no mention of it in any of their creeds or councils, or catechetical discourses, in which the other articles of their faith are set down and explained. The fifth General Council, which condemned Origen for his errors concerning the pains after death, never mentioned any other purgatory in opposition to that which he had heretically invented. But that which shews it yet more plainly to have been unknown to them is, that not only St. Austin, but Pope Gregory himself, the great patron of this error, yet spoke of it with some doubt; not as they use to do of a point firmly believed by the Church, but as a peculiar thing, in which they were not themselves very well resolved. When the Fathers disputed against Origen, they none of them mention any of the purgatory pains which the orthodox faith taught, to distinguish them from those which he erroneously had invented. When Epiphanius disputed against Aerius, concerning the reason and benefit of praying for the dead, is it to be imagined he could then have forgot the great concern of delivering the souls departed out of purgatory, had the Church then believed any such thing? To all which if we finally add, that the Greek Church neither at this day does, nor ever did receive this doctrine, I cannot tell what clearer evidence we can desire to shew, that this whole business of purgatory is but an error of the Latin Church, not an article of the Catholic Faith.

Thirdly, for reason.

I shall only offer this one reflection: Whether there can be any reason to think there should be such a place, and such punishments as purgatory, for no end or purpose in the world. They who go thither must be perfect in charity, in the grace of God, secure of their salvation; their satisfaction must have been made by Christ's blood, and so God's justice satisfied. Now when all this is already done, to what end is it that they should be tormented? Had there been any means by such a purgatory, either to fit them for Heaven or to satisfy the Divine justice, there might then have been some pretence for it. But to think that God punishes men only for punishing sake, and this too His own servants, men who are in His favour, that have lived well, and upon that account are justified by Him through the blood of Christ; this is such an idea of an infinite love, mercy, and goodness, as sure can never be the dictate of right reason; I think I may say, is utterly inconsistent with it.

# X. THE CHRISTIAN MINISTRY

# (1) PRINCIPLES

## No. 148.  RICHARD HOOKER

[From *The Laws of Ecclesiastical Polity*, Book V, Chapter lxxvii, §§ 1, 2, 8 ; Chapter lxxviii, §§ 4, 5, 12.  *Works*, ed. J. Keble, Vol. II, pp. 455 f., 462 f., 473 f., 482.  Cp. note on No. **150**.  In 1591 Hooker had been presented by Whitgift to the living of Boscombe, near Salisbury, and he immediately set to work on the *Ecclesiastical Polity*. The first four books were finished in less than two years, though they were not published until 1594.  The main theme of these four books is the nature of " law " ; " they lay foundations upon which the later [books] build " (L. S. Thornton, *Richard Hooker*, p. 25).  It was not until 1597 that the much larger Fifth Book saw the light.  In this Book Hooker draws out his teaching about the Incarnation and its implications for the Doctrine of the Sacraments.  See F. Paget, *An Introduction to the Fifth Book of Hooker's Treatise of the Laws of Ecclesiastical Polity*, Oxford (Clarendon Press), 1899.]

THE Ministry of things divine is a function which as God did Himself institute, so neither may men undertake the same but by authority and power given them in lawful manner.  That God Which is no way deficient or wanting unto man in necessaries, and hath therefore given us the light of His heavenly truth, because without that inestimable benefit we must needs have wandered in darkness to our endless perdition and woe, hath in the like abundance of mercies ordained certain to attend upon the due execution of requisite parts and offices therein prescribed for the good of the whole world, which men thereunto assigned do hold their authority from Him, whether they be such as Himself immediately or as the Church in His Name investeth, it being neither possible for all nor for every man without distinction convenient to take upon Him a charge of so great importance.  They are therefore ministers of God, not only by way of subordination as princes and civil magistrates whose execution of judgement and justice the supreme hand of divine providence doth uphold, but ministers of God as from Whom their authority is derived, and not from men.  For in that they are Christ's ambassadors and His labourers, who should give them their commission but He Whose most inward affairs they manage ?  Is not God alone the Father of spirits ?  Are not souls the purchase of Jesus Christ ?  What Angel in Heaven could have said to man as Our Lord did unto Peter, *Feed My sheep : Preach : Baptize : Do this in remembrance of Me : Whose sins ye retain they are retained : and their offences in heaven pardoned whose faults you shall on earth forgive ?*  What think we ?  Are these terrestrial sounds, or else are they voices uttered out of the clouds above ?  The power of the ministry of God translateth out of darkness into glory, it raiseth men from the earth and bringeth

345

God Himself down from Heaven, by blessing visible elements it maketh them invisible grace, it giveth daily the Holy Ghost, it hath to dispose of that flesh which was given for the life of the world and that blood which was poured out to redeem souls, when it poureth malediction upon the heads of the wicked they perish, when it revoketh the same they revive.  O wretched blindness if we admire not so great power, more wretched if we consider it aright and notwithstanding imagine that any but God can bestow it !

To whom Christ hath imparted power both over that mystical Body which is the society of souls, and over that natural which is Himself for the knitting of both in one,—a work which Antiquity doth call the making of Christ's body,—the same power is in such not amiss both termed a kind of mark or character and acknowledged to be indelible. Ministerial power is a mark of separation, because it severeth them that have it from other men, and maketh them a special *order* conse-crated unto the service of the Most High in things wherewith others may not meddle.  Their difference therefore from other men is in that they are a distinct *order*.  So Tertullian calleth them. . . .

Now, besides that the power and authority delivered with those words is itself χάρισμα, a gracious donation which the Spirit of God doth bestow, we may most assuredly persuade ourselves that the hand which imposeth upon us the function of our ministry doth under the same form of words so tie itself thereunto, that he which receiveth the burden is thereby for ever warranted to have the Spirit with him and in him for his assistance, aid, countenance and support in whatsoever he faithfully doth to discharge duty.  Knowing therefore that when we take Ordination we also receive the presence of the Holy Ghost, partly to guide, direct and strengthen us in all our ways, and partly to assume unto itself for the more authority those actions that appertain to our place and calling, can our ears admit such a speech uttered in the reverend performance of that solemnity, or can we at any time renew the memory and enter into serious cogitation thereof but with much admiration and joy ?  Remove what these foolish words do imply, and what hath the ministry of God besides wherein to glory ?  Whereas now, forasmuch as the Holy Ghost which Our Saviour in His first Ordinations gave doth no less concur with spiritual vocations throughout all ages, than the Spirit which God derived from Moses to them that assisted him in his government did descend from them to their successors in like authority and place, we have for the least and meanest duties performed by virtue of ministerial power, that to dignify, grace and authorize them, which no other offices on earth can challenge.  Whether we preach, pray, baptize, communicate, condemn, give absolution, or whatsoever, as disposers of God's mysteries, our words, judgements, acts and deeds, are not ours but the Holy Ghost's.  Enough, if unfeignedly and in heart we did believe it, enough to banish whatsoever may justly be thought corrupt, either in bestowing, or in using, or in esteeming the same otherwise than is meet. For profanely to bestow, or loosely to use, or vilely to esteem of the Holy Ghost we all in show and profession abhor. . . .

Of Presbyters some were greater some less in power, and that by Our Saviour's own appointment; the greater they which received fullness of spiritual power, the less they to whom less was granted. The Apostles' peculiar charge was to publish the Gospel of Christ unto all nations, and to deliver them His ordinances received by *immediate revelation from Himself*. Which pre-eminence excepted, to all other offices and duties incident into their order it was in them to ordain and consecrate whomsoever they thought meet, even as Our Saviour did Himself assign seventy other of His Own Disciples inferior Presbyters, whose commission to preach and baptize was the same which the Apostles had. Whereas therefore we find that the very first sermon which the Apostles did publicly make was the conversion of above three thousand souls, unto whom there were every day more and more added, they having no open place permitted them for the exercise of Christian Religion, think we that twelve were sufficient to teach and administer sacraments in so many private places as so great a multitude of people did require? This harvest Our Saviour no doubt foreseeing provided accordingly labourers for it beforehand. By which means it came to pass that the growth of that Church being so great and so sudden, they had notwithstanding in a readiness Presbyters enough to furnish it. And therefore the history doth make no mention by what occasion Presbyters were instituted in Jerusalem, only we read of things which they did, and how the like were made afterwards elsewhere.

To these two degrees appointed of Our Lord and Saviour Christ His Apostles soon after annexed Deacons. Deacons therefore must know, saith Cyprian, that Our Lord Himself did elect Apostles, but Deacons after His ascension into Heaven the Apostles ordained. Deacons were stewards of the Church, unto whom at the first was committed the distribution of Church goods, the care of providing therewith for the poor, and the charge to see that all things of expense might be religiously and faithfully dealt in. A part also of their office was attendance upon their Presbyters at the time of Divine Service. For which cause Ignatius to set forth the dignity of their calling saith, that they are in such case to the Bishop as if Angelical powers did serve him. . . .

The ancientest therefore of the Fathers mention those three degrees of ecclesiastical order specified and no more. "When your captains," saith Tertullian, " that is to say the Deacons, Presbyters and Bishops fly, who shall teach the laity that they must be constant?" Again, "What should I mention laymen," saith Optatus, "yea or divers of the ministry itself ? To what purpose Deacons which are in the third, or Presbyters in the second degree of Priesthood, when the very heads and princes of all even certain of the Bishops themselves were content to redeem life with the loss of heaven ? " Heaps of allegations in a case so evident and plain are needless. I may securely therefore conclude that there are at this day in the Church of England no other than the same degrees of ecclesiastical order, namely Bishops, Presbyters, and Deacons, which had their beginning from Christ and His blessed Apostles themselves.

### No. 149.  JOSEPH MEDE

[From *Diatribae. Discourses on Divers Texts of Scripture, Delivered upon several Occasions*, Book I, No. 5 (on 1 *Cor.* iv, 1). *Works*, ed. J. Worthington (1672), p. 26. The *Diatribae* of the " pious and profoundly learned Joseph Mede " were first published at London in 1642.]

There are properly but two orders ecclesiastical, *Presbyteri* and *Diaconi*,—the one the Masters, Priests; the other the Ministers, Deacons. The rest are but divers degrees of these two. As Bishops are a degree of Presbyters of Divine ordinance, to be as heads, chiefs, and presidents, of their brethren, so Subdeacons, Lectors, and indeed any other kind of ecclesiastical ministers, whether *in Ecclesia* or *Foro Ecclesiastico* (I mean whether they attend Divine duties in the Church, or jurisdiction in Ecclesiastical Courts) are all a kind of Deacons, being to the Presbyters, either single or episcopal, as the Levites were to the *Sacerdotes* in the Old Testament, namely to minister unto or for them. Thus, when we say Bishops, Presbyters, and Deacons, we name but two Orders, yet three degrees.

# (2) EPISCOPACY

## No. 150.  RICHARD HOOKER

[From *The Laws of Ecclesiastical Polity*, Book VII, Chapters i, § 4; ii, §§ 1, 2, 3; iii, § i; iv, §§ 1, 3, 4; v, §§ 1, 3, 9; vi, § 3.  *Works*, ed. J. Keble, Vol. III, pp. 143 f., 145–147, 148 f., 149, 151, 153–155, 155, 157 f., 166 f., 169.  Cp. note on No. **148**. As is well known, the authenticity of Books VI to VIII of the *Ecclesiastical Polity* is a matter of considerable doubt.  Hooker had died in 1600; but Books VI and VIII were not published until 1651, and Book VII not until 1662.  They were probably based upon rough notes which Hooker had written, but only after considerable re-arrangement, and perhaps some modification in doctrinal matters.  Apparently Hooker himself had almost completed his MS. of Books VI to VIII.  His final draft, however, has never been recovered.  On the subject, see the ' Editor's Preface ' to J. Keble's edition, pp. xx–xliv; also F. Paget, *An Introduction to the Fifth Book of Hooker's Treatise of the Laws of Ecclesiastical Polity*, Appendix VII.]

A THOUSAND five hundred years and upward the Church of Christ hath now continued under the sacred regiment of Bishops.  Neither for so long hath Christianity been ever planted in any kingdom throughout the world but with this kind of government alone ; which to have been ordained of God, I am for mine own part even as resolutely persuaded, as that any other kind of government in the world whatsoever is of God.  In this realm of England, before Normans, yea before Saxons, there being Christians, the chief pastors of their souls were Bishops.  This Order from about the first establishment of Christian Religion, which was publicly begun through the virtuous disposition of King Lucie not fully two hundred years after Christ, continued till the coming in of the Saxons, by whom Paganism being everywhere else replanted, only one part of the island, whereinto the ancient natural inhabitants the Britons were driven, retained constantly the Faith of Christ, together with the same form of spiritual regiment, which their fathers had before received.  Wherefore in the histories of the Church we find very ancient mention made of our own Bishops.  At the Council of Ariminum, about the year three hundred and fifty-nine, Britain had three of her Bishops present.  At the arrival of Augustine, the monk whom Gregory sent hither to reclaim the Saxons from Gentility about six hundred years after Christ, the Britons he found observers still of the selfsame government by Bishops over the rest of the clergy ; under this form Christianity took root again, where it had been exiled.  Under the selfsame form it remained till the days of the Norman Conqueror. By him and his successors thereunto sworn, it hath from that time till now by the space of five hundred years more been upheld. . . .

For whatsoever we bring from Antiquity, by way of defence in this cause of Bishops, it is cast off as impertinent matter, all is wiped away with an odd kind of shifting answer, " That the Bishops which now are be not like unto them which were." We therefore beseech all indifferent judges to weigh sincerely with themselves how the case doth stand. If it should be at this day a controversy whether kingly regiment were lawful or no, peradventure in defence thereof the long continuance which it hath had sithence the first beginning might be alleged. Mention perhaps might be made what kings there were of old, even in Abraham's time, what sovereign princes both before and after. Suppose that herein some man purposely bending his wit against sovereignty should think to elude all such allegations by making ample discovery through a number of particularities, wherein the kings that are do differ from those that have been, and should therefore in the end conclude that such ancient examples are no convenient proofs of that royalty that is now in use. Surely for decision of truth in this case there were no remedy, but only to show the nature of sovereignty, to sever it from accidental properties, make it clear that ancient and present regality are one and the same in substance, how great odds soever otherwise may seem to be between them. In like manner, whereas a question of late hath grown, whether Ecclesiastical Regiment by Bishops be lawful in the Church of Christ or no; in which question, they that hold the negative, being pressed with that general received order, according whereunto the most renowned lights of the Christian world have governed the same in every age of Bishops; seeing their manner is to reply, that such Bishops as those ancient were, ours are not; there is no remedy but to show, that to be a Bishop is now the selfsame thing which it hath been; that one definition agreeth fully and truly as well to those elder, as to these latter Bishops. Sundry dissimilitudes we grant there are, which notwithstanding are not such that they cause any equivocation in the name, whereby we should think a Bishop in those times to have had a clean other definition than doth rightly agree unto Bishops as they are now. Many things there are in the state of Bishops which the times have changed; many a parsonage at this day is larger than some ancient Bishoprics were; many an ancient Bishop poorer than at this day sundry under them in degree. The simple, hereupon lacking judgement and knowledge to discern between the nature of things which changeth not and these outward variable accidents, are made believe that a Bishop heretofore and now are things in their very nature so distinct that they cannot be judged the same. Yet to men that have any part of skill, what more evident and plain in Bishops, than that augmentation or diminution in their precincts, allowances, privileges, and such like, do make a difference indeed, but no essential difference between one Bishop and another? As for those things in regard whereof we use properly to term them Bishops, those things whereby they essentially differ from other pastors, those things which the natural definition of a Bishop must contain, what one of them is there more or less appliable unto Bishops now than of old ?

The name ' Bishop ' hath been borrowed from the Grecians, with whom it signifieth one which hath principal charge to guide and oversee others. The same word in Ecclesiastical writings being applied unto Church Governors, at the first unto all and not unto the chiefest only, grew in short time peculiar and proper to signify such Episcopal authority alone as the chiefest governors exercised over the rest. For with all names this is usual, that inasmuch as they are not given till the things whereunto they are given have been sometime first observed therefore generally things are ancienter than the names whereby they are called. . . .

But to let go the name, and come to the very nature of that thing which is thereby signified. In all kinds of regiment whether ecclesiastical or civil, as there are sundry operations public, so likewise great inequality there is in the same operations, some being of principal respect, and therefore not fit to be dealt in by everyone to whom public actions, and those of good importance, are notwithstanding well and fitly enough committed. From hence have grown those different degrees of magistrates or public persons even ecclesiastical as well as civil. Amongst ecclesiastical persons therefore Bishops being chief ones, a Bishop's function must be defined by that wherein his chiefty consisteth.

A Bishop is a minister of God, unto whom with permanent continuance there is given not only power of administering the Word and Sacraments, which power other Presbyters have, but also a further power to ordain ecclesiastical persons and a power of chiefty in government over Presbyters as well as Laymen a power to be by way of jurisdiction a Pastor even to Pastors themselves. So that this office, as he is a Presbyter or Pastor, consisteth in those things which are common unto him with other pastors, as in ministering the Word and Sacraments : but those things incident unto his office, which do properly make him a Bishop, cannot be common unto him with other Pastors.

Now even as pastors, so likewise Bishops being principal pastors, are either at large or else with restraint : at large, when the subject of their regiment is indefinite, and not tied to any certain place ; Bishops with restraint are they whose regiment over the Church is contained within some definite, local compass, beyond which compass their jurisdiction reacheth not. Such therefore we always mean when we speak of that regiment by Bishops which we hold a thing most lawful, divine, and holy in the Church of Christ.

In our present regiment by Bishops two things there are complained of, the one their great authority, and the other their great honour. Touching the authority of our Bishops, the first thing which therein displeaseth their adversaries is their superiority which Bishops have over other ministers.  They which cannot brook the superiority which Bishops have, do notwithstanding themselves admit that some kind of difference and inequality there may be lawfully amongst ministers. Inequality as touching gifts and graces they grant, because this is so plain that no mist in the world can be cast before men's eyes so thick, but that they needs must discern through it that one minister of the Gospel may be more learneder, holier, and wiser, better able to instruct, more apt to rule and guide them than another : unless thus much were confessed, those men should lose their fame and glory whom they themselves do entitle the lights and grand worthies of this present age. Again, a priority of order they deny not but that there may be, yea such a priority as maketh one man amongst many a principal actor in those things whereunto sundry of them must necessarily concur, so that the same be admitted only during the time of such actions and no longer ; that is to say, just so much superiority, and neither more nor less may be liked of, than it hath pleased them in their own kind of regiment to set down.  The inequality which they complain of is, " That one minister of the Word and Sacraments should have a permanent superiority above another, or in any sort a superiority of power mandatory, judicial, and coercive over other ministers."  By us on the contrary side, " Inequality, even such inequality as unto Bishops being ministers of the Word and Sacraments granteth a superiority permanent above ministers, yea a permanent superiority of power mandatory, judicial and coercive over them," is maintained a thing allowable, lawful and good. . . .

The first Bishops in the Church of Christ were His Blessed Apostles ; for the office whereunto Matthias was chosen the sacred history doth term ἐπισκοπὴν, an episcopal office.  Which being spoken expressly of one, agreeth no less unto them all than unto him.  For which cause St. Cyprian speaking generally of them all doth call them Bishops. They which were termed Apostles, as being sent of Christ to publish His Gospel throughout the world, and were named likewise Bishops, in that the care of government was also committed unto them, did no less perform the offices of their episcopal authority by governing, than of their apostolical by teaching.  The word ἐπισκοπή, expressing that part of their office which did consist in regiment, proveth not (I grant) their chiefty in regiment over others, because as then that name was common unto the function of their inferiors, and not peculiar unto theirs. But the history of their action showeth plainly enough how the thing itself which that name appropriated importeth, that is to say, even such spiritual chiefty as we have already defined to be properly episcopal, was in the holy Apostles of Christ.  Bishops therefore they were at large. . . .

For in process of time the Apostles gave episcopal authority, and that to continue always with them which had it. "We are able to number up them," saith Irenaeus, "who by the Apostles were made Bishops." In Rome he affirmeth that the Apostles themselves made Linus the first Bishop. Again of Polycarp he saith likewise, that the Apostles made him Bishop of the Church of Smyrna. Of Antioch they made Evodius Bishop, as Ignatius witnesseth, exhorting that Church to tread in his holy steps, and to follow his virtuous example.

The Apostles therefore were the first which had such authority, and all others who have it after them in orderly sort are their lawful successors, whether they succeed in any particular Church, where before them some Apostle hath been seated, as Simon succeeded James in Jerusalem; or else be otherwise endued with the same kind of Bishoply power, although it be not where any Apostle before hath been. For to succeed them, is after them to have that episcopal kind of power which was first given to them. "All Bishops are," saith Jerome, "the Apostles' successors." In like sort Cyprian doth term Bishops *Praepositos qui Apostolis vicaria ordinatione succedunt.* From hence it may haply seem to have grown that they whom we now call Bishops were usually termed at the first Apostles, and so did carry their very names in whose rooms of spiritual authority they succeeded.

Such as deny Apostles to have any successors at all in the office of their Apostleship may hold that opinion without contradiction to this of ours, if they well explain themselves in declaring what truly and properly Apostleship is. In some things every Presbyter, in some things only Bishops, in some things neither the one nor the other, are the Apostles' successors. The Apostles were sent as special chosen eyewitnesses of Jesus Christ, from Whom immediately they received their whole embassage and their commission to be the principal first founders of an House of God, consisting as well of Gentiles as of Jews. In this there are not after them any other like unto them; and yet the Apostles have now their successors upon earth, their true successors, if not in the largeness, surely in the kind of that episcopal function, whereby they had power to sit as spiritual ordinary judges, both over laity and over clergy where Churches Christian were established.

The Apostles of Our Lord did, according unto those directions which were given them from above, erect Churches in all such cities as received the Word of Truth, the Gospel of God. All Churches by them erected received from them the same Faith, the same Sacraments, the same form of public regiment. The form of regiment by them established at first was that the laity or people should be subject unto a college of ecclesiastical persons which were in every such city appointed for that purpose. These in their writings they term sometime Presbyters, sometime Bishops. . . .

That so the ancient Fathers did think of episcopal regiment; that they held this order as a thing received from the blessed Apostles themselves, and authorized even from heaven, we may perhaps more easily prove, than obtain that they all shall grant it who see it proved. St. Augustine setteth it down for a principle, that whatsoever positive order the whole Church everywhere doth observe, the same it must needs have received from the very Apostles themselves, unless perhaps some General Council were the authors of it. And he saw that the ruling superiority of Bishops was a thing universally established, not by the force of any Council (for Councils do all presuppose Bishops, nor can there any Council be named so ancient, either General, or as much as Provincial, sithence the Apostles' own times, but we can show that Bishops had their authority before it, and not from it). Wherefore St. Augustine, knowing this, could not choose but reverence the authority of Bishops as a thing to him apparently and most clearly Apostolical. . . .

Another argument that the regiment of Churches by one Bishop over many Presbyters hath been always held Apostolical may be this. We find that throughout all those cities where the Apostles did plant Christianity, the history of times hath noted succession of pastors in the seat of one, not of many (there being in every such Church evermore many pastors), and the first one in every rank of succession we find to have been, if not some Apostle, yet some Apostle's disciple. By Epiphanius the Bishops of Jerusalem are reckoned down from James to Hilarion then Bishop. Of them which boasted that they held the same things which they received of such as lived with the Apostles themselves, Tertullian speaketh after this sort: " Let them therefore shew the beginnings of their Churches, let them recite their Bishops one by one, each in such sort succeeding other, that the first Bishop of them hath had for his author and predecessor some Apostle, or at least some Apostolical person who persevered with the Apostles. For so Apostolical Churches are wont to bring forth the evidence of their estates. So doth the Church of Smyrna, having Polycarp whom John did consecrate." Catalogues of Bishops in a number of other Churches, Bishops, and succeeding one another from the very Apostles' times, are by Eusebius and Socrates collected; whereby it appeareth so clear, as nothing in the world more, that under them and by their appointment this order began, which maketh many Presbyters subject unto the regiment of some one Bishop. For as in Rome while the civil ordering of the commonwealth was jointly and equally in the hands of two consuls, historical records concerning them did evermore mention them both, and note which two as colleagues succeeded from time to time; so there is no doubt but Ecclesiastical Antiquity had done the very like, had not one pastor's place and calling been always so eminent above the rest in the same Church. . . .

Again, the power of ordaining both Deacons and Presbyters, the power to give the power of Order unto others, this also hath been always peculiar unto Bishops. It hath not been heard of that inferior Presbyters were ever authorized to ordain. And concerning Ordination, so great force and dignity it hath, that whereas Presbyters, by such power as they have received for Administration of the Sacraments, are able only to beget children unto God, Bishops having power to ordain, do by virtue thereof create fathers to the people of God, as Epiphanius fitly disputeth. There are which hold that between a Bishop and a Presbyter, touching power of Order, there is no difference. The reason of which conceit is, for that they see Presbyters no less than Bishops authorized to offer up the prayers of the Church, to preach the Gospel, to baptize, to administer the Holy Eucharist, but they considered not withal as they should, that the Presbyter's authority to do these things is derived from the Bishop which doth ordain him thereunto, so that even in those things which are common unto both, yet the power of the one is as it were a certain light borrowed from the other's lamp. The Apostles, being Bishops at large, ordained every-where Presbyters. Titus and Timothy having received Episcopal power as Apostolic ambassadors or legates, the one in Greece, the other in Ephesus, they both did by virtue thereof likewise ordain throughout all Churches Deacons and Presbyters within the circuits allotted unto them. As for Bishops by restraint, their power this way incommunicable unto Presbyters, which of the Ancients do not acknowledge?

## No. 151. RICHARD HOOKER

[From *The Laws of Ecclesiastical Polity*, Book VII, Chapter xxiii, § 11. *Works*, ed. J. Keble, Vol. III, pp. 300–302. Cp. note on No. 150.]

Now whereas against the present estate of Bishops and the greatness of their port and the largeness of their expenses at this day, there is not anything more commonly objected than those ancient Canons, whereby they are restrained unto a far more sparing life, their houses, their retinue, their diet limited within a far more narrow compass than is now kept; we must know that those laws and orders were made when Bishops lived of the same purse which served as well for a number of others as them, and yet all at their disposing. So that convenient it was to provide that there might be a moderate stint appointed to measure their expenses by, lest others should be injured by their wastefulness. Contrariwise there is now no cause wherefore any such law should be urged when Bishops live only of that which hath been peculiarly allotted unto them. They having therefore temporalities and other revenues to bestow for their own private use, according to that which their state requireth, and no other having with them any such common interest therein, their own discretion is to be their law for this matter ; neither are they to be pressed with the rigour of such ancient Canons as were framed for other times, much less so odiously to be upbraided with unconformity unto the pattern of Our Lord and Saviour's estate, in such circumstances as Himself did never mind to require that the rest of the world should of necessity be like Him. Thus against the wealth of the clergy they allege how meanly Christ Himself was provided for ; against Bishop's palaces, His want of a hole to hide His Head in ; against the service done unto them, that *He came to minister, not to be ministered unto in the world.* Which things, as they are not unfit to control covetous, proud, or ambitious desires of the ministers of Christ, and even of all Christians, whatsoever they be ; and to teach men contentment of mind, how mean soever their estate is, considering that they are but servants to Him Whose condition was far more abased than theirs is, or can be ; so to prove such difference in state between us and Him unlawful, they are of no force or strength at all. If one convented before their consistories, when he standeth to make his answer, should break out into invectives against their authority and tell them that Christ, when He was on earth, did not sit to judge, but stand to be judged, would they hereupon think it requisite to dissolve their eldership, and to permit no tribunals, no judges at all, for fear of swerving from Our Saviour's example ? If those men, who have nothing in their mouths more usual than the poverty of Jesus Christ and His Apostles, allege not this as Julian sometime did *beati pauperes* unto Christians, when his meaning was to spoil them of that they had ; our hope is then, that as they seriously and sincerely wish that Our Saviour Christ in this point may be followed, and to that end only propose His blessed example ; so at our hands again they will be content to hear with like willingness the holy Apostle's exhortation made unto them of the laity also, *Be ye followers of us, even as we are of Christ ; let us be your example, even as the Lord Jesus Christ is ours, that we may all proceed by one and the same rule.*

## No. 152.  JOHN DAVENANT

[From *Determinationes Quaestionum Quarundam Theologicarum*, Quaestio XLII (" Diversitas Graduum in Ministris Evangelicis Verbo Dei non repugnat "), Cambridge, 1634, pp. 187–193.   The translation is based upon that of Dr. Morris Fuller in his *Life, Letters, and Writings of John Davenant, D.D., 1572–1641, Lord Bishop of Salisbury* (1897), pp. 209–212 ; but many alterations and corrections have been made.   Davenant's Forty Nine *Determinationes*, which the author defended when Margaret Professor of Divinity at Cambridge, treat of a great variety of controverted subjects.]

Of Bishops there are three peculiar marks (*insignia propria*) by which they are readily distinguished from other presbyters and recognized as superior to them.

The first is that in cities, however large and populous, and wherein many Presbyters were created, the Apostles ordained one Bishop only, at whose decease another succeeded singly in the same see.  Hence that decree of the Council of Nicaea, " Let there not be two Bishops in one city." Hence Cornelius, Bishop of Rome, reproaches Novatus with ignorance for not acknowledging the singleness of Episcopal succession: "This vindicator of the Gospel is ignorant that there must be but one Bishop in that very Church in which he is not ignorant there are forty-six Presbyters, etc." If the Apostles had approved of a parity of all ministers, why should they have wanted one to be distinguished from all the rest by this singleness of succession? Jerome, one who is accounted but little favourable to the Episcopal dignity, nevertheless confesses that with this singleness of succession a singular eminence and dignity was conjoined. For thus he writes concerning the Bishop of Alexandria: "At Alexandria, from the Evangelist Mark down to the Bishops Heraclas and Dionysius, the Presbyters, when they had always elected one from themselves and placed him in a higher degree, named him Bishop." Upon this outstanding authority of a single Bishop in one city or diocese, the most wise and holy fathers saw that the external peace and unity of the Church depended, and of this they have left their testimony to us. Cyprian, a man altogether unmoved by pride and ambition, shows that this sacerdotal authority of one Bishop was confirmed by the Divine approval, and immediately adds, "For in very truth heresies and schisms have no other source but this, that no obedience is paid to the Bishop (*sacerdoti Dei*), nor is it considered that there is but one Bishop (*sacerdos*) at a time in a Church, and but one who judges in Christ's stead." Which words are most impudently wrested by the Romanists to establish the monarchy of the Pope, when it is clearer than the noon-day light that the blessed Martyr was speaking of himself and not of the Roman Pontiff. If, in the cause of Bishops, the testimony of a Bishop be suspicious, let us again hear St. Jerome, who was not wont unduly to depress Presbyters or to exalt Bishops. Thus speaks he against the Luciferians: "The safety of the Church depends on the dignity of the Chief Priest, to whom if a certain peculiar and eminent power be not granted by all, there will be formed in the Churches as many schisms as there are Priests." This very singleness of Episcopal succession, joined as it always is with a considerable extent of authority (*cum amplitudine quadam authoritatis*), is sufficient of itself to crush the modern error (*errorem nuper natum*) of the parity of all ministers.

But there follows a second mark of the dignity of Bishops, namely the right and power of Ordination, which was transmitted by the Apostles themselves to Bishops, but denied to inferior Presbyters. Both these things are clear from the consideration that we find that the Apostles sent Timothy and Titus to Churches in which there were many Presbyters, *viz.*, to Ephesus and Crete, that they might ordain Presbyters where there was need. *Lay hands suddenly on no man* is the admonition of Paul to Timothy who was endued with the power of Ordination. *For this cause left I thee in Crete, that thou shouldest set in order the things*

28

*that are wanting and ordain Presbyters in every city* are the words of the
same Apostle to Titus, with reference to the same subject. Why could
not the Ephesian Presbyters ordain others before Timothy's arrival?
Why was it not lawful for the ministers of Crete to do the like before
Titus came? No adequate reason for this can be given, unless the power
of ordaining resides in those alone who exercise Episcopal functions.
Jerome, whom some suppose to have agreed with Aerius, admits none
the less that Ordination is so characteristic of Bishops that it is not
lawful for Presbyters to exercise it. " What does a Bishop do, Ordination alone excepted, which a Presbyter does not ? " In this Apostolic
institution the Catholic Church has always acquiesced, and has recognized no other Ordination as lawful but that which was solemnized by
a lawful Bishop. We find a remarkable example of this in the works of
Athanasius. One Colluthus, a Presbyter in the Church of Alexandria,
presumed to ordain other Presbyters. But what was afterwards done to
them ? " This Ordination of his was rescinded, and all those made
Presbyters by him were reduced to the rank of laymen." It is certain,
therefore, that the power of ordaining belongs to the office of Bishops
only, and does not belong to inferior Presbyters,—which is a manifest
proof of Episcopal dignity and Presbyteral inferiority.

But here in passing we may resolve a doubt which was not omitted
even by the Schoolmen. For they were wont to raise the question
whether in addition to a Bishop, who by virtue of his office (*ex officio*)
dispenses Sacred Orders, anyone inferior to a Bishop can confer the
same in case of necessity ? To which I answer, Seeing that to confer
Holy Orders is by Apostolical institution an act of the Episcopal office,
if Presbyters in a well-constituted (*bene instituta*) Church do so, this
their act is not only unlawful but null and void (*irritum et inanem*).
For here obtains the axiom of Hugo, " What is performed contrary to
the institution is accounted null." But in a disturbed (*turbata*) Church,
wherein all the Bishops have fallen into heresy or idolatry, wherein they
refuse to ordain orthodox ministers, or wherein they account those alone
to be worthy of Holy Orders who participate in their error or faction,
if orthodox Presbyters be compelled to ordain other Presbyters that the
Church may not perish, I could not venture to pronounce Ordination
of this kind null and void. For if the danger that threatens a single
infant be sufficient to transfer to any layman the office of baptizing
which by institution belongs to Ministers alone, why is not the danger
impending over any particular Church sufficient to transfer to simple
Priests the office of ordaining which by institution belongs to Bishops
alone ? Necessity has aptly been termed " temporary law " (*lex
temporis*), and in such a case it defends what it requires. It is the
opinion of Armachanus [? of Richard Fitzralph] that if all the Bishops
had died, the lower Priests could then ordain ; and certainly the situation
is not dissimilar, when they have all proved to be sworn enemies to the

truth. For just as any commonwealth, so too any particular Church, has a certain extraordinary power for the necessary preservation of itself. If then certain Protestant Churches which could not look for Ordination from Popish Bishops have under this necessity ordained Presbyters with the consent of their own Presbyters, they are not on that account to be judged as having injured the Episcopal dignity, but to have yielded to their Church's necessity.

There remains the last mark of Episcopal dignity which raises [Bishops] above Presbyters,—a mark which utterly forbids them to be accounted their equals in status. This is their power of jurisdiction not only over the laity, but over the clergy, who are also by Apostolical institution subject to Bishops. It is a saying both true and common that "Equal hath not power over equal." But Bishops have power over the clergy; not indeed a Regal (*Regale*) or Lordly (*Herile*) power, but a Pastoral (*Pastorale*) or Paternal (*Paternale*) power,—one such as is inconsistent with any kind of parity or equality. To say nothing of other powers, excommunication, which is the spiritual staff, is delivered into the Bishop's hand so that he may chastise not only the vicious or contumacious of the laity, but also Presbyters that deserve this censure. This is very evident from the Epistles to Timothy and Titus, one of whom was constituted by St. Paul Bishop of the Church of Ephesus, and the other of the Church of Crete. They are commanded to charge certain [Presbyters] not to preach strange doctrines, to stop the mouths of deceivers, to reject heretics, and to do other things of that kind implying jurisdiction and authority. The same is also evident from the language of Christ Himself to the Angels of the Asiatic Churches. The Angel, that is, the Bishop, of the Church of Pergamos is reproved because he had in his Church some who held the doctrine of the Nicolaitans; so likewise the Angel of the Church of Thyatira, because he permitted the woman Jezebel to teach and seduce the people. Therefore, in the judgement of Christ Himself, the Bishop hath authority to restrain heretics and to cast them out of the Church.

I do not say that a Bishop was accustomed to do this without the counsel of his Presbyters; for what Cyprian declares of himself,—that "from the beginning of his episcopate he had determined to do nothing of his own private opinion without advice,"—was probably observed also by other pious Bishops. But it is none the less manifest that the censure proceeded from the Episcopal authority alone, and passed as an act of Episcopal jurisdiction upon the offenders. For excommunication is termed "the Episcopal Sword." In the case of excommunication, there was an appeal from the Bishop's judgement to a Synod, and this confirmed the Bishop's censure if it had been rightly pronounced, or rescinded it if otherwise. Therefore in the act of excommunication, neither the people nor the Presbyters are the acknowledged judges, but the Bishop alone. That this was the discipline of the Primitive Church can be made clear from ancient Councils. Let the Council of Nice, canon 5, of Antioch, canon 6, of Sardica, canon 14, be examined. Nay, Jerome himself does not doubt that the power of excommunicating Presbyters belongs to the Bishops. Hence he writes thus to Riparius concerning Vigilantius, an heretical Presbyter : " I wonder that the holy Bishop in whose diocese he is said to be a Presbyter sits quiet at the frenzy of the man, and does not break this unprofitable vessel with the Apostolical and iron rod, and deliver him to the destruction of the flesh, that his spirit may be saved." These things shew clearly enough that from the times of the very Apostles, Bishops were superior in power and degree to Presbyters, and that a parity among ministers of the Gospel never obtained.

## No. 153. JOHN COSIN

[From a Sermon at the Consecration of Dr. Francis White to the See of Carlisle. *Works*, ed. *L. A. C. T.*, Vol. I, pp. 94–101. This sermon, on *John* xx, 21, 22, was preached on Advent Sunday (December 3) 1626 at Durham House Chapel in London, where the Consecration took place.]

The Apostles then were sent, as all other Bishops and Priests are. What commission have they with them ? For at large they are not sent, either to teach and to govern as they list themselves, but they have a *sicut* and a *sic* with them to keep all right. *As My Father sent Me, so send I you.*

We demand then, How was Christ sent ? And He was sent for two ends. The first, to be the Redeemer of our souls and to reconcile God unto men, which He did by His death ; the second, to be the Bishop of our souls, and to reconcile men unto God, which He did by leaving us a Gospel, His life and doctrine, in a Church behind Him. In the first sense the Apostles were not sent, they were to be no redeemers nor mediators neither. For it cost more to redeem men's souls, and both they and their successors must let that *sicut* alone for ever. And yet there is a *sicut similitudinis* in it for all that, though there be no *sicut aequalitatis* ; there is some likeness in their sendings this way. He, sent by His Father to be a Mediator for mankind, and to reconcile the world by His death and sacrifice upon the cross ; they, sent by Him, to mediate and to pray for the people, to be ministers of the reconciliation, as St. Paul speaks, and in a manner, to be sacrificers too, representers at the Altar here, and appliers of the Sacrifice once made for all ; without which last act, the first will do us no good.

But then in the second sense more properly. And here the *sicut* runs many ways ; we will choose them only which are the chief, and for which the Scripture is plain, Christ was of purpose sent.

First then, Christ was sent to preach the Gospel to the poor ; and of the same errand are His Apostles and Bishops sent, *Go ye and teach all nations.* The Priests' office not so large, who preach too, but yet under the Bishop's licence only ; they then to be the great pastors of the Diocese, and we [Priests] but as servants and substitutes under them, to preach by their commission and not by our own. For by virtue of our Orders we are only put to offer up the prayers and sacrifices of the Church, to administer the Sacraments, to bind and to loose, and not to preach " unless we be thereunto appointed," says the Book. And indeed, so went the old Canons and the Stories of the ancient Church. For Canons, I name the Sixth in Trullo and the Decree of Damasus the Pope, one whom St. Jerome made much esteem of, that otherwhiles presbyters were not to preach at all, as Balsamon there observes of them in Alexandria. For Stories, I name Sozomen, and Nicephorus, and St. Chrysostom himself, that was much troubled about it, and would fain have given over preaching (as in his Second Homily upon Esay), when he saw the Bishop come into the Church, he being then but a Priest. Good men ; they thought priests had a deal to do besides, to say their hours, to sing their service, to visit the sick, to reconcile penitents, and not to preach so much, though they neglected not this neither. But then it was when the Bishop set them a-work, when he was otherwise employed and could not so often attend it ; for there must be preaching howsoever. I would not be mistaken, I come not here to preach down preaching ; but this I wonder at, that preaching now-a-days should be counted our only office, as if we had nothing else to do, and an office independent too, as if we were all Bishops when we preach. But let them preach, they have licence perhaps to do it.

Then would both Bishops and they be put in mind of a second *sicut* here, that we may keep us to the text. For secondly, Christ was sent, as the Scripture many times tells us, not to preach His Own Will, but His Father's ; *As My Father said unto Me, so I speak.* Nor were the Apostles sent to preach what they would themselves, but whatsoever Christ had commanded them ; that they, which preach as voluntary as the organ plays, or the sudden motions of a spirit, as their fancy leads them, that call it speaking by the spirit when never a wise word is spoken, and they which preach us up new doctrines, or a new faith, which was never heard on since the world began afore, may go seek some other commission to make good what they do, for from Christ here have they none.

Christ was sent to preach a law, as we read in the Second Psalm : *I will preach the law whereof the Lord spake unto Me* ; and they that are sent by Him are sent to make men observe a law and to do what He hath commanded. If we love not to hear of a law,—of a working and a doing religion,—we must go to some other Church, for in Christ's Church men are to preach us a law, set us somewhat to do, and hold us or keep us in with a law ; that they now which preach us all Gospel and put no law among it, Bishops and Priests that will tell the people all is well if they can but say their Catechism and hear Sermons, make them believe that there is nothing to be done more but to believe and so be saved, these men, they preach by some other pattern sure ; for Christ, He is sent not to preach down the old law so much as to preach up a new.   Now to make men observe and do what the Church teaches them is, or should be, in the Bishop's hands.   We suffer scandal from them of the Church of Rome in many things ; in nothing more than this, that we are sent to preach sermons to the people, as men that had some pretty commodities to sell them which, if they liked, they might buy and use ; if not, they might let them alone ; that we talk of devotion but live like the careless ; that we have a service, but no servants at it ; that we have Churches but keep them not like the Houses of God ; that we have the Sacraments, but few to frequent them ; Confession but few to practise it ; finally, that we have all religious duties (for they cannot deny it), but seldom observed ; all good laws and Canons of the Church, but few or none kept ; the people are made to do nothing ; the old discipline is neglected, and men do what they list.   It should be otherwise, and our Church intends it otherwise. Enough to free her from slander, let them condemn them that will not obey her ; but enough to free her, and to stir up men, specially them whom it concerns, to make others active, for therefore are they sent, even as Christ also was.

And to make this take the better effect we say, fourthly, that Christ was sent to preach by His Own Life, and to give an example to others, *exemplum dedi vobis*, which is the best kind of preaching, when all is done ; that they which stand like idols and statues, to point out the way to others, and yet stir not themselves to lead the way, they are by this very mark known to be none of Christ's ambassadors.

And now I come to another *sicut* ; *sicut oves* saith Christ, *Behold I send you as sheep among wolves.   As sheep among wolves?*   Now above all other *sicuts* let us have none of that.   For will the comparison hold here too, trow we ?   Yes, Christ was sent so Himself, *sicut ovis* saith the Prophet, as a sheep to the slaughter, and *sicut agnus inter lupos*, as a lamb among the wolves.   A lesson this which my lord Bishop of Rome hath, it seems, long ago forgot ; for he has turned the text now quite another way and made it run backwards.   *Sicut lupus inter agnos* comes he, like a wolf among the sheep that is ready to devour them, and like a lion among the lambs that is greedy of his prey.   Christ came not so, and the Apostles came not so.   I wonder of whose sending he should be that comes after this manner.

But if the Pope on the one side has forgotten how St. Peter was sent, there are the common people on the other side that will remember it well enough, how he and all the rest were sent ; and they mean, it seems, to take an order for it that their successors shall never be sent otherwise, never but as sheep among wolves. Let us be sheep and they will be sure to be wolves, keen enough to prey upon the Church and to prey upon Churchmen too, leave them by their good will neither goods nor good name behind them. We know the world has studied this text well; and though they keep never a saying of Christ's besides, yet will they be sure to keep this. Since Christ has said it, they will take Him at His Word; we shall be sheep still, and they will be wolves. Christ told the clergy that they were the salt of the earth, and the world has taken Him; because He has said it, it shall be made good. Account made of us as of salt indeed? a poor contemptible thing, salt, ye may buy enough of it for a farthing. This is their jest; but as contemptible as it is, ye can savour nothing without it, and this is our answer. But what do I pleading for account, or for any good words from the world, whenas Christ here has bidden us to look for none beforehand? Not but that we should have them, but because we are never like to have them. Men speak well of their clergy? No. There is a saying of His which spoiled that long ago, *They shall speak all manner of evil against you*: and so they do. I know no saying in all the Bible studied better than this. But since Christ was willing to bear it, we must be content to endure it too. In the meanwhile we would desire all men to remember Whose ambassadors they are that are thus used; assuring them that any, the least injury done to them, reflects upon Christ their Lord and Master.

Who, to make them amends for this, hath not sent them without another *sicut*, a *sicut* of honour and dignity, whereas He sent them to be the ambassadors of God and the dispensers of His sacred mysteries. This shall be the last. In Priests this to consecrate the Sacrament and to meddle with the keys; but I meddle not with them, as being not proper for the day. In Bishops (*opus diei*) to send, ordain, and govern others, as He sent and governed them. For it was the High-Priest of old and not the Presbytery; it is the Bishop now and not the Vestry-man, nor the Priest neither, that hath authority to put into the Priest-hood or to give any Orders at all. It is the full consent of reverend Antiquity to distinguish the ministers of the Gospel into three degrees, answerable to the triple order under the Law, as servants to the same Trinity, the God both of Law and Gospel. There are Bishops, successors to the Apostles, answerable to the High-Priest; Presbyters succeeding the seventy disciples, answerable to the Priests; and Deacons, instituted by the Apostles, answerable to the Levites. I gather then, that as the putting into the Priest's office was *penes Ponti-ficem*, in the High-Priest's power alone, so the Consecration of Bishops, the Ordination of Priests and Deacons, and the putting of them into office or place within the Church, was, and is, in the authority and jurisdiction of Bishops only, who are the height and the princes of the clergy, as Optatus said, and said it from Ignatius, the oldest Father that is, and St. John's own scholar. If Fathers would do it, we could bring two juries of them; but this place is clear, and St. Paul is clear, what need we any more witnesses? *Propter hanc causam, for this cause*, saith St. Paul to Titus, *have I set thee in Crete* (not anybody else) *that thou shouldest ordain Presbyters.* Neither is there any one example to be found in all the Stories of the Church of any Holy Orders that were ever given but by a Bishop. I will shew you all that may be found. There was an old Arian heretic, they called him Ischyras, a fellow suborned by a faction to accuse Athanasius in the great Council of Nice, and he was ordained a priest indeed by Colluthus, an imaginary Bishop; but because it was afterwards proved that the one was no Bishop, the Council concluded that the other was no Priest, and so put them both off with contempt and scorn. This was one. There is but another example to be had, and it is out of the Second Council of Seville, where the Priest takes upon him to give Orders like a Bishop. You shall see what came of it. The Priest dies presently, or they had met with them; and his imaginary clergy-men were by that Council turned back again to their lay-brethren with shame enough.

Yet starts me up Aerius, and he would have Bishops and Priests to be all one, held for so holding as little better than mad; but ye should have given him a Bishopric, saith St. Austin, and then the heretic would have been quiet. Forsooth, Bishops and Priests had otherwhiles been both one name; so had Bishops and Angels too, were they therefore both one order? I may call the Bishop a Priest when he consecrates the Sacrament, and the Priest a Bishop when he looks to his charge; but what makes this to the power of Ordination? *Cum de re constat, qui fit de nomine pugna?* Let the Priests submit themselves then, saith St. Ignatius, it is none of theirs; they were not sent for this purpose.

And if not they, much less the consistory, and the verdict of the vestry, to whom they say the Spirit is lately gone, and departed from the whole Church besides. But I will not here vouchsafe to confute them, not to name them, more than that they are a tumultuous faction, and despise dominions, and speak evil of dignities; and that we own them not.

To the Bishops' power of Ordaining, then, add their power of setting Church matters in order by virtue of St. Paul's *ordinabo cetera*; their votes in council, by virtue of that in the *Acts*; their power to correct, deprive, suspend, excommunicate, and stop the mouths of offenders, specially of those that speak perverse things and draw disciples after them, by virtue of the Apostle's charge to Timothy; and then you have their full commission with all the *sicuts* and extents of it, drawn up at large. And now it wants nothing but the seal, which we will set to with expedition, and make an end.

It follows then, *When He had spoken these words He breathed on them and said, Receive the Holy Ghost.*

## No. 154. JOHN GAUDEN

[From *Hieraspistes, A Defence by Way of Apology for the Ministry and Ministers of the Church of England, humbly presented to the Consciences of all those that excel in Virtue*, London, 1653, pp. 273–276. Gauden published two treatises on the Christian Ministry in the year 1653; the other one was entitled *The Case of Ministers' Maintenance by Tithes (as in England) plainly discussed in Conscience and Prudence.* Neither of them has been reprinted.]

If any man ask me then what kind of Bishop I would have, I answer, Such an one for age, as may be a Father; for wisdom, a Senator; for gravity, a Stoic; for light, an Angel; for innocency, a Saint; for industry, a Labourer; for constancy, a Confessor; for zeal, a Martyr; for charity, a Brother; for humility, a Servant to all the faithful ministers and other Christians under his charge. I would have him venerable for those several excellencies which are most remarkable in the ancient and most imitable Bishops,—the devotion of St. Gregory, the indefatigableness of St. Austin, the courage of St. Ambrose, the learning of Nazianzen, the generosity of Basil, the eloquence of Chrysostom, the gentleness of Cyprian, the holy flames of Ignatius, the invincible constancy of Polycarp,—that so he may come nearest to the Apostolical pattern, and resemble the most of any Christian or minister the grace and glory of Our Lord Jesus Christ. I would have him (yet not I, but the vote of all pious Antiquity requires a Bishop) to be among men the most moral; among Christians the most faithful; among preachers, the most painful; among orators, the most persuasive; among governors, the most moderate; among devotionaries, the most fervent; among professors, the most forward; among practicers, the most exact; among sufferers, the most patient; among perseverants, the most constant. He should be as the Holy of Holies was, both to the inward court of those that are truly sanctified and converted; and to the outward court of those that are called Christians only in visible profession. I would have nothing in him that is justly to be blamed or sinisterly suspected, and all things that are most deservedly commended by wise and sober Christians. I would have a Bishop of all men the most complete, as having on him the greatest care, that of the Church and of souls; and this in a more public and eminent inspection, as one daily remembering the strictness of God's account and expecting either a most glorious crown or a most grievous curse to all eternity.

I would have him most deserve and most able to use well, but yet least esteeming, coveting, or ambitionating, the riches, pomp, glory, and honour of the world. One that knows how to own himself in persecution as well as in prosperity, and dares to do his duty as a Bishop in both estates. I do not much consider the secular parade and equipage, further than as public encouragements of merit, as excitations to excel, as noble rewards of learning, and as extern decencies or solemnities which do much set off and embroider authority in the sight of the vulgar. I wish him duly chosen with judgement, accepting with modesty, esteemed with honour, reverenced with love, overseeing with vigilance, ruling with joint-counsel, not levelled with younger preachers and novices, not too much exalted above the graver and elder presbyters; neither despised of the one nor despising of the other. I wish him an honourable competency, if it may be had, with his eminency, that he may have wherewith to exercise a large heart and a liberal hand, which everywhere carry respect and conciliate love. If this cannot be had, yet I wish him that in true worth which is denied him in wealth; that his virtue and piety may still preserve the authority of his place, and this in the order, peace, and dignity of the Church; that he may be the touchstone of truth, the loadstone of love, the standard of faith, the pattern of holiness, the pillar of stability, and the centre of unity in the Church.

Nor are these to be esteemed as characters of an Eutopian Prelate, only to be had in the abstract of fancy and speculation. Many such Bishops have been anciently in the Church and not a few here in England. Some still are such in their merits amidst their ruins and obscurings, and more might constantly and easily be supplied to the Church's good order, peace, and honour,—if reason and not passion, religion and not superstition, judgement and not prejudice, calmness and not fierceness, learning and not idiotism, gravity and not giddiness, wisdom and not vulgarity, prudence and not precipitancy, impartial antiquity and not interested novelty, may be the judge of true Episcopacy.

I think nothing further from a true Bishop than idleness set off with pomp, than ignorance decked with solemnity, than pride blazoned with power, than covetousness gilded with empire, than sordidness smothered with state, than vanity dressed up with great formalities. Bishops should not be like blazing comets in their dioceses, having more of distance, terror, and pernicious influence than of light or celestial virtue. But rather, as fixed stars of the prime magnitude, shining most usefully and remarkably in the Church, during this night of Christ's absence, Who is the only Sun for His light and Spouse for His love to the Church. Yet hath He appointed some proxies to woo for Him, and messengers to convey love-tokens from Him, among whom the holy Bishops of the Church were ever accounted as the chiefest Fathers next the Apostles, when they were indeed such as evil men most feared, good men most loved, schismatics most envied, and heretics most hated. Right Episcopacy is so great an advantage to the Church's happiness and so unblamable in its due constitution and exercise, that it is no small blemish to any godly man's judgement not to approve it; and nothing (as to imprudence) is I think more blameworthy than not to desire, esteem, love, and honour it. Since such Prelature is as lawful as it is useful, and it is as useful as either reason or religion, polity or piety can propound in any thing of that nature which, if not absolutely necessary, yet certainly most convenient for the Church, and commendable in the Church, (so far as it stands in a visible polity and society,) being no way either sinful in itself or contrary to any positive law of God, any more than it is for Christians in civil government to have mayors in their cities, colonels in their armies, masters in their colleges, wardens in their fraternities, captains or pilots in their ships, or fathers in their families.

Nor is indeed the venerable face of true Episcopacy so deformed by some man's late ridiculous dresses and disguises, but that wise and learned men still see the many reverend and excellent lineaments of it, not only of pious and prime antiquity, but of beauty, order, symmetry, and benefit, such as flow from both human and Divine wisdom. If popular contempt and prejudices in some of the vulgar be any measure of things, or any argument against anything in religion or in the Church of Christ, it will serve as well to vilify and nullify all presbytery and all ministry, as all Episcopacy. Indeed, neither of them can preserve their honour, use, and comeliness, if they exceed their proportions, and either dash against or encroach upon each other,—contrary to those bounds and methods which primitive wisdom observed between power and counsel, order and authority, community and unity. It is very probable that a few years' experience of the want of good Bishops will so reconcile the minds of sober and impartial Christians to them, that few will be against them, save only such who think the best security for some of their estates to be the utter exploding and perpetual extirpation of Episcopacy,—a thing which one of the wisest of mortals so much abhorred and for which he was able to give so good an account in reason, piety, and true polity, that it appears to have been not pertinacity and interest, but judgement and conscience that so long sustained that unhappy controversy which I have no mind to revive, but only, if possible, to reconcile, which is no hard matter where clear truths meet with moderate affections and peaceable inclinations. For I find by the proportion of all polity and order, that if Episcopal eminency be not the main weight and carriage of ecclesiastical government, yet it is as the axis or wheel which puts the whole frame of Church society and communion into a fit order and aptitude for motion, especially in greater associations of Christians which make the most firm and best constituted Churches.

This being then the true figure of a learned, grave, godly, and industrious Bishop, there need not more be said to redeem episcopacy from prejudices; or to assert it against those trivial objections which are not with truth and judgement, so much as with spite and partiality made against it.

## No. 155. KING CHARLES I

[From *The King's Majesty's Answer to the Paper Delivered in by the Reverend Divines Attending the Honorable Commissioners Concerning Church Government.* London, October 12th, 1648, pp. 3 f. On October 2, 1648, Charles I had presented to the Parliamentary Divines at Newport *His Majesty's Reason Why He Cannot in Conscience consent to Abolish the Episcopal Government.* The Divines had delivered their *Answer* in writing to the King on the following day; and the above treatise was the King's reply.]

For the name *Episcopus* or Bishop, His Majesty hath long since learnt from those that are skilful in the Greek tongue that it imports properly no more than an 'overseer,' one that hath the charge or inspection of something committed unto him, as he that is set to watch a beacon or to keep sheep. Whence in the New Testament and in the ecclesiastical use, it is applied to such persons as have the care and inspection of the Churches of Christ committed unto them *in spiritualibus*; as both Bishops and Presbyters have in some sort, but with this difference,—that mere Presbyters are *Episcopi gregis* only, they have the oversight of the flock in the duties of preaching, Administration of the Sacraments, Public Prayer, exhorting, rebuking, etc.; but Bishops are *Episcopi gregis et pastorum* within their several precincts in the acts of external government. So that the common work of both functions is the Ministry of the Gospel. But that which is peculiar to the function of Bishops as distinguished from Presbyters is Church Government. It is not therefore to be wondered if it should happen in the New Testament the word *Episcopus* to be usually applied unto Presbyters, who were indeed overseers of the flock, rather than unto Church Government, who had then a title of greater eminency whereby to distinguish them from ordinary Presbyters,—to wit, that of 'Apostles.' But when the government of Churches came into the hands of their successors, the names were by common usage (which is the best master of words) very soon appropriated, that of *Episcopus* to the Ecclesiastical Government or Bishop of a Diocese, and that of Presbyter to the ordinary Minister or Priests.

His Majesty hath rather cause to wonder that upon such premises you should [conclude] with so much confidence as if the point were rendered most clear to the judgement of most men, both ancient and of latter times, that there is no such officer to be found in the Scriptures of the New Testament as a Bishop distinct from a Presbyter, when as His Majesty remembereth to have seen cited by such authors as he hath no reason to suspect, both out of the Ancient Fathers and Councils, and out of sundry modern writers even of these Reformed Churches that want Bishops, great variety of testimonies to the contrary.

# (3) PRIESTHOOD

## No. 156.  RICHARD HOOKER

[From *The Laws of Ecclesiastical Polity*, Book V, Chapter lxxiii, §§ 2, 3.  *Works*, ed. J. Keble, Vol. II, pp. 471–473.  Cp. note on No. **148**.]

SEEING then that Sacrifice is now no part of the Church Ministry how should the name of Priesthood be thereunto rightly applied ? Surely even as St. Paul applieth the name of Flesh unto that very substance of fishes which hath a proportionable correspondence to flesh, although it be in nature another thing.  Whereupon when philosophers will speak warily, they make a difference between flesh in one sort of living creatures and that other substance in the rest which hath but a kind of analogy to flesh : the Apostle contrariwise having matter of greater importance whereof to speak nameth indifferently both flesh.  The Fathers of the Church of Christ with like security of speech call usually the ministry of the Gospel *Priesthood* in regard of that which the Gospel hath *proportionable* to ancient sacrifices, namely the Communion of the blessed Body and Blood of Christ, although it have properly now no sacrifice.  As for the people when they hear the name it draweth no more *their minds* to any cogitation of sacrifice, than the name of a senator or of an alderman causeth them to think upon old age or to imagine that every one so termed must needs be ancient because years were respected in the first nomination of both.

Wherefore to pass by the name, let them use what dialect they will, whether we call it a Priesthood, a Presbytership, or a Ministry it skilleth not : Although in truth the word *Presbyter* doth seem more fit, and in propriety of speech more agreeable than *Priest* with the drift of the whole Gospel of Jesus Christ.  For what are they that embrace the Gospel but sons of God ?  What are Churches but His families ? Seeing therefore we receive the adoption and state of sons by their ministry whom God hath chosen out for that purpose, seeing also that when we are the sons of God, our continuance is still under their care which were our progenitors, what better title could there be given them than the reverend name of *Presbyters* or fatherly guides ?  The Holy Ghost throughout the body of the New Testament making so much mention of them doth not any where call them Priests.  The prophet Esay I grant doth ; but in such sort as the ancient Fathers, by way of analogy. A Presbyter according to the proper meaning of the New Testament is "he unto whom Our Saviour Christ hath communicated the power of spiritual procreation." Out of twelve patriarchs issued the whole multitude of Israel according to the flesh. And according to the mystery of heavenly birth our Lord's Apostles we all acknowledge to be the patriarchs of His whole Church. St. John therefore beheld sitting about the throne of God in heaven four and twenty Presbyters, the one half fathers of the Old, the other of the New Jerusalem. In which respect the Apostles likewise gave themselves the same title, albeit that name were not proper but common unto them with others.

## No. 157.  JOSEPH MEDE

[From *Diatribae. Discourses on Divers Texts of Scripture, Delivered upon several Occasions.* Book I, No. 5 (on 1 *Cor.* iv, 1).  *Works*, ed. J. Worthington (1672), p. 27. Cp. note on No. **149**.]

I come now to a second assertion which is, that howsoever any ecclesiastical person may be rightly called a Minister (so it be in a proper relation to Godward), yet the word Minister is again most unfitly used by us for a name of distinction of one ecclesiastical order from another; as when we call them which are Presbyters, Ministers by way of distinction from Deacons; for so we speak Ministers and Deacons, instead of Priests and Deacons. The reason we thus speak is to avoid the name Priest, which we conceive to signify *Sacerdos*, that is, one that sacrificeth, such as were those in the Law; but our curates of holy things in the Gospel are not to offer Sacrifice, and therefore ought not to be called *Sacerdotes*, and consequently not Priests. This is the reason.  But if it be well examined, "Priest" is the English of "Presbyter" and not of "*Sacerdos*," there being in our tongue no word in use for *Sacerdos*,—"Priest," which we use for both, being improperly used for a Sacrificer, but naturally expressing a Presbyter, the name whereby the Apostles call both themselves and those which succeed them in their charge.  For who can deny that our word Priest is corrupted of Presbyter?  Our ancestors the Saxons first used *Preoster*, whence, by a farther contraction, came *Preste* and *Priest*.  The High and Low Dutch have *Priester*, the French *Prestre*, the Italian *Prete*; but the Spaniard only speaks full *Presbytero*.

# (4) THE APOSTOLICAL SUCCESSION

## No. 158.  JOHN OVERALL

[From *The Convocation Book of 1606*, usually known as *Bishop Overall's Convocation Book Concerning the Government of God's Catholic Church and the Kingdoms of the Whole World*.  Ed. *L. A. C. T.*, pp. 147 f.   Cp. note on No. **61**.]

FURTHERMORE, it is most apparent by the testimonies of all Antiquity, Fathers, and Ecclesiastical Histories, that all the Churches in Christendom that were planted and governed by the Apostles, and by such their coadjutors, apostolical persons, as unto whom the Apostles had to that end fully communicated their apostolical authority, did think that after the death, either of any of the Apostles, which ruled amongst them, or of any other the said Bishops ordained by them, it was the meaning of the Holy Ghost, testified sufficiently by the practice of the Apostles, that the same order and form of ecclesiastical government should continue in the Church 'for ever.  And therefore upon the death of any of them, either Apostles or Bishops, they, the said Churches, did always supply their places with others the most worthy and eminent persons amongst them ; who, with the like power and authority that their predecessors had, did ever succeed them.  Insomuch as in every city and episcopal see, where there were divers priests and ministers of the Word and Sacraments and but one Bishop only, the catalogues of the names, not of their Priests but of their Bishops, were very carefully kept from time to time, together with the names of the Apostles or Apostolical persons, the Bishops their predecessors, from whom they derived their succession.  Of which succession of Bishops, whilst the succession of truth continued with it, the ancient Fathers made great account and use when any false teachers did broach new doctrine, as if they had received the same from the Apostles ; choking them with this, that they were not able to shew any Apostolical Church that ever taught as they did.   Upon such an occasion Irenaeus, Bishop of Lyons, within seventy-five years, or thereabout, after St. John's death, doth write in this sort : *Habemus annumerare eos, qui ab Apostolis instituti sunt episcopi in ecclesiis, et successores eorum usque ad nos, qui nihil tale docuerunt, neque cognoverunt, quale ab his deliratur.*   And so likewise, not long after him, Tertullian, to oppress some who, as it seemeth, drew companies after them, saith thus : *Edant origines ecclesiarum suarum ; evolvant ordinem episcoporum suorum, ita per successiones ab initio decurrentem, ut primus ille episcopus aliquem ex Apostolis, aut apostolicis viris, qui tamen cum Apostolis perseveraverit, habuerit autorem et antecessorem ; hoc enim modo Ecclesiae Catholicae sensus suos deferunt.*   And St. Augustine, *Radix Christianae societatis per sedes Apostolorum et successores episcoporum certa per orbem propagatione diffunditur.*

### No. 159.   WILLIAM BEVERIDGE

[From *Sermons.* " The True Nature of the Christian Church, the Office of its Ministers, and the Means of Grace Administered by them, Explained in Twelve Sermons.  Sermon I [on] *Christ's Presence with His Ministers." Works,* ed. *L. A. C. T.,* Vol. I, pp. 10–12, 16 f., 23 f.   The text of this sermon was *Matt.* xxviii, 20.]

Hence the Apostles, being thus ordained and instructed by Our Lord, took special care to transfer the same Spirit to others which they had received from Him.   But this they could not do after the same manner as Christ had done it to them, even by breathing upon them : for that way was peculiar to Christ, from Whom the Spirit proceedeth. Wherefore, they being doubtless directed thereto by the same Spirit, transmitted it to others by laying their hands upon them, which was the old way that had been used in the Church before : for so Moses communicated the Spirit of Wisdom to Joshua, thereby constituting him his successor in the government of Israel, even by laying his hands upon him, *Deut.* xxxiv, 9.   Thus Paul and Barnabas were ordained by the special appointment of the Holy Ghost Himself, *Acts* xiii, 3 ; for it is said that they, having *fasted and prayed, laid their hands upon them,* and so sent them out,—who, thereupon, are said in the next verse to be sent by the Holy Ghost, it being now conferred upon them by the imposition of hands.   Thus St. Paul communicated χάρισμα τοῦ θεοῦ, as he calls it, the gift of the Spirit, unto Timothy, *II Tim.* i, 6.   And wheresoever we read that the Apostles ordained any, they still did it after this manner, even by laying their hands upon them : and that too, whether they ordained them into their whole office, or else into any part of it.   For the whole care of the Church being committed unto them, they had power to constitute what officers they thought fit under them.   But still they did it by laying their hands upon them, and so communicating of the same Spirit unto them, Which they had received from Christ. As when they found it necessary to have Deacons in the Church, to take care of the widows, they ordained them by laying their hands upon them, *Acts* vi, 6, thereby transferring so much of the Spirit upon them as was necessary for that office.   And when they afterwards saw it very necessary that there should be other officers in the Church, which we now call Presbyters, that should have power under them to preach the Gospel and administer the Sacraments in places where they themselves could not be always present, upon these also they laid their hands, and by that means communicated so much of the Spirit unto them as was necessary for the due and effectual execution of the said office.

Thus therefore it is that the Apostolical Office hath been handed down from one to another ever since the Apostles' days to our time, and so will be to the end of the world, Christ Himself being continually present at such imposition of hands ; thereby transferring the same Spirit, which He had first breathed into His Apostles, upon others successively after them, as really as He was present with the Apostles themselves, when He first breathed it into them. Insomuch, that they who are thus ordained are said to be made Bishops by the Holy Ghost Himself, as well as the Apostles were, *Acts* xx, 28. By which means the Holy Catholic Church always hath been, and still is, truly Apostolical, as it is called in the Nicene Creed. And the several parts of the Apostolical Office are now as effectually performed by their successors, and others ordained under them, as they were while the Apostles themselves lived. For it was not the persons of the Apostles but their Office, influenced and assisted by the Spirit of God, that made the Sacraments they administered to be valid, and their preaching the Gospel so prevalent upon those that heard it. Though Paul himself planted, and Apollos watered, it was God only that gave the increase.

And so it is to this day. All the efficacy that there is or can be in the administration of any ecclesiastical office depends altogether upon the Spirit of God going along with the office, and assisting at the execution of it. Without which, the Sacraments we administer would be but empty signs and our preaching no more than beating of the air. Where-as, on the other side, Christ, according to His promise, being always present by His Holy Spirit at the administration of the several offices which He has ordained in His Church, they can never fail of their designed effect, if the persons to whom they are administered be but rightly disposed and qualified for it. By this means, they that are duly baptized are *born again, not only of water, but of the Spirit also (John* iii, 5) ; and so together with the *washing of regeneration, they have the renewing of the Holy Ghost (Tit.* iii, 5). Hence also, in the Sacrament of the Lord's Supper, the worthy receiver does really by faith partake of the mystical Body and Blood of Christ and of such influences of the Holy Spirit as shall enable him to walk as becomes a member of Christ. And whensoever we read, preach, or publish the Gospel as Christ taught it, the Holy Spirit goes along with it, so that it becomes the power of God unto salvation to every one that believeth. And seeing Our Lord thus continually accompanies the Apostles and their successors, so as to vouchsafe His Spirit to those on whom they lay their hands, and to co-operate by the same Spirit with those who are so ordained by them, in their administration of the Word and Sacraments ; hence He may well be said to be always with them, according to the promise He makes them in my text. . . .

Hence, therefore, in the first place I observe how much we are all bound to acknowledge the goodness, to praise, magnify, and adore the

Name of the Most High God, in that we were born and bred, and still live in a Church, wherein the Apostolical line hath through all ages been preserved entire, there having been a constant succession of such Bishops in it, as were truly and properly successors to the Apostles, by virtue of that Apostolical imposition of hands, which, being begun by the Apostles, hath been continued from one to another ever since their time down to ours. By which means the same Spirit which was breathed by Our Lord into His Apostles is, together with their Office, transmitted to their lawful successors, the pastors and governors of our Church at this time, and acts, moves, and assists at the administration of the several parts of the Apostolical Office in our days, as much as ever. From whence it follows, that the means of grace which we now enjoy are in themselves as powerful and effectual as they were in the Apostles' days ; and if they prove not always so successful now as they were then, that cannot be imputed to any want of efficacy in them, but to some defect or other in those who use them. For they who are duly prepared cannot but always find the same effect from them, because there is always the same cause, even the Spirit of God moving upon His Word and Sacraments, when administered by our Church, as well as when administered by the Apostles to whom It was first given. . . .

As for schism, they certainly hazard their salvation at a strange rate, who separate themselves from such a Church as ours is, wherein the Apostolical Succession, the root of all Christian Communion, hath been so entirely preserved, and the Word and Sacraments are so effectually administered ; and all to go into such assemblies and meetings, as can have no pretence to the great promise in my text [i.e. *Matt.* xxviii, 20]. For it is manifest that this promise was made only to the Apostles and their successors to the end of the world. Whereas, in the private meetings, where their teachers have no Apostolical or Episcopal imposition of hands, they have no ground to pretend to succeed the Apostles, nor by consequence any right to the Spirit which Our Lord here promiseth ; without Which, although they preach their hearts out, I do not see what spiritual advantage can accrue to their hearers by it. And therefore whatsoever they may think of it, for my own part I would not be without this promise of Our Saviour for all the world, as knowing that not only myself, but the whole Catholic Church, is highly concerned in it ; it being by virtue of this promise that the Church is continually acted, guided, and assisted by the Spirit of God, and so the ordinary means of grace are made effectual to salvation, which otherwise would be of no force or efficacy at all. And therefore, to speak modestly, they must needs run a very great hazard who cut themselves off from ours, and by consequence from the Catholic Church, and so render themselves uncapable of receiving any benefit from this promise, or from the means of grace which they do or may enjoy.

# (5) HOLY ORDERS AS A SACRAMENT

## No. 160.  RICHARD MONTAGUE

[From *Appello Caesarem. A Just Appeal from Two Unjust Informers.* Part II, Chapter xxxiii. London, 1625, pp. 305 f. Cp. note on No. **3**.]

HE [*i.e.* Calvin] admitteth it [*i.e.* Ordination] a Sacrament, but not an ordinary Sacrament. No Papist living, I think, will say or desire more. It is not for all, but for some. Which saying of his is semblably expressed in that short, small, but perfect, Catechism in our Communion Book, where the question being asked " How many Sacraments are there ? " the answer is made " Two only as generally necessary unto salvation " ; not excluding others from that name and designation, though from the prerogative and degree. For touching Sacramental Unction, it is observed out of Mr. Hooker that, in the writings of the ancient Fathers, all articles peculiar unto Christian faith, all duties of religion containing that which sense or natural reason cannot of itself discern, are commonly called Sacraments. And this is not denied by Bishop Morton. " For if we should speak of ' improper ' Sacraments," saith he, " which are mentioned by the ancient Fathers, our adversaries would not deny that not only seven, but seventy times seven, Sacraments might be named."

## No. 161.  HUMPHREY PRIDEAUX

[From *The Validity of the Orders of the Church of England, made out against the Objections of the Papists, in Several Letters to a Gentleman of Norwich that desired Satisfaction therein,* London, 1688, pp. 53-55. The " Gentleman of Norwich " was one Anthony Norris, who became converted to Roman Catholicism. They were occasioned by a conference between an Anglican (Earbury) and a Jesuit (Acton) on the subject of Anglican Orders. Norris had been present at this conference and had professed himself unsatisfied by its conclusion, and was thus led to write to Humphrey Prideaux on the subject. This treatise begins with a narration of this conference.]

If you please to read the Eighth Chapter of *Leviticus*, you will there find that Aaron and his sons were consecrated to the Levitical priesthood by the outward ceremony only, without as much as any one word spoken by Moses, the consecrator signifying the holy office to which they were set apart. And Maimonides, the most authentic writer among the Rabbis, gives us an account that in after times the Consecration of the High Priest among the Jews was performed only by the anointing with the holy oil, and vesting with the High Priest's vestments ; and after the destruction of the first Temple, in which the holy oil was lost, by vesting him only. For outward signs can by general institution be made as expressive of anything of this nature as a form of words. For words are only sounds, appointed by the common consent of those that use them to be the signs of things ; and when outward actions are appointed to signify the same things, they are altogether as expressive. And the King of France, by delivering the sword to the Constable and a staff to the Marshal of France, doth as effectually create those officers by that outward ceremony only, as if he had done it by a form of words, the most expressive of the authority and power given that could be devised, because the laws of the kingdom and the long received customs of it have made these ceremonies alone the well known manner of constituting those officers. And had the laws of the Christian Church, or the long received usages of it, made any outward ceremony whatever, in like manner, the well known Rite of Ordaining a Priest, it would be altogether as valid for this purpose without any form of words whatever. For Ordination, being only a ministerial act of delegating that office to another which was received from Christ, anything that is sufficient to express this delegation, whether words or signs, doth sufficiently do the thing. For if Forms be so necessary to Ordination, what is it that makes them so ? It must be either the Institution of Christ, or the nature of the thing itself. Any other reason for it, I know not. If it be from the Institution of Christ let us but be convinced of that, and have done. For in this case either to omit the Form or alter in the least from its first Institution would make the whole performance culpable. But if there be no Institution of Christ for any such Form (as I have already abundantly demonstrated that there is not), all the necessity of such a Form must be from the nature of the thing itself. Now if the nature of Ordination doth not necessarily require any such Form, but that any of the offices of the Church may be as well conferred by an outward ceremony only, by public Institution made significant and expressive of the thing done, there appears no necessity for the use of any such Forms at all, so as to invalidate those Orders that are conferred without them. That which makes the Church of Rome so much insist upon the Matter and Form of Ordination is that they have made it a Sacrament ; and they, observing the Sacrament of the Lord's Supper and the Sacrament of Baptism, which are really Sacraments of Christ's Own Institution, to consist each of them, as prescribed in Scripture, of an outward sign and a form of words annexed, the former of which they call the Matter and the latter the Form of the Sacrament, from hence they do infer that they are both essentially necessary to all those other Rites which they will have to be Sacraments also ; and because they find none such instituted in Scripture for them (as they themselves acknowledge), that they may not be without them, introduce Matters and Forms (as they call them) of their own making. And hence it is that they talk so much of the Matter and Form of Orders, and will have both so essentially necessary to the conferring of them ; whereas, would they argue aright this point, they ought not so much to have inferred the necessity of what they call the Matter and Form for Ordination from that it is a Sacrament, as that for this very reason it can be no Sacrament because it hath neither the one nor the other, by Divine Institution, belonging thereto. For the nature of a Sacrament according to their own definitions consists in this, that it is an outward ceremony consisting of things and words, instituted and enjoined by Christ Himself, with a promise of saving grace annexed to the performance of it.  And since nothing of this can be made out to us from Scripture, it doth hence follow that, although Orders be enrolled among the Sacraments in the Church of Rome, it was never so in the Church of Christ.  For where have we in Scripture any external sign, where any Form of words commanded to be made use of in the Administration of Orders ?  Or where any promise of saving grace annexed thereto ?  All that we find instituted in Scripture concerning this matter is that, as Christ sent the Apostles, so they should send others and that none should preach except they were sent.  But as to the manner of this mission or sending, nothing is at all instituted or prescribed unto us in Holy Writ ; but the whole of this is left to the Church, and those chief pastors of it which have the authority of giving those missions committed to them, so to order and appoint it according to the various circumstances of times, places, and things, as they shall judge will be most fitting, provided it be agreeable in all things to the Word of God and sufficiently declarative of the thing intended.

## No. 162.  WILLIAM WAKE

[From *An Exposition of the Doctrine of the Church of England in the Several Articles proposed by Monsieur de Meaux, Late Bishop of Condom* [i.e. J. B. Bossuet], *in his Exposition of the Doctrine of the Catholic Church*, Article XV (" Of Holy Orders "). London, 1686, pp. 45 f.  Cp. note on No. **258.**]

The imposition of hands in Holy Orders, being accompanied with a blessing of the Holy Spirit, may perhaps upon that account be called a kind of particular Sacrament.  Yet since that grace which is thereby conferred, whatever it be, is not common to all Christians, nor by consequence any part of that federal blessing which Our Blessed Saviour has purchased for us, but only a separation of him who receives it to a special employ, we think it ought not to be esteemed a common Sacrament of the whole Church, as Baptism and the Lord's Supper are.

# (6) ANGLICAN ORDERS

## No. 163. FRANCIS MASON

[From *Of the Consecration of the Bishops in the Church of England, With their Succession, Jurisdiction, and other Things incident to their Calling ; as also of the Ordination of Priests and Deacons. Five Books ; Wherein they are cleared from the Slanders and Odious Imputations of Bellarmine, Sanders, Bristow, Harding, Allen, Stapleton, Parsons, Kellison, Eudemon, Becanus, and other Romanists ; and justified to contain Nothing contrary to the Scriptures, Councils, Fathers, or approved Examples of Primitive Antiquity*, London, 1613. Book I, chs. i, vii, ii, iii, vii (*bis*); Book II, chs. vi, ix, x, xi (*bis*); Book III, ch. iv; Book V, chs. i, ii. Pp. 7, 34, 9 f., 20, 37, 38; 63 f., 78 f., 88, 95 f., 96 f.; 121, 123, 123 f., 126, 126 f.; 207 f. This treatise contains the first systematic refutation of the Nag's Head Fable. It is written in the form of a dialogue between " Philodox " and " Orthodox." It was reprinted in 1728 under the title *A Vindication of the Church of England*.]

ORTHODOX. For that Faith and Religion which is agreeable to the Scripture is true, holy, ancient, Catholic and Apostolic; but the Faith and Religion publicly professed at this day in England is in every article and branch thereof agreeable to the Scripture; therefore it is in every article and branch thereof, true, holy, ancient, Catholic and Apostolic. Moreover where the Gospel is truly preached, and the Holy Sacraments rightly administered, there is a true Christian visible Church. But both these duties are religiously performed in England. What reason have you to say then, that we have no Church ?

PHILODOX. Because you have no Ministry : for there cannot be a Church without Pastors and Bishops, as St. Cyprian teacheth, who defineth the Church to be a people united to a Bishop, and St. Hierome, when he saith, that it is no Church which hath not Priests. This doth appear evidently by St. Paul, who declareth that *Christ gave pastors and teachers for the consummation of the Saints, the work of the Ministry, and the edification of the Body of Christ, until we meet all in the unity of faith into a perfect man, and the measure of the age of the fulness of Christ.* In which place as our learned Cardinal [*i.e.* Bellarmine] hath observed, the Apostle teacheth, that there shall be Pastors in the Church till the Day of Judgement, for then we shall meet the Lord in the unity of faith. Behold, saith Father Hessius, *till the number of the elect be accomplished in the end of the world, the Church shall always have pastors and teachers.* Neither doth Luther deny this, but rather put it among the Notes of the Church; and Calvin affirmeth, That the Church can never want Pastors and teachers. From this plain approved principle, thus I dispute. Where there is no true Ministry, there is no true Church;

378

but among the Protestants in England there is no true Ministry; therefore among them there is no true Church. . . .

PHILODOX. That Ordination is a Sacrament truly and properly is rightly defined by the Council of Trent. For there are three things only required to a Sacrament, as yourselves confess, an external sign, a promise of grace, and a commandment or Divine institution,—All which are found in ordination as our learned Cardinal [*i.e.* Bellarmine] hath proved out of the Scripture; who hath also declared that those Scriptures whereby Catholics do prove Ordination to be a Sacrament are understood of Episcopal Ordination. Whereupon he affirmeth, that if Episcopal Ordination be not a Sacrament, we cannot prove evidently out of the Scriptures, that Ordination is a Sacrament.

ORTHODOX. If the word Sacrament be taken somewhat largely, for any external sign instituted of God, whereto is annexed a promise of grace, then we will grant with St. Austin that Order may be called a Sacrament; but if it be taken strictly for such a sign as is a seal of the righteousness of faith, whereto is annexed a promise of the grace of Justification and Remission of Sins, in which sense Baptism and the Lord's Supper are Sacraments, then we may not admit it for a Sacrament. For in Baptism and the Lord's Supper, the saving grace of Justification and the Remission of sins is signified, sealed, and exhibited to the worthy receiver. But the grace given in Ordination is of another nature, respecting not so much the good of the receiver as of the flock, for which he receiveth it. For the Ministers of the Gospel are salt to season others, candles to shine unto others, pipes and conduits to convey the water of life unto others. . . .

ORTHODOX. You please yourselves, and beat the air with a sound of idle and empty words; but leave your vain flourishes, and let us hear what you can say against our calling.

PHILODOX. Then I demand whether you have an inward or an outward calling?

ORTHODOX. We have both.

PHILODOX. An outward calling must either be immediately by the voice of Christ, as was the calling of the Apostles, or mediately by the Church.

ORTHODOX. We are called of God by the Church; for it is He which giveth Pastors and teachers for the consummation of the Saints.

PHILODOX. All that are called of God by the Church derive their authority by lawful succession from Christ and His Apostles. If you do so, then let it appear, show us your descent, let us see your pedigree. If you cannot then what are you, whence come you? If you tell us that God hath raised you in extraordinary manner, you must pardon us if we be slow in believing such things. There are many deceivers gone out into the world, and *Satan can transform himself into an Angel of*

*Light.* In a word, every lawful calling is either ordinary or extraordinary; if yours be ordinary, let us see your authority; if extraordinary, let us see your miracles. If one take upon him extraordinary authority as an Ambassador from a King, he must produce his commission under the King's seal. If you will challenge the like from God, then we require a miracle, that is, the Seal of the King of Heaven. But (to use the words of Doctor Stapleton) in the hatching of the Protestants' brood, no ordinary vocation nor sending extraordinary appeareth; so the ground and foundation being naught, all which they have builded upon it falleth down.

ORTHODOX. The Ministers of England receive imposition of hands in lawful manner from lawful Bishops, endued with lawful authority; and therefore their calling is Ordinary.

PHILODOX. Your Bishops themselves, whence have they this authority?

ORTHODOX. They received it from God, by the hands of such Bishops as went before them.

PHILODOX. But your first Reformers, whence do they derive their succession?

ORTHODOX. Archbishop Cranmer, and other heroical spirits whom the Lord used as His instruments to reform Religion in England, had the very self-same Ordination and succession whereof you so glory; and therefore if these argue that your calling is Ordinary, you must confess that theirs likewise was Ordinary.

PHILODOX. We must not only examine Cranmer, and such others consecrated in King Henry's time, but them also that were in King Edward's, and in the beginning of Queen Elizabeth's, as Parker, Grindal, Sandys, Horne, and the like, which were Priests after the Roman rite, but leaped out of the Church before they were Bishops.

ORTHODOX. As the first Bishops consecrated in King Edward's time derived their spiritual power by succession from those that were in King Henry's, so the first that were advanced under the reign of Queen Elizabeth received theirs from such as were formerly created, partly in King Henry's days, partly in King Edward's; and the Bishops at this day under our gracious Sovereign King James have the like succession from their predecessors, as may be justified by records in particular, and is confessed in general by Cudsemius who came into England in the year of our Lord 1608 to observe the state of our Church and the orders of our Universities. . . .

ORTHODOX. What reason have you to say that our Bishops are not consecrated by three? The Canon hath always been observed in our Church, neither can all the Papists in the world give any one instance to the contrary since the time of Reformation.

PHILODOX. Doctor Sanders declareth that there was a time when you had neither three nor two Bishops, and yet at the same time your new Superintendents invaded the Ecclesiastical Chairs, and were glad to seek their confirmation from the Prince and Parliament, after they had enjoyed the Episcopal Office certain years without any Episcopal Consecration. And therefore all the water in the Thames cannot clear the Clergy of England from being usurpers.

ORTHODOX. But if this be false, then all the water in the Tiber, though it were turned into Holy-Water, cannot purge the Papists from being slanderers. And how false it is shall hereafter be declared out of authentical records, by which it shall appear, that the Queen's Letters Patents of Commission concerning the Confirmation and Consecration of the very first Bishop made in her time, were directed to seven Bishops, and also that the Consecration was accomplished by four Bishops, whose names and titles shall be specified. In the meantime this only I say; in lying and slandering many Papists have had an admirable dexterity, but Sanders surmounted them all. For as his *Book of Schism* is truly called by a learned Bishop, *Sterquilinium Mendaciorum*, a dunghill of lies; so it might be justly termed, *sterquilinium calumniarum*, a very dunghill of slanders, insomuch that for his noble faculty that way, he deserveth no more to be called M. Doctor Sanders, but M. Doctor Slanders. . . .

ORTHODOX. Hitherto of three. Now I will prove that two are not required of absolute necessity. For Evagrius, Patriarch of Antioch, was ordained by Paulinus alone, and yet was allowed for a lawful Bishop. . . . Finally I will add some testimonies of your own writers. Johannes Major : *Dico esse constitutionem humanam quod Episcopus ordinetur a tribus,* " I say that it is a human constitution that a Bishop should be ordained of three." Petrus de palude : *In Ecclesia unus Episcopus sufficit ad alium consecrandum : nec est nisi propter solemnitatem ab Ecclesia inventum, ut tres concurrant,* " In the Church one Bishop is sufficient to consecrate another; and it is nothing else but for the solemnity of the matter that the Church hath devised that three Bishops should meet together." Cardinal Turrecremata is plentiful in this point and proveth it by fourteen arguments. . . .

ORTHODOX. It remaineth that we consider the Consecration of that most reverend Father and blessed Martyr, Thomas Cranmer, Archbishop of Canterbury, concerning whom I expect your judgement.

PHILODOX. My judgement is, that he was a principal cause of all those lamentable alterations, which happened in the days of King Henry the Eighth and Edward the Sixth.

ORTHODOX. Do you call them lamentable ? Therein you resemble Envy in the poet which lamented because she saw nothing worthy of lamentation. For those alterations which ye call lamentable were a gracious beginning of a thousand blessings both to the Church and

Commonwealth of England. But speak directly to the point in question, whether Cranmer were a Canonical Bishop. Why do you not answer? You are like the one which holdeth a wolf by the ears, who neither knoweth how to hold him, nor how to let him go. Fain would you infringe the Consecration of Cranmer, but alas you cannot. . . .

PHILODOX. Wherefore, though Cranmer had a lawful consecration, yet it seemeth, when he fell into schism and heresy, he lost his order and power of Ordination. Therefore the Bishops in King Edward's time consecrated by Cranmer received nothing, because Cranmer had nothing to give. And the Bishops in Queen Elizabeth's time consecrated by those whom Cranmer did consecrate, received nothing, because their consecrators had nothing to give. And those which now succeed them received nothing because their predecessors had nothing to give.

ORTHODOX. Take heed, Philodox, lest while you go about to put out our eyes, you put out your own. For if your allegations be found, what shall become of Bonner, Bishop of London? What shall become of Nicolas Heath, whom Queen Mary made Archbishop of York, and after the death of Gardiner, Lord Chancellor of England? What shall become of Thirlby, whom Queen Mary translated from Norwich to Ely? For all these were consecrated at such time, when in your judgement both the consecrators and consecrated were stained with schism and heresy. Did all these receive nothing because their consecrators had nothing to give? If they were no Bishops, then what becomes of the Bishops in Queen Mary's reign, whom these did consecrate? If they all received nothing, then you must confess that the Priests whom they ordained were no Priests; if they were no Priests, then though they used the words of Consecration, they could not consecrate the host; if this be true then all that worshipped the host which they did consecrate were idolators.

PHILODOX. Edmund Bonner, and the rest of our Bishops and Priests were Reverend and Canonical, whatsoever you esteem of them.

ORTHODOX. Can there be a Bishop without effectual Consecration?

PHILODOX. It is impossible.

ORTHODOX. And other Consecration they had none, but that which we have mentioned; for I hope they were not reordained in Queen Mary's time.

PHILODOX. Reordained? I do not think so; for as rebaptizations so reordinations were forbidden in the Council of Capua. And Gregory saith, as he which is once baptised ought not to be baptised again, so he which is once Consecrated ought not to be Consecrated again in the same order. Therefore undoubtedly they were not reordained; but Cardinal Poole, the Pope's legate, absolved them from Schism and heresy, so they were confirmed for lawful Bishops.

ORTHODOX. You hold that it is impossible to be a Bishop without

effectual Consecration. Therefore seeing they had no other Consecration but that mentioned, and yet were Bishops, it followeth that
their Consecration was effectual. Wherefore you are forced to confess
that if a schismatical and heretical Bishop give orders, the orders were
effectual. . . .

ORTHODOX. Then at last to gather into brief heads that which hath
been discoursed at large, you grant that Archbishop Cranmer was a
Canonical Bishop.

PHILODOX. I grant it, for the reasons before alleged.

ORTHODOX. And you make no doubt of any of the Bishops of
England before Cranmer ?

PHILODOX. None at all, as you heard before.

ORTHODOX. And you say that every Canonical Bishop hath an
Episcopal character ?

PHILODOX. We say so.

ORTHODOX. And that this character is so indelible, that no schism,
no sin, no heresy, no censures of the Church, no excommunication,
suspension, interdiction, degradation, nothing, nothing at all saving
only death, if death, can dissolve it ; otherwise it is everlasting ?

PHILODOX. All this was proved out of the most famous Councils
of Florence and Trent.

ORTHODOX. And that every Bishop by virtue of his Episcopal
character, hath power to give Holy orders, yea even the order of a
Bishop ?

PHILODOX. Very true, so he be assisted by a sufficient number of
Bishops, and impose hands upon a capable person, according to the
form of the Church.

ORTHODOX. Then to proceed to the rest of the Bishops, consecrated
in King Henry's days, in the time of the pretended schism. Were not
they capable of the Episcopal function ?

PHILODOX. Though King Henry abolished the authority of the
Pope, yet the Sacrifice of the Mass continued till the end of his reign.
So we make no doubt, but the Priesthood then in use was a sacrificing
Priesthood, complete in all points, and consequently capable of the
Episcopal character, notwithstanding the crime of schism and
heresy. . . .

ORTHODOX. What meaneth Kellison by the Matter of Ordination ?

PHILODOX. According to the doctrine of the Catholic Church, Holy
Order is a Sacrament ; and every Sacrament of the new Law consisteth
of things and words, as the matter and the form, which are so certain
and determined of God, that it is not lawful to change them. Now in
Ordination the matter is a sensible sign ; as for example, imposition of
hands, which Bellarmine calleth the matter essential.

ORTHODOX. Others of your own men are of another opinion. For

Salmeron the Jesuit having proposed the question bringeth reasons for both sides, but seemeth to incline to the contrary. Fabius Incarnatus asketh this question, ' How many things are of the substance of order ? ' and answereth that six. But imposition of hands is none of the six. Navarrus speaking of imposition of hands, saith *Illa non est de substantia Sacramenti*, that is, " it is not of the substance of the Sacrament." For which opinion he allegeth Scotus. But if imposition of hands be the Matter of Ordination, then Kellison is guilty of lying and slandering, when he saith that in King Edward's days the Matter of Ordination was not used. For Sanders himself, though a shameless fellow, yet confesseth that in the days of King Edward the former law, concerning the number of Bishops which should impose hands upon the ordained, was always observed—a point so clear, that it might be justified by many records. But what need we go to records, seeing it is a plain case, that the very Book of Ordination which was made and established in the days of King Edward, commandeth imposition of hands ? Wherefore if the essential matter be imposition of hands, then I must conclude out of your own principles that in King Edward's days, the essential matter was used.

PHILODOX. In the ordering of a Deacon there is not only imposition of hands, but also the reaching of the Gospels ; so in ordering of a Priest, not only imposition of hands, but also the reaching of the instruments, that is, of the Paten and Chalice : and both these Ceremonies are essential, as Bellarmine proveth. Therefore why may we not say, that in Episcopal Consecration, not only the imposition of hands, but other ceremonies also belong to the essential matter ?

ORTHODOX. What other ceremonies I beseech you ? Do you mean the holy oil, wherewith the head of the consecrated is anointed with these words : ' Let thy head be anointed and consecrated with celestial benediction ' ? Or the ring which is blessed with prayer and holy water, and put upon his finger with these words, *Accipe annulum, fidei signaculum :* ' Receive the ring, the seal of faith ' ? Or the crosier, delivered in these words, ' Receive the staff of the Pastoral office ' ? If you mean these or the like, and urge them as essential, you must give us leave to reject them, because they are only human inventions. You told us before out of Bellarmine that the Matter of Ordination is certain and determined of God. Now where shall we find the determinations of God but in the Book of God ? We find in Holy Scripture imposition of hands, and we embrace it as Apostolical. As for your rings and crosiers, when you can demonstrate them out of the Book of God, we will then accept them as the determinations of God. In the meantime we cannot acknowledge them for the essential Matter of Ordination. But now from the Matter, let us come to the Form.

PHILODOX. It is agreed upon that the Form consisteth in the words which are uttered, while the sensible sign is used, and they are the very same whereby the spiritual power is given.

ORTHODOX.  I hope you will not say that these words, " Receive the ring," or, " Receive the staff," concern the essential Form.  Tell us therefore in what words the true Form consisteth, that so we may the better examine the speech of Kellison.

PHILODOX.  The words may be divers, yet the sense the same, and this diversity of words may severally signify the substance of the Sacrament. . . .

ORTHODOX.  By what words is the Episcopal power given in the Church of Rome ?

PHILODOX.  By these words, " *Receive the Holy Ghost*," because they are used when the Bishop imposeth hands.  And therefore as Priests in their Ordination receive the Holy Ghost, that is (as Bellarmine expounds it out of Chrysostom and Cyril) " a ghostly power consisting in forgiving and retaining of sins " ;  so a Bishop in his Consecration receiveth the Holy Ghost, that is a ghostly power consisting in the performance of those things which are reserved properly to Bishops, amongst which the power of Ordination is most eminent.

ORTHODOX.  If you call these words the Form of Consecration, then you must acknowledge that not only the Matter, but also the right Form of Consecration, was used in the days of King Edward ;  for these words were then used while the Bishops imposed hands, as appeareth by the book.  And consequently you must confess that Ridley, Hooper, and Ferrar, were rightly ordained Bishops, and moreover, that Kellison is a notorious slanderer.  Thus much of the second rank.  Now come we to the third, wherein we may place such (if any such be found) as were made both Priests and Bishops, in the days of King Edward.

PHILODOX.  We think that no man can possibly have the order of a Bishop which hath not the right order of Priesthood.  But the Priesthood conferred in King Edward's time was no Priesthood, because they wanted the authority to offer the blessed Sacrifice of the Mass ;  therefore those Priests were not capable of the Episcopal order.

ORTHODOX.  I answer first, that seeing that King Edward reigned but six years and five months, it is likely that most of them which were advanced in his time to be Bishops were before his time in the order of Priesthood.  Secondly, if any be produced that were not, yet it shall be justified (God willing) when we come to the point, that the order of Priesthood conferred in the days of King Edward, Queen Elizabeth, and King James is the true ministry of the Gospel, and that your sacrificing Priesthood is sacrilegious and abominable.  In the meantime, you must give us leave to hold that the Ministry of the Church of England is holy in the sight of God, and justifiable in the sight of man. . . .

ORTHODOX.  These shameless Papists would make the world

believe that our Bishops derive not their Consecration from Bishops, but from Kings and Queens, which is an impudent slander; for our Kings do that which belongeth to Kings, and our Bishops do that which belongeth to Bishops. In the vacancy of any Archbishopric or Bishopric, the king granteth to the Dean and Chapter a licence under the Great Seal, as of old time hath been accustomed, to proceed to an election, with a letter missive, containing the name of the person which they shall elect and choose, which being duly performed and signified to the King, under the common seal of the electors, the King giveth his royal assent; and signifying and presenting the person elected to the Archbishop and Bishops, as the law requireth, he giveth them commission, and withal requireth and commandeth them, to confirm the said election, and to invest and consecrate the said person, using all ceremonies and other things requisite for the same. Whereupon the Archbishop and Bishops, proceeding according to the ancient form in those cases used, do cause all such as can object or take exception, either in general or particular, either against the manner of the election or the person elected, to be cited publicly and peremptorily to make their appearance. When the validity of the election and the sufficiency of the person are by public acts and due proceedings judicially approved, then followeth Consecration, which is performed by a lawful number of lawful Bishops, and that in such form as is required by the ancient Canons. . . .

PHILODOX. If you can justify your Bishops, produce their Consecrations; make it appear to the world when, by whom, and how they were consecrated, beginning with the first which was made in the Queen's time, that is, with Matthew Parker who did bear the name of the Archbishop of Canterbury.

ORTHODOX. You learned this disdainful speech of Nicholas Sanders, who dedicated his *Rock of the Church* to that reverend Archbishop in this unreverend manner: " To the Right Worshipful Master Doctor Parker, bearing the Name of the Archbishop of Canterbury." Wherein (to let pass that right worshipful and right scornful title) he doth not stile him " Archbishop," but " Bearing the Name of Archbishop," as though our Bishops were Bishops only in name. But what can you say against him?

PHILODOX. I would feign learn of you the place where he was consecrated. I have read that Maximus was consecrated in the house of a minstrel, and it seemeth that Matthew Parker was consecrated in a Tavern. For Doctor Kellison saith that " he heard it credibly reported, that some of your new Superintendents were made Bishops at the Nag's Head in Cheape. A fit Church for such a Consecration! " And it is most likely that Matthew Parker was one of them because he was the first.

ORTHODOX. This of the Nag's Head doth call to my remembrance Pope John XII, who ordained a deacon in a stable amongst his horses. A fit sanctuary for such a saint. . . . But whereas you say that Kellison heard this credibly reported, I must tell you, that you are very forward in spreading false reports against the Protestants. It is credibly reported in Rome that we in England have wrapped some Papists in bear skins, and baited them with dogs; that we enclose dormice in basins and lay them to the sides of the Catholics to eat out their bowels; that we bind them in mangers, and feed them with hay like horses. These are shining lies, fit carbuncles for the Pope's Mitre. Neither do they report them only, but print them, and paint them, and publish them with the Pope's privilege. They need a privilege which tell such glorious lies. This of the Nag's Head, though it go current at Rome, and be blazed for truth through the world by men of your rank, is cousin-germane to the former, as appeareth by the records of the Archbishopric, which declare, that he was consecrated *in Capella intra manerium suum de Lambeth*, that is, in the Chapel within his manor of Lambeth. Thus you see the falsehood of this fable, which was devised to no other purpose, but only to make our Ministry and Religion seem odious to all men. Is not this strange dealing, for men that make such great ostentation of sincerity and gravity? But for my own part, I do not marvel at it, your proceedings are but answerable to your doctrines. For you teach that an officious lie is but a venial sin. And again, that the Church of Rome is the holy mother Church: therefore to whom should kind offices rather be performed than to the Church of Rome? And what office will she take more kindly than the discrediting of those whom she accounteth heretics? Therefore I do not wonder that you put it in practice. I fear nothing, but that shortly it shall grow with you a point meritorious. Well, the stripe of the rod maketh marks on the flesh, but the stripe of the tongue breaketh the bones. But let them remember, that the tongue which lieth, slayeth the soul; and that all liars shall have their portion (except they repent) in the lake that burneth with fire and brimstone. . . .

ORTHODOX. Queen Mary died in the year 1558 the 17th of November: and the selfsame day died Cardinal Poole, Archbishop of Canterbury, and the very same day was Queen Elizabeth proclaimed. The 15th of January next following was the day of Queen Elizabeth's Coronation when Doctor Oglethorpe, Bishop of Carlisle, was so happy as to set the diadem of the kingdom upon her royal head. Now the See of Canterbury continued void till December following, about which time the Dean and Chapter having received the *Congé d'élire*, elected Master Doctor Parker for their Archbishop. *Iuxta morem antiquum et laudabilem consuetudinem Ecclesiae praedictae ab antiquo usitatam et inconcusse observatam*, *i.e.* proceeding in this election according to the ancient manner, and the laudable custom of the foresaid Church, anciently used and inviolably observed. After which election, orderly performed and signified according to the law, it pleased her Highness to send her Letters Patents of commission for his Confirmation and Consecration to seven Bishops (six whereof were lately returned from exile), whose names with so much of the commission as concerneth this present purpose, I will here set down for your better satisfaction.

*Elizabeth Dei gratia, etc., Reverendis in Christo patribus.*

> *Anth. Landavensi.*
> *Will. Barlow quondam Bath.*
> *Episcopo nunc Cicestrensi electo.*
> *Joh. Scory quondam Cicestrensi Episcopo, nunc Herefordensi electo.*
> *Miloni Coverdale, quondam Exoniensi Episcopo.*
> *Joh., Suffraganeo Bedford.*
> *Joh., Suffraganeo Thetford.*
> *Joh. Bale, Ossorensi Episcopo. . . .*

PHILODOX.  But was the consecration accordingly performed ?

ORTHODOX.  You need not doubt of it.  For first, the Bishops to whom the Letters Patents were directed had reason to set their hands cheerfully to so good a work, so much tending to the advancing of the true religion which they all embraced, and for which all of them, except one, had been in exile.  Secondly, how durst they do otherwise, seeing it was enacted by a statute made in the 25th. year of King Henry VIII, and still in force, that " if any Archbishop or Bishop within the King's dominions after any such election, nomination, or presentation signified unto them by the King's Letters Patents, should refuse and not confirm, invest and consecrate with all due circumstance within twenty days after the King's Letters Patents of such signification or presentation should come to their hands, then he or they, so offending, should run in the dangers, pains and penalties of the *Statute of Provision and Premunire* made in the twenty fifth year of the reign of King Edward III, and in the sixteenth of King Richard II " ? . . .

PHILODOX.  Whatsoever you have as yet said is nothing, because to the very being of a Bishop the order of Priesthood is essentially re-quired, which is not to be found in the Church of England.  For there are two principal functions of Priesthood,—the first is the power of Sacrificing, the second of Absolution ; but you have neither, as I will prove in order.  To begin with the first, it is given in Holy Church by these words : *Accipe potestatem offerre sacrificium Deo, missasque cele-brare, tam pro vivis quam pro defunctis in nomine Domini.*  That is, " Receive power to offer sacrifice to God, and to celebrate Mass as well for the quick as for the dead in the name of the Lord."  But you use neither these words nor any equivalent in your Ordination of Priests, as may appear by the Book. Therefore you want the principal function of Priesthood.

ORTHODOX. If you mean no more by 'Priest', than the Holy Ghost doeth by 'Presbyter', that is, a Minister of the New Testament, then we profess and are ready to prove that we are Priests, as we are called in the Book of Common Prayers and the Form of Ordering, because we receive in our ordination, authority to preach the Word of God, and to minister His Holy Sacraments. Secondly, [if] by Priests you mean Sacrificing Priests, and would expound yourselves of Spiritual Sacrifices, then as this name belongeth to all Christians, so it may be applied by an excellency to the Ministers of the Gospel. Thirdly, although in this name you have a relation to bodily Sacrifices, yet even so we may be called Priests, by way of allusion. For as Deacons are not of the tribe of Levi, yet the ancient Fathers do commonly call them Levites, alluding to their office because they come in place of Levites, so the ministers of the New Testament may be called Sacrificers, because they succeed the sons of Aaron, and come in place of Levites. Fourthly, forasmuch as we have authority to minister the Sacraments, and consequently the Eucharist, which is a representation of the sacrifice of Christ, therefore we may be said to offer Christ in a mystery, and to sacrifice Him by way of commemoration. Is not this sufficient? If it be not, what other sacrificing is required?

PHILODOX. There is required sacrificing properly so called, which is an external oblation made only to God by a lawful Minister whereby some sensible and permanent thing is consecrated and changed with Mystical rite, for the acknowledgement of human infirmity, and for the profession of the Divine Majesty.

ORTHODOX. What is the sensible and permanent thing you offer?

PHILODOX. It is the very Body and Blood of Christ.

ORTHODOX. The Church of England teacheth thus according to the Scripture: "The offering of Christ once made is that perfect redemption, propitiation, and satisfaction, for all the sins of the whole world, both original and actual, and there is no other satisfaction for sin, but that alone," and consequently it condemneth your " masses for the quick and the dead, as blasphemous fables and dangerous deceits ".

## No. 164.  JOHN BRAMHALL

[From *The Consecration and Succession of Protestant Bishops Justified ; the Bishop of Duresme Vindicated ; and that Infamous Fable of the Ordination at the Nag's Head Clearly Confuted.* Passages from Chapters III, IV, V, VI. *Works*, ed. L. A. C. T., Vol. III, pp. 41 f., 45 f., 49f.; 50–53, 63 f.; 67, 71 ; 94–96, 96, 97 f. The occasion of this work was the anonymous appearance at Rouen or Antwerp in 1657 of *A Treatise of the Nature of Catholic Faith and Heresy*, by N. N., the author being the Jesuit, Peter Talbot. In it, Talbot asserted that the Nag's Head Fable had been openly admitted by the Bishop of Durham (Thomas Morton) in the House of Lords. Bramhall published his reply at the Hague in the following year (1658). He was able conclusively to refute Talbot by a declaration of the aged Bishop of Durham, in which he asserted solemnly : " I do here in the presence of Almighty God solemnly protest and declare to all the world that what [Talbot] there affirms concerning me is a most notorious untruth and a gross slander."]

I. The first reason which I bring against this ridiculous fable [*i.e.*, the Nag's Head Fable], is taken from the palpable contradictions and gross absurdities and defects of those Roman Catholic writers who have related this silly tale of a tub, and agree in nothing but in their common malice against the Church of England.

It is no strange matter for such as write upon hearsay, or rely upon the exact truth of other men's notes or memories, to mistake in some inconsiderable circumstance ; as to set down the name of a place amiss, which may be the transcriber's fault, or the printer's as well as the author's ; or to say twó suffragans for one, when there were two named in the commission and but one present at the consecration. Such immaterial differences, which are so remote from the heart of the cause, about indifferent circumstances, may bring the exactness of the relation into question, but not the substantial truth of it. Such petty unsignificant variations do rather prove, that the relations were not made upon compact or confederacy, especially where there are original records taken upon the place by sworn notaries, whose names and hands and acts are as well known to every man versed in the records of those times, as a man knoweth his own house ; to which all relaters and relations must submit, and are ready to submit, as to an infallible rule. But he who should give credit to such a silly, senseless fable as this is, which is wholly composed of absurd, improbable, incoherent, inconsistent, contradictory fictions, had need to have a very implicit faith. . . .

II. My second reason against this senseless fable, is the late discovery of it to the world and the long concealing of it in holes and corners before they durst adventure to present it to the view of the world. Can any man who is in his right wits be so stupid as to imagine that the Nag's Head Ordination happened in the year 1559, and (if these Fathers say truly) was " notoriously known to all the world," and that it should never once peep into the light for almost a whole age after it was pretended to have been done, that is, till after the year sixteen hundred ? We use to say, a monster is but nine days' wonder ; but this ugly monster was not taken notice of in the world until after forty years. The reason is evident ; either it was then but newly hatched, or it had been kept all that time at dry nurse in a closet. If it had been so " notorious to all the world " from the year 1559 as the Fathers fain, all the windows in the Nag's Head would have been full of it, and the room would have been shewed to all their guests, where such a prodigious pageant had been acted.

I dare to appeal to the judgements of these Fathers themselves, whether it be credible, that this story should be notoriously known to the world in the beginning of Queen Elizabeth's reign, and yet neither Stapleton, nor Harding, nor Bristow, nor Alan, nor Reynolds, nor Parsons, nor any one of all their Roman Catholic writers, should so much as mention it for forty years ensuing ; especially writing so much as they did upon that very subject, the validity or invalidity of our Ordination. How could their silence have been excused from betraying of their cause, to lose such an egregious advantage ? Was it peradventure out of affection to us, to conceal the defects of the Protestants ? No, they had will enough. But they durst not avouch such a monstrous untruth in earnest (if ever they did hear of such a vain rumour, which I cannot easily believe), so contrary to the knowledge of that age. . . .

III. A third reason against this ridiculous libel of the Nag's Head Consecration is taken from the strictness of our laws, which allow no man to consecrate, or be consecrated, but in a sacred place, with due Matter and Form, and all the Rites and Ceremonies prescribed by the Church of England. No man must be consecrated by fewer than four Bishops, or three at least, and that after the election of the Dean and Chapter is duly confirmed, and upon the mandate or commission of the King under the Great Seal of England, under the pain of a *praemunire*, that is, the forfeiture of lands, and goods, and livings, and liberty, and protection. They allow not Consecration in a tavern, without due Matter and Form, without the ceremonies and solemnity prescribed by the Church, without election, without confirmation, without Letters Patent, by one single Bishop, or two at the most ; such as they feign the Nag's Head Ordination to have been. Who can believe, that two Archbishops, and thirteen Bishops, having the reputation of learning and prudence, should wilfully thrust themselves into an apparent *praemunire*, to forfeit not only their Archbishoprics and Bishoprics but all their estates and all their hopes, for a fantastic form and scandalous Consecration ; when the Queen and Kingdom were favourable to them, when the Form prescribed by the Church did please them well enough, when there were Protestant Bishops of their own communion enough to consecrate them, when all the Churches in the kingdom were open to them ? unless it had been Midsummer-Moon in December, and they were all stark mad, and then it is no matter where they were consecrated. . . .

IV. My fourth plea is, because there was no need to play this counterfeit pageant. We use to say, necessity hath no law, that is, regardeth no law. In time of war the laws are silent. But this was a time of peace. First, there could be no necessity why they should have a clandestine Consecration, without a register or public notary, when they might have had an army of public notaries ready upon their whistle, even under their elbows at Bow's Church, out of the Courts of the Arches, and the Audience, and Prerogative. Secondly, there was no necessity why they should anticipate the Queen's Letters Patents for their Consecration, by whose gracious favour they were elected ; and of the accomplishment whereof in due time they could not doubt, unless they would wilfully destroy their own hopes by such a mad prank as this had been ; that is, unless they would themselves hew down the bough whereupon they stood. Thirdly, there was no necessity that they should choose a common tavern for the place of their Consecration, when the keys of all the Churches in the kingdom were at their command. Fourthly, there could be no necessity why they should desert the Form of Ordination prescribed by the law, which was agreeable both to their judgements, and to their desires, and to their duties ; and to omit the essentials of Ordination, both Matter and Form, which they knew well enough, to be consecrated after a new brain-sick manner.

Then all the necessity which can be pretended, is want of a competent number of ordainers. Suppose there had been such a necessity to be ordained by two Bishops, or by one Bishop, this very necessity had been a sufficient dispensation with the rigour of the Canons, and had justified the act. As St. Gregory pleadeth to Augustine, " In the English Church, wherein there is no other Bishop but thyself, thou canst not ordain a Bishop otherwise than alone." And after this manner our first English Bishops were ordained. And so might these Protestant Bishops have been validly ordained, if they received the essentials of Ordination. But what a remedy is this,—because they could not have a competent number of Bishops according to the Canons of the Church and the Laws of England, therefore to reject the essentials of Ordination, for a defect which was not essential, and to cast off obedience to their superiors, both civil and ecclesiastical ? This had been just like little children, which because they cannot have some toy which they desire, cast away their garments, and whatsoever their parents had provided for them. Want of three Bishops might in some cases make a Consecration illegal or uncanonical, but it could not have rendered it invalid, as this silly pretended Ordination had.

But now I come up close to the ground-work of the fable, and I deny positively that there was any such want of a competent number of Bishops, as they pretend. And for proof hereof, I bring no vain rumours or uncertain conjectures, but the evident and authentic testimony of the Great Seal of England, affixed to the Queen's Letters Patents for authorizing the Confirmation and Consecration of Archbishop Parker, dated the sixth day of December, *anno* 1559, directed to seven Protestant Bishops, namely, Anthony Bishop of Llandaff, William Barlow sometimes Bishop of Bath and Wells and then elect

Bishop of Chichester, John Scory sometimes Bishop of Chichester then elect Bishop of Hereford, Miles Coverdale sometimes Bishop of Exeter, John Suffragan Bishop of Bedford, John Suffragan Bishop of Thetford, and John Bale Bishop of Ossory in Ireland.  Three are a canonical number;  if there were choice of seven, then there was no want of a competent number to ordain canonically.  I add, that if it had been needful, they might have had seven more out of Ireland, Archbishops and Bishops, for such a work as a Consecration.  Ireland never wanted store of ordainers;  nor ever yet did any man object want of a competent number of Consecraters to an Irish Protestant Bishop.  They who concurred freely in the Consecration of Protestant Bishops at home, would not have denied their concurrence in England, if they had been commanded.  Which makes me give no credit to that vain report, of an Irish Archbishop prisoner in the Tower, who refused to comply with the desires of the Protestant Bishops, " for his liberty and a large reward."  But the Archbishop wanteth a name, and the fable wanteth a ground ; the witnesses and persuaders are all unknown.  And if there had been a grain of truth in this relation, yet in this case one man is no man ; one man's refusal signifieth nothing. . . .

V. The fifth reason is drawn from that well-known principle in rhetoric—" *Cui bono*,"—or what advantage could such a Consecration, as the Nag's Head Consecration is pretended to have been, bring to the consecraters, or the persons consecrated.  God and nature never made any thing in vain.  The hair of the head, the nails upon the fingers' ends, do serve both for ornament and muniment.  The leaves defend the blossoms, the blossoms produce the fruit, which is nature's end.  In sensitives, the spider doth not weave her webs, nor the silly bee make her cells, in vain.  But especially intellectual creatures have always some end of their actions.  Now consider, what good such a mock-Consecration could do the persons so consecrated ? Could it help them to the possession of their Bishoprics by the law of England ?  Nothing less.  There is such a concatenation of our English customs and records, that the counterfeiting of any one can do no good except they could counterfeit them all, which is impossible.

When any Bishop's See becometh void, there issueth a writ out of the Exchequer to seize the temporalities into the King's hand, as being the ancient and well-known patron of the English Church, leaving the spiritualities to the Archbishop, or to the Dean and Chapter, according to the custom of the place. . . .

VI. My sixth reason is taken from the diametrical opposition which is between this fabulous relation of the Nag's Head Ordination, and all the records of England, both ecclesiastical and civil. . . .

VII. Thus we have seen, how the records of England, civil and ecclesiastical, do contradict this tale of a tub.  My seventh reason

sheweth, how the same records do confirm and establish our relation. . . .

VIII. The eighth reason to prove the Nag's Head Ordination to
be a fable, is taken from the authority of the statute in the eighth year
of Queen Elizabeth; which is thus entitled, " An Act declaring the
manner of making and Consecrating of the Archbishops and Bishops
of this Realm to be good, lawful, and perfect." " An Act declaring,"—
not enacting or making,—" the manner of making and Consecrating
the Archbishops and Bishops of this Realm,"—that is, those in the
beginning of Queen Elizabeth's time, as appeareth by the whole body
of the Act,—" to be good, lawful, and perfect." The title of the statute
alone is sufficient to confute this fable. But there is much more in the
body of the statute, as where it " approveth the making and Consecrating of the same Archbishops and Bishops to be duly and orderly
done, according to the laws of this realm." If it was " done duly and
orderly according to the laws of this realm," then it was not done at
the Nag's Head, nor after such a silly ridiculous manner as these Fathers
do relate it. That Form differeth from our Form in all things. In the
consecrater, or minister of the Consecration;—we must have three
Bishops at the least, there was but one. In the Matter;—our Matter
is imposition of hands, their Matter was the laying the Bible upon
the head or shoulders of the person consecrated. In the Form;—
our Form is " Receive the Holy Ghost," etc.; their Form was " Take
thou authority to preach the Word of God sincerely."

The statute proceedeth, that " they were elected, made, and consecrated Archbishops and Bishops, according to such Order and Form,
and with such Ceremonies in and about their Consecrations, as were
allowed and set forth by the said Acts, Statutes, and Orders, annexed
to the said Book of Common Prayer before mentioned." This is plain
enough. If the Parliament say truly, then they were consecrated in a
Church, not in a tavern; not according to the brainsick whimsies of a
self-conceited fool, or rather the ludubrious device of an arch-enemy,
but according to the Form prescribed by the Church and Kingdom.
The Parliament had more reason to know the truth than these Fathers;
for there were personally present both the persons who did consecrate,
and the persons who were consecrated, and many Lords and gentlemen
who were eye-witnesses of the Consecration. Choose, reader, whether
thou wilt trust the tale of a single, obscure, malicious spy, tattling in a
corner, or the asseveration of the Parliament of England, in the face
of the sun, published to the world in print. . . .

IX. My ninth reason to prove that Nag's Head relation fabulous and
counterfeit, is taken from the testimony of that book formerly mentioned[1]

---

[1] [The *De Antiquitate Britannicae Ecclesiae*, said to be by John Jocelyn, the
secretary of Archbishop Parker.]

of the Lives of the seventy Archbishops of Canterbury; wherein the Consecrations of Archbishop Parker and all the rest are particularly related. . . .

X. The tenth and last reason to prove our relation true, and theirs fabulous, is taken from all sorts of witnesses, ours and theirs indifferently. Mr. Mason reckoneth up seven of our writers, who had justified the legality of our Ordinations and cited our registers as authentic records, before himself: Bishop Jewel, Bishop Hall, Bishop Godwin, Dr. Collins, Mr. Camden, Mr. Sheldon, and one who was then living when this question was so hotly debated in King James his time, and had been an eye-witness of Archbishop Parker's Consecrations at Lambeth, that was, the Earl of Nottingham. One that was well stored with our English writers in Queen Elizabeth's time might add many more; but that cannot well be expected from me at this distance. . . .

## No. 165. HUMPHREY PRIDEAUX

[From *The Validity of the Orders of the Church of England*, London, 1688, pp. 45 f. Cp. note on No. **161**. The treatise referred to in the first sentence of the extract was a folio published by Peter Walsh in 1674. The quotation itself is from the same writer's *Four Letters on several Subjects to Persons of Quality, the Fourth being an Answer to the Bishop of Lincoln's* [i.e. Thomas Barlow's] *Book entitled " Popery, etc."*; Walsh sought to defend himself in the eyes of his co-religionists for calling the (Anglican) Bishop of Lincoln " Most Illustrious and Most Reverend."]

" I had about twelve years since in the Preface to my *History of the Irish Remonstrance* publicly in print acknowledged my opinion to be that the Ordination of the Protestant Church of England is valid, meaning it undoubtedly to be so, according both to the public doctrine of the Roman Church Schools themselves and the ancient Rituals of all Catholic Churches, Latin and Greek, nay, and to those Rituals of all the Oriental Heterodox Churches too, as Morinus, a learned Oratorian, hath recorded them." Thus far Father Walsh. . . . But he is not the only man of that religion [*i.e.* Roman Catholicism] that allows our Orders to be good and valid; abundance more are of his mind herein, and several have taken the same freedom of expressing it, although to the disadvantage of their own cause. Father Davenport, alias Sancta Clara, another priest of the Romish Church, is altogether as express in this matter as Father Walsh; for in his Exposition of the 36th Article of our Church he proves from Vasquez, Coninck, Arcudius, and Innocent IV, that our Church hath all the essentials of Ordination required in Scripture; and, as to our Form of Ordination, he plainly says, that if the difference of the words herein from their Form do annul our Ordinations, it must annul those of the Greek Church too; for the Form of the Greek Church altogether differs as much from the Form of the Roman, as doth that of the English. And Cudsemius, one that writes violently enough against us, speaks also to the same purpose, which he would never have done but that the manifest certainty of the thing extorted this confession from him.  For he, coming into England in the year 1608 to observe the state of our Church and the order of our Universities, was so far convinced of the validity of our Orders by his inquiring into this particular, that in a book printed two years after, on his return home, he hath these words :  " Concerning the state of the Calvinian sect in England, it so standeth that either it may endure long, or be changed suddenly, or in a trice.  In regard of the Catholic Order there in a perpetual line of their Bishops, and the lawful succession of pastors received from the Church, for the honour whereof we use to call the English Calvinists by a milder term, not Heretics but Schismatics." [1]  And in the late times, when one Goffe went over unto the Church of Rome, a question arising about the validity of our Orders, on his taking upon him at Paris to say Mass by virtue of his Orders received in our Church, it was referred to the Sorbonne to examine the matter ;  where it being fully discussed they gave in their opinion that our Orders were good.  And this I have by the testimony of one now eminent Papist, who some years since told me the whole story from his own knowledge, he being then in Paris, when the whole matter was there transacted.  And although afterwards, as he told me, the Pope determined otherwise of this matter, and ordered the Archbishop of Paris to reordain him, yet the Sorbonnists still stuck to their opinion that he was a good priest by his first Ordination.  And if you will know whence this difference in the determination arose, it was that the one proceeded according to the merits of the cause, and the other as would best suit with his own interest and the interest of the party he was to support.

[1] Cudsemius, *De Desperata Calvini causa*, cap. 11, page 108.  [This treatise was published at Mainz in 1609.  On Petrus Cudsemius, cp. H. Hurter, *Nomenclator Literarius*, i, 423.]

## (7) NON-EPISCOPAL ORDERS

### No. 166.  RICHARD HOOKER

[From *The Laws of Ecclesiastical Polity*, Book VII, Chapter xiv, § 11.  *Works,*
ed. J. Keble, Vol. III, pp. 231 f.  Cp. note on No. **148**.]

THE whole Church visible being the true original subject of all
power, it hath not ordinarily allowed any other than Bishops alone
to ordain.   Howbeit, as the ordinary course is ordinarily in all things
to be observed, so it may be in some cases not unnecessary that we
decline from the ordinary ways.

Men may be extraordinarily, yet allowably, two ways admitted unto
spiritual functions in the Church.   One is, when God Himself doth
of Himself raise up any, whose labour He useth without requiring that
men should authorize them; but then He doth ratify their calling
by manifest signs and tokens Himself from Heaven, and thus even
such as believed not Our Saviour's teaching did yet acknowledge
Him a lawful teacher sent from God : *Thou art a teacher sent from God,
otherwise none could do those things which Thou doest.*   Luther did but
reasonably, therefore, in declaring that the senate of Mulheuse should
do well to ask of Muncer, from whence he received power to teach,
who it was that had called him; and if his answer were that God had
given him his charge, then to require at his hands some evident sign
thereof for men's satisfaction,—because God is so wont, when He
Himself is the author of any extraordinary calling.

Another extraordinary kind of vocation is, when the exigence of
necessity doth constrain to leave the usual ways of the Church, which
otherwise we would willingly keep; where the Church must needs
have some ordained, and neither hath nor can have possibly a Bishop
to ordain.   In case of such necessity, the ordinary institution of God
hath given oftentimes, and may give, place.   And therefore we are
not simply without exception to urge a lineal descent of power from
the Apostles by continued Succession of Bishops in every effectual
Ordination.   These cases of inevitable necessity excepted, none may
ordain but only Bishops.   By the imposition of their hands it is,
that the Church giveth power of Order, both unto Presbyters and
Deacons.

## No. 167.  JOHN COSIN

[*A Letter from Cosin to Mr. Cordel at Blois.  Works*, ed. L. A. C. T., Vol. IV, pp. 401–408.  It was first published by William Fleetwood, in his *Judgement of the Church of England in the Case of Lay Baptism* (1712, anonymous).  The isolation of the Anglican exiles on the Continent naturally led them to look as favorably as they could upon the Protestant Churches with which they were brought into contact. Nothing seems known of the Mr. Cordel to whom the letter was addressed.]

*To Mr. Cordel at Blois.*

Paris, Feb. 7, 1650.

I like your moderation well, in giving so fair and calm an answer to Monsieur Testard's motion for communicating in their Church, which truly (to speak my mind freely to you) I would not wish to any of ours absolutely to refuse, or determine to be unlawful, for fear of a greater scandal that may thereupon arise, than we can tell how to answer or excuse : especially if any of us should renounce it upon these two grounds which you allege for them, 1. that they have no Priests, 2. that they have no consecration of the elements.

I. For, as to the first, though we may safely say, and maintain it, that their ministers are not so duly and rightly ordained, as they should be, by those Prelates and Bishops of the Church, who since the Apostles' time have only had the ordinary power and authority to make and constitute a Priest, yet, that by reason of this defect there is a total *nullity* in their ordination, or that they be therefore no Priests or Ministers of the Church at all, because they are ordained by those only who are no more but Priests or Ministers among them, for my part, I would be loath to affirm and determine against them.  And these are my reasons :

First, I conceive that the power of Ordination was restrained to Bishops, rather by *Apostolical practice*, and the perpetual custom and canons of the Church, than by any *absolute precept*, that either Christ or His Apostles gave about it.  Nor can I yet meet with any convincing argument to set it upon a more high and divine institution.  From which customs and laws of the universal Church, (therein following the example of the Apostles,) though I reckon it to be a great presumption and fault for any particular Church to recede, and may truly say that *fieri non oportuit*, (when the college of mere Presbyters shall ordain and make a Priest,) yet I cannot so peremptorily say that *factum non valet*, and pronounce the ordination to be utterly void.  For as, in the case of *Baptism* we take just exceptions against a layman, or a woman, that presumes to give it, and may as justly punish them by the censures of the Church wherein they live for taking upon them to do that office, which was never committed unto them, yet, if once they have done it, we make not their act and administration of Baptism void, nor presume we to iterate the Sacrament after them,—so may it well be in the case of *Ordination*, and the ministers of the reformed congregations in France : who are liable to give an account, both to God and His Church in general, for taking upon them to exercise that power, which by the perpetual practice and laws of His Church they were never permitted to exercise, and may justly be faulted for it, both by the verdict of all others who are members of the Catholic Church, (as we are that adhere to the laws of it more strictly and peaceably than they do,) and by the censures of a lawful meeting or general council of that Church, which at anytime shall come to have authority over them. And yet, all this while, the act which they do, though it be *disorderly* done, and the ordinations which they make, though they make them *unlawfully*, shall not be altogether null and invalid, no more than the act of baptizing before mentioned, or the act of consecrating or administering the Eucharist by a Priest that is suspended, and restrained from exercising his power and office in the Church. Therefore, if at any time a minister so ordained in these French Churches came to incorporate himself in ours, and to receive a public charge or cure of souls among us in the Church of England, (as I have known some of them to have so done of late, and can instance in many other before my time,) our Bishops did not re-ordain him before they admitted [him] to his charge, as they would have done if his former ordination here in France had been void. Nor did our laws require more of him than to declare his public consent to the religion received amongst us, and to subscribe the articles established. And I love not to be herein more wise, or harder, than our own Church is ; which because it hath never publicly condemned and pronounced the ordinations of the other reformed Churches to be void, as it doth not those of the unreformed Churches neither among the Papists, (though I hear that the ministers here (see note A.) in France and Geneva use so to do, who will not admit a Papist Priest himself to exercise the office of a minister among them, till they have re-ordained him,) for my part, as to that particular, I dare not take upon me to condemn, or determine a nullity of their own ordinations against them : though, in the interim, I take it to be utterly a fault among them, and a great presumption, deserving a great censure to be inflicted on them by such a power of the Church as may, by the grace of God, be at any time duly gathered together hereafter against them, as well for the amendment of many other disorders and defects in their Church, as for this particular *inorderly ordination* and defect of Episcopacy amongst them.

Secondly, Besides that this their boldness, presumption, and novelty, (in setting up themselves, without any invincible necessity that they had so to do, against the Apostolical practice and perpetual order of God's Church till their days,) was always faulted and reserved for further censure in due time, which they have justly merited, there have been both learned and eminent men, (as well in former ages as in this, and even among the Roman Catholics as well as Protestants,) who have held and maintained it for good and passable divinity, that Presbyters have the intrinsical power of ordination *in actu primo*, though for the avoiding of schism (as St. Hierome speaks) and preserving order and discipline in the Church, they have been restrained ever since the first times, and still are (but where they take a liberty to themselves that was never duly given them) from exercising their power *in actu secundo* ; and therefore that, however their act of ordaining other presbyters shall be void according to the strictness of the canon, (in regard they were universally prohibited from executing that act, and breaking the order and discipline of the Church), yet that the same act shall not be simply void in the nature of the thing, in regard that the intrinsical power remained, when the exercise of it was suspended, and taken from them. Of this opinion and judgement in old time were St. Hierome, and his followers, alleged by Gratian, *Dist.*, 93 ; and, of later times, the Master of the Sentences, lib. iv. dist. 24 ; Bonavent., *ibid.* 93, art. 2 ; with other schoolmen, as Aureol., *ibid.*, art. 2 ; and Anton. de Rosellis, *de Potest. Imper. et Papali*, part iv, c. 18 ; and, in this latter age, not only Armachanus in *Sum. ad quaest. Arm.*, lib. xi. c. 2, 3, etc., and c. 7 ; Alphons. a Castro, verb. *Episcopus* ; Mich. Medina, *De Sacr. Hom. Orig.*, lib. i, c. 5 ; among the Roman Catholics : but likewise Cassander, *In Consult.*, art. 14 ; besides Melancthon, Clementias, Gerardus, and Calixtus, amongst the Protestants ; and Bishop Jewel (*Def.*, p. ii, c. iii, d. 1, and c. ix, div. 1.) ; Dr. Field, *Of the Church*, lib. iii, c. 39 ; Hooker, *Eccles. Pol.*, lib. iii. 3 ult. ; and Mason, among the divines of our own Church. All which authors are of so great credit with you and me, that, though we are not altogether of their mind, yet we would be loath to let the world see, that we contradict them all, and condemn their judgement openly ; as needs we must, if we hold the contrary, and say that the ministers of the reformed French Churches, for want of episcopal ordination, have no order at all.

Thirdly, If upon this ground we renounce the French, we must for the very same reason renounce all the ministers of Germany besides, (for the superintendents, that make and ordain ministers there, have no new ordination beyond their own presbytery at all,) and then what will become of the Protestant party ?

Fourthly, If the Church and kingdom of England have acknowledged them, (as they did in admitting of them, when they fled thither for refuge, and placing them by public authority in divers of the most eminent cities among us, without prohibiting to any of our people to go and communicate with them,) why should we, that are but private persons, utterly disclaim their communion in their own country ?

Fifthly, St. Cyprian's error, in re-baptizing heretics, was as scandalous to other Churches abroad, as the French error is in their ordaining of ministers here; and yet, those other Churches abroad did not renounce communion with them, but Cornelius and his clergy could well agree with him and his followers, notwithstanding the difference between them in that particular; which is a fair pattern for ourselves, though they in the meanwhile be in the wrong, as St. Cyprian then was, (and so we may tell them, without disclaiming their communion,) and we in the right, as Cornelius then was.

Sixthly, Somewhat it is, that they do not absolutely disclaim Episcopacy, nor ever did; but say and hold, that their Presbyters are Bishops, especially the chief Presbyters that preside at their ordinations and their courts of jurisdiction. So that the true question between us and them is not so much whether there ought to be Bishops in the Church or no, as whether their Presbyters be true Bishops: wherein I think they will have more to do, to defend themselves for want of *subordination*, than of *ordination* itself. For, where the clergy are any great multitude, order doth necessarily require that they be distinguished by degrees: and therefore, as they have ever been, so we hold (and, as I believe, we hold most truly) there ever ought to be, at least two sorts of ecclesiastical persons besides Deacons, the one subordinate to the other, as inferior ministers were to the Apostles at the beginning, and to the Bishops always since: which we find plainly set forth in the Scripture, and all ecclesiastical records that followed after.

Thus, by all that I have said in this first point, you see my mind; wherein I seek the ways of peace with others, without prejudice to the truth and right that we have among ourselves. And therefore, under that *protestation* (see note B.) which Monsieur Testard offers you a permission to make, and considering there is no prohibition of our Church against it, (as there is against our communicating with the Papists, and *that* well grounded upon the Scripture and Will of God,) I do not see but that both you and others that are with you may (either in case of necessity, when you cannot have the Sacrament among yourselves, or in regard of declaring your unity in professing the same religion, which you and they do) go otherwhiles to communicate reverently with them of the French Church. Only I could wish, that, as you shall be admitted to your protestation *before* you do it, so you may be likewise admitted to receive that blessed Eucharist devoutly upon your knees, and have the words pronounced to you, *when* they deliver it, which even in Scotland they omit not, and which in effect the ministers here in France say before, both in their exhortation or declaration to the people, and in their prayers to God: " *Prenez, mangez les vivandes sacrées de notre Seigneur Jésus Christ, qui nous veut vraiment faire participants de Son Corps et de Son Sang : le pain céleste pour vous repaître et nourrir à vie éternelle : la Communion de Jésus Christ notre Seigneur, livré pour nous à mort, et nous donné en viande et nourriture de vie éternelle, en certaine foi que nous jouissons de Son Corps et de Son Sang, voire de Lui, tout entièrement : Jésus Christ, étant vrai Dieu et vrai homme, est véritablement le saint pain céleste pour nous vivifier.*" Any of which sentences (being their own already) if you could obtain to be particularly said to you, when you receive the Sacrament in both kinds, it would be more agreeable to the institution and nature of that holy action and service, and more efficacious to the elevating of your devout souls at that instant time, than barely to pass by, and have nothing said to you, but what was generally said before in the declaration to all the people. Nor know I any reason, why they may not as well satisfy your desires in these two particulars, (without alleging the order of their Church against it,) as suffer you to make your *protestation*, which is no less against their order than the others are : though we hold not either of them so material, as that without them there may be no communion at all.

II. Now, as to the second point of consecrating the Sacrament, I shall need to say no more, but that, whether you take it after the way of the Greek Church by prayers and invocations, or after the way of the Latin, by repeating the words of our Saviour in the institution of the Sacrament, it cannot be denied but that these French Churches have them both : as you may see in their public books appointed for that purpose, though disposed after another order than ours is. And if it be *idem*, though it be *idem alio modo*, it alters not the substance or nature of the thing itself. Which is as much as at the present I can say to both your demands : and which you may communicate to whom you please, (to Monsieur Testard and all, if you will,) but specially to my noble friend Sir Ralph Verney, whose servant I am, as I am likewise truly yours,

J. C.

*Note A.*

A. Monsieur Testard can tell you whether this be true or no ; and, if it be true, I know not how they will be able to justify it.

*Note B.*

B. Which was, not to recede in any wise from the doctrine and discipline of the Church of England ; nor thereby to approve this discipline of the French Churches for a rule to others ; or to join with them that renounce Episcopacy, and condemn the proceedings of our own Church, or the laws of our own kingdom.

## No. 168.  JOHN BRAMHALL

[From *A Vindication of Himself and the Episcopal Clergy from the Presbyterian Charge of Popery, as it is managed by Mr. Baxter in his ' Treatise of the Grotian Religion,'* Chapter III.  *Works,* Vol. III, ed. *L. A. C. T.,* p. 518.  Cp. note on No. **263**.]

Episcopal Divines will readily subscribe to the determination of the learned Bishop of Winchester [Andrewes], in His Answer to the Second Epistle of Molinaeus.—" Nevertheless, if our form [*viz.*, Episcopacy] be of Divine right, it doth not follow from thence that there is no salvation without it, or that a Church cannot consist without it.  He is blind who does not see Churches consisting without it ; he is hard-hearted who denieth them salvation.  We are none of those hard-hearted persons ; we put a great difference between these things.  There may be something absent in the exterior regiment, which is of Divine right, and yet salvation be to be had."  This mistake proceedeth from not distinguishing between the true nature and essence of the Church, which we do readily grant them, and the integrity or perfection of a Church, which we cannot grant them without swerving from the judgement of the Catholic Church.

# XI. THE SACRAMENTS

# (1) PRINCIPLES

## No. 169.  RICHARD HOOKER

[From *The Laws of Ecclesiastical Polity*, Book V, Chapter i, §§ 2, 3 ;  Chapter lvii,
§§ 1, 3, 5 ; Chapter lviii, § 2.  *Works*, ed. J. Keble, Vol. II, pp. 219 f. ;  255, 256 f.,
258 ;  259 f.  Cp. note on No. 148.]

WE all admire and honour the Holy Sacraments, not respecting so
much the service which we do unto God in receiving them, as the dignity
of that sacred and secret gift which we thereby receive from God.  Seeing
that Sacraments therefore consist altogether in relation to some such
gift or grace supernatural as only God can bestow, how should any but
the Church administer those ceremonies as Sacraments which are not
thought to be Sacraments by any but by the Church ?

There is in Sacraments to be observed their force and their form of
administration.  Upon their force their necessity dependeth.  So that
how they are necessary we cannot discern till we see how effectual they
are.  When Sacraments are said to be visible signs of invisible grace,
we thereby conceive how grace is indeed the very end for which these
heavenly mysteries were instituted, and besides sundry other properties
observed in them, the matter whereof they consist is such as signifieth,
figureth, and representeth their end.  But still their efficacy resteth
obscure to our understanding, except we search somewhat more
distinctly what grace in particular that is whereunto they are referred,
and what manner of operation they have towards it.

The use of Sacraments is but only in this life, yet so that here they
concern a far better life than this, and are for that cause accompanied
with *grace which worketh Salvation*.  Sacraments are the powerful
instruments of God to eternal life.  For as our natural life consisteth
in the union of the body with the soul, so our life supernatural in the
union of the soul with God.  And forasmuch as there is no union of
God with man without that mean between both which is both, it seemeth
requisite that we first consider how God is in Christ, then how Christ
is in us, and how the Sacraments do serve to make us partakers of
Christ.  In other things we may be more brief, but the weight of these
requireth largeness. . . .

It greatly offendeth that some, when they labour to shew the use of
the holy Sacraments, assign unto them no end but only *to teach* the
mind, by other senses, that which the Word doth teach by hearing.
Whereupon, how easily neglect and careless regard of so heavenly

mysteries may follow, we see in part by some experience had of those men with whom that opinion is most strong. For where the Word of God may be heard, which teacheth with much more expedition and more full explication any thing we have to learn, if all the benefit we reap by Sacraments be instruction, they which at all times have opportunity of using the better mean to that purpose, will surely hold the worse in less estimation. And unto infants which are not capable of instruction, who would not think it a mere superfluity that any Sacrament is administered, if to administer the Sacraments be but to teach receivers what God doth for them? There is of Sacraments therefore undoubtedly some other more excellent and heavenly use. . . .

But their chiefest force and virtue consisteth . . . in that they are heavenly ceremonies, which God hath sanctified and ordained to be administered in His Church, first, as marks whereby to know when God doth impart the vital or saving grace of Christ unto all that are capable thereof, and secondly as means conditional which God requireth in them unto whom He imparteth grace. For sith God in Himself is invisible, and cannot by us be discerned working, therefore when it seemeth good in the eyes of His heavenly wisdom, that men for some special intent and purpose should take notice of His glorious presence, He giveth them some plain and sensible token whereby to know what they cannot see. For Moses to see God and live was impossible, yet Moses by fire knew where the glory of God extraordinarily was present. The angel, by whom God endued the waters of the pool called Bethesda with supernatural virtue to heal, was not seen of any, yet the time of the angel's presence known by the troubled motions of the waters themselves. The Apostles by fiery tongues which they saw were admonished when the Spirit, which they could not behold, was upon them. In like manner it is with us. Christ and His Holy Spirit with all their blessed effects, though entering into the soul of man we are not able to apprehend or express how, do notwithstanding give notice of the times when they use to make their access, because it pleaseth Almighty God to communicate by sensible means those blessings which are incomprehensible. . . .

This is therefore the necessity of Sacraments. That saving grace which Christ originally is or hath for the general good of His whole Church, by sacraments He severally deriveth into every member thereof. Sacraments serve as the instruments of God to that end and purpose, moral instruments, the use whereof is in our hands, the effect in His; for the use we have His express commandment, for the effect His conditional promise: so that without our obedience to the one, there is of the other no apparent assurance, as contrariwise where the signs and sacraments of His grace are not either through contempt unreceived, or received with contempt, we are not to doubt but that they really give what they promise, and are what they signify. For we take not Baptism nor the Eucharist for bare *resemblances* or memorials of things absent, neither for *naked signs* and testimonies assuring us of grace received before, but (as they are indeed and in verity) for means effectual whereby God when we take the sacraments delivereth into our hands that grace available unto eternal life, which grace the sacraments represent or signify. . . .

In writing and speaking of the blessed sacraments we use for the most part under the name of their Substance not only to comprise that whereof they outwardly and sensibly consist, but also the secret grace which they signify and exhibit. This is the reason wherefore commonly in definitions, whether they be framed larger to augment, or stricter to abridge the number of sacraments, we find grace expressly mentioned as their true essential form, elements as the matter whereunto that form doth adjoin itself. But if that be separated which is secret, and that considered alone which is seen, as of necessity it must in all those speeches that make distinction of sacraments from sacramental grace, the name of a sacrament in such speeches can imply no more than what the *outward substance* thereof doth comprehend. And to make complete the outward substance of a sacrament, there is required an outward form, which form sacramental elements receive from sacramental words. Hereupon it groweth, that many times there are three things said to make up the substance of a sacrament, namely, the grace which is thereby offered, the element which shadoweth or signifieth grace, and the word which expresseth what is done by the element. So that whether we consider the outward by itself alone, or both the outward and inward substance of any sacrament, there are in the one respect but two essential parts, and in the other but three that concur to give sacraments their full being.

## No. 170. EDWARD REYNOLDS

[From *Meditations on the Holy Sacrament of the Lord's Last Supper*, Chapter II. *Works*, ed. London (1826), Vol. III, pp. 7–9. This treatise was published in 1638. But Reynolds had written it, as he says, " with respect only to mine own private use many years since, when I was a young student in the University, as my first theological essay." An attempt, without the consent of the author, to issue the *Meditations* surreptitiously led him to publish them himself.]

The promises and Word of Grace with the Sacraments are all but as so many sealed deeds, to make over unto all successions of the Church,—so long as they continue legitimate children and observe the laws on their part required,—an infallible claim and title unto that good which is not yet revealed, unto that inheritance which is as yet laid up unto that life which is hid with God and was never yet fully opened or let shine upon the earth. Even in Paradise there was a Sacrament,—a tree of life indeed it was, but there was but one.

Whereas Adam was to eat of all the fruits in the garden, he was there but to taste *sometimes* of life; it was not to be his perpetual and only food. We read of *a tree of life* in the beginning of the Bible, and of *a tree of life* in the end too; that was in Adam's Paradise on earth, this in St. John's Paradise in Heaven. But that did bear but the first-fruits of life, the earnest of an after-fulness; this bare life in abundance, for it bare twelve manner of fruits, and that every month,—which shews both the completeness and eternity of that glory which we expect. And as the tree of Paradise was but a Sacrament of life in Heaven, so Paradise itself was but a Sacrament of Heaven. Certainly, Adam was placed among the dark and shady trees of the garden that he might, in an emblem, acknowledge that he was as yet but in the shadow of life, the substance whereof he was elsewhere to receive. Even when the Church was pure, it was not perfect; it had an age of infancy, when it had a state of innocence. Glory was not communicated unto Adam himself, without the veil of a Sacrament. The light of God did not shine on Paradise with a spreading and immediate ray. Even there it was mixed with shadows, and represented only in a sacramental reflex, not in its own direct and proper brightness. The Israelites in the wilderness had light indeed, but it was in a cloud; and they had the presence of God in the Ark, but it was under several coverings; and they had the light of God shining on the face of Moses, but it was under the veil; and Moses himself did see God, but it was in a cloud;—so incapable is the Church, while encompassed with a body of sin, to see the lustre of that glory which is expected. Certainly, as the Son of God did admirably humble Himself, in His hypostatical union, unto a visible flesh,—so doth He still, with equal wonder and lowliness, humble Himself in a sacramental union, unto visible elements. Strange it is, that that mercy which is so wonderful that the Angels desire to look into it,—so unconceivable, as that it hath not entered into the thought of man; of such height and length and breadth and depth as passeth knowledge,—should yet be made the object of our lowest faculties, that that which is hid from the wise and prudent in man's little world, his mind and spirit,—should be revealed unto the babes, his senses. It were almost a contradiction in anything, save God's mercy, to be so deep as that no thought can fathom it, and yet so obvious that each eye may see it. " *Handle Me and see ;* for a spiritual substance hath not flesh,"—was sometimes the argument of Christ; and yet " *Handle and see, take and eat,* for a spiritual grace is conveyed by flesh " is the Sacrament of Christ. So humble is His mercy, that, since we cannot raise our understandings to the compre- hension of Divine mysteries, He will bring down and submit those mysteries to the apprehension of our senses. Hereafter our bodies shall be over-clothed with a spiritual glory, by a real union unto Christ in His Kingdom. Meantime, that special glory which we groan after is here over-clothed with weak and visible elements, by a sacramental union at His Table. Then shall sense be exalted and made a fit subject of glory; here is glory humbled and made a fit object of sense. *Then shall we see as we are seen, face to face; here we see but as in a glass, darkly,*—in the glass of the creature, in the glass of the Word, in the glass of the Sacraments. And surely these are in themselves clear and bright glasses; yet we see even in them but darkly in regard of that vapour and steam which exhaleth from our corrupt nature, when we use them; and even on these doth our soul look through other dark glasses, the windows of sense. But yet, at the best, they are but glasses, whose properties are to present nothing but the pattern, the shadow, the type of those things which are in their substance quite behind us, and therefore out of sight. So then, in general, the nature of a Sacrament is to be the representative of a substance, the sign of a covenant, the seal of a purchase, the figure of a body, the witness of our faith, the earnest of our hope, the presence of things distant, the sight of things absent, the taste of things unconceivable, and the knowledge of things that are past knowledge.

# (2) THE NUMBER OF THE SACRAMENTS

## No. 171.  JOSEPH HALL

[From *The Old Religion*, Chapter XI (" Of the Seven Sacraments "), §§ 2, 3. *Works*, ed. Peter Hall (1837), Vol. IX, pp. 370 f.  Cp. note on No. **231**.]

### Seven Sacraments beside Scripture.

NOT to scan particulars, which all yield ample exceptions, but to wind them all up in one bottom, whosoever shall look into the Scripture shall find it apparent that as in the time of man's innocence there were but two Sacraments, the Tree of Life and the Tree of Knowledge, so, before and under the Law, however they had infinite rites, yet in the proper sense they had but two Sacraments,—the same, in effect, with those under the Gospel; the one, the Sacrament of Initiation, which was their Circumcision, paralleled by that Baptism which succeeded it, the other, the Sacrament of our Holy Communion, that spiritual meat and drink which was their Paschal Lamb and Manna and water from the rock, pre-figuring the true Lamb of God and Bread of Life and Blood of our Redemption.

The great Apostle of the Gentiles that well knew the analogy hath compared both : *Moreover, brethren, I would not have you ignorant, how that all our fathers were under the cloud, and all passed through the sea, and all were baptized in the cloud, and in the sea, and all did eat the same spiritual meat, and all did drink the same spiritual drink ; for they drank of that spiritual rock, that followed them, and that rock was Christ* (*I Cor.* x, 1–4).

What is this in any just construction but that the same two Sacraments of Baptism and the Lord's Supper, which we celebrate under the Gospel, were the very same with those which were celebrated by God's ancient people under the Law,—they two and no more ? *Hoc facite, Do this*, is our warrant for the one ; and, *Ite, baptizate, etc., Go, teach and baptize*, for the other.  There is deep silence in the rest.

### Seven Sacraments against Reason.

In Reason it must be yielded that no man hath power to set a seal, but he whose the writing is.

Sacraments, then, being the seals of God's gracious evidences whereby He hath conveyed to us eternal life, can be instituted by no other than the same power that can assure and perform life to His creature.

In every Sacrament, therefore, must be a Divine institution and command of an element that signifies, of a grace that is signified, of a word adjoined to that element, of a holy act adjoined to that word. Where these concur not, there can be no true Sacrament,—and they are palpably missing in these five adjections of the Church of Rome.

Lastly, the Sacraments of the New Law, as St. Austin often, flowed out of the side of Christ. None flowed thence but the Sacrament of Water, which is Baptism, and the Sacrament of Blood, in the Supper, whereof the Author saith *This cup is the New Testament in My Blood, which is shed for you*. The rest, never flowing either from the side or from the lips of Christ, are as new and misnamed Sacraments justly rejected by us; and we thereupon as unjustly censured.

### No. 172. RICHARD BAXTER

[From *Confirmation and Restauration, The Necessary Means of Reformation and Reconciliation for the Healing of the Corruptions and Divisions of the Churches*. Under "Proposition 10". *Works*, ed. W. Orme (1830), Vol. XIV, pp. 449 f.; ed. London, 1838, Vol. IV, p. 305. In this treatise, which appeared in 1658, Baxter opposed restricting the administration of the Rite to Bishops.]

The Papists tell us of Seven Sacraments,—Baptism, Confirmation, Penance, Orders, the Eucharist, Matrimony, and Extreme Unction. Calvin sticks not to yield them three. The name "Sacrament" being not in Scripture, but of mere Ecclesiastic use, and being a word that will stretch, I distinguish between three sorts of Sacraments: (1) For any Divine institution which notably signifieth spiritual grace; and so, though I think Extreme Unction none as being now no duty, yet I doubt not but there are more than seven. (2) For any solemn investiture of a person by ministerial delivery in a state of Church privileges, or some special Gospel mercy. And so I grant that there are five Sacraments,—Baptism, Confirmation, Absolution, the Lord's Supper, and Ordination. As a man that delivereth possession of a house doth deliver the key to him that enters; and as we are invested in the possession of land by the delivery of a twig or turf; and as ministers are wont to be invested, or have induction into the Churches, by giving them the books and the bell-ropes, and as women were wont to be married with a ring; and as a prince doth knight a man by a sword; so Christ by His ministers doth first by Baptism invest us in our Church state and infant privileges; and by Confirmation confirm us in our Church state and invest us with a right to the privileges of the adult; and by Absolution reinvest us in the privileges that we had forfeited; and by the Lord's Supper deliver to us Christ and His benefits for our ordinary nourishment and growth in grace; and by Ordination He investeth the person ordained with ministerial power. (3) But taking the word "Sacrament" in that strictest sense, as our

Divines define a Sacrament, as it is an outward sign of Christ's institution for the obsignation of the full covenant of grace betwixt Him and the covenanter, and a delivery, representation, and investiture of the grace or benefits of that covenant; thus we have only two Sacraments, Baptism, and the Lord's Supper. But truly, I would not quarrel with them for the mere name as to the five which I mentioned.

## No. 173.  EDWARD GEE

[From *The Texts Examined which Papists cite out of the Bible for the Proof of their Doctrine concerning Seven Sacraments and the Efficacy of them*, Part I, beginning. *Enchiridion Theologicum Anti-Romanum* (Oxford, University Press, 1837), pp. 460 f. Gee's treatise was issued in two separate parts, both of which were published in 1688.]

We have two Sacraments which are certainly of our Blessed Saviour's institution, for which we are thankful and with which we are satisfied. Had our Saviour instituted more sacraments, we should have been more thankful and should have had greater obligations to gratitude. And this should satisfy the gentlemen of the Church of Rome and abate their wrath and severities against us, since though we reject those five additional Sacraments which they would be obtruding upon the world, yet we do it not because they are Sacraments we do not like, but because they are not Sacraments at all,—because they are not Christ's Sacraments, Who never appointed them, but the Church of Rome's Sacraments, which did appoint them, or advance them to the dignity of Sacraments. And this we take to be a sufficient reason why we should reject the five additional Sacraments, since neither the Church of Rome herself, nor all the Churches of the world together, are able to institute one Sacrament, and this is what their learned men dare not deny. And therefore they are careful always to lay claim to the Scriptures and to affirm that in the New Testament we find the institution of every one of those Sacraments, which they teach, and we of the Church of England refuse.

## No. 174.  LANCELOT ANDREWES

[From *Two Answers to Cardinal Perron*.  *Minor Works*, ed. L. A. C. T., pp. 25 f. Cp. note on No. 218.]

We deny not but that the title of *Sacrament* hath sometimes been given by the Fathers unto all these five [1] in a larger signification. But so is it also to many things more : and, namely, (as it is alleged after by the Cardinal, in the XVII Head,) *salt* is called a *Sacrament : Sacramentum Catechumenis non detur, nisi solitum sal*. But *pour vrai et propre Sacrament*, there is not any of the Fathers so affirms any of the five. The whole matter is a mere λογομαχία. If the thing were agreed upon, we should not strive for the name.

---

[1] [*I.e.*, the "five commonly called Sacraments" of Article XXV.]

# (3) THE UNWORTHINESS OF THE MINISTER

## No. 175. FRANCIS WHITE

[From *A Reply to Jesuit Fisher's Answer*, p. 52. Cp. note on No. **228**.]

THE promises of Christ made to the Church concerning His presence and assistance to His Word and Sacraments, preached and administered according to His commandment, are fulfilled when wicked persons execute the office and perform the work of outward ministry. For although wicked persons, like the carpenters of Noah's Ark, reap no benefit to themselves, yet God Almighty concurreth with their ministry (being His own Ordinance) for the salvation of all devout and worthy communicants.

# (4) THE DOCTRINE OF INTENTION

## No. 176. JOHN BRAMHALL

[From *Protestant Ordinations Defended; or An Answer to the Twentieth Chapter of the ' Guide of Faith, or the Third Part of the Antidote of S.N., Doctor of Divinity,'* § 3. *Works,* ed. *L. A. C. T.,* Vol. V, pp. 210–214. The *Guide of Faith*, the work of an English Jesuit, Sylvester Norris (*d.* 1630), was issued in 1615; a second and much fuller edition appeared in 1621. Bramhall's reply was written between the years 1644 and 1654 when he was abroad. It is thus an earlier writing than his *Consecration and Succession of Protestants Bishops Justified* (cp. note on No. **164**). But it was first published in the posthumous folio edition of Bramhall's *Works*, which appeared at Dublin in 1676.]

His [*i.e.* Norris'] third argument is contained in the 6th. section. The " English superintendents, after their fall from the Roman Church, neither intended to give those Holy Orders instituted by Christ, neither did the ordained intend to receive them. . . . For . . . the Priesthood instituted by Christ " comprehended " two " functions : " the one appertaining to the . . . Real Body of Christ, to complete it and offer it to God ; . . . the other, over the Mystical Body of Christ, to remit sins." But with the Protestants, the consecrating Bishops " do not intend to give, nor the consecrated ministers to receive " either of these two functions ; but on the contrary do " deny " them, and " disclaim " them. Therefore, " notwithstanding their character," they " have not those Sacred Orders which were instituted by Christ : " but " their Ordination is a mere profanation of that Sacrament."

There is no opinion of the Roman Catholics of more desperate consequence than this, of the necessity of the minister's intention to the being of a Sacrament, especially according to the literal sense of the word. First, for Baptism, it leaves no man certain whether he be a Christian or not. It puts it in the power of an atheistical Priest, or such an one as Judas was, to exclude out of the Church Triumphant any or all those souls, which should be admitted by him into the Communion of the Militant Church. For if he intend not to baptize them at all, or intend to baptize them amiss, they perish irreparably according to their doctrine, since Baptism cannot be iterated, and the nullity of this hypocritical action cannot be discovered by man, but is known to God alone, Who is the seacher of hearts. Secondly, in the Holy Eucharist, it subjects every Roman Catholic to manifest peril of idolatry, to adore bread instead of Christ,—that is, if the consecrator either maliciously or negligently intend not to consecrate (of which delinquency some Romish Priests have confessed themselves culpable, and have suffered for it) ; or if the consecrator be no Priest, which may easily happen, for want of the like intention in any one of those Bishops, from whom he derives his Holy Orders, throughout a whole series or succession of sixteen hundred years' continuance. Thirdly, in their Ordination. It leaves no Church, not Rome itself, certain whether they have Holy Orders or not ; that is as much as to say, whether they be a Church or not. For as the failing of any one link breaks a chain in sunder, so the want of this intention in any one Bishop, in a long row of seventy or eighty predecessors, breaks in sunder the chain of their succession, and leaves all those, who pretend to derive from thence downwards, without Holy Orders.

This is *the measure wherewith* they *mete out* to us ; but forgetting that *a false balance is an abomination to the Lord,* they have another measure to receive in for themselves. Here they mitigate and mollify the rigour of their tenet, and plane it so long with their distinctions until they leave nothing of it remaining. First, they distinguish an intention into explicit, that is, particular or determinate, and implicit, that is, general—to do what the Church doth, or what Christ instituted. The Councils of Florence and Trent require only an implicit intention as necessary. If they would allow the same favour to the Protestants which they assume to themselves, this argument were at an end ; for the Protestants intend to do what Christ instituted. But their Schools go yet further, and distinguish an implicit intention into actual and habitual ; actual, that is, to consider really what they do, whilst they are celebrating the Sacraments ; habitual is that, which they have sometimes actually had, though they have it not in present then when they celebrate the Sacrament. They say an actual intention is not necessary, neither do those distractions which creep upon us, whilst we are celebrating those Holy Mysteries, render the act done invalid ; but an habitual or virtual intention, that is, an impression left in the imagination, is sufficient. Many of their authors rest not here, but distinguish an intention into internal, which they say is not absolutely necessary, and external, which is nothing else but an actual application of the due matter, with an actual expression of the words prescribed by the authority of Christ. This intention the Protestants allow, and never want. If the one be acknowledged to be Catholics, why are the other censured as heretics ?

To his argument then I answer :—

First, that the interior intention of the consecrant is not necessary to make the ordination valid. If a prince send a present to a friend by an untrusty servant, who envieth his master's bounty, or wisheth that the gift might do his friend no good, yet this shall not deprive him of the fruit of the prince's bounty. God's grace is not annihilated by the malice, much less by the negligence, of a sinful man.

Secondly, I answer, that the Protestants have an implicit intention in their Ordinations to do what the Catholic Church doth, and to do whatsoever Christ instituted, though they are far from believing, that the Roman Church is the Catholic Church ; and this is sufficient, our adversaries being judges, to the validity of Holy Orders.  Differences in opinion about the manner or extent of believing, do not evacuate the grace of the Sacraments.  One intends to produce the Body of Christ out of the bread ; another intends to adduce it to the bread.  The former cries out, that adduction implies only a transubiation, not a transubstantiation ; the latter thunders it out aloud that the Body which is produced of bread is not the same Body which was born of a Virgin. Thus their greatest champions gore one another.  Yet they do not believe, that this doth invalidate the Sacraments.

Thirdly, to his two functions, of consecrating and remitting sin, Protestants do intend to confer them both, so far as either Christ did confer them or the Blessed Apostles execute them.  Doubtless they know their own intentions better than S[ylvester] N[orris].  He who saith, " Take thou authority to exercise the Office of a Priest in the Church of God " (as the Protestant consecrators do) doth intend all things requisite to the Priestly function, and amongst the rest, to offer a representative Sacrifice, to commemorate and to apply the Sacrifice which Christ made upon the Cross.  But for any other Sacrifice, distinct from that, which is propitiatory, meritorious, and satisfactory by its proper virtue and power, the Scriptures do not authorize, the Fathers did not believe, the Protestants do not receive, any such.  This is a certain truth, that the Passion of Christ is the only ransom and propitiation for sin.  He who saith, *Whose sins thou dost remit they are remitted, whose sins thou dost retain are retained* (which are the very words used in the Protestants' Form of Ordination) surely intends to confer a power to remit sins.  We acknowledge that he who is ordained is enabled by his office many ways to put away sins.  1. By Baptism ;—" I believe one Baptism for the remission of sins " ; so saith the Creed.  2. By the Sacrament of the Lord's Supper ;—*This is My Blood, which is shed for you and for many, for remission of sins* ; so said our Saviour.  3. By prayer ;—*Call for the presbyters of the Church ; the prayer of faith shall save the sick ; and if he have committed sins, they shall be forgiven him.* 4. By preaching the word of reconciliation ;—*God was in Christ, reconciling the world unto Himself, not imputing their trespasses unto them ; and hath committed unto us the word of reconciliation.*  5. By special absolution ;—*Whose sins ye remit, they are remitted.*  To forgive sins is no more proper to God than to work wonders above the course of nature.  The one is communicable as the other.  The Priest absolves, or, to say more properly, God absolves by the Priest.  Therefore he saith, " I absolve thee in the Name of the Father, and of the Son, and of the Holy Ghost." God remits sovereignly, imperially, primitively, absolutely; the Priest's power is derivative, delegate, dependent, ministerial, conditional. It is true the Protestants differ amongst themselves whether the Absolution of the Priest be declarative or operative; that is, about the manner. And so do the Romanists, likewise one with another. Yea, I dare say, that their Schools do scarcely ever run more [into] division than about this; which they make the Sacrament of Reconciliation.

# XII. BAPTISM AND CONFIRMATION

# (1) BAPTISM

## No. 177.  HENRY MORE

[From a letter from Henry More to William Penn.  Richard Ward, *The Life of the Learned and Pious Dr. Henry More*, London, 1710, pp. 316–318.  The subject of the whole letter was " Baptism and the Lord's Supper and some Usages of the Quakers "; it was printed by Richard Ward for the first time (pp. 311–350).]

IT is plain, therefore, that the making of disciples to Christ and entering them into His flock by Water-Baptism is an Institution of Christ.  And from this passage of *John* iv, 1, where Christ is said πλείονας μαθητὰς ποιεῖν καὶ βαπτίζειν, *to make and baptize more disciples than John*, is most easily and naturally understood that precept Christ gives to His Apostles, *Matt.* xxviii, [19], *Go therefore* μαθητεύσατε (*i.e.* μαθητὰς ποιεῖτε) *make* disciples of all nations (now promiscuously, as you did of *Jews* only at first), *baptizing them in the Name of the Father, Son, and Holy Ghost*.  But as you baptized them with water then, to bear My name and profess themselves My disciples, so now I enjoin the same Sacrament or Ceremony, but with a more explicit Form,— *In the Name of the Father, the Son and the Holy Ghost*.  Of the *Father*, the Creator and Original of All; of the *Son*, that is the Messias, or the Christ of God, in Whom the Eternal Logos became Man; and of the *Holy Spirit*, by Whose Illumination and Sanctification all true believers in the Messias (by virtue of this Regeneration through this Spirit, which the Messias promised should perpetually assist His Church) become the Sons of God.  This is the profession that, by the external ceremony of water, all nations that were converted to Christ were to be baptized into; and I think no man will be so extravagant as to think that this Form of Words was used without the ceremony of Water-Baptism accompanying it.  And there is no Baptism now that is available to mankind but this, namely that *One Baptism* that is into this *One Faith* and *One Lord*, the Christ of God the Father, Who has promised al requisite aids of His Spirit to them that rightly believe in Him.  And in this regard is it said, there is but *One Baptism*, because both the Water-Baptism and that of the Spirit signified thereby terminate in this one point, that is the profession of that *One Faith* and that *One Lord*, namely the Lord Christ, God and Man; the soul and body of the Messias being united with the Logos and so continuing as a gracious and powerful Intercessor for His Church with the Father for ever, according as He has promised, *Behold I am with you to the end of the World*.

But though this Baptism be truly One in one respect, and that a main one, as I have declared, yet it is not absurd in another sense to say there are Two, namely that of the Spirit and that of the Water ; *Flaminis et Fluminis*, as some have expressed it.   And the Author to the *Hebrews* seems to allude to some such thing, where he reckons amongst the first rudiments or principles of the Christian religion the doctrine of Baptisms,—this Water Baptism and that of the Spirit ; plainly acknowledging Two in this sense, that one is exterior and elementary, the other spiritual and interior.   But they drive at one thing, as the sense of a word and the sound of a word, though two things, are counted one, they reaching at one and the same mark.

## No. 178.   JOHN HACKET

[From *Christian Consolations; Taught from Five Heads in Religion*, Chapter V. The Five Heads, each of which has a Chapter devoted to it, are (1) Faith, (2) Hope, (3) The Holy Spirit, (4) Prayer, (5) The Sacraments.   This writing is included in Vol. I of Heber's edition of the *Works* of Jeremy Taylor, to whom Heber attributed it. The extract is from pp. 154–156 of that Volume.   The *Christian Consolations* was first published in 1671, and reprinted in 1840.]

Our Common Prayer-Book (a store-house of rare divinity) tells us what is to be expected at that laver for them that come to be baptized.

1. That God hath promised to be the Father of the faithful and of their seed, and will most surely perform and keep His promise with them ; and by this introduction we are incorporated into the Holy Congregation.   Behold, they whom we love above all others by nature, our children, are naturalized to be the citizens of the heavenly kingdom, and enter into it through this door of grace.

2. Secondly ; as God did save Noah and his family from perishing by water, and safely led the children of Israel through the Red Sea while their enemies were drowned ; so the millions of the nations whom God hath not given to Christ for His inheritance are drowned in their own lusts and corruptions.   But, O what a privilege it is to be among those few that are received into the ark of Christ's Church, to be exempted from the common deluge, and to be the faithful seed of Abraham, led through the channel of the sea, and baptized in the cloud that went along with them when the armies of the mighty are mightily consumed !

3. Thirdly ; we may gather out of our Church-office for Baptism, that the everlasting benediction of heavenly washing affords two comforts.   It signifies the Blood of Christ to cleanse us *per modum pretii*, as the price that was paid to ransom us from death ; and the sanctifying of the Holy Spirit to cleanse us *per modum habitus*, by His inbeing and celestial infusion : and both are put together in one collect, " that all that are baptized, may receive remission of sins by spiritual regeneration." *There is no remission of sin without blood*, says the Apostle, meaning the

invaluable Blood of the Lamb of God. And the heavenly thing is represented by the visible element of water; for there must be some aptitude between the sign and the thing signified, else it were not a Sacrament;—that as water washeth away the filth of the body, so the Blood of Christ delivereth our souls from the guilt and damnableness of sin. *The Blood of Christ, His Son, cleanseth us from all sin.* The metaphor of cleaning must have respect to baptismal water. Again, *Who loved us, and washed us from our sins in His Blood.* Where the Scripture speaks of washing from sin, it must be taken from the water of Baptism, figuring the virtue of Christ's Blood, that in the sight of His Father makes us white as snow. The Scriptures indeed strike most upon the other string, and more directly, as *Christ loved the Church, and gave Himself for it, that He might sanctify and cleanse it with the washing of water by the Word. He saved us by the washing of regeneration, and the renewing of the Holy Ghost,* and in many other places. Therefore, our Liturgy falls most upon the purifying operation of the Spirit, to be shadowed in the outward washing of water,—as when it prays, " Send Thy Holy Spirit to these infants, and grant that they may be baptized with water and with the Holy Ghost," and " Grant that all that are baptized may receive the fulness of Thy grace." Spiritual regeneration is that which the Gospel hath set forth to be the principal correlative of Baptism. O happy it is for us to be born again by water and the Holy Ghost! For better it were never to be born than not to be born twice.

God put a good mind unto us and reform one great fault in us; which is, that our Baptism being past over a great while ago, we cast it out of our memory, and meditate but little upon the benefits and comforts of it. We are got into the Church, and do in a sort forget how we got in. Whereas the whole life of a Christian man and woman should be a continual reflection how in Baptism we entered into covenant with Christ, " to believe in Him, to serve Him, to forsake the devil, the vanities of the world, and all sinful desires of the flesh." Water is a pellucid element to look through it to the bottom. So often look through the sanctified water, to see what Christ hath done for you, and what you have engaged to do for Christ. And there is no heart so full of blackness and melancholy, but will recover upon it, and be as fresh in sound health, as if it were filled with marrow and fatness.

## No. 179. JOHN HACKET

[From *A Century of Sermons upon several remarkable Subjects* (London, 1675), pp. 154, 155. This colossal folio is said to be a work of great rarity. There is a copy of it in the Bodleian. The text of the sermon from which the extract is taken, was *Matt.* iii, 13.]

The next part of my remonstrance is that the Baptism of John hath the same virtue with the Baptism of Christ. Take my reasons briefly.

1. It was the Baptism of Repentance, and Repentance cannot be taught without faith in Christ and remission of sins in His Blood. Take them two away, and repentance is but a lesson of heathen philosophy ; put them both together, and is there not all the benefit of Christ's Baptism, faith and forgiveness of sins ? Nay, directly, *Mark* i, 4, *John did preach the Baptism of Repentance for the remission of sins.* And indeed no man can separate true repentance from remission of sins, *At what time soever a sinner doth repent him, etc.* 2. The scope of his Baptism was to warn men to fly from the wrath to come ; that is the true washing of the Spirit. Says he to the Pharisees when they came to him to Jordan, *O ye generation of vipers, who hath warned ye to flee from the wrath to come ?* 3. Our Saviour foretelling to His disciples that the time was coming at the Feast of Pentecost when they should have a greater blessing from Heaven than ever they had before, *Acts* xv [*sic* ; *Acts* i, 15], *John truly baptized with water but ye shall be baptized with the Holy Ghost not many days hence ;* then the disciples had no other Baptism but John's until they were baptized with fire, and surely they had a true and an efficacious baptism. So Apollos knew of no other baptism but John's (*Acts* xviii, 25), and yet we do not find that he was sprinkled with any other Baptism. 4. This reason is of great weight. If John's were not the true Baptism of the Spirit which Christ received, then either all we have received a Baptism divers from Our Saviour, which were very comfortless ; or else we have not received the Baptism of the Spirit, which were every whit as comfortless. 5. John baptized at the same time while the disciples of Christ did baptize, even till the time that he was shut up in prison by Herod. And this he ought not to have done if his washing had been uneffectual, but to have it laid down when a more perfect Sacrament was afoot. These are the reasons, sufficient as I suppose, to prove that the Baptism of John had the same substantial virtue with the Baptism of Christ.

This is that opinion against which the Tridentine Council doth thunder forth *Anathema*. . . .

Though so ancient Fathers may seem to dissent from me, yet they are not so uncharitable to bid *Anathema* to any in so disputable a point. I am sure St. Austin, having disputed on both sides, concludes he would not strive eagerly with him that should say sins were remitted in the Baptism of John, meaning it did not essentially differ from the Baptism of Christ. Yet I will end with this . . . observation, that in some less principal respects, the Baptism of Christ doth exceed the Baptism of John. I will name five distinctions :—

1. *In forma verborum.* John baptized in the name of the Messias that came after him, *Acts* xix, 4, and it was more advantage to teach it to every of the Jews as he baptized them, one by one, than to proclaim it to the whole multitude. But Christ bade His disciples choose another

form, and for that He would not take all honour to Himself,—it must be the Name of the Father, and of the Son, and of the Holy Ghost.

2. They differ *in amplitudine nationum*. John meddled with none but such as were within the regions of Judaea, Christ bade His disciples to except no people, but to wash all nations from their sins.

3. Christ's Baptism transcends John's *in varietate personarum*. For it sounds not to likelihood that John baptized infants. They could not confess their sins nor learn the doctrine of repentance nor be taught the coming of the Messias; such only came to him. But Christ's Baptism pertains to little ones and *His Spirit was poured out upon all flesh, your sons and daughters shall prophecy, and your young men see visions*.

4. Christ's Baptism hath the upper hand *in gradibus efficaciae*. The Spirit is more operative in [His] Baptism, since Christ did go to His Father to send us His Comforter, than ever it was before.

5. It is greater than John's Baptism *in modo necessitatis*. The Sacraments of the New Testament had the seeds of life in them from the first institution and they were good to the receiver. But they were not imposed by necessary commandment till the old Law was quite abolished and that was at the Resurrection, says Leo; or at the farthest, in other men's opinions, at the Feast of Pentecost. So John's Baptism was always good, never necessary; Christ's Baptism is always good, is and ever will be necessary unto the end of the world.

# (2) INFANT BAPTISM

## No. 180. JEREMY TAYLOR

[From *The Great Exemplar. The History of the Life and Death of the Holy Jesus.* Part I, Section ix (Discourse vi, § 16). *Works*, ed. R. Heber, Vol. II, pp. 275 f. Vol. II, pp. 260 f. (ed. C. P. Eden, Vol. II, pp. 260 f.). Cp. note on No. 212.]

IN Baptism we are born again ; and this infants need in the present circumstances and for the same great reason that men of age and reason do. For our natural birth is either of itself insufficient, or is made so by the Fall of Adam and the consequent evils, that nature alone, or our first birth, cannot bring us to Heaven, which is a supernatural end,—that is, an end above all the power of our nature as now it is. So that if nature cannot bring us to Heaven, grace must, or we can never get thither ; if the first birth cannot, a second must. But the second birth spoken of in Scripture is Baptism. *A man must be born of water and the Spirit.* And therefore Baptism is λουτρὸν παλιγγενεσίας, *the laver of a new birth.* Either then infants cannot go to Heaven any way that we know of, or they must be baptized. To say they are to be left to God is an excuse, and no answer. For when God hath opened the door and calls that " the entrance into Heaven ", we do not leave them to God when we will not carry them to Him in the way which He hath described and at the door which Himself hath opened. We leave them, indeed, but it is but helpless and destitute. And though God is better than man, yet that is no warrant to us ; what it will be to the children, that we cannot warrant or conjecture. And if it be objected that to the new birth are required dispositions of our own which are to be wrought by and in them that have the use of reason, besides that this is wholly against the analogy of a new birth, in which the person to be born is wholly a passive and hath put into him the principle that in time will produce its proper actions, it is certain that they that can receive the new birth are capable of it. The effect of it is a possibility of being saved, and arriving to a supernatural felicity. If infants can receive this effect, then also the new birth, without which they cannot receive the effect. And if they can receive salvation, the effect of the new birth, what hinders them but they may receive that that is in order to that effect and ordained only for it, and which is nothing of itself, but in its institution and relation, and which may be received by the same capacity in which one may be created, that is, a passivity, or a capacity obediential ?

## No. 181. GEORGE HICKES

[From *The Case of Infant Baptism, in Five Questions.* London, 1683, pp. 29 f. This tract, published anonymously, was reprinted in 1685 in *A Collection of Cases and Other Discourses lately written to recover Dissenters to the Communion of the Church of England.* At the date of publication Hickes was Vicar of All Hallows', Barking.]

Wherefore, if the relative nature of circumcision, considered as a Sacrament, was the same under the Law that Baptism is under the Gospel, it must needs follow that children under the Gospel are as capable of this (supposing no new command to exclude them) as under the Law they were of that. If Infant Church-membership, or the initiation of infants was then no absurdity, surely it can be none now. If God under the Old Testament vouchsafed it as a gracious privilege unto children to be incorporated with actual believers, and with them to be made members of His Church, without a prohibition to the contrary, they must needs be capable of the same privilege still. Nay, if Infants were admitted into the Church, when the entrance into it was more grievous, and not without blood, how unreasonable is it to assert that they are now uncapable of admission into it, when the entrance into it is made more easy and more agreeable to the natural weakness of a young and tender child? Certainly if the Jewish infants were circumcised with the most painful and bloody circumcision made with hands, Christian infants, without a special countermand from God, must be deemed capable of the circumcision made without hands, I mean of Baptism, which is the circumcision of Christ. What God hath sanctified and adopted and made a member of His Church, let no man presume to think it uncapable of sanctification, adoption, and Church-membership. But yet so rash and extravagant have the professed adversaries of Infant Baptism been, as to pronounce little infants as uncapable of Baptism, as the young ones of unreasonable creatures, and that it is as vain to call upon God to send His Holy Spirit upon them as to pray Him to illuminate a stone or a tree.

# (3) THE SIGN OF THE CROSS IN BAPTISM

## No. 182.  THE CANONS OF 1604

[From *The Constitutions and Canons Ecclesiastical . . . Agreed upon with the King's Majesty's Licence in* [*the*] *Synod Begun at London, Anno Domini*, 1603.  Canon XXX. E. Cardwell, *Synodalia*, Vol. I, pp. 260–264.  These famous Canons are printed in full, both in Latin and English, in the work just mentioned.  The Archiepiscopal See being vacant at the time, Bancroft, then Bishop of London, presided over the Convocation of Canterbury, and delivered to the Prolocutor in the eleventh session these 141 Canons.  They were accepted by the Convocation of York in 1606.  Their enactment has been described as " the principal legislative achievement of the English Church since the breach with Rome ".(Gordon Crosse, in *Dict. Eng. Ch. Hist.*, *s.v.* ' Canon Law in the English Church from 1534.')  Cp. also note on No. **230**.]

WE are sorry that His Majesty's most princely care and pains taken in the Conference at Hampton Court, amongst many other points, touching this one of the Cross in Baptism, hath taken no better effect with many but that still the use of it in Baptism is so greatly stuck at and impugned.  For the further declaration therefore of the true use of this ceremony, and for the removing of all such scruple as might any ways trouble the consciences of them who are indeed rightly religious, following the Royal steps of our most worthy King, because he therein followeth the rules of the Scriptures and the practice of the primitive Church, we do commend to all the true members of the Church of England these our directions and observations ensuing.

First, it is to be observed, that although the Jews and Ethnics derided both the Apostles and the rest of the Christians for preaching and believing in Him Who was crucified upon the Cross ; yet all, both Apostles and Christians, were so far from being discouraged from their profession by the ignominy of the Cross, as they rather rejoiced and triumphed in it.  Yea, the Holy Ghost by the mouths of the Apostles did honour the name of the Cross (being hateful among the Jews) so far, that under it He comprehended not only Christ crucified, but the force, effects, and merits of His Death and Passion, with all the comforts, fruits, and promises, which we receive or expect thereby.

Secondly, the honour and dignity of the name of the Cross begat a reverend estimation even in the Apostles' times (for aught that is known to the contrary) of the Sign of the Cross which the Christians shortly after used in all their actions,—thereby making an outward show and profession, even to the astonishment of the Jews, that they were not ashamed to acknowledge Him for their Lord and Saviour, Who died for them upon the Cross.  And this Sign they did not only use themselves with a kind of glory, when they met with any Jews, but signed therewith their children when they were christened, to dedicate them by that badge to His service, Whose benefits bestowed upon them in Baptism the name of the Cross did represent. And this use of the Sign of the Cross in Baptism was held in the primitive Church, as well by the Greeks as the Latins, with one consent and great applause. At what time, if any had opposed themselves against it, they would certainly have been censured as enemies of the name of the Cross, and consequently of Christ's merits, the Sign whereof they could no better endure. This continual and general use of the Sign of the Cross is evident by many testimonies of the ancient Fathers.

Thirdly, it must be confessed, that in process of time the Sign of the Cross was greatly abused in the Church of Rome, especially after that corruption of Popery had once possessed it. But the abuse of a thing doth not take away the lawful use of it. Nay, so far was it from the purpose of the Church of England to forsake and reject the Churches of Italy, France, Spain, Germany, or any such like Churches, in all things which they held and practised, that, as the *Apology of the Church of England* [*i.e.* of Jewel] confesseth, it doth with reverence retain those ceremonies which doth neither endamage the Church of God nor offend the minds of sober men ; and only departed from them in those particular points, wherein they were fallen both from themselves in their ancient integrity and from the Apostolical Churches, which were their first founders. In which respect, amongst some other very ancient ceremonies, the Sign of the Cross in Baptism hath been retained in this Church, both by the judgement and practice of those reverend Fathers and great Divines in the days of King Edward the Sixth, of whom some constantly suffered for the profession of the truth ; and others, being exiled in the time of Queen Mary, did after their return, in the beginning of the reign of our late dread Sovereign, continually defend and use the same. This resolution and practice of our Church hath been allowed and approved by the censure upon the Communion Book in King Edward the Sixth his days, and by the harmony of Confessions of later years ; because indeed the use of this Sign in Baptism was ever accompanied here with such sufficient cautions and exceptions against all Popish superstition and error, as in the like cases are either fit or convenient.

First, the Church of England, since the abolishing of Popery, hath ever held and taught, and so doth hold and teach still, that the Sign of the Cross used in Baptism is no part of the substance of that Sacrament. For when the Minister, dipping the infant in water, or laying water upon the face of it (as the manner also is), hath pronounced these words, *I baptize thee in the Name of the Father, and of the Son, and of the Holy Ghost,* the infant is fully and perfectly baptized, so as the Sign of the

Cross being afterwards used doth neither add any thing to the virtue and perfection of Baptism, nor being omitted doth detract any thing from the effect and substance of it.

Secondly, it is apparent in the Communion Book, that the infant baptized is by virtue of Baptism, before it be signed with the Sign of the Cross, received into the congregation of Christ's flock, as a perfect member thereof, and not by any power ascribed unto the Sign of the Cross. So that for the very remembrance of the Cross, which is very precious to all them that rightly believe in Jesus Christ, and in the other respects mentioned, the Church of England hath retained still the Sign of it in Baptism; following therein the Primitive and Apostolical Churches and accounting it a lawful outward ceremony and honourable badge, whereby the infant is dedicated to the service of Him that died upon the Cross, as by the words used in the Book of Common Prayer it may appear.

Lastly, the use of the Sign of the Cross in Baptism, being thus purged from all Popish superstition and error, and reduced in the Church of England to the primary institution of it, upon those true rules of doctrine concerning things indifferent, which are consonant to the Word of God and the judgement of all the ancient Fathers, we hold it the part of every private man, both Minister and other, reverently to retain the true use of it prescribed by public authority : considering that things of themselves indifferent do in some sort alter their natures, when they are either commanded or forbidden by a lawful magistrate ; and may not be omitted at every man's pleasure, contrary to the law, when they be commanded, nor used when they are prohibited.

### No. 183. RICHARD HOOKER

[From *The Laws of Ecclesiastical Polity*, Book V, Chapter lxv, 6–8, 11, 19–21. *Works*, ed. J. Keble, Vol. II, pp. 321–325, 327 f., 334–337. Cp. note on No. 148.]

Now the cause why Antiquity did the more in actions of common life honour the ceremony of the Cross might be for that they lived with infidels. But that which they did in the Sacrament of Baptism was for the selfsame good of believers which is thereby intended still. The Cross is for us an admonition no less necessary than for them to glory in the service of Jesus Christ, and not to hang down our heads as men ashamed thereof although it procure us reproach and obloquy at the hands of this wretched world.

Shame is a kind of fear to incur disgrace and ignominy. Now whereas some things are worthy of reproach, some things ignominious only through a false opinion which men have conceived of them, nature that generally feareth opprobrious reprehension must by reason and religion be taught what it should be ashamed of and what not. But be we never so well instructed what our duty is in this behalf, without some present admonition at the very instant of practice, what we know is many times not called to mind till that be done whereupon our just confusion ensueth. To supply the absence of such as that way might do us good when they see us in danger of sliding, there are judicious and wise men which think we may greatly relieve ourselves by a bare imagined presence of some, whose authority we fear and would be loth to offend, if indeed they were present with us. " Witnesses at hand are a bridle unto many offences. Let the mind have always some whom it feareth, some whose authority may keep even secret thoughts under awe. Take Cato, or if he be too harsh and rugged, choose some other of a softer mettle, whose gravity of life and speech thou lovest, his mind and countenance carry with thee, set him always before thine eyes either as a watch or as a pattern. That which is crooked we cannot straighten but by some such level " [Seneca].

If men of so good experience and insight in the maims of our weak flesh have thought these fancied remembrances available to awaken shamefacedness, that so the boldness of sin may be stayed ere it look abroad, surely the wisdom of the Church of Christ which hath to that use converted the ceremony of the Cross in Baptism it is no Christian man's part to despise, especially seeing that by this mean where nature doth earnestly implore aid, religion yieldeth her that ready assistance than which there can be no help more forcible serving only to relieve memory, and to bring to our cogitation that which should most make ashamed of sin.

The mind while we are in this present life, whether it contemplate, meditate, deliberate, or howsoever exercise itself, worketh nothing without continual recourse unto imagination, the only storehouse of wit and peculiar chair of memory. On this anvil it ceaseth not day and night to strike, by means whereof as the pulse declareth how the heart doth work, so the very thoughts and cogitations of man's mind be they good or bad do no where sooner bewray themselves, than through the crevices of that wall wherewith nature hath compassed the cells and closets of fancy. In the forehead nothing more plain to be seen than the fear of contumely and disgrace. For which cause the Scripture (as with great probability it may be thought) describeth them marked of God in the forehead, whom His mercy hath undertaken to keep from final confusion and shame. Not that God doth set any corporal mark on His chosen, but to note that He giveth His elect security of preservation from reproach, the fear whereof doth use to shew itself in that part. Shall I say, that the Sign of the Cross (as we use it) is in some sort a mean to work our preservation from reproach ? Surely the mind which as yet hath not hardened itself in sin is seldom provoked thereunto in any gross and grievous manner, but nature's secret suggestion objecteth against it ignominy as a bar. Which conceit being entered into that palace of man's fancy, the gates whereof hath imprinted in them that holy sign which bringeth forthwith to mind whatsoever Christ hath wrought and we vowed against sin, it cometh hereby to pass that Christian men never want a most effectual though a silent teacher to avoid whatsoever may deservedly procure shame. So that in things which we should be ashamed of we are by the Cross admonished faithfully of our duty at the very moment when admonition doth most need.

Other things there are which deserve honour and yet do purchase many times our disgrace in this present world, as of old the very truth of religion itself, till God by His own outstretched arm made the glory thereof to shine over all the earth. Whereupon St. Cyprian, exhorting to martyrdom in times of heathenish persecution and cruelty, thought it not vain to allege unto them with other arguments the very ceremony of that Cross whereof we speak. Never let that hand offer sacrifice to idols which hath already received the Body of our Saviour Christ, and shall hereafter the crown of His glory. " Arm your foreheads " unto all boldness, that the " Sign of God " may be kept safe.

Again, when it pleased God that the fury of their enemies being bridled the Church had some little rest and quietness (if so small a liberty but only to breathe between troubles may be termed quietness and rest), to such as fell not away from Christ through former persecutions, He giveth due and deserved praise in the selfsame manner. " You that were ready to endure imprisonment, and were resolute to suffer death ; you that have courageously withstood the world, ye have made yourselves both a glorious spectacle for God to behold, and a worthy example for the rest of your brethren to follow. Those mouths which had sanctified themselves with food coming down from heaven loathed after Christ's own Body and Blood to taste the poisoned and contagious scraps of idols ; those foreheads which the Sign of God had purified kept themselves to be crowned by Him, the touch of the garlands of Satan they abhorred." Thus was the memory of that sign which they had in Baptism, a kind of bar or prevention to keep them even from apostasy, whereinto the frailty of flesh and blood, overmuch fearing to endure shame, might peradventure the more easily otherwise have drawn them. . . .

But to prevent some inconveniences which might ensue if the over ordinary use thereof (as it fareth with such rites when they are too common) should cause it to be of less observation or regard where it most availeth, we neither omit it in that place, nor altogether make it so vulgar as the custom heretofore hath been : although to condemn the whole Church of God when it most flourished in zeal and piety, to mark that age with the brand of error and superstition only because they had this ceremony more in use than we now think needful, boldly to affirm that this their practice grew so soon through a fearful malediction of

God upon the ceremony of the Cross, as if we knew that His purpose was thereby to make it manifest in all men's eyes how execrable those things are in His sight which have proceeded from human invention, is as we take it a censure of greater zeal than knowledge. . . .

In all persuasions which ground themselves upon example, we are not so much to respect what is done, as the causes and secret inducements leading thereunto.   The question being therefore whether this ceremony supposed to have been *sometimes* scandalous and offensive ought for that cause to be *now* removed, there is no reason we should forthwith yield ourselves to be carried away with examples, no not of them whose acts the highest judgement approveth for having reformed in that manner any public evil : but before we either attempt any thing or resolve, the state and condition as well of our own affairs as those whose example presseth us, is advisedly to be examined ; because some things are of their own nature scandalous, and cannot choose but breed offence, as those sinks of execrable filth which Josias did overwhelm ; some things albeit not by nature and of themselves, are notwithstanding so generally turned to evil by reason of an evil corrupt habit grown and through long continuance incurably settled in the minds of the greatest part, that no redress can be well hoped for without removal of that wherein they have ruined themselves, which plainly was the state of the Jewish people, and the cause why Ezechias did with such sudden indignation destroy what he saw worshipped ; finally some things are as the Sign of the Cross though subject either almost or altogether to as great abuse, yet curable with more facility and ease.   And to speak as the truth is, our very nature doth hardly yield to destroy that which may be fruitfully kept, and without any great difficulty clean scoured from the rust of evil which by some accident hath grown into it.   Wherefore to that which they build in this question upon the example of Ezechias let this suffice.

When heathens despised Christian religion, because of the sufferings of Jesus Christ, the Fathers to testify how little such contumelies and contempts prevailed with them chose rather the Sign of the Cross than any other outward mark, whereby the world might most easily discern always what they were.   On the contrary side now, whereas they which do all profess the Christian religion are divided amongst themselves, and the fault of the one part is that in zeal to the sufferings of Christ they admire too much and over-superstitiously adore the visible Sign of His Cross, if you ask what we that mislike them should do, we are here advised to cure one contrary by another.   Which art or method is not yet so current as they imagine.

For if, as their practice for the most part sheweth, it be their meaning that the scope and drift of reformation when things are faulty should be to *settle* the Church in the contrary, it standeth them upon to beware of this rule, because seeing vices have not only virtues but other vices also in nature opposite unto them, it may be dangerous in these cases to seek but that which we find contrary to present evils.    For in sores and sicknesses of the mind we are not simply to measure good by distance from evil, because one vice may in some respect be more opposite to another than either of them to that virtue which holdeth the mean between them both.    Liberality and covetousness, the one a virtue and the other a vice, are not so contrary as the vices of covetousness and prodigality ; religion and superstition have more affiance, though the one be light and the other darkness, than superstition and profaneness which both are vicious extremities.    By means whereof it cometh also to pass that the mean which is virtue seemeth in the eyes of each extreme an extremity ; the liberal hearted man is by the opinion of the prodigal miserable, and by the judgement of the miserable lavish ; impiety for the most part upbraideth religion as superstitious, which superstition often accuseth as impious, both so conceiving thereof because it doth seem more to participate each extreme, than one extreme doth another, and is by consequent less contrary to either of them, than they mutually between themselves.    Now if he that seeketh to reform covetousness or superstition should but labour to induce the contrary, it were but to draw men out of lime into coal-dust.    So that their course which will remedy the superstitious abuse of things profitable in the Church is not still to abolish utterly the use thereof, because not using at all is most opposite to ill using, but rather if it may be to bring them back to a right perfect and religious usage, which albeit less contrary to the present sore is notwithstanding the better and by many degrees the sounder way of recovery.

And unto this effect that very precedent itself which they propose may be best followed.    For as the Fathers when the Cross of Christ was in utter contempt did not superstitiously adore the same, but rather declare that they so esteemed it as was meet, in like manner where we find the Cross to have that honour which is due to Christ, is it not as lawful for us to retain it in that estimation which it ought to have and in that use which it had of old without offence, as by taking it clean away to seem followers of their example which cure wilfully by abscission that which they might both preserve and heal ?

Touching therefore the sign and ceremony of the Cross, we no way find ourselves bound to relinquish it, neither because the first inventors thereof were but mortal men, nor lest the sense and signification we give unto it should burden us as authors of a new gospel in the house of God, nor in respect of some cause which the Fathers had more than we have to use the same, nor finally for any such offence or scandal as heretofore it hath been subject unto by error now reformed in the minds of men.

## No. 184.  FRANCIS WHITE

[From *The Orthodox Faith and Way to the Church Explained and Justified; in Answer to a Popish Treatise Entitled " White Dyed Black "; wherein T. W., P[riest], in his triple Accusation of D[octor John] White for Impostures, Untruths, and Absurd Illations, is proved a Trifler; and the present Controversies between us and the Romanists are more fully delivered and cleared*, London, 1617, p. 61.  The T. W. referred to in the title was Thomas Worthington, the full title of whose work was *Whyte Dyed Black; or a Discovery of many most foul Blemishes, Impostures, and Deceits, which D. White hath practiced in his Book entitled " The Way to the True Church "*.  Worthington's treatise was published at Douai in 1615.  Dr. John White, the author of *The Way to the True Church* (1608), was the brother of Francis White; he had died in 1615.  On John White's treatise, cp. the note on No. **270**.]

The signing of the body with the Sign of the Cross,—as it was anciently used by the prime Christians to these ends, 1. to profess that they were not ashamed of Christ crucified, nor of the persecutions and crosses which befell them for His sake; 2. that they hoped for salvation and redemption by Christ Jesus crucified, Whom the Jews and Gentiles despised,—our divines acknowledge to be lawful.  But the Papists, not contenting themselves with the lawful use thereof, have sundry ways abused the same.  1. They make it an instrument of miracles, after that the gift of miracles was ceased in the Church.  2. They ascribe unto it a virtue to sanctify men's persons and the creatures of God; to expel and repel devils; to deliver from dangers and evils; and to perform some of these effects by force of the very outward deed, or *ex opere operato*.

In regard of these abuses our Church observeth not so common an use of the Sign of the Cross as was in former ages.  Nevertheless we condemn not the same sign in regard of itself, but use it in the Sacrament of Baptism and abstain from the more frequent use of it, because you have so foully abused it to superstition.  And we follow herein the rule of Canon Law, warranted by the Scripture and Primitive Church.

# (4) THE DESTINY OF THE UNBAPTIZED

## No. 185. JOSEPH HALL

[From *Epistles*, Fifth Decade, No iv. *Works*, ed. Peter Hall (1837), Vol. VI, pp. 248 f. This Epistle, which is entitled " Discoursing of the Necessity of Baptism ; and the Estate of those which necessarily want it ", was addressed to " My Lady Honoria Hay." Hall's Epistles, which extended to Six Decades, were published in three volumes of two decades each in 1608, 1608, and 1611 respectively, all of them dedicated to Henry, Prince of Wales, who died in 1612. They are said to be the first collection of letters to have been published in the English tongue.]

THAT the contempt of Baptism damneth is past all doubt; but, that the constrained absence thereof should send infants to hell, is a cruel rashness. It is not their sin to die early : death is a punishment, not an offence, an effect of sin, not a cause of torment. They want nothing but time, which they could not command. Because they could not live a while longer, that therefore they should die everlastingly, is the hard sentence of a bloody religion.

I am only sorry that so harsh an opinion should be graced with the name of a Father, so reverend, so divine,—whose sentence yet let no man plead by halves. He, who held it impossible for a child to be saved unless the baptismal water were poured on his face, held it also as impossible, for the same infant, unless the sacramental bread were received into his mouth. There is the same ground for both, the same error in both, a weakness fit for forgetfulness. See yet how ignorant or ill-meaning posterity could single out the one half of the opinion for truth, and condemn the other of falsehood; in spite of whom, one part shall easily convince the other,—yea, without all force. Since both cannot stand, both will fall together for company. The same mouth which said, Unless ye be born again of water, and the Holy Ghost, said also, Except ye eat the flesh of the Son of Man, and drink His blood ;—an equal necessity of both. And, lest any should plead different interpretations, the same St. Austin avers this latter opinion also concerning the necessary communicating of children to have been once the common judgement of the Church of Rome,—a sentence so displeasing that you shall find the memory of it noted with a black coal, and wiped out in that infamous bill of Expurgations.

Had the ancient Church held this desperate sequel, what strange and yet wilful cruelty had it been in them, to defer Baptism a whole year long : till Easter ; or that Sunday, which hath his name, I think, from the white robes of the baptized ! Yea, what an adventure was it in some to adjourn it till their age with Constantine if, being unsure of their life, they had been sure the prevention of death would have inferred damnation !

Look unto that Legal Sacrament of Circumcision which, contrary to the fancies of our Anabaptists, directly answers this Evangelical. Before the eighth day, they could not be circumcised : before the eighth day, they might die. If, dying the seventh day, they were necessarily condemned, either the want of a day is a sin, or God sometimes condemneth not for sin. Neither of them possible ; neither according with the justice of the Lawgiver.

## No. 186.  JOHN BRAMHALL

[From *A Short Discourse to Sir Henry de Vic about a Passage at his Table, after the Christening of his Daughter, Anne Charlotte, Of Persons Dying without Baptism. Works*, ed. *L. A. C. T.*, Vol. V, pp. 176–180.  Sir Henry de Vic was British Ambassador to the States.  The subject of the *Discourse* had been raised by a discussion at the Ambassador's table, and Bramhall sent the *Discourse* to him subsequently.  It was first published in the folio edition of Bramhall's works (1676).]

If infants which die unbaptized be excluded from all hope of salvation, then it is by reason of that original corruption which they derive by propagation from their parents, because " no polluted thing can enter into Heaven " [1]; for we know, that infants are not capable of any actual sins.  But this reason is not sufficient ; for the Jewish infants were as subject to original sin and had a remedy appointed for it by God, as well as Christians, that is, the Sacrament of Circumcision ; which though it should be admitted that it did not causally produce grace, yet it is confessed by the Romanists that it did certainly procure grace, and was as strictly enjoined to them as Baptism is to us.  *The uncircumcised male child . . . shall be cut off from his people.*  But this notwithstanding, the Jewish infants, dying without Circumcision, might be saved.  Neither is God more propitious to the Jewish infants than to the Christian, for *He hath loved the tents of Sion above all the tabernacles of Jacob.*  Therefore Christian infants may be saved likewise without Baptism.  That the Jewish children might be saved without Circumcision is thus proved by the institution of God.  Circumcision was not celebrated till the eighth day after the nativity ; but many thousand Jewish infants died before the eighth day, and consequently without Circumcision ; to exclude all those from hope of salvation for want of Circumcision, which by God's own ordinance they might not have, intrencheth too much upon the goodness of God.  More particularly, David's child died upon the seventh day, and yet David doubted not to say, *I shall go to him, but he shall not return to me.*  David could not go to him either in Hell or in *Limbus Infantum.*  And of this opinion St. Gregory seemeth to be, as he is cited by the Master of Sentences [*i.e.*, Peter Lombard] ;—" That which Baptism doth with us,

---

[1] [So Bonaventura, Alexander of Hales, etc.  Cp. A. W. Haddan's note.]

that same the faith of the parents performed in the law of nature." If " in the law of nature," why not as well in the Law of Moses and of Christ ?    Most certainly, if infants might be saved in any one of these three states without some Sacrament or other, then in all the three without exception. . . .

It is confessed that in the Primitive times Baptism was administered ordinarily but twice in the year, that is, at Easter and at Whitsuntide ; and many did defer their baptization till the hour of death that they might depart more undefiled out of this world.    But considering those infinite dangers which hang continually over the heads of mortal men whilst they are in this vale of misery, and how many are swept away out of this life, even in an instant, by sudden death, by sickness, or other casualties, some sleeping, some eating, some walking, this practice had been the most unsafe and dangerous in the whole world and the loss of millions of souls if all persons dying unbaptized were infallibly excluded out of Heaven : especially little infants who, being incapable of reason, cannot supply the want of actual Baptism by their hearty desires.    I do not examine the grounds of this delay neither do I justify the practice ;  but it argues strongly that they did not esteem the only want of Baptism, without contempt (or as they conceived, neglect), to deprive all sorts of persons from hope of salvation.

You may be pleased to remember how it was urged that St. Austin was of the same faith with the Church of Rome in this particular. And it was then answered that he did neither agree with them nor us in this question.    St. Austin is in this a hard father to little infants, and innocents from actual sins, in that he concludes all who die unbaptized in Hell.    The Church of Rome teacheth contrarily that they are not in Hell, but in a certain *Limbus Infantum*.    The Protestants leave them to the mercy of God, and doubt not but that many of them are in Heaven.    St. Austin saith, they are certainly damned.  The Protestants say, they may be saved.    The Romanists say, they cannot be saved, and yet they are not damned.    The Romanists say, they suffer *poenam damni*, but not *poenam sensus* ;  a privative, but not positive punishment.    St. Austin saith, they suffer, both privatively and positively, the very fire of Hell.    The Protestants believe, that many of them do suffer neither.

Observe the words of St. Austin :—

*Hypognosticon* lib. v.—" The first place the faith of Catholics doth believe, by Divine authority, to be the Kingdom of Heaven, from whence he that is not baptized, is excepted ;  the second, Hell, where every apostate or stranger from the faith of Christ, shall prove eternal torments ;  the third, we know not at all, yea, we do not find it to be in the Holy Scriptures."

*Liber de Meritis et Remissione Peccatorum.*—" Neither is there any middle place to any person ; that he can be anywhere but with the Devil, who is not with Christ."

And in his Eighteenth *Sermon upon the Words of the Apostle* :— " He that is such an one, let him choose now where he desires to dwell, when the time is that he may be changed ; for there are two habitations, the one in the eternal kingdom, the other in eternal fire."

And *Sermon* 232 [ = 295, App.] :—" Let no man deceive himself, brethren ; for there are two places, and there is not any third. He that shall not merit to reign with Christ without doubt shall perish with the Devil."

The like he doth [urge] *De Civitate Dei*, lib. xxi, cap. 25.

When we urge these places against Purgatory, they answer that St. Austin " speaks of eternal places against Pelagius, who had invented a third place besides Heaven and Hell, for children which died unbaptized." And in the two first places, indeed, St. Austin speaketh expressly against Pelagius ; but the other are general, neither distinguishing infants nor old men, temporal nor eternal mansions.

But leaving Purgatory for the present, as not concerning the question which is now in hand, this makes more strongly against the Romish *Limbus Infantum* ; which they themselves do make to be eternal and against which (by their own confession in this answer) St. Austin disputeth. St. Austin saith he " knew no " such place, he did " not find it in Holy Scripture." He saith, " He that is not with Christ " (that is in Heaven, where Christ is), " is with the Devil," that is, in Hell. He makes no mean between an " eternal kingdom " and " eternal fire," between " reigning with Christ " and " perishing with the Devil."

To conclude. Infants unbaptized, according to St. Austin, must either be sheep or goats, either stand upon the right hand or upon the left, either hear *Come ye blessed*, or *Go ye cursed*, either inherit a kingdom or be cast into *eternal fire prepared for the Devil and his angels*. This is more than a mere loss of blessedness. But the Romanists do not, dare not, say that all infants unbaptized are " with the Devil," that they " perish with the Devil," that they are " in eternal fire." And therefore we may conclude, on the other side, that they are " with Christ," that they enjoy an " eternal kingdom " where they reign with their Saviour ; or at least that some of them are crowned, some tormented, according to the good pleasure of God, Whose extraordinary help is then often found when the help of man doth fail.

## No. 187. FRANCIS WHITE

[From *A Reply to Jesuit Fisher's Answer*, p. 177. Cp. note on No. 228.]

Whereas the objector [*i.e.* Jesuit Fisher] addeth that Protestants deny the necessity of Baptism for infants, granting them Salvation without Baptism, he must understand that necessity is either absolute, or else of precept and supposition. We verily maintain the latter necessity of Baptism for the salvation of infants, against the Pelagians and Anabaptists ; and the contempt and wilful neglect of this Holy Sacrament is damnable to such as are guilty of this contempt ; and our Church provideth diligently that all infants (if it be possible) may receive Baptism before they depart this life. But if it fall out inevitable that new born babes, descending of Christian parents, cannot receive this Sacrament, not only Protestants, but the ancient Church itself, and discreeter Papists, have thought it more pious to hope of God's indulgence towards such infants, than to aggravate His vengeance with such rigour and extremity as the Trent Fathers and their disciples do.

# (5) CONFIRMATION

## No. 188. JOHN COSIN

[The form of the Rite of Confirmation proposed by Cosin for the Revision of the Prayer Book in 1661. *The Correspondence of John Cosin, D.D., Lord Bishop of Durham, together with other papers Illustrative of his Life and Times*, Part II. Surtees Society [1872, for] 1870, pp. 69–72. These notes were discovered in a copy of the Book of Common Prayer of the year 1619 which had been altered in Cosin's own hand, and which is now in the Cathedral Library at Durham. Several of Cosin's proposals as recorded in this Book were adopted, but not the following one.]

" *Upon the day appointed, after Morning or Evening Prayer is ended, the Bishop shall go to the Lord's Table, and all that are to be then confirmed being placed and standing in order before him, near unto the same, he or his chaplain, or some other Minister appointed by him, shall read this Preface following.*"

Confirmation is by the Church of Rome, that now is corrupted with many errors and novelties in religion, held to be a Sacrament. But we who by the grace of God are numbered among the Reformed Churches, whereof this Church of England is both for doctrine and discipline the most eminent and the most pure, the most agreeable to Scripture and Antiquity of all others, we hold it to be none.

And yet we hold it to be a sacred and a solemn action of religion, which being accompanied with fervent prayer will be a special means to convey the graces of God's Holy Spirit upon those persons that have duly prepared themselves to receive it, that thereby they may be established in their faith and the better fitted to every good word and work, as all true Christians ought to be.

The ancient custom of the Church of Christ was, after that persons were once baptized, to add unto their Baptism Imposition of hands, with earnest prayer for the gifts of God's graces to be bestowed upon them, whereby they might be confirmed and strengthened in that holy profession which, in the Sacrament of Baptism, they had first begun to make.

For our means to obtain the graces which God doth bestow are our prayers; and our prayers to that intent are available as well for others as for ourselves.

When we thus pray for others (as now in this action we shall do for you that come to be confirmed), we implore God's blessing upon them for whom we pray; and thereby we do actually bless them, because our prayers and imposition of hands in those prayers are an especial means

443

ordained by God to procure that Blessing from Him upon them whom, by this solemn rite, we present unto Him for that purpose.

So Israel blessed the sons of Joseph and imposed his hands upon them, and the like custom was usually observed from the time of Moses to Christ, Who used it Himself and His Apostles after Him, as His Church has done after them in all ages.

And the reason why the Church hath always continued it is for the great benefit which every member of the Church thereby enjoyeth, or may at least enjoy, if it be not their own fault, and want of true preparation and devotion that hindreth them.

And therefore the ancient Fathers and Bishops of the Church everywhere in their learned, godly, and Christian writings impute unto it those gifts and graces of the Holy Ghost, which doth not make men and women Christians, as they were at first in their Baptism, but, when they are made such there, assisteth them in all virtue, and armeth them the better against all the several temptations of the world and the devil, to resist the wiles of the flesh.

When Baptism was at first administered to them of full age who in their infancy were either Jews or heathens, there was no reason to sever Confirmation from it. But when it was administered to infants (as it was to you) though they might very well be admitted to live in the family of Christ (as you have been), yet forasmuch as to fight in the Army of God, and to discharge the duties of a Christian man or woman, to bring forth the fruits of their religion, and to do the works of the Holy Ghost, their time of liability was not yet come, their Confirmation was deferred till they arrived to riper years (as yours now is) that in the meanwhile they might be seasoned with the principles of true Religion (as we hope well now you are), and a good foundation laid betimes for the better direction of your lives ever after.

For that which in our Baptism we first performed by others, being Infants without any understanding of our own, when we come afterwards to acknowledge ourselves (as now you do), what do we else but only bring to ripeness that very seed which was sown in us before ?

Whereunto imposition of hands and prayer being added (as now we intend to do), our warrant and trust for the good effect thereof is the same which the Patriarchs, the Prophets, the Apostles, and men of God have practised and found before us.

Nor is there any cause that we should doubt of the benefit, if it be not our own fault ; but truly there is great cause to make complaint of the great and general neglect of this Christian duty. Let no man take it in evil part ; the small regard hereof hath done much harm in the Church of God ; and the frequency of it may do much good.

To the end therefore that Confirmation may be ministered, etc., none, etc., shall be confirmed but such as [the Ministers of the several parishes have first instructed, and examined in the Catechism following, and shall testify and undertake for them that they are come to years of discretion and] [1] can say, etc., in the prescribed Catechism are contained, wherein the Bishop, or such as he shall appoint, shall by his discretion examine them etc.[2]

## No. 189.  JOSEPH HALL

[From Χειροθεσία; or the Apostolic Institution of Imposition of Hands for Confirmation Revived. Sections 2–5. Works, ed. Peter Hall (1837), Vol. X, pp. 442–447. This small treatise was published anonymously as a pamphlet in 1649, the author describing himself as a " Lover of Peace."]

Besides that extraordinary act of laying on the hand for curing of diseases and infirmities, practised by Our Blessed Saviour and His Apostles and for conveying the Holy Ghost in a miraculous way, in the Primitive Times there were three occasions and usages of Imposition of Hands,—in cases of 1. Confirmation; 2. of Ordination; 3. of Absolution and Readmission of Penitents.

That the first of these is here [in Heb. vi, 2] intended, not only all Antiquity, but all late interpreters except some few stragglers do unanimously agree.   Neither indeed can it with any probability be taken with either of the other.

Not of Ordination.   What should novices have to do with that business, now, in the Primer of their Christianity?  Their teachers were only concerned therein, not the Puisnes in that School of Christ.

Not of Readmission of Penitents, the ceremony whereof, for aught we can find, began not till after the Apostles.

Doubtless, therefore, of Confirmation.   For which cause also, as Calvin well noteth, it is paired together with Baptism, as an ordinary subsequent thereof; so as this practice, thus hinted by the Apostle, and made good . . . by the constant tradition of all following times, is plainly denied even by Mr. Calvin's own confession, from no less than Apostolical Institution.

It hath been the lot of this sacred rite [i.e. of Confirmation] to fall into ill hands and to be foully wronged by a double extreme; the one, of Excess, the other, of Defect.   The Excess, in a superstitious over-doing and over-valuing it, the Defect, in a neglective disestimation; both which must be clearly evicted and quit ere we can present this holy ordinance to the beholder in its native beauty and perfection.

First, then, it is an injurious Excess of respect that is given to

[1] [These words in brackets have had a pen drawn through them in the original. It is apparently impossible to say whether this, and many other similar alterations in this " Arrangement " were the expression of Cosin's own revised judgement, or the record of modifications which did not meet with the approval of the Bishops.]

[2] [Bishop Cosin intended that the remaining part of the Preface in the Confirmation Service of the Prayer-book of 1604 should stand, usque ad " to the Will of God."— EDITOR'S NOTE.]

Confirmation by them who have advanced it into the rank of Sacraments, forcing upon it that honour which it never originally affected and which it utterly, with due modesty, refused to undergo.

To make up a Christian Sacrament, Cardinal Bellarmine himself sticks not to profess three things to be necessarily required. First, a promise of grace; secondly, a sensible sign, together with a word, whereby that promise is applied; thirdly, a command from God, enjoining the ministration of it. Now, after all his confident undertaking, where are all, where are any, of these to be found in this business of Confirmation?

For the promise, he tells us of the Comforter, Whom Our Lord Jesus pre-engaged Himself to send, and of that gracious word at His last farewell, *Ye shall receive power, after that the Holy Ghost is come upon you* (*Acts* i, 8). But what is this to the particular act of Confirmation? All this might well have been, and yet no hands imposed, no Confirmation implied. Well might this promise confirm the Apostles in a confident expectation of some miraculous work to be wrought upon them, but could give no intimation of a new Sacrament to be erected, no specialty of their hands to be employed in an Imposition. That distinction, therefore, of Alphonsus Vivaldus, That Christ instituted this Sacrament though not *exhibendo*, yet *promittendo*, is no better than frivolous, unless he can .shew that Our Saviour applied that general promise to this special institution; which he shall never be able to perform.

For the sensible sign, here were hands indeed laid on, but not with any intention of acting or constituting a Sacrament. And where is the solemn word whereby that promise is applied and that sign actuated? Surely, here God is silent. Men may speak; for that Set Form, which they bind their tongues unto, " I sign thee with the Sign of the Cross, and confirm thee with the Chrism of Salvation, in the Name of the Father, Son, and Holy Ghost," whose is it? They dare not father it upon Christ, Who is the sole Author of Sacraments. It is a device of their own, and thereupon subject to much variation of expression, as their casuists stick not to confess.

As for any command, it is as far to seek as either of the other. What Scripture can be pretended to carry the least colour of a mandate? It is a poor shift of the Cardinal, instead of a word of injunction, to flap us off with the execution of the act. It is true, hands were laid on by the Apostles; the Holy Ghost was given. But was this done with either purpose or charge to make this a perpetual Sacrament unto the Church? Or, if this were anywhere to be found, yet what were all this to the warrant of the rites used in the Church of Rome in the administration of this pretended Sacrament? Wherein, as if the Apostles' act were quite forgotten, there is no Imposition of Hands at all; only some strange and uncouth rites are foisted in, which the Apostles were never guilty of thinking of. For in what Scripture shall we look for the chrism, compounded, as it needs must be, of oil and balsam? Where shall we look for the consignation with the cross in the forehead? For the box on the ear, given to the confirmed, with the rest of the complements of that pretendedly sacramental action?

So as now, the Cardinal [Bellarmine] may spread before us the testimony of " Ten Popes, nine Councils, nine Greek Fathers, ten Latin," besides Middle-Aged Authors and Schoolmen, for the avowing of this their Sacrament and the Antiquity of the holy appendances of it. But all these fall too short for the proof of a true and genuine Sacrament of the Christian Church,—a truth that was well seen by the quick and piercing eyes of our Alexander of Hales, the Father of the Schoolmen, whom they styled the " Irrefragable Doctor " and the " Fountain of Life "; as also by his acute disciple, Cardinal Bonaventure, whom they have honoured with the title of a Saint. Both which flatly deny any such Sacrament instituted by Christ, or so much as by His Apostles, sending us, for the first rise of it, to a French Council held at Melde, which was not till the year of grace 845. So as the Roman Catechism, which from the counterfeit authority of their Fabian would cast their holy Chrism upon Christ Himself, and Scotus, who yet suffers for stooping so low as to fetch it from the Apostles, are quite beside the cushion.

Yet a far more injurious degree of excess it is that Confirmation is not only ranged together with the Holy Sacraments, but also equalled and, not without a high and intolerable affront, preferred to Baptism itself.

Not so much in respect of the dignity of the person, whose hand was wont to be employed in this action, held, commonly and of old, in a key above Presbytery, or as *Primus Presbyterorum*, in the lowest style; as of the virtue and efficacy of the act itself,—without which, the eminence of the agent could avail little to the dignifying of the work. We know the very Angels are content to condescend to mean offices for the good of us wretched men; yet those acts, to which they have stooped, have been never the more ennobled in themselves. And if an Emperor shall be designed to hold a Pope's stirrup, the act is never the less servile, because the agent is royal.

It is not for us in this case to stand upon the person; to whom, if it were appropriated of old, as Jerome speaks, *propter honorem Sacerdotii*, I fear it is now by some denied, *propter invidiam Sacerdotii*. The case is herein much altered. Once, men could have been content, with the Galatians, to have pulled out their eyes and to have given them to us, but in these last times too many could be content to lose one of their own eyes that we might lose both ours. However, it were great pity and sin, that so holy an act should lie still, as dead, while we strain courtesy who should take it up.

But it is not, as I said, so much the dignity of the agent that is insisted upon, as the power and energy of the act of Confirmation, which is by our Romish Doctors set up proudly to contest with and overtop the acknowledged Sacrament of Baptism. " If Baptism be yielded to begin our Christendom, Confirmation," they say, " perfects it," and all the praises, which they, from their Urban, Melchiades, Clemens, Fabian, and others, yield unto their Confirmation, are understood, as Chemnitius well construes them, as antithetical,—so many derogations from the power of Baptism. " In Baptism," say they, " we are regenerated to life ; in Confirmation, we are armed to fight. In Baptism, there is only preparation made for God's in-dwelling in our hearts ; in Confirmation, He actually takes up the house-room for Himself." Yea, in flat terms, they dare say " He shall never be a Christian that is not anointed by Episcopal Confirmation," and it is the title of one of the chapters of their *Decretum*, " *Manus impositionis sacramentum, etc.*" " The Sacrament of the Imposition of Hands, is more worthy than the Sacrament of Baptism."

These, and whatever other excesses of titles and prerogatives have been cast upon this holy institution to the disparagement of other more noble ordinances, have not a little blemished the face of it in some undistinguishing eyes.

To which may be added, the over-eager and tumultuous affectation, wherewith it was wont, not very long since, to be prosecuted in some parts, the Western especially, of this Church. It cannot be spoken with what fervour and violence of desire that people were wont to sue for this sacred ceremony. What Fair-like confluences have we there seen of zealous ambients ! How have we been tired with the importunity of suitors, impatient of either denial or delay ! How have we been oppressed with the throngs of the multitude, striving for the first admission ! Insomuch as we have been forced to call for the help of officers to our rescue from that well-meant impetuousness. Yea, so hath that people been formerly devoted to this religious institution that the want of it was one of the causes of their insurrection, in the days of King Edward the Sixth, falling out, as then, by reason of the absence or willing forbearance of Miles Coverdale, their elected Bishop.

Now I must be pardoned if I impute some part of this height of zeal in those our modern clients to an ungrounded over-weening of opinion, which they have conceived of this godly ordinance, traduced unto them by their fore-fathers ; whereof, if need were, I could give too sufficient an account to the reader, an error which, by good counsel, might in good time be redressed.

But leaving the consideration of an excessive over-valuation, whereof (I dare undertake) the greatest part of this nation at this day are far enough from being guilty, we descend to that other extreme, of Defect ; whereof, I fear, there are not too many free.

What an universal neglect is there of this holy duty, in all the Churches that profess Reformation ! What a willing forgetfulness of it ! As if there had never been any such matter practised in the Church of God ; never any such ceremony so much as intimated by any Apostle ; never any mention or memory of it in the succeeding ages ; lastly, as if there never had been, never could be, any profitable or godly use of it amongst Christians.

Yea rather, on the contrary, how odious is the very name of it grown to the ears of those, who profess the strictest godliness ! How is the practice of it cried down and hooted at, as merely superstitious and Anti-Christian !

Who can but wonder at this strange partiality ? That men who profess so awful an observance and so strict and punctual imitation of all the Apostolical ordinations and actions should willingly abandon and carelessly slight one of their prime and most apparent institutions ! Fain would I know what they can say to this irrefragable text [viz. *Heb.* vi, 2]. Was there not such a thing in the Apostolic Times as the Imposition of Hands ? Was not the doctrine and practice of it held so useful as that it was singled out for one of the principles of Christian Religion ? Is there not as much occasion and need of the use of it, as ever ? Was this only a temporary institution, soon after to be abrogated ? What need was there then to trouble the heads and to clog the Catechism of Christian Novices, with a vanishing and now already gasping ceremony ? And why is it ranked in the style of Faith, Repentance, Baptism, etc., whose use and practice must be perpetual ? Surely, to coop up the Doctrine of Baptism and Imposition of Hands in a parenthesis, as some have poorly devised, is both very unreasonable and injurious to the Spirit of God, Which would have this Scripture to run freely, in all equal relations, to the foregoing and following clauses. What God will have laid open, it is high presumption in any man to enclose.

## No. 190. RICHARD BAXTER

[From *Confirmation and Restauration, The Necessary Means of Reformation and Reconciliation.* Under ' Proposition 19 '. *Works,* ed. W. Orme (1830), Vol. XIV, pp. 481 f. ; ed. London, 1838, Vol. IV, pp. 315 f. Cp. note on No. 172.]

When I was a schoolboy about fifteen years of age, the Bishop coming into the country, many went to him to be confirmed. We that were boys ran out to see the Bishop among the rest, not knowing anything of the meaning of the business. When we came thither, we met about thirty or forty in all, of our own stature and temper, that had come for to be " bishopped," as then it was called. The Bishop examined us not at all in one article of the Faith ; but in a church-yard in haste we were set in a rank, and he passed hastily over us, laying his hands on our head, and saying a few words, which neither I nor any that I spoke with, understood ; so hastily were they uttered, and a very short prayer recited, and there was an end. But whether we were Christians or infidels, or knew so much as that there was a God, the Bishop little knew nor inquired. And yet he was esteemed one of the best Bishops in England. And though the Canons require that the Curate or Minister send a certificate that children have learned the Catechism, yet there was no such thing done, but we ran of our own accord to see the Bishop only ; and almost all the rest of the country had not this much. This was the old, careless practice of this excellent duty of Confirmation.

## No. 191.  HAMON L'ESTRANGE

[From *The Alliance of Divine Offices*, Annotation A upon Chapter IX. Ed. L. A. C. T., pp. 389 f.  Cp. note on No. 232.]

Confirmation is by the Church of Rome held for a Sacrament, and so some of the ancient Fathers represent it. St. Cyprian, speaking of Baptism and Confirmation : *tunc esse filii Dei possunt, si Sacramento utroque nascantur.* " Then are they made the sons of God, when they are born again by both Sacraments." So St. Augustine mentions *chrismatis Sacramentum*, and in both their senses (they applying that title to all things of mysterious import in a large construction, as Augustine not less than nineteen times in his *De Celebratione Paschæ*) we will allow this for a Sacrament. But that it is so in true propriety of speech our adversaries shall never obtain from us, until they can find *verbum et elementum*, and both of Christ's institution, to meet in it ; neither of which, as they confess, are yet to be found, their great Cardinal [*i.e.* Bellarmine] putting us off for both to " tradition unwritten." But although we entertain it not as a Sacrament, yet being of Apostolical practice, and exercised with the product of such marvellous effects and operations, we, who pretend not to any such miraculous gifts, have not yet so slight a value for it as absolutely to reject it, being well persuaded that, accompanied with such fervent prayers, it will be the readier way to convey those graces of the Holy Spirit into the soul of the party baptized, which are necessary to " establish him in every good word and work." For the gift of the Holy Ghost, in order to which this rite is used, is not so much an effect of the hands imposed as of the invocation then applied : *ad invocationem sacerdotis Spiritus Sanctus infunditur,* saith St. Ambrose very well.   " At the invocation of the Bishop the Holy Ghost is infused."

## No. 192.   JEREMY TAYLOR

[From Χρῖσις Τελειωτική ; *A Discourse of Confirmation,* Section vii (" Of Preparation to Confirmation and the Circumstances of Receiving it "). *Works,* ed. R. Heber, Vol. XI, pp. 290 f. (ed. C. P. Eden, Vol. V, pp. 663 f.)   Cp. note on No. 193.]

But therefore there is a third way [1] which the Church of England and Ireland follows, and that is, that after infancy, but yet before they understand too much of sin, and when they can competently understand the fundamentals of religion, then it is good to bring them to be confirmed, that the Spirit of God may prevent their youthful sins and Christ by His Word and by His Spirit may enter and take possession at the same time.   And thus it was in the Church of England long since provided and commanded by the laws of King Edgar, cap. 15, *ut nullus ab episcopo confirmari diu nimium detrectarit,* " that none should too long put off his being confirmed by the Bishop "; that is, as is best expounded by the perpetual practice almost ever since, as soon as ever, by Catechism and competent instruction, they were prepared, it should not be deferred.   If it have been omitted (as of late years it hath been too much), as we do in Baptism, so in this also, it may be taken at any age, even after they have received the Lord's Supper ; as I observed before in the practice and example of the Apostles themselves, which in this is an abundant warrant.   But still the sooner the better,—I mean, after that reason begins to dawn.   But ever it must be taken care of that the parents and godfathers, the ministers and masters, see that the children be catechised and well instructed in the fundamentals of their religion.

## No. 193.   JEREMY TAYLOR

[From Χρῖσις Τελειωτική ; *A Discourse of Confirmation,* Section IV (" The Bishops were always and the only Ministers of Confirmation "). *Works,* ed. R. Heber, Vol. XI, pp. 273 f. (ed. C. P. Eden, Vol. V, p. 650.)   This treatise was published in 1663 with a dedication to the Duke of Ormond.   It is one of the earliest treatises to have been written in English on the subject.]

It [*i.e.* Confirmation] was ever called *confirmatio episcopalis, et impositio manuum episcoporum,* which our English word well expresses, and perfectly retains the use ; we know it by the common name of " bishopping of children."   I shall no further insist upon it, only I shall observe that there is a vain distinction brought into the Schools and glosses of the Canon Law of a Minister Ordinary and Extraordinary ; all allowing that the Bishop is appointed the Ordinary minister of Confirmation, but they would fain innovate, and pretend, that in some cases others may be Ministers Extraordinary.   This device is of infinite

---

[1] [*I.e.* besides that of Infant Confirmation and the restriction of the Rite to such as are " of Riper Years."]

danger to the destruction of the whole Sacred Order of the Ministry, and disparks the enclosures, and lays all in common, and makes men supreme controllers of the orders of God, and lies upon a false principle; for in true Divinity, and by the economy of the Spirit of God, as there can be no Minister of any Divine ordinance but he that is of Divine appointment, there can be none but the Ordinary Minister. I do not say that God is tied to this way. He cannot be tied but by Himself; and therefore Christ gave a special commission to Ananias to baptize and to confirm St. Paul, and He gave the Spirit to Cornelius even before he was baptized, and He ordained St. Paul to be an Apostle without the ministry of man. But this I say, that though God can make Ministers Extraordinary, yet man cannot; and they that go about to do so, usurp the power of Christ, and snatch from His hand what He never intended to part with. The Apostles admitted others into a part of their care and of their power; but when they intended to employ them in any Ministry, they gave them so much of their order as would enable them. But a person of a lower order could never be deputed Minister of actions appropriate to the higher; which is the case of Confirmation, by the practice and tradition of the Apostles, and by the universal practice and doctrine of the primitive Catholic Church, by which Bishops only, the successors of the Apostles, were alone the Ministers of Confirmation. And therefore if any man else usurp it, let them answer it; they do hurt indeed to themselves, but do no benefit to others, to whom they minister shadows instead of substances.

## No. 194.  EDWARD BOUGHEN

[From *A Sermon of Confirmation* (London, 1620), pp. 11 f. This sermon was delivered at Oxford on September 27, 1619, at the first Episcopal Visitation of John Howson. The Text was *Acts* viii, 17.]

Here is one ceremony more, added (as it seems) by the Church before St. Cyprian's time, namely, to conclude Confirmation with the sign of the Cross,—a sign so generally received in Saint Austin's time, that he makes it a wonder if any man should be ignorant of it. *Quid est, quod omnes noverunt* (saith he) *signum Christi, nisi crux Christi?* What is that, which all the world takes notice of? That sign of Christ, what is it but the Cross of Christ? And so highly was it esteemed by him and the holy men of that age, that he professeth, unless it be added *sive frontibus credentium, sive ipsi aquæ qua regenerantur, sive oleo quo Chrismate unguntur,*—unless, saith he, the Sign of the Cross be used in Baptism and in Confirmation,—*nihil eorum rite perficitur*—none of them are rightly performed,—that is, according to the orders and rites of the Church.

So Saint Austin. The Cross, therefore, upon this or the like consideration, is enjoined to be used in Confirmation, in the Book of

Common Prayer set forth and allowed in Edward the Sixth's Reign, and I find it not at any time revoked. But it is left (as it seems) to the Bishop's discretion to use or not use the Cross in Confirmation.

## No. 195. JEREMY TAYLOR

[From Χρίσις Τελειωτική; *A Discourse of Confirmation*, Section V (" The Whole Procedure or Ritual of Confirmation is by Prayer and Imposition of Hands "). *Works*, ed. R. Heber, Vol. XI, pp. 277 f. (ed. C. P. Eden, Vol. V, p. 653.) Cp. note on No. **193**.]

That this [*i.e.* Anointing] was the ancient ceremony [*i.e.* in Confirmation] is without doubt, and that the Church had power to do so hath no question; and I add, it was not unreasonable. For if ever the Scripture expresses the mysteriousness of a grace conferred by an exterior ministry (as this is, by imposition of hands), and represents it besides in the expression and analogy of any sensible thing, that expression drawn into a ceremony will not improperly signify the grace, since the Holy Ghost did choose that for His own expression and represent-ment. In Baptism we are said to be *buried with Christ*. The Church does according to the analogy of that expression, when she immerges the catechumen in the font; for then she represents the same thing which the Holy Ghost would have to be represented in that Sacrament. The Church did but the same thing when she used Chrism in this ministration. This I speak in justification of that ancient practice. But because there was no command for it, λόγος γεγραμμένος οὐκ ἔστι, said St. Basil, " concerning Chrism there is no written word," that is, of the ceremony there is not; he said it not of the whole rite of Con-firmation. Therefore though to this we are all bound,—yet as to the anointing, the Church is at liberty, and hath with sufficient authority omitted it in our ministrations.

In the Liturgy of King Edward the Sixth, the Bishops used the Sign of the Cross upon the foreheads of them that were to be confirmed. I do not find it since forbidden, or revoked by any expression or intima-tion, saving only that it is omitted in our later offices; and therefore it may seem to be permitted to the discretion of the Bishops, but yet not to be used unless where it may be for edification, and where it may be by the consent of the Church, at least by interpretation. Concerning which I have nothing else to interpose, but that neither this, nor any thing else which is not of the nature and institution of the rite, ought to be done by private authority, nor ever at all but according to the Apostle's rule, εὐσχημόνως καὶ κατὰ τάξιν, " whatsoever is decent, and whatsoever is according to order," that is to be done, and nothing else. For prayer and imposition of hands for the invocating and giving the Holy Spirit are all that are in the foundation and institution.

34

# XIII. THE EUCHARIST

# (1) INTRODUCTORY

## No. 196. THOMAS KEN

[From *An Exposition on the Church Catechism; or, The Practice of Divine Love.* Exposition of "the Lord's Supper." London, 1685, pp. 75 f. *Prose Works*, ed. W. Benham ('Ancient and Modern Library of Theological Literature'), pp. 184 f. This work, which quickly went through a number of editions, became remarkably popular. A French translation of it appeared in 1703 and an Italian translation in 1865. There is a copy of the uncommon first edition in the British Museum.]

GLORY be to Thee, O adorable Jesus, Who under the outward and visible part, the Bread and Wine, things obvious and easily prepared, both which Thou hast commanded to be received, dost communicate to our souls the mystery of Divine Love, the inward and invisible grace, Thy Own most blessed Body and Blood, which are verily and indeed taken and received by the faithful in Thy supper, for which all Love, all Glory, be to Thee.

O [1] God Incarnate, how Thou canst give us Thy flesh to eat and Thy Blood to drink, how Thy flesh is meat indeed and Thy Blood is drink indeed, how he that eateth Thy flesh and drinketh Thy Blood dwelleth in Thee, and Thou in him, how he shall live by Thee and shall be raised up by Thee to life eternal, how Thou Who art in heaven art present on the altar, I can by no means explain; but I firmly believe it all, because Thou hast said it, and I firmly rely on Thy Love and on Thy Omnipotence to make good Thy Word, though the manner of doing it I cannot comprehend.

I believe, O Crucified Lord, that the Bread which we break in the celebration of the Holy Mysteries is the Communication of Thy Body, and the cup of Blessing which we bless, is the Communication of Thy Blood, and that Thou dost as effectually and really convey Thy Body and Blood to our souls by the bread and wine, as Thou didst Thy Holy Spirit by Thy Breath to Thy disciples; for which all Love, all Glory be to Thee.

Lord, what need I labour in vain to search out the manner of Thy mysterious presence in the Sacrament, when my Love assures me Thou art there? All the faithful who approach Thee with prepared hearts, they well know Thou art there; they feel the virtue of Divine Love going out of Thee, to heal their infirmities and to enflame their affections, for which all Love, all Glory be to Thee.

---

[1] [The text of this paragraph as it stood in the first edition is printed here. It was modified considerably in later editions in a Receptionist direction.]

O Holy Jesu, when at Thy Altar I see the Bread broken and the Wine poured out, O teach me to discern Thy Body there.   O let those sacred and significant actions create in me a most lively remembrance of Thy sufferings, how Thy most blessed Body was scourged and wounded and bruised and tormented, how Thy most precious Blood was shed for my sins ;  and set all my powers on work to love Thee and to celebrate Thy love in thus dying for me.

Glory be to Thee, O Jesu, Who didst institute the Holy Eucharist in both kinds and hast commanded both to be received, both the Bread and the Wine, both Thy Body broken and Thy Blood shed. Thy love, O Lord, has given me both, and both are equally significative and productive of Thy Love.   I do as much thirst after the one as I hunger after the other ;  I equally want both, and it would be grievous to my love to be deprived of either.

Ah Lord, who is there that truly loves Thee, when Thou givest him two distinct pledges of Thy Love, can be content with one only ? What lover can endure to have one half of Thy Love withheld from him ? And therefore all Love, all Glory be to Thee for giving both.

## No. 197.  " THE WHOLE DUTY OF MAN "

[From *The Whole Duty of Man*, Sunday III, §§ 12, 24–29. Edit. London, 1684, pp. 81 f., 90–95.  It is not known with certainty who was the author of this very widely used devotional manual.  Among those to whom it has been ascribed are Richard Allestree, John Fell, and Henry Hammond.  As the title page informs the reader, the work " is divided into xvii chapters, one whereof being read every Lord's Day, the whole may be read over thrice in the year."  It made its first appearance in 1658 or 1659, with a prefatory letter by H[enry] H[ammond], who was thus undoubtedly aware of the identity of its author.]

Concerning the particulars of this resolution [*i.e.* of Obedience], I need say no more but that it must answer every part and branch of our duty ;  that is, we must not only in general resolve that we will observe God's Commandments, but we must resolve it for every Commandment by itself, and especially where we have found ourselves most to have failed heretofore, there especially to renew our resolutions. And herein it nearly concerns us to look that these resolutions be sincere and unfeigned, and not only such slight ones as people use out of custom to put on at their coming to the Sacrament, which they never think of keeping afterwards.  For this is a certain truth, that whosoever comes to this Holy Table without an entire hatred of every sin comes unworthily ;  and it is as sure, that he that doth entirely hate all sin, will resolve to forsake it ;  for you know forsaking naturally follows hatred, no man willingly abides with a thing or person he hates. And therefore he that doth not so resolve as that God the Searcher of hearts may approve it as sincere, cannot be supposed to hate sin, and so cannot be a worthy receiver of that Holy Sacrament.   Therefore try your resolutions thoroughly, that you deceive not yourselves in them; it is your own great danger, if you do; for it is certain you cannot deceive God, nor gain acceptation from Him by any thing which is not perfectly hearty and unfeigned. . . .

I have now gone through those several parts of duty we are to perform before our receiving. In the next place, I am to tell you, what is to be done at the time of receiving. When thou art at the Holy Table, first humble thyself in an unfeigned acknowledgment of thy great unworthiness to be admitted there; and to that purpose remember again between God and thine own soul some of thy greatest and foulest sins, thy breaches of former vows made at that Table, especially since thy last receiving. Then meditate on those bitter sufferings of Christ which are set out to us in the Sacrament. When thou seest the bread broken, remember how His blessed Body was torn with nails upon the Cross; when thou seest the Wine poured out, remember how His precious Blood was spilt there; and then consider, it was thy sins that caused both. And here think how unworthy a wretch thou art to have done that which occasioned such torments to Him: how much worse than His very crucifiers! They crucified Him once, but thou hast, as much as in thee lay, crucified Him daily. They crucified Him because they knew Him not, but thou hast known both what He is in Himself, the Lord of Glory, and what He is to thee, a most tender and merciful Saviour; and yet thou hast still continued thus to crucify Him afresh. Consider this, and let it work in thee, first a great sorrow for thy sins past, and then a great hatred and a firm resolution against them for the time to come.

When thou hast a while thus thought on these sufferings of Christ for the increasing thy humility and contrition, then in the second place think of them again to stir up thy faith. Look on Him as the Sacrifice offered up for thy sins, for the appeasing of God's wrath, and procuring His favour and mercies toward thee. And therefore believingly, yet humbly, beg of God to accept of that Satisfaction made by His innocent and beloved Son, and for the merits thereof to pardon thee whatever is past, and to be fully reconciled to thee.

In the third place, consider them again to raise thy thankfulness. Think how much both of shame and pain He there endured, but especially those great agonies of His Soul which drew from Him that bitter cry, *My God, My God, why hast Thou forsaken Me?* Now all this He suffered only to keep thee from perishing. And therefore consider what unexpressible thanks thou owest Him, and endeavour to raise thy soul to the most hearty and zealous thanksgiving; for this is a principal part of duty at this time, the praising and magnifying that mercy which hath redeemed us by so dear a price. Therefore it will here well become thee to say with David, *I will take the Cup of Salvation, and will call upon the Name of the Lord.*

Fourthly, look on these sufferings of Christ to stir up this love. And surely there cannot be a more effectual means of doing it; for here the Love of Christ is to thee most manifest, according to that of the Apostle, *I John iii, 16, Hereby perceive we the love of God towards us, because He laid down His life for us*; and that even the highest degree of love, for as Himself tells us, *John xv, 13, Greater love than this hath no man, that a man lay down his life for his friend.* Yet even greater love than this had He; for He not only died, but died the most painful and most reproachful death, and that not for His friends, but for His utter enemies. And therefore if after all this love on His part there be no return of love on ours, we are worse than the vilest sort of men, for even the *Publicans love those that love them (Matth.* v, 46). Here therefore chide and reproach thyself that thy love to Him is so faint and cool, when His to thee was so zealous and affectionate. And endeavour to enkindle this holy flame in thy soul, to love Him in such a degree that thou mayst be ready to copy out His example, to part with all things, yea, even life itself whenever He calls for it; that is whensoever thy obedience to any command of His shall lay thee open to those sufferings. But in the meantime to resolve never again to make any league with His enemies, to entertain or harbour any sin in thy breast. But if there have any such hitherto remained with thee, make this the season to kill and crucify it; offer it up at this instant a sacrifice to Him who was sacrificed for thee, and particularly for that very end that *He might redeem thee from all iniquity.* Therefore here make thy solemn resolutions to forsake every sin, particularly those into which thou hast most frequently fallen. And that thou mayest indeed perform those resolutions, earnestly beg of this crucified Saviour, that He will, by the power of His Death, mortify and kill all thy corruptions.

When thou art about to receive the Consecrated Bread and Wine, remember that God now offers to seal to thee that New Covenant made with mankind in His Son. For since He gives that His Son in the Sacrament, He gives with Him all the benefits of that Covenant, to wit, pardon of sins, sanctifying grace, and a title to an eternal inheritance. And here be astonished at the infinite goodness of God Who reaches out to thee so precious a treasure. But then remember that this is all but on condition that thou perform thy part of the Covenant. And therefore settle in thy soul the most serious purpose of obedience, and then with all possible devotion join with the Minister in that short but excellent prayer, used at the instant of giving the Sacrament, "The body of our Lord, etc."

So soon as thou hast received, offer up thy devoutest praises for that great mercy, together with thy most earnest prayers for such assistance of God's Spirit as may enable thee to perform the vow

thou hast now made. Then remembering that Christ is a " propitiation not for our sins only, but also for the sins of the whole world,"
let thy charity reach as far as His hath done, and pray for all mankind,
that everyone may receive the benefit of that Sacrifice of His ; commend
also to God the estate of the Church, that particularly whereof thou art
a member. And forget not to pray for all to whom thou owest
obedience, both in Church and State ; and so go on to pray for such
particular persons as either thy relations or their wants shall present
to thee. If there be any collection for the poor (as there always ought
to be at this time) give freely according to thy ability ; or if by the
default of others there be no such collection, yet do thou privately
design something towards the relief of thy poor brethren, and be sure
to give it the next fitting opportunity that offers itself. All this thou
must contrive to do in the time that others are receiving, that so when
the public prayers after the Administration begin, thou mayest be ready
to join in them, which thou must likewise take care to do with all
devotion. Thus much for behaviour at the time of Receiving.

## No. 198.  HENRY HAMMOND

[From *Of Fundamentals in a Notion referring to Practice*, Chapter xix, §§ 16–21.
*Miscellaneous Theological Works*, ed. L. A. C. T., pp. 178–180.  Cp. note on No. 62.]

Those which are thus confirmed are thereby supposed to be fit for
admission to that other Sacrament [1] of the Body and Blood of Christ,
instituted in the close of His Last Supper. And that, whether it be
considered, 1. as an Institution of Christ for the solemn Commemorating
of His death ; or 2. as a Sacrifice Eucharistical performed by the
Christian to God ; or 3. as the κοινωνία ' Communication ' of the Body
and Blood of Christ, the means of conveying all the benefits of the
crucified Saviour unto all that come fitly prepared and qualified for
them ; or whether 4. as a Federal Rite betwixt the soul and Christ,
eating and drinking at His Table, and thereby engaging our obedience
to Him ; or lastly, as an Emblem of the most perfect Divine charity to
be observed among all Christians, in all and every of these respects, I
say, it is doubtless an instrument of great virtue that hath a peculiar
propriety to engage the receiver to persevere in all piety ; and that yet
further improved by the frequent iteration and repetition of that
Sacrament.

First, as it is the commemorating the death of Christ, so it is the
professing ourselves the disciples of the crucified Saviour ; and that
engageth us to *take up His cross and follow Him*, and not to fall off from
Him for any temptations, or terrors of death itself, but to resist to
blood, as Christ did, in our spiritual ἀγῶνες, our Olympics or combats
against sin.

[1] [*I.e.* than Baptism, the Sacrament previously referred to.]

Secondly, as it is the Eucharistical Christian Sacrifice, so it is formally the practising of several acts of Christian virtue; 1. of prayer, of thanksgiving, of all kind of piety towards God; 2. of charity to our brethren, both that spiritual of *interceding for all men, for Kings, etc.,* and corporal in the offertory, for the relief of those that want; and 3. the offering up and so consecrating *ourselves, our souls and bodies, to be a holy, lively, acceptable, sacrifice* to God, the devoting ourselves to His service all our days; and this last a large comprehensive act of piety, which contains all particular branches under it, and is again the repeating of the baptismal vow, and the yet closer binding of this engagement on us.

Thirdly, as it is by God designed, and as an institution of His, blessed and consecrated by Him into a Sacrament, a holy rite, a means of conveying and communicating to the worthy receiver the benefits of the Body and Blood of Christ, that pardon of sin and sufficiency of strength and grace which were purchased by His Death and typified and consigned to us by the Sacramental elements, so it is again the ridding us of all our discouraging fears, and the animating and obliging of us to make use of that grace which will carry us, if we do not wilfully betray our succours, victoriously through all difficulties.

Fourthly, as it is a federal rite betwixt God and us, as eating and drinking both among the Jews and heathens was wont to be, so it is on our part the solemn undertaking of the condition required of us to make us capable of the benefit of God's new evangelical covenant, and that is sincere performance of all duties prescribed the Christian by Christ; and he that doth no longer expect good from God than he performs that condition is *ipso facto* divested of all those fallacious flattering hopes, which pretended to make purifying unnecessary, and must now either live purely and piously, or else disclaim ever seeing of God.

Lastly, as this Supper of the Lord is a token and engagement of charity among the disciples of Christ, so it is the supplanting of all the most diabolical sins, the filthiness of the spirit, the hatred, variance, emulation, strife, revenge, faction, schism, that have been the tearing and rending of the Church of God,—ofttimes upon pretence of the greatest piety,—but were by Christ of all other things most passionately disclaimed, and cast out of His temple. And if by the admonitions which this emblem is ready to afford us, we can think ourselves obliged to return to that charity and peaceable-mindedness which Christ so frequently and vehemently recommends to us, we have His own promise that the *whole body shall be full of light*, that all other Christian virtues will by way of concomitance or annexation accompany or attend them in our hearts.

# (2) THE EUCHARISTIC PRESENCE

## No. 199.  RICHARD HOOKER

[From *The Laws of Ecclesiastical Polity*, Book V, Chapter lxvii, § 12.  *Works*, ed. J. Keble, Vol. II, pp. 359 f.  Cp. note on No. 148.]

VARIETY of judgements and opinions argueth obscurity in those things whereabout they differ.  But that which all parts receive for truth, that which every one having sifted is by no one denied or doubted of, must needs be matter of infallible certainty.  Whereas therefore there are but three expositions made of *This is My Body*: the first, ' this is in itself before participation *really and truly the natural substance of My Body by reason of the coexistence which My omnipotent Body hath with the sanctified element of bread,*' which is the Lutherans' interpretation ; the second, ' this is itself and before participation *the very true and natural substance of My Body, by force of that Deity which with the Words of Consecration abolisheth the substance of bread and substituteth in the place thereof My Body,*' which is the Popish construction ; the last, ' *this hallowed food, through concurrence of divine power, is in verity and truth unto faithful receivers instrumentally a cause of that mystical participation, whereby, as I make Myself wholly theirs, so I give them in hand an actual possession of all such saving grace as My sacrificed Body can yield, and as their souls do presently need, this is* to them and in them *My Body.*'  Of these three rehearsed interpretations the last hath in it nothing but what the rest do all approve and acknowledge to be most true, nothing but that which the Words of Christ are on all sides confessed to enforce, nothing but that which the Church of God hath always thought necessary, nothing but that which alone is sufficient for every Christian man to believe concerning the use and force of this Sacrament, finally nothing but that wherewith the writings of all antiquity are consonant and all Christian confessions agreeable.  And as truth in what kind soever is by no kind of truth gainsayed, so the mind which resteth itself on this is never troubled with those perplexities which the other do both find, by means of so great contradiction between their opinions and true principles of reason grounded upon experience, nature and sense.

## No. 200.  LANCELOT ANDREWES

[From *Responsio ad Apologiam Cardinalis Bellarmini.*  Ed. *L. A. C. T.*, pp. 13, 262, 265, 266 f., 250 f. ; the first passage is from the reply to Chapter I of the *Apologia*, the remainder from that to Chapter VIII.  The new Oath of Allegiance, occasioned by the Gunpowder Plot of 1605, led James I to become engaged in controversy with Cardinal Bellarmine. Andrewes was drawn into the fray, and wrote two important books against the Cardinal. The first, entitled *Tortura Torti*, was an answer to a work which Bellarmine had written under the pseudonym *Matthaeus Tortus*; the other was the *Responsio*, from which the extract is taken. For the translation of these passages we are indebted to D. Stone, *A History of the Doctrine of the Holy Eucharist*, ii, 264–266.]

Christ said, " This is My Body." He did not say, " This is My Body in this way." We are in agreement with you as to the end; the whole controversy is as to the method. As to the " This is," we hold with firm faith that it is. As to the " This is in this way " (namely, by the Transubstantiation of the bread into the Body), as to the method whereby it happens that it is, by means of In or With or Under or By transition, there is no word expressed. And because there is no word, we rightly make it not of faith; we place it perhaps among the theories of the school, but not among the articles of the faith. . . . We believe no less than you that the presence is real. Concerning the method of the presence, we define nothing rashly, and, I add, we do not anxiously inquire, any more than how the Blood of Christ washes us in our Baptism, any more than how the Human and Divine Natures are united in one Person in the Incarnation of Christ. . . .

It is perfectly clear that Transubstantiation, which has lately been born in the last four hundred years, never existed in the first four hundred. . . . In opposition to the Jesuit, our men deny that the Fathers had anything to do with the fact of Transubstantiation, any more than with the name. He regards the fact of Transubstantiation as a change in substance (*substantialis transmutatio*). And he calls certain witnesses to prove this. And yet on this point, whether there is there a conversion in substance, not long before the Lateran Council the Master of the Sentences himself says " I am not able to define." But all his witnesses speak of some kind of change (*pro mutatione, immutatione, transmutatione*). But there is no mention there of a change in substance, or of the substance. But neither do we deny in this matter the preposition *trans*; and we allow that the elements are changed (*transmutari*). But a change in substance we look for, and we find it nowhere. . . .

At the coming of the almighty power of the Word, the nature is changed so that what before was the mere element now becomes a Divine Sacrament, the substance nevertheless remaining what it was before. . . . There is that kind of union between the visible Sacrament and the invisible reality (*rem*) of the Sacrament which there is between the manhood and the Godhead of Christ, where unless you want to smack of Eutyches, the Manhood is not transubstantiated into the Godhead. . . .

About the adoration of the Sacrament he stumbles badly at the very threshold. He says " of the Sacrament, that is, of Christ the

Lord present by a wonderful but real way in the Sacrament." Away with this. Who will allow him this? "Of the Sacrament, that is, of Christ in the Sacrament." Surely, Christ Himself, the reality (*res*) of the Sacrament, in and with the Sacrament, outside and without the Sacrament, wherever He is, is to be adored. Now the King [*i.e.* James I] laid down that Christ is really present in the Eucharist, and is really to be adored, that is, the reality (*rem*) of the Sacrament; but not the Sacrament, that is, the "earthly part," as Irenæus says, the "visible," as Augustine says. We also, like Ambrose, "adore the flesh of Christ in the mysteries," and yet not it but Him Who is worshipped on the altar. For the Cardinal puts his question badly, "What is there worshipped?" since he ought to ask, "Who?", as Nazianzen says, "Him," not "it." And, like Augustine, we "do not eat the flesh without first adoring." And yet we none of us adore the Sacrament. . . .

Our men believe that the Eucharist was instituted by the Lord for a memorial of Himself, even of His Sacrifice, and, if it be lawful so to speak, to be a commemorative sacrifice, not only to be a Sacrament and for spiritual nourishment. Though they allow this, yet they deny that either of these uses (thus instituted by the Lord together) can be divided from the other by man, either because of the negligence of the people or because of the avarice of the priests. The Sacrifice which is there is Eucharistic, of which Sacrifice the law is that he who offers it is to partake of it, and that he partake by receiving and eating, as the Saviour ordered. For to "partake by sharing in the prayer," that indeed is a fresh and novel way of partaking, much more even than the private Mass itself. . . . Do you take away from the Mass your Transubstantiation; and there will not long be any strife with us about the Sacrifice. Willingly we allow that a memory of the Sacrifice is made there. That your Christ made of bread is sacrificed there we will never allow.

## No. 201. LANCELOT ANDREWES

[From *Sermons of the Nativity*, Sermon XVI. *Works*, ed. *L. A. C. T.*, *Sermons*, Vol. I, pp. 281 f. The whole series of Ninety-Six Sermons was first published in 1629, under the editorship of Laud and Buckeridge. Perhaps the set of seventeen on the Nativity are the most renowned in this collection. Every one of this set was preached on a Christmas Day, before James I at Whitehall, the first in 1605 and the last in 1624. The sermon from which the extract is taken was delivered on December 25, 1623; the text was *Eph.* i, 10. In the extract, Andrewes expresses his belief on the nature of the Sacramental Presence and Indwelling.]

There we do not gather to Christ or of Christ, but we gather Christ Himself; and, gathering Him, we shall gather the tree and fruit and all upon it. For, as there is a recapitulation of all in Heaven and earth in Christ, so there is a recapitulation of all in Christ in the Holy Sacrament. You may see it clearly. There is in Christ the Word eternal, for things in Heaven ; there is also flesh, for things on earth. Semblably, the Sacrament consisteth of a Heavenly and of a terrene part (it is Irenæus' own words) ; the Heavenly—there the Word too, the abstract of the other ; the earthly—the element.

And in the elements, you may observe there is a fulness of the seasons of the natural year ; of the corn-flour or harvest in the one, bread ; of the wine-press or vintage in the other, wine. And in the Heavenly, of the " wheat-corn " whereto He compareth Himself—bread, even *the Living Bread* (or, *Bread of life*) *that came down from Heaven* ; the true Manna, whereof we may gather each his gomer. And again, of Him, the true Vine as He calls Himself,—the blood of the grapes of that Vine. Both these issuing out of this day's recapitulation, both in *corpus autem aptasti Mihi* of this day.

And the gathering or vintage of these two in the Blessed Eucharist is, as I may say, a kind of hypostatical union of the sign and the thing signified, so united together, as are the two Natures of Christ. And even from this Sacramental union do the Fathers borrow their resemblance, to illustrate by it the personal union in Christ,—I name Theodoret for the Greek, and Gelasius for the Latin Church, that insist upon it both, and press it against Eutyches ; that even as in the Eucharist neither part is evacuate or turned into the other, but abide each still in his former nature and substance, no more is either of Christ's Natures annulled, or one of them converted into the other, as Eutyches held, but each Nature remaineth still full and whole in his own kind. And backwards ; as the two Natures in Christ, so the *signum* and *signatum* in the Sacrament *e converso*. And this latter device, of the substance of the bread and wine to be flown away and gone, and in the room of it a remainder of nothing else but accidents to stay behind, was to them not known, and had it been true, had made for Eutyches and against them. And this for the likeness of union in both.

## No. 202. NATHANIEL EATON

[From *De Fastis Anglicis, sive Calendarium Sacrum. The Holy Calendar, being a treble Series of Epigrams upon all the Feasts Observed by the Church of England; to which is added the like Number of Epigrams upon some other more especial Days which have either their Footsteps in Scripture, or are more remarkable in this Kingdom*, London, 1661, p. 29. The extract is Epigram No. 2 for Ascension Day. *The Holy Calendar* was reprinted in 1888 by J. Tasker at Shrewsbury. The following passage is also contained in W. Lock, *John Keble*, pp. 51 f.]

Look in what sense the Son of Man was said
To be in Heaven whilst yet on earth He stayed.
In the same sense we grant His Body, though
In Heaven, may still be said to be below.
He is ascended all agree, that same
Material Flesh and Blood of His that came

From the pure Virgin's womb, Heavens now retain,
And until all things be restored again,
Must still retain it ; yet it is confesst
That when the holy Elements are blest
By the Priest's powerful lips, though nothing there
To outward sense but bread and wine appear,
Yet doth there under those dark forms reside
The Body of the Son of Man that died.
This, what bold tongue soever doth deny
Gives in effect even Christ Himself the lie.
Yet this whoe'er too grossly doth maintain
Pulls His ascended Lord from Heaven again.
A middle course 'twixt these two rocks to steer,
Is that becomes the Christian Mariner.
So to believe the Ascension as to grant
His real Presence in the Sacrament ;
Yet so His Real Presence there to own
As not to make void His Ascension.

## No. 203. JOHN COSIN

[From the *Historia Transubstantiationis Papalis, Cui Praemittitur atque Opponitur tum S. Scripturae, tum Veterum Patrum et Reformatorum Ecclesiarum Doctrina Catholica De Sacris Symbolis et Praesentia Christi in Sacramento Eucharistiae*, Chap. I ; Chap. IV, §§ 2, 5. *Works*, ed. L. A. C. T., Vol. IV, pp. 155–157 ; 172 f. ; 174 f. This work was written in 1656, while Cosin was in exile at Paris. It was circulated originally in MS., and not published until 1675, Cosin having died in 1672. An English translation, by Luke de Beaulieu, appeared in 1676 ; it is this translation which is here used.]

Those words which Our Blessed Saviour used in the institution of the Blessed Sacrament of the Eucharist, *This is My Body, which is given for you, This is My Blood which is shed for you, for the remission of sins*, are held and acknowledged by the Universal Church to be most true and infallible ; and, if any one dares oppose them, or call in question Christ's veracity, or the truth of His words, or refuse to yield his sincere assent to them except he be allowed to make a mere figment or a bare figure of them, we cannot, and ought not, either excuse or suffer him in our Churches ; for we must embrace and hold for an undoubted truth whatever is taught by Divine Scripture. And therefore we can as little doubt of what Christ saith, *My Flesh is meat indeed, and My Blood is drink indeed*, which, according to St. Paul, are both given to us by the consecrated elements. For he calls the bread *the communion of Christ's Body*, and the cup *the communion of His Blood*.

Hence it is most evident that the bread and wine (which, according to St. Paul, are the elements of the Holy Eucharist) are neither changed as to their substance, nor vanished, nor reduced to nothing, but are solemnly consecrated by the Words of Christ, that by them His Blessed Body and Blood may be communicated to us.

And further it appears from the same words, that the expression of Christ and the Apostle is to be understood in a Sacramental and mystic sense; and that no gross and carnal presence of Body and Blood can be maintained by them.

And, though the word *Sacrament* be no where used in Scripture to signify the Blessed Eucharist, yet the Christian Church ever since its primitive ages hath given it that name, and always called the presence of Christ's Body and Blood therein mystic and Sacramental.  Now a Sacramental expression doth, without any inconvenience, give to the sign the name of the thing signified.  And such is as well the usual way of speaking, as the nature of Sacraments, that not only the names, but even the properties and effects of what they represent and exhibit, are given to the outward elements.  Hence (as I said before) the bread is as clearly as positively called by the Apostle *the communion of the Body of Christ*.

This also seems very plain, that Our Blessed Saviour's design was not so much to teach what the elements of bread and wine are by nature and substance, as what is their use and office and signification in this mystery.  For the Body and Blood of Our Saviour are not only fitly represented by the elements, but also by virtue of His institution really offered to all by them, and so eaten by the faithful mystically and Sacramentally; whence it is, that *He truly is and abides in us, and we in Him*.

This is the spiritual (and yet no less true and undoubted than if it were corporal) eating of Christ's Flesh, not indeed simply as it is flesh, without any other respect (for so it is not given, neither would it profit us), but as it is crucified, and given for the redemption of the world. Neither doth it hinder the truth and substance of the thing that this eating of Christ's Body is spiritual, and that by it the souls of the faithful, and not their stomachs, are fed by the operation of the Holy Ghost; for this none can deny but they who, being strangers to the Spirit and the Divine virtue, can savour only carnal things, and to whom what is spiritual and Sacramental is the same as if a mere nothing.

As to the manner of the presence of the Body and Blood of Our Lord in the Blessed Sacrament, we that are Protestant and Reformed according to the ancient Catholic Church do not search into the manner of it with perplexing inquiries; but, after the example of the primitive and purest Church of Christ, we leave it to the power and wisdom of Our Lord, yielding a full and unfeigned assent to His words.  Had the Romish maintainers of Transubstantiation done the same, they would not have determined and decreed, and then imposed as an article of faith absolutely necessary to salvation, a manner of presence newly by them invented, under pain of the most direful curse; and there would have been in the Church less wrangling, and more peace and unity, than now is. . . .

There is no reason why we should dispute concerning God's Omnipotency, whether it can do this or that, presuming to measure an infinite power by our poor ability which is but weakness. We may grant that He is able to do beyond what we can think or apprehend and resolve His most wonderful acts into His absolute will and power; but we may not charge Him with working contradictions. And, though God's almightiness were able in this mystery to destroy the substance of bread and wine, and essentially to change it into the Body and Blood of Christ, while the accidents of bread and wine subsist of themselves without a subject, yet we desire to have it proved that God will have it so, and that it is so indeed. For that God doth it, because He can, is no argument; and, that He wills it, we have no other proof but the confident assertion of our adversaries. Tertullian against Praxeas declared, "that we should not conclude God doth things because He is able, but that we should inquire what He hath done." For God will never own that praise of His omnipotency, whereby His unchangeableness and His truth are impaired, and those things overthrown and destroyed which in His word He affirms to be: for take away the bread and wine, and there remains no Sacrament. . . .

It appears that this whole controversy may be reduced to four heads:—1, Concerning the signs; 2, Concerning the things signified; 3, Concerning the union of both; and 4, Concerning their participation. As for the first, the Protestants differ from the Papists in this, that, according to the nature of Sacraments, and the doctrine of Holy Scripture, we make the substance of bread and wine, and they accidents only, to be signs. In the second, they, not understanding our opinion, do misrepresent it: for we do not hold (as they say we do) that only the merits of the death of Christ are represented by the blessed elements, but also that His very Body which was crucified and His Blood which was shed for us, are truly signified and offered, that our souls may receive and possess Christ as truly and certainly as the material and visible signs are by us seen and received. And so, in the third place, because the thing signified is offered and given to us as truly as the sign itself, in this respect we own the union betwixt the Body and Blood of Christ and the elements, whose use and office we hold to be changed from what it was before. But we deny what the Papists affirm, that the substance of bread and wine are quite abolished and changed into the Body and Blood of Our Lord, in such sort that the bare accidents of the elements do alone remain united with Christ's

35

Body and Blood. And we also deny that the elements still retain the nature of Sacraments, when not used according to Divine institution, that is, given by Christ's ministers and received by His people ; so that Christ in the consecrated bread ought not, cannot, be kept and preserved to be carried about, because He is present only to the communicants. As for the fourth and last point, we do not say that in the Lord's Supper we receive only the benefits of Christ's Death and Passion, but we join the ground with its fruits, that is, Christ with those advantages we receive from Him ; affirming with St. Paul, that *the bread which we break is κοινωνία, the communion of the Body of Christ, and the cup which we bless the communion of His Blood,*—of that very substance which He took of the Blessed Virgin, and afterwards carried into heaven ; differing from those of Rome only in this, that they will have our union with Christ to be corporal and our eating of Him likewise, and we, on the contrary, maintain it to be indeed as true, but not carnal or natural. And, as he that receives unworthily (that is, with the mouth only, but not with a faithful heart) eats and drinks his own damnation, so he that doth it worthily receives his absolution and justification,—that is, he that discerns, and then receives the Lord's Body as torn and His Blood as shed for the redemption of the world. But, that Christ (as the Papists affirm) should give His Flesh and Blood to be received with the mouth and ground with the teeth, so that not only the most wicked and infidels, but even rats and mice, should swallow Him down,—this our words and our hearts do utterly deny.

### No. 204. WILLIAM NICHOLSON

[From *A Plain but Full Exposition of the Catechism of the Church of England,* " Of the Lord's Supper." Ed. *L. A. C. T.*, p. 179. This treatise was first published in 1655, and was dedicated to his parishioners of Llandilo-Vawr. A new edition appeared in 1663 after the author's consecration to the see of Gloucester in 1661 ; this edition contained a dedication to Gilbert Sheldon, then Bishop of London.]

Christ is said to be present four manner of ways :—

1. Divinely, as God, and so He is present in all places. *Whither shall I fly from Thy presence ? I, the Lord, fill heaven and earth.*

2. Spiritually, and so He is present in the hearts of true believers. *Christ dwells in our hearts by faith.*

3. Sacramentally, and so is He present in the Sacrament, because He hath ordained the Sacrament to represent and communicate Christ's death unto us. *The cup of blessing which we bless, is it not the communion of the blood of Christ, etc.?*

4. Corporally ; so present in Judæa in the days of His flesh.

And as the word ' presence,' so the word ' really,' is diversely taken : for sometimes,

1. It is opposed to that which is feigned, and is but imaginary, and imports as much as ' truly.'

2. It is opposed to that which is merely figurative, and barely representative, and imports as much as ' effectually.'

3. It is opposed to that which is spiritual, and imports as much as ' corporally ' or ' bodily.'

We then believe Christ to be present in the Eucharist Divinely after a special manner, Spiritually in the hearts of the communicants, Sacramentally or relatively in the elements. And this presence of His is real, in the two former acceptions of ' real '; but not in the last, for He is truly and effectually there present, though not corporally, bodily, carnally, locally.

### No. 205. WILLIAM FORBES

[From *Considerationes Modestae et Pacificae Controversiarum de Justificatione, Purgatorio, Invocatione Sanctorum, Christo Mediatore, et Eucharistia,* De Eucharistia, Book I, ch. i, 2 (*bis*); I, i, 7; I, i, 27; I, ii, 1; I, iii (chapter-heading); I, iv, 12; II, ii, 8; II, ii, 9; III, i, 10, 12; III, ii, 2; III, ii, 17. This collection of passages has been borrowed from Darwell Stone, *A History of the Doctrine of the Holy Eucharist,* Vol. II, pp. 305–308, of whose translation we have availed ourselves. The *Considerationes Modestae* were first edited by Bishop Sydserf and published in London in 1658, over 20 years after the author's death. On the title page, it was described as an *Opus Posthumum Diu Desideratum.* A very careful edition, with an English translation, was prepared for the *L. A. C. T.* by George Hay Forbes (two vols. 1850 and 1856 respectively).]

The opinion of Zwingli which the Divines of Zurich tenaciously maintained and defended, namely that ' Christ is present in the Eucharist only by the contemplation of faith; that there is no place to be given here to a miracle, since we know in what way Christ is present to His Supper, namely, by the quickening Spirit, spiritually and efficaciously; that Sacramental union consists wholly in signification,' etc., is by no means to be approved, since it is most clearly contrary to Scripture and the common opinion of all the Fathers. . . .

The holy Fathers . . . most firmly believed that he who worthily receives these mysteries of the Body and Blood of Christ really and actually receives into himself the Body and Blood of Christ, but in a certain spiritual, miraculous, and imperceptible way. . . .

The opinion of those Protestants and others seems to be most safe and most right who think, nay, who most firmly believe, that the Body and Blood of Christ are really and actually and substantially present and taken in the Eucharist, but in a way which the human mind cannot understand and much more beyond the power of man to express, which is known to God alone and is not revealed to us in the Scriptures,—a way indeed not by bodily or oral reception, but not only by the understanding and merely by faith, but in another way known, as has been said, to God alone, and to be left to His omnipotence. . . .

In the Supper by the wonderful power of the Holy Ghost we invisibly partake of the substance of the Body and Blood of Christ, of which we are made recipients no otherwise than if we visibly ate and drank His Flesh and Blood. . . .

As regards Transubstantiation, many Protestants very perilously and too rashly deny that God is able to convert the bread substantially into the Body of the Lord. For Almighty God can do many things above the understanding of all men, nay, even of the angels. All indeed allow that what implies contradiction cannot be done. But inasmuch as in the particular case it is not clear to any one what the essence of each thing is and therefore what implies or does not imply a contradiction, it is certainly a mark of great rashness, on account of the weakness of our blind understanding, to prescribe limits to God, and stubbornly to deny that He can do this or that by His Omnipotence. . . .

Transubstantiation is not of faith, nay, is contrary to the Scriptures and the more ancient Fathers, yet is by no means to be condemned as heretical. . . .

The reasons by which the more-rigid Protestants seem to themselves to have proved most clearly that each doctrine, both that of the Romanists and that of the Lutherans, is contrary to the Articles of the Faith and therefore heretical, impious, and blasphemous, have been abundantly refuted both by the maintainers of these opinions and by others who are anxious for the unity of the Church. . . .

Gigantic is the error of the more rigid Protestants who deny that Christ is to be adored in the Eucharist with any but inward and mental adoration, and contend that He is not to be adored with any outward rite of worship, as by kneeling or some other like position of the body. Almost all these hold wrong views about the presence of Christ the Lord in the Sacrament, Who is present in a wonderful but real manner. . . .

As regards the first assertion of Bellarmine about venerating the symbols with a kind of lesser worship, we admit it. But as regards his saying that the adoration of supreme worship, though in itself and properly it is due and given to Christ, yet belongs also to the symbols insofar as they are apprehended as one with Christ Himself, Whom they contain and Whom they cover and conceal like garments, it is false and is contrary to the opinion of many others. . . .

The holy Fathers say very often that the Body of Christ itself is offered and sacrificed in the Eucharist, as is clear from almost numberless places ; but not in such a way that all the properties of a sacrifice are properly and actually preserved, but by way of commemoration and representation of that which was performed once for all in that One Only Sacrifice of the Cross whereby Christ our High Priest consummated all other sacrifices, and by way of pious prayer whereby the Ministers of the Church most humbly beseech God the Father on account of the abiding Victim of that One Sacrifice, Who is seated in Heaven on the right hand of the Father and is present on the Holy

Table in an ineffable manner, to grant that the virtue and grace of this perpetual Victim may be efficacious and healthful to His Church for all the necessitites of body and soul. . . . Assuredly, in every real Sacrifice that is properly so called, it is necessary that the victim should be consumed by a certain destructive change, as Romanists themselves universally admit. But in the Mass the Body of Christ is neither destroyed nor changed, as is clear. . . .

The more moderate Romanists rightly affirm that the Mass is not only a sacrifice of thanksgiving and service or honour, but that it can also be called hilastic or propitiatory in a sound sense ; not indeed as if it effected the propitiation and forgiveness of sins, for that pertains to the Sacrifice of the Cross, but as impetrating the propitiation which has already been made, as prayer, of which this Sacrifice is a kind, can be called propitiatory. . . .

The Sacrifice which is offered in the Supper is not merely of thanksgiving, but is also propitiatory in a sound sense, and is profitable to very many not only of the living but also of the departed.

## No. 206.  THOMAS MORTON

[From *Of the Institution of the Sacrament of the Blessed Body and Blood of Christ,* by some called the " *Mass of Christ,*" *Discovering the Superstitious, Sacrilegious and Idolatrous Abominations of the Romish Mass, Together with the Consequent Obstinacies, Overtures of Perjuries, and the Heresies discernable in the Defenders thereof,* Book III, Chap i, § 1 ;  Book IV, Chapter i, § 2 ;  Book IV, Chapter i, § 1.  London, 1631, pp. 103, 148–150, 147 f.  This folio work reached a second edition in 1635 ; it was one of a whole series of treatises which Morton wrote against Rome.]

There lieth a charge upon every soul that shall communicate and participate of this Sacrament that herein he *discern the Lord's Body* ; which office of discerning (according to the judgement of Protestants) is not only in the use but also in the nature to distinguish the object of faith from the object of sense.  The first object of Christian faith is the Divine alteration and change of natural bread into a Sacrament of Christ's Body ;  this we call a Divine change, because none but the same Omnipotent Power that made the creature and element of bread can change it into a Sacrament.  The second object of faith is the Body of Christ itself Sacramentally represented and verily exhibited to the faithful communicants.  There are then three objects in all to be distinguished.  The first is before consecration, the bread merely natural ;  secondly, after consecration, bread Sacramental ;  thirdly, Christ's own Body, which is the spiritual and supersubstantial bread truly exhibited by this Sacrament to the nourishment of the souls of the faithful. . . .

There may be observed four kinds of truths of Christ His presence in this Sacrament.  One is *veritas signi*, that is, truth of representation of Christ His Body ;  the next is *veritas revelationis*, truth of revelation ; the third is *veritas obsignationis*, that is, a truth of seal, for better assur-

ance ; the last is *veritas exhibitionis*, the truth of exhibiting and deliverance of the real Body of Christ to the faithful communicants. The
truth of the sign in respect of the thing signified is to be acknowledged
so far as in the signs of bread and wine is represented the true and real
Body and Blood of Christ, which truth and reality is celebrated by us
and taught by ancient Fathers in contradiction to Manichees, Marcionites, and other old heretics, who held that Christ had in Himself no true
body but merely phantastical. . . . A second truth and reality in
this Sacrament is called *veritas revelationis*, as it is a sign in respect of
the typical signs of the same Body and Blood of Christ in the rites of
the Old Testament, yet not absolutely in respect of the matter itself
but of the manner, because the faithful under the Law had the same
faith in Christ, and therefore their Sacraments had relation to the same
Body and Blood of Christ, but in a difference of manner. . . . As,
therefore, the truth of history is held to be more real than the truth of
prophecy because it is a declaration of a real performance of that which
was promised, so the evangelical Sacrament may be said to contain in it a
more real verity than the Levitical. . . . Besides the former two,
there is *veritas obsignationis*, a truth sealed, which maketh this Sacrament
more than a sign, even a seal of God's promises in Christ. . . . A
fourth reason to be observed herein, as more special, is *veritas exhibitionis*, a truth exhibiting and delivering to the faithful communicants
the thing signified and sealed. . . . Vain therefore is the objection
made by your Cardinal [*i.e.* Bellarmine] in urging us with the testimony
of Athanasius to prove that Christ His body is exhibited to the receivers
as though there were not a truth in a mystical and Sacramental deliverance of Christ His body except it were by a corporal and material
presence thereof ; which is a transparent falsity, as any may perceive
by any deed of gift which by writing, seal, and delivery conveyeth any
land or possession from man to man, yet this far more effectually. . . .

It would be a wonder to us to hear any of our own profession to be
so extremely indifferent concerning the different opinions of the manner
of the Presence of Christ's Body in the Sacrament as to think the
Romish sect therefore either tolerable or reconcilable, upon pretence
that the question is only *de modo*, that is, of the manner of being, and
that consequently all controversy about this is but vain jangling. Such
an one ought to enter into his second thoughts, to consider the necessity
that lieth upon every Christian to abandon divers heresies, albeit their
difference from the orthodox profession were only *de modo* . . . . That
the Romish manner of eating Christ His Body is Capernaitical ; her
manner of sacrifice sacrilegious ; her manner of Divine adoration
thereof idolatrous ; and all these manners irreconciliable to the manner
of our Church, is copiously declared in the books following.

## No. 207.   JOHN BRAMHALL

[From *An Answer to M. de la Milletière, His Impertinent Dedication of His Imaginary Triumph ; or His Epistle to the King of Great Britain, Wherein he inviteth His Majesty to forsake the Church of England and to embrace the Roman Catholic Religion,* Init. *Works,* ed. *L. A. C. T.,* Vol. I, pp. 7–23. The occasion of this small treatise, first printed at The Hague in 1653, is indicated by the title. Théophile Brachet de la Milletière, after a varied experience as a French Huguenot, became he converted to Roman Catholicism. In 1651 he published at Paris *La Victorie de la Vérité pour la Paix de l'Eglise, au Roy de la Grande Brétagne. Pour convier Sa Majesté d'embrasser la Foy Catholique.* The instructive Dedicatory Epistle to this work,—instructive because it presents the judgement of a foreigner upon the character of the Church of England,—is printed (in an English translation) in the *L. A. C. T.* edition of Bramhall's *Works,* Vol. I, pp. cxix-cl ; Bramhall directs his reply against this part of de la Milletière's treatise.]

Sir, You might long have disputed your question of Transubstantiation with your learned adversary[1] and proclaimed your own triumph on a silver trumpet to the world, before any member of the Church of England had interposed in this present exigence of our affairs. I know no necessity that Christians must be like cocks that " when one crows, all the rest must crow for company." Monsieur Aubertin will not want a surviving friend, to teach you what it is " to sound a triumph before you have gained the victory." He was no fool that desired no other epitaph on his tomb than this, " Here lies [Sir Henry Wotton,] the author of this sentence, *Prurigo disputandi scabies Ecclesiae*—The itch of disputing is the scab of the Church."

Having viewed all your strength with a single eye, I find not one of your arguments that comes home to Transubstantiation, but only to a true Real Presence ; which no genuine son of the Church of England did ever deny, no, nor your adversary himself. Christ said *This is My Body* ; what He said, we do steadfastly believe. He said not, after this or that manner, *neque con, neque sub, neque trans.* And therefore we place it among the opinions of the schools, not among the Articles of our Faith. The Holy Eucharist, which is the Sacrament of peace and unity, ought not to be made the matter of strife and contention.

There wanted not abuses in the administration of this Sacrament in the most pure and primitive times, as profaneness and uncharitableness among the Corinthians. The Simonians, and Menandrians, and some other such imps of Satan, unworthy the name of Christians, did wholly forbear the use of the Eucharist ; but it was not for any difference about the Sacrament itself but about the Natural Body of Christ ; they held that His flesh and Blood and Passion were not true and real, but imaginary and phantastical things. The Manichees did forbear the Cup ; but it was not for any difference about the Sacrament itself ; they made two Gods,—a good God, whom they called $\Phi \hat{\omega}_s$ or

---

[1] [*I.e.,* Edmund Aubertin, referred to just below. He was a distinguished theologian of the French Reformed Church in the Seventeenth Century. B., 1595 ; d. 1652.]

Light, and an evil God, whom they termed Σκότος or Darkness ; which evil God, they said, did make some creatures of the dreg or more feculent parts of the matter, which were evil and impure ; and among these evil creatures they esteemed wine, which they called ' the gall of the dragon.' For this cause, not upon any other scruple, they wholly abstained from the Cup, or used water in the place of wine ; which Epiphanius recordeth among the errors of the Ebionites and Tatians, and St. Augustine, of the Aquarians. Still we do not find any clashing, either in word or writing, directly about this Sacrament in the Universal Church of Christ, much less about the Presence of Christ in the Sacrament. " *Neque ullus veterum disputat contra hunc errorem primis sexcentis annis* " (Bellarmine).

The first that are supposed by Bellarmine to have broached any error in the Church about the Real Presence were the Iconomachi, after seven hundred years. " *Primi qui veritatem Corporis Domini in Eucharistia in quaestionem vocarunt, fuerunt Iconomachi post annum Domini* 700 ; "—only because they called the Bread and Wine the Image of Christ's Body. This is as great a mistake as the former. Their difference was merely about images, not at all about the Eucharist. So much Vasquez confesseth that, " in his judgement, they were not to be numbered with those who deny the Presence of Christ in the Eucharist."

We may well find different observations in those days, as one Church consecrating leavened bread, another unleavened ; one Church making use of pure wine, another of wine mixed with water ; one Church admitting infants to the Communion, another not admitting them ; but without controversies or censures or animosity one against the other. We find no debates or disputes concerning the Presence of Christ's Body in the Sacrament, and much less concerning the manner of His Presence, for the first eight hundred years.

Yet all the time we find as different expressions among those primitive Fathers, as among our modern writers at this day ; some calling the Sacrament " the Sign of Christ's Body," " the Figure of His Body," " the Symbol of His Body," " the Mystery of His Body," " the Exemplar," " Type," and " Representation, of His Body " ; saying " that the Elements do not recede from their first nature " ; others naming it " the true Body and Blood of Christ," " changed, not in shape, but in nature" ; yea, doubting not to say that in this Sacrament " we see Christ," " we touch Christ," " we eat Christ," " that we fasten our teeth in His very Flesh and make our tongues red in His Blood." Yet, notwithstanding, there were no questions, no quarrels, no contentions amongst them ; there needed no Councils to order them, no conferences to reconcile them, because they contented themselves to believe what Christ had said,—*This is My Body*—without presuming on their own heads to determine the manner how it is His Body, neither weighing all their own words so exactly before any controversy was raised nor expounding the sayings of other men contrary to the analogy of Faith.

The first doubt about the Presence of Christ's Body in the Sacrament seems to have been moved not long before the year 900 in the days of Bertram and Paschasius ; but the controversy was not well formed, nor this new article of Transubstantiation sufficiently concocted, in the days of Berengarius, after the year 1050, as appeareth by the gross mistaking and misstating of the question on both sides. First Berengarius, if we may trust his adversaries, knew no mean between a naked figure or empty sign of Christ's Presence and a corporeal or local Presence, and afterwards fell into another extreme of *impanation*. On the other side, the Pope and the Council made no difference between Consubstantiation and Transubstantiation,—they understood nothing of the spiritual or indivisible being of the Flesh and Blood of Christ in the Sacrament, as appeareth by that ignorant and " Capernaitical " retractation and abjuration which they impose upon Berengarius, penned by Umbertus, a Cardinal, approved by Pope Nicholas and a Council :—" *Ego Berengarius, etc.*," " I, Berengarius, do consent to the Holy Roman Apostolic See, and profess with my mouth and my heart to hold the same Faith of the Sacrament of the Lord's Supper with Pope Nicholas and this holy Synod, etc." And what the Faith of Pope Nicholas and this Synod was follows in the next words : " That the Bread and Wine, which are set upon the Altar after Consecration are not only the Sacrament, but the very Body and Blood of Christ." This seems to favour Consubstantiation, rather than Transubstantiation. If the Bread and Wine be the Body and Blood of Christ, then they remain Bread and Wine still ; if the Bread be not only the Sacrament, but also the thing of the Sacrament, if it be both the sign and the thing signified, how is it now to be made nothing ?

It follows in the retractation, " That the Body and Blood of Christ is sensibly, not only in the Sacrament, but in truth, handled and broken by the hand of the Priest, and bruised by the teeth of the faithful." If it be even so, there needs no more but feel and be satisfied. To this they made Berengarius swear " by the Consubstantial Trinity and the Holy Gospels," and accurse and anathematize all those who held the contrary ; yet these words did so much scandalize and offend the Glosser upon Gratian, that he could not forbear to admonish the reader that " unless he understood those words in a sound sense, he would fall into a greater heresy than that of Berengarius." Not without reason, for the most favourable of the Schoolmen do confess that these words are not properly and literally true, but figuratively and metonymically, understanding the thing containing by the thing contained ; as to say the Body of Christ is broken or bruised, because the quantity or *species* of Bread are broken and bruised. They might as well say, that the Body and Blood of Christ becomes fusty and sour, as often as the *species* of Bread and Wine before their corruption become fusty and sour. But the retractation of Berengarius can admit no such figurative sense,—that " the Body and Blood of Christ in the Sacrament are divided and bruised sensibly, not only in the Sacrament " (that is the species) " but also in truth,"—a most ignorant Capernaitical assertion. For the Body of Christ, being not in the Sacrament *modo quantitativo*, according to their own tenet, but indivisibly, after a spiritual manner, without extrinsecal extension of parts, cannot in itself or in truth be either divided or bruised. Therefore others of the Schoolmen go more roundly and ingenuously to work, and confess, that " it is an abusive and excessive expression," " not to be held or defended," and that " it happened to Berengarius " (they should have said to Pope Nicholas and Cardinal Umbertus), " as it doth with those who out of a detestation of one error incline to another." Neither will it avail them any thing at all, that the Fathers have sometimes used such expressions of " seeing Christ," of " touching Christ " in the Sacrament, of " fastening our teeth in His Flesh," and " making our tongues red in His Blood." There is a great difference between a sermon to the people and a solemn retractation before a judge. The Fathers do not say that such expressions are true, not only Sacramentally or figuratively (as they made Berengarius both say and accurse all others that held otherwise),—but also properly and in the things themselves. The Fathers never meant by these forms of speech to determine the manner of the Presence (which was not dreamt of in their days), but to raise the devotion of their hearers and readers, to advertise the people of God that they should not rest in the external symbols, or signs, but principally be intent upon the invisible grace; which was both lawful and commendable for them to do. Leave us their primitive liberty, and we will not refrain from the like expressions.

I urge this to shew that the new doctrine of Transubstantiation is so far from being an old article of Faith, that it was not well digested, nor rightly understood, in any tolerable measure, by the greatest clerks, and most concerned, above a thousand years after Christ.

The first definition or determination of this manner of the Presence was yet later, in the Council of Lateran, in the days of Innocent the Third, after the year 1200. " *Ante Lateranense Concilium Transubstantiatio non fuit dogma fidei* " (Duns Scotus). And what the fruit of it was let Vasquez bear witness,—" *Audito nomine Transubstantiationis, etc.*" " The very name of Transubstantiation being but heard, so great a controversy did arise among the later Schoolmen concerning the nature thereof that the more they endeavoured to wind themselves out, the more they wrapped themselves in greater difficulties, whereby the mystery of Faith became more difficult both to be explained and to be understood, and more exposed to the cavils of its adversaries." He adds, that "the name of Conversion and Transubstantiation gave occasion to these controversies."

No sooner was this bell rung out, no sooner was this fatal sentence given, but, as if Pandora's box had been newly set wide open, whole swarms of noisome questions and debates did fill the Schools.

Then it began to be disputed by what means this change comes, whether by the Benediction of the Elements, or by the repetition of these words of Christ, *This is My Body*. The common current of your Schools is for the latter; but your judicious Archbishop of Caesarea,[1] since the Council of Trent, in a book dedicated to Sixtus the Fifth, produceth great reason to the contrary.

Then was the question started, What the demonstrative pronoun *Hoc* signifies in these words, *This is My Body*,—whether this thing, or this substance, or this Bread, or this Body, or this meat, or these accidents, or that which is contained under these *species*, or this *individuum vagum*, or lastly (which seems stranger than all the rest) this nothing.

Then it began to be argued whether the Elements were annihilated; whether the matter and form of them being destroyed, their essence did yet remain; or the essence being converted, the existence remained; whether the Sacramental existence of the Body and Blood of Christ do depend upon its natural existence; whether the whole Host were transubstantiated, or only some parts of it, that is, such parts as should be distributed to worthy communicants; or whether in those parts of the Host, which were distributed unto unworthy communicants, the matter of Bread and Wine did not return; whether the Deity did assume the Bread, or the *species* thereof, by a new hypostatical union, called *impanation*, either absolutely, or respectively *mediante Corpore*; whether the Body and Blood of Christ might be present in the Sacrament without Transubstantiation, with the Bread or without the Bread; whether a body may be transubstantiated into a Spirit; and (which is most strange) whether a creature might be transubstantiated into the Deity.

Then the Schoolmen began to wrangle what manner of change this was, whether a material change, or a formal change, or a change of the whole substance, both matter and form; and if it were a conversion of the whole substance, then whether it was by way of *production*, or by *adduction*, or by *conservation*; each of which greater squadrons are subdivided into several lesser parties, speaking as different languages as the builders of Babel, pestering and perplexing one another with inextricable difficulties.

It cannot be a new *production* (saith one), because the Body of

---

[1] [Christopher de Capite Fontium.]

Christ, whereinto the Elements are supposed to be converted, did pre-exist before the change ; neither can that Body which is made of Bread be the same Body with that Which was born of a Virgin.

If it be not by production (say others), but only by *adduction*, then it is not a tran*substanti*ation, but a tran*subia*tion ; not a change of natures, but a local succession. Then the Priest is not the " maker of his Maker " (as they use to brag), but only puts Him into a new Positure or Presence under the *species* of Bread and Wine.

Howbeit this way by adduction be " the more common and the safer way " (if we may trust Bellarmine), yet of all conversions or changes it hath least affinity with Transubstantiation. Suppose the water had not been turned into wine at Cana of Galilee by Our Saviour but poured out or utterly destroyed, and wine new created or adduced by miracle into the water-pots, in such a manner that the introduction of the wine should be the expulsion of the water not only *comitanter* but *causaliter* ; in such case it had been no Transubstantiation. Moses his rod was truly changed into a serpent, but it was by production ; if his rod had been conveyed away invisibly by legerdemain, and a serpent had been adduced into the place of it, what Transubstantiation had this been ? None at all ; no, though the adduction of the serpent had been the means of the expulsion and destruction of the rod. It is so far from Transubstantiation, that it is no conversion at all. The substance of the Elements is not converted, for that is supposed to be destroyed. The accidents are not converted, but remain the same ʰthey were. It is no adduction at all when the Body of Christ (which is the thing supposed to be adduced) remains still in Heaven where it was before.

It cannot be a *conservative* conversion (say others) ; for the same individual thing cannot be conserved by two total distinct conservations ; but if this were a conservative conversion, the Body of Christ should be conserved by two total distinct conservations, the one in Heaven, the other in earth ; yea, by ten thousand distinct total conservations upon earth, even as many as there are consecrated Hosts : " which seems to be ridiculous, and without any necessity administers great occasion to the adversaries of Christian Religion of jesting and deriding the mysteries of our Faith."

So here we have a Transubstantiation without Transubstantiation ; a production of a *modus* or manner of being, for a production of a substance ; an annihilation supposed, yet no annihilation confessed ; an adduction, without any adduction ; a *terminus ad quem*, without a *terminus a quo*. Who shall reconcile us to ourselves ? But the end is not yet.

Then grew up the question, what is the proper adequate Body which is contained under the *species* or accidents ; whether a material Body, or a substantial Body, or a living Body, or an organical Body, or a human Body; whether it have weight or not, and why it is not perceived; whether it can be seen by the eye of mortal man; whether it can act or suffer any thing; whether it be moveable or immoveable, whether by itself, or by accident, or by both; whether it can move in one place and rest in another, or be moved with two contrary motions, as upwards and downwards, southwards and northwards, at the same time.

Add to these, whether the Soul of Christ and the Deity and the whole Trinity do follow the Body and Blood of Christ under either species by concomitance; whether the Sacramental Body must have suffered the same things with the Natural Body,—as, supposing that an Host, consecrated at Christ's Last Supper, had been reserved until after His Passion, whether Christ must have died and His Blood have been actually shed in the Sacrament; yea, whether those wounds, that were imprinted by the whips in His Natural Body, might and should have been found in His Sacramental Body without flagellation.

Likewise, what Blood of Christ is in the Sacrament, whether that Blood only which was shed, or that Blood only which remained in the Body, or both the one and the other; and whether that Blood which was shed was assumed again by the Humanity in the Resurrection.

Then began those paradoxical questions to be first agitated in the Schools; whether the same individual body, without division or discontinuation from itself, can be locally in ten thousand places, yea, in Heaven and in earth, at the same time; or if not locally, yet whether it can be spiritually and indivisibly; and whether it be not the same as to this purpose, whether a body be locally or spiritually present in more places than one. Bellarmine seems to incline to the affirmative :—" Though to be any where sacramentally doth not imply the taking up of a place, yet it implies a true and real Presence; and if it be in more Hosts or Altars than one, it seems no less opposite unto indivisibility, than the filling up of many places." Nay, he is past seeming positive, that " without doubt, if a body cannot be in two places locally, it cannot be sacramentally in two places." Compare this of Bellarmine with that of Aquinas, that " it is not possible for one body to be in more places than one locally, no, not by miracle, because it implies a contradiction ; " and consider upon what tottering foundations you build articles of Faith. It is impossible, and implies a contradiction, for the Body of Christ to be locally in more Hosts than one at the same time (saith Aquinas). But it is as impossible, and implies a contradiction as much for the Body of Christ to be Sacramentally in more Hosts than one at the same time as to be locally (saith Bellarmine). The inference is plain and obvious.

And many such strange questions are moved :—as whether it be possible the thing contained should be a thousand times greater than the thing containing; whether a definitive being in a place do not imply a not-being out of that place; whether more bodies than one can be in one and the same place; whether there can be a penetration of dimensions; whether a body can subsist after a spiritual manner so as to take up no place at all, but to be wholly in the whole and wholly in every part: moreover, whether the whole Body and Blood of Christ be in every particle of the Bread and of the Cup; and if it be, then whether only after the division of the Bread and Wine or before division also; and in how many parts, and in which parts, is the whole Body and Blood of Christ; whether in the least parts; and if in the least parts, then whether in the least in kind, or the least in quantity, that is, so long as the *species* may retain the name of Bread and Wine, or so long as the matter is divisible; and whether the Body and Blood of Christ be also in the indivisible parts, as points, and lines, and superficies; lastly, whether accidents can subsist without their subjects, that is, whether they can be both accidents and no accidents; whether all the accidents of the elements do remain, and particularly whether the quantity doth remain; whether the other accidents do inhere in the quantity as their subject, that is, whether an accident can have an accident; whether the quantity of Christ's Body be there; and whether it be there after a quantitative manner, with extension of parts, either extrinsecal or intrinsecal; and whether the quantity of the Body of Christ be distinct and figured, or indistinct and unfigured; whether the accidents can nourish or make drunken, or corrupt and a new Body be generated of them; and what supplies the place of the matter in such generation,—whether the quantity, or the Body of Christ, or the old matter of the Bread and Wine restored by miracle, or new matter created by God; and how long in such corruption doth the Body of Christ continue.

Whosoever is but moderately versed in your great doctors, must needs know that these questions are not the private doubts or debates of single Schoolmen, but the common garboils and general engagements of your whole Schools. Wherefore it had been a mere vanity to cite every particular author for each question, and would have made the margin swell ten times greater than the text.

From this bold determination of the manner of the Presence how, have flowed two other differences:

I. First, the detention of the Cup from the laity, merely upon presumption of concomitance, first decreed in the Council of Constance, after the year 1400. Let what will become of concomitance, whilst we keep ourselves to the Institution of Christ and the universal practice of the Primitive Church. It was not for nothing that our Saviour did distinguish His Body from His Blood, not only in the consecration, but also in the distribution, of the Sacrament.

By the way, give me leave to represent a contradiction in Bellarmine which I am not able to reconcile. In one place he saith, " The providence of God is marvellous in Holy Scripture : for St. Luke hath put these words *Do you this* after the Sacrament given under the form of Bread, but he repeated it not after the giving of the Cup ; that we might understand, that the Lord commanded that the Sacrament should be distributed unto all under the form of Bread, but not under the form of Wine." And yet in the next chapter but one of the same Book, he doth positively determine the contrary, upon the ground of concomitance,—that " the Bread may be taken away if the Cup be given, but both cannot be taken away together." Can that be taken away which Christ hath expressly commanded to be given to all ?

II. A second difference flowing from Transubstantiation is about the adoration of the Sacrament, one of those impediments which hinder our communication with you in the celebration of Divine Offices. We deny not a venerable respect unto the consecrate Elements, not only as love-tokens sent us by our best Friend, but as the instruments ordained by our Saviour to convey to us the Merits of His Passion ; but [and ?] for the Person of Christ, God forbid that we should deny Him Divine worship at any time, and especially in the use of this Holy Sacrament. We believe with St. Austin that " no man eats of that Flesh, but first he adores." But that which offends us is this, that you teach and require all men to adore the very Sacrament with Divine Honour. To this end you hold it out to the people. To this end *Corpus Christi* Day was instituted about three hundred years since. Yet we know that even upon your own grounds you cannot, without a particular revelation, have any infallible assurance that any Host is consecrated ; and consequently you have no assurance that you do not commit material idolatry. But that which weighs most with us is this, that we dare not give Divine worship unto any creature, no, not to the very Humanity of Christ in the abstract (much less to the Host), but to the *Whole* Person of Christ, God and Man, by reason of the hypostatical union between the Child of the Blessed Virgin Mary and the Eternal Son, *Who is God over all, Blessed for ever*. Shew us such an union betwixt the Deity and the Elements, or accidents, and you say something. But you pretend no such things. The highest that you dare go is this :—" As they that adored Christ when He was upon earth, did after a certain kind of manner adore His garments " (Bellarmine). Is this all ? This is " after a certain kind of manner " indeed. We have enough. There is no more adoration due to the Sacrament than to the garments which Christ did wear upon earth. Exact no more.

Thus the seamless Coat of Christ is torn in pieces ; thus Faith is

minced into shreds and spun up into niceties more subtle than the
webs of spiders :—

> " *Fidem minutis dissecant ambagibus,*
> " *Ut quisque est lingua nequior* " [Prudentius] ;

because curious wits cannot content themselves to touch hot coals with
tongs but they must take them up with their naked fingers ; nor to
apprehend mysteries of religion by Faith, without descanting upon
them and determining them by reason, whilst themselves confess that
they are incomprehensible by human reason, and imperceptible by
man's imagination ;—how Christ is present in the Sacrament, " can
neither be perceived by sense, nor by imagination " (Aquinas). The
more inexcusable is their presumption to anatomize mysteries and to
determine supernatural not-revealed truths upon their own heads,
which, if they were revealed, were not possible to be comprehended by
mortal man. As vain an attempt as if a child should think to lade out
all the water out of the sea with a cockle-shell. *Secret things belong to
the Lord our God, but things revealed unto us, and our children for ever.*

This is the reason why we rest in the Words of Christ, *This is My
Body*, leaving the manner to Him that made the Sacrament. We know
it is Sacramental, and therefore efficacious, because God was never
wanting to His own ordinances where man did not set a bar against
himself ; but whether it be corporeally or spiritually (I mean not only
after the manner of a Spirit, but in a spiritual sense) ; whether it be in the
soul only, or in the Host also ; and if in the Host, whether by Consubstantiation or Transubstantiation ; whether by Production, or Adduction, or Conservation, or Assumption, or by whatsoever other way bold
and blind men dare conjecture ; we determine not. " *Motum sentimus,
Modum nescimus, Praesentiam credimus.*" [1]

This was the belief of the Primitive Church, this was the Faith
of the ancient Fathers, who were never acquainted with these modern
questions *de modo*, which edify not, but expose Christian religion to
contempt. We know what to think and what to say with probability,
modesty, and submission, in the Schools ; but we dare neither screw
up the question to such a height, nor dictate our opinions to others so
magisterially as Articles of Faith.

> " *Nescire velle quae Magister maximus*
> " *Docere non vult, erudita est inscitia.*"

O ! how happy had the Christian world been, if scholars could have
sat down contented with a latitude of general, sufficient, saving truth
(which when all is done must be the olive-branch of peace, to shew
that the deluge of ecclesiastical division is abated), without wading too

---

[1] [Attributed to] Durandus.

far into particular subtilties, or *doting about questions and logomachies, whereof cometh envy, strife, railings, evil surmisings, perverse disputings.* Old controversies evermore raise up new controversies, and yet more controversies, as circles in the water do produce other circles.

Now especially these Scholastical quarrels seem to be unseasonable when Zeno's school is newly opened in the world, who " sometimes wanted opinions, but never wanted arguments." Now, when atheism and sacrilege are become the mode of the times ; now, when all the fundamentals of theology, morality, and policy, are undermined and ready to be blown up ; now, when the unhappy contentions of great princes, or their ministers, have hazarded the very being of monarchy and Christianity ; now, when Bellona shakes her bloody whip over this kingdom ;—it becometh well all good Christians and subjects to leave their litigious questions, and to bring water to quench the fire of civil dissension already kindled, rather than to blow the coals of discord, and to render themselves censurable by all discreet persons ; like that half-witted fellow personated in the orator, " *Qui cum capiti mederi debuisset, reduviam curavit* "—" when his head was extremely distempered, he busied himself about a small push on his finger's end " (Cicero).

## No. 208. ROBERT NELSON

[From *Transubstantiation Contrary to Scripture; or The Protestant's Answer to the Seeker's Request.* London, 1688, pp. 19–22. Nelson's wife had become converted to Roman Catholicism ; and in 1686 a treatise was published with the title *A Discourse Concerning a Judge of Controversy in Matters of Religion*, which was ascribed to her. Nelson thus became implicated in the Roman Controversy. In the following year there appeared *A Seeker's Request to Catholic Priests and Protestant Ministers, for satisfying his Conscience in the Truth of what he ought to believe of the Lord's Supper;* and it was to this work that Nelson replied (anonymously) in his pamphlet.]

I will make bold to sum up what hath been said on both sides and which both have attempted to prove from Scripture, and then leave you and everyone to judge which has the Bible (the Rule, as well as the Evidence, of Faith) for them.

| *THE CHURCH OF ROME* | *THE CHURCH OF ENGLAND* |
|---|---|
| Jesus the same night He was betrayed took Bread, and when He had given thanks, etc., He said, *Take Eat, This is My Body* ; This somewhat, This Bread or This Species, This figure, form, or appearance of Bread, is My Body, is really, truly and substantially, My true Body and Blood, Bones and Sinews, together with My Soul | Jesus the same night He was betrayed took Bread, and when He had given thanks, etc., He said, *Take eat, This is My Body* ; this bread and the breaking of it, this cup and the pouring out of the Wine and the distribution of both among you is (as the Lamb we have just now eaten is the Passover) the Memorial, Figure, and |

36

and Divinity, and in the very substance wherein I was born of My Mother and shall sit down at the Right Hand of My Heavenly Father. Nay, as much is This My Body as that body you see before you, and which delivers and speaks this to you ; and this that I myself now take and eat and give to each of you to eat is the same entire and undivided Body and as fully and entirely so, as if it was but one. And though I depart and shall bodily ascend into Heaven and am there bodily to continue to the end of the world, yet as often as you and the Catholic Church after you celebrate this supper, by virtue of these words, *This is My Body*, the Bread and Wine you celebrate it in shall be substantially changed into My proper flesh and Blood, wheresoever and whensoever it is ; and I shall be as truly present in My Body at all times and in all places in the Eucharist as I am now with you, and shall be as properly offered up upon the Altar by the priest for a propitiation, under the form of a wafer, as I shall be tomorrow upon the Cross in My own Form and Substance. And now My Command is, that as oft as you do this, you would do it in remembrance of Me, that am thus bodily present with you, wherever you do remember Me.

Representation of My Body and My sufferings in it that I am now to undergo, and of that Blood I am to shed for the Remission of sins. And because I shall leave you and you may be apt to forget Me and My sufferings, I do appoint this Supper to be continued to the end of the world for the remembrance of Me. For as often as ye eat this bread and drink this cup, ye do shew forth My death and your belief of it. And as this cup is the sign and seal of the New Testament or Covenant which is to be confirmed by My Blood, so this is a pledge of it to you and of all the benefits thereby purchased, and which, in the worthy participation of this, ye shall receive ; for the Bread which you break is the Communion or Communication of My Body ; and the cup of blessing which is blessed is the Communion of My Blood, in all the spiritual fruits, advantages, and blessings of it. And all this I shall as certainly give and you as certainly by faith receive, as if I was bodily present and you were to receive them as you do these elements, from My own hands.

I hope by this time it appears that Transubstantiation (or the change of the substance of Bread and Wine) in the Supper of the Lord, cannot, as our Church says, be proved by Holy Writ ; as is evident from the whole account of the Institution, and from the practice of the Apostles where we find it recorded.

## No. 209. GEORGE MORLEY

[From *A Vindication of the Argument Drawn from Sense Against Transubstantiation, From a pretended Answer to it by the Author of a Pamphlet called ' A Treatise of the Nature of Catholic Faith and Heresy,*' pp. 24 f. Morley's original pamphlet which was entitled *An Argument Drawn from the Evidence and Certainty of Sense Against the Doctrine of Transubstantiation,* is said to have been written while the author was ' beyond sea.' The *Treatise* referred to has not been traced. Both the *Argument* and the *Vindication* were included in Morley's *Several Treatises Written upon Several Occasions,* London, 1683 (cp. note on No. **43**).]

There can be no such miracle as Transubstantiation ; because all miracles are possible, but Transubstantiation is impossible, as implying many real and formal contradictions, as the being of Accidents without Subjects, the nourishing of Substances by Accidents, and the generation of other Substances out of the corruption of Accidents ; as likewise that there should be a body without quantity, or quantity without extension, or extension without extending itself in any space or place. Or lastly, that one and the same body should be in divers places at one time, and yet not fill any place, nor be in any of the spaces betwixt those places, and consequently to be united and not united, divided and not divided ; nay, that the same body which is in Heaven *circumscriptive* or *tanquam in loco proprie dicto* should be at the same time out of that place, and consequently *in loco* and *extra locum*, that is, circumscribed and not circumscribed, or circumscribed in one place and not circumscribed in another ; besides many other the like inconsistencies and contradictions which you may see demonstrated at large in Dr. Whitaker, Bishop Morton, and Mr. Chillingworth. Now that whatsoever implies a contradiction cannot be done, no not by miracle, is their doctrine as well as ours, because this would rather argue an impotency than an omnipotency in God.

## No. 210. WILLIAM BEVERIDGE

[From *Sermon LXII. Works*, ed. L. A. C. T., Vol. III, p. 188. The subject of this sermon was " The Preference of Things Invisible and Eternal to Visible and Temporal," and the text *II Cor.* iv, 18.]

This is the way to use the means of grace so as really to obtain grace by them ; neither can it be done any other way. He that looks only at the things which are seen can never pray to any purpose ; for he doth not see Him he prays to ; he cannot hear the Word of God as such, in that he doth not look upon Him Whose Word it is. And in the Sacrament of the Lord's Supper, though he may eat the bread and drink the wine which he doth see, he cannot possibly receive the Body and Blood of Christ ; for they are not seen. Whereas they who look at the things which are not seen, they find and feel wonderful life and vigour and efficacy in these holy institutions. All the while they are upon their knees, their eyes and their hearts are wholly upon God, to Whom they pray, and upon their Advocate at His right hand, in Whose Name

they do it.    All the while they are singing psalms or hymns or spiritual
songs, they join with all the invisible Host of Heaven in praising and
glorifying their Almighty Creator, and most merciful Redeemer.    All
the while they are hearing the Word of God read or expounded to them,
though they see only a man speaking, they *receive it not as the word of
man, but as it is in truth, the Word of God, which effectually worketh in
them who thus believe.*    And when they are at our Lord's Table, looking
not at the bread and wine or any thing else they see, but only at Christ
Whom they do not see, they verily and indeed receive His most blessed
Body and Blood, to preserve both their souls and bodies to eternal life.

### No. 211.   JAMES USSHER

[From *A Sermon Preached before the Commons House of Parliament in St. Margaret's
Church, at Westminster, the 18th. of February*, 1620.   First printed in 1621.   *Works*,
ed. C. R. Elrington (1864), Vol. II, pp. 426 f., 428–437.   The text was *I Cor.* x, 17.]

It is a lamentable thing to behold how this Holy Sacrament, which
was ordained by Christ to be a bond whereby we should be knit together in unity, is, by Satan's malice and the corruption of man's
disposition, so strangely perverted the contrary way, that it is made the
principal occasion of that woeful distraction which we see amongst
Christians at this day, and the very fuel of endless strifes and implacable
contentions.    And forasmuch as these mischiefs have proceeded from
the inconsiderate confounding of those things which in their own nature
are as different as may be, for the clearer distinguishing of matters we
are in the first place to consider that a Sacrament, taken in its full extent,
comprehendeth two things in it,—that which is outward and visible,
which the Schools call properly *Sacramentum*, in a more strict acceptation of the word ; and that which is inward and invisible, which they
term *rem sacramenti*, the principal thing exhibited in the Sacrament.
Thus in the Lord's Supper the outward thing, which we see with our
eyes, is bread and wine ; the inward thing which we apprehend by
faith is the Body and Blood of Christ.    In the outward part of this
mystical action, which reacheth to that which is *sacramentum* only, we
receive this Body and Blood but Sacramentally ; in the inward, that
containeth *rem*, the thing itself in it, we receive them really.    And consequently the presence of these in the one is relative and symbolical, in
the other real and substantial. . . .

We acknowledge Sacraments to be signs ; but bare signs we deny
them to be.    Seals they are, as well as signs, of the Covenant of Grace.
As it was therefore said of John the Baptist that he was *a prophet and
more than a prophet*, so we must say of Sacraments that they be signs and
more than signs—even pledges and assurances of the interest which
we have in the heavenly things that are represented by them.    He that
hath in his chamber the picture of the French King hath but a bare sign,

which possibly may make him think of that King when he looketh on it, but sheweth not that he hath any manner of interest in him. It is otherwise with him that hath the King's Great Seal for the confirmation of the title which he hath unto all the lands and livelihood which he doth enjoy. And as here the wax that is affixed to those Letters Patent, howsoever for substance it be the very same with that which is to be found everywhere, yet, being applied to this use, is of more worth to the patentee than all the wax in the country beside,—so standeth it with the outward elements in the matter of the Sacrament. The Bread and Wine are not changed in substance from being the same with that which is served at ordinary tables. But in respect of the sacred use whereunto they are consecrated, such a change is made that now they differ as much from common bread and wine, as heaven from earth. Neither are they to be accounted barely significative, but truly exhibitive also, of those heavenly things whereto they have relation, as being appointed by God to be a means of conveying the same unto us, and putting us in actual possession thereof. So that in the use of this holy ordinance, as verily as a man with his bodily hand and mouth receiveth the earthly creatures, so verily doth he with his spiritual hand and mouth, if any such he have, receive the Body and Blood of Christ.

And this is that real and substantial presence which we affirmed to be in the inward part of this sacred action. For the better conceiving of which mystery, we are to enquire, first, what the thing is which we do here receive, secondly, how and in what manner we are made partakers of it. Touching the first, the truth which must be held is this: that we do not here receive only the benefits that flow from Christ, but the very Body and Blood of Christ, that is, Christ Himself crucified. For as none can be made partaker of the virtue of the Bread and Wine to his bodily sustenance, unless he first do receive the substance of those creatures, so neither can any participate in the benefits arising from Christ to his spiritual relief, except he first have communion with Christ Himself. We must have the Son before we have life: and therefore eat Him we must, as Himself speaketh; that is, as truly be made partakers of Him as we are of our ordinary food, if we will live by Him. As there is a giving of Him on God's part, for *unto us a Son is given*, so there must be a receiving of Him on our part, for *as many as received Him, to them gave He power to become the Sons of God*. And as we are called by God unto the communion of His Son Jesus Christ Our Lord, so if we do hear His voice and not harden our hearts by unbelief we are indeed made partakers of Christ. This is that great mystery, for so the Apostle termeth it, of our union with Christ, whereby we are made members of His Body, of His Flesh, and of His Bones; and this is that eating of the Flesh of the Son of Man and drinking of His Blood which Our Saviour insisteth so much upon in the Sixth [chapter] of *John*.

Where if any man shall demand (that I may now come into the second point of our enquiry) *How can this man give us His flesh to eat?*, he must beware that he come not preoccupied with such dull conceits as they were possessed withal who moved that question there. He must not think that we cannot truly feed on Christ unless we receive Him within our jaws; for that is as gross an imagination as that of Nicodemus, who could not conceive how a man could be born again, unless he should *enter the second time into his mother's womb*; but must consider that the eating and drinking, which Our Saviour speaketh of, must be answerable to the hungering and thirsting, for the quenching whereof this heavenly banquet is provided. Mark well the words which He useth, toward the beginning of His discourse, concerning this argument. *I am the Bread of life; he that cometh to Me shall never hunger; and he that believeth on Me shall never thirst. But I said unto you, that ye also have seen Me, and believe not.* And compare them with those in the end, *It is the Spirit that quickeneth, the flesh profiteth nothing; the words that I speak unto you, they are spirit and they are life. But there are some of you that believe not.* Now observe, that such as our hungering is, such is our eating. But everyone will confess that the hunger here spoken of is not corporal, but spiritual. Why then should any man dream here of a corporal eating? Again the corporal eating, if a man might have it, would not avail anything to the slaking of this hunger; nay we are expressly told that the flesh thus taken, for so we must understand it, profiteth nothing; a man should never be the better, nor one jot the holier, nor any whit further from the second death, if he had filled his belly with it. But that manner of feeding on this flesh, which Christ Himself commendeth unto us, is of such profit that it preserveth the eater from death and maketh him to live for ever. It is not therefore such an eating that every man who bringeth a bodily mouth with him may attain unto; but it is of a far higher nature, namely a spiritual uniting of us unto Christ, whereby He dwelleth in us and we live by Him.

If any do further enquire how it is possible that any such union should be, seeing the Body of Christ is in Heaven and we are upon earth, I answer that if the manner of this conjunction were carnal and corporal, it would be indeed necessary that the things conjoined should be admitted to be in the same place; but it being altogether spiritual and supernatural, no local presence, no physical nor mathematical continuity or contiguity, is any way requisite thereunto. It is sufficient for the making of a real union in this kind, that Christ and we, though never so far distant in place each from other, be knit together by those spiritual ligatures which are intimated unto us in the words alleged out of the Sixth of *John*; to wit, the quickening Spirit descending downward from the Head, to be in us a fountain of supernatural life; and a lively faith, wrought by the same Spirit, ascending from us upward, to lay fast hold upon Him, *Who, having by Himself purged our sins, sitteth on the right hand of the Majesty on high.*

First, therefore, for the communion of the Spirit, which is the ground and foundation of this spiritual union, let us call to mind what we have read in God's Book,—that Christ, the second Adam, was made *a quickening spirit*, and that He *quickeneth whom He will*; that unto Him *God hath given the Spirit without measure*; and *of His fulness have all we received*; that *He that is joined unto the Lord is One Spirit*; and that *Hereby we know that we dwell in Him and He in us, because He hath given us of His Spirit.* By all which it doth appear that the mystery of our union with Christ consisteth mainly in this, that the self-same Spirit which is in Him, as in the Head, is so derived from Him into every one of His true members that thereby they are animated and quickened to a spiritual life. We read in the First of *Ezekiel* of four living creatures and of four wheels standing by them. *When those went*, saith the text, *these went ; and when those stood, these stood ; and when those were lifted up from the earth, the wheels were lifted up over against them.* He that should behold such a vision as this would easily conclude by that which he saw that some invisible bands there were, by which these wheels and living creatures were joined together, howsoever none did outwardly appear unto the eye ; and the Holy Ghost, to give us satisfaction herein, discovereth the secret, by yielding this for the reason of this strange connexion,—that *the spirit of the living creature was in the wheels.* From whence we may infer that things may be truly conjoined together, though the manner of the conjunction be not corporal ; and that things distant in place may be united together, by having the spirit of the one communicated unto the other.

Nay, if we mark it well, we shall find it to be thus in every of our own bodies, that the formal reason of the union of the members consisteth not in the continuity of the parts (though that also be requisite to the unity of a natural body), but in the animation thereof by one and the same Spirit. If we should suppose a body to be as high as the heavens, then the head thereof should be where Christ our Head is, and the feet where we His members are ; no sooner could that head think of moving one of the toes, but instantly the thing would be done, without any impediment given by that huge distance of the one from the other. And why ? Because the same soul that is in the head, as in the fountain of sense and motion, is present likewise in the lowest member of the body. But if it should so fall out, that this or any other member proved to be mortified, it presently would cease to be a member of that body, the corporal conjunction and continuity with the other parts notwithstanding. And even thus is it in Christ. Although in regard of His corporal presence, the *heaven must receive Him until the times of the restitution of all things*, yet is He here *with us alway, even unto the end of the world*, in respect of the presence of His Spirit; by the vital influence whereof from Him, as from the Head, *the whole body is fitly joined together, and compacted by that which every joint supplieth, according to the effectual working in the measure of every part.* Which quickening Spirit, if it be wanting in any, no external communion with Christ or His Church can make him a true member of this mystical Body,—this being a most sure principle that *he which hath not the Spirit of Christ is none of His.*

Now, among all the graces that are wrought in us by the Spirit of Christ, the soul as it were of all the rest, and that whereby the *just doth live* is *faith.* *For we through the Spirit wait for the hope of righteousness by faith,* saith St. Paul to the Galatians. And again: *I live, yet not I, but Christ liveth in me ; and the life which I now live in the flesh, I live by the faith of the Son of God Who loved me, and gave Himself for me.* By faith it is that we do *receive Christ*; and so likewise *Christ dwelleth in our hearts by faith.* Faith, therefore, is that spiritual mouth in us, whereby we *eat the flesh of the Son of Man and drink His Blood*, that is, as the Apostle expresseth it without the trope, *are made partakers of Christ*, He being by this means as truly and every way as effectually made ours, as the meat and drink which we receive into our natural bodies.

But you will say, If this be all the matter, what do we get by coming to the Sacrament, seeing we have faith and the quickening Spirit of Christ before we come thither? To this I answer: that the Spirit is received in divers measures, and faith bestowed upon us in different degrees; by reason whereof our conjunction with Christ may every day be made straiter, and the hold which we take of Him firmer. To receive the Spirit *not by measure* is the privilege of our Head; we that *receive out of His fulness* have not our portion of grace delivered unto us all at once, but must daily look for the *supply of the Spirit of Jesus Christ.* So also, while we are in this world, *the righteousness of God is revealed unto us from faith to faith*, that is from one degree and measure of it to another; and consequently, we must still labour to perfect that which is lacking in our faith and evermore pray with the Apostles *Lord, increase our faith.* As we have therefore *received Christ Jesus the Lord, so must we walk in Him ; rooted and built up in Him and stablished in the faith ; that we may grow up into Him in all things, Which is the Head.* And to this end God hath ordained public officers in His Church, *for the perfecting of the saints, for the work of the ministry, for the edifying of the Body of Christ ; till we all come in the unity of the faith and of the knowledge of the Son of God, unto a perfect man, unto the measure of the stature of the fulness of Christ ;* and hath accordingly *made them able ministers of the Spirit that quickeneth*, and *ministers by whom we should believe, even as the Lord shall give to every man.* When we have therefore received the Spirit and faith, and so spiritual life, by their ministry, we are not there to rest; but *as new-born babes we must desire the sincere milk of the Word, that we may grow thereby*, and as grown men too, we must desire to be fed at the Lord's Table that by the strength of that spiritual repast we may be enabled to do the Lord's work; and may continually be nourished up thereby in the life of grace, unto the life of glory.

Neither must we here with a fleshly eye look upon the meanness of the outward elements; and have this faithless thought in our hearts, that there is no likelihood a bit of bread and a draught of wine should be able to produce such heavenly effects as these. For so we should prove ourselves to be no wiser than Naaman the Syrian was, who having received direction from the man of God that he should wash in Jordan seven times, to be cleansed of his leprosy, replied with indignation, *Are not Abana and Pharpar, rivers of Damascus, better than all the waters of Israel? May I not wash in them and be clean?* But as his servants did soberly advise him then, *If the prophet had bid thee do some great thing, wouldst thou not have done it? How much rather then, when he saith to thee, Wash and be clean?* so give me leave to say unto you now: If the Lord had commanded us to do some great thing, for the attaining of so high a good, should not we willingly have done it? How much rather then when He biddeth us to eat the Bread and drink the Wine that He hath provided for us at His Own Table; that by His blessing thereupon we may grow in grace and be preserved both in body and soul unto everlasting life?

True it is indeed these outward creatures have no natural power in them to effect so great a work as this is, no more than the water of Jordan had to recover the leper. But the work wrought by these means is supernatural; and God hath been pleased in the dispensation both of the Word and of the Sacraments so to ordain it, that these heavenly treasures should be presented unto us *in earthen vessels, that the excellency of the power might be of God.* As therefore in the preaching of the Gospel, the minister doth not *dare verba*, and beat the air with a fruitless sound, but the words that he speaketh unto us are Spirit and life, *God being pleased by the foolishness of preaching to save them that believe*; so likewise in the Administration of the Lord's Supper, He doth not feed us with bare Bread and Wine, but, if we have the life of faith in us (for still we must remember that this table is provided not for the dead but for the living), and come worthily, *the cup of blessing which He blesseth* will be unto us *the Communion of the Blood of Christ*, and *the Bread which He breaketh the Communion of the Body of Christ*; of which precious Body and Blood we being really made partakers (that is, in truth and indeed, and not in imagination only), although in a spiritual and not a corporal manner, the Lord doth *grant us according to the riches of His glory, to be strengthened with might by His Spirit in the inner man, that we may be filled with all the fulness of God.* For the Sacraments, as well as the Word, be a part of that *ministration of the Spirit*, which is committed to the *ministers of the New Testament*; forasmuch as *by one Spirit* (as before we have heard from the Apostle) *we have been all baptized into one Body, and have been all made to drink into one Spirit.*

# (3) THE EUCHARISTIC SACRIFICE

## No. 212. JEREMY TAYLOR

[From *The Great Exemplar, The History of the Life and Death of the Holy Jesus.*
Part III, Section xv (Discourse xix). *Works*, ed. R. Heber, Vol. III, pp. 296, 297 f.
(ed. C. P. Eden, Vol. II, pp. 642 f., 643 f.). This long treatise first appeared in 1649.
It is made up largely of discourses of a devotional character which have no direct
bearing upon the Life of Christ; its merits are mainly doctrinal and spiritual. It was
dedicated to Lord Hatton. On its publication, the Roman controversialist John
Sergeant (cp. note on Nos. **28, 57**) accused Taylor of plagiarizing from the *Vita Jesu
Christi Redemptoris Nostri* of Ludolphus of Saxony; it seems likely that it was at least
very much influenced by this work.]

As it is a Commemoration and Representation of Christ's death, so
it is a Commemorative Sacrifice. As we receive the symbols and the
mystery, so it is a Sacrament. In both capacities, the benefit is next
to infinite. First, for whatsoever Christ did at the Institution, the
same He commanded the Church to do in remembrance and repeated
rites; and Himself also does the same thing in Heaven for us, making
perpetual intercession for His Church, the Body of His redeemed ones,
by representing to His Father His Death and Sacrifice. There He
sits, a High Priest continually, and offers still the same one perfect
Sacrifice; that is, still represents it as having been once finished and
consummate, in order to perpetual and never failing events. And this
also His ministers do on earth. They offer up the same Sacrifice to
God, the Sacrifice of the Cross by prayers, and a commemorating rite
and representment, according to His holy Institution. . . . Our very
holding up the Son of God and representing Him to His Father is the
doing an act of mediation and advantage to ourselves in the virtue and
efficacy of the Mediator. As Christ is a Priest in Heaven for ever and
yet does not sacrifice Himself afresh nor yet without a Sacrifice could
He be a Priest, but by a daily ministration and intercession represents
His Sacrifice to God and offers Himself as sacrificed, so He does upon
earth by the ministry of His servants. He is offered to God; that is,
He is by prayers and the Sacrament represented or offered up to God
as sacrificed, which in effect is a celebration of His Death, and the
applying it to the present and future necessities of the Church as we
are capable by a ministry like to His in Heaven. It follows, then, that
the celebration of this Sacrifice be in its proportion an instrument of
applying the proper Sacrifice to all the purposes which it first designed.
It is ministerially and by application an instrument propitiatory; it is
eucharistical; it is an homage and an act of adoration; and it is
impetratory and obtains for us and for the whole Church all the benefits
of the Sacrifice, which is now celebrated and applied. That is, as this

rite is the remembrance and ministerial celebration of Christ's Sacrifice, so it is destined to do honour to God, to express the homage and duty of His servants, to acknowledge His supreme dominion, to give Him thanks and worship, to beg pardon, blessings, and supply of all our needs. And its profit is enlarged not only to the persons celebrating, but to all to whom they design it, according to the nature of sacrifices and prayers and all such solemn actions of religion.

### No. 213. JOHN BRAMHALL

[From *An Answer to M. de la Milletière, His Impertinent Dedication of His Imaginary Triumph*, Med. *Works*, ed. *L. A. C. T.*, Vol. I, p. 54. Cp. note on No. 207.]

You say we have renounced your Sacrifice of the Mass. If the Sacrifice of the Mass be the same with the Sacrifice of the Cross, we attribute more unto it than yourselves; we place our whole hope of salvation in it. If you understand another Propitiatory Sacrifice distinct from that (as this of the Mass seems to be; for confessedly the priest is not the same, the altar is not the same, the temple is not the same), if you think of any new meritorious satisfaction to God for the sins of the world, or of any new supplement to the merits of Christ's Passion, you must give us leave to renounce your sacrifice indeed and to adhere to the Apostle *By one offering He hath perfected for ever them that are sanctified.*

### No. 214. JOHN BRAMHALL

[From *A Replication to the Bishop of Chalcedon's Survey of the Vindication of the Church of England from Criminous Schism*, Chapter II, section vii; Chapter IX, section vi. *Works*, ed *L. A. C. T.*, Vol. II, pp. 88, 276. In 1654, the year after his reply to de la Milletière (cp. note on No. 207), Bramhall published at London his *Just Vindication of the Church of England from the Unjust Aspersion of Criminal Schism*. To this Richard Smith, titular Bishop of Chalcedon, replied with *R*[ichard] *C*[halcedon]'s *Brief Survey of the Lord of Derry, His Treatise of Schism* (Paris, 1654 or 1655). Bramhall's *Replication* appeared at London in 1656.]

The Holy Eucharist is a commemoration, a representation, an application of the all-sufficient propitiatory Sacrifice of the Cross. If his Sacrifice of the Mass have any other propitiatory power or virtue in it than to commemorate, represent, and apply the merit of the Sacrifice of the Cross, let him speak plainly what it is. . . .

We acknowledge an Eucharistical Sacrifice of praise and thanksgiving; a commemorative Sacrifice or a memorial of the Sacrifice of the Cross; a representative Sacrifice, or a representation of the Passion of Christ before the eyes of His Heavenly Father; an impetrative Sacrifice, or an impetration of the fruit and benefit of His Passion by way of real prayer; and, lastly, an applicative Sacrifice, or an application of His Merits unto our souls. Let him that dare go one step further than we do; and say that it is a suppletory Sacrifice, to supply the defects of the Sacrifice of the Cross. Or else let them hold their peace and speak no more against us in this point of sacrifice for ever.

## No. 215.  LANCELOT ANDREWES

[From *Two Answers to Cardinal Perron.  Minor Works*, ed. L. A. C. T., pp. 20 f. Cp. note on No. 218.]

If we agree about the matter of Sacrifice, there will be no difference about the Altar.   The Holy Eucharist being considered as a *Sacrifice* (in the representation of the Breaking the Bread and pouring forth the Cup), the same is fitly called an *Altar*;  which again is as fitly called a *Table*, the Eucharist being considered as a *Sacrament*, which is nothing else but a distribution and an application of the Sacrifice to the several receivers.   The same Saint Augustine that in the place alleged doth term it an Altar saith in another place, *Christus quotidie pascit.   Mensa Ipsius est illa in medio constituta.   Quid causae est, o audientes, ut mensam videatis, et ad epulas non accedatis ?*   The same Nyssen in the place cited, with one breath calleth it θυσιαστήριον, that is an *Altar*, and ἱερὰ τράπεζα that is, the *Holy Table*.

Which is agreeable also to the Scriptures ;  for the *Altar*, in the Old Testament, is by Malachi called *Mensa Domini*.   And of the *Table*, in the New Testament, by the Apostle it is said, *Habemus Altare*. Which, of what matter it be,—whether of stone, as Nyssen, or of wood, as Optatus,—it skills not.   So that the matter of Altars makes no difference in the face of our Church.

# (4) COMMUNION IN TWO KINDS

## No. 216. THOMAS JACKSON

[From *The Third Book of Commentaries Upon the Apostles' Creed; Containing the Blasphemous Positions of Jesuits and Other later Romanists concerning the Authority of their Church*, Chapter V, §§ 18 f. *Works*, ed. London (1673), Vol. I, pp. 395 f.; ed. Oxford (1844), Vol. II, pp. 224–226. The publication of Jackson's grandly planned series of *Commentaries on the Apostles' Creed* was spread over a series of years. The present one was first issued in 1614.]

IF the Cup be an essential and substantial part of this Sacrament, the Council [of Trent] by their own confession did foully err in prohibiting Communion under both kinds. If no such part it be, they might by their own rule have altogether denied the use of it so much as to the Sacrificer or Conficient; but so the very use and end, on which the essence of the Sacrament (as of all other matters of moral practice) immediately depends, and by whose expiration instantly must determine, should utterly have perished. The end and use of this sacred Institution, as Our Saviour expressly teacheth and the Council grants, was to represent the Testator's Death, yea so to represent it, as we might be partakers of His Body and Blood, not spiritually only, but withal (as the Trent Fathers contend) Sacramentally. Admitting then all they can pretend against the necessity of the Cup,—*that the whole Christ were in the bread alone*,—yet this will not preserve the true and fruitful use of the Sacrament, nor salve that deadly wound, the essence of it must perforce receive from frustration of the end, necessarily ensuing the Cup's absence. For this Sacrament was ordained, as to represent, so to exhibit, Christ's Body unto all faithful Communicants,—not as entire and whole; His Blood, not as it was inclosed in the veins; but the one as torn and rent, the other as shed and poured out upon the Cross. *This is My Blood of the New Testament* (saith Our Saviour) *which is shed for many* (for all that receive it faithfully) *for the remission of sins*. His Blood then, as shed and poured out, is as the loadstar of penitent and contrite hearts, whereon the eyes of their faith, that seek remission of sins in this Sacrament, must be fastened; for (as the Apostle saith) *without shedding of blood is no remission*. This was the complement of that inestimable all-sufficient Sacrifice, that which represents His precious Blood thus poured out, the principal part of this Sacrament, as well in respect of representing His death, as in applying remission of sins thereby in general purchased, and by this Sacramental Type sealed to every one in particular; especially if the

Trent Council's Doctrine be true, that Christ's very Blood, which was shed upon the Cross, is really present in the Chalice, and might be as immediately sprinkled at least upon the lips or doors of every faithful receiver's heart, as the blood of the Paschal Lamb was upon the door-posts of the Israelites. Thus as Satan [is] the Father of lies, so false opinions suggested by him draw men with pleasure into those evils, for whose practice in the end they become their chief accusers. That opinion which at first brought in neglect of the Chalice, and, as the Trent Council presumed, would have warranted them in making this decree, doth most condemn them; for the measure of their iniquity could not have been so fully accomplished, unless they had held a Transubstantiation of the wine into Christ's Blood.

What part of Scripture can we presume they will spare, that dare thus countermand the most principal of all God's Commandments? What reckoning may we think they make of Our Saviour Christ, that adventure thus shamefully to disannul and cancel His Last Will and Testament, defrauding almost the whole Christian World of half their Lord and Master's Royal allowance; partly without any show of Scriptures, either to restrain or otherwise interpret these Sovereign precepts, partly upon such idle and frivolous allegations, as may further witness their slight estimate of God's Word, save only so far as it may be wrested to serve their turns.

### No. 217. WILLIAM LAUD

[From *A Relation of the Conference between William Laud and Mr. Fisher the Jesuit*, Section XXXV. Ed. C. H. Simpkinson (1901), pp. 356 f. Cp. note on No. 54.]

That Christ instituted [the Sacrament in both kinds] is confessed by both Churches [*i.e.* by the Church of England and the Church of Rome]. That the ancient Churches received it so is agreed by both Churches. Therefore, according to the former rule, and here in truth too, it is safest for a man to receive this Sacrament in both kinds. And yet here this ground of A.C. [*i.e.* " Fisher the Jesuit "] must not stand for good—no, not at Rome; but to receive in one kind is enough for the laity. And the poor Bohemians must have a dispensation that it may be lawful for them to receive the Sacrament as Christ commanded them. And this must not be granted to them neither, " unless they will acknowledge,"—most opposite to truth,—" that they are not bound by Divine law to receive it in both kinds." And here their building *with untempered mortar* appears most manifestly. For they have no show to maintain this but the fiction of Thomas of Aquin, " That he which receives the Body of Christ receives also His Blood *per concomitantiam*," " by concomitancy," because the Blood goes always with the Body; of which term, Thomas was the first author I can yet find. First, then, If this be true, I hope Christ knew it: and then why did He so unusefully institute it in both kinds ? Next, If this be true, " concomitancy " accompanies the priest as well as the people : and then why may not he receive it in one kind also ? Thirdly, This is apparently not true ; for the Eucharist is a Sacrament *sanguinis effusi,* " of Blood shed ", and poured out ; and Blood poured out, and so severed from the Body, goes not along with the Body *per concomitantiam.* And yet Christ must rather err, or proceed I know not how, in the Institution of the Sacrament in both kinds, rather than the " holy unerring Church of Rome " may do amiss in the determination for it, and the administration of it in one kind. Nor will the distinction, " That Christ instituted this as a Sacrifice, to which both kinds were necessary," serve the turn ; for suppose that true, yet He instituted it as a Sacrament also, or else that Sacrament had no institution from Christ ; which I presume A.C. dares not affirm. And that institution which this Sacrament had from Christ was in both kinds.

# (5) RESERVATION OF THE EUCHARIST

## No. 218.  LANCELOT ANDREWES

[From *Two Answers to Cardinal Perron*  *Minor Works*, ed. *L. A. C. T.*, pp. 17–19. The circumstances which led to the composition of this work, first published in 1629 after Andrewes' death, are somewhat complicated.  An account of them will be found in the *L. A. C. T.* edition, pp. 5 f.; in fuller detail, in Dupin's *Ecclesiastical History*, Century XVII, Book v, *s.v.* 'Cardinal Perron.'  Perron having asserted that James I could not claim the title of a " Catholic " prince, Isaac Casaubon wrote a letter to the Cardinal vindicating the King's claim.  Perron's *Replique à la Response du serenissime Roy de la Grande Bretagne* was published at Paris in 1620, two years after the author's death.  Andrewes' reply was only of the nature of a fragment.]

It cannot be denied but reserving the Sacrament was suffered a long time in the Primitive Church.

1. In time of Persecution they were permitted to carry away how great a part they would, and to keep it by them, and to take it at times to comfort them, because they knew not when they should, or whether ever they should, meet at the Sacrament again.

2. And those that lived as Anchorites and Hermits, in remote desert places, were likewise permitted to carry away with them how much they thought good, to take at times; because a long time together they were not to come back to places where any Churches were.

Having it then with them in their own hands and power, they might and did *keep it in their chests, eat it at home, carry it about with them in their journey.*

For, as for *sending it into far countries,* Eusebius hath no word of *far countries*: but that, such as held not their Fasts, or keep not their Easter, as the Church of Rome did, notwithstanding, when they came to Rome, had it sent them by the Deacon, as others there had.

But all this is from the matter.  For it is well known, this is not now the face or fashion of the Church of Rome.  For no man, there, may carry the Sacrament home, and eat it to breakfast, or carry it to sea, or tie it up in his *orarium*.  For, this of *carrying it home*, and there *reserving* it, was long since taken away; and order taken, that every man, what was delivered him, he should receive and take it down in the church.  And it is to be noted that this was done, Saint Augustine living, both by the Council of Saragossa, Can. iii, in the year 381, upon pain of anathema: and by the First Council of Toledo, Can. xiv, in the year 405, upon pain of *being cast out as a sacrilegious person*.  Which was so ordered, because of divers and sundry evil practices, whereto the Priscillianists and other heretics and bad persons were known to abuse it. So that this pertaineth nothing to the face of the Church now, either as it is with them or as it is with us.

But for the *Sick*, it was always sent them home, were the distance never so great. And against the time of extremity it was thought not amiss to have it *reserved*; that, if the priest should not then be in state to go to the sick party, and there to consecrate it for him, yet at least it might be sent him, as in the case of Serapion. For it is sure they made far greater account of the receiving it as their *viaticum* than some do now.

But neither doth this touch us, who at the desire of any that is in that case may not refuse but go to him, and minister it him. So that *Reservation* needeth not; the intent is had without it.

## No. 219. WILLIAM FORBES

[From *Considerationes Modestae et Pacificae*, De Eucharistia, Book II, Chapter ii, § 6. D. Stone, *A History of the Doctrine of the Holy Eucharist*, Vol. II, p. 307. Cp. note on No. 205.]

Take away the abuse of the modern Roman Church in reserving the Host, which has been consecrated once for all, in ciboria for processions and theatrical pomp, as a thing which, not less apart from Communion than in Communion itself or in relation to it, is the real and substantial Body of Christ, and continues such as long as the species endure (on the corruption of which, if so be, the Body and Blood of the Lord cease to be there); and this controversy may be removed without condemning the practice of the Ancient Church as to Reservation which was then usual.

## No. 220. ANTHONY SPARROW

[From *A Rationale or Practical Exposition of the Book of Common Prayer* (" Of the Communion of the Sick "). Ed. Samuel Downes (1722), pp. 223 f. Cp. note on No. 234.]

The Rubric at the Communion of the Sick directs the Priest to deliver the Communion to the sick, but does not there [*i.e.* in the pre-1662 Book of Common Prayer] set down how much of the Communion Service shall be used at the delivering of the Communion to the sick; and therefore seems to me to refer us to former directions in times past. Now the direction formerly was this :—

" If the same day [that the sick is to receive the Communion] there be a Celebration of the Holy Communion in the Church, then shall the Priest reserve, at the open Communion, so much of the Sacrament of the Body and Blood, as shall serve the sick person and so many as shall communicate with him [ ]. And as soon as he may conveniently, after the open Communion ended in the Church, shall go and minister the same, first to them that are appointed to communicate with the sick, if there be any; and last of all to the sick [person himself]. . . .

" But if the day [wherein the sick person is to receive the Communion] be not appointed for the open Communion in the Church then, upon convenient warning given, the curate shall come and visit the sick person aforenoon." And cutting off the Form of the Visitation [of the Sick] at the Psalm, *In Thee, O Lord*, shall go straight to the Communion (Rubr. 3, Communion of the Sick); that is, after he hath said the Collect, Epistle, and Gospel there directed, he shall go to the Communion Service (*King Edward VI's First Liturgy*).

## No. 221. HERBERT THORNDIKE

[From *The Reformation of the Church of England Better than that of the Council of Trent; or a Short Resolution of the Controversies between the Church of England and the Church of Rome*, Chapter xxxix, § 4. *Works*, ed. *L. A. C. T.*, Vol. V, p. 578. Cp. note on No. **318**.]

And thus far I will particularize as concerning the Eucharist, that the Church is to endeavour the celebrating of it so frequently that it may be reserved to the next Communion. For in the meantime it ought to be so ready for them that pass into the other world, that they need not stay for the consecrating of it on purpose for everyone. The reason of the necessity of it for all, which hath been delivered, aggravates it very much in danger of death. And the practice of the Church attests it to the utmost. Neither will there be any necessity of giving it in one kind only; as by some passages of Antiquity may be collected, if common reason could deceive [? decide] in a subject of this nature.

# (6) FREQUENCY OF COMMUNION

## No. 222.   ISAAC BARROW

[From *A Brief Exposition of the Lord's Prayer and Decalogue; to which is added The Doctrine of the Sacraments* (" The Eucharist "). *Works*, ed. Oxford, 1818, Vol. V, pp. 606–608; ed. A. Napier (Cambridge), 1859, Vol. VII, pp. 524–527. This treatise was first issued, posthumously, in 1681.]

THERE is one duty which I should not forbear to touch concerning this Sacrament, that is, our gladly embracing any opportunity presented of communicating therein; the doing so being not only our duty, but a great aid and instrument of piety; the neglecting it a grievous sin, and productive of great mischiefs to us.

The primitive Christians did very frequently use it, partaking therein, as it seems, at every time of their meeting for God's service. It is said of them by St. Luke that *they continued steadfastly in the Apostles' doctrine and communion, and in breaking of bread, and in prayers*, and *When you meet together, it is not* (as according to the intent and duty of meeting it should be) *to eat the Lord's Supper*, saith St. Paul; and Justin Martyr in his *Second Apology*, describing the religious service of God in their assemblies, mentioneth it as a constant part thereof; and Epiphanius reporteth it a custom in the Church, derived from Apostolical institution, to celebrate the Eucharist thrice every week, that is, so often as they did meet to pray and praise God. Which practice may well be conceived a great means of kindling and preserving in them that holy fervour of piety, which they so illustriously expressed in their conversation and in their gladsome suffering for Christ's sake; and the remitting of that frequency, as it is certainly a sign and an effect, so in part it may possibly be reckoned a cause, of the degeneracy of Christian practice into that great coldness and slackness which afterward did seize upon it, and now doth apparently keep it in a languishing and half-dying state.

The rarer occasions therefore we now have of performing this duty (the which indeed was always esteemed the principal office of God's service), of enjoying this benefit,—the being deprived whereof was also deemed the greatest punishment and infelicity that could arrive to a Christian,—the more ready we should be to embrace them. If we dread God's displeasure, if we value Our Lord and His benefits, if we tender the life, health, and welfare of our souls, we shall not neglect it. For how can we but extremely offend God by so extreme rudeness, that when He kindly invites us to His Table, we are averse from coming thither, or utterly refuse it? That when He calleth us into His Presence, we run from Him? That when He, with His own Hand, offereth us inestimable mercies and blessings, we reject them? It is not only the breach of God's command, Who enjoined us to do this, but a direct contempt of His favour and goodness, most clearly and largely exhibited in this office. And how can we bear any regard to Our Lord, or be anywise sensible of His gracious performances in our behalf, if we are unwilling to join in thankful and joyful commemoration of them? How little do we love our own souls, if we suffer them to pine and starve for want of that food which God here dispenseth for their sustenance and comfort, if we bereave them of enjoying so high a privilege, so inestimable a benefit, so incomparable pleasures as are to be found and felt in this service, or do spring and flow from it? What reasonable excuse can we frame for such neglect? Are we otherwise employed? What business can there be more important than serving God and saving our own souls? Is it wisdom, in pursuance of any the greatest affair here, to disregard the principal concern of our souls? Do we think ourselves unfit and unworthy to appear in God's Presence? But is any man unworthy to obey God's commands? Is any man unfit to implore and partake of God's mercy, if he be not unwilling to do it? What unworthiness should hinder us from remembering Our Lord's excessive charity towards us, and thanking Him for it, from praying for His grace, from resolving to amend our lives? Must we, because we are unworthy, continue so still, by shunning the means of correcting and curing us? Must we increase our unworthiness, by transgressing our duty? If we esteem things well, the conscience of our sinfulness should rather drive us to it, as to our medicine, than detain us from it. There is no man indeed who must not conceive and confess himself unworthy; therefore must no man come thither at God's call? If we have a sense of our sins and a mind to leave them; if we have a sense of God's goodness and a heart to thank Him for it, we are so worthy that we shall be kindly received there and graciously rewarded. If we will not take a little care to work these dispositions in us, we are indeed unworthy; but the being so, from our own perverse negligence, is a bad excuse for the neglect of our duty. In fine, I dare say, that he who, with an honest meaning (although with an imperfect devotion) doth address himself to the performance of this duty, is far more excusable than he that upon whatever score declineth it. No scrupulous shyness can ward us from blame. What then shall we say, if supine sloth or profane contempt are the causes of such neglect?

# (7) FASTING COMMUNION

## No. 223.  JEREMY TAYLOR

[From *The Rule and Exercises of Holy Living*, Chapter IV, Section x, § 9.  *Works*, ed. R. Heber, Vol. IV, pp. 270 f. (ed. C. P. Eden, Vol. III, pp. 217 f.).  This very famous devotional manual appeared in 1650; the companion volume on *Holy Dying* followed in 1661.  They passed through 19 editions within little over fifty years from their publication; and probably they are still the most widely known writings of any Anglican Seventeenth Century Divine.]

THESE Holy Mysteries are offered to our senses but not to be placed under our feet.  They are sensible, but not common.  And therefore as the weakness of the elements adds wonder to the excellency of the Sacrament, so let our reverence and venerable usages of them add honour to the elements, and acknowledge the glory of the Mystery and the Divinity of the mercy.  Let us receive the Consecrated Elements with all devotion and humility of body and spirit ; and do this honour to it, that it be the first food we eat, and the first beverage we drink that day, unless it be in case of sickness or other great necessity ; and that your body and soul both be prepared to its reception with abstinence from secular pleasures, that you may better have attended fastings and preparatory prayers.  For if ever it be seasonable to observe the counsel of St. Paul, that married persons by consent should abstain for a time that they may attend to solemn religion, it is now.  It was not by St. Paul nor the after-ages of the Church called a duty so to do ; but it is most reasonable that the more solemn actions of religion should be attended to without the mixture of anything that may discompose the mind, and make it more secular or less religious.

# (8) KNEELING RECEPTION

## No. 224. THOMAS JACKSON

[From *Christ's Answer unto John's Question* [*i.e.*, that in *Matt.* xi, 3]; *or an Introduction to the Knowledge of Jesus Christ and Him Crucified, Delivered in certain Sermons in the Famous Town of Newcastle Upon Tyne*, §§ 92, 94. *Works*, ed. London (1673), Vol. II, pp. 559 f., 561; ed. Oxford (1844), Vol. VI, pp. 488–490, 492. This treatise first appeared in 1625.]

IN all cases of this nature [*i.e.* such as the question of kneeling at Communion], that is, in all cases wherein the thing itself or action is expressly commanded to be done and the manner or circumstances of doing it not so expressly commanded, the authority of superiors must rule our affections or opinions for the manner or circumstance of doing what is commanded. Whosoever in this case heareth not his lawful pastor or governor, heareth not Christ. Whosoever in this case despiseth the Canons and Constitutions of the Church wherein he liveth, despiseth Christ. Whosoever in this case wilfully offendeth against the Canons of the Church, is offended in Christ, and puts a stumbling-block in his own way; yea, he bars himself out of the Kingdom of Grace, expressly promised here in my text [*Matt.* xi, 4–6] to all that are not offended in Christ and in more special sort really exhibited to all that worthily receive this Blessed Sacrament of His Body and Blood. But haply it will be farther replied that, albeit Our Saviour did not expressly forbid us to receive the Sacrament kneeling, yet He hath taught us by His example to receive it after another manner and gesture; and it is more convenient to follow His example than the ordinance of the Church. To this I answer that Our Saviour did not at all receive the Sacrament, because He had no sins to be remitted by it. His Apostles had, and did receive it; but whether standing, sitting, or kneeling, it is not expressed. All that can be gathered out of the Evangelist is this, that as they were eating Our Saviour *took Bread and blessed it and brake it, and gave it to His disciples; so He did the Cup likewise.* But whether they received the Bread or the Cup still sitting after the same manner as they did at their meat is not expressed, nor can hence be gathered. For so a man may truly say that whilst we are at Service and Prayers, we receive the Communion, yet it will not follow that because all or most of us sit in time of Service, we therefore sit at the receiving of the Communion. But be it granted that the Apostles ate the Bread and drank the Wine after the selfsame manner that they ate the Passover, yet it would be very hard to express the particular manner of their eating the Passover. I am persuaded that there is never a joiner in this Kingdom that could make us seats and tables of the same fashion that the tables and seats were of at which Our Saviour and His Apostles did eat the Passover ; or in case we had such seats or tables made to our hands, for aught I can imagine we must have some famous Antiquary or Master of Ceremonies to instruct us how to sit or lie, or to dispose of our bodies at them. . . .

If a man should ask whether the rite or custom observed in the Greek Church or in our Church be in itself the more decent or significant, or better befitting the use or end of this Sacrament, I dare confidently affirm that the ceremony or gesture observed and commanded by our Church doth much better befit the use and end of the Sacrament than the rite or ceremony observed by the Greek Church doth ; better than any other rite or manner can do, though otherwise as decent and fitting, or more decent and fitting, in all other parts of God's service. And my reason which I commend unto your impartial consideration is this, that this Sacrament was not instituted in remembrance of the first institution of it or to represent the Apostles' manner of receiving of it, but in remembrance of Our Saviour's Death and Passion. Whence I would request such as urge Our Saviour's example for a pattern of their behaviour or deportment at the Sacrament to look upon Our Saviour's bodily gesture or deportment in the heat and extremity of His Passion, wherein He presented Himself before His Father, in His Agony and Bloody Sweat in the garden. Being in His Agony, as St. Luke saith, He presented these supplications unto His Father : *Father, if Thou be willing, remove this cup from Me ; nevertheless, not My Will but Thy Will be done.* But after what manner or gesture of body did His perplexed soul utter these earnest supplications ?—θεὶς τὰ γόνατα, *kneeling or fixing His knees upon the ground.*

# (9) THE EPICLESIS

## No. 225.  THE 1637 CONSECRATION PRAYER

[The Consecration Prayer at the Eucharist in *The Book of Common Prayer and Administration of the Sacraments, and other Parts of Divine Service for the Use of the Church of Scotland*, Edinburgh, 1637.  This was reprinted at London in 1844 by William Pickering.  As is well known, Laud was mainly instrumental in the compilation of this Prayer Book, though at an earlier stage he had strongly advocated the introduction of the English Book into Scotland.  See F. Procter and W. H. Frere, *A New History of the Book of Common Prayer*, pp. 143–151.]

ALMIGHTY God, Our heavenly Father, Which of Thy tender mercy didst give Thine only Son Jesus Christ to suffer death upon the Cross for our redemption ; Who made there (by His one oblation of Himself once offered) a full, perfect, and sufficient sacrifice, oblation, and satisfaction for the sins of the whole world, and did institute, and in His Holy Gospel command us to continue, a perpetual memory of that His precious death and sacrifice, until His coming again.  Hear us, O merciful Father, we most humbly beseech Thee, and of Thy Almighty goodness vouchsafe so to bless and sanctify with Thy Word and Holy Spirit these Thy gifts and creatures of Bread and Wine, that they may be unto us the Body and Blood of Thy most dearly beloved Son ; so that we, receiving them according to Thy Son Our Saviour Jesus Christ's holy institution, in remembrance of His Death and Passion, may be partakers of the same His most precious Body and Blood.  Who, in the night that He was betrayed, *took bread*, and when He has given thanks, He brake it, and gave it to His disciples, saying, *Take eat, this is My body, which is given for you ; do this in remembrance of Me.*  Likewise, after supper, He *took the cup*, and when He had given thanks, He gave it to them, saying, *Drink ye all of this, for this is My Blood of the New Testament, which is shed for you and for many, for the remission of sins ; do this, as oft as ye shall drink it, in remembrance of Me.*

## No. 226.  WILLIAM LAUD

[From *The History of the Troubles and Trial of . . . Laud*, Chapter III (Reply to Art. III, § 3).  *Works*, ed L. A. C. T., Vol. III, pp. 353–355.  Cp. note on No. 80.]

They [*i.e.* the Scottish Commissioners] say, " The Corporal Presence of Christ's Body in the Sacrament is to be found in this Service Book." But they must pardon me.  I know it is not there.  I cannot be myself of a contrary judgement, and yet suffer that to pass.  But let's see their proof.  " The words of the Mass Book serving to that purpose, which are sharply censured by Bucer in King Edward's Liturgy, and are not to be found in the Book of England, yet are taken into this Service

Book." I know no words tending to this purpose in King Edward's Liturgy, fit for Bucer to censure sharply, and therefore not tending to that purpose; for did they tend to that, they could not be censured too sharply. The words, it seems, are these: " O merciful Father, of Thy almighty goodness, vouchsafe so to bless and sanctify with Thy Word and Holy Spirit these Thy gifts and creatures of bread and wine that they may be unto us the Body and Blood of Thy most dearly beloved Son." Well, if these be the words, how will they squeeze Corporal Presence out of them? Why, first, " The change here is made a work of God's Omnipotency." Well, and a work of omnipotency it is, whatever the change be. For less than Omnipotence cannot change those elements, either in nature or use, to so high a service as they are put in that great Sacrament. And therefore the invocating of God's Almighty Goodness to effect this by them is no proof at all of intending the " Corporal Presence of Christ in this Sacrament." It is true this passage is not in the Prayer of Consecration in the Service Book of England; but I wish with all my heart it were. For though the consecration of the elements may be without it, yet it is much more solemn and full by that invocation.

Secondly, " these words," they say, " intend the Corporal Presence of Christ in the Sacrament because the words in the Mass are *ut fiant nobis*," " that they may be unto us the Body and the Blood of Christ." Now for the good of Christendom I would with all my heart that these words *ut fiant nobis*,—that these elements might be " to us," worthy receivers, the blessed Body and Blood of Our Saviour,—were the worst error in the Mass. For then I would hope that this great controversy, which to all men that are out of the Church is the shame, and among all that are within the Church is the division of Christendom, might have some good accommodation. For if it be only *ut fiant nobis*, that they may be to us, the Body and the Blood of Christ, it implies clearly that they " are to us "; but are not transubstantiated in themselves into the Body and Blood of Christ, nor that there is any Corporal Presence in or under the elements. And then nothing can more cross the doctrine of the present Church of Rome than their own Service. For as the elements after the benediction or consecration are, and may be called, the Body and Blood of Christ without any addition in that real and true sense in which they are so called in Scripture; so, when they are said to become the Body and Blood of Christ *nobis*, to us that communicate as we ought, there is by this addition, *fiant nobis*, an allay in the proper signification of the Body and Blood; and the true sense, so well signified and expressed that the words cannot well be understood otherwise than to imply not the corporal substance but the real and yet the spiritual use of them. And so the words *ut fiant nobis* import quite contrary to that which they are brought to prove.

# XIV. OTHER RELIGIOUS PRACTICES

# (1) AURICULAR CONFESSION

## No. 227. "THE WHOLE DUTY OF MAN"

[From *The Whole Duty of Man*, Sunday III, §§ 21–23. Edit. London, 1684, pp. 87–90. Cp. note on No. 197.]

I SHALL add but one thing more concerning the things which are to be done before the Sacrament [*i.e.* Holy Communion], and that is an advice, that if any person upon a serious view of himself cannot satisfy his own soul of his sincerity, and so doubts whether he may come to the Sacrament, he do not rest wholly on his own judgement in the case. For if he be a truly humbled soul, it is likely he may judge too hardly of himself; if he be not, it is odds, but if he be left to the satisfying his own doubts, he will quickly bring himself to pass too favourable a sentence. Or whether he be the one or the other, if he come to the Sacrament in that doubt, he certainly plunges himself into further doubts and scruples, if not into sin; on the other side if he forbear because of it, if that fear be a causeless one, then he groundlessly absents himself from that holy ordinance, and so deprives his soul of the benefits of it. Therefore in the midst of so many dangers which attend the mistake of himself, I would, as I said before, exhort him not to trust to his own judgement, but to make known his case to some discreet and godly Minister, and rather be guided by his, who will probably (if the case be duly and without any disguise discovered to him) be better able to judge of him than he of himself. This is the counsel the Church gives in the Exhortation before the Communion, where it is advised that if any by other means there fore-mentioned " cannot quiet his own conscience, but require further counsel and comfort, then let him go to some discreet and learned Minister of God's Word and open his grief, that he may receive such ghostly counsel, advice, and comfort that his conscience may be relieved, etc."

This is surely such advice as should not be neglected, neither at the time of coming to the Sacrament nor any other when we are under any fear or reasons of doubt concerning the state of our souls. And for want of this many have run into very great mischief, having let the doubt fester so long, that it hath either plunged them into deep distresses of conscience, or which is worse they have, to still that disquiet within them, betaken themselves to all sinful pleasures, and so quite cast off all care of their souls.

But to all this it will perhaps be said, that this cannot be done without discovering the nakedness and blemishes of the soul, and there is shame in that, and therefore men are unwilling to do it. But, to that I answer, that it is very unreasonable that should be a hindrance. For first, I suppose you are to choose only such a person as will faithfully keep any secret you shall commit to him, and so it can be no public shame you can fear. And if it be in respect of that single person, you need not fear that neither; for supposing him a godly man, he will not think the worse of you, but the better, that you are so desirous to set all right between God and your soul. But if indeed there were shame in it, yet as long as it may be a means to cure both your trouble and your sin too (as certainly godly and faithful counsel may tend much to both) that shame ought to be despised; and it is sure it would, if we loved our souls as well as our bodies. For in bodily diseases, be they never so foul or shameful, we count him a fool who would rather miss the cure than discover it; and then it must here be so much a greater folly, by how much the soul is more precious than the body.

But God knows it is not only doubtful persons to whom this advice might be useful. There are others of another sort, whose confidence is their disease, who presume very groundlessly of the goodness of their estates: and for those it were most happy if they could be brought to hear some more equal judgements than their own in this so weighty a business. The truth is, we are generally so apt to favour ourselves, that it might be very useful for the most, especially the most ignorant sort, sometimes to advise with a spiritual Guide, to enable them to pass right judgements on themselves; and not only so, but to receive directions how to subdue and mortify those sins they are most inclined to, which is a matter of so much difficulty, that we have no reason to despise any means that may help us in it.

### No. 228.  FRANCIS WHITE

[From *A Reply to Jesuit Fisher's Answer to Certain Questions Propounded by His Most Gracious Majesty, King James*. London, 1624, pp. 187–189. In 1622 Francis White was employed by James I to dispute against " John Fisher " (whose real name was apparently " Percy "), in order to hinder the Roman Catholic tendencies of the Countess of Buckingham. White took part in two ' conferences '; they were followed by a third and more famous ' conference,' in which Laud was the Anglican protagonist. (Cp. note on No. **54.**) An independent dispute between White and Fisher took place in the following year, and an account of this was published under the title *The Fisher Catched in His Own Net* (1623). The *Reply* was a much fuller answer to Fisher, which, with a supplement, extended to nearly 700 folio pages.]

The difference then between Papals and us in this question is not about the thing itself, considered without abuses, but concerning the manner and also the obligation and necessity thereof.

First, they require of all persons, being of age, a private and distinct Confession of all and every known mortal sin, open and secret, of outward deed and inward consent, together with the circumstances thereof, though obscene and odious to Christian ears, to be made at the least annually to some Roman priest authorized. And they affirm the same to be simply necessary, either in act or in desire, by Divine precept for the obtaining remission of sins committed after Baptism. And they teach that this Confession, and Absolution upon it, is one of the proper Sacraments of the New Testament, having an operative virtue to confer grace and to change attrition, or imperfect sorrow for sins past, into contrition.

Secondly, our tenet is, that auricular Confession is not absolutely necessary to remission of sins after Baptism, neither is the same generally in respect of all persons commanded or imposed by Divine law, and the rigorous urging thereof according to the Popish Doctrine is not Orthodoxal or Catholic Faith. Neither is Penance a Sacrament of the New Testament like unto Baptism and the Holy Eucharist.

The true ends of private Confession are these which follow : First, to inform, instruct, and counsel Christian people in their particular actions. Secondly, if they be delinquents, to reprove them and make them understand the danger of their sin. Thirdly, to comfort those that are afflicted, and truly penitent, and to assure them of remission of sins by the word of Absolution. Fourthly, to prepare people to the worthy receiving of the Holy Communion. And if private Confession be referred and used to these ends it is a work of godly discipline, consonant to the Holy Scripture and anciently practised by the Primitive Church. Bishops and Ministers of the Church are Shepherds, Stewards, and Overseers of God's people committed to their charge (*I Pet.* v, 1, 2 ; *Acts* xx, 28). They have received the keys of the Kingdom of Heaven and power to loose and bind sinners (*Matt.* xvi, 19 ; *Matt.* xviii, 18 ; *Joh.* xx, 23). They have power to direct and govern their whole flock and every sheep and member of the same in things concerning their salvation. The people are subject to them in such offices and actions as concern their spiritual state (*Heb.* xiii, 17 ; *I Thess.* v, 12). And if Christian people must confess and acknowledge their faults one to another (*James* v, 16), then also when there is cause why should they not do the same to the Pastors of their souls ?

But the precise and strict law of Confession, imposed upon all Christians as a necessary means of remission of sins, is neither commanded in the New Testament nor hath warrant from the Primitive Church.

## No. 229. JOHN COSIN

[From the Notes appended to Nicholls' *Commentary on the Book of Common Prayer.* Cosin's *Works*, ed. L. A. C. T., Vol. V, pp. 163 f. Cp. note on No. **287**.]

The Church of England, howsoever it holdeth not Confession and Absolution Sacramental that is made unto and received from a Priest to be so absolutely necessary, as without it there can be no remission of sins, yet by this place[1] it is manifest what she teacheth concerning the virtue and force of this sacred action. The Confession is commanded to be special. The Absolution is the same that the ancient Church and the present Church of Rome useth. What would they more? Maldonate, their greatest divine that I meet with, *de Paenit.*, p. 19, saith thus *Ego autem sic respondendum puto, non esse necesse, ut semper peccata remittantur per sacramentum paenitentiae, sed ut ipsum sacramentum natura sua possit peccata remittere, si inveniat peccata, et non inveniat contrarium impedimentum.* And so much we acknowledge. Our " if he feel his conscience troubled " is no more than his *si inveniat peccata* ; for if he be not troubled with sin, what needs either Confession or Absolution ? Venial sins that separate not from the grace of God need not so much to trouble a man's conscience ; if he hath committed any mortal sin, then we require Confession of it to a Priest, who may give him, upon his true contrition and repentance, the benefit of Absolution, which takes effect according to his disposition that is absolved. And therefore the Church of Rome adds to the Form of Absolution, *Quantum in me est, et de jure possum, ego te absolvo* ; not absolutely, lest the doctrine should get head, that some of their ignorant people believe, that be the party confessed never so void of contrition the very act of Absolution forgives him his sins. The truth is, that in the Priest's Absolution there is the true power and virtue of forgiveness, which will most certainly take effect, *Nisi ponitur obex*, as in Baptism.

## No. 230.  THE IRISH CANONS OF 1634

[From *Constitutions and Canons Ecclesiastical treated Upon by the Archbishops and Bishops and the Rest of the Clergy of Ireland . . . in their Synod begun and holden at Dublin, Anno Domini MDCXXXIV*.  These Canons were reprinted in David Wilkins, *Concilia Magnae Britanniae et Hiberniae*, Vol. IV, pp. 496–516 ; Canon XIX is on p. 501.  They were based on the English Canons of 1603 ; but in order to shew her independence, the Church of Ireland remodelled those current in England and reduced the number of them from 141 to 100.  The task of revising them was entrusted to John Bramhall, who was at the time Bishop of Derry.]

XIX.  *Warning to be given beforehand for the Communion.*  Whereas every lay person is bound to receive the Holy Communion thrice every year, and many notwithstanding do not receive that Sacrament once in a year, we do require every minister to give warning to his parishioners publicly in the Church at Morning Prayer the Sunday before every time of his administering the Holy Sacrament, for the better preparation of themselves.  Which said warning we enjoin the said parishioners to accept and obey, under the penalty of danger of the law.  And the minister of every parish, and in Cathedral and Collegiate Churches some public minister of the Church, shall the afternoon before the said administration give warning by the tolling of the bell or otherwise, to the intent that if any have any scruple of conscience, or desire the

---

[1] [*i.e.* in the Rubric urging Confession in the Office for the Visitation of the Sick.]

special ministry of reconciliation, he may afford it to those that need it. And to this end the people are often to be exhorted to enter into a special examination of the state of their own souls ; and that finding themselves either extreme dull or much troubled in mind, they do resort unto God's ministers to receive from them as well advice and counsel for the quickening of their dead hearts and the subduing of those corruptions whereunto they have been subject, as the benefit of Absolution likewise for the quieting of their consciences, by the power of the keys which Christ hath committed to His ministers for that purpose.

## No. 231. JOSEPH HALL

[From *The Old Religion. A Treatise Wherein is laid down the true State of the Difference betwixt the Reformed and Roman Church, and the Blame of this Schism is cast upon the True Authors, Serving for the Vindication of our Innocence, for the Settling of Wavering Minds, for a Preservative against Popish Insinuations*, Chapter XIII (" Of Full and Forced Sacramental Confession "), §§ 2–4. *Works*, ed. Peter Hall (1837), Vol. IX, pp. 361–363. The treatise was published in 1628, immediately after Hall had been made Bishop of Exeter (Dec. 23, 1627). As the title indicates, Hall (in spite of his Puritan sympathies) was among those who believed that the Church of Rome was a part, though a corrupt part, of the Church. The treatise was reprinted in Edmund Gibson's *Preservative Against Popery*.]

### Full and Forced Sacramental Confession not warranted by Scripture.

Since our quarrel is not with the Confession itself, which may be of singular use and behoof, but with some tyrannous strains in the practice of it, which are the violent forcing and perfect fulness thereof, it shall be sufficient for us herein to stand upon our negative, That there is no Scripture, in the whole Book of God, wherein either such necessity or such entireness of confession is commanded,—a truth so clear that it is generally confessed by their own Canonists.

Did we question the lawfulness of Confession, we should be justly accountable for our grounds from the Scriptures of God. Now that we cry down only some injurious circumstances therein, well may we require from the fautors thereof their warrants from God ; which, if they cannot shew, they are sufficiently convinced of a presumptuous obtrusion.

Indeed, Our Saviour said to His Apostles and their successors *Whose sins ye remit, they are remitted ; and whose sins ye retain, they are retained* (*John* xx, 23) ; but did He say, " No sin but what *ye* remit ? " or " No sin shall be remitted by you, but what is particularly numbered unto you " ?

St. James bids, *Confess your sins one to another* (*James* v, 16) ; but would they have the Priest ? This act must be mutual, not single.

Many believing Ephesians *came, and confessed, and shewed their deeds* (*Acts* xix, 18) ; many, but not all, not *omnes utriusque sexus*. They confessed their deeds ; some, that were notorious, not all their sins.

38

Contrarily, rather, so did Christ send His Apostles as the Father sent Him (*John* xx, 21). He was both their warrant and their pattern. But that gracious Saviour of ours many a time gave absolution where was no particular confession of sins. Only the sight of the paralytic's faith fetched from Him, *Son, be of good cheer, thy sins be forgiven thee* (*Matt.* ix, 2). The noted sinner in Simon's house, approving the truth of her repentance by the humble and costly testimonies of her love, without any enumeration of her sins heard, *Thy sins are forgiven thee.*

### Full and Forced Sacramental Confession against Reason.

In true Divine Reason, this supposed duty is needless, dangerous, impossible.

Needless; in respect of all sins, not in respect of some. For, however, in the cases of a burthened conscience, nothing can be more useful, more sovereign; yet, in all, our peace doth not depend upon our lips. *Being justified by faith, we have peace with God, through Jesus Christ our Lord* (*Rom.* v, 1).

Dangerous; in respect both of exprobation, as St. Chrysostom worthily; and of infection, for *Delectabile carnis etc.* as a Casuist confesseth, " Fleshly pleasures, the more they are called into particular mention, the more they move the appetite." I do willingly conceal from chaste eyes and ears what effects have followed this pretended act of devotion in wanton and unstaid Confessors.

Impossible; for, who can tell how oft he offendeth ? He is poor in sin, that can count his stock; and he sins always, that so presumes upon his innocence, as to think he can number his sins; and if he say of any sin, as Lot of Zoar, Is it not a little one ? as if, therefore, it may safely escape the reckoning. It is a true word of Isaac the Syrian, *Qui delicta etc.*, " He that thinks any of his offences small, even in so thinking falls into greater."

This doctrine and practice, therefore, both as new and erroneous, full of usurpation, danger, impossibility, is justly rejected by us; and we, for so doing, unjustly ejected.

### The Novelty of Absolution before Satisfaction.

Lest anything in the Roman Church should retain the old form, how absurd is that innovation which they have made in the order of their Penance and Absolution.

The ancient course, as Cassander and Lindanus truly witness, was that absolution and reconciliation and right to the communion of the Church was not given by imposition of hands unto the penitent, till he had given due satisfaction, by performing of such penal acts, as were enjoined by the discreet Penitentiary. " Yea, those works of penance," saith he, " when they were done out of faith, and a heart truly sorrowful, and by the motion of the Holy Spirit preventing the mind of man with the help of His Divine Grace, were thought not a little available to obtain remission of sin, and to pacify the displeasure of God for sin. Not that they could merit it, by any dignity of theirs ; but, that thereby the mind of man is in a sort fitted to the receipt of God's grace. But, now, immediately upon the Confession made, the hand is laid upon the penitent and he is received to his right of Communion, and after his Absolution certain works of piety are enjoined him, for the chastisement of the flesh and expurgation of the remainders of sin." Thus Cassander.

In common apprehension, this new order can be no other than preposterous ; and, as our learned Bishop of Carlisle, like Easter before Lent. But, for this, *ipsi viderint* ; it shall not trouble us, how they nurture their own child.

## No. 232. HAMON L'ESTRANGE

[From *The Alliance of Divine Offices, exhibiting all the Liturgies of the Church of England since the Reformation ; as also the late Scotch Service-Book, with all their respective Variations; and upon them all Annotations, Vindicating the Book of Common Prayer from the main objections of its Adversaries, explicating many parcels thereof hitherto not clearly understood, shewing the Conformity it beareth with the Primitive Practice, and giving a fair Prospect into the Usages of the Ancient Church*, Annotation S upon Chapter X. Ed. *L. A. C. T.*, pp. 448 f. This treatise, the scope of which is fully indicated in its programmatic title, appeared in 1659, *i.e.*, shortly before the revision of the Prayer Book at the Restoration. A second edition appeared in 1690.]

The Church [of England] approveth of, though she doth not command, Auricular Confession. Many times poor souls lie labouring under the pangs of a horrid reflex upon the number or greatness of their sins and the dreadful wrath of God deservedly expected for them. In this case, no remedy [? is] comparable to an humble and sincere confession at large, common to all, and sometimes restrained to some one particular predominant sin, of whose pressure he finds the greatest weight. Upon which Confession, mixed with a vehement and earnest plying the Throne of God for mercy, it becomes the Minister instantly to interpose, to lay before him the inexhaustible treasure of God's infinite mercies, to assure him of his interest therein, and, upon the hypothesis of his contrition to be serious and unfeigned, to give him Absolution. Not that at the moment of such Absolution, and not before, the sinner's pardon is sealed in Heaven, which is done at the very first minute of his repentance, if to the great Critic of Hearts, as He calls Himself, the all-seeing God, it appeareth cordial ; but that that pardon be evidenced to him, and manifested by unspeakable comforts usually flowing into a disconsolate soul upon the pronouncing of such Absolution, God thereby countenancing and giving reputation both to His Word and Ministry. But there being two Absolutions mentioned in the former offices, one at Morning Prayer, and the other in the Communion Service, it may be demanded why only this is in the first person, " I absolve thee " ?  The answer is, there are three opinions concerning Absolution.  The first, entertained by a few, conceive it optative, precarious, or by petition only, as praying for the pardon of the sins of the penitent.  The second think it declaratory only, that is, pronouncing the penitent absolved, by applying God's promises to the signs of his contrition.  Lastly, some contend that it is authoritative, as deriving power and commission from God, not to declare the party absolved, but for the priest to do it in words denoting the first person. All these three opinions our Church seemeth in part to favour.  The first under these words, " Almighty God have mercy upon you, pardon and deliver you," etc. (Absolution for the Communion).  The second under these words, " Hath given charge and command to His Ministers, to declare and pronounce to His people, being penitent, the absolution and remission of their sins."  The last by these words, " I absolve thee."  Which authoritative Absolution is rather proper here, because where the priest absolves in his own person, his Absolution is not fitly applicable to any but such as have given him evident tokens of hearty sorrow for their sins, such as Divine chastisement usually causeth. Extendible it is not to whole congregations (as in the former instances) where the confession is too general to be conceived in all real ; and a confession at large can at most pretend but to an Absolution at large, effectual only to such as truly and sincerely repent.

## No. 233.  JEREMY TAYLOR

[From *A Dissuasive from Popery, Part I.*  Chapter ii, § 4 (" The Roman Doctors differ as to the Efficiency of Indulgences ").  *Works,* ed. R. Heber, Vol. X, p. 206 (ed. C. P. Eden, Vol. VI, p. 241).  Cp. note on No. 260.]

" Confession " might be made of excellent use and is so among the pious children of the Church of England ; but by the doctrines and practices in the Church of Rome it is made, not the remedy of sins by proper energy, but the excuse, the alleviation, the confidence, the ritual, external, and Sacramental remedy, and serves instead of the labours of a holy and a regular life ; and yet is so entangled with innumerable and inextricable cases of conscience, orders, human prescripts, and great and little artifices, that scruples are more increased than sins are lessened.

# (2) THE VISITATION AND UNCTION OF THE SICK

## No. 234. ANTHONY SPARROW

[From *A Rationale or Practical Exposition of the Book of Common Prayer* (" Of the Communion of the Sick "), Ed. Samual Downes (1722), pp. 221 f. This treatise appeared in 1657, and thus was based on the pre-Restoration form of the Book of Common Prayer. The views expressed in it are of great weight in view of the fact that Sparrow was to become one of the leading advocates of the Episcopal attitude at the Savoy Conference. The *Rationale* was reprinted by J. H. N[ewman] in 1839.]

WE have seen the Church's care to provide all necessaries for [the] sick person's salvation. It were an happy thing to see in the people an answerable diligence in the use of these ghostly offices; that they would, when they are sick, send for the priest; not verbally only to comfort them by rehearsing to them comfortable texts of Scripture, whether they belong to them or not (which is not to heal the sick, but to tell them that they have no need of the spiritual physician, by which means precious souls perish, for whom Christ died); but to search and examine the state of their souls, to shew them their sins, to prepare them by ghostly counsel and exercises of penance, for Absolution and the Holy Communion; whereby they might indeed find comfort, remission of sins, and the Holy Ghost the Comforter. . . . There is an excellent Canon to this purpose, *Decretal.*, lib. 5, tit. 38, c. 13. " By this present Decree we strictly charge and command all physicians, that when they shall be called to sick persons, they first of all admonish and persuade them to send for the physicians of souls, that after provision hath been made for the spiritual health of the soul, they may the more hopefully proceed to the use of corporal medicine. For when the cause is taken away, the effect may follow." That which chiefly occasioned the making of this good law was the supine carelessness of some sick persons, who never used to call for the physician of the soul till the physician of the body had given them over. And if the physician did, as his duty was, timely admonish them to provide for their soul's health, they took it for a sentence of death and despaired of remedy, which hastened their end and hindered both the bodily physician from working any cure upon their body and the ghostly physician from applying any effectual means to their soul's health. It is good counsel that *Ecclesiasticus* gives (xxxviii, 9), where we are advised not first to send for the physician and when we despair of his help and are breathing our last then to send for the priest, when our weakness hath made him useless; but first to

521

make our peace with God by ghostly offices of the priest, and then give place to the physician. Which method Our Saviour hath taught us also by His method of cure; Who, when any came to Him for bodily cures, first cured the soul of sin before He healed the bodily infirmity, teaching us that sin is the cause of sickness and that cure first to be looked after. And by thus doing we may possibly save the body without the physician, *James* v, 14. *Is any sick, let him send for the elders or priests of the Church to pray over him ; and the prayer of faith shall save the sick.* But if he fails of that bodily cure by these means, yet he may be sure to obtain remission of sins by their means. *If he hath committed sins, they shall be forgiven him,* v. 15, by the benefit of Absolution ; so the words import. For ἁμαρτίαι, *sins,* being a feminine plural, seems not to agree with the verb ἀφεθήσεται, *it shall be forgiven,* of the singular number, and therefore this word more properly seems to be rendered impersonally thus, *If he hath committed sins, pardon or absolution shall be given him.* And so by this means the sick person shall be sure, if not to save his body, yet at least to save his soul.

### No. 235. JOHN GILBERT

[From *An Answer to the Bishop of Condom* (*Now of Meaux*) [*i.e.* J. B. Bossuet] *His Exposition of the Catholic Faith,* etc., *Wherein the Doctrine of the Church of Rome is Detected, and that of the Church of England Expressed, from the Public Acts of both Churches.* Section ix (" Of the Sacraments, Extreme Unction "). London, 1686, pp. 63 f. On Bossuet's *Exposition,* cp. note on No. 258.]

Extreme Unction being pretended to derive its institution from St. James, if we consider his words we shall better apprehend whether the Church of England be in the right in excluding it from the Sacraments, *James* v, 14. *Is any sick among you ? Let him call for the elders of the Church and let them pray over him, and anoint him with oil in the Name of the Lord ; and the prayer of faith shall save the sick, and the Lord shall raise him up ; and if he have committed sins they shall be forgiven him.* Here the Apostle directs the sick to call for the elders of the Church, whom we allow to be the Ministers ; and this questionless for their assistance to those effects which the Apostle orders them to assist them in. The means to which he directs are two, to pray over them, and anoint them with oil in the name of the Lord ; and this in order to two ends, the recovery of the sick and the remission of sins. Now to both these effects I suppose the Church of England does allow the help of the elders of the Church, useful to the sick ; and therefore has provided that none lack this assistance. But inasmuch as the promises relating to these effects are different, the promise to one effect being perpetual and common to the Church in all ages, to the other temporary whilst God empowered it to work such effects, the Church, which thinks she can only ground her faith upon God's promises, does still retain and declare her power in the cure of sin, having a continued promise of God's grace to go along with its ministry in effecting of it. But not being assured nor having any promise to assure it that its ministry shall be effectual to the recovery of bodily health, it dares not warrant it to her children, and therefore does not think fit to use the ceremony of anointing the sick with oil, which was then used as a sign effective of their recovery. Not that she is not ready to pray for this on their behalf, grounding herself upon the general promise God has made to hear the prayers of His Church. But not having any sure word of promise to ground a firm faith upon, as to the absolute recovery of the sick, and it being the prayer of faith, to which the Apostle here attributes this recovery (as faith indeed, and that special and extraordinary, was always necessary to all miraculous effects), she therefore thinks she cannot use that sign which was then applied to the sick, to assure him of his recovery by that power which God was then pleased to give for the working such cures.

That this reason is not inconsiderable, the Church of Rome herself is forced to allow, and thereupon is greatly perplexed to find out a reason why the first of these effects, the forgiveness of sins, being provided for by the Sacrament of Penance, there should be another Sacrament provided for this purpose. To solve which she has invented a distinction (not to be found in the Apostle's words, I am sure) that the grace of this Sacrament is to extinguish our venial sins, the other being chiefly provided for the forgiveness of deadly sins. No less is she perplexed as to the other. For seeing *de facto* that the ministry of the Church does not take effect to the bodily recovery and withal knowing it necessary that all who come to a Sacrament ought to come with a faith that they shall receive the benefit tendered by it, she orders that the Priest shall labour to persuade the sick to offer himself to this Unction with no less a faith than those tendered themselves who were miraculously cured by the Apostles. "That if the sick reap not so much benefit by it at this time as of old, this must not be ascribed to any defect in the Sacrament, but we are to believe it so happens for this cause rather, that faith is weaker in the greatest part of those that are anointed with this sacred oil, or in those that administer it, the Gospel telling us that Our Lord did not many mighty works in His Own country because of their unbelief." And yet for all this, at last she is forced to confess the true reason, "That miracles do not seem so necessary now, since Christianity has taken so wide and deep a root, as they were in the beginning of the Church." Which reason, as it shews that we ought not to expect the like effects now as then, does likewise fully justify the practice of the Church of England in not using Unction to warrant the recovery of the sick, though she be ready to assist them with her prayers, which may be hoped effectual in an ordinary way to all that is consistent with the Divine Will.

# (3) INVOCATION OF THE SAINTS

## No. 236.  JOSEPH HALL

[From *The Old Religion*, Chapter X (" On the Invocation of Saints "), § 3.  *Works*, ed. Peter Hall (1837), Vol. IX, p. 368.  Cp. note on No. **231**.]

### *Invocation of Saints, against Reason.*

How absurd, therefore, is it in reason, when the King of Heaven calls us to Him, to run with our petitions to the guard or pages of the court !  Had we to do with a finite prince, whose ears must be his best informers, or whose will to help us were justly questionable, we might have reason to present our suits by second hands.  But since it is an Omnipresent and Omniscious God with Whom we deal, from Whom the saints and angels receive all their light and love to His Church, how extreme folly is it to sue to those courtiers of heaven, and not to come immediately to the Throne of Grace !  That one Mediator *is able*, and willing also, *to save them to the utmost, that come unto God by Him* ; *seeing He ever liveth to make intercession for them* (*Heb.* vii, 25).

Besides, how uncertain must our devotions needs be, when we can have no possible assurance of their audience !  For who can know that a Saint hears him ?  That God ever hears us, we are as sure, as we are unsure to be heard of Saints.  Nay, we are sure we cannot be all heard of them.  For what finite nature can divide itself betwixt ten thousand suppliants, at one instant, in several regions of the world, much less impart itself whole to each ?  Either, therefore, we must turn the Saints into so many Deities, or we must yield that some of our prayers are unheard.  And *whatsoever is not of faith, is sin*.

As for that heavenly glass of St. Gregory, wherein the Saints see us and our suits, confuted long since by Hugo de Sancto Victore, it is as pleasing a fiction as if we imagined therefore to see all the corners of the earth, because we see that sun which sees them.  And the same eyes that see in God the particular necessities of His Saints below, see in the same God such infinite grace and mercy for their relief, as may save the labour of their reflecting upon that Divine mirror in their special intercessions.

This doctrine, therefore, and practice of the Romish Invocation of Saints, both as new and erroneous, against Scripture and Reason, we have justly rejected.

## No. 237.  RICHARD MONTAGUE

[From *Immediate Address Unto God Alone, First Delivered in a Sermon before His Majesty at Windsor, Since Revised and Enlarged to a Just Treatise of Invocation of Saints, Occasioned by a False Imputation of M. Antonius De Dominis upon the Author, Richard Montague*, London, 1624, pp. 107–109. The Sermon referred to had been preached before King James I three years previously. The text was *Psalm* l, 15. De Dominis, who was present, charged Montague with teaching the Doctrine of the Invocation of Saints, and in the present work Montague sought to vindicate himself from this charge.]

Peradventure some Saint or Saints departed may have more special care of, interest in, charge over, some men or man, country or countries, than is used ordinarily, or others commonly have by usual disposition ; out of some special dispensation, some peculiar deputation, out of ardent affection, religious devotion, or some other like regard best known and approved unto God, in His secret council and purpose in some extraordinary course.   Leo had this opinion of St. Peter, as appeareth in his Epistles in sundry places, as specially supervising and patronizing the Church of Rome.  *Nos experti sumus*, saith he, *et nostri probavere majores, credimus et confidimus inter omnes labores istius vitae, ad obtinendam misericordiam Dei semper nos specialium Patronorum orationibus adjuvandos.*   And it may be admitted that, as opinion hath been, some certain Saints have more special care and a peculiar patronage, custody, and protecting power, as Angels also have, over certain persons and countries by especial deputation.   Not for employment, to be sent *e tabernaculis beatorum*, the office of Angels in their ministry ; but for advancement of their good, in general intercession for the Body,[1] not in special mediation for any part or member occasionally.   Examples hereof are frequent and many :—St. George is accounted the Patron of England ; Saint Andrew of Scotland ; Saint James for Spain ; others for other peoples and countries anciently chosen and deputed.   It needs not be tendered or held as *de fide*.   It is no point of necessity to salvation. It may be true.   There is no impiety in believing so or so.   Nor doth this opinion of a general protection infer any special intercession.   This I am sure, the ancients supposed it, and were of opinion, yet never said to any such patron saint, *Ora pro nobis* or *pro me*.   Leo had that opinion for St. Peter over Rome.   Basil imagined the like for those forty martyrs of Caesarea.   Nazianzen relateth a story done, whereby the most blessed Mother of God may seem to have special care of holy virgins.   And St. Augustine supposeth not much differently.  *Deus suorum merita Martyrum ubi vult, quando vult, quomodo vult, maxime per eorum memorias, quoniam hoc novit nobis expedire ad aedificandam fidem Christi, pro cuius illi confessione passi sunt bonitate mirabili et ineffabili commendat.* So St. Augustine opined, and I see nothing to the contrary but so may we. For no support is hence, no direction, no colour at all for call upon them

[1] [Evidently = ' the Church.']

ordinarily. Incident occasions newly arriving every day have no dependency upon, nor correspondency with, these *precedents*.

## No. 238.  HERBERT THORNDIKE

[From *An Epilogue to the Tragedy of the Church of England*, Book III (" The Laws of the Church "), Chapter xxxi, §§ 21–30.  *Works*, ed. *L. A. C. T.*, Vol. IV, Part ii, pp. 768–779.  Cp. note on No. 69.]

I will distinguish three sorts of prayers to Saints, whether taught or allowed to be taught in the Church of Rome.

The First is of those that are made to God, but to desire His blessings by and through the merits and intercession of His Saints.  I cannot give so fit an example, as out of the Canon of the Mass, which all the Western Churches of that Communion do now use.  There it is said . . . " Communicating in and reverencing the memory of such and such and of all Thy Saints, by whose merit and prayer grant that in all things we may be guarded by Thy protection and help."  There is also a short prayer for the Priest to say when he comes to the altar, as he finds opportunity . . . " We pray Thee, Lord, by the merits of the Saints, whose relics are here, and all Saints, that Thou wouldest vouchsafe to release me all my sins."  And on the First Sunday in Advent mentioning the Blessed Virgin, they pray . . . " That we who believe her truly the Mother of God, may be helped by her intercessions with Thee."

The Second is that which their Litanies contain, which, though I do not undertake to know how they are used or how they ought to be used by particular Christians,—that is, how far voluntary, how far obligatory,—yet the form of them is manifest, that whereas you have in them sometimes, " Lord, have mercy upon us," " Christ, have mercy upon us," " Holy Trinity, One God, have mercy upon us," you have much oftener the Blessed Virgin repeated again and again, under a number of her attributes.  You have also all the Saints and Angels, or such as the present occasion pretends for the object of the devotion which a man tenders, named and spoken to with, " *Ora pro nobis*," i.e. " Pray for us."  The Blessed Virgin sometimes with " *Te rogamus audi nos*," " We beseech thee to hear us."  One thing I must not forget to observe, that the prayers which follow those Litanies are almost always of the first kind ; that is to say, addressed directly to God, but mentioning the intercession of Saints or Angels for the means to obtain our prayers at His hands.

The Third is when they desire immediately of them the same blessings, spiritual and temporal, which all Christians desire of God.  There is a Psalter to be seen, with the name of God changed every where into the name of the Blessed Virgin.  There is a book of devotion in French with this title : *Moyen de Bien Servir, Prier, et Adorer la Vierge*

*Marie*, i.e., *The Way Well to Serve, Pray to, and Adore the Blessed Virgin*. There are divers forms of prayer, as well as excessive speeches, concerning her especially and other Saints, quoted in the *Answer to the Jesuit's Challenge*,[1] pp. 330–345.

Of these, then, the First kind seems to me utterly agreeable with Christianity, importing only the exercise of that Communion which all members of God's Church hold with all members of it, ordained by God, for the means to obtain for one another the grace which the obedience of Our Lord Jesus Christ hath purchased for us without difference, whether dead or alive ; because we stand assured that they have the same affection for us, dead or alive, so far as they know us and our estate, and are obliged to desire and esteem their prayers for us, as for all the members of Christ's mystical Body. Neither is it in reason conceivable that all Christians from the beginning should make them the occasion of their devotions as I said, out of any consideration but this. For, as concerning the term of ' merit ' perpetually frequented in these prayers, it hath been always maintained by those of the Reformation that it is not used by the Latin Fathers in any other sense than that which they allow. Therefore the Canon of the Mass and probably other prayers which are still in use, being more ancient than the greatest part of the Latin Fathers, there is no reason to make any difficulty of admitting it in that sense, the ground whereof I have maintained in the Second Book.[2]

The Third, taking them at the foot of the letter, and valuing the intent of those that use them by nothing but the words of them, are mere idolatries ; as desiring of the creature that which God only gives, which is the worship of the creature for the Creator, *God blessed for evermore*. And were we bound to make the acts of them that teach these prayers the acts of the Church, because it tolerates them and maintains them in it, instead of casting them out, it would be hard to free that Church from idolatry ; which whoso admitteth, can by no means grant it to be a Church, the being whereof supposeth the worship of One God, exclusive to any thing else. But the words of them are capable of the same limitation that I gave to the words of Our Lord when I said [3] that they whom Christians do good to here, may be said to receive them into everlasting habitations, because God does it in consideration of them, and of the good done them. And so when Irenaeus calls the Virgin Mary the advocate of Eve (v. 19), he that considers his words there and iii. 33, shall find that he saith it, not because she prayed for her, but because she believed the Angel's message and submitted to God's Will, and so became the means of saving all, though by Our Lord Christ, Who pleadeth even for her as well as for Eve. Ground enough

---

[1] [By James Ussher.]   [2] [*i.e.* in *The Covenant of Grace*.]
[3] [Earlier in the chapter.]

there is for such a construction ; even the belief of One God alone, that stands at the head of our Creed, which we have no reason to think the Church allows them secretly to renounce, whom she alloweth to make these prayers. And therefore no ground to construe them so, as if the Church, by allowing them, did renounce the ground of all her Christianity. But not ground enough to satisfy a reasonable man that all that make them do hold that infinite distance between God and His Saints and Angels, of whom they demand the same effects, which if they hold not, they are idolaters as the Heathen were ; who, being convinced of one Godhead, as the Fathers challenge to their faces, divided it into One Principal and divers that by His gift are such. How shall I presume that simple Christians, in the devotions of their hearts, understand that distance of God from His creatures which their words signify not, which the wisest of their teachers will be much troubled to say, by what figure of speech they can allow it ? Especially if it be considered how little reason or interest in religion there can be to advance the reverence of Christian people towards the Saints or Angels so far above the reason and ground, which ought to be the spring-head of it. For so far are we from any tradition of the Catholic Church for this, that the admonition of Epiphanius to the Collyridians takes hold of it. . . . So doth the admonition of St. Ambrose (*In Romanos*, i.) to them who reserve nothing to God that they give not to His servants. So doth that of St. Augustine (*De Vera Religione*, cap. lv.) that our religion is not to consist in worshipping the dead ; and that an Angel forbad St. John to worship him, but only God, Whose fellow-servants they were. So doth the argument of St. Gregory Nyssen (*Contra Eunomium*, iv.) and Athanasius (*Contra Arianos*, iii.), concluding our Lord to be God, because He is worshipped, which Cornelius was forbid by St. Peter, St. John by the Angel, to do to them, saith Athanasius.

In fine, so dangerous is the case, that whoso communicateth in it is no way reasonably assured that he communicateth not in the worship of idols. Only the Church of England having acknowledged the Church of Rome a true Church, though corrupt, ever since the Reformation, I am obliged so to interpret the prayers thereof, as to acknowledge the corruption so great, that the prayers which it alloweth, may be idolatries, if they be made in that sense which they may properly signify : but not that they are necessarily idolatries. For if they were necessarily idolatries, then were the Church of Rome necessarily no Church, the being of Christianity presupposing the worship of One true God. And though, to confute the heretics, the style of modern devotions leaves nothing to God which is not attributed to and desired of His Saints, yet it cannot be denied they may be the words of them who believe that God alone can give that which they desire.

The Second sort, it is confessed, had the beginning in the flourishing times of the Church after Constantine. The lights of the Greek and Latin Church, Basil, Nazianzen, Nyssen, Ambrose, Jerome, Augustine, Chrysostom, Cyrils both, Theodoret, Fulgentius, Gregory the Great, Leo, more or rather all after that time, have all of them spoken to the Saints departed and desired their assistance. But neither is this enough to make a tradition of the Church. For the Church had been three hundred years before it began. Irenaeus is mistaken, when he is alleged for it, as I said even now. Cardinal Bellarmine alleges out of Eusebius (*De Preparatione*, xiii. 10) . . . "We make our prayers to them." But the Greek bears only, "We make our prayers to God at their monuments." Athanasius, *De Sanctissima Deipara*, whom he quotes, is certainly of a later date than Athanasius. Out of St. Hilary I see nothing brought nor remember any thing to be brought to that purpose. In fine, after Constantine, when the Festivals of the Saints, being publicly celebrated, occasioned the confluence of Gentiles as well as Christians, and innumerable things were done which seemed miracles done by God to attest the honour done them, and the truth of Christianity which it supposed, I acknowledge those great lights did think fit to address themselves to them as petitioners ; but so at the first, as those that were no ways assured by our common Christianity that their petitions arrived at their knowledge. You have seen St. Augustine acknowledge that they must come by such means as God is no way tied to furnish. Gregory Nazianzen speaks to Gorgonia in his Oration upon her, and to Constantine, in his First Oration against Julian, but under a doubtful condition, if they were sensible of what he spake. Enough to distinguish praying to God from any address to a creature, though religion be the ground of it. And when the apparitions about their monuments were held unquestionable, yet was it questioned whether the same soul could be present at once in places of so much distance or Angels appear like them, as you may see in the *Answer* [of Ussher] aforesaid. Nay, Hugo de S. Victore (in Cassander, *Epist.* xix.) hath enabled him to hold, that the Litanies do not suppose that the Saints hear them, and therefore are expounded by some to signify conditional desires, if God grant them to come to their knowledge. But of that I speak not yet, only as it enables me to conclude that this kind of prayer is not idolatry. This necessarily follows from the premises, because a man cannot take that Saint or Angel for God whose prayers he desires ; but manifestly shews that his desire is grounded upon the relation which he thinks he hath to him by Our Lord Christ and by His Church. Nevertheless, though it be not idolatry, the consequence and production of it not being distinguishable from idolatry, the Church must needs stand obliged to give it those bounds that may prevent such mischief as that which shall make it no Church.

## No. 239. JOHN COSIN

[From a Sermon preached at Brancepath in 1632. *Works*, ed L. A. C. T., Vol. I, pp. 146–148. The extract is from Sermon No. 10 ; and the text was *Exodus* xx, 3.]

The Spaniards call upon St. James, and the French upon St. Denis ; the Germans they call upon St. Martin, and the Hungars upon St. Lewis, as of old the Scots did upon St. Andrew, and the English here upon St. George. These for countries. In cities, at Milan, St. Ambrose is their patron, and at Colon [*i.e.* Cologne] the Three Kings ; at Auspurg [*i.e.* Augsburg], St. Hulderic ; and otherwhere St. Quintine, St. Valentine, St. Thomas, St. John ; here at home, St. Brandon and St. Cuthbert have been deified.

The mariners they call upon St. Nicholas, and St. Christopher ; the physicians upon St. Luke ; the lawyers upon Ivo, the gentlemen upon St. George, the tradesmen upon St. Loy, St. Crispin, St. Gutman, St. Eustace, and a hundred more besides.

The care of their vineyards they commend to St. Urban, of their horse to St. Loy, of their hogs to St. Anthony, of their oxen to Pelagius, and of their pullaine [*i.e.* poultry] to Wendelin.

When they would not have their corn hurt by tempest, they hold up and fall down to St. John the Evangelist ; when they fear burning by fire, St. Agatha is their goddess ; and when they fear the plague, they run to St. Sebastian for mercy and pity to be shewn upon them ; when they are troubled with a fever, they call upon St. Petronelle ; and when their teeth pain them, they bemoan themselves to St. Apoline. St. Felicitie is called upon for children, St. Margaret for safe delivery, and St. Barbarie for a good departure out of the world. It were infinite to number up all. But I trow this is sufficient to shew their vanity, their impiety, their manifest contempt and breach of this precept, when they have so many gods to run to, so many helpers to trust to besides One ; and let no man deceive you, they that hold of this religion, they hold of a wrong one, and one that will deceive them all at last.

Neither shall their distinction of ' oblique ' and ' relative,' of indirect and transitory, of secondary and mediate prayers, serve their turn ; for the world can never be got to believe that oblique and relative prayers (such as we would use to holy men here upon earth) is all that is sought for, seeing it is most evident, both by their practice abroad and their continual use here at home, to pray directly, absolutely, and finally to their saints, as to them that had as much power as God Himself, to give and forgive them what they will ask. They say to the Blessed Virgin, ' O Holy Mother of God, vouchsafe and keep us, we worship thy name, and that world without end ; let thy mercy lighten upon us, as our trust is in thee.' And again, ' In thee only ' (and what can be said more to God ?) ' In thee only have I trusted, let me never be confounded.' This to her. And to others, *Tu dona cœlum, Tu perduc ad gloriam, pestem fuga, solve a peccatis,* in direct and plain terms, so absolute that I know not what can be more; and sure I am, that we have no more for God, and for Christ Himself. Insomuch that we may be bold to conclude and to assure you all, that whoever they be that practise themselves, or persuade any other to use this kind of religion, they do it by some other precept, for precept of God have they none. Nay this precept, this command of His, is directly set up against them. And though the memory of the saints be precious among us, and ought so to be, though we honour their glorified persons, though we sing, and praise, and magnify their virtues, though we teach all generations to call them blessed, yet for all this, the commandment of God, and the glory of God, of their God and ours, is precious to us above them all, and so let it be for ever; and let all the people say Amen.

## No. 240. JEREMY TAYLOR

[From *A Dissuasive from Popery, Part I.* Chapter ii, § 8. (" The Roman Church prays to the Dead.") *Works,* ed. R. Heber, Vol. X, pp. 223 f. (ed. C. P. Eden, Vol. VI, pp. 254 f. [§ 9]). Cp. note on No. 260.]

The Church of Rome in her public and allowed offices prays to dead men and women who are, or whom they suppose to be, beatified, and these they invocate as preservers, helpers, guardians, deliverers in their necessity, and they expressly call them " their refuge, their guard and defence, their life and health "; which is so formidable a devotion that we, for them, and for ourselves too, if we should imitate them, are to dread the words of Scripture, *Cursed is the man that trusteth in man.* We are commanded to *call upon God in the time of trouble,* and it is promised, *that He will deliver us and we shall glorify Him.* We find no such command to call upon Saints, neither do we know who are Saints, excepting a very few; and in what present state they are, we cannot know, nor how our prayers can come to their knowledge; and yet if we did know all this, it cannot be endured at all that Christians, who are commanded to call upon God and upon none else, and to make all our prayers "through Jesus Christ," and never so much as warranted to make our prayers " through Saints departed," should yet choose Saints for their particular patrons, or at all rely upon them, and make prayers to them in such forms of words which are only fit to be spoken to God; prayers which have no testimony, command, or promise, in the Word of God, and therefore which cannot be made in faith or prudent hope.

Neither will it be enough to say that they only desire the Saints to pray for them. For though that be of itself a matter indifferent, if we were sure they do hear us when we pray and that we should not by that means secretly destroy our confidence in God or lessen the honour of

Christ our Advocate,—of which because we cannot be sure, but much rather the contrary, it is not a matter indifferent ; yet besides this, in the public offices of the Church of Rome, there are prayers to Saints made with confidence in them, with derogation to God's glory and prerogative, with diminution to the honour of Christ, with words in sound and in all appearance the same with the highest that are usually expressed in our prayers to God and His Christ ; and this is it we insist upon and reprove, as being a direct destruction of our sole confidence in God, and too near to blasphemy to be endured in the devotions of Christians.

## No. 241. WILLIAM CLAGETT

[From *A Discourse Concerning the Worship of the Blessed Virgin and the Saints ; With an Account of the Beginnings and Rise of it amongst Christians, In Answer to M. de Meaux's Appeal to the Fourth Age, in his " Exposition " and " Pastoral Letter,"* London, 1686, §§ 3, 1. *Enchiridion Theologicum Anti-Romanum* (ed. E. Cardwell, Oxford, 1837), Vol. III, pp. 375 f., 377–379 ; 368–371. The former work referred to in the title is J. B. Bossuet's famous *Exposition de la Foi Catholique* (Cp. note on No. 258.]

But to all that we can say, they give this plausible answer, That it makes no more against their practice in desiring the prayers of their brethren in Heaven, than against theirs and ours, in desiring the prayers of our brethren upon earth ; and, as Monsieur de M[eaux] says, that it " is profitable to pray to the Saints, in the same spirit of charity, and according to the same order of fraternal society, which moves us to demand assistance of our brethren living upon earth."

Now this is a very popular way to save themselves from blame, but by no means sufficient. For there is a concurrence of other reasons to make it profitable to desire the prayers of our brethren upon earth besides these two, that *they are our brethren* and that *we love one another*. God has manifestly approved it in the Holy Scriptures ; that is one reason. Besides, we are also sure that when we desire our brethren upon earth to pray for us, they hear us ; that is another reason. But neither of these reasons can be justly produced to shew the profitableness of praying to the Saints departed.

But because this is the most common and colourable defence they make, I shall further shew what may and ought to be replied to it by the people of our Communion. They say, we may as lawfully desire those in Heaven to pray for us, as those on earth : but let us then tell them, that when we ask of one another things proper to be asked, these requests are by no means that which we understand by prayer or religious invocation ; and that themselves do not so account them. Monsieur de M[eaux] clearly gives them another name ; he called it, "beseeching or demanding the assistance of our brethren." But men of all religions do agree this to be quite a different thing from that part of religion which we call *prayer*. . . .

Now if you desire to know what it is in this case that makes the difference, I think the answer is very plain. For the difference is not to be taken 1, from the matter of the request, for that is the same ; nor 2, from the persons themselves to whom the request is made. For if the Saint departed were here, why would my requesting of the same thing be prayer to him and not to the priest? And therefore 3, it must necessarily lie in the different circumstances of the priest and the Saint ; that the former is with me, and the latter is absent from me. Requests made to the faithful are made to those that are within the compass of civil conversation ; but the same requests made to the Blessed Virgin and the Saints are made to those that are departed out of the compass of civil conversation. And this is that which makes them not to be prayer in the former case, and to be prayer in the latter.

But if it be further inquired, Why it is prayer to ask the same things of those that are distant from civil conversation, which to ask of those that are within the compass of it is not prayer ? the reason seems plainly to be this,—That when I address myself to one that is within the compass of civil conversation, in which men use to hear or to understand one another, my assurance that he hears me does no way ascribe to him a knowledge or a presence which is above the condition of a creature. But if I invoke the Saints every where, with assurance that they hear me, I have no other reasonable ground of such assurance than that they are every where present at the same time. For if I acknowledge that there is a certain limited compass within which they can hear and know, let this limit be never so wide, how can I be assured that they are not out of that compass when I speak to them ? But the Romanists pray every where to every Saint, believing that they are heard. " It is certain," says one of them, " that the Saints know what we bring forth by the affection of the heart only." " It is of faith," saith another, " that the blessed know our prayers which we pour out to them, else it were in vain to make them." Now a request does undoubtedly become prayer or religious invocation when the making of it attributes any Divine prerogative or perfection to the being that is called upon ; and therefore because immensity of presence is an incommunicable perfection of God, and because also requests made to those that are out of all lines of civil communication, being made in faith, do ascribe that power to them which is proper to God only, therefore such requests are proper prayer, or religious invocation.

It is indeed very possible that he that prays to the Blessed Virgin and to the Saints may not believe that they are omnipresent ; but if he prays, as they pretend to do in the Roman Church, with assurance that they hear him, his prayer implies it, and himself, by construction of the fact, ascribes it to them. For let him, if he can, produce any other reasonable ground of assurance that they hear him, wheresoever and

**39**

whensoever he addresses to them.   But instead of that, M. de Meaux
tells us that " the Church contents herself to teach, with all Antiquity
(not *all* Antiquity I am sure), those prayers to be very profitable to such
who make them, whether it be the Saints know them by the ministry
and communication of Angels who, according to the testimony of the
Scripture, know what passes amongst us, etc. ; whether it be that God
Himself makes known to them our desires by a particular revelation ;
or lastly, whether it be that He discovers the secret to them in His
Divine essence, in which all truth is comprised."   Now if his Church
could have taught us upon what grounds they are assured that the
Saints do hear them, either this way or that way ; or that God has in
general revealed to us that they hear or know the prayers we make to
them, one way or other, and therefore that it is profitable to pray to them,
she had not been content to teach that the Saints do know them some
way or other, though she knows not how or why.   For what foundation
that they hear us can be gathered from such uncertain and loose conjectures as these are ?   Can any man convince me that a thing is done
by telling me that it might be done, by some way or other, for any thing
he knows to the contrary?   And is this kind of arguing a sufficient
ground to establish so solemn a part of religion as the Invocation of
Saints ?   I know it is possible for God to reveal to my friend in the East
Indies what I say here in England ; but am I sure that if I say to him an
*Ora pro nobis*, at this distance, it reaches him forthwith ?   It were no
difficult matter, if it were needful, to find them trouble enough to clear
these very conjectures from absurdity ; but as long as they are only
conjectures, they can be no foundation of a certain persuasion.   Whereas therefore M. de Meaux says " It is manifest that to say a creature may
have the knowledge of these prayers, by a light communicated to him
by God, is not to elevate a creature above his condition," I say, it is as
manifest that this is no ground of certainty that the Saints hear our
prayers at all ; and if this be all they have to say, and yet will pretend to
pray to them with faith, there is but one ground left for that faith, viz.,
that the Saints are everywhere present, and are therefore elevated above
the condition of creatures : which though some of themselves do not
believe, yet their assurance to be heard being altogether unreasonable
without that belief, their prayers do give the omnipresence of God to
creatures ; which is indeed the great reason why their addresses to
the Saints are properly prayers.

This therefore I lay down, and let them remove it if they can : That
to invocate any creature who is out of the compass of civil conversation
—i.e., with whom I cannot converse as we do with one another, by
speaking within the known distances of hearing, or by writing, or messages, or the like,—is in itself a vain and foolish thing, because he is out
of distance.   But if I pretend that it is profitable to invoke the Saints,

and this upon assurance that they hear me, though I can neither tell which way in particular, nor can shew in general that they do certainly hear me some way that does not infer their omnipresence, there is no remedy but my invocation of them must by consequence confess that they are omnipresent. . . .

But let no man think that in this cause we are engaged against the Saints departed, because we contend with their worshippers. Let no man take our refusal to honour them as their worshippers honour them, for an argument that we do not honour them at all. We are content to be tried by that known rule of St. Austin that " they are to be honoured for imitation, not to be adored for religion." We believe that the highest honour we can do them is to follow their examples. We love their memories; we celebrate anniversary commemorations of their piety and virtues, especially of their sufferings for righteousness' sake; we congratulate their victories over the world; we rejoice in their glory and happiness; we propound their examples to the imitation of the faithful, exciting them to live as the Saints once lived, that they at length may inherit those promises, which, by their faith and patience in this world, the Saints now inherit in the other; we praise God for them as often as we meet together at the Holy Table of Our Lord; and when we meet to inter our Christian brethren, we pray to God " to hasten His Kingdom, that we, with all those that are departed in the true faith of His Holy Name, may have our perfect consummation and bliss, both in body and soul, in His everlasting glory."

Thus we honour the departed Saints, remembering all along, that though they are highly exalted above us who are here below imprisoned in earthly bodies and struggling in a sinful world with infirmities and temptations, we yet belong to the same body of which they are members, and that they are still our fellow-servants. We are persuaded they have not less but rather more charity for us than they had for the Church when they lived upon the earth; but whether they know us in particular or not, or in what instances they express their charity towards us, God having made no revelations of these things, we can define nothing about them; and therefore we dare not give them those honours, which suppose such an assurance of these things as God hath thought fit to deny us.

As to the Virgin Mary in particular, we do with men and Angels acknowledge that she was *blessed amongst women*, since she brought forth the Saviour of mankind and the Lord of Heaven and earth; since she was not the Mother only, but the Virgin Mother also of Our Lord, and conceived Him by the power of the Holy Ghost. Which confession so honourable to her, being inseparable from a right belief concerning Our Lord Jesus, we do not only set it forth upon the anniversary of the Annunciation, but frequently also in our sermons and daily in the Creed.   Moreover, we take these singular graces of God towards her, in conjunction with other things of a more common quality.   We doubt not but she was an excellently pious and virtuous person.   We see by her behaviour when the Angel Gabriel came to her, that she was not apt to be imposed upon by counterfeit visions and revelations, nor forward to believe great things of herself, nor lifted up with pride, because she was so highly favoured; but that upon this extraordinary occasion, she wholly resigned herself to the disposal of God, with a wisdom and humility that could not but be habitual.   But if nothing at all had been said of her personal qualities in the Scriptures (as indeed there is but very little), we might have presumed without rashness that because God (Who has no less regard to a holy mind than to a pure body) would have the Mother of Our Lord to retain the purity of a Virgin, He would also choose a most holy Virgin to be His Mother; and since He was pleased to send us so heavenly a treasure in an earthen vessel, He would choose one of the greatest honour.   For which reason likewise we might have concluded, without other testimony, that she became afterwards a faithful disciple of her Son.   For when one, in admiration of Him, cried out, *Blessed is the womb that bare Thee, and the paps that gave Thee suck.   Yea rather*, said He, *blessed are they that hear the word of God, and keep it.*   Without which blessedness, she that bore Him in her womb, and nourished Him at her breasts, would have been justly esteemed by all generations the most unhappy and miserable creature in the world.   Finally, from all this we cannot but conclude that she is very happy and glorious in the Kingdom of Heaven.   For though we have no particular revelations concerning this, to warrant any comparisons of her state with that of Angels and Archangels, yet upon general reasons we may say with sufficient assurance that her rewards and glories in Heaven are exceeding great, and such as hold proportion, not only with her faith and patience (for as some think she suffered martyrdom), but likewise with that honour which God was pleased to confer upon her in this world.

Now if anything remains whereby to express the tenderness we have for the honour of the Blessed Virgin it is this, that we should do what we can to redeem her name from that dishonourable imputation of affecting glories that cannot belong to the most excellent creature, that is but a creature.   For they who by most solemn rites of religious service address to her, as to the " queen of heaven and earth," would make us believe, and pretend to believe themselves, that she is pleased with that worship which they offer to her.   But if, as we say, they yield to her those services which no creature is to receive, they do by consequence represent her as a lady that aspires to the glory of the Most High; which is by no means for the glory of the Blessed Virgin.   And if their Saint-worship be liable to the same charge, thus also they represent the other Saints. Now though, in opposing their doctrine and practice, we are principally moved by that concern we ought to have for the glory of our Creator and Saviour; yet it is some inducement to us so to do, that we shall thereby vindicate the Blessed Virgin also, and all the glorified Saints. For if she knows what passes amongst mortals, she cannot but be displeased at those services that have been and still are paid to her by some of her Son's disciples; and if she said any thing at all to them, she should say to her votaries, but with greater indignation, what the Angel said to St. John, falling at his feet to worship him: *See thou do it not. I am thy fellowservant. Worship God.* (*Rev.* xix, 10).

The same I say of the Angels, the Apostles, the Martyrs, and all the Saints, whom they honour with the same kind of worship that they give to the Blessed Virgin. Only the degree of her worship and the frequency of their addresses to her and the strength of their confidence in her is so much greater, that they have thought fit to invent a word of art to express it by. *Hyperdulia* they call it,—a word which our people cannot understand better, than by knowing the practice which it is a name for.

It is so vast a proportion of religious service which they render to her, it consists of so many parts and diversities, that it were a labour to recount them as particularly as the case would bear. It shall suffice to mention some of the principal heads. They worship her with religious prayers and vows. They erect Churches and oratories for her service, where they worship her very images and pictures and pretended relics. They make rosaries and compose Hours, Psalters, and other forms of devotion, to her. They ask things of her that are proper to be asked of God only. They burn incense to her images, and offer their very Sacrifice of the Mass in her honour.

Now as to this and all the rest, we cannot but stand amazed that this service of the Blessed Virgin should grow to be one of the principal parts of their religion, when the Holy Scriptures have not given us the least intimation of rule or example for it, or of any doctrine or practice that leads to it; that it should be a main design of their Catechisms to instruct youth in the worship of the Blessed Virgin; of their sermons to excite the people to put confidence in her, and to call upon her for the present occasion; of their books of devotion to direct them how to pray to her, and magnify her in formal invocations; of their confessors to enjoin penitents to say so many Ave Maries, in satisfaction for their sins, and to make at least as frequent applications to Mary as to Jesus Himself for deliverance from sins and dangers;—when not one word, not one intimation of anything, like to anything of all this, is left upon record in the writings of the Evangelists and Apostles, from whom those men pretend to derive their religion, whose books are large enough for this so famous a service to have been at least mentioned somewhere or other, and who, without all doubt, would have more than mentioned it, if it had been the religion of those times. This is that we must always wonder at; and so much the more, because the constant tenor of the Holy Scriptures bears against such practices as these, agreeably to that precept of both Testaments, *Thou shalt worship the Lord thy God, and Him only shalt thou serve.*

## No. 242. JOHN PEARSON

[From *An Exposition of the Creed.* On the words of Article III, " Born of the Virgin Mary." Ed. Oxford (E. Burton), 1864, p. 321. Cp. note on No. 13.]

In respect of her [*i.e.* of the Blessed Virgin] it was therefore necessary that we might perpetually preserve an esteem of her person, proportionable to so high a dignity. It was her own prediction, *From henceforth all generations shall call me blessed*; but the obligation is ours to call her, to esteem her so. If Elizabeth cried out *with so loud a voice, Blessed art thou among women,* when Christ was but newly conceived in her womb, what expressions of honour and admiration can we think sufficient now that Christ is in Heaven, and that Mother with Him ! Far be it from any Christian to derogate from that special privilege granted her, which is incommunicable to any other. We cannot bear too reverend a regard unto the *Mother of Our Lord,* so long as we give her not that worship which is due unto the Lord Himself. Let us keep the language of the Primitive Church. Let her be honoured and esteemed, let Him be worshipped and adored.

## No. 243. GEORGE HICKES

[From *Speculum Beatae Virginis. A Discourse of the Due Praise and Honour of the Virgin Mary. By a True Catholic of the Church of England.* London, 1686, pp. 9 f., 38 f. This anonymous Discourse was as exposition of *Luke* i, 28. A second edition was called for in the year of its first appearance.]

It is our duty, who have the benefit of her example, to honour and celebrate her name and commemorate her virtues and set forth her praises, in whom there was a concurrence of so many Divine virtues, such a strong faith, such abasing humility, such pure chastity and all other graces in as much perfection as was consistent with human frailty.

So divine, so righteous a person ought to be had in everlasting remembrance and blessed among women from generation to generation. We ought not to mention her name without honour, her name which ought to be like precious ointment wheresoever the Gospel is preached and written in the biggest and most conspicuous character in the Diptychs of the Church.

If the names of other Saints are distinguished with miniature, hers ought to shine with gold. Especially if we consider that she, of all the Virgin daughters of Israel, had the honour to be chosen by the Holy Trinity for the Mother of God. What shall be done to the woman whom the King of Kings delighteth to honour ?   Certainly if we should hold our peace and refuse to praise her among women, the stones of the Church would cry out, *the stone shall cry out of the wall and the beam out of the timber shall answer it*.   If what the woman did, who poured forth a box of precious ointment upon the head of our Saviour, was to be spoken of for a memorial of her, wheresoever the Gospel should be preached throughout the whole world, surely that most Blessed Virgin, who had the honour to bring forth and breed up the Son of God, ought to have a festival and be mentioned with all due reverence and esteem in all the Churches of the Saints.   Wheresoever the Gospel is preached, that which she hath done and suffered for Our Lord ought to be spoken of for a memorial of her, from whom He took that very Body which was crucified, and that precious Blood, which was shed for the remission of our sins.

But . . . though we ought to honour her, and have honourable thoughts and make honourable mention of her, yet we ought to take care that we do not honour her too much, in thinking and speaking more highly of her than we ought to think and speak of an human creature. Indeed, there is a particular respect due unto her, upon the account of her eminent graces, and as she is the Mother of God.   And so we find her cousin Elizabeth treated her with a particular respect unto that character.   *Whence is this to me that the Mother of my Lord should come unto me ?*   But then we must not let our respect for her commence into worship, nor romance her into a deity because it was her lot to be that happy Virgin of whom Christ was born.   We must not treat her upon the account of her singular relation to Immanuel, as if she were an infinite Majesty, or as if her graces were indeed Divine attributes and " her prerogatives of grace and glory ", as a late book [1] asserts, " one and the same with those of her Son ".   We ought not to pay such homage and veneration to her under the character of the Queen, as is only due to the King of Heaven.   But we must carefully keep our respects to her person and memory within due bounds and limits, lest transgressing herein, we should fall into those unwarrantable excesses and abuses which a great part of Christendom is too justly chargeable with. . . .

Wherefore, my brethren of this truly Catholic and Apostolic Church of England, let us take care to keep within the bounds and limits which our pure and holy mother, after the example of the Primitive Church, hath set to the praise and honour of the Blessed Virgin.   Let us cheerfully and respectfully give her the honourable titles of Holy, and Blessed, and Perpetual Virgin, and call her without scruple the Holy and Blessed Mother of God.   Nay, let us for peace sake go as far as we can with our fellow-Christians of the Latin Communion, so we go with caution and circumspection in honouring of this glorious Saint.   Let us acknow-

[1] Epist. Dedic. to *The Contemplations of the Virgin Mary*.

ledge with them that she is to be honoured above all Saints.   But let us not honour her with religious honour nor pray unto her either as a donor or as an intercessor in the presence of God.   Let us acknowledge with them her perpetual Virginity, according to ancient tradition.   And if it will gain or oblige any of them, let us not oppose them in the opinion they have, that she promised and vowed her virginity to God ; for it is an innocent opinion, though it is precarious and hath no ground in Scripture or Primitive Antiquity.   In a word, let us admire her singular purity and holiness, though we cannot admit her innocence. Let us give her all the honour that is due to so great a Saint, but not one jot more than is allowed to a creature.   And if by doing so much and no more, you offend on the left hand and on the right, the offence will be taken and not given ; but if by refusing to do so much you offend, the offence will be given, to both Churches, and that will be a great offence. To conclude, let us always mention her with respect.   Let her Name still perfume the air like precious ointment.   Let us celebrate her great virtues.   Let us keep her Festivals, as it becomes true sons of the Primitive Church of England.   Let us imitate her blessed example and thank God for the benefit of it.   Let us endeavour as she did, to hear the Word of God and keep it, and to do the will of our Heavenly Father ; and then we shall all become κεχαριτωμένοι, high favourites of Heaven, even the Mother, and Sister, and Brethren of Christ.

## No. 244.  ANTHONY STAFFORD

[From *The Female Glory ; or the Life and Death of Our Blessed Lady, the Holy Virgin Mary, God's Own Immaculate Mother*, " to whose Sacred Memory the author dedicates these his humble endeavours," London, 1635.   From the (unpaged) Preface " To the Masculine Reader."   Ed. Orby Shipley (1869), pp. cxxv f.   This treatise must be unique in the devotional literature of the Seventeenth Century ; among other things it contained an engraving depicting the Assumption of the Virgin.   As the author doubtless expected, the work created a storm among the Puritans.   Laud stood up in defence of the writer.]

I am the first, to my knowledge, who hath written in our vulgar tongue on this our Blessed Virgin, drawn thereto, I confess, by the strength rather of affection than of ability.   Yet withal I profess that I am her admirer, not her idolater ; and that I no way allow of their profane custom, who rob God of His honour and bestow it on her.   But this I will say, that though I impute not the late troubles and afflictions of the Protestant party in Germany to the small reverence there paid her (many of God's judgements, according to Saint Austin, being secret, none unjust), yet truly I believe the undervaluing of one so great and dear in Christ's esteem cannot but be displeasing to Him ; and that the more we ascribe to her (setting Invocation apart) the more gracious we appear in His sight.

# (4) CEREMONIES

## No. 245.  RICHARD HOOKER

[From *The Laws of Ecclesiastical Polity*, Book V, Chapter vi, § 2 ; vii, §§ 1, 3, 4 ; viii, §§ 1, 2, 5.  *Works*, ed. J. Keble, Vol. II, pp. 30, 32–34, 35 f.  Cp. note on No. 148.]

LET our first demand be therefore, that in the external form of religion such things as are apparently, or can be sufficiently proved, effectual and generally fit to set forward godliness, either as betokening the greatness of God or as beseeming the dignity of religion or as concurring with celestial impressions in the minds of men, may be reverently thought of ; some few, rare, casual, and tolerable, or otherwise curable inconveniences notwithstanding.

Neither may we in this case lightly esteem what hath been allowed as fit in the judgement of Antiquity, and by the long continued practice of the whole Church ; from which unnecessarily to swerve, experience hath never as yet found it safe.  For wisdom's sake we reverence them no less that are young, or not much less, than if they were stricken in years. . . .

In which consideration there is cause why we should be slow and unwilling to change, without very urgent necessity, the ancient ordinances, rites, and long approved customs, of our venerable predecessors.  The love of things ancient doth argue staidness, but levity and want of experience maketh apt unto innovations.  That which wisdom did first begin, and hath been with good men long continued, challengeth allowance of them that succeed, although it plead for itself nothing.  That which is new, if it promise not much, doth fear condemnation before trial ; till trial, no man doth acquit or trust it, what good soever it pretend and promise.  So that in this kind there are few things known to be good, till such time as they grow to be ancient.  The vain pretence of those glorious names, where they could not be with any truth, neither in reason ought to have been so much alleged, hath wrought such a prejudice against them in the minds of the common sort, as if they had utterly no force at all ; whereas (especially for these observances which concern our present question) antiquity, custom, and consent in the Church of God, making with that which law doth establish, are themselves most sufficient reasons to uphold the same, unless some notable public inconvenience enforce the contrary.  For a small thing in the eye of law is as nothing.

We are therefore bold to make our second petition this, That in things the fitness whereof is not of itself apparent, nor easy to be made sufficiently manifest unto all, yet the judgement of Antiquity concurring with that which is received may induce them to think it not unfit, who are not able to allege any known weighty inconvenience which it hath, or to take any strong exception against it.

All things cannot be of ancient continuance, which are expedient and needful for the ordering of spiritual affairs : but the Church being a body which dieth not hath always power, as occasion requireth, no less to ordain that which never was, than to ratify what hath been before. To prescribe the order of doing in all things, is a peculiar prerogative which Wisdom hath, as queen or sovereign commandress over other virtues. This in every several man's actions of common life appertaineth unto Moral, in public and politic secular affairs unto Civil wisdom. In like manner, to devise any certain form for the outward administration of public duties in the service of God, or things belonging thereunto, and to find out the most convenient for that use, is a point of wisdom Ecclesiastical.

It is not for a man which doth know or should know what order is, and what peaceable government requireth, to ask, " why we should hang our judgement upon the Church's sleeve ; " and " why in matters of order, more than in matters of doctrine." [1] The Church hath authority to establish that for an order at one time, which at another time it may abolish, and in both it may do well. But that which in doctrine the Church doth now deliver rightly as a truth, no man will say that it may hereafter recall, and as rightly avouch the contrary. Laws touching matter of order are changeable, by the power of the Church ; articles concerning doctrine not so. We read often in the writings of Catholic and holy men touching matters of doctrine, " This we believe, This we hold, This the Prophets and Evangelists have declared, This the Apostles have delivered, This Martyrs have sealed with their blood, and confessed in the midst of torments, To this we cleave as to the anchor of our souls, Against this, though an Angel from heaven should preach unto us, we would not believe." But did we ever in any of them read, touching matters of mere comeliness, order, and decency, neither commanded nor prohibited by any Prophet, any Evangelist, any Apostle, " Although the Church wherein we live, do ordain them to be kept, Although they be never so generally observed, Though all the Churches in the world should command them, Though Angels from heaven should require our subjection thereunto, *I would hold him accursed* that doth obey " ? Be it in matter of the one kind or of the other, what Scripture doth plainly deliver, to that the first place both of credit and obedience is due ; the next whereunto is whatsoever any man can necessarily conclude by force of reason ; after these the voice of the Church succeedeth.

[1] Aristotle, *Ethics*, Book II, ch. 9.

That which the Church by her ecclesiastical authority shall probably think and define to be true or good must in congruity of reason overrule all other inferior judgements whatsoever. . . .

We therefore crave . . . to have it granted, That where neither the evidence of any law divine, nor the strength of any invincible argument otherwise found out by the light of reason, nor any notable public inconvenience, doth make against that which our own laws ecclesiastical have although but newly instituted for the ordering of these affairs, the very authority of the Church itself, at the least in such cases, may give so much credit to her own laws, as to make their sentence touching fitness and conveniency weightier than any bare and naked conceit to the contrary, especially in them who can owe no less than child-like obedience to her that hath more than motherly power.

## No. 246. JOSEPH HALL

[From *Holy Decency in the Worship of God*, near the beginning. *Works*, ed. Peter Hall (1837), Vol. VI, p. 464.]

But, surely, I fear these men are not more faulty in the one extreme than many Christians are in the other, who place a kind of holiness in a slovenly neglect, and so order themselves as if they thought a nasty carelessness in God's services were most acceptable to Him. Hence it is that they affect homely places for His worship, abandoning all magnificence and cost, in all the acts and appendances of their devotion ; clay and sticks please them better than marble and cedars. Hence it is that their dresses make no difference of festivals ; all stuffs, all colours are alike to them in all sacred solemnities. Hence, that they stumble into God's House, without all care or show of reverence ; and sit them down at His Table, like His fellows, with their hats on their heads. Hence, that they make no difference of coming with full paunches to that heavenly banquet, and that the very dogs are allowed free access and leave to lift up their legs at those Holy Tables, where we partake of the Son of God.

For the rectifying of which misconceits and practices, let it be laid down as an undoubted rule,—that it is a thing well-pleasing to God that there should be all outward cleanliness, gravity, reverent and comely postures, meet furniture, utensils, places, used and observed in the service of the Almighty,—a truth, sufficiently grounded upon that irrefragable canon of the Apostle, *Let all things be done decently, and in order* (*I Cor.* xiv, 40) ; whereof order refers to persons and actions, decency to the things done and the fashion of doing them.

## No. 247. JOSEPH HALL

[From *Epistles*, Fifth Decade, No. ii. *Works*, ed. Peter Hall, (1837), Vol. VI, p. 242. This Epistle is entitled " Shewing the Difference of the Present Church from the Apostolical; and the Needlessness of our Conformity thereto in All Things," and was addressed to " My Lord Bishop of Worcester " (Gervase Babington was Bp. of Worcester 1597–1610; Henry Parry, 1610–1617). Cp. note on No. **185.**]

I fear not to say those men are but superstitiously curious, Right Reverend and Honourable, which would call back all circumstances to their first patterns. The Spouse of Christ hath been ever clothed with her own rites : and, as apparel, so religion hath her fashions, variable according to ages and places. To reduce us to the same observations which were in Apostolical use were no better than to tie us to the sandals of the disciples or seamless coat of Our Saviour. In these cases, they did what we need not ; and we may, what they did not. God meant us no bondage in their example. Their Canons bind us, whether for manners or doctrine ; not their Ceremonies.

Neither Christ nor His Apostles did all things for imitation. I speak not of miraculous acts. We need not be silent before a judge, as Christ was. We need not take a towel, and gird ourselves and wash our servants' feet, as Christ did. We need not make tents for our living, as Paul ; nor go armed, as Peter ; nor carry about our wives, as he and the other Apostles.

I acknowledge the ground, not only of Separation, but Anabaptism ; and wonder that these conceits do not answer themselves. Who can choose but see a manifest difference betwixt those laws, which Christ and His great ambassadors made for eternal use, and those ritual matters which were confined to place and time ? Every nation, every person sins, that observes not those. These, for the most part, are not kept of the most ; and are as well left without sin by us, as used without prescription or necessity by the authors.

### No. 248.  JOHN BRAMHALL

[From *The Consecration and Succession of Protestant Bishops Justified.* Chapter XI. *Works,* ed. L. A. C. T., Vol. III, p. 170, Cp. note on No. **164.**]

If Mr. Mason did commend the wisdom of the English Church for paring away superfluous ceremonies in Ordination, he did well. Ceremonies are advancements of order, decency, modesty, and gravity in the service of God, expressions of those heavenly desires and dispositions which we ought to bring along with us to God's House, adjuments of attention and devotion, furtherances of edification, visible instructors, helps of memory, exercises of faith, the shell that preserves the kernel of religion from contempt, the leaves that defend the blossoms and the fruit ; but if they grow over thick and rank, they hinder the fruit from coming to maturity, and then the gardener plucks them off. There is great difference between the hearty expressions of a faithful friend and the mimical gestures of a fawning flatterer ; between the unaffected comeliness of a grave matron, and the fantastical paintings and patchings and powderings of a garish courtesan. When ceremonies become burdensome by excessive superfluity, or unlawful ceremonies are obtruded, or the substance of Divine worship is placed in circumstances, or the service of God is more respected for human ornaments than for the Divine ordinance, it is high time to pare away excesses and reduce things to the ancient mean. These Fathers are quite out, where they make it lawful at some times to add, but never to pare away; yet we have pared away nothing which is either prescribed or practised by the true Catholic Church. If our ancestors have pared away any such things out of any mistake (which we do not believe), let it be made appear evidently to us, and we are more ready to welcome it again at the fore-door than our ancestors were to cast it out at the back-door. *Errare possumus, haeretici esse nolumus.*

### No. 249. WILLIAM BEVERIDGE

[From *Ecclesia Anglicana Ecclesia Catholica* [= On the Thirty-Nine Articles], on Article XXXIV. *Works*, ed. *L. A. C. T.*, Vol. VII, pp. 533 f. Cp. note on No. 52.]

That the Church in general hath power to decree Rites and Ceremonies, we have before proved, *Art.* XX; that the same power is granted to every national Church in particular, we have here asserted: and truly if the Church in general as a Church be acknowledged to have such a power, every particular Church, in that it is a Church also, cannot be denied it. So that as the Universal Church, gathered together in an Œcumenical Council, may ordain and decree Rites and Ceremonies to be observed, not only by particular, but by the Universal Church, so have all provincial or particular Churches power to decree Rites and Ceremonies for themselves, though not for the Universal Church, nor yet for other particular Churches. And therefore did our Reformers of ever blessed memory, giving the reasons why they abolished some Ceremonies and retained others, profess, saying, " In these our doings we condemn no other nations, nor prescribe any thing but to our own people only." But though any particular or provincial Church cannot prescribe ceremonies for other Churches, yet it may for itself; and if it may decree and ordain some, it must needs follow that it may also change and abolish others; and indeed it is often necessary it should do so, as in particular before our Reformation, when as our Reformers, in the place before cited, observe, " Ceremonies were so far abused, partly by the superstitious blindness of the rude and unlearned, and partly by the unsatiable avarice of such as sought more their own lucre than the glory of God, that the abuses could not well be taken away, the thing still remaining." So that it is often necessary, when Ceremonies are abused, not only to take off the abuses, but to abolish the Ceremonies. I say it is often, yet not always, so necessary; for in some Ceremonies the abuses may be so taken off as the Ceremonies may still be retained without the abuses. And in such cases, though it may seem better to abolish them, yet in St. Augustine's judgement it is better to retain them rather than to bring in new ones which at the first may seem to be preferred before them ; and the reason he gives is, " Because the change of a custom, though it may help by its utility, yet it hurts by its novelty." And this was the reason why in our Reformation some were still retained as well as others abolished.

## No. 250. WILLIAM SHERLOCK

[From *A Vindication of the Rights of Ecclesiastical Authority; Being an Answer to the First Part of "The Protestant Reconciler,"* London, 1685, pp. 52 f. In the year that Sherlock wrote this treatise he became Master of the Temple. *The Protestant Reconciler Humbly Pleading for Condescension to Dissenting Brethren in Things Indifferent and Unnecessary* was the title of a treatise written by Daniel Whitby under the anonym of " A Well Wisher to the Church's Peace." It came out in two separate parts, which appeared in 1682 and 1683 respectively. Whitby's plea for a measure of toleration provoked strong hostility, and the University of Oxford condemned his book in Convocation on July 21, 1683.]

The Apostle, it seems, thought it a piece of decency that their external garb and habit, when they worshipped God, should be proper and suitable to their state and condition ; [that it] should represent and signify the authority and government of the man, and the subjection of the woman.[1] And then I would fain know a reason why this is not decent for the Ministers of religion too, that they should perform the public offices of religion in such a distinct habit as may both signify the peculiarity of their function and that holiness and purity of mind, which becomes those who minister in holy things. A white linen garment has always been thought very proper for this purpose. The twenty four elders who sat about the Throne are represented as clothed in white linen garments ; nay, that great multitude who stood before the Throne and before the Lamb were clothed with white robes. Nay, this is one privilege which was granted to the wife of the Lamb, that she should be clothed with fine linen clean and white. Which I allege only for this purpose, to shew that a white linen garment is very proper for the ministries of religion, and very expressive both of the honour and purity of the ministerial function ; for otherwise it would not be represented as the habit of those elders who sat round the Throne, nor as the habit of the Lamb's Wife. For all these prophetical descriptions must borrow their figures and resemblances from earthly things. And if a white linen garment were not proper to signify the dignity and honour and holiness of such persons, it could not properly be used to represent and signify that in Heaven which it does not signify on earth. And if a white linen garment do very aptly signify both the honour and purity of such a function, and it be a piece of decency to use such habits in religious worship as are proper to the state, condition, or relation of the worshippers, we may certainly conclude that a surplice or a white linen garment is a very decent habit for the ministers of religion when they perform the public offices of religion.

[1] [Cp. *I Cor.* xi.]

# (5) CEREMONIAL IN PRACTICE

## No. 251.  LANCELOT ANDREWES

[This Form was first printed in 1854 in *Two Answers to Cardinal Perron, and Other Miscellaneous Works*, pp. 160–163, which constituted a volume of the *L. A. C. T.* edition of Andrewes' *Works*.  The original is said to be among the MS. collections of Henry Wharton in the Lambeth Library (MS. Lamb, 577, pp. 113–115), and a collation of it to be in MSS. Harl. No. 3795.  Art. 8.  The Form was used by Andrewes for the Consecration of the Communion Plate in Worcester Cathedral; but the circumstances which led him to perform this office are not recorded.  Apart from its intrinsic interest, the Form is noteworthy as an instance of the construction of a special form of service for an occasion not covered by the *Book of Common Prayer*.]

## THE ORDER OF CONSECRATING PLATE FOR THE ALTAR.

*The plate to be consecrated is placed upon a Table about the middle of the quire before the beginning of Divine Service.*

*Immediately after the Nicene Creed, and the Pronouncing of this sentence, " Let your light so shine before men, etc.," the Presenter of the plate being in his choral habit (if he be a Churchman) cometh forth, and standing by the said Table after obeisance first to God, and to the Bishop, saith :—*

*Presenter.*  Reverend Father in God, in the name of the Dean and Chapter of the Cathedral Church of Worcester, I humbly beseech your Lordship that some vessels prepared for the use of that Church here ready may be presented unto the Lord, and by your Sacred Office may receive an holy dedication unto godly Divine service.

*The Bishop.*  We are ready to do what you desire in a matter so well becoming them in whose name you come, and (as we assure ourselves) so acceptable unto God for the service of His Holy Church.  First therefore, let us begin with prayer.

O Eternal God, Lord of all power and·glory, prostrate here before Thy Throne of Grace, we beg Thy heavenly mercy, and humbly call upon Thee for Thy Divine acceptance.  Lord, bow down Thine ear and hear us.  Open, Lord, Thine eyes, and behold Thy poor servants, and have respect unto the supplications which, in full assurance of Thy Blessed Son's merits, we presume to make before Thee.  Take away the stony heart out of the midst of us, and give us hearts truly sensible of Thy Divine Majesty.  Let Thy Holy Spirit help our infirmities.  Lord, increase our faith, order our devotions, make us zealous for Thy glory, and give us to revive in the service of Thy most Blessed Name, through Jesus Christ our Lord.  Amen.

*The said Presenter taketh in his hands first the paten, and (after obeisance) cometh up to the Bishop standing before the midst of the Altar, and kneeling down saith :—*

I offer this unto Thee and Thy Holy Service, O Lord God Almighty.

*The Bishop receiveth them and turneth to set them on the Altar, his Chaplains standing on each side of the Altar in their formalities, and in the meantime saying alternatim :—*

*a.* He rained down manna on them for to eat, and gave them bread from Heaven.

*b.* So man did eat Angels' food, and He sent them meat enough.

*In the meanwhile the Presenter is ready again with the chalices covered, and kneeling down, saith,* (ut prius).

*Whiles the Bishop sets them on, the Chaplains pronounce :—*

*a.* That He may bring food out of the earth, and wine that maketh glad the heart of man.

*b.* We will be glad and rejoice in Thee : we will remember Thy love more than wine.

*The Presenter as before offereth the Flagons which, while the Bishop sets on, the Chaplains say :—*

*a.* They shall be satisfied with the plenteousness of Thy house, and Thou shalt give them drink of Thy pleasures as out of the river.

*b.* Eat, O friends, drink and be replenished, O beloved.

*The basin is offered next by the Presenter, which, when the Bishop hath taken, the Chaplains say :—*

*a.* An offering of a free heart will I give Thee and praise Thy name, O Lord, because it is so comfortable.

*b.* Let the freewill offering of my mouth please Thee, O Lord, and teach me Thy judgements.

*The Presenter bringeth the candlesticks, and the Bishop setteth them on ; the Chaplains say :—*

*a.* Thy Word is a lantern unto my feet, and a light unto my path.

*b.* For in Thee is the fountain of light, and in Thy light shall we see light.

*Lastly he bringeth the censer, which the Bishop likewise sets on, and the Chaplains say :—*

*a.* While the King sitteth at His Table, my spikenard sendeth out the smell thereof.

*b.* Let my prayer be set forth before Thee as the incense, and let the lifting up of my hands be as the evening sacrifice.

*Then the Bishop layeth his hands upon every piece again, and, standing, saith :—*

O Lord, Heavenly Father, we most meekly beseech Thee favourably to accept these holy offerings now presented unto Thee. Thine, O Lord, be all the glory in all our approaching unto Thee, ·the honour Thine alone in all our service of Thee. Grant, most gracious Lord, that what we have now faithfully offered unto Thee in the uprightness of our hearts, may be religiously preserved from all profane and secular uses, and may ever continue in that holy service whereunto they are now dedicated, through Jesus Christ our Lord. Amen.

### The Benediction.

We bless Thee, O Lord, for Thy blessings upon us, and for that it hath pleased Thee to put into the hearts of Thy humble servants to make these holy dedications unto Thy Divine Majesty. Look down, Lord, in mercy upon them, and bless them with the riches of Thy goodness. Bless them in their persons and in their substance, and in all that belongs unto them, or that they give their hands unto. And grant, we beseech Thee, that by the reverend and holy use of these offerings, Thy praise and glory may now and ever be set forth in Thy Church, and that Thy daily service may therein be performed in the beauty of holiness, as becometh so holy and glorious a God; through Jesus Christ our Lord. Amen.

*This done they proceed to read the other sentences for the ordinary offerings, and so go on with the rest of the Communion.*

### No. 252. LANCELOT ANDREWES

[From *Two Answers to Cardinal Perron. Minor Works*, ed. L. A. C. T., p. 25. Cp. note on No. 218.]

### *Mingling of Wine with Water in the Eucharist.*

St. Chrysostom against the *Hydroparastatae*, or *Aquarii*, seemeth to oppose it. We hold it a matter not worth the standing on ; so all else were agreed, we would not stick with them [*i.e.* the Roman Catholics] to put as much water in as the Priests use to do.

### No. 253. LANCELOT ANDREWES

[From *Notes on the Book of Common Prayer. Minor Works*, ed. L. A. C. T., pp. 156 f. These notes, derived ultimately from Andrewes' own copy of the Book of Common Prayer, were transcribed by a number of hands ; the original has been lost. They were reprinted in William Nicholls' *Comment on the Book of Common Prayer* (cp. note on No. 287). For a full account of these notes, see the *L. A. C. T.* edition, pp. 143 f. The following note is appended to the words in the Order for Holy Communion " The Priest, standing up, shall say the Prayer of Consecration,"—a position in the Rite surprising to those familiar with modern Eucharistic ceremonial.]

Here the priest, having made adoration, poureth water upon the napkin ready for that purpose and cleanseth his hands, mystice respiciens illud Psalmi, *Lavabo in innocentia manus meas, et sic introibo ad altare Dei, ut annuncièm vocem* εὐχαριστίας, *Ps.* xxvi, 6. Moraliter et decore, uti cum magnatibus accubituri sumus.

Postea panes e canistro in patinam ponit : dein vinum e doliolo, adinstar Sanguinis erumpentis, in calicem haurit : tum aquam e triconali scypho immiscet; postremo omnibus rite, et quam fieri potest decentissime atque aptissime compositis, stans pergit et peragit.

In rariore solennitate hic pergit Episcopus et consecrat.

## No. 254. PETER SMART

[From *The Vanity and Downfall of Superstitious Popish Ceremonies; Or a Sermon preached in the Cathedral Church of Durham by one Mr. Peter Smart, a Prebend there, July 27, 1628; Containing not only an historical Relation of all those several Popish Ceremonies and Practices which Mr. John Cosens hath lately brought into the said Cathedral Church; But likewise a Punctual Confutation of them, Especially of erecting Altars and Cringing to them* (a Practice much in Use of late) *and of praying towards the East.* Edinburgh, 1628. The following " Narration " is the Introduction to this work. Appropriately to the occasion of it, the text of the sermon was *Psalm* xxxi, 6. It appears to have been issued originally without the Introduction. The very day on which the sermon was preached proceedings were initiated against him by the High Commission of the Province of York. He was suspended on September 2, 1628. The case was transferred to the High Commission of Canterbury, but ultimately referred back to that of York; and Smart in 1631 was deposed, degraded, and fined £500.]

*A brief but true historical Narration of some notorious Acts and Speeches of Mr. John Cosens and some other of his Companions, Contracted into Articles.*

We doubt not but the world hath heard of Mr. John Cosens his speculative and theorical Popery, which he hath audaciously broached in his *Book of Private Devotions, or The Hours of Prayer*, which book one Mr. Burton, a zealous minister, and Mr. Prynne, a private gentleman, have largely answered, though we hear they were but ill rewarded for their pains; both of them being troubled for these their orthodox books by your High Commissioners, who strain, it seems, at harmless gnats, yet swallow camels. We have therefore thought it our bounden duty as to publish this worthy sermon, so to inform the world in particular how this Cosens hath turned these his Popish theories and speculations into practice.

*Inprimis*, the said Mr. Cosens hath uttered these traitorous speeches in an open and affirmative manner: That the King's Highness is no more Supreme Head of the Church of England, than the boy that rubs his horse's heels (a coarse comparison for a loyal subject), and this as we are credibly informed hath been proved against him by the oaths of two sufficient witnesses.

Secondly, this Cosens in a sermon of his upon the Parable of the Tares uttered these Popish and Anti-Christian speeches: That the Reformers of our Church, when they took away the Mass, they took away all religion, and the whole service of God; [that] they called it a Reformation, but it was indeed a Deformation. He likewise said to one that swore by the Mass, in a frowning manner: That he wist not what he said; and that he sware by a better thing than he was aware of; the Mass is a good thing and a good word. The author of this sermon telling him upon occasion the Mass is disallowed, he replied roundly

" Will you deny that our service is a Mass ? " These are his speeches. Now behold his actions.

Thirdly, this Cosens hath set up 50 glittering Angels round about the choir of Durham Church, in long scarlet gowns, with golden wings and gilded heads, together with three other images over the Bishop's Throne, one of them being the image of Christ, with a golden beard, a glorious blue cap with rays like the sun's beams : which betokens in the Pope's School some deity in the head which it covereth, if it might be known to be an extraordinary idol to be worshipped, as this image hath been by some Popish people which came to see it.

Fourthly, on Candlemas Day last past Mr. Cosens, in renewing that Popish ceremony of burning candles to the honour of Our Lady, busied himself from two of the clock in the afternoon till four in climbing long ladders to stick up wax candles in the said Cathedral Church. The number of all the candles burnt that evening was 220, besides 16 torches, 60 of those burning tapers and torches standing upon and near the High Altar (as he calls it), where no man came nigh.

Fifthly, he hath brought in a new custom of bowing the body down to the ground before the Altar (on which he hath set Candlesticks, Basons, and Crosses, Crucifixes and Tapers which stand there for a dumb show) ; he hath taught and enjoined all such as come near the Altar to cringe and bow unto it ; he hath commanded the choristers to make low legs unto it, when they go to light the tapers that are on it in the winter nights ; and in their return from it, he hath enjoined them to make low legs unto it again, going backwards with their faces towards the East, till they are out of the inclosure where they stand.

Sixthly, he enjoins all them that come to the Cathedral Church to pray with their faces towards the East, scolding and brawling with them, even in time of Divine Service, which refuse to do it, and bidding them either to pray towards the East, or to be packing out of the Church. Himself hath praying and reading, his face always turned towards the East. When he ministers the Sacrament, he stands at the West side of the Altar (as he terms and makes it), not at the North as the Common Prayer Book enjoins him : that so his face may be East and his backward parts to the people's faces, who can neither hear nor understand him. He hath removed the reader's ancient desk and pew, together with all the seats and the Dean's pew which stood on the East side of the Church, to the West side, that so their faces might stand Eastward. He sends the vergerers about the Church to remove all those, both strangers and others, which sit down with their backs to the East. So devoted is he to this Eastern superstition.

Seventhly, he hath divided the Morning Service into two parts ; the six of clock service, which was used to be read only and not sung, he chants with organs, sackbuts, and cornets which yield an hideous noise, and makes that service which was scarce one quarter of an hour long before, one hour and a half at least,—and this he calls Mattins. The second service at ten of the clock he calls Mass, which consists of Epistles and Gospels, the Ten Commandments and the Nicene Creed, which are only to be read on Sundays and Holy days, by the Order in the Common Prayer Book.

Eighthly, he enjoins all the people to stand up at the Nicene Creed (a ceremony which your Church enjoins not), which he commands to be sung with organs, sackbuts and cornets and all other instruments of music, which were used at the Consecration of Nabuchadonozer's golden image (unfit instruments for Christian Churches, where men come for to pray and not for to chant or hear a sound or consort [= concert] of they know not what). Each who refuse to stand during this musical cries (sic) (which lasts for half an hour) Mr. Cosens himself hath gone and raised them up during Divine Service, to the great disturbance of all there present, bidding them to depart out of the Church, and nailing up their pew-doors in despite of the Dean and other Prebends, that so they might not come into their seats.

Ninthly, he hath turned most of the Service into piping and singing, so that the people understand it not, no more than they do Greek or Hebrew. He hath brought mere ballads and jigs into the Church, and commanded them to be sung for anthems; and among many other, the three Kings of Colen [= Cologne],—Jasper, Melchior and Balthaser. He will not suffer so much as the Holy Communion to be administered without an hideous noise of vocal and instrumental music (the tunes whereof are all taken out of the Mass-books), whereby the people's minds are wholly withdrawn from the holy duty which they are about, and from the meditation of Christ's bitter Death and Passion. On the Fast Day after Easter last, he commanded the last prayer at the end of the Communion to be sung with the organ as an anthem so that no man could understand one word, in so much that the people rising up and sitting when it began to be sung, Mr. Cosens called to them that sat near about them, saying, " You must kneel, you must kneel, it is a prayer." Then all the congregation kneeled down and prayed very devoutly they knew not what. It was the fondest Fast that ever any man saw, it being rather a triumph than any fast or humiliation.

Tenthly, he hath brought divers old copes which have been used in May-games heretofore, one of them having the picture of the Trinity embroidered upon it, and these copes he would enjoin the prebends constantly to wear.

Eleventhly, he hath employed divers Recusant Papists (and such only) in making of wax candles, Crucifixes, and glass windows, in gilding and painting of Images and the Altar, fit workmen for such idolatrous works, and incite (sic) instruments to revive and set up Popery once again.

Twelfthly, he hath violently enforced the observation of those ceremonies, going about the Church like a madman, thrusting some out by the head and shoulders, calling them pagans when they stood quietly hearing service and refusing to observe his Popish ceremonies. He hath likewise gone about the Altar (for so he calls it) before the Communion, crossing the cushions, kissing the Altar cloths, and smacking them with his lips; in so much as some seeing him so ridiculously occupied, said one to another: " Look! Look! Is not the man mad? Look I pray, is he not mad? "

These and sundry other Popish innovations hath Mr. Cosens brought into the Church of Durham. And now see their fruits. One, Mr. Francis Burgonie [*sic*, = Burgoine [1]], Parson of Wearmouth, following Mr. Cosens his practices, hath taken away the Communion Table out of his Parish Church, and instead thereof hath erected an Altar in the East End of the Chancel, made of a gravestone. This stone he hath laid upon a wall, not on a frame. He hath adorned it with gilded hangings round about it, contrary to the Communion Book. This Altar he worshippeth with the bowing of his knees unto it; and there both he and his curate read part of the service, so that most of the people on both sides can neither hear nor see them. This example of Mr. Burgonie, many Parish Churches else are reported to follow, to the great offence of religious people, the great advancement of Popery and superstition, which are like to overthrow the whole Bishopric of Durham if they are not in time suppressed; in so much that the Papists of Durham say openly " The Protestants need not labour to bring us to them, for they are coming apace to us." Thus, thus, alas *Grex totus in agris unius scabie cadit*. Our prayer, our desire, therefore, to this present Assembly of Parliament is but this: *Pereat unus ne pereamus omnes.* Let Mr. Cosens with all his great abettors and disciples rather perish with their Pardons (which we hear his potent Bishop patron, who should have rather procured them an helter [= halter] than a pardon, had he any spark of love to your religion in him, hath of late procured), than that both you and we, with both our States and Churches, should perish by their Pardons, which can never expiate nor disannul these great offences.

[1] [On him, see *Bishop Cosin's Correspondence, etc.*, Vol. I (Surtees Soc. for 1868), p. 73 n.]

# (6) RELICS AND SUPERSTITIONS

## No. 255. JEREMY TAYLOR

[From *A Dissuasive from Popery, Part I.* Chapter ii, § 10. (" Roman Sacramentals.") *Works*, ed. R. Heber, Vol. X, pp. 239–241 (ed. C. P. Eden, Vol. VI, pp. 267 f. [§ 11]). Cp. note on No. 260.]

To put our trust and confidence in God only and to use ministries of His own appointment and sanctification, is so essential a duty owing by us to God, that whoever trusts in any thing but God is a breaker of the First Commandment; and he that invents instrumental supports of his own head and puts a subordinate ministerial confidence in them, usurps the rights of God, and does not pursue the interests of true religion, whose very essence and formality is to glorify God in all His attributes and to do good to man and to advance the honour and Kingdom of Christ. Now how greatly the Church of Rome prevaricates in this great soul of religion appears by too evident and notorious demonstration: for she hath invented sacramentals of her own, without a Divine warrant. Δεῖ γάρ, περὶ τῶν θείων καὶ ἁγίων τῆς πίστεως μυστηρίων, μηδὲν τὸ τυχὸν ἄνευ τῶν θείων παραδίδοσθαι γραφῶν, said St. Cyril, " Concerning the Holy and Divine Mysteries of faith or religion, we ought to do nothing by chance, or of our own heads, nothing without the authority of the Divine Scriptures." But the Church of Rome does otherwise; invents things of her own, and imputes spiritual effects to these sacramentals; and promises not only temporal blessings and immunities and benedictions, but the collation or increment of spiritual graces, and remission of venial sins, and alleviation of pains due to mortal sins, to them who shall use these sacramentals; which because God did not institute, and did not sanctify, they use them without faith, and rely upon them without a promise, and make themselves the fountains of these graces, and produce confidences, whose last resort is not upon God, Who neither was the author, nor is an approver of them.

Of this nature are holy water, the paschal wax, oil, palm-boughs, holy bread (not eucharistical), Agnus Dei's, medals, swords, bells, and roses hallowed upon the Sunday called *Laetare Jerusalem* such as Pope Pius II. sent to James II. of Scotland, and Sixtus Quintus to the Prince of Parma; concerning which their doctrine is this, that the Blood of Christ is by these applied unto us, that they do not only signify but produce spiritual effects, that they blot out venial sins, that they drive

away devils, that they cure diseases, and that though these things do not
operate infallibly, as do the Sacraments, and that God hath made no
express covenant concerning them, yet by the devotion of them that
use them and the prayers of the Church they do prevail.

Now though it be easy to say, and it is notoriously true in Theology,
that the prayers of the Church can never prevail but according to the
grace which God has promised ; and either can only procure a blessing
upon natural things, in order to their natural effects, or else an extraordinary supernatural effect, by virtue of a Divine promise ; and that
these things are pretended to work beyond their natural force, and yet
God hath not promised to them a supernatural blessing, as themselves
confess ; yet besides the falseness of the doctrine, on which these
superstitions do rely, it is also as evident, that these instrumentalities
produce an affiance and confidence in the creature and estrange men's
hearts from the true religion and trust in God, while they think themselves blessed in their own inventions, and in digging to themselves
cisterns of their own, and leaving the fountain of blessing and eternal life.

To this purpose the Roman priests abuse the people with romantic
stories out of the Dialogues of St. Gregory and Venerable Bede, making
them believe that St. Fortunatus cured a man's broken thigh with holy
water, and that St. Malachias, the Bishop of Down and Connor, cured a
madman with the same medicine ; and that St. Hilarion cured many sick
persons with holy bread and oil (which indeed is the most likely of them
all, as being good food and good medicine).   And although not so much
as a chicken is now-a-days cured of the pip by holy water, yet upon all
occasions they use it, and the common people throw it upon children's
cradles and sick cows' horns and upon them that are blasted ; and if
they recover by any means, it is imputed to the holy water.   And so the
simplicity of Christian Religion, the glory of our dependence on God, the
wise order and economy of blessings in the Gospel, the sacredness and
mysteriousness of Sacraments and Divine institutions, are disordered
and dishonoured ; the Bishops and Priests inventing both the word
and the element, institute a kind of Sacrament, in great derogation to
the supreme prerogative of Christ ; and men are taught to go in ways
which superstition hath invented, and interest does support.

## No. 256.  JOSEPH HALL

[From *Sacred Polemics, Part the First.   No Peace with Rome*, Chapter III, Section
iii (II, 3).   *Works*, ed. Peter Hall (1837), Vol. XI, pp. 368, 370 (Latin Text, pp. 369,
371).   Cp. note on No. **305**.]

We honour, as we ought, the dear and happy memory of the Saints,
and chiefly the leader of that heavenly choir, the Blessed Virgin, " the
Mother of God " : and whatsoever she can think not too dishonourable
to herself and her Lord and Saviour, we will most gladly give it her to
the full.

Neither will we only glorify God in His Saints, as Augustine hath taught Durand to speak ; but we will magnify the Saints, as opportunity serves, for their excellent graces and worthy acts, both in God and in themselves. We will admire, extol, and, what we may, imitate their singular constancy, faith, sanctity ; as Sidonius said of his Claudian,

> " No tomb can either soul or glory shroud."

But to dig up their holy bones, that I may borrow Luther's word, out of their quiet graves and to fall down before these worm-eaten monuments of the Saints, to expect from them a divine power, whether of cure or of sanctification, equally to respect Francis's cowl, Anna's comb, Joseph's breeches, Thomas's shoe, as Erasmus complains, with the Son of God Himself, can seem no better to us than a horrible impiety.

Neither can we abide, either to deify men or to canonize beasts. It seems that Cardinal could abide it well in whose garden is yet to be seen this epitaph which he wrote upon his too-dearly-beloved bitch :

> " This tomb for thee, dear bitch, I builded have,
> " That worthier wert of heaven, than a grave."

## No. 257.  JEREMY TAYLOR

[From *A Dissuasive from Popery, Part I*, Chapter i, § 9 (" Of Picturing God and the Trinity "). *Works*, ed. R. Heber, Vol. X, pp. 175–177 (ed. C. P. Eden, Vol. VI, pp. 217 f.)  Cp. note on No. 260.]

We greatly reprove the custom of the Church of Rome in picturing God the Father and the Most Holy and Undivided Trinity ; which, besides that it ministers infinite scandal to all sober-minded men and gives the new Arians in Polonia and Anti-Trinitarians great and ridiculous entertainment, exposing that Sacred Mystery to derision and scandalous contempt, it is also (which at present we have undertaken particularly to remark) against the doctrine and practice of the primitive Catholic Church.

St. Clemens of Alexandria says, " In the discipline of Moses, God was not to be represented in the shape of a man or of any other thing " ; and that Christians understood themselves to be bound by the same law, we find it expressly taught by Origen, Tertullian, Eusebius, Athanasius, St. Jerome, St. Austin, St. Theodoret, Damascene, and the Synod of Constantinople as is reported in the sixth action of the Second Nicene Council. And certainly, if there were not a strange spirit of contradiction or superstition or deflection from the Christian rule greatly prevailing in the Church of Rome, it were impossible that this practice should be so countenanced by them, and defended so to no purpose with so much scandal and against the natural reason of mankind and the very law of nature itself; for the heathens were sufficiently, by the light of nature, taught to abominate all pictures or images of God.

*Sed nulla effigies, simulacraque nota Deorum*
*Majestate locum et sacro implevere timore.*

They, in their earliest ages, had " no pictures, no images of their gods; their temples were filled with majesty and a sacred fear." And the reason is given by Macrobius : " Antiquity made no image," viz. of God; " because the Supreme God, and the Mind that is born of Him," that is His Son, the Eternal Word, " as it is beyond the soul, so it is above nature, and therefore it is not lawful that figments should come thither."

Nicephorus Callistus, relating the heresy of the Armenians and Jacobites, says they made images of the Father, Son, and Holy Ghost. " *Quod perquam absurdum est.*" " Nothing is more absurd " than to make pictures or images of the persons of the Holy and Adorable Trinity. And yet they do this in the Church of Rome. For in the windows of their churches, even in country villages, where the danger cannot be denied to be great and the scandal insupportable, nay, in their books of devotion, in their very Mass-books and Breviaries, in their Portuises and Manuals, they picture the Holy Trinity with three noses, and four eyes, and three faces, in a knot, to the great dishonour of God and scandal of Christianity itself. We add no more (for the case is too evidently bad), but reprove the error with the words of their own Polydore Virgil : " Since the world began, never was anything more foolish than to picture God, Who is present every where."

## No. 258. WILLIAM WAKE

[From *An Exposition of the Doctrine of the Church of England in the Several Articles proposed by Monsieur de Meaux, Late Bishop of Condom* [i.e. J. B. Bossuet], *In his " Exposition of the Doctrine of the Catholic Church,"* Article IV (" Of Images and Relics "), London, 1686, pp. 17 f. Bossuet's *Exposition de la Foi Catholique* (in MS.) claimed to have brought about Turenne's adhesion to the Catholic Church in 1668. Some circumstances connected with the publication of this treatise in 1671 were revealed by Wake in his Preface. Bossuet, having issued a draft of his manual in that year, sent it to the Sorbonne for their approval. They expressed themselves very critically of some of its contents ; and in consequence such copies as had been printed were suppressed as far as possible, though Wake had access to a copy of this edition. A revision of Bossuet's original composition was produced in the same year, purporting to be the " first " impression.
Wake's *Exposition* drew the author into an extended controversy. He wrote a *Defence of the Exposition*, also in 1686 ; and a *Second Defence of the Exposition*, in two parts, in 1687.]

When therefore all these abuses which we have named, and which Monsieur de Meaux seems content to allow with us to be such, shall be corrected ; When in the matter of Images, 1. The Hymns and Addresses that teach us, so contrary to the Spirit of Christianity, to demand graces of them and to put our trust in them shall be reformed, St. Thomas and his abettors censured, and all other marks of an unwarrantable Worship be forbidden ; 2. When the Pictures of God the Father, and of the Holy Trinity, so directly contrary both to the Second Commandment and to St. Paul's doctrine, shall be taken away, and those of Our Saviour and the Blessed Saints be by all necessary cautions rendered truly the books, not snares of the ignorant ; When in points of Relics, 3. they shall be declared to have no sanctifying value in them ; 4. Nor that they ought to be sought to for any assistance spiritual or temporal to be expected from them ; 5. When it shall be resolved to be no matter of merit to go to visit them ; 6. Nor any more extravagant Indulgences to be set forth for Pilgrimages unto them ; When all these things which Monsieur de Meaux passes over, and which yet are undeniably their practice and our scandal, shall be corrected, then will we both believe and submit to the rest which he desires of us.  We will honour the Relics of the Saints as the Primitive Church did.  We will respect the Images of Our Saviour and the Blessed Virgin.  And, as some of us now bow towards the Altar, and all of us are enjoined to do so at the name of the Lord Jesus, so will we not fail to testify all due respect to His Representation.  In the meantime, if the outcries of their own Church at these abuses cannot prevail with them to redress them, yet at least they will confirm us in the reformation we have made of them. And whilst we find Hezekiah commended in the Holy Scripture for destroying the brazen serpent, though made by God's express command, and in some sort deservedly honourable for that great deliverance it brought to the Jews, *Because the children of Israel offered incense unto it,* we shall conclude ourselves to be by so much the more justifiable in that the Images we have removed were due only to the folly and superstition of men, and have been more scandalously abused to a worser and greater dishonour of God.

# (7) INDULGENCES

## No. 259. FRANCIS WHITE

[From *A Reply to Jesuit Fisher's Answer*, p. 534. Cp. note on No. **228**.]

To the constitution of Pope's Pardons, three things are required by the Papals and rejected by us. First, superfluous and redundant satisfactions of Saints ; Secondly, a vast treasury in the Church Militant to receive and contain the same ; Thirdly, an eminent authority and power in the Popes and Prelates of the Roman Church to communicate and apply the same to the living and defunct. Protestants deny that any member of this doctrine is Catholic and Orthodoxal, or that the Holy Apostles or Primitive Church maintained the same by teaching or practice. We affirm also that the said doctrine is novel and devised by Roman prelates for filthy lucre.

## No. 260. JEREMY TAYLOR

[From *A Dissuasive from Popery to the People of Ireland, Part I*, Chapter i, § 3 (" On the Roman Doctrine of Indulgences "). *Works*, ed. R. Heber, Vol. X, pp. 138–145 (ed. C. P. Eden, Vol. VI, pp. 188–193). Taylor wrote this treatise after he became Bishop of Down, Connor, and Dromore, whereby he was brought into immediate relationship with Roman Catholicism in Ireland. It was published in 1664. Not unnaturally, it provoked several replies, with which Taylor dealt in a second Part of the Treatise. Cp. note on No. **50**.]

The Roman doctrine of Indulgences was the first occasion of the great change and Reformation of the Western Churches begun by the preachings of Martin Luther and others. And besides that it grew to that intolerable abuse that it became a shame to itself and a reproach to Christendom, it was also so very an innovation that their great Antoninus confesses that " concerning them we have nothing expressly, either in the Scriptures or in the sayings of the ancient Doctors ; " and the same is affirmed by Sylvester Prierias. Bishop Fisher, of Rochester, says that in the beginning of the Church there was no use of Indulgences, and that they began after the people were awhile affrighted with the torments of purgatory ; and many of the Schoolmen confess that the use of indulgences began in the time of Pope Alexander III. towards the end of the Twelfth Century. But Agrippa imputes the beginning of them to Boniface VIII. who lived in the reign of King Edward I. of England, one thousand three hundred years after Christ. But that in his time the first Jubilee was kept, we are assured by Crantzius. This Pope lived and died with great infamy, and therefore was not likely from himself to transfer much honour and reputation to the new institution. But that about this time indulgences began, is more than probable; much before, it is certain they were not. For, in the whole Canon Law written by Gratian and in the *Sentences* of Peter Lombard, there is nothing spoken of Indulgences. Now because they lived in the time of Pope Alexander III., if he had introduced them, and much rather if they had been as ancient as St. Gregory (as some vainly and weakly pretend, from no greater authority than their own legends), it is probable that these great men, writing bodies of divinity and law, would have made mention of so considerable a point and so great a part of the Roman religion as things are now ordered. If they had been doctrines of the Church then, as they are now, it is certain they must have come under their cognizance and discourses.

Now lest the Roman emissaries should deceive any of the good sons of the Church, we think fit to acquaint them that in the Primitive Church, when the Bishops imposed severe penances, and that they were almost quite performed, and a great cause of pity intervened, or danger of death, or an excellent repentance, or that the martyrs interceded, the Bishop did sometimes indulge the penitent, and relax some of the remaining parts of his penance; and according to the example of St. Paul in the case of the incestuous Corinthian, gave them ease *lest they should be swallowed up with too much sorrow.* But the Roman doctrine of Indulgences is wholly another thing; nothing of it but the abused name remains. For in the Church of Rome they now pretend that there is an infinite of degrees of Christ's merits and satisfaction beyond what is necessary for the salvation of His servants: and (for fear Christ should not have enough) the Saints have a surplusage of merits, or at least of satisfactions,—more than they can spend, or themselves do need; and out of these the Church hath made her a treasure, a kind of poor man's box; and out of this, a power to take as much as they list, to apply to the poor souls in purgatory; who, because they did not satisfy for their venial sins, or perform all their penances which were imposed, or which might have been imposed, and which were due to be paid to God for the temporal pains reserved upon them, after He had forgiven them the guilt of their deadly sins, are forced sadly to roar in pains not inferior to the pains of Hell, excepting only that they are not eternal. That this is the true state of their article of indulgences, we appeal to Bellarmine.

Now, concerning their new foundation of Indulgences, the first stone of it was laid by Pope Clement VI. in his Extravagant, *Unigenitus de poenitentiis et remissionibus*, A.D. 1350. This constitution was published fifty years after the First Jubilee, and was a new device to bring in customers to Rome at the Second Jubilee, which was kept in Rome in this Pope's time. What ends of profit and interest it served, we are not much concerned to inquire. But this we know, that it had not yet passed into a Catholic doctrine, for it was disputed against by Franciscus de Mayronis and Durandus, not long before this Extravagant; and that it was not rightly formed to their purposes till the stirs in Germany raised upon the occasion of Indulgences made Leo X. set his clerks on work to study the point, and make something of it.

But as to the thing itself. It is so wholly new, so merely devised and forged by themselves, so newly created out of nothing, from great mistakes of Scripture and dreams of shadows from Antiquity, that we are to admonish our charges that they cannot reasonably expect many sayings of the primitive doctors against them, any more than against the new fancies of the Quakers, which were born but yesterday. That which is not cannot be numbered; and that which was not could not be confuted. But the perfect silence of Antiquity in this whole matter is an abundant demonstration that this new nothing was made in the later laboratories of Rome. For, as Durandus said, the Holy Fathers, Ambrose, Hilary, Jerome, Austin, speak nothing of Indulgences. And whereas it is said that St. Gregory, six hundred years after Christ, gave Indulgences at Rome in the stations, Magister Angularis, who lived about two hundred since, says he " never read of any such any where ; " and it is certain there is no such thing in the writings of St. Gregory, nor in any history of that age, nor any other that is authentic ; and we could never see any history pretended for it by the Roman writers, but a legend of Ledgerus brought to us the other day by Surius, which is so ridiculous and weak that even their own parties dare not avow it as a true story ; and therefore they are fain to make use of Thomas Aquinas upon the *Sentences*, and *Altisiodorensis*, for story and record. And it were strange that if the power of giving Indulgences to take off the punishment, reserved by God after the sin is pardoned, were given by Christ to His Church, that no one of the ancient doctors should tell any thing of it : insomuch that there is no one writer of authority and credit, not the more ancient doctors we have named nor those who were much later, Rupertus Tuitiensis, Anselm, or St. Bernard, ever took notice of it ; but it was a doctrine wholly unknown to the Church for about one thousand two hundred years after Christ : and Cardinal Cajetan told Pope Adrian VI. that to him that readeth the Decretals, it plainly appears that " an Indulgence is nothing else but an absolution from that penance which the confessor hath imposed " ; and therefore can be nothing of that which is now-a-days pretended.

True it is that the canonical penances were, about the time of Burchard, lessened and altered by commutations ; and the ancient discipline of the Church, in imposing penances, was made so loose, that the Indulgence was more than the imposition, and began not to be an act of mercy, but remissness and absolution without amends. It became a trumpet and a levy for the Holy War in Pope Urban II's. time, for he gave a Plenary Indulgence and remission of all sins to them that should go and fight against the Saracens.   And yet no man could tell how much they were the better for these Indulgences ;   for concerning the value of Indulgences, the complaint is both old and doubtful, said Pope Adrian, and he cites a famous gloss, which tells of four opinions all Catholic and yet vastly differing in this particular.   But the *Summa Angelica* reckons seven opinions concerning what that penalty is which is taken off by Indulgences.   No man could tell then, and the point was but in the infancy ;   and since that, they have made it what they please.   But it is at last turned into a doctrine, and they have devised new propositions, as well as they can, to make sense of it.   And yet it is a very strange thing, a Solution not an Absolution (it is the distinction of Bellarmine) ;   that is, the sinner is let to go free without punishment in this world or in the world to come ;   and in the end, it grew to be that which Christendom could not suffer, a heap of doctrines without grounds of Scripture or Catholic Tradition.   And not only so, but they have introduced a way of remitting sins, that Christ and His Apostles taught not, a way destructive to the repentance and remission of sins, which was preached in the name of Jesus.   It brought into the Church false and fantastic hopes, *a hope that will make men ashamed*, a hope that does not glorify the merits and perfect satisfaction of Christ ;   a doctrine expressly dishonourable to the full and free pardon given us by God through Jesus Christ ;   a practice that supposes a new bunch of keys given to the Church besides that which the Apostles received to open and shut the Kingdom of Heaven ;   a doctrine that introduces pride amongst the Saints and advances the opinion of their works beyond the measures of Christ, Who taught us that *when we have done all that is commanded, we are unprofitable servants*, and therefore certainly cannot supererogate, or do more than what is infinitely recompensed by the Kingdom of Glory, to which all our doings and all our sufferings are not worthy to be compared ;   especially since the greatest Saint cannot but say with David, *Enter not into judgement with Thy servant ; for in Thy sight no flesh living can be justified.*   It is a practice that hath turned penances into a fair, and the court of conscience into a lombard, and the labours of love into the labours of pilgrimages,—superstitious and useless wanderings from place to place,—and religion into vanity, and our hope in God to a confidence in man, and our fears of Hell to be a mere scarecrow to rich and confident sinners.   And at last it was frugally employed by a great Pope to raise a portion for a lady, the wife of Franceschetto Cibo, bastard son of pope Innocent VIII. ;   and the merchandise itself became the stakes of gamesters at dice and cards, and men did vile actions that they might win Indulgences,—by gaming, making their way to heaven easier.

Now although the Holy Fathers of the Church could not be supposed, in direct terms, to speak against this new doctrine of Indulgences, because in their days it was not ; yet they have said many things, which do perfectly destroy this new doctrine and these unchristian practices. For besides that they teach repentance wholly reducing us to a good life ; a faith that entirely relies upon Christ's merits and satisfactions ; a hope wholly depending upon the plain promises of the Gospel ; a service perfectly consisting in the works of a good conscience ; a labour of love ; a religion of justice and piety and moral virtues ; they do also expressly teach that pilgrimages to holy places and such like inventions, which are now the earnings and price of Indulgences, are not required of us, and are not the way of salvation, as is to be seen in an Oration made by St. Gregory Nyssen, wholly against pilgrimages to Jerusalem, in St. Chrysostom, St. Austin, and St. Bernard. The sense of these Fathers is this, in the words of St. Austin : " God said not, Go to the East, and seek righteousness ; sail to the West, that you may receive Indulgence. But indulge thy brother, and it shall be indulged to thee. You have need to inquire for no other indulgence to thy sins. If thou wilt retire into the closet of thy heart, there thou shalt find it." That is, all our hope of indulgence is from God through Jesus Christ, and is wholly to be obtained by faith in Christ, and perseverance in good works, and entire mortification of all our sins.

To conclude this particular : Though the gains which the Church of Rome makes of Indulgences be a heap almost as great as the abuses themselves, yet the greatest patrons of this new doctrine could never give any certainty or reasonable comfort to the conscience of any person that could inquire into it. They never durst determine whether they were absolutions or compensations ; whether they only take off the penances actually imposed by the confessor, or potentially, and all that which might have been imposed ; whether all that may be in the court of men, or all that can or will be required by the laws and severity of God. Neither can they speak rationally to the great question, Whether the treasure of the Church consists of the satisfactions of Christ only, or of the Saints ?—For if of Saints, it will by all men be acknowledged to be a defeasible estate and, being finite and limited, will be spent sooner than the needs of the Church can be served ; and if, therefore, it be necessary to add the merits and satisfaction of Christ, since they are an ocean of infinity and can supply more than all our needs, to what purpose is it to add the little minutes and droppings of the Saints ? They cannot tell whether they may be given, if the receiver do nothing or give nothing for them. And although this last particular could better be resolved by the Court of Rome than by the Church of Rome, yet all the doctrines, which built up the new fabric of Indulgences were so dangerous to determine, so improbable, so unreasonable, or, at best, so uncertain and invidious, that, according to the advice of the

Bishop of Modena, the Council of Trent left all the doctrines and all the cases of conscience quite alone, and slubbered the whole matter both in the question of Indulgences and Purgatory in general and recommendatory terms ; affirming, that the power of giving Indulgence is in the Church, and that the use is wholesome ; and that all hard and subtle questions, viz. concerning Purgatory, which although (if it be at all) it is a fire, yet it is the fuel of Indulgences, and maintains them wholly, all that is suspected to be false, and all that is uncertain, and whatsoever is curious and superstitious, scandalous, or for filthy lucre, be laid aside.  And in the mean time, they tell us not what is, and what is not, superstitious, nor what is scandalous, nor what they mean by the general term of " Indulgence " ;  and they establish no doctrine, neither curious nor incurious ;  nor durst they decree the very foundation of this whole matter, the Church's treasure ; neither durst they meddle with it, but left it as they found it and continued in the abuses and proceeded in the practice and set their doctors, as well as they can, to defend all the new and curious and scandalous questions, and to uphold the gainful trade.  But however it be with them, the doctrine itself is proved to be a direct innovation in the matter of Christian Religion ;  and that was it, which we have undertaken to demonstrate.

# (8) SUNDAY OBSERVANCE

## No. 261. "THE DECLARATION ON SPORTS"

[The *King's Majesty's Declaration to His Subjects Concerning Lawful Sports to be used.* E. Cardwell, *Documentary Annals of the Reformed Church of England*, Vol. II, pp. 188–193. This, the so-called "Book of Sports," was first issued by James I in 1618 and republished with the additions at the beginning and end reprinted here by Charles I in 1633. Its republication created fierce resentment among the Puritanically minded. On the Declaration, cp. Max Levy, *Der Sabbath in England. Wesen and Entwicklung des englischen Sontags* (Leipsig, 1933), pp, 211–223.]

### By the King.

OUR dear Father of blessed memory, in His return from Scotland coming through Lancashire, found that His subjects were debarred from lawful recreations upon Sundays after evening prayers ended, and upon Holy Days ; and he prudently considered, that if these times were taken from them, the meaner sort who labour hard all the week should have no recreations at all to refresh their spirits. And after His return He further saw that His loyal subjects in all other parts of the Kingdom did suffer in the same kind, though perhaps not in the same degree, and did therefore in His Princely Wisdom publish a Declaration to all His loving subjects concerning lawful sports to be used at such times, which was printed and published by His Royal Commandment in the year MDCXVIII in the tenour which hereafter followeth :

### By the King.

Whereas upon Our Return the last year out of Scotland we did publish Our Pleasure touching the recreations of Our People in those parts under Our Hand, for some causes us thereunto moving We have thought good to command these Our Directions, then given in Lancashire with a few words thereunto added, and most applicable to these parts of the realms, to be published to all Our Subjects.

Whereas We did justly in Our Progress through Lancashire rebuke some Puritans and precise people, and took order that the like unlawful carriage should not be used by any of them hereafter, in the prohibiting and unlawful punishing of Our good People for using their lawful recreations and honest exercises upon Sundays and other Holidays after the afternoon sermon or service, We now find that two sorts of people, wherewith that country is much infected (we mean Papists and Puritans) have maliciously traduced and calumniated those Our Just and Honourable Proceedings. And therefore, lest Our Reputation might upon the one side (though innocently) have some aspersion laid upon it, and that upon the other part Our Good People in that country be misled by the mistaking and misrepresentation of Our Meaning, We have therefore thought good hereby to clear and make Our Pleasure to be manifested to all Our Good People in those parts.

It is true, that at Our First Entry to this Crown and Kingdom we were informed, and that too truly, that Our County in Lancashire abounded more in Popish Recusants than any county of England ; and hath still continued to Our Great Regret with little amendment, save that now of late in Our Last Riding through Our Said County We find both by the report of the judges, and of the bishop of the diocese, that there is some amendment now daily beginning, which is no small contentment to Us.

The report of this growing amendment amongst them made Us the more sorry, when with Our Own Ears We heard the general complaint of Our People that they were barred from all lawful recreation and exercise upon the Sunday afternoon, after the ending of all divine service, which cannot but produce two evils ; the one the hindering of the conversion of many, whom their priests will take occasion hereby to vex, persuading them that no honest mirth or recreation is lawful on those days, which cannot but breed a great discontent in Our People's Hearts, especially of such as are peradventure upon the point of turning ; the other inconveniency is, that this prohibition barreth the common and meaner sort of people from using such exercises as may make their bodies more able for war, whenever We or Our Successors shall have occasion to use them ; and in place thereof, set up filthy tiplings and drunkenness, and breed a number of idle and discontented speeches in their alehouses. For when shall the common people have leave to exercise, if not upon Sundays and Holy-days, seeing that they must live by their labour, and win their living in all working days ?

Our Express Pleasure therefore is, that the Laws of Our Kingdom and Canons of Our Church be as well observed in that county, as in all other places of this Our Kingdom. And on the other part that no lawful recreations shall be barred to Our Good People, which shall not tend to the breach of the aforesaid Laws and Canons of Our Church ; which to express more particularly, Our Pleasure is, that the Bishops and all other inferior clergymen and church-wardens shall for their parts be careful and diligent both to instruct the ignorant, and convince and reform them that are misled in religion, presenting them that will not conform themselves but obstinately stand out, to Our Judges and Justices whom We likewise command to put the Laws in due execution against them. Our Pleasure likewise is, that the Bishop of the diocese take the like strait order with all the Puritans and precisians within the same, either constraining them to conform themselves, or to leave the county according to the Laws of Our Kingdom and Canon of Our Church, and so to strike equally on both hands against the contemners of Our Authority and adversaries of Our Church. And as for Our Good People's Lawful Recreation, Our Pleasure likewise is, that after the end of Divine service Our Good People be not disturbed, letted, or discouraged from any lawful recreation, such as dancing, either men or women, archery for men, leaping, vaulting, or any other such harmless recreation, nor from having of May-games, Whitsun-ales, and morris-dances, and the setting up of May-poles, and other sports therewith used, so as the same be had in due and convenient time without impediment or neglect of Divine service ; and that women shall have leave to carry rushes to Church for the decoring of it, according to their old custom. But withal We do here account still as prohibited all unlawful games to be used on Sundays only as bear and bull baitings, interludes, and at all times in the meaner sort of people by Law prohibited bowling.

And likewise We bar from the benefit and liberty all such known Recusants, either men or women, as will abstain from coming to Church or Divine service, being therefore unworthy of any lawful recreation after the said service, that will not first come to Church and serve God. Prohibiting in like sort the said recreations to any that, though conform in religion, are not present in the Church at the service of God, before their going to the said recreations. Our Pleasure likewise is, that they, to whom it belongeth in office, shall present and sharply punish all such, as in abuse of this Our Liberty will use their exercises before the end of all Divine services for that day. And we likewise straitly command that every person shall resort to his own parish Church to hear Divine service, and each parish by itself to use the said recreations after Divine service. Prohibiting likewise any offensive weapons to be carried or used in the said times of recreations. And Our Pleasure is, that this Our Declaration shall be published by order from the Bishop of the diocese through all the parish Churches, and that both Our Judges of Our Circuits, and Our Justices of Our Peace be informed thereof. Given at Our Manor of Greenwich the 24th day of May, in the 16th year of Our Reign of England, France, and Ireland, and of Scotland the 51st.

Now out of a like pious care for the service of God, and for suppressing of any humours that oppose truth, and for the ease, comfort, and recreation of Our Well-Deserving People, We do ratify and publish this Our Blessed Father's Declaration, the rather because of late in some counties of Our Kingdom We find, that under pretence of taking away abuses there hath been a general forbidding not only of ordinary meetings, but of the Feasts of the Dedication of the Churches, commonly called " Wakes." Now Our Express Will and Pleasure is, that the

Feasts with others shall be observed, and that Our Justices of the Peace in their several divisions shall look to it, both that all disorders there may be prevented or punished, and that all neighbourhood and freedom with manlike and lawful exercises be used. And We further command Our Justices of the Assize in their several circuits to see that no man do trouble or molest any of Our Loyal and Dutiful People in or for their lawful recreations, having first done their duty to God, and continuing in obedience to Us and Our Laws. And of this We command all Our Judges, Justices of the Peace, as well within liberties as without, mayors, bailiffs, constables, and other officers to take notice of and see observed, as they tender Our Displeasure. And We further will that publication of this Our Command be made by order from the Bishops through all the parish Churches of their several dioceses respectively. Given at our Palace of Westminster the 18th day of October, in the 9th year of Our Reign.

*God Save the King.*

## No. 262. DAVID PRIMEROSE

[From *A Treatise of the Sabbath and the Lord's Day* . . . *Wherein is declared both the Nature, Original, and Observation as well of the One under the Old as of the Other under the New Testament, Written in French, by David Primerose, Bachelor in Divinity in the University of Oxford and Minister of the Gospel in the Protestant Church of Rouen, Englished out of his French Manuscript by his Father* G[ilbert] P[rimerose], *D.D.,* Part III, Chapter i. London, 1636, pp. 199 f. This was one of the many treatises occasioned by the reissue of the " Book of Sports " in 1633 (cp. note on No. **261**).]

Here beginneth a new question, Whether the institution thereof [*i.e.* of Sunday] be Divine or Apostolical,—If it was Our Lord Jesus Christ that ordained it after His Resurrection to be kept by all Christians during the whole time of the New Testament, if the Apostles also enjoined it to all the faithful till the end of the world, so that they are all bound to the observation thereof by the Institution of Christ or of His Apostles ; Or whether the faithful did not, of themselves, without any commandment, through respect to the Resurrection of Our Lord Jesus Christ, keep the day wherein it came to pass, as also to make a distinction thereby between them and the Jews, and to shew that they were made free from all Jewish observations, types, and figures, amongst which was the Sabbath day ; and that they observed not a day in quality of type and figure, but only for order's sake and for Ecclesiastical government, to apply themselves together to the exercises of religion, and for that cause had changed the seventh day of the Jews into another ; which usage and custom, as very fit and convenient, being begun first amongst a few, fare [= ' prospered '] and softly prevailed, and was established with the Christian Religion amongst all those that embraced it, and since that time hath continued in the Christian Church till this day.

Although the first of these opinions were true, it cannot enforce the

Morality [1] of a Seventh Day of rest, but only that the First Day of the weeks was instituted by Jesus Christ or His Apostles as a point of order whereunto, in such a case, the faithful should be bound by the necessity of a Divine and Apostolical commandment. But I see not that this opinion hath any solid ground, whereas the second is well founded. For there is nothing found in the New Testament, concerning the observation of the First Day of the week, importing a commandment of Christ or of His Apostles. Neither is there any such commandment inferred, but by remote and most weak consequences. And it is more likely that all the places alleged to that purpose denote only a single usage among some Christians in those days, which by succession of time hath been settled and is become universal.

Indeed, if Jesus Christ, or His Apostles by express commandment from Him or by Divine inspiration, had ordained that day as a point so necessary as it is thought to be, I doubt not but that their commandment should have been expressly set down in the Books of the New Testament, as are all other ordinances of necessary things, and that in them we should find reprehension against those that had neglected the observation of that day, as in them there are reprehensions against all kind of sinners. But seeing there is no such commandment to be found in them, that it cannot be gathered from them but by consequences which are of no force, that no man is blamed in them for the inobservation of that day, whereas under the Old Testament God taxed so often and so sharply those that kept not His Sabbaths, this is to me a most firm and assured proof, that neither Jesus Christ nor His Apostles have ordained it.

## No. 263. JOHN BRAMHALL

[From *A Vindication of Himself and the Episcopal Clergy from the Presbyterian Charge of Popery, as it is managed by Mr. Baxter in his ' Treatise of the Grotian Religion,'* Chapter IX. *Works,* ed. L. A. C. T., Vol. III, pp. 576 f. In 1658 Baxter issued *The Grotian Religion Discovered.* Baxter, while expressing his sympathy with Grotius' concilatory spirit, contended that the famous Dutch Divine went much too far in a Romeward direction, and attacked his partiality towards Episcopacy. Bramhall, having been introduced by name into Baxter's treatise, wrote the reply named. It was first published in 1672 by Samuel Parker, nine years after the author's death; Bramhall composed it in the winter of 1659–1660.]

If Mr. Baxter think that no recreations of the body at all are lawful or may be permitted upon the Lord's Day, he may call himself a " Catholic " if he please; but he will find very few Churches of any communion whatsoever, old or new, reformed or unreformed, to bear him company.

No, no. Even among the Churches of his own communion, which he calleth " the holiest parts of the Church upon earth," he will find none at all to join with him, except the Churches of New England and

---

[1] [*i.e.* its 'moral,'—and therefore permanent—character (as opposed to its 'ceremonial' character).]

old England and Scotland whereinto this opinion hath been creeping by degrees this last half century of years or somewhat more. Before that time even our greatest disciplinarians in England abhorred not private recreations, so they could practise them without scandal. And Calvin himself disdained not to countenance and encourage the burghers of Geneva by his own presence and example to their public recreations, as bowling and shooting upon the Lord's Day after their devotions at Church were ended. In Germany, Switzerland, France, and the Low Countries, all the Churches of his own communion do enjoy their recreations. And in sundry of them their prayers and sermons on the afternoon of the Lord's Day are but lately introduced, whereas formerly not the vulgar only, but the most eminent persons, did use to bestow the whole afternoon upon their recreations.

But it may be his pick is not against recreations in general, but against dancing in particular. Indeed dancing was disliked at Geneva, not only upon the Lord's Days, but upon the other days of the week; and if their manner of dancing there or anywhere else was so obscene, as hath been in use in former ages, in some places, not undeservedly. No man can be so absurd as to affirm all sorts of dancing to be unlawful, as Miriam's dance, and that of the virgins of Shiloh, and Jephtha's daughter, and David. There is no time for any thing that is absolutely unlawful; but there is *a time to dance*. On the other side, it is as great an extreme to affirm that all sorts of dances are lawful. Not only conscientious Christians, but even modest heathens, have disliked some sorts of dances. And as there are some sorts of dances unlawful, so there may be great danger of abuse in the use of lawful dances. But where there is no lawful or direct prohibition either of God or man, we may advise a brother or a friend to beware of danger, but we have no authority to restrain him except he will of his own accord. As for the public dances of our youth on country greens, upon Sundays after the duties of the day were done, I see nothing in them but innocent, and agreeable to that under sort of people. But if any man out of prudence, or conscience, or scrupulosity, do disaffect them, either because they were sometimes used promiscuously, or for any other reasons, I think it easier to regulate those recreations which should be allowed, than to brawl about them perpetually until the end of the world.

## No. 264.  JOHN COSIN

[From a Letter to one Mr. Wood, preserved among the Cosin MSS. at Durham. *Works*, ed. *L. A. C. T.*, Vol. IV, pp. 462 f.]

The Church never had a custom to fast upon Sundays, neither Greek nor Latin. I honour my Lord Morton, but he saith nothing against it. The difference between the Roman and Greek Church was about the custom of fasting upon the *Saturdays*, and the words of the

Sixth Council (*in Sabbatis Quadragesimae*) meant no more. The Greeks were so far from fasting upon the Sundays, that *in honorem Resurrectionis* (as you say your books quote it) they would not fast upon the Evens neither, that is, upon the Saturdays before Easter and Pentecost. The Latin Church, *in memoriam Luctus Apostolorum*, they would fast upon the Saturday: for upon Saturday was their *Luctus*, when Christ was taken from them and laid in His grave. So you see the reason of both Churches for fasting, and not fasting, upon Saturdays (there was the same difference between Milan and Rome in St. Ambrose his days, who followed the custom of the Greeks); but all this is nothing to a *Sunday* fast, concerning which this saying of Tertullian was the general rule of all Churches: *Jejunare Die Dominico nefas ducimus.* And it was but within this last age that *Dies Sabbati* became Latin for *Sunday.*

# (9) HOLY DAYS

## No. 265.  RICHARD HOOKER

[From *The Laws of Ecclesiastical Polity*, Book V, Chapter lxx, §§ 1, 8.  *Works*, ed. J. Keble, Vol. II, pp. 384, 388–390.  Cp. note on No. 148.]

THE sanctification of days and times is a token of that thankfulness and a part of that public honour which we owe to God for admirable benefits, whereof it doth not suffice that we keep a secret calendar, taking thereby our private occasions as we list ourselves to think how much God hath done for all men, but the days which are chosen out to serve as public memorials of such His mercies ought to be clothed with those outward robes of holiness whereby their difference from other days may be made sensible.  But because time in itself as hath been already proved can receive no alteration, the hallowing of festival days must consist in the shape or countenance which we put upon the affairs that are incident into those days. . . .

Generally therefore touching Feasts in the Church of Christ, they have that profitable use whereof St. Augustine speaketh, " By festival solemnities and set days we dedicate and sanctify to God the memory of His benefits, lest unthankful forgetfulness thereof should creep upon us in course of time."

And concerning particulars, their Sabbath the Church hath changed into our Lord's day, that as the one did continually bring to mind the former world finished by creation, so the other might keep us in perpetual remembrance of a far better world begun by Him Which came to restore all things, to make both heaven and earth new.  For which cause they honoured the last day, we the first, in every seven throughout the year.

The rest of the days and times which we celebrate have relation all unto one head.  We begin therefore our ecclesiastical year with the glorious Annunciation of His Birth by angelical embassage.  There being hereunto added His Blessed Nativity itself, the Mystery of His legal Circumcision, the testification of His true Incarnation by the Purification of her which brought Him into the world, His Resurrection, His Ascension into heaven, the admirable sending down of His Spirit upon His chosen, and (which consequently ensued) the notice of that Incomprehensible Trinity thereby given to the Church of God ; again forasmuch as we know that Christ hath not only been manifested great in Himself, but great in other His Saints also, the days of whose departure out of the world are to the Church of Christ as the birth and coronation days of kings or emperors, therefore especial choice being made of the very flower of all occasions in this kind, there are annual selected times to meditate of Christ glorified in them which had the honour to suffer for His sake, before they had age and ability to know Him; glorified in them which knowing Him as Stephen had the sight of that before death whereinto so acceptable death did lead; glorified in those sages of the East that came from far to adore Him and were conducted by strange light; glorified in the second Elias of the world sent before Him to prepare His way; glorified in every of those Apostles whom it pleased Him to use as founders of His Kingdom here; glorified in the Angels as in Michael; glorified in all those happy souls that are already possessed of Heaven. Over and besides which number not great, the rest be but four other days heretofore annexed to the feast of Easter and Pentecost by reason of general Baptism usual at those two feasts, which also is the cause why they had not as other days any proper name given them. Their first institution was therefore through necessity, and their present continuance is now for the greater honour of the principals whereupon they still attend.

## No. 266. FRANCIS WHITE

[From *A Treatise of the Sabbath Day*, pp. 265 f. Cp. note on No. 67.]

Under the Gospel, Christian people are prohibited only worldly actions *respectively*, that is, so far forth as they are impediments of performing evangelical duties upon the Lord's Holy Days. And men are not now obliged, by the space of a whole natural day, or a whole artificial day, to an actual exercise of religious offices (for there is no Divine, Ecclesiastical, or temporal, law commanding this); but they must be prepared in the habitual disposition of their minds to exercise these duties, so far forth, and in such manner, and for such space of time, as the equity of the Fourth Commandment and the laws of superiors shall require; and likewise they are obliged in conscience actually to exercise them at such time of the day as either equity of Divine Law or lawful superiors doth enjoin.

Now the natural equity of Divine Law and the positive precepts of superiors command no longer space of time for actual performance of religious offices upon the Lord's Holy Days than such as both is necessary for God's solemn worship and for the spiritual edification of Christian people; and likewise such as may be performed of all well-affected persons, without surcharging or exceeding the natural strength and ability of body or mind. For people must serve the Lord with a free and joyful heart (*Psalm* c, 2; *II. Chron.* xxx, 23). But the imposing such a quantity and continuance of spiritual actions as exceedeth the ordinary hability of human faculties, choketh rejoicing and comfort in the services which men perform, and makes the same a tedious burden.

And this seemeth to me to have been a prime motive to our religious governors of allowing the people of the land some recreations (not prohibited by our laws) upon the Holy Days. For if they should (upon Puritan principles) restrain them wholly from all repast, the Holy Day would be more unwelcome to them than the plough day; and besides it might engender in people's minds a distaste of their present religion and manner of serving God.

# (10) CHRISTMAS

## No. 267. HENRY HAMMOND

[From *A Practical Catechism*, Book II, Section xii. Ed. *L. A. C. T.*, pp. 193–196. This famous manual was first published anonymously in, it seems, 1644, on the urgent persuasion of Dr. Christopher Potter, then Provost of Queen's (cp. J. Fell, *Life of Hammond*; in the *L. A. C. T.* edition of the *Practical Catechism*, pp. xxx–xxxii). Its merits were soon appreciated. Charles I held it in such estimation that when at Carisbrooke he entrusted a copy of it to Sir Thomas Herbert to be given to his son, the Duke of Gloucester. A second edition of it was issued in 1646, with the author's name attached to it. By 1683 a twelfth edition was reached.]

*Scholar. Please you now to proceed to inform me what that authority is by which this festivity* [of Christmas] *pretends to stand in the Church of Christ ; for that will be necessary to be superadded to the bare lawfulness of it, to render it either necessary or fit to be observed by us.*

*Catechist.* The authority by which it stands in the whole Church is that of the practice of the Primitive Universal Christian Church ; not that we have any certain evidence of the time of its beginning, but that the immemorial observation of it is an argument of the Primitive, if not Apostolic, institution of it. And thus indeed do the ancient Fathers, in their homilies upon that day, speak of it, as of a most ancient usage. Thus the very ancient author of the *Constitutions* mentions a day solemnized in remembrance of Christ's Birth. And Origen, one of our first writers, doth not only vindicate that place of *Gal.* iv. from having anything contrary to the Christian Feasts, which were ridiculous, if there were none such, but also mentions the Feast of the Innocent Infants, (which is now attendant on the Nativity and cannot be imagined ancienter than that) as that which was by the Holy Fathers, according to the will of God, commanded to be for ever celebrated in the Church. Soon after him St. Cyprian hath a treatise on this day. And Ammianus Marcellinus, speaking of Julian the Apostate, above thirteen hundred years ago, mentions it, as the design to cover his apostatical intentions, that he went solemnly to the Christians' Church, and worshipped God on that Holy Day in January which the Christians call Epiphany ; which day being mentioned so anciently as a known Festival of the Christian Church, gives not only to that day, but to Christmas, which that concludes, a far greater antiquity than that time of Julian's on occasion of which it is there mentioned. And so saith St. Chrysostom that, though till his time the observation of it on December the twenty-fifth was not fixed at Antioch, yet from Rome over all the West it had been so observed from the most ancient records of Christianity.

By this and much more that might be produced, it appears to be at the least an ecclesiastical institution, very early received over all the West and the far greatest part of Christendom, and within four hundred years universally solemnized. And sure this is a very competent authority,—when withal it is so probable, that it may be more according to a rule of the Fathers, " that every ancient and general usage, whose beginnings are unknown, may be resolved to be of apostolical institution or practice,"—to oblige the continuance of so pious a solemnity in the Church, according to that of St. Augustine, " that all that acknowledge themselves sons of the Church observe the Festivals of the Church " (in which number he places this of the Nativity in the front) ; to which it is consequent, that they which observe them not, disclaim this sonship and cast themselves out of this family, upon a temptation much too slight to own or excuse an act of such unkindness to themselves, and ingratitude to the Christian Church which designed it so much to their advantage. To this head of the ancientness of this institution in the universal Church I shall add but one evidence more, and it is this, that as most of the first customs or institutions of Christianity were taken by some light change from the customs of the Jews, (Christ's Baptism from their washings at the initiation of Jews and proselytes in the Temple, the Sacrament of the Lord's Supper from their loaf and cup of benediction after supper, our Easter from their Passover, the Christian from the Jewish Pentecost, and many other the like), so it was in this matter also. The beginnings of all months, and seasons, and years, were kept festival among the Jews ; in like manner the Feast of the Dedication of the Temple, the anniversary commemorating of the beginning or birth, as it were, of that House of God, as among other people the birthdays of cities, the day wherein the trench was first cast up, hath usually been solemnized. And then, as the Temple was a type of Christ, and He said by Himself to be greater than the Temple, as the substance which the Temple foreshadowed, His flesh the walls, and His Divinity the glory which inhabited it, so are these two, the type and antitype, the Feast of Dedication among them and the Nativity among Christians, most perfectly answerable the one to the other. And proportionably as among them the beginnings or calends of every month were kept holy, so here twelve days together, one for every month, are joined to attend the calends or Nativity of Christ. And all this, as it is a fair compliance with God's institution among the Jews, so sure is it an argument of the antiquity of the observation, that it is thus imitated from the Jews ; for that signifies it to have been begun about that great time of reformation, before the Jewish ceremonies were quite abolished, as the Egyptians' jewels were then taken from them, when the Israelites departed out of the land, and began their journey toward Canaan. As for this particular Church wherein we live, there is little doubt but that this festivity is of the same standing with the first plantation of Christian religion among us. If we reckon that from the conversion of the Saxons, to which the name of English is properly affixed, it is then most clear by the records of King Ethelbert. But if we speak of the Britons, then as their conversion is much more ancient, and Tertullian's testimony is clear that the British islands were converted to Christianity before his time, so if there be any truth in that objection which some men have made against the celebration of this Feast among us, viz. that some heathen usages are retained in it, this will be yet a higher evidence of the antiquity of this Festival in this nation, so far as to render the original of it, if not Apostolical, yet very primitive and near the Apostles' Age,—that being the time of the conversion of the nation from heathenism. And if it were not of the usage of this festivity also, it is not imaginable how any heathen custom should come to be adherent to it. This, I suppose, may help to recover this festivity to some competent part of that reverence which in reason is due to Christian Antiquity in point of ceremony or observation, in a kingdom especially where common usage is common law, the best that any man holds his estate by, and awake us to a more pious, Christian, spiritual, and not to a more voluptuous carnal, heathenish, observance of it.

## No. 268. JOSEPH HALL

[From a *Letter for the Observation of the Feast of Christ's Nativity. Works*, ed. Peter Hall (1837), Vol. X, pp. 126–131. No indication is given in the 1837 edition as to who the gentleman was to whom this letter was addressed.]

For the Celebration of the solemn Feasts of our Saviour's Nativity, Resurrection, Ascension, and the Coming Down of the Holy Ghost, which you say is cried down by your zealous Lecturer, one would think there should be reason enough in those wonderful and unspeakable benefits which those days serve to commemorate unto us.

For, to instance in the late Feast of the Nativity, when the Angel brought the news of that blessed Birth to the Jewish shepherds, *Behold*, saith he, *I bring good tidings of great joy, which shall be to all people ; for unto you is born this day a Saviour.* If, then, the report of this blessing were the best tidings of the greatest joy that ever was or ever could be possibly incident into mankind, why should not the commemoration thereof be answerable ? Where we conceive the greatest joy, what should hinder us to express it in a joyful festivity ?

But, you are taught to say, the day conferred nothing to the blessing ; that, every day, we should, with equal thankfulness, remember this inestimable benefit of the Incarnation of the Son of God ; so as a set anniversary day is altogether needless.

Know, then, and consider, that the All-Wise God, who knew it fit that His people should every day think of the great work of the creation and of the miraculous deliverance out of the Egyptian servitude and should daily give honour to the Almighty Creator and Deliverer, yet ordained one day of seven for the more special recognition of these marvellous works, as well knowing how apt we are to forget those duties, wherewith we are only encharged in common, without the designment of a particular rememoration. Besides, the same reason will hold proportionably against any monthly or annual celebration whatsoever. The Jews should have been much to blame, if they had not every day thankfully remembered the great deliverance, which God wrought for them from the bloody design of cruel Haman; yet it was thought requisite, if not necessary, that there should be two special days of Purim set apart for the anniversary memorial of that wonderful preservation. The like may be said for the English Purim, of our November. It is well if, besides the general tie of our thankfulness, a precise day, ordained by authority, can enough quicken our unthankful dulness to give God His own for so great a mercy. Shall we say now, " It is the work of the year, what needs a day ? " As, therefore, no day should pass over our head without a grateful acknowledgement of the great mystery of God Incarnate, so withal the wisdom of the Primitive Church, no doubt by the direction of the Holy Ghost, hath pitched upon one special day, wherein we should entirely devote our thoughts to the meditation of this work, which the Angels of Heaven cannot enough admire.

But, you are told, that perhaps we miss of the day since the season is litigious, uncertain, unknown; and, in likelihood, other than our December; and, that it is purposely not revealed, that it may not be kept.

As to the first, I deny not, that the just day is not certainly known. The great Saviour of the World, that would have His Second Coming without observation going before it, would have His First Coming without observation following it. He meant to come down without noise, without a recorded notice. Even in the second hundred (so ancient we are sure this festivity is) there was question and different opinions of the season : the just knowledge and determination whereof matters nothing at all to the duty of our celebration. Most sure we are that such a day there was ; and no less sure that it was the happiest day that ever looked forth into the world. It is all one to us whether this day or that. We content ourselves with this, that it hath pleased the Church for many hundred years to ordain this day for the commemoration of that transcendent blessing. What care we to stand upon those twelve hours, that made up the artificial day, wherein this wonderful work was wrought which we are sure cannot but be much changed by so many intercalations ? So long and constant a practice of the Christian Church, upon so holy grounds, is no less warrant to us than if an Angel from Heaven should have revealed unto us the just hour of this Blessed Nativity.

As to the second, surely, whosoever shall tell you that God did purposely hide this day from us that it might escape a celebration, as He concealed the burial of Moses to avoid the danger of an idolatrous adoration, makes himself a presumptuous commenter upon the actions of the Almighty. Where did God tell him so? Or what revelation can he pretend for so bold an assertion? If this were the matter, why then did not the same God with equal caution conceal the day of the Passion, Resurrection, Ascension of our Blessed Saviour, and of the Descent of the Holy Ghost?,—the observation of all which days is, with no less vehemence and upon the same danger, cried down by these scrupulous persons. Either, therefore, let him say that God would have these other Feast Days observed, because He would have them known to the world; or yield that He did not therefore conceal the day of the Nativity of Christ because He would not have it observed.

But, you hear it said, " There is Popery and Superstition in keeping that day."

Tell those that suggest so, that they cast a foul slander upon the Saints of God in the Primitive Times, upon the holy and learned Fathers of the Church, who preached, and wrote for, and kept the Feast of Christ's Nativity with sacred solemnity many hundred years before Popery was hatched; and that they little know what wrong they do to religion and themselves, and what honour they put upon that superstition which they profess to detest, in ascribing that to Popery which was the mere act of holy and devout Christianity.

But, to colour this plea, you are taught that the Mystery of Iniquity began early to work, even in the very Apostolic Times, and that Antichrist did secretly put in his claw before his whole body appeared.

Surely, there is singular use wont to be made of this shift by those which would avoid the countenance of all Primitive authority to any displeasing (however lawful and laudable) institutions and practices. So the Anabaptist tells us that the baptizing of children is one of the timely workings of the Mystery of Iniquity; so the blasphemous Nearians [= Neo-Arians] of our time tell us that the mystery of the Blessed Trinity of Persons in the Unity of One Godhead is but an ancient device of Antichrist, working underhand before his formal exhibition. Every sect is apt to make this challenge; and therefore it behoves us wisely to distinguish betwixt those things which men did as good Christians and those which they did as engaged to their own private or to the more common interest of others. What advantage can we conceive it might be to Antichrist, that Christ should have a day celebrated to the memory of His Blessed Birth, and that devout Christians should meet together in their holy assemblies to praise God for the benefit of that happy Incarnation? And what other effect could be expected from so religious a work, but glory to God and edification to men? Who can suppose that the enemy of Christ should gain by the honour done to Christ? Away, therefore, with this groundless imagination: and let us be so popish, so superstitious as those Holy Fathers and Doctors of the Primitive Church, famous for learning and piety, who lived and died devout observers of this Christian Festival.

But, you are bidden to ask, what warrant we find in the Word of God, which is to be the rule of all our actions, for the solemn keeping of this day.

In answer, you may, if you please, tell that questionist, that to argue from Scripture negatively in things of this nature is somewhat un-theological. Ask you him again, with better reason, what Scripture he finds to forbid it: for if it be unlawful to be done, which is not in God's Word commanded, then much rather that which is not there forbidden cannot be unlawful to be done. General grounds of edifica-tion, decency, expedience, peaceable conformity to the injunctions of our spiritual governors, are, in these cases, more than enough to build our practice upon.

If it be replied that we are enjoined six days to labour, and for-bidden to observe days and times, as being a part of the Jewish paeda-gogue,—two common pretences, wherewith the eyes of the ignorant are wont to be bleared,—know, that, for the first, it is not so much preceptive as permissive: neither was it the intention of the Almighty to intersperse the command of human affairs in the First Table of His Royal Law, wherein Himself and His service is immediately concerned. In such like expressions, 'mayest' and 'shalt' are equivalent, and promiscuously used. That instance is clear and pregnant, *Gen.* ii, 16. *The Lord*, saith the text, *commanded the man, saying, Eating thou shalt eat of every tree in the garden*; which our last Version renders well to the sense, *Thou mayest freely eat of every tree in the garden.* And, if the charge in that Fourth Commandment were absolute and peremptory, what human authority could dispense with those large shreds of time which are usually cut out of the six days for sacred occasions? What warrant could we have to intermit our work for a daily lecture, or a monthly fast, or for an Anniversary Fifth of November? And if notwithstanding this command of God, it be allowed to be in the power of man, whether sovereign (as Con-stantine appropriated it) or spiritual, to ordain the setting apart of some set parcels of time to holy uses, why should it be stuck at in the requiring and observing the pious and useful celebrity of this Festival?

As for that other suggestion of the Apostle's taxation of observing days and times, any one that hath but half an eye may see that it hath

respect to those Judaical Holy-Days which were part of the Ceremonial Law, now long since out of date as being of typical signification
and shadows of things to come. Should we, therefore, go about to
revive those Jewish Feasts, or did we erect any new day to an essential
part of the worship of God, or place holiness in it as such, we should
justly incur that blame which the Apostle casts upon the Galatian
and Colossian false-teachers. But, to wrest this forbiddance to a
Christian Solemnity which is merely commemorative of a blessing
received, without any prefiguration of things to come, without any
opinion of holiness annexed to the day, is no other than an injurious
violence.

Upon all this which hath been said, and upon a serious weighing
of whatever may be further alleged to the contrary, I dare confidently
affirm, that there is no just reason why good Christians should not,
with all godly cheerfulness, observe this which that holy Father styled
the Metropolis of all Feasts. To which I add that those which by
their example and doctrine slight this day, causing their people to
dishonour it with their worst clothes, with shops open, with servile
works, stand guilty before God of a high and sinful contempt of that
lawful authority under which they live; forasmuch as, by the statutes
of our land, made by the full concurrence of King and State, this day
is commanded to be kept holy by all English subjects, and this power
is backed by the charge of God, *Submit yourselves to every ordinance
of man, for the Lord's sake.*

If now, after all this, I should let my pen loose to the suffragant
testimonies, whether of Antiquity, or of modern Divines and Reformed
Churches, I should try your patience and, instead of a letter, send
you a volume.

Let it suffice that ever since the second hundred year after Christ,
this Feast hath without contradiction obtained in the Church of God,
and hath received many noble eulogies and passionate enforcements
from the learned and holy Fathers of the Church.

Amongst the rest, that of Gregory Nazianzen is so remarkable,
that I may not omit it; as that which sets forth the excess of joyful
respect wherewith the Ancient Christians were wont to keep this
day. " Let us," saith he, " celebrate this Feast; not in a panegyrical
but divine, not in a worldly but supersecular manner: not so much
regarding ourselves or ours, as the worship of Christ, etc. And how
shall we effect this? Not by crowning our doors with garlands, nor
by leading of dances, nor adorning our streets; not by feeding our
eyes; not by delighting our ears with songs; not by effeminating
our smell with perfumes; not with humouring our taste with dainties;
not with pleasing our touch; not with silken and costly clothes, etc.;
not with the sparkling of jewels; not with the lustre of gold; not

42

with the artifice of counterfeit colours, etc.  Let us leave these things to Pagans for their pomps, etc.  But we who adore the Word of the Father, if we think fit to affect delicacies, let us feed ourselves with the dainties of the Law of God and with those discourses especially, which are fitting for this present Festival." So that learned and eloquent Father, to his auditors of Constantinople.

Whereto let me, if you please, have leave to add one or two practical instances.

One shall be of the good Emperor Theodosius, lying now, for eight months, under the severe censure of Bishop Ambrose.  When the Feast of the Nativity drew near, what moan did that religious Prince make to his courtiers that he was, by that resolute Bishop, shut out (for his blood-guiltiness) from partaking with the assembly in that holy service !  And what importunate means did he make for his admission !  Had that gracious Emperor been of the diet of these new Divines, he would have slighted that repulse, and gladly taken this occasion of absence from that superstitious solemnity.  Or had one of these grave monitors been at his elbow, he might have saved that pious Prince the expence of many sighs and tears, which now he bestowed upon his abstention from that dearly affected devotion.

The other shall be a history of as much note as horror, too clear a proof of the ancient celebration of this Festival.  It was under the tyranny of Diocletian and his co-partner Maximinus that twenty thousand Christians, which were met to celebrate the Feast of this Blessed Nativity in the large Church of Nicomedia, were made a holocaust, and burnt, together with that goodly fabric, to ashes on that day.  Lo, so great a multitude as twenty thousand Christians, of all ages, of both sexes, had not thus met together in a time of so mortal a danger to celebrate this Feast, if the holy zeal of their duty had not told them they ought to keep that day, which these novellers teach us to contemn.  Now let these bold men see of how contrary a disposition they are to these blessed Martyrs which, as this day, sent up their souls, like to Manoah's Angel, to Heaven in those flames.

After thus much said, I should be glad to know, since reason there can be none, what authority induces these gainsayers to oppose so ancient and received a custom in the Church of God.

# (11) FASTING

## No. 269.  WILLIAM BEVERIDGE

[*Sermon XXXIX.  Works*, ed. *L. A. C. T.*, Vol. II, pp. 235–254.  The text of the following sermon was *I Cor.* ix, 27.]

## THE USEFULNESS OF FASTING

" *But I keep under my body and bring it into subjection, lest that by any means, when I have preached to others, I myself should be a cast-away.*"

From your presence here at this time I cannot but in charity infer three things.  First, that you all believe a future state; and that as really as you are now in this, it is not long but you will all be in another world, either in a world of happiness, or else in a world of misery; for if you do not believe this, it is to no purpose for you to come hither, this place and work having a peculiar reference to the other world, and not to this where we now are.  Secondly, hence I infer likewise that you are fully persuaded that your condition in the other world will be according to your behaviour in this, that if you continue in your sins here you will there be miserable, but if you repent and turn to God, you will be happy for ever; for certainly you would not come hither to learn what to do in order to your future happiness, unless you were fully persuaded beforehand that you must do something in order to it.  Hence therefore, in the third place, I conclude also that you all desire when you leave this, to go to a better world, even to Heaven, the only place of real and eternal happiness; for what need you come hither to know how to get to Heaven, if you do not care whether you ever come there or no?

Taking it therefore for granted that your minds are possessed with a firm belief of another world, with a full persuasion that you shall live there in happiness or misery, according as you live here in holiness or sin, and with hearty desires to carry yourselves so while you live that when you die you may go to Heaven, this, I say, being taken for granted, it cannot but be very seasonable and suitable to your design in coming hither to explain these words of the Apostle which I have now read unto you; wherein you have the great end which the Apostle did, and you, I suppose, do aim at in all your actions, even how to get to Heaven; and then secondly, one of the means whereby he did,

583

and you, by the blessing of God, may attain that end, even by keeping the body under and bringing it into subjection: *I keep under my body*, saith he, *and bring it into subjection, lest that by any means, when I have preached unto others, I myself should be a cast-away.*

As for the first, it is plain from these words that one of the great ends St. Paul aimed at, the great designs he carried on in all he did, was to save himself as well as those that heard him. He was conscious to himself that the efficacy of the Word and Sacraments which he administered did not depend upon his own personal holiness, but upon his Apostolical Office and the promise of the Spirit annexed to it; and therefore that it was very possible for him to be an instrument in God's hand to save others, and yet he himself be damned; that he might shew others the way to Heaven, and yet he himself not walk in it. Hence he took special care all along lest that by any means when he had preached to others and taught them how to obtain the crown of glory, he himself should lose it, by being ἀδόκιμος, a 'cast-away,' a reprobate, one not approved of as fit to have it set upon his head.

And if St. Paul himself used so much care and diligence lest after all the pains he had taken for salvation of others, he himself should miss of it, what cause have we to do so, who are now entrusted with the administration of the Word and Sacraments? Certainly we had need to look about us, lest after all our preaching unto others, we ourselves should perish everlastingly, especially considering that we cannot but be all sensible that it is far easier to preach the Gospel than to practise it; to tell others what to do, than to do it ourselves. And therefore whatsoever pains we take in the one, we had need to take as much, if not much more, to do the other too: for what a sad thing will it be, to see many converted by our ministry shining in Heaven's glory, and we ourselves lie scorching in eternal flame! To see them with Lazarus in Abraham's bosom, solacing themselves in those rivers of pleasure which are at *God's right hand for evermore*, and ourselves in the meanwhile with Dives in Hell torments, without so much as a drop of water to cool our enflamed tongues! And yet St. Paul foresaw this would be the consequence of his preaching the Gospel to others unless he himself lived up unto it; and therefore we may be confident it will be so unto us too. But I would not have you think that this concerns us of the clergy only; the same argument holds good as to all others. For if so holy a person as we must all acknowledge St. Paul to have been, after all his preaching Salvation unto others, was so solicitous about his own, what cause then have you to fear, lest after all your reading and hearing the Word of God, after all your public and private devotions, after all your receiving the Sacrament of the Lord's Supper, you at last be cast-aways, and so lose all your pains and labour! And by consequence, how much doth it concern you all to take as much care if possible, as St. Paul himself did, of your future happiness! I am sure all that are wise amongst you cannot but look upon this as a matter of the greatest importance that you have or can have in this world; and howsoever any of you may think otherwise at present, it is not long but you will all be of the same mind. Which that you may be before it be too late, I pray and beseech you all seriously to consider that you have another world to live in as well as this, an eternal world where you must abide either in the height of happiness or else in the depth of misery for evermore, so that as really as you now live amongst men, you will there live either with Christ and His Holy Angels, or else with the devil and his damned fiends unto all eternity.

Do but seriously consider this, and you will need no other arguments to persuade you to follow the example of this great Apostle in this particular, even to make it your daily, your constant, your only care and business in this world, to prepare and fit yourselves for the other, that when you come to die you may then begin to live, to live with God, to live in light, in love, in rest, in peace, in joy, in Heaven itself; in Heaven, I say, where we shall be freed from all those griefs and troubles, from all those cares and fears, that here distract our minds and make us restless and uneasy; in Heaven, where we shall trample upon this lower world and ride in triumph over both sin and Satan, so as never to be tempted or disturbed more; in Heaven where our souls shall be reduced to their primitive frame and temper, and be made so perfectly happy, as to be perfectly holy; in Heaven, where our thoughts shall be always pure, our minds serene, and our hearts transported with love and joy in the chiefest good; where we shall always behold the glory, admire the perfections, and enjoy the presence of the great Jehovah, so as always to apprehend Him as well pleased with us, rejoicing over us, and manifesting His infinite love and goodness to us; which is so great, so exceeding great an happiness, that it may justly strike us into admiration, how it is possible for such silly creatures as we are to enjoy and bear it. Yet how great soever it be, there is never a soul here present but as yet is capable of it and invited to it; and if you be not failing to yourselves, you may all ere long be admitted into the actual possession of it.

But for that end you must still remember that as Heaven is the highest happiness you can attain to, so it is the hardest matter in the world to attain unto it. I speak not this to discourage any of you, but I would not have you fooled by the Devil and his emissaries into a groundless conceit that it is easy to get to Heaven; for Christ Himself, by Whom alone it is possible for any of you to come there, hath told you the contrary, assuring you with His own mouth *That the gate is strait, and the way narrow which leadeth unto life, and few there be that find it.* And you cannot but all acknowledge as much, if you do but consider what is necessary in order to it; for what must you do that you may inherit eternal life? Or rather what must you not do? You must mortify every lust, for one sin will keep you out of Heaven, as well as twenty. You must exercise every grace and perform every duty that is required of you both to God and man. You must *walk in all the commandments of God blameless*, to the utmost of your knowledge and power, so as to be sincerely, entirely, and constantly holy in all manner of conversation; for it is the irrevocable decree of Heaven, that *without holiness no man shall see the Lord.* And therefore, if ever you desire to see the Lord in glory, you must live above the world whilst you are in it, and contemn it while you use it. You must gather up all your scattered affections from all things here below, and fix them upon God, so that all the inclinations of your souls must meet and rest in Him as their only centre, otherwise you will not be *meet to be partakers of the inheritance of the saints in light*, nor capable of those pure and spiritual joys, which are there prepared for you.

But if these things be so, you may say to me, as the Apostles said to Our Lord, *Who then can be saved? For who is sufficient for these things?* To that I answer, It is true, if we look no further than ourselves, we may justly despair of ever knowing what Heaven is. But our comfort is that *our sufficiency is of God*, Who is always ready to assist us in the use of those means that are appointed by Himself; amongst which we are now, in the second place, to consider one of the most effectual, even that which the Apostle tells us he himself used, saying, *I keep under my body, and bring it into subjection.*

In speaking to which, I shall not trouble you with any critical observations about the Greek words ὑπωπιάζω καὶ δουλαγωγῶ here used; for our English translation gives you the full sense and meaning of them, as well as any words are able to express it: *I keep under my body, and bring it into subjection*; as if he should have said, " I being still in the body and finding by experience that that is very apt to resist and rebel against my soul, to tempt me to vice, and to hinder me in the exercise of virtue, I therefore take care to keep it under, in such a temper as that it may be always subject unto, and ready to observe the dictates of my reason, and the motions of God's Spirit within me, and so be no hindrance, but rather a furtherance to me in my progress to Heaven."

But for our better understanding of this we shall consider two things :—

1. How the Apostle did, and we may, keep our bodies under, and bring them into subjection.

2. How much this conduceth to our being so holy here, that we may be happy hereafter, and so not be cast-aways, as the Apostle here speaks.

The first will be soon dispatched; for it is plain that the Apostle kept his body under, and brought it into subjection, by fasting and abstinence, as the Fathers frequently observe. For as for the corporal chastisements by whipping and scourging of themselves, so commonly and ridiculously used by the Papists in their solemn processions, St. Paul never makes any mention of them. He saith, indeed, that he *was thrice beaten with rods, and five times received forty stripes save one*. But he received them not from himself or his confessor, as the Papists do, but from his implacable enemies, the Jews. But when he afterwards saith, that *he was in hunger and thirst often, in fastings often*, by the former the Fathers generally understand the hunger and thirst which he was forced to undergo in his travels and imprisonments; by the latter those voluntary fastings which he undertook himself, whereby to *keep his body under, and to bring it into subjection*, this being indeed the most, if not the only, effectual means to do it. Forasmuch as indulging the appetite, and constant feeding to the full, though without excess, swells the veins, and breeds those petulant and noxious humours in the body, which make it rampant and ungovernable,—whereas, on the other side, fasting and frequent abstinence withdraws the fuel which foments those combustions and tumults, those wars and rebellions which the body raiseth against the soul, the inferior against the superior powers. And therefore, as it was by fasting that St. Paul did it, so it is by fasting that we must keep our bodies under, if we ever desire to do it effectually.

And so I come to the other thing to be considered, even how much this keeping the body under by fasting and abstinence, conduceth to our being holy here, and by consequence happy hereafter; which being a thing so seldom thought of in our age, and yet of greater importance than can easily be imagined, for the better explication of it, I shall lay down these propositions.

1. First, therefore, true holiness, we must know, is seated only in the soul and is indeed nothing else, but the right disposition of the several faculties of the soul, and their acting conformably to the law and nature of God; and therefore, though the soul can perform many acts of holiness without the body, the body can perform none without the soul; and although to some acts, both parts are required to put forth themselves in their several capacities, yet they are no further acts of holiness than as they proceed from the soul. Hence the soul may be perfectly holy, and perfectly happy too without the body, as in the state of separation when the body is capable of neither.

2. Although the soul be a distinct substance from the body, and so

is capable of acting separately from it, even whilst it is in it, yet so long as it is tied to the body and actually informs it so as to be but one part of that composition which we call man, it ordinarily makes use of the organs of the body, especially of the animal spirits, in all its actions; and those only are properly called human actions which are thus performed even by the whole man, which therefore cannot but depend very much upon the temper of the body that concurs to the performance of them, as we find by daily experience they do; for if our bodies be out of tune, so are our minds too. If anything affects our heads, disturbs our brains, and so disorders the animal spirits which the soul makes use of in its operations, they are likewise disorderly and irregular: as in music, though the artist be never so skilful, yet if his instrument be out of tune there can be no harmony or melody in what he plays upon it. Yea, none of us but may easily observe, that whatsoever humour prevails most in the body, as phlegm, choler, melancholy, or the like, our actions are usually tainted with it, in so much that by them we may discover what that humour is which is most predominant; from whence it plainly appears, that so long as the soul is in the body, although it was designed to rule and govern it, yet it is apt to be governed by it, and to humour it so far as to follow not its own reason and judgement, but the more impetuous inclinations of the sensitive part, although it be to its ruin and destruction.

3. Seeing therefore that the soul is the proper seat of holiness and yet, so long as it is in the body, it makes more or less use of it in all human actions and is very apt to be swayed by it; hence it necessarily follows in the third place, that the keeping the body under by fasting, and so bringing it into subjection to the soul, cannot but conduce very much to the exercise of all true holiness; for by this means the soul being kept always in its throne, with full power and authority over its subjects, the inferior faculties, being under no restraint, its reasonings would be clear, its judgements sound, its counsels deliberate, it would act like itself, a rational and spiritual substance, and so would be as free from all sensual vices as when separate from the body, which inclines it to them; and then it will begin to relish spiritual objects as suitable to its own nature. For it will look upon virtue and vice, not as they are falsely represented by the imagination, corrupted with the humours of the body, but as they are in themselves, and so discern how lovely and amiable the former is, how odious and detestable the latter, and by consequence exert all its power, to follow the one, and avoid the other.

To explain this more fully to ordinary capacities, I might descend down to particulars and shew how keeping the body under, by fasting and abstinence, does of itself conduce to the mortifying of most lusts and to the quickening the contrary graces in us. For which end I need not instance in gluttony and drunkenness, for these being directly contrary, yea contradictory to true fasting; where this is rightly observed, those vices must needs cease of their own accord, and the contrary virtues of temperance and sobriety take their place. The same may be said of luxury and uncleanness, for that proceeding only from too great a plenitude and luxuriancy of humours in the body, if your bodies be kept under as they ought to be, you will be as much averse from such sins, as ever you were inclined to them.

But I shall chiefly consider some other vices, which at first sight may seem more remote to our present purpose as not depending so much upon the temper of the body; as for example, Are you apt to be angry and peevish, to fret and to be disturbed at eveıy little thing that happens, as many are? This commonly proceeds from immoderate diet, or constant feeding to the full, which breeds abundance of choler, and over-heats the animal spirits, whereby they are apt to take fire and to be enflamed at every thing that occurs contrary to our present desires. But by constant abstinence the choler would be abated, the spirit cooled, and so the mind reduced into a sedate, meek, and gentle temper.

Are you addicted to pride? Although there be a spiritual pride, which degenerate souls are subject to, as well as fallen Angels, yet that which mostly puffs up mankind with vain and foolish conceits of themselves usually springs from the corruption of the fancy, caused by those malign vapours, which by reason of over much eating are exhaled from the stomach into the head, and there disturb the imagination. But fasting prevents the very engendering of such fumes, and by consequence the corruption of the fancy by them, by which means the mind is able to judge of things as they are, and to see clearly that we neither have nor can have any thing in the world to be proud of, but many things to be humbled for; and therefore the keeping the body under, is certainly the best way in the world to keep the mind humble and lowly.

Are you inclined to covetousness? To dote upon the toys and trifles of this lower world? This also must be ascribed very much to the depraved imagination, representing these little things as in a magnifying glass, and so making them seem to be what they really are not, great and amiable; and therefore as fasting frees the imagination from such exhalations as corrupt it, so it must needs help to the mind's looking upon things as it were with its naked eye, and so passing a right judgement upon them, by which means it is soon brought to contemn and despise the world as much as ever it admired or loved it.

Are you dull and heavy at your devotions, not able to pray, to hear, to meditate, or serve the Lord without distractions? Whence comes that dulness? Whence these distractions but from that hurry of gross

vapours in the brain, which obstruct its passages and crowd about it
so disorderly, that the soul cannot without much time and pains rally
them together, and reduce them to such an order, as to make any
tolerable use of them ?   And therefore as these distractions are caused
by overmuch eating, so they may be cured by fasting.   Hence it is
that none of you but may find by experience that you can never perform any spiritual exercise with that life and vigour, that cheerfulness
and alacrity, that constant presence and composure of mind, as when
your bodies are empty, and so kept under as to be in a due subjection
to the soul.

I might instance in many other particulars from whence to shew
how fasting doth of itself conduce much to the extirpation of most
vices and to the planting and growth of true virtue and goodness in
us ;  but most others depend upon, or at least may be referred to these
already mentioned, therefore there is the same reason for them, as
there is for those.   So that we may justly conclude this, with a remarkable passage of St. Hierome in his Epistle to Celantia, where speaking
of the very words of my text he saith, " That fasting and abstinence,"
*non castitati tantummodo, sed omnibus omnino virtutibus opitulatur*,
" helps not only to chastity, but to all manner of virtues whatsoever."

But the great and principal reason of all why it doth so is still
behind, and that is because that fasting is so pleasing and acceptable
to Almighty God, that He hath promised a blessing, a reward to it,
whensoever it is rightly performed, and that too not by the mouth
of a Prophet, an Apostle, or an Angel, but by His own Divine mouth
when He was here upon earth.   For Our Lord Himself saith, *When
thou fastest, anoint thine head, and wash thy face, that thou appear not
unto men to fast, but to thy Father which is in secret ; and thy Father
which seeth in secret shall reward thee openly.*   From whence it is plain,
that if a man fast not out of vain ostentation to be seen of men and
thought holy, but out of a sincere design to keep his body under, and
so fit himself the better for the service of God, that man shall certainly
be rewarded for it.   But what reward shall we have ?   Why, God will
bless and sanctify it to the great ends and purposes for which it is
designed.   Fasting, as I have shewn, doth conduce much to our being
holy, but it cannot make us so ;  that is only in the power of God,
the only Fountain of all true grace and holiness.   But He being well
pleased with fasting, where it is duly observed, doth by His own
Grace and Spirit make it effectual for the subduing our lusts and for
our performance of all holy and good works.

For our better understanding of this, we must consider, that
although God can work with means, or without means, or by contrary
means, as He Himself sees good, yet He ordinarily makes use of the
most fit and proper means that can be used for the effecting whatsoever

He designs; and it is presumption in us to expect He should do otherwise. But fasting, as we have shewn already, is a very fit and proper means as of itself conducing much to an holy and virtuous life; and therefore they who give themselves to fasting and abstinence as they ought to do are always in God's way, using the proper means for the obtaining of true grace and virtue, and so need not doubt but He will bestow it upon them; whereas they who refuse or neglect such means have no more ground to expect His blessing and assistance, than they have to expect He should work miracles for them.

And besides that, although the most High God, the chiefest, the only good, be always ready and free to communicate of Himself, and distribute the graces of His Holy Spirit, it is to those who are rightly disposed for the receipt of them, whose bodies are fitted and prepared for the inhabitation of the Spirit, or as the Apostle words it, *To be the temple of the Holy Ghost.* But certainly no bodies are so fit and proper for so Divine, so pure a Guest, as those which by fasting and abstinence are kept in continual subjection to the soul; for it being the soul that is primarily inspired and sanctified by the Spirit, unless the body be subject to the soul, it will not be subject to the Spirit that is in it, *But the flesh will lust against the Spirit.* Whereas if the body be kept clean and pure, at the beck of the soul, always ready and willing to observe its commands, then the Spirit that enlightens, actuates and quickens the soul, will with great facility diffuse its influences over the whole man, so as to sanctify it throughout; for then the body being subject to the soul, and the soul to the Spirit, as the Spirit is, so will both soul and body be in their capacities, pure and holy.

Hence it is that the greatest discoveries that God hath made of Himself to men, and the most powerful effects of the Spirit upon them, have usually been when they were fasting, and so in a right disposition for them. Thus Moses was fasting forty days and forty nights, even all the while that he conversed with God upon Mount Sinai and received the Law from Him. Elias had fasted forty days and forty nights, when God discoursed so familiarly with him upon Mount Horeb. Our Lord Himself also, though He had no need of it, His body being always perfectly subject to His soul without it, yet He also for our example and imitation fasted forty days and forty nights, even all the while that He was overcoming the Devil and had the Angels to minister unto Him in the wilderness. Daniel was fasting when the Angel Gabriel was sent unto him, to acquaint him with the precise time of the Messiah's Coming. The disciples at Antioch were fasting when the Holy Ghost in a miraculous manner spake unto them, saying, *Separate Me Saul and Barnabas for the work whereunto I have called them.* To name no more, Cornelius, by whose conversion the door of Salvation was opened to the Gentiles, was also fasting when the Angel was sent to instruct him how to get to Heaven. By all which it appears, that when men are fasting, and so their bodies are subject to their souls, then God takes the opportunity of manifesting Himself and His Will and pleasure to them, and also of directing and assisting them in the way to bliss; and by consequence, that fasting is of greater moment to our being holy than it is commonly thought to be.

Nay, after all, it is very observable that it is so necessary to our being holy, that we can never be perfectly holy, until we fast perpetually, I mean in Heaven, where our *bodies shall be fashioned like unto Christ's glorious Body*, and reduced to such an excellent temper, as neither to want nor desire food. Then, and not till then, will our bodies be brought into perfect subjection to our souls, and our souls to God; so that instead of eating and drinking, we shall be always loving, always rejoicing, always praising, always honouring and obeying Him. And seeing that we can never arrive at the perfection of holiness, until we come to fasting altogether, we cannot surely but from thence conclude, that fasting must needs contribute much not only to our being as near as we can like to the Saints in Heaven, but likewise to our coming to them; and so, that the Fathers did not more commonly than truly observe, that as it was by eating that we were cast out of Paradise, so it is by fasting that we are restored to it.

Thus I have briefly touched upon some of those many arguments which might be produced to demonstrate the excellency and usefulness of fasting. I am very sensible that this will seem strange doctrine to many in our age, like those St. Chrysostom speaks of, who προσχήματι τελειότητος, under a pretence of greater light and perfection, look upon themselves as far above so low a dispensation as this is, and therefore indulge their appetites, and laugh at such pitiful, mean Christians as are forced to give themselves to fasting; and I fear that many of you who hear me at this time are of the same mind, and therefore think that fasting perhaps may be very good and needful for others, but not at all for themselves.

But what? Are you not commanded to fast as well as pray? And how come you to be disobliged from one duty more than from the other? Did not Christ Himself say, *That when He, the Bridegroom, was taken from them, then His disciples should fast*? And are not you in the number of His disciples? Hath not He, your Master, taught you how to fast, as well as how to pray, and to give your alms? And do you think that He would teach you anything, but what you are bound to do? Nay, are you not therefore bound to do it, because He hath taught you it? Did not He Himself do it? Have not all the Saints, both in the Old and New Testament, and in all ages ever since, given themselves to fasting? Did not St. Paul himself do so? And do you think yourselves more pure, more holy, more perfect than St. Paul was?

Men and brethren, I heartily wish that every soul here present was so, even that you were all greater Saints, more eminent Christians than that great, that eminent Apostle himself was; that you were all so free from vice, so full of grace, so sure of Heaven, that you had not that occasion as he had to keep your bodies under, lest after all you be cast-aways; that you had all got that perfect conquest over yourselves and lusts, as never more to be inclined or tempted to sin or vanity! Then I must confess you would not have so much need of fasting, as St. Paul had, and therefore might be better excused from it than he was.

But I beseech you not to flatter yourselves with such groundless conceits as these are, as if you were more holy and spiritual than St. Paul was. Do but deal faithfully with yourselves, and you cannot but believe that you come far short of him in every point, in your love to God, in your faith in Christ, in your zeal for the Gospel, in every true Christian grace and virtue whatsoever; and therefore you must needs acknowledge, that if he, one of the strongest, most pious and famous Christians that ever lived upon the face of the earth, if he, I say, was forced to keep his body under, and to bring it into subjection by fasting, lest after all he should be a cast-away, certainly you have all the reason in the world to fear, that you should be cast-aways indeed, unless you do so.

Do but consider these things seriously, and I am confident you will not blame but thank our Church for putting you in mind of this great duty. You will admire her prudence, and commend her care of those that live in her Communion, in that she, in conformity to the Primitive and Universal Church, hath appointed several days every year for the performance of this duty, which otherwise you would be too apt to forget. And although some may think them too many, yet the greatest part of Christians in the world would rather judge them to be too few, especially those that live in the East, for they observe many more. But our Church, in this as in all other things, keeps still in the mean. And therefore besides the nights or Eves before some Holy Days, she hath appointed for days of fasting or abstinence only one day every week, to wit, Friday, which hath always been observed in the Church; one week in every quarter, viz. Ember Week, in imitation of the Apostles, who always fasted before they ordained any to the ministry; and lastly, the three Rogation Days, and this great fast of Lent once every year, which was observed, if not by the Apostles themselves, yet at least by Apostolical men, or those who lived in the very next ages to the Apostles, and so hath been continued as a time of fasting by all Churches in all ages and places ever since,—which questionless would not have been, had not Christians all along found extraordinary benefit and advantage by it. And I do not doubt in the least but that if all you that hear me at this time would be persuaded to observe all these fasts as you ought to do, you would find yourselves otherguess Christians at the year's end than you are now. For supposing you to be always temperate, without which you deserve not to be called Christians, and besides that, to observe these several fasts as they recur: as your constant temperance would keep your bodies always in health, so your frequent abstinence would keep them always under, and bring them into subjection to your souls; by which means you would be every day more averse from your former lust, more inclined to God and goodness, more capable of His Divine illuminations and assistances, more ready and able to serve God here, and more fit to go to Heaven and enjoy Him for ever.

Now these things being duly weighed, you cannot surely but look upon yourselves, as concerned in interest as well as duty, to fast; and therefore cannot but be very solicitous to know how you may do it aright, even so as to make it effectual to the purposes aforesaid, which therefore I shall endeavour to resolve you in, as briefly as I can. For which end we must first know in general, that there can be no certain rules laid down as necessary to be observed by all men in this case; for some require more fasting, some less, some none at all, even such as are weak and sickly, for to them their sickness supplies the use of fasting, in keeping their bodies under; hence it is that we commonly see sickly people have a deeper sense of God and religion than others, because their bodies, by reason of their often infirmities, are constantly kept in subjection to their souls; and they also who are of strong and healthful constitutions, are not bound to abstain for any long time from any manner of food, but only from such, both for quantity and quality, as is apt to pamper the body and to make it rebel against the soul; and if we do but attain the end of fasting, even to keep our bodies under, and bring them into subjection to the soul, we need not, we ought not to be too scrupulous about other things.

This being premised in general, I think it is not amiss to mind you of some particular rules which I think necessary to be observed, in order to the attaining our ends in fasting.

1. Make no distinction at such times betwixt flesh and fish, as the Papists do, who if they do but abstain from flesh, and what proceeds from it, think they fast sufficiently, how much soever they eat or drink of other things. But neither the Scriptures, nor the Primitive Church ever observed any such distinction, neither doth it consist with the nature and end of fasting; but the old Catholic way was, that when

they fasted they abstained from all manner of food until the evening, and still observed Daniel's rule, who when he fasted *ate no pleasant* or desirable *food, neither did flesh nor wine come into his mouth.* This the Primitive Christians observed very strictly, that when they fasted they ate neither more nor better food than, as we use to say, to keep soul and body together; and as for wine, they would not so much as touch it; which, I think, is still necessary to be observed by all that would fast to any purpose.

2. Have a care of those superstitious ends which the Papists propound to themselves in fasting, who think they worship God by it, and that they thereby make Him satisfaction for their former sins, and merit His grace and favour for the future. But you, when you fast, do it only for that end which the Apostle here mentions in my text, *Even to keep your bodies under, and bring them into subjection to your souls, that so you may not at the last be cast-away.*

3. Have a care of falling into the other extreme, even of fasting too much, as well as too little. For as St. Chrysostom observes from my text, the Apostle kept his body under, but he did not kill it; he brought it into subjection, but not to destruction; he used it as a servant, not as an enemy, and therefore would not starve it, for then he could expect no other service from it. Yea, it is St. Basil's observation upon these words, that they, who fast too much, and so weaken and distemper their bodies, violate the Apostle's rule; for he by fasting brought his body into subjection to his soul, they fast so as to bring their souls into subjection to their bodies, forcing them to spend their time in looking after their bodies and serving them instead of being served by them. Hence the same Apostle elsewhere commands us, not simply to *make no provision for the flesh,* but not so, as *to fulfil the lusts thereof.* I suppose there are not many that need this caution, but there are some, and therefore I durst not omit it.

4. To your fasting always join prayer. These two frequently go together in Scripture and ought not to be separated by us, for they strongly excite and quicken one another, in so much that Our Lord Himself tells us, *There are some kind of Devils that cannot be cast out but by prayer and fasting.* Some may be cast out by one, some by the other, some by neither alone; but there is no devil so powerful but he may be expelled, no sin so strong but it may be subdued by both together. And therefore when you fast, spend more time than ordinary in your private devotions, at least as much as you use to spend upon other days in eating, by which means you will lose no time from your particular, but gain much for your general calling.

5. To fasting and prayer add alms also, for these three Christ joined together in His preaching, and Cornelius in his practice. And so must we too. In so much that the ancients scarce ever speak of

fasting, but they prescribe this as necessary to the due performance of it; and the general rule they lay down for it is this, that what you save by fasting yourselves, you must give away to the relief of others; by which means, without either the loss of time or the impairing your estates, you may perform the three great duties of the Gospel, fast, and pray, and give alms; which even severally are very acceptable to Almighty God, much more when they go together.

Lastly, When you have performed this duty as exactly as you can, have a care lest you place any confidence in it, but trust on Christ and Him alone to bless and sanctify it to the great ends for which you use it; for Christ Himself hath told you, that *without Him you can do nothing*. But by Him there is nothing but you may do, as St. Paul long ago experienced, saying, *I can do all things through Christ Which strengtheneth me*. And therefore whensoever you fast, as you must pray to God, so you must trust in Christ for His assistance of you, and then you need not fear but it shall most effectually conduce to *the keeping your bodies under, and the bringing them into subjection, so that you shall not be cast-aways, but happy for ever*. These are the rules which I judge necessary to be observed in fasting; and therefore whensoever I speak of fasting, I desire to be understood of fasting according to those rules, and no otherwise.

Thus now I have done my duty in acquainting you with yours. What effect a sermon of this nature will have upon you, I know not, but fear, it will meet with the same fate that sermons nowadays use to do. Some will like one thing, some another, some nothing at all in it, but dislike and censure the whole; and such will be so far from resolving to practise what they have heard, that they are resolved already not to practise it, and such may now go out of the Church, for I have no more to say unto them, but only this, that this sermon will one day rise up in judgement against them, and then they will wish they had observed it better, when it is too late. But as for such amongst you as seriously mind the concerns of another life, I have a few more words to speak to you, which I desire you to hear with patience and attention.

Beloved in the Lord, you cannot but all ascribe it to the infinite goodness and mercy of the Most High God that you are still alive, and not in Hell, but in the capacity as yet of getting to Heaven whither, I suppose, you all desire to go when you die. But Heaven, you know, is a place where but few come, nor indeed any but real and true Saints; and therefore as ever you desire to go thither when you die, you must while you live be sanctified wholly, you must mortify all your lusts and subdue your passions, you must love and fear God above all things, you must serve, honour, and obey Him with a perfect heart and a willing mind, and do all such good works as He hath prepared for you to walk in, which being no easy matter to do, you must lose no time, spare no costs, neglect no means that may be any way helpful to you in it; especially you must be sure to take St. Paul's course, *You must keep your bodies under, and bring them into subjection*, otherwise you can expect no other but to be cast-aways and undone for ever.

Hence, therefore, I beseech you as your friend, I advise and exhort you as a Minister of Christ, as you tender your eternal Salvation by Him, that you would now set upon this work, this great work, so long neglected by you, even upon fasting, not after a careless, customary, or hypocritical manner, but in good earnest, so as that it may be effectual to the keeping of your bodies in continual subjection to your souls; for which end, I suppose, the strict observation of the days prescribed by our Church, may be sufficient for most people. But if any of you find that that will not do your business, fast oftener, but still observing the rules laid down before, and never leave off till you have brought your bodies to such a temper as no way to obstruct your passage to Heaven, till you have *mortified all your members that are upon the earth*; till you find *no sin reigning in your mortal bodies, so as to fulfil the lusts thereof*; for till then you may be sure you have not fasted enough, or at least not aright; for God is so ready to assist the constant and conscientious performance of this duty according to the aforesaid rules, that no sin, no devil is able to withstand it.

And do not say or think within yourselves, that this is an hard work, who can bear it? For if you cannot deny yourselves a meal's meat, or a little wine now and then for Christ's sake, how is it possible for you to deny yourselves any thing at all for Him? And then with what face can you call yourselves His disciples, when you have not so much as learnt the first part of the first lesson that He hath taught all those that come to Him, even self-denial? And besides, how hard soever this duty may seem at first, by custom it will soon grow easy; when you have been once used to it for a while, you will find that comfort and satisfaction in it, and reap that spiritual benefit and advantage from it, that not only itself, but all other duties will be both easy and pleasant to you.

How happy therefore should I think myself, would it please Almighty God to make me an instrument in His hand to persuade all you that hear me at this time, to the diligent performance of this duty! For how happy then should we all be. Then our minds, being no way disturbed by our bodies, would be always kept in so fine, so delicate a temper that we should think ourselves in another world. Then we should despise the pleasures of this world, and leave them for brute beasts and such men as live as if they were all body and no soul. Then we should not be affrighted at the approach of any evil, as knowing that all things shall work together for our good. Nay,

43

death itself would then be no terror to us, for we should not fear, but *desire to be dissolved, and to be with Christ.*

And when that blessed time shall once come, being freed from these lumps of clay, which now put us to all this trouble, we shall be made like to the glorious Angels themselves, and then we shall never be troubled with eating or drinking more, but yet shall feast continually upon glory, goodness, all-sufficiency, pleasure itself; always enjoying, praising, adoring and magnifying the Eternal God, and our dear and ever blessed Saviour Jesus Christ, Who hath purchased this grace and glory for us: to Whom therefore with the Father and the Holy Spirit, three Persons, one glorious and Eternal God, be all honour, praise, and glory from this time forth, and for evermore. Amen.

## No. 270. JOHN WHITE

[From *The Way to the True Church; Wherein the principal Motives persuading to Romanism and Questions touching the Nature and Authority of the Church and Scriptures are familiarly disputed and driven to their issues where this Day they stick between the Papists and us.* Digression 32 (" Touching Fasting, and how we differ from the Papists therein; and whether the Doctrine of our Church be against it, as the Papists charge us "). Ed. London, 1610, pp. 223–226. This treatise was first issued in 1608. Other editions appeared in 1612 and 1616. It took the form of an answer, section by section, to *A Brief Discourse Concerning Faith, By Which is evidently declared how every one that hath a Desire to please God and a Care to save his Soul . . . ought to resolve and settle himself in all Points, Questions, and Controversies of Faith.* This is said to have been the work of " Fisher " (cp. note on No. 228), and published in London in 1600; a revised edition of it was issued at St. Omer in 1614, with the title *A Treatise of Faith.* The author of the *Treatise* wrote under the pseudonym " A.D., Student in Divinity."]

The first point objected against us is merely false. For we have no doctrine that teaches to break fasting days, but the contrary; that fasting is a Christian exercise, needful to be used for the humbling and ennobling of ourselves to the duties of prayer and repentance, as often as the time shall require; and we hold him no good Christian that omits it. Yea, our Church hath public fasts in the danger of any general affliction, and our people are taught to exercise themselves in fasting privately as much as any Papist whatsoever, setting hypocrisy and superstition aside. The difference is, that we reject their set days and their manner of fast upon those days, by distinction of meats for conscience sake, wherein they place the worship of God by way of Merit and Satisfaction; for the most part also neglecting such exercises of religion by prayer, contemplation, and repentance, as of right ought to be joined with the outward abstinence. Yea, they place and practise fasting only in forbearing flesh and things coming of flesh on certain days; allowing themselves instead thereof not only fish, which is as good as flesh, but that which is daintier,—wine, conserves, sweet meats, and such like, in as great measure as can be, as the experience of this our country shews among such as are Popishly affected.

And suppose we had omitted all fasting indeed, and allowed no time for it, yet some Papists would have borne us company herein that so themselves might be guilty of breaking fasting days as well as we. For Cajetan holdeth, " It is nowhere commanded, but only by custom was brought in, and is necessary neither for the service of God nor the love of our neighbour." Wherein, though we refuse his judgement, yet touching our putting away the distinction of meats and days we are not to be blamed. For what liberty or looseness can possibly be imagined to proceed from eating flesh more than from eating fish, sweet meats, spices, and other things finer than flesh, which the Church of Rome alloweth ? And how may it be conceived to be such disorder on a Friday or in Lent or on a Saint's Even to eat butter or eggs or a bit of flesh, when they that are busiest in controlling it the same days will drink strong wine and other drinks, and eat confections of better stuff and warmer operations ? Or why should a man be censured for eating his meat on an Ember Day, that fasts carefully and zealously upon any day without respect of difference ? Especially our adversaries confessing, there is no kind of nourishment, either of plants or living creatures, but by the law of God and nature, we may lawfully use it. Nothing can be objected but the precept of the Church, for Durand's reason is too gross, " that fish is eaten and not flesh, because God cursed the earth, but not the waters, in that His Spirit moved on them." But what such authority hath a particular Church to make a general law against that which God and nature left at large ? And what jurisdiction hath Rome of late obtained that it should forbid that which the Church in old time permitted ?

For all Antiquity can witness that in the Primitive Church fasting was held " an indifferent thing, and every man was left to his own mind therein, no law binding him to this or that manner," as Cajetan confesseth ; Montanus, a condemned heretic, being the first that ever brought in the Laws of Fasting, from whom the Papists have borrowed them. For Irenaeus that lived fourteen hundred years ago testifieth concerning the keeping of Lent in his time that " some fasted before Easter one day only, some two days, some more ; and the unity of faith was well maintained, notwithstanding all this variety." Basil mentioneth only five days. And Socrates writeth how " it was observed one way in one place and another way in another." . . . Spiridion, the Bishop of Cyprus, though he kept Lent, yet was it " but upon certain days that he fasted " ; and when a stranger came to him upon one of those same days, he set swine's flesh before him, and ate thereof with him. Yea, they kept a Lent before the Feast of Christ's Nativity also, which we do not. And touching Saturdays, some utterly condemned fasting that day, yet others observed it. And Epiphanius thought it an Apostolical tradition to fast Wednesdays and Fridays, excepting those between Easter and Whitsuntide, which yet the Church of Rome observeth not. And as for Ember Days and Saints Evens, we find no use of them for fasting till of late times. And touching the whole question of fasting days, let it be marked what Saint Augustine writeth to a friend of his, " If " (saith he) " you ask my opinion concerning the matter, I find in writings of the Evangelists and Apostles and all the New Testament, that we are commanded to fast; but what days we must fast and what days we must not, I find it not determined by any commandment of Christ or His Apostles." So that if we be faulty because we fast not after the Romish manner, then themselves are likewise faulty because they fast not after the Primitive manner; there being no greater reason why they should condemn us for neglecting their fasts, than why we should condemn them for neglecting the fasts of the ancient Church; nor any cause why our liberty in the use of meats and days should be taken in worse part now, than the same liberty used of old in the Primitive Church, when these things depended upon the will of him that fasted.

And possibly our accusers break fasting days in the same manner that we do. For first, *they eat as often and as good* as we do, when they fast. Next, they have *Dispensations* which exempt them from fasting so commonly and of course, that any man may see the Pope defined fasting by meats and days for no other cause but to vent his pardons. Thirdly, they have *Collations*, which they hold by prescription, which are equal to set feasts. For in Spain, on the Even of the Nativity for example, they have a bountiful supper, exceeding the measure of fasting, made of fruits, conserves, marchpanes, and such like, which they think is lawful, though it hold not the nature of fasting. Fourthly, they have *Customs*, allowing them on fasting days to do as much as we do. For in divers places of Spain and Castile they use eggs, cheese, butter, yea the lard of swine's flesh. And generally on Saturdays they eat the inwards of any beast, with the head and feet; yea, any part of a swine, the buttock excepted. Might it please the Papists now, either to give us leave to do what they do themselves, or else to invite us to their table on fasting days, seeing they bind us out from feasting at home? That is it which a Bishop [John of Salisbury] noted in them long ago and is worth the marking, " They undertake strict professions and shew us difficult things, and being more familiarly favourable to themselves when it comes to performance, they do things gentle and possible."

## No. 271.  THOMAS KEN

[From *A Sermon Preached in the King's Chapel at Whitehall in the Year*, 1685. *Prose Works*, ed. W. Benham ('Ancient and Modern Library of Theological Literature'), pp. 85 f. This sermon was preached on March 8, the First Sunday in Lent, and the text was *Daniel* x, 11. The King, who had recently opened an Oratory at Whitehall, had ceased to attend the official sermons.]

For what is Lent, in its original institution, but a spiritual conflict to subdue the flesh to the spirit, to beat down our bodies, and to bring

them into subjection ?   What is it but a penitential martyrdom for so
many weeks together, which we suffer for our own and others' sins ?
A devout soul, that is able duly to observe it, fastens himself to the
Cross on Ash Wednesday, and hangs crucified by contrition all the
Lent long ; that, having felt in his closet the burthen and the anguish,
the nails and the thorns, and tasted the gall of his own sins, he may
by his own crucifixion be better disposed to be crucified with Christ
on Good Friday, and most tenderly sympathize with all the dolors
and pressures and anguish and torments and desertion, infinite,
unknown, and unspeakable, which God Incarnate endured when He
bled upon the Cross for the sins of the world ; that being purified by
repentance and made conformable to Christ crucified, he may offer
up a pure oblation at Easter and feel the power and the joys and the
triumph of his Saviour's Resurrection.   And to encourage you to
such a devotion, thus enforced with fasting, and mourning, and alms,
as was this of Daniel, reflect on the wonderful success he found.   For
when he began his supplications the angel Gabriel was sent to him by
God, and arrived before he had ended them ; and by that heavenly
messenger God then honoured him with that glorious prophecy of
the seventy weeks.   And the prophet Ezekiel joins Daniel with Noah
and Job, as the three greatest instances of prevalence with God that
ever prayed.

## No. 272.  GEORGE BUDDLE

[From *A Short and Plain Discourse, fully containing the Whole Doctrine of Evangelical Fasts* (London, 1609), Chapter IV (" The Peroration or Hortatory Conclusion of
this Discourse "), pp. 85–87.   This treatise is an exposition of *Matt.* ix, 15.   It was
dedicated to William Barlow, Bishop of Lincoln.]

If we cannot fast with one spare and homely meal a day all the
week-days of Lent, so long as Lent lasteth (as our Church would
have us), yet at the least let us hear the Word of God read or preached
unto us, and let us in truth and no longer in profane and childish
hypocrisy (according to the words of our Common Liturgy) " turn
unto the Lord by weeping, fasting, and praying " this whole last week
of Lent, which we call *Hebdomadam paenosam*, the Passion Week, in
which we ought, if ever, to redeem our ill-kept Lent and to prepare
ourselves by nailing our sinful flesh unto Christ's Cross of mortification, to the end we may rise again with Him at Easter unto justification
with Whom we have died by mortification, that also after our suffering
with Him, we may one day ascend and enter into glory with Him.
As Leo saith truly of the whole Lent Fast, *Quanto sanctius quisque hos
dies invenietur egisse, tanto probabitur pascha Domini honorasse religiosius*,
—the more holily a man shall be found to have kept all the fasting
days of Lent, the more devoutly will he be found and find himself by
experience to have honoured the Feast of Easter or of the Resurrection,

which followeth and endeth Lent.   So the same also may be said even
of the holy and devout keeping of this last week of Lent.   For surely
now the devil is most busy to draw us from our worthy celebration of
this week unto all profaneness, worldliness, security, and wantonness,
and at no time of the year doth he so earnestly seek our destruction by
forgetfulness of God and of our duties of love one toward another as
he doth this week of Christ's Passion, to the end that he may still in
the same week crucify Christ in His members, and make us altogether
unworthy through our profanations and fleshly contentions both of the
merits of Christ's death and of the virtue of Christ's Resurrection;
as the same Leo therefore saith of the whole time of Lent, That *Parum
religiosus alio tempore demonstratur, qui in his diebus religiosior non
invenitur*,—" he hath little or no religion in him at other times who
is not more religious on the Lent days than he was other common
days."   So I may truly say that he hath little, or rather no religion
at all, who is not now contented with those Capernaits in the Sixth
of *John*, in so short a time before the Feast of the Passover, to fast
three days and three nights together, or at least to fast every twenty-
four hours for the space of six days in hearing Christ preach unto
him,—that after such humiliation Christ may by His Spirit testify and
comfortably say unto him, as He testified and said unto them, " Cause
this man to sit down, who is faint with hunger after righteousness, and
hath followed Me fasting now six days together " that I may refresh
him with food at My table, because I have compassion on him.   To
conclude, a chief cause,—I say it again,—of pride in magistrates, of
wantonness in rich folk, of self-wilfulness and worse than heathenish
disobedience and stubbornness in rude people amongst us at this day,
is this our common, unregarded, undisciplined, wanton, humorous,
irreligious, rude disobeying of Christ and His Church, their con-
sultatory commands of this Fast of Lent, and other Fasts whatsoever.

## (12) CHURCHES

### No. 273.  RICHARD HOOKER

[From *The Laws of Ecclesiastical Polity*, Book V, Chapters xxv, §§ 1–3, 4, 5 ; xii, §§ 3, 6; xiii, § 1 ; xvi, § 2.  *Works*, ed. J. Keble, Vol. II, pp. 118 f., 121 ; 47, 48 f. ; 57 f.  Cp. note on No. 148.]

A GREAT part of the cause wherefore religious minds are so inflamed with the love of public devotion is that virtue, force, and efficacy, which by experience they find that the very form and reverend solemnity of common prayer duly ordered hath to help that imbecility and weakness in us, by means whereof we are otherwise of ourselves the less apt to perform unto God so heavenly a service, with such affection of heart and disposition in the powers of our souls as is requisite.  To this end therefore all things hereunto appertaining have been ever thought convenient to be done with the most solemnity and majesty that the wisest could devise.  It is not with public as with private prayer.  In this rather secrecy is commended than outward show, whereas that being the public act of a whole society, requireth accordingly more care to be had of external appearance.  The very assembling of men therefore unto this service hath been ever solemn.

And concerning the place of assembly, although it serve for other uses as well as this, yet seeing that Our Lord Himself hath to this as to the chiefest of all other plainly sanctified His Own Temple, by entitling it " the House of Prayer," what pre-eminence of dignity soever hath been either by the ordinance or through the special favour and providence of God annexed unto His Sanctuary, the principal cause thereof must needs be in regard of Common Prayer.  For the honour and furtherance whereof, if it be as the gravest of the ancient Fathers seriously were persuaded and do oftentimes plainly teach, affirming that the house of prayer is a Court beautified with the presence of celestial powers ; that there we stand, we pray, we sound forth hymns unto God, having His Angels intermingled as our associates ; and that with reference hereunto the Apostle doth require so great care to be had of decency for the Angels' sake ; how can we come to the house of prayer, and not be moved with the very glory of the place itself so to frame our affections praying, as doth best beseem them, whose suits the Almighty doth there sit to hear, and His Angels attend to further ?  When this was ingrafted in the minds of men, there needed no penal statutes to draw them unto public prayer.  The warning sound was no sooner heard, but the Churches were presently filled, the pavements covered with bodies prostrate, and washed with their tears of devout joy.

And as the place of public prayer is a circumstance in the outward form thereof, which hath moment to help devotion, so the person much more with whom the people of God do join themselves in this action, as with him that standeth and speaketh in the presence of God for them. The authority of his place, the fervour of his zeal, the piety and gravity of his whole behaviour must needs exceedingly both grace and set forward the service he doth. . . .

But of all helps for due performance of this service the greatest is that very set and standing order itself, which framed with common advice, hath both for matter and form prescribed whatsoever is herein publicly done. No doubt from God it hath proceeded, and by us it must be acknowledged a work of His singular care and providence, that the Church hath evermore held a prescript form of Common Prayer, although not in all things every where the same, yet for the most part retaining still the same analogy. So that if the liturgies of all ancient Churches throughout the world be compared amongst themselves, it may be easily perceived they had all one original mould, and that the public prayers of the people of God in Churches thoroughly settled did never use to be voluntary dictates proceeding from any man's extemporal wit.

To him which considereth the grievous and scandalous inconveniences whereunto they make themselves daily subject, with whom any blind and secret corner is judged a fit house of Common Prayer, the manifold confusions which they fall into where every man's private spirit and gift (as they term it) is the only Bishop that ordaineth him to this ministry, the irksome deformities whereby through endless and senseless effusions of indigested prayers they oftentimes disgrace in most unsufferable manner the worthiest part of Christian duty towards God, who herein are subject to no certain order, but pray both what and how they list; to him I say which weigheth duly all these things the reasons cannot be obscure, why God doth in public prayer so much respect the solemnity of places where, the authority and calling of persons by whom, and the precise appointment even with what words or sentences His name should be called on amongst His people. . . .

Nor doth the solemn dedication of Churches serve only to make them public, but farther also to surrender up that right which otherwise their founders might have in them, and to make God Himself their owner. For which cause at the erection and consecration as well of the Tabernacle as of the Temple, it pleased the Almighty to give a manifest sign that He took possession of both. Finally, it notifieth in solemn manner the holy and religious use whereunto it is intended such houses shall be put. . . .

When therefore we sanctify or hallow Churches, that which we do is only to testify that we make them places of public resort, that we invest God Himself with them, that we sever them from common uses. In which action, other solemnities than such as are decent and fit for that purpose we approve none.

Indeed we condemn not all as unmeet, the like whereunto have been either devised or used haply amongst idolaters. For why should conformity with them in matter of opinion be lawful when they think that which is true, if in action when they do that which is meet it be not lawful to be like unto them? Are we to forsake any true opinion because idolaters have maintained it? Nor to shun any requisite action only because we have in the practice thereof been prevented by idolaters. It is no impossible thing but that sometimes they may judge as rightly what is decent about such external affairs of God, as in greater things what is true. Not therefore whatsoever idolaters have either thought or done, but let whatsoever they have either thought or done *idolatrously* be *so far forth* abhorred. For of that which is good even in evil things God is Author.

Touching the name of Angels and Saints whereby the most of our Churches are called, as the custom of so naming them is very ancient, so neither was the cause thereof at the first, nor is the use and continuance with us at this present, hurtful. That Churches were consecrated unto none but the Lord only, the very general name itself doth sufficiently shew, inasmuch as by plain grammatical construction " Church " doth signify no other thing than " the Lord's House." And because the multitude as of persons so of things particular causeth variety of proper names to be devised for distinction sake, founders of Churches did herein that which best liked their own conceit at the present time, yet each intending that as oft as those buildings came to be mentioned, the name should put men in mind of some memorable thing or person. Thus therefore it cometh to pass that all Churches have had their names, some as memorials of Peace, some of Wisdom, some in memory of the Trinity itself, some of Christ under sundry titles, of the blessed Virgin not a few, many of one Apostle, Saint, or Martyr, many of all. . . .

Again, albeit the true worship of God be to God in itself acceptable, Who respecteth not so much in what place as with what affection He is served, and therefore Moses in the midst of the sea, Job on the dunghill, Ezechias in bed, Jeremy in mire, Jonas in the whale, Daniel in the den, the children in the furnace, the thief on the Cross, Peter and Paul in prison, calling unto God were heard, as St. Basil noteth; manifest notwithstanding it is, that the very majesty and holiness of the place, where God is worshipped, hath *in regard of us* great virtue, force, and efficacy, for that it serveth as a sensible help to stir up devotion, and *in that respect* no doubt *bettereth* even our holiest and best actions in this kind. As therefore we every where exhort all men to worship God, even so for performance of this service by the people of God assembled, we think not any place *so good* as the Church, neither any exhortation so fit as that of David, *O worship the Lord in the beauty of holiness.*

## No. 274.  WILLIAM HARDWICK

[From *Conformity With Piety Requisite in God's Service*, London, 1638, pp. 12–15. This was a Visitation Sermon delivered at Kingston-on-Thames on September 8, 1638. The author (of whom we have been unable to find any further particulars) is described on the title-page as " Priest and Curate of Reigate, in Surrey."]

There is a conclusion highly cried up amongst us and which hath oftentimes been objected to me, and it is this : That Churches are none other than ordinary and common places, but only in time of Divine Service. For my part, I confess ingenuously, I cannot but blush to hear such an unsavoury assertion to proceed from any mouth which makes a profession of Christ and Christian Religion. O Beloved ! Shall we who are Christians belch out that against the House of our God which never any pagan did against the Temple of his feigned Deity ? Blessed Brethren ! Are not these houses always separated to a holy use, set apart to a holy employment ? Do not sins of theft or of uncleanness, etc., committed in them appear with a far more ghastly and horrid countenance than if they had been committed in other places ? In a word, when we set our feet on these sacred pavements, do not these stones we tread on put us in mind of our duty, as that we have holy thoughts, holy gestures ? It were a happiness not to be expressed, could we at all times and in all places have holy thoughts of our God ; which because our weakness is such that we cannot, Almighty God hath appointed set times and set places for the performing these holy duties. Now the place appointed for God's public worship is the Church. Now what a Church is, Saint Chrysostom tells us, *Non est Ecclesia tonstrina aut unguentária taberna aut officina forensis ; sed locus Angelorum, Regia Caeli, Coelum ipsum.* " The Church is no Barber's or Apothecary's shop ; it is no Westminster or Guildhall ; but the place of Angels, the Court of Heaven, yea, Heaven itself." Into the which, when the Saints heretofore entered, what prostrations, what incurvations did they use ! O, how they did bedew the pavements with their tears ! Thus reverent were the Saints, the servants of God, in the House of their gracious Master. And, indeed, why should they not ? For nature itself teacheth no less. Never pagan entered into the Temple of his idol, but with reverence. And what now ? Shall idols have this, and not the living God ? Shall heathens be reverent, and not Christians ? Let no man torture himself with a causeless fear of superstition in being thus reverent in the holy assemblies. Indeed, were our reverence tendered to the walls, or to some image, or crucifix, or the like, there were too apparent cause of fear. But whereas our reverence is tendered only to God Himself, I see no reason at all in the world why we should not use all reverence that possibly may be in this House of God. Wherefore, ye that are fearful of superstition, let me desire you to be as fearful of profaneness; fall not into the one, by flying from the other. Now for Christians to tread in God's courts without putting off their hats, bending their bodies, bowing their knees, and other the like gestures of reverence, if this be not outward profaneness, I seriously profess, I know not what profaneness is.

Yea, but may some say, this outward reverence may shelter much hypocrisy and therefore why should it be so much urged as nowadays it is?

I answer, Suppose it doth. Suppose many may draw near to God with their lips, when their hearts are far from Him, as also sit here with their heads uncovered, when their hearts are at home shut up in their chests or otherwise gone after their covetousness. What of all this? Shall (say I) the hypocrisy of some make others irreverent? God forbid. For my part, when I come into a Church and there behold a poor sinner kneeling upon his knees, weeping with his eyes, and with a humble and lowly reverence both petitioning and hearing his God, my charity bids me think the best, as how that these shews are not without substance, because I know no other,—it being a peculiar privilege and prerogative of Almighty God to be $\kappa\alpha\rho\delta\iota\sigma\gamma\nu\omega\sigma\tau\eta\varsigma$, a Knower, a Searcher of the heart. But again, let me see a man here sitting in his Master's house, in his Master's presence, as if he were rather God Almighty's fellow than His servant, seldom uncovering his head, seldomer bending his knee, or saucily lolling on his elbows; let such a man make never so many protestations that his heart is upright to Godward, I shall hardly be brought to believe him. For, if there were any zeal, any reverence in the inward man, it would appear and shew itself in the outward man. Well, I say no more but this, Know that ye are servants, and then ye cannot but be obedient, ye cannot but be reverent.

### No. 275. WILLIAM LAUD

[From *A Speech Delivered in the Star Chamber on Wednesday, the xiv. of June MDCXXXVII, at the Censure of John Bastwick, Henry Burton, and William Prynne, Concerning Pretended Innovations in the Church. Works*, ed. L. A. C. T., Vol. VI, Part i, pp. 56 f. This speech was published at London in the year of its delivery; the dedication to Charles I begins " I had no purpose to come in print, but your Majesty commands it and I obey."]

For my own part, I take myself bound to worship with body as well as in soul, whenever I come where God is worshipped. And were this kingdom such as would allow no Holy Table standing in its proper place (and such places some there are), yet I would worship God when I came into His House. And were the times such as should beat down Churches, and all the *curious carved work thereof*, *with axes and hammers*, as in *Psal.* lxxiv, 6 (and such times have been), yet would I worship in what place soever I came to pray, though there were not so much as a stone laid for Bethel. But this is the misery, it is superstition nowadays for any man to come with more reverence into a Church, than a tinker and his bitch come into an ale-house. The comparison is too homely, but my just indignation at the profaneness of the times makes me speak it.

And you, my honourable Lords of the Garter, in your great solemnities, you do your reverence, and to Almighty God, I doubt not; but yet it is *versus altare*, " towards His Altar," as the greatest place of God's residence upon earth. I say the greatest, yea, greater than the pulpit; for there it is *Hoc est corpus meum*, " This is My Body "; but in the pulpit it is at most but *Hoc est verbum meum*, " This is My Word." And a greater reverence, no doubt, is due to the Body than to the Word of Our Lord. And so, in relation answerably to the throne where His Body is usually present, than to the seat whence His Word useth to be proclaimed. And God hold it there, at His Word. For as too many men use the matter, it is *Hoc est verbum Diaboli*, " This is the word of the Devil," in too many places; witness sedition, and the like to it. And this reverence ye do when ye enter the chapel, and when you approach nearer to offer. And this is no innovation, for you are bound to it by your order, and that is not new.

## No. 276.  JAMES USSHER

[From a letter written by Ussher (when Bishop of Meath) to John Selden. Ussher's *Works*, ed. C. R. Elrington (1864), Vol. XV, pp. 175 f. The letter is dated ' Dublin, April 16, 1622 '.]

Touching that which you move concerning the situation of Churches in the elder times of Christianity, Walafridus Strabo telleth us *Non magnopere curabant illius temporis justi, quam in partem orationis loca converterent.* Yet his conclusion is, *Sed tamen usus frequentior, et rationi vicinior habet, in orientem orantes converti, et pluralitatem maximam ecclesiarum eo tenore constitui.* Which doth further also appear by the testimony of Paulinus, Bishop of Nola, in his Twelfth Epistle to Severus, *Prospectus vero basilicae non, ut usitatior mos, orientem spectat.* And particularly with us here in Ireland, Joceline in the Life of St. Patrick observeth that a Church was built by him in Sabul, hard by Down, in Ulster, *Ab aquilonali parte versus meridianam plagam.* Add hereunto that place of Socrates, Ἐν Ἀντιοχείᾳ τῆς Συρίας, ἡ Ἐκκλησία ἀντίστροφον ἔχει τὴν θέσιν· οὐ γὰρ πρὸς ἀνατολὰς τὸ θυσιαστήριον, ἀλλὰ πρὸς δύσιν ὁρᾷ, and compare it with that other place of Walafridus Strabo, where he sheweth both in the Church that Constantine and Helena builded at Jerusalem and at Rome also in the Church of All Saints' (which before was the Pantheon) and St. Peter's, *Altaria non tantum ad orientem, sed etiam in alias partes esse distributa.*

## No. 277. THE CANONS OF 1640

[From the *Constitutions and Canons Ecclesiastical . . . Agreed Upon with the King's Majesty's Licence in [the] Several Synods begun at London and York MDCXL,* Canon VII. E. Cardwell, *Synodalia,* Vol. I, pp. 404 f. The Short Parliament sat from April 13 until May 5, 1640. On its dissolution, the Convocations did not dissolve, but continued to sit in contrast to long-established custom. Their continuance was provided for by a special warrant from Charles I. The Canons from which the extract is taken were issued later in the same year. A Bill was introduced into Parliament in 1641 with a view to making the Canons void ; but it was not passed.]

The Synod declareth as followeth : That the standing of the Communion Table sideway under the east window of every Chancel or Chapel is in its own nature indifferent, neither commanded nor condemned by the Word of God, either expressly or by immediate deduction, and therefore that no religion is to be placed therein or scruple to be made thereon. And albeit at the time of reforming this Church from that gross superstition of Popery, it was carefully provided that all means should be used to root out of the minds of the people both the inclination thereunto and memory thereof, especially of the idolatry committed in the Mass, for which cause all Popish Altars were demolished : yet notwithstanding it was then ordered by the injunctions and advertisements of Queen Elizabeth of blessed memory, that the Holy Tables should stand in the place where the Altars stood, and accordingly have been continued in the Royal Chapels of three famous and pious Princes, and in most Cathedral and some Parochial Churches, which doth sufficiently acquit the manner of placing the said Tables from any illegality or just suspicion of Popish superstition or innovation. And therefore we judge it fit and convenient that all Churches and Chapels do conform themselves in this particular to the example of the Cathedral or Mother Churches, saving always the general liberty left to the Bishop by law, during the time of administration of the Holy Communion. And we declare that this situation of the Holy Table doth not imply that it is, or ought to be esteemed a true and proper Altar, whereon Christ is again really sacrificed ; but it is and may be called an Altar by us, in that sense in which the Primitive Church called it an Altar, and in no other.

And because experience hath shewed us how irreverent the behaviour of many people is in many places, some leaning, others casting their hats, and some sitting upon, some standing, and others sitting under the Communion Table in time of Divine Service ; for the avoiding of these and the like abuses, it is thought meet and convenient by this present Synod, that the said Communion Tables in all Chancels or Chapels be decently severed with rails, to preserve them from such or worse profanations.

# (13) CHURCH MUSIC

## No. 278. THOMAS BROWNE

[From *Religio Medici*, Part II.   Ed. Everyman's Library, pp. 79 f.   Cp. note on No. 4.]

THERE is a music wherever there is a harmony, order, or proportion, and thus far we may maintain the Music of the Spheres; for those well-ordered motions and regular paces, though they give no sound unto the ear, yet to the understanding they strike a note most full of harmony.   Whosoever is harmonically composed delights in harmony; which makes me much distrust the symmetry of those heads which declaim against all Church-Music:   For myself, not only from my obedience, but my particular genius, I do embrace it; for even that vulgar and tavern-music, which makes one man merry, another mad, strikes in me a deep fit of devotion, and a profound contemplation of the First Composer.   There is something in it of Divinity more than the ear discovers.   It is an hieroglyphical and shadowed lesson of the whole world and creatures of God; such a melody to the ear, as the whole world, well understood, would afford the understanding.   In brief, it is a sensible fit of that harmony which intellectually sounds in the ears of God.

## No. 279.  JOHN GAUDEN

[From *Hieraspistes.   A Defence by Way of Apology for the Ministry and Ministers of the Church of England* (1653), pp. 254–256.   Cp. note on No. 154.]

It is true the Most Blessed God . . . is not immediately and for itself delighted with any singing or melody of sense, any more than with other expressions of a reasonable soul, in eloquence, praying, or preaching.   Yet since the use of harmonious sounds is a gift which the Creator hath given to man above all creatures, and wherewith man may be so pleased and exercised in the use of it as thereby to be better disposed and more affected, even to serve the Creator, either in more spiritual, holy, humble, calm affections, or in more flaming devotions and sweet meditations (which are the usual effects of good and grave music on sober and devout souls; who, though they do not dwell and stay on this ladder of sensible melody, yet they may be still ascending and descending by the staves of it in fervency, charity, and humility to God, others, and themselves); I conceive no true religion, but such as is flatted with vulgar fears, can forbid Christians to make the best (which is a religious) use even of music, referring it, as all honest and comely things, to God's glory. And this, not only in reading or hearing such Psalms and Hymns and Spiritual Hymns in which the Divine truth of the matter affects the enlightened judgement and the quieted conscience with the nearest conformity to the holy minds and spirits of those sacred writers who have left us the matter so endited (*sic*), though we have lost the ancient tunes of their holy psalmodies; but also in that audible singing, and melodious delectation, which is sensible in good music, and which hath a secret, sweet, and heavenly virtue to allay the passions of the soul and to raise up our spirits to angelical exaltations by which we may more glorify and praise God, which is a part of our worship of Him; and wherein the Spirit of God in David and other holy men of the ancient Church hath set us allowable, commendable, imitable examples; wherein the immusical rusticity of some men of more ferine spirits which no harp can calm or cause to depart from them, as Saul's did, must not prejudice the use and liberty of those Christians who are of more sweet and harmonious tempers, even in this particular gift and excellency of music, than which nothing hath a more sensible and nothing a less sensual delectation. So that if there be not music in Heaven, sure there is a kind of heaven in music; yet even in this so sweet and harmless a thing, we see that the immoderation and violence of Christians (which hath in it a vein of the old Picts' and Scythian barbarity) is an enemy, even to humanity, as well as to Divinity, while it seeks to deprive men and Christians of one of the Divinest ornaments, most harmless contentments and indulgences, which in this world they can enjoy. I the rather insist in this most innocent particular of singing and music, because no instance can shew more those rude and unreasonable transports to which men are subject in what they call Religious Reformations, if they do not carry all things with very wise hearts and wary hands, that so the leaven of unnecessary vigours and severities may not make the mass or lump of religion more sour and heavy than God in His Word hath required, Who cannot be an enemy to the right and sanctified use of melody or music, since He commands singing to His praises and loves a cheerful temper in His service. Certainly Music is of all sensible human beauty the most harmless and Divine. Nor did I ever see any reason why it should be thought to deform us Christians, or be wholly excluded from making a part in the beauty of holiness.

# (14) 'THE PRECEPTS OF THE CHURCH'

## No. 280. JOHN COSIN

[From *A Collection of Private Devotions; in the Practice of the Ancient Church called the 'Hours of Prayer'*; *as they were after this Manner published by Authority of Queen Elizabeth*, 1560, *taken out of the Holy Scriptures, the Ancient Fathers, and the Divine Service of our own Church.* Works, ed. L. A. C. T., Vol. II, p. 121. This famous devotional book appeared in 1627.]

### *The Precepts of the Church*

1. To observe the Festivals and Holy Days appointed.

2. To keep the Fasting Days with devotion and abstinence.

3. To observe the Ecclesiastical Customs and Ceremonies established, and that without frowardness or contradiction.

4. To repair unto the public service of the Church for Matins and Evensong, with other Holy Offices at times appointed, unless there be a just and an unfeigned cause to the contrary.

5. To receive the Blessed Sacrament of the Body and Blood of Christ with frequent devotion, and three times a year at least, of which times Easter to be always one. And for better preparation thereunto, as occasion is, to disburthen and quit our consciences of those sins that may grieve us, or scruples that may trouble us, to a learned and discreet Priest, and from him to receive advice, and the benefit of Absolution.

# XV. PRAYER

# (1) PRAYER IN GENERAL

## No. 281.  JEREMY TAYLOR

[From *A Letter to a Person Newly Converted to the Church of England.  Works*, ed. R. Heber, Vol. XI, pp. 206 f. (ed. C. P. Eden, Vol. VI, p. 664).]

PRAY frequently and effectually; I had rather your prayers should be often than long.  It was well said of Petrarch, *Magno verborum fraeno uti decet, cum superiore colloquentem*, " When you speak to your superior, you ought to have a bridle on your tongue; " much more when you speak to God.  I speak of what is decent in respect of ourselves and our infinite distances from God.  But if love makes you speak, speak on, so shall your prayers be full of charity and devotion.  *Nullus est amore superior; ille te coget ad veniam, qui me ad multiloquium.*  Love makes God to be our friend and our approaches more united and acceptable; and therefore you may say to God, " The same love which made me speak, will also move Thee to hear and pardon."  Love and devotion may enlarge your litanies, but nothing else can, unless authority does interpose.

## No. 282.  JOSEPH HALL

[From *Meditations and Vows, Divine and Moral, Serving for Directions in Christian and Civil Practice.  Century I, No. lxxxv.  Works*, ed. Peter Hall (1837), Vol. VIII, p. 24.  There were three " Centuries " of these *Meditations and Vows*, the first of them being dedicated to Sir Robert Drury.  They were all issued in 1606, the third century separately from the first two.]

There is none like to Luther's three masters: Prayer, Temptation, Meditation.  Temptation stirs up holy meditation; meditation prepares to prayer; and prayer makes profit of temptation and fetcheth all Divine knowledge from Heaven.  Of others I may learn the theory of Divinity, of these only, the practice.  Other masters teach me, by rote, to speak, parrot-like of Heavenly things; these alone, with feeling and understanding.

## No. 283.  JOSEPH HALL

[From *The Devout Soul; or Rules of Heavenly Devotion*, Sections II [= Chap. I], VIII–XI [= Chaps. III f.].  *Works*, ed. Peter Hall (1837), Vol. VI, pp. 477–479, 485– 489.  This treatise was published in 1643 at a time, as the author says in the Preface, " when we hear no noise but of drums and trumpets, and talk of nothing but arms and sieges and battles."  " Blessed be my God," he adds, " Who in the midst of these woeful tumults hath vouchsafed to give me these calm and holy thoughts."]

If you tell me (by way of instance in a particular act of Devotion) that there is a gift of Prayer and that the Spirit of God is not tied to rules, I yield both these; but withal, I must say there are also helps of Prayer, and that we must not expect immediate inspirations. I find the world much mistaken in both. They think that man hath the gift of Prayer that can utter the thoughts of his heart roundly unto God, that can express himself smoothly in the phrase of the Holy Ghost and press God with most proper words and passionate vehemence; and surely this is a commendable faculty wheresoever it is. But this is not the gift of Prayer; you may call it, if you will, the gift of elocution. Do we say that man hath the gift of pleading, that can talk eloquently at the bar, that can in good terms loud and earnestly importune the judge for his client, and not rather he that brings the strongest reason, and quotes his books and precedents with most truth and clearest evidence, so as may convince the jury and persuade the judge? Do we say he hath the gift of preaching, that can deliver himself in a flowing manner of speech to his hearers, that can cite Scriptures or Fathers, that can please his auditory with the flowers of rhetoric, or, rather, he that can divide the word aright, interpret it soundly, apply it judiciously, put it home to the conscience, speaking in the evidence of the Spirit, powerfully convincing the gainsayers, comforting the dejected, and drawing every soul nearer to Heaven? The like must we say for Prayer; the gift whereof he may be truly said to have, not that hath the most rennible tongue (for Prayer is not so much a matter of the lips as of the heart), but he that hath the most illuminated apprehension of the God to Whom he speaks, the deepest sense of his own wants, the most eager longings after grace, the ferventest desires of supplies from Heaven, and in a word, whose heart sends up the strongest groans and cries to the Father of Mercies.

Neither may we look for enthusiasms and immediate inspirations, putting ourselves upon God's Spirit, in the solemn exercises of our invocation without heed or meditation; the dangerous inconvenience whereof hath been too often found in the rash and unwarrantable expressions that have fallen from the mouths of unwary suppliants. But we must address ourselves with due preparation to that holy work. We must digest our suits and fore-order our supplications to the Almighty, so that there may be excellent and necessary use of meet rules of our devotion.

He Whose Spirit helps us to pray, and Whose lips taught us how to pray, is an all-sufficient Example for us. All the skill of men and angels cannot afford a more exquisite model of supplicatory Devotion than that Blessed Saviour of ours gave us in the Mount, led in by a Divine and heart-raising preface, carried out with a strong and heavenly enforcement; wherein an awful compellation makes way for petition, and petition makes way for thanksgiving; the petitions marshalled in a most exact order, for spiritual Blessings, which have an immediate concernment of God, in the first place; then for temporal favours, which concern ourselves, in the second. So punctual a method had not been observed by Him that heareth prayers, if it had been all one to Him to have had our devotions confused and tumultuary. . . .

Occasional ejaculations are such as are moved upon the presence of some such object as carries a kind of relation or analogy to that holy thought which we have entertained. Of this nature I find that which was practised in St. Basil's time; that, upon the lighting of candles, the manner was to bless God in these words, " Praise be to God the Father, and the Son, and the Holy Ghost," which that Father says was anciently used; but who was the author of it he professeth to be unknown. To the same purpose was the *Lucernarium*, which was a part of the Evening Office of old. For which, there may seem to be more colour of reason, than for the ordinary fashion of apprecation upon occasion of our sneezing, which is expected, and practised by many, out of civility. Old and reverend Beza was wont to move his hat with the rest of the company, but to say withal, *Gramercy Madam la Super-stition.* Now howsoever in this or any other practice which may seem to carry with it a smack of superstition, our devotion may be groundless and unseasonable, yet nothing hinders but that we may take just and holy hints of raising up our hearts to our God; as when we do first look forth, and see the Heavens over our heads, to think, *The Heavens declare Thy Glory, O God.* When we see the Day breaking, or the Sun rising, *The Day is Thine, and the Night is Thine, Thou hast prepared the Light and the Sun.* When the Light shines in our faces, *Thou deckest Thyself with Light as with a garment*; or, *Light is sprung up for the righteous.* When we see our garden embellished with flowers, *The Earth is full of the goodness of the Lord.* When we see a rough sea, *The waves of the sea rage horribly, and are mighty ; but the Lord that dwelleth on high is mightier than they.* When we see the darkness of the night, *The darkness is no darkness unto Thee.* When we rise up from our bed, or our seat, *Lord, Thou knowest my down-sitting and my up-rising ; Thou understandest my thoughts afar off.* When we wash our hands, *Wash Thou me, O Lord, and I shall be whiter than snow.* When we are walking forth, *O hold Thou up my goings in Thy paths, that my footsteps slip not.* When we hear a passing bell, *O teach me to number my days, that I may apply my heart to wisdom*; or, *Lord, let me know my end, and the number of my days.*

Thus may we dart out our holy desires to God, upon all occasions; wherein, heed must be taken that our ejaculations be not, on the one side, so rare, that our hearts grow to be hard and strange to God, but that they may be held on in continual acknowledgment of Him and acquaintance with Him; and, on the other side, that they be not so over-frequent in their perpetual reiteration, as that they grow to be (like that of the Romish Votaries) fashionable; which, if great care be not taken, will fall out, to the utter frustrating of our devotion. Shortly, let the measure of these devout glances be the preserving our hearts in a constant tenderness and godly disposition, which shall be further actuated upon all opportunities by the exercises of our more enlarged and fixed devotion : whereof there is the same variety that there is in God's services, about which it is conversant.

There are three main businesses wherein God accounts His service, here below, to consist.  The first is our address to the Throne of Grace and the pouring out of our souls before Him in our Prayers; the second is, the reading and hearing His most Holy Word; the third is, the receipt of His Blessed Sacraments; in all which there is place and use for a settled devotion.

To begin with the first work of our actual and enlarged devotion. Some things are pre-required of us, to make us capable of the comfortable performance of so holy and Heavenly a duty, namely, that the heart be clean first, and then that it be clear : clean from the defilement of any known sin; clear from all entanglements and distractions.  What do we in our prayers but converse with the Almighty, and either carry our souls up to Him or bring Him down to us?  Now it is no hoping that we can entertain God in an impure heart.  Even we men loath a nasty and sluttish lodging.  How much more will the Holy God abhor an habitation spiritually filthy?  I find that even the *unclean spirit* made that a motive of his repossession, that he found *the house swept and garnished.*  Satan's cleanliness is pollution, and his garnishment disorder and wickedness; without this he finds no welcome; each spirit looks for an entertainment answerable to his nature. How much more will that God of Spirits, Who is purity itself, look to be harboured in a cleanly room?  *Into a malicious soul Wisdom shall not enter, nor dwell in the body that is subject unto sin.*  What Friend would be pleased that we should lodge him in a Lazarhouse?  Or, who would abide to have a toad lie in his bosom?  Surely, it is not in the verge of created nature to yield any thing that can be so noisome and odious to the sense of man, as sin is to that absolute and essential Goodness.  His pure eyes cannot endure the sight of sin, neither can He endure that the sinner should come within the sight of Him.  *Away from me ye wicked*, is His charge both here and hereafter.  It is the privilege and happiness of the pure in heart that they shall see God, see Him both in the end and in the way, enjoying the vision of Him both in grace and in glory; this is no object for impure eyes.  Descend into thyself therefore, and ransack thy heart, who ever wouldst be a true client of devotion.  Search all the close windings of it with the torches of the Law of God, and if there be any iniquity found lurking in the secret corners thereof, drag it out and abandon it.  And when thou hast done, that thy fingers may retain no pollution, say with the holy Psalmist, *I will wash my hands in innocency, so will I go to Thine Altar.* Presume not to approach the Altar of God, there to offer the sacrifice of thy devotion with unclean hands; else thine offering shall be so far from winning an acceptance for thee from the Hands of God, as that thou shalt make thine offering abominable. *And if a beast touch the Mount it shall die.*

As the soul must be clean from sin, so it must be clear and free from distractions. The intent of our devotion is to welcome God to our hearts; now where shall we entertain Him if the rooms be full, thronged with cares and turbulent passions? The Spirit of God will not endure to be crowded up together with the world in our straight lodgings; an holy vacuity must make way for Him in our bosoms. The Divine Pattern of Devotion, in Whom the Godhead dwelt bodily, retires into the Mount to pray. He that carried Heaven with Him, would even thus leave the world below Him. Alas, how can we hope to mount up to Heaven in our thoughts, if we have the clogs of earthly cares hanging at our heels? Yea not only must there be a shutting out of all distractive cares and passions, which are professed enemies to our quiet conversing with God in our devotion, but there must be also a denudation of the mind from all those images of our phantasy (how pleasing soever) that may carry our thoughts aside from those better Objects. We are like to foolish children, who when they should be stedfastly looking on their books are apt to gaze after every butterfly that passeth by them. Here must be therefore a careful intention of our thoughts, a restraint from all vain and idle rovings, and an holding ourselves close to our Divine task. Whilst Martha is troubled about many things, her devouter sister, having chosen the better part, plies the one thing necessary, which shall never be taken from her; and whilst Martha would feast Christ with bodily fare, she is feasted of Christ with heavenly delicacies.

After the heart is thus cleansed and thus cleared, it must be in the next place decked with true humility, the cheapest, yet best ornament of the soul. If the Wise Man tells us that *Pride is the beginning of Sin,* surely all gracious dispositions must begin in humility. The foundation of all high and stately buildings must be laid low; they are the lowly valleys that soak in the showers of Heaven, which the steep hills shelve off, and prove dry and fruitless. *To that man will I look* (saith God) *that is poor, and of a contrite spirit, and trembleth at My Word.* Hence it is, that the more eminent any man is in grace, the more he is dejected in the sight of God; the Father of the Faithful comes to God under the style of *dust and ashes;* David under the style of *a worm and no man;* Agur, the son of Jakeh, under the title of *more brutish than any man. and one that hath not the understanding of a man;* John Baptist, *as not worthy to carry the shoes of Christ after Him;* Paul, *as the least of saints, and chief of sinners.* On the contrary, the more vile any man is in his own eyes and the more dejected in the sight of God, the higher he is exalted in God's favour; like as the conduit-water, by how much lower it falls, the higher it riseth. When therefore we would appear before God in our solemn devotions, we must see that we empty ourselves of all proud conceits, and find our hearts fully convinced of our own vileness, yea, nothingness in His sight. Down, down with all our high thoughts. Fall we low before our great and holy God, not to the earth only, but to the very brim of Hell, in the conscience of our own guiltiness; for though the miserable wretchedness of our nature may be a sufficient cause of our humiliation, yet the consideration of our detestable sinfulness is that which will depress us lowest in the sight of God.

## No. 284. RICHARD BAXTER

[From *The Saint's Everlasting Rest*. Part IV, ch. xiii, § 1. *Works*, ed. W. Orme (1830), Vol. XXIII, pp. 406 f.; ed. London, 1838, Vol. III, pp. 329 f. Cp. note on No. **141**.]

As thou makest conscience of praying daily, so do thou of the acting of thy graces in meditation; and more especially in meditating on the joys of Heaven. To this end, set apart one hour or half hour every day wherein thou mayst lay aside all worldly thoughts, and with all possible seriousness and reverence, as if thou wert going to speak with God Himself or to have a sight of Christ or of that blessed place, so do thou withdraw thyself into some secret place, and set thyself wholly to the following work. If thou canst, take Isaac's time and place who went forth into the field in the evening to meditate; but if thou be a servant, or poor man, that cannot have that leisure, take the fittest time and place that thou canst, though it be when thou art private about thy labours.

When thou settest to the work, look up toward Heaven. Let thine eye lead thee as near as it can. Remember that there is thine Everlasting Rest. Study its excellency, study its reality, till thy unbelief be silenced and thy faith prevail. If thy judgement be not yet drawn to admiration, use those sensible helps and advantages which were even now laid down. Compare thy heavenly joys with the choicest on earth, and so rise up from sense to faith. If yet this mere consideration prevail not (which yet hath much force, as is before expressed), then fall a pleading the case with thy heart. Preach upon this text of Heaven to thyself; convince, inform, confute, instruct, reprove, examine, admonish, encourage, and comfort thy own soul from this celestial doctrine; draw forth those several considerations of thy Rest, on which thy several affections may work, especially that affection or grace which thou intendest to act. If it be love which thou wouldst act, show it the loveliness of Heaven, and how suitable it is to thy condition;

if it be desire, consider of thy absence from this lovely object; if it be hope, consider the possibility and probability of obtaining it; if it be courage, consider the singular assistance and encouragements which thou mayst receive from God, the weakness of thy enemy and the necessity of prevailing; if it be joy, consider of its excellent ravishing glory, of the interest in it, and of its certainty, and the nearness of the time when thou mayst possess it. Urge these considerations home to thy heart. Whet them with all possible seriousness upon each affection. If thy heart draw back, force it to the work; if it loiter, spur it on; if it step aside, command it in again; if it would slip away and leave the work, use thine authority. Keep it close to the business till thou have obtained thine end. Stir not away, if it may be, till thy love do flame, till thy joy be raised, or till thy desire or other graces be lively acted. Call in assistance also from God; mix ejaculations with thy cogitations and soliloquies; till having seriously pleaded the case with thy heart, and reverently pleaded the case with God, thou hast pleaded thyself from a clod to a flame, from a forgetful sinner to a mindful lover; from a lover of the world to a thirster after God, from a fearful coward to a resolved Christian, from an unfruitful sadness to a joyful life. In a word, what will not be done one day, do it the next, till thou have pleaded thy heart from earth to Heaven, from conversing below to a walking with God; and till thou canst lay thy heart to rest, as in the bosom of Christ, in this meditation of thy full and Everlasting Rest.

# (2) THE VALUE OF SET FORMS OF PRAYER

## No. 285. "EIKON BASILIKE"

[From the Εἰκὼν Βασιλική, *The Portraiture of His Sacred Majesty in His Solitudes and Sufferings*, § 16 (" Upon the Ordinance against the Common-Prayer Book "), ed. 1648, pp. 96–100. This famous Royalist treatise was published soon after Charles I's execution on January 30, 1648/9. The author is unknown, but it was quite possibly John Gauden, who became Bishop of Exeter at the Restoration. Christopher Words-worth (" *Who wrote* 'Εικὼν Βασιλική *?* " *Considered and Answered in Two Letters*, 1824) contended strongly for its attribution to Charles I. See *D. N. B.*, *s. v.* ' John Gauden ' (Bibliography), for references to further discussion on the authorship. The treatise evoked John Milton's *Eikonoklastes* (1649) in reply.]

FOR the manner of using set and prescribed forms, there is no doubt but that wholesome words, being known and fitted to men's understandings, are soonest received into their hearts, and aptest to excite and carry along with them judicious and fervent affections.

Nor do I see any reason why Christians should be weary of a well-composed Liturgy (as I hold this [1] to be) more than of all other things, wherein the constancy abates nothing of the excellency and usefulness.

I could never see any reason why any Christian should abhor, or be forbidden to use, the same forms of prayer, since he prays to the same God, believes in the same Saviour, professeth the same Truths, reads the same Scriptures, hath the same duties upon him, and feels the same daily wants for the most part, both inward and outward, which are common to the whole Church.

Sure we may as well before-hand know what we pray as to Whom we pray; and in what words, as to what sense. When we desire the same things, what hinders we may not use the same words? Our appetite and digestion too may be good when we use, as we pray for, *our daily bread*.

Some men, I hear, are so impatient not to use in all their devotions their own invention and gifts, that they not only disuse (as too many), but wholly cast away and contemn the Lord's Prayer; whose great guilt is, that it is the warrant and original pattern of all set Liturgies in the Christian Church.

I ever thought that the proud ostentation of men's abilities for invention, and the vain affectations of variety for expressions, or [=either] in public prayer, or in any sacred administrations, merits a greater brand of sin than that which they call coldness and barrenness. Nor are men in these novelties less subject to formal and superficial tempers

[1] [*I.e.* the Book of Common Prayer.]

(as to their hearts) than in the use of constant forms, where not the words but men's hearts are to blame.

I make no doubt but a man may be very formal in the most extemporary variety and very fervently devout in the most wonted expressions. Nor is God more a God of Variety than of Constancy. Nor are constant forms of prayer more likely to flat and hinder the spirit of prayer and devotion than unpremeditated and confused variety to distract and lose it.

Though I am not against a grave, modest, discreet and humble use of ministers' gifts, even in public, the better to fit and excite their own and the people's affections to the present occasions, yet I know no necessity why private and single abilities should quite justle out and deprive the Church of the joint abilities and concurrent gifts of many learned and godly men, such as the composers of the Service-Book were; who may in all reason be thought to have more gifts and graces enabling them to compose with serious deliberation and concurrent advice such Forms of Prayers as may best fit the Church's common wants, inform the hearers' understanding, and stir up that fiduciary and fervent application of their spirits (wherein consists the very life and soul of prayer, and that so much pretended spirit of prayer), that [= than ?] any private man by his solitary abilities can be presumed to have; which, that [= what ?] they are many times (even there, where they make a great noise and shew) the affectations, emptiness, impertinency, rudeness, confusions, flatness, levity, obscurity, vain and ridiculous repetitions, the senseless and ofttimes blasphemous expressions (all these burthened with a most tedious and intolerable length) do sufficiently convince all men but those who glory in that Pharisaic way.

Wherein men must be strangely impudent and flatterers of themselves not to have an infinite shame of what they so do and say, in things so sacred a nature before God and the Church, after so ridiculous, and indeed, profane a manner.

Nor can it be expected that in duties of frequent performance, as Sacramental administrations and the like, which are still the same, ministers must either come to use their own forms constantly, which are not like to be so sound or comprehensive of the nature of the duty as forms of public composure; or else they must every time affect new expressions when the subject is the same, which can hardly be presumed in any man's greatest sufficiencies not to want (many times) much of that completeness, order, and gravity becoming those duties; which by this means are exposed at every celebration to every minister's private infirmities, indispositions, errors, disorders, and defects, both for judgement and expression.

A serious sense of which inconvenience in the Church unavoidably following every man's several manner of officiating, no doubt, first occasioned the wisdom and piety of the Ancient Churches to remedy those mischiefs by the use of constant Liturgies of public composure.

The want of which I believe this Church will sufficiently feel when the unhappy fruits of many men's ungoverned ignorance and confident defects shall be discovered in more errors, schisms, disorders, and uncharitable distractions in Religion, which are already but too many, the more is the pity.

However, if violence must needs bring in and abet those innovations (that men may not seem to have nothing to do) which law, reason, and religion forbids at least to be so obtruded as wholly to justle out the public Liturgy ;

Yet nothing can excuse that most unjust and partial severity of those men who either lately had subscribed to, used, and maintained the Service Book ; or refused [= refusing ?] to use it, cried out of the rigour of Laws and Bishops, which suffered them not to use the liberty of their consciences in not using it.

That these men (I say) should so suddenly change the Liturgy into a Directory, as if the Spirit needed help for invention, though not for expressions ; or as if matter prescribed did not as much stint and obstruct the Spirit as if it were clothed in, and confined to, fit words,—so slight and easy is that legerdemain which will serve to delude the vulgar ;

That, further, they should use such severity as not to suffer without penalty any to use the Common Prayer Book publicly, although their consciences bind them to it, as a duty of piety to God and obedience to the Laws ;

Thus I see no men are prone to be greater tyrants and more rigorous exacters upon others to conform to their illegal novelties than such whose pride was formerly least disposed to the obedience of lawful constitutions.

## No. 286.  WILLIAM BEVERIDGE

[From *A Sermon on the Excellency and Usefulness of the Common Prayer*. *Works*, ed. *L. A. C. T.*, Vol. VI, pp. 370–373.  This Sermon was preached at the Parish Church of St. Peter's, Cornhill, on November 27, 1681.  Its text was *I Cor.* xiv, 26.  The sermon was published as a quarto pamphlet in 1682 and constantly reprinted.  Cp. note on No. 269.]

The words being thus briefly explained, I shall now apply them to our present purpose, and shew that that form of religious worship, which is prescribed by our Church, established by the laws of the land, and therefore to be used now in this place, agrees exactly with this rule or canon of the Holy Apostle, even that *all things in it are done to edifying*.

But before we prove that that form in particular which our Church has prescribed is agreeable to this Apostolical rule, it is necessary to prove first that the prescribing a form in general is so.  For unless the prescribing a form in general be according to this rule, no form in particular that is prescribed can possibly agree with it. But now, that this rule admits, yea, requires the prescribing of some form, is evident from the rule itself; for the Apostle here commands the Church of Corinth, and so all provincial Churches, to take care that in their religious assemblies *all things be done to edifying*. But how is it possible for any provincial Church to see that this be done, except she prescribes some certain form for the doing of it? If every minister of a parish should be left to his own liberty to do what he pleaseth in his own congregation, although some, perhaps, might be so prudent as to observe this rule as well as they could, yet, considering the corruption of human nature, we have much cause to fear that others would not; at least, the Church could be no way secured that all would and, therefore, must needs be obliged to consider of and appoint some such form to be used in all her congregations, by which she may be fully assured that this Apostolical rule is everywhere observed, as it ought to be. And although we should suppose, what can never be expected, that all the clergy in every province should be as wise and as good as they ought to be, yet it cannot be supposed that every one of them should understand what is for the edification of the people as well as all together. And, therefore, it must needs be acknowledged, that the surest way to have this rule observed is for the governors of every Church and the whole clergy to meet together by their representatives in a synod or convocation; and there, upon mature deliberation, agree upon some such form, which they, in their prudence and consciences, judge to be according to this rule, which the Apostle here lays down before them.

And, besides that the prescribing a form in general is more for our edifying, than to leave everyone to do what seems good in his own eyes, we have the concurrent testimony, experience, and practice of the Universal Church; for we never read or heard of any Church in the world, from the Apostles' days to ours, but what took this course. Though all have not used the same, yet no Church but have used some form or other. And, therefore, for any man to say that it is not lawful, or not expedient, or not to edifying, to use a form of prayer in the public worship of God, is to contradict the general sense of Christianity, to condemn the Holy Catholic Church, and to make himself wiser than all Christians that ever were before him; which, whatsoever it may be thought now, was always heretofore reckoned one of the greatest sins and follies that a man could be guilty of.

Nay, more than all this too. For this is not only to make a man's self wiser than all Christians, but wiser than Christ Himself; for it is impossible to prescribe any form of prayer in more plain and express terms than He hath done it, where He saith, *When ye pray, say, Our Father Which art in Heaven*, etc. And I hope none here present but will acknowledge that Christ, by Whom alone we can be edified, knows better what is or what is not for our edification, than we, or all the men in the world, can do.   And therefore, seeing He have not only prescribed a form of prayer for His Disciples to use, but hath expressly commanded them to use it, we, who profess ourselves to be His Disciples, ought to rest fully satisfied in our minds, that using of a form of prayer is not only lawful, but much more for our edifying, than it is possible for any other way of praying to be.

The same may be proved also from the nature of the thing itself, by such arguments which do not only demonstrate that it is so, but likewise shew how it comes to be so.   For, first, in order to our being edified, so as to be made better and holier, whensoever we meet together upon a religious account, it is necessary that the same good and holy things be always inculcated and pressed upon us, after one and the same manner.   For we cannot but all find by our own experience how difficult it is to fasten anything that is truly good, either upon ourselves or others ; and that it is rarely, if ever, effected without frequent repetitions of it. Whatsoever good things we hear only once, or now and then, though, perhaps, upon the hearing of them, they may swim for awhile in our brains, yet they seldom sink down into our hearts, so as to move and sway the affections, as it is necessary they should do, in order to our being edified by them.   Whereas, by a set form of public devotions rightly composed, as we are continually put in mind of all things necessary for us to know or do, so that is always done by the same words and expressions, which, by their constant use, will imprint the things themselves so firmly in our minds, that it will be no easy matter to obliterate or rase them out ; but, do what we can, they will still occur upon all occasions ; which cannot but be very much for our Christian edification.

Moreover, that which conduceth to the quickening our souls and to the raising up our affections in our public devotions must needs be acknowledged to conduce much to our edification.   But it is plain that as to such purposes a set form of prayer is an extraordinary help to us.   For if I hear another pray, and know not beforehand what he will say, I must first listen to what he will say next ; then I am to consider whether what he saith be agreeable to sound doctrine, and whether it be proper and lawful for me to join with him in the petitions he puts up to God Almighty ; and if I think it is so, then I am to do it.   But before I can well do that, he is got to another thing ; by which means it is very difficult, if not morally impossible, to join with him in every thing so regularly as I ought to do.   But by a set form of prayer all this trouble is prevented ; for having the form continually in my mind, being thoroughly acquainted with it, fully approving of every thing in it, and always knowing beforehand what will come next, I have nothing else to do, whilst the words are sounding in mine ears, but to move my heart and affections suitably to them, to raise up my desires of those good things which are prayed for, to fix my mind wholly upon God, whilst I am praising of Him, and so to employ, quicken, and lift up my whole soul in performing my devotions to Him. No man that hath been accustomed to a set form for any considerable time, but may easily find this to be true by his own experience, and by consequence, that this way of praying is a greater help to us than they can imagine that never made trial of it.

To this may also be added, that if we hear another praying a prayer of his own composition or voluntary effusion, our minds are wholly bound up and confined to his words and expressions, and to his requests and petitions, be they what they will: so that, at the best, we can but pray his prayer. Whereas, when we pray by a form prescribed by the Church, we pray the prayers of the whole Church we live in, which are common to the minister and people, to ourselves, and to all the members of the same Church, so that we have all the devout and pious souls that are in it concurring and joining with us in them; which cannot, surely, but be more effectual for the edifying, not only of ourselves in particular, but of the Church in general, than any private prayer can be.

# (3) THE RECITATION OF THE DAILY SERVICES

## No. 287.  JOHN COSIN

[From Cosin's *Works*, ed. *L. A. C. T.*, Vol. V, pp. 9-11.  The authorship of the extract is uncertain.  It is taken from the first of five series of notes which were appended to William Nicholls' *Comment[ary] on the Book of Common Prayer*, first published in 1710.  (The extract is on p. 6 of this edition.)  The second and third of these series of notes are undoubtedly the work of John Cosin, and J. Barrow, the editor of the *L. A. C. T.* reprint of Cosin, believes that the first series was also written by him.  On the grounds for attributing them to a Mr. Hayward of Coton, a nephew of Bishop Overall, see some correspondence in the *Guardian*, September 26–October 24, 1900.]

WE are also bound, as all Priests are in the Church of Rome, daily to repeat and say the public prayers of the Church.  And it is a precept the most useful and necessary of any other that belong to the ministers of God and such as have cure of other men's souls, would men regard it and practise it a little more than they do among us.  We are all for preaching now; and for attending the service and prayers appointed by the Church for God's worship and the good of all men, we think that too mean an office for us; and, therefore, as if it were not worth our labour, we commonly hire others under us to do it, more to satisfy the law than to be answerable to our duties.  Here is a command that binds us every day to say the Morning and Evening Prayer.  How many are the men that are noted to do it?  It is well they have a back door for an excuse to come out at here; for, good men! they are so belaboured with studying of Divinity and preaching the Word, that they have no leisure to read these same Common Prayers, as if this were not the chief part of their office and charge committed unto them.  Certainly, the people whose souls they have care of reap as great benefit, and more too, by these prayers, which their pastors are daily to make unto God for them, either privately or publicly, as they can do by their preaching.  For God is more respective to the prayers which they make for the people than ever the people are to the sermons which they make to them.  And in this respect are the Priests called God's remembrancers, because they put God in mind of His people, desiring Him to keep and bless them daily with things needful both for their bodies and their souls.  And whatsoever the world makes of it, no doubt but God hath a greater regard to the prayers of His Priests, men that are near Him and appointed for the offering up of that Daily Sacrifice, than to the prayers of other common Christians whatsoever.  And so God tells Abimelech that He would have him to deal well with Abraham, because he was a prophet and *should pray for him*. And to Job's friends, *that His servant Job should pray for them, and He would accept him*. And it was the office that was appointed the priests in the Law, *He shall make an atonement for the people*,not so much to teach and preach to the people (as men now-a-days think all the office lays in doing that), but *to offer sacrifice and incense unto the Lord*, which was but a figure of that which the ministers of Christ were to do in the Gospel. Therefore Samuel professes it openly, to the shame of all others, that he should sin no less in neglecting to pray for the people, than he should in leaving off to teach them the right way of God's commandments; both which are needful, but to them that are already converted prayer is more necessary than preaching. Howsoever we are to remember, that we which are Priests are called *angeli Domini*, and it is the Angel's office not only to descend to the people and teach them God's will, but to ascend also to the presence of God to make intercession for the people, and to carry up the daily prayers of the Church in their behalf, as here they are bound to do.

As we are common Christians we should go to our prayers three times a day; *At evening, and morning, and at noon-day will I praise Thee*. But as we are specially separated from other Christians to be priests and prophets, we should go to them seven times a day, *Seven times a day do I praise Thee*.

And of old, this daily and continual prayer made by the Priests in the behalf of the people, was so much accounted and made on, that they took order to have no intermission of prayer; and because the same Priests could not always attend it, therefore they were to do it in their courses, some at the first watches, some at the second, and others at the third; that so whilst some rested, the others might pray. And of this David speaks, when he saith *Mine eyes prevent the night watches*; and Christ mentions the second and third watches; and David's diligence in performing his duty for the good of the people was such, as that he professes it, *At midnight I will rise up to give thanks unto Thee*; so Paul and Silas rose at midnight to sing praises unto God. It were therefore well to be wished that the like order were taken in the Church now, and that the Sacrifice of Prayer might be continually offered up unto God among Christians, as well as it was in the synagogues of the Jews.

### No. 288. JOHN FELL

[From *The Life of the Most Learned, Reverend, and Pious Dr. Henry Hammond*, Section II. In the *L. A. C. T.* edition of Hammond's *Practical Catechism*, pp. lxx f. Cp. note on No. 341.]

When we reckon up and audit the expenses of the Doctor's [*i.e.* Dr. Hammond's] time, we cannot pass his constant tribute of it paid by him to Heaven in the offices of prayer, which took up so liberal propor-

45

tions of each day unto itself, for the ten last years of his life, and probably the preceding.   Besides occasional and supernumerary addresses,
his certain perpetual returns exceeded David's *seven times a day*.   As
soon as he was ready, which was usually early, he prayed in his chamber
with his servant, in a peculiar form composed for that purpose.   After
this he retired to his own more secret devotions in his closet.   Betwixt
ten and eleven in the morning he had a solemn intercession in reference
to the national calamities ; to this, after a little distance, succeeded the
morning office of the Church, which he particularly desired to perform
in his own person and would by no means accept the ease of having it
read by any other.   In the afternoon he had another hour of private
prayer, which on Sundays he enlarged. . . . About five of the clock,
the solemn private prayers for the nation, and the evening service of
the Church returned.   At bed-time his private prayers closed the day ;
and after all, even the night was not without its office, the Fifty First
Psalm being his designed midnight entertainment.

## No. 289.  IZAAK WALTON

[From *The Life of Sir Henry Wotton, late Provost of Eaton College*, ed. " World's
Classics " (G. Saintsbury, 1927), pp. 138 f.   Walton published his biography of Wotton
(1568–1639) in 1651 ; it was reissued together with the lives of Donne, Hooker, and
Herbert, in a single volume in 1670.]

In both which places [*i.e.* at Eton and Kilmore], his [*i.e.* William
Bedell's] life was so holy as seemed to equal the Primitive Christians ;
for as they, so he kept all the Ember Weeks, observed besides his
private devotions the Canonical Hours of Prayer very strictly, and so
he did all the Feasts and Fast-days of his Mother, the Church of
England.

# (4) PRAYERS FOR THE DEAD

## No. 290. THOMAS BROWNE

[From *Religio Medici*, Part I, Ed. Everyman's Library, p. 9. Cp. note on No. **4**.]

A THIRD there is, which I did never positively maintain or practise, but have often wished it had been consonant to truth and not offensive to my religion, and that is, the Prayer for the Dead; whereunto I was inclined from some charitable inducements, whereby I could scarce contain my Prayers for a friend at the ringing of a bell, or behold his corpse without an orison for his soul. It was a good way, methought, to be remembered by posterity, and far more noble than an history.

## No. 291. JEREMY TAYLOR

[From *A Dissuasive from Popery, Part I*.   Chapter i, § 4 (" Doctrine of Purgatory "). *Works*, ed. R. Heber, Vol. X, pp. 147–149 (ed. C. P. Eden, Vol. VI, pp. 195 f.).   Cp. note on No. 260.]

Before we say any more in this question, we are to premonish that there are two great causes of their mistaken pretensions in this article from Antiquity.

The first is, that the ancient Churches in their Offices and the Fathers in their writings did teach and practise respectively Prayer for the Dead. Now because the Church of Rome does so too, and, more than so, relates her prayers to the doctrine of purgatory and for the souls there detained, her doctors vainly suppose that whenever the holy Fathers speak of Prayer for the Dead that they conclude for purgatory; which vain conjecture is as false as it is unreasonable. For it is true the Fathers did pray for the dead. But how? " That God should show them mercy, and hasten the resurrection, and give a blessed sentence in the great day." But then it is also to be remembered that they made prayers, and offered for those, who, by the confession of all sides, never were in purgatory, even for the patriarchs and prophets, for the Apostles and Evangelists, for Martyrs and Confessors, and especially for the Blessed Virgin Mary. So we find it in Epiphanius, St. Cyril, and in the canon of the Greeks, and so it is acknowledged by their own Durandus; and in their mass-book anciently they prayed for the soul of St. Leo, of which because by their latter doctrines they grew ashamed, they have changed the prayer for him into a prayer to God by the intercession of St. Leo, in behalf of themselves; so by their new doctrine, making him an intercessor for us, who, by their old doctrine, was supposed to need our prayers to intercede for him; of which Pope Innocent, being asked a reason, makes a most pitiful excuse.

Upon what accounts the Fathers did pray for the Saints departed and indeed generally for all, it is not now seasonable to discourse, but to say this only, that such general prayers for the dead as those above reckoned, the Church of England never did condemn by any express article, but left it in the middle; and by her practice declares her faith of the Resurrection of the Dead and her interest in the Communion of Saints, and that the Saints departed are a portion of the Catholic Church, parts and members of the Body of Christ; but expressly condemns the doctrine of purgatory, and consequently all Prayers for the Dead relating to it. And how vainly the Church of Rome from Prayer for the Dead infers the belief of purgatory, every man may satisfy himself, by seeing the writings of the Fathers, where they cannot meet with one collect or clause for praying for the delivery of souls out of that imaginary place. Which thing is so certain, that in the very Roman Offices, we mean the Vigils said for the Dead, which are Psalms and Lessons taken from the Scripture speaking of the miseries of this world, repentance and reconciliation with God, the bliss after this life of them that die in Christ, and the resurrection of the dead, and in the anthems, versicles, and responses, there are prayers made recommending to God the soul of the newly defunct, praying, " he may be freed from hell and eternal death," that " in the day of judgement he be not judged and condemned according to his sins, but that he may appear among the elect in the glory of the resurrection "; but not one word of purgatory or its pains.

### No. 292. HERBERT THORNDIKE

[From *Just Weights and Measures; That is, The Present State of Religion Weighed in the Balance, and Measured by the Standard of the Sanctuary*, Chapter XVI, §§ 1-3. *Works*, ed. L. A. C. T., Vol. V, pp. 186 f. This treatise was first published in 1662; a second edition of it appeared in 1680. Thorndike had been as " assistant " in the Committee which revised the Book of Common Prayer. He was disappointed that fewer changes were not made in a Catholic direction; and in the present work, many of his feelings on this subject found expression.]

The practice of the Church in interceding for them [*i.e.* for the Departed] at the Celebration of the Eucharist is so general and so ancient, that it cannot be thought to have come in upon imposture, but that the same aspersion will seem to take hold of the common Christianity.

But to what effect this intercession was made, that is, indeed, the due point of difference. For they, who think that the ancient Church prayed, and do themselves pray, for the removing of them from a place of purgatory-pains into perfect happiness by the clear sight of God, offend against the ancient Church, as well as against the Scripture, both ways. For Justin Martyr makes it a part of the Gnostics' heresy, that the soul without the body is in perfect happiness. They indeed held it, because they denied the resurrection. But the Church therefore, believing the resurrection, believes no perfect happiness of the soul before it. And the great consent of the ancient Church in this point is acknowledged by divers learned writers in the Church of Rome. Neither is the consent of it less evident in this, that there is no translating of souls into a new estate before the great trial of the general judgement.

In the meantime, then, what hinders them to receive comfort and refreshment, rest and peace and light (by the visitation of God, by the consolation of His Spirit, by His good Angels), to sustain them in the expectation of their trial, and the anxieties they are to pass through during the time of it? And though there be hope for those that are most solicitous to live and die good Christians, that they are in no such suspense, but within the bounds of the Heavenly Jerusalem, yet because their condition is uncertain and where there is hope of the better there is fear of the worse, therefore the Church hath always assisted them with the prayers of the living, both for their speedy trial (which all blessed souls desire), and for their easy absolution and discharge with glory before God, together with the accomplishment of their happiness in the receiving of their bodies.

# (5) PRAYING IN LATIN

## No. 293.  FRANCIS WHITE

[From *A Reply to Jesuit Fisher's Answer*, pp. 367 f.  (P. 367 is wrongly numbered 357.)  Cp. note on No. **228**.]

IT is repugnant to the nature and end of vocal prayer that the same should be exercised in a form of words which people that pray together understand not.  For prayer is an ascending of the mind to God ; and according to Aquinas and other Schoolmen it is an action of the understanding faculty.  And in the same, people confess their sins, and request of God such things as they have need of.  They give thanks for benefits spiritual and temporal, general and special, conferred upon them ; and the effect of prayer dependeth upon their inward humiliation and sense of their wants (*II Chron.* xxxiv, 27 ; *Ps.* li, 19) and upon their special faith in the Divine promises (*Matt.* ix, 28 ; *Mark* ix, 23 ; and *Mark* xi, 29).  And Tertullian saith, *God is not so much an hearer of the voice, as of the heart.*  But these things cannot be performed where people understand not what they confess, request, or praise God for.  And words are appointed to instruct, excite, and edify men ; and if they understand them not, to what use serveth vocal prayer ?  For we use not words to teach God, but to instruct and excite ourselves.  And hereby the Popish evasion is answered wherein they affirm that even as when a supplication is preferred to a king or judge which the suppliant understandeth not, it is all one in what language soever the same be preferred, the judge understands it, so likewise because God understandeth all languages, it mattereth not though people pray to Him in a strange tongue.  For our words in vocal prayer concern ourselves mutually and principally ; but God Himself requireth the understanding and affection of our heart.

## No. 294.  DANIEL WHITBY

[From *A Treatise in Confutation of the Latin Service Practiced, and by the Order of the Trent Council Continued, in the Church of Rome.*  Chapters I, VI.  London, 1687, pp. 8 f., 104.  This treatise was published anonymously.]

Now that it may be evident to all indifferent persons how repugnant is that established practice of the Church of Rome to the avowed practice of the Church of Christ for many ages, confirmed by Scripture and by Reason, I shall endeavour to demonstrate :—

1. That the public service of Singing, Praying, Reading, was for the

first six centuries and more performed by the Church of God, in a tongue understood by the people ;

2. That the Fathers do expressly teach that it was necessary that the public service of Prayer, Singing, and Reading, should be so performed ;

3. That they condemned the contrary practice of celebrating the Public Worship in a tongue not understood by the common people, as opposite unto the Word of God and to the ends for which the public service was appointed ;

4. That this practice may be disproved by most evident and cogent reasons, built upon the assertions of the holy Fathers ; in a word, that they most plainly do condemn all that the Church of Rome doth practise and hath decreed in this matter, and justify all that the Protestants assert in opposition to her determinations. . . .

The prevailing prayer must, saith St. James, be δέησις ἐνεργουμένη, a prayer put up with great devotion, intention, and inward working of the heart ; and suitably the Fathers generally tell us this intention of the mind is necessary, because God is not the hearer of the voice but of the heart, or, as St. Gregory, " true prayer consists not in the words of the mouth but in the thoughts of the heart," that we must knock with a pious excitation and " fervent intention of the heart in prayer," with many things of a like nature. But what possibility is there that the illiterate, who knows not in the least the meaning of the words the Mass-Priest utters, should thus join with him in his prayer, serving God with all his heart, soul, and mind, engaging and lifting up his heart to God, and praying with the understanding ? He indeed may think of other good things at the same time or use some other prayers with which he is acquainted. But join with the Mass-Priest in his he cannot, for his heart knows nothing of it, conceives nothing of the sense of the words spoken, and so is not affected with them or moved by them to desire anything. He therefore loseth all the advantages he might receive by these prayers, spoken in a language understood,—the excellency of devotion, the passion of desires, the ascent of the mind to God, the intellectual conversation with Him, the actings of his faith, affiance, hopes, compunction, humiliation, upon occasion of the prayers recited ; and whether it be reasonable that in the public Service all these advantages should be lost to the greatest part of the Catholic Church, to them who chiefly need, and might entirely enjoy them from the Service ministered in their Mother-tongue, let any reasonable man judge.

# (6) SEVENTEENTH CENTURY PRAYERS

## No. 295. THE BOOK OF COMMON PRAYER

[From the *Book of Common Prayer*. The Collects for the Third Sunday in Advent, the Sixth Sunday after Epiphany, and Easter Even; and the first Ember Collect. All of these Collects were new to the 1661 Book, and all of them are attributed to Cosin. That for Advent III is certainly Cosin's composition and was substituted for a colourless collect derived from the Roman Rite; that for Easter Even is an adaptation of that contained in the Scottish Liturgy of 1637, which was probably written by Laud; the Ember Collect is to be found in Cosin's *Private Devotions*.]

O LORD JESU CHRIST, Who at Thy first Coming didst send Thy messenger to prepare Thy way before Thee; Grant that the ministers and stewards of Thy mysteries may likewise so prepare and make ready Thy way, by turning the hearts of the disobedient to the wisdom of the just, that at Thy second Coming to judge the world we may be found an acceptable people in Thy sight, Who livest and reignest with the Father and the Holy Spirit, ever one God, world without end. Amen.

O God, whose blessed Son was manifested that He might destroy the works of the devil, and make us the sons of God, and heirs of eternal life; Grant us, we beseech Thee, that, having this hope, we may purify ourselves, even as He is pure; that, when He shall appear again, with power and great glory, we may be made like unto Him in His eternal and glorious Kingdom; where with Thee, O Father, and Thee, O Holy Ghost, He liveth and reigneth, ever one God, world without end. Amen.

Grant, O Lord, that as we are baptized into the death of Thy Blessed Son our Saviour Jesus Christ, so by continual mortifying our corrupt affections we may be buried with Him; and that through the grave and gate of death, we may pass to our joyful resurrection; for His merits, Who died, and was buried, and rose again for us, Thy Son Jesus Christ our Lord. Amen.

Almighty God, our Heavenly Father, Who hast purchased to Thyself an Universal Church by the precious Blood of Thy dear Son, Mercifully look upon the same, and at this time so guide and govern the minds of Thy servants, the Bishops and Pastors of Thy flock, that they may lay hands suddenly on no man, but faithfully and wisely make choice of fit persons to serve in the sacred Ministry of Thy Church. And to those which shall be ordained to any holy function give Thy grace and Heavenly benediction; that both by their life and doctrine they may set forth Thy glory and set forward the salvation of all men; through Jesus Christ our Lord. Amen.

## No. 296.  THE BOOK OF COMMON PRAYER

[From the Service for January 30, the day of Charles I's Martyrdom, annexed until 1859 to the *Book of Common Prayer*. In that year an Act of Parliament was passed which repealed the annual observance of this day. Hitherto a Royal Mandate had been issued at the beginning of every reign authorizing the inclusion of the Service (as well as the services for May 29 and November 5) in the *Book of Common Prayer*. The text of the following prayer suffered a number of modifications as time went on.]

Blessed Lord, in Whose sight the death of Thy Saints is precious, We magnify Thy Name for that abundant grace bestowed on our late martyred Sovereign, by which he was enabled so cheerfully to follow the steps of His Blessed Master and Saviour, in a constant meek suffering of all barbarous indignities, and at last resisting unto blood; and even then, according to the same pattern, praying for his murderers. Let his memory, O Lord, be ever blessed among us, that we may follow the example of his patience and charity. And grant that this our land may be freed from the vengeance of his blood, and Thy mercy glorified in the forgiveness of our sins. And all for Jesus Christ His Sake. Amen.

## No. 297.  LANCELOT ANDREWES

[From *Preces Privatae, Pars Prima* (Diei Primae, Intercessio). Ed. *L. A. C. T.*, p. 55; English translation ed. F. E. Brightman (1903), p. 49. The *Preces Privatae* were compiled for Andrewes' own devotional use and apparently never intended for publication. They were first printed in 1648 by Richard Drake. Drake, however, was dependent upon an incomplete MS., and he contended himself with a translation. The full ('Laudian') text was first edited by P. G. Medd (*S.P.C.K.*, 1892). On the history of the text, see the Introduction and Preface to F. E. Brightman's careful edition, especially pp. xiii–xxv.]

O Rex Nationum, usque ad terminos terræ,

 Robora omnia totius Terræ Regna et Politias, utpote ordinationem tuam, etsi humanam creaturam.

 Dissipa gentes quæ bella volunt.

 Tolle bella usque ad terminos terræ.

O Domine, sustentatio insularum et earum spes,

 Libera insulam hanc, et totam regionem in qua habitamus,

 Ab omni afflictione, periculo, et extrema necessitate.

## No. 298.  JOHN COSIN

[From *A Collection of Private Devotions*. Part of "A Devout Prayer which may be used at all Times"—this constituting a kind of appendix to "Matins"; §§ ii, iii. *Works*, ed. *L. A. C. T.*, Vol. II, p. 166. Cp. note on No. **280**.]

Be Thou a light unto mine eyes, music to mine ears, sweetness to my taste, and a full contentment to my heart. Be Thou my sunshine in the day, my food at the table, my repose in the night, my clothing in nakedness, and my succour in all necessities.

Lord Jesu, I give Thee my body, my soul, my substance, my fame, my friends, my liberty, and my life. Dispose of me and of all that is mine, as it seemeth best to Thee and to the glory of Thy Blessed Name.

## No. 299. WILLIAM LAUD

[From *A Summary of Devotions Compiled and Used by Dr. William Laud, Sometime Lord Archbishop of Canterbury, Now Published according to the Copy written with his own Hand and reserved in the Archives of St. John Baptist's College Library in Oxon.* (Oxford, 1667), *s.v.* "Ecclesia." *Works*, ed. L. A. C. T., Vol. III, p. 67.]

Gracious Father, I humbly beseech Thee for Thy Holy Catholic Church. Fill it with all truth, in all truth, with all peace. Where it is corrupt, purge it. Where it is in error, direct it. Where it is superstitious, rectify it. Where anything is amiss, reform it. Where it is right, strengthen and confirm it. Where it is in want, furnish it. Where it is divided and rent asunder, make up the breaches of it, O Thou Holy One of Israel.

## No. 300. THOMAS KEN

[From *A Manual of Prayers for the Use of the Scholars of Winchester College and all other devout Christians, to which are added Three Hymns for Morning, Evening and Midnight*, "Directions for Receiving the Holy Eucharist." *Prose Works*, ed. W. Benham ("Ancient and Modern Library of Theological Literature"), p. 224. The extract is headed "Motives to Examination." The first edition of this treatise was published in 1674, Ken having been elected a Fellow of Winchester College in 1666.]

O my soul, thou art now in the presence of the great Judge of Heaven and Earth, before Whose dreadful tribunal thou must certainly appear at the Day of Judgement, to give a strict account of all thy actions and every idle word, of every evil thought, and thine own conscience will then be thy accuser.

Think, O my soul, think if thou canst what unimaginable horrors will seize an impenitent sinner when the last trump calls him out of the grave, and the devils begin to drag him to God's Judgement-Seat! What would such a wretch give to purchase one such opportunity of repentance as God now in great mercy gives thee? If ever thou hopest to escape those horrors, O my soul, make thy peace with God, judge thyself here, lest thou be condemned hereafter.

XVI. ETHICS

# (1) CHRISTIAN MORALS

## No. 301.  THOMAS BROWNE

[From *Christian Morals*, Part I, § 12.   Ed. Everyman's Library (*The Religio Medici and other Writings*), p. 238.   This treatise was first published posthumously by John Jeffery, Archdeacon of Norwich, in 1716.   It is apparently a continuation of the *Religio Medici* (cp. note on No. 4), but probably Browne himself would not have issued it without considerable revision.]

LIVE by old ethics and the classical rules of honesty.   Put no new names or notions upon authentic virtues and vices.   Think not that morality is ambulatory; that vices in one age are not vices in another, or that virtues, which are under the everlasting seal of right reason, may be stamped by opinion.   And therefore, though vicious times invert the opinions of things, and set up new ethics against virtue, yet hold thou unto old morality; and rather than follow a multitude to do evil, stand like Pompey's pillar conspicuous by thyself, and single in integrity.   And since the worst of times afford imitable examples of virtue, since no deluge of vice is like to be so general but more than eight will escape, eye well those heroes who have held their heads above water, who have touched pitch, and not been defiled, and in the common contagion have remained uncorrupted.

## No. 302.  HENRY MORE

[From *An Explanation of the Grand Mystery of Godliness ; Or a True and Faithful Representation of the Everlasting Gospel of Our Lord and Saviour Jesus Christ, the Only Begotten Son of God and Sovereign over Men and Angels*, Book II, Chapters xi f. London, 1660, pp. 51, 53–56.   In spite of the author's expression of his averseness from the writing of books, "the common disease of this Scripturient age," ('To the Reader,' p. vii) this work alone extends to over 550 folio pages.   It is a sort of *summa* of the Christian Religion, based on the Gospels.]

We have now competently set out the nature of the *Animal Life*. But before we pass to the *Divine*, it will be needful to us to take notice of a *Middle Life*, or faculty of the soul of man betwixt the Divine and Animal, which, if we might name by the general principle or common root thereof, we may call it Reason; which is a power or faculty of the soul, whereby either from her innate ideas or common notions, or else from the assurance of her own senses, or upon the relation or tradition of another, she unravels a further clue of knowledge, enlarging her sphere of intellectual light, by laying open to herself the close connexion and cohesion of the conceptions she has of things, whereby inferring one

641

thing from another, she is able to deduce multifarious conclusions, as well for the pleasure of speculation as the necessity of practice.

From this single faculty or common root of improved knowledge shoot out many branches, but I shall name only some main ones, such as are the skill of Natural Philosophy, of Arithmetic and Geometry; the power of speech, whether merely grammatical or also rhetorical; a capacity of civil education; and an ability of discoursing and acting also after an exterior way in matters of religion.

This is a short description of the Middle life which is neither Animal nor Divine, but is really (what the Astrologians fancy Mercury to be) such as that with which it is conjoined, whether good or bad, Divine or Animal. . . .

But this *Holy and Divine Life* to such as have an eye to see will be most perceptible in the branches thereof, though to the Natural man they will look very witheredly and contemptibly. These branches are three, whose names, though trivial and vulgar, yet if rightly understood they bear such a sense with them, that nothing more weighty can be pronounced by the tongue of men or Seraphims; and, in brief, they are these, Charity, Humility, and Purity; which, wherever they are found, are the sure and infallible marks or signs of either an unfallen Angel or a regenerate soul.

These we call Divine Virtues, not so much because they imitate in some things the Holy Attributes of the Eternal Deity, but because they are such as are proper to a creature to whom God communicates His Own Nature so far forth as it is capable of receiving it, whether that creature be man or Angel, and so becomes θεάνθρωπος or θεοδαίμων, that is θεάγγελος. For such a creature as this (and Christ was such a creature in the highest manner conceivable) has conspicuously in it these three Divine Virtues, namely Humility, Charity, and Purity.

By *Humility*, I understand such a spirit or gracious property in the soul of man or any intellectual creature as that hereby he does sensibly and affectionately attribute all that he has or is or can do to God the Author and Giver of every good and perfect gift. This is the highest piece of holiness, and the truest and most acceptable sacrifice we can offer to God, thus lively and freely to acknowledge that all we have is from Him. From whence we do not arrogate anything to ourselves, nor contemptuously lord it over others. In this grace is comprehended an ingenuous Gratitude, which is the freest and most noble kind of justice, that is, a full renouncing of all self-dependency, a firm and profound submission to the will of God in all things, and a disgust, or at least a deadness, to the glory of the world and the applause of men.

By *Charity*, I understand an intellectual love, by which we are enamoured of the Divine Perfections, such as His Goodness, Equity,

Benignity, His Wisdom also, His Justice, and His Power, as they are graciously actuated and modified by the forenamed attributes. And I say that to be truly transformed into these Divine Perfections, so far forth as they are communicable to human nature, and out of the real sense of them in ourselves, to love and admire God in Whom they infinitely and immeasurably reside, is the truest and highest kind of adoration, and the most grateful praising and glorifying God that the soul of man can exhibit to her Maker. But in being thus transformed into this Divine image of intellectual love, our minds are not only raised in holy devotions towards God, but descend also in very full and free streams of dearest affection to our fellow-creatures, rejoicing in their good as if it were our own, and compassionating their misery as if it were ourselves did suffer, and according to our best judgement and power ever endeavouring to promote the one and to remove the other. And this most eminently contains in it whatever good is driven at by Civil Justice or Moral Honesty. For how should we injure those for whose real welfare we could be content to die ?

By *Purity* I understand a due moderation and rule over all the joys and pleasures of the flesh, bearing so strict an hand and having so watchful an eye over their subtle enticements and allurements, and so firm and loyal affection to that idea of celestial beauty set up in our minds, that neither the pains of the body nor the pleasures of the Animal life shall ever work us below our spiritual happiness and all the competible enjoyments of that life that is truly Divine. And in this conspicuously is contained whatever either Moral Temperance or Fortitude can pretend to. For ordinarily he is held temperate enough that can but save his brains from gross sottishness and his body from diseases ; but this Purity respects the Divine Life itself, and requires such a moderation in all the affairs of the flesh, that our bodies may still remain unpolluted temples and meet habitations for the Spirit of God to dwell in and act in, whether by way of Illumination, or Sanctification and Animation to interior duties of Holiness. And as for Fortitude, it is plain that this Purity of the soul, having mortified and tamed the exorbitant lusts and pleasures of the body, death will seem less formidable by far, and this mortal life of lesser value.

But the greatest *Fortitude* of all is when Love proves stronger than death itself even in the deepest and most bitter sense of it ; and not so much the weakness and insensibleness of the body, nor yet the full career or furious heat and hurry of the natural spirits makes pain and death more tolerable ; but the pure courage of the soul herself animated only by an unrelinquishable love of the Divine Life, and whatever design is imposed upon her by that principle.

The example of this Fortitude is admirable in Our Blessed Saviour, and transcends as much the general valour recorded by the pens of poets and historians, as the valour of those heroes does exceed the savage fierceness and boldness of bears, wolves, and lions. For a man to encounter death in an exalted heat and fire of his agitated spirits is not much unlike a mere drunken fray where their blood being heated with the excess of wine, the combatants become unsensible of those mortal gashes they make in one another's bodies. But to fight in cold blood is true valour indeed, and the greater by how much more the occasion of the enterprise approves itself noble and the parties are not at first engaged by any rage or passion. For then they sacrifice their lives but to a rash fit of choler or at least to that tyrant in them, pride, which they for the better credit of the business ordinarily call 'The Sense of Honour,' else they could willingly upon better thoughts save themselves the pains and danger of the combat.

But to speak of valour more lawful and laudable, which is to meet the enemy in the field, where their minds are enraged and heightened by the sound of the drum and the trumpet (which are able to put but an ordinarily-metalled man out of his wits), it is yet counted a very valiant and honourable act, if a man in this hurry and tumult of his spirits makes his sword fat with the blood of the slain, and mows down his enemies on every side as a sacrifice to his country and friends, I mean to his wife and children, and all that are near unto him. Which yet may be paralleled with the courage and rage of wolves and tigers, who will fiercely enough defend their young by that innate valour and animosity in them, without help of any external artifice to heighten their boldness. But the valour and fortitude of the ever-blessed Captain of our Salvation has no parallel, but is transcendently above whatever can be named. For what comparison is there betwixt that courage which is inspired from the pomp of war or single combat, from the heat and height of the natural spirits, from the rage and hatred against an enemy, or from the love to a friend; and such a fortitude as being destitute of all the advantages of the Animal Life, nay clogged with the disadvantages thereof, as with a deep sense of death, fear, agony, and horror, yet notwithstanding all this, in an humble submission to the Will of God and a dear respect to that lovely Image of the Divine Life, wades through with an unyielding constancy and this (which is not to be thought on without astonishment and amazement) not to rescue or right a friend, but to save and deliver a malevolent enemy?

We have seen how Justice, Temperance, and Fortitude are in a supereminent manner comprehended in the Divine Life, which taking possession of the Middle Life or Rational Powers, must needs beget also in the soul the truest ground of Prudence that may be. For this Divine Life is both the Light and the Purification of the Eye of the Mind, whereby Reason becomes truly illuminated in all Divine and Moral concernments. Which Mystery, though it cannot be declared according to the worthiness of the matter, yet some more external intimations may serve for a pledge of the truth thereof. As for example in that it does remove Pride, Self-interest, and Intemperance that clog the body and cloud the soul, it is plain from hence of what great advantage the Divine Life is for the rectifying and ruling our judgements and understandings in all things.

I have endeavoured according to the best of my abilities briefly to set before you the excellency of that Life which we call Divine. But it is impossible by words to convey it to that soul that has not in her in some measure the sense of it aforehand. Which if she have, it is to her the truest key to the Mystery of Christianity that can be found; and in this light a man shall clearly discern how decorous and just a thing it is that this Life, which is transcendently better than all, should at last after long trials and conflicts triumph over all; and that for this purpose Jesus Christ should come into the world, Who is the Author and Finisher of this more than noble and heroical enterprise.

## No. 303.   JOSEPH HALL

[From *Susurrium Cum Deo,* [*i.e.*] *Soliloquies, or Holy Self-Conferences of the Devout Soul upon Sundry Choice Occasions with Humble Addresses to the Throne of Grace.* Soliloquy No. LI.   *Works*, ed. Peter Hall (1837), Vol. VIII, pp. 274 f.   Cp. note on No. 346.]

### The Power of Conscience.

It is a true word of the Apostle, *God is greater than our conscience*, and surely none but He. Under that great God, the supreme power on earth is the conscience. Every man is a little world within himself; and, in this little world, there is a court of judicature erected, wherein, next under God, the conscience sits as the supreme judge from whom there is no appeal; that passeth sentence upon us, upon all our actions, upon all our intentions; for our persons, absolving one, condemning another; for our actions, allowing one, forbidding another. If that condemn us, in vain shall all the world beside acquit us; and, if that clear us, the doom which the world passeth upon us is frivolous and ineffectual. I grant this judge is sometimes corrupted with the bribes of hope, with the weak fears of loss, with an undue respect of persons, with powerful importunities, with false witnesses, with forged evidences, to pass a wrong sentence upon the person or cause, for which he shall be answerable to Him, that is higher than the highest; but yet this doom, though reversible by the tribunal of Heaven, is still obligatory on earth. So as it is my fault, that my conscience is misled; but it is not my fault to follow my conscience. How much need have I therefore, O my God, to pray that Thou wouldst guide my conscience aright, and keep this great judge in my bosom from corruption and error! And what need hath this intestine arbiter of mine to take special care

46

that he may avoid all misinformations that may mislead his judgement; and all the base suggestions of outward advantage or loss, that may deprave his affections! And, O Thou, That only art greater than my conscience, keep me from doing ought against my conscience. I cannot disobey that, but I must offend Thee; since that is but Thine officer under Thee, and only commands for Thee.

# (2) SIN

## No. 304. JEREMY TAYLOR

[From *Unum Necessarium*, Chapter III, Section i (" Of Sins called Mortal and Venial "), §§ 1–3. *Works*, ed. R. Heber, Vol. VIII, pp. 335–337 (ed. C. P. Eden, Vol. VII, pp. 83 f.). Cp. note on No. **307**.]

MEN have not been satisfied with devising infinite retirements and disguises of their follies to hide them from the world, but finding themselves open and discerned by God, have endeavoured to discover means of escaping from that eye, from which nothing can escape but innocence, and from which nothing can be hid but under the cover of mercy. For besides that we expound the Divine Laws to our own purposes of ease and ambition, we give to our sins gentle censures, and adorn them with good words, and refuse to load them with their proper characters and punishments ; and at last are come to that state of things, that since we cannot allow to ourselves a liberty of doing every sin, we have distinguished the questions of sins into several orders and have taken one half to ourselves. For we have found rest to our fancies in the permissions of one whole kind, having distinguished sins into ' mortal ' and ' venial ' in their own nature; that is, sins which may, and sins which may not be done, without danger; so that all the difference is, that some sins must be taken heed of, but others there are, and they the most in number and the most frequent in their instances and returns, which we have leave to commit, without being affrighted with the fearful noises of damnation ; by which doctrine, iniquity and confidence have much increased and grown upon the ruins and declension of the Spirit.

And this one article hath almost an infinite influence to the disparagement of religion in the determination of cases of conscience. For supposing the distinction to be believed, experience and certain reason will evince that it is impossible to prescribe proper limits and measures to the several kinds; and between the least mortal and the greatest venial sin, no man is able with certainty to distinguish. And therefore (as we see it daily happen, and in every page written by the casuists) men call what they please venial, take what measures of them they like, appoint what expiation of them they fancy, and consequently give what allowance they list to those whom they please to mislead. For in innumerable cases of conscience it is oftener enquired whether a thing be venial or mortal than whether it be lawful or not lawful;

and as purgatory is to hell, so venial is to sin, a thing which men fear not, because the main stake they think to be secured : for, if they may have Heaven at last, they care not what comes between. And as many men of the Roman persuasion will rather choose purgatory, than suffer here an inconsiderable penance or do those little services which themselves think will prevent it, so they choose venial sins and hug the pleasures of trifles, warming themselves at fantastic fires and dancing in the light of the glow-worms; and they love them so well, that rather than quit those little things, they will suffer the intolerable pains of a temporary hell (for so they believe); which is the testimony of a great evil and a mighty danger. For it gives testimony that little sins can be beloved passionately, and therefore can minister such a delight as is thought a price great enough to pay for the sufferance of temporal evils and purgatory itself.

But the evil is worse yet, when it is reduced to practice. For in the decision of very many questions, the answer is, It is a venial sin; that is, though it be a sin, yet there is in it no danger of losing the favour of God by that, but you may do it and you may do it again a thousand thousand times; and "all the venial sins of the world put together, can never do what one mortal sin can, that is, make God to be your enemy,"—so Bellarmine expressly affirms. But because there are many doctors who write Cases of Conscience, and there is no measure to limit the parts of this distinction (for that which is not at all, cannot be measured), the doctors differ infinitely in their sentences; some calling that mortal which others call venial (as you may see in the little summaries of Navarre and Emmanuel Sa); the poor souls of the laity and the vulgar clergy who believe what is told them by the authors or confessors they choose to follow must needs be in infinite danger, and the whole body of practical divinity, in which the life of religion and of all our hopes depends, shall be rendered dangerous and uncertain and their confidence shall betray them unto death.

## No. 305. JOSEPH HALL

[From *Sacred Polemics, Part the First. No Peace With Rome. Wherein is Proved that as Terms now stand, there can be no Reconciliation of the Reformed Religion with the Romish ; and that the Romanists are in all the Fault*, Chapter III, Section iii (1, 7). *Works*, ed. Peter Hall (1837), Vol. XI, p. 342 (Latin text, p. 343). This treatise was published in Latin in 1611 as *Polemices Sacrae Pars Prior. Roma Irreconciliabilis*; later Hall translated it into English. There never was more than a " first part."]

Pardons do both imply and presuppose that known distinction of Mortal and Venial Sin, which neither hath God ever allowed, neither while He gainsays it will ever the Protestants.

That there are certain degrees of evil, we both acknowledge and teach. So as we may here justly tax the dishonesty and shamelessness of Campion, Duræus, Coccius, and the Monks of Bourdeaux, who have upbraided us with the opinion of a certain Stoical and Jovinianish parity of sins; yea, Bellarmine himself hath already done this kind office for us.

Some offences are more heinous than other, yet all, in the malignity of their nature, deadly: as of poisons, some kill more gently and lingeringly, others more violently and speedily, yet both kill.

Moreover, if we have respect unto the infinite mercy of God and to the object of this mercy, the penitent and faithful heart, there is no sin which, to borrow the word of Prudentius, is not venial; but in respect of the anomy or disorder there is no sin which is not worthy of eternal death.

## No. 306.  JAMES USSHER

[From *Eighteen Sermons Preached in Oxford*, 1640; *of Conversion unto God, Of Redemption, and Justification by Christ*, London, 1660.  "Published by John Crabb, William Ball, and Thomas Lye, Ministers of the Gospel, who writ them from his mouth, and compared their copies together."  Sermon No. II.  *Works*, ed. C. R. Elrington (1864), Vol. XIV, pp. 24 f.  The text of this Sermon was *Heb.* iv, 7.  Cp. note on No. 126.]

Think not all will be surely well, because thou hasteth to shake hands with God at thy journey's end, when thou hast not walked with Him all the way.

*Objection.*  But did not the thief repent at the last on the Cross, and why not I on my death-bed?

*Solution.*  This is no good warrant for thy delay, for Christ might work this miraculously, for the glory of His Passion.  Dost thou think, when in thy health and strength, thou hast for several years despised the riches of God's goodness and forbearance and long suffering that leads thee to repentance, that as soon as thou art cast on thy death-bed and ready to breathe out thy soul, the rocks shall be rent again, and the graves opened, to quicken thy repentance and beget in thee a saving faith?  Trust not, therefore, on this, nor content thyself with good intentions but set about the business in good earnest and presently.

## No. 307.  JEREMY TAYLOR

[From *Unum Necessarium, or The Doctrine and Practice of Repentance, Describing the Necessities and Measures of a Strict, a Holy, and a Christian Life, and Rescued from Popular Errors.*  Chapter VI, Section v (" Of Liberty of Election remaining after Adam's Fall "), §§ 71 f., 73–76.  *Works*, ed. R. Heber, Vol. IX, pp. 45–47, 47–49 (ed. C. P. Eden, Vol. VII, pp. 279 f., 280–282).  This treatise, which was published in the autumn of 1655, occasioned great offence.  In it, Taylor criticized the current teaching on Original Sin, contending that it was not sin at all in the strict connotation of the word.  Adam's Fall was merely the loss of certain supernatural gifts with which he had previously been endowed.]

Besides that the causes of a universal impiety are apparent without any need of laying Adam in blame for all our follies and miseries, or rather without charging them upon God, Who so ordered all things as we see and feel, the universal wickedness of man is no argument to prove our will servile, and the powers of election to be quite lost in us, excepting only that we can choose evil.  For admitting this proposition, that there can be no liberty where there is no variety, yet that all men choose sin is not any testimony that there is no variety in our choice. If there were but one sin in the world, and all men did choose that, it were a shrewd suspicion that they were naturally determined or strongly precipitated. But every man does not choose the same sin, nor for the same cause, neither does he choose it always, but frequently declines it, hates it, and repents of it. Many men, even among the heathens, did so. So that the objection hinders not, but that choice and election still remain to man, and that he is not naturally sinful, as he is naturally heavy, or upright, apt to laugh, or weep. For these he is always, and unavoidably.

And indeed the contrary doctrine is a destruction of all laws. It takes away reward and punishment, and we have nothing whereby we can serve God. And precepts of holiness might as well be preached to a wolf as to a man, if man were naturally and inevitably wicked.

*Improbitas nullo flectitur obsequio.*

There would be no use of reason or of discourse, no deliberation or counsel; and it were impossible for the wit of man to make sense of thousands of places of Scripture which speak to us as if we could hear and obey, or could refuse. Why are promises made and threatenings recorded? Why are God's judgements registered? To what purpose is our reason above, and our affections below, if they were not to administer to and attend upon the will? But upon this account, it is so far from being true that man after his Fall did forfeit his natural power of election that it seems rather to be increased. For as a man's knowledge grows, so his will becomes better attended and ministered unto. But after his Fall, his knowledge was more than before; he knew what nakedness was and had experience of the difference of things, he perceived the evil and mischief of disobedience and the Divine anger; he knew fear and flight, new apprehensions and the trouble of a guilty conscience. By all which and many other things, he grew better able, and instructed with arguments to obey God, and to refuse sin for the time to come. And it is every man's case; a repenting man is wiser and hath oftentimes more perfect hatred of sin than the innocent, and is made more wary by his fall. But of this thing God Himself is witness. *Ecce homo tanquam singularis, ex se ipso habet scire bonum et malum*; so the Chaldee paraphrase reads *Gen.* iii, 22. Our Bibles read thus: *And the Lord God said, Behold, the man is become as one of us, to know good and evil.* Now as a consequent of this knowledge, God was pleased, by ejecting him out of Paradise, to prevent his *eating of the tree of life,—Ne forte mittat manum suam in arborem vitæ*; meaning, that now he was grown wise and apt to provide himself and use all such remedies as were before him. He knew more after his Fall than before;

therefore ignorance was not the punishment of that sin. And he that knows more is better enabled to choose, and lest he should choose that which might prevent the sentence of death put upon him, God cast him from thence where the remedy did grow. . . .

I might be infinite in this, but I shall only add this one thing,—that to deny to the will of man powers of choice and election, or the use of it in the actions of our life, destroys the immortality of the soul. Κινδυνεύει γὰρ εἰς τὸ μὴ εἶναι ὑποφέρεσθαι ἡ ἀνθρωπίνη ψυχὴ διὰ τῆς εἰς τὸ παρὰ φύσιν ἐκτροπῆς, said Hierocles: "Human nature is in danger to be lost, if it diverts to that which is against nature." For if it be immortal, it can never die in its noblest faculty. But if the will be destroyed, that is, disabled from choosing (which is all the work the will hath to do), then it is dead. For to live, and to be able to operate, in philosophy are all one. If the will therefore cannot operate, how is it immortal? And we may as well suppose an understanding that can never understand, and passions that can never desire or refuse, and a memory that can never remember, as a will that cannot choose. Indeed all the faculties of the soul that operate by way of nature can be hindered in individuals; but in the whole species never. But the will is not impedible; it cannot be restrained at all, if there be any acts of life. And when all the other faculties are weakest, the will is strongest and does not all depend upon the body. Indeed it often follows the inclination and affections of the body, but it can choose against them, and it can work without them. And indeed since sin is the action of a free faculty, it can no more take away the freedom of that faculty, than virtue can; for that also is the action of the same free faculty. If sin be considered in its formality, as it is an inordination or irregularity, so it is contrary to virtue; but if you consider it as an effect or action of the will, it is not at all contrary to the will, and therefore it is impossible it should be destructive of that faculty from whence it comes.

Now to say that the will is not dead, because it can choose sin but not virtue, is an escape too slight. For besides that it is against an infinite experience, it is also contrary to the very being and manner of a man and his whole economy in this world. For men indeed, sometimes by evil habits, and by choosing vile things for a long time together, make it morally impossible to choose and to love that good in particular which is contrary to their evil customs. Ἡράκλειτος ἔφη ὡς ἦθος ἀνθρώπῳ δαίμων. Custom is the devil that brings in new natures upon us; for nature is innocent in this particular. *Nulli nos vitio natura conciliat : nos illa integros ac liberos genuit.* "Nature does not engage us upon vice. She made us entire, she left us free" (Seneca). But we make ourselves prisoners and slaves by vicious habits; or, as St. Cyril expresses it, ἐλθόντες ἀναμάρτητοι, νῦν ἐκ προαιρέσεως ἁμαρτάνομεν. "We came into the world without sin," meaning, without sin properly

so called, " but now we sin by choice," and by election bring a kind of
necessity upon us.   But this is not so in all men, and scarcely in any
man in all instances ;  and as it is, it is but an approach to that state in
which men shall work by will without choice, or by choice without
contrariety of objects.   In Heaven and Hell men will do so.   The
Saints love God so fully, that they cannot hate Him nor desire to dis-
please Him.   And in Hell the accursed spirits so perfectly hate Him,
that they can never love Him.   But in this life, which is *status viæ*,
a middle condition between both and a passage to one or the other,
it cannot be supposed to be so, unless here also a man be already saved
or damned.

But then I consider this also, that since it is almost by all men
acknowledged to be unjust that infants should be eternally tormented
in the flames of hell for original sin, yet we do not say that it is unjust
that men of age and reason should so perish, if they be vicious and disobedient.   Which difference can have no ground but this, that infants
could not choose at all, much less that, which not they, but their father
did long before they were born.   But men can choose, and do what
they are commanded, and abstain from what is forbidden.   For if they
could not, they ought no more to perish for this than infants for that.

And this is so necessary a truth that it is one of the great grounds
and necessities of obedience and holy living ;  and if, after the Fall of
Adam, it be not by God permitted to us to choose or refuse, there is
nothing left whereby man can serve God or offer Him a sacrifice.
It is no service ;  it is not rewardable if it could not be avoided, nor the
omission punishable if it could not be done.   All things else are
determined, and fixed by the Divine Providence, even all the actions
of men.   But the inward act of the will is left under the command of
laws only, and under the arrests of threatenings, and the invitation
of promises.   And that this is left for man, can no ways impede any of
the Divine decrees, because the outward act being overruled by the
Divine Providence, it is strange if the Schools will leave nothing to man
whereby He can glorify God.

# (3) INSTANCES OF CASUISTRY

## No. 308. ROBERT SANDERSON

[From the latter of *Two Sermons*; the *Former* [on *I Pet.* ii, 16] *Concerning the Right Use of Christian Liberty*; the *Later* [on *Rom.* xiv, 23] *Concerning the Persuasion of Conscience*, London, 1635. *Sermons*, ed. R. Montgomery (1841), Vol. I, pp. 208–214, 218; *Works*, ed. W. Jacobson (1854), Vol. II, pp. 127–134, 139. It is numbered ' Sermon IV *Ad Clerum* ' (§§ 22–28, 33). It was preached on the text *Rom.* xiv, 23, at a Metropolitical Visitation at Grantham, Lincoln, on August 22, 1634. It will be remembered that it was in the Diocese of Lincoln that Laud conducted the First of his Metropolitical Visitations : John Williams was Bishop of Lincoln at the time.]

It may be demanded, fourthly, suppose a man would fain do something of the lawfulness whereof he is not in his conscience sufficiently resolved, whether he may in any case do it, notwithstanding the reluctancy of his conscience, yea or no ?

As they write of Cyrus, that to make a passage for his army he cut the great river Gyndes into many smaller channels, which in one entire stream was not passable, so to make a clear and distinct answer to this great question, I must divide it into some lesser ones ; for there are sundry things considerable in it, whether we respect the conscience, or the person of the doer, or the action to be done. As namely, and especially in respect of the conscience, whether the reluctancy thereof proceed from a settled and steadfast resolution, or from some doubtfulness only, or but from some scruple ? And in respect of the person, whether he be *sui juris*, his own master, and have power to dispose of himself at his own choice in the things questioned, or he be under the command, and at the appointment of another ? And in respect of the action, or thing to be done, whether it be a necessary thing, or an unlawful thing, or a thing indifferent and arbitrary ? Any of which circumstances may quite alter the case and so beget new questions. But I shall reduce all to three questions ; whereof the first shall concern a resolved conscience, the second a doubtful conscience, and the third a scrupulous conscience.

The first question then is, If the conscience be firmly resolved that the thing proposed to be done is unlawful, whether it may then be done or no ? Whereunto I answer in these two conclusions. The first conclusion, If the conscience be firmly so resolved, and that upon a true ground (that is to say, if the thing be indeed unlawful, and judged so to be), it may not in any case or for any respect in the world be done. There cannot be imagined a higher contempt of God than for a man to despise the power of his own conscience, which is the highest sovereignty under Heaven, as being God's most immediate deputy for the ordering of his life and ways. βροτοῖς ἅπασιν ἡ συνείδησις θεός, a heathen man could say. Woeful is the state of those men (unless they repent) who for filthy lucre, or vain pleasure, or spiteful malice, or tottering honour, or lazy ease, or any other reigning lust, dare lie or swear or cheat or oppress or commit filthiness or steal or kill or slander or flatter or betray or do any thing that may advance their base ends; nothing at all regarding the secret whisperings, or murmurings, no nor yet the loud roarings and bellowings of their own consciences there against. *Stat contra ratio, et secretam gannit in aurem.* It doth so; but yet they turn a deaf ear to it, and despise it. Wonder not, if when they out of the terrors of their troubled consciences shall howl and roar in the ears of the Almighty for mercy, or for some mitigation at least of their torment, He then turn a deaf ear against them and despise them. *To him that knoweth to do good, and doeth it not, to him it is sin,* sin not to be excused by any plea or colour. But how much more inexcusably then is it sin to him, that knoweth the evil he should not do, and yet will do it? There is not a proner way to hell, than to sin against conscience. *Happy is he which condemneth not himself in that which he alloweth*; but most wretched is he that alloweth himself to the practice of that which in his judgement he cannot but condemn. Neither maketh it any difference at all here whether a man be otherwise *sui juris* or not. For although there be a great respect due to the higher powers in doubtful cases (as I shall touch anon), yet where the thing required is simply unlawful and understood so to be, inferiors must absolutely resolve to disobey, whatsoever come of it. God's faithful servants have ever been most resolute in such exigents. *We are not careful to answer thee in this matter,*—belike in a matter of another nature they would have taken care to have given the king a more satisfactory, at least a more respective answer; but in this matter: *Be it known to thee, O king, that we will not serve thy gods. Da veniam, imperator,* etc. You know whose answers they were. If we be sure God hath forbidden it, we sin against our own consciences if we do it at the command of any mortal man whosoever, or upon any worldly inducement whatsoever. That is the first conclusion.

The second is this. If a man be in his conscience fully persuaded that a thing is evil and unlawful, which yet in truth is not so, but lawful, the thing by him so judged unlawful cannot by him be done without sin. Even an erroneous conscience bindeth thus far, that a man cannot go against it and be guiltless; because his practice should then run cross to his judgement, and so the thing done could not be of faith. For if his reason judge it to be evil, and yet he will do it, it argueth manifestly that he hath a will to do evil, and so becometh a transgressor of that general law which bindeth all men to eschew all evil. Yet in this case we must admit of some difference, according to the different nature of the things, and the different condition of the persons. For if the things so judged unlawful be in their own nature not necessary, but indifferent, so as they may either be done or left undone without sin, and the person withal be *sui juris* in respect of such things, no superior power having determined his liberty therein,—then, although he may not do any of these things by reason of the contrary persuasion of his conscience without sin, yet he may without sin leave them undone. As for example :—Say a man should hold it utterly unlawful (as some errone-ously do) to play at cards or dice, or to lay a wager, or to cast lots in trivial matters,—if it be in truth lawful to do every of these things, (as I make no question but it is, so they be done with sobriety and with due circumstances) yet he that is otherwise persuaded of them, cannot by reason of that persuasion do any of them without sin. Yet, forso-much as they are things no way necessary, but indifferent, both in their nature and for their use also, no superior power having enjoined any man to use them ; therefore he that judgeth them unlawful, may abstain from them without sin, and so indeed he is in conscience bound to do, so long as he continueth to be of that opinion. But now on the other side, if the things so misjudged to be unlawful be any way neces-sary, either in respect of their own nature, or by the injunction of authority, then the person is by that his error brought into such a strait between two sins, as he can by no possible means avoid both, so long as he persisteth in that his error ; for both, if he do the thing, he goeth against the persuasion of his conscience, and that is a great sin, and if he do it not, either he omitteth a necessary duty, or else disobeyeth lawful authority ; and to do either of both is a sin too. Out of which snare, since there is no way of escape but one, which is to rectify his judgement and to quit his pernicious error, it concerneth every man, therefore, that unfeignedly desireth to do his duty in the fear of God, and to keep a good conscience, not to be too stiff in his present apprehensions, but to examine well the principles and grounds of his opinions, strongly sus-pecting that wind that driveth him upon such rocks, to be but a blast of his own fancy, rather than a breathing of the Holy Spirit of truth,— once this is most certain, that whosoever shall adventure to do any thing repugnant to the judgement of his own conscience (be that judge-ment true or be it false), shall commit a grievous sin in so doing, ὅτι οὐκ ἐκ πίστεως, because it cannot be of faith, and whatsoever is not of faith is sin.

That is now where the conscience apparently inclineth the one way. But say the scales hang even, so as a man cannot well resolve whether way he should rather take,—now he is in one mind, by and by in another, but constant in neither ; right St. James his ἀνὴρ δίψυχος, a double minded man. This is it we call a doubting conscience, concerning which the second question is, what a man ought to do in case of doubtfulness. Perfect directions here (as in most deliberatives) would require a large discourse because there are so many considerable circumstances that may vary the case, especially in respect of the cause from which that doubtfulness of mind may spring. Many times it ariseth from mere fickleness of mind or weakness of judgement, as the lightest things are soonest driven out of their place by the wind ; even as St. James saith, *a double minded man is wavering in all his ways*, and St. Paul speaketh of some that were like children, off and on, soon wherried about with every blast of doctrine. Sometimes it proceedeth from tenderness of conscience, which is indeed a very blessed and gracious thing : but yet (as tender things may soon miscarry, if they be not the more choicely handled) very obnoxious through Satan's diligence and subtilty to be wrought upon to dangerous inconveniences. Sometimes it may proceed from the probability of those reasons that seem to stand on either side, betwixt which it is not easy to judge which are strongest, or from the differing judgements and opinions of learned and godly men thereabout, and from many other causes. But for some general resolution of the question,—What is to be done where the conscience is doubtful ? I answer :—

First, that if the doubtfulness be not concerning the lawfulness of any of the things to be done, considered simply and in themselves, but of the expediency of them as they are compared one with another (as when of two things proposed at once, whereof one must, and but one can be done, I am sufficiently persuaded of the lawfulness of either, but am doubtful whether of the two rather to pitch upon) ; in such a case the party ought first to weigh the conveniences and inconveniences of both, as well and advisedly as he can by himself alone, and to do that which then shall appear to him to be subject to the fewer and lesser inconveniences. Or if the reasons seem so equally strong on both sides that he cannot of himself decide the doubt, then, secondly, if the matter be of weight and worth the while, he should do well to make his doubts known to some prudent and pious man (especially to his own spiritual pastor, if he be a man meetly qualified for it), resolving to rest upon his judgement, and to follow his direction. Or if the matter be of small moment, he may then thirdly, do whether of both he hath best liking to (as the Apostle saith in one particular case, and it may be applied to many more, *let him do what he will he sinneth not*), resting his conscience upon this persuasion that so long as he is unfeignedly desirous to do for the best, and hath not been negligent to use all requisite diligence to inform himself aright, God will accept of his good intention therein and pardon his error if he shall be mistaken in his choice.

But secondly, if the question be concerning the very lawfulness of the thing itself, whether it may be lawfully done or no, and the conscience stand in doubt, because reasons seem to be probable both *pro* and *contra*, and there are learned men as well of the one opinion as of the other, etc., as we see it is (for instance) in the question of usury, and of second marriage after divorce, and in sundry other doubtful cases in moral divinity ; in such a case the person (if he be *sui juris*) is certainly bound to forbear the doing of that thing of the lawfulness where he so doubteth ; and if he forbear it not, he sinneth. It is the very point the Apostle in this verse intendeth to teach, and for the confirming whereof he voucheth this rule of the text,—*he that doubteth*, saith he, *is damned if he eat* : he is αὐτοκατάκριτος, condemned of his own conscience, because he doth that willingly whereof he doubteth when he hath free liberty to let it alone, no necessity urging him thereunto. And the reason why he ought rather to forbear than to adventure the doing of that whereof he doubteth, is because in doubtful cases wisdom would that the safer part should be chosen. And that part is safer which, if we choose, we are sure we shall do well, than that which, if we choose, we know not but we may do ill. As for example, in the instances now proposed : If I doubt of the lawfulness of usury, or of marrying after divorce, I am sure that if I marry not nor let out my money, I shall not sin in so abstaining ; but if I shall do either of both doubtingly, I cannot be without some fear lest I should sin in so doing ; and so those actions of mine being not done in faith, must needs be sin, even by the rule of the text ὅτι οὐκ ἐκ πίστεως, *for whatsoever is not of faith is sin.*

But then, thirdly, if the liberty of the agent be determined by the command of some superior power to whom be oweth obedience, so as he is not now *sui juris ad hoc*, to do or not to do at his own choice, but to do what he is commanded, this one circumstance quite altereth the whole case, and now he is bound in conscience to do the thing commanded, his doubtfulness of mind whether that thing be lawful or no notwithstanding. To do that whereof he doubteth where he hath free liberty to leave it undone bringeth upon him (as we have already shown) the guilt of wilful transgression ; but not so where he is not left at his own liberty. And where lawful authority prescribeth *in alterutram partem*, there the liberty *ad utramque partem contradictionis* is taken away from so many as are under that authority. If they that are over them have determined it one way, it is not thenceforth any more at their choice whether they will take that way or the contrary, but they must go the way that is appointed them without gainsaying or grudging. And if in the deed done at the command of one that is endued with lawful authority there be a sin, it must go on his score that requireth it wrongfully, not on his that doth but his duty in obeying. A prince commandeth his subject to serve in his wars,—it may be the quarrel is unjust, it may be there may appear to the understanding of the subject great likelihoods of such injustice, yet may the subject for all that fight in the quarrel, yea he is bound in conscience so to do,— nay he is deep in disloyalty and treason if he refuse the service, whatsoever pretensions he may make of conscience for such refusal. Neither need that fear trouble him, lest he should bring upon himself the guilt of innocent blood ; for the blood that is unrighteously shed in that quarrel, he must answer for that set him on work, not he that spilt it. And truly it is a great wonder to me that any man endued with understanding and that is able in any measure to weigh the force of those precepts and reasons which bind inferiors to yield obedience to their superiors should be otherwise minded in cases of like nature. Whatsoever is commanded us by those whom God hath set over us, either in Church, commonwealth, or family (*quod non sit tamen certum displicere Deo*, saith St. Bernard), which is not evidently contrary to the Law and Will of God, ought to be of us received and obeyed no otherwise than if God Himself had commanded it, because God Himself hath commanded us to obey the higher powers, and to submit ourselves to their ordinances. Say it be not well done of them to command it,—*sed enim quid hoc refert tua?* saith he,—what is that to thee ? Let them look to that whom it concerneth ; *tolle quod tuum est, et vade.* Do thou what is thine own part faithfully, and never trouble thyself further. *Ipsum quem pro Deo habemus, tanquam Deum, in his quae aperte non sunt contra Deum, audire debemus,*—Bernard still. God's vicegerents must be heard and obeyed in all things that are not manifestly contrary to the revealed Will of God. . .

There remaineth but one other question, and that of far smaller difficulty,—What is to be done when the conscience is scrupulous ? I call that a scruple when a man is reasonably well persuaded of the lawfulness of a thing, yet hath withal some jealousies and fears lest perhaps it should prove unlawful. Such scruples are most incident to men of melancholy dispositions, or of timorous spirits, especially if they be tender conscienced withal ; and they are much increased by the false suggestions of Satan, by reading the books, or hearing the sermons, or frequenting the company of men more strict, precise, and austere in sundry points than they need or ought to be, and by sundry other means which I now mention not. Of which scruples it behoveth every man, First to be wary that he do not at all admit them if he can choose ; or, if he cannot wholly avoid them, that, Secondly, he endeavour, as far as may be, to eject them speedily out of his thoughts as Satan's snares and things that may breed him worse inconveniences ; or, if he cannot be so rid of them, that then, Thirdly, he resolve to go on according to the more probable persuasion of his mind and despise those scruples. And this he may do with a good conscience, not only in things commanded him by lawful authority, but even in things indifferent and arbitrary, and wherein he is left to his own liberty.

## No. 309. JEREMY TAYLOR

[From *Ductor Dubitantium, or the Rule of Conscience*, Book I, Chapter v (" Of a Doubtful Conscience "). *Works*, ed. R. Heber, Vol. XII, pp. 127 f. (ed. C. P. Eden, Vol. IX, p. 227). This prodigious piece of learning was first published in 1660 with a dedication to Charles II. It can claim to be its author's *magnum opus*, and is the most erudite treatise in moral theology which the Church of England has produced.]

### *In Doubts the safer Part is to be chosen.*

When the conscience is doubtful, neither part can be chosen till the doubt be laid down. But to choose the safer part is an extrinsical means instrumental to the deposition of the doubt and changing the conscience from doubtful to probable. This rule, therefore, does properly belong to the probable conscience ; for that the conscience is positively doubtful is but accidental to the question and appendant to the person. For the reasons on either side make the conscience probable, unless fear, or some other accident, make the man not able to rest on either side. For in matters of conscience, it is as hard to find a case so equally probable that a man shall find nothing without or within to determine him as it is to find that which the philosophers call *temperamentum ad pondus*, " a constitution so equal that no part shall excel the other." For if there were nothing in the things to distinguish them, yet in the man there is a natural propensity which will make him love one sort of arguments more than another. What can be more indifferent than to see two dogs fight ? and yet no man sees their cruelty, but he wishes better to one than to another. And although no opinions are so very even, yet if they were, the man hath an acquisite, or else a natural bias, or something of contingency that will determine him ; and if the conscience remains undetermined, so that he may not, or dare not, venture upon either part, it is certainly a disease, or a direct infirmity.

## No. 310. JEREMY TAYLOR

[From *Ductor Dubitantium, or the Rule of Conscience*, Book I, Chapter iv (" Of the Probable, or Thinking Conscience "), Rule viii. *Works*, ed. R. Heber, Vol. XII, pp. 87 f. (ed. C. P. Eden, Vol. IX, pp. 194 f.). Cp. note on No. 309.]

### *An Opinion relying upon very slender Probability is not to be followed, except in the Cases of great Necessity or great Charity.*

That it is not ordinarily to be followed is therefore certain, because it cannot be supposed but that its contradictory hath greater probability ; and either he that follows this trifle is light of belief, or unreasonable in his choice, or his reason is to him but as eyes to an owl or bat, half sighted and imperfect, and, at the best, no fit motive to the will. And if it could be lawful to follow every degree of probability, it were perfectly in any man's choice to do almost what he pleased, especially if he meets with an ill counsellor and a witty advocate. For, at this rate, all marriages may be dissolved, all vices excused, upon pretence of some little probable necessity; and drunkenness will be entertained as physic, and fornication as a thing allowed by some vicious persons whose wit is better than their manners; and all books of conscience shall become patrons or *indices* of sins and teach men what they pretend against; and there shall be no such thing as checks of conscience, because few men sin without some excuse, and it were no excuse unless it were mingled with some little probabilities; and there were, in very many cases, no rule for conscience but a witty inventor of pretty little inducements, which rather than a man shall want, his enemy will supply to him out of his magazine of fallacies.

# (4) DIVORCE

## No. 311.  THE CANONS OF 1604

[Canon 107 of the *Constitutions and Canons Ecclesiastical*, agreed upon in the Convocation of Canterbury in the year 1604.  E. Cardwell, *Synodalia*, Vol. I, 307 f. Cp. note on No. **182**.]

*In all sentences for Divorce, Bond to be taken for not marrying during each other's Life.*

In all sentences pronounced only for divorce and separation *a thoro et mensa*, there shall be a caution and restraint inserted in the act of the said sentence, That the parties so separated shall live chastely and continently; neither shall they, during each other's life, contract matrimony with any other person.  And, for the better observation of this last clause, the said sentence of divorce shall not be pronounced until the party or parties requiring the same shall have given good and sufficient caution and security into the court that they will not any way break or transgress the said restraint or prohibition.

## No. 312.  LANCELOT ANDREWES

[From *A Discourse . . . Against Second Marriage, after Sentence of Divorce with a Former Match, the Party then living.  Minor Works*, ed. *L. A. C. T.*, pp. 106 f., where it was printed for the first time from a British Museum MS. (Birch MSS. 4149, art. 38, p. 320).  This discourse is dated 1601, the year in which Andrewes was made Dean of Westminster.]

The question is, Whether upon adultery proved, or sentence recorded, a man be set at liberty that he may proceed to contract with another.

First, I take the act of adultery doth not dissolve the bond of marriage; for then it would follow that the party offending would not, upon reconciliation, be received again by the innocent to former society of life without a new solemnising of marriage, insomuch as the former marriage is quite dissolved, which is never heard of, and contrary to the practice of all Churches.

Secondly, the sentence, as I take it, doth not relieve, for there is no lawful sentence of any court in case of divorce but it ever containeth an express inhibition to either party to marry with another, with intimation in flat terms, that from the time that either of them shall go about any other marriage, *quod ex tunc prout ex nunc, et ex nunc prout ex tunc,* (it is the style of the court), that present sentence shall be void to all purposes, and they in the same case as if it had never been given.

661

These both failing, the Word of God is sought to, where, let me tell you first, that during the Primitive Church, ever till now of late, the judgement of the Divines and the present practice of the Law Ecclesiastical were both one.  And great reason why; for well known it is, that the authority of the Fathers was the ground of the ancient Canons by which the law in this case is ruled.  So that but for the conceit of some latter Divines, there need not be sought any opposition between Law and Divinity in this question, nor that pitiful distraction happen which we daily see, Divines to give their hands for licence to that for which Law will convent men, and censure them too.

But, in my opinion, second marriages (where either party is living) are not warranted by the Word of God.  The ground of which opinion is, that one may not in any wise have two wives at once; for by the original institution, there can be but two in one flesh.  But a man having one wife already, which, notwithstanding she hath profaned marriage with another, is not thereby become the wife of him with whom she now liveth, but remaineth his wife whose first she was, and whose only she can be while she liveth.

## No. 313.  HENRY HAMMOND

[From *A Practical Catechism*, Book II, Section vii.  Ed. *L. A. C. T.*, pp. 139 f. Cp. note on No. 267.  Observe that in the following extract no permission for remarriage after divorce " in case of fornication " is given.]

*Scholar*.  What doth Christ now in His new law in this matter of divorce ?

*Catechist*.  He repealeth that whole commandment and imposeth a stricter yoke on His disciples.  For coming now to give more grace than the law brought with it to the Jews, He thinks not fit to yield so much to any considerations, particularly to the hardness of men's hearts, as to allow Christians that liberty, so contrary to the first institution of wedlock, but raiseth them higher to that pitch which, when it was not commanded, was yet most excellent and principally approved by God and all good men, and now becomes necessary by being commanded by Him.  And therefore now He clearly affirms of all such divorces, that whosoever thus puts away his wife, as the Jews frequently did, causeth her to commit adultery, and he that marrieth her committeth adultery; and if after such divorcement he himself marry again, he committeth adultery, and is in that respect sadly liable. That is, in brief, that the bond of wedlock now under Christ is so indissoluble, that it is not the husband's dislikes which can excuse him for putting away his wife, nor his giving her a bill of divorce which can make it lawful for her to marry any other, nor for any other to marry her, who is for all this bill still indissolubly another man's wife.

*Scholar*.  But what, is no kind of divorce now lawful under Christ ?

*Catechist*.  Yes clearly, that which is here named, in case of fornication, *i.e.* if the wife prove false to the husband's bed, and take in any other man, it will then be lawful by Christ's law for the husband to give her a bill of divorce, *i.e.* legally to sue it out, and so put her away. The reason being because of the great inconveniences and mischiefs that such falseness brings into the family; children of another's body to inherit with, or perhaps before, his own, etc. Which sort of reasons it is, together with the dominion of the husband over the wife, that this matter of divorce now, under Christ, is chiefly built on (and not only, as might be imagined, that of the conjugal contract; for that, being mutual, would as well make it lawful for the wife to put away the husband, which is nowhere permitted in the Old or New Testament), this liberty being peculiar to the husband against the wife, and not common to the wife against her husband; because, I say, those family inconveniences do not follow the falseness of the husband as they do that of the wife; and because the wife hath by promise of obedience made herself a subject, and owned him as lord, and so hath none of that authority over him (an act of which putting away seemeth to be) which he by being lord hath over her.

*Scholar.* Is there no other cause of divorce now pleadable or justifiable among Christians, but that in case of fornication?

*Catechist.* I cannot define any, because Christ hath named no other.

### No. 314. JOHN COSIN

[From a paper, " *Proving that Adultery works a Dissolution of the Marriage.*" *Works*, ed. L. A. C. T., Vol. IV, pp. 489–493. The notes constituting these papers were the substance of a number of speeches in the House of Lords in connexion with the Lord Ross Divorce Case. Cosin was one of the two Bishops in the House of Lords who, in 1669, voted in favour of the Divorce Bill.]

The question is indefinitely to be spoken of whether a man being divorced from his wife who hath committed adultery, and is convicted of it, may marry himself to another wife or no during the life of her which is divorced.

The place in *St. Matthew* the 5th, repeated again *St. Matthew* the 19th, has great perspicuity. If it be not lawful for any man to put away his wife and marry again, except it be in the case of fornication (for the displacing the words by putting the exception before the marriage cannot alter the sense), then *a contrario* it must of necessity follow that, if the wife be put away for fornication, the husband by the tenor of Christ's words is left free to marry again; which freedom is not allowed the adulteress herself, nor to any man else that shall marry her.

*St. Mark* and *St. Luke* have been opposed to *St. Matthew*; and it has been said that Christ's words in *St. Matthew* did not properly belong to Christ's disciples or the Christian Church, as the words of *St. Mark* and *St. Luke*, which are absolute, do; which is a saying that neither I nor, I think, nobody else ever heard of before. For Christ's

Sermon in the Mount was spoken to His disciples, and especially belonged to Christians.

It is clear they are spoken to His disciples ; for He says to them that they are the salt of the earth, and the light of the world, and that they are blessed when they suffer persecution for His Name's sake, which no man will say or apply to the Jews.

It is true that, in the 19th chapter of *St. Matthew*, Christ answers the Scribes and Pharisees who came to tempt Him with their question whether it was lawful for a man to put away his wife for any cause, as they said Moses had permitted them to do. But the answer that Christ gave them, that it was not lawful, but only in the case of adultery, for men to put away their wives and to marry another, was a rule which concerned all Christians to observe for ever after, and for that reason was recorded by *St. Matthew*.

The words in *St. Mark* and *St. Luke* are not to be taken absolutely ; but to be supplied and understood by His words in *St. Matthew*, as in many other cases is clear, viz., the thief upon the cross, Baptism in the Name of the Father, Son, and Holy Ghost, etc. ; whereof many instances may be brought, as the destruction of Nineveh, etc.

But, for Christ's words, the exception confirms the rule and infers a concession that, in the case of fornication, the putting away one wife and marrying another is allowed. It is alike with divers other His exceptions, which are found in Scripture ; for brevity, I will instance in this one, viz., *Except ye repent, ye shall all likewise perish.* Upon which text if I or any Bishop else were to preach, I believe we should not discharge our duty unless we should tell the people, that, if by the Grace of God they did repent, they should not perish.

The exception here, εἰ μή, *nisi*, ' unless,' is parallel with *I Kings* iii, 18. *None were in the house, except we twain* ; they two therefore were, others were not.

Such exceptions, proceeding from natural equity, are tacitly implied in laws, though pronounced in general terms.

But, as to the exception here, the words are not capable of any other sense than as I have observed. For except that restraint be referred to marrying again, the sense would run thus, *Whoever puts away his wife commits adultery* : which stands not with truth or reason, since it is not the dismission that is adulterous, but the marriage of another. It is, therefore, the plain drift of Our Saviour to teach the Pharisee that the marriage of a second wife after a dismission of a former, upon any other cause except for fornication, is no less than adultery, thereby inferring that, upon a just dismission for fornication, a second marriage cannot be branded with adultery.

Besides, the Pharisee's question *Is it lawful for a man to put away his wife for every cause?* was not without a plain implication of liberty to marry another. Which Our Saviour well knowing gives a full answer, as well to what He meant, as what He said; which had not been perfectly satisfactory, if He had only determined that one part concerning dismission, and not the other concerning marriage; which clause if two Evangelists express not, yet it must be fetched necessarily from the third, since it is a sure and irrefragable rule, that all four Evangelists make up one perfect Gospel.

The Rheimists and College of Douay urge for the popish doctrine, *Rom.* vii, 2 : *The woman which hath an husband is bound by the law to her husband as long as he liveth.* But,

1. This place is to be expounded by Christ's words.

2. St. Paul hath no occasion here to speak of divorce, but of marriage whole and sound as it stands by God's ordinance.

3. He speaks of a woman who is under an husband; so is not she that is divorced from him.

4. St. Paul useth this to his purpose of the law being dead, to which we are not bound.

Nor is their doctrine more favoured by *I Cor.* vii, 10, *Let not the woman depart*, as being in her choice whether she would depart or not. But in the case of fornication she was to depart, or rather be put away, whether she would or not.

The bond of the marriage is to be inquired into, what it properly is. Being a conjugal promise, solemnly made between a man and his wife, that each of them will live together, according to God's holy ordinance, notwithstanding poverty or infirmity or such other things as may happen during their lives, separation from bed and board, which is part of their promise so to live together, doth plainly break that part of the bond, whereby they are tied to live together both as to bed and to board. The distinction betwixt bed and board and the bond is new, never mentioned in the Scripture, and unknown in the Ancient Church, devised only by the Canonists and the Schoolmen in the Latin Church (for the Greek Church knows it not) to serve the Pope's turn the better, till he got it established in the Council of Trent; at which time, and never before, he laid his *anathema* upon all them that were of another mind, forbidding all men to marry, and not to make any use of Christ's concession.

Bed and board, or cohabitation, belong to the essence and substance of matrimony; which made Erasmus and Bishop Hall say that the distinction of those two from the bond is merely chimerical, and fancy.

The promise of constancy and mutual forbearance, if it hinders divorce as to the bond, hinders it also as to bed and board, because the same bed and the same table were promised in the marriage contract. But the promise does not extend even to tolerating adultery, or malicious desertion, which according to God's ordinance dissolves the marriage.

Our Saviour speaks of divorces instituted by the Mosaical law ; but they were no other than divorces from the bond.

## No. 315.  JOSEPH HALL

[From *Resolutions and Decisions of Divers Practical Cases of Conscience, in Continual Use among Men*, Fourth Decade (" Cases Matrimonial "), Case iii (" Whether, after a lawful divorce for adultery, the innocent party may marry again "). *Works*, ed. Peter Hall (1837), Vol. VII, p. 474.  Cp. note on No. **324**.]

Shortly, then, I doubt not but I may, notwithstanding great authorities to the contrary, safely resolve that, in the case of divorce, it is lawful for the innocent person to marry.   But for that I find the Church of England hitherto somewhat tender in the point ; and this practice, where it rarely falls, generally held, though not sinful, yet of ill report and obnoxious to various censures.   I should therefore earnestly advise and exhort those whom it may concern, carefully and effectually to apply themselves to the fore-mentioned remedies : reconciliation if it be possible to prevent a divorce ; holy endeavours of a continued continence, if it may be obtained, to prevent a second marriage after divorce.   But, if these prevail not, I dare not lay a load upon any man's conscience, which God hath not burthened.   I dare not ensnare those whom God will have free.

# (5) CLERICAL CELIBACY AND MONASTICISM

## No. 316.  RICHARD HOOKER

[From *The Laws of Ecclesiastical Polity*, Book VI, Chapter xv, § 12.  *Works*, ed.
J. Keble, Vol. III, pp. 247 f.  Cp. note on No. 150.]

ST. PAUL indeed doth exhort Timothy after this manner: *Suffer
thou evil as a noble soldier of Jesus Christ.  No man warring is entangled
with the affairs of life, because he must serve such as have pressed him unto
warfare* (*II Tim.* ii, 3, 4).  The sense and meaning whereof is plain,
that soldiers may not be nice and tender, that they must be able to endure
hardness, that no man betaking himself unto wars continueth entangled
with such kind of businesses as tend only unto the ease and quiet
felicity of this life, but if the service of him who hath taken them under
his banner require the hazard, yea the loss of their lives, to please him
they must be content and willing with any difficulty, any peril, be it
never so much against the natural desire which they have to live in
safety.  And at this point the clergy of God must always stand.  Thus
it behoveth them to be affected as oft as their Lord and captain leadeth
them into the field, whatsoever conflicts, perils, or evils they are to
endure.  Which duty being not such but that therewith the civil
dignities which ecclesiastical persons amongst us do enjoy may enough
stand, the exhortation of Paul to Timothy is but a slender allegation
against them.

As well might we gather out of this place that men having children
or wives are not fit to be ministers (which also hath been collected,
and that by sundry of the ancients), and that it is requisite the clergy
be utterly forbidden marriage.  For as the burden of civil regiment
doth make them who bear it the less able to attend their ecclesiastical
charge, even so St. Paul doth say that the married are careful for the
world, the unmarried freer to give themselves wholly to the service of
God.  Howbeit, both experience hath found it safer that the clergy
should bear the cares of honest marriage than be subject to the inconveniences which single life imposed upon them would draw after it;
and as many as are of sound judgement know it to be far better for this
present age that the detriment be borne which haply may grow through
the lessening of some few men's spiritual labours, than that the clergy
and commonwealth should lack the benefit which both the one and
the other may reap through their dealing in civil affairs.  In which

consideration, that men consecrated into the spiritual service of God be licensed so far forth to meddle with the secular affairs of the world, as doth seem for some special good cause requisite and may be without any grievous prejudice unto the Church, surely there is not in the Apostles, being rightly understood, any let.

## No. 317.   JOSEPH HALL

[From *The Honour of the Married Clergy, Maintained against the Malicious Challenges of C. E.* [i.e. *Edward Coffin,* a] *Mass-Priest ; or the Apology written some years since for the Marriage of Persons Ecclesiastical, Made Good against the Cavils of C. E.* [i.e. *Edward Coffin*], *Pseudo-Catholic Priest,* Book I, Section iii. *Works,* ed. Peter Hall (1837), Vol. IX, pp. 169 f.   This treatise was published in 1620.   Some twelve years previously Hall had written a letter to one John Whiting on the " Marriage of Ecclesiastical Persons " ;  it is to this letter that reference is made in the second subtitle of the treatise, and it is to be found among Hall's *Epistles,* Decade II, Epistle iii (In Peter Hall's edition, Vol. VI, pp. 155–162).   Edward Coffin, who published his attack on Hall at St. Omer, entitled it *A Refutation of Mr. Joseph Hall, His Apologetical Discourse for the Marriage of Ecclesiastical Persons by C. E., a Catholic Priest* ; it appeared in 1619. Hall dedicated his treatise to Abbot, the Archbishop of Canterbury.]

As for the vow [of Celibacy], it is so far from being essential to Holy Orders as that it is made by some learned Papists a difference betwixt the obligation of their Religious and their Priests,—that their Religious are bound by a solemn vow to single life in the very intrinsical nature of their profession, their priests only by a Church-Constitution without vow.   And those that go further with their famous Cardinal [Cajetan], and teach that it is expressly forbidden to Bishops to ordain any without the promise of single life, ground this but upon an Epistle of Pope Gregory, a late and weak foundation ;  and, besides, hold that their vow is but semi-solemn and accidentally incident into this profession, forasmuch as here is neither a direct exhibition of the body to this purpose in the offerer, nor a direct consecration to this end in the admitter ;  both which make up the solemnity of the vow.   Upon which reason, according to them, a Religious Order, because it yields over the body unto an estate repugnant to matrimony, doth of itself, in its own nature, both hinder marriage and nullify it ;  not so the Ecclesiastical.   To which we may add, that according to their own Doctors, solemnity and simplicity make no difference of the vow before God, though before the Church,—a distinction, too slight, too newly upstart, to overturn an ancient and well-grounded institution.   Neither need we any better or other proof of the inconnexion of this vow with Holy Orders than that of their own Dominicus a Soto, *Non est de essentia sacerdotis, etc.*   " It is not of the essence of a priest," saith he, " to keep single ;  for that the Grecian clergy are permitted, even by the Roman Church, to continue in the estate of marriage."   What can be more clear ?   If there were a necessary and inseparable connexion of a vowed continency with Holy Orders, then would not, neither could, the Roman Church acknowledge a true priesthood where it finds conjugal society. Their act of allowance to the Greek Church implies a fair independency of these two, which some of their clamorous clients plead to have indivisibly coupled.

So as now, all the strength of this necessary Celibate is resolved into the power of a Church-Statute; and of what Church, but the Roman? All other Churches in the world, as of Armenia, Grecia, Syria, Ethiopia, Russia, the Georgians, etc., allow the conjunction of ministry and marriage, and are so far from requiring a vow of necessary continency that they rather erroneously pre-require a necessity of marriage in the persons to be ordained. It is only the Church of Rome, the great and imperious mistress of the world, that imposes the yoke of this vow upon her vassals. Imposes it, but *ad libitum*; so as her great paramour, in whose vast bosom that whole Church lies, may dispense with it as he lists.

## No. 318.  HERBERT THORNDIKE

[From *The Reformation of the Church of England Better than that of the Council o, Trent ; or a Short Resolution of the Controversies between the Church of England and the Church of Rome*, Chapter xxxvii. *Works*, ed. L. A. C. T., Vol. V, pp. 570-573. This treatise, which is said to have been composed between the years 1670 and 1672, was first published in the *L. A. C. T.* edition of Thorndike's works. The author had died in July, 1672. This, perhaps the least ponderous of Thorndike's writings, deals briefly with a large range of subjects.]

Opposite to the state of Marriage is the state of Continence. And having resolved afore that it is advised by Our Lord in the Gospel, and therefore hath the promise of His grace, to them that embrace it as Christians, it is in the next place to be said that it is most acceptable to God and honourable to Christianity. But as the best things, when they are corrupted, turn the worst; so is the danger greatest, now the world is come into the Church, that they who choose the most sublime course for low and mean reasons will not be able to hold their choice. And therefore seeing the whole order and course of monastical life is introduced by the Church, and rather by sufferance than by law, the want of it cannot be a bar to the salvation of them that live in the Church that hath it not. But seeing it is a perfection to Christianity, it is certainly a blot in the Reformation which we profess, that we are without it.

The difficulties that have hindered the effect of it seem to be chiefly two : the one, the study of princes and great persons in Christendom to propagate their names by heaping riches upon large foundations of abbeys and nunneries; the other, proper to the Western Church, of exempting them from the jurisdiction of their ordinaries to the immediate government of the see of Rome; which in the late Orders of Friars is original, because they subsist by allowance and privilege of it. Whether of these is more prejudicial to the profession, it is hard to say. For all monks being originally mere lay persons, and having no privilege of clergy further than necessity requires that they should have some clergy to minister to them the offices of Christianity according to the order of the Church, what reason can be imagined, why they should be exempt from ordinary jurisdiction? They that profess retirement from the world, why should they be brought into the world, to make the noise in it which for divers hundreds of years they have done? I grant that it is to be wished that some may be employed in learning, as well as others in the labour of their hands; according as their breeding may have been when they leave the world. But neither is any learning, no, not that of the Scriptures, acceptable to God or beneficial to His Church that is not subject to the government of it. Neither can they that only distinguish the intervals of their devotions by the work of their bodies create occasions to employ extraordinary power in the Church.

But when great persons took up a fashion to vie with one another in the greatness and riches of their monastical foundations, first, they laid as fit a foundation as the devil could have wished to corrupt the sublimity of that profession, which they pretended to propagate. Secondly that gave a very colourable pretence to their successors to find fault with their love to their country in mortifying so much of the goods of them from the service of it. Whosoever will look into their histories shall find this to have been a continual temptation to sacrilege on the part of the laity; and, on the part of the clergy, the justest plea that ever they had, to conspire to advance the temporal power of the Church, which could not be secure from sacrilege otherwise. Lastly, there is in this course an appearance of want of trust to the salvation of souls in the clergy. For we know that prayer with fasting and alms is the means to recover the favour of God and to reconcile a sinner to Him, as performing and demonstrating true contrition and conversion of heart. But when Christian people were taught the redemption of purgatory-pains and were not taught how to regain a well-grounded assurance of grace, how easy was it for flesh and blood, being taught to redeem purgatory-pains by their goods, to think God's grace was regained into the bargain. And so not only the profession of monastical life, but the founding and endowing or furthering of it, make commutation for sin, without the change of the inward man.

But setting aside these corruptions, how great an advantage is it to Christianity to have before the eyes of the world the examples of them that wholly forego it; to warn them that live in it, to use it as if they used it not,—that is, for the service of God, not for the satisfaction of themselves. How great a benefit to the world that they who are shipwrecked in it, being taught by their afflictions to love it no more, may have a haven to retire to the service of God, being uncapable to serve Him any longer in serving their generations. How great a provision for the discipline of penance to have the convenience of such places to confine penitents to, either for a time or during life, that they be not cast away. Lastly, how great an encouragement to youth to choose the highest pitch and to run such a course as may bring them back into the world to serve the Church in the clergy, being furnished with that resolution against the snares of it which that education furnisheth.

Which being so, how much is it to be wished that the public faith may be engaged in the protection and maintenance of the institution; providing, first, that the public suffer neither in the persons nor goods that shall be mortified to the maintenance of it,—and that is best done, when provision is made that it be so moderate as to create no envy;— that the time, which is spared from the works of devotion be employed in the exercises either of the body or of the mind, according to men's education and capacities; and that this employment may turn to an account of charity, according to the Orders recounted in St. Basil and Cassian. For upon these terms there will be no cause why the direction and correction of such places should not resort, in the first place, to the Bishop of the Diocese, having his clergy to assist him in it; and then to the respective synods, whereof the Bishops are members.

I will add one thing:—that some of the Fathers are of opinion to excuse them that upon trial find themselves unable to go through with the rigour of that monastical life, which they had professed, and to admit them to marriage without penance: though others are more rigorous. Which seems to argue that,—now the world is come into the Church, and a necessity has followed of abating the rigour of primitive discipline, that Christianity may be maintained without hypocrisy, though not without defect,—there is very great reason to allow it, and to make the profession signify, according to the signification of *votum* in Latin, an earnest desire to go through with that which we profess, though for human infirmity and the difficulties of the world not irrevocable. For when the sincerity of men's intentions is left to God alone to be judged, a great temptation of our first parents is taken off; of desiring things prohibited, because prohibited.

# (6) OATHS

## No. 319.  JOHN TILLOTSON

[From *The Lawfulness and Obligation of Oaths. A Sermon preached at the Assizes held at Kingston upon Thames, July* 21, 1681. London, 1681, pp. 7 f., 13–15, 15 f., 16 f. The text was *Heb.* vi, 16.]

THE third thing I proposed was to vindicate the lawfulness of oaths, where they are necessary. And it is a very strong inducement to believe the lawfulness of them, that the unavoidable condition of human affairs hath made them so necessary. The Apostle takes it for granted that an oath is not only of great use in human affairs, but in many cases of great necessity to confirm a doubtful thing and to put an end to controversies which cannot otherwise be decided to the satisfaction of the parties contending : *An oath for confirmation is to them an end of all strife.* And indeed it is hardly imaginable that God should not have left that lawful, which is so evidently necessary to the peace and security of mankind.

But because there is a sect [*i.e.* the Quakers] sprung up in our memory which hath called in question the lawfulness of all oaths, to the great mischief and disturbance of human society, I shall endeavour to search this matter to the bottom and to manifest how unreasonable and groundless this opinion is. . . .

Our Saviour seems altogether to forbid swearing in any case. *Ye have heard that it hath been said to them of old time, Thou shalt not forswear thyself ; but I say unto you swear not at all, neither by Heaven, etc. But let your communication be Yea, Yea, and Nay, Nay ; for whatsoever is more than these cometh of evil.* And this law St. James recites as that which Christians ought to have a very particular and principal regard to : *Above all things, my brethren, swear not.* And he makes the breach of this law a damning sin,—*lest ye fall into condemnation.* But the authority of Our Saviour alone is sufficient, and therefore I shall only consider that text.

And because here lies the main strength of this opinion of the unlawfulness of oaths, it is very fit that this text be fully considered and that it be made very evident that it was not Our Saviour's meaning by this prohibition wholly to forbid the use of oaths.

But before I enter upon this matter I will readily grant that there is scarce any error whatsoever that hath a more plausible colour from Scripture than this,—which makes the case of those who are seduced into it the more pitiable. But then it ought to be considered how much this doctrine of the unlawfulness of oaths reflects upon the Christian religion, since it is so evidently prejudicial both to human society in general, and particularly to those persons that entertain it, neither of which ought rashly to be supposed and taken for granted concerning any law delivered by Our Saviour; because upon these terms it will be very hard for us to vindicate the Divine Wisdom of Our Saviour's doctrine and the reasonableness of the Christian Religion. Of the inconvenience of this doctrine to human society, I have spoken already. But besides this it is very prejudicial to them that believe it. It renders them suspected to Government and in many cases incapable of the common benefits of justice and other privileges of human society, and exposeth them to great penalties as the constitution of all Laws and Governments at present is; and it is not easy to imagine how they should be otherwise. And which is very considerable in this matter, it sets those who refuse oaths upon very unequal terms with the rest of mankind, if where the estates and lives of men are equally concerned, their bare testimonies shall be admitted without an oath, and others shall be obliged to speak upon oath,—nothing being more certain in experience than that many men will lie for their interest when they will not be perjured, God having planted in the natural consciences of men a secret dread of perjury above most other sins. And this inconvenience is so great as to render those who refuse oaths in all cases almost intolerable to human society. I speak not this either to bring them into trouble or to persuade them to measure truth by their interest. But on the other hand I must needs say that it is no argument either of a wise or good man to take up any opinion, especially such a one as is greatly to his prejudice, upon slight grounds. And this very consideration, that it is so much to their inconvenience, may justly move them to be very careful in the examination of it. . . .

Several circumstances of these words of Our Saviour do manifestly shew that they ought to be interpreted in a limited sense, as only forbidding swearing in common conversation,—needless and heedless oaths (as one expresseth it),—and in general all voluntary swearing unless upon some great and weighty cause in which the glory of God and the good of the souls of men is concerned. For that in such cases a voluntary oath may be lawful, I am induced to believe from the example of St. Paul, who useth it more than once upon such occasions. . . .

That this prohibition of Our Saviour's ought to be understood of oaths in ordinary conversation appears from the opposition which Our Saviour makes, *Swear not at all; but let your communication be Yea, Yea,*—that is, in your ordinary commerce and affairs do not interpose oaths, but say and do. And this is very much confirmed in that Our Saviour does not under this general prohibition instance in (*sic*) such oaths as are expressly by the Name of God; the reason whereof is this, The Jews thought it unlawful in ordinary communication to swear expressly by the Name of God, but lawful to swear by the creatures, as by Heaven and earth, etc. So that Our Saviour's meaning is as if He had said: You think you may swear in common conversation, provided you do not swear by the Name of God. But I say unto you, Let your communication be without oaths of any kind. You shall not so much as swear by Heaven or by earth, because God is virtually invoked in every oath. And unless we suppose this to be Our Saviour's meaning, I do not see what good reason can be given why Our Saviour should only forbid them to swear by the creatures, and not much rather by the Name of God,—such oaths being surely of all others most to be avoided, as being the most direct abuse and profanation of the Name of God.

## No. 320. JEREMY TAYLOR

[From *The Great Exemplar*, Part II, Section xii (Discourse x; § 20). *Works*, ed. R. Heber, Vol. III, pp. 21 f. (ed. C. P. Eden, Vol. II, pp. 425 f.). Cp. note on No. 212.]

The sum is this. Since the whole subject matter of this precept [*i.e.* of the Third Commandment] is Oaths Promissory or Vows, all promises with Oaths are regularly forbidden to Christians, unless they be made to God or God's vicegerent, in a matter not trifling. For, in the first case, a promise made to God and a swearing by God to perform the promise to Him is all one; for the Name of God being the instrument and determination of all our addresses, we cannot be supposed to speak to God without using of His Name explicitly or by implication; and therefore he that promises to God makes a promise and uses God's Name in the promise, and the promise itself being in the nature of a prayer or solemn invocation of God. In the second case, when the public necessity requires it, of which we are not judges, but are under authority, we find the lawfulness by being bound to believe, or not to contradict, the pretence of its necessity. Only care is to be taken that the matter be grave or religious, that is, it is to be esteemed and presumed so by us, if the Oath be imposed by our lawful superiors, and to be cared for by them; or else it is so to be provided for by ourselves, when our intercourse is with God, as in vows and promises passed to God,—being careful that we do not offer to God goat's hair, or the fumes of mushrooms, or the blood of swine, that is, things either impious or vain. But in our communication, that is, in our ordinary intercourse with men, we must promise by simple testimony not by religious adjurations, though a creature be the instrument of the Oath.

## No. 321. WILLIAM BEVERIDGE

[From *Ecclesia Anglicana Ecclesia Catholica* [= On the Thirty-Nine Articles]. On Article XXXIX. *Works*, ed. *L. A. C. T.*, Vol. VII, pp. 617–619. Cp. note on No. 52.]

That Our Saviour doth not forbid all manner of swearing when He commands us not to *swear at all* is plain also from the practice and example of the Apostle St. Paul. For that St. Paul understood the meaning of Our Saviour in these words better than any one doth or can in these days, I hope there is none as yet so sottishly ignorant and so highly presumptuous as to deny. Yet we find him often swearing and calling upon God to witness what he saith : *For God is my record*, saith he, *how greatly I long after you all* (*Phil.* i, 8). . . . So full, so clear is Scripture, both in precepts and precedents, to assure us that it is as lawful to swear in itself as it is sinful to swear in vain.

Neither doth Scripture only, but reason also, proclaim this doctrine for a truth. For, first, that which is part of God's honour must needs be lawful. But now to swear lawfully is part of His honour, and therefore is serving God and swearing by His Name joined together (*Deut.* vi, 13) ; indeed, from swearing by His Name lawfully, according to His will, there is much honour redounding to Him, for hereby we acknowledge Him to be an all-seeing God, Who seeth what I think, as well as men hear what I speak. Hereby we acknowledge Him to be a God that loveth justice and truth, and will severely revenge all such as take His Name in vain ; so that to deny this truth is to rob God of a great part of His honour. Secondly, if we consider the nature of a lawful oath, we shall easily see that it is lawful to take an oath ; for a lawful oath is nothing but a calling upon God to witness what is true. Now to call upon God is no sin ; and to call upon God to do good, even to defend the truth, by bearing witness to it, cannot possibly be accounted any sin, there being no law transgressed by it. Lastly, to this we may also add, that an oath is the end of strife ; and so the end of an oath is to be the end of strife, and to establish peace and equity betwixt man and man : and so the end of it cannot possibly but be acknowledged as lawful in its nature. And seeing the nature and end of it is lawful, itself cannot be sinful, but a man may swear when the magistrate requireth him, and not sin ; nay, but rather sin if he doth not swear, in not obeying the magistrate in such things which he may lawfully do.

# (7) USURY

## No. 322.  JOSEPH HALL

[From *Resolutions and Decisions of Divers Practical Cases of Conscience, in Continual Use among Men.* First Decade (" Cases of Profit and Traffic "), Case i.  *Works,* ed. Peter Hall (1837), Vol. VII, pp. 372–375.  Cp. note on No. **324.**]

*Whether is it lawful for me, to raise any profit by the loan of money?*

You may not expect a positive answer either way.  Many circumstances are considerable, ere any thing can be determined.

First, who is it that borrows ?   A poor neighbour, that is constrained out of need ?   Or a merchant, that takes up money for a freer trade ? Or a rich man, that lays it out upon superfluous occasions ?   If a poor man borrow out of necessity, you may not expect any profit for the loan (*Deut.* xv, 7, 8, 9).   To the poorest of all, we must give and not lend ; to the next rank of poor, we must lend freely.   But if a man will borrow that money which you could improve for the enriching of himself or, out of wanton expence, will be laying out that which might otherwise be useful to you, for his mere pleasure, the case is different.   For God hath not commanded you to love any man more than yourself ; and there can be no reason why you should veil your own just advantage to another man's excess.

Secondly, Upon what terms do you lend ?   Whether upon an absolute compact for a set increment, whatever become of the principal, or upon a friendly trust to a voluntary satisfaction, according to the good improvement of the sum lent ?   The former is not safe ; and, where there hath been an honest endeavour of a just benefit disappointed, either by unavoidable casualty or force, may not be rigorously urged without manifest oppression.   The latter can be no other than lawful ; and, with those that are truly faithful and conscionable, the bond of gratitude is no less strong than that of law and justice.

Thirdly, if upon absolute compact, is it upon a certainty or an adventure ?   For where you are willing to hazard the principal, there can be no reason but you should expect to take part of the advantage.

Fourthly, where the trade is ordinarily certain, there are yet farther considerations to be had.   To which I shall make way by these undeniable grounds :—

That the value of moneys or other commodities is arbitrary, according to the sovereign authority and use of several kingdoms and countries.

That whatsoever commodity is saleable is capable of a profit in the loan of it, as a horse or an ox, being that it may be sold, may be let out for profit.

Money itself is not only the price of all commodities in all civil nations, but it is also, in some cases, a trafficable commodity: the price whereof rises and falls in several countries upon occasion, and yieldeth either profit or loss in the exchange.

There can be no doubt, therefore, but that money, thus considered, and as it were turned merchandise, may be bought and sold, and improved to a just profit.

But the main doubt is whether money, merely considered as the price of all other commodities, may be let forth for profit, and be capable of a warrantable increase.

For the resolving whereof, be it determined

1. That all usury which is an absolute contract for the mere loan of money is unlawful, both by law natural and positive, both Divine and human.

Nature teacheth us that metals are not a thing capable of a super-fœtation; that no man ought to set a price on that which is not his own time; that the use of the stock once received is not the lender's, but the borrower's, for the power and right of disposing the principal is by contract transferred for the time to the hands of him that receives it, so as he that takes the interest by virtue of such transaction doth but in a mannerly and legal fashion rob the borrower.

How frequent the Scripture is in the prohibition of this practice, no Christian can be ignorant. And as for human laws, raised even from the mere light of nature amongst heathen nations, how odious and severely interdicted usurary contracts have been in all times, it appears sufficiently by the records which we have of the Decrees of Egypt, of Athens, of Rome; and not only by the restraint of the Twelve Tables and of Claudius and Vespasian, but by the absolute forbiddance of many popular statutes condemning this usage. Tiberius himself, though otherwise wicked enough, yet would rather furnish the Banks with his own stock to be freely let out for three years to the citizens upon only security of the sum doubled in the forfeiture, than he would endure this griping and oppressive transaction. And how wise Cato drove all usurers out of Sicily and Lucullus freed all Asia from this pressure of Interest, history hath sufficiently recorded.

As for Laws Ecclesiastical, let it be enough that a Council[1] hath defined that to say usury is not a sin is no better than heresy. And in succeeding times how liable the usurer hath ever been to the highest censures of the Church, and how excluded from the favour of Christian burial, is more manifest than to need any proof.

[1] [The Council of Vienne, 1311.]

48

2. However it is unlawful to covenant for a certain profit for the mere loan of money, yet there may be and are circumstances appending to the loan which may admit of some benefit to be lawfully made by the lender for the use of his money; and especially these two,—the loss that he sustains, and the gain that he misses, by the want of the sum lent. For what reason can there be, that to pleasure another man I should hurt myself? That I should enrich another by my own loss?

If, then, I shall incur a real loss or forfeiture by the delayed payment of the sum lent, I may justly look for a satisfaction from the borrower; yea, if there be a true danger of loss to me imminent, when the transaction is made, nothing hinders but that I may by compact make sure such a sum as may be sufficient for my indemnity.

And if I see an opportunity of an apparent profit that I could make fairly by disbursing of such a sum *bona fide*, and another that hath a more gainful bargain in chase shall sue to me to borrow my money out of my hand for his own greater advantage, there can be no reason why, in such a case, I should have more respect to his profit than my own; and why should I not, even upon pact, secure unto myself such a moderate sum as may be somewhat answerable to the gain which I do willingly forego, for his greater profit?—since it is a true ground, which Lessius, with other Casuists, maintains against Sotus and Durand, that even our hopes of an evident commodity are valuable, and that no less than the fears of our loss.

Shortly, for the guidance of our either caution or liberty, in matter of borrowing or lending, the only cynosure is our charity. For in all human and civil acts of commerce, it is a sure rule that whatsoever is not a violation of charity cannot be unlawful, and whatsoever is not agreeable to charity can be no other than sinful. And as charity must be your rule, so yourself must be the rule of your charity: Look what you could wish to be done to you by others, Do but the same to others,—you cannot be guilty of the breach of charity. The maxims of traffic are almost infinite; only charity, but ever inseparable from justice, must make the application of them. That will teach you that every increase by loan of money is not usury, and that those which are absolutely such are damnable. That will teach you to distinguish betwixt the one improvement of loan and the other, and will tell you that if you can find out a way, whether by loan or sale, to advance your stock that may be free from all oppression and extortion and beneficial as well to others as to yourself, you need not fear to walk in it with all honest security. But, in the mean time take good heed that your heart beguile you not in misapplications: for we are naturally too apt out of our self-love, to flatter ourselves with fair glozes of bad intentions, and rather to draw the rule to us than ourselves to the rule.

But, while I give you this short solution, I must profess to lament the common ignorance or mistaking of too many Christians, whose zeal justly cries down usury as a most hateful and abominable practice, but in the mean time makes no bones of actions no less biting and oppressive. They care not how high they sell any of their commodities, at how unreasonable rates they set their grounds, how they circumvent the buyer in their bargains, and think any price just, any gain lawful, that they can make in their markets; not considering, that there is neither less, nor less odious usury, in selling and letting, than there is in lending. It is the extortion in both that makes the sin, without which the kind or terms of the transaction could not be guilty. Surely, it must needs be a great weakness to think that the same God, Who requires mercy and favour in lending, will allow us to be cruel in selling. Rigour and excess in both equally violates the law of communicative justice, equally crosses the law of charity. Let those, therefore, that make scruple of an usurious lending, learn to make no less conscience of a racking bargain. Otherwise, their partial obedience will argue a gross hypocrisy, and they shall prove themselves the worse kind of what they hate, usurers: for in the ordinary loan-usury, the borrower hath yet time to boot for his money, but here the buyer pays down an excessive interest, without any consideration at all but the seller's cruelty.

## No. 323. HENRY HAMMOND

[From *A Practical Catechism*, Book IV, Section ii. Ed. *L. A. C. T.*, pp. 297–302. Cp. note on No. 267.]

*Scholar.* I shall take leave to put you in mind of one thing which may perhaps cost you some time, and yet belonging directly to this matter of just dealing betwixt man and man, I cannot but think it seasonable for me to demand, and for you to give, your judgement of it.

*Catechist.* What is that?

*Scholar.* The known famous business of usury, of which there are various and distinct opinions, and perhaps the reasons given for any of them not very satisfactory. I shall expect your opinion of it.

*Catechist.* You shall have it as clearly and briefly as I can. And first, I must tell you that the business of usury is not so clearly stated in the New Testament (and for that among the Jews in the Old, it is both obscure, and only to a fellow Jew, and so belongs not unto Christians, who are not obliged by their judicial laws any further than the equity of them is imitable by us) as that I can set strict and certain laws to all any man's actions from thence, which you will believe with me when I tell you the one only ground of objection I have against usury from the New Testament. It is from an observation which I made in comparing the Hebrew with the Septuagint's interpretation of the Book of Nehemiah, in which generally the phrase which we render

' to exact usury ' is rendered by the Greek ' to exact ' simply, without any substantive added to it; and· so the Greek noun for ' requiring ' or ' exacting ' signifies there ' requiring of use ': and so *II Macc.* iv, 27, that which is rendered ' required it,' most probably signifies this ' receiving of use,' the period being best rendered thus : *As for the money, etc., he put it not into any good course, but Sostratus, etc., took the use of it ; for unto him belonged the managing of the moneys.* From whence, knowing what sympathy or consent there is between the Greek of the New Testament and of the Old, I presently thought that that place of the Gospel *Luke* vi, 30, might be explained, where Christ speaking of acts of mercy, *giving to every one that asketh*, addeth in our translating, *And from him that taketh away thy goods, ask them not again* : where I conceive the most proper and commodious sense, and that which will be most agreeable to the context concerning giving, will be this, *From him that receiveth* (not ' taketh by force,' but all one with the word which we render ' receiving ') *by way of loan any of thy goods, require no usury* (according to that notion in Nehemiah, of ' requiring ' for ' exacting of usury ') *of him.* Which being, as I said, joined with *giving to them that ask*, denoteth a work of mercy, as indeed lending is a prime way of mercy. *The good man is merciful and lendeth*, and *he that is merciful will lend to his neighbour*, and many the like. And I remember a most excellent obliging Roman exercised himself especially in this kind of mercy, lending and strictly requiring the payment on the day. And Cornelius Nepos saith he did more good that way than by giving he could have done—teaching men to be thrifty and laborious, whereas giving or suffering them not to repay would have made them sluggish and beggars. Which being supposed, it will follow that this of not requiring of use, being an act of mercy, must I conceive, be extended no farther than the former precept of giving was to be extended. Now though the words are in an unlimited latitude, *Give to every one that asketh*, yet ordinary prudence will interpret them so, that if a covetous rich man ask of me, I am not bound to give to him, but only to him whose wants set him on asking. And so consequently in like manner the prohibition or forbidding to exact, take, or require use of him that borrows, belongs not again to the poor or mean creditor when a rich man borrows of him, but only when the rich lends to the poor man, to whom a free loan is a seasonable mercy. From whence, as I should conclude without any demur, that when I lend a poor man, I must not require use, any more than I must deny alms to him that wants it, when I have it to spare ; so I cannot conclude it unlawful from hence to receive from a rich man (I mean, who wants not that alms) what interest or increase he is willing to give me, which is, I suppose, the question resolved. All I conceive necessary to be added by way of caution is, first, that I take care that such lending to the rich do not disable me from assisting the poor. Secondly, that I am, as far as morally I can be, sure that he who pays me this use is able to do it without eating out or hurting himself, but that he makes greater gain of it by trading, or the like. Thirdly, that it be not so done as that it may bring reproach or censure of worldly-mindedness or illiberality upon me, especially if I be a clergyman,—for by the Canons of ancient Councils, they are forbidden many things of this nature which were permitted others; much more that it be not an act of a covetous mind, but only a way of subsisting on that small portion my friends have left me.

*Scholar.* But what must I do in case the person to whom I thus lent upon use (and in so doing observed, as well as I could, the second caution,—conceived him very probable to make gain by that loan), either by misadventure or by his own neglects lose by my loan, or be eaten out by paying me interest?

*Catechist.* I answer, that in that case it is the safest course to forbear the interest, and in matters of this nature, I conceive it is my duty to take the safest course; and the thinking myself obliged to do so will make me more circumspect than perhaps otherwise I should be, in examining the condition of the person of whom I adventure to take use, and being as sure as I can that I take it not from any that could need my charity, *i.e.* my lending without use. In all this you must not think that I am so positive as in other things I have been, but only that I set you down my opinion and the grounds on which I build it, and shall expect your assent no farther than my grounds convince you. For the truth is, after all this which I have said upon that ground, from that passage of St. Luke so interpreted, I must confess that the word which I render ' requiring of use ' may signify somewhat else, viz. to exact or require back the loan, when it is lent without use, for so the word to ' require back that which is lent ' (contrary to release) is rendered *Deut.* xv, 2 and 3; and so *Wisd.* xv, 8, and *Ecclus.* xx, 15, the Greek word is used for calling back a loan, and so indeed the word more usual is ' to lend ' simply, as well as ' to lend upon use.' And then the meaning of the verse in Luke will be: That as I must *give to him that asketh*, so of him that borroweth of me, I must not exact repayment, when he is not through poverty able to do it, for that were an act of oppression or very contrary to charity; and therefore *Isa.* ix, 4, the word signifies *oppressors*, and *Ecclus.* xx, 15, it is set down as the character of an illiberal fool, *To-day he lendeth, and to-morrow he asketh again.* And if this be the sense, then it will be still pertinent to the business of liberality or charity in giving and lending, and so no farther belong to the matter of usury than by analogy may be inferred from thence, viz. that if from a poor man I must not hasten or exact the repayment of his debt, but continue the loan to him as long as his distress requires, then surely I must not sell that loan, *i.e.* take use of him. But this still must belong only to the rich man lending to the poor.   As for the case of the rich man's lending to the rich, there hath appeared nothing in either of these interpretations which will oblige to it, or if he do, which will prohibit the taking interest of him; and there is as little to that purpose in a third possible interpretation of the words, according to the sound of our English, of not requiring the legal fourfold of him that hath robbed me,—which though it be not the importance of the word 'taketh,' which notes only 'receiving' not 'rapine,' yet is no very improbable rendering of the word 'require,' if we compare it with a place in an ancient human author.   But as this still belongs not to usury at all by any analogy, but only concludes that the not requiring the legal fourfold of the thief will by analogy with the former part of the verse be restrained only to the case of the poor (not rich) thief that by necessity is enforced to take away ought from thee; so do I not know any other so much as colour of text in the New Testament which forbids it, nor indeed reason nor analogy, either from that great rule in hand of *doing as I would be done to* (for if I were a rich man, I would, in case of convenience or advantage that a loan would probably bring into me, be willing to pay use for it) or of *loving my neighbour as myself*; nor consequently can I yet affirm it unlawful, still supposing that the cautions which I mentioned be observed uprightly.

*Scholar.*   I shall rest in your present directions and draw you on no farther in this business of justice, because I conceive the prime thing designed in the rule on which we have built these discourses is indeed that duty of mercifulness.

# (8) DUELLING

## No. 324.  JOSEPH HALL

[From *Resolutions and Decisions of Divers Practical Cases of Conscience, in Continual Use among Men*, Second Decade (" Cases of Life and Liberty "), Case ii.  *Works*, ed. Peter Hall (1837), Vol. VII, pp. 398–400.  This treatise was published in 1649; there was a second edition in 1650 and a third edition in 1654.  It is noteworthy that, after a period of several years occupied with doctrinal controversies, Hall in his old age returned to ' practical ' subjects.]

*Whether may I lawfully make use of a duel, for the deciding of my right or the vindication of mine honour ?*

I HAVE long ago spent my opinion upon this point in a large epistolar discourse,[1] which I find no reason to alter.  Thither I might refer you to spare my labour; but lest, perhaps, that should not be at hand, shortly thus :—

The sword in a private hand was never ordained to be a decider of any controversies, save this one, whether of the two is the better fencer; nor yet that always, since *the race is not to the swift, nor the battle to the strong*, as Solomon hath observed.

It can be no better, therefore, than a mere tempting of God, as Rodriguez justly censures it, to put ourselves or our cause upon so unwarranted a trial.

I find but two practices of it in the records of Scripture.

The one, that famous challenge of Goliath, which that proud Philistine had not made if he had not presumed of his giantly strength and stature, so utterly unmatchable by all Israel, that the whole host was ready to give back upon his appearance.  He knew the advantage so palpable that none would dare to undertake the quarrel, and had still gone on to triumph over that trembling army, had not God's inexpected champion, by Divine instinct, taken up the monster and vanquished him, leaving all but his head to bedung that earth which had lately shaken at his terror.

The other was in that mortal quarrel betwixt Joab and Abner, on the behalf of their two masters, David and Ishbosheth, wherein Abner invites his rival in honour to a tragical play, as he terms it, a monomachy of twelve single combatants, on either part, which was so acted that no man went victor away from that bloody theatre.

Only it is observable that in both these conflicts still the challengers had the worst.

[1] [See *Epistles*; Decade IV, Epistle 2.]

683

In imitation of which latter, I cannot allow that which I find frequently done in the managing of public hostility, that some confident cavalier out of mere bravery of spirit craves leave to put himself forth before both armies and, as in way of preface to an ensuing battle, bids defiance to any antagonist;—an act of more valour than judgement, whereof the undertaking is void of warrant and the issue (lightly) of success; while it pleaseth God commonly to punish presumption with a foil, and the ominous miscarriage of one proves a sad discouragement to many.

And if single fortitude be not triable this way, much less justice in causes litigious. To make the sword arbiter of such differences were no better than to revive the old Ordalian trial, used by our Heathen Ancestors, since God hath no more ordained, nor promised, to bless the one than the other. And reason itself tells us, in how ill a condition that righteous cause is, which must be carried by the sharper weapon, the stronger arm, the skilfuller fencer.

Now, whereas there are two acts, as introductions into the field, a challenge and an acceptation, both of them have their guilt: but the former so much more, as it hath in it more provocation to evil.

I cannot, therefore, but wonder at and cry down the opinion of Bannez and Cajetan that a man, slandered by an unjust accuser, may justly challenge him in the field, and vindicate himself by the sword: a doctrine, which, if it were allowed and accordingly practised, besides that it would destroy the course of justice and wrest revenge out of the hands of the Almighty, were enough to make the world an Aceldama: for, who would not be his own judge, for the accusation; and his own executioner for the revenge?

There may yet seem more innocence in the acceptation, which makes shew of a mere passive nature, and appears to be extorted by the insolence of a provoking adversary, whose pressures are wont to receive such construction, as that the challenged party refusing, upon what ground soever, is, in the vulgar opinion, proclaimed for base and recreant; and I must needs confess, the irritation diminisheth the offence. But, withal, however the Spanish and Italian Casuists, whose nations are wont to stand a little too highly upon the points of a mis-called honour, are wont to pass fair interpretations of the matter, I cannot but find it deeply guilty also: for, what is this other, than a consent to sin by engaging in blood? which, by a man wise and conscionable, might be turned off with a just contempt, without imputation of cowardice, since the plea of conscience is able to bear down the vain fancies of idle sword-men: or, if that will not be taken, the false blurs, that are cast upon a worthy man's reputation by vulgar breath, deserve no entertainment but scorn: or, lastly, other means lie open to both parts, for the proof of a questioned valour, which in a lawful way the challenged is ready to embrace. He walks, not unprovided, about the business of his calling: if he be fairly set upon on equal terms, he shall make no doubt to defend himself. But, to make a formal business of a quarrel on either part, and to agree upon a bargain of blood-shedding, is wicked and damnable; and, though both should come fairly off, yet the very intention to kill is murder.

This case is so clear, that the Council of Trent hath thought fit to denounce heavy sentences, and inflict sharp censures upon Emperors, Kings, States, and Potentates, that shall give allowance to duels within their dominions; pronouncing them, *ipso jure*, excommunicate, and depriving them of those towns, cities, lands, if held of the Church, where such unlawful acts are made: and that those, who either act or patronize, and by their presence assist, countenance, or abet such combats, shall incur the sentence of excommunication, the loss of all their goods, and perpetual infamy; and, if they die in such quarrel, shall, as self-murderers, be debarred the privilege of Christian burial.

Briefly, therefore, neither your justice nor your honour may depend upon the point of private swords; and, if there can be no other remedy, you must rather suffer in either, than hazard your soul.

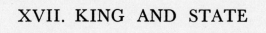

XVII. KING AND STATE

## (1) THE MONARCHY

### No. 325.  RICHARD HOOKER

[From *The Laws of Ecclesiastical Polity*, Book VIII, Chapter ii, § 13.  *Works*, ed.
J. Keble, Vol. III, p. 353.  Cp. note on No. 150.]

IN which respect, I cannot choose but commend highly their wisdom,
by whom the foundations of this Commonwealth [of England] have
been laid; wherein though no manner, person, or cause, be unsubject
to the King's power, yet so is the power of the King over all and in all
limited, that unto all his proceedings the law itself is a rule.  The
axioms of our regal government are these : *Lex facit regem* ; the King's
grant of any favour made contrary to the law is void, *Rex nihil potest
nisi quod jure potest*.  Our Kings, therefore, when they take possession
of the room they are called unto, have it painted out before their eyes,
even by the very solemnities and rites of their inauguration, to what
affairs by the said law their supreme authority and power reacheth.
Crowned we see they are, and enthronized, and anointed : the crown
a sign of military, the throne, of sedentary or judicial, the oil, of religious
or sacred power.

### No. 326.  WILLIAM LAUD

[From *The Answer of the Most Reverend Father in God William, Lord Archbishop of
Canterbury, to the Speech of the Lord Saye and Sele, touching the Liturgy*.  *Works*, ed.
*L. A. C. T.*, Vol. VI, Part i, pp. 142–145.  This Answer was first printed in 1695 by
Henry Wharton at the end of the *History of Laud's Troubles and Trial*.]

I will not dispute it here, what power a lay assembly (and such a
Parliament is) hath to determine matters of religion, primely and originally by and of themselves, before the Church hath first agreed upon
them.  Then, indeed, they may confirm or refuse.  And this course was
held in the Reformation.  But originally to take this power over religion
into lay hands, is that which hath not been thus assumed since Christ to
these unhappy days : and I pray God this chair of religion do not prove
*cathedra pestilentiae*, as the Vulgar reads it in *Ps.* i, 1, to the infecting of
this whole nation with schism and heresy, and in the end bring all to
confusion.

I meddle not here with the King's power.  For he may be present in
Convocation when he pleases, and take or leave any canons as he pleases,
which are for the peace and well ordering of the Church; as well as in
Parliament, take or leave any laws made ready for him, for the good and

689

quiet of his people.   But if it come to be matter of faith, though in his absolute power he may do what he will, and answer God for it after ;  yet he cannot commit the ordering of that to any lay assembly, Parliament or other, for them to determine that which God hath intrusted into the hands of His priests.   Though, if he will do this, the clergy must do their duty to inform him and help that dangerous error if they can :  but if they cannot, they must suffer an unjust violence how far soever it proceed ;  but they may not break the duty of their allegiance.

It is true Constantius the Emperor, a great patron of the Arians, was by them interested in their cause, and meddled *in decernendo*, in determining, and that beforehand, what the prelates should do ;  and sometimes in commanding the orthodox prelate to communicate with the Arians.   This they refused to do, as being against the Canons of the Council of Nice.

And then his answer was, " Yea, but that which I will shall go for Canon." · But then we must know withal, that Athanasius reckoned him for this, as that Antichrist which Daniel prophesied of.   Hosius also, the famous confessor of those times, condemned in him that kind of meddling in and with religion.   And so doth St. Hilary of Poictiers. Valentinian also, the younger, took upon him to judge of religion at the like persuasion of Auxentius the Arian, but he likewise was sharply reproved for it by St. Ambrose.   In like manner, Maximus the tyrant took upon him to judge in matters of religion, as in the case of Priscillian and his associates.   But this also was checked by St. Martin, Bishop of Tours :  where it is again to be observed, that though these emperors were too busy in venturing upon the determination of points of faith, yet no one of them went so far as to take power from the synods, and give it to the senate.   And the orthodox and understanding emperors did neither the one nor the other.   For Valentinian the elder left this great Church-work to be done by Churchmen.   And though the power to call Councils was in the emperor, and though the emperors were sometimes personally present in the Councils, and sometimes by their deputies, both to see order kept, and to inform themselves, yet the decisive voices were in the clergy only.   And this will plainly appear in the instructions given by the Emperor Theodosius to Candidianus, whom he sent to supply his place in the Council of Ephesus ; which were, " That he should not meddle with matters of faith if any came to be debated."   And gives this reason for it :  " Because it is unlawful for any but bishops to mingle himself with them in those consultations."   And Basilius, the emperor, long after this, in the eighth General Council, held at Constantinople, 870, affirms it of the laity in general, " that it is no way lawful for them to meddle with these things.   But that it is proper for the patriarchs, bishops, and priests, which have the office of government in the Church, to enquire into these things." And more of this argument might easily be added, were that needful, or I among my books, and my thoughts at liberty. And yet this crosses not the supremacy which the King of England hath in causes ecclesiastical : as it is acknowledged both by the Church and law. For that reaches not to the giving of him power to determine points of faith, either in Parliament or out ; or to the acknowledgment of any such power residing in him ; or to give him power to make Liturgies, and public forms of prayer ; or to preach or administer sacraments ; or to do anything which is merely spiritual. But in all things which are of a mixed cognisance, such as are all those which are properly called ecclesiastical and belong to the bishops' external jurisdiction, the supremacy there, and in all things of like nature, is the king's. And if at any time the emperor or his deputy sit judge in a point of faith, it is not because he hath any right to judge it, or that the Church hath not right ; but merely in case of contumacy, where the heretic is wilful, and will not submit to the Church's power. And this the heretics sometimes did ; and then the bishops were forced to appeal thither also ; but not for any resolution in the point of faith, but for aid and assistance to the just power of the Church.

## No. 327.  JAMES USSHER

[From *The Power Communicated by God to the Prince, and the Obedience Required of the Subject, Briefly laid down and confirmed out of the Holy Scriptures, the Testimony of the Primitive Church, the Dictates of Right Reason, and the Opinions of the Wisest Among the Heathen Writers*, Part II, " The Obedience of the Subject." *Works*, ed. C. R. Elrington (1864), Vol. XI, pp. 357 f. This treatise, which was written for the most part in 1639 at the request of the Earl of Strafford, Ussher sent to London with a view to its publication, but unfortunately the MS. was lost. After his death, the original draft of the work was found among Ussher's papers ; and it was prepared for publication by James Tyrrell, the Archbishop's grandson. The work which appeared in 1661 was dedicated to Charles II, and it contained a preface by Robert Sanderson, Bishop of Lincoln.]

But those stiff spirits that will not stoop unto this passive kind of obedience if they can help it, think they have stricken the matter dead by proposing this case unto us : " Suppose," say they, " the king should command us to worship the Devil. Would you wish us here to lay down our heads upon the block, and not give us leave to stand upon our guard and to the utmost of our power repel the violence of such a miscreant ? If not, what would become of God's Church and His religion ? " As if this had been a new case, never heard of before, and the Apostle had not sufficiently declared unto us that *the things which the Gentiles sacrificed, they sacrificed to devils and not to God.* And yet when this devil-worship was so vehemently urged by the cruel edicts of the persecuting emperors, did the Christians ever take arms against them for the matter ? or betook themselves to any other refuge but fervent prayers unto Almighty God, Whom they acknowledged to be their prince's only superior, and patient suffering of what disgrace or punishment

soever should be imposed upon them ?  To the cheerful undergoing
whereof, see how St. Peter . . . doth animate and encourage them:
*Beloved, think it not strange concerning the fiery trial, which is to try you,
as though some strange thing happened to you.  But rejoice, inasmuch as
ye are partakers of Christ's sufferings, that when His glory shall be revealed,
ye may be glad also with exceeding joy.   If ye be reproached for the name of
Christ, happy are ye ; for the spirit of glory and of God resteth on you ;
Who on their part is evil spoken, but on your part He is glorified.   But
let none of you suffer as a murderer, or as a thief, or as an evil doer, or as
a busybody in other men's matters.   Yet if any suffer as a Christian, let
him not be ashamed ; but let him glorify God on this behalf.*

## No. 328.  ROBERT SANDERSON

[From the Preface to James Ussher's *The Power Communicated by God to the
Prince and the Obedience Required of the Subject*, § XV.   Sanderson's *Works*, ed. W.
Jacobson (1854), Vol. V, p. 210.   On the circumstances connected with the publication
of this treatise, cp. note on No. **327**.]

As for those . . . that would derive the original of all Government
from the people by way of pact and contract, it may suffice to say that
they take that for granted which never yet was proved nor (I dare say)
ever will be proved while the world standeth, either from Scripture,
Reason, or History.   *Jus gladii*, the right and power of the sword (which
is really the Sovereign Power) belongeth, we know, to Kings.   But it
is *by the ordinance of God*, not the donation of the people ; for *he beareth
the sword*, St. Paul telleth us, as God's minister from Whom he received
it, and not as the people's minister, who had no right to give it because
they never had it themselves.   If any shall say they had, the proof
lieth on their part to show how they came by it ; whether God gave it
them, or they took it themselves.   If God gave it them, let it be made
appear when and where the first grant was made ; let some evidence
be produced to justify the claim, or at least some credible testimony,
or pregnant presumption to render it probable that there was some such
thing done, though the records be lost.   If none of all this can be done,
it remaineth that if they had it they took it.   And if they so did, it
was saucily and sacrilegiously done at the first ; and by Our Saviour's
presage (*Matt.* xxvi, 52) like enough to prosper with them accordingly at
the last.

## No. 329.  ROBERT SANDERSON

[From *Episcopacy as established by Law in England not Prejudicial to Regal Power*,
Section II, § xii.   *Works*, ed. W. Jacobson (1854), Vol. V, pp. 157 f.   This treatise was
first published in 1661, the year that Sanderson was chosen 'Moderator' of the Savoy
Conference which rejected the Presbyterian polity.]

All power to the exercise whereof our Bishops have pretended
cometh under one of the two heads,—of Order or of Jurisdiction.   The

power of Order consisteth partly in Preaching the Word and other Offices of Public Worship, common to them with their fellow-ministers; partly in Ordaining Priests and Deacons, admitting them to their particular cures, and other things of like nature, peculiar to them alone. The power of Jurisdiction is either Internal, in retaining and remitting sins *in foro conscientiae*, common to them also (for the substance of the authority, though with some difference of degree) with other Ministers; or External for the outward government of the Church in some parts thereof peculiar to them alone. For that External Power is either Directive in prescribing rules and orders to those under their Jurisdictions, and making Canons and Constitutions to be observed by the Church,—wherein the inferior Clergy by their Representatives in Convocation have their votes, as well as the Bishops, and both dependently upon the King (for they cannot either meet without his Writ, or treat without his Commission, or establish without his Royal Assent); or Judiciary and Coercive, in giving sentence *in foro exteriori* in matters of Ecclesiastical cognisance, excommunicating, fining, imprisoning offenders, and the like. Of these powers, some branches, not only in the exercise thereof, but even in the very substance of the Power itself, (as namely that of External Jurisdiction Coercive), are by the Laws declared, and by the Clergy acknowledged to be wholly and entirely derived from the King, as the sole Fountain of all Authority of External Jurisdiction whether Spiritual or Temporal within the Realm; and consequently not of Divine Right. Other-some, although the substance of the power itself be immediately from God and not from the King, as those of Preaching, Ordaining, Absolving, etc., yet are they so subject to be inhibited, limited, or otherwise regulated in the outward exercise of that power by the Laws and Customs of the Land, as that the whole execution thereof still dependeth upon the Regal Authority.

## No. 330. ROBERT SANDERSON

[From *De Obligatione Conscientiae Praelectiones Decem, Oxonii in Schola Theologica Habitae, Anno Domini MDCXLVII*, Prael. VII (on *Prov.* viii, 15), §§ 29 f. *Works*, ed. W. Jacobson (1854), Vol. IV, pp. 168–170. The translation reprinted here is that contained in the edition of Christopher Wordsworth, issued at Lincoln in 1877 under the title of *Bishop Sanderson's Lectures on Conscience and Human Law* (pp. 224–226). These lectures were first published at London in 1660. Sanderson had been appointed Regius Professor of Divinity at Oxford on July 19, 1642. Owing to the troubled state of the University at the time, however, he could not enter upon the duties of his office until 1646; while in 1648 he was turned out of his Professorship by the Parliamentary Visitors. These lectures were thus the chief fruit of his labours as Regius Professor.]

Our fifth inquiry relates to Ecclesiastical Laws in particular. That new laws may be made concerning rites and ecclesiastical matters and persons, with regard to the circumstances of outward worship, and promoting order, decency, and edification, besides those delivered by Christ and His Apostles in Scripture, is a case so evident and agreeable

49

to reason that it would be a glaring proof of prejudice and obstinacy seriously to deny it; but to whom the right of making Ecclesiastical Laws does properly belong, has been eagerly controverted by Divines.

The Romanists, who would exempt the clergy from all jurisdiction of the civil magistrate (concerning which controversy this is not the place to dispute), contend that Bishops only, and especially the Pope, whom they call the Oecumenical Bishop, have a right and power to make laws, which not only oblige the consciences of the clergy, but of the laity also, and that without the leave or consent of the civil magistrate.

The Puritanical Reformers of the present age, who profess themselves the most bitter enemies of Popery, but at the same time turn all things into confusion, among many other doctrines of the Papists, embrace this tenet,—from whom they differ in persons, not in opinion, —and they take away all power, authority, and ecclesiastical jurisdiction from the Crown, and confine it wholly to their own classes and conventions. The Erastians, on the contrary, who also set up for Reformers (Good heavens! what strange names and opinions, alike ill-shapen and dire, but otherwise monstrously diverse, have these last seven years, fruitful of prodigies, brought forth into the world, and nursed and cherished under pretence of Reformation!), the disciples of Erastus, I say, would rob the spiritualty of all ecclesiastical jurisdiction, and give up the outward government of the Church absolutely into the hands of the civil magistrate.

I have no desire nor leisure (unless I should be willing to trespass unduly on your patience) to engage with both these adversaries. But in this, as in many other debates, the mean between the two extremes seems to be the truer opinion, and safer to follow; and I am confident that you will be more easily led to concur in my sentiments, because they are as agreeable to the Doctrine of the Church of England and to the Laws of the Realm. My assertion is, that the right of making Ecclesiastical Laws is vested in the Bishops and Presbyters and other persons duly elected by the whole body of the clergy of the whole realm, and assembled duly in a lawful synod; yet so, that the exercise of this right and power ought to depend, in every Christian state, upon the authority of the Supreme Civil Magistrate, and this both *a parte ante, et a parte post*, i.e. previously and subsequently to deliberation, so that they cannot, without his permission first obtained, and being summoned by his mandate, or at least by his authority, either meet in order to make Ecclesiastical Canons; nor after they are thus called and authorized are the Canons, which may be agreed to in such a convention, of any force to oblige till the assent of the Supreme Magistrate be obtained; by whose public authority and approbation so soon as they are confirmed, they immediately obtain the force of laws, and oblige the conscience of the subject.

## No. 331. JOHN LAKE

[From *A Defence of the Profession which the Right Reverend Father in God, John, late Lord Bishop of Chichester, made upon his Death-bed Concerning Passive Obedience and the New Oaths ; together with an Account of some Passages of His Lordship's Life.* London, 1690, pp. 10 f. This treatise was published anonymously by Robert Jenkin, a former chaplain of the bishop, who on August 27, 1689, had dictated to him a " Profession " of faith from which the following extract is taken. See J. H. Overton *The Non-Jurors. Their Lives, Principles, and Writings* (1902), pp. 79–81.]

Being called by a sick and I think a dying bed, and the good hand of God upon me in it, to take the last and best Viaticum, the Sacrament of my dear Lord's Body and Blood, I take myself obliged to make this short recognition and profession.

That whereas I was baptized into the Religion of the Church of England, and sucked it in with my milk, I have constantly adhered to it through the whole course of my life, and now, if so be the Will of God, shall die in it ; and I had resolved, through God's grace assisting me, to have died so, though at a stake.

And whereas that Religion of the Church of England taught me the doctrine of Non-Resistance and Passive Obedience, which I have accordingly inculcated upon others, and which I took to be the distinguishing character of the Church of England, I adhere no less firmly and steadfastly to that, and in consequence of it have incurred a suspension from the exercise of my office and expected a deprivation. I find in so doing much inward satisfaction, and if the Oath had been tendered at the peril of my life, I could only have obeyed by suffering.

## (2) ECCLESIASTICAL AND CIVIL LAWS

### No. 332. WILLIAM BEVERIDGE

[From Συνοδικόν, *Sive Pandectae Canonum Sanctorum Apostolorum et Conciliorum ab Ecclesia Graeca receptorum.* Two volumes, Oxford, 1672. Prolegomena, §§ I, II. This treatise still remains a standard work, though its scholarship is open to criticism. Soon after publication, an attack was made upon it, and Beveridge replied in *Codex Canonum Ecclesiae Primitivae Vindicatus ac Illustratus* (1678); this treatise was reprinted in the *L. A. C. T.* edition of Beveridge's *Works* (Vols. XI and XII).]

ETIAMSI Ecclesia in Imperio sit, unumque cum eo in singulis regnis caput commune habeat, reapse nihilominus ab eo distinguitur, non secus atque anima a corpore; hoc enim medici, illa Theologi curae committitur: proinde homo ex duabus istis conflatus partibus, commune est utriusque regiminis subjectum, sub diverso tamen respectu, Imperio quidem quatenus ζῶον πολιτικόν est, Ecclesiae autem quatenus ζῶον ἀθάνατον, sempiternae scilicet felicitatis, vel miseriae capax. Enimvero homo convenientis sibi societatis ex natura appetens, istiusmodi necesse est subjiciatur legibus, quibus talis societas conservetur; ad eam autem integre conservandam nihil amplius requiritur, quam ut caveatur, ne unus alteri noceat, sed singuli sibi invicem prospiciant, et suum cuique tribuatur. Huic itaque rei ab Imperio consultum est: quod propterea externis tantum hominum actionibus, per corporea scilicet exertis organa, advigilat, ut eae nimirum suos intra limites ita coerceantur, ut nihil ex iis mali, sed quantum fieri potest boni commodique, et aliis singulis et toti communitati emergat, ut ita quisque se, et suis, et aliorum etiam societate, quiete et tranquille gaudeat. Verumenimvero homo non hominum tantum, sed ipsius etiam Dei creatoris summique boni communione frui, eumque colere, et ad summam, quae in creaturam conferri potest, felicitatem evehi ex natura comparatus est. Cum is autem et veram erga Deum pietatem, et suam in eo beatitudinem neglectui habere plus nimio propensus sit; imprimis necessarium est, ut harum etiam rerum cura ei habeatur. Haec autem Ecclesiae concreditur: cui propterea, quoad ejus fieri potest, cavere incumbit, ut et debitus Deo omnipotenti honor a singulis exhibeatur, et ipsi suprema illa quibus nati apti sunt gaudia consequantur. Imperium igitur externis tantum hominum erga se invicem actionibus, Ecclesia omnibus eorum erga ipsum etiam Deum gestibus intenta est: illud corpora, haec animas administrat. Christiani, fateor, cives utrique subjiciuntur, sed ei quatenus cives, huic quatenus Christiani: et illud proinde praesentia tantum mala ab iis propulsare,

haec perpetua iis bona conciliare studet.   Vel ut summatim dicam,
Imperium publicae tantum in terris hominum quieti, Ecclesia aeternae
etiam in coelis eorum saluti consulit.

Vel me tacente, nemo non videat quare haec praemissa sunt, et
quid ex iis consequetur.   Ut enim ad praescriptos Imperii consequendos
fines, leges ab eo ferantur necesse est, quibus singuli constringimur,
et quarum servi omnes idcirco sumus, ut liberi vivere possimus : sic
etiam Ecclesia praestitutos sibi fines nunquam assequetur, nisi suas
habeat leges, quibus omnes teneantur, qui in spiritualem istam societa-
tem admissi sunt.   Et quidem inter Ecclesiasticas hasce et civiles
leges, non minus quam inter Ecclesiam ipsam et Imperium interest.
Primo enim quantum ad poenas iis annexas, leges civiles morte saepe
puniunt, Ecclesiasticae nunquam, ut quibus vitam non eripere, sed
servare propositum est.   Corpora ab utrisque castigantur, sed ab illis
externe, per verbera ;  ab his interne, per jejunia et luctus.   Quinetiam
leges Politicae per publicam bonorum confiscationem in delinquentes
animadvertunt ;   Ecclesiasticae autem  per depositionem si Clerici
sint, a gradu suscepto ;  sin laïci, per segregationem a spirituali coetu ;
et per anathemata iis inflicta :  quae sane talia sunt supplicia, quorum
exigendi potestatem nullus unquam Imperator sibi arrogavit ;  nec
jure arrogare potuit ;  siquidem omnis ista ligandi et solvendi potestas,
in Apostolis solis et ipsorum successoribus ab ipso Deo, a quo omnis
autoritas derivatur, sita sit, nulla regum mentione facta.   Si autem de
fide loquamur Christiana, et legibus ad Ecclesiasticam spectantibus
disciplinam, ipsi etiam Imperatores Christiani ingenue multoties
professi sunt, nihil sibi juris in istiusmodi sanciendis rebus tributum
esse.   Sic Constantinus Magnus, Valentinianus, Marcianus, Theodosius, aliique quorum verba alibi retulimus.   Quin ipse etiam omnium
peritissimus legum Imperator Justinianus, in ea fuit sententia, leges
nempe Civiles non praecedere debere, sed sequi Ecclesiasticas, idque
sine dedignatione : *Secundum sacras*, inquit, *et divinas regulas, quas
etiam nostrae sequi non dedignantur leges*. Novel. LXXXIII.  Hinc
est, quod etiamsi Imperatores multa de Ecclesiasticis personis et rebus
in Constitutionibus suis ediderint, nihil tamen de novo constituerunt,
sed ea tantum, quae ab Ecclesiasticis synodis prius constituta fuerant,
ipsi sua etiam autoritate confirmarunt ;  adeo ut quaecunque in Codice,
aut in novellis, de personis causisve Ecclesiasticis asserantur, ab
Ecclesiastica aliqua potestate antea sancita fuerint, quam illuc relata,
ut ex singulorum istiusmodi locorum inductione cuivis Canonici pariter
atque Politici perito juris facile patebit.   Quod etiam ex eo ulterius
elucescit, quod ad Ecclesiasticas, quae emerserunt, dirimendas lites,
et leges instituendas, ipsi etiam Imperatores concilia Ecclesiastica
convocare soliti fuerunt.   Sic enim Nicaenum primum Oecumenicum
a Constantino Magno ;  Constantinopolitanum a Theodosio seniore ;

Ephesinum a Theodosio juniore : et ut reliqua taceam, Chalcedonense a Marciano Imperatore congregatum est : Neque ullus ex hisce Imperatoribus causam aliquam a synodo, quam convocavit, discutiendam prius determinavit, quam ab ipsa synodo judicata est. Quicquid autem a synodis Ecclesiasticis decretum est, a civili etiam potestate confirmari solenne fuit. Unde et omnes propemodum Canones qui hoc libro continentur, ab Imperatore Justiniano Rhinotmeto iis subscribente corroborati sunt. Nimirum Principes Christiani, ut ad Ecclesiae praesidium, aeque ac ad Imperii regimen, civilem sibi commissam habentes potestatem, ea Ecclesiasticam per imperii sui provincias stabilire autoritatem, Canonicas tueri leges, et cavere ut Ecclesia pace sub suo fruatur patricinio, et autoritatem ipsi concreditam libere exerceat, ex officio suo tenentur ; ut veteres etiam Ecclesiae Patres docuerunt. Et idcirco, etiamsi ipsi Imperatores inconsulta Ecclesia Ecclesiasticas nunquam ferant leges, ut latae tamen in imperio cujusque conserventur, ipsis etiam per civilem suam autoritatem providere incumbit.

# XVIII. VISITATIONS

# (1) THEIR USEFULNESS

## No. 333.  RICHARD HOOKER

[From *The Laws of Ecclesiastical Polity*, Book VII, Chapter xxiv, § 9.  *Works*, ed. J. Keble, Vol. III, p. 309.  Cp. note on No. 150.]

TOUCHING Bishops' Visitations, the first institution of them was profitable, to the end that the state and condition of Churches being known, there might be for evils growing convenient remedies provided in due time.  The observation of Church Laws, the correction of faults in the service of God and manners of men, these are things that visitors should seek.  When these things are inquired of formally, and but for custom's sake, fees and pensions being the only thing which is sought and little else done by Visitations, we are not to marvel if the baseness of the end doth make the action itself loathsome.  The good which Bishops may do not only by these Visitations belonging ordinarily to their office, but also in respect of that power which the founders of colleges have given them of special trust, charging even fearfully their consciences therewith,—the good, I say, which they might do by this their authority, both within their own Dioceses, and in the well-springs themselves, the Universities, is plainly such as cannot choose but add weight to their heavy accounts in that dreadful day if they do it not.

# (2) LAUD'S VISITATION ARTICLES, 1635

## 334. WILLIAM LAUD

[In 1634, Laud, acting on pre-Reformation precedent, instituted a Visitation of all the dioceses within his Province. The form taken by the Articles of Inquiry varied according to the circumstances of the particular dioceses. The set which follows bore the title *Articles to be Inquired of in the Metropolitical Visitation of the Most Reverend Father William, By God's Providence Lord Archbishop of Canterbury, Primate of all England, and Metropolitan, In and for the Diocese of Winchester, in the Year of Our Lord God 1635, and in the Second Year of his Grace's Translation*; they were circulated in print at the time. Walter Curll was then Bishop of Winchester. As is well known, the Visitation was fiercely opposed.]

*Concerning the Church, the Ornaments thereof, and the Church's Possessions*

*Imprimis.* Whether have you in your several Churches and Chapels the whole Bible of the largest volume and the Book of Common Prayer, both fairly and substantially bound; a font of stone, set up in the ancient usual place; a convenient and decent Communion Table, with a carpet of silk or some other decent stuff, continually laid upon the same at time of Divine Service, and a fair linen cloth thereon at the time of the receiving of the Holy Communion? And whether is the same Table placed in such convenient sort within the Chancel or Church, as that the minister may be best heard in his prayer and administration and that the greatest number may communicate? And whether is it so used out of time of Divine Service as is not agreeable to the holy use of it, as by sitting on it, throwing hats on it, writing on it, or is it abused to other profaner uses? And are the Ten Commandments set upon the East End of your Church or Chapel where the people may best see and read them, and other sentences of Holy Scripture, written on the walls likewise for that purpose?

2. Whether are the afternoon sermons, in your several parishes turned into catechizing by question and answer, according to the form prescribed in the Book of Common Prayer? And whether doth every lecturer read Divine Service, according to the Liturgy printed by authority, in his surplice and hood before the lecture? And whether are his Majesty's instructions in all things duly observed?

3. Whether have you in your said Church or Chapel a convenient seat for your minister to read service in, together with a comely pulpit set up in a convenient place, with a decent cloth or cushion for the same, a comely large surplice, a fair communion cup with a cover of silver,

a flagon of silver, tin, or pewter, to put the wine in, whereby it may be set upon the Communion Table, at the time of the blessing thereof, with all other things and ornaments necessary for the celebration of Divine Service and Administration of the Sacraments? And whether have you a strong chest for alms for the poor, with three locks and keys, and another chest for keeping the books, and ornaments of the Church, and the Register Book? And whether have you a Register Book in parchment, for Christenings, Weddings, and Burials, and whether the same be kept in all points according to the Canons in that behalf provided? And is the mother's Christian name therein registered as well as the father's, and a transcript thereof brought in yearly within one month after the 25th of March, into the Lord Archbishop, or Bishop of the Diocese, his principal Register? And whether have you in your said Church or Chancel a table set of the degrees wherein by law men are prohibited to marry?

4. Whether are your Church and Chapels, with the chancels thereof, and your parsonage or vicarage house, your parish almshouse and Church House, in good reparations? And are they employed to godly and their right holy uses? Is your Church, chancel, and Chapel decently and comely kept, as well within as without, and the seats well maintained, according to the 85th Canon, in that behalf provided? Or have any patrons or others decayed the parsonage houses, and kept a stipendiary priest or curate in place where an incumbent should be provided? Whether is your churchyard well fenced with walls, rails, or pales, and by whom? And if not, in whose default the same is, and what the defect or fault is? And whether any person have encroached upon the ground of the churchyard, or whether any person or persons have used any thing or place consecrated to holy use, profanely or wickedly?

5. Is your Church or Chapel decently paved, and is your churchyard well and orderly kept without abuse? Are the bones of the dead decently interred or laid up in some fit place, as beseemeth Christians? And is the whole consecrated ground kept free from swine and all other nastiness, as becometh the place so dedicated?

6. Whether have any ancient monuments or glass windows been defaced, or any brass inscriptions, lead, stone, or anything else belonging to your Church or Chapel been at any time purloined, and by whom?

7. Whether have you the terrier of all the glebe-lands, meadows, gardens, orchards, houses, stocks, implements, tenements, and portions of tithes (whether within your parish or without) belonging unto your parsonage or vicarage, taken by the view of honest men in your said parish? And whether the said terrier be laid up in the Bishop's Registry, and in whose hands any of them are now? And if you have no terrier already made in parchment, you the churchwardens and sidemen, together with your parson or vicar, or in his absence with your minister,

are to make diligent enquiry and presentment of the several particulars following, and make, subscribe, and sign the said terrier, as aforesaid.

1. How many several parcels of glebe-land, do you know, or have you credibly heard to belong unto your rectory, Church, parsonage, vicarage, etc.; and by what names are they (or any of them) commonly called and known? And what yearly rent have you known or heard to have been paid, unto the parson, vicar, or to his or their assigns, for every, or any of the said parcels?

2. In whose occupation are the said parcels at this present? How much doth each parcel contain by measure of the sixteen foot pole? How is each parcel butted, on every part? And who is to repair the fences on each side thereof?

3. What hedge, ditch, meere, tree, thorn, doole,[1] or distinction is there now, at this present, whereby the said parcels of Church lands may be apparently known and distinguished from the lands of other men, upon whom they do abut?

4. What cartway, horseway, footway, gates, or stiles, do lead from your parsonage or vicarage house unto every of the said parcels of glebe-land? Declare your knowledge therein.

5. Whether you do know, or have you credibly heard, that some stiles, gates, hedges, ditch, meere, tree, thorn, or other doole (formerly growing or being between the said parcels of glebe, or some of them, and the lands of other men) have been digged up, felled down, destroyed, put by or defaced? And who hath the said parcel (so wronged) in occupation, when the said stile, gate, hedge, ditch, meere, tree, thorn, or other ancient doole, was so digged up, felled down, destroyed, put by or defaced?

### Concerning the Clergy

1. Whether doth your parson, vicar, or curate, distinctly and reverently say Divine Service upon Sundays and Holydays, and other days appointed to be observed by the Book of Common Prayer, as Wednesdays and Fridays and the Eves of every Sunday and Holyday, at fit and usual times? And doth he duly observe the orders, rites, and ceremonies, prescribed in the said Book of Common Prayer, as well in reading public prayers and the Litany, as also in administering the Sacraments, Solemnization of Matrimony, Visiting the Sick, Burying the Dead, Churching of Women, and all other like rites and Offices of the Church, in such manner and form as in the said Book of Common Prayer he is enjoined, without any omission or addition? And doth he read the Book of the Last Canons yearly, and wear a surplice according to the said Canons?

2. Whether have you any lecturer in your parish, who hath preached in his cloke and not in his gown, and whether you have any lecturer who

---

[1] [A boundary stake, marking the limits of Church lands.]

will not profess his willingness and readiness to take upon him a living or benefice, with cure of souls, or who hath refused a benefice when it hath been offered unto him ?

3. Doth your minister bid Holydays and Fasting Days, as by the Book of Common Prayer is appointed ? And doth he give warning beforehand to the parishioners for the receiving of the Holy Communion, as the Two-and-Twentieth Canon requireth ? And whether he doth administer the Holy Communion so often, and at such times as that every parishioner may receive the same, at the least three times in every year, whereof once at Easter, as by the Book of Common Prayer is appointed ? And doth your minister receive the same himself, on every day that he administereth it to others, and use the words of institution according to the Book at every time that the bread and wine is renewed, according as by the proviso of the 21st Canon is directed ? And doth he deliver the bread and wine to every communicant severally, and kneeling ? Whether he hath admitted to the Holy Communion any notorious offender or schismatic, contrary to the 26th and 27th Constitutions, or received any to the Communion being not of his own cure, or put any from the Communion who are not publicly infamous for any notorious crime ? Doth he use the Sign of the Cross in Baptism, or baptize in any basin or other vessel and not in the usual font ; or admit any father to be godfather to his own child or such who have not received the Holy Communion ; or baptize any children that were not born in the parish, or wilfully refuse to baptize any infant in his parish, being in danger, having been informed of the weakness of the said child : and whether the child dieth through his default without baptism ?

4. Whether hath your minister married any without a ring, or without banns published three several Sundays or Holydays in time of Divine Service, in the several Churches or Chapels of their several abodes, according to the Book of Common Prayer, or in times prohibited, albeit the banns were thrice published, without a licence or dispensation from the Archbishop, or Bishop of the Diocese, or his chancellor, first obtained in that behalf ? Or not betwixt the hours of eight and twelve in the forenoon, or have married any in any private house, or if the party be under the age of twenty-one years, before their parents or governors have signified their consent unto him ?

5. Doth he refuse to bury any which ought to be interred in Christian burial, or defer the same longer than he should ? Or bury any in Christian burial, which by the constitutions of the Church of England, or laws of the land, ought not to be so interred ?

6. Is your minister a preacher allowed ? If yea, then by whom ? If not, whether doth he procure some who are lawfully licensed to preach monthly among you at the least ?

7. Doth your minister (being licensed) preach usually according

to the Canons, either in his own cure or in some other Church or Chapel near adjoining, where no other preacher is, and how often hath he been negligent in that behalf, and doth he preach standing, and with his hat off? Or whether doth he or his curate upon every Sunday, when there is no sermon, read an homily, or some part thereof, according as he ought to do? Or in case he be not licensed to preach, doth he take upon him to preach or expound the Scriptures in his own cure, or elsewhere? If so, then you are to present the same, the time and place, when and where he doth it.

8. Doth your minister use to pray for the King's Majesty, King Charles, and for the Queen's Majesty, Prince Charles, and all the royal progeny, with addition of such style and titles as are due to his highness, and exhort the people to obedience to His Majesty and all magistrates in authority under him? And doth he also pray for all Archbishops, Bishops, and other ecclesiastical persons?

9. Is your minister continually resident upon his benefice, and how long time hath he been absent; and in case he be licensed to be absent, whether doth he cause his cure to be sufficiently supplied, according to the Canons? Or in case he hath another benefice, whether doth he supply his absence by a curate sufficiently licensed to preach in that cure where he himself is not resident? Or otherwise, in case the smallness of the living cannot find a preaching minister, doth he preach at both his benefices usually?

10. Doth your minister or curate serve any more cures than one? If yea, then what other cure doth he serve, and how far are they distant?

11. Doth your minister or curate every Sunday and Holyday, before Evening Prayer, for half an hour or more, examine and instruct the youth and ignorant persons of his parish in the Ten Commandments, Articles of the Belief, and in the Lord's Prayer, and the Sacraments, according as it is prescribed in the Catechism, set forth in the Book of Common Prayer, only? And if he do not, where is the fault, either in the parents and masters of the children, or in the curate neglecting his duty? And is he careful to tender all such youths of his parish as have been well instructed in their Catechism, to be confirmed by the Bishop in his visitation, or any other convenient time, as is appointed by the Book aforesaid?

12. Doth your minister in the Rogation Days go in perambulation of the circuit of the parish, saying and using the prayers, suffrages, and thanksgiving to God, appointed by law, according to his duty, thanking God for His blessings, if there be plenty on the earth; or otherwise, to pray for His grace and favour, if there be a fear of scarcity?

13. Hath your minister admitted any woman, begotten with child in adultery, or fornication, to be churched without licence of the ordinary?

14. Hath your minister, or any other preacher, baptized children, churched any woman, or ministered Holy Communion in any private house, otherwise than by law is allowed?

15. Doth your minister endeavour and labour diligently to reclaim the popish recusants in his parish from their errors (if there be any such abiding in your parish)? Or whether is your parson, vicar, or curate, over conversant with, or a favourer of recusants, whereby he is suspected not to be sincere in religion?

16. Hath your minister taken upon him to appoint any public or private fasts, prophecies, or exercises, not approved by law or public authority, or hath used to meet in any private house or place with any person or persons, there to consult how to impeach or deprave the Book of Common Prayer, or the doctrine or discipline of the Church of England? If yea, then you shall present them all.

17. Hath your minister stayed the publication of any excommunications or suspensions, or doth he every half year denounce in his parish Church all such of his parish as are excommunicated, and persevere therein without seeking to be absolved; or doth he wittingly and willingly keep company with such as are excommunicate; and hath he admitted into your Church any person excommunicate, without a certificate of his Absolution from the ordinary or other competent judge?

18. Doth your minister carefully look to the relief of the poor and from time to time call upon his parishioners to give somewhat as they can spare to godly and charitable uses, especially when they make their testaments?

19. Whether your minister, or any having taken Holy Orders, being now silenced or suspended, or any other person of your knowledge or as you have heard, hold any conventicles, or doth preach in any place, or use any other form of Divine Service than is appointed in the Book of Common Prayer? If yea, then you are to present their names, and with whom.

20. Whether is your curate licensed to serve by the Bishop of this Diocese, or by any other, and by whom?

21. Doth your minister use such decency and comeliness in his apparel, as by the 47th Canon is enjoined? Is he of sober behaviour, and one that doth not use such bodily labour, as is not seemly for his function and calling?

22. Is your minister noted or defamed to have obtained his benefice or his Orders, by simony, or any other way defamed to be a simoniacal person, or any way noted to be a schismatic, or schismatically affected, or reputed to be an incontinent person, or doth table or lodge any such in his house? Or is he a frequenter of taverns, inns, or alehouses, or any place suspected for ill rule? Or is he a common drunkard,

a common gamester, or player at dice, a swearer, or one that applieth himself not at his study, or is otherwise offensive and scandalous to his function or ministry?

23. Doth your preacher or lecturer read Divine Service before his sermon, or lecture and minister the Sacraments twice a year at least in his own person, according to the Canons?

24. When any person hath been dangerously sick in your parish, hath he neglected to visit him, and when any have been parting out of this life, hath he omitted to do his last duty in that behalf?

25. Doth your minister, curate, or lecturer in his or their sermons deliver such doctrine as tends to obedience and the edifying of their auditory in faith and religion, without intermeddling with matters of state, not fit to be handled in the pulpit, but to be discussed by the wisdom of His Majesty and His Council? And if you find any fault herein, you shall present them.

### Schoolmasters

1. Doth any in your parish openly or privately take upon him to teach school, without licence of the ordinary, and is he conformable to the religion now established? And doth he bring his scholars to the Church to hear Divine Service and sermons? And doth he instruct his scholars in the grounds of the religion now established in this Church of England, and is he careful and diligent to benefit his scholars in learning?

2. Doth your schoolmaster teach and instruct his youth in any other Catechism than is allowed by public authority? And what Catechism is it that he so teacheth?

3. Is any living or means given towards the erection or maintenance of the school withholden back or otherwise employed, and by whom?

4. Doth any keep school in the chancel or Church, by which means that holy place and the Communion Table are many ways profaned, and the windows broken?

### Parish Clerks and Sextons

1. Have you a fit parish clerk, aged twenty years at least, of honest conversation, able to read and write? Whether are his and the sexton's wages paid without fraud, according to the ancient custom of your parish? If not, then by whom are they so defrauded or denied? By whom are they chosen? And whether the said clerk is approved by the Ordinary? And hath he taken an oath, as in such cases is fitly required? And is he diligent in his office and serviceable to the minister? And doth he take upon him to meddle with anything above his office, as Churching of Women, Burying the Dead, or such like?

2. Doth your clerk or sexton keep the Church clean, the doors

locked at fit times? Is anything lost or spoiled in the Church through his default? Are the Communion Table, font, books, and other ornaments of the Church kept fair and clean? Doth he suffer any unseasonable ringing, or any profane exercise in your church? Or doth he, when any is passing out of this life, neglect to toll a bell, having notice thereof?

### Concerning the Parishioners

1. Whether any of your parishioners being sixteen years of age or upwards, or others lodging or commonly resorting to any house within your parish, do wilfully absent themselves from your parish Church, upon Sundays or Holydays at Morning and Evening prayers? Or who come late to Church, and depart from Church before service be done upon the said days? Or who do not reverently behave themselves during the time of Divine Service, devoutly kneeling when the General Confession of sins, the Litany, the Ten Commandments, and all Prayers and Collects are read, and using all due and lowly reverence, when the blessed Name of the Lord Jesus Christ is mentioned, and standing up when the Articles of the Belief are read? Or who do cover their heads in the Church during the time of Divine Service, unless it be in case of necessity, in which case they may wear a night-cap or coif? Or who do give themselves to babbling, talking, or walking, and are not attentive to hear the word preached or read? Whether any of your parish, being of sixteen years of age or upwards, do not receive the Holy Communion in your Church thrice every year, whereof once at Easter; and whether they do not devoutly kneel at the receiving thereof? And whether any having divers houses of remove do shift from place to place, of purpose to defeat the performance of their Christian duties in that behalf?

2. Whether any of your parishioners, being admonished thereof, do not send their children, servants, and apprentices to the minister, to be catechized upon such Sundays and Holydays as are appointed? Or whether any of them do refuse to come; or if they come, refuse to learn those instructions set forth in the Book of Common Prayer?

3. Whether any of your parish do entertain within their house any sojourner, common guests, or other persons who refuse to frequent Divine Service or receive the Holy Communion, as aforesaid? Present their names, their qualities, or conditions.

4. What Recusant Papists are there in your parish or other sectaries? Present their names, qualities, or conditions. Whether they keep any schoolmaster in their house which cometh not to Church to hear Divine Service and receive the Communion? What is his name, and how long hath he taught there or elsewhere?

5. Whether any of the said Popish Recusants or other schismatics do labour to seduce and withdraw others from the religion now estab-

50

lished ? Or instruct their families or children in Popish Religion ? Or refuse to entertain any, especially in place of greatest service or trust, but such as concur with them in their opinions ?

6. How long have the said Popish Recusants abstained from Divine Service, or from the Communion, as aforesaid ?

7. Is there any in your parish that retain, sell, utter, or disperse any Popish books, writings, or other books, libraries, or writings of any sectaries, touching the religion, state, or government ecclesiastical of this Kingdom of England, or keep any monuments of superstition uncancelled or undefaced ?

8. Whether have you any in your parish, which heretofore being Popish Recusants or sectaries have since reformed themselves, and come to Church to hear Divine Service and to receive the Sacraments ? If yea, then who are they ? And how long since they so reformed themselves ? And whether they still remain and abide in that conformity ?

9. Is there any in your parish that refuse to have their children baptized, or themselves to receive the Communion at the hands of your minister, taking exception against him, and what causes or exceptions do they allege ? Or have any married wives refused to come to Church, according to the Book of Common Prayer, to give God thanks after their child-birth for their safe deliverance ? And whether do any of or in your parish refuse to have their children baptized in your parish Church, according to the Form prescribed in the Book of Common Prayer ?

10. Do any of your parish usually go to other parish Churches to hear Divine Service or sermons ? Or do they communicate, or baptize their children in any other parish ?

11. Whether there be any in your parish who will come to hear the sermon, but who will not come to public prayers appointed by the Book of Common Prayer, making a schism or division (as it were) between the use of public prayer and preaching ?

12. What persons within your parish for any offence, contumacy, or crime of ecclesiastical cognizance, do stand excommunicate ? Present their names, and for what cause they are excommunicated, and how long they have so stood, and what person or persons do wittingly and usually keep them company.

13. Whether any, not being in Orders, do execute any Priestly or Ministerial Office, in your Church, Chapel, or churchyard, and what be their names ?

14. Whether any in your parish that having heretofore taken upon him the Order of Priesthood or Deacon hath since relinquished the same, and lives as a layman neglecting his vocation ?

15. Hath any person in your parish quarrelled, or stricken, or used any violence to your minister, or have stricken or quarrelled with any

other person within your Church or churchyard, or demeaned himself disorderly in the Church, by filthy or profane talk or any other base or immodest behaviour ?   Or hath disturbed the minister in time of Divine Service ?   Or hath libelled or spoken slanderous words against your minister, to the scandal of his vocation, or defamed any of his neighbours touching any crime of ecclesiastical cognizance ?

16. Whether any of or in your parish, without consent of the Ordinary or other lawful authority, have caused any to do penance, or to be censured or punished for any matter of ecclesiastical cognizance, by any vestry meetings or otherwise by their own authority ?   Or have taken any money or commutation for the same ?   Present their names that have done it.   And who have been so punished ?   On what manner and upon what cause ?

17. Whether any person in your parish do exercise any trade or labour, buy or sell, or keep open shops or warehouses upon any Sunday or Holyday, by themselves or their servants or apprentices, or have otherwise profaned the said days, contrary to the orders of the Church of England ?   And whether there be any innkeepers, alehouse keepers, victuallers, or other persons, that permit any persons in their houses to eat, drink, or play, during the time of Divine Service or sermon, or reading the homilies in the forenoon or afternoon, upon those days ?

18. Whether the fifth day of November be kept holy, and thanksgiving made to God for His Majesty's and this state's happy deliverance, according to the ordinance in that behalf ?

19. Whether any of your parish hold or frequent any conventicles or private congregations, or make or maintain any constitutions agreed upon in any such assemblies ?   Or any that do write, or publicly or privately speak against the Book of Common Prayer or anything therein contained, or against any of the Articles of Religion, agreed upon *in anno* 1562, or against the King's Supremacy in causes ecclesiastical, or against the Oath of Supremacy or of Allegiance, as pretending the same to be unlawful and not warrantable by the Word of God ?   Or against any of the rites or ceremonies of the Church of England, now established ?   Or against the government of the Church of England under the King's Most Excellent Majesty, by Archbishops, Bishops, Deans, Archdeacons, and other officers of the same ; affirming that the same is repugnant to the Word of God and that the said ecclesiastical officers are not lawfully ordained ?   Or whether there be any authors, maintainers, or favourers of heresy or schism, or there be suspected to be Anabaptists, Libertines, Brownists, of the Family of Love, or of any other schisms ?   Present their names.

20. Whether any in your parish have married within the degrees by law prohibited, and where, and by whom ?   And whether any

couple in your parish being lawfully married live apart one from the other, without due separation by the Law? Or any that have been divorced, that keep company with any other at bed or at board?

21. Whether do any persons administer the goods of the dead without lawful authority, or suppress the last will of the dead? Or are there in your parish any wills not yet proved, or goods of the dead (dying intestate) left unadministered? By authority in that behalf you shall not fail to present the executors and all others faulty therein; and also how many persons being possessed of any goods and chattels, have died within your parish since the 10th day of February, 1634.

22. Whether any withhold the stock of the Church, or any goods or other things given to good and charitable uses?

23. Whether your hospitals and almshouses and other such houses and corporations, founded to good and charitable uses, and the lands, possessions, and goods of the same, be ordered and disposed of as they should be? And do the masters, governors, fellows, and others of the said houses and corporations behave and demean themselves according to the godly ordinances and statutes of their several foundations?

24. Whether have you any in your parish to your knowledge or by common fame or report, which have committed adultery, fornication, or incest? Or any which have imprudently bragged or boasted that he or they have lived incontinently with any person or persons whatever? Or any that have attempted the chastity of any woman or solicited any woman to have the carnal knowledge of her body? Or which are commonly reputed to be common drunkards, blasphemers of God's holy Name, common swearers, common slanderers of their neighbours, and sowers of discord, filthy and lascivious talkers, usurers, simoniacal persons, bawds or harbourers of women with child, which be unmarried, or conveying or suffering them to go away before they have made satisfaction to the Church? Or any that having heretofore been presented or suspected of any of the aforesaid crimes, have for that cause departed your parish, and are now returned again? Or any which have used any enchantments, sorceries, incantations, or witchcrafts, which are not made felony by the statutes of this realm, or any which have committed any perjury in any ecclesiastical court, in an ecclesiastical cause, or which have committed any forgery, punishable by the ecclesiastical laws, and the procurors and abettors of the said offences; you shall truly present the names of all and singular the said offenders, and with whom they have committed the said offences, in case they have not been publicly punished to your knowledge for the same crimes.

### Physicians, Chirurgeons, and Midwives

1. How many physicians, chirurgeons, or midwives, have you in your parish? How long have they used their several sciences or

offices, and by what authority? And how have they demeaned themselves therein, and of what skill accounted to be in their profession?

### Touching the Churchwardens and Sidemen

1. Whether you and the churchwardens, questmen, or sidemen from time to time do, and have done their diligence, in not suffering any idle person to abide either in the churchyard or Church porch, in service or sermon-time, but causing them either to come into the Church to hear Divine Service, or to depart and not disturb such as be hearers there? And whether they have, and you do diligently see the parishioners duly resort to the Church every Sunday and Holyday and there to remain during Divine Service and sermon? And whether you or your predecessors, churchwardens there, suffer any plays, feasts, drinkings, or any other profane usages, to be kept in your Church, Chapel, or churchyard, or have suffered to your and their uttermost power and endeavour, any person or persons to be tippling or drinking in any inn or victualling house in your parish, during the time of Divine Service or sermon on Sundays and Holydays?

2. Whether, and how often have you admitted any to preach within your Church or Chapel, which was not sufficiently licensed? And whether you, together with your minister, have not taken diligent heed and care that every parishioner being of sixteen years of age or upwards, have received thrice every year as aforesaid? And also that no strangers have usually come to your Church from their own parish Church?

3. Whether have there been provided against every Communion, a sufficient quantity of white bread and good wholesome wine for the communicants that shall receive? And whether that wine be brought in a clean and sweet standing pot of pewter, or of other purer metal?

4. Whether were you chosen by the consent of the minister and the parishioners? And have the late churchwardens given up a just account for their time and delivered to their successors, by bill indented, the money and other things belonging to the Church which was in their hands? And are the alms of the Church faithfully distributed to the use of the poor?

5. Whether do you see the names of all preachers which are strangers and preach in your parish Churches to be noted in a book for that purpose, and whether every preacher do subscribe his name, and of whom he had his licence?

6. Whether there be any legacies withholden given to the Church, or poor people, or to the mending of highways, or otherwise by the testators? In whose name it is, by whom it was given, and by whom it is withholden?

7. Do you know of anything that hath been complained of, that is not yet redressed?

## Concerning Ecclesiastical Magistrates and Officers

1. Whether do you know or have heard of any payment, composition, or agreement, to or with any ecclesiastical magistrate, judge, or officer for winking at or sparing to punish any person for any offence of ecclesiastical cognizance, or for suppressing or concealing of any excommunication, or any other ecclesiastical censure of or against any recusant, or any other offender in the cases aforesaid ? What sum of money, or other consideration hath been received or promised, by, or to any of them, in that respect, by whom, and with whom ?

2. Hath any person within your parish paid or promised any sum of money or other reward, for commutation of penance, for any crime of ecclesiastical cognizance ? If so, then with whom ? When, and for what, and how hath the same been employed ?

3. Are your ecclesiastical judges and their substitutes Masters of Arts, or Bachelors of the Laws at least, learned and practised in the civil and ecclesiastical laws ; men of good life and fame, zealously affected in religion, and just and upright in executing their offices ? Have they heard any matter of office privately in their chambers, without their sworn registers' or their deputies' presence ?

4. Do you know, or have you heard, that any ecclesiastical judge, officer, or minister, hath received or taken any extraordinary fees, or other rewards or promises, by any ways or means, directly or indirectly, of any person or persons whatsoever, either for the granting of the administration of the goods and chattels of those that have died intestate, to one before another, or for allotting of larger portions of the goods and chattels of those that have died intestate to one more than to another : or for allowing larger and unreasonable account, made by executors or administrators, or for giving them *quietus est*, or discharges, without inventory or account, to defraud creditors, legataries, or those who are to have portions ? And what sums of money do you know, or have you heard, that any ecclesiastical judge or officer hath taken out of the estate of any dying intestate upon pretence to bestow the same *in pios usus* ? And how have the same been bestowed ?

5. Hath any ecclesiastical magistrate, judge, officer, or any exercising ecclesiastical jurisdiction within this your Diocese, or any advocate, register, proctor, clerks, apparitors, or other minister belonging to the same ecclesiastical courts, exacted or taken by any ways or means, directly or indirectly, extraordinary or greater fees than are due and accustomed ? And whether is there a table for the rates of all fees, set up in their several courts and offices ? And whether they have sent or suffered any process to go out of the ecclesiastical courts otherwise than by law they ought ? Or have they taken upon them the offices of informers or promoters to the said courts, or any other way abused themselves in their offices, contrary to the law and canons in that behalf provided ?

6. What number of apparitors have every several judge ecclesiastical? And wherein, and in what manner is the country overburdened by them? And wherein have they caused or summoned any to appear in the said courts, without a presentment or citation first had? Or whether have they threatened any to prosecute them in the said courts, if they would not give them some rewards and what bribes in that behalf have they taken?

7. What reward or fees hath any of the apparitors taken to save the journeys to the ecclesiastical court of any persons, and what (after composition so made) have they or any of them taken and received, and what acquittance or discharge have they given or promised them and whether have they not cited some to appear before the Archdeacon or his official, after they have been ordered by the commissary, and done their penance accordingly? And whom have they so cited and troubled, and what hath it cost them, as you know or have heard, or by enquiry can find?

If you know of any other default or crime of ecclesiastical cognizance you are to present the same by virtue of your oaths.

The minister of every parish may and ought to join in the present-ment with the churchwardens and sidemen; and if they will not present, the minister may and ought himself to present the defaults and crimes aforesaid. And there must be several presentments made to every several article. And the minister, churchwardens, and swornmen, are to meet and confer about the said presentments, and answering of every of the aforesaid articles.

# XIX. CAROLINE PIETY

# (1) "THE COUNTRY PARSON"

## No. 335.  GEORGE HERBERT

[From *A Priest to the Temple ; or the Country Parson, His Character and Rule of Holy Life*, Chapters iii, iv, v, viii, ix, xxii. *Works*, ed. G. H. Palmer (1905), Vol. I, pp. 213 f., 215–217, 218 f., 228–230, 231–234, 270–273.  This famous work appeared posthumously in 1652 as a piece in a volume entitled *Herbert's Remains, or Sundry Pieces of that Sweet Singer of the Temple*, Mr. George Herbert.  It was edited by Barnabas Oley, who wrote for the volume " A Prefatory View of the Life and Virtues of the Author and the Excellencies of this Book."  A separate edition of *The Country Parson* first appeared in 1671.  G. H. Palmer, *op. cit.*, I, 196, conjectures that " the title, *A Priest to the Temple*, is a happy invention of Oley's."]

## The Parson's Life

THE Country Parson is exceeding exact in his life, being holy, just, prudent, temperate, bold, grave in all his ways.  And because the two highest points of life wherein a Christian is most seen are patience and mortification,—patience in regard of afflictions, mortification in regard of lusts and affections and the stupifying and deading of all the clamorous powers of the soul, therefore he hath thoroughly studied these, that he may be an absolute master and commander of himself for all the purposes which God hath ordained him.  Yet in these points he labours most in those things which are most apt to scandalize his parish.  And first, because country people live hardly and therefore, as feeling their own sweat and consequently knowing the price of money, are offended much with any, who by hard usage increase their travail, the country parson is very circumspect in avoiding all covetousness, neither being greedy to get, nor niggardly to keep, nor troubled to lose any worldly wealth ; but in all his words and actions slighting and disesteeming it, even to a wondering that the world should so much value wealth, which in the day of wrath hath not one dram of comfort for us. Secondly, because luxury is a very visible sin, the parson is very careful to avoid all the kinds thereof, but especially that of drinking, because it is the most popular vice ; into which if he come, he prostitutes himself both to shame and sin, and by having *fellowship with the unfruitful works of darkness* he disableth himself of authority to reprove them ;  for sins make all equal, whom they find together, and then they are worst who ought to be best.  Neither is it for the servant of Christ to haunt inns, or taverns, or alehouses, to the dishonour of his person and office.  The parson doth not so, but orders his life in such a fashion that when death takes him, as the Jews and Judas did

Christ, he may say as He did, *I sat daily with you teaching in the temple*. Thirdly, because country people (as indeed all honest men) do much esteem their word, it being the life of buying and selling and dealing in the world; therefore the parson is very strict in keeping his word, though it be to his own hindrance, as knowing that if he be not so, he will quickly be discovered and disregarded; neither will they believe him in the pulpit, whom they cannot trust in his conversation. As for oaths and apparel, the disorders thereof are also very manifest. The parson's *yea is yea, and nay nay*; and his apparel plain, but reverend and clean, without spots or dust or smell, the purity of his mind breaking out and dilating itself even to his body, clothes, and habitation.

### The Parson's Knowledge

The Country Parson is full of all knowledge. They say it is an ill mason that refuseth any stone: and there is no knowledge but, in a skilful hand, serves either positively as it is, or else to illustrate some other knowledge. He condescends even to the knowledge of tillage and pasturage, and makes great use of them in teaching, because people by what they understand are best led to what they understand not. But the chief and top of his knowledge consists in the Book of Books, the storehouse and magazine of life and comfort, the Holy Scriptures. There he sucks and lives. In the Scriptures he finds four things: precepts for life, doctrines for knowledge, examples for illustration, and promises for comfort. These he hath digested severally. But for the understanding of these, the means he useth are, first, a holy life, remembering what his Master saith, that *If any do God's Will, he shall know of the doctrine* and assuring himself, that wicked men, however learned, do not know the Scriptures, because they feel them not, and because they are not understood but with the same Spirit that writ them. The second means is prayer, which if it be necessary even in temporal things, how much more in things of another world, where the well is deep and we have nothing of ourselves to draw with? Wherefore he ever begins the reading of the Scripture with some short inward ejaculation, as, *Lord, open mine eyes, that I may see the wondrous things of Thy law, etc.* The third means is a diligent collation of Scripture with Scripture. For all truth being consonant to itself, and all being penned by one and the self-same Spirit, it cannot be but that an industrious and judicious comparing of place with place must be a singular help for the right understanding of the Scriptures. To this may be added the consideration of any text with the coherence thereof, touching what goes before, and what follows after, as also the scope of the Holy Ghost. When the Apostles would have called down fire from Heaven, they were reproved, as ignorant of what spirit they were. For the Law required one thing and the Gospel another: yet as diverse, not as repugnant. Therefore the spirit of both is to be considered and weighed. The fourth means are commenters and Fathers, who have handled the places controverted which the parson by no means refuseth. As he doth not so study others as to neglect the grace of God in himself and what the Holy Spirit teacheth him, so doth he assure himself that God in all ages hath had His servants, to whom He hath revealed His truth, as well as to him; and that as one country doth not bear all things, that there may be a commerce, so neither hath God opened, or will open, all to one, that there may be a traffic in knowledge between the servants of God, for the planting both of love and humility. Wherefore he hath one comment at least upon every Book of Scripture, and ploughing with this and his own meditations he enters into the secrets of God treasured in the Holy Scripture.

### The Parson's Accessory Knowledges

The Country Parson hath read the Fathers also, and the Schoolmen and the later writers, or a good proportion of all, out of all which he hath compiled a book, and body of Divinity, which is the storehouse of his sermons and which he preacheth all his life, but diversely clothed, illustrated, and enlarged. For though the world is full of such composures, yet every man's own is fittest, readiest, and most savoury to him. Besides, this being to be done in his younger and preparatory times, it is an honest joy ever after to look upon his well-spent hours. This body he made by way of expounding the Church Catechism, to which all Divinity may easily be reduced. For it being indifferent in itself to choose any method, that is best to be chosen, of which there is likeliest to be most use. Now catechizing being a work of singular and admirable benefit to the Church of God, and a thing required under canonical obedience, the expounding of our Catechism must needs be the most useful form. Yet hath the parson, besides this laborious work, a slighter form of catechizing, fitter for country people; according as his audience is, so he useth one or other, or sometimes both, if his audience be intermixed. He greatly esteems also of cases of conscience, wherein he is much versed. And indeed, herein is the greatest ability of a parson, to lead his people exactly in the ways of truth, so that they neither decline to the right hand nor to the left. Neither let any think this is a slight thing. For everyone hath not digested, when it is a sin to take something for money lent, or when not; when it is a fault to discover another's fault, or when not; when the affections of the soul in desiring and procuring increase of means or honour, be a sin of covetousness or ambition, and when not; when the appetites of the body in eating, drinking, sleep, and the pleasure that comes with sleep, be sins of gluttony, drunkenness, sloth, lust, and when not; and so in many circumstances of actions. Now if a shepherd know not which grass will bane, or which not, how is he fit to be a shepherd? Wherefore the parson hath throughly canvassed all the particulars of human actions, at least all those which he observeth are most incident to his parish. . . .

## The Parson on Sundays

The Country Parson, as soon as he awakes on Sunday morning, presently falls to work, and seems to himself so as a market-man is when the market-day comes, or a shop-keeper when customers use to come in. His thoughts are full of making the best of the day, and contriving it to his best gains. To this end, besides his ordinary prayers, he makes a peculiar one for a blessing on the exercises of the day, that nothing befall him unworthy of that Majesty before which he is to present himself, but that all may be done with reverence to His glory, and with edification to his flock, humbly beseeching his Master, that how or whenever He punish him, it be not in his ministry. Then he turns to request for his people, that the Lord would be pleased to sanctify them all, that they may come with holy hearts and awful minds into the congregation, and that the good God would pardon all those who come with less prepared hearts than they ought. This done, he sets himself to the consideration of the duties of the day, and if there be any extraordinary addition to the customary exercises, either from the time of year, or from the State, or from God by a child born or dead, or any other accident, he contrives how and in what manner to induce it to the best advantage. Afterwards when the hour calls, with his family attending him, he goes to church, at his first entrance humbly adoring and worshipping the invisible majesty and presence of Almighty God, and blessing the people either openly or to himself. Then having read divine service twice fully, and preached in the morning, and catechised in the afternoon, he thinks he hath in some measure, according to poor and frail man, discharged the public duties of the congregation. The rest of the day he spends either in reconciling neighbours that are at variance, or in visiting the sick, or in exhortations to some of his flock by themselves, whom his sermons cannot or do not reach. And everyone is more awaked, when we come and say, *Thou art the man.* This way he finds exceeding useful and winning; and these exhortations he calls his privy purse, even as princes have theirs, besides their public disbursements. At night he thinks it a very fit time, both suitable to the joy of the day and without hindrance to public duties, either to entertain some of his neighbours, or to be entertained of them, where he takes occasion to discourse of such things as are both profitable and pleasant, and to raise up their minds to apprehend God's good blessing to our Church and State; that order is kept in the one, and peace in the other, without disturbance or interruption of public divine offices. As he opened the day with prayer, so he closeth it, humbly beseeching the Almighty to pardon and accept our poor services, and to improve them, that we may grow therein, and that our feet may be like hinds' feet, ever climbing up higher and higher unto Him.

## The Parson's State of Life

The Country Parson considering that virginity is an higher state than matrimony, and that the ministry requires the best and highest things, is rather unmarried than married. But, yet, as the temper of his body may be or as the temper of his parish may be, where he may have occasion to converse with women and that amongst suspicious men and other like circumstances considered, he is rather married than unmarried. Let him communicate the thing often by prayer to God, and as His grace shall direct him, so let him proceed. If he be unmarried and keep house, he hath not a woman in his house, but finds opportunities of having his meat dressed and other services done by menservants at home, and his linen washed abroad. If he be unmarried and sojourn, he never talks with any woman alone, but in the audience of others, and that seldom, and then also in a serious manner, never jestingly or sportfully. He is very circumspect in all companies, both of his behaviour, speech, and very looks, knowing himself to be suspected and envied. If he stand steadfast in his heart, having no necessity, but hath power over his own will and hath so decreed in his heart that he will keep himself a virgin, he spends his days in fasting and prayer, and blesseth God for the gift of continency, knowing that it can no way be preserved, but only by those means by which it was at first obtained. He therefore thinks it not enough for him to observe the fasting days of the Church and the daily prayers enjoined him by authority, which he observeth out of humble conformity and obedience; but adds to them, out of choice and devotion, some other days for fasting and hours for prayers; and by these he keeps his body tame, serviceable, and healthful; and his soul fervent, active, *young, and lusty as an eagle.* He often readeth the life of the primitive monks, hermits, and virgins, and wondereth not so much at their patient suffering and cheerful dying under persecuting emperors, though that indeed be very admirable, as at their daily temperance, abstinence, watchings, and constant prayers, and mortifications in the times of peace and prosperity. To put on the profound humility and the exact temperance of Our Lord Jesus, with other exemplary virtues of that sort, and to keep them on in the sunshine and noon of prosperity, he findeth to be as necessary and as difficult at least as to be clothed with perfect patience and Christian fortitude in the cold

midnight storms of persecution and adversity.   He keepeth his watch
and ward, night and day, against the proper and peculiar temptations
of his state of life, which are principally these two, spiritual pride and
impurity of heart.   Against these ghostly enemies he girdeth up his
loins, keeps the imagination from roving, puts on the whole armour
of God, and by the virtue of the shield of faith he is not afraid of *the
pestilence that walketh in the darkness* (carnal impurity), nor of *the sickness that destroyeth at noonday* (ghostly pride and self-conceit).   Other
temptations he hath, which, like mortal enemies, may sometimes
disquiet him likewise;  for the human soul being bounded and kept in,
in her sensitive faculty, will run out more or less in her intellectual.
Original concupiscence is such an active thing, by reason of continual
inward or outward temptations, that it is ever attempting or doing one
mischief or other.   Ambition, or untimely desire of promotion to a
higher state or place, under colour of accommodation or necessary
provision, is a common temptation to men of any eminency, especially
being single men.   Curiosity in prying into high speculative and unprofitable questions is another great stumbling-block to the holiness
of scholars.  These and many other *spiritual wickednesses in high
places* doth the parson fear, or experiment, or both;  and that much
more being single than if he were married, for then commonly the
stream of temptations is turned another way, into covetousness, love
of pleasure, or ease, or the like.   If the parson be unmarried and means
to continue so, he doth at least as much as hath been said.   If he be
married, the choice of his wife was made rather by his ear than by his
eye;  his judgement, not his affection, found out a fit wife for him,
whose humble and liberal disposition, he preferred before beauty,
riches, or honour.   He knew that (the good instrument of God to
bring women to Heaven) a wise and loving husband could out of
humility produce any special grace of faith, patience, meekness, love,
obedience, etc., and out of liberality make her fruitful in all good works.
As he is just in all things, so is he to his wife also, counting nothing so
much his own as that he may be unjust to it.   Therefore he gives her
respect both before her servants and others, and half at least of the
government of the house, reserving so much of the affairs as serve
for a diversion for him;  yet never so giving over the reins, but that he
sometimes looks how things go, demanding an account, but not by
the way of an account.   And this must be done the oftener, or the
seldomer, according as he is satisfied of his wife's discretion. . . .

### The Parson in Sacraments

The Country Parson being to administer the Sacraments is at a
stand with himself, how or what behaviour to assume for so holy things.
Especially at Communion times he is in a great confusion, as being

not only to receive God, but to break and administer Him. Neither finds he any issue in this but to throw himself down at the throne of grace, saying, " Lord Thou knowest what Thou didst, when Thou appointedst it to be done thus. Therefore do Thou fulfil what Thou didst appoint ; for Thou art not only the feast but the way to it." At Baptism, being himself in white, he requires the presence of all, and baptiseth not willingly, but on Sundays or great days. He admits no vain or idle names, but such as are usual and accustomed. He says that prayer with great devotion where God is thanked for calling us to the knowledge of His grace, Baptism being a blessing that the world hath not the like. He willingly and cheerfully crosseth the child, and thinketh the ceremony not only innocent, but reverend. He instructeth the godfathers and godmothers, that it is no complimental or light thing to sustain that place, but a great honour and no less burden, as being done both in the presence of God and His saints, and by way of undertaking for a Christian soul. He adviseth all to call to mind their Baptism often ; for if wise men have thought it the best way of preserving a state to reduce it to its principles by which it grew great, certainly it is the safest course for Christians to meditate often (being the first step into their great and glorious calling), and upon what terms and with what vows they were baptised. At the times of the Holy Communion, he first takes order with the churchwardens, that the elements be of the best, not cheap or coarse, much less ill-tasted or unwholesome. Secondly, he considers and looks into the ignorance or carelessness of his flock, and accordingly applies himself with catechizing and lively exhortations, not on the Sunday of the Communion only (for then it is too late), but the Sunday or Sundays before the Communion, or on the eves of all those days. If there be any who, having not yet received, are to enter into this great work, he takes the more pains with them, that he may lay the foundation of future blessings. The time of everyone's first receiving is not so much by years as by understanding ; particularly, the rule may be this : When anyone can distinguish the sacramental from common bread, knowing the institution and the difference, he ought to receive, of what age soever. Children and youths are usually deferred too long, under pretence of devotion to the Sacrament ; but it is for want of instruction, their understandings being ripe enough for ill things, and why not then for better ? But parents and masters should make haste in this, as to a great purchase for their children and servants, which while they defer, both sides suffer ; the one, in wanting many excitings of grace ; the other, in being worse served and obeyed. The saying of the Catechism is necessary, but not enough, because to answer in form may still admit ignorance ; but the questions must be propounded loosely and widely, and then the answerer will discover what he is. Thirdly, for the manner

51

of receiving, as the parson useth all reverence himself, so he administers to none but to the reverent. The feast indeed requires sitting, because it is a feast; but man's unpreparedness asks kneeling. He that comes to the Sacrament hath the confidence of a guest; and he that kneels confesseth himself an unworthy one, and therefore differs from other feasters. But he that sits, or lies, puts up to an Apostle. Contentiousness in a feast of charity is more scandal than any posture. Fourthly, touching the frequency of the Communion, the parson celebrates it, if not duly once a month, yet at least five or six times in the year, as at Easter, Christmas, Whitsuntide, afore and after harvest, and the beginning of Lent. And this he doth, not only for the benefit of the work, but also for the discharge of the churchwardens; who being to present all that receive not thrice a year, if there be but three Communions, neither can all the people so order their affairs as to receive just at those times, nor the churchwardens so well take notice who receive thrice, and who not.

# (2) THE SAINTLINESS OF INDIVIDUALS

## No. 336.  JOHN EARLE

[From *Microcosmography ; Or, A Piece of the World Discovered, in Essays and Characters*, § 3 (" A Grave Divine "), ed. Cambridge, 1903, pp. 5–7. This singular work appeared in 1628, and made the writer famous ; for though it was published anonymously by Edward Blount, the identity of its author was soon discovered. It went through ten editions before Earle's death in 1665. Fifty-four ' characters ' were described in the first edition, and more in the later ones.]

### A Grave Divine

Is one that knows the burden of his calling and hath studied to make his shoulders sufficient ; for which he hath not been hasty to launch forth of his port, the University, but expected the ballast of learning and the wind of opportunity. Divinity is not the beginning but the end of his studies, to which he takes the ordinary stair and makes the Arts his way. He counts it not profaneness to be polished with human reading, or to smooth his way by Aristotle to School-Divinity. He has sounded both religions, and anchored in the best, and is a Protestant out of judgement, not faction ; not because his country, but his reason, is on this side. The Ministry is his choice, not refuge ; and yet the pulpit not his itch, but fear. His discourse there is substance, not all rhetoric ; and he utters more things than words. His speech is not helped with enforced action, but the matter acts itself. He shoots all his meditations at one butt ; and beats upon his text, not the cushion, making his hearers, not the pulpit, groan. Inciting of Popish errors, he cuts them with arguments, not cudgels them with barren invectives ; and labours more to shew the truth of his cause than the spleen. His sermon is limited by the method, not the hour-glass ; and his devotion goes along with him out of the pulpit. He comes not up thrice a week because he would not be idle, nor talks three hours together because he would not talk nothing ; but his tongue preaches at fit times, and his conversation is the every day's exercise. In matters of ceremony he is not ceremonious, but thinks how he owes that reverence to the Church to bow his judgement to it, and make more conscience of schism than a surplice. He esteems the Church's hierarchy as the Church's glory, and however we jar with Rome would not have our confusion distinguish us. In Simoniacal purchases he thinks his soul goes in the bargain, and is loath to come by promotion so dear. Yet his worth at the length advances him, and the price of his own merit buys him a living. He is no base grater of his tithes and will not wrangle for the odd egg. The lawyer is the only man he hinders, by whom he is spited for taking up quarrels. He is a main pillar of our Church, though not yet Dean or Canon, and his life our religion's best apology. His death is his last sermon, where in the pulpit of his bed he instructs men to die by his example.

## No. 337.   HENRY ISAACSON (on ANDREWES)

[From *An Exact Narration of the Life and Death of the Late Reverend and Learned Prelate and Painful Divine, Lancelot Andrewes, Late Bishop of Winchester, Which may serve as a Pattern of Piety and Charity to all godly disposed Christians.* Andrewes' *Miscellaneous Works*, ed. L. A. C. T., pp. xxii f., xxiii f., xxv f. This memoir of Andrewes was published in 1650. The author was born in 1581, and had acted as Andrewes' amanuensis.]

From the first time of his preferment to means of any considerable value, even to his dying day, [Andrewes] was ever hospitable, and free in entertainment to all people of quality and worthy of respect, especially to scholars and strangers, his table being ever bountifully and neatly furnished with provisions, and attendants answerable, to whom he committed the care of providing and expending in a plentiful yet orderly way,—himself seldom knowing what meat he had, till he came from his study to dinner, at which he would show himself so noble in his entertainment and so gravely facetious, that his guests would often profess they never came to any man's table where they received better satisfaction in all points, and that his Lordship kept Christmas all the year in respect of the plenty they ever found there. And yet, by the way, take this, that he ever strictly observed in his provisions of diet the time of Lent, Embers, and other fasting days, according to the laws of this kingdom and the orders of the Church. . . .

The seventh [of Andrewes' virtues] is his humanity and affability, not only to the last mentioned, his guests, but to every one that did converse with him; for which, not only divers famous scholars and others of this kingdom, but others of foreign parts, as they had just cause, have admired him. As, not to mention natives, Master Casaubon, Master Cluverius, Master Vossius, Master Grotius, Master Moulin, Master Barclay, and, besides many others, Master Erpenius, to whom he tendered an annual stipend, to have read and taught here the Oriental tongues, wherein, long before his death, he himself had been well versed, as may appear by his Commencement verses; the experienced professors whereof he much delighted in and did much for them, as Master Bedwell, to whom he gave the Vicarage of Tottenham in Middlesex, if living, among others would testify. And the reason for this a late reverend Father of this Church [Buckeridge] hath given, *Omnes quid in se amant, in aliis venerantur,*—" loving and honouring those gifts in others, which he had in himself." For among the other parts of his profound learning, he by his industry had attained to the knowledge of fifteen tongues, if not more.

To these former may be added his modesty, which was ever such that although the whole Christian world took especial notice of his profound and deep learning, yet was he so far from acknowledging it in himself that he would often complain of his defects, even to the extenuating, yea vilifying of his own worth and abilities; professing many times, that he was but *inutilis servus*, nay, *inutile pondus*. Insomuch that being preferred by King James to the Bishopric of Chichester, and pretending his own imperfections and insufficiency to undergo such a charge, as also that he might have not only his Clergy, but all others to take notice thereof, he caused to be engraven about the seal of his Bishopric those words of St. Paul, *Et ad haec quis idoneus?* "And who is sufficient for these things?" (*II Cor.* ii, 16). . . .

His indefatigability in study cannot be paralleled, if we consider him from his childhood to his old age. Never any man took such pains, or at least spent so much time in study, as this Reverend Prelate; for even in those days when it might have been supposed he would have taken some ease for his former pains, then also from the hour he arose, his private devotions finished, to the time he was called to dinner, which, by his own order, was not till twelve at noon at the soonest, he kept close at his book, and would not be interrupted by any that came to speak with him, or upon any occasion, public prayer excepted. Insomuch that he would be so displeased with scholars that attempted to speak with him in a morning, that he would say "He doubted they were no true scholars that came to speak with him before noon."

After dinner, for two or three hours space, he would willingly pass the time either in discourse with his guests or other friends, or in despatch of his own temporal affairs or of those who, by reason of his Episcopal jurisdiction, attended him; and being quit of these and the like occasions, he would return to his study, where he spent the rest of the afternoon even till bedtime, except some friend took him off to supper, and then did he eat but sparingly.

Of the fruit of this his seed-time, the world, especially this land, hath reaped a plentiful harvest in his Sermons and Writings. Never went any beyond him in the first of these, his preaching, wherein he had such a dexterity, that some would say of him, that he was quick again as soon as delivered; and in this faculty he hath left a pattern unimitable. So that he was truly styled, *Stella praedicantium* and "an angel in the pulpit." And his late Majesty took especial care in causing that volume of his sermons to be divulged, though but a handful of those which he preached, by enjoying whereof this kingdom hath an inestimable treasure.

And for his acuteness and profundity in writing against the adversary, he so excelled all others of his time that neither Bellarmine, champion to the Romanists, nor any other of them, was ever able to answer what he wrote; so that as his sermons were unimitable, his writings were unanswerable.

To draw to an end of deciphering his virtues and endowments. It may truly be said of him that he had those gifts and graces, both of art and nature, so fixed in him, as that this age cannot parallel him; for his profundity and abyss of learning was accompanied with wit, memory, judgement, languages, gravity, and humility, insomuch that if he had been contemporary with the ancient Fathers of the Primitive Church, he would have been, and that worthily, reputed not inferior to the chiefest among them.

## No. 338.  IZAAK WALTON (on HERBERT)

[From *The Life of Mr. George Herbert*, ed. " World's Classics " (G. Saintsbury, 1927), pp. 295–303.  Walton's *Life* of Herbert (1593–1633) was the fourth of his famous five biographies to be written.  Barnabas Oley's *Life* of Herbert had already come out in 1652, prefixed to Herbert's *Remains*.  Walton's appeared first as a separate volume in 1670, in which year it was also reissued as a single work together with its three predecessors.  The biography of Robert Sanderson did not see the light until 1678.]

The Texts for all [Herbert's] future Sermons (which God knows were not many) were constantly taken out of the Gospel for the day; and he did as constantly declare why the Church did appoint that portion of Scripture to be that day read, and in what manner the Collect for every Sunday does refer to the Gospel, or to the Epistle then read to them.  And that they might pray with understanding, he did usually take occasion to explain not only the Collect for every particular Sunday, but the reasons of all the other Collects and Responses in our Church-Service; and made it appear to them that the whole Service of the Church was a reasonable, and therefore an acceptable, sacrifice to God; as namely, that we begin with Confession of ourselves to be vile, miserable sinners; and that we begin so because till we have confessed ourselves to be such, we are not capable of that mercy which we acknowledge we need and pray for.  But having in the Prayer of Our Lord begged pardon for those sins which we have confessed, and hoping that as the Priest hath declared our absolution, so by our public confession and real repentance, we have obtained that pardon, then we dare and do proceed to beg of the Lord, to open our lips, that our mouths may shew forth His praise; for, till then, we are neither able nor worthy to praise Him.  But this being supposed, we are then fit to say, " Glory be to the Father, and to the Son, and to the Holy Ghost "; and fit to proceed to a further service of our God, in the Collects, and Psalms, and Lauds that follow in the Service.

And as to these Psalms and Lauds, he proceeded to inform them why there were so often, and some of them daily repeated in our Church-service : namely, the Psalms every month, because they be an historical and thankful repetition of mercies past; and such a composition of prayers and praises, as ought to be repeated often and publicly; for with such sacrifices, God is honoured, and well-pleased. This, for the Psalms.

And for the Hymns and Lauds, appointed to be daily repeated or sung after the First and Second Lessons are read to the congregation, he proceeded to inform them that it was most reasonable, after they have heard the will and goodness of God declared or preached by the Priest in his reading the two chapters, that it was then a seasonable duty to rise up and express their gratitude to Almighty God for those His mercies to them and to all mankind; and then to say with the Blessed Virgin, That their Souls do magnify the Lord, and that their spirits do also rejoice in God their Saviour. And that it was their duty also to rejoice with Simeon in his Song and say with him, That their eyes have also seen their salvation, for they have seen that salvation which was but prophesied till his time; and he then broke out into those expressions of joy that he did see it, but they live to see it daily in the history of it, and therefore ought daily to rejoice, and daily to offer up their Sacrifices of praise to their God, for that particular mercy. A service, which is now the constant employment of that Blessed Virgin, and Simeon, and all those blessed Saints that are possessed of Heaven, and where they are at this time interchangeably and constantly singing, " Hoiy, Holy, Holy, Lord God, Glory be to God on High, and on Earth peace." And he taught them that to do this was an acceptable service to God, because the Prophet David says in his Psalms, *He that praiseth the Lord, honoureth Him.*

He made them to understand how happy they be that are freed from the incumbrances of that Law which our forefathers groaned under, namely, from the legal sacrifices and from the many ceremonies of the Levitical Law; freed from Circumcision and from the strict observation of the Jewish Sabbath and the like. And he made them know that having received so many, and so great blessings, by being born since the days of Our Saviour, it must be an acceptable sacrifice to Almighty God for them to acknowledge those blessings daily, and stand up and worship, and say as Zacharias did, *Blessed be the Lord God of Israel, for He hath* (in our days) *visited and redeemed His people ; and* (He hath in our days) *remembered, and shewed that mercy which by the mouth of the prophets, He promised to our forefathers : and this He hath done, according to his Holy Covenant made with them :* and he made them to understand that we live to see and enjoy the benefit of it, in His Birth, in His Life, His Passion, His Resurrection and Ascension into Heaven, where He now sits sensible of all our temptations and infirmities, and where He is at this present time making intercession for us, to His and Our Father. And therefore they ought daily to express their public gratulations, and say daily with Zacharias, " Blessed be that Lord God of Israel, that hath thus visited, and thus redeemed His people."—These were some of the reasons by which Mr. Herbert instructed his congregation for the use of the Psalms and the Hymns appointed to be daily sung or said in the Church-service.

He informed them also when the Priest did pray only for the congregation, and not for himself, and when they did only pray for him ; as namely, after the repetition of the Creed, before he proceeds to pray the Lord's Prayer or any of the appointed Collects, the Priest is directed to kneel down, and pray for them, saying—" The Lord be with you." And when they pray for him, saying—" And with Thy spirit." And then they join together in the following Collects, and he assured them that when there is such mutual love and such joint prayers offered for each other, then the holy Angels look down from Heaven, and are ready to carry such charitable desires to God Almighty, and He as ready to receive them ; and that a Christian congregation calling thus upon God, with one heart and one voice, and in one reverend and humble posture, look as beautifully as Jerusalem, that is at peace with itself.

He instructed them also why the prayer of Our Lord was prayed often in every full service of the Church, namely at the conclusion of the several parts of that Service ; and prayed then, not only because it was composed and commanded by our Jesus that made it, but as a perfect pattern for our less perfect forms of prayer and therefore fittest to sum up and conclude all our imperfect petitions.

He instructed them also that as by the Second Commandment we are required not to bow down or worship an idol, or false God, so, by the contrary rule, we are to bow down and kneel, or stand up and worship the true God. And he instructed them why the Church, required the congregation to stand up at the repetition of the Creeds, namely, because they did thereby declare both their obedience to the Church, and an assent to that Faith into which they had been baptized. And he taught them that in that shorter Creed, or Doxology so often repeated daily, they also stood up to testify their belief to be, That the God that they trusted in was one God, and three Persons, the Father, the Son, and the Holy Ghost, to Whom they and the Priest gave glory. And because there had been heretics that had denied some of these three Persons to be God ; therefore the congregation stood up and honoured Him by confessing and saying, " It was so in the beginning, is now so, and shall ever be so world without end." And all gave their assent to this belief by standing up and saying " Amen."

He instructed them also what benefit they had by the Church's appointing the celebration of Holy-days, and the excellent use of them ; namely, that they were set apart for particular commemorations of particular mercies received from Almighty God ; and (as Reverend Mr. Hooker says) to be the landmarks to distinguish times. For by them we are taught to take notice how time passes by us ; and that we ought not to let the years pass without a celebration of praise for those mercies which those days give us occasion to remember. And therefore they were to note that the Year is appointed to begin the 25th. Day of March, a day in which we commemorate the Angel's appearing to the Blessed Virgin with the joyful tidings that she should conceive and bear a Son, that should be the Redeemer of mankind ; and she did so forty weeks after this joyful salutation, namely, at our Christmas, a day in which we commemorate His Birth, with joy and praise ; and that eight days after this happy Birth, we celebrate His Circumcision ; namely, in that which we call New-year's Day. And that upon that day which we call Twelfth-Day, we commemorate the manifestation of the unsearchable riches of Jesus to the Gentiles. And that that day we also celebrate the memory of His goodness in sending a star to guide the three wise men from the East to Bethlehem, that they might there worship, and present Him with their oblations of gold, frank-incense, and myrrh. And he (Mr. Herbert) instructed them that Jesus was forty days after His Birth presented by His Blessed Mother in the Temple ; namely, on that day which we call, " the Purification of the Blessed Virgin, Saint Mary." And he instructed them that by the Lent-Fast we imitate and commemorate our Saviour's humiliation in fasting forty days ; and, that we ought to endeavour to be like Him in purity. And, that on Good-Friday we commemorate and condole His Crucifixion. And at Easter, commemorate His glorious Resur-rection. And he taught them, that after Jesus had manifested Himself to His Disciples to be that Christ that was crucified, dead and buried ; and by His appearing and conversing with His Disciples for the space of forty days after His Resurrection, He then, and not till then, ascended into Heaven, in the sight of those Disciples,—namely, on that day which we call the Ascension, or Holy Thursday. And that we then celebrate the performance of the promise which He made to His Disciples, at or before His Ascension,—namely, that though He left them, yet He would send them the Holy Ghost to be their Comforter ; and that he did so on that day which the Church calls Whitsunday. Thus the Church keeps an historical and circular commemoration of times, as they pass by us, of such times as ought to incline us to occa-sional praises, for the particular blessings which we do, or might, receive by those holy Commemorations.

He made them know also why the Church hath appointed Ember Weeks ; and to know the reason why the Commandments and the

Epistles and Gospels were to be read at the Altar or Communion Table; why the Priest was to pray the Litany kneeling, and why to pray some Collects standing; and he gave them many other observations, fit for his plain congregation, but not fit for me now to mention; for I must set limits to my pen, and not make that a treatise, which I intended to be a much shorter account than I have made it. But I have done, when I have told the reader that he was constant in catechizing every Sunday in the afternoon, and that his catechizing was after his Second Lesson, and in the Pulpit, and that he never exceeded his half hour, and was always so happy as to have an obedient and a full congregation.

And to this I must add, That if he were at any time too zealous in his Sermons, it was in reproving the indecencies of the people's behaviour in the time of Divine Service, and of those Ministers that huddled up the Church prayers without a visible reverence and affection; namely, such as seemed to say the Lord's Prayer or a Collect in a breath. But for himself, his custom was to stop betwixt every Collect, and give the people time to consider what they had prayed, and to force their desires affectionately to God, before he engaged them into new petitions.

And by this account of his diligence to make his parishioners understand what they prayed, and why they praised and adored their Creator, I hope I shall the more easily obtain the reader's belief to the following account of Mr. Herbert's own practice; which was, to appear constantly with his wife and three nieces (the daughters of a deceased sister) and his whole family twice every day at the Church prayers, in the chapel which does almost join to his Parsonage House. And for the time of his appearing, it was strictly at the Canonical Hours of 10 and 4; and then and there he lifted up pure and charitable hands to God in the midst of the congregation. And he would joy to have spent that time in that place where the honour of his Master Jesus dwelleth; and there, by that inward devotion which he testified constantly by an humble behaviour and visible adoration he, like Joshua, brought not only *his own household thus to serve the Lord*; but brought most of his parishioners and many gentlemen in the neighbourhood constantly to make a part of his congregation twice a day; and some of the meaner sort of his parish did so love and reverence Mr. Herbert, that they would let their plough rest when Mr. Herbert's Saints'-Bell rung to prayers, that they might also offer their devotions to God with him; and would then return back to their plough. And his most holy life was such that it begot such reverence to God and to him, that they thought themselves the happier, when they carried Mr. Herbert's blessing back with them to their labour. Thus powerful was his reason and example to persuade others to a practical piety and devotion.

And his constant public prayers did never make him to neglect his own private devotions, nor those prayers that he thought himself bound to perform with his family, which always were a set-form, and not long.   And he did always conclude them with that Collect which the Church hath appointed for the day or week.   Thus he made every day's sanctity a step towards that Kingdom where impurity cannot enter.

His chiefest recreation was music, in which heavenly art he was a most excellent master and did himself compose many Divine Hymns and Anthems, which he set and sung to his lute or viol; and, though he was a lover of retiredness, yet his love to music was such that he went usually twice every week on certain appointed days to the Cathedral Church in Salisbury; and at his return would say, That his time spent in prayer and Cathedral music elevated his soul, and was his Heaven upon earth.   But before his return thence to Bemerton, he would usually sing and play his part at an appointed private music-meeting; and, to justify this practice, he would often say, Religion does not banish mirth, but only moderates and sets rules to it.

## No. 339.   IZAAK WALTON (on FERRAR)

[From *The Life of Mr. George Herbert*, ed. " World's Classics " (G. Saintsbury, 1927), pp. 309–312.   Cp. note on No. 338.]

Mr. Nicholas Farrer (who got the reputation of being called Saint Nicholas at the age of six years) was born in London, and doubtless had good education in his youth; but certainly was at an early age made Fellow of Clare Hall in Cambridge, where he continued to be eminent for his piety, temperance, and learning.   About the 26th year of his age, he betook himself to travel, in which he added to his Latin and Greek a perfect knowledge of all the Languages spoken in the Western parts of our Christian world; and understood well the principles of their Religion and of their manner and the reasons of their worship.   In this his travel he met with many persuasions to come into a communion with that Church which calls itself Catholic, but he returned from his travels as he went, eminent for his obedience to his Mother, the Church of England.   In his absence from England, Mr. Farrer's father (who was a merchant) allowed him a liberal maintenance; and, not long after his return into England, Mr. Farrer had by the death of his father, or an elder brother, or both, an estate left him that enabled him to purchase land to the value of four or five hundred pounds a year,—the greatest part of which land was at Little Gidding, four or six miles from Huntingdon and about eighteen from Cambridge; which place he chose for the privacy of it, and for the Hall, which had the Parish-Church, or Chapel, belonging and adjoining near to it.   For Mr. Farrer, having seen the manners and vanities of the world and found them to be, as Mr. Herbert says, " A nothing between two dishes," did so contemn it, that he resolved to spend the remainder of his life in mortifications and in devotion and charity, and to be always prepared for death. And his life was spent thus.

He and his family, which were like a little College and about thirty in number, did most of them keep Lent and all Ember-Weeks strictly, both in fasting and using all those mortifications and prayers that the Church hath appointed to be then used. And he and they did the like constantly on Fridays, and on the Vigils or Eves appointed to be fasted before the Saints' Days; and this frugality and abstinence turned to the relief of the poor. But this was but a part of his charity; none but God and he knew the rest.

This family, which I have said to be in number about thirty, were a part of them his kindred and the rest chosen to be of a temper fit to be moulded into a devout life; and all of them were for their dispositions serviceable and quiet, and humble, and free from scandal. Having thus fitted himself for his family, he did about the year 1630 betake himself to a constant and methodical service of God, and it was in this manner. He being accompanied with most of his family, did himself use to read the Common Prayers (for he was a Deacon) every day at the appointed hours of Ten and Four in the Parish Church, which was very near his house and which he had both repaired and adorned,—for it was fallen into a great ruin by reason of a depopulation of the village before Mr. Farrer bought the Manor. And he did also constantly read the Mattins every morning at the hour of six, either in the Church, or in an oratory which was within his own house. And many of the family did there continue with him after the prayers were ended, and there they spent some hours in singing Hymns or Anthems, sometimes in the Church, and often to an organ in the oratory. And there they sometimes betook themselves to meditate, or to pray privately, or to read a part of the New Testament to themselves, or to continue their praying or reading the Psalms. And in case the Psalms were not all always read in the day, then Mr. Farrer and others of the congregation did at night, at the ring of a watch-bell, repair to the Church or oratory, and there betake themselves to prayers, and lauding God, and reading the Psalms that had not been read in the day. And when these, or any part of the congregation, grew weary or faint, the watch-bell was rung, sometimes before and sometimes after midnight; and then another part of the family rose, and maintained the watch, sometimes by praying, or singing lauds to God, or reading the Psalms; and when after some hours they also grew weary or faint, then they rung the watch-bell, and were also relieved by some of the former, or by a new part of the society, which continued their devotions (as hath been mentioned) until morning. And it is to be noted that in this continued serving of God, the Psalter, or whole *Book of Psalms*, was in every four and twenty hours sung or read over, from the first to the last verse : and this was done as constantly as the sun runs his circle every day about the world, and then begins again the same instant that it ended.

Thus did Mr. Farrer, and his happy family, serve God day and night. Thus did they always behave themselves, as in His presence. And they did always eat and drink by the strictest rules of temperance, —eat and drink so, as to be ready to rise at midnight or at the call of a watch-bell, and perform their devotions to God. And it is fit to tell the reader that many of the clergy that were more inclined to practical piety and devotion than to doubtful and needless disputations, did often come to Gidding Hall, and make themselves a part of that happy society, and stay a week or more, and then join with Mr. Farrer and the family in these devotions, and assist and ease him or them in their watch by night. And these various devotions had never less than two of the domestic family in the night, and the watch was always kept in the Church or oratory, unless in extreme cold winter nights, and then it was maintained in a parlour which had a fire in it ; and the parlour was fitted for that purpose. And this course of piety and great liberality to his poor neighbours, Mr. Farrer maintained till his death, which was in the year 1639.

## No. 340. "THE ARMINIAN NUNNERY"

[From *The Arminian Nunnery, or A Brief Description and Relation of the late Erected Monastical Place called ' The Arminian Nunnery ' at Little Gidding in Huntingdonshire*, pp. 6–8. This scarce pamphlet of ten small quarto pages was a Puritan attack upon the establishment of Nicholas Ferrar.]

This Prolocutor [*i.e.* Nicholas Ferrar] confessed himself to be about 42 years old, was a Fellow in a House in Cambridge (he named not what House), and that he had taken Orders of a Deacon. But he said nothing of his having been at Rome, as it is well known he hath been.

Now I was invited by this Deacon to go with him into the Chapel of their devotion, at the entrance whereof this priestlike deft Deacon made a low obeisance ; a few paces farther, lower ; and coming to the half-pace which is at the East end, where the ' Altered-table ' stood, he bowed and prostrated himself to the ground. Then he went up into a fair large reading place (having placed me above with a fair large window cushion of green velvet before me). The Mother Matron with all her train, which were her daughters and daughters' daughters, who with four sons kneeled all the while on the body of the half-pace, all being in black gowns, and as they came to Church in round Monmouth Caps, all I say in black, save one of the daughters who was in a friar's grey gown.

We being all placed before the Deacon (for now so we must call him) with a very loud and shrill voice began and trolled out the Litany and read divers other Prayers and Collects in the Book of Common Prayer and Athanasius his Creed; and concluded with the Form of words, " The Peace of God, etc." . . .

I observed the Chapel in general to be fairly and speciously adorned with herbs and flowers natural and artificial, and upon every pillar along both sides of the Chapel (such as are in Cathedral Churches) tapers (I mean great Virgin-wax candles on every pillar). The half-pace at the upper end (for there was no other division betwixt the body of the Chapel and the East end) was all covered with tapestry and upon that half-pace stood the Altar-like Table, with a rich carpet hanging very large on the half-pace, and some plate, as a chalice and candlesticks with wax candles in them. By the preaching place stood the font, a leg laver and cover, all of brass, cut and carved with imagery work, the laver of the bigness of a barber's bason, and the cover had a cross erected on it. And this is all I had leisure to observe in the Chapel.

Then I made bold in temperate terms to ask the Deacon what use they made of so many tapers on the Table and in the Chapel. He answered (forsooth) to give them light when they could not see without them. And having formerly, as I said before, obtained leave to say what I listed, I asked him to whom he made all these courtesies, bowings and prostrations. He said " To God." I told him the Papists make no other answer for their bowing to images and crucifixes, yet we account them idolaters for so doing, as justly we may. He said we have no such warrant for the one, but for the other we had a precept (forsooth) to do all things with decency and order, as he took this to be. I demanded then why he used not the same solemnity in his house and whether he thought the Chapel more holy than his house. He said " No "; but that God was more immediately present in the Chapel than in the house whilst we were worshipping Him.

## No. 341. JOHN FELL (on HAMMOND)

[From *The Life of the Most Learned, Reverend, and Pious Dr. Henry Hammond*, the concluding paragraphs. In the *L. A. C. T.* edition of Hammond, this *Life* is in the same volume as his *Practical Catechism*; the extract which follows is from pp. cxiii–cxv. It was first published in 1661 and reprinted in the following year. John Fell also wrote a life of Richard Allestree.]

Having thus given a faithful though imperfect draught of this excellent person [Henry Hammond], whose virtues are so far from imitation by practice that they exercise and strain the comprehension of words, and having shewed how much he has merited of this nation in its most pressing exigents, both by his writings and by his example, and perchance above both these by his unwearied intercession in devotion, it may possibly be neither useless nor unacceptable to offer a request unto the reader in his behalf, and shew him an expedient whereby he may pay his debt of gratitude, and eminently oblige this holy saint though now with God.

It is this, to add unto his account in the day of retribution by taking benefit by his performances : and as he being dead yet speaks, so let him persuade likewise.

That the covetous reader would now at his request put off his sordid vice and take courage to be liberal, assured by his example, that if in the worst of times profuseness could make rich, charity shall never bring to beggary.

That the proud opinionated person on the same terms would in civility to him descend from his fond heights, instructed here that lowly meekness shall compass great respects, and instead of hate or flattery be waited on with love and veneration.

That the debauched or idle would leave upon this score his lewd unwarrantable joys, convinced that strict and rugged virtue made an age of sunshine, a life of constant smiles amidst the dreadfullest tempests ; taught the gout, the stone, the cramp, the colic, to be treatable companions, and made it eligible to live in bad times and die in flourishing.

That the angry man, who calls passion at least justice, possibly zeal and duty, would for his sake assume a different temper, believe that arguments may be answered by saying reason, calumnies by saying No, and railings by saying nothing.

The coward and disloyal that durst not own in words, much less by service and relief, his Prince, that complimented his apostasy and treason by the soft terms of changing an interest, will from hence learn that the surest way to safety is to have but one interest, and that espoused so firmly as never to be changed ; since such a constancy was that which a Cromwell durst not persecute.

That the employed in business would from hence dismiss their fears of regular piety, their suspicion that devotion would hinder all dispatch and manage of affairs ; since it appeared his constant office (like the prayer of Joshua, which made the sun stand still) seemed to have rendered unto him each day as long as two.

That the ambitious person, especially the ecclesiastic, would think employment and high place a stewardship that renders debtors both to God and man ; a residence at once of constant labour and attendance too ; a precipice that equally exposes both to envy and to ruin ; and consequently to be that which should become our greatest fear and terror, but at no hand our choice, since it was that which this heroic constancy was not ashamed to own a dread of, and whose appearance did render death itself relief and rescue.

Lastly, that the narrow self-designing person, who understands no kindness but advantage ; the sensual, that knows no love but lust ;

the intemperate, that owns no companion but drink ; may all at once from him reform their brutish errors : since he has made it evident that a friend does fully satisfy these distant and importunate desires, being as the most innocent and certainly ingenuous entertainment, so besides that the highest mirth, the greatest interest and surest pleasure in the world.

They that had the happiness of a personal acquaintance with this best of men, this saint, who seems in our decays of ancient virtue lent us by special Providence even for this end and purpose, that we might not disbelieve the faith of history, delivering the excellency of primitive Christians, know with what thirst and eagerness of soul he sought the spiritual advantage of any single man how mean soever, with what enjoyment he beheld the recovery of any such from an ill course and habit. And whatever apprehensions other men may have, they will be easily induced to think that if blessed spirits have commerce with earth,—as surely we have reason to believe it somewhat more than possible,—they, I say, will resolve it a connatural and highly agreeable accession unto his fruitions, that when there is joy in the presence of the angels of God for a sinner that repents, he may be an immediate accessory to that blessed triumph and be concerned beyond the rate of a bare spectator.

Persuasions to piety now-a-days are usually in scorn called preaching. But it is to be hoped that this, how contemptible an office soever it be grown, will be no indecency in this instance ; that it will not be absurd if his history, who deservedly was reckoned among the best preachers, whose life was the best of sermons, should bear a correspondence to its subject, and professedly close with an application : that it adjures all persons to be what they promised God Almighty they would be in their Baptismal vows, what they see the glorious Saints and Martyrs and Confessors, and in particular this holy man, has been before them ; be what is most honourable, most easy and advantageous to be at present ; and, in a word, to render themselves such as they desire to be upon their death-beds, before they leave the world, and then would be for ever.

Which blessed achievement as it was the great design of the excellent Doctor's both words and writings, his thoughts and actions, is also (besides the payment of a debt to friendship and to virtue) the only aim of this imperfect, but yet affectionate and well meant, account. And may Almighty God by the assistance of His grace give all of these this their most earnestly desired effect and issue.

## No. 342. JEREMY TAYLOR (on BRAMHALL)

[From *A Sermon Preached in Christ's Church, Dublin, July* 16, 1663, *at the Funeral of the Most Reverend Father in God, John* [Bramhall], *Late Lord Archbishop of Armagh, and Primate of All Ireland. Works*, ed. R. Heber, Vol. VI, pp. 444 f. (ed. C. P. Eden,

Vol. VIII, pp. 422 f. ; Bramhall's *Works*, ed. *L. A. C. T.*, Vol. I, pp. lxxiv–lxxvi).   This is the Seventh Sermon of the ten constituting Taylor's Δεκὰς Ἐμβολιμαῖος, which were first published as a Supplement to the Ἐνιαντός in the year 1663 ; they were dedicated to the Duchess of Ormond.   The text of this particular sermon was *I Cor.* xv, 23.]

To sum up all.   [Bramhall] was a wise prelate, a learned doctor, a just man, a true friend, a great benefactor to others, a thankful bene-ficiary where he was obliged himself.   He was a faithful servant to his masters, a loyal subject to the king, a zealous assertor of his religion against popery on the one side and fanaticism on the other.   The practice of his religion was not so much in forms and exterior ministries, though he was a great observer of all the public rites and ministries of the Church, as it was in doing good for others.   He was like Myson, whom the Scythian Anacharsis so greatly praised, ὁ Μύσων ἦν οἶκον οἰκήσας καλῶς, " he governed his family well."   He gave to all their due of mainte-nance and duty ; he did great benefit to mankind ; he had the fate of the Apostle St. Paul, he passed *through evil report and good report, as a deceiver, and yet true.*   He was a man of great business and great resort : *Semper aliquis in Cyronis domo*, as the Corinthians said : " There was always somebody in Cydon's house."   He was μερίζων τὸν βίον ἔργῳ καὶ βίβλῳ " he divided his life into labour and his book."   He took care of his Churches when he was alive, and even after his death, having left five hundred pounds for the repair of his Cathedral of Armagh and St. Peter's Church in Drogheda.   He was an excellent scholar, and rarely well accomplished, first instructed to great excel-lency by natural parts and then consummated by study and experience. Melancthon was use to say, that himself was a logician ; Pomeranus, a grammarian ; Justus Jonas, an orator ; but that Luther was all these. It was greatly true of him that the single perfections which make many men eminent were united in this Primate and made him illustrious.

> *Ergo Quinctilium perpetuus sopor*
> *Urget ? cui Pudor, et, Justitiae soror,*
> *Incorrupta Fides, nudaque Veritas,*
> *Quando ullum invenient parem ?*

It will be hard to find his equal in all things : *Fortasse tanquam Phoenix anno quingentesimo nascitur* (that I may use the words of Seneca) *nec est mirum ex intervallo magna generari* ; *mediocria et in turbam nascentia saepe fortuna producit; eximia vero ipsa raritate commendat.*   For in him were visible the great lines of Hooker's judiciousness, of Jewel's learning, of the acuteness of Bishop Andrewes.   He was skilled in more great things than one ; and, as one said of Phidias, he could not only make excellent statues of ivory, but he could work in stone and brass.   He showed his equanimity in poverty and his justice in riches ; he was useful in his country and profitable in his banishment ;

52

for, as Paraeus was at Anvilla, Luther at Wittenberg, St. Athanasius and St. Chrysostom in their banishment, St. Jerome in his retirement at Bethlehem, they were oracles to them that needed it. So was he in Holland and France, where he was abroad ; and beside the particular endearments which his friends received from him, for he did do relief to his brethren that wanted and supplied the soldiers out of his store in Yorkshire when himself could but ill spare it. But he received public thanks from the Convocation of which he was President and public justification from the Parliament where he was speaker ; so that although, as one said, *Miraculi instar vitae iter, si longum, sine offensione percurrere*, yet no man had greater enemies, and no man had greater justifications.

But God hath taken our Elijah from our heads this day. I pray God that at least his mantle may be left behind and that his spirit may be doubled upon his successor ; and that we may all meet together with him at the right hand of the Lamb, where every man shall receive according to his deeds, whether they be good or whether they be evil. I conclude with the words of Caius Plinius : *Equidem beatos puto quibus Deorum munere datum est, aut facere scribenda, aut scribere legenda.* " He wrote many things fit to be read, and did very many things worthy to be written." Which if we wisely imitate, we may hope to meet him in the resurrection of the just, and feast with him in the Eternal Supper of the Lamb, there to sing perpetual anthems to the honour of God the Father, Son, and Holy Ghost.

## No. 343. EDWARD HYDE (on FALKLAND)

[From *The History of the Rebellion and Civil Wars in England, begun in* 1641, *with the precedent Passages and Actions that contributed thereto, and the happy End and Conclusion thereof by the King's Blessed Restoration*, Book VII, §§ 219-221. Ed. by W. D. Macray (Oxford, Clarendon Press), 1888, Vol. III, pp. 179-181. The writing of this great work was spread over a long number of years. Between 1646 and 1648, Hyde wrote a " History of the Rebellion " down to the defeat of Hopton at Alresford in March 1644. This was expanded and continued, and other projected writings incorporated into it. It was not until 1702-4 that the work was first published, at Oxford, in three folio volumes. From the profits derived from it, the Clarendon Printing House, now the Old Clarendon Building, was constructed in 1713.]

[Lucius Cary] was a great cherisher of wit and fancy and good parts in any man and, if he found them clouded with poverty or want, a most liberal and bountiful patron towards them, even above his fortune ; of which in those administrations he was such a dispenser as if he had been trusted with it to such uses, and if there had been the least of vice in his expense he might have been thought too prodigal. He was constant and pertinacious in whatsoever he resolved to do, and not to be wearied by any pains that were necessary to that end. And therefore, having once resolved not to see London (which he loved above all places) till he had perfectly learned the Greek tongue, he went to his own house in the country, and pursued it with that indefatigable industry that it will not be believed in how short a time he was master of it, and accurately read all the Greek historians.

In this time, his house being within ten miles of Oxford,[1] he contracted familiarity and friendship with the most polite and accurate men of that University, who found such an immenseness of wit and such a solidity of judgement in him, so infinite a fancy bound in by a most logical ratiocination, such a vast knowledge that he was not ignorant in anything, yet such an excessive humility as if he had known nothing, that they frequently resorted and dwelt with him, as in a college situated in a purer air; so that his house was a university bound in a lesser volume, whither they came not so much for repose as study, and to examine and refine those grosser propositions which laziness and consent made current in vulgar conversation.

Many attempts were made upon him by the instigation of his mother (who was a lady of another persuasion in religion, and of a most masculine understanding, allayed with the passion and infirmities of her own sex) to pervert him in his piety to the Church of England, and to reconcile him to that of Rome; which they prosecuted with the more confidence, because he declined no opportunity or occasion of conference with those of that religion, whether priest or laics, having diligently studied the controversies, and exactly read all or the choicest of the Greek and Latin Fathers, and having a memory so stupendous that he remembered on all occasions whatsoever he read. And he was so great an enemy to that passion and uncharitableness which he saw produced by difference of opinion in matters of religion, that in all those disputations with priests and others of the Roman Church he affected to manifest all possible civility to their persons, and estimation of their parts; which made them retain still some hope of his reduction, even when they had given over offering farther reasons to him to that purpose. But this charity towards them was much lessened, and any correspondence with them quite declined, when by sinister arts they had corrupted his two younger brothers, being both children, and stolen them from his house, and transported them beyond seas, and perverted his sisters. Upon which occasion he writ two large discourses against the principal positions of that religion, with that sharpness of style and full weight of reason, that the Church is deprived of great jewels in the concealment of them, and that they are not published to the world.[2]

---

[1] [At Great Tew, sixteen miles from Oxford (Macray's note).]

[2] [If one of these was the *Discourse of Infallibility*, it had already been two years in print when Hyde wrote this passage, having been published in 1645. The other may be the answer to a *Reply*, which was first printed in 1651 (Macray's note).]

## (3) THE RELIGIOUS TEMPER OF THE AGE

### No. 344.  ISAAC BARROW

[Sermon on " The Profitableness of Godliness." *Works*, ed. A. Napier (Cambridge), 1859, Vol. I, pp. 202–233 ; ed. Oxford (1818), Vol. I, pp. 40–63.  This magnificent discourse is the latter of a pair of sermons on the same text and subject.  Barrow's fame as a preacher is posthumous rather than contemporary.  For the impression his sermons made upon John Locke, Warburton, the two Pitts, and others, see *D. N. B. s.v.* " Barrow."]

### THE PROFITABLENESS OF GODLINESS
*" But godliness is profitable for all things."  I Tim.* iv, 8.

IN discoursing formerly upon these words, I did propound divers general considerations serving to confirm and recommend this assertion of St. Paul.  I shall now insist upon some others more particular, which yet seem much conducible to the same purpose, declaring the vast utility of religion or piety.

I. We may consider that religion doth prescribe the truest and best rules of action, thence enlightening our mind and rectifying our practice in all matters and upon all occasions, so that whatever is performed according to it is done well and wisely, with a comely grace in regard to others, with a cheerful satisfaction in our own mind, with the best assurance, that things are here capable of, to find happy success and beneficial fruit.

Of all things in the world there is nothing more generally profitable than light.  By it we converse with the world and have all things set before us ; by it we truly and easily discern things in their right magnitude, shape and colour ; by it we guide our steps safely in prosecution of what is good and shunning what is noxious ; by it our spirits are comfortably warmed and cheered, our life consequently, our health, our vigour, and activity are preserved.  The like benefits doth religion, which is the light of our soul, yield to it.  Pious men are *children of the light* ; pious works are works of *light shining before men*.  God's Word (or true religion) is *a lamp unto our feet, and a light unto our path*, enabling us to perceive things and judge rightly of them ; teaching us to walk straightly and surely, without erring or stumbling ; qualifying us to embrace what is useful and to avoid hurtful things ; preserving our spiritual life and disposing us to act well with a vigorous alacrity. Without it a man is stark blind and utterly benighted, gropeth in doubt,

744

wandereth in mistake, trippeth upon all occasions, and often falleth into mischief. *The path of the just,* saith the Wise Man, *is as the shining light. The way of the wicked is as darkness, they know not at what they stumble. Righteousness keepeth him that is upright in the way ; but wickedness overthroweth the sinner.*

Again, it is a fair ornament of a man, and a grand convenience both to himself and to others with whom he converseth or dealeth, to act regularly, uniformly, and consistently ; freeing a man's self from distraction and irresolution in his mind, from change and confusion in his proceedings ; securing others from delusion and disappointment in their transactions with him. Even a bad rule constantly observed is therefore better than none. Order and perseverance in any way seemeth more convenient than roving and tossing about in uncertainties. But secluding a regard to the precepts of religion, there can hardly be any sure or settled rule, which firmly can engage a man to, or effectually restrain a man from, any thing.

There is scarce in nature anything so wild, so untractable, so unintelligible, as a man who hath no bridle of conscience to guide or check him. A profane man is like a ship, without anchor to stay him, or rudder to steer him, or compass to guide him ; so that he is tossed with any wind, and driven with any wave, none knoweth whither,—whither bodily temper doth sway him, or passion doth hurry him, or interest doth pull him, or example leadeth him, or company enveigleth and haleth him, or humour transporteth him ; whither any such variable and unaccountable causes determine him, or divers of them together distract him : whence he so rambleth and hovereth, that he can seldom himself tell what in any case he should do, nor can another guess it ; so that you cannot at any time know where to find him or how to deal with him ; you cannot with reason ever rely upon him, so *unstable he is in all his ways.* He is in effect a mere child, all humour and giddiness, somewhat worse than a beast, which, following the instinct of its nature, is constant and regular, and thence tractable, or at least so untractable, that no man will be deceived in meddling with him. Nothing therefore can be more unmanly than such a person, nothing can be more unpleasant than to have to do with him.

But a pious man, being steadily governed by conscience and a regard to certain principles, doth both understand himself and is intelligible to others. He presently descrieth what in any case he is to do, and can render an account of his acting. You may know him clearly, and assuredly tell what he will do, and may therefore fully confide in him.

What therefore law and government are to the public, things necessary to preserve the world in order, peace, and safety (that men may know what to do, and distinguish what is their own), that is piety to each man's private state, and to ordinary conversation. It freeth a man's own life from disorder and distraction; it prompteth men how to behave themselves towards one another with security and confidence.

This it doth by confining our practice within settled bounds. But this advantage appeareth greater, considering that the rules which it prescribeth are the best that can be. Such they must needs be, as proceeding from infallible wisdom and immense goodness; being indeed no other than laws, which the allwise and most gracious Lord and Maker of the world, out of tender kindness to His subjects and creatures, with especial regard to our welfare, hath been pleased to enact and declare. What of old He said to the Israelites concerning their laws may with greater advantage be applied to those, which should regulate our lives: *And now, Israel, what doth the Lord thy God require of thee, but to fear the Lord thy God, to walk in all His ways, and to love Him, and to serve the Lord thy God with all thy heart, and with all thy soul ; to keep the commandments of the Lord, and His statutes, which I command thee this day for thy good ?* (For thy good ; that was the design of their being commanded, thereto the observance of them did tend.) And that commendation, which by the Levites in *Nehemiah* is given to that, doth more clearly and fully agree to the Christian (general and perfect) institution : *Thou camest down from Mount Sinai, and spakest with them from Heaven, and gavest them right judgements, and true laws, good statutes and commandments.* And *The law* saith the Apostle Paul, *is holy ; the commandment is holy, just and good.* As such it is recommended to us by its Author, so we Christians are by many great arguments assured that it is, and that it is such even our natural reason dictateth. So (as to the chief instances thereof) the most wise and sober men always have acknowledged ; so the general consent doth avow, and so even common experience doth attest. For heartily to love and reverence the Maker of all things Who by everything apparent before us demonstrateth Himself incomprehensibly powerful, wise, and good, to be kind and charitable to our neighbours, to be just and faithful in our dealings, to be sober and modest in our minds, to be meek and gentle in our demeanours, to be staunch and temperate in our enjoyments, and the like principal rules of duty, are such that the common reason of man and continual experience do approve them as hugely conducible to the public good of men and to each man's private welfare. So notoriously beneficial they appear, that for the justification of them we might appeal even to the judgement and conscience of those persons, who are most concerned to derogate from them. For hardly can any man be so senseless or so lewd, as seriously to disapprove or condemn them, as inwardly to blame or slight those who truly act according to them. The will of men sometimes may be so depraved that dissolute persons wantonly and heedlessly may scoff at and seem to disparage goodness ; that good men by very bad men for doing well may be envied and hated (their being so treated is commonly an argument of the goodness of their persons and their ways); but the understanding of men can hardly be so corrupted that piety, charity, justice, temperance, meekness, can in good earnest considerately by any man be disallowed, or that persons apparently practising them can be despised; but rather, in spite of all contrary prejudice and disaffections, such things and such persons cannot but in judgement and heart be esteemed by all men. The lustre of them by natural and necessary efficacy (like that of Heaven's glorious light) dazzleth the sight and charmeth the spirits of all men living. The beauty of them irresistibly conquereth and commandeth in the apprehensions of men. The more they are observed the more useful and needful they appear for the good of men, all the fruits which grow from the observance of them being to all men's tastes very pleasant, to all men's experience very wholesome. Indeed, all the good, whereby common life is adorned, is sweetened, is rendered pleasant and desirable, doth spring thence; all the mischiefs which infest particular men, and which disturb the world, palpably do arise from the transgression or neglect thereof.

If we look on a person sticking to those rules, we shall perceive him to have a cheerful mind and composed passions, to be at peace within and satisfied with himself, to live in comely order, in good repute, in fair correspondence, and firm concord with his neighbours. If we mark what preserveth the body sound and lusty, what keepeth the mind vigorous and brisk, what saveth and improveth the estate, what upholdeth the good name, what guardeth and graceth a man's whole life, it is nothing else but proceeding in our demeanour and dealings according to the honest and wise rules of piety. If we view a place where these commonly in good measure are observed, we shall discern that peace and prosperity do flourish there; that all things proceed on sweetly and fairly; that men generally drive on conversation and commerce together contentedly, delightfully, advantageously, yielding friendly advice and aid mutually, striving to render one another happy; that few clamours or complaints are heard there, few contentions or stirs do appear, few disasters or tragedies do occur; that such a place hath indeed much of the face, much of the substance of Paradise.

But if you mind a person who neglecteth them, you will find his mind galled with sore remorse, racked with anxious fears and doubts, agitated with storms of passion and lust, living in disorder and disgrace, jarring with others, and no less dissatisfied with himself. If you observe what doth impair the health, doth weaken and fret the mind, doth waste the estate, doth blemish the reputation, doth expose the whole life to danger and trouble, what is it but thwarting these good rules? If you consider a place where these are much neglected, it will appear like a wilderness of savage beasts, or a sty of foul swine, or a hell of cursed

fiends, full of roaring and tearing, of factions and feuds, of distractions
and confusions, of pitiful objects, of doleful moans, of tragical events.
Men are there wallowing in filth, wildly revelling, bickering and squab-
bling, defaming, circumventing, disturbing and vexing one another;
as if they affected nothing more than to render one another as miserable
as they can.  It is from lust and luxury, from ambition and avarice,
from envy and spite, and the like dispositions, which religion doth
chiefly interdict, that all such horrid mischiefs do spring.

In fine, the precepts of religion are no other than such as physicians
would prescribe for the health of our bodies, as politicians would avow
needful for the peace of the state, as Epicurean philosophers do recommend for the tranquillity of our mind and pleasure of our lives; such
as common reason dictateth and daily trial sheweth conducible to our
welfare in all respects : which consequently, were there no law exacting
them of us, we should in wisdom choose to observe, and voluntarily
impose on ourselves, confessing them to be fit matters of law, as
most advantageous and requisite to the good (general and particular)
of mankind.  So that what Plutarch reporteth Solon to have said,
that " he had so squared his laws to the citizens, that all of them might
clearly perceive that to observe them was more for their benefit and interest than to violate them," is far more true concerning the Divine laws.

II.  We may consider more particularly that piety yieldeth to the prac-
tiser all kind of interior content, peace, and joy ; freeth him from all
kinds of dissatisfaction, regret, and disquiet, which is an inestimably great
advantage.  For certainly the happiness and misery of men are wholly
or chiefly seated and founded in the mind.  If that is in a good state
of health, rest and cheerfulness, whatever the person's outward condition
or circumstances be, he cannot be wretched : if that be distempered
or disturbed, he cannot be happy.  For what if a man seem very poor,
if he be abundantly satisfied in his own possessions and enjoyments ?
What if he tasteth not the pleasures of sense, if he enjoyeth purer and
sweeter delights of mind ?  What if tempests of fortune surround him,
if his mind be calm and serene ?  What if he have few or no friends,
if he yet be thoroughly in peace and amity with himself, and can delightfully converse with his own thoughts ?  What if men slight, censure
or revile him, if he doth value his own state, doth approve his own
actions, doth acquit himself of blame in his own conscience ?  Such
external contingencies can surely no more prejudice a man's real happiness than winds blustering abroad can harm or trouble him that
abideth in a good room within doors, than storms and fluctuations at
sea can molest him who standeth firm upon the shore.  On the other
hand the greatest affluence of seeming goods will avail nothing, if real
content of mind be wanting.  For what will the highest eminence of
outward state import to him that is dejected in his own conceit ?  What

if the world court and bless him, or if all people do admire and applaud him, if he be displeased with, if he condemneth, if he despiseth himself? What if the weather look fair and bright without, if storms rage in his breast, if black clouds do overcast his soul? What if he do abound with friends, and enjoy peace abroad, if he find distraction at home, and is at cruel variance with himself? How can a man enjoy any satisfaction, or relish any pleasure, while sore remorse doth sting him, or solicitous doubts and fears do rack him?

Now that from the practice of religion, and from it alone, such inward content and pleasure do spring; that it only ministereth reason of content, and disposeth the mind to enjoy it; that it extirpateth the grounds and roots of discontent; that it is the only mother of true, sober alacrity and tranquillity of mind, will, upon considering things, be manifest.

There is no other thing here in this world that can yield any solid or stable content to our mind. For all present enjoyments are transient and evanid; and of any future thing, in this kingdom of change and contingency, there can be no assurance. There is nothing below large enough to fill our vast capacities, or to satiate our boundless desires, or to appease our squeamish delicacy. There is nothing whose sweetness we do not presently exhaust and suck dry, whereof thence we do not soon grow weary, quite loathing or faintly liking it. There is not anything that is not slippery and fleeting so that we can for a long time hope to possess it or for any time can enjoy it, without restless care in keeping it, and anxious fear of losing it. Nothing there is, in the pursuance, the custody, the defence and maintenance whereof we are not liable to disappointments and crosses. Nothing consequently there is productive of any sound content to the fastidious, impatient, greedy, and restless heart of man. The greatest confluence of present, corporeal, secular things (of all the health, the riches, the dignity, the power, the friendships and dependencies, the wit, the learning and wisdom, the reputation and renown in this world) will not afford much of it; which yet is but an imaginary supposition, for in effect hardly do all such accommodations of life concur in any state. There is ever some *dead fly* in our box, which marreth our *ointment*; some adherent inconvenience, which soureth the gust of our enjoyments. There is always some good thing absent, which we do want or long for; some ill thing present, or in prospect, which we abhor, would avoid, do fear may come. If therefore we would find content, we must not seek it here; we must want it, or have it from another world: it must come hither from Heaven, and thence only piety can fetch it down. This instead of these unsatisfying, uncertain, and unstable things, supplieth us with goods adequate to our most outstretched wishes, infallibly sure, incessantly durable; *an indefectible treasure, an incorruptible inheritance, an unshakable kingdom,* a perfect and endless joy, capable to replenish the vastest heart ; which he that hath a good title to, or a confident hope of, how can he be otherwise than extremely pleased, than fully content ? It assureth the favour and friendship of God, of Him that is Absolute Lord and Disposer of all things ; the which he that hath, and confideth in, what can he want or wish more ? What can he fear ? What can annoy or dismay him ? What can hap to him worthy to be deemed evil or sad ? What is poverty to him, for whom God is concerned to provide ? What is disgrace to him, that hath the regard and approbation of God ? What is danger to him, whom God continually protecteth ? What can any distress work on him, whom God doth comfort and will relieve ? What is any thing to him, who is sensible that all things are purposely disposed to him by that Wisdom which perfectly knoweth what is best, by that Goodness which entirely loveth him ? In fine, he that is conscious to himself of being well affected in mind, and acting the best way, who is satisfied in the state of his soul, secure from God's displeasure and hopeful of His favour, what can make any grievous impression on him ? What other affections than such as are most grateful and pleasant can lodge in his soul ? Joy and peace have natural seeds in such a mind, and necessarily must spring up there ; in proportion, I mean, and according to the degrees of piety resident therein.

The Epicureans did conceit and boast, that having, by their atheistical explications of natural effects and common events here, discarded the belief and dread of religion, they had laid a strong foundation for tranquillity of mind, had driven away all the causes of grief and fear, so that nothing then remained troublesome or terrible unto us ; and consequently, what, said they, could forbid, but that we should be entirely contented, glad and happy ? *Nos exæquat victoria cœlo ;* no God then surely could be more happy than we. But their attempt in many respects was vain and lame. They presumed of a victory which it is impossible to obtain : and supposing they had got it, their triumph would not have been so glorious, their success would not have been so great, as they pretended. For seeing no Epicurean discourse can baffle the potent arguments which persuade religion (those arguments, which the visible constitution of nature, the current tradition of all ages, the general consent of man, the pregnant attestations of history and experience concerning supernatural and miraculous events, do afford) ; since the being and providence of God have proofs so clear and valid, that no subtlety of man can so far evade them, as not to be shaken with them, as wholly to be freed from doubt and suspicion of their truth ; since there can be no means of evincing the negative part in those questions to be true or probable, it is impossible that any considering man, in this cause against religion, should suppose himself to have acquired an absolute and secure victory or that he should reap substantial fruit of comfort thence. It cannot be, that any man should enjoy any perfect quiet, without acting so as to get some good hope of avoiding those dreadful mischiefs, which religion threateneth to the transgressors of its precepts. Were there indeed but reason enough to stir, if not to stagger, an infidel; were it somewhat dubious whether, yea, were it great odds that there are not reserved any punishments for impiety, as indeed there is, if not the perfectest assurance imaginable, yet vast advantage on the contrary side; were there but any small reason for a judgement to come, as there are apparently very many and great ones; had most men conspired in denying Providence, as ever generally they have consented in avowing it; were there a pretence of miracles for establishing the mortality and impunity of souls, as there have been numberless strongly testified by good witnesses and great events, to confirm the opposite doctrines; did most wise and sober men judge in favour of irreligion, as commonly they ever did and still do otherwise; yet wisdom would require that men should choose to be pious, since otherwise no man can be thoroughly secure. It is a wildness not to dread the least possibility of incurring such horrible mischiefs. Any hazard of such importance cannot but startle a man in his wits. To be in the least obnoxious to eternal torments, if men would think upon it as men (that is, as rational and provident creatures), could not but disturb them. And indeed so it is in experience; for whatever they say, or seem, all atheists and profane men are inwardly suspicious and fearful; they care not to die, and would gladly escape the trial of what shall follow death. But let us grant or imagine the Epicurean successful as he could wish in this enterprise of subduing religion. Yet except therewith he can also trample down reason, new mould human nature, subjugate all natural appetites and passions, alter the state of things here, and transform the world, he will yet in the greatest part fail of his conceited advantages; very short he will fall of triumphing in a contented and quiet mind. That which accrueth thence will at most be no more than some negative content, or a partial indolency, arising from his being rescued from some particular cares and fears; which exceedeth not the tranquillity of a beast, or the stupidity of one that is out of his senses; that is all he can claim, which yet is more than he can ever compass. For he cannot be as a beast, or a mere sot, if he would. Reason, reflecting on present evils and boding others future, will afflict him. His own unsatiable desires, unavoidable fears, and untameable passions, will disquiet him. Were the other world quite out of his faith or his thought, yet this world would yield trouble sufficient to render him void of any steady rest or solid joy. All men ever have, and ever will complain, that the burdens, crosses, satieties of this life do much surpass the conveniences and comforts

of it. So that, were no other to be expected or feared, this of itself
would become grievous and nauseous; we should soon have enough or
too much of it, without a support and supply from other-where.
In the largest affluence of things, in the deepest calm of our state,
we are apt to nauseate and are weary even of our prosperity itself;
the which indeed commonly hath ingredients not only somewhat
unsavoury, but very bitter and loathsome. We may add, that had
those profane attempters quite banished religion they with it must have
driven away all the benefits and comforts of it; which, even supposing
them imaginary, are yet the greatest which common life doth need or
can desire. With it they would send packing justice, charity, sobriety,
and all solid virtue, things which cannot firmly subsist without
conscience; which being gone, human life would be the most disorderly, most unsafe, most wretched and contemptible thing that can
be. Nothing but insipid and flashy sensualities would be left behind
to comfort a man with; and those hardly any man (by reason of com-
petitions and contentions for them, nowise restrainable) could enjoy
quietly or safely. It is therefore piety alone which, by raising hopes
of blessings and joys incomparably superior to any here, that cannot be
taken from us, can lay any ground of true content, of substantial and
positive content; such as consisteth not only in removing the objects
and causes of vexatious passions, but in employing the most pleasant
affections (love, hope, joy) with a delightful complacence upon their
proper and most noble objects. *The Kingdom of God* (and that only, no
other kingdom hath that privilege) *consisteth in righteousness* (first; then
in) *peace and spiritual joy*. No philosopher, with truth and reason, can
make that overture to us which Our Lord doth: *Come unto Me, all ye
that are weary and heavy laden, and ye shall find rest to your souls*. Out of
religion there can be no aphorism pretended like to that of the Prophet,
*Thou shalt keep him in perfect peace, whose mind is stayed on Thee*.

If indeed we distinctly survey all the grounds and sources of content,
it will appear that religion only can afford it.

Doth it result from a well governing and ordering our passions?
Then it is plain that only a pious man is capable thereof. For piety
only can effect that. It alone, with the powerful aid of Divine grace,
doth guide our passions by exact rules, doth set them upon worthy
objects, doth temper and tune them in just harmony, doth seasonably
curb and check them, doth rightly correct and reform them.

This no bare reason (which naturally is so dim and so feeble in man)
can achieve; much less can unreasonableness do it, which is ever
prevalent in irreligious persons. Their passions do ever run wildly
and at random, in no good pace, within no good compass, towards the
meanest and basest objects; whence they can have no rest or quiet
in their minds. As they are constantly offending, so will they ever be

punishing themselves, with intestine broils and conflicts, with dis-
satisfactions and regrets.    Hence, *there is no peace to the wicked.    He is
like the troubled sea, which cannot rest.*    God (as St. Austin speaketh)
hath said it and so it is:  " Every inordinate mind is a punishment to
itself."

Doth content spring from a hearty approbation of, or a complacence
in, a man's own actions; from reflexion that he constantly doth act
according to reason and wisdom, to justice and duty ?    Then can the
pious man alone pretend to it, who knoweth that he walketh *inoffensively
toward God and man* ;  that he consulteth his own best interests and welfare ;  that assuredly no bad consequence can attend his unblameable
behaviour ;  that most wise men have declared their approbation of his
proceedings ;  that if he prove in his chief design mistaken, yet no
mischief can thence befall him ;  yea, that he is not thereby quite disappointed, seeing even much present satisfaction and  convenience
do arise up to him from his practice.

Doth content grow from a sound and healthful constitution of soul ?
It is the pious man alone that hath that, whose mind is clear from
distempers of vice and passion.    The impious man is infirm, out of
order, full of disease and pain ; according to the Prophet's description
of him, *The whole head is sick, and the whole heart faint : from the sole
of the foot even unto the head there is no soundness in it ;  but wounds, and
bruises, and putrefying sores.*

Doth content arise specially from good success in our attempts or
from prosperous events befalling us ?    Then it is the pious man who
is most capable thereof.    For he only is secure that what seemeth
good and prosperous is really such to him, as meant for his good by
the Divine goodness, as tending thereto by the guidance of infallible
wisdom.    As he only hath ground to hope for success, because he
confideth in God, because he dutifully seeketh God's help, because
God is favourably disposed toward him, because God *ordereth his
steps,* because God is by promise engaged to bless him, because he is
conscious of intentions to render God thanks and praise for it, to employ
his success to God's honour and service :  so he only can be satisfied
with the appearance of success, being able with assurance to say after
St. Paul, *We know that to those who love God all things cooperate for good.*

Is security from danger, from trouble, from want, from all evil,
a source or matter of content ?    It certainly doth attend the pious
man, God being his especial protector, his comforter, his purveyor.
*There shall no evil befall the just : there shall no plague come near his
dwelling.    God keepeth all his bones, not one of them is broken.    He
delivereth the righteous out of their troubles.    The desire of the righteous
shall be granted.    There is no want to them that fear God.*    So do the
holy oracles assure us.

Doth contentedness spring from sufficiency, real or apprehended ? This appertaineth peculiarly to the pious man. For, having God, the Master of All, for *his portion*, he hath the richest estate that can be ; he hath all that he can desire, he cannot but take himself to have enough. Hence *Godliness with contentedness* (μετ' αὐταρκείας, with sufficiency) is, as St. Paul saith, μέγας πορισμός, *the great way of gaining*. He saith it not, as supposing godliness and contentedness to be separable ; but rather as implying godliness therefore to be the most gainful, because sufficiency and contentedness do ever attend it. In fine, if that saying of Seneca be true that, " If to any man the things he possesseth do not seem most ample, although he be master of the whole world, he is yet miserable," then assuredly the pious man only can be happy ; for to him alone his possessions can seem the largest and best, such as there can be no possible accession to, or amendment of. For nothing can be greater or better than God, in Whom he hath a steadfast propriety, Whose infinite power and wisdom are engaged to do him the utmost good that he is capable of. And farther,

III. Seeing we have mentioned happiness, or the *Summum Bonum*, the utmost scope of human desire, we do add, that piety doth surely confer it. Happiness, whatever it be, hath certainly an essential coherence with piety. These are reciprocal propositions, both of them infallibly true : He that is pious is happy, and he that is happy is pious. No man doth undertake or prosecute anything which he doth not apprehend in some order or degree conducing to that which all men under a confused notion regard and tend to, which they call happiness, the highest good, the chiefest desirable thing. But in their judgements about this thing or the means of attaining it, as men dissent much, so of necessity most of them must be mistaken. Most, indeed, do aim and shoot at a mere shadow of profit or at that which is very little considerable, and in comparison nothing at all ; which little conduceth to the perfection of their nature or the satisfaction of their desire. If they miss the mark, they are disappointed ; if they hit it, they are no less, and in effect hit nothing. But whatever this grand matter is, in whatever it consisteth, however it be procured, be it the possession and fruition of some special choice goods, or an aggregation and affluence of all goods, piety surely is the main ingredient and principal cause thereof. All other goods without it are insignificant and unuseful thereto ; and it cannot be wanting, where piety is. Be a man never so rich, so powerful, so learned and knowing, so prosperous in his affairs, so honourable in the opinions and affections of men, yet nowise happy can he be, if he is not pious ; being he wanteth the best goods, and is subject to the worst evils ; being he wanteth the love and favour of God, he wanteth peace and satisfaction of conscience, he wanteth a right enjoyment of present things, he wanteth security concerning his final welfare. Be he never so poor, so low in the eyes of men, so forlorn and destitute of worldly conveniences; yet if he be pious, he cannot be wretched. For he hath an interest in goods incomparably more precious, and is safe from all considerable evils; he hath a free resort to the inexhaustible foundation of all happiness, he hath a right to immense and endless felicity, the which eminently containeth all the goods we are capable of. He is possessed thereof in hope and certain reversion, there is but a moment to pass before his complete fruition of it. The want of all other petty things no more can maim the integrity of his felicity, than cutting the hair or paring the nails do mutilate a man : all other things are but superfluities or excrescences in regard to the constitution of happiness. Whatever happeneth, that will assuredly be true, which is so much inculcated in Holy Scripture, *Blessed is everyone that feareth the Lord, that walketh in His ways ; happy shall he be, and it shall be well with him.* Piety is indeed fraught with beatitudes, every part thereof yieldeth peculiar blessedness. To the love of God, to charity toward our neighbour, to purity of heart, to meekness, to humility, to patience, to merciful-ness, to peaceableness, beatitude is ascribed by Our Lord, the great Judge and Dispenser of it. Each religious performance hath happy fruits growing from it, and blissful rewards assigned thereto. All pious dispositions are fountains of pleasant streams, which by their confluence do make up a full sea of felicity.

IV. It is a peculiar advantage of piety that it furnisheth employment fit for us, worthy of us, hugely grateful, and highly beneficial to us. Man is a very busy and active creature which cannot live and do nothing, whose thoughts are in restless motion, whose desires are ever stretching at somewhat, who perpetually will be working either good or evil to himself. Wherefore greatly profitable must that thing be which deter-mineth him to act well, to spend his care and pain on that which is truly advantageous to him ; and that is religion only. It alone fasteneth our thoughts, affections, and endeavours upon occupations worthy the dignity of our nature, suiting the excellency of our natural capacities and endowments, tending to the perfection and advancement of our reason, to the enriching and ennobling of our souls. Secluding that, we have nothing in the world to study, to affect, to pursue, not very mean and below us, not very base and misbecoming us, as men of reason and judgement. What have we to do but to eat and drink, like horses or like swine; but to sport and play, like children or apes ; but to bicker and scuffle about trifles and impertinences, like idiots ? What but to scrape or scramble for useless pelf ; to hunt after empty shows and shadows of honour, or the vain fancies and dreams of men ? What, but to wallow or bask in sordid pleasures, the which soon degenerate into remorse and bitterness ? To which sort of employments were a man confined, what a pitiful thing would he be, and how inconsiderable his life ! Were a man designed only like a fly, to buzz about here for a time, sucking in the air and licking the dew, then soon to vanish back into nothing or to be transformed into worms ; how sorry and despicable a thing were he ! And such without religion we should be. But it supplieth us with business of a most worthy nature and lofty importance ; it setteth us upon doing things great and noble as can be ; it engageth us to free our minds from all fond conceits, and cleanse our hearts from all corrupt affections ; to curb our brutish appetites, to tame our wild passions, to correct our perverse inclinations, to conform the dispositions of our soul and the actions of our life to the eternal laws of righteousness and goodness. It putteth us upon the imitation of God and aiming at the resemblance of His perfections ; upon obtaining a friendship and maintaining a correspondence with the High and Holy One ; upon fitting our minds for conversation and society with the wisest and purest spirits above ; upon providing for an immortal state, upon the acquist of joy and glory everlasting. It employeth us in the divinest actions, of promoting virtue, of performing beneficence, of serving the public, and doing good to all ; the being exercised in which things doth indeed render a man highly considerable, and his life excellently valuable.

It is an employment most proper to us as reasonable men. For what more proper entertainments can our mind have, than to be purifying and beautifying itself, to be keeping itself and its subordinate faculties in order, to be attending upon the management of thoughts, of passions, of words, of actions, depending upon its governance ?

It is an employment most beneficial to us : in pursuing which we greatly better ourselves and improve our condition. We benefit and oblige others. We procure sound reputation and steady friendships. We decline many irksome mischiefs and annoyances. We do not, like those in the Prophet, *spend our labour for that which satisfieth not, nor spend our money for that which is not bread* : for both temporal prosperity and eternal felicity are the wages of the labour which we take herein.

It is an employment most constant, never allowing sloth or listlessness to creep in, incessantly busying all our faculties with earnest contention ; according to that profession of St. Paul, declaring the nature thereof, *Herein always do I exercise myself, to have a conscience void of offence toward God and toward man.* Whence it is called a " fight," and a " race," implying the continual earnestness of attention and activity, which is to be spent thereon.

It is withal a sweet and grateful business. For it is a pious man's character, that *he delighteth greatly in God's commandments* ; that *the commandments are not grevious to him* ; that it is *his meat and drink to do God's will* ; that *God's Words* (or precepts) *are sweeter than honey to his taste* ; that *the ways of* religious *wisdom are ways of pleasantness, and all her paths are peace.* Whereas all other employments are wearisome and soon become loathsome, this, the farther we proceed in it, the more pleasant and satisfactory it groweth. There is perpetual matter of victory over bad inclinations pestering us within, and strong temptations assailing us without: which to combat hath much delight, to master breedeth unexpressible content. The sense, also, of God's love, the influences of His grace and comfort, communicated in the performances of devotion and all duty, the satisfaction of good conscience, the assured hope of reward, the foretastes of future bliss, do season and sweeten all the labours taken, and all the difficulties undergone therein.

In fine, the bare light of nature hath discerned that were it not for such matters as these to spend a man's care and pains upon, this would be a lamentable world to live in. There was, for instance, an Emperor great and mighty as ever did wield sceptre on earth, whose excellent virtue coupled with wisdom (inferior, perhaps, to none that any man ever without special inspiration hath been endowed with) did qualify him with most advantage to examine and rightly to judge of things here; who, notwithstanding all the conveniences which his royal estate and well settled prosperity might afford (the which fully he had tasted and tried) did yet thus express his thoughts: τί μοι ζῆν ἐν κόσμῳ κενῷ θεῶν ἢ προνοίας κενῷ; "What doth it concern me to live in a world void of God or void of Providence?" To govern the greatest Empire that ever was, in the deepest calm; to enjoy the largest affluences of wealth, of splendour, of respect, of pleasure; to be loved, to be dreaded, to be served, to be adored by so many nations; to have the whole civil world obsequious to his will and nod; all these things seemed vain and idle, not worthy of a man's regard, affection, or choice, in case there were no God to worship, no providence to observe, no piety to be exercised. So little worth the while common sense hath adjudged it to live without religion.

V. It is a considerable benefit of piety, that it affordeth the best friendships and sweetest society. Man is framed for society and cannot live well without it. Many of his faculties would be useless, many of his appetites would rest unsatisfied in solitude. To have a friend wise and able, honest and good, unto whom upon all occasions we may have recourse for advice, for assistance, for consolation, is a great convenience of life; and this benefit we owe to religion, which supplieth us with various friendships of the best kind, most beneficial and most sweet unto us.

It maketh God our friend, a friend infinitely better than all friends, most affectionate and kind, most faithful and sure, most able and willing, and ever most ready to perform all friendly offices, to yield advice on all our doubts, succour in all our needs, comfort in all our troubles, satisfaction to all our desires. Unto him it ministereth a free address upon

53

all occasions; with him it alloweth us continually a most sweet and pleasant intercourse. The pious man hath always the all-wise God to counsel him, to guide his actions, and order his steps; he hath the Almighty to protect, support, and relieve him; he hath the immense Goodness to commiserate and comfort him. Unto Him he is not only encouraged, but obliged to resort in need. Upon Him he may, he ought to discharge all his cares and burdens.

It consequently doth engage all creatures in the world to be our friends, or instruments of good to us, according to their several capacities, by the direction and disposal of God. All the servants of our great Friend will, in compliance to Him, be serviceable to us. *Thou shalt be in league with the stones of the field, and the beasts of the field shall be in league with thee* : so Job's friend promiseth him upon condition of piety. And God Himself confirmeth that promise: *In that day*, saith He in the Prophet, *will I make a covenant for them with the beasts of the field and with the fowls of Heaven, and with the creeping things of the ground.* And again, *When thou passest through the waters, I will be with thee ; and through the rivers, they shall not overflow thee. When thou walkest through the fire, thou shalt not be burnt ; neither shall the flame kindle upon thee.* And, *The sun shall not smite thee by day, nor the moon by night. Thou shalt tread upon the lion and the adder, the young lion and the dragon shalt thou trample under foot. They shall take up scorpions ; and if they drink any deadly thing, it shall not hurt them.* So Our Lord promised to His Disciples. Not only the Heavens shall dispense their kindly influences, and the earth yield her plentiful stores, and all the elements discharge their natural and ordinary good offices; nor only the tame and sociable creatures shall upon this condition faithfully serve us; but even the most wild, most fierce, most ravenous, most venomous creatures shall, if there be need, prove friendly and helpful, or at least harmless to us; as were the ravens to Elias, the lions to Daniel, the viper to St. Paul, the fire to the three children.

But especially piety doth procure the friendship of the good angels, that puissant host of glorious and happy spirits. They all do tenderly love the pious person; they are ever ready to serve and do him good, to protect him from danger, to aid him in his undertakings, to rescue him from mischiefs. What an honour, what a blessing is this, to have such an innumerable company of noble friends (the courtiers and favourites of Heaven) deeply concerned and constantly vigilant for our welfare !

It also engageth the blessed saints in glory, *the spirits of just men perfected, the Church of the first-born*, to bear dearest affection to us, to further our prosperity with their good wishes and earnest prayers, mightly prevalent with God.

It rendereth all sorts of men our friends. To good men it uniteth us in holy communion; the communion of brotherly charity and hearty good will, attended with all the good offices they are able to perform. To other men it reconcileth and endeareth us; for that innocent and inoffensive, courteous and benign, charitable and beneficent demeanour, such as piety doth require and produce, are apt to conciliate respect and affection from the worst men. For, *Vincit malos pertinax bonitas*; men hardly can persist enemies to him whom they perceive to be their friend: and such the pious man in disposition of mind, and in effect when occasion serveth, is toward all men, being sensible of his obligation to love all men, and *as he hath opportunity, to do good to all men.* It assureth and more strictly endeareth our friends to us. For, as it maketh us hearty, faithful, constant friends to others, so it reciprocally tieth others to us in the like sincerity and fastness of good will.

It reconcileth enemies. For, *when a man's ways do please the Lord, He maketh his enemies to be at peace with him.* It hath a natural efficacy to that purpose, and Divine blessing promoteth it.

By it all conversation becometh tolerable, grateful, and useful. For a pious man is not easily disturbed with any crossness or perverseness, any infirmity or impertinency of those he converseth with. He can bear the weaknesses and failings of his company; he can by wholesome reflexions upon all occurrences advantage and please himself.

In fine, piety rendereth a man a true friend and a good companion to himself; satisfied in himself, able to converse freely and pleasantly with his own thoughts. It is for the want of pious inclinations and dispositions that solitude (a thing which sometimes cannot be avoided, which often should be embraced) is to most men so irksome and tedious, that men do carefully shun themselves, and fly from their own thoughts; that they decline all converse with their own souls, and hardly dare look upon their own hearts and consciences, whence they become aliens from home, wholly unacquainted with themselves, most ignorant of their own nearest concernments, no faithful friends or pleasant companions to themselves. So for refuge and ease they unseasonably run into idle or lewd conversation, where they disorder and defile themselves. But the pious man is, like Scipio, " never less alone than when alone." His solitude and retirement is not only tolerable, but commonly the most grateful and fruitful part of his life. He can ever with much pleasure and more advantage converse with himself; digesting and marshalling his thoughts, his affections, his purposes into good order; searching and discussing his heart, reflecting on his past ways, enforcing his former good resolutions, and framing new ones; inquiring after edifying truths; stretching his meditations toward the best and sublimest objects; raising his hopes and warming his affections toward spiritual and heavenly things; asking himself pertinent questions, and resolving incident doubts concerning his practice; in fine conversing with his best friend in devotion; with admiration and love contemplating the Divine perfections displayed in the works of nature, of providence, of grace; praising God for His excellent benefits and mercies; confessing his defects and offences; deprecating wrath and imploring pardon, with grace and ability to amend; praying for the supply of all his wants. All which performances yield both unconceivable benefit and unexpressible comfort. So that solitude (that which is to common nature so offensive, to corrupt nature so abominable) is to the pious man extremely commodious and comfortable: which is a great advantage peculiar to piety, and the last which I shall mention.

So many, and many more than I can express, vastly great and precious advantages do accrue from piety; so that well may we conclude with St. Paul that *Godliness is profitable for all things.*

It remaineth that, if we be wise, we should if we yet have it not ingraffed in us, labour to acquire it. If we have it, that we should endeavour to improve it, by constant exercise, to the praise of God, the good of our neighbour, and our own comfort. Which that we may effectually perform, Almighty God in mercy vouchsafe, by His grace, through Jesus Christ Our Lord; to Whom for ever be all glory and praise. *Amen.*

## No. 345. JOSEPH HALL

[From *Epistles,* Fourth Decade, No. iii. *Works,* ed. Peter Hall (1837), Vol. VI, pp. 214 f. This Epistle is entitled " A Discourse of the Pleasure of Study and Contemplation; with the varieties of Scholar-like Employments; not without Incitation of others thereto; and a Censure of their Neglect," and was addressed to " Mr. Matthew Milward." Cp. note on No. 185.]

I can wonder at nothing more than how a man can be idle; but of all other a Scholar, in so many improvements of reason, in such sweetness of knowledge, in such variety of studies, in such importunity of thoughts.

Other artizans do but practise; we, still learn. Others run still in the same gyre, to weariness, to satiety; our choice is infinite. Other labours require recreations; our very labour recreates our sports. We can never want either somewhat to do, or somewhat that we would do.

How numberless are those volumes which men have written of arts, of tongues! How endless is that volume, which God hath written of the world, wherein every creature is a letter, every day a new page! Who can be weary of either of these? To find wit in poetry; in philosophy, profoundness; in mathematics, acuteness; in history, wonder of events; in oratory, sweet eloquence; in Divinity, supernatural light and holy devotion; as so many rich metals in their proper mines, whom would it not ravish with delight?

After all these, let us but open our eyes, we cannot look beside a lesson, in this universal Book of our Maker, worth our study, worth taking out. What creature hath not his miracle? What event doth not challenge his observation? And if, weary of foreign employment, we list to look home into ourselves, there we find a more private world of thoughts, which set us on work anew, more busily, not less profitably. Now our silence is vocal, our solitariness popular, and we are shut up to do good unto many.

And, if once we be cloyed with our own company, the door of conference is open. Here interchange of discourse, besides pleasure, benefits us; and he is a weak companion, from whom we return not wiser.

I could envy, if I could believe, that Anchorite who, secluded from the world and pent up in his voluntary prison-walls, denied that he thought the day long, while yet he wanted learning to vary his thoughts. Not to be cloyed with the same conceit is difficult above human strength; but, to a man so furnished with all sorts of knowledge that, according to his dispositions, he can change his studies, I should wonder that ever the sun should seem to pace slowly. How many busy tongues chase away good hours, in pleasant chat, and complain of the haste of night! What ingenuous mind can be soon weary of talking with learned authors, the most harmless and sweetest of companions? What a heaven lives a scholar in, that at once, in one close room, can daily converse with all the glorious Martyrs and Fathers, that can single out, at pleasure, either sententious Tertullian, or grave Cyprian, or resolute Jerome, or flowing Chrysostom, or divine Ambrose, or devout Bernard, or, who alone is all these, heavenly Augustine; and talk with them and hear their wise and holy counsels, verdicts, resolutions: yea, to rise higher, with courtly Isaiah, with learned Paul, with all their fellow-Prophets, Apostles: yet more, like another Moses, with God Himself, in them both! Let the world contemn us. While we have these delights, we cannot envy them: we cannot wish ourselves other than we are.

Besides, the way to all other contentments is troublesome: the only recompence is in the end. To delve in the mines, to scorch in the fire, for the getting, for the fining of gold, is a slavish toil: the comfort is in the wedge, to the owner, not the labourers; where our very search of knowledge is delightsome. Study itself is our life, from which we would not be barred for a world. How much sweeter then is the fruit of study, the conscience of knowledge! In comparison whereof, the soul that hath once tasted it, easily contemns all human comforts.

## No. 346. JOSEPH HALL

[From *Susurrium Cum Deo*, [*i.e.*] *Soliloquies, or Holy Self-Conferences of the Devout Soul upon Sundry Choice Occasions ; with Humble Addresses to the Throne of Grace*, Soliloquy No. XXIII. *Works*, ed. Peter Hall (1837), Vol. VIII, p. 252. This delightful collection of meditations was first published in 1651, when the author was 77 years of age; a second edition was called for in the same year.]

## The Body of Subjection

*Bodily exercise*, saith the Apostle, *profits little*,—little, sure, in respect of any worth that it hath in itself, or any thank that it can expect from the Almighty. For, what is it, to that good and great God, whether I be full or fasting; whether I wake or sleep; whether my skin be smooth or rough, ruddy or pale, white or discoloured; whether my hand be hard with labour or soft with ease; whether my bed be hard or yielding; whether my diet be coarse or delicate? But, though in itself it avail little, yet so it may be, and hath been, and ought to be improved, as that it may be found exceedingly beneficial to the soul. Else the same Apostle would not have said, *I keep under my body, and bring it into subjection, lest that by any means, when I have preached to others, I myself should be a cast-away.* In all the records of history, whom do we find more noted for holiness than those who have been most austere in the restraints of bodily pleasures and contentments? In the Mount of Tabor, who should meet with our Saviour in His Transfiguration but those two eminent Saints, which had fasted an equal number of days with Himself? And, our experience tells us that what is detracted from the body is added to the soul: for the flesh and spirit are not more partners than enemies, one gains by the other's loss. The pampering of the flesh is the starving of the soul. I find an unavoidable emulation between these two parts of myself. O God, teach me to hold an equal hand betwixt them both. Let me so use them, as holding the one my favourite, the other my drudge, not so humouring the worse part, as to discontent the better, nor so wholly regarding the better, as altogether to discourage the worse. Both are Thine, both by gift and purchase. Enable Thou me to give each of them their dues, so as the one may be fitted, with all humble obsequiousness to serve; the other, to rule and command, with all just authority and moderation.

## No. 347. JOSEPH HALL

[From *Occasional Meditations*, No. 44 (" Upon Hearing of Music by Night "). *Works*, ed. Peter Hall (1837), Vol. XI, p. 94. These *Meditations* were edited, when their author was occupied with his Episcopal duties as Bishop of Exeter, by his son, Robert Hall; they were published in 1630, and dedicated to the Viscount Doncaster. Joseph Hall later translated them into Latin with the title Αὐτοσχεδιάσματα, *vel Meditatiunculae Subitaneae èque re nata subortae*. The preface to this Latin Version is dated 1634. In Peter Hall's edition, the Latin is printed on the opposite page to the English.]

How sweetly doth this music sound, in this dead season! In the day-time, it would not, it could not, so much affect the ear. All harmonious sounds are advanced by a silent darkness.

Thus it is with the glad tidings of salvation. The Gospel never sounds so sweet, as in the night of persecution or of our own private affliction. It is ever the same. The difference is, in our disposition to receive it.

O God, Whose praise it is to give songs in the night, make my prosperity conscionable and my crosses cheerful.

## No. 348. JOSEPH HALL

[From *Christian Moderation, in Two Books.* " Introduction " to Book I (" Of Moderation in Matter of Practice "). *Works*, ed. Peter Hall (1837), Vol. VI, pp. 367 f. This treatise was first published in 1639, at a period in the author's life during which he was engaged in fierce controversy. It was dedicated " To all Christian people wheresoever, but especially to those of this Western Diocese [*i.e.* Exeter]."]

I cannot but second and commend that great Clerk of Paris, who (as our witty countryman Bromiard reports), when King Lewis of France required him to write down the best word that ever he had learnt, called for a fair skin of parchment, and in the midst of it wrote this one word MEASURE, and sent it sealed up to the King. The King, opening the sheet and 'finding no other inscription, thought himself mocked by his Philosopher, and calling for him expostulated the matter. But when it was shewed him, that all virtues and all religious and worthy actions were regulated by this one word, and that without this, virtue itself turned vicious, he rested well satisfied. And so he well might, for it was a word well worthy of one of the seven sages of Greece, from whom indeed it was borrowed, and only put into a new coat. . . . Neither could aught be spoken of more use or excellency ; for, what goodness can there be in the world without moderation, whether in the use of God's creatures or in our own disposition and carriage ? Without this, justice is no other than cruel rigour ; mercy, unjust remissness ; pleasure, brutish sensuality ; love, frensy ; anger, fury ; sorrow, desperate mopishness ; joy, distempered wildness ; knowledge, saucy curiosity ; piety, superstition ; care, wracking distraction ; courage, mad rashness. Shortly, there can be nothing under Heaven without it, but mere vice and confusion : like as in Nature, if the Elements should forget the temper of their due mixture, and encroach upon each other by excess, what could follow but universal ruin ? Or what is it that shall put an end to this great frame of the world, but the predominancy of that last devouring fire ? It is therefore Moderation by which this inferior world stands, since that wise and great God, Who hath ordained the continuance of it, hath decreed so to contemper all the parts thereof that none of them should exceed the bounds of their own proportion and degree, to the prejudice of the other. Yea, what is the Heaven itself, but (as Gerson compares it well) as a great clock regularly moving in an equal sway of all the orbs, without difference of poise, without variation of minutes in a constant state of eviternal evenness, both of being and motion ; neither is it any other, by which this little world of ours (whether of body or mind) is upheld in any safe or tolerable estate. When humours pass their stint, the body sickens; when passions, the mind.

There is nothing therefore in the world more wholesome or more necessary for us to learn than this gracious lesson of Moderation, without which, in very truth a man is so far from being a Christian, that he is not himself. This is the centre wherein all, both Divine and moral Philosophy meet; the rule of life, the governess of manners, the silken string that runs through the pearl-chain of all virtues, the very ecliptic-line, under which reason and religion move without any deviation, and therefore most worthy of our best thoughts, of our most careful observance.

### No. 349. THOMAS FULLER

[From *The Holy and Profane State*, Book III, ch. 20. Ed. 1652, p. 201. This work appeared in 1642. A transcription of it was made by the members of the Community at Little Gidding; the discovery of one such copy led *The Holy and Profane State* to be wrongly ascribed by Peckard to Ferrar.]

Moderation is like the silken string running through the pearl chain of all virtues. It appears both in practice and judgement. We will insist on the latter, and describe it first negatively.

Moderation is not an halting betwixt two opinions, when the thorough-believing of one of them is necessary to salvation. No pity is to be shewn to such voluntary cripples. We read (*Acts* xxvii, 12) of an haven in Crete *which lay toward the South-West and towards the North-West*; strange that it could have part of two opposite points, North and South,—sure, it must be very winding. And thus some men's souls are in such intricate postures, they lay towards the Papists and towards the Protestants. Such we count not of a moderate judgement, but of an immoderate unsettledness.

Nor is it a lukewarmness in those things wherein God's glory is concerned. Herein it is true a rule, *Non amat qui non zelat*. And they that are thus lukewarm here shall be too hot hereafter in that oven wherein dough-baked cakes shall be burnt.

But it is a mixture of discretion and charity in one's judgement. Discretion puts on a difference betwixt things absolutely necessary to salvation to be done and believed, and those which are of a second sort and lower form, wherein more liberty and latitude is allowed. In maintaining whereof, the stiffness of the judgement is abated and suppled with charity towards his neighbour. The lukewarm man eyes only his own ends and particular profit. The moderate man aims at the good of others and unity of the Church.

### No. 350. ROBERT BOYLE

[From *Some Motives and Incentives to the Love of God, Pathetically Discoursed of in a Letter to a Friend* (= " Seraphic Love "). *Works*, ed. London (1772), Vol. I, pp. 281 f. Cp. note on No. 124.]

But, Lindamor, before I proceed to set forth to you the greatness of the felicity reserved for us in heaven, it will, I fear, be requisite to mind you of the lawfulness of having an eye to it. For many not undeservedly applauded preachers have of .late been pleased to teach the people, that to hope for heaven is a mercenary, legal, and therefore unfilial affection. Indeed, to hope for heaven as wages for work performed or by way of merit, in the proper and strict acception of that term were a presumption, to which none of the Divines we dissent from, can be too much an enemy, nor perhaps more so than I am. But to take in God's blessings among the motives of loving God is but to do as he did, who said *I love the Lord because He hath heard my voice and my supplications* ; and to look upon the joys of heaven to comfort and support us in the hardships and losses to be undergone in our journey thitherward, is to imitate no worse a man than Moses, of whom it is said, that *he esteemed the reproach of Christ greater riches than the treasures in Egypt ; for he had respect* or ' turned his eye ' (ἀπέβλεπε) *unto the recompence of the reward.* It is indeed, Lindamor, a happy frame of mind to be able to love God purely for Himself, without any glance at our own advantages. But though I dare not deny that it is possible to attain to so high and disinterested a kind of love, yet I think that that excellency supposed to be vouchsafed to some men is not by the Scripture exacted as a duty from all men. Were all the recompense of piety of a worldly nature and to be here received, the actions invited to, by the intuition of it, might pass for mercenary. But when Heaven is chiefly hoped for as it will admit us unto the fruition of God Himself in Christ, and the other joys expected there are so far from being of a sensual or a worldly nature that they are known not to be˙attainable till by death the senses and bodies themselves and all the merely animal faculties be abolished, for a Heaven so considered, I say, to forego readily all the pleasures of the senses, and undergo cheerfully all the hardships and dangers that are wont to attend a holy life is, Lindamor, such a kind of mercenariness as none but a resigned, noble, and believing soul is likely to be guilty of. If I should say that fear itself, and even the fear of hell, may be one justifiable motive of men's actions, though I should propose what those I am reasoning with would think a paradox : yet I should perhaps hold forth therein no more than Scripture does, *Let us therefore fear* (says the writer to the Hebrews) *lest a promise being left us of entering into His rest, any of you shall seem to come short of it.*

## No. 351.  ROBERT BOYLE

[From *The Excellency of Theology Compared With Natural Philosophy* (*As both are Objects of Men's Study*), *Discoursed of in a Letter to a Friend ; To which are Annexed some Occasional Thoughts about the Excellency and Grounds of the Mechanical Hypothesis*, Part I, Section iii. *Works*, ed. London (1772), Vol. IV, pp. 31 f. This work was written in 1665, when the author was in retirement in the country, to avoid the Plague which was then raging in London. It was first published in 1674.]

And this leads me to the mention of the last advantage belonging to the study I would persuade you to, and indeed, the highest advantage that can recommend any study, or invite men to any undertaking. For this is no less than the everlasting fruition of the Divine objects of our studies hereafter, and the comfortable expectation of it here. For the employing of one's time and parts to admire the nature and providence of God and contemplate the Divine mysteries of religion, as it is one of the chief of those homages and services whereby we venerate and obey God, so it is one of those to which He hath been pleased to apportion no less a recompence than (that which can have no greater) the enjoyment of Himself. The Saints and Angels in Heaven have divers of them been employed to convey the truths of theology, and are solicitous to look into those sacred mysteries; and God hath been pleased to appoint that those men who study the same lessons that they do here, shall study them in their company hereafter. And doubtless, though Heaven abound with unexpressible joys, yet it will be none of the least that shall make up the happiness, even of that place, that the knowledge of Divine things, that was here so zealously pursued, shall there be completely attained. For those things that do here most excite our desires and quicken the curiosity and industry of our searches, will not only there continue, but be improved to a far greater measure of attractiveness and influence. For all those interests, and passions, and lusts, that here below either hinder us from clearly discerning, or keep us from sufficiently valuing, or divert us from attentively enough considering, the beauty and harmony of Divine truths, will there be either abolished or transfigured; and as the object will be unveiled, so our eye will be enlightened, that is, as God will there disclose those worthy objects of the Angels' curiosity, so He will enlarge our faculties to enable us to gaze, without being dazzled, upon those sublime and radiant truths, whose harmony, as well as splendour, we shall be then qualified to discover, and consequently with transports to admire. And this enlargement and elevation of our faculties will, proportionably to its own measure, increase our satisfaction at the discoveries it will enable us to make. For Theology is like a heaven, which wants not more stars than appear in it, but we want eyes, quick-sighted and piercing enough to reach them. And as the Milky Way and other whiter parts of the firmament have been full of immortal lights from the beginning, and our new telescopes have not placed, but found them, there; so, when Our Saviour, after His glorious Resurrection, instructed His Apostles to teach the Gospel, it is not said that He altered anything in the Scriptures of Moses and the Prophets, but only opened and enlarged their intellects that they might understand the Scriptures. And the royal Prophet makes it his prayer *That God would be pleased to open his eyes, that he might see wonderful things out of the Law*, being (as was above intimated) so well satisfied that the Word of God wanted not admirable things, that he is only solicitous for the improvement of his own eyes, that they might be qualified to discern them.

## No. 352.  RICHARD BAXTER

[From *The Divine Life*.  Part II, ch. v.  *Works*, ed. W. Orme (1830), Vol. XIII, pp. 223–225, 227 f.  Ed. London, 1838, Vol. IV, pp. 833 f., 834 f.  This treatise was first published in 1664.]

*Objection.*  But it may be the objector will be ready to think that if it be indeed our duty to walk with God, yet thoughts are no considerable part of it.  What more uncertain or mutable than our thoughts ?  It is deeds and not thoughts that God regardeth.  To do no harm to any but to do good to all, this is indeed to walk with God.  You set a man upon a troublesome and impossible work, while you set him upon so strict a guard, and so much exercise of his thoughts.  What cares the Almighty for my thoughts ?

*Answer* 1.  If God know better than you and be to be believed, then thoughts are not so inconsiderable as you suppose.  Doth He not say that *the thoughts of the wicked are an abomination to the Lord?* (*Prov.* xv, 26).  It is the work of the Gospel by its power, to *pull down strong holds, casting down imaginations, and every high thing that exalteth itself against the knowledge of God, and bringing into captivity every thought to the obedience of Christ* (*II Cor.* x, 4, 5).  The unrighteous man's forsaking his thoughts is part of his necessary conversion (*Isa.* lv, 7).  It was the description of the deplorate state of the old world, *God saw that the wickedness of man was great in the earth, and that every imagination of the thoughts of his heart was only evil continually ; and it repented the Lord that He had made man on the earth, and it grieved Him at His heart* (*Gen.* vi, 5 f.)  Judge by this whether thoughts be so little regarded by God, as you imagine.  David saith of himself *I hate vain thoughts* (*Psal.* cxix, 113).  Solomon saith *The thoughts of the righteous are right* (*Prov.* xii, 5).  Paul saith that *Charity thinketh not evil* (*I Cor.* xiii, 5).

2.  Thoughts are the issue of a rational soul.  And if its operations be contemptible, its essence is contemptible ; if its essence be noble, its operations are considerable.  If the soul be more excellent than the body, its operations must be more excellent.  To neglect our thoughts and not employ them upon God and for God, is to vilify our noblest faculties, and deny God, Who is a Spirit, that spiritual service which He requireth.

3.  Our thoughts are commonly our most cordial, voluntary acts, and show the temper and inclination of the heart ; and therefore are regardable to God that *searcheth the heart*, and calleth first for the service of the heart.

4. Our thoughts are radical and instrumental acts. Such as they are, such are the actions of our lives. Christ telleth us that *out of the heart proceed evil thoughts, murders, adulteries, fornications, thefts, false witness, blasphemies, which defile the man* (*Matt.* xv, 19, 20).

5. Our thoughts are under a law, as well as words and deeds. *The thought of foolishness is sin* (*Prov.* xxiv, 9). And *Matt.* v, 28, etc., Christ extendeth the Law even to the thoughts and desires of the heart. And under the Law it is said, *Beware that there be not a thought in thy wicked heart,* etc. (*Deut.* xv, 9), viz. of unmercifulness towards thy brother.

6. Thoughts can reach higher much than sense and may be employed upon the most excellent and invisible objects; and therefore are fit instruments to elevate the soul that would converse with God. Though God be infinitely above us, our thoughts may be exercised on Him; our persons never were in heaven and yet our conversation must be in heaven (*Phil.* iii, 20). And how is that but by our thoughts? Though we see not Christ, yet by the exercise of believing thoughts on Him we love Him, and rejoice with joy unspeakable and full of glory. Though God be invisible, yet our *meditations of Him may be sweet, and we may delight in the Lord* (*Psal.* civ, 34). Say not that all this is but fantastical and delusory as long as thoughts of things unseen are fitter to actuate and elevate the love, desires, and delights of the soul, and to move and guide us in a regular and holy life, than the sense of lesser present good. The thoughts are not vain or delusory, unless the object of them be false and vain, or delusory. Where the object is great and sure and excellent, the thoughts of such things are excellent operations of the soul. If the thoughts of vain-glory, wealth, and pleasure, can delight the ambitious, covetous, and sensual, no wonder if the thoughts of God and life eternal afford us solid, high delights.

7. The thoughts are not so liable to be counterfeit and hypercritical as are the words and outward deeds, and therefore they show more what the man is and what is in his heart. For as Solomon saith, *As he thinketh in his heart, so is he* (*Prov.* xxiii, 7).

8. Our thoughts may exercise the highest graces of God in man; and also show those graces, as being their effects. How is our faith and love and desire and trust and joy and hope to be exercised but by our thoughts? If grace were not necessary and excellent, it would not be wrought by the Spirit of God, and called the Divine Nature and the Image of God. And if the grace be excellent, the use and exercise of it is excellent: and therefore our thoughts by which it is exercised must needs have their excellency too. . . .

12. Lastly, The thoughts are the most constant actions of a man, and therefore most of the man is in them. We are not always reading or hearing or praying or working; but we are always thinking. And

therefore it doth especially concern us to see that this constant breath of the soul be sweet, and that this constant stream be pure, and run in the right channel. Well therefore did David make this his request: *Search me, O God, and know my heart : try me, and know my thoughts ; and see if there be any wicked way in me, and lead me in the way everlasting* (*Psal.* cxxxix, 23, 24). I say therefore to those that insist on this irrational objection, that these very thoughts of theirs concerning the inconsiderableness of thoughts are so foolish and ungodly, that when they understand the evil even of these, they will know that thoughts were more to be regarded. "If therefore thou hast done foolishly in lifting up thyself, or if thou hast thought evil, lay thy hand upon thy mouth."

## No. 353. EDWARD REYNOLDS

[From *The Staves of Beauty and Bands, Opened in a Sermon preached at Yarmouth, August* 23, 1663. *Works,* ed. London (1826), Vol. V, pp. 410–414. The text was *Zech.* xi, 7. It was published separately in the year in which it was delivered.]

As we read of Moses that his face shined when he came down from the Mount, to signify the glory and lustre of the legal ministry, as the Apostle teacheth us, so likewise do we read of Christ that His face shined as the sun in His Transfiguration on the Mount, to signify the far more excellent glory of the evangelical ministry of life and righteousness. In which respect He is called *the glory of His people,* and *a diadem of beauty unto the residue of them.* For where Christ walketh in the midst of the golden candlesticks, having His ordinances in their vigour and efficacy duly administered, He thereby rendereth His Church beautiful in these four respects :—

1. By the verity of His heavenly doctrine. When a people are taught of the Lord, then their stones are laid with fair colours and their foundations with sapphires, their windows of agates, their gates of carbuncles, and their borders of precious stones (*Isa.* liv, 11, 12, 13). When the earth is full of knowledge of the Lord, then is His rest, or the place of His abode, glorious (*Isa.* xi, 9, 10). And therefore when Christ was ascended up on high, far above all heavens, that He might fill all things, He gave unto His Church, Apostles, Prophets, Evangelists, Pastors, and Teachers, in order to the perfecting and edifying of His Body and carrying it on unto the measure of the stature of His fulness, wherein alone the beauty thereof consisteth.

2. By the purity of spiritual worship. When sacrifices are offered with acceptance upon God's altar (and none are so but spiritual sacrifices) then doth He glorify the House of His Glory and beautify the place of His Sanctuary and make it an eternal excellency; then doth He give gold for brass and silver for iron; then doth He call the walls of the Church salvation, and her gates praise (*Isa.* lx, 7, and xiii, 15, 17, 18). Therefore the Second Temple, though far inferior in outward

splendour to the former, is said to exceed that in glory; because unto it the *Desire of all Nations* should come and set up therein His spiritual worship (*Hag.* ii, 3, 7, 8, 9). For as the soul, which is the breath of life, puts beauty into the body, so the Spirit of Christ, poured out upon His Church, doth enliven and beautify that, and turn the wilderness into a fruitful field.

3. By sanctity of life, renewing them after the image of Christ. For when the Church is sanctified and cleansed with the washing of water by the Word, then it is fit to be presented unto Christ as a glorious Church (*Eph.* v, 26, 27). Holiness is called by the Apostle *the renewing of the Holy Ghost, the forming of Christ in us, the quickening and creating us in Him unto good works.* Look what beauty the renewing of a ruinous and decayed building bringeth upon that; what beauty the re-union of a living soul unto a ghastly body doth restore unto that; what beauty the creation brought upon the void and indigested chaos, when it was wrought unto that goodly frame and structure which we now behold. The same, and much more, doth the forming of Christ and the Spirit of Holiness bring upon our deformed and defiled nature by the efficacy of the ordinances.

4. By decency of order, rendering the Church *beautiful as Tirzah, comely as Jerusalem, terrible as an army with banners* (*Cant.* vi, 4). Thus the Church of Israel marched in the wilderness in the manner of a formed camp, with exquisite beauty and order, whereof we have an ample description (*Numb.* ii). In like manner, the New Jerusalem which descended out of heaven, beautified with the glory of God, whose street was pure gold as transparent glass, whose foundation was garnished with all manner of precious stones, is said to be four-square, having an accurate proportion and a symmetry in all the parts thereof (*Rev.* xxi, 16). And thus the Apostle directed *all things to be done* in the Church of Christ *with decency and order* (*I Cor.* xiv, 40), and rejoiced to see the order which was in the Church of the Colossians (*Col.* ii, 5). When every member keepeth his own rank and every officer doth his proper duty according to the pattern and·commission given him by Christ, then is the pastoral office administered with the *staff of Beauty*.

In one word, the ordinances are thus the beauty of a Church, because in and by them Christ is spiritually present therein, and the treasures of His grace are unfolded unto it. He Who is the chiefest among ten thousand and altogether lovely, Who was the Desire of all Nations and the hope of glory to His people, in comparison of Whose excellencies all other things are but loss and dung, Whose very afflictions and reproaches are preferred before the pleasure and riches of the world, in Whose very sufferings there is joy, He is in His ordinances evidently set forth before our eyes, His righteousness the robe wherewith His Church is clothed, His comeliness the beauty wherewith she is adorned and made high above all the people in praise, and in Name, and in honour, by her interest in Him, and relation unto Him. She hath a new Name given her, *Hephzibah*, " the Lord's delight," Who delighteth over her as the bridegroom over the bride, esteeming her His rest, His dwelling-place, His desire, so that glorious things are spoken of her.

These beauties of Christ in His ordinances, and in His Church by means of them, were typified and prefigured by the glorious garments of the priests; with allusion whereunto we are said in Baptism " to put on Christ," whose righteousness is unto His Church a garment of praise. By the splendour of the tabernacle and of Solomon's Temple and all the vessels and utensils belonging unto the worship of God therein, all which were exceeding glorious and magnificent, for the building and providing whereof, David prepared as immense a treasure as we shall likely read of in any history, in which respect that holy House is called the *throne of God's glory* (*Jer.* xiv, 21); by the city Jerusalem, the mountain of the Lord's holiness and the joy of the whole earth; by the holy oil, wherewith the tabernacle, the ark, the holy vessels and priests were anointed, compounded of the principal spices after the art of the apothecary; by the beautiful order which was in Solomon's family; by the dressing and preparing of a bride for the bridegroom, as we read of the long and costly purification of the virgins to go unto King Ahasuerus (*Esther* ii, 12). So here, in the ordinances, the spouse of Christ is attired and made ready, being arrayed in fine linen, clean and white, and thereby prepared unto glory and unto every good work. Lastly, by a straight, smooth, even, and pleasant path, wherein is no crookedness, from whence all stumbling-blocks and offences are removed.

The Author and Efficient of all this beauty is the Lord, all Whose works are perfect, Who hath made everything beautiful in His time. The sum and total of all God's works are the World and the Church; the world is called κόσμος, for the beauty and comeliness of it; in which, everything was very good when the Lord took a view of it. But the Lord hath chosen His Church, upon which to bestow more abundant glory. It is called a land of ornament (*Dan.* xi, 16), a land of desire (*Jer.* iii, 1); in the building whereof the Lord is said to appear in His glory (*Psal.* cii, 16). The World is beautified with the power and wisdom of God; the Church, besides that, with His love and grace. In the World we have the foot-prints of His greatness; but in the Church we have the image of His holiness. The World was made by Him, the Church like Him; the World to show forth His glory, the Church to enjoy it; the World a tenement for His creatures to dwell in, the Church a palace for Himself to dwell in. He hath desired it for His habitation; it is His rest for ever. Above all excellencies, holiness is the beauty of a creature; and therefore the Angels, who excel in all created perfection, are, above all other appellations, honoured with the name of 'Saints' (*Deut.* xxxiii, 2). They differ not in nature from devils; in holiness, they do. Derived holiness consisteth in conformity to primitive holiness. The Lord is most holy in Himself; and our holiness standeth in His Image and likeness, so far forth as He hath, by a holy law, made His holiness a pattern for ours. And when we threw away that Image of God wherein our created holiness consisted, and the Lord was pleased in any of us to renew it again, He did it by the pattern of His Beloved Son, Who is the Image of the invisible God and the character of His person, full of grace and truth. Now then, according to the excellency of the pattern, we are to measure and take an estimate of that beauty, wherein we are conformable unto that pattern; and what pattern more glorious than the blessed God, and the holy Son of God, the chiefest of ten thousand?,—unto Whom, therefore, the conformity of a creature must be its chief and principal beauty.

## No. 354.　EDWARD REYNOLDS

[From *The Brand Plucked Out of the Fire*. *Works*, ed. London (1826), Vol. V, pp. 189 f. This was a Sermon preached at St. Paul's before the Lord Mayor, Alder-men, and Companies of London, on November 5, 1659, and published in the same year. The text was *Zech.* iii, 1 f.]

We live in failing times. We have found men of low degree vanity, and men of high degree a lie. We have leaned on our house, but it did not stand; we have leaned on our staff, and it hath gone into our hand. We trusted too much in Parliaments, and they have been broken; in Princes, and they have given up the ghost: *Nec vitia nec remedia ferre possumus.* We have been afflicted both with our diseases and with our remedies. Fear, and the pit, and the snare have been upon us. We have been changed from vessel to vessel, and we break every vessel we are put into. Our ships have been broken, our trade broken, our estates broken, our government broken, our hopes broken, our Church broken; nothing but our hearts and our sins, unbroken. A sad thing, that a people will be quite fatherless, before they will think of going to God; that they will have their way hedged up with thorns, before they will resolve to return to their first husband; that they will be brought to husks, before they will come to themselves and go to their Father; that they will be brought to such extremities as not to know what to do, before they will have their eyes upon the Lord. Well; it hath been our sin, and our folly, to trust in broken reeds, in dying and perishing comforts. Let it, at last, before the Ephah be sealed, before the decree bring forth, be our wisdom and our faith to trust in the living God; and, by repentance and humiliation, to remove our sins from between God and us. And then no other impossibilities can obstruct the passage of mercy unto us; nothing can any more hinder the fulfilling of an Evangelical promise than of a prophetical vision.

## No. 355.  WILLIAM SANCROFT

[From *A Sermon preached in St. Peter's Westminster on the First Sunday in Advent* [December 2, 1660], *at the Consecration of the Right Reverend Fathers in God, John* [Cosin], *Lord Bishop of Durham, William* [Lucy], *Lord Bishop of St. David's, Benjamin* [Laney], *Lord Bishop of Peterborough, Hugh* [Lloyd], *Lord Bishop of Llandaff, Richard* [Sterne], *Lord Bishop of Carlisle, Brian* [Walton], *Lord Bishop of Chester, and John* [Gauden], *Lord Bishop of Exeter.* This sermon is reprinted in G. D'Oyly, *Life of William Sancroft* (London, 1821), Vol. II, Appendix iv. The extract is from pp. 347 f. The occasion, of course, was a very famous one, when several of the sees which had been vacant for some years were filled again. The text of the sermon, which was dedicated to Cosin, was *Titus* i, 5.]

Blest be the mercies of God, we are at last returned, and Titus is come back into Crete; and there are elders ordained for every city. But *hic Rhodus, hic Saltus.* Reverend Father, this is your Crete, adorn it as you can. The province is hard, and the task weighty and formidable, even to an Angel's shoulders. That we mistake not, Titus was not left behind in Crete to take his ease, or to sleep out the storm which soon after overtook St. Paul at sea; he might well expect a worse at land (*naufragium terrestre*) and a more tempestuous Euroclydon. Believe it, a Bishop's robe is *Tunica molesta* (as the martyr's pitched coat was called of old), and sits perhaps more uneasy upon the shoulders. The mitre is not Ὅρκου γαλέη, to render invisible or invulnerable, but rather exposeth to enemies; the rotchet and the surplice, emblems of innocence indeed, but marks of envy too; and it is in those whites that malice sticks all her darts. And, therefore, St. Paul was fain to intreat Timothy into this dignity. *For this cause besought I thee, to abide at Ephesus*; for there were beasts to be fought with there, and the Apostle had tried them, both tooth and paw. So that I cannot wonder if our Bishops say *nolo episcopari* in good earnest. And if any of our Zarahs thrust forth a hasty hand and be laid hold on, and the scarlet thread cast about his finger, it is not strange if he draw back his hand and refuse the primogeniture; choosing rather to lie hid in obscurity, *quam vinctus purpura progredi*, as the great [Baronius] wittily alludes. As in Crete new founded, so in England new restored, there must needs be many things wanting, and much amiss, not so easily to be supplied or amended.

## No. 356.  GILBERT SHELDON

[From a letter written by Sheldon to an absentee Bishop. Vernon Staley, *The Life and Times of Gilbert Sheldon* (London, 1913), pp. 118 f.; the original letter is in the Tanner MSS. (Vol. xxxvi, fol. 190) at the Bodleian. Staley states that the exact date of the letter is not known, though it must have been after Sheldon's elevation to the See of Canterbury in 1663.]

My Lord,—Since neither the duty you owe to your Diocese as you are a Bishop, nor anything that I have said to you by word of mouth, has been prevalent to carry you down to your Bishopric, to make your personal residence there that thereby the several ends for which you were ordained a Bishop might be fulfilled, but that you still remain in and about London without any just cause that you have made appear to me, I have thought fit by writing to you at this time upon the same subject to shew how serious I am in that particular and to tell you once more that I do expect you should forthwith and without any delay go down to your Bishopric and make your residence there; for if you will not perform that Episcopal duty that is incumbent upon you, yet I must and ought to do that which lies upon me as I am your Metropolitan, which is to see that done by you which you do so grossly neglect and which your Episcopal function requires at your hands. Since, therefore, I do hereby require no more from you than· what by the nature of your function or the Laws Ecclesiastical of this nation you are to perform, I do expect that you should comply therewith and put the same presently in execution. And albeit I should be very unwilling to take any public rigorous course with you, yet if this which I now require from you be not obeyed forthwith you must expect to hear further from me in another way which if it puts you to any open shame it is your own fault when gentler means were used that could not prevail.

## No. 357. JOHN DONNE

[From *Divine Poems*, " The Cross." *The Poems of John Donne*, ed. H. J. C. Grierson, Oxford (1929), pp. 302–304. This poem was probably written about the year 1609 (Grierson, ' Introduction,' p. xli).]

### The Cross.

Since Christ embraced the Cross itself, dare I
His image, th'image of His Cross deny?
Would I have profit by the sacrifice
And dare the chosen Altar to despise?
It bore all other sins, but is it fit
That it should bear the sin of scorning it?
Who from the picture would avert his eye,
How would he fly His pains, Who there did die?
From me, no Pulpit, nor misgrounded law,
Nor scandal taken, shall this Cross withdraw.
It shall not, for it cannot; for the loss
Of this Cross, were to me another Cross.
Better were worse, for no affliction,
No Cross is so extreme, as to have none.
Who can blot out the Cross, which th'instrument
Of God, dewed on me in the Sacrament?
Who can deny me power and liberty

To stretch mine arms, and mine own Cross to be ?
Swim, and at every stroke thou art thy Cross ;
The Mast and Yard make one, where seas do toss ;
Look down, thou spiest out Crosses in small things ;
Look up, thou seest birds raised on crossed wings ;
All the globe's frame, and sphere's, is nothing else
But the meridians crossing parallels.
Material Crosses, then, good physic be
But yet spiritual have chief dignity.
These for extracted chimique medicine serve,
And cure much better, and as well preserve ;
Then are you your own physic, or need none,
When stilled, or purged by tribulation.
For when that Cross ungrudged unto you sticks,
Then are you to yourself a Crucifix.
As perchance, carvers do not faces make
But that away, which hid them there, do take.
Let Crosses, so, take what hid Christ in thee,
And be His Image, or not His, but He.
But as oft alchemists do coiners prove,
So may a self-despising get self-love ;
And then as worst surfeits of best meats be,
So is pride, issued from humility,
For 'tis no child, but monster ; therefore cross
Your joy in Crosses, else 'tis double loss
And cross thy senses else both they and thou
Must perish soon, and to destruction bow.
For if th'eye seek good objects, and will take
No Cross from bad, we cannot scape a snake.
So with harsh, hard, sour, stinking, cross the rest,
Make them indifferent all ; call nothing best.
But most the eye needs crossing, that can roam
And move ; to th'other th'objects must come home.
And cross thy heart ; for that in man alone
Points downwards and hath palpitation.
Cross those dejections, when it downward tends,
And when it to forbidden heights pretends.
And as the brain through bony walls doth vent
By sutures, which a Cross's form present,
So when thy brain works, ere thou utter it,
Cross and correct concupiscence of wit.
Be covetous of Crosses, let none fall.
Cross no man else, but cross thyself in all.
Then doth the Cross of Christ work fruitfully

Within our hearts, when we love harmlessly
That Cross's pictures much, and with more care
That Cross's children, which our Crosses are.

## No. 358.  THOMAS TRAHERNE

[From *Centuries of Meditations* (ed. 1927), First Century, No. 93 (pp. 68 f.) ; Third Century, No. 46 (p. 186).   These Meditations were not discovered until about thirty years ago ;  they were edited by Bertram Dobell and published in 1908.  See B. Dobell's ' Introduction ' in his edition.]

As my body without my soul is a carcase, so is my soul without Thy Spirit a Chaos, a dark, obscure heap of empty faculties ; ignorant of itself, unsensible of Thy goodness, blind to Thy glory ;  dead in sins and trespasses.  Having eyes I see not, having ears I hear not, having an heart I understand not the glory of Thy works and the glory of Thy Kingdom.  O Thou Who art the root of my being and the Captain of my salvation, look upon me.  Quicken me, O Thou life-giving and quickening seed.  Visit me with Thy light and Thy truth ; let them lead me to Thy Holy Hill and make me to see the greatness of Thy love in all its excellencies, effects, emanations, gifts, and operations. O my Wisdom !  O my Righteousness, Sanctification, and Redemption ! Let Thy wisdom enlighten me, let Thy knowledge illuminate me, let Thy Blood redeem me, wash me and clean me, let Thy merits justify me, O Thou Who art equal unto God, and didst suffer for me.  Let Thy righteousness clothe me.  Let Thy Will imprint the form of itself upon mine ;  and let my will become conformable to Thine, that Thy Will and mine may be united, and made one for evermore.

When I came into the country, and being seated among silent trees and meads and hills had all my time in mine own hands, I resolved to spend it all, whatever it cost me, in search of happiness and to satiate that burning thirst which Nature had enkindled in me from my youth. In which I was so resolute, that I chose rather to live upon ten pounds a year, and to go in leather clothes, and feed upon bread and water, so that I might have all my time clearly to myself, than to keep many thousands per annum in an estate of life where my time would be devoured in care and labour.  And God was so pleased to accept of that desire, that from that time to this I have had all things plentifully provided for me, without any care at all, my very study of Felicity making me more to prosper than all the care in the whole world. So that through His blessing I live a free and a kingly life as if the world were turned again into Eden, or much more, as it is at this day.

## No. 359. ANTHONY HORNECK

[From *The Fire of the Altar ; or Certain Directions How to raise the Soul into Holy Flames Before, At, and After the Receiving the Blessed Sacrament of the Lord's Supper, With suitable Prayers and Devotions ; To which is prefixed a Dialogue betwixt a Christian and his own Conscience concerning the true Nature of the Christian Religion*, London, 1683, pp. 34 f. (From the section headed " Conscience.") The fact that this devotional manual was " intended chiefly for the inhabitants of St. Mary le Strand and the precinct of the Savoy " (title-page) did not hinder it from securing a very wide circulation. By 1718 it had reached a thirteenth edition.]

O whither shall I go but to Thee, Who hast words of Eternal Life ! Thou art my Sun ; by Thee I shall be enlightened, by Thee my soul shall be warmed. O how comfortable are Thy beams ! What a progress must that soul make on which Thou shinest, and dartest Thy glorious rays ! Thou art that lofty cedar, whose boughs overspread the believing world !

Under the shadow of that tree will I rest. It is for the healing of the nations. I will be glad in the Lord and rejoice in my bleeding Jesus. While the world despises Thee, I will honour Thee. While great men pass by and regard Thee not, I that am poor and needy will wait to be refreshed by Thee.

Go ye fools ! Be enamoured with your trifles. Admire your butterflies. Doat on your sensual pleasures. Here is One that looks charming in His tears, lovely in His blood, amiable in His wounds, and is more beautiful in the midst of all His distresses than the brightest virgin's face, adorned with all the glittering treasures of the East !

## No. 360. ROBERT SOUTH

[From *Twelve Sermons Upon Several Subjects and Occasions* (Vol. III of South's *Sermons*), London (1698), pp. 174-182. From the Sermon entitled " False Foundations Removed and True Ones laid for Such Wise Builders as design to build for Eternity." It was preached before the University of Oxford on December 10, 1661, in St. Mary the Virgin's. The text was *Matt.* vii, 26 f.]

But that the very life of Religion consists in practice will appear yet further from those subordinate ends to which it is designed in this world, and which are as really, though not as principally, the purpose of it as the utmost attainment of the beatific vision and the very last period of our Salvation. And these are two.

First, The honouring of God before the world. God will not have His Worship, like His Nature, invisible. Next to authority itself is the pomp and manifestation of it. And to be acknowledged is something more than to be obeyed. For what is Sovereignty unknown, or Majesty unobserved ? What glory were it for the sun to direct the affairs, if he did not also attract the eyes, of the world ? It is his open and universal light more than his occult influence that we love and admire him for. Religion, if confined to the heart, is not so much entertained, as imprisoned. That indeed is to be its fountain, but not its channel.

The water arises in one place, but it streams in another; and fountains would not be so much valued if they did not produce rivers.

One great end of Religion is to proclaim and publish God's Sovereignty, and there is no such way to cause men to *glorify our Heavenly Father*, as by *causing our light to shine before them*; which, I am sure, it cannot do, but as it beams through our good works. When a man leads a pious and good life, every hour he lives is virtually an act of worship. But if inward grace is not exerted and drawn forth into outward practice, men have no inspection into our hearts to discern it there. And let this be fixed upon as a standing principle, That it is not possible for us to honour God before men, but only by those acts of worship that are observeable by men. It is our faith indeed that recognizes Him for Our God, but it is our obedience only that declares Him to be Our Lord.

Secondly, The other end of Religion in this world, is the good and mutual advantage of mankind in the way of society. And herein did the admirable Wisdom and the Goodness of God appear, that He was pleased to calculate and contrive such an instrument to govern as might also benefit the world. God planted Religion amongst men as a Tree of Life; which, though it was to spring upwards directly to Himself, yet it was to spread its branches to the benefit of all below.

There is hardly any necessity or convenience of mankind, but what is in a large measure served and provided for by this great blessing (as well as business) of the world, religion. And he who is a Christian is not only a better man, but also a better neighbour, a better subject, and a truer friend than he that is not so. For was ever anything more for the good of mankind than to forgive injuries, to love and caress our mortal adversaries, and instead of our enemy, to hate only our revenge?

Of such a double yet benign aspect is Christianity, both to God and Man. Like incense, while it ascends to Heaven, it perfumes all about it; at the same time both instrumental to God's Worship, and the worshippers' refreshment. As it holds up one hand in supplication, so it reaches forth the other in benefaction.

But now, if it be one great end of Religion, thus to contribute to the support and benefit of society, surely it must needs consist in the active piety of our lives, not in empty thoughts and fruitless persuasions. For what can one man be the better for what another thinks or believes? When a poor man begs an alms of me, can I *believe* my bread into his mouth, or my money into his hand? Believing without Doing is a very cheap and easy, but withal a very worthless way of being religious.

And thus, having given the reasons why the active part of Religion is the only sure bottom for us to build upon, I now proceed to the second thing proposed, namely to shew those false and sandy foundations, which many venture to build upon, and are accordingly deceived by. Which though they are exceedingly various and, according to the multiplicity of men's tempers, businesses, and occasions, almost infinite, and like the sand mentioned in my text [i.e. *Matt.* vii, 26 f.], not only infirm, but numberless also ; yet according to the best of my poor judgement and observance, I shall reduce them to these . . . heads.

The First of which, is a naked, unoperative, faith. Ask but some upon what grounds they look to be saved, and they will answer, " Because they firmly believe, that through the merits of Christ their sins are forgiven them." But since it is hard for a man in his right wits to be confident of a thing, which he does not at all know, such as are more cautious will tell you further, " That to desire to believe is to believe, and to desire to repent is to repent." But as this is absurd and impossible, since no act can be its own object without being not itself, forasmuch as the act and the object are distinct things, and consequently a desire to believe can no more be belief, than a desire to be saved can be salvation ; so it is further intolerable upon this account that it quite dispirits Religion, by placing it in languid, abortive velleities, and so cuts the nerves of all endeavour, by rating glory at a bare desire, and eternity at a wish.

But because the poison of this opinion does so easily enter and so strangely intoxicate, I shall presume to give an antidote against it in this one observation, namely, That all along the Scripture where Justification is ascribed to Faith alone, there the word " Faith " is still used by a metonymy of the antecedent for the consequent, and does not signify abstractedly a mere persuasion, but the obedience of an holy life performed in the strength and virtue of such a persuasion. Not that this justifies *meritoriously* by any inherent worth or value in itself, but *instrumentally* as a condition appointed by God, upon the performance of which He freely imputes to us Christ's Righteousness, which is the sole, proper and formal cause of our Justification. So that, that Instrumentality which some, in the business of Justification, attribute to one single act of credence, is by this ascribed to the whole aggregate series of Gospel Obedience, as being that which gives us a title to a perfect Righteousness without us, by which alone we stand justified before God. And this seems with full accord both to Scripture and Reason to state the business of justification by an equal poise both against the arrogant assertions of Self-Justiciaries on the one hand and the wild opinions of the Antinomians on the other.

But whether the obedience of a pious life, performed out of a belief or persuasion of the truth of the Gospel, ought to pass for that faith which justifies, or only for the effect or consequent of it, yet certainly it is such an effect as issues by a kind of con-natural, constant efficiency

and result from it.   So that how much so ever they are distinguishable
by their respective actions from one another, they are absolutely inseparable by a mutual and a necessary connexion ; it belonging no less
to the faith which justifies to be operative than to justify,—indeed,
upon an essential account, more ; forasmuch as it is operative by its
nature, but justifies only by institution.

Secondly, The second false ground which some build upon is a
fond reliance upon the goodness of their heart and the honesty of their
intention.   A profitable, and therefore a very prevailing fallacy, and
such an one as the Devil seldom uses but with success ; it being one of
his old and long experimental fetches, by the pretences of a good heart
to supplant the necessity of a good life.   But to allege the honesty of
the mind against the charge of an evil course is a protestation against
the fact which does not excuse, but enhance its guilt.   As it would look
like a very strange and odd commendation of a tree to apologize for
the sourness of its fruit, by pleading that all its goodness lay in the root.

### No. 361.  JOHN EVELYN

[From *The History of Religion ;   A Rational Account of the True Religion*, Vol. I,
ch. v, § 1.   Pp. 260 f., 264.   This treatise remained unpublished until it was edited, with
notes, by the Reverend R. M. Evanson in two volumes in 1850.   Evelyn began to write
it in 1657.]

Religion, as being the highest reason, is that alone which makes
mankind to differ from brute animals,—because it renders him like his
great Creator, rectifying the depravity of his nature which, if unculti-
vated by religion, becomes fierce and sensual.   But religion and the
sense of a Deity, or some transcendently excellent being, purifies the
soul and refines our nature by virtue of its precepts,—there being no
creature besides that can actually and intentionally address its powers
and faculties to God.   Wherefore to be religious is more truly the formal distinction between men and beasts than all that the philosophers
have furnished to its definition ;   and therefore more adequate to his
character than either polity, society, risibility, without which he were
no reasonable creature, but a mere brute, the very worst of the kind.
There is, indeed, among brute animals some imperfect traces of all the
perfections and qualities of man, excepting that of religion.   But with
all this, they apprehend neither God, angel, or intelligence.   And therefore Gesner, I remember, concludes that pygmies (those diminutive
people, or sort of apes or satyrs, so much resembling the little men
storied under that name) are therefore not of human race because they
have no religion.

It is true that all entities and beings whatsoever love that which is
good, and does them good.   And, as David says, *there is none good but
God* ;  and therefore those who love good do consequently love God,
metaphysically speaking ;  and the love of God being the sum of all

religion, all who love that which is good **are** religious.   But if this love
of good flows not from an intellectual principle, it is not properly
religion, which is among all nations and people competent only to
mankind,—that is, such an impression as enables him to offer the Deity
a rational and spiritual worship. . . .

Thus religion qualifies the Christian and enlarges the understanding,
enabling us to discern beyond the narrow confines and scantling of
brutish sense and stupid ignorance, to behold and contemplate things
invisible and spiritual.   And this creates an habitual reverence to some
Superior Being, more excellent than ourselves, and incites us to such
devotion and services as we apprehend to be most agreeable to His
nature.   And this, since it cannot be performed without some rites and
solemnities, lies in a system of all those mysteries which concern the
knowledge and service of the Deity to be worshipped, and in that
manner and way alone He prescribes.

## No. 362.  RALPH CUDWORTH

[From *Mr. Cudworth's Sermon preached before the House of Commons at Westminster*,
*March* 31, 1647.   Cambridge, 1852, pp. 16–21.   The text of this sermon was *I John*,
ii, 3 f., and it was published with a dedication to the House of Commons.   In it
Cudworth issued a timely protest against the importance which the Puritans attached to
dogmatic *minutiae*.]

If hereby we are to judge whether we truly know Christ, by our
keeping of His commandments, so that *he that saith he knoweth Him
and keepeth not His commandments is a liar*, then this was not the plot
and design of the Gospel, to give the world an indulgence to sin, upon
what pretence soever ; though we are too prone to make such mis-
constructions of it as if God had intended nothing else in it, but to
dandle our corrupt nature and contrive a smooth and easy way for us to
come to happiness, without the toilsome labour of subduing our lusts
and sinful affections.   Or, as if the Gospel were nothing else but a
declaration to the world of God's engaging His affections from all
eternity on some particular persons, in such a manner as that He would
resolve to love them and dearly embrace them, though He never made
them partakers of His Image in righteousness and true holiness ; and
though they should remain under the power of all their lusts, yet they
should still continue His beloved ones and He would, notwithstanding,
at last bring them undoubtedly into heaven.   Which is nothing else but
to make the God that we worship, the God of the New Testament, a
προσωπολήπτης, an Accepter of Persons ;  and one that should encourage
that in the world which is diametrally opposite to God's own life and
being.   And indeed nothing is more ordinary than for us to shape out
such monstrous and deformed notions of God unto ourselves, by
looking upon Him through the coloured medium of our own corrupt
hearts, and having the eye of our soul tinctured by the suffusions

of our own lusts. And therefore, because we mortals can fondly love and hate, and sometimes hug the very vices of those to whom our affections are engaged and kiss their very deformities, we are so ready to shape out a Deity like unto ourselves and to fashion out such a God as will in Christ at least hug the very wickedness of the world ; and in those that be once His own, by I know not what fond affection, appropriated to Himself, connive at their very sins so that they shall not make the least breach betwixt Himself and them. Truly, I know not whether of the two be the worse idolatry and of the deeper stain, for a man to make a God out of a piece of wood, and *fall down unto it and worship it and say " Deliver me, for thou art my God,"* as it is expressed in the Prophet Isaiah, or to set up such an idol-god of our own imagination as this is, fashioned out according to the similitude of our own fondness and wickedness ; and when we should paint out God with the liveliest colours that we can possibly borrow from any created being, with the purest perfections that we can abstract from them, to draw Him out thus with the blackest coal of our own corrupt hearts, and to make the very blots and blurs of our own souls to be the letters which we spell out His name by. Thus do we that are Children of the Night, made [= " make "] black and ugly representations of God unto ourselves as the Ethiopians were wont to do, copying Him out according to our own likeness, and setting up that unto ourselves for a God which we love most dearly in ourselves, that is, our lusts. But there is no such God as this anywhere in the world but only in some men's false imaginations, who know not all this while that they look upon themselves instead of God, and make an idol of themselves which they worship and adore for Him ; being so full of themselves that whatsoever they see round about them, even God Himself, they colour with their own tincture, like him that Aristotle speaks of, that wheresoever he went and whatsoever he looked upon, he saw still his own face, as in a glass, represented to him. And therefore it is no wonder if men seem naturally more devoutly affected towards such an imaginary God as we have now described, than to the true real God, clothed with His own proper attributes ; since it is nothing but an image of themselves which, Narcissus-like, they fall in love with. No wonder if they kiss and dandle such a baby-god as this which like little children they have dressed up out of the clouts of their own fond fancies, according to their own likeness, of purpose that they might play and sport with it. But God will ever dwell in spotless light, howsoever we paint Him and disfigure Him here below. He will still be circled about with His own rays of unstained and immaculate glory. And though the Gospel be not God, as He is in His own brightness, but God veiled and masked to us, God in a state of humiliation and condescendent as the sun in a rainbow, yet it is nothing else but a clear and unspotted mirror of Divine holiness, goodness, purity, in which attributes lies the very life and essence of God Himself. The Gospel is nothing else but God, descending into the world in our form and conversing with us in our likeness, that He might allure and draw us up to God and make us partakers of His Divine form. Θεὸς γέγονεν ἄνθρωπος (as Athanasius speaks) ἵνα ἡμᾶς ἐν ἑαυτῷ θεοποιήσῃ ; " God was therefore incarnated and made man, that He might deify us," that is (as St. Peter expresseth it), *make us partakers of the Divine Nature*.

Now, I say, the very proper character and essential tincture of God Himself is nothing else but goodness. Nay, I may be bold to add that God is therefore God because He is the highest and most perfect good ; and good is not therefore good, because God out of an arbitrary Will of His would have it so. Whatsoever God doth in the world, He doth it as it is suitable to the highest goodness, the first idea and fairest copy of which is His own essence. Virtue and holiness in creatures, as Plato well discourseth in his *Euthyphro*, are not therefore good because God loveth them and will have them be accounted such, but rather God therefore loveth them because they are in themselves simply good. Some of our own authors go a little further yet and tell us that God doth not fondly love Himself because He is Himself, but therefore He loveth Himself because He is the highest and most absolute goodness ; so that if there could be anything in the world better than God, God would love that better than Himself. But because He is essentially the most perfect good, therefore He cannot but love His own goodness infinitely above all other things. And it is another mistake which sometimes we have of God by shaping Him out according to the model of ourselves, when we make Him nothing but a blind, dark, impetuous self-will, running through the world, such as we ourselves are furiously acted with that have not the ballast of absolute goodness to poise and settle us. That I may therefore come nearer to the thing in hand, God Who is absolute goodness cannot love any of His creatures and take pleasure in them without bestowing a communication of His goodness and likeness upon them. God cannot make a Gospel to promise men life and happiness hereafter without being regenerated and made partakers of His holiness. As soon may heaven and hell be reconciled together, and lovingly shake hands with one another, as God can be fondly indulgent to any sin in whomsoever it be. As soon may light and darkness be espoused together and midnight be married to the noon-day, as God can be joined in a league of friendship to any wicked soul.

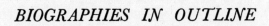

*BIOGRAPHIES IN OUTLINE*

[*These Biographies have been compiled for the convenience of students, in most cases from the standard works of reference. It has not been possible to verify from contemporary sources all the facts referred to, though it is believed that the information contained in them will be found reasonably accurate. The numbered references to the extracts at the beginning of each entry are intended to serve the purpose of an index of authors.*]

## ANDREWES, Lancelot (1555–1626). Nos. 91, 174, 200, 201, 215, 218, 251, 252, 253, 297, 312.

Born at Barking. Educated at Merchant Taylors' and Pembroke Hall, Cambridge. Elected Fellow, 1576, and Fellow of Jesus College, Oxford, in the same year. Ordained, and appointed Catechist at Pembroke College, 1580. Presented to the living of St. Giles', Cripplegate; Prebendary of St. Paul's; and Master of Pembroke, 1589. Prebendary of Westminster, 1597. Dean of Westminster, 1601. Bishop of Chichester, 1605; of Ely, 1609; of Winchester, 1619. Buried in St. Saviour's, Southwark.

*Works.* *Tortura Torti* (1609); *Responsio ad Apologiam Cardinalis Bellarmini* (1610; cp. No. **200**); *Ninety-Six Sermons* (1629, first collected edition; cp. No. **201**); *Two Answers to Cardinal Perron* (1629, posthumous; cp. No. **218**); *A Pattern of Catechistical Doctrine* (1630, posthumous; cp. No. **91**); *Preces Privatae* (1648; ed. by Richard Drake). Also drew up a number of Forms of Service; cp. No. **251**.

*Collected Edition, L. A. C. T.*

## [Arminian Nunnery, The. No. 340.]

## BACON, Francis (1561–1626). No. 97.

Son of Sir Nicholas Bacon, Lord Keeper of the Great Seal. Educated at Trinity College, Cambridge. Entered Gray's Inn, 1576. M.P., 1584. Knighted and appointed King's Counsel by James I, 1603. Attorney-General, 1613. Privy Councillor, 1616. Created Lord Chancellor and Baron Verulam, 1618. Led Prosecutions of Raleigh, 1618, and of Suffolk, 1619. Viscount St. Alban's, 1621. Charged before House of Lords with bribery, and admitted " corruption and neglect." Deprived of all his offices and committed to the Tower, 1621; but soon afterwards released.

*Works.* Include his *Essays* (1597; cp. No. **97**); *The Advancement of Learning* (1605); *Novum Organon* (1620). Numerous editions.

*Lives.* J. Spedding (1861); T. Fowler (1881); R. W. Church (1884).

## BARLOW, Thomas (1607–1691). No. 75.

Born at Orton, Westmoreland. Educated at Appleby Grammar School and Queen's College, Oxford. B.A., 1630. Fellow, 1633. Bodley's Librarian, 1642. Provost of Queen's, 1657. Lady Margaret Professor and Canon of Worcester (the Canonry was then annexed to the Professorship), 1660. Archdeacon of Oxford, 1661. Bishop of Lincoln, 1675. Died at Buckden, and buried in the Parish Church.

*Works.* *Exercitationes aliquot Metaphysicae de Deo* (1637); *Pegasus, or the Flying Horse from Oxford* (1648); *Concerning the Invocation of Saints*

(1679); *Plain Reasons why a Protestant of the Church of England should not turn Roman Catholic* (1688; cp. No. **75**); *Cases of Conscience* (1692, posthumous).

**BARROW, Isaac (1630–1677). Nos. 27, 101, 115, 120, 121, 127, 128, 131, 222, 344.**

Born in London. Son of the Linendraper to Charles I. Educated at Charterhouse and Felstead; and at Trinity College, Cambridge. Scholar, 1647. B.A., 1648. Fellow, 1649. Travelled, 1655–9. Ordained by Bishop Brownrigg, 1659. Regius Professor of Greek, Cambridge, 1660. Professor of Geometry at Gresham College. First Lucasian Professor of Mathematics, 1663; resigned in favour of Isaac Newton, 1669. Chaplain to Charles II, and D.D. by Royal Mandate, 1670. Master of Trinity, 1672. Buried in Westminster Abbey.

*Works.* *A Treatise of the Pope's Supremacy* (1680, posthumous; cp. No. **27**); Many *Sermons* (cp. Nos. **101, 115, 121, 127, 128, 131, 344**) and *Lectures* (cp. Nos. **120, 222**). Also famous scientific works.

*Collected Editions.* By Tillotson, 4 vols., folio, 1683–9; *Theological Works*, Oxford, 1818; also by A. Napier, Cambridge, 1859.

**BAXTER, Richard (1615–1691). Nos. 44, 141, 172, 190, 284, 352.**

Born at Rowton, near High Ercall, Shropshire. Educated at the free school at Wroxeter, and by the Chaplain to the Council of Ludlow Castle. Ordained at Worcester, 1638, and licensed to the school at Dudley. Minister at Bridgnorth, 1640; at Kidderminster, 1641. Ejected, 1642, and removed to Coventry. Returned to Kidderminster, 1649. Removed to London, 1660. Member of the Savoy Conference. Finally left the Church of England, May 16th, 1662, and retired to Acton, Middlesex. Tried before Judge Jeffreys for libel and imprisoned, 1684. Released, 1686. Buried in Christ Church, London.

*Works.* Exceedingly numerous. Include *The Saint's Everlasting Rest* (1650; cp. No. **141**); *The Right Method for Peace and Conscience and Spiritual Comfort* (1653); *Making Light of Christ* (1655); *A Call to the Unconverted* (1657); *Confirmation and Restauration* (1658; cp. No. **172**); *A Treatise of Self-Denial* (1659); *The True Catholic and Catholic Church Described* (1660; cp. No. **44**); *The Divine Life* (1664; cp. No. **352**); *A Sheet for the Instruction of the Sick during the Plague* (1665); *Family Catechism* (1683).

*Collected Edition.* W. Orme; 1830, in 23 vols. ("Practical Works" only).

*Life.* *Reliquiae Baxterianae*, published by Matthew Sylvester, 1696 (Everyman's Library, 1931). Later *Lives* by John Hamilton Davies (1887); F. J. Powicke (1924), A. R. Ladell (1925). Cp. also F. J. Powicke, *The Reverend Richard Baxter under the Cross, 1662–1691* (1927).

**BEVERIDGE, William (1637–1708). Nos. 42, 51, 52, 53, 135, 159, 210, 249, 269, 286, 321, 332.**

Baptized at Barrow, Leicestershire. Sizar at St. John's College, Cambridge, 1653. Became deeply interested in Oriental languages. Ordained Deacon, January 1661; and priest in the same month. Vicar of Ealing, Middlesex, 1661. Vicar of St. Peter's, Cornhill, 1672, where he had the daily service and a Eucharist every Sunday. Archdeacon of Colchester,

1681. Prebendary of Canterbury, 1684. Offered the See of Bath and Wells from which Ken had been deprived, 1691; but declined. Not invited again to become a Bishop till 1704, when he accepted the See of St. Asaph. Opposed Union with Scotland.

*Works. Excellency and Use of the Oriental Tongues* (1658); Συνοδικόν (1672; cp. No. **332**); *Vindication of his Collection of Canons* (1679); *Excellency and Usefulness of the Common Prayer* (1681, a sermon; cp. No. **286**); *Private Thoughts upon Religion* (1709, posthumous); *Exposition of the Thirty-Nine Articles* (1710, also posthumous; cp. No. **52**); and a large collection of Sermons (cp. Nos. **42, 159, 210, 269**).

*Collected Editions.* Folio ed., 2 vols., 1720. Also by T. Hartwell Horne, 9 vols., London, 1824; by J. Bliss, *L. A. C. T.*, 12 vols., 1842–1846.

[**Book of Common Prayer, The. Nos. 78, 295, 296.**]

**BOUGHEN, Edward (1587–1660?). No. 194.**

Born in Buckinghamshire. Educated at Westminster School and Christ Church, Oxford. Chaplain to Howson, Bishop of Oxford. Rector of Woodchurch, Kent, 1633. D.D., 1646.

*Works.* Several sermons, including *A Sermon of Confirmation* (1620; cp. No. **194**). Also *Principles of Religion* (1646; on the Prayer Book Catechism).

**BOYLE, The Hon. Robert (1627–1691). Nos. 56, 89, 103, 104, 124, 350, 351.**

Son of Richard Boyle, the First Earl of Cork. Educated at Eton. Travelled on the Continent until 1644. Settled at Oxford and erected a laboratory, 1654. Published his discovery of " Boyle's Law," 1662. Also a keen student of Oriental languages. Governor of the Corporation for the Spread of the Gospel in New England, 1661–89. Took a leading part in the foundation of the Royal Society.

*Works.* Very diffusely written. Include *Some Motives and Incentives to the Love of God* (1659; cp. No. **124**); *New Experiments Physico-Mechanical touching the Spring of the Air and its Effects* (1660); *Some Considerations touching the Style of the Holy Scriptures* (1661; cp. No. **56**); *Some Considerations touching the Usefulness of Experimental Natural Philosophy* (1663; cp. No. **89**); *A Hydrostatical Discourse* (1672; cp. No. **104**); *The Excellency of Theology Compared with Natural Philosophy* (1673; cp. No. **351**); *A Disquisition Concerning the Final Causes of Natural Things* (1688); *The Christian Virtuoso* (1690; cp. No. **103**).

*Collected Edition.* By T. Birch in 5 folio vols., 1744; reprinted 1772 in 6 large quarto vols. This edition also contains a *Life*.

**BRAMHALL, John (1594–1663). Nos. 28, 40, 86, 164, 168, 176, 186, 207, 213, 214, 248, 263.**

Baptized and educated at Pontefract. Entered Sidney Sussex College, Cambridge, 1609. B.A., 1612. M.A., 1616. D.D., 1630. Ordained about 1616, and presented to the Rectory of Elvington, Yorks. After a dispute at Northallerton with two Roman Catholics, Hungate and Houghton, appointed Chaplain to Tobias Matthew, Archbishop of York, 1623. Sub-dean of Ripon, 1623. Resigned, and accepted the post of Chaplain to Wentworth, 1633. Archdeacon of Meath, 1633. Bishop of Derry, 1634. Impeached by the Irish Commons, March 4th, 1641; but liberated. Fled to England, thence to the Continent, 1644. Returned to Ireland for a short period, 1648–9; but soon left again for the Continent. Translated to the Archiepiscopal See of Armagh, 1661.

*Works.* Include *A Fair Warning to take heed of the Scottish Discipline* (1649; cp. No. **40**); *An Answer to de la Milletière* (The Hague, 1653; cp. No. **207**); *A Just Vindication of the Church of England from the Unjust Aspersion of Criminal Schism* (1654); *A. Replication to the Bishop of Chalcedon's Survey* (1656; cp. No. **214**); *Schism Guarded* (1658; cp. No. **28**); *The Consecration of Protestant Bishops Vindicated* (1658; cp. No. **164**); *The Catching of Leviathan* (1658); *A Vindication from the Presbyterian Charge of Popery* (1672, posthumous; cp. No. **263**); *Protestant Ordinations Vindicated* (1676, posthumous; cp. No. **176**); *Of Persons dying without Baptism* (1676, posthumous; cp. No. **186**).

*Collected Editions.* Folio edition, Dublin, 1676. Reprinted, with additions, by A. W. Haddan, in the *L. A. C. T.*

### BROWNE, Sir Thomas (1605–1682). Nos. 4, 88, 92, 102, 146, 278, 290, 301.

Born in Cheapside. Educated at Winchester and Pembroke College, Oxford. B.A., 1626. Travelled on the Continent and in Ireland. M.D. at Leyden, 1633. Physician at Shipden Hall, near Halifax. Removed to Norwich, 1637. M.D. at Oxford, 1637. Knighted, 1671. Corresponded with John Evelyn. Buried in St. Peter Mancroft, Norwich.

*Works.* *Religio Medici* (1642, 1643; cp. No. **4**); *Pseudodoxia Epidemica* (1646); *Hydriotaphia or Urn-Burial* (1658); *Christian Morals* (1716, posthumous; cp. No. **301**).

*Collected Editions.* 1686 (said to have been edited by Tenison); Simon Wilkin, 1835–6; W. C. Hazlitt (with a *Life* of Browne), 2 vols., 1868; G. Keynes, 1928–1931, 6 vols.

### BUDDLE, George. No. 272.

Nothing further has been ascertained of the author of *A Short and Plain Discourse of Evangelical Fasts* (1609; cp. No. **272**).

### BULL, George (1634–1710). Nos. 11, 109, 110, 129, 134, 138.

Born at Wells, Somerset. Educated at Wells Grammar School, at Tiverton, and at Exeter College, Oxford. Left Oxford, with his tutor Mr. Ackland, owing to his refusal to take Oath to Commonwealth, 1649, and settled at North Cadbury, Somerset. Ordained Deacon and Priest by Dr. Skinner, the ejected Bishop of Oxford, 1655. Presented to the living of St. George's, near Bristol. Rector of Suddington St. Mary, near Cirencester, 1658; plus St. Peter's, 1662. Rector of Avening, 1685. Archdeacon of Llandaff, 1686. Bishop of St. David's, 1705.

*Works.* *Harmonia Apostolica* (1670; cp. No. **129**); *Examen Censurae* (1675; cp. No. **11**); *Defensio Fidei Nicaenae* (1685; cp. No. **109**); *Judicium Ecclesiae Catholicae* (1694); *Primitiva et Apostolica Traditio* (1710).

*Collected Editions.* An admirable edition in 7 vols. by the Clarendon Press, 1827; also *L. A. C. T.* (contains translations).

*Life.* By Robert Nelson (1713; cp. No. **77**).

### BURNET, Gilbert (1643–1715). Nos. 29, 105.

Son of Presbyterian lawyer. Born in Edinburgh. Educated at Marischal College, Aberdeen. Probationer of Scottish Church, 1661. Visited Oxford,

London, and Cambridge (where he was much influenced by Cudworth and More), 1663; then studied in Paris and Amsterdam, 1664. Minister of Saltoun, East Lothian, 1665; Clerk of Haddington Presbytery, 1667. Employed by Archbishop Leighton to negotiate with the Presbyterians, 1669. Divinity Professor at Glasgow, 1669. Chaplain to Charles II, and refused Bishopric of Edinburgh, 1671. Withdrew to Continent, 1683–1688. Accompanied William of Orange to England, 1688. Preached Coronation Sermon and appointed Bishop of Salisbury, 1689. Obtained " Queen Anne's Bounty " for the Church, 1704. Buried in the parish of St. James', Clerkenwell.

*Works. Memoirs of the Lives and Actions of James and William, Dukes of Hamilton and Castleherald* (1677); *History of the Reformation in England* (in three parts: 1679, 1682, 1715); *A Discourse of the Opposition of the Church of Rome* (1688; cp. No. **105**); *Exposition of the Thirty-Nine Articles* (1699); *History of His Own Time* (in two parts, posthumously; 1724, 1734).

*Lives.* By Sir Thomas Burnet (son), in the *History of His Own Time*; T. E. S. Clarke and H. C. Foxcroft (1907).

**[Canons of 1604, The. Nos. 182, 311.]**

**[Canons of 1640, The. No. 277.]**

## CHARLES I (1600–1649). No. 155.

Born at Dunfermline, Nov. 19, 1600. Became Heir Apparent on death of Prince Henry, 1612. Secret expedition with Buckingham to Spain with a view to a marriage alliance, 1623. Succeeded to English throne, March 27, 1625. Married to Henrietta Maria, the Roman Catholic daughter of Henry IV of France. Supported Richard Montague's attack on Calvinism. Dissolved Parliament, March 1629, which did not reassemble until 1640. " Book of Sports " reissued 1633. Attempt to impose Laud's revision of the *Book of Common Prayer* upon Scotland, 1637. Outbreak of Civil War, 1642. Executed, Jan. 30th, 1648/9.

*Attributed to Charles I*: Εἰκὼν Βασιλική, published immediately after his execution; but probably this book was the work of John Gauden (see Note on No. **285**).

## CHILLINGWORTH, William (1602–1644). Nos. 55, 64.

Born at Oxford. Scholar of Trinity College, Oxford, 1618. Fellow, 1628. Converted by " Fisher " to Roman Catholicism in about 1629, and proceeded to the Jesuit College at Douai. Left Douai in 1631; came back to Oxford; and at length on theological grounds returned to the Church of England. Declined preferment because he felt unable to subscribe to the Thirty-Nine Articles (he particularly objected to belief that Fourth Commandment was binding upon Christians and the damnatory clauses in Athanasian Creed). Having overcome his scruples against the Articles, he was appointed to Chancellorship of the Church of Sarum, 1638, supported the King during the Siege of Gloucester (1643) and accompanied Lord Hopton in his campaign. Taken ill at Arundel Castle; captured by Waller, and brought to Chichester, where he died, Jan. 1644.

*Works. The Religion of Protestants, a Safe Way of Salvation* (1637; cp. No. **55**). Also Sermons (cp. No. **64**).

*Collected Editions.* London, 1719, folio; Oxford, 1838, 3 vols.

*Life.* By T. Birch in the 1742 edition of Chillingworth's *Works*.

### CLAGETT, William (1646-1688).   No. 241.

Born at Bury St. Edmunds.   Admitted to Emmanuel College, Cambridge, 1659.   M.A., 1667.   D.D., 1683.   Preacher at Gray's Inn, 1680. Rector of Farnham Royal, Bucks., 1683.

*Works.   A Discourse Concerning the Operations of the Holy Spirit* (1677, 1680); *An Answer to the Dissenters' Objections against the Liturgy of the Church of England* (1683); *Discourse Concerning the Worship of the Blessed Virgin and the Saints* (1686; cp. No. **241**); and other works.

[Consecration Prayer of 1637, The.   No. 225.]

[Contemplations on the State of Man.   No. 145.]

### COSIN, John (1594-1672).   Nos. 8, 24, 59, 153, 167, 188, 203, 229, 239, 264, 280, 287, 298, 314.

Born at Norwich.   Educated at Norwich Grammar School, and at Caius College, Cambridge, where he afterwards became a Fellow.   Secretary and Librarian to Overall, Bishop of Coventry and Lichfield, till 1619, when he became Chaplain to Neile, Bishop of Durham.   Master of Greatham Hospital and Prebendary of Durham, 1624.   Archdeacon of East Riding of Yorkshire, 1625.   Rector of Brancepeth, 1626.   Indicted before the Archbishop of York for ritualistic practices in Durham Cathedral, 1628 and 1629.   Master of Peterhouse, Cambridge, 1634.   Vice-Chancellor, 1639.   Dean of Peterborough, and Chaplain to Charles I, 1640.   Upon a petition to the House of Commons by Peter Smart, sequestrated from all his livings, 1641.   Ejected from Peterhouse, 1644.   Retired to Paris and officiated in the household of Henrietta Maria.   Restored to Deanery of Peterborough, 1660.   Consecrated Bishop of Durham, Dec. 2nd, 1660.   One of the leading Revisers at the Savoy Conference, 1661-2.   Died in London; buried at Bishop Auckland.

*Works.   Collection of Private Devotions* (1627; cp. No. **280**); *Regiae Angliae Religio Catholica* (1652); *Historia Transubstantionis Papalis* (1656; cp. No. **203**); *A Scholastical History of the Canon of Holy Scripture* (1657; cp. No. **59**); *Notes and Collections on the Book of Common Prayer* (1710; cp. No. **287**).   Also *Letters* (cp. Nos. **24, 167, 264**) and *Sermons* (cp. Nos. **153, 239**).   For notes of a speech, cp. No. **314**; for his Will, cp. No. **8**.

*Collected Edition, L. A. C. T.*; Correspondence edited by the Surtees Society (2 vols., 1868-1870; cp. No. **188**).

### CUDWORTH, Ralph (1617-1688).   Nos. 132, 362.

Born at Aller, Somerset.   Admitted as Pensioner to Emmanuel College, 1630.   Matriculated, 1632.   Master of Clare Hall and B.D., 1645.   Regius Professor of Hebrew, also 1645.   Apparently presented to living of North Cadbury, 1650 (but it is not certain that he ever left Cambridge to reside there).   Master of Christ's, 1654.   Prebendary of Gloucester, 1678.   Died at Cambridge, and buried in Christ's College Chapel.

*Works.   A Discourse concerning the True Nature of the Lord's Supper* (1632); *A Sermon Preached before the House of Commons* (1647; cp. No. **362**); *The True Intellectual System of the Universe* (1678, though finished in 1671).

Posthumous : *Treatise concerning Eternal and Mutable Morality* (1731); *Treatise of Freewill* (1838).

## DAVENANT, John (1572–1641). No. 152.

Born in London. Admitted to Queens' College, Cambridge, 1587. Ordained about 1597. B.D., 1601. D.D., 1609. Lady Margaret Professor of Divinity, 1609. President of Queens', 1614. One of the representatives of James I at the Synod of Dort (Dordrecht), 1618. Bishop of Salisbury, 1621.

*Works.* *Expositio Epistolae ad Colossenses* (1627); *Praelectiones de duobus in theologia controversis capitibus* (1631); *Determinationes quaestionum quarundam theologicarum* (1634; cp. No. **152**).

[Declaration on Sports, The. No. 261.]

## DODWELL, Henry (1641–1711). No. 34.

Born at Dublin. Entered Trinity College, Dublin, 1656. Subsequently Scholar and then Fellow. Owing to conscientious objections to taking Holy Orders, he resigned his Fellowship in 1666. Camden Professor of History, Oxford, 1688. Deprived of Professorship because of his refusal to take Oath of Allegiance, 1691. Retired to Shottesbrooke in Berkshire, where he resided until his death.

*Works.* *A Discourse concerning Sanchoniathon's Phœnician History* (1681); *An Account of the Fundamental Principle of Popery* (1688; cp. No. **34**); *De Veteribus Graecorum Romanorumque cyclis* (1701).

## DOMINIS, Marco Antonio de (1566–1624). No. 36.

Born in the island of Arbe off the Dalmatian coast. Educated by Jesuits. Lectured at Verona, Padua (Mathematics), and Brescia (Rhetoric and Philosophy). Bishop of Segni in Dalmatia, 1596; Archbishop of Spalato, 1598. Quarrelled with Papacy. Resigned See, 1616. Welcomed in England and appointed Master of Savoy, 1618; Dean of Windsor, 1618. Published in London, with Dedication to James I, Paolo Sarpi's *Historia del Concilio Tridentino*, 1619. Received back into Roman Catholic Church, 1621. Proceeded against by the Inquisition. Though he died in Rome in prison before the case was concluded, he was later found guilty, and his body was publicly burnt in the Campo di Fiore.

*Works.* *Papatus Romanus* (1617, anon.); *De republica ecclesiastica* (1618); *Sui Reditus ex Anglia Consilium* (1623).

## DONNE, John (1571 ?–1631). Nos. 144, 357.

Educated in the Roman Catholic religion. Entered Hart Hall, Oxford, 1584. Admitted to Lincoln's Inn, 1592. Member of Essex's expedition to Cadiz, 1596. Secretary to Sir Thomas Egerton, 1596–1601. Hon. M.A., Oxford, 1610. Ordained to the ministry of the Anglican Church, 1615. Chaplain to James I, also 1615. Rector of Keyston, Huntingdon, and Sevenoaks, Kent, and D.D., Cambridge, 1616. Dean of St. Paul's, 1621. Prolocutor of Convocation, 1623 and 1624.

*Works.* A large number of Sermons (cp. No. **144**) and Poems (cp. No. **357**). Also *Pseudo-Martyr* (1610; against Bellarmine); *Devotions upon Emergent Occasions* (1624); *Biathanatos* (1644, posthumous).

*Collected Poems* 1633, and many later editions, notably H. J. C. Grierson (1912, also 1929) and by J. Hayward (1929).

*Selection of Prose.* L. P. Smith (1919).

*Life.* By Izaak Walton (1640).

**DUREL, John (1625–1683). No. 83.**

Born at St. Heliers, Jersey. Entered Merton College, Oxford, 1640. M.A. of Sylvanian College, Caen, 1644. Founded Savoy French Episcopal Chapel, and became its first Minister, 1660. Chaplain to Charles II, 1662. Prebendary of Salisbury, 1663; of Windsor, 1664. Translated Revised Prayer Book into French, 1661–1667. Prebendary of Durham, 1668. Also translated (in conjunction with others) Revised Prayer Book into Latin. D.D. of Oxford, 1670. Dean of Windsor and Wolverhampton, 1677.

*Works.* *The Liturgy of the Church of England* (1662; cp. No. **83**); *A View of the Government and Public Worship of God in the Reformed Churches beyond the Seas* (1662); *Sanctae Ecclesiae Anglicanae . . . Vindiciae* (1669).

**EARLE, John (1601 ?–1665). No. 336.**

Born at York. Educated at Christ Church and Merton College, Oxford. Chaplain and Tutor to Prince Charles, 1641. Elected member of Westminster Assembly, 1643; but owing to his strongly Royalist sympathies he refused to sit. After the Battle of Worcester (1651) he went abroad, and later joined the Duke of York (James II) on the Continent. Dean of Westminster, 1660. Bishop of Worcester, 1662; of Salisbury, 1663. Strongly opposed the Conventicle and Five-Mile Acts.

*Works.* *Microcosmography* (1628, anon.; cp. No. **336**); Latin translation of Εἰκὼν Βασιλική (1649).

**EATON, Nathaniel (1609?–1674). No. 202.**

Educated at Westminster and at Trinity College, Cambridge. Having taken Orders, he accompanied his two elder brothers to America, 1637. Became President-Designate of Harvard College; but owing to the severity and cruelty of his methods and the consequent proceedings taken against him in the courts, he fled to New Hampshire, and eventually found his way back to Europe. In possession of the living of Bishop's Castle, Shropshire, 1661. Rector of Bideford, 1668.

*Works.* *Oratio habita a Nathanaele Eatono . . . im Academia Patavina* (1647); *De Fastis Anglicis sive Calendarium Sacrum* (1661; cp. No. **202**).

**[Eikon Basilike. No. 285.]**

**EVELYN, John (1620–1706). No. 361.**

Born at Wotton House, near Dorking, Surrey. Admitted to the Middle Temple, 1637, and subsequently to Balliol College, also 1637. Took part in the Civil War, 1642. Left England for some years abroad, Oct. 1643. Married daughter of Sir Thomas Browne, 1647. Visited Charles I at Hampton Court, 1647. One of the promoters of the Royal Society, of which he became Secretary in 1672. Supported the Revolution of 1688. Died at Wotton.

*Works.* His famous *Diary*, which covers the years 1640–1706, was not published till 1818. He wrote on many subjects, including Gardening, Architecture, and Numismatics. Cp. note on No. **361**.

**FELL, John (1625–1686). Nos. 288, 341.**

Son of Samuel Fell, Dean of Christ Church. Born at Longworth. Student of Christ Church, 1636. Deacon, 1647; priest, 1649. Deprived of his Studentship by the Parliamentary Visitors, 1648. During Commonwealth maintained Prayer Book Services at Oxford in a house opposite Merton College. Dean of Christ Church, 1660. Vice-Chancellor, 1666–1669. Bishop of Oxford (continuing to hold the Deanery *in commendam*), 1676.

*Works.* Include many famous editions of the Fathers and the classics : *Clement of Rome* (1677); *Cyprian* (1682); *Athenagoras* (1682); *Clement of Alexandria* (1683); *Theophilus of Antioch* (1684). Also *Life* of Henry Hammond (1661; cp. No. **341**); of Richard Allestree (1684). Perhaps part of *The Whole Duty of Man* is to be ascribed to John Fell (cp. No. **197**).

## FIELD, Richard (1561–1616). Nos. 18, 20, 72, 116.

Born at Hemel Hempstead, Herts. Educated at Berkhampstead and Magdalen College, Oxford. Divinity Reader in Winchester Cathedral, 1592. Divinity Reader at Lincoln's Inn, 1594. Rector of Burghclere, 1594. Prebendary of Windsor, 1604. Dean of Gloucester, 1610.

He wrote : *Of the Church* (1606, 1610; cp. No. **72**).

## FORBES, William (1585–1634). Nos. 205, 219.

Born at Aberdeen. Graduated at Marischal College, Aberdeen, 1601. Travelled widely on the Continent. Returned to Scotland, where he was ordained. Appointed one of the ministers of Aberdeen, 1616; of Edinburgh, 1621. Zealous in enforcing the observance of the Perth Articles. Returned to Aberdeen, 1626. Preached at Holyrood before Charles I on his visit to Scotland, 1633. First Bishop of Edinburgh, 1634.

*Works. Considerationes Modestae et Pacificae* (1658, posthumous; cp. No. **205**). He wrote also *Animadversions on the Works of Bellarmine*, but the MS. has perished.

## FULLER, Thomas (1608–1661). No. 349.

Born at Aldwincle St. Peter's, Northamptonshire. Entered Queens' College, Cambridge, 1621 or 1622. Curate of St. Benet's, Cambridge, 1630. Prebendary of Salisbury, 1631. Rector of Broadwindsor, 1634. B.D., 1635. Supported the Royalist Cause during the Civil War, though accused of moderation by the more ardent supporters of the King. Lampooned by Robert South on the ground that he was constantly seeking patronage for his literary works. Chaplain to George Berkeley of Cranford House and Rector of Cranford, 1658. Died at Covent Garden. Buried in Cranford Church.

*Works. David's Heinous Sin* (1631); *History of the Holy War* (1639); *The Holy and Profane State* (1642; cp. No. **349**); *Cause and Cure of a Wounded Conscience* (1647); *Church History of Britain* (1655); *History of Worthies of England* (posthumous, 1662).

*Lives.* Anon. (1661); J. E. Bailey (1874).

## GAUDEN, John (1605–1662). Nos. 7, 41, 82, 154, 279.

Born at Mayland, Essex. Educated at St. John's College, Cambridge. M.A., 1626. Entered Wadham College, Oxford, 1630. Vicar of Chippenham, 1640. Dean of Bocking, 1642. Retained his preferment during the Commonwealth. Bishop of Exeter, 1660; of Worcester, 1662.

*Works.* Probably the author of Εἰκὼν Βασιλική (1649; cp. No. **285**). Also wrote *Cromwell's Bloody Slaughter House* (1649; not published till 1660); *Hieraspistes* (1653; cp. No. **154**); *The Case of Ministers' Maintenance by Tithes* (1653); Ἱερὰ Δάκρυα (1659; cp. No. **41**); ᾽Ανάλυσις (1660); and other works.

## GEE, Edward (1657–1730). No. 173.

Born at Manchester. Educated at Manchester Grammar School and St. John's College, Cambridge. B.A., 1679. M.A., 1683. Took an important part in the controversy with Rome in James II's reign. Rector of St. Benet's, Paul's Wharf, London, 1688. Prebendary of Westminster, 1701. Dean of Peterborough, 1721; of Lincoln, 1722. Buried in Westminster Abbey.

*Works.* Many, including *Veteres Vindicati* (1687); *Primitive Fathers no Papists* (1688); *The Texts Examined Concerning Seven Sacraments* (1688; cp. No. **173**).

## GILBERT, John (1659–?). No. 235.

Son of John Gilbert of Salisbury. Entered Hart Hall, Oxford, 1674. B.A., 1677. M.A., 1680. Incumbent at Peterborough. Very little is known of him.

*Works.* *Answer to the Bishop of Condom* [i.e. Bossuet] (1686; cp. No. **235**); *Reflexions on* [Bossuet's] *Pastoral Letter* (published with the preceding).

## GLANVILL (or GLANVIL), Joseph (1636–1680). No. 139.

Born at Plymouth. Educated at Exeter and Lincoln Colleges, Oxford. M.A., 1658. Successively Rector of Wimbish in Essex (1660); Vicar of Frome Selwood, Somerset (1662); and Rector of Streat and Walton (1672). Incumbent also of Abbey Church, Bath, 1666. Chaplain-in-Ordinary to Charles II, 1672. Prebendary of Worcester, 1678. Died at Bath.

*Works.* *The Vanity of Dogmatizing* (1661,—familiar through Matthew Arnold's *Scholar Gipsy*); *Lux Orientalis* (1662; cp. No. **139**); *Philosophical Considerations touching the Being of Witches and Witchcraft* (1667); *The Way of Happiness* (1670).

## GUNNING, Peter (1614–1684). No. 49.

Born at Hoo in Kent. Educated at Clare Hall, Cambridge. Fellow, 1633. Chaplain of New College, Oxford, 1644–1646. D.D. by Royal Mandate, Master of Clare, and Lady Margaret Professor of Divinity, 1660. Head of St. John's College, Cambridge, and Regius Professor of Divinity, 1661. Bishop of Chichester, 1669. Bishop of Ely, 1674/5.

*Works.* *Schism Unmasked* (Paris, 1658); *Sermon on the Lent Fast* (1662; cp. No. **49**).

## HACKET, John (1592–1670). Nos. 178, 179.

Born at London. Educated at Westminster School and Trinity College, Cambridge (where he was subsequently Fellow). Ordained, 1618. Rector of Stoke Hammond, Bucks, 1621. Chaplain to James I, 1623. Presented to the livings of St. Andrew's, Holborn, and of Cheam, Surrey, 1624. Pleaded for continuance of Cathedral Establishments in the House of Commons, 1641. Living of St. Andrew's, Holborn, sequestered, 1645. Bishop of Lichfield and Coventry, 1661.

*Works.* *Christian Consolations* (attributed to Hacket; cp. No. **178**); *A Century of Sermons* (1675; cp. No. **179**); *Scrinia Reserata* (Life of Bishop John Williams, posthumous, 1693).

**HALES, John (1584–1656). No. 23.**

Known as "the ever-memorable." Born at Bath. Educated at Bath Grammar School and Corpus Christi College, Oxford. Fellow of Merton, 1605. Public Lecturer in Greek at Oxford, 1612. Fellow of Eton, 1613. Pronounced Funeral Oration on Sir Thomas Bodley, 1613. Present at the Synod of Dort, 1618. Retired to Eton, 1619. Chaplain to Archbishop Laud and Canon of Windsor, 1639. Dispossessed of Fellowship, 1649. Died at Eton.

*Works.* *Schism and Schismatics* (1636; first published, 1642); *The Golden Remains* (1659); *Miscellanies* (? posthumous; cp. No. 23).

*Collected Edition.* In 3 vols., edited by Lord Hailes, Glasgow, 1765.

**HALL, Joseph (1574–1656):** **Nos. 19, 39, 93, 142, 143, 171, 185, 189, 231, 236, 246, 247, 256, 268, 282, 283, 303, 305, 315, 317, 322, 324, 345, 346, 347, 348.**

Born at Bristow Park, near Ashby-de-la-Zouch. Educated at Ashby School and Emmanuel College, Cambridge. Presented to the benefice of Halsted, Suffolk, 1601. Accompanied Sir Edmund Bacon to Spa, 1605. Chaplain to Prince Henry, 1608. Vicar of Waltham, Essex, 1608. Prebend of Willenhall in the Collegiate Church of Wolverhampton, 1610. Dean of Worcester, 1616. Sent by James I to represent him at Synod of Dort, 1618. Consecrated Bishop of Exeter, 1627; translated to Norwich, 1641. Ejected by Puritans, and retired to Higham, Norfolk, where he died.

*Works.* Numerous. *Meditations and Vows* (1606; cp. No. **282**); *Epistles* (1608–1611; Nos. **185, 247, 345**); *Sacred Polemics* (1611; cp. No. **305**); *The Honour of the Married Clergy Maintained* (1620; cp. No. **317**); *The Old Religion* (1628; cp. No. **231**); *Occasional Meditations* (1630; cp. No. **347**); *A Paraphrase of all the hard Texts of Scripture* (1633; cp. No. **19**); *Christian Moderation* (1639; cp. No. **348**); *Episcopacy by Divine Right Asserted* (1641; cp. No. **39**); *The Devout Soul* (1643; cp. No. **283**); *A Treatise of Christ Mystical* (1647; cp. No. **143**); *Resolutions and Decisions of Cases of Conscience* (1649; cp. No. **324**); Χειροθεσία (1649; cp. No. **189**); *Sussurium Cum Deo, or Soliloquies* (1651; cp. No. **346**); *Holy Decency in the Worship of God* (? posthumous; cp. No. **246**); also *Letters* (cp. No. **268**).

*Collected Editions.* Many. Among the more recent, those of Josiah Pratt (1808, 10 vols.); Peter Hall (1837, 12 vols.); and Philip Wynter (1863, 10 vols.).

**HAMMOND, Henry (1605–1660). Nos. 62, 94, 133, 198, 267, 313, 323.**

Born at Chertsey. Educated at Eton and at Magdalen College, Oxford. Fellow of Magdalen, 1625. Ordained deacon, 1629. Presented to living of Penshurst, Kent, and resigned his Fellowship, 1633. Archdeacon of Chichester, 1643. Canon of Christ Church and Public Orator, Oxford, 1645. Chaplain to Charles I, 1647. Deprived and imprisoned, 1647. After being released, he lived privately till his death at Westwood, Worcestershire.

*Works.* *Practical Catechism* (1644; cp. No. **267**); *Of a Late and Death-Bed Repentance* (1645); *View of the Directory and Vindication of the Ancient Liturgy* (1645); *Of the Reasonableness of Christian Religion* (1650; cp. No. **94**); *Of Fundamentals* (1654; cp. No. **62**). Also many Sermons.

*Collected Edition* (far from complete): *L. A. C. T.*, with John Fell's *Life*.

**HARDWICK, William. No. 274.**

Nothing further has been discovered of the author of *Conformity with Piety Requisite in God's Service* (1638; cp. No. **274**); he is described on the title-page as " Curate of Reigate."

**HERBERT, George (1593–1633). Nos. 5, 335.**

Born at Montgomery Castle. Fifth son of Sir Richard Herbert, and brother of Lord Herbert of Cherbury. Educated at Westminster School and Trinity College, Cambridge. B.A., 1613. M.A. and Major Fellow, 1616. Public Orator, 1619. Among his friends were Donne, Wotton, Izaak Walton, Andrewes, and Francis Bacon. Prebendary of Layton Ecclesia (only two miles from Little Gidding), 1626. Incumbent of Bemerton, near Salisbury, and ordained priest, 1630. Buried in Bemerton Church.

*Works.* *The Temple,—Sacred Poems and Private Ejaculations* (1633, published by Nicholas Ferrar immediately after his death; cp. No. **5**); *The Country Parson* (also posthumous, 1651; cp. No. **335**).

*Life.* By Izaak Walton (1670; cp. No. **338**).

**HEYLYN, Peter (1600–1662). Nos. 63, 85, 119, 136.**

Born at Burford. Educated at Hart Hall and Magdalen College, Oxford. Fellow of Magdalen, 1618. Ordained, 1624. Chaplain to Charles I, 1630. Appointed Rector of Hemingford, 1630; but owing to his Laudian sympathies, John Williams, Bishop of Lincoln, declined to institute him. Charles accordingly made him Prebendary of Westminster, and allowed him to hold the Deanery *in commendam*. Vicar of South Warnborough, 1637. Assisted in the preparation of the case against Prynne, who had published the *Histriomastix*. During the Civil War he edited the *Mercurius Aulicus* at Oxford.

*Works.* Numerous. Include *History of St. George of Cappadocia* (1631); *History of Sabbath* (1636); *Theologia Veterum* (1654; cp. No. **63**); *Historia Quinquarticularis* (1660; cp. No. **85**); *Ecclesia Restaurata* (1661); *Cyprianus Anglicus* (Life of Laud; 1668, posthumous); *Aerius Redivivus* (attack on Presbyterianism; 1670, also posthumous).

*Life.* By J. Barnard, etc. (1681) and by G. Vernon (1682). See *D.N.B.* *s.v.* Heylyn.

**HICKES, George (1642–1715). Nos. 30, 31, 45, 181, 243.**

Born at Newsham, near Thirsk, Yorks. Successively at St. John's College (1659), Magdalen College, and Magdalen Hall, Oxford; Fellow of Lincoln, 1664. Rector of St. Ebbe's, Oxford, 1675. Vicar of All Hallows', Barking, London, 1680. Chaplain to Charles II, 1681. Dean of Worcester, 1683. At the Revolution, refused to take Oaths of Allegiance to William III and Mary, and accordingly deprived of his Deanery. A leading " Non-Juror." Was consecrated Suffragan Bishop of Thetford, 1694.

*Works.* Many. *The Spirit of Enthusiam Exorcized* (1680, a sermon; cp. No. **30**); *The Case of Infant Baptism* (1683; cp. No. **181**); *Speculum Beatae Virginis* (1686; cp. No. **243**); *Institutiones Grammaticae Anglo-Saxonicae et Moeso-Gothicae* (1689); *Linguarum veterum Septentrionalium Thesaurus Grammatico-criticus et Archaeologicus* (1703–1705); *Of the Christian Priesthood* (1707); *Of the Dignity of the Episcopal Order* (1707).

**HOOKER, Richard (1554 ?–1600). Nos. 17, 47, 48, 106, 108, 112, 148, 150, 151, 156, 166, 169, 183, 199, 245, 265, 273, 316, 325, 333.**

Born at Heavitree, Exeter. Educated at Exeter Grammar School and Corpus Christi College, Oxford. Fellow, 1577. Ordained Deacon, 1581. Resigned Fellowship and accepted living of Drayton-Beauchamp, Bucks, 1584. Master of the Temple, March 1585. Controversy with Travers. Rector of Boscombe, Wilts, and Minor Prebend of Salisbury, 1591. Rector of Bishopsbourne, near Canterbury, 1595. Buried at Bishopsbourne.

*Works.* *The Laws of Ecclesiastical Polity* (1594, 1597, and posthumous; cp. Nos. **148, 150**). Also Sermons.

*Collected Editions.* By J. Keble, Oxford, 1836; 3 vols. Seventh edition, revised by R. W. Church and F. Paget, Oxford, 1888.

*Lives.* By Izaak Walton (1665; cp. note on Nos. **289, 338**). Also by L. S. Thornton (S.P.C.K., 1924). Cp. also F. Paget, *An Introduction to the Fifth Book of Hooker's Treatise of the Laws of Ecclesiastical Polity*, Oxford, 1899.

**HORNECK, Anthony (1641–1697). No. 359.**

Of German descent; born at Bacharach-am-Rhein. Studied at Heidelberg. Came to England, 1661. Entered Queen's College, Oxford, 1664. Vicar of All Saints', Oxford. Preacher at the Savoy, 1671, where he became a very popular pulpit-orator. Prebendary of Westminster, 1693; of Wells, 1694. Buried in Westminster Abbey.

*Works.* *The Great Law of Consideration* (1676); *Delight and Judgement* (1683); *The Fire of the Altar* (1683; cp. No. **359**); *The Crucified Jesus* (1686); *Several Sermons upon the Fifth of St. Matthew* (1698).

**HYDE, Edward (1609–1674). No. 343.**

Born at Norbury. Educated at Magdalen Hall, Oxford. Entered Middle Temple, 1625. Called to the Bar, 1633. Member for Wootton Bassett in the Short Parliament; for Saltash in the Long Parliament. Supported Strafford's impeachment. Successfully obstructed Root and Branch Bill, 1641. Expelled from House of Commons, 1642, and used his active influence in support of Royalist Cause. Appointed by Charles as Chancellor of the Exchequer, 1643. Became one of chief advisers of Charles II during the Commonwealth. Lord Chancellor, 1658. Chancellor of Oxford University, 1660–1667. Created Earl of Clarendon, 1661. Advocated policy of repression of Nonconformity, known as the " Clarendon Code." Dismissed, 1667. The remainder of his life was spent in exile.

*Works.* *History of the Great Rebellion* (posthumous, 1702–1704; cp. No. **343**); and several other writings.

*Life.* By Thomas Lister (1837).

**[Irish Canons of 1634, The. No. 230.]**

**ISAACSON, Henry (1581–1654). No. 337.**

Born in London. Educated at Pembroke College, Cambridge. Intimate friend of Andrewes until his death in 1626. Benefactor of the parish of St. Catherine, Coleman Street. He described himself in his will as a " citizen and painter-stainer of London."

*Works.* *Saturni Ephemerides* (1633); *An Exact Narrative of the Life and Death of Lancelot Andrewes* (1650; cp. No. **337**). Probably also several devotional manuals initialled " H. I.", including *Jacob's Ladder* (1637).

**JACKSON, Thomas (1579-1640). Nos. 216, 224.**

Born at Witton-le-Wear, Durham. Educated at Oxford. Fellow of Corpus, 1606. Incumbent of St. Nicholas, Newcastle, 1623, and of Winston, Durham, 1625. President of Corpus Christi College, Oxford, 1630. Prebendary of Winchester, 1635. Dean of Peterborough, 1639.

*Works.* Commentaries on the Apostles' Creed, the first complete edition (1673) being entitled *The Works of Thomas Jackson, D.D.* (cp. Nos. 216, 224).

*Editions.* Reprinted, Oxford, 1844, in 12 vols.

**JAMES I (1566-1625). No. 1.**

Born in Edinburgh Castle, June 19th, 1566. Crowned King James VI of Scotland upon his mother's abdication, July 29th, 1567. Succeeded to the English throne, March 24th, 1603. Summoned the Hampton Court Conference, 1604. Commanded publication of the Authorised Version of the Bible which appeared in 1611. Died in London, March 27th, 1625, and buried in Westminster Abbey.

*Works. Demonology* (1597); Βασιλικὸν Δῶρον (1599); *The True Law of Free Monarchies* (1603); *A Counterblast to Tobacco* (1604); *Triplici Nodo Triplex Cuneus* (1607; an apology for the Oath of Allegiance, against Cardinal Bellarmine); *A Premonition to all Most Mighty Monarchs* (1609, Basle; cp. No. 1).

*Collected Works,* published by Bishop James Montague, 1616 (in English); 1619 (in Latin).

**KEN, Thomas (1637-1711). Nos. 12, 196, 271, 300.**

Born at Little Berkhampstead, Herts. Entered Winchester College, 1652. Student of Hart Hall, 1656. Fellow of New College, 1657. Ordained, 1662. Held successively the livings of Little Easton, Essex; Brightstone in the Isle of Wight; and East Woodhay, Hants. Fellow of Winchester, 1666. Returned to live at Winchester, 1672. Appointed Chaplain to Princess (later Queen) Mary at The Hague, 1679. Bishop of Bath and Wells, 1684. Attended Charles II on his death-bed. Refused to publish the "Declaration of Indulgence," 1688. Declining Oath of Allegiance to William III and Mary he was deprived; and was succeeded in his Bishopric by Kidder (Dean of Peterborough). Lived in retirement for the remainder of his life at Longleat.

*Works. Ichabod* (1663; doubtful, cp. No. 12); *The Practice of Divine Love ; being an Exposition of the Church Catechism* (1685; cp. No. 196). Many famous hymns; also *Prayers* (cp. No. 300) and some Sermons (cp. No. 271).

**LAKE, John (1624-1689). No. 331.**

Born at Halifax, Yorks. Educated at Halifax Grammar School and St. John's College, Cambridge. Served in the Royalist forces during the Civil War. Ordained (probably by Skinner, Bishop of Oxford), 1647. Vicar of Leeds, 1660. D.D. by Royal Mandate, 1661. Presented to St. Botolph's, Bishopsgate, 1663; and to living of Prestwich, Lancs, 1669. Bishop of Sodor and Man, 1682; of Bristol, 1684; and of Chichester, 1685. Refused to take Oath of Allegiance to William and Mary ; but died before he could be deprived. Buried in St. Botolph's, Bishopsgate.

*Sermon.* A funeral sermon, entitled Στέφανος πιστοῦ, on William Cade (1671).

**LAUD, William (1573–1645). Nos. 25, 35, 54, 73, 74, 80, 122, 217, 226, 275, 299, 326, 334.**

Born at Reading. Educated at Reading School and at St. John's College, Oxford. Elected Fellow, 1593. Deacon, Jan. 4th, 1601; Priest, April 5th of same year. Vicar of Stanford, Northamptonshire, 1607. Cuxton, Kent, 1610. President of St. John's College, Oxford, 1611. Prebend of Buckden, 1615. Archdeacon of Huntingdon, 1615. Dean of Gloucester, 1616. Prebendary of Westminster, 1621. Bishop of St. David's, 1621. Dean of the Chapel Royal, 1626. Privy Councillor, 1627. Bishop of London, 1628. Chancellor of Oxford University, 1628. Archbishop of Canterbury, 1633. Impeached by the Long Parliament, 1640, and committed to the Tower, 1641. Tried by a Bill of Attainder, 1644. Executed, Jan. 10th, 1645, and buried at All Hallows', Barking.

*Works.* Relatively few. *A Relation of the Conference* [1622] *between William Laud and Mr. Fisher the Jesuit* (1639; cp. No. **54**); *A Summary of Devotions* (1667, posthumous; cp. No. **299**). Also Visitation Articles (cp. No. **334**), Sermons and Speeches (cp. Nos. **275, 326**).

*Lives. A History of the Troubles and Trials of William Laud* (1694, autobiography; cp. No. **80**). W. H. Hutton (1895).

*Collected Edition.* First collection of Sermons, 1651. Also *L. A. C. T.*

**L'ESTRANGE, Hamon (1605–1660). Nos. 191, 232.**

Baptized at Sedgeford, Norfolk. Admitted to Gray's Inn, 1617; but apparently never called to the Bar. Sided with the King in the Civil War. Buried at Pakenham, Suffolk.

*Works. God's Sabbath before and under the Law and under the Gospel* (1641); *Reign of King Charles* (1655, anon.); *The Alliance of Divine Offices* (1659; cp. No. **232**).

**MASON, Francis (1566?–1621). No. 163.**

Born of poor parents in County of Durham. Matriculated at Oriel College, Oxford, 1583. Elected probationer Fellow of Merton, 1586. Presented to the Rectory of Sudbourne, with the chapel of Orford in Suffolk, 1599. Installed Archdeacon of Norfolk, after a petition from his wife, supported by Archbishop Abbot, and Williams, Bishop of London, 1619. Died and buried at Oxford.

*Work. Of the Consecration of the Bishops in the Church of England* (1613, a work which earned its author the title *Vindex Ecclesiae Anglicanae*; cp. No. **163**. It was translated into Latin, 1620. New English edition, 1728).

**MEDE (or MEAD), Joseph (1586–1638). Nos. 149, 157.**

Born at Berden, Essex. Entered Christ's College, Cambridge, 1602. Fellow, 1613. Greek Lecturer, 1619. Of extraordinary learning, he interested himself especially in the prophecies of the Apocalypse. Buried in the inner chapel of his College.

*Works. Clavis Apocalyptica* (1627); *In Sancti Joannis Apocalypsin Commentarius* (1632); *Of the Name Altar or* θυσιαστήριον (1635); *Diatribae* (1642, posthumous; cp. No. **149**).

*Editions.* First collected "Works," 1648 (ed. J. Worthington); enlarged to 2 vols. 1663–4; further enlarged, 1672.

**MONTAGUE, Richard (1577–1641). Nos. 3, 137, 160, 237.**

Born at Dorney, Bucks. Educated at Eton College and at King's College, Cambridge. Received living of Wootton Courtenay, Somerset, 1610. Fellow of Eton, 1613. Rector of Stanford Rivers, Essex, 1613. Dean of Hereford, 1616, exchanged for Canonry of Windsor, 1617. Archdeacon of Hereford, 1617, also Rector of Petworth, Sussex, and Chaplain to James I. Accused before Parliament in 1625. Appointed Chaplain to Charles I. Bishop of Chichester, 1628. Translated to Norwich, 1638. Buried in Norwich Cathedral.

*Works.* *A New Gag for an old Goose* (1624); *Immediate Address unto God Alone* (1624; cp. No. **237**); *Appello Caesarem* (1625; cp. No. **3**); *De Originibus Ecclesiasticis Commentationes* (1636, 1640).

**MORE, Henry (1614–1687). Nos. 177, 302.**

Born at Grantham. Educated at Eton, and at Christ's College, Cambridge. B.A., 1635. Fellow, 1639. Declined all preferments. Died at Cambridge, and buried in his College Chapel. Member of company of Cambridge Platonists, and author of many philosophical works.

*Works.* *Philosophical Poems* (1647); *Antidote Against Atheism* (1652); *Enthusiasmus Triumphatus* (1656); *An Explanation of the Grand Mystery of Godliness* (1660; cp. No. **302**); *Enchiridion Ethicum* (1666); *Enchiridion Metaphysicum* (1679).

*Collected Edition.* *Opera Omnia* (1679, *i.e.* during More's lifetime).

*Life.* By Richard Ward (1710; cp. No. **177**). See also J. Tulloch, *Rational Theology in England in the Seventeenth Century*, Vol. II, pp. 303–409.

**MORLEY, George (1597–1684). Nos. 43, 209.**

Born at London. Educated at Westminster and Oxford. Canon of Christ Church, 1641. Deprived of his Canonry, owing to his resistance to the Parliamentary Visitation of Oxford University, 1647. During Commonwealth at The Hague. Dean of Christ Church, and later Bishop of Worcester, 1660. Chief representative of Bishops at Savoy Conference, 1661. Bishop of Winchester, 1662.

*Works.* Few. *The Bishop of Worcester's Letter to a Friend for Vindication of Himself from the Calumnies of Mr. Richard Baxter* (1662); *Several Treatises Written upon Several Occasions* (1683; cp. Nos. **43, 209**).

**MORTON, Thomas (1564–1659). No. 206.**

Born at York. Educated at, and subsequently Fellow of, St. John's College, Cambridge. Ordained, 1592. Incumbent of Long Marston, Yorks, 1598. Dean of Gloucester, 1606. Dean of Winchester, 1609. Bishop of Chester, 1616; of Lichfield and Coventry, 1618; and of Durham, 1632. After the abolition of Episcopacy (1646) he spent the remainder of his life in retirement.

*Works.* Numerous, chiefly against Roman Catholicism. *Apologia Catholica* (1605); *A Catholic Appeal* (1609); *Of the Institution of the Sacrament* (1631; cp. No. **206**).

**NELSON, Robert (1665–1715). Nos. 77, 208.**

Educated as private pupil of George Bull. Possessed of a large fortune he did not follow a profession, but travelled widely until 1691, in which year he settled at Blackheath. Intimate with Archbishop Tillotson and the astronomer Halley. Jacobite and Non-juring sympathies. Active supporter of S.P.C.K. and S.P.G.

*Works. Transubstantiation Contrary to Scripture* (1688; cp. No. **208**); *Companion for the Festivals and Fasts of the Church of England* (1704); *Life of Bull* (1710; cp. No. **77**); *Address to Persons of Quality and Estate* (1715).

## NEWTON, Isaac (1642–1727). No. 100.

Born at Woolsthorpe. Educated at Grantham Grammar School and Trinity College, Cambridge. B.A., 1665. Elected Fellow of Trinity, 1667; and Lucasian Professor in succession to Isaac Barrow, 1669. Submitted his discoveries in the field of optics to the Royal Society, and elected Fellow, 1672. Constructed reflecting telescope. Involved in many scientific controversies, notably with Richard Hooke and (later, over the claim to priority in the discovery of the Infinitesimal Calculus) with Leibniz. Discovery of the Law of Gravitation published in the *Principia*, 1686. Warden of the Mint, 1695. President of the Royal Society, 1703 (annually re-elected until his death). Buried in Westminster Abbey.

*Works. Philosophiae Naturalis Principia Mathematica* (1686; cp. No. **100**); *Optics* (1704); *Observations on the Prophecies of Daniel and the Apocalypse of St. John* (posthumous, 1743).

*Life.* By D. Brewster (1855); and by L. T. More (New York, 1934).

## NICHOLSON, William (1591–1672). Nos. 14, 204.

Born at Stratford St. Mary, Suffolk. Chorister of Magdalen College, Oxford, 1598. Bible Clerk at Magdalen, 1612; Chaplain, 1616. Rector of Llandilo-Vawr, Carmarthen, 1626. Nominated member of Westminster Assembly, 1643; but soon withdrew. Archdeacon of Brecon, 1644. After deprivation, he carried on a private school with Jeremy Taylor. Returned to his parish at Restoration. Bishop of Gloucester, 1661.

*Works. A Plain Exposition of the Church Catechism* (1655; cp. No. **204**); *An Apology for the Discipline of the Ancient Church* (1659); *An Exposition of the Apostles' Creed* (1661).

## OVERALL, John (1560–1619). Nos. 61, 158.

Born at Hadleigh, Suffolk. Entered St. John's College, Cambridge, 1575. Migrated to Trinity College, 1578, where he held a succession of offices until Senior Fellow, 1596. Ordained, 1592. Regius Professor of Divinity, 1596. Opposed the theology of the "Lambeth Articles." Master of Catherine Hall, Cambridge, 1598. Dean of St. Paul's, 1602. At the instigation of the Hampton Court Conference, enlarged the " Church Catechism." Prolocutor of Lower House of Convocation of Canterbury, 1605, in which capacity he was perhaps responsible for the Canons in the so-called *Bishop Overall's Convocation Book* (cp. note on No. **61**). Bishop of Coventry and Lichfield, 1614; of Norwich, 1618.

*Works.* Besides those mentioned, *Sententia Ecclesiae Anglicanae de Praedestinatione* (1631), and other posthumous writings.

## PATRICK, Simon (1626–1707). Nos. 6, 71.

Born at Gainsborough. Entered Queens' College, Cambridge, 1644. Ordained, 1651. Rector of St. Paul's, Covent Gauden, 1662. Dean of Peterborough, 1679. Bishop of Chichester, 1689. Bishop of Ely, 1691.

*Works.* Numerous, including several Commentaries on the Books of the Old Testament. Also *An Account of the New Sect of Latitude Men* (1662, apparently by S. Patrick; cp. No. **6**); *A Friendly Debate between a Conformist and a Non-Conformist* (1668); *The Second Note of the Church Examined* (1687; cp. No. **71**). He contributed to *Poems upon Divine and Moral Subjects* (1719; posthumous).

### PAYNE, William (1650–1696). No. 70.

Born at Hutton, Essex. Entered Magdalene College, Cambridge, 1665; Fellow, 1671. Rector of Whitechapel, 1681. Took active part in the anti-Roman Catholic agitation raised by the " Popish Plot " of 1678. Strongly supported the comprehension scheme of 1689. Appointed, under the Great Seal, " Visitor Royal " of several London churches. Defended Sherlock against South in his controversy on the Trinity.

*Works. A Discourse of the Adoration of the Host* (1685); *The Sixth Note of the Church Examined* (1688; cp. No. **70**); *Family Religion* (1691).

### PEARSON, John (1612–1686). Nos. 13, 60, 107, 125, 140, 242.

Born at Great Snoring, Norfolk. Educated at Eton, and at Queens' and at King's Colleges, Cambridge. Fellow of King's, 1634. Ordained, 1639. Chaplain to George Goring's forces during the Civil War. Appointed weekly preacher at St. Clement's, Eastcheap, 1654. Published in 1659 the *Golden Remains of the Ever-Memorable Mr. John Hales of Eton.* Master of Jesus College, Cambridge, 1660. Lady Margaret Professor of Divinity, 1661. Master of Trinity College, Cambridge, 1662. F.R.S., 1667. Bishop of Chester, 1673. Died at Chester.

*Works. Exposition of the Creed* (1659; cp. No. **13**); *Vindiciae Epistolarum S. Ignatii* (1672); *Annales Cyprianici* (1682). Also posthumous works, ed. by H. Dodwell.

*Life.* By E. Churton, prefixed to " Minor Theological Works," 1844.

### PRIDEAUX, Humphrey (1648–1724). Nos. 84, 161, 165.

Born at Place in Cornwall. Educated at Westminster (under Busby) and at Christ Church, Oxford. B.A., 1672; B.D., 1682; D.D., 1686. Rector of St. Clement's, Oxford, and Hebrew Lecturer at Christ Church, 1679. Incumbent of Saham, Norfolk, 1686. Archdeacon of Suffolk, 1688. Dean of Norwich, 1702. Died at Norwich.

*Works.* Some important pamphlets (cp. notes on Nos. **84, 161**). Also *Life of Mahomet* (1697, anti-Deist); *The Old and New Testament connected in the History of the Jews* (1716).

*Life.* Anonymous (? by T. Birch), 1748.

### PRIMEROSE (or PRIMROSE), David. No. 262.

Son of Gilbert Primerose, D.D. (1580 ?–1641; cp. *D.N.B.*). Born at St. Jean d'Angely in France. Educated at Bordeaux and at Exeter College, Oxford. Incorporated M.A., Oxford, 1623. B.D., *c.* 1624. After leaving Oxford he exercised his Ministry in Normandy.

*Works. Theses Theologicae de peccato in genere et specie* (1620, Geneva); *Disputatio Theologica de divina Praedestinatione* (1621, Basle); *A Treatise of the Sabbath and the Lord's Day* (1636; cp. No. **262**).

**REYNOLDS, Edward (1599-1676).  Nos. 33, 170, 353, 354.**

Educated at Southampton Grammar School and Merton College, Oxford.  Fellow of Merton, 1619.  Preacher at Lincoln's Inn, 1622.  Supported John Prideaux against Peter Heylyn.  Vicar of All Saints', Nottingham, 1628.  Took 'up moderate Anglican position during Civil War.  Vicar of St. Lawrence, Jewry, 1645.  Parliamentary Visitor of Oxford, 1647.  Dean of Christ Church, 1648-1650, and again in 1659.  Warden of Merton, 1660.  Bishop of Norwich, 1661—in which capacity he treated Dissenters with great moderation.

*Works.*  Many sermons (cp. Nos. **353, 354**) and devotional works which were widely read and used.  They include *Explication of Psalm* 110 (1632; cp. No. **33**); *Israel's Prayer in Time of Trouble* (1645); *Meditations on the Holy Sacrament of the Lord's Last Supper* (1638; cp. No. **170**).

*Collected Edition,* 1658.  In 6 vols., 1826.

**RICAUT (or RYCAUT), Paul (1628-1700).  No. 37.**

Born at Aylesford, Kent.  Entered Trinity College, Cambridge, 1647.  Abroad during most of the Commonwealth.  Accompanied the embassy of Heneage Finch to Turkey in 1661.  Appointed by the Levant Company Consul in Smyrna, 1667.  Returned to England, 1679.  Secretary to Earl of Clarendon and knighted, 1685.  Appointed Resident in Hamburg and the Hansa Towns, 1689.  Buried in Aylesford Church.

*Works.*  Mainly historical.  *The Capitulations and Articles of Peace between England and the Porte* (1663); *The Present State of the Ottoman Empire* (1668); *The Present State of the Greek and Armenian Churches, Anno Christi,* 1678 (1679; cp. No. **37**).

**SANCROFT, William (1617-1693).  No. 355.**

Born at Fressingfield, Suffolk.  Educated at the Grammar School of Bury St. Edmunds, and Emmanuel College, Cambridge, where he was elected Fellow, 1642, and Bursar, 1644.  Held Fellowship until 1649.  Then retired to Fressingfield, and afterwards travelled through Germany to Italy, where he became a student of Padua University.  Chosen Select Preacher at Cambridge, and Chaplain to Cosin, Bishop of Durham, 1660.  Assisted in Revision of Prayer Book 1661-2.  Prebendary in Durham Cathedral, 1662.  Master of Emmanuel College, Cambridge, 1662.  Dean of York, January 1664.  Dean of St. Paul's, December 1664, where he devoted himself to rebuilding the church after the Great Fire.  Archdeacon of Canterbury, 1668-1670.  Consecrated Archbishop of Canterbury, Jan. 27th, 1678.  Signed petition against Declaration of Indulgence; committed to the Tower; tried and acquitted, 1688.  Refused to take Oaths of Allegiance to William and Mary.  Deprived August 1st, 1689.  Retired to Fressingfield.  Buried in Fressingfield Churchyard.

*Works.*  *Fur Praedestinatus* (1651); *Modern Politics* (1652); *Three Sermons* (1694).

*Life.*  By G. D'Oyly, with Sermons (cp. No. **355**).

**SANDERSON, Robert (1587-1663).  Nos. 9, 98, 308, 328, 329, 330.**

Educated at Rotherham Grammar School, and at Lincoln College, Oxford, where he became Fellow, 1606.  Reader in Logic, 1608.  Ordained Deacon and Priest, 1611.  Presented to Rectory of Wyberton, Lincolnshire, 1618, which he exchanged for that of Boothby Pagnell, 1619.  Prebendary of South-

56

well, also 1619. Prebendary of Farrendon-cum-Balderton in Lincoln Cathedral, 1629. Chaplain to Charles I, 1631. Rector of Muston, Leicestershire, 1633. Regius Professor of Divinity at Oxford, 1642. Deprived of his Professorship, 1648; restored, 1660. Consecrated Bishop of Lincoln, October 28th, 1660. One of the prominent members of the Savoy Conference, 1661-2. Buried at Buckden.

*Works.* Especially on Moral Theology. *De Obligatione Conscientiae* (1660; cp. No. 330); *Episcopacy not Prejudicial to Regal Power* (posthumous; cp. No. 329); *Cases of Conscience* (also posthumous). Also *Sermons* (cp. Nos. 98, 308). He edited J. Ussher's *Power Communicated by God to the Prince* (1661; cp. No. 328).

*Collected Edition.* By W. Jacobson (1854; 6 vols.).

*Life.* By I. Walton (1678).

### SELDEN, John (1584-1654). Nos. 81, 117, 130.

Born at West Tarring, Sussex. Educated at Chichester Grammar School and Hart Hall, Oxford. Admitted to Inner Temple, 1604. Called to the Bar, 1612. Probably instigated protestation on the rights and privileges of the House of Commons, 1621; and subsequently imprisoned. M.P. for Lancaster, 1623. In Charles I's reign his sympathies became more Royalist than hitherto. Sat in Long Parliament as M.P. for Oxford University. Opposed resolution against Episcopacy. Took part in discussions of Westminster Divines, 1643. Subscribed Solemn League and Covenant, 1646. Died at Friary House in Whitefriars; buried in the Temple Church.

*Works.* Numerous and very learned. *De Diis Syriis* (1617); *History of Tithes* (1618); *De Successione in Pontificatum Ebraeorum* (1631); *Mare Clausum* (1635, a reply to Grotius' *Mare Liberum*, 1609); *Uxor Ebraica* (1636). *Table Talk* (1689, recorded by R. Milward; cp. note on 117).

### SHARP, John (1645-1714). No. 15.

Born at Bradford. Educated at Christ's College, Cambridge. Ordained deacon and priest, August 12th, 1667. Archdeacon of Berkshire, 1673. Dean of Norwich, 1681. In bad odour with James II. Succeeded Tillotson as Dean of Canterbury, 1689. Archbishop of York, 1691. Preached at the Coronation of Queen Anne. Welcomed the Armenian Bishops who visited England in 1706. Died at Bath.

*Works.* Chiefly sermons (cp. No. 15).

*Collected Edition,* 1754. Reprinted at Oxford, in 5 vols., 1829.

*Life.* By his son Thomas Sharp (edited and first printed by T. Newcome, 1825).

### SHELDON, Gilbert (1598-1677). No. 356.

Born at Stanton in parish of Ellastone, Staffordshire. Educated at Oxford. Ordained, 1622. Warden of All Souls', 1626. Took part on the Royalist side in the negotiations for the Treaty of Uxbridge, 1644. Ejected from All Souls', 1648, and imprisoned. Bishop of London and Master of the Savoy, 1660. At his lodgings was held the Savoy Conference (1661). Consecrated Archbishop of Canterbury, 1663. Chancellor of the University of Oxford, 1667. He wrote practically nothing.

### SHERLOCK, William (1641 ?-1707). Nos. 16, 58, 113, 123, 250.

Born at Southwark. Educated at Eton and Peterhouse, Cambridge. Rector of St. George's, Botolph Lane, London, 1669. Prebendary of St.

Paul's, 1681. At first refused to take Oaths of Allegiance to William and Mary, but gave way. Dean of St. Paul's, 1691. Died at Hampstead.

*Works. The Knowledge of Jesus Christ and Union with Him* (1674; an attack on John Owen); *A Vindication of the Rights of Ecclesiastical Authority* (1685; cp. No. **250**); *A Practical Discourse concerning Death* (1689); *A Vindication of the Doctrine of the Trinity* (1690; cp. No. **58**); *The Case of the Allegiance due to Sovereign Powers Stated and Resolved* (1691).

## SMART, Peter (1569–1652 ?). No. 254.

Born in Warwickshire. Educated at Westminster and at Broadgates Hall (Pembroke College), Oxford. Subsequently, Student of Christ Church. M.A., 1595. Rector of Boldon, Durham, 1609. Prebendary of Durham, also 1609. Strongly opposed to the ceremonial innovations of Richard Neile and John Cosin in Durham Cathedral; he was proceeded against in the Court of High Commission for a sermon in which he attacked their changes. Gave evidence against Laud, 1644. Rector of Bishopstoke, Hants, 1645.

*Works. The Vanity and Downfall of Superstitious Popish Ceremonies* (1628; cp. No. **254**); *A Short Treatise of Altars* (? 1641); *Septuagenarii Senis Iterantis Cantus Epithalamicus* (1643).

## SMITH, John (1618–1652). No. 96.

Born at Achurch, near Oundle. Entered Emmanuel College, Cambridge, 1636, where his tutor was **Benjamin WHICHCOTE** (*q.v.*). Transferred by the Earl of Manchester to Queens' College, 1644. Died of consumption, and buried in Queens' College Chapel. His Funeral Sermon was preached by **Simon PATRICK** (*q.v.*).

*Works. Select Discourses* (1660, posthumous; second edition, 1673; cp. No. 96).

## SOUTH, Robert (1634–1716). Nos. 46, 114, 360.

Born at Hackney, Middlesex. Educated at Westminster and at Christ Church, Oxford. Ordained, 1658. Public Orator of Oxford University, 1660. Domestic Chaplain to Lord Clarendon, 1661. Prebendary of Westminster, 1663. Chaplain to Duke of York, 1667. Rector of Islip, Oxon., 1678. Declined See of Rochester and Deanery of Westminster, 1713.

*Works.* Chiefly Sermons; cp. Nos. **46, 114, 360**. Also *Animadversions on Dr. Sherlock's Book, entitled " A Vindication of the Holy and Ever Blessed Trinity "* (1693); *Tritheism Charged upon Dr. Sherlock's New Notion of the Trinity, and the Charge Made Good* (1695).

*Reprints.* Oxford, 1823, in 7 vols.; Oxford, 1842, in 5 vols.

## SPARROW, Anthony (1612–1685). Nos. 220, 234.

Born at Depden, near Bury St. Edmunds. Scholar of Queens' College, Cambridge, 1629. Fellow, 1633. Held several University appointments, 1638–1643. Ejected from his Fellowship on the ground of his Royalism, 1644. Presented to Rectory of Hawkedon in Suffolk, 1648; but ejected after five weeks for using the *Book of Common Prayer.* Reinstated, 1660. D.D. *per litteras regias*, 1660. Prebendary of Ely, 1661. President of Queens', 1662, a royal mandamus over-riding the appointment of **Simon PATRICK** (*q.v.*), who had been elected by a majority of the Fellows. Bishop of Exeter, 1667; of Norwich, 1676. Died at Norwich.

*Works. A Rationale upon the Book of Common Prayer* (1655 ?,—no extant copies older than 1657; cp. No. **234**); *A Collection of Articles, Injunctions, Canons of the Church of England* (1661).

### STAFFORD, Anthony (1587–1645 ?). No. 244.

Educated at Oriel College, Oxford. Also entered at the Inner Temple, 1606. Very fiercely attacked by the Puritans, owing to his writings on the subject of Invocation ; supported by Laud.

*Works.* *Meditations and Resolutions, Moral, Divine and Political* (1612) ; *Stafford's Heavenly Dog* (1615) ; *Guide of Honour* (undated) ; *The Day of Salvation* (1635) ; *The Female Glory* (1635 ; cp. No. 244).

### STILLINGFLEET, Edward (1635–1699). No 38.

Born at Cranborne, Dorset. Educated at St. John's College, Cambridge. Fellow, 1653. Presented to the living of Sutton in Bedfordshire, 1657. Leaned towards toleration after 1660. Prebendary of St. Paul's Cathedral, 1667. Dean of St. Paul's, 1678. Resisted proposed Declaration of Indulgence, 1688. Bishop of Worcester, 1689. Controversy with John Locke. Buried at Worcester.

*Works.* *Irenicum* (1659) ; *Origines Sacrae* (1662) ; *A Rational Account of the Grounds of the Protestant Religion* (1664 ; cp. No. 38) ; *The Unreasonableness of Separation* (1680) ; *Origines Britannicae* (1685).

*Collected Edition,* London, 1710, with *Life* by Richard Bentley.

### TAYLOR, Jeremy (1613–1667). Nos. 10, 22, 50, 65, 76, 79, 87, 180, 192, 193, 195, 212, 223, 233, 240, 255, 257, 260, 281, 291, 304, 307, 309, 310, 320, 342.

Baptized at Cambridge. Educated at Perse Grammar School, Cambridge, and at Gonville and Caius College. Fellow of his College, 1633. Ordained, 1633. Nominated by Laud to a Fellowship at All Souls' College, Oxford, 1635. Rector of Uppingham, 1638. Intimate with Christopher Davenport (*alias* Francis a Sancta Clara), a learned Franciscan friar. Zealous supporter of Royal cause during Civil War. Deprived of his preferments and became private chaplain to the Earl of Carbery at Golden Grove in Carmarthenshire. Three times imprisoned during the Commonwealth, on one occasion in Chepstow Castle and on another in the Tower. Bishop of Down, Connor, and Dromore, 1661, where he had a very troubled episcopate.

*Works.* Numerous. *A Discourse of the Liberty of Prophesying* (1647 ; cp. No. 87) ; *An Apology for Authorized and Set Forms of Liturgy* (1647 ; cp. No. 79) ; *The Great Exemplar* (1649 ; cp. No. 212) ; *Holy Living* (1650 ; cp. No. 223) ; *Holy Dying* (1651) ; *The Golden Grove* (1655) ; *Unum Necessarium* (1665 ; cp. No. 307) ; *Ductor Dubitantium* (1660 ; cp. No. 309) ; *A Discourse of Confirmation* (1663 ; cp. No. 193) ; *Dissuasive from Popery* (1664 ; 1667 ; cp. Nos. 50, 260). Also many Letters (cp. No. 10), and Sermons (cp. No. 342).

*Editions.* R. Heber, 15 vols., London, 1828 ; C. P. Eden, 10 vols., London, 1850.

*Lives.* By R. Heber (1828) ; E. Gosse (1904) ; W. J. Brown (S.P.C.K., 1925).

### THORNDIKE, Herbert (1598–1672). Nos. 69, 221, 238, 292, 318.

Son of a Lincolnshire gentleman. Educated at Trinity College, Cambridge. Minor Fellow, 1618 ; Major Fellow, 1620. Prebendary of Layton Ecclesia in Lincoln Cathedral, 1636. Hebrew Lecturer at Trinity College,

1640. Nearly elected Master of Sidney Sussex College, Cambridge, 1643; but Cromwell intervened, causing one of Thorndike's supporters to be arrested, and thus leaving him without a majority of votes. Retired to the living of Barley, 1644; but deprived of this also in the ensuing troubles. Took a keen interest in the production of Brian Walton's *Polyglott*. Reinstated in his living and his Fellowship at the Restoration. Prebendary of Westminster, 1661.

*Works.* Many. Include *Epitome Lexici Hebraici, Syriaci, Rabinici, et Arabici* (1635); *The Right of the Church in a Christian State* (1649); *An Epilogue to the Tragedy of the Church of England* (1659; cp. No. **69**); *Just Weights and Measures* (1662; cp. No. **292**); *The Reformation of the Church of England better than that of the Council of Trent* (written 1670–1672; first published in *L. A. C. T.* ed.; cp. No. **318**).

*Collected Edition. L. A. C. T.*

## TILLOTSON, John (1630–1694). Nos. 99, 319.

Born at Old Haugh End, in the parish of Halifax. Educated at Clare Hall, Cambridge. Elected Fellow, 1651 (having previously been nominated a Probationer Fellow by the Government). Elected to succeed Calamy at St. Mary, Aldermanbury, 1662; but declined. Preacher at Lincoln's Inn, 1664. Became famous as pulpit orator. D.D., 1666. Dean of Canterbury, 1672. Dean of St. Paul's, 1689. Archbishop of Canterbury, 1691.

*Works.* Chiefly Sermons. Among them, *The Wisdom of Being Religious* (1664; cp. No. **99**); *The Lawfulness and Obligation of Oaths* (1681; cp. No. **319**). Also *The Rule of Faith* (1666; against Roman Catholicism).

*Collected Edition*, 1752, with *Life* by Thomas Birch.

## TRAHERNE, Thomas (1637 ?–1674). No. 358.

Born at Hereford. Entered Brasenose College, Oxford, 1652. Rector of Credenhill, near Hereford, 1657. Domestic Chaplain to Sir Orlando Bridgeman. Died at Teddington.

*Works. Roman Forgeries* (1673); *Christian Ethics* (1675); *A Serious and Pathetical Contemplation of the Mercies of God* (1699). His *Poetical Works* (1906) and his *Centuries of Meditations* (1908; cp. No. **358**), the MS. of both of which had a very remarkable history, were edited by Mr. B. Dobell.

## USSHER (or USHER), James (1581–1656). Nos. 32, 68, 111, 126, 211, 276, 306, 327.

Born in Dublin. Educated at the newly-founded University of Dublin. Catechetical Lecturer in the University, 1600. Ordained deacon and priest on the same day, 1601. Chancellor of St. Patrick's Cathedral, 1606. Regius Professor of Divinity, 1607. Intimate with many famous English scholars, notably Camden, Selden, Bodley, and Cotton. Sought to impose a Calvinistic set of Articles upon the Irish Church, 1615. Bishop of Meath, 1621. While in England nominated Archbishop of Armagh, early in 1625; but did not return to Ireland till August 1626. Defeated Bramhall's attempt in 1634 to impose upon the Church of Ireland doctrinal standards identical with those of the Church of England. Left Ireland for England 1640, never to return. Preacher at Lincoln's Inn, 1647. Buried in Westminster Abbey.

*Works.* Many learned archæological and chronological writings, including *A Discourse of the Religion Anciently Professed by the Irish and British*

(1622), *Britannicarum Ecclesiarum Antiquitates* (1639), *Annales Veteris et Novi Testamenti* (1650–1654; cp. No. **111**). Also *An Answer to a Challenge made by a Jesuit* (1625; cp. No. **68**); *The Power Communicated by God to the Prince* (1661, posthumous; cp. No. **327**); and many *Sermons* (cp. Nos. **126, 211,** and **306**). On *A Body of Divinity*, attributed to Ussher, cp. note on No. **32**.

*Collected Edition.* Edited by C. R. Elrington, Dublin, 1864, 17 vols.

## WAKE, William (1657–1737). Nos. 147, 162, 258.

Born at Blandford. Educated at Christ Church, Oxford. Went to Paris as Chaplain to the Ambassador, Richard Graham, 1682. Returned to England, 1685. Canon of Christ Church, 1689. Rector of St. James', Westminster, 1693. Dean of Exeter, 1703. Bishop of Lincoln, 1705. Archbishop of Canterbury, 1716. Negotiated with French Church on possibilities of reunion, 1718.

*Works.* Numerous, including *An Exposition of the Doctrine of the Church of England* (1686; cp. No. **258**); *A Discourse of Purgatory* (1687; cp. No. **147**); *A Discourse of Prayers for the Dead* (1687); *The Genuine Epistles of the Apostolical Fathers* (1693); *The State of the Church and Clergy of England, historically deduced* (1703).

## WALTON, Izaak (1593–1683). Nos. 289, 338, 339.

Born at Stafford. Moved to London, where he kept shops successively in Cornhill and Fleet Street. Retired from business after Royalist defeat at Marston Moor. Spent most of the latter part of his life " in the families of the eminent clergymen of England, of whom he was much beloved " (Anthony Wood).

*Works.* *The Complete Angler* (1653). Also *Lives* of *John Donne* (1640), *Sir Henry Wotton* (1651; cp. No. **289**), *Richard Hooker* (1662), *George Herbert* (1670; cp. No. **338**), and *Robert Sanderson* (1678).

## WHICHCOTE (or WHITCHCOTE), Benjamin (1609–1683). No. 90.

Born at Stoke, Shropshire. Educated at Emmanuel College, Cambridge. Fellow, 1633. Ordained, 1636. Rector of North Cadbury, 1643. Provost of King's College, Cambridge, 1644. Vice-Chancellor of Cambridge, 1650. Consulted by Cromwell on the question of granting toleration to Jews, 1655. Lost Provostship of King's at Restoration on account of his sympathies with the Commonwealth. Presented to St. Anne's, Blackfriars, 1662; and to St. Lawrence, Jewry, 1668.

*Works.* All posthumous. *Select Sermons* (1698); *Several* [viz. ten] *Discourses* (1701; cp. No. **90**).

*Collected Editions.* Aberdeen, 1751, in 4 vols.; *Moral and Religious Aphorisms*, London, 1753.

## WHITBY, Daniel (1638–1726). Nos. 57, 95, 118, 294.

Born at Rushden, Northamptonshire. Educated at Trinity College, Oxford. Fellow, 1664. Rector of St. Edmund's, Salisbury, 1669. D.D., 1672. Pleaded for toleration of Nonconformists, and condemned accordingly by the University of Oxford in Convocation. Advocated Oaths to William and Mary, 1689. Wrote in defence of Hoadly in Bangorian Controversy (1714 and 1718).

*Works.* Very numerous. Include Δὸς ποῦ στῶ (1666; cp. No. **57**); Λόγος τῆς Πίστεως (1671; cp. No. **118**); *Treatise in Confutation of the Latin Service* (1684; cp. No. **294**); *A Discourse Concerning Election and Reprobation* (1710); *A Confutation of the Doctrine of the Sabellians* (1716).

## WHITE, Francis (1564 ?–1638). Nos. 2, 21, 26, 66, 67, 175, 184, 187, 228, 259, 266, 293.

Born at Eaton Socon, Bedfordshire. Elder brother of **John WHITE** (*q.v.*). Gonville and Caius College, Cambridge, 1578. Ordained 1588. Rector of St. Peter's, Cornhill. Disputed with " John Fisher " (1622; cp. note on No. **228**). Bishop of Carlisle, 1626; of Norwich, 1629; and of Ely, 1631. Held a Conference with Brabourne about the observance of the Sabbath (cp. note on No. **67**). Died at Ely House.

*Works.* *The Orthodox Faith and Way to the Church* (1617; cp. No. **184**); *A Reply to Jesuit Fisher's Answer* (1624; cp. No. **228**); *A Treatise of the Sabbath Day* (1635; cp. No. **67**).

## WHITE, John (1570–1615). No. 270.

Born at Eaton Socon. Younger brother of **Francis WHITE** (*q.v.*). Entered Gonville and Caius College, Cambridge, 1586. M.A., 1593. D.D., 1612. Fellow of the Collegiate Church, Manchester, 1606. Rector of Barsham, 1609. Chaplain-in-Ordinary to James I, 1614 or 1615. Died in Lombard Street, London.

*Works.* *The Way to the True Church* (1608; cp. No. **270**); *English Paradise* (1612).

[**Whole Duty of Man, The.** Nos. 197, 227.]

[*L. A. C. T. = Library of Anglo-Catholic Theology.*]